THE SCOUTING REPORT: 1997

Doug Myers
David Srinivasan
Editors

Produced by Mountain Lion, Inc.

HarperPerennial
A Division of HarperCollins*Publishers*

The player photos in this book were provided by the 28 individual Major League Baseball teams and are used with their permission.

HarperCollins books may be purchased for educational, business, or sales promotional use. For information, please write to: Special Markets Department, HarperCollins Publishers, Inc., 10 East 53rd Street, New York, NY 10022.

FIRST EDITION

ISSN 0743-1309
ISBN 0-06-273055-X

96 97 98 99 00 ❖/RRD 10 9 8 7 6 5 4 3 2 1

Doug Byron contributed to the White Sox, Indians, Royals, Blue Jays, Cubs, Mets, and Cardinals.

Todd Willoughby contributed to the Orioles, Red Sox, Tigers, Brewers, Twins, Rangers, and Reds.

Evan Rentschler contributed to the A's, Dodgers, and Pirates.

Veteran major-league and minor-league scouts, all of whom chose to remain anonymous, contributed scouting reports and opinions.

John Monteleone, Randy Voorhees, Mark Gola, and Joan Mohan at Mountain Lion were instrumental in pulling all the pieces together.

Margaret Trejo of Trejo Production made it look better than ever.

William Drennan copyedited the text.

Robert Wilson, former minor-league player and our editor at HarperCollins, supported the development of the new format and new approach to this book.

Jim Keller and Jay Virshbo of Howe Sportsdata provided the minor league statistics.

Members of the Media Relations departments at all 28 major league baseball teams provided the mug shots.

Evan Ashworth, Andrew O'Sullivan, and John Spanos offered their US$.02 at various stages of the process. So did Pat Walker, who contributed some great one-liners to the Brewers.

CONTENTS

ORGANIZATION

This book is organized alphabetically by team, and alphabetically by player within the team. 1,281 players are listed in the **Free Agents** and **Looking for a Game** section after the 28 teams. All players are listed in the index at the back of the book.

PLAYERS

We don't follow a rigid formula in selecting the players we choose to present. We present 99% of all major leaguers who saw significant time last year, though we have deep-sixed a few bench veterans to make room for a few extra prospects. If Mike Kingery knocks in 90 runs in '97, we'll issue a formal apology to him. As for the prospects, we've included 456 of them in this book. Most of them were in Double-A or Triple-A last season, but we've included plenty of Class-A and Rookie League players, as well, if we were particularly excited about their future.

TABS

We've tabbed certain players with descriptive phrases like *Superstar* (rarely) or *Young Gun*. Most are self-explanatory, but a few merit more detail. Minor leaguers about whose futures we're very optimistic have been tabbed a *Grade-A Prospect*, which means we think they could be impact players in the big leagues. A notch below a *Grade-A Prospect* is a *Solid Prospect*—players we think will make it to the big leagues someday and get some playing time. If we think this could happen as soon as '97, we include that in his write-up. A *Sleeper* is either a minor leaguer no one is talking too much about yet (usually a low round draft pick); a former top prospect who's just now getting it back on the rails; or a big leaguer we think could come "out of nowhere" to contribute in '97. There are 172 Sleepers in this book and, obviously, not all will wake up. However, these are the players we think have the *best* chance of surprising.

INFO LINES

Major Leaguers vs. Minor Leaguers

Here's Jack McDowell's info and stat lines:

SP • BR • TR • 6'5 • 180 • 31 • CHA87/1

	G	GS	IP	H	HR	BB	K	W	L	S	ERA	K/BB	K9	HW9
CHA94	25	25	181	186	12	42	127	10	9	0	3.73	3.0	6.3	11.34
NYA95	30	30	217	211	25	78	157	15	10	0	3.93	2.0	6.5	11.99
CLE96	30	30	192	214	22	67	141	13	9	0	5.11	2.1	6.6	13.17
CAREER	251	251	1753	1683	152	564	1216	119	77	0	3.73	2.2	6.2	11.54

SP (starting pitcher) is his primary position. BR and TR mean that he bats and throws right-handed. He is 6'5" and weighs 180 pounds. He will be 31 years old on 4/1/97 and was drafted by the White Sox in 1987 with their first pick. He played for the White Sox in 1994, the Yankees in 1995, and the Indians in 1996. Most of the stat abbreviations you're already familiar with: G (games), GS (games started), IP (innings pitched), H (hits allowed), HR home runs allowed), BB (walks), K (strikeouts), W (wins), L (losses), S (saves), ERA (earned run average), K/BB (strikeout-to-walk ratio), K9 (strikeouts per 9 innings), HW9 (hits and walks per 9 innings).

Here's Brooks Kieschnick:

OF • BL • TR • 6'4 • 225 • 24 • CHN93/1

	AB	R	H	2B	3B	HR	RBI	BB	SO	SB	CS	BA	OB	SA
AAA	441	47	114	20	1	18	64	37	108	0	1	.259	.315	.431

Outfield (OF) is his primary position. BL and TR means that he bats left and throws right. He is 6'4" and weighs 225 pounds. He will be 24 years old on 4/1/97 and was drafted by the Cubs in 1993 with their first pick. He played in Triple-A in 1996. Again, you'll be familiar with most of the stat abbreviations already: AB (at bats), R (runs), H (hits), 2B (doubles), 3B (triples), HR (home runs), RBI (runs batted in), BB (walks), SO (strikeouts), SB (stolen bases), CS (caught stealing), BA (batting average), OB (on-base percentage), SA (slugging average).

For big league veterans, we've presented a stat line from 1994 through 1996 and career totals. For first- or second-year players, we've presented their 1995 and/or 1996 seasons. For players who split time between the major and minor leagues last year, we've presented their big league stats if they got at least 50 at bats or 20 innings. For those who played

in different levels of the minor leagues, we presented the highest level attained, provided they got a significant amount of playing time there.

MINOR LEAGUES

Here are the levels: AAA (American Association, International League, and Pacific Coast League); AA (Eastern League, Southern League, and Texas League); A+ (California League, Carolina League, Florida State League); A (Midwest League, South Atlantic League); A- (Northwest League, New York-Penn League); R+ (Appalachian League, Pioneer League); R (Arizona League, Gulf Coast League).

Here are some league averages, so you can tell which are hitters' leagues and which are pitchers' leagues. We've taken these into account when gauging a player's potential. If a pitcher puts up an ERA of 4.20 in the California League, we take notice. We're not as impressed with that kind of ERA in any other Class-A league. A batting average of .280 is very good in the American Association, but only average in the PCL.

AAA	**BA**	**SA**	**ERA**
American Association	.260	.410	4.07
International League	.269	.427	4.57
Pacific Coast League	.279	.423	4.58
AA			
Eastern League	.260	.399	4.09
Southern League	.263	.401	4.25
Texas League	.272	.416	4.29
A+			
California League	.276	.420	4.81
Carolina League	.260	.388	3.97
Florida State League	.256	.360	3.63
A			
Midwest League	.254	.367	3.94
South Atlantic League	.241	.350	3.59
A-			
Northwest League	.252	.379	4.13
New York-Penn League	.246	.348	3.75
R+			
Appalachian League	.252	.376	4.45
Pioneer League	.290	.432	5.70
R			
Arizona League	.253	.354	3.93
Gulf Coast League	.245	.335	3.53

WRITE-UPS

The team write-ups offer a month-by-month review of the highlights and lowlights of the '96 season (**1996 Autopsy**), and a snapshot of how things looked for '97 as we went to press in late November (**1997 Diagnosis**).

A sage once said, "The only constant in life is change." So, while we realize that professional baseball players are the best at what they do, and that major leaguers are the best of the best, we've compiled our reports with an eye toward discerning who is changing, and in what direction—getting better, or slipping? Accordingly, we have tossed our accolades toward the former and verbal grenades toward the latter. The player write-ups do not follow a rigid formula. They range from extensive (Ken Griffey) to seven words (Jon Zuber). They may be reverent (Jeff Bagwell), tongue-in-cheek (Jim Edmonds), or vicious (Gregg Jefferies)—the only thing they all have in common is that they strive to be both insightful, informative, and entertaining.

Is there something you like? Something you'd like us to add? Drop us a line (there's a survey on the back page of the book), or e-mail us at scouting97@aol.com. And if you're related to Gregg Jefferies, we apologize in advance for the facts we've gathered and opinions we've posited.

— Doug Myers

INTRODUCTION

There are a lot of changes to this year's *Scouting Report.* As always, the detailed information you want on the strengths and weaknesses of 1,281 major league and minor league players is here. But with a new attitude and a different format, we've been able to produce not just the most informative baseball book on the market, but the most entertaining and thought-provoking, as well.

Here are some of the changes:

STATS

We provided even more stats for both the big leaguers and the prospects. We give you three year's worth of stats and career totals for the veterans. We give you numbers for minor leaguers that aren't always available, but that will help you better gauge their prospects: walks, strikeouts, and caught stealing for the hitters; strikeouts-to-walk ratio, strikeouts per 9 inning, and hits/walks per 9 innings for the pitchers. Time and again, minor leaguers with gaudy home run, batting average, or stolen base numbers haven't been able to make it in the big leagues, while pitchers with outrageous won-loss records have struggled as well. A lot of this could have been anticipated (see David McCarty) if some less popular statistics had been considered.

PLAYERS

We continue to present the strengths and weaknesses of every player, to analyze trends in their stat lines, and to offer our assessment of their outlook for 1997. Derek Bell is a good example of one whose write-up should come as a surprise. This year, we've gathered quotes that are telling (see Jim Edmonds) or humorous (see Alex Cole) or informative (see Francisco Cordova), and that will help show what the numbers can't. We do the same with tangents (see John Jaha and Jose Valentin) and anecdotes (see Jason Varitek of the Seattle Mariners and R.A. Dickey of the Texas Rangers), weaving them in wherever appropriate, and making this year's *Scouting Report* the most fun to read yet.

TEAMS

In the past, we've looked at players exclusively. This year, we look at how the teams did in 1996 and how they look going into 1997. We provide a month-by-month breakdown of the 1996 season, offering the highlights and lowlights of last year's campaign. For 1997, we offer our assessment of the team's offense, defense, and pitching; its farm system; and how well it's being run—in the owner's box, the front office, and down on the field. We conclude each section with a brief essay on something we think you might find interesting. Some examples:

The Dark Side of the Mouse (California Angels). What baseball may look like after Disney has its way with it.

Kirby Baseball (Minnesota Twins). An assessment of Kirby Puckett's Hall of Fame credentials, as well as that of another player who has similar credentials and a tragically abbreviated career—but who has received little to no consideration in the dozen or so years he's been eligible.

A Rod and Mel Ott (Seattle Mariners). The greatest 20 year old ballplayers in recent years, and the greatest teenage ballplayer of all time.

The Curse of the Senators (Texas Rangers). A look back at 35 years in Arlington; not for the faint of heart.

Come Back and Go Away (Chicago Cubs). Ryne Sandberg and the countless other un-expected comebacks in '96 . . . as well as Doug Jones and others who wore out their welcomes very quickly.

Schott in the Dark (Cincinnati Reds). Our take on that daffy broad in Cincinnati.

Lies, Damned Lies, and Statistics (Houston Astros). Eight hitters (a catcher, an infield, and an outfield) who aren't as good as some of their numbers suggest. To keep it interesting, we limited ourselves to only one member of the Colorado Rockies.

FREE AGENTS

To help you evaluate how well a team has ended up doing in the rotisserie draft that is the annual free agent signings, we've put into a separate section all the players who remained free agents as we went to press. In addition to our **Free Agents** section, we have another section called **Looking for a Game**—the players who became free agents involuntarily. If you can't find someone, check the index.

We think you'll enjoy this new approach to the 16th edition of the first (and oft imitated) book of its kind. Tell us what you think. There's a survey on the back page you can mail to us, or you can send us an e-mail at scouting97@aol.com. We've had our chance to state our opinion, now here's your opportunity for rebuttal!

— Doug Myers

American League

■ 1996 AUTOPSY

The Orioles entered the '96 season picked by most observers to compete neck-and-neck with the Yankees for the division title. The club had made significant moves in the off-season and were led by a new manager, Davey Johnson. Roberto Alomar got all the headlines as the Orioles' biggest acquisition, and the double-play combination of Alomar and Cal Ripken was heralded as possibly the best ever. B. J. Surhoff had been signed to play third. Bobby Bonilla was added to play right field or third. All the new bats were expected to ignite an offense that had been sluggish in '95. Kent Mercker was the big addition to the starting rotation and Randy Myers had been signed to handle the closing duties. They'd lost Kevin Brown for their rotation, but that didn't seem like a big deal. Davey Johnson faced the difficult task of bringing all the superstars together in one clubhouse and make them play as a team, but that didn't seem like it would be that big a deal either.

April 14-12 (14-12, half-game back)
The club rolled to an 11-2 record, jumping out to an early 4½ game lead. The starting rotation pitched well, but more impressive was the bullpen. For the first 13 games, they allowed 1 earned run in 34.2 innings. Then the Orioles went into Texas on the 19th and lost 26-7, the worst defeat in the club's history. Mercker was gone after 4.1 innings and the bullpen surrendered 16 runs in the 8th inning! The team ERA went from 3.00 to 4.52. The loss sent them on a 6-game losing streak, and they would lose 10 of their next 13. Brady Anderson tied the A.L. record for homers in April with 11, drove in 21 runs, and scored 25. No one counted on that continuing.

May 14-10 (28-22, 1 game back)
In May, Johnson must have been having fond thoughts of working for Marge Schott. The club started the month playing .500 ball, and the frustration began to mount. Johnson dropped Mercker to the no. 5 spot in the rotation, and suggested the bullpen as a possibility. Mercker didn't sound too confident: "If he thinks we have no chance of winning with me out there, I guess I have to go with that. But if I'm not good enough right now to start, I'm not good enough to pitch out of the bullpen in a game that's important." Meanwhile, Bonilla was critical of Johnson's decision to use him as a designated hitter. His hitting was suffering and he wanted out. Then Johnson told reporters that he had asked Cal Ripken to move to third temporarily—though Ripken, who is the real boss in Baltimore, didn't sound too keen about the idea.

June 14-14 (42-36, 4½ games back)
Johnson relented to Bobby Bonilla's complaints and finally moved him into right field. Bonilla responded immediately, breaking out of his season-long slump to hit .355 with 22 RBI for the month. Manny Alexander got tired of waiting for a shot at playing shortstop and told reporters that the Orioles were holding him back because of his ethnicity. Armando Benitez threatened to quit baseball when the club asked him to go down to their minor-league facility as he recuperated from an injured elbow. Rafael Palmeiro wondered what he had to do to get a few All-Star votes.

July 11-16 (53-52, 10 games back)
Ripken got even more headlines in July than he had in June. Peter Angelos told reporters that Ripken needed to step up and be a leader. "This team is in desperate need of leadership on the field and around the clubhouse, and no one is more qualified than Cal Ripken to provide that leadership." Cal went to the All-Star game and got his nose broken inadvertently by White Sox closer Roberto Hernandez during a photo session. And when he returned, Davey Johnson tried to appease Manny Alexander by giving him a try at short, moving Ripken to third for the first time in 14 years. Alexander folded under the pressure, though, and the experiment lasted only 6 games. Broadcaster Jim Palmer, a respected opinion on all things Oriole, blasted the team for lackadaisical play. "When I pitched, you never saw this kind of laziness in the major leagues," he said. "But then, the inmates didn't run the asylum back then." The Orioles got Eddie Murray back for Mercker, but more trade rumors circulated as the club contemplated throwing it in and building for the future.

August 19-11 (72-63, 4 games back)
Angelos put an end to any speculation that the Orioles had given up by forbidding GM Pat Gillick to trade away their stars. "We're still going to do everything we can to keep the team competitive and make it a winner," Angelos said. "Which leaves us with nothing at the bottom line, and might even leave a deficiency. But that is a policy that we've adopted and that is a policy we will maintain." On the field, the club started playing ball, even if they were beating up on also-rans Oakland, Minnesota, and Milwaukee. The offense got in gear and scored 154 runs with 34 home runs. Mike Mussina enjoyed his best month, going 5-1 with a 3.77 ERA. The Orioles went after more power at the end of the month, acquiring right-handed sluggers Pete Incaviglia and Todd Zeile from the Phillies for a couple of pitching prospects. By the end of the month they had clawed their way back into contention for the division title.

September 16-11 (88-74, 4 games back, clinched wild-card)
On the 6th, Eddie Murray belted his 500th home run, off the Tigers Felipe Lira. Murray joined Hank Aaron and Willie Mays as the only players with 3,000 hits and 500 homers. The Orioles opened the month with a 12-4 record against Detroit, California, and Chicago. After the 15th, they were 2½ games out and heading into the Bronx for the crucial showdown. The Orioles need to win 2 of 3 to have a chance. They dropped 2 of 3, salvaging the nightcap of a doubleheader. It continued a pattern of losing to the better teams in the bigger games, while beating up on the weak sisters. The Orioles played the Blue Jays 7 out of their last 10 games, and went 4-3 to clinch the wild-card spot. Roberto Alomar spit in the face of umpire John Hirschbeck, but was on the field to hit a game-winning home run to put them in the playoffs. In the locker room victory celebration, some Orioles players spit beer in each other's faces as a tribute to Alomar.

October (lost in Championship Series to Yankees)
Roberto Alomar was given a hero's welcome in Baltimore for the first 2 games of the series against the Indians, but the outrage in every other part of the country apparently was getting to him. He didn't do much in the series, until he tied Game 4 in the 9th inning with a 2 strike, 2 out single off José Mesa, then won it in extra innings with a home run. The Orioles returned to the Bronx for another showdown with the Yankees, losing Game 1 when a 12-year-old fan reached out over the right-field wall to turn a fly-ball out—or a possible double—into a Derek Jeter home run. Most baseball fans weren't willing to give the Orioles much sympathy, especially since few felt Roberto Alomar should be playing in the postseason. If anything, it seemed as if the baseball gods were doing their part to do what the baseball establishment wouldn't do. And to remind everyone that it was, after all, just a kids' game. The Orioles hadn't beaten the Yankees at Camden Yards al' season, and couldn't beat them in the playoffs either. They melted down in Game 3 when the ball slipped out of Todd Zeile's hand on a fake throw to second, allowing the lead run to score. Mike Mussina, who hadn't pitched well in any big games all year, lost his composure and served up a dinger to Cecil Fielder that put the game out of reach. The Orioles were buried by 5 Yankee dingers in Game 4, then surprised most fans by actually showing up for Game 5. In some wonderfully poetic justice, a Little League error by Roberto Alomar opened the flood-gates for 5 unearned runs in the 3rd that were the difference in the game. Angelos had bought himself a lot of talent. In '97 he'll have to try to buy his team some character if he wants to go any farther.

■ 1997 DIAGNOSIS

Offense
There was never any doubt that the Orioles could score a lot of runs. They shattered the major-league season record for home runs with 257. They had 9 players with 20 or more homers. They scored 914 runs, good for third place in the A.L. The offense won't be as productive in '97. Bobby Bonilla is gone and Todd Zeile will likely follow. The team wants Cal Ripken to play third base, and a gloveman is likely to take his spot at shortstop. Chris Hoiles will also give way to a better defensive catcher. Brady Anderson can't be expected to repeat his '96 performance in '97. But if the Orioles can play even better defense and show more guts, they might hit 100 fewer home runs and win a World Series. The Yankees did.

Defense
The Orioles' defense last season was very good. They were among only 4 A.L. teams to make fewer than 100 errors. Rafael Palmeiro is sure-handed at first and Roberto Alomar is very good at second. Cal Ripken is overrated at short, though he continues to make all the routine plays. He will be better at third, as will the team—if he stops fighting it and just accepts it. Brady Anderson doesn't have great range and should probably be moved back to left field, if they can find a legitimate center fielder. B.J. Surhoff did as well as could be expected in the outfield. The weakest link is behind the plate, where Hoiles played like a DH.

Pitching
The rotation was inconsistent, and they (like most teams) never found a solid no. 5 starter. Johnson put them into a four-man rotation in the second half until September, which seemed to work. Mussina almost got 20 victories, despite posting his worst ERA ever. Of course, just about every pitcher posted his worst ERA last year—except ex-Oriole Kevin Brown, that is. David Wells and Scott Erickson were shaky during stretches, and there's no guarantee that Wells will be re-signed. Rocky Coppinger emerged as a major-leaguer. He will be a dominant starter, just not yet. Jimmy Haynes struggled horribly last year, but he's talented. If he isn't still suffering from shell shock, he could contribute.

The bullpen caused problems early in the season, but they turned it around in the second half with the recoveries of Armando Benitez and Alan Mills. Benitez emerged as a potential closer, though Randy Myers will still serve in that role in '97. Johnson may need to find another left-handed reliever, since Jesse Orosco will soon be eligible for Social Security.

Farm System
Baltimore's minor-league system is thin, a fact that has weighed heavily on their minds as they mull over their options in the free-agent market. They simply don't have much talent on the horizon, and they need to spend a great deal to keep and acquire quality players. Pat Gillick isn't used to having to do business this way.

Management and Ownership
Owner Peter Angelos has certainly been willing to spend the bucks on big-name players in an effort to build a winning team. He endeared himself to the players during the strike. And the fans loved him last year for nixing any trades that would have left the team less competitive in the short haul. His spat with Johnson and Gillick in October was probably inevitable after the turbulent season the Orioles endured. But then even Steinbrenner got off to a good start with Yankee fans, too, 20 years ago.

GM Pat Gillick built a formidable offense in the 1995–96 off-season and even found help for the pitching staff. But the deals he made during the '96 season didn't address their immediate needs. The Mercker/Murray deal helped both clubs in the short term but did not address the Orioles' pitching concerns. And the Zeile/Incaviglia deal cost them a quality pitching prospect in Calvin Maduro, something they very much need. The minor leagues are paper-thin, and nothing was done last year to change that. Gillick was hamstrung by Angelos when he tried to trade stars and salaries for prospects, so it is difficult to say what else he could have done.

Davey Johnson probably took this group of individuals as far as any manager could. It remains to be seen whether any manager can turn these stars into a team.

. . . and whatnot: Alomar
Roberto Alomar spit in an umpire's face and, for that, he will be suspended for 5 games in April, with pay (that was part of the last collective bargaining agreement, one of those owner givebacks).

Perhaps no event has more accurately captured all the problems currently facing baseball. A baseball establishment full of men with big mouths and no guts—and no leadership, unless you believe that Bud Selig and Gene Budig could get anyone to follow them anywhere. A players' union that refuses to acknowledge any wrongdoing by one of its members and will fight every battle, regardless of the cost, if for no other reason than to flex its muscle—oblivious to the damage they are doing to the sport and themselves in the process. Baseball owners who set no standards of personal conduct for their employees—at least not during postseason.

After all, Peter Angelos could have solved this entire problem by choosing to suspend Alomar himself. Yet the pro-union owner didn't seem to have any problem with an employee who behaved like Alomar had—nor with the idea of scab umpires taking the field at Camden Yards.

But perhaps most disturbing in this entire mess was the reaction of Baltimore's fans to Alomar. These fans are regarded by players around the league as the best in baseball, and have earned a reputation for being knowledgeable and fair. But by cheering Alomar during the playoffs—some even standing to do so—they sent a clear message to athletes around the country. If you play for us, you can do just about anything, short of murder, and we will still cheer for you. Winning is that important to us. And if this kind of attitude exists in Baltimore, it more than likely exists in every major-league city in the country.

Fans recognize that the players and owners will continue to threaten strikes and lockouts unless they hit them in the turnstiles, as they did, albeit briefly, in 1995. It's time for fans to recognize that players will continue to behave abominably unless they are willing to turn on one of their own. The truth hurts, but the two-headed monster that baseball owners and players have become is a creation of the fans. Too many people don't know how to amuse themselves without spectator sports, or to feel good about themselves without their team winning. And when something is in such desperate need, the providers can pretty much set their own terms.

With baseball, we get what we pay for—and who we cheer for—and too often these days it ain't that pretty at all. Alomar is just the first . . .

MANNY ALEXANDER

SS • BR • TR • 5'10 • 165 • 26 • BAL88

	AB	R	H	2B	3B	HR	RBI	BB	SO	SB	CS	BA	OB	SA
BAL95	242	35	57	9	1	3	23	20	30	11	4	.236	.299	.318
BAL96	68	6	7	0	0	0	4	3	27	3	3	.103	.141	.103

There's been a lot of hard-luck stories in baseball, but Manny's is a classic. So little time, so much Ripken. He saw his first major-league action back in '92, but has been the Orioles' shortstop of the future for much longer. He finally got tired of waiting and began asking for a trade at midseason. His frustration reached the point that he began telling reporters that the Orioles weren't playing him because he was Hispanic. The team wisely decided not to reprimand him. Johnson: "When you can't play a person at the position he was bred to play, it would be hard to get excited. He's the one guy on the club who has to play behind Ripken." Johnson moved Ripken to third and gave Manny a 6-game audition in July. It didn't go well. He committed 4 errors and went 1 for 18, including 9 strikeouts. Alexander admitted he was too nervous, and a "little afraid" of upsetting Cal. Ironically, Ripken will be moving to third in '97, but Alexander won't be the one to replace him at shortstop. ■

ROBBY ALOMAR

AL ELITE

2B • BB • TR • 6'0 • 185 • 29 • SD85

	AB	R	H	2B	3B	HR	RBI	BB	SO	SB	CS	BA	OB	SA
TOR94	392	78	120	25	4	8	38	51	41	19	8	.306	.386	.452
BAL95	517	71	155	24	7	13	66	47	45	30	3	.300	.354	.449
BAL96	588	132	193	43	4	22	94	90	65	17	6	.328	.411	.527
CAREER	5048	829	1522	273	52	99	593	560	587	313	82	.302	.371	.435

Before the inevitable discussion of Alomar the citizen, let's take a look at his season. He entered the season being heralded as one-half of the greatest double play combination of all time. After flirting with .400 most of the first half, he led the club in hitting and broke the club record for runs scored. Now, *the incident.* If you weren't comatose in September, you know what happened. When Alomar sees how he's greeted in

visiting parks throughout '97, he'll wish he'd been suspended for the playoffs. After all, in most of those games, he didn't show up anyway. Along with Chuck Knoblauch's, Alomar's game is head and shoulders above that of every other second baseman in the major leagues. But that isn't how he will be remembered, and he's got no one to blame but himself. ■

BRADY ANDERSON — CONSISTENT STAR

OF • BL • TL • 6'1 • 195 • 33 • BOS85/10

	AB	R	H	2B	3B	HR	RBI	BB	SO	SB	CS	BA	OB	SA
BAL94	543	78	119	25	5	12	48	57	75	31	1	.219	.356	.350
BAL95	554	108	145	33	10	16	64	87	111	26	7	.262	.371	.444
BAL96	579	117	172	37	5	50	110	76	106	21	8	.297	.396	.637
CAREER	3850	629	989	201	49	122	456	535	699	208	61	.257	.356	.430

Anderson was everything a ball player should be last season. He showed up, as always, in excellent shape, and shocked everyone by tying an A.L. record with 11 home runs in April. He hustled all year, which resulted in a few nicks and scrapes, but his physical condition allowed him to heal quickly. And he played through the pain of appendicitis, avoiding surgery that could have ended his season and the Orioles' playoff hopes.

Anderson has often been derided as a poor leadoff hitter. Last season, his on-base percentage was .379, with 79 walks, and he set the major-league record for leadoff home runs with 12. That record, incidentally, came on the last game of the season, one which he could have taken off to rest for the playoffs. Instead, he suited up and took Pat Hentgen deep in the 1st inning. That homer also broke Frank Robinson's Oriole's season record.

Of course, many are saying his season was a flash in the pan, and it may have been. But that's some flash. ■

ARMANDO BENITEZ — YOUNG GUN

RP • BR • TR • 6'4 • 180 • 24 • BAL90

	G	GS	IP	H	HR	BB	K	W	L	S	ERA	K/BB	K9	HW9
BAL94	3	0	10	8	0	4	14	0	0	0	.90	3.5	12.6	10.80
BAL95	44	0	47	37	8	37	56	1	5	2	5.66	1.5	10.7	14.17
BAL96	18	0	14	7	2	6	20	1	0	4	3.77	3.3	12.8	8.34
CAREER	65	0	71	52	10	47	90	2	5	6	4.68	1.9	11.4	12.53

By the end of the season, Benitez was reminding everyone of a young Mark Wohlers—and not just

because of his high-90s fastball. His frustrating inability to do anything with it also prompted the comparison. At the beginning of the season, the Orioles were unhappy with his work ethic and his physical condition. Perhaps as a result of this, he sprained an elbow ligament early on that kept him out until late August. When he returned, he was unhittable. Johnson was impressed with his poise and started using him in close and late situations, during which he gave up 2 hits to 21 batters. Johnson likes him a lot and could use him as a setup man this year. Benitez will become the closer in the not-too-distant future. ■

BOBBY BONILLA (see Free Agents)

BRENT BOWERS

OF • BL • TR • 6'3 • 200 • 25

	AB	R	H	2B	3B	HR	RBI	BB	SO	SB	CS	BA	OB	SA
AAA	206	40	67	8	4	4	19	14	41	9	3	.325	.368	.461

Bowers came over from the Blue Jays last year, and the change of scenery did him good. He was a .255 career hitter until he landed in Double-A Bowie. Suddenly he's a .300+ hitter with decent speed and moderate power. The Orioles will want to know if he's for real before they bring him up. But no one else locked down the backup role in the outfield last year. If he gets a hot start, he could find himself in the majors by midseason. ■

ROCKY COPPINGER — YOUNG GUN

SP • BR • TR • 6'5 • 245 • 23 • BAL93/19

	G	GS	IP	H	HR	BB	K	W	L	S	ERA	K/BB	K9	HW9
EAL	96	23	22	125	126	25	60	104	10	60	5.18	1.7	7.5	13.39

It's hard to believe, but Coppinger started the '95 season in Single-A. By May last year, he was in the majors to stay. In spring training of '96 the Orioles assembled their minor-league pitchers and asked who among them was ready for the big leagues. Coppinger was the only one who raised his hand. The Orioles felt he had tremendous poise and an attitude that spelled team leader from the first day

he arrived in Baltimore. He has an excellent fastball, a decent change-up, and a good slider that is somewhat inconsistent. The fast move up the levels adversely affected his control, but that is to be expected. Once he gets adjusted, those problems should disappear. He recorded 10 victories for Davey Johnson, despite the fact that he was thrown into a 4-man rotation. Johnson thought he should be considered for Rookie Pitcher of the Year. "If you look at what he's had to do, as opposed to what a normal rookie has to do, there's a difference," Johnson said. "Normally, you never put in a rookie on 3 days rest. He's come in at times and overthrown, but as far as a rookie year, he's been as good or even better than some awfully good pitchers I've had." ■

ARCHIE CORBIN

RP • BR • TR • 6′4 • 190 • 29

	G	GS	IP	H	HR	BB	K	W	L	S	ERA	K/BB	K9	HW9
BAL96	18	0	27	22	2	22	20	2	0	0	2.30	.9	6.7	14.65

Talk about coming out of nowhere! The Orioles signed Corbin in the spring after he was cut by a team in the Mexican League. His fastball was considered the best in the International League, and he earned himself a call-up in early August. And Johnson was impressed with his arm. His control wasn't the best, but he threw as hard as anyone on the team. ■

DAVID DELLUCCI

OF • BL • TL • 5′10 • 180 • 23 • BAL95/10

	AB	R	H	2B	3B	HR	RBI	BB	SO	SB	CS	BA	OB	SA
AA	251	27	73	14	1	2	33	28	56	2	7	.291	.363	.378

Dellucci is a pure hitter who's moved up quickly. His promotion to Double-A Bowie last year made it 4 levels in 2 years of professional ball. Obviously he found the pitching there a little tougher, but he's shown outstanding plate discipline at the lower levels. Once he makes the adjustment he should be hitting at or above .300. Don't look for much power out of him, but he's a good contact hitter. ■

CESAR DEVAREZ

C • BR • TR • 5′10 • 175 • 27 • BAL88

	AB	R	H	2B	3B	HR	RBI	BB	SO	SB	CS	BA	OB	SA
AAA	223	24	64	9	1	4	27	9	26	5	1	.287	.312	.390

Devarez was bounced between Triple-A Rochester and Baltimore last season, but he ended up with some significant major-league experience. He was there at the end of the year, and Johnson was pleased with his performance. He has developed well as a hitter, is capable behind the plate, and could find himself on the roster early in the season. ■

MIKE DEVEREAUX (see Free Agents)

SCOTT ERICKSON

SP • BR • TR • 6′4 • 220 • 29 • MIN89/4

	G	GS	IP	H	HR	BB	K	W	L	S	ERA	K/BB	K9	HW9
MIN94	23	23	144	173	15	59	104	8	11	0	5.44	1.8	6.5	14.50
MIN/BAL95	32	31	196	213	18	67	106	13	10	0	4.81	1.6	4.9	12.86
BAL96	34	34	222	262	21	66	100	13	12	0	5.02	1.5	4.1	13.30
CAREER	206	203	1310	1408	111	468	688	83	76	0	4.34	1.5	4.7	12.89

What a roller-coaster career. Erickson went from a 20-8 season in '91 to an 8-19 season in '93. He's now returned to above-average form. Observers feel Erickson is still learning to pitch, and many question his guts. He didn't do much against the Yankees to dispel these doubts about his ability to handle adversity. His big problem remains the long ball. He didn't let many guys on base, but when he made mistakes, they really hurt. The Orioles shouldn't expect much more from him. He's gone 22-16 in a year and a half with the club and gave them 34 starts last year. He averaged 6.5 innings per start. But he's only a no. 3 or 4 starter and shouldn't be asked to be any more than that. ■

CHRIS FUSSELL

SOLID PROSPECT

SP • BR • TR • 6′2 • 185 • 20 • BAL94/9

	G	GS	IP	H	HR	BB	SO	W	L	S	ERA	K/BB	K9	HW9
A	15	14	86	71	8	44	94	5	2	0	2.81	2.1	9.8	11.99

If you think Fussell had a sweet strikeout rate last year, he fanned 98 in 65.2 innings for rookie league Bluefield in '95. Syd Thrift, the Orioles' director of player development, likes Fussell better than Coppinger. And there's a lot to like. He has an excellent curveball, a couple of fastballs, and a good change-up—and has great location with all 4. He's been

compared to Greg Maddux, a quiet guy with a bulldog attitude who also happens to be good at changing speeds. ■

JEFFREY HAMMONDS

OF • BR • TR • 6'0 • 195 • 26 • BAL92/1

	AB	R	H	2B	3B	HR	RBI	BB	SO	SB	CS	BA	OB	SA
BAL94	250	45	74	18	2	8	31	17	39	5	0	.296	.339	.480
BAL95	178	18	43	9	1	4	23	9	30	4	2	.242	.279	.371
BAL96	248	38	56	10	1	9	27	23	53	3	3	.226	.301	.383
CAREER	781	111	205	45	4	24	100	51	138	16	5	.262	.310	.423

After reconstructive knee surgery in the off-season, Hammonds faced a difficult task breaking into the Orioles' lineup. They gave him the chance, but by mid-June he was hitting .237 with only 19 RBI in 194 at-bats. The club sent him down to Triple-A to find himself. "It's an opportunity to go down and find out what kind of player he wants to be," said Davey Johnson. "He needs to go down there and express his talent." Hammonds took it like a man. "I had an opportunity and I haven't fulfilled it . . . yet," he said. "I was supposed to be not only a ballplayer, but sort of a leader. I was slotting myself to be a role player." But he didn't recover quickly in Triple-A. When he made it back in late July, the knee was reinjured, and he played only 15 more games. The injuries have certainly slowed his development, if they haven't already taken his career. ■

JIMMY HAYNES

SLEEPER

SP • BR • TR • 6'4 • 185 • 24 • BAL91/7

	G	GS	IP	H	HR	BB	K	W	L	S	ERA	K/BB	K9	HW9
BAL95	4	3	24	11	2	12	22	2	1	0	2.25	1.8	8.3	8.63
BAL96	26	11	89	122	14	58	65	3	6	1	8.29	1.1	6.6	18.20

Before you evaluate Haynes's season, consider his résumé. He led the International League in strikeouts in '95 and the Eastern League in strikeouts in '94. He was impressive in a 24-inning stint in the majors in '95 and was listed among Rookie of the Year candidates. He has a 90-mph fastball and two excellent curveballs, a tight-breaker and a slow-breaker. But he stunk last year. His control went south, and he just couldn't get anybody out. The Orioles were a little desperate for starting pitching during stretches and kept him around. Now they think they kept him too long. He was shelled in September (7 runs and 9 hits in 1.2 innings), and the club is concerned that they may have screwed up his confidence. They still feel he's a major-leaguer, and all indications up until last season suggest he is. They'll have him pitch in winter ball just to get him back in the groove. Haynes should be a fine pitcher once he makes the mental adjustments to the big leagues. He's still a youngster and the Orioles aren't about to hit the panic button just yet. They just hope Haynes won't, either. ■

CHRIS HOILES

C-DH • BR • TR • 6'0 • 195 • 32 • DET86/19

	AB	R	H	2B	3B	HR	RBI	BB	SO	SB	CS	BA	OB	SA
BAL94	332	45	82	10	0	19	53	63	73	2	0	.247	.371	.449
BAL95	352	53	88	15	1	19	58	67	80	1	0	.250	.373	.460
BAL96	407	64	105	13	0	25	73	57	97	0	1	.258	.356	.474
CAREER	2233	334	586	95	2	124	344	346	480	4	6	.262	.366	.473

The Orioles began the season knowing they would have trouble stopping base stealers. Sure enough, Hoiles and backup Greg Zaun threw out only 5 in 31 attempts in April. Hoiles played with a bum shoulder all season and never had much success throwing the ball. He threw out only 23% for the year. But he hit well in the second half, finally looking more like the hitter he was in '93. He may be moving into a new phase of his career. Several teams inquired about his availability, and he may become a designated hitter for a different club this season. His defensive skills have declined, but he can still hit with power. ■

PETE INCAVIGLIA (see Looking for a Game)

EUGENE KINGSALE

OF • BB • TR • 6'3 • 170 • 20

	AB	R	H	2B	3B	HR	RBI	BB	SO	SB	CS	BA	OB	SA
A+	166	26	45	6	4	0	9	19	32	23	4	.271	.363	.355

Kingsale became the first man from Aruba to play in the major leagues. Kingsale was the fastest runner in the Carolina League last year, possibly the fastest in the minors. Johnson brought him up to pinch run,

which he did, but he never got to the plate. He can handle the bat and has good plate discipline, but don't expect any power. The club would like him to improve his bunting so he can take better advantage of his speed. ■

RICK KRIVDA

SP • BR • TL • 6'1 • 180 • 27 • BAL91/23

	G	GS	IP	H	HR	BB	K	W	L	S	ERA	K/BB	K9	HW9
BAL95	13	13	75	76	9	25	53	2	7	0	4.54	2.1	6.4	12.12
BAL96	22	11	81	89	14	39	54	3	5	0	4.96	1.4	6.0	14.21

While a 3-5 record may not look like a breakthrough year, Krivda cemented himself in the Orioles' plans with good performances in key spot starts. The most important came in late September with the playoffs on the line. He pitched 6 strong innings in Fenway, giving up 4 hits, and allowed the club to rest the other starters. The next night, Coppinger beat the Sox again, virtually locking down the wild-card berth. Krivda was in flux between the rotation and the bullpen all year and handled the uncertainty well for a young pitcher. This year he will get the chance to be a regular starter. If that doesn't work out, he is also effective in long relief. ■

TERRY MATHEWS

RP • BL • TR • 6'2 • 225 • 32 • TEX87/7

	G	GS	IP	H	HR	BB	K	W	L	S	ERA	K/BB	K9	HW9
FLA94	24	2	43	45	4	9	21	2	1	0	3.35	2.3	4.4	11.30
FLA95	57	0	82	70	9	27	72	4	4	3	3.38	2.7	7.9	10.65
FLA/BAL96	71	0	73	79	10	34	62	4	6	4	4.56	1.8	7.6	13.92
CAREER	226	4	298	296	32	119	232	16	15	8	4.08	1.9	7.0	12.53

Mathews got the ball more in '96, though he'd become less effective. With the emergence of Mills and Benitez, Mathews will be pushed into the 5th and 6th innings of close games and the 3rd and 4th innings of blow-outs. His better days may be in his rear-view mirror. ■

SCOTT MCCLAIN

SLEEPER

3B • BR • TR • 6'3 • 210 • 24 • BAL90/23

	AB	R	H	2B	3B	HR	RBI	BB	SO	SB	CS	BA	OB	SA
AAA	463	76	130	23	4	17	69	61	109	8	6	.281	.361	.458

McClain was the best defensive third baseman in the International League last year. He has very good range and soft hands. He's improved a great deal at the plate as well. The club would like him to work on hitting to all fields and improve his plate discipline, but he has good power and decent speed. The Orioles have Cal Ripken to hold down third, so they can give McClain more time to work on his hitting. But don't be surprised to see McClain in the majors by midseason. Maybe he'll be the answer to the inevitable Ripken trivia question when the streak comes to an end, the Babe Dahlgren of the '90s. ■

ROGER MCDOWELL

RP • BR • TR • 6'1 • 175 • 36 • NYN82/3

	G	GS	IP	H	HR	BB	K	W	L	S	ERA	K/BB	K9	HW9
LA94	32	0	41	50	3	22	29	0	3	0	5.23	1.3	6.4	15.79
TEX95	64	0	85	86	5	34	49	7	4	4	4.02	1.4	5.2	12.71
BAL96	41	0	59	69	7	23	20	1	1	4	4.25	.9	3.0	14.03
CAREER	723	2	1049	1045	50	410	524	70	70	159	3.29	1.3	4.5	12.48

McDowell was a workhorse for the Orioles early in the season, the only consistent right-hander Johnson had to throw in there. In April and May he threw 40 innings with a 2.48 ERA. That proved to be too much for his veteran arm, and he struggled with injuries the rest of the season. He was very effective when he was healthy, but Mills and Benitez eventually stepped up in his absence. ■

ALAN MILLS

RP • BB • TR • 6'1 • 190 • CAL86 • 30

	G	GS	IP	H	HR	BB	K	W	L	S	ERA	K/BB	K9	HW9
BAL94	47	0	45	43	7	24	44	3	3	2	5.16	1.8	8.8	13.39
BAL95	21	0	23	30	4	18	16	3	0	0	7.43	.9	6.3	18.78
BAL96	49	0	54	40	10	35	50	3	2	3	4.28	1.4	8.3	12.48
CAREER	239	5	384	335	45	223	273	26	19	11	3.84	1.2	6.4	13.08

After a couple of disappointing seasons, Mills worked himself back into a front-line pitcher. He's had arm problems that reduced his velocity earlier in the year, but by the end of the season he'd been clocked regularly in the high 90s. With the arm fully recovered, he got into a few late-inning situations, and Johnson was pleased with the results. He started using Mills to spell closer Randy Myers late in the season, which didn't sit too well with Myers.

One month does not a season make, but Mills looks to have regained much of his old form. If he can maintain that velocity this year, he'll be an integral part of an improved bullpen. ■

RYAN MINOR

3B • BAL96/3 • UNIVERSITY OF OKLAHOMA

	AB	R	H	2B	3B	HR	RBI	BB	SO	SB	CS	BA	OB	SA
R+	87	14	22	6	0	4	9	7	32	1	0	.253	.330	.460

Basketball fans will remember Minor as an honorable mention All-American from Oklahoma. The Orioles drafted him in the 3d round last year; the '76ers took him in the 2nd. He struggled early in the Appalachian League, but found his bat down the stretch. *Baseball America* named him one of the top prospects in the league after he hit a couple of home runs in the playoffs. ■

EDDIE MURRAY

1B-DH • BB • TR • 6'2 • 200 • 41 • BAL73/3

	AB	R	H	2B	3B	HR	RBI	BB	SO	SB	CS	BA	OB	SA
CLE94	433	57	110	21	1	17	76	31	53	8	4	.254	.302	.425
CLE95	436	68	141	21	0	21	82	39	65	5	1	.323	.375	.516
CLE/BAL96	566	69	147	21	1	22	79	61	87	4	0	.288	.361	.478
CAREER	11169	1614	3218	553	35	501	1899	1318	1490	109	43	.288	.361	.478

Even though he started the season with the Indians, Murray's season didn't seem to start until mid-July when the Orioles brought him back home. He was hitting .262 at the time and his playing time had been squeezed by Jeromy Burnitz. The move was intended to bring some energy to the Orioles as they prepared for the stretch drive. The publicity that was sure to follow Murray in his quest for his 500th homer couldn't hurt. Murray became the 3rd player with 3,000 hits and 500 homers; Hank Aaron and Willie Mays are the others. Murray actually spoke to the media about that: "It's hard to see yourself being mentioned in the same voice with those guys. They're people everybody knows. You say baseball, and you say those guys."

In the aftermath, Psychic Friends Network founder Michael Laskey bought the ball Murray hit for $500,000 from the fan who caught it. $500,000? Would you call up for advice from that guy? ■

MIKE MUSSINA

AL ELITE

SP • BR • TR • 6'2 • 185 • 28 • BAL90/1

	G	GS	IP	H	HR	BB	K	W	L	S	ERA	K/BB	K9	HW9
BAL94	24	24	176	163	19	42	99	16	5	0	3.06	2.4	5.1	10.48
BAL95	32	32	221	187	24	50	158	19	9	0	3.29	3.2	6.4	9.65
BAL96	36	36	243	264	31	69	204	19	11	0	4.81	3.0	7.6	12.33
CAREER	161	161	1137	1066	117	274	760	90	41	0	3.56	2.8	6.0	10.61

Concerned about the lack of rest for his arm, Mussina was openly critical of Davey Johnson when he mulled over and later went with a 4-man rotation. When asked how many pitchers Johnson had in the rotation, Johnson replied, "Four and a half." The situation caused some to question Mussina's dedication to the team.

He pulled a stomach muscle in the spring and struggled for stretches throughout the season. Despite the fact that he has arguably the best off-speed stuff in baseball, Johnson thought he relied too much on the fastball. "I think there have been some times when Mike has located his fastball so well that he would get to just using it, and hitters were making adjustments," Johnson said. "When he uses all his pitches, he can frustrate some very good hitters."

Still, he was Baltimore's most reliable starter. The rotation as a whole was inconsistent at best, and Mussina was the only guy with an ERA below the league average. Last year's mediocre season was an anomaly—Mussina is one of baseball's best, and he should rebound this season. Perhaps he might even pitch well in a big game—after getting bombed by the White Sox, Yankees, and Brewers in consecutive starts in crucial September games, yielding 15 earned runs and 19 hits in 12.2 innings.

RANDY MYERS

CONSISTENT STAR

CL • BL • TL • 6'1 • 190 • 34 • NYN82

	G	GS	IP	H	HR	BB	K	W	L	S	ERA	K/BB	K9	HW9
CHN94	38	0	40	40	3	16	32	1	5	21	3.79	2.0	7.2	12.59
CHN95	57	0	55	49	7	28	59	1	2	38	3.88	2.1	9.7	12.60
BAL96	62	0	58	60	7	29	74	4	4	31	3.53	2.6	11.5	13.79
CAREER	605	12	767	652	61	348	787	38	53	274	3.20	2.3	9.2	11.73

Myers didn't exactly have a dominating year. He wasn't bad, but he did blow 7 saves, allowed a lot of baserunners, and wasn't exactly dominating in October. Worse yet, he ruffled a few feathers. He blasted ace Mike Mussina in July when Mussina was

reluctant to go to a 4-man rotation at Davey Johnson's suggestion. Myers said Mussina wasn't a team player. Team player Myers then complained about the way Johnson was using *him* in September when the manager started putting Alan Mills in to close. Myers told reporters that the Orioles were going to trade him to cut their payroll, which the club denied. The next night, Myers entered a game in the 9th and walked the first couple of batters. Johnson pulled him after he got an out, and Myers complained again. The Orioles do want to cut their payroll, and they couldn't have been too happy with Myers' antics. And the emergence of Benitez and Mills may have made him expendable. ■

JESSE OROSCO

RP • BR • TL • 6′2 • 185 • 39 • MIN78/2

	G	GS	IP	H	HR	BB	K	W	L	S	ERA	K/BB	K9	HW9
MIL94	40	0	39	32	4	26	36	3	1	0	5.08	1.4	8.3	13.38
BAL95	65	0	49	28	4	27	58	2	4	3	3.26	2.1	10.7	10.10
BAL96	66	0	55	42	5	28	52	3	1	0	3.40	1.9	8.5	11.44
CAREER	885	4	1076	867	84	460	972	74	69	133	3.93	2.1	8.1	11.10

Orosco still throws an 85-87-mph fastball, and it was clocked as high as 89 last year. Not bad for a guy at his age. He did a fine job for the Orioles in spot relief and led the bullpen in appearances. Johnson knew he could go to him when he needed to get a lefty out. The development of other, younger arms may reduce his time, but he will once again play a major role this year. ■

RAFAEL PALMEIRO

AL ELITE

1B • BL • TL • 6′0 • 190 • 32 • CHN85/1

	AB	R	H	2B	3B	HR	RBI	BB	SO	SB	CS	BA	OB	SA
BAL94	436	82	139	32	0	23	76	54	63	7	3	.319	.392	.550
BAL95	554	89	172	30	2	39	104	62	65	3	1	.310	.380	.583
BAL96	626	110	181	40	2	39	142	95	96	8	0	.289	.381	.546
CAREER	5483	868	1636	336	29	233	848	589	637	68	24	.298	.367	.498

What does Palmeiro have to do to get some respect? He was one of the finest hitters in the game last year, as he has been this entire decade. In the 1990s he leads the majors in doubles, is second to Paul

Molitor in hits, and has the 4th-highest home-run total among left-handed hitters. Yet he hasn't been to an All-Star game since 1991. In June, as the early ballots were first being counted, Palmeiro was in 8th place. Two designated hitters, Eddie Murray and Paul Molitor, were ahead of him. "I don't expect to be first," Palmeiro said. "There are guys more worthy than I am. But I don't expect guys that are DHs to get more votes than me. I guess I'll just take my three days rest and do what I always do during the All-Star break."

But it isn't easy to make it into that lineup going against Frank Thomas and Mo Vaughn. The average A.L. first baseman hit .292 with 30 home runs and 110 RBI, so the field is loaded with tremendous hitters. Plus, Palmeiro played on the same team as Ripken, Alomar, and A.L. home-run leader Brady Anderson. He shouldn't need those honors to recognize his contribution to his team. He's one of the best defensive first basemen in the league and was the Orioles' steadiest performer last year. ■

CALVIN PICKERING

1B • BL • TL • 6′3 • 285 • 20 • BAL95/35

	AB	R	H	2B	3B	HR	RBI	BB	SO	SB	CS	BA	OB	SA
R+	200	45	65	14	1	18	66	28	64	8	2	.325	.411	.675

Cecil Fielder, move over. Bigger Daddy tips the scales at 300 pounds and reportedly weighed 340 before the Orioles got hold of him. Pickering led the minor leagues with 13 homers in August, and finished with 18 in 200 at-bats. If he can stay off the doughnuts, he could be a good one. Or, at the very least, a gate attraction. ■

ARTHUR LEE RHODES

RP-SP • BL • TL • 6′2 • 190 • 27 • BAL88/3

	G	GS	IP	H	HR	BB	K	W	L	S	ERA	K/BB	K9	HW9
BAL94	10	10	52	51	8	30	47	3	5	0	5.81	1.6	8.1	14.00
BAL95	19	9	75	68	13	48	77	2	5	0	6.21	1.6	9.2	13.92
BAL96	28	2	53	48	6	23	62	9	1	1	4.08	2.7	10.5	12.06
CAREER	97	61	397	392	53	211	335	26	25	1	5.49	1.6	7.6	13.67

Rhodes seems to have found a home in the bullpen. Heading into the All-Star break, he won his first 9 decisions as a reliever with a 3.06 ERA. At the time,

there was speculation that he could become a closer in the mold of his friend José Mesa. Rhodes broke down in the second half, though, and missed most of the rest of the season. He may still get a spot start now and again if he returns healthy, but he'll get the bulk of his innings from the bullpen. ■

BILLY RIPKEN

UT • BR • TR • 6'1 • 185 • 32 • BAL82/11

	AB	R	H	2B	3B	HR	RBI	BB	SO	SB	CS	BA	OB	SA
BAL96	135	19	31	8	0	2	12	9	18	0	0	.230	.281	.333
CAREER	2452	261	598	109	5	17	200	160	290	22	13	.244	.293	.313

The Orioles brought Billy back into the fold last year after a 3-year absence from the team. Critics have derided him as merely "Cal's little brother," but he's more than that. He's an excellent defender and held down the starting role at second for the Orioles for several years. They knew they were getting a fine backup when they signed him. It must be hard playing in Cal's shadow, yet they complement each other well. Billy hit 2 homers last year. One came on the same night Cal hit 3 over the fence, which made for a great human-interest story. But there was the little brother, overshadowed again. He filled in brilliantly for the injured B. J. Surhoff at third in May. At the time, Johnson was asserting himself by threatening to move Cal Ripken to the hot corner, but Billy's play made the move unnecessary. He didn't do much at the plate, but no one expects him to. He's valuable for his glove and his versatility. He's also one of the few people in their clubhouse who has a sunny disposition. ■

CAL RIPKEN

AL ELITE

SS-3B • BR • TR • 6'4 • 215 • 36 • BAL78/4

	AB	R	H	2B	3B	HR	RBI	BB	SO	SB	CS	BA	OB	SA
BAL94	444	71	140	19	2	13	75	32	41	1	0	.315	.364	.455
BAL95	550	71	144	33	2	17	88	52	59	0	1	.262	.324	.422
BAL96	640	94	178	40	1	26	102	59	78	1	2	.278	.341	.466
CAREER	9217	1366	2549	487	43	353	1369	960	1033	35	34	.277	.345	.454

After all the attention that surrounded his streak over the past couple of years, Cal probably hoped he could return to quietly playing ball in his dogged fashion. There was still the international consecutive-games record to conquer, but that was it.

Instead, he faced several challenges from within the organization. Davey Johnson asserted his presence early by publicly considering moving Cal to third. He removed Cal for a pinch runner late in a close game, and he moved him down to 7th in the batting order for a time. Some saw these moves as efforts to show Ripken who was in charge—while others saw Ripken's irritation at them, blasphemous as it sounded, as him thinking he was bigger than the game. Peter Angelos wasn't afraid to criticize him, urging him to be more of a leader. And in July, Johnson yielded to Manny Alexander's complaints and gave him an audition at short, bumping Cal to third base. "It's not really a sad day for me," said Ripken. "I'm playing a baseball game. I'm going to be in there in the lineup like I always am. I'm going to look at it as a challenge, to see if third base is as comfortable as it was years ago." For the season, Ripken turned in his best year at the plate since '91. He'll end up back at third base in '97. And he'll excel. ■

NERIO RODRIGUEZ

SLEEPER

SP-RP • BR • TR • 6'1 • 195 • 24

	G	GS	IP	H	HR	BB	SO	W	L	S	ERA	K/BB	K9	HW9
A+	24	17	111	83	10	40	114	8	7	2	2.26	2.9	9.2	9.94

If you're a struggling minor-league catcher, try the other end of the battery. It worked for Nerio. Last year was his first full season as a pitcher, and already he was considered the second-best pitching prospect in his league. He even made it the majors briefly and got a start. Obviously, he's developed quickly. Rodriguez has good velocity and throws a hard slurve. His strikeout rate last year was outstanding, and he had great control for a first-year pitcher. He's on the fast track and could be quite a story. ■

MELVIN ROSARIO

C • BB • TR • 6'0 • 190 • 23

	AB	R	H	2B	3B	HR	RBI	BB	SO	SB	CS	BA	OB	SA
AA	162	14	34	10	0	2	17	6	43	3	2	.210	.257	.309

Rosario was initially with the Padres, but when they picked up Ben Davis, he was expendable. The Orioles definitely liked his improvement at High

Desert and jumped him up to Double-A Bowie. He had a hard time making the adjustment, but they haven't given up on him. Rosario has an exceptional arm, and he likes to make throws down to first. The organization likes his aggressive style. ■

MARK SMITH

SLEEPER

OF • BR • TR • 6'3 • 205 • 26 • BAL91/1

	AB	R	H	2B	3B	HR	RBI	BB	SO	SB	CS	BA	OB	SA
BAL95	104	11	24	5	0	3	15	12	22	3	0	.231	.314	.365
BAL96	78	9	19	2	0	4	10	3	20	0	2	.244	.298	.423

Smith was incensed when he was left off the roster after spring training. He was Baltimore's no. 1 pick in '91 and has spent the better part of the past 3 years being so close he could taste it. But once again, the Orioles had guys they wanted to try first, such as Tony Tarasco and Luis Polonia. Smith got a shot in June, but they sent him down after only 20 games despite a game-winning, 9th inning dinger, prompting him to ask for a trade. Instead, they brought him back up in July, whereupon he hurt his shin and missed most of the remainder of the season. Sounds like he needs a change of scenery. ■

B.J. SURHOFF

3B-OF • BL • TR • 6'1 • 190 • 32 • MIL85/1

	AB	R	H	2B	3B	HR	RBI	BB	SO	SB	CS	BA	OB	SA
MIL94	134	20	35	11	2	5	22	16	14	0	1	.261	.336	.485
MIL95	415	72	133	26	3	13	73	37	43	7	3	.320	.378	.492
BAL96	537	74	157	27	6	21	82	47	79	0	1	.292	.352	.482
CAREER	4421	546	1221	221	30	78	606	341	402	102	65	.276	.326	.393

Surhoff is a jack-of-all-trades and the Orioles signed him last year to play third base. He struggled a bit with nagging injuries, but he held down the position admirably most of the season until the team acquired Todd Zeile. Surhoff, then moved to left field. Johnson thought he was a tremendous worker and competitor: "It'd be like pulling teeth trying to get him out of there," he said. He swung the bat well all year and set career highs for home runs and RBI. Overall, the Orioles were very impressed, and here's a testament to how much. Surhoff's contract included a $100,000 bonus based on plate appearances, but he fell 14 appearances short. GM Pat Gillick spotted him the 14 and cut the check. With Ripken going to third, Surhoff's move to left could be permanent. He could care less. He just wants to play. ■

TONY TARASCO

OF • BL • TR • 6'0 • 185 • 26 • ATL88/17

	AB	R	H	2B	3B	HR	RBI	BB	SO	SB	CS	BA	OB	SA
ATL94	132	16	36	6	0	5	19	9	17	5	0	.273	.313	.432
MON95	438	64	109	18	4	14	40	51	78	24	3	.249	.329	.404
BAL96	84	14	20	3	0	1	9	7	15	5	3	.238	.297	.310
CAREER	689	100	173	29	4	20	70	67	115	34	7	.251	.318	.392

After years as a Braves' prospect, Tarasco went to Montreal early in '95 and cracked the starting lineup. He was hoping to do the same in Baltimore—but he was getting the chance only because the Expos had quickly tired of his uninspired defense and his questionable attitude. He struggled through April, hitting only .192. And just when he got on a little hot streak (.321 and 6 RBI in 8 games), the Orioles sent him down. He made it back in September, but sat out the divisional series with Cleveland. He went on to be part of history in the A.L.C.S., though. He'll be remembered as the guy who might've caught the ball if New York's favorite 12-year-old hadn't interfered—pointing up at him and jumping up and down like . . . well, like a 12-year-old. Yankees fans shrugged it off and said of the fan, "At least he didn't spit on him." ■

B. J. WAZSGIS

C • BR • TR • 6'2 • 210 • 26 • BAL91/10

	AB	R	H	2B	3B	HR	RBI	BB	SO	SB	CS	BA	OB	SA
AAA	304	37	81	16	0	11	48	41	87	2	3	.266	.360	.428

Wazsgis has progressed steadily the past few years. He's moved up a level per season and has been remarkably consistent at the plate—which isn't to say he's a great hitter, but his numbers have been pretty much the same regardless of the quality of pitching he's faced. The Orioles like his defense and he has a little power. The club may be ready for some youth behind the plate; they definitely need better defense. Wazsgis will get a long look in the spring and could land the no. 2 slot. ■

DAVID WELLS (see Free Agents)

TODD ZEILE (see Free Agents)

■ 1996 AUTOPSY

After winning the division handily in '95, the Red Sox watched all the preseason attention going to the free-spending Yankees and the Orioles. They weren't complaining, though—they'd been picked to finish 4th in '95 and took the division going away.

But this was a different team. Gone were Rick Aguilera, Erik Hanson, Rheal Cormier, and Lee Tinsley. New faces included Wil Cordero, Tom Gordon, Kevin Mitchell, Heathcliff Slocumb, Jamie Moyer, and Mike Stanley. With the signing of Mitchell, the Red Sox felt they had a slugging lineup that could match up with the Indians, who had swept them in the divisional series the previous year. José Canseco was back and healthy, and Mo Vaughn was coming off an MVP season. John Valentin and Tim Naehring were two of the best hitters at their infield positions. Dwayne Hosey, a good-hitting prospect, had been claimed from waivers to play center, and their stalwart veteran Mike Greenwell was in left. Stanley, one of the better slugging catchers in the game, was behind the plate. The team figured to score a lot of runs.

And they were going to have to. Their team defense, which had been the worst in the league in '95, had gone unaddressed in the off-season. GM Dan Duquette figured if they didn't need it in '95 to be successful, they wouldn't need it now with an even better offense.

April 7-19 (7-19, 7½ games back)
The team stumbled off to a 2-12 record, the worst start in franchise history. In the first 12 games, the club hit .215 with only 7 homers and led the league with 17 errors and 19 unearned runs. If they weren't questioning the fence-bashing, no-defense philosophy they'd pursued in the off-season, the rest of the league was. Manager Kevin Kennedy: "It's a mystery. It's baffling. If this was a new team I might understand it. But this is a team of veterans and a team that won last year. . . . We've had meetings, we've had no meetings, we've had private meetings. The bottom line is the results aren't there."

No one was hitting, no one was fielding, and no one was pitching. Clemens was 0-4 for the first time ever, Tom Gordon had a 9.97 ERA in 5 starts, Slocumb had blown 2 of his 6 save opportunities, and Cordero had committed 10 errors at second. The club salvaged 5 wins to finish out the month. They didn't expect an easy time defending the division title, but they didn't figure to be 7½ games back after a month.

May 14-12 (21-31, 9 games back)
There's nothing like a little blood-letting to cure what ails you, or so Duquette thought. Pitching coach Al Nipper was the designated scapegoat, and he was replaced by minor-league pitching instructor Sammy Ellis. Ellis became Duquette's 4th pitching coach in less than a year. The 5th would be hired at year end. The move angered many of the players, but it wouldn't be the last time. Duquette made it clear that other changes were possible if things didn't turn around—though he wasn't looking in the mirror when he said it. By the end of the month the club was playing decent ball but was still losing ground to the Yankees—who, in a quirk of the schedule, they wouldn't play until July.

June 13-14 (34-45, 13 games back)
The team continued to play .500 ball, but the real action took place in the clubhouse. After missing 37 of the team's first 54 games, Kevin Mitchell apologized to his teammates and their fans: "I feel guilty. I feel funny walking around the clubhouse because I'm not playing. If I could have been in there we would have been in first place." Then Vaughn lashed out at Duquette's management of the team and called for CEO John Harrington to take a more active role. Naehring complained that some teammates had attitude problems. Clemens said the team wasn't hustling. And in a local newspaper article, Kevin Kennedy was accused of dividing the team. Kennedy was fuming: "Fabrications written by a coward who's never sat down with me and talked. You can question moves I make and criticize me for them but don't question a man's integrity or character. Dan [Duquette] and I are very close, nobody's going to drive a wedge between us." Except Duquette, that is.

July 13-13 (47-58, 16 games back)
Mo Vaughn was named the Red Sox only All-Star and some teams began using the Ted Williams shift on him. Reggie Jefferson was named player of the week for the first time in his career in mid-July. Roger Clemens recorded his first victory since May

23. Kevin Mitchell was supposed to join the club in Detroit but didn't show up. On the 30th he was traded to the Reds for Roberto Mejia, who hadn't even been able to hit in Denver. The club played .500 once again, but the pitching staff was very quietly putting together a little consistency—especially Wakefield, who had won his last 3 decisions, including a victory over the Yankees and a shutout of the Orioles. Jamie Moyer, who won 3 consecutive starts to go 7-1, earned a ticket out of town—going to Seattle for Darren Bragg, an outfielder who wasn't a regular in the between-innings blooper reels.

August 22-9 (69-67, 7½ games back)
The pendulum finally began to swing the other way for the Sox, and they started putting wins back to back and belly to belly. By the 26th they had charged to within 3 games of wild-card leader Chicago. On the 30th they were 6 games behind the Yankees. Vaughn: "We're not thinking wild card, we're thinking 6 games. . . . I'm going to tell you right now I'm as optimistic as I've ever been about playing. To get where we are from where we've been is an amazing accomplishment."

And they were winning on the strength of good pitching. For the first time all year, the entire rotation, with the notable exception of Aaron Sele, was pitching well at the same time. Clemens pitched 27.1 scoreless innings in a row and went 4-1 with a 1.88 ERA for the month. Gordon struck out 41 batters in 44.1 innings, going 2-1 with a 3.25 ERA. Wakefield went 3-2 with a 3.78 ERA. And Mike Maddux returned from the disabled list to go 2-1 in 4 starts. Heathcliff Slocumb saved 9 games out of 10 chances. The offense went through one of its worst months of the season, but it didn't matter. The staff was hot. Hard to believe that the Sox of April would be winning games 3-1, 3-2, 4-1, 3-2, 2-0, 4-3, 2-1, 4-1, and 2-1 in August.

September 16-10 (85-77, 7 games back)
The Sox fought through series with contenders Chicago and Seattle and scratched out a .500 record for the first two weeks. Meanwhile, Baltimore was tearing up Detroit and Chicago to take the lead and then widen it. When Boston lost Naehring, Stanley, and Valentin, all within the space of a couple of weeks, they were doomed—but they didn't go quietly. Clemens struck out 20 in a 4-0 victory over the Tigers on the 18th, just before their big showdown in the Bronx with the division leaders. They came to Yankee Stadium for a 4-game series and gutted out a split—including a ninth-inning rally against the untouchable Yankee bullpen, sparked by 3 broken-bat singles off John Wetteland—to keep them alive into the final week.

When they were finally eliminated, it just left them some time for more clubhouse hi-jinks. Clemens debated skipping his last start so he wouldn't strain his arm and lower his market value. Greenwell cleared out his locker before the last game had been played and called a press conference to announce his departure on his terms—a respect Dwight Evans was never accorded. Valentin let the club know he didn't want to move to third for Nomar Garciaparra. Duquette let the deadline for renewing Kennedy's contract go by, even though the team had gone 78-58 after April.

■ 1997 DIAGNOSIS

Offense
It's no surprise that Fenway Park is a pitcher's nightmare—though it's been singles, doubles, and triples it's been generating lately, not dingers. Weird things have been happening to the home run counts at Fenway, ever since they raised the grandstand behind home plate to cram in some luxury seats. Some blame it on the wind patterns, others on the baseball gods. But Fenway's been doing weird things to the Red Sox for a long time. The case can be made that the biggest park effect is on double plays and GMs: double plays from right-handed power hitters trying to jerk every pitch onto the screen (fans in the mid-80s used to chant 6-4-3 at Jim Rice and Tony Armas every time they came to the plate with a runner on first); and GMs who continually overrate their hitters and underrate their pitchers (especially the lefties, Bob Ojeda and John Tudor the most notable examples). There is very serious talk of the Red Sox leaving Fenway, and the natives are not as outraged as you'd expect. Babe Ruth was a pitcher the last time they won it all, so maybe it is time to pave paradise and put up a parking lot.

Despite their off-season push to sign sluggers and run-producers—and considering their ballpark—the

Sox had a very average offense last year. Adjusted for park effects, they had the 8th-best offense in the league. Mo Vaughn doesn't show any signs of slowing down. But who can forecast what José Canseco will do when José himself has barely half a clue? After that, it depends entirely on what they do in the free-agent market, how their youngsters adjust to major-league pitching, and what veterans insist on an exit visa rather than having anything to do with reputed genius Dan Duquette. As the suits go, he's more cold, smug, and empty than most, and is about as popular with his ballplayers right now as an IRS man with questions about card show income.

Defense

The Sox had the worst defense in the league in '95 and had done nothing to correct the problem. It should get better in '97, simply because it cannot get any worse. Nomar Garciaparra should be outstanding at shortstop, and a full season with Darren Bragg in the outfield should give the fans less reason to cringe on pop flies. But the rest of the team, at the moment, is composed of hitters who own gloves and know, for the most part, where they're supposed to stand on the field.

Pitching

The starting rotation is a testament to the deception of averages. The team's ERA was 5.01, just above the league average of 4.99—but rarely at this level during the year. They were either very good or very bad, so stick one hand in ice, the other in boiling water, and you average out to be comfortable. They threw 17 complete games, which tied them with Kansas City for the 3rd-highest total, and pitched 1,003.1 innings, the 4th-highest. They'll most likely have to do it again without Roger Clemens, who must have figured out by now that the only way he's going to see the field at a World Series is to pull a Wade Boggs, swallow his pride, and don the pinstripes. Without him, it's hope for the best—and even that might not be enough. Tom Gordon should have a better season this year with some of the distractions that seemed to bother him removed. Tim Wakefield's success follows the flight of his knuckleball, which is equally unpredictable. Aaron Sele hasn't looked like a front-line starter since his rookie year in '93, but they haven't given up on him yet. Jeff Suppan will become an important part of the rotation this season. He may not tear up the league in his first full year, but he's an excellent pitcher. Carl Pavano and Brian Rose may also be there by September. Not exactly Eck, Torrez, Tiant, and Lee.

The bullpen was considered very deep going into the season and one of the team's strengths, provided they stayed healthy. Their ERA was 3rd-worst among the bullpens in the league. They walked more batters than only Oakland and Detroit. And it wasn't as if it was a group of wild pitchers with nasty stuff—they only struck out 385, 9th-best in the league. They couldn't get any consistency and injuries played a big part in that. They also couldn't find a reliable closer until Slocumb finally came around in the second half. They did acquire some youngsters along the way—Mark Brandenburg, Reggie Harris and Kerry Lacy—who look like they can help immediately. There are others from their own farm who look promising, so the bullpen should be more effective this season.

Farm System

Boston's farm system is generally considered one of the deepest in baseball. At the top, they have outstanding prospects in Suppan, Garciaparra, Pavano, and Donnie Sadler. There are a number of very good pitching prospects: Juan Peña, Josh Garrett, Rose, Chris Reitsma, Chuck Ricci, and Andy Yount. The majority of the position players who stand out at this point are older players who could contribute shortly. The organization has drafted outstanding athletes rather than focusing on accomplished baseball players—so there are a number of talented youngsters in their system with a lot to learn. The effectiveness of this strategy remains to be seen. Duquette's future with the team is riding on it.

Management and Ownership

Owner John Harrington appears to be preoccupied with the task of gearing up for his imminent stadium battle. Despite pleas from players, most notably Mo Vaughn, he did little to clean up the mess that was Boston's clubhouse last year. He left it to GM Dan Duquette, though most of it was his doing in the first place.

In terms of player acquisitions, Duquette made some solid moves last year but also made some dis-

astrous ones. As for handling internal personnel issues, his actions were almost cataclysmic. His team spun out of control and he was continually looking for somebody else to blame. He had to settle for Jimy Williams in the duguot, with Terry Francona rebuffing him to go to the Phillies. *The Phillies.* That speaks volumes.

. . . and whatnot: The Bean-Counter and the Jocks
The Red Sox went through one of the most tumultuous seasons in recent memory, characterized by inconsistent play on the field and constant back-biting behind the scenes. And GM Dan Duquette wasted no time letting his handpicked field manager take the fall for him. Duquette would have the fans believe that manager Kevin Kennedy was an ineffectual field leader who was unable to mold a collection of veterans and youngsters into a cohesive unit. And that he failed to keep the players in line, allowing them to publicly criticize upper management.

But Duquette had the table set for the club's failure before the season even started. In the off-season, his biggest acquisitions were Kevin Mitchell, Wil Cordero, and Heathcliff Slocumb. Mitchell was loaded up with incentives, but remained fat, lazy, and injured throughout his entire stay in Boston, and had to be unloaded in late July. Slocumb, with only one season as a closer under his belt, struggled early in the season, creating chaos in the bullpen. He played better in the second half, but he was never a solid replacement for Rick Aguilera, whom Duquette let slip back to the Twins—after giving up Frankie Rodriguez to rent him for a few months. Cordero was so inadequate a shortstop that the Expos were trying to turn into an outfielder, but Duquette gave him to Kennedy to try to work him into the mix in the infield at a new position—perhaps so Cordero could be both inadequate and inexperienced.

None of these acquisitions addressed the team's biggest problem in '95: abysmal defense. In fact, they made a bad situation worse. He continued to neglect that minor detail of a center fielder, and was actually operating under the assumption that either Mitchell, Jefferson, or Canseco—*if not two of them at once*—were viable options in the outfield. His plan was simply to score more runs than the defense could give up—which, as strategies go, is astonishingly stupid. It's no different than building a team by completely neglecting hitting or pitching. This was one of the most poorly constructed teams in recent baseball history, and that Duquette could deflect so much of the blame for the team's dismal early-season play is astounding. That he seemed personally offended that the team played like a hungover beer league team is reason enough to understand why at least half a dozen players wanted five minutes alone with him in the Fenway boiler room.

After playing a club-record 53 players in '95, Duquette brought 63 players into spring training for Kennedy to audition and sort out. Hampered by an unusual exhibition schedule, Kennedy was unable to bring the survivors together as a team. Duquette didn't think the roster was a problem. "We got off to a slow start because our team wasn't ready to start the season," he said. "At the end of the year, everybody should take a look at what he could have done better . . . that includes a lot of everybodys." The Sox used 55 everybodys in '96, and Duquette battled with Kennedy most of the season over how those players should be used. A former accountant—and once a bean-counter, always a bean-counter—he seems to treat players like entries in the debit and credit columns. He shuffles players in and out at will, attempts to make them play where he sees fit, gets annoyed when they struggle in unfamiliar roles, and sows the seeds of discontent in his ruthless contractual dealings with players and coaches. There is no continuity on this team, but plenty of uncertainty, insecurity, and ill will. Greenwell: "He's all about power. He wants to be the only voice."

Duquette angered players when he demoted Al Nipper, his 4th pitching coach in less than a year. He failed to secure longtime veterans Greenwell and Clemens immediately with new contracts. In the case of Greenwell, that may have been a wise decision, but he made it in a way that let his players know how little he values loyalty and commitment. But in the case of Clemens, it was just plain stupid. It led to a situation where veteran players were complaining about their contract status in the middle of a wild-card race rather than concentrating on the game.

It got so bad that one of the nicest guys in baseball, Mo Vaughn, was on him in the press after

Kennedy was fired. "They'll probably hire someone who's a dictator because that's what the GM wants," Mo said. "He wants someone who will run back and tell him everything. . . . I feel bad for all the professional people on that staff who have been let go." When Canseco says he wants out because Kennedy's been fired, you consider his twisted history and discount it. But Vaughn is as straight-up as any professional athlete you can find, so things with the Red Sox must really be bad for him to go off like this.

Stay tuned. Mo is nobody's fool. He knows that Duquette won't win in a showdown with him. Vaughn is the most popular athlete in Boston today, and no. 2 isn't even close. Duquette has painted himself into a corner. If he doesn't get Vaughn on his side, Mo can make his life in Boston miserable. If Duquette is fool enough to decide he wants a piece of him, Mo can make his life in Boston short. And if Vaughn ever does decide to leave, and he ends up with the team he rooted for as a kid—the hated Yankees—Duquette will have to enter the witness protection program.

The situation in Boston is out of control. Duquette has blamed the players and fired most of the coaching staff, so there aren't many more places left to point the finger. He's Steinbrenner without the cash or the three rings. Makes you wonder whether he's still harboring some bitterness over always being picked last for the team as a kid. Now he's grown up and all those jocks who beat him up are under his thumb.

Indeed, Dan-o, there are a lot of everybodys who can take some responsibility for this mess. And you're at the top of the list.

STAN BELINDA (see Free Agents)

RICH BETTI — SLEEPER

RP-SP • BR • TL • 5′11 • 170 • 23 • ATL93/26

	G	GS	IP	H	HR	BB	SO	W	L	S	ERA	K/BB	K9	HW9
AA	31	8	81	70	7	44	65	9	1	1	3.67	1.5	7.2	12.67

The Braves compared Betti to Mike Stanton, but apparently overcrowded with arms, could afford to release him in '94. The Sox picked him up and were amazed with his stuff. He's a lefty and throws a 90+ mph heater for strikes. He's working on a change-up. Betti was phenomenal in the lower levels and looked great after jumping to Double-A Trenton. A lot of teams could build an entire staff from Braves rejects. Betti could be a real find. ■

DARREN BRAGG — YOUNG GUN

OF • BL • TR • 5′9 • 180 • 27 • SEA91/22

	AB	R	H	2B	3B	HR	RBI	BB	SO	SB	CS	BA	OB	SA
SEA95	145	20	34	5	1	3	12	18	37	9	0	.234	.331	.345
SEA/BOS96	417	74	109	26	2	10	47	69	74	14	9	.261	.366	.405

Bragg showed an improved attitude going into spring training in '96 and hit .433 with 2 homers in exhibition play. The Mariners bounced him between Triple-A and the majors early in the season until he settled down and earned a job platooning in left with Rich Amaral. Bragg proved more than competent as a leadoff man. He showed fine plate discipline, good speed, and decent power. The Red Sox traded Jamie Moyer for him in late July, and Kennedy fell in love with him. He was everything Duquette hadn't given him to work with at the beginning of the year. ■

MARK BRANDENBURG

RF • BR • TR • 6′0 • 170 • 26 • TEX92/26

	G	GS	IP	H	HR	BB	K	W	L	S	ERA	K/BB	K9	HW9
TEX95	11	0	27	36	5	7	21	0	1	0	5.93	3.0	7.0	14.33
TEX/BOS96	55	0	75	76	8	33	66	5	5	0	3.48	2.0	7.9	13.06

Hoping to get some immediate impact out of the trade that sent Mike Stanton to Texas, the Red Sox tried Brandenburg at closer in August. In his debut, he gave up back-to-back homers to Milwaukee. He settled down in spot relief appearances for the club. He has a good strikeout rate and had one of the lowest ERAs in the bullpen. He probably won't get another shot at the closer role, but the Sox picked up a good right-hander. ■

JOSÉ CANSECO

DH-OF • BR • TR • 6′3 • 240 • 32 • OAK82/14

	AB	R	H	2B	3B	HR	RBI	BB	SO	SB	CS	BA	OB	SA
TEX94	429	88	121	19	2	31	90	69	114	15	8	.282	.386	.552
BOS95	396	64	121	25	1	24	81	42	93	4	0	.306	.378	.556
BOS96	360	68	104	22	1	28	82	63	82	3	1	.289	.400	.589
CAREER	5071	864	1379	251	13	328	1033	623	1349	156	68	.272	.355	.521

When Canseco was in the lineup batting after Mo Vaughn, he caused some serious problems for

opposing managers. In one series against Seattle, Piniella intentionally walked Vaughn to load the bases. Canseco didn't take this lightly and cranked a grand slam. Two days later, with runners on second and third, Piniella pitched to Vaughn, who belted one into the upper deck. Choose your poison.

Canseco fought a painful back injury all year, a ruptured disc above a herniated one. For the most part, he could be used at designated hitter, but standing in the outfield caused his back to tighten up and ache—not to mention what it did to his manager's stomach lining. He eventually had surgery in late July and was thought to be done for the year. He made it back in September but didn't contribute much.

Canseco was a terror when he was healthy, though. He hit 23 homers in his first 223 at-bats, which is a Mark McGwire-like pace, and ended up with the best slugging percentage of his career. After the firing of Kevin Kennedy at the end of the season, Canseco demanded a trade. "The only reason I came to the Boston Red Sox was because of Kevin Kennedy," Canseco said. "I wouldn't play for anyone else." Apparently no one has handled him as a relief pitcher as effectively. His days in Beantown may be over and the fans can go back to hurling obscenities at him and chanting "Ster-roids!" ▪

ROGER CLEMENS (see Free Agents)

ALEX COLE

OF • BL • TL • 6′2 • 170 • 31 • SL85/2

	AB	R	H	2B	3B	HR	RBI	BB	SO	SB	CS	BA	OB	SA
MIN94	345	68	102	15	5	4	23	44	60	29	8	.296	.375	.403
MIN95	79	10	27	3	2	1	14	8	15	1	3	.342	.409	.468
BOS96	72	13	16	5	1	0	7	8	11	5	3	.222	.296	.319
CAREER	1760	286	493	58	26	5	117	217	296	148	59	.280	.284	.351

Cole had one good season and one broken leg in Minnesota before the Red Sox signed him in '96. When he was called up to take Dwayne Hosey's spot on the roster in May, he changed his goggles to spectacles because Boston has so many colleges. "I wanted to look more intelligent." ▪

MICHAEL COLEMAN

OF • BR • TR • 5′11 • 210 • 21 • BOS94/18

	AB	R	H	2B	3B	HR	RBI	BB	SO	SB	CS	BA	OB	SA
A+	407	54	100	20	5	1	36	38	86	24	5	.246	.320	.327

Coleman is considered the top athlete in Boston's system, but he's raw. He was Tennessee's Mr. Football in '94. He has excellent range in center and speed on the basepaths. He has little power at this point, though, and needs time to develop his hitting. It used to be that the Red Sox didn't have a single player like this in their entire system. Now they're tripping over them. ▪

WIL CORDERO

SLEEPER

2B • BR • TR • 6′2 • 185 • 25 • MON88

	AB	R	H	2B	3B	HR	RBI	BB	SO	SB	CS	BA	OB	SA
MON94	415	65	122	30	3	15	63	41	62	16	3	.294	.363	.489
MON95	514	64	147	35	2	10	49	36	88	9	5	.286	.341	.420
BOS96	198	29	57	14	0	3	37	11	31	2	1	.288	.330	.404
CAREER	1728	231	482	115	8	40	215	131	272	39	12	.279	.337	.424

The Expos soured on Cordero in '95, feeling he'd gotten sloppy defensively at short, so they shifted him to left field. In the off-season they shipped him off to Boston to let them pay him the big arbitration money. The Red Sox figured he was good enough to play second. He didn't do the club any favors during their slow start, especially in the field, but started to get it going in May, when he hit .345 with 14 RBI. But late in the month he suffered a fractured tibia when Oakland's George Williams took him out with a hard slide with Boston up 16-4 in the ninth inning. Cordero returned August 12, but he continued to experience pain in his leg. His replacement, Jeff Frye, was playing well, anyway, and Kennedy didn't want to push his recovery. So he used him sparingly at DH for the remainder of the season. His brief and rocky career isn't over, but the injury opened the door for Frye to step in, and Cordero will have to beat him out to get the job back. Hard to believe that a man who hit nearly .300 and hit 15 dingers in two-thirds of a season at age 22 would have to duke it out with a 30-year-old journeyman, but the Red Sox seem to bring that out in players. ▪

MILT CUYLER (see Looking for a Game)

BO DODSON

1B • BL • TL • 6'2 • 195 • 26

	AB	R	H	2B	3B	HR	RBI	BB	SO	SB	CS	BA	OB	SA
AAA	276	37	95	20	0	11	43	32	50	4	0	.344	.410	.536

Dodson spent several years in the Brewers' system. He's been inconsistent with the bat, although he's impressive when he gets it going, and he has a big-time ballplayer's name. Last season was his best ever and the Sox protected him on their 40-man roster after the season. ■

VAUGHN ESHELMAN

RP-SP • BL • TL • 6'3 • 205 • 27 • BAL91/4

	G	GS	IP	H	HR	BB	K	W	L	S	ERA	K/BB	K9	HW9
BOS95	23	14	81	86	3	36	41	6	3	0	4.85	1.1	4.6	13.56
BOS96	39	10	87	112	13	58	59	6	3	0	7.08	1.0	6.1	17.57

Eshelman was called up to replace Stan Belinda in May. In his first outing, he faced 9 batters, gave up 2 homers, a double, 2 singles, 2 walks, and left the game with an 81.00 ERA. They sent him down briefly, but he came back and pitched much better in the second half. Eshelman's been a starter his entire career, but the Sox have used his left-handed slop in relief extensively the past couple of years. His minor-league numbers suggest he could be a decent, though not overpowering, starter in the major leagues—probably a no. 4 or 5, though his product line fares much better anywhere but Fenway. But with a fastball that couldn't break glass, he should be grateful for any kind of work he can get. ■

JEFF FRYE

2B • BR • TR • 5'9 • 180 • 30 • TEX88/30

	AB	R	H	2B	3B	HR	RBI	BB	SO	SB	CS	BA	OB	SA
TEX94	205	37	67	20	3	0	18	29	23	6	1	.327	.408	.454
TEX95	313	38	87	15	2	4	29	24	45	3	3	.278	.335	.377
BOS96	419	74	120	27	2	4	41	54	57	18	4	.286	.372	.389
CAREER	1136	173	325	71	8	9	100	123	152	28	11	.286	.360	.386

The Red Sox signed Frye in June, hoping to fill holes at second base and in the leadoff spot. Wil Cordero had broken his leg and, at that time, looked to be out for the season. Frye stepped in and had his best

year at the plate, setting career highs for batting average, runs, stolen bases, and RBI. He had some problems in the field, but played well enough to hold off Cordero when he returned in August—but then Jerry Remy would have been able to do that. Frye has a decent chance at holding on to the job this year. Even though Cordero is five years younger, it could be Arquimedez Pozo who poses a bigger threat. ■

RICH GARCES

RP • BR • TR • 6'0 • 215 • 25 • MIN87

	G	GS	IP	H	HR	BB	K	W	L	S	ERA	K/BB	K9	HW9
CHN/FLA95	18	0	24	25	1	11	22	0	2	0	4.44	2.0	8.3	13.50
BOS96	37	0	44	42	5	33	55	3	2	0	4.91	1.7	11.3	15.34
CAREER	63	0	78	75	6	50	81	3	4	2	4.27	1.6	9.3	14.42

Garces is awfully young to be in his 4th organization already. His control has never been good, and occasionally stomach-turning, but the Red Sox were really impressed with his performance in winter ball in '95 and kept him with the club to start the season. He's got strikeout stuff, but Wakefield's got a better idea of where his pitches are going. ■

NOMAR GARCIAPARRA — SOLID PROSPECT

SS • BR • TR • 6'1 • 175 • 23 • BOS94/1

	AB	R	H	2B	3B	HR	RBI	BB	SO	SB	CS	BA	OB	SA
BOS96	87	11	21	2	3	4	16	4	14	5	0	.241	.272	.471

The list of outstanding young shortstops keeps getting longer. The Red Sox introduced their fans to Garciaparra, their shortstop of the future, at the end of August. At the beginning of the year, it didn't look like that would happen. He tore up his left knee early on at Triple-A Pawtucket and was thought to be gone for the season. He returned by late June and hit the first pitch he faced for a homer. He went on to an outstanding year at Pawtucket and was named the top prospect in the International League. He's an outstanding defensive shortstop with an excellent work ethic and is also a very good hitter with line-drive power. He doesn't sting the ball

quite like Alex Rodriguez, but how many shortstops do? Now that he's arrived in Boston, there will be changes in the infield. He's there to stay. ■

JOSH GARRETT

SP-RP • BOS96/1 • SOUTH SPENCER H.S. (IN)

	G	GS	IP	H	HR	BB	SO	W	L	S	ERA	K/BB	K9	HW9
R	7	5	27	22	0	5	17	1	1	0	1.67	3.4	5.7	9.00

The Red Sox took Garrett with the 26th overall pick in '96. He's a Mets fan who remembers celebrating wildly when Bill Buckner let the ball go through his legs in '86. At 6'4", Garrett was an all-state basketball player in Indiana and his class valedictorian. His coaches love his work ethic and his poise. He has a lively fastball that has been clocked at 90-92 mph, and he has excellent control. He was the top pitching prospect in the Gulf Coast League last year. He started the season late and didn't get many appearances, but the Sox were impressed with what they saw. ■

TOM GORDON

SP • BR • TR • 5'9 • 160 • 29 • KC86/6

	G	GS	IP	H	HR	BB	K	W	L	S	ERA	K/BB	K9	HW9
KC94	24	24	155	136	15	87	126	11	7	0	4.35	1.4	7.3	12.95
KC95	31	31	189	204	12	89	119	12	12	0	4.43	1.3	5.7	13.95
BOS96	34	34	215	249	28	105	171	12	9	0	5.59	1.6	7.2	14.81
CAREER	308	178	1364	1289	119	692	1170	91	80	3	4.27	1.7	7.7	13.07

He's not doing much to dispel the conventional wisdom about short pitchers. It was feast or famine last year for Gordon. He was streaky and pitched very effectively for stretches when his knee-buckling bender was on. When he couldn't throw it for strikes, he was dog food. During their disastrous April, Gordon went 1-2 with a 9.67 ERA and gave up more than 20 baserunners per 9 innings. On the 24th, against Texas, he lasted 1.1 innings and surrendered 8 hits and 6 runs. In May he was 4-0 with a 3.60 ERA. On the 30th, in Seattle, he threw a complete-game 2-hitter for a 10-1 victory. All or nothing all year.

For the season, Gordon had the best winning percentage on the rotation and recorded double-digit victories for the 4th straight year. But he gave Kevin Kennedy headaches, always unhappy when the manager pulled him, even when he was getting crushed. He complained that players were whispering behind his back about his pitching and felt that Kennedy always had the bullpen warming up when he pitched. He was probably right. Paranoia, after all, is just having all the facts. ■

MIKE GREENWELL (see Free Agents)

GREG HANSELL

RP • BR • TR • 6'5 • 215 • 26 • BOS89/10

	G	GS	IP	H	HR	BB	K	W	L	S	ERA	K/BB	K9	HW9
LA95	20	0	19	29	5	6	13	0	1	0	7.45	2.2	6.2	16.58
MIN96	50	0	74	83	14	31	46	3	0	3	5.69	1.5	5.6	13.86

Hansell is back in Boston, after being traded to the Mets for Mike Marshall (recently voted Best in Show at the Westchester Kennel Club's annual competition). The Dodgers gave up Hansell to rent Kevin Tapani for the second half of '95. Hansell struggled as a starter in L.A. until they moved him to the bullpen in '94. The move, and some personal coaching from Luis Tiant in Minnesota, improved his game dramatically. But not enough to keep him off waivers, and the Red Sox claimed him in October. He's still got a way to go, but a decent staff could be formed with Dodger castoffs: Mike James, Jim Poole, Juan Guzman, Sid Fernandez, Darren Holmes, Mike Muñoz, Tim Scott, John Franco, Jeff Nelson, and some guy named John Wetteland, who struggled as a starter. ■

REGGIE HARRIS

RP • BR • TR • 6'1 • 190 • 28

	G	GS	IP	H	HR	BB	SO	W	L	S	ERA	K/BB	K9	HW9
AA	33	0	37	17	2	19	43	2	1	17	1.46	2.3	10.5	8.76

Harris made the switch to the bullpen in '95 after 8 years in the minors. He reached the majors briefly in '90 and '91 for Oakland, but he wasn't going to make it as a starter. In his debut as a closer for the Sox last year—a role just about everyone got a chance at in '96 except Tom Burgmeier—he was overpowering. He crashed hard soon after, and was sent down to Double-A to try to grow into the role. ■

BILL HASELMAN

SLEEPER

C • BR • TR • 6′3 • 205 • 30 • TEX87/2

	AB	R	H	2B	3B	HR	RBI	BB	SO	SB	CS	BA	OB	SA
BOS95	152	22	37	6	1	5	23	17	30	0	2	.243	.322	.395
BOS96	237	33	65	13	1	8	34	19	52	4	2	.274	.331	.439
CAREER	641	88	160	34	3	19	84	52	124	7	5	.250	.309	.401

Haselman spent most of the year as Boston's no. 2 behind Mike Stanley. He actually hit a bit better than Stanley, though not with the same power. When he played more regularly at the end of the season, he hit .306 with 5 homers and 20 RBI in his last 85 at-bats. His 237 at-bats last year were by far his highest total ever, so it's difficult to say whether he could sustain that kind of pace over a full year. A guy named Mike Stanley was in the same situation for 6 years before he finally got a chance to play everyday at the age of 30. Maybe lightning strikes twice. ▪

JOE HUDSON

RP • BR • TR • 6′1 • 175 • 26 • BOS92/26

	G	GS	IP	H	HR	BB	K	W	L	S	ERA	K/BB	K9	HW9
BOS95	39	0	46	53	2	23	29	0	1	1	4.11	1.3	5.7	14.87
BOS96	36	0	45	57	4	32	19	3	5	1	5.40	.6	3.8	17.80

You don't need to go very far inside the numbers—nor would you want to—to realize that Hudson's stuff was so lame in '96 that he was afraid to throw a strike. And when, as a random event, he did screw up and throw a pitch over the plate, it was warmly received. Nothing he has done as a pro suggests that this is as much of an aberration as his friends, family, and agent might want to believe. ▪

ADAM HYZDU

SLEEPER

OF • BR • TR • 6′2 • 210 • 25 • SF90/1

	AB	R	H	2B	3B	HR	RBI	BB	SO	SB	CS	BA	OB	SA
AA	374	71	126	24	3	25	80	56	75	1	8	.337	.424	.618

What Hyzdu did in Double-A Trenton's cavernous ballpark last year was truly amazing. He didn't even sign with the Sox until a month into the season and still hit 24 homers in a park that eats up sluggers. He led the team in virtually every offensive category. He was the Giants' no. 1 pick in 1990, but he never hit for average or great power in their organization. Last year was a breakout season for him, and that's the only reason he isn't rated a solid prospect as yet. If he can repeat these numbers in '97, he'll be in the majors by the end of the season. ▪

REGGIE JEFFERSON

DH-OF • BL • TL • 6′4 • 215 • 28 • CIN86/3

	AB	R	H	2B	3B	HR	RBI	BB	SO	SB	CS	BA	OB	SA
SEA94	162	24	53	11	0	8	32	17	32	0	0	.327	.392	.543
BOS95	121	21	35	8	0	5	26	9	24	0	0	.289	.333	.479
BOS96	386	67	134	30	4	19	74	25	89	0	0	.347	.388	.593
CAREER	1232	166	364	69	8	46	185	84	264	1	3	.295	.343	.476

I guess the moral of this story is to never, ever give up on big, left-handed sluggers named Reggie. The Red Sox used Jefferson at first, DH, and in left last year; basically anywhere they could fit his bat into the lineup. The injuries to Canseco and Mitchell left him with plenty of opportunities, and he didn't waste them. In April he hit .432 and went on to finish the first half with a .376 average and .653 slugging percentage. He set career-highs in every category. He did a lot of his damage against the Hapless (suburb of Detroit) Tigers. In 10 games and 36 at-bats, he hit .500 with 6 home runs, 16 RBIs, and a 1.194 slugging percentage! 1.194! They call him the Tiger-killer in Detroit, and he'd be well advised not to leave his hotel after dark. Of course, that goes for just about anybody. Mitchell's gone and Canseco's on his way, so Jefferson is looking at 500 at-bats in '97 for the first time in his career. ▪

KERRY LACY

RP • BR • TR • 6′2 • 195 • 24 • TEX91/15

	G	GS	IP	H	HR	BB	SO	W	L	S	ERA	K/BB	K9	HW9
AAA	44	0	64	49	2	17	39	3	3	10	2.53	2.3	5.5	9.28

Lacy came over in the Stanton trade with Texas last year. He was overpowering at Triple-A and got his first taste of the majors in mid-August when Aaron Sele went on the disabled list. He blew a couple of saves for the Sox, but that probably just helped him fit in with the rest of the guys. He looks more promising than his brief stint in Boston indicates. ▪

MIKE MADDUX

RP-SP • BL • TR • 6′2 • 180 • 35 • PHI82/5

	G	GS	IP	H	HR	BB	K	W	L	S	ERA	K/BB	K9	HW9
NYN94	27	0	44	45	7	13	32	2	1	2	5.11	2.5	6.5	11.86
PIT/BOS95	44	4	98	100	5	18	69	5	1	1	4.10	3.8	6.3	10.84
BOS96	23	7	64	76	12	27	32	3	2	0	4.48	1.2	4.5	14.48
CAREER	341	48	708	709	51	227	462	32	30	19	3.93	2.0	5.9	11.90

After a rough start in April, Maddux suffered an elbow injury in May and didn't return until August. On the way to his first start after rejoining the team, he and Tim Wakefield were slightly injured when a car ran a red light and smashed into Wakefield's Blazer. Maddux had to be scratched. Two days later he took the mound and got his first victory of the season. Asked if he took any precautions getting to the game, Maddux replied, "I rented a tank." He pitched well for the remainder of the season, as did Wakefield—which could have given Kennedy yet another reason for running down Aaron Sele outside Fenway. ■

PAT MAHOMES

RP-SP • BR • TR • 6′1 • 175 • 26 • MIN88/6

	G	GS	IP	H	HR	BB	K	W	L	S	ERA	K/BB	K9	HW9
MIN94	21	21	120	121	22	62	53	9	5	0	4.73	.9	4.0	13.73
MIN95	47	7	94	100	22	47	67	4	10	3	6.37	1.4	6.4	14.07
MIN/BOS96	31	5	57	72	13	33	36	3	4	2	6.94	1.1	5.7	16.57
CAREER	125	51	378	413	70	195	223	20	28	5	5.83	1.1	5.3	14.47

The Red Sox acquired Mahomes from the Twins in August. He was one of their finer prospects from '90 to '93 and turned in a fine year for the Twins as a starter in '94. But after a disappointing '95, he was moved to the bullpen. He couldn't have given up more dingers if he'd let the hitters set the ball up on a tee. Mahomes has a lot of potential—but, you know, that's one of those things you lose if you use it. A DWI was featured in 1994, a demotion for oversleeping in 1995. He has a decent fastball, a good change-up, and the requisite breaking pitches—and no clue how lucky he is to get the opportunities he's been throwing away. His last chance may be in 1997. ■

JOSÉ MALAVE

OF • BR • TR • 6′2 • 195 • 25 • BOS89

	AB	R	H	2B	3B	HR	RBI	BB	SO	SB	CS	BA	OB	SA
BOS96	102	12	24	3	0	4	17	2	25	0	0	.235	.257	.382

Malave has been slipping downward since leading the Eastern League in slugging in '94. In a couple of years in Pawtucket, he hasn't made the adjustment to Triple-A pitching. He was bothered early in the season by a nerve irritation between his toes, and that may have affected his production. His toes? Somewhere, Ken Caminiti would laugh—if it didn't hurt so much just to breathe. Malave's once-prodigious power has diminished. There are jobs to be had in Boston if he can get it back on the rails. ■

WALT MCKEEL

C • BR • TR • 6′0 • 200 • 25 • BOS90/2

	AB	R	H	2B	3B	HR	RBI	BB	SO	SB	CS	BA	OB	SA
AA	464	86	140	19	1	16	78	60	52	2	4	.302	.385	.450

McKeel seemed baffled by his September call-up—"It boggled my mind"—even though he was an Eastern League All-Star last year and hit 16 homers in a park that doesn't yield many. He's an aggressive catcher with excellent power and has improved his average a great deal over his career. After last year's experience, he could be in the majors for good in a short time. ■

ROBERTO MEJIA

2B • BR • TR • 5′11 • 165 • 24 • LA88

	AB	R	H	2B	3B	HR	RBI	BB	SO	SB	CS	BA	OB	SA
AAA	448	64	128	28	9	13	62	34	97	17	6	.286	.475	.475

The Red Sox acquired Mejia at the end of July in a trade with the Reds for Kevin Mitchell. He hit for a good average in the Rockies' organization with occasional flashes of power. They brought him up for extended periods over 3 years, but he never got it going at the plate in Denver—which gives him and Jason Bates something to talk about, but no one else is joining that particular group therapy session. The second-base situation in Boston's system is getting crowded. If they move Sadler to second, it gets even more so. So the chances are the Red Sox took Mejia in exchange for Mitchell because league

rules forbid the outright donation of players to another team. ■

TIM NAEHRING

3B • BR • TR • 6'2 • 205 • 30 • BOS88/8

	AB	R	H	2B	3B	HR	RBI	BB	SO	SB	CS	BA	OB	SA
BOS94	297	41	82	18	1	7	42	30	56	1	3	.276	.349	.414
BOS95	433	61	133	27	2	10	57	77	66	0	2	.307	.415	.448
BOS96	430	77	124	16	0	17	65	49	63	2	1	.288	.363	.444
CAREER	1613	216	453	86	3	40	210	198	272	4	6	.281	.363	.412

The Red Sox really felt that Naehring should have been on the All-Star team last year. A hamstring injury slowed him in April, but he played extremely well through the rest of the first half. At the break, he was hitting .324 with 42 RBI and had played excellent defense all season. Perhaps his biggest moment came in June. In a town like Boston, history is very important—after all, it's a town of masochists. The Red Sox have never been swept by any team in a single season, but Cleveland had beaten them in their first 11 games. In their last meeting, Tim singled in the tying run in the 9th to send it into extra innings and then homered in the 15th to win it.

He went on to endure an epic slump through July and August. He suffered from a sore shoulder and knee, but refused to blame his troubles on the injuries that eventually shut him down in September. He turned in his second straight year of solid play at third. He was a service time free agent, and the Red Sox would like to move Valentin to third to make room for Garciaparra, so Naehring may be on his way out. ■

TROT NIXON

SLEEPER

OF • BL • TL • 6'2 • 195 • 22 • BOS93/1

	AB	R	H	2B	3B	HR	RBI	BB	SO	SB	CS	BA	OB	SA
AA	438	55	110	11	4	11	63	50	65	7	9	.251	.329	.370

The Red Sox feel Nixon is an outstanding hitter with incredible intensity. He's been hampered by back trouble and hasn't been able to cut loose. He has good speed and can run the bases. Defensively he has a strong arm, and the Sox think he'll make an excellent right fielder. They called him up from Double-A in mid-September just to give him a look. If he can stay healthy, they figure he'll be a major part of their outfield in a short time. If not, it could be Ellis Burks all over again. ■

TROY O'LEARY

OF • BL • TL • 6'0 • 175 • 27 • MIL87/14

	AB	R	H	2B	3B	HR	RBI	BB	SO	SB	CS	BA	OB	SA
MIL94	66	9	18	1	1	2	7	5	12	1	1	.273	.329	.409
BOS95	399	60	123	31	6	10	49	29	64	5	3	.308	.355	.491
BOS96	497	68	129	28	5	15	81	47	80	3	2	.260	.327	.427
CAREER	1003	140	282	63	12	27	140	86	165	9	6	.281	.340	.449

O'Leary followed up his strong '95 season with an inconsistent but, at times, impressive '96. He started off hot in April, hitting 4 dingers and knocking in 12 runs in limited play. He hit for a lower average in May but still managed 20 RBI on 21 hits. He disappeared in June and July, but many contending teams were after him as the trading deadline neared. He was one of the more extreme hitters in baseball—below .200 against lefties; in the .270s against righties; .300 at home; in the 2-teens on the road; in the low .200s with the bases empty; and well over .300 with men on base. Take your best guess on which O'Leary will show up next year—the one who hit .318 in August with 7 dingers and 26 RBI, or the one who hit .186 in September. ■

RAFAEL ORELLANO

SP • BL • TL • 6'2 • 160 • 23 • BOS92

	G	GS	IP	H	HR	BB	SO	W	L	S	ERA	K/BB	K9	HW9
AAA	22	20	99	124	20	62	66	4	11	0	7.88	1.1	6.0	16.89

Orellano was the Red Sox organization's Pitcher of the Year in '95 and is considered their top left-handed prospect. He led the Eastern League in strikeouts and innings a couple of years ago. Then how do you explain the shelling he endured last year in Triple-A? If you have any idea, let the Sox know, because they're stumped. He threw well in spring training, but once the season started, his strikeout rate plummeted and he just got clocked. He went 0-5 with a 16.47 ERA in his first 6 starts. The club sent him down to Single-A, and he seemed to work things out.

Orellano throws hard and has a good change-up, which is more of a fosh. It works well against right-handers, tailing down and away from them. He also has a mediocre curveball, which the organization wants him to improve to use against left-handed hitters. Anything could happen in '97—a return to form, or a Steve Blass-like exit from professional baseball. ■

CARL PAVANO — GRADE-A PROSPECT

SP • BR • TR • 6'5 • 225 • 21 • BOS94/12

	G	GS	IP	H	HR	BB	SO	W	L	S	ERA	K/BB	K9	HW9
AA	27	26	185	154	16	47	146	16	5	0	2.63	3.1	7.1	9.78

Together with Brian Rose, Pavano was part of a great 1-2 punch for Trenton last year in the Double-A Eastern League. He has a sinking fastball that is generally 88–92 mph and sometimes reaches 94. He also has a good slider and change-up and has good control with all three. The club has him working on a curveball. Pavano's coaches loved his attitude and his workhorse mentality. He pitched 185 innings last year despite missing a couple of weeks with shoulder tendinitis. When he returned in June, he allowed 2 runs in his first 16 innings back. During another stretch, he pitched 25 consecutive scoreless innings. Any concern about him tiring out in September? He went 7-0 with a 0.83 ERA in his final 10 starts. ■

RUDY PEMBERTON — SLEEPER

OF • BR • TR • 6'1 • 185 • 27 • DET87

	AB	R	H	2B	3B	HR	RBI	BB	SO	SB	CS	BA	OB	SA
BOS96	41	11	21	8	0	1	10	2	4	3	1	.512	.556	.780

Pemberton is one of several players who rotted for years in Detroit's system and didn't truly blossom until they left. He earned a call-up in September and saw 12 games in right field. Check the numbers—that's called making your chances count. Last time the Red Sox got that kind of production from a September call-up it was Ted Cox—and they promptly parlayed that into an ace, dealing him to the Indians for Dennis Eckersley. Eck is going to the Hall of Fame; Cox went on to hit 9 home runs in 4 years. ■

JUAN PEÑA — SOLID PROSPECT

SP • BR • TR • 6'5 • 210 • 19 • BOS95/27

	G	GS	IP	H	HR	BB	SO	W	L	S	ERA	K/BB	K9	HW9
A	26	26	188	149	16	34	156	12	10	0	2.97	4.6	7.5	8.78

Peña started the year going 8-4 with a 2.51 ERA in his first 12 decisions on his way to the Midwest League All-Star game. He didn't let up much in the other half either. Peña has outstanding control for such a youngster and an excellent strikeout rate. And he was virtually unhittable, as he was in '95. If he can do it again in the Eastern League this year, you'll be hearing a lot about him. ■

ARQUIMEDEZ POZO — SLEEPER

2B-3B • BR • TR • 5'10 • 160 • 23 • SEA90

	AB	R	H	2B	3B	HR	RBI	BB	SO	SB	CS	BA	OB	SA
BOS96	58	4	10	3	1	1	11	2	10	1	0	.172	.210	.310

Boston picked up Pozo in July in a trade with Seattle for Jeff Manto, which shows how far Pozo's stock has fallen. A couple of years ago, he was touted as one of the top infield prospects in all of baseball after hitting .300 wih 10 dingers in Triple-A. He's still an excellent prospect, but the Mariners don't think they need him—despite a mediocre Joey Cora in the majors and not much on the farm. Pozo is a natural second baseman, but he worked extensively at third in the Mariners' system. The Red Sox used him as a backup at both. He didn't get many at-bats in Boston and didn't do much with them, but his numbers at Tacoma were pretty good. He's always been a very good hitter with fine power for a middle infielder, and has excellent ability in the field. The Red Sox got away with larceny on this one. ■

CHRIS REITSMA

SP • BOS96/1 • CHRISTIAN HIGH SCHOOL (CANADA)

	G	GS	IP	H	HR	BB	SO	W	L	S	ERA	K/BB	K9	HW9
R	7	6	27	24	0	1	32	3	1	0	1.35	32.0	10.8	8.44

Reitsma was taken with the supplemental first round pick the Red Sox received for losing Erik Hanson to free agency. Reitsma is often compared to teammate Josh Garrett. In fact, he was the second-best prospect in the Gulf Coast League, behind Garrett. His fastball has a lot of movement, and he throws it in the low 90s. He also has a good curve. Check his K/BB ratio—reason enough to remember the name. ■

CHUCK RICCI

SLEEPER

RP • BR • TR • 6'2 • 180 • 28 • BAL87/4

	G	GS	IP	H	HR	BB	SO	W	L	S	ERA	K/BB	K9	HW9
AAA	60	0	80	56	12	32	79	8	4	13	3.01	2.5	8.9	9.88

Ricci was a welcome addition to Pawtucket's bullpen last season. Previously, he was a starter on Baltimore's farm and made it to the majors briefly for the Phillies in '95. He wasn't going to make it as a starter, but he's been unhittable as a closer for the past couple of years. He is a sinker-slider type who relies heavily on location. He misses now and again and give up a few walks, but nobody hits him. Sounds like what Greg McMichael used to be. ■

BRIAN ROSE

GRADE-A PROSPECT

SP • BR • TR • 6'2 • 190 • 21 • BOS94/3

	G	GS	IP	H	HR	BB	SO	W	L	S	ERA	K/BB	K9	HW9
AA	27	27	163	157	21	45	115	12	7	0	4.01	2.6	6.3	11.14

According to one scout, Rose and Pavano were the best pitchers in the Eastern League. They are both fine prospects, and Eastern League managers felt Rose had the best control in the league. Rose throws 89–92 mph with good movement, and the Sox expect him to throw 95 when he finally matures physically. He has a decent curveball and is developing a change-up and slider. All three still need work. The club thinks all he needs are innings. ■

DONNIE SADLER

SOLID PROSPECT

SS • BR • TR • 5'7 • 160 • 21 • BOS94/10

	AB	R	H	2B	3B	HR	RBI	BB	SO	SB	CS	BA	OB	SA
AA	454	68	121	20	8	6	46	38	75	34	8	.267	.329	.385

The Red Sox claim that Sadler is the fastest man ever to play for their organization—which is not saying much, quite frankly, when in the past 20 years your team's been led in stolen bases by Jeff Frye, John Valentin, a Medicare-eligible Otis Nixon, Scott Fletcher, Jody Reed (with 7), Mike Greenwell, Ellis Burks, Marty Barrett, Bill Buckner (yup, Bill Buckner), Jackie Gutierrez, Jerry Remy, Carney Lansford (yup, Carney Lansford), Rick Burleson, Fred Lynn, and Jim Rice (yup, 6-4-3 Rice). Sadler is a sure bet to lead off for them someday. They say he's another Lofton. At this point, *James* Lofton would be an improvement.

Sadler had a tremendous season in '95, and the Sox were so impressed they jumped him from the Midwest League to the Eastern League. At the same time, Duquette decided he wanted him to try center field, since Tony Armas wasn't taking his calls. Sadler couldn't cope with both adjustments at the same time, and his hitting suffered greatly. He didn't like the outfield anyway, and the experiment ended in June.

Under normal conditions, he looks like he could be a very good hitter with moderate power. Defensively, he has excellent range and a strong arm. Now the Sox seem intent on moving Sadler to second this year, in an attempt to get him and Garciaparra in the same infield. That seems a more reasonable move to make than to the outfield—and it looks good on paper. But it could also result in a repeat of last season's Cordero disaster. ■

AARON SELE

SP • BR • TR • 6'5 • 205 • 26 • BOS91/1

	G	GS	IP	H	HR	BB	K	W	L	S	ERA	K/BB	K9	HW9
BOS94	22	22	143	140	13	60	105	8	7	0	3.83	1.8	6.6	12.58
BOS95	6	6	32	32	3	14	21	3	1	0	3.06	1.5	5.9	12.94
BOS96	29	29	157	192	14	67	137	7	11	0	5.32	2.0	7.9	14.84
CAREER	75	75	444	464	35	189	356	25	21	0	4.03	1.9	7.2	13.23

The past couple of seasons have been very disappointing after Sele's brilliant debut in '93. On the other hand, after missing most of '95, last season wasn't a bad comeback. Sele came into the spring in the best shape of his life, but struggled with his control throughout the first half. At the break he was 3-5 with a 5.99 ERA, and people were beginning to question his mental toughness. Clemens said Sele was at the point of his career where he had to decide if he wanted to be a no. 2 man or just another pitcher. He turned it around in the second half, despite a rib-cage injury that sidelined him in August, which suggests that Clemens's lasting gift to this team might have been getting through to a talented underachiever. ■

HEATHCLIFF SLOCUMB

CL • BR • TR • 6'3 • 210 • 30 • NYN84

	G	GS	IP	H	HR	BB	K	W	L	S	ERA	K/BB	K9	HW9
PHI94	52	0	72	75	0	28	58	5	1	0	2.86	2.1	7.2	12.87
PHI95	61	0	65	64	2	35	63	5	6	32	2.89	1.8	8.7	13.71
BOS96	75	0	83	68	2	55	88	5	5	31	3.02	1.6	9.5	13.33
CAREER	300	0	357	347	13	189	292	21	17	65	3.50	1.5	7.4	13.51

Slocumb is one of the good guys in the league, but that didn't earn him any favors when he struggled

early. He blew 3 saves in his first 10 chances with 12 walks in 23.1 innings. Kennedy replaced him as closer with Mike Stanton in May. Slocumb pitched much better in the second half and returned to closing. After the break, he saved 20 of 23 chances with a 2.68 ERA. He control was still a problem, though. The Red Sox didn't get what they were looking for out of the Slocumb/Ken Ryan deal—but then Slocumb had been a one-year wonder coming into '96. Boston has a few closer prospects on the horizon, and that's where they may look next. ■

MIKE STANLEY

C • BR • TR • 6'1 • 185 • 33 • TEX85/15

	AB	R	H	2B	3B	HR	RBI	BB	SO	SB	CS	BA	OB	SA
NYA94	290	54	87	20	0	17	57	39	56	0	0	.300	.384	.545
NYA95	399	63	107	29	1	18	83	57	106	1	1	.268	.360	.481
BOS96	397	73	107	20	1	24	69	69	62	2	0	.270	.383	.506
CAREER	2669	398	721	136	7	109	440	402	569	10	2	.270	.367	.449

Stanley signed with the Red Sox after 4 years with the Yankees. His defense wasn't so hot for the Red Sox last year, baserunners stole at will off him, but his hitting was an improvement over Mike Macfarlane. He hit especially well in the second half as the Red Sox climbed back in the pennant race. In July and August, he hit .282 with 13 homers and 30 RBI—only to go down in September, along with half the team, with a herniated disc in his lower neck. Look for him to lose some playing time to a more solid defender like Haselman. ■

JEFF SUPPAN

SOLID PROSPECT

SP • BR • TR • 6'1 • 200 • 22 • BOS93/2

	G	GS	IP	H	HR	BB	K	W	L	S	ERA	K/BB	K9	HW9
BOS95	8	3	22	29	4	5	19	1	2	0	5.96	3.8	7.8	13.91
BOS96	8	4	22	29	3	13	13	1	1	0	7.54	1.0	5.3	17.13

Suppan was considered the second-best pitching prospect in the International League last year, trailing only Detroit's Justin Thompson. He's often compared to Greg Maddux for his polish, poise, and pitching instincts—which is like comparing left-handed fastball pitchers to Sandy Koufax. Nothing

quite like setting the bar so high for someone that he won't even be able to get high enough to knock it over. Suppan has a good fastball, a cutter, a curveball he can throw for strikes, and a change-up—and he mixes his pitches well. There was some sentiment among Red Sox management to use him in the majors all season, but they decided to be cautious, even when their rotation struggled. Suppan was eventually called up in August when Stan Belinda was injured. He pitched 5 scoreless innings in his debut against the Twins before running out of gas. Everything indicates he has the potential and ability to be a dominant starter. ■

LEE TINSLEY

OF • BB • TR • 5'10 • 185 • 28 • OAK87/1

	AB	R	H	2B	3B	HR	RBI	BB	SO	SB	CS	BA	OB	SA
BOS94	144	27	32	4	0	2	14	19	36	13	0	.222	.315	.292
BOS95	341	61	97	17	1	7	41	39	74	18	8	.284	.359	.402
PHI/BOS96	244	29	54	6	1	3	16	17	78	8	12	.221	.277	.291
CAREER	748	119	186	28	2	13	73	77	197	39	20	.249	.321	.344

Boston traded Tinsley to Philly in the off-season, and he boomeranged back to them on on June 6. It took Tinsley until June 28 (his 17th game) to get his first RBI. Tinsley: "I couldn't drive in Miss Daisy." He actually hit well immediately after the trade—.318 for the month. But that was end of his hot streak. Tinsley struggled at the plate the rest of the year and lost his job to new arrival and Kennedy favorite Darren Bragg. If the Red Sox keep him around, it will be as a spare part. ■

BRAD TWEEDLIE

RP • BR • TR • 6'2 • 215 • 25 • CIN93/3

	G	GS	IP	H	HR	BB	SO	W	L	S	ERA	K/BB	K9	HW9
A+	44	0	41	41	6	25	31	3	5	18	5.05	1.2	6.8	14.49

The Red Sox acquired Tweedlie from the Reds for Kevin Mitchell at the end of July. He was basically a throw-in with Robert Mejia after a lackluster '95 in low-Class-A Charleston—and perhaps the intent was to inflict on Mitchell the indignity of being traded

for a man named Tweedlie. But he impressed the Sox in his brief stint in high-Class-A Sarasota. They moved him into the closer role with excellent results. He's raw material at this point, but his fastball's been clocked at 97 mph on the fast gun. Come to think of it, Dibble sounded like a really stupid name back in 1988. ■

JOHN VALENTIN

SS • BR • TR • 6′0 • 180 • 30 • BOS88/5

	AB	R	H	2B	3B	HR	RBI	BB	SO	SB	CS	BA	OB	SA
BOS94	301	53	95	26	2	9	49	42	38	3	1	.316	.400	.505
BOS95	520	108	155	37	2	27	102	81	67	20	5	.298	.399	.533
BOS96	527	84	156	29	3	13	59	63	59	9	10	.296	.374	.436
CAREER	2001	316	587	145	10	65	301	255	258	36	20	.293	.376	.473

Valentin played through a shoulder injury most of the season until it forced him onto the disabled list in August. At the time, he was hitting .306 with 11 homers and 66 runs scored. He returned quickly, but things went downhill from there. On the 31st the inevitable happened, and Nomar Garciaparra was called up. The same day, Valentin gave his take on the situation. "I am not ready to move. I want to stay with the Red Sox as a shortstop. But I'm not ruling out any options." With Naehring ailing, Kennedy moved Valentin to third and used Garciaparra at short several times, which is the combination the club would like to see in the future. Valentin has made it clear that he doesn't like the idea and he has some decisions to make. If he won't move to third, they will try to sign Naehring again and trade Valentin.

And what is so emotionally disturbing about these position movements that make solid veterans such as Valentin, Tim Wallach, and Cal Ripken treat them like sex-change operations? They sign the checks, you play where they put you. If Valentin keeps balking, Duquette should take less just to dump him in Philadelphia. ■

MO VAUGHN

AL ELITE

1B • EL • TR • 6′1 • 225 • 29 • BOS89/2

	AB	R	H	2B	3B	HR	RBI	BB	SO	SB	CS	BA	OB	SA
BOS94	394	65	122	25	1	26	82	57	112	4	4	.310	.408	.576
BOS95	550	98	165	28	3	39	126	68	150	11	4	.300	.388	.575
BOS96	635	118	207	29	1	44	143	95	154	2	0	.326	.420	.583
CAREER	2692	430	794	144	8	155	541	372	656	26	15	.295	.387	.527

Vaughn entered the season on a mission to prove that last year's MVP was no fluke. Vaughn: "People said Mo won the MVP because he's a nice guy. Well, I am a nice guy at times but I play as good as anybody!" While not singling anyone out, he reportedly wasn't too happy with Albert Belle's off-season comments about the award. Mo was incredible in the first half of the season. In April, he tied Fred Lynn's team record with 8 homers and set the mark for RBI with 28. In May he shattered the homer record with 12. He repeated the 28 RBI and was honored as the player of the month for the first time in his career. For the first couple of months he was about the only player on the team who bothered to show up. His torrid pace slowed after the All-Star break, due in part to a hand injury, but Vaughn bettered his MVP '95 numbers in almost every category. There's a lot of blame to go around for the Red Sox disappointing '96 season, but none of it goes to Vaughn. ■

TIM WAKEFIELD

SP • BR • TR • 6′2 • 195 • 30 • PIT88/8

	G	GS	IP	H	HR	BB	K	W	L	S	ERA	K/BB	K9	HW9
BOS95	27	27	195	163	22	68	119	16	8	0	2.95	1.8	5.5	10.66
BOS96	32	32	211	238	38	90	140	14	13	0	5.14	1.6	6.0	13.99
CAREER	96	92	626	622	77	268	369	44	33	0	4.13	1.4	5.3	12.79

Wakefield slumped horribly during the early part of last season. The slide bottomed out in June, when he was 2-3 with an 8.72 ERA and gave up 54 hits in 32 innings. Kennedy and his staff pored over films and analyzed his mechanics, but they couldn't find the problem. Rumors circulated that he would soon be released. Kennedy stood by him, but the team did consider sending him for another training session with legendary knuckleballer Phil Niekro. On August 4, the

night after his car accident, Wakefield threw a 6-hit, complete-game victory over the Blue Jays. He went on to hit his stride in August and pitched very well down the stretch, which was key in the club's resurgence. Wakefield said his recovery was due to a tip from Mike Greenwell. "Greenie talked to Haselman . . . and told him it looked like I was throwing the knuckleball harder this year."

Knowing knuckleballers, it could just as easily have been the accident. ■

ANDY YOUNT

SOLID PROSPECT

SP • BR • TR • 6'2 • 185 • 20 • BOS95/1

	G	GS	IP	H	HR	BB	SO	W	L	S	ERA	K/BB	K9	HW9
A-	8	8	34	38	0	38	30	1	2	0	6.29	.8	7.9	19.92

Yount didn't have much of a season, getting shut down early with arm trouble. He has a 95–98-mph fastball—the best in the '95 draft—and the Red Sox took him with the 15th pick. He worked hard in the instructional league on a fosh change-up to complement the fastball and a good curve. His coaches praise him for his poise and mechanics. The club was anxious to get a full season out of him so he could work on his control. Then again, the Red Sox have plenty of experience with waiting until next year. ■

■ 1996 AUTOPSY

Going into the season, the Angels were looked at as the team to beat in the A.L. West. They had a great offense, led by Chili Davis, Tim Salmon, and Jim Edmonds, and followed by Garret Anderson and J. T. Snow. The bullpen had 3 good arms: closer Lee Smith, setup man Mike James, and the most intimidating reliever in the league, Troy Percival. The rotation had 3 proven starters, Mark Langston, Jim Abbott and Chuck Finley to match up against Seattle's Randy Johnson and whatever Lou Piniella had left lying around the clubhouse. Team leader Tony Phillips had split for Chicago, but the team still appeared stacked and prepared to challenge Cleveland for the title of top team in the league. But if it was a prizefight, it would have been stopped—and the investigation into the fix would have begun.

April 13-12 (13-12, 2½ games back)
As the season started, the Angels seemed sluggish but unconcerned. The pitching was a crime, and the blood evidence pointed to Shawn Boskie (5.76 ERA in 25 innings) and Finley (7.44 ERA in 32.2 innings). These two were able to offset the excellence of James (4-2, 2.16), Percival (0.00, 8 saves in 10 innings), and Langston (2-1, 3.65). Hot starts by Davis (.325-6-15) and Edmonds (.319-8-23) were doused by Anderson, Snow and Salmon. Offense was up throughout the league, but the Angels team wasn't taking part in the surge.

May 13-14 (26-26, 7½ games back)
The Angels continued to tread water in May. Their 26-26 record wasn't matching up with their lofty ambitions and inflated self-image, and many in the clubhouse might have wanted to believe they were unlucky. They were anything but. The team had scored 243 runs and allowed 278, and a team with those totals should have been 23-29, not 26-26. That may sound trivial, but over the course of a season, that's the difference between going 81-81 and drawing pennant race crowds late into September, and going 70-92 and salary dumping in late August. The Angels were 11-6 in 1-run games, a tribute to Percival's bullpen dominance. Finley was exceptional, going 4-0 with a 0.79 ERA in 45.2 innings, and Rex Hudler was incredible off the bench (.353-8-17). Just as it appeared that California was ready to make a run, Langston went down with knee trouble and no one stepped up to replace him. The team had already used 9 starters, backing up its "Big Three" with the likes of Boskie, Jason Grimsley, Phil Leftwich, Scott Sanderson, Dennis Springer, and Shad Williams. The highlight of the month was the unloading of the unhappy Lee Smith, who had been insisting on closing games rather than recognizing that he was old and in the way and just being grateful to cash a $10,000 check every gameday.

June 15-14 (41-40, 7½ games back)
As summer came, the offense started putting some crooked numbers on the board. Unfortunately, so did the pitching. On the offense, Jim Edmonds went down for the first time, but Tim Salmon picked up the slack (.318-13-26). They finally gave up on Jim Abbott, demoting him to the bullpen after he went 0-3 with a 12.06 ERA, 1-11 and 7.92 for the year at this point. The Angels continued to win their well-pitched games (10-3 when they gave up fewer than 5 runs) and getting blown out in their losses (14-1, 14-3, 18-2). But few teams can do that for an entire season—and if one did and only managed to go .500 in the process, it would be a criminal waste of good luck.

July 10-16 (51-56, 10 games back)
This is the month when reality sneaked up and bit Club Disney right in its hindquarters. Darin Erstad had come up in June and sparked the Angels after Edmonds' injury, but his play in July was no substitute for a 30-homer hitter. The team hit .299 for the month, but the power went out. Garret Anderson's performance typified the offense: .351 with no homers and 11 RBI (not even Tony Gwynn would slug only .433 while hitting .351). Langston returned from the DL, but should have stayed on, going 0-1, 6.46 in 23.2 innings. The staff as a whole was at 6.06. No September collapse for the Angels this year—they were down and out in July.

August 11-18 (62-74, 15½ games back)
Boskie: "I've been on teams that weren't good, but I've never been through anything like this." During one stretch, they lost 11 of 12, by scores such as 13-5, 13-5, and 18-3—to the Tigers, Twins, and Royals respectively! GM Bill Bavasi: "We've got a

player or two that we may have overrated, and a few players that we definitely rated correctly, but they just aren't playing up to their potential. That's a bad combination." The club president, Tony Tavares, was a bit more to the point: "This team has too many players who look like they came from Newport Beach, where their daddies and mommies gave them everything they wanted." The front office was deluged with complaint letters from the residents of Newport Beach—no doubt most of them from people irate that their community be associated in any way with this ballclub.

Manager Marcel Lachemannn, talked out of it a month earlier, finally quit in disgust. Perhaps the breaking point was in a game against Seattle when Rich Amaral was walked 3 times in front of Alex Rodriguez and Junior. Or maybe it was the backbiting from some of his players after J. T. Snow was benched for *one game* against a lefty in favor of Rex Hudler. First, Snow—who can't hit 50-year-old lefties in b.p.—whined about sitting and threatened to stop working on his switch-hitting if this continued. Then Snow's replacement, Hudler, made an error and took it out on the manager. Hudler: "We have a Gold Glover sitting on the bench. If (Lachemannn) is looking for at-bats for me, I don't need that. He's overused me already." It's amazing that Lachemann stuck with this bunch as long as he did, and that he didn't Patton-slap a few of these whiners on his way out. Finley had already observed that the manager took losses too hard, so maybe Lachemann could have learned something from his players: how to accept—and even revel in—failure.

September 9-17 (71-91, 19½ games back)
Interim manager John McNamara ended up in the hospital with a blood clot in his leg. McNamara: "The good thing about watching the game on TV, especially watching this team, is that you can get up and go to another room." Responding to criticism from his former players, Lachemann said: "I've heard how they're a lot more comfortable and relaxed now. I never felt like I caused guys to tense up, but I guess I did. But it's not like I can change the way I am. I'm just not a guy who can laugh his way through a game." In their new, stress-free environment, the club was able to calmly and peacefully drop 10 of 11 on their way through a wretched September. In fact, the only thing that pulled the Rangers out of their Angelic tailspin was a 3-game series against California in the second-to-last week of the season, in which Texas took 2 out of 3 by a combined score of 11-2.

■ 1997 DIAGNOSIS

Offense
In '96 the Angels' offense was one of the worst in the league. They finished 11th in the league in on-base percentage, 10th in slugging percentage and 13th in runs scored. But the numbers don't tell the whole story. Based on their hitting line, they should have scored 828 runs, not 762. If you choose to believe that is due to bad luck—and if you choose to ignore conditional probabilities—you might expect the reverse in the following season. But consider one law of math and one intangible. Luck evens out over a long period of time, but that period is a lot longer than one year—as any Red Sox fan will tell you. And as long as the Angels run out the Newport Beach Fratboys day in and day out as their starting lineup, underachievement will have a lot more to do with character than fortune.

Defense
This was an excellent defensive infield in '96 and '97 should be more of the same. J. T. Snow, considered by some observers to be the finest defensive first baseman in baseball, is overrated but still good. George Arias has the tools at third, though he looked shaky at times in '96. His range is excellent, his arm is good, and he is brilliant on the double play—but 10 errors at third base in a half season of work are too many for someone with his skills. Randy Velarde was superb at second base, and Gary DiSarcina is one of the best at short. The outfield is as good as the infield. Edmonds, Salmon, and Erstad all have above-average range, with Anderson the only weak link. Salmon has a gun and Edmonds has a decent arm, too. Erstad's throwing comes with favorable reviews, but he hasn't had much chance to show it in his two trials in the majors. With Erstad in left instead of Anderson, this would be one of the better defensive outfields in baseball. Catching is a problem, and the Angels even resorted to bringing in Pat Borders rather than have to watch Jorge Fabregas behind the plate every day. Rookie Todd

Greene will be an improvement, especially in cutting down on the baserunners who have been strolling down to second with impunity.

Pitching

The Angels starters had an ERA of 5.57, third-worst in the A.L. Finley was very good, Langston was decent when he was healthy, Boskie was effective in the first half of the season, but the rest of the staff was wall-to-wall brutal, day, night, home, away, spring, summer, and fall. Springer, Grimsley, and Abbott were shuffled between the rotation and the bullpen, finishing the season at 12-31, yielding 61 dingers and 590 baserunners in 367 innings. Makes you wonder how they even managed 12 wins. In addition to off-season acquisition, Mark Gubicza, here are some human sacrifices on the menu for '97: Jason Dickson, Phil Leftwich, Ryan Hancock, and three long shots—Jarrod Washburn, Matt Perisho and Scott Schoeneweiss. But if Marcel Lachemannn doesn't agree to work with these guys (would you?), don't expect any of them to do much more than throw b.p. to the opposition without a protective cage.

Despite Troy Percival, Mike James, Chuck McElroy, and Mike Holtz—who threw 221 innings with an ERA of 2.57, 13 wins and 37 saves—this was one of the worst bullpens in baseball. Is that possible? They had one of the top closers in the game and three fine setup men, but the rest of the bullpen—the guys who had to come get the starters in the third—had an ERA around 7.00. In many ways, the key to the bullpen in '97 is the starting rotation. If Percival, James, McElroy, and Holtz do what they did in '96 *and* if the starters can keep the nos. 5 and 6 guys in the bullpen *out* of the game, the bullpen's numbers will improve dramatically.

Farm System

The farm system is bereft of Grade-A players. Larry Barnes, Todd Greene, Ben Molina, and Keith Luuloa are good young players, but none will be mistaken for the Pirates' Chad Hermansen or the Tigers' Richard Almanzar. Scott Schoeneweiss, Jarrod Washburn, and Jeremy Blevins are decent young pitchers, but the Cardinals won't be trading Braden Looper for any or all of them.

Management and Ownership

Disney Sports Enterprises. That's an unnerving proposition. See the essay at the end of this section (*The Dark Side of the Mouse*) for an extended discussion of what baseball may look like after the scariest company in America has its way with it.

GM Bill Bavasi got a four-year contract extension in mid-August. Does he deserve it? During the '95 off-season the Angels started gutting their scouting budget and fired 14 of 18 international scouts. According to *Baseball America*, the Angels hadn't produced a Latin American player in 10 seasons. The team *has* developed Tim Salmon, Jim Edmonds, Troy Percival, Chuck Finley, and Bryan Harvey. Darin Erstad's name will be added to that list shortly. The $3.5 million he could have given Tony Phillips, the team leader during '95, ended up with Jim Abbott to go 2-18, and Harvey and Steve Ontiveros to sit on the disabled list all season. Park renovations will limit cash flow in '97, with seating capacity reduced to 27,000—so Charlie Sheen will now be able to buy out the entire stadium, rather than just the left field bleachers, in an effort to get his mitts on a game ball. The future direction of this team will be determined in large part by the deal Bavasi makes—probably J. T. Snow or Garret Anderson, though Jim Edmonds and Tim Salmon weren't untouchable.

Marcel Lachemannn had an integral role in the development of Jim Abbott, Chuck Finley, Troy Percival, and Mike James. Consider this:

1. Despite no minor-league experience, Abbott made the jump to the majors in 1989 and had a decent season. He soon developed into one of the best left-handers in baseball before losing a tremendous amount of velocity.

2. With 41 career minor-league innings split between the short-season Northwest League and the low Class-A Midwest League—even Gooden put in 270 innings down on the farm—Finley was promoted to California. He was an average major-league pitcher for 2 seasons before exploding into an All-Star in 1989.

3. Percival throws 100 mph, but at Triple-A his ERA (4.13) and his control (4.3 walks per 9 innings) were pretty poor for such a good pitcher's park. Percival came to the majors and improved his ERA

to 1.95, his control to 3.2 walks per 9 innings, and his strikeouts per 9 rose from 10.8 to 11.4.

4. James had bounced around the minors for 7 years with Los Angeles. His career ERA as a Dodgers farmhand was 5.03. He followed this up with a 5.22 ERA at Vancouver in 91.1 innings in '94. In '95 he had a 9.53 ERA in 6 innings at Class-A Lake Elsinore before he made the majors. He cut his major-league ERA that season to 3.88.

Lachemannn has a unique ability to work with raw power pitchers and help them succeed. If Marcel wasn't such a nice guy and was actually a bit vindictive, he would go to some other team in the A.L. West and be Club Disney's worst nightmare.

The Angels decision to hire a manager who has a reputation for being too easy on his players is questionable. Terry Collins is a good manager, but this cries out as a right-man-wrong-place situations. The front office should have taken this team's performance personally and dropped someone more paranoid and anti-social into the clubhouse—perhaps trying to lure Mike Keenan away from the St. Louis Blues or Frank Kush from the NCAA Football Dictators retirement home.

. . . and whatnot: The Dark Side of the Mouse

"Hello, Disney Sports."

That's how they answer the phone these days in Anaheim. Gene Autry got no more enjoyment out of playing with this toy, didn't want to inflict it on his wife after he passed, so he sold it to Disney. The Mouse has deep pockets, but there isn't much talk of increasing the scouting budget or dipping into the free-agent market for some character. What's being done is much more . . . well, Disney.

The team will be called the Anaheim Angels in '97 and will be dressed in the teal and "eggplant" of the Mighty Ducks of the NHL and HBO. There will be cheerleaders over the dugout in hot pants. Roving bands in the stands playing music. Home runs greeted with some bizarre water display in the outfield. All of it sounds too twisted for words.

Tony Tavares, team president: "It's all about trying to give the fans a better time. We'll try a variety of things and see how they're received. I'm sure some of the purists will absolutely despise some of the things we're doing. At least initially. And a lot of people will think they're absolute fun. We hope to achieve a balance." Distract the fans with enough lights, noise, and babes, and maybe they won't notice how badly the team is playing. That's what the suits might be hoping for, but that won't work—not even in Southern California, where Dodgers fans leave extra-inning playoff games with the score tied. Disney certainly hasn't grown broke underestimating the taste of the American public, but this time they're aiming low even by their standards

As bad as their good intentions are, take a look behind the curtain and you'll find that The Mouse has a dark side. Disney was actually running things by May, and one of its first acts was to fire the entire front-office staff and force these people to interview for the jobs they used to hold. Nearly half would be sent packing. Now rumors abound that only players, the manager, the GM, and the president are to be interviewed—and that it will be a hanging offense if an Angels scout or coach is caught talking to the press. So much for family fun at the Magic Kingdom. When the camera goes off, Mickey's wearing jackboots.

It comes as no surprise that Jim Leyland took one look and said, thank you, no. That man is substance over style, which is as un-Disney as it gets. And even after spending that much time in Pittsburgh, there isn't enough money in the world to join this Disney cast of characters.

JIM ABBOTT

SP • BL • TL • 6'3 • 200 • 29 • CAL88/1

	G	GS	IP	H	HR	BB	K	W	L	S	ERA	K/BB	K9	HW9
NYA94	24	24	160	167	24	64	90	9	8	0	4.55	1.4	5.1	12.99
CHA/CAL95	30	30	197	209	14	64	86	11	8	0	3.70	1.3	3.9	12.47
CAL96	27	23	142	171	23	78	58	2	18	0	7.48	.7	3.7	15.78
CAREER	238	234	1560	1634	138	566	837	80	100	0	4.11	1.5	4.8	12.69

Abbott lost velocity in 1993, continues to do so, and short of bionic surgery, he's never going to get it back. He threw 89–91 mph when he was drafted—excellent for a left-hander—and now throws in the low 80s. Some games he didn't break 80. Some say he could work in the minors and learn how to get by with junk. Is this possible? Yes. Is it probable? No. Name 10 other pitchers who survive with low-80s fastballs. Now remove the knuckleballers. Not much there besides Frank Tanana and Tommy John.

The love his teammates feel for him can't be overstated. They even used Percival for 2 innings late in the year to get him his second win. He couldn't even have survived as a left handed relief specialist. Lefties slaughtered him last season. Gehrig-like numbers: .336 with a .393 on-base percentage and a .689 slugging average. No pleasure can be taken in concluding that Jim Abbott is washed up. He has 2 more years left on a $7.8 million contract, but maybe it will help just to have him around so the rest of the team can watch someone who refuses to give up. ■

GARRET ANDERSON — OVERRATED

LF • BL • TL • 6'3 • 190 • 24 • CAL90/3

	AB	R	H	2B	3B	HR	RBI	BB	SO	SB	CS	BA	OB	SA
CAL95	374	50	120	19	1	16	69	19	65	6	2	.321	.352	.505
CAL96	607	79	173	33	2	12	72	27	84	7	9	.285	.314	.405

Coming into '96, some were comparing Anderson's swing (and talent) to Ken Griffey's. Apparently the fact that Anderson was only a year younger than Griffey and had 177 fewer home runs wasn't factored into the equation. Anderson does have talent, but he shouldn't be mentioned in the same sentence as Junior unless he's hitting a fly ball to him. He's a solid hitter, but even as offensive totals skyrocketed last season, his offense plummeted. He's a good bet to do better in '97, but he's not likely to be a superstar. If he wants to make a big step forward, he must learn the strike zone—and that's highly unlikely at Anderson's age.

His growth in '95 was a little too dramatic—he'd hit only 22 home runs in 5 years in the minors—to be for real. And though he hit .321, he didn't display additional plate discipline. He was hitting .282 with 2 strikes, which is in a higher-rent district than even Molitor and Boggs. But he struck out 65 times with only 6 walks, which is an astonishingly bad ratio that would shame even Andujar Cedeño. In '96 his average with two strikes dropped to the .220s with Belle, Thome, and Salmon, his batting average stayed the same in other situations, and he ended up in the .280s, where he belongs. What Anderson did with 2 strikes in '95 was a fluke, and impossible to sustain for anyone other than Gwynn or Boggs in his prime. He did improve his plate discipline, drawing 27 walks while striking out 84 times—which isn't very good, either, but consider the depths from which he's risen.

Anderson wasn't thrilled with the 4-outfielder system the Angels used briefly when Erstad was up and Edmonds was healthy. Anderson: "All baseball people know platoon systems don't work if you want to win." Evidently Casey Stengel and Earl Weaver weren't covered when Garret took Baseball 101. Or perhaps he missed the second half of the sentence: "Platoon systems don't work . . . when you have selfish players concerned more with individual statistics than team performance." Anderson wants a multiyear deal calling for Marty Cordova money. If the Angels give it to him, they have no one to blame but themselves. ■

GEORGE ARIAS — SLEEPER

3B • BR • TR • 5'11 • 190 • 25 • CAL93/7

	AB	R	H	2B	3B	HR	RBI	BB	SO	SB	CS	BA	OB	SA
CAL96	252	19	60	8	1	6	28	16	38	2	1	.238	.284	.349

In the off-season before '96, Arias was sent to Venezuela to improve his plate discipline and learn to hit to the opposite field. He certainly showed it in AAA Vancouver, where he hit .338 and cut down dramatically on his strikeouts—which had been in

the century club the past 2 seasons. His numbers in Anaheim looked like someone different was stepping off the plane from British Columbia. His performance will improve if the Angels commit to him at third base and let him see a full season of major-league pitching. He could hit 25 homers eventually—much closer to Tim Wallach than Mike Schmidt, but good enough to have a long career. In the field, he has good range and a strong arm and was named best defensive third baseman in the PCL last season—skills he showed, at times, in Anaheim, though his fielding percentage wouldn't suggest that. Now he just needs to cut down on the number of balls he kicks or airmails. ■

LARRY BARNES — SOLID PROSPECT

1B • BL • TL • 6'1 • 195 • 22

	AB	R	H	2B	3B	HR	RBI	BB	SO	SB	CS	BA	OB	SA
A	489	84	155	36	5	27	112	58	101	9	6	.317	.392	.577

The Midwest League is not a hitter's league, and Cedar Rapids does not have a hitter's park, so Barnes' numbers are legit. If he explodes—though that's very unlikely—Barnes could make the majors this season. He'll probably start the season at Class A Lake Elsinore and get a shot at moving to Double-A later. His only weakness is his strikeout rate, and it isn't *that* bad. In addition, he's pretty smooth defensively. Looks like the Angels have themselves a fine young hitter here. ETA: midseason 1998. ■

MATT BEAUMONT

SP • BL • TL • 6'3 • 210 • 23 • CAL94/4

	G	GS	IP	H	HR	BB	K	W	L	S	ERA	K/BB	K9	HW9
AA	28	28	162	198	20	71	132	7	16	0	5.85	1.9	7.3	14.98

Beaumont has average velocity and throws the basic 4 pitches for strikes. He's not overpowering and was clubbed at Double-A. Obviously he's not Steve Carlton, but Midland is brutal on pitchers, and this guy does have some ability (he was 16-9 with a 3.29 ERA in '95). ■

JEREMY BLEVINS — SOLID PROSPECT

SP • BR • TR • 6'3 • 195 • 19 • CAL95/3

	G	GS	IP	H	HR	BB	K	W	L	S	ERA	K/BB	K9	HW9
A-	14	13	59	54	4	58	39	2	3	0	6.60	.7	6.0	17.18

Blevins has a good fastball that hits 92 mph now, and the Angels think it could eventually reach 95. He also has a good curveball. In addition to his control problems, he can't change speeds and doesn't even pretend to have a change-up. It shows in the numbers. But this kid is so young and raw that anything is possible—he could be Roger Clemens, he could be Clemente Nunez. ■

SHAWN BOSKIE (see Free Agents)

MIKE BOVEE

SP • BR • TR • 5'10 • 200 • 23 • KC91/6

	G	GS	IP	H	HR	BB	K	W	L	S	ERA	K/BB	K9	HW9
AA	27	27	177	223	21	40	102	10	11	0	4.84	2.6	5.2	13.40

Bovee came over to the Angels with Gubicza in the Chili Davis trade. He's a stocky curveball specialist with good control. Bovee, 23, enjoyed great strikeout ratios in his first 4 seasons after being drafted in '91, and even won the Carolina League ERA title in '94. But since his promotion to Wichita in '95, he's lost the ability to bait hitters with the bender, and his strikeouts have dropped precipitously. This is not a good sign. Last season was his second in Double-A, and he allowed an ungodly number of hits. If he doesn't regain command and make a successful transition to Triple-A now, he will have missed the boat on his career. ■

BRIAN COOPER — SOLID PROSPECT

SP • BR • TR • 6'1 • 175 • 22 • CAL95/4

	G	GS	IP	H	HR	BB	K	W	L	S	ERA	K/BB	K9	HW9
A+	26	23	162	177	17	39	155	7	9	0	4.21	4.0	8.6	11.98

Cooper is considered the best control pitcher in the California League. Lake Elsinore's stadium is kind to pitchers, but anyone who can post these kinds of numbers in a league like this is a prospect. The Angels took notice not just of his control, but of his strikeout numbers and his stock has risen accordingly. ■

JASON DICKSON — SLEEPER

SP • BL • TR • 6'0 • 190 • 24 • CAL94/4

	G	GS	IP	H	HR	BB	K	W	L	S	ERA	K/BB	K9	HW9
CAL96	7	7	43	52	6	18	20	1	4	0	4.57	1.1	4.2	14.64

Dickson has good but unexceptional stuff. His fastball peaks at 92 mph and has good movement. He also has a curveball, a change-up, and a power slider. Scouts think he's a bit small, but California loves him and his bulldog attitude. He survived the Pacific Coast League meat grinder, though it certainly helped to pitch in a park that was friendly to pitchers. His strikeout rate was poor (70 Ks in 130 innings in Vancouver), but he has the tools to be a good pitcher, if not a dominating one, in the majors. ■

GARY DISARCINA

SS • BR • TR • 6'1 • 170 • 29 • CAL88/5

	AB	R	H	2B	3B	HR	RBI	BB	SO	SB	CS	BA	OB	SA
CAL94	389	53	101	14	2	3	33	18	28	3	7	.260	.294	.329
CAL95	362	61	111	28	6	5	41	20	25	7	4	.307	.344	.459
CAL96	536	62	137	26	4	5	48	21	36	2	1	.256	.286	.347
Career	2335	281	596	110	14	19	212	100	191	27	26	.255	.291	.339

DiSarcina's defense is a thing of beauty and, with Vizquel's injury problems, he was probably the best defensive infielder in the league in '96. He was definitely poured from his position's classic mold. Like Mark Belanger, Marty Marion, and Roy McMillan, his excellence in the field overcomes any hitting weaknesses. The Angels recognize his value, signing him to a 4-year extension through 2000. ■

JIM EDMONDS — AL ELITE

CF • BL • TL • 6'1 • 190 • 26 • CAL88/6

	AB	R	H	2B	3B	HR	RBI	BB	SO	SB	CS	BA	OB	SA
CAL94	289	35	79	13	1	5	37	30	72	4	2	.273	.343	.377
CAL95	558	120	162	30	4	33	107	51	130	1	4	.290	.352	.536
CAL96	431	73	131	28	3	27	66	46	101	4	0	.304	.375	.571
Career	1339	233	387	75	9	65	214	129	319	9	8	.289	.354	.504

Edmonds missed significant time last season because of a torn thumb ligament, a pulled stomach muscle, a strained groin, and a slight muscle tear in his left shoulder. Despite the injuries, he proved

1995 was no fluke and established himself as one of the best center fielders in baseball. He is a superb fielder and a fine hitter. Four years ago he was a decent defensive player and a middling line-drive hitter. He owes his offensive improvements to Rod Carew's tutelage and careful weight training. He retained his ability to hit for average while pulling the ball more—which is essentially what Kirby Puckett did in 1986.

The Angels—a team that thought it could throw its gloves out on the field and make the playoffs—want Edmonds to be more of a team leader. He can hit and he can field, but he's no Kirk Gibson. Listen to him complaining about the first bumps in the road in early June: "People talk about the dog days of July and August, but these are the dog days, too. People say it's still early in the season, but it's not early for me. We've been going at it since February 15. It gets tough. Maybe we should play a 140-game season. Why not? What can you prove in 162 games that you can't prove in 140? I don't want anyone to feel sorry for us, but we're working 7 days a week."

Hmmm. Where to begin? (1) If this is the best you can do from a team "leader," your ballclub will be mailing it in by the All-Star break. (2) Jim's right about what can be proven in 140 games. The Angels played only 144 games in '95 thanks to the labor unrest but still found a way to blow one of the biggest leads in history—as impressive a feat in a shortened season as Belle's 50 dingers. It only took 144 games in '95 to prove how soft this team is, and they showed it sooner than that in '96. (3) As we shorten this season by 15% to cut down on the wear and tear of this vicious contact sport, is the Major League Baseball Players' Association willing to take a 15% across-the-board pay cut? Didn't think so. And finally, (4) don't worry, Jim, no one is going to feel sorry for you. There's a finite amount of sympathy to go around, and there isn't much left for hopelessly-out-of-touch professional baseball players crying in their sports drinks about how tough they've got it. ■

DARIN ERSTAD

YOUNG GUN

OF • BL • TL • 6′2 • 195 • 22 • CAL95/1

	AB	R	H	2B	3B	HR	RBI	BB	SO	SB	CS	BA	OB	SA
CAL96	208	34	59	5	1	4	20	17	29	3	3	.284	.333	.375

Erstad came into spring training 1996 like he was the second coming of George Brett, displaying great hustle in center field and an exceptional line-drive bat. But when he didn't make the team and was sent to Triple-A Vancouver, he took a step backward, hitting for average but with little power. Then the Angels decided to promote him in mid-June when Jim Edmonds tore up his thumb. Erstad played well initially, but was demoted around the time Lachemannn quit. This understandably infuriated Erstad. He looks like a legitimate .300 hitter and should show more power in the majors. In addition, many Angels officials say Erstad has the finest bat speed they've ever seen. They want him as a full-time lead off man. ■

JORGE FABREGAS

C • BL • TR • 6′3 • 205 • 27 • CAL91/2

	AB	R	H	2B	3B	HR	RBI	BB	SO	SB	CS	BA	OB	SA
CAL94	127	12	36	3	0	0	16	7	18	2	1	.283	.321	.307
CAL95	227	24	56	10	0	1	22	17	28	0	2	.247	.298	.304
CAL96	254	18	73	6	0	2	26	17	27	0	1	.287	.326	.335
Career	608	54	165	19	0	3	64	41	73	2	4	.271	.315	.317

Fabregas doesn't get on base, has little power, the league runs wild on him, and the Angels grew so dissatisfied with his handling of the pitchers that they brought in Pat Borders for a while. He was one of the worst catchers in the American League in '96, though that's not to say he underachieved. He could be even more notorious: He's the guy who almost ended Cal Ripken's streak at 2,129 with an awkward slide trying to break up a double play. ■

CHUCK FINLEY

CONSISTENT STAR

SP • BL • TL • 6′6 • 220 • 34 • CAL85

	G	GS	IP	H	HR	BB	K	W	L	S	ERA	K/BB	K9	HW9
CAL94	25	25	183	178	21	71	148	10	10	0	4.32	2.1	7.3	12.24
CAL95	32	32	203	192	20	93	195	15	12	0	4.21	2.1	8.6	12.64
CAL96	35	35	238	241	27	94	215	15	16	0	4.16	2.3	8.1	12.67
CAREER	344	287	2074	1985	191	850	1584	129	114	0	3.65	1.9	6.9	12.30

If nothing else, Finley is modest. After being named A.L. player of the week in late July, he said: "That just shows how this league has gone to hell." When he gets his curveball over, it makes his fastball, and forkball that much more effective. When he doesn't, hitters sit on hi fastball which now peaks at 90. Finley still has more good days than bad—especially if you adjust for the explosion in offense the past 3 seasons. Because he's adjusted as he's lost velocity, he should be solid for another season or two and may find his way to the Yankees yet. ■

GREG GOHR

P • BR • TR • 6′3 • 205 • 29 • DET89/21

	G	GS	IP	H	HR	BB	K	W	L	S	ERA	K/BB	K9	HW9
DET94	8	6	34	36	3	21	21	2	2	0	4.50	1.0	5.6	15.09
DET95	10	0	10	9	0	3	12	1	0	0	.87	4.0	10.8	10.80
DET/CAL96	32	16	115	163	31	44	75	5	9	1	7.27	1.7	5.9	16.19
CAREER	66	22	182	234	35	82	131	8	11	1	6.23	1.6	6.5	15.62

Things were so bad for the Tigers, they were talking about making Tipper their closer after 67 major-league innings in which his ERA was 4.43 and his HW9 was 14.64. He split his season between starting and mopping up, and the results were unspeakably wretched. The case could be made that his numbers were worse than Jim Abbott's. Only in the A.L. would a guy going this bad still get to throw well over 1,000 pitches to major league hitters. ■

TODD GREENE

SOLID PROSPECT

C • BR • TR • 5′10 • 195 • 25 • CAL93/12

	AB	R	H	2B	3B	HR	RBI	BB	SO	SB	CS	BA	OB	SA
CAL96	79	9	15	1	0	2	9	4	11	2	0	.190	.238	.278

Greene was *Baseball Weekly*'s top prospect in '95, and the first minor-leaguer to hit 40 homers since Danny Tartabull in '85. His swing is so powerful that he broke a bone in his wrist on a checked swing in early '96. He started the season on the DL, but he came back strong. He's slow, vulnerable to

breaking balls away, and is a mediocre catcher at the moment. But he managed to throw out 35% of runners in Triple-A, was in the majors before the summer was over, and says he wants to earn a Gold Glove. Given his work ethic, don't bet against him. There's certainly nothing blocking his path in Anaheim. ■

MARK GUBICZA

SP • BR • TR • 6′6 • 215 • 34 • KC81/2

	G	GS	IP	H	HR	BB	K	W	L	S	ERA	K/BB	K9	HW9
KC94	22	22	130	158	11	26	59	7	9	0	4.50	2.3	4.1	12.74
KC95	33	33	213	222	21	62	81	12	14	0	3.75	1.3	3.4	12.00
KC96	19	19	119	132	22	34	55	4	12	0	5.13	1.6	4.2	12.55
CAREER	382	327	2218	2226	153	783	1366	132	135	2	3.92	1.7	5.5	12.21

Gubicza got career strikeout 1,325 May 4 to move him past Dennis Leonard as the Royals' career leader. That was about it for bright spots. His season was ended by a Paul Molitor line drive up the box that fractured his left tibia on July 5. He still has a late-breaking slider that is especially rough on right-handers, and he was about league-average last season, but it's obvious that his career is in its twilight. The last link to the champion '85 Royals, he came over from Kansas City for Chili Davis. ■

RYAN HANCOCK

SLEEPER

SP • BR • TR • 6′2 • 220 • 25 • CAL93/2

	G	GS	IP	H	HR	BB	K	W	L	S	ERA	K/BB	K9	HW9
CAL96	11	4	27	34	2	17	19	4	1	0	7.48	1.1	6.3	16.96

Hancock had a 92 mph fastball and a hard slider, but he lost both after tearing up his knee playing quarterback for Brigham Young. He's tough, so he could get his stuff back. The Angels should trade him to the Yankees, so the debate for the best quarterback in New York can be between him and the Knicks' point guard Charlie Ward. ■

MIKE HOLTZ

YOUNG GUN

RP • BL • TL • 5′9 • 175 • 24 • CAL94/17

	G	GS	IP	H	HR	BB	K	W	L	S	ERA	K/BB	K9	HW9
CAL96	30	0	29	21	1	19	31	3	3	0	2.45	1.6	9.6	12.40

Holtz has had his share of adversity. A 17th-round pick from Clemson in '94, he had Tommy John surgery when he was 19. Despite this and his small frame, he throws 90+ with a good curveball. He came to the majors, and despite poor control, dominated—pitching effectively against lefties and mulching right-handers. He demonstrated excellent command in the minors and has good stuff. Anyone who refuses to be set back by what he faced is made for late-inning relief. ■

REX HUDLER (see Free Agents)

MIKE JAMES

RP • BR • TR • 6′4 • 215 • 29 • LA87/43

	G	GS	IP	H	HR	BB	K	W	L	S	ERA	K/BB	K9	HW9
CAL95	46	0	55	49	6	26	36	3	0	1	3.88	1.4	5.9	12.27
CAL96	69	0	81	62	7	42	65	5	5	1	2.67	1.5	7.2	11.56

James throws in the mid-90s and has a decent slider. He doesn't have Percival's command or his strikeout rate, but he's an excellent middle reliever. James is murder on right-handers and adequate against left-handers. He had a major problem last season with his inherited runners, allowing about half of them to score. He should be effective for the next 4 to 6 years. If he wants to get a nice free-agent deal when he gets enough service time—which is what it's all about, right?—he has to consolidate his 1995–96 gains, improve his control, and increase his strikeout rate. ■

PETE JANICKI

SP • BR • TR • 6′4 • 190 • 26 • CAL92/1

	G	GS	IP	H	HR	BB	K	W	L	S	ERA	K/BB	K9	HW9
AAA	31	14	104	135	15	37	86	2	9	1	6.75	2.3	7.4	14.88

Janicki is a former 1st round pick, but he is old, has a history of arm trouble, and was shelled last year in both Double-A (6.39) and Triple-A, going 3-12 combined. But he has a 91-mph fastball, a hard curveball, a good change-up, and a forkball he uses against lefties. Too bad it looks like Marcel Lachemann won't be around to work with him. This is just the kind of guy he's worked wonders with in the past. ■

MARK LANGSTON

HEADED FOR A FALL

SP • BR • TL • 6′2 • 190 • 36 • SEA81/3

	G	GS	IP	H	HR	BB	K	W	L	S	ERA	K/BB	K9	HW9
CAL94	18	18	119	121	19	54	109	7	8	0	4.68	2.0	8.2	13.23
CAL95	31	31	200	212	21	64	142	15	7	0	4.63	2.2	6.4	12.42
CAL96	18	18	123	116	18	45	83	6	5	0	4.82	1.8	6.1	11.78
CAREER	401	398	2771	2486	283	1190	2335	172	146	0	3.86	2.0	7.6	11.94

There are no pitchers more physically dissimilar than Mark Langston and Randy Johnson, yet their careers continue to be entertwined. They were traded for one another, faced off against each other in a single game playoff in '95, and after relatively injury-free careers, both were on the DL for most of '96. Recurring knee injuries limited Langston to 123 innings, and he was done by August. After 13 seasons, he's lost 2 or 3 feet off his fastball—down to 88–89 mph from 95–96. If he doesn't have strong legs underneath him in '97, his pitches will be up in the zone, and he could get tattooed. He still has his excellent curve and change-up, but he's at the age where any pitch could be his last. ■

PHIL LEFTWICH

SP • BR • TR • 6′5 • 205 • 27 • CAL90/1

	G	GS	IP	H	HR	BB	K	W	L	S	ERA	K/BB	K9	HW9
CAL96	2	2	7	12	1	3	4	0	1	0	7.36	1.3	4.9	18.42

Leftwich missed most of '96 after shoulder surgery, depriving him of the chance to contribute any more than a single dinger to the 214 served up by the staff. He has an adequate fastball and a good breaking ball. If he can stay healthy, he could be an asset—especially on a team as desperate for pitching as the Angels. Yet another in a long line of disappointing 1st round picks by the Angels: Leftwich, Eduardo Perez, Janicki, and Brian Anderson from 1990–93. McKay Christensen was taken in 1994, and promptly went on a Mormon mission until '96 and is now in the White Sox organization. Erstad looks to break this string of futility. He'll have to; they didn't have a 1st round pick in '96, sending it to the Yankees as compensation for signing aging free agent and utility infielder, Randy Velarde. ■

KEITH LUULOA

SOLID PROSPECT

2B • BR • TR • 6′1 • 185 • 22

	AB	R	H	2B	3B	HR	RBI	BB	SO	SB	CS	BA	OB	SA
AA	531	80	138	24	2	7	44	47	54	4	6	.260	.325	.352

Luuloa, Louie Lou-i, is very young and a decent hitter. If his hitting can continue to develop, he's looking at a major-league audition in September. There's not much in front of him in the minors, and Velarde is 34. ■

CHUCK MCELROY

RP • BL • TL • 6′0 • 160 • 29 • PHI86/8

	G	GS	IP	H	HR	BB	K	W	L	S	ERA	K/BB	K9	HW9
CIN94	52	0	57	52	3	15	38	1	2	5	2.34	2.5	6.0	10.57
CIN95	44	0	40	46	5	15	27	3	4	0	6.02	1.8	6.1	13.73
CIN/CAL96	52	0	48	45	4	23	45	7	1	0	3.93	2.0	8.4	12.72
CAREER	367	0	403	376	29	200	340	23	19	14	3.49	1.7	7.6	12.87

McElroy got fat and lost something off his fastball in '95. He rebounded last season, pitching well against righties and lefties despite the lively ball. He isn't a star, but he's the kind of guy a bullpen needs—and getting him for a washed-up and unhappy Lee Smith was more than the Angels should have had any right to expect. ■

BEN MOLINA

SOLID PROSPECT

C • BR • TR • 5′11 • 190 • 22

	AB	R	H	2B	3B	HR	RBI	BB	SO	SB	CS	BA	OB	SA
AA	365	45	100	21	2	8	54	25	25	0	1	.274	.327	.408

Like many of the Angels' minor-leaguers, Molina hasn't hit much yet, but has consistently been young for his league. And he has only struck out 60 tmes in 847 career at bats in the minors. He should start this season in Triple-A and will likely get a chance to play at Anaheim at some point in '97. ■

BRAD PENNINGTON

RP • BL • TL • 6′5 • 215 • 27 • BAL89/12

	G	GS	IP	H	HR	BB	K	W	L	S	ERA	K/BB	K9	HW9
BAL94	8	0	6	9	2	8	7	0	1	0	12.00	.9	10.5	25.50
BAL/CIN95	14	0	16	12	1	22	17	0	1	0	6.61	.8	9.6	19.13
BOS/CAL96	22	0	20	11	2	31	20	0	2	0	6.29	.6	9.0	18.87
CAREER	78	0	75	66	12	86	83	3	6	4	6.95	1.0	10.0	18.22

He *is* Nuke Laloosh. He could blow a double baconburger by Bill Clinton, but walks a guy an inning and is onto his 4th team in 2 years. At Triple-A he struck out 14.2 per 9 innings, far better than Goose Gossage in his prime. Pennington will be on

someone's minor-league roster until he blows his arm out. If a pitching coach can ever get between his ears, he will dominate. ■

TROY PERCIVAL

AL ELITE

RP • BR • TR • 6′3 • 200 • 27 • CAL90/5

	G	GS	IP	H	HR	BB	K	W	L	S	ERA	K/BB	K9	HW9
CAL95	62	0	74	37	6	26	94	3	2	3	1.95	3.6	11.4	7.66
CAL96	62	0	74	38	8	31	100	0	2	36	2.31	3.2	12.2	8.39

For 2 seasons, Percival has been the most dominant relief pitcher in baseball. But his questionable mechanics and injury problems in the minors make him a cuff tear candidate. They said that about Dibble and were right; they've been saying the same thing about Kevin Appier for 8 years and he's been on the disabled list only once. Percival is one of the few homegrown closers in baseball (see Jose Mesa's write-up in the Cleveland Indians).

As if his stuff isn't intimidating enough on its own—Nen's fastball and Kile's curve—apparently his vision is bad and he powers down 7 cups of coffee a day. He also has a healthy dislike for hitters, avoiding them at the All-Star Game in Philadelphia, and has a feud brewing with Frank Thomas. Not bad for a guy with the preppiest name in baseball. ■

TIM SALMON

AL ELITE

RF • BR • TR • 6′3 • 200 • 28 • CAL89/3

	AB	R	H	2B	3B	HR	RBI	BB	SO	SB	CS	BA	OB	SA
CAL94	373	67	107	18	2	23	70	54	102	1	3	.287	.382	.531
CAL95	537	111	177	34	3	34	105	91	111	5	5	.330	.429	.594
CAL96	581	90	166	27	4	30	98	93	125	4	2	.286	.386	.501
CAREER	2085	369	610	115	10	120	374	331	496	16	17	.293	.392	.530

Salmon dominated during the second half of 1995—hitting .364 with 19 homers and 63 RBI. That didn't carry over into '96, but with the help of an exceptional June (.318-13-26), he ended up with respectable numbers. But with the large increase in offense in the American League last season, the difference between his '95 and '96 performances was dramatic. Salmon was still one of the better players in the league last year, but he wasn't anything remotely resembling an MVP candidate, as he was in '95. Unless they raise the mound, call strikes, and loosen up the ball, expect Salmon to improve his offense and reestablish himself as the best right fielder in the league. ■

JEFF SCHMIDT

SLEEPER

RP • BR • TR • 6′5 • 210 • 26 • CAL92/2

	G	GS	IP	H	HR	BB	K	W	L	S	ERA	K/BB	K9	HW9
AAA	35	0	38	29	0	25	19	0	1	19	2.87	.8	4.5	12.90

Schmidt was named the outstanding reliever in the Pacific Coast League, saving 19 games with a 2.87 ERA despite a surprisingly bad strikeout rate. It was even worse at Midland in '95. He's a big boy with the best fastball in the Angels minor-league system and a slider that could be excellent once he masters it, so there's something's wrong with this picture. More cause for pessimism: He's not that young and he'll have to beat out Mike James just to get a setup job. ■

SCOTT SCHOENEWEISS

SOLID PROSPECT

SP • CAL96/3 • DUKE UNIVERSITY

	G	GS	IP	H	HR	BB	K	W	L	S	ERA	K/BB	K9	HW9
A+	14	12	94	86	6	27	83	8	3	0	3.94	3.1	7.9	11.63

The Angels have left-handers who've dealt with more than a little adversity. First there was Jim Abbott, then there was Mike Holtz, now there's Schoeneweiss. He's had Tommy John surgery *and* cancer. Neither has kept him from throwing 91 with a good slider and an improving change-up. He has a good delivery, and scouts like his courage and the way he challenges hitters—so, other than Abbott and Holtz, it doesn't look like there'll be anyone in Anaheim who can relate to him. ■

J. T. SNOW

1B • BB • TL • 6′2 • 200 • 29 • NYA89/4

	AB	R	H	2B	3B	HR	RBI	BB	SO	SB	CS	BA	OB	SA
CAL94	223	22	49	4	0	8	30	19	48	0	1	.220	.289	.345
CAL95	544	80	157	22	1	24	102	52	91	2	1	.289	.353	.465
CAL96	575	69	148	20	1	17	67	56	96	1	6	.257	.327	.384
CAREER	1775	232	457	65	4	65	258	187	328	6	8	.257	.331	.408

After his solid 1995, Snow started 1996 in wretched fashion, hitting a very soft .244. He improved a bit in May, but he was stuck in the slow lane all season

and was hopeless against left-handers. In '95 he hit .267 with a .351 OBP and a .404 slugging percentage against lefties; in '96 it was down to .199 with a .249 OBP and a .274 slugging percentage. That's the difference between hitting .290 and hitting .250 overall. If he can handle lefties, he's a good player. Otherwise, he's a Greg Colbrunn who makes flashier plays in the field. ■

DENNIS SPRINGER

SP • BR • TR • 5′10 • 190 • 32 • LA87/21

	G	GS	IP	H	HR	BB	K	W	L	S	ERA	K/BB	K9	HW9
PHI95	4	4	22	21	3	9	15	0	3	0	4.84	1.7	6.1	12.27
CAL96	20	15	94	91	24	43	64	5	6	0	5.51	1.5	6.1	12.82

Springer's a knuckleballer who pitched competently last season. He didn't load the bases too much, but he did hang his pitches at an unbelievable rate. Not even fellow knuckleballers Sparks and Wakefield were tagged as frequently. He needs to keep the ball in the park and continue to make sure he keeps the walks under control. If he doesn't, he won't even last with the Angels' staff and California might finally realize why a team like the Phillies could afford to let him go. ■

RANDY VELARDE

2B • BR • TR • 6′0 • 185 • 34 • CHA85/19

	AB	R	H	2B	3B	HR	RBI	BB	SO	SB	CS	BA	OB	SA
NYA94	280	47	78	16	1	9	34	22	61	4	2	.279	.338	.439
NYA95	367	60	102	19	1	7	46	55	64	5	1	.278	.375	.392
CAL96	530	82	151	27	3	14	54	70	118	7	7	.285	.372	.426
CAREER	2465	345	662	126	13	57	262	256	500	29	22	.269	.342	.400

He played well as the right-handed part of the Angels' platoon at second, while filling in at short and third. He hit for a decent average, got on base well, and had some power. A former Yankee, he was one of the few players to be disgusted with what the Angels produced in '96. Velarde: "It's embarrassing what we're putting on the field. I'm glad [team president Tony Tavares] is ticked because the guy in New York [Steinbrenner] wouldn't put up with this. . . . Playing here is like playing in a country club." He got a standing ovation when he hit a home run in his first at-bat in Yankee Stadium. But Slam Duncan went on to hit .340 in his place, so they won't know him in The Bronx in '97. ■

JARROD WASHBURN — SOLID PROSPECT

SP • BL • TL • 6′1 • 185 • 22 • CAL95/2

	G	GS	IP	H	HR	BB	K	W	L	S	ERA	K/BB	K9	HW9
AA	13	13	88	77	11	25	58	5	6	0	4.40	2.3	5.9	10.43

Washburn throws a hard-moving 93-mph fastball and has a good slider, but his curveball is a work in progress. Some of his effectiveness can be attributed to the deceptive arm angle on his release. Going into '96 he had little knowledge of changing speeds; he played his college ball at the University of Wisconsin at Oshkosh, where he could keep it simple and blow away Division III hitters with the hard stuff. Last season he made it to Double-A, where he wasn't too bad at Midland. If he pitches well at Triple-A Vancouver he could see some major-league action this season. ■

SHAD WILLIAMS

SP • BR • TR • 6′0 • 185 • 26 • CAL91/18

	G	GS	IP	H	HR	BB	K	W	L	S	ERA	K/BB	K9	HW9
CAL96	13	2	28	42	7	21	26	0	2	0	8.89	1.2	8.3	20.23

He's got a good first name for a team composed primarily of fratboys. Williams is an off-speed/ breaking-ball pitcher who relies on his curveball to succeed. He's nothing special, but because he has good control, and has survived at Triple-A, he earned a shot in '96. But on one of the worst staffs in baseball, he took the honors of highest ERA for anyone with at least 10 innings pitched. ■

■ 1996 AUTOPSY

The White Sox lost two-thirds of their starting outfield to the Big Apple during the off-season. They traded Tim Raines to the Yankees, and the Mets signed Lance Johnson. But GM Ron Schueler acquired ageless wonders Tony Phillips and Harold Baines; the sub-of-the-gods, Dave Martinez; and Danny Tartabull to replace their bats—and Darren Lewis to replace Johnson's defense. Added to the bats of Frank Thomas, Robin Ventura, and Ray Durham, it was considered an upgrade over the '95 lineup. With their corps of talented young pitchers, all the White Sox had to do to improve on their 68-76 record in '95 was play to their ability.

March 0-1 (½ game back)
The White Sox were given the honor of playing the earliest game in major-league history. Unfortunately, that honor came with facing Randy Johnson in the Kingdome, and the White Sox started the season in the hole.

April 15-9, (15-10, 1½ games back)
The White Sox were looking like contenders despite slow starts by Tartabull, Lewis, and Martinez. The offense rode the backs of Frank Thomas (the A.L. player of the month—he hit .378-8-23) and Harold Baines, who hit .311 with 5 homers. Overall, they scored a respectable number of runs in April, but the pitching staff carried the day. The rotation looked good, even though the starters weren't pitching deep into games. Fernandez (4-1, 3.60 ERA) and Alvarez (2-2, 3.52 ERA) were fantastic. James Baldwin, called up in place of the dreadful Jason Bere, won both his starts and had a 3.60 ERA. Wilson Alvarez had just a 2-2 record to show for his 3.52 ERA. Their short outings strained the bullpen, but the late-inning relief stood out. Roberto Hernandez blew his first save opportunity but settled down, converting his next 9 with 14 scoreless innings.

May 17-10 (32-20, 3 games back)
The White Sox couldn't gain any ground on the Indians, no matter how well they hit. Comparing the two teams, the White Sox scored 30 more runs than the Indians and gave up 26 fewer runs. The Sox should have been able to make up a couple of games, but they actually lost ground. The Tribe went 19-9 to increase their lead in the Central, while the White Sox were very wasteful with their offense. They won 11-5, 11-2, 20-8, 12-1, and 9-0, and, in a 3-game series in Detroit, 41-13—only to lose 6 games by 2 runs or less.

Though Fernandez went 1-2 in his starts, Kevin Tapani and Alvarez each won 4 games to give the rotation respectability. Baldwin pitched decently enough in the 4th spot. Where the rotation got into trouble, though, was when a 5th starter was needed. Kirk McCaskill and Joe Magrane (evidently Britt Burns, Ken Kravec, and Ross Baumgarten weren't available for duty) served in that capacity for the time being—and not very well. But you get what you pay for. A sore spot was also festering in the bullpen. Larry Thomas, Bill Simas, and Matt Karchner were used so often to get the ball to Roberto Hernandez that they were all in the league's top 10 in appearances

June 14-14 (46-34, 3 games back)
Chicago ran in place in June, but the Indians helped them out, going 14-14 as well. Wilson Alvarez had a 6-game winning streak into mid-June and Roberto Hernandez stretched his consecutive saves streak to 20. Meanwhile, a few miles back and stuck in the ditch were McCaskill and Magrane. They went 2-6, and both had ERAs in the mid-5.00 range by the end of the month, sending urgent signals to the front office to step up their search for a starter. Mike Sirotka was called up from Triple-A Nashville to bolster the bullpen, which was still going strong. They were second in the league (behind the Yankees) in ERA with the All-Star game approaching.

Thomas kept up his torrid hitting (he reached base in the team's first 49 games!) with a .361 average and 7 homers for the month. And Tony Phillips, Robin Ventura, and Dave Martinez joined Thomas in leading the offense. Coming off their slamfest against the A.L. East, the Sox suffered an 8-game losing streak at the hands of the Mariners and the Angels in mid-June. Not a good sign considering they had a pair of 4-game series with the Indians just before the break. They missed a chance to close the gap by splitting the first series.

July 12-15 (58-49, 7 games back)
The White Sox went to Jacobs Field just before the All-Star break, took 3 of 4 from the Indians, and went into the break 2 games out, leading the league in ERA and fielding percentage and 4th in runs scored. It would prove to be the high-water mark of the season. Frank Thomas went on the shelf with a stress fracture in his left foot. Schueler: "We're about to see what we're made of." What is: clay. Underachievers for 500, Alex. The White Sox went 7-12 during the 3 weeks Thomas was on the DL, dropping 5 more games in the standings. Without Thomas the White Sox dropped from 5.7 runs per game to 4.6.

The bullpen finally wore down. Manager Terry Bevington's relievers had a month-long stretch when Hernandez, Simas, Karchner, and Brian Keyser combined for 9 losses. The Indians, in turn, went 16-11 during the month and led the Sox by 7 games. The Sox still talked about winning the division, but the wild-card would be their only route to the playoffs.

August 15-15 (73-64, 8 games back)
Thomas returned after three weeks, saying, "We've got work to do." He then went out and hit .400 with 3 home runs in his first 15 games back. But in mid-August the White Sox started to slide, losing their 4½ game lead in the wild-card race despite playing sub-.500 teams. Tapani had tendinitis in his pitching hand and suddenly lost effectiveness. Baldwin was poor as well, giving up 11 home runs in 6 starts. Even Alvarez, who previously had winning streaks of 6 and 4 games, couldn't buy a victory. Bevington kept trotting rookies such as Simas (5.23 ERA) and Karchner (6.17 ERA, 3 blown saves) out of the bullpen, even though they turned close games into groaners. Schueler acquired Tony Castillo from the Blue Jays on the 22nd, but the supplies had been airlifted in too late. The inexperienced bullpen blew 5 saves (and quite possibly the wild-card) in August.

Things got so bad that Bevington was booed at Comiskey every time he made a pitching change. Trouble was, he couldn't figure out why. The crowds at Comiskey weren't huge last season, but they knew the team's weakness and weren't in an understanding mood. Yuppies don't do Comiskey—a boring park in a bad neighborhood in the Cubs' town. Only baseball fans do.

September 12-13 (85-77, 14½ games back)
The rotation, with the exception of Fernandez (who went 4-1), continued to sputter. Alvarez, Tapani, and Baldwin were 2-7 with an ERA over 7.00. Roberto Hernandez, who had been consistent all season, blew 2 saves and lost 4 games in his final 12 appearances. Matt Karchner and Larry Thomas were injured and rookies Alan Levine, Mike Sirotka, and Mike Bertotti got creamed in their stead.

In the wild-card race, the White Sox held a 4½ game lead over the Orioles on August 15, then went 18-23 over the final 6 weeks of the season while Baltimore went 25-18. Losing the division by 14½ games was disappointing. But it couldn't have hurt half as much as watching Baltimore pass them as if they were standing still. Since the White Sox won the division in '93 with one of the best young pitching staffs in years (see *Sympathy for the GM* in the Philadelphia Phillies section), they've had the plug pulled on another playoff run by the strike, were inexcusably bad in '95, and collapsed in '96. Take a look around the garage, because someone must have taken this team apart, put it back together again, and left a few key pieces lying around on the floor.

■ 1997 DIAGNOSIS

A few players have taken a run at Maris's 61 in the past 35 years, but Maris's and Mantle's 115 hasn't ever really been in reach. Until now.

Offense

The 1996 season was one of the best offensive years in White Sox history. Caught up in the homer hysteria that defined last season, the Sox hit 195 dingers, surpassing the team record set by the 1977 Sox of Jorge Orta, Alan Bannister, Eric Soderholm, Oscar Gamble, and "Pitch at Risk to" Richie Zisk. Sox hitters set records for runs, RBI, and slugging average as well. Tony Phillips was a first-rate table-setter, and the team got the most out of Baines, Tartabull, and Martinez. And Ventura finally had his career year. Thomas was able to offset the drain of having two regulars hitting in the .220s—Karkovice and Lewis. Only the Royals' David Howard, the Expos' Shane Andrews, the Marlins' Charles Johnson, and the mother of all outmakers (451 for the season!), Delino DeShields had more at-bats and

as little to show for them as Karkovice and Lewis. Free agents Harold Baines and Danny Tartabull may be out of the mix in '97, but Jeff Abbott and Mike Cameron could step in and challenge for the Rookie of the Year award. Oh, yeah, and this Belle guy looks like he could have the inside track on the clean-up spot.

Defense

Thomas isn't much of a fielder. Yes, and Trevor Hoffman isn't much of a hitter. Ray Durham has enough range to cover the entire right side anyway. Ozzie Guillen is a fine fielder, though his reconstructed knee limits his range and other assorted injuries are starting to keep him out of the lineup. Chris Snopek wouldn't be near the same caliber in the field, but the Sox are looking for him to be Guillen's successor anyway. Ventura was snake-bit in the field in '95, but he returned to form last year, winning his fourth Gold Glove. Dave Martinez and Darren Lewis were both very slick in the field. Tony Phillips was steady in left, which wasn't a surprise—but his 13 assists last season were. Stay tuned to see if Albert insists on playing the field, no doubt so he can feel the love in the bleachers. Considered a defensive liability, Tartabull rediscovered his drive and improved his defense dramatically. Cameron will be much better. Karkovice's outstanding throwing arm will continue to keep his anemic bat in the lineup.

Pitchings

Alvarez, Fernandez, and Bere went into '96 with something to prove. In '94 the three combined for a 36-16 record. But they fell to 28-34 in '95. Bere didn't pitch all year because of a muscle-fiber tear in his elbow—though he may have a few tears in his mental fiber, too. The elbow didn't require surgery, but it puts his status in question all the same. Fernandez and Alvarez came back strong in '96, giving the rotation a solid one-two punch. Kevin Tapani was a good pickup, though he faltered down the stretch because of a chronic hand injury. After a disappointing trial in '95, Baldwin broke through with 11 victories. The 5th spot was a black hole. A number of pitchers were shuffled in and out all season, going 3-12. With or without service-time free agent Alex Fernandez, they were looking to add a starter who could eat some innings and spare their bullpen in '97.

Relievers were their strength in the first half of the season, keeping pace with the Yankees' celebrated bullpen. But the starters went the distance only 7 times last season, putting a strain on the middle relievers. As a result, rookies Karchner, Simas, and Thomas folded in the second half. By the time the club traded for Tony Castillo, it was too late. Roberto Hernandez, effective most of the season, fell apart in September. The bullpen ended up blowing a major-league record 33 saves in '96, and the Sox lost a league-worst 34 one-run games. The bullpen should be better in '97 for a couple of reasons: the young arms aren't nearly as bad as they appeared to be, and Bevington probably won't work them as hard as early.

Farm System

The system is top-heavy with position prospects who will need jobs soon. Outfielders Jeff Abbott and Mike Cameron look great and are probably ready. Third basemen Olmedo Saenz and Jeff Liefer are also fine hitters. Saenz is a step behind Chris Snopek now, and Liefer has the bat to push the issue within a couple of years. The Sox have a year to figure out how they'll fit a trio of third basemen into the lineup. Pitchers in the system are in much shorter supply, and most have already been called up in '96.

Management and Ownership

Jerry Reinsdorf is the power behind the commissioner's office. Reinsdorf led the movement to install Fay Vincent after Bart Giamatti's death. Then, after Vincent blunderbussed his way through the first attempt at divisional realignment, Reinsdorf led the insurrection against him. When the dust cleared, Reinsdorf's friend, Bud Selig, was in power, and Reinsdorf was in perfect position to influence the upcoming labor negotiations. It was a masterful palace coup. The revolution might not have been televised, but the White Sox fans know what's going on and are staying away in droves from the worst new ballpark in baseball. They know that he doesn't have the best interests of anything except himself in that small lump of coal that passes for his heart. Reinsdorf will find the economics of his own team taking up more of his time in '97. His payroll, near the top of the league at $42 million in '96, isn't getting any smaller, even though attendance for

White Sox home games averaged only 21,220, a 34% drop since the strike in '94.

GM Ron Schueler has always had a keen eye for free-agent signings. His acquisitions of Phillips, Tapani, Baines, and Tartabull all turned out to be big factors in the team's success. But he drew a tremendous amount of fire for ignoring the troubles Bevington was having with the 5th starter and his bullpen depth. He said at the beginning of June that he was going to try to land a starter, but he wouldn't part with Mike Cameron (most team's asking price) to get one. That may prove to be the best trade he never made, though Tony Phillips didn't see it that way. Phillips retired and unretired twice before completing this statement: "Opportunities to go to the World Series don't come around all the time. When they come around, you've got to do whatever it takes to win games." Easy for a veteran to say when he's going to be on *Celebrity Skeet-Shooting* on ESPN when Cameron is standing on the foul line at the All-Star game.

The White Sox didn't exactly give manager Terry Bevington a resounding vote of confidence in '95 by speaking with Tony LaRussa in the off-season. But when they put out feelers for Jim Leyland in '96, it seemed that Bevington's brakes were being greased for a slide out the door. But he somehow survived, signing a contract through '98. Bevington is a fiery personality, and his grouchiness hasn't made him many friends in the media. He snapped at questions he didn't like, and he hates to be second-guessed or reminded of his team's weaknesses. His handling of the bullpen earned him a steady round of boos in September. He'll either learn his lesson—or he'll snap and charge the stands with a fungo bat. Either one ought to be more fun to watch than yet another overmatched rookie pitcher sweating gravy and walking in runs.

. . . and whatnot: Bag Man or Big Hurt

You hear these arguments in schoolyards all the time. "Superman would beat Batman in a fight to the death." "Ali would knock out Tyson." "My mommy could beat up your daddy." The comparison of Frank Thomas and Jeff Bagwell is equally troublesome, albeit less violent. Each player is unanimously considered the best first baseman in his league. And in some circles, each player is considered the best hitter in his league. Here's each hitter's batting line. **RC** stand for runs created—it's how many runs each player contributed single-handedly. For these guys, it's about a run per game.

Player	AB	R	H	2B	3B	HR	RBI	BB	SO	BA	OBP	SLG	RC
Bagwell	568	111	179	48	2	31	120	135	114	.315	.447	.570	145
Thomas	527	108	182	27	0	40	134	109	70	.349	.461	.626	152

In the real world, Thomas jumps out to an early lead. Even though Bagwell played more, reached base more often, and scored more runs, Thomas created more runs. He hit for much more power than Bagwell, and that, combined with his huge batting average, is enough to tip the scale. While nobody ever said the real world was fair, there is an advantage going to Thomas that can, and should, be compensated for: The Astrodome has an even more stifling effect on a hitter's statistics than Comiskey II (the pointless sequel). Here are the same stats for each player, this time "pasteurized" for his home-park effect.

Player	AB	R	H	2B	3B	HR	RBI	BB	SO	BA	OBP	SLG	RC
Bagwell	576	122	193	51	0	33	132	135	110	.335	.461	.593	157.5
Thomas	529	108	182	27	0	40	132	111	72	.344	.477	.620	150.3

Basically, when you put each player's offensive season in the context of a neutral hitting environment, Bagwell comes out with a slight edge in runs created. But there's another comparison that can be made between the two. We've seen how the hitters stack up against each other. Now let's see how they stack up against the average hitter in their respective leagues, with the impact of the DH and the pitchers removed.

Player	AB	R	H	2B	3B	HR	RBI	BB	SO	BA	OBP	SLG	RC
Bagwell	576	122	193	51	0	33	132	135	110	.335	.461	.593	157.5
N.L. Avg.	576	82	157	29	3	18	77	57	105	.272	.338	.425	82.7
Thomas	529	108	182	27	0	40	132	111	72	.344	.477	.620	150.3
A.L. Avg.	529	82	148	28	3	18	76	56	93	.277	.348	.442	80.9

Thomas is 70 runs better than the average A.L. hitter, but Bagwell is 75 runs better than the average in the National League. We could look at them park-neutralized on the Sabbath against left-handed Gentiles, but it's obvious that the two are going to be extremely close in terms of overall offensive production no matter how the cake gets cut. Both deserve to be MVP candidates. Both made decent players hitting behind them look better than they are

(Derek Bell and Harold Baines, respectively). But even if the offense is called a draw, Bagwell gets the slight edge over Thomas as the best first baseman in baseball in '96 for three reasons:

1. Bagwell played all season.
2. Bagwell's defense is dramatically better
3. Bagwell stole 21 bases in 28 attempts, so give him 65 doubles to Thomas's 27.

Bagwell's better, but it's not an argument you should try to make on a South Side playground.

JEFF ABBOTT — SOLID PROSPECT

OF • BR • TL • 6'2 • 190 • 24 • CHA94/6

	AB	R	H	2B	3B	HR	RBI	BB	SO	SB	CS	BA	OB	SA
AAA	440	64	143	27	1	14	60	32	50	12	4	.325	.373	.486

The White Sox spent their 4th-round draft pick on Abbott in 1994, and they practically stole him. His stock dropped considerably because he missed his junior year at Kentucky because of a bad case of mono. If it wasn't for that, he may have been a 1st- or 2nd-round pick the previous year. If you're thinking his .325 average at Triple-A Nashville looks good, consider what he did the two previous seasons. In 1994, his first pro season, Abbott hit .393 and slugged .598 for short-season Class-A Hickory. In '95 Abbott hit .348 and slugged .454 for Class-A Prince William and was promoted to Double-A Birmingham. There he hit .320 and slugged .431 before the season ended. He drives the ball all over the yard and makes adjustments like a big-leaguer. He has a smooth swing with line-drive power, and it's difficult to find a weakness. Defensively, he might need a little work. He played center field in the minors, but scouts say he has a little trouble tracking fly balls hit right at him. ■

WILSON ALVAREZ — YOUNG GUN

SP • BL • TL • 6'1 • 175 • 27 • TEX86

	G	GS	IP	H	HR	BB	K	W	L	S	ERA	K/BB	K9	HW9
CHA94	24	24	161	147	16	62	108	12	8	0	3.45	1.7	6.0	11.68
CHA95	29	29	175	171	21	93	118	8	11	0	4.32	1.3	6.1	13.58
CHA96	35	35	217	216	21	97	181	15	10	0	4.22	1.9	7.5	12.98
CAREER	164	138	918	855	95	470	660	58	43	1	3.91	1.4	6.5	12.99

Alvarez still hasn't conquered his control problems. He allowed nearly 13 baserunners per 9 innings last season. But he won 15 games, due in large part to the outrageous run support he received. White Sox hitters averaged 6.3 runs every time Alvarez took the mound, by far the best support on the team. In fact, during one stretch from mid-May into June, Alvarez won 6 straight; his ERA for that span was 4.53, but his hitters scored 11.5 runs a game for him. He got more support than Ivana Trump.

Alvarez has excellent stuff. His fastball, which he throws in the low 90s, has excellent late movement. His curve is hard and nasty. The biggest knock against him, other than his conditioning, is that he allows too many bases on balls. The White Sox think it's because he loses concentration. Ozzie Guillen calls time out frequently to walk to the mound and wake him up. ■

HAROLD BAINES (see Free Agents)

JAMES BALDWIN — YOUNG GUN

SP • BR • TR • 6'4 • 210 • 25 • CHA90/5

	G	GS	IP	H	HR	BB	K	W	L	S	ERA	K/BB	K9	HW9
CHA95	6	4	14	32	6	9	10	0	1	0	12.89	1.1	6.4	26.36
CHA96	28	28	169	168	24	57	127	11	6	0	4.42	2.2	6.8	11.98

Baldwin has the stuff to be a winner. All he needs to dominate is a little experience and he should be getting plenty in the coming years. His power curve buckles knees. It's been referred to as the best breaking pitch in almost every league he has played. His fastball is above average, and his change-up is improving daily. Baldwin went 3-0 after his promotion, beating the Angels, Yankees and Orioles. That put the league on notice that 1996 was going to be the breakthrough

season that Chicago expected out of him in '95—when Baldwin was supposed to rule the American League, but instead got spanked all the way down to the American Association. He won't be going back. ■

ALBERT BELLE

AL ELITE

LF • BR • TR • 6′2 • 210 • 30 • CLE87/2

	AB	R	H	2B	3B	HR	RBI	BB	SO	SB	CS	BA	OB	SA
CLE94	412	90	147	35	2	36	101	58	71	9	6	.357	.438	.714
CLE95	546	121	173	52	1	50	126	73	80	5	2	.317	.401	.690
CLE96	602	124	187	38	3	48	148	99	87	11	0	.311	.410	.623
CAREER	3441	592	1014	223	16	242	751	396	622	61	25	.295	.369	.580

Is there any way to comprehend the season Belle had? Maybe, but first you'd have to walk a mile in his shoes and nobody seems to be lining up for that ride. The statistical accomplishments he had in 1996 are up there with the immortals. Even though he barely missed becoming the only player since Ruth to hit 50 home runs in consecutive seasons, his 148 RBI were the most by an A.L. outfielder since Ted Williams' 159 in 1949. But in ten years, will Albert Belle's '95–96 seasons be remembered for the statistical company he kept or will it be remembered for throwing a ball at a photographer, nearly decapitating a puny second baseman in Milwaukee, and trying to run down some brats with his Jeep on Halloween?

Welcome to Albert's universe, population 1. If you're not Albert Belle, you're an intruder. He thought the world was out to get him, and now his prophecy has been self-fulfilled. If you listen to him—which is harder to do these days since the only "journalist" he'll speak to is Spike Lee—you'll hear that all he wants is to be left alone. Well, it's getting harder to understand this Garbo act when his own actions embroil him in the center of a new controversy every other week.

While Belle is one of the American League's top three right-handed hitters (Frank Thomas and Edgar Martinez are the others), he has never been the best player in the league. He turned down two attempts by the Indians to re-sign him, one of which would have made him the highest-paid player in the game, because he wanted to be the first $10 million player. A lot to ask when you aren't much with the glove, on the bases, or in the clubhouse. His idea of leadership is to keep the locker room cold and smash the thermostats with his bats after teammates try to turn it up—and to glare at a gimpy-kneed Kevin Seitzer for failing to get Belle an RBI by scoring a meaningless run in a meaningless late season game.

Now that the White Sox have Belle, club officials have to hope that the home runs and RBIs Belle supplies are worth the collateral damage he is sure to cause. And they can forget about the players they could have bought with the millions they'll be paying Belle. The White Sox, drooling at the thought of Frank Thomas and Belle back-to-back, were willing to risk $11 million a year. It remains to be seen whether Thomas will be thinking about wins, or battling the intruders to Belle's world. ■

JASON BERE

SP • BR • TR • 6′3 • 185 • 25 • CHA90/37

	G	GS	IP	H	HR	BB	K	W	L	S	ERA	K/BB	K9	HW9
CHA94	24	24	141	119	17	80	127	12	2	0	3.81	1.6	8.1	12.70
CHA95	27	27	137	151	21	106	110	8	15	0	7.19	1.0	7.2	16.88
CHA96	5	5	16	26	3	18	19	0	1	0	10.26	1.1	10.6	24.65
CAREER	80	80	438	405	53	285	385	32	23	0	4.99	1.4	7.9	14.18

If he continues to follow the above trends, he may never retire another batter. Little did the Sox know how much they would miss Bere. He went on the DL June 5 with tendinitis in his elbow and never made it back. And while Bere rehabbed and soft-tossed the rest of the season, Chicago's 5th starters combined to go 3-12. The lack of a quality arm in that spot, coupled with the ineffectiveness of the bullpen, contributed greatly to their fall from wild-card contention in September. A healthy Bere might have given the White Sox five pitchers with double-digit victories and a chance to challenge Baltimore.

When he was healthy, Bere was considered the best arm on the White Sox staff. His fastball reaches 94-95 and explodes into the strike zone. He also throws a hard breaking ball that bores into hitters and a "fosh" change-up. Trouble is, he hasn't shown much command, and he makes Scottie Pippen and Mike Mussina look mentally tough. Even if his elbow has recovered, he's got a lost '96 and a wretched '95 to live down. He's the type of pitcher who, if he finds his control, could once again excel.

Or he could get filed away in the "Didn't You Used to Be" bin—the kind of pitcher who gets heckled at Old-Timers games if they bother to invite him back at all. ■

PAT BORDERS (see Looking for a Game)

MIKE CAMERON — GRADE-A PROSPECT

OF • BR • TR • 6'1 • 170 • 24 • CHI91/18

	AB	R	H	2B	3B	HR	RBI	BB	SO	SB	CS	BA	OB	SA
AA	473	120	142	34	12	28	77	71	117	39	15	.300	.402	.600

Cameron's season at Double-A Birmingham can only be described as dominating. Always considered a fine defensive player with great athletic skills that didn't translate into baseball, he put it all together and had the season of his life in the Southern League last year. He always had the strength; it just never showed up in his extra-base-hit totals. Cameron spent his '95 off-season in the Mexican Winter League, learning to hit the breaking ball. He made a lot of progress south of the border, so he was primed when the regular season started.

Cameron is considered a 5-tool player. He's got outstanding speed and range in the field, his throwing arm was the best in the Southern League last year, his bat speed is impressive, and he has an incredible vertical leap. He was also voted Most Exciting Player in the Southern League. Scouts most often compare him to Ellis Burks, but he might actually be a better hitter. Unless Terry Bevington forgets to take his medication, he'll give Cameron every opportunity to win the starting right-field job in '97. If he stays focused and gets a few breaks, he could be the Rookie of the Year. ■

CARLOS CASTILLO — SOLID PROSPECT

RP • BR • TR • 6'2 • 225 • 25 • CHA93/3

	G	GS	IP	H	HR	BB	SO	W	L	S	ERA	K/BB	K9	HW9
A	20	19	133	131	12	29	128	9	9	0	4.05	4.4	8.6	10.80

Castillo has walked only 63 batters, while striking out 299, over a span of 327 innings in his professional career. That's 1.7 walks and 8.2 strikeouts per 9 innings. He's not considered one of the best prospects in the organization at this point, but if he pitches in Double-A the way he's pitched in Class-A, the suits may have to start taking his agent's calls. ■

TONY CASTILLO

RP • BL • TL • 5'10 • 175 • 34 • TOR83

	G	GS	IP	H	HR	BB	K	W	L	S	ERA	K/BB	K9	HW9
TOR94	41	0	68	66	7	28	43	5	2	1	2.51	1.5	5.7	12.44
TOR95	55	0	72	64	7	24	38	1	5	13	3.22	1.6	4.8	11.00
TOR/CHA96	55	0	94	95	10	24	57	5	4	2	3.63	2.4	5.5	11.38
CAREER	314	6	436	443	39	145	277	23	17	18	3.55	1.9	5.7	12.13

Ron Schueler swapped pitchers Luis Andujar and Allen Halley to the Blue Jays August 22 to land Castillo. He immediately became Bevington's setup man, supplanting Simas, but by then it was a case of trying to dress an open chest wound with a cotton ball. At his age, and with his build, Castillo has to rely on his pitching smarts to survive. His primary weapon is a sweeping curveball, and he lives on the corners with a slider and an average fastball. ■

DOMINGO CEDEÑO

2B • BB • TR • 6'0 • 170 • 28 • TOR87

	AB	R	H	2B	3B	HR	RBI	BB	SO	SB	CS	BA	OB	SA
TOR94	97	14	19	2	3	0	10	10	31	1	2	.196	.261	.278
TOR95	161	18	38	6	1	4	14	10	35	0	1	.236	.289	.360
TOR/CHA96	301	46	82	12	2	2	20	15	64	6	3	.272	.308	.346
CAREER	605	83	147	20	6	6	51	36	140	8	6	.243	.286	.326

The Blue Jays shipped Cedeño to Chicago at a time when his trade value was at its peak. He was hitting about .278 when the Sox acquired him in August along with Castillo. He didn't get much playing time for the Sox in '96, and the role of defensive sub is the job Cedeño will be asked to fill in '97. Even though he played a lot of second base for the Blue Jays, shortstop is his natural position. He's basically an insurance policy in case Guillen gets hurt and Snopek can't handle the position switch. Cedeño is a defensive whiz, but he would have to fill his bat with a trainload of cork to put up any numbers. ■

MCKAY CHRISTENSEN

OF • 21 • CAL94/1

	AB	R	H	2B	3B	HR	RBI	BB	SO	SB	CS	BA	OB	SA
R	133	17	35	7	5	1	16	10	23	10	3	.263	.327	.414

The Angels drafted Christensen with their no. 1 pick in '94 and signed him knowing he was going to spend 2 years on a Mormon mission in Japan before he would ever play a game for them. That should give you an idea of the kind of talent he possesses. Christensen is a fine athlete with great speed, who was recruited by Brigham Young as a running back. His quick swing has some pop in it, and is geared toward hitting line drives. Schueler, who got him

cheap in the '95 Abbott trade, says he reminds him of a young Brett Butler. Christensen has missed a lot of time. As a matter of fact, it's quite possible he could be challenging for a job in the spring if he had started playing after the draft. So when did BYU alum Jim McMahon find the time between golfing naked and shutting down the bars on Rush Street to fulfill *his* Mormon mission? ■

CHRIS CLEMONS

SP • BR • TR • 6'4 • 220 • 24 • CHA94/1

	G	GS	IP	H	HR	BB	SO	W	L	S	ERA	K/BB	K9	HW9
AA	19	16	94	91	7	40	69	5	2	0	3.15	1.7	6.6	12.53

A 1st round pick in '94 out of Texas A&M—a supplemental pick as compensation for losing Ellis Burks to free agency—Clemons has a power-pitcher's build and a pretty good fastball. However, a lack of command has hampered his progress. After allowing 8 walks in 6 starts for Class-A Prince William, Clemons earned a promotion to Double-A Birmingham in June. He lost some control after the jump, but it was an improvement over his early seasons. Clemons is no Clemens, but then who is? ■

JEFF DARWIN

SLEEPER

RP • BR • TR • 6'3 • 180 • 27 • SEA88/13

	G	GS	IP	H	HR	BB	K	W	L	S	ERA	K/BB	K9	HW9
CHA96	22	0	30	26	5	9	15	0	1	0	2.93	1.7	4.5	10.48

He's Danny Darwin's baby brother, and he came over from Seattle, where he served as their Triple-A closer the previous couple of seasons. His stuff isn't incredible, but he has excellent control. He throws an average fastball, but it has a tailing motion to it. He also has a sharp slider. He performed very well in his 22 appearances last season, limiting hitters to a .232 average overall, and manhandling lefties. That should earn him a trip back for '97. Darwin won't be taking any save situations away from Hernandez but is a pretty good bet to get a lot of innings in long relief. And if he has his brother's longevity, the Darwin family will have had their children in the majors from 1978 to 2014. ■

RAY DURHAM

YOUNG GUN

2B • BB • TR • 5'8 • 170 • 25 • CHA90/6

	AB	R	H	2B	3B	HR	RBI	BB	SO	SB	CS	BA	OB	SA
CHA95	471	68	121	27	6	7	51	31	83	18	5	.257	.309	.384
CHA96	557	79	153	33	5	10	65	58	95	30	4	.275	.350	.406

Durham had problems in '95 hitting from the left side, but he worked with hitting coach Bill Buckner in early April and found out that he was crouching too much in his stance and getting ahead of the ball. He was trying to generate more bat speed, as his right-handed swing is quicker—short and compact, compared by some to Joe Morgan's.

Durham has great speed that translates into both stolen bases and excellent range in the field. He can also turn the double play. His hands aren't the softest, but they're good enough to make all the routine plays. Durham will improve in '97. He's young, but has already shown a line-drive swing and a good batting eye and he could develop 15-20 home-run power. He gives the White Sox excellent production for a second baseman. At least half of their keystone combo can hit. ■

ALEX FERNANDEZ

AL ELITE

SP • BR • TR • 6'2 • 200 • 27 • CHA90/1

	G	GS	IP	H	HR	BB	K	W	L	S	ERA	K/BB	K9	HW9
CHA94	24	24	170	163	25	50	122	11	7	0	3.86	2.4	6.5	11.27
CHA95	30	30	203	200	19	65	159	12	8	0	3.80	2.4	7.0	11.75
CHA96	35	35	258	248	34	72	200	16	10	0	3.45	2.8	7.0	11.16
CAREER	199	197	1346	1306	148	426	951	79	63	0	3.78	2.2	6.4	11.58

Fernandez joined the pitching elite in '96, finishing in the top 10 in 6 important categories. He was tied for 5th in victories (despite receiving the worst run support on the staff), ranked 4th in the league in ERA, 5th with a .253 batting average allowed, 5th in hits per nine innings, 5th in strikeouts, and 9th in strikeouts per 9 innings. Fernandez was awesome in his 16 victories, allowing 104 hits and a 1.97 ERA in 128 innings. But one way to judge a starter's season is to see what he did in his no-decisions—he had a 3.28 ERA in his 9.

His wins were split evenly between the halves of the season. He went 8-5 with a 4.10 ERA before the break and 8-5 with a 2.81 ERA after the break. He should have won more games in the second half of the season, but his offense, which scored 98 fewer runs after the break, didn't support him, and his

bullpen fell apart. Fernandez has a no. 1 starter's stuff. His heater consistently clocks in at 92 with good riding action. He also has a quick slider and a curve that he uses more as a change of pace than anything else. He gets into trouble sometimes because he tends to leave his fastball high in the strike zone, yielding 34 homers in the process.

Most significantly, Fernandez could be the reason the owners wouldn't ratify a labor agreement during the season. His free-agent status depended on whether the new deal included service time lost to the strike. Jerry Reinsdorf was betting that the players would give up the issue to get a deal done, so he refused to offer Fernandez a deal during the season. Knowing Fernandez would walk if liberated (the pitcher was upset about a bitter arbitration loss in '95) set Reinsdorf's fillings to aching. So when it looked like a deal would be cut allowing service time, he stepped into the labor negotiations just as talk of a settlement started hitting the press. In a 3½-hour conference call August 12, Reinsdorf helped convince enough of his fellow owners to vote against the proposal and stall the agreement. If so, Dante may need to concoct a 10th ring of Hell for this beast. ■

TOM FORDHAM — SOLID PROSPECT

SP • BL • TL • 6'2 • 210 • 23 • CHA93/11

	G	GS	IP	H	HR	BB	SO	W	L	S	ERA	K/BB	K9	HW9
AAA	22	22	140	117	15	69	118	10	8	0	3.45	1.7	7.6	11.94

Fordham was out of shape his first pro season and finished with a 5-4 record. But since then, he's averaged almost 14 victories a season. Last season he went a combined 12-9 with a 3.28 ERA as he climbed from Double-A to Triple-A. After his promotion he allowed a .229 average to American Association hitters. His fastball is below average, but his curve and change-up are solid. He's been so successful because he changes speeds, has excellent poise, and good location. Fordham doesn't have the arm of a prospect such as Ruffcorn, but he's got to be considered one of the better pitching prospects in the White Sox system. ■

OZZIE GUILLEN

SS • BL • TR • 5'11 • 150 • 33 • SD80

	AB	R	H	2B	3B	HR	RBI	BB	SO	SB	CS	BA	OB	SA
CHA94	365	46	105	9	5	1	39	14	35	5	4	.288	.311	.348
CHA95	415	50	103	20	3	1	41	13	25	6	7	.248	.270	.318
CHA96	499	62	131	24	8	4	45	10	27	6	5	.263	.273	.367
CAREER	5577	634	1488	219	62	20	513	171	436	158	98	.267	.287	.339

Guillen has lost a lot of range and hasn't turned the double play with quite the same precision since his knee surgery in '93. But he makes up for the lack of range by positioning himself intelligently. And when he gets to the balls, his soft hands and accurate arm do the rest. His arm is strong enough that he hardly ever has to plant and throw. Sometimes he tries to be a little too flashy in the field, though. As a hitter, he's a lost cause. As he says, "If I hit .300, people will expect it from me every year. My destiny is .240." He's signed through '97, but if his fielding keeps slipping as it has the past two years, his destiny will be .240 as a part-time player. ■

ROBERTO HERNANDEZ — AL ELITE

CL • BR • TR • 6'4 • 220 • 32 • CAL86/1

	G	GS	IP	H	HR	BB	K	W	L	S	ERA	K/BB	K9	HW9
CHA94	45	0	47	44	5	19	50	4	4	14	4.91	2.6	9.6	12.05
CHA95	60	0	59	63	9	28	84	3	7	32	3.92	3.0	12.8	13.88
CHA96	72	0	84	65	2	38	85	6	5	38	1.91	2.2	9.1	11.03
CAREER	299	3	356	301	27	132	364	24	23	134	2.93	2.8	9.2	10.94

Hernandez has one of the best fastballs in the league, rated 7+, on a scale of 1-8, by the scouts. There were times when it was clocked at 99–100 mph last season, but it normally hovers around the 96–97 mph mark. Hernandez also throws a hard split-finger pitch that breaks straight down as it crosses the plate. He tends to be wild in the strike zone and can get hit hard when he tries to aim his heat. But when he just rocks and fires, he's as dominant a pitcher as there is.

The big knock about Hernandez's pitching is that his wildness causes him to go through streaks of ineffectiveness that can last weeks. Last year his streak couldn't have come at a worse time. Hernandez lost 4 games, blew 2 saves, and had a 6.59 ERA in September, just when the Sox were fighting

to stay in the wild-card race. He took his performance hard, too—even harder than when he accidentally broke Cal Ripken's nose at the All-Star team photo session. ■

JIMMY HURST

OF • BR • TR • 6'6 • 225 • 25 • CHA90/13

	AB	R	H	2B	3B	HR	RBI	BB	SO	SB	CS	BA	OB	SA
AA	472	62	125	23	1	18	88	53	128	19	11	.265	.338	.432

In the not-too-distant past, Hurst was considered to have the highest ceiling among all White Sox outfielders. But he broke his wrist during winter ball in '95 and couldn't get his stroke back when he returned to action. He's since been eclipsed by Mike Cameron. Hurst has great power potential and decent speed. But what has slowed his advancement is a long swing that's good for about 140 whiffs a year. He also needs to improve his defense despite his solid progress of late. Hurst played with Latrell Sprewell on Three Rivers Junior College's Division III national champion basketball team, which makes him the second best basketball playing outfielder who's been through Birmingham in recent years. Except Hurst didn't provide his own bus. ■

MATT KARCHNER

RP • BR • TR • 6'4 • 245 • 29 • KC89/9

	G	GS	IP	H	HR	BB	K	W	L	S	ERA	K/BB	K9	HW9
CHA95	31	0	32	33	2	12	24	4	2	0	1.69	2.0	6.8	12.66
CHA96	50	0	59	61	10	41	46	7	4	1	5.76	1.1	7.0	15.55

Karchner won the setup job on the strength of his brilliant rookie performance in '95. But the fact that he made his major-league debut at age 28 should have been an omen that it wouldn't get much better than that. Karchner went 4-0 with a 2.87 ERA in his first 23 games, but from June on, he was 3-4 with a 9.45 ERA. Bevington kept running him out there, even though it was obvious he had nothing. Despite Karchner's imposing size, his fastball only hits the upper 80s. He couples it with a hard slider. When he's on, he keeps the ball low and induces a lot of ground balls. But his stuff doesn't blow anybody away, and when his control left him in June, he got rocked. He could be over about as quickly as he'd begun. ■

RON KARKOVICE

C • BR • TR • 6'1 • 215 • 33 • CHA82/1

	AB	R	H	2B	3B	HR	RBI	BB	SO	SB	CS	BA	OB	SA
CHA94	207	33	44	9	1	11	29	36	68	0	3	.213	.325	.425
CHA95	323	44	70	14	1	13	51	39	84	2	3	.217	.306	.387
CHA96	355	44	78	22	0	10	38	24	93	0	0	.220	.270	.366
CAREER	2459	326	549	117	6	90	317	222	717	24	14	.223	.291	.386

Karkovice's value to the White Sox lies almost solely with his defense. He did a wonderful job handling the team's young pitching staff last season. He moves well behind the plate, and he's a gritty player who takes charge of the defense. He improved his throwing a great deal, but that was largely due to the fact that he didn't have to throw out runners on pitches he was lunging for, as he did much of '95.

He'll never help his team much with his swing-hard-three-times-and-make-a-left-turn offense, but it's hard to find a catcher of his defensive quality. Karkovice has had some knee problems in the past, but he began a weight-training regimen in June last season, and he plans to continue it all winter. Hopefully he'll be able to build up the strength in his knees he needs to catch another full season. ■

CHAD KREUTER (see Looking for a Game)

DARREN LEWIS

CF • BR • TR • 6'0 • 180 • 29 • OAK88/19

	AB	R	H	2B	3B	HR	RBI	BB	SO	SB	CS	BA	OB	SA
SF94	451	70	116	15	9	4	29	53	50	30	13	.257	.340	.357
SF/CIN95	472	66	118	13	3	1	24	34	57	32	18	.250	.311	.297
CHA96	337	55	77	12	2	4	53	45	40	21	5	.228	.321	.312
CAREER	2359	358	580	70	25	13	188	234	267	172	66	.246	.320	.313

The White Sox lost a lot of team speed when they let Lance Johnson go in the 1995 off-season, so they went out and signed his defensive clone, Darren Lewis. But his work at the plate left the Sox without a no. 2 hitter who could swing the bat. Lewis went from the 2nd spot in the batting order to the bottom as the season wore on. That's not to say that the Sox didn't know what they were getting at the plate. Lewis's reputation as a Punch-and-Judy hitter with an ability

to make contact and leg out infield hits is well known. But they didn't expect him to skate the Mendoza Line all season, either. The Sox have some pretty good outfield prospects in the minors, so they'll look long and hard at Lewis's trade value. If he does return, he'll only be a stopgap measure. ■

JEFF LIEFER

SOLID PROSPECT

3B • BL • TR • 23 • CHA95/1

	AB	R	H	2B	3B	HR	RBI	BB	SO	SB	CS	BA	OB	SA
A+	147	17	33	6	0	1	13	11	27	0	0	.224	.277	.286

Liefer, out of Long Beach State, was the 25th pick in the '95 draft, but didn't play that year because he signed late. He made his debut last season at full-season Class-A South Bend and impressed managers enough in his half season there that they considered him the 2nd-best prospect in the Midwest League. Liefer was also selected MVP of the Midwest League All-Star game. He was promoted to the Carolina League shortly after midseason, but he hit just .224 the rest of the way. He is a left-handed third baseman with a powerful swing that enables him to jack the ball to all fields. One example of his power: He became the first player to hit a home run over the center-field wall (an equipment shack that stands 30 feet high and is 405 feet from the plate) at South Bend's Covaleski Stadium. He was considered the best-hitting prospect in the Midwest League, bar none. Many people compared him to Robin Ventura.

Despite a strong arm, Liefer has shown himself to be error-prone at third base. He booted quite a few balls early in the season and blamed it on the cold weather. Nevertheless, the Sox have a bunch of third basemen in the system, so a switch to the outfield is probably inevitable. No matter what position he plays, Liefer will move quickly through the system. It wouldn't be a surprise to see him play a full season in Double-A in '97, with a chance to make the majors by late '98. ■

NORBERTO MARTIN

UT • BR • TR • 5'10 • 175 • 30 • CHA84

	AB	R	H	2B	3B	HR	RBI	BB	SO	SB	CS	BA	OB	SA
CHA94	131	19	36	7	1	1	16	9	16	4	2	.275	.317	.366
CHA95	160	17	43	7	4	2	17	3	25	5	0	.269	.281	.400
CHA96	140	30	49	7	0	1	14	6	17	10	2	.350	.374	.421
CAREER	445	69	133	21	5	4	49	19	59	19	4	.299	.325	.396

Martin missed the first couple of months of the season after undergoing facial surgery to repair

multiple fractures below his left eye suffered on a bunt play that went wrong. "Paco" is a Comiskey Park favorite. He doesn't hit much, and is a notorious hacker at the plate. But Bevington keeps him around for his versatility, his speed, his attitude, and his bat off the bench. He says of Martin, "I love the way 'Paco' plays. He's the kind, with that body, who could still be playing when he's 40." Martin hustles all the time and can play all over the infield. Because of this, he is a good backup to have around for Durham and Guillen. ■

DAVE MARTINEZ

OF-1B • BL • TL • 5'10 • 150 • 32 • TOR84

	AB	R	H	2B	3B	HR	RBI	BB	SO	SB	CS	BA	OB	SA
SF94	235	23	58	9	3	4	27	21	22	3	4	.247	.314	.362
CHA95	303	49	93	16	4	5	37	32	41	8	2	.307	.371	.436
CHA96	440	85	140	20	8	10	53	52	52	15	7	.318	.393	.468
CAREER	3774	514	1037	156	53	63	372	346	579	139	65	.275	.336	.394

A career .269 hitter coming into the season, his amnesia continued in '96. Forgetting his career trends, he hit over .300 for the 2nd consecutive season. Martinez has long been considered a weak hitter, and that has kept him from landing a starting job. As an 11-year veteran, he may not be able to change his reputation enough to be anything but a 4th outfielder. But what he brings to the table as a spare part is enough to get him plenty of playing time. It's getting harder and harder to take him out of the lineup. ■

LYLE MOUTON

OF • BR • TR • 6'4 • 240 • 27 • NYA91/5

	AB	R	H	2B	3B	HR	RBI	BB	SO	SB	CS	BA	OB	SA
CHA95	179	23	54	16	0	5	27	19	46	1	0	.302	.373	.475
CHA96	214	25	63	8	1	7	39	22	50	3	0	.294	.361	.439

Mouton spent 4 seasons in the Yankees system before the White Sox picked him up as the player to be named later in the Jack McDowell trade. The Yanks might have given up on him because of a reputation he earned for not hustling in the minors, something he admits. "As a high draft choice, I

didn't work hard . . . I'll never squander opportunities again."

Mouton has a long swing and he has trouble hitting the breaking ball, but he didn't seem to have a problem hitting last season. He hit equally well against both lefties and righties. Defensively, Mouton isn't a superstar, but he's solid enough to play both right and left. He doesn't run very well, but his arm is a cannon, and it's very accurate. He had a single assist last season, but that was because runners were afraid of him. Mouton has proven to be a savvy acquisition for the White Sox so far. He could step into a starting job next season, if either Abbott or Cameron have difficult adjustments to the majors. ■

TONY PHILLIPS — HEADED FOR A FALL

OF • BB • TR • 5'10 • 160 • 37 • MON78

	AB	R	H	2B	3B	HR	RBI	BB	SO	SB	CS	BA	OB	SA
DET94	438	91	123	19	3	19	61	95	105	13	5	.281	.409	.468
CAL95	525	119	137	21	1	27	61	113	135	13	10	.261	.394	.459
CHA96	581	119	161	29	3	12	63	125	132	13	8	.277	.404	.399
CAREER	6441	1094	1718	286	44	133	692	1099	1237	152	100	.267	.374	.387

Despite his age, Phillips proved to be one of the best free-agent acquisitions the White Sox have made in quite some time. He replaced Lance Johnson in the leadoff spot and ended up eclipsing Johnson's walk total from the previous season by nearly 100. In all, Phillips reached base 286 times, setting the table for the Big Hurt with bone china and sterling silver. It's evident just from looking at the stats, but Phillips works the count better than anyone in the league. That's what makes him such a great leadoff hitter. He doesn't steal much, but that's not because of his age. He never swiped many bases in the first place.

Phillips hasn't lost anything in the field. He didn't play much in the infield because the Sox were already set there. His range in left field is still excellent, and he nailed 13 baserunners who tried to run on him. Phillips isn't ready to hang up his spikes yet, but his skills will inevitably start declining. Expect it sooner rather than later. ■

SCOTT RUFFCORN — SLEEPER

RP • BR • TR • 6'4 • 215 • 27 • CHA91/1

	G	GS	IP	H	HR	BB	K	W	L	S	ERA	K/BB	K9	HW9
AAA	24	24	149	142	18	61	129	13	4	0	3.87	2.1	7.8	12.26

Ruffcorn's 1996 season looked just like all the others. Once again, he pitched very well in Triple-A. Once again, he got a call-up after the All-Star break. Once again, he struggled in a very limited trial. Once again, he was sent back to the minors. The White Sox have called him up each of the past 4 seasons, and Ruffcorn has yet to get in more than 4 big-league appearances in each of them. They've got to give him more of a chance to prove himself.

Ruffcorn had lost some velocity in the past due to shoulder problems. But his fastball started returning last season. Regardless of how hard he throws it, Ruffcorn's heater has a tremendous amount of movement on it. It was voted best in the American Association last year and helped him pitch his way into the Triple-A All-Star game. He also throws a circle change and an average slider.

The White Sox have speculated that Ruffcorn is lacking the mental toughness to make it in the majors. That might be true. But how is he supposed to learn what it takes to succeed in the big leagues if the White Sox do everything short of demoting him during his 8 warm-up pitches? Ruffcorn needs a trade to jump-start a once-promising career, though the Sox won't get as much for him as they would have 4 years ago. ■

OLMEDO SAENZ — SLEEPER

3B • BB • TR • 6'0 • 185 • 26 • CHA90

	AB	R	H	2B	3B	HR	RBI	BB	SO	SB	CS	BA	OB	SA
AAA	476	86	124	29	1	18	63	53	80	4	2	.261	.350	.439

He's no spring chicken, and 1996 was his 3rd season in Triple-A, but Saenz is a good prospect just the same. He knows what he's doing at the plate, has a quick bat, and solid power. Defensively, he was considered the best third baseman in the American Association. Chris Snopek was moved from third to short to keep from being stockpiled behind Ventura. Now it's Saenz's turn to sit and wait. ■

BILL SIMAS

RP • BL • TR • 6′3 • 220 • 25 • CAL92/9

	G	GS	IP	H	HR	BB	K	W	L	S	ERA	K/BB	K9	HW9
CHA95	14	0	14	15	1	10	16	1	1	0	2.57	1.6	10.3	16.07
CHA96	64	0	72	75	5	39	65	2	8	2	4.58	1.7	8.1	14.24

Simas was acquired by the White Sox in the Abbott trade with the Angels. His fastball approaches 90 mph, and his slider is solid. But last year he didn't have much command of either and the league had a .358 on-base average against him. Simas was being groomed as a closer in the Angels organization before the trade. The White Sox felt they could use him to close games if Hernandez struggled, but Simas responded by blowing 6 of his 8 save opportunities. ■

BRIAN SIMMONS — SLEEPER

OF • BB • TR • 6′2 • 190 • 23 • CHA95/2

	AB	R	H	2B	3B	HR	RBI	BB	SO	SB	CS	BA	OB	SA
A+	131	17	26	4	3	4	14	9	39	2	0	.198	.250	.366

Simmons didn't do much in his debut, but he turned on the jets last year in the Midwest League—(17-58-.298 in 92 games)—where he was named the circuit's second-best hitting prospect, behind teammate Jeff Liefer. He's a pure athlete with a great combination of speed and power. He was promoted to South Bend at mid-season and struggled, but his manager said he had the best tools of any player in the league. A trip to Double-A Birmingham in '97 wouldn't be out of the question either. Simmons could be a good one. ■

MIKE SIROTKA

RP-SP • BL • TL • 6′1 • 190 • 25 • CHA93/15

	G	GS	IP	H	HR	BB	K	W	L	S	ERA	K/BB	K9	HW9
CHA95	6	6	34	39	2	17	19	1	2	0	4.19	1.1	5.0	14.82
CHA96	15	4	26	34	3	12	11	1	2	0	7.18	.9	3.8	15.90

Sirotka, 26, was called up to take a turn as the 5th starter last season, but after just 4 starts, the White Sox demoted him to the bullpen. He was very ineffective in the majors last year, but his stats don't indicate his true quality. His fastball tops out in the high 80s, but it has life. He throws the standard complementary pitches as well—a curve, slider, and change-up. He has good control and is known for painting the corners, drawing the inevitable comparisons to Tom Glavine. Sirotka has come a long way in a very short time. Not many pitchers make it to the show within 3 years of being drafted. But Sirotka is a left-handed pitcher. Everyone knows the rules get bent for lefties who can throw strikes. ■

CHRIS SNOPEK — YOUNG GUN

3B-SS • BR • TR • 6′1 • 185 • 26 • CHA92/6

	AB	R	H	2B	3B	HR	RBI	BB	SO	SB	CS	BA	OB	SA
CHA95	68	12	22	4	0	1	7	9	12	1	0	.324	.403	.426
CHA96	104	18	27	6	1	6	18	6	16	0	1	.260	.304	.510

Snopek has fantastic defensive skills as a third baseman and is merely competent at shortstop. The White Sox will eventually find a position for him in the majors. There was speculation that Ventura would be moved to first base with Thomas becoming the full-time DH, but the Sox are now leaning toward grooming Snopek as Guillen's successor. That would be the most likely scenario, as Snopek doesn't have the 30-homer potential desired of a third baseman. That's not to say that Snopek is a weak hitter. He's got a great bat and has hit everywhere he has gone in the minors. He's gotten limited playing time in the majors, but has displayed an ability to make adjustments. He hit just .200 in 60 first-half at-bats. But then he hit .341 in 44 at-bats over the second half. The White Sox see him as a .290-.300 hitter with 15–20 homers. He has the instincts and the bulldog attitude to be a full-time player as soon as this year. ■

KEVIN TAPANI (see Free Agents)

DANNY TARTABULL (see Free Agents)

FRANK THOMAS — SUPERSTAR

1B • BR • TR • 6′5 • 240 • 28 • CHA89/1

	AB	R	H	2B	3B	HR	RBI	BB	SO	SB	CS	BA	OB	SA
CHA94	399	106	141	34	1	38	101	109	61	2	3	.353	.487	.729
CHA95	493	102	152	27	0	40	111	136	74	3	2	.308	.454	.606
CHA96	527	110	184	26	0	40	134	109	70	1	1	.349	.459	.626
CAREER	3291	675	1077	211	8	222	729	770	513	17	14	.327	.452	.599

This Thomas guy could be something.

He ranked in the top 10 in just about every offensive category last season: 2nd in batting average, 3rd in on-base percentage, 5th in walks, 6th in slugging, 7th in RBI, and 8th in home runs. Now consider that

Thomas missed 3 weeks with a stress fracture in his left foot. Would he have made a run at the Triple Crown had he stayed healthy? Well, his batting line would have looked something like this:

AB	R	H	2B	3B	HR	RBI	BB	SO	BA
605	126	211	30	0	46	154	125	80	.349

While his RBI total would have led the league, his home runs would have fallen short. Still, Thomas had an amazing offensive season. One of the keys to his hitting is that he has such exceptional plate discipline that he can afford to let the marginal pitches go by and make the pitcher throw a ball in his prime hitting zone. This is a rare quality for a big man with such a ferocious swing. There is a major flaw in his hitting though: NORAD reports that his home runs didn't leave the yard with the same escape velocity they once did. He'll have to work on that in the off-season.

Thomas is the driving force behind the White Sox offense. One telling fact about the Big Hurt's season: The day he was injured (July 11) the White Sox were 50-37, just 2 games behind the Indians. When he returned to the lineup 3 weeks later, they were 6 games back and, if the Indians had played better, they could have been buried 10 games back.

The only knock against Thomas is that his defense isn't up to par. His hands are good enough to play the position, but he doesn't have much range. Eventually the White Sox may wish to make him a DH. But any discussion of his defensive shortcomings becomes moot. If Thomas declared he wanted to play shortstop full time, Ozzie Guillen would be looking for work the next day.

Thomas joined Canseco and McGwire last season as the only active players to reach 200 home runs within 6 seasons of their debut. If he can avoid the potholes Canseco and McGwire have hit, Thomas will careen right into Cooperstown on the first ballot. ■

LARRY THOMAS

RP • BR • TL • 6'1 • 190 • CHA91/2

	G	GS	IP	H	HR	BB	K	W	L	S	ERA	K/BB	K9	HW9
CHA95	17	0	13	8	1	6	12	0	0	0	1.32	2.0	8.3	9.69
CHA96	57	0	30	32	1	14	20	2	3	0	3.23	1.4	6.0	13.77

Thomas used to be one of the Sox' better starting pitcher prospects. But he hit the wall when he made it to Triple-A in 1993 because he got tentative and started trying to nibble at the corners. A conversion to the bullpen in '95 suited him because he didn't have to worry about pacing himself or facing hitters more than once. His '96 season in the White Sox bullpen was, on the whole, successful, and his career is no longer in jeopardy. Thomas doesn't have much velocity on his fastball—it reaches just 85–87 mph. But his slider is sharp, and he's pretty good at upsetting hitters' timing. He isn't afraid to back hitters off the plate either. Thomas will probably find himself as the main left-handed setup man in the bullpen again this season. It's a role he can handle. ■

ROBIN VENTURA

AL ELITE

3B • BL • TR • 6'1 • 185 • 29 • CHA88/1

	AB	R	H	2B	3B	HR	RBI	BB	SO	SB	CS	BA	OB	SA
CHA94	401	57	113	15	1	18	78	61	69	3	1	.282	.373	.459
CHA95	492	79	145	22	0	26	93	75	98	4	3	.295	.384	.498
CHA96	586	96	168	31	2	34	105	78	81	1	3	.287	.368	.520
CAREER	3769	547	1041	178	7	144	624	555	527	14	25	.276	.367	.442

Ventura's career year was one of the more underreported stories of the season. He kept his batting average stable while beefing up his power numbers in a big way. He attained career highs in home runs, RBI, and slugging percentage last season despite seeing significant numbers of at-bats in 3 different spots in the batting order. Ventura uses the whole field when hitting. Pitchers can get him out if they pound him inside or get him to climb the ladder. But the latter is hard to do because Ventura has good plate discipline and will lay off the high pitches. No matter how you pitch him, though, he'll eventually make the necessary adjustments to avoid a prolonged slump. Still, trade rumors persist—fed, in part, by all the third base prospects in the organization. Stay tuned. ■

■ 1996 AUTOPSY

The Indians strolled into the regular season as confident as the dealer in a rigged game. Little retooling took place, and little was needed. GM John Hart signed Julio Franco to replace Paul Sorrento, and Jack McDowell to bolster an aging rotation. The Indians still weren't considered a great fundamental team—but it was their offense that intimidated their opposition, not their glovework. Manager Mike Hargrove knew that the suits and the fans would settle for nothing less than a World Series rematch with the Braves.

April 16-8 (16-8, 1½ games)

The Indians started the season on a sour note, dropping 2 in a row to New York and a game to Toronto, being outscored 19-3 in those losses. The Indians would eventually lose 5 of their first 7 games before setting the offense on cruise control and piling up the victories. But with the victories came turmoil. Albert Belle took exception with a *Sports Illustrated* photographer snapping away during workouts and nailed him with a throw from the outfield. The league investigated the matter and no suspension was handed down, but Belle was ordered to undergo counseling for his temper. Belle didn't let the furor surrounding him affect his hitting—this time—going .330-9-23.

May 19-9 (35-17, 3 games ahead)

In winning 19 times in May, the Indians compiled a 6-game winning streak and won 12 of 14 between May 11 and 26. Nagy won 6 in a row in May, lowering his ERA to 3.53 (he was 9-1 overall), and Dennis Martinez won 4 games. Orel Hershiser continued to be inconsistent, and the team still searched for a 5th starter. Belle produced incredible numbers in May, hitting .365 with 12 homers and 33 RBI. For good measure, he hit safely in 21 consecutive games. By the end of the month Belle had 21 home runs, putting him on pace to hit 67.

But every silver lining had a cloud. Omar Vizquel's injured shoulder was starting to manifest itself in throwing errors. Manny Ramirez started drawing fire from Hargrove for defensive and baserunning lapses. Carlos Baerga had reported to spring training overweight and was having trouble shedding it. By the end of May, Baerga's game was heading downhill fast, and the Indians were starting to get worried.

And there was Albert's big night in Milwaukee. Belle, on base after being hit with a pitch, was running from first to second in the eighth. Fernando Viña, for the second time in the game, chose to tag Belle in the basepaths on a double-play ball, and this time got a forearm to the face for his trouble. The incident sparked retaliation from both teams' pitchers (Belle was plunked his next time up), and a bench-clearing brawl finally erupted when Julian Tavarez threw behind Mike Matheny. In the middle of the brouhaha, Tavarez put a kung-fu move on umpire Joe Brinkman, flipping him after Brinkman grabbed him from behind. Tavarez and Belle would initially be suspended for 5 games by A.L. president Gene Budig, but it eventually was reduced to 2 games and a $25,000 fine after a well-prepared defense launched by the team and the players' union.

June 14-14 (49-31, 3 games ahead)

There seemed to be a cost to Belle's actions this time. They lost the mid-month doubleheader with the Yankees that Belle had to sit out—in the process of dropping the season series at home to New York. Belle hit .222 with 16 RBI for the month as the team played .500 ball. Was the team out of control, as some reporters suggested? Hargrove: "I resent that. I resent the hell out of that."

Nagy continued to shine and was joined by a suddenly effective Hershiser. But McDowell, who was expected to virtually guarantee a pennant single-handedly, had a subpar month, and Dennis Martinez wasn't winning games. Compounding the rotation's problems was the pitching of José Mesa, who lost his closer job to Paul Shuey after allowing 13 earned runs in 10 innings.

The offense homered in 20 consecutive games and scored in droves, but Hargrove wasn't satisfied. He saw a lack of clutch hitting and an almost nonchalant attitude regarding fundamentals. Baerga, especially, continued to struggle. The embattled second baseman was bumped from the third spot in the order to seventh in mid-June, and a trade rumor late in the month had him going to the Marlins for Jeff Conine.

July 16-11 (65-42, 7 games ahead)
Limping into the break, the Indians held a 2-game lead in the Central Division despite losing 5 of 8 to the White Sox between June 27 and July 7. Inconsistent pitching and a lack of hitting and fundamentals contributed greatly to the mini-slide that saw them lose 7 of 8 games at one point. Dennis Martinez landed on the DL June 29 with a strained elbow and Julio Franco followed suit July 7 with a pulled hamstring. Losing Franco really hurt since Eddie Murray refused to play first because of a sore shoulder and Herbert Perry, the primary backup, was lost to knee surgery. Sensing the team was getting flat, John Hart pulled off three gutsy moves to bolster the lineup for the stretch run. On July 9 he dealt lefty reliever Jim Poole to the Giants for first baseman Mark Carreon. Then, on July 21, the day McDowell went on the DL with a strained forearm, he traded Murray to the Orioles for Kent Mercker. The finishing blow came on the July 31 trading deadline, when Hart dumped Carlos Baerga and Alvaro Espinoza on the Mets for Jeff Kent and José Vizcaino. But with McDowell and Martinez both hurting, Hart left some observers wondering why he didn't acquire a serviceable starter for all the talent he shipped away—like perhaps getting Mark Clark back from the Mets after he gave him away in the spring for Ryan Thompson.

August 15-13 (80-55, 8 games ahead)
The Indians chugged along in August, never coming close to losing their cushion over the White Sox or the rest of the division. The rotation continued to be a problem. Nagy, Hershiser and Chad Ogea pitched well, winning 7 games among them, with a combined 3.56 ERA. But Martinez failed in his comeback bid and McDowell pitched like he was still hurt, giving up 26 runs in 22 innings.

The powerful offense kept them afloat, averaging almost 6 runs a game during August. Jim Thome responded to a switch to the no. 3 spot in the batting order with a .407 average and 11 homers. Injuries still cut into their depth, though. Julio Franco spent most of the month nursing his hamstring. Mark Carreon hit a foul ball off his knee August 23 and landed on the DL. Hart acquired Kevin Seitzer on August 30 to replace Carreon at first base, and Martinez's absence had the Indians jumping into the Denny Neagle sweepstakes. They eventually lost out to the Braves on the deal, but it showed their level of confidence about going into the postseason with their existing rotation.

September 19-7 (99-62, 14½ games ahead)
The Indians were inconsistent at the beginning of September, but they finally kicked into gear and walked away with the Central Division title thanks, in part, to a dismal finish by White Sox. Hargrove was most proud of his team's attitude: "The personality of this team has changed in the last month or so. The chemistry of this club is as good as I've ever seen it. I think the players are more supportive of each other. There's a real feeling of closeness now that was missing at times this season."

October 1-3 (lost division series in 4 games to the Orioles)
The closeness lasted 4 games. Charles Nagy gave up 3 home runs in a 10-4 Game 1 loss, including 2 dingers to B.J. Surhoff. The Indians' 7-4 Game 2 loss turned on a botched double-play attempt—ironic, considering how much work Hart had put into upgrading the defense. The Indians rode an Albert Belle grand slam in the seventh inning to a 9-4 victory in Game 3. But the Indians were ushered out of the playoffs by Robby Alomar in a 12-inning Game 4 loss. Nagy pitched his guts out, giving up 2 runs and striking out 12 in 6 innings. But José Mesa allowed a two-out, two-strike, game-tying single to Roberto Alomar in the 9th and Ogea served up a winning homer to Alomar in the 12th.

Their offense didn't really show up in the playoffs other than in Game 3, and the defense, pitching, and bullpen weren't there to bail them out. They had the league's 2nd-best offense, 2nd-best rotation, and best bullpen and they hit the postseason wall in 4 games. Unlike the Braves, who were built for 162 games, not 7, the Indians can't use that as an excuse. Like the Yankees, they had 3 strong starters, a deep bullpen, and bench depth on offense. They would have been well positioned to exploit the Braves' weaknesses, but they couldn't get past a team built on dingers and little else. For Cleveland fans, this has to be as tough as losing the Browns—if not worse. At least they know they'll be getting a football team again. They don't have that kind of guarantee on the Indians playing baseball in October.

■ 1997 OUTLOOK

Offense

The Indians led the league in batting average and on-base average, and finished second to the Mariners in slugging percentage. They scored a club-record 952 runs and belted a club-record 218 home runs. Three Indians hit 30 homers and drove in 100 runs. Without Belle, they'll still have Lofton, Thome, and Ramirez to drive the offense, and that's more than most teams have. They'll also have $10 million—or, essentially, all gate receipts from the first 20 home games—to spend on starting pitching and a well-rounded, well-adjusted left fielder.

Defense

For a team to win, as the saying goes, it must be strong up the middle. Last year, the Indians weren't. Vizquel's defense at short slipped quite a bit, but most of his problems were tied to his bum shoulder. It's been repaired, so his defense could return to extraordinary. They'll be in the market for a second baseman and, unless they settle on Jack Brohamer or Duane Kuiper, he'll be better than Baerga. Thome should be able to handle first, if he ends up there, though the gap between former Gold Glover Matt Williams and Jim Thome is nowhere near as great as it used to be at third. There are few better center fielders than Kenny Lofton, despite his 10 errors. He has the range to play his position, plus a good chunk of left and right field, as well as the first three rows of the bleachers. Belle was an average left fielder, at best, and the team's defense will most likely improve without him. Manny Ramirez has the ability to be a great defender, but it depends on if his mind is in the game. Opposing baserunners were testing the outfield all season, and Belle, Lofton, and Ramirez all ended up with double digit assists.

Pitching

The '95 rotation led the league in ERA (4.21). The '96 version finished second in the league, with a 4.59 ERA. Charles Nagy was brilliant. Hershiser, after he worked out his mechanical problems, pitched effectively in June, July and August, but was crusty around the edges of the season. Jack McDowell's season was interrupted by injury for the first time in his career, leading to a subpar performance. Chad Ogea stepped in for Martinez and pitched well from July on. The Indians shuttled several pitchers in and out of the 5th starter's spot, most notably left-hander Brian Anderson and Albie Lopez. Nagy, Hershiser, and Black Jack look to be coming back, and Ogea is the favorite to fill the no. 5 spot. But Martinez will not be back, so Hart will need to add an arm to the rotation.

The '96 bullpen again led the league in ERA (3.80). Of the pitchers who put in significant time in the Indians' bullpen, only ex-Indian Julian Tavarez and Alan Embree had ERAs over 3.75. The Indians were fortunate. When José Mesa hit a rough stretch in July, Paul Shuey stepped in to take the reins. Mesa shouldn't have the same problem again, but if he does, he'll have a backup. Paul Assenmacher and free agent Eric Plunk are both veteran pitchers who know what they're doing in a setup role. Kent Mercker, if the Indians re-sign him and can resist the temptation to try to make him a starter, could be a pleasant surprise in '97, especially if his lost velocity is found.

Farm System

The mainstays of their '96 team—Belle, Ramirez, Thome, and Nagy—were all homegrown products. There's more on the way. The system is weighted toward position prospects, especially first basemen. Richie Sexson and Sean Casey have good offensive potential, and '96 1st-rounder Danny Peoples, if he recovers from rotator cuff surgery, has exceptional hitting skills, though he hasn't had a chance to show them off yet. Third baseman Russ Branyan has big-league power, but he plays the field like a natural-born DH. Shortstop Enrique Wilson is polished defensively and may see time at second. Catcher Einar Diaz is also polished defensively, but he hasn't shown much with the bat.

Two pitchers of note in the organization are Bartolo Colon and Jaret Wright. Colon has had injuries and stamina problems and will be converted to closer. Wright is a couple of years away. But both throw in the mid-to-upper 90s and have the killer instinct to succeed. Casey Whitten is also a very solid pitcher worth watching.

Management and Ownership

Richard Jacobs made his fortune in real estate and is well known in the community as a fan-oriented

civic leader. Other than that, what's there to know about him? He provides plenty of capital for the team and, for the most part, stays out of the parlor politics so prevalent in ownership circles these days. What more could a baseball fan ask from his team's owner?

GM John Hart is an innovator. A few years back, he decided that arbitration was a no-win situation. To save a few bucks, a team has to tear down a player's performance in the hearing *in front of the player.* Hart figured that process only fostered animosity and started signing all his young arbitration-eligible players to long-term contracts. That is basically how the Indians have been able to keep, until now, a core of players such as Lofton, Thome, and Belle. When the season starts, Hart is not afraid to upgrade his team at any time. Unlike reputed genius John Schuerholz, Hart does not send his team into the postseason with glaring weaknesses year after year. And although the trade of Baerga to the Mets raised a big stink, the trades he pulled off in '96 all helped the club one way or another, and the deal for Matt Williams should just be more of the same.

Hargrove tries to maintain a stable, professional environment for his players to perform in. But that doesn't mean he has this team under control. Maybe he did as well he could with children like Baerga and Belle. Both of these sweethearts will be someone else's problem in '97, and it will be interesting to see what another manager gets out of them.

. . . and whatnot: Bye-bye, Baerga

The trade of Carlos Baerga to the Mets July 31 knocked the stuffing out of many a Cleveland Indians fan. They knew Carlos as a 3-time All-Star, a lifetime .300 hitter, and a hero. They felt GM John Hart was giving up on him just when he needed the support the most. They took it out on Hart the next day, booing the new arrivals and carrying signs that read, "Trade Hart, Not Carlos."

If anything, Hart was *too* patient. Baerga reported to spring training at 227 pounds, 15 pounds heavier than his playing weight from the previous season. Hart: "Carlos will have to pay attention to himself physically if he is going to stay at this level. He's not 22 years old anymore." Though he was quick to add, "I want to emphasize we're not upset with Carlos. We love him." It also didn't help that Baerga had a cellular phone in his hand more often than a glove or a bat during warm-ups. Carlos, it seems, was a getting a bit too into that "star thing."

Baerga hit 2 homers in his first 171 at-bats and Hargrove eventually moved him from 2nd in the order down to 7th, saying he didn't think the move would be permanent. "I think this will take some of the pressure off Carlos. I've never really seen him struggle like this except for a time during his rookie year." But a couple of days later, John Hart had to deny a report that he was discussing a trade with the Marlins. "It's not happening. Carlos is going nowhere. . . . Nowhere. The whole thing is bizarre. . . . Bizarre." Actually it made perfect sense. The only thing bizarre about the situation was Hart's weird habit of repeating words. . . . Words.

Baerga was hitting .267 with 10 homers before the trade—after 4 consecutive seasons over .310. He also had 15 errors—his previous high for a season was 19. So Hart pulled the trigger on a deal for Jeff Kent and José Vizcaino, essentially a pair of utility infielders. Hart: "We felt we were limited at second base and the big offense we were used to seeing from Carlos wasn't there this season."

Limited at second base? Was that a cryptic reference to his weight?

Baerga on the weight issue: "That was bull. I've been like that all my career. I came to camp 5 pounds lighter than I was last season. I was working hard every day. You didn't hear anybody in San Diego talk about Tony Gwynn's weight when he hit .300 every year. I don't know what they want." It's simple, Carlos. They want you to hit .300 every year like Tony, not just to be overweight like Tony.

Baerga offered his own explanation of the reasons for the trade. He said Hart approached him in the off-season about a position switch to third base so the Indians could pursue free agent Robby Alomar. Baerga refused to move, and the Indians never did get into the bidding for Alomar. "I told them that wasn't what they needed. I told them they needed pitching and then they got Jack McDowell."

The Indians traded Baerga because he was killing them at the plate and in the field—regardless of whether or not he was fat or liked to play GM when

the team had a chance to sign a future Hall of Famer. It's all about performance. Just ask Cecil Fielder. If you can hit, nobody cares if you're as big as a house. And if Baerga continues to mail it in for the Mets—he hit .193 and seemed very content spending most of his time sitting out due to an abdominal strain—they'll probably start vilifying Hart for not getting Matt Williams for him sooner.

SANDY ALOMAR

C • BR • TR • 6'5 • 200 • 30 • SD83

	AB	R	H	2B	3B	HR	RBI	BB	SO	SB	CS	BA	OB	SA
CLE94	292	44	84	15	1	14	43	25	31	8	4	.288	.347	.490
CLE95	203	32	61	6	0	10	35	7	26	3	1	.300	.332	.478
CLE96	418	53	110	23	0	11	50	19	42	1	0	.263	.299	.397
CAREER	2076	246	561	103	4	53	265	111	233	22	14	.270	.313	.400

His season totals were below his career averages, but Alomar's got to be happy nonetheless. For the first time since his rookie season, he contributed for the long haul. The Indians will never need to depend on his bat. They do, however, depend on his defense. Alomar is one of the better-fielding catchers in the game. His size and his knee injuries have robbed him of some mobility behind the plate, but he blocks pitches well, he's a pretty decent-throwing catcher, and he's very adept at handling pitchers. His '96 production, give or take a few at-bats, is exactly what to expect from him if he beats the odds and stays healthy again. ■

BRIAN ANDERSON

SP • BL • TL • 6'1 • 190 • 24 • CAL93/1

	G	GS	IP	H	HR	BB	K	W	L	S	ERA	K/BB	K9	HW9
CAL94	18	18	101	120	13	27	47	7	5	0	5.22	1.7	4.2	13.09
CAL95	18	17	99	110	24	30	45	6	8	0	5.87	1.5	4.1	12.73
CLE96	10	9	51	58	9	14	21	3	1	0	4.91	1.5	3.7	12.70
CAREER	50	45	263	299	47	73	117	16	14	0	5.37	1.6	4.0	12.73

The Angels gave up on him after a couple of years of trying to fit him into their rotation. Giving up 24 homers in 99 innings in '95 didn't help. But Hart took a chance on him because he's young, he's a lefty, and he has an adequate fastball and a nice change-up. The Indians gave him a chance to break into the rotation in mid-May, and he threw well in his first 3 starts. But he gave up 11 runs in his next 2 starts and was optioned to Triple-A Buffalo. He came back up again in August and pitched well enough down the stretch to earn consideration for a playoff roster spot, going 3-0 with a 3.63 ERA after his recall. Anderson doesn't have a consistent breaking pitch, so the Indians want to see him develop his curve. But he's earned a chance to try to fill a rotation slot in the spring, and he could surprise. A lot of pitchers have built careers on weaker stuff than his. ■

PAUL ASSENMACHER

RP • BL • TL • 6'3 • 195 • 36 • ATL83

	G	GS	IP	H	HR	BB	K	W	L	S	ERA	K/BB	K9	HW9
CHA94	44	0	33	26	2	13	29	1	2	1	3.55	2.2	7.9	10.64
CLE95	47	0	38	32	3	12	40	6	2	0	2.82	3.3	9.5	10.42
CLE96	63	0	46	46	1	14	44	4	2	1	3.09	3.1	8.6	11.72
CAREER	685	1	726	670	57	264	682	52	38	49	3.38	2.6	8.5	11.58

Assenmacher's workload has diminished greatly since 1993 and he will probably never pitch more than 50 innings a season again. But if you need to get a tough left-hander out, anytime, anyplace, he is as safe a bet as anybody to get it. Last year was a perfect example. He allowed a .333 average when there were no runners on and no outs. But with runners in scoring position, the batting average against him dropped to .254. He remains effective because he has excellent command of his big, sweeping curve. Assenmacher is signed through the end of this season, with a club option for '98. As long as he stays healthy, there's no reason to expect anything less than 40 to 50 solid innings of relief out of him. ■

RUSS BRANYAN

SOLID PROSPECT

3B • BB • TR • 6'3 • 195 • 21 • CLE94/7

	AB	R	H	2B	3B	HR	RBI	BB	SO	SB	CS	BA	OB	SA
A	482	102	129	20	4	40	106	62	166	7	4	.268	.320	.473

A switch-hitting third baseman with incredible power, Branyan's 40 home runs last season set a South Atlantic League record. What's even more impressive is that he had that kind of season at 20. His 166 strikeouts prove that he still has some work to do, though. Defensively, he is also a work in progress. He's much more interested in hitting home

runs than in fielding sharp grounders cleanly. He also irks pitchers because he stands at the plate, admiring his tape-measure shots. Some attitude adjustments are needed. Branyan's got awfully impressive power. He will surely be moved up to Double-A Canton/Akron to begin the '97 season. ■

MARK CARREON (see Free Agents)

SEAN CASEY — SOLID PROSPECT

1B • BL • TR • 6'4 • 215 • 22 • CLE95/2

	AB	R	H	2B	3B	HR	RBI	BB	SO	SB	CS	BA	OB	SA
A+	344	62	114	31	3	12	57	36	47	1	1	.331	.402	.544

After winning the NCAA batting title with the Richmond Spiders in '95, the Indians selected him with their 2nd-round pick. They considered him the best pure hitter available in the draft, and he went on to win the Carolina League batting title last season. He didn't hit for much power for a guy his size, but his manager thought it was merely the result of not being aggressive enough in hitter's counts. There's a glut of first basemen in the Cleveland system, but Casey could turn out to be the best of the lot. He wasn't challenged by the Carolina League last season. As soon as he shows more power, he'll be in Triple-A. That could be as early as this season. ■

BARTOLO COLON — SOLID PROSPECT

SP-RP • BR • TR • 6'0 • 185 • 21 • CLE93

	G	GS	IP	H	HR	BB	SO	W	L	S	ERA	K/BB	K9	HW9
AA	13	12	62	44	2	25	56	2	2	0	1.74	2.2	8.1	10.02

Colon was considered the Indians' best starting pitching prospect going into the '96 season. But 6 weeks on the DL with a strained elbow (his second elbow injury in 2 years) forced a change in his role. He'll be converted to closer because of the concerns his injury raised. Colon's stuff is impressive. He throws a fastball clocked as high as 97 mph and an effective change-up. But his managers have noticed he hits the wall after 80 to 90 pitches. His mechanics go and limbs start flying all over the place, which is what causes the stress on his elbow. The Indians believe the switch to the bullpen will keep his elbow healthy, but they haven't ruled out making him a starter again if his mechanics improve. Regardless of his role, he still has the best arm in the organization. If he avoids injury, the Indians will find a job for him as early as '98. ■

MAXIMO DE LA ROSA

RP-SP • BR • TR • 5'11 • 170 • 25

	G	GS	IP	H	HR	BB	SO	W	L	S	ERA	K/BB	K9	HW9
AA	40	15	120	104	7	81	109	11	5	3	3.91	1.3	8.2	13.91

Originally signed as an outfielder out of the Dominican Republic, de la Rosa was converted to the mound in '93. He has a plus arm and proved it in both starting and relief roles last season. De la Rosa's fastball is his best pitch. He throws it in the mid-90s with excellent movement. But Maximo has "Minimo" command of his breaking ball at this point in his career. The walks he has allowed are simply unacceptable. He's got a long road ahead of him. ■

EINAR DIAZ — SOLID PROSPECT

C • BR • TR • 5'10 • 165 • 24 • CLE90

	AB	R	H	2B	3B	HR	RBI	BB	SO	SB	CS	BA	OB	SA
AA	395	47	111	26	2	3	35	12	22	3	2	.281	.317	.380

Diaz is a 23-year-old catching prospect the Indians would like to see develop into Alomar's backup by '98. His defensive skills are quite polished, and he showcases a rifle arm frequently. He's been bereft of power at the plate since '94, when he hit 16 homers, but he's tough to strike out. He hits whatever he swings at, just not very hard and not very far. Diaz will be in Triple-A in '97, and he has a chance to see big-league time before the year is out. But his development at the plate will always be overshadowed by his play behind the plate. ■

TRAVIS DRISKILL

SP-RP • BR • TR • 6'0 • 185 • 25 • CLE93/4

	G	GS	IP	H	HR	BB	SO	W	L	S	ERA	K/BB	K9	HW9
AA	29	24	172	169	8	63	148	13	7	0	3.61	2.3	7.7	12.14

Originally a 4th round pick out of Texas Tech in '93, Driskill had put in 3 seasons pitching out of the bullpen, earning 35 saves for Class-A Columbus in '94. But last season the Indians moved him into the rotation at Double-A Canton/Akron, and Driskill responded with a 13-7 record. He's not a great prospect, but the Indians sent him to the Arizona Fall League during the off-season, so it's evident

they have plans for him. He'll pitch in Triple-A Buffalo where he could emerge as this year's sleeper. ■

ALAN EMBREE

SLEEPER

RP • BL • TL • 6'2 • 190 • 27 • CLE89/4

	G	GS	IP	H	HR	BB	K	W	L	S	ERA	K/BB	K9	HW9
CLE95	23	0	24	23	2	16	23	3	2	1	5.11	1.4	8.6	14.63
CLE96	24	0	31	30	10	21	33	1	1	0	6.39	1.6	9.6	14.81

After Embree made the successful transition to the bullpen in '95, his star was once again on the rise in Cleveland. He impressed the front office with his performance during the '95 World Series, which left some Braves hitters saying he was the best lefty reliever they saw that season. (Bear in mind, the best the N.L. had to offer, based on appearances, were an aging Randy Myers, an aging John Franco, Yorkis Perez, Mike Muñoz, Jason Christiansen, Dan Plesac, Tony Fossas, and Shawn Barton.) But Embree's success didn't carry over into the '96 season, and he found himself spending as much time in Triple-A Buffalo as he did in the majors.

Embree has to live down being a 1-pitch wonder. He possesses a devastating fastball, but he's never has been able to develop a consistent breaking pitch to go along with it. He's spent the past couple of years trying to develop a slider. He's come a long way from elbow-ligament transplant surgery in '93. Just regaining the velocity he once had is a victory. But Embree's struggles in '96 have caused some within the organization to question his mental toughness. The '97 season will determine whether his future is in Cleveland. ■

JULIO FRANCO

1B • BR • TR • 6'1 • 190 • 35 • PHI78

	AB	R	H	2B	3B	HR	RBI	BB	SO	SB	CS	BA	OB	SA
CHA94	433	72	138	19	2	20	98	62	75	8	1	.319	.406	.510
CLE96	432	72	139	20	1	14	76	61	82	8	8	.322	.407	.470
CAREER	6813	1036	2061	319	46	134	937	684	889	245	95	.303	.366	.422

Franco could be one of the wisest major-leaguers around. After all, he had the sense to flee to Japan as soon as the labor strife started, didn't he? And he didn't come back looking like Kevin Mitchell. The Indians envisioned a big year from him. Sandwiched

between Lofton and Belle, he would have threatened his career highs in home runs and RBI, but he came up lame running the bases in July and spent nearly 2 months on the DL with a hamstring pull. He'd been on the DL only 3 times before, all in 1992.

Franco draws a good amount of walks and can hit for power. The Indians will hold on to him in '97, hoping he will play the entire season—and will work him into the DH role to help him do just that. ■

BRIAN GILES

SLEEPER

OF • BL • TL • 5'11 • 195 • 26 • CLE89/17

	AB	R	H	2B	3B	HR	RBI	BB	SO	SB	CS	BA	OB	SA
CLE96	121	26	43	14	1	5	27	19	13	3	0	.355	.434	.612

Giles was promoted to the major-league roster in July. In his first at-bat he had a pinch-hit home run with 2 out in the 9th to spark a come-from-behind victory against the Twins. He hit .355 the rest of the way and walked more than he struck out. He's been hitting like that for 3 seasons now in Double- and Triple-A. He has a short, compact swing that generates solid power. And he's only 17 months older than Manny Ramirez. Giles would be a competent, economical, and behaviorally sound replacement for Belle in left field. ■

DANNY GRAVES

SOLID PROSPECT

RP • BR • TR • 5'11 • 200 • 23 • CLE94/3

	G	GS	IP	H	HR	BB	K	W	L	S	ERA	K/BB	K9	HW9
CLE96	15	0	29	29	2	10	22	2	0	0	4.55	2.2	6.8	12.08

The Indians took Graves in the 4th round of the '94 draft, after he blew out his knee in the College World Series just a few days earlier. That shows how much they liked him. Above all else, Graves has an excellent makeup for a relief prospect. He generates ground-ball outs by the dozen with a good sinking fastball that hits 90–93 mph. He's also developing a sharp slider to complement it.

Graves finished 3rd in the American Association in saves last season despite spending 3 months in

the big leagues. He's been one of the best pitchers in the organization since he started his pro career in '95, and the Indians will give him every chance to hold a job in the bullpen in '97. He could be José Mesa's replacement within a few years. ■

OREL HERSHISER

SP • BR • TR • 6'3 • 190 • 38 • LA79/18

	G	GS	IP	H	HR	BB	K	W	L	S	ERA	K/BB	K9	HW9
LA94	21	21	135	146	15	42	72	6	6	0	3.79	1.7	4.8	12.53
CLE95	26	26	167	151	21	51	111	16	6	0	3.87	2.2	6.0	10.89
CLE96	33	33	206	238	21	58	125	15	9	0	4.24	2.2	5.5	12.93
CAREER	402	362	2529	2323	168	762	1679	165	117	5	3.16	2.2	6.0	10.98

Hershiser's stuff isn't even close to what it used to be—his slider barely hits the 80-mph mark. But he was able to win 15 games with the Indians last year using a combination of moxie, run support, and durability. He sandwiched decent starts with bad ones over the first couple of months of the season. In his first 12 starts he was 4-4 with a 6.64 ERA. But for the remainder of the season, he went 11-5 with a 3.19 ERA in 144 innings. His best pitching came in a 9-game stretch from June 8 though July 22. In that span he won 6 out of 9, including 5 in a row, and compiled a 0.85 ERA over 64 innings.

Hershiser insists he was healthy all season and that his early-season troubles were caused by a minute flaw in his mechanics. But he is so competitive that even if his arm were hanging by a thread, he'd still find a way to convince his manager he could go 9 innings. Hershiser should have at least one more good season left in him. With the kind of run support he gets from the Indians, another 10 to 15 victories wouldn't be out of the question. Even now, he's on the short list of pitchers you'd want out there in Game 7. ■

DAMIAN JACKSON

SS • BR • TR • 5'10 • 160 • 23 • CLE91/44

	AB	R	H	2B	3B	HR	RBI	BB	SO	SB	CS	BA	OB	SA
AAA	452	77	116	15	1	12	49	48	78	24	7	.257	.333	.374

Jackson is a 23-year-old shortstop prospect and paradox. His strong suit is his speed, but he insists on swinging for the fences instead of trying to hit the ball on the ground and leg out hits. He has shown flashes of brilliance on defense as well, but his error totals the past few seasons have been scary. His error rate in Buffalo dropped last season, so there's hope he can come around eventually on the rest of his game. But until he gives up his dream of hitting 30 homers in the big leagues, Jackson will continue to struggle. ■

DARON KIRKREIT

SLEEPER

SP • BR • TR • 6'6 • 225 • 24 • CLE93/1

	G	GS	IP	H	HR	BB	SO	W	L	S	ERA	K/BB	K9	HW9
A+	6	6	33	23	3	10	19	2	0	0	1.93	1.9	5.2	9.09

Kirkreit was considered one of the best arms in the system as recently as a couple of seasons ago. But he tried to pitch through a rotator-cuff injury in '95 and wound up having major arm surgery during the off-season. When healthy, he throws a hard, sinking fastball and a slider that's close to major-league caliber. He returned to start 6 games for Class-A Kinston late last season, but he's got to be considered a question mark. ■

KENNY LOFTON

SUPERSTAR

CF • BL • TL • 6'0 • 180 • 29 • HOU88/18

	AB	R	H	2B	3B	HR	RBI	BB	SO	SB	CS	BA	OB	SA
CLE94	459	105	160	32	9	12	57	52	56	60	12	.349	.412	.536
CLE95	481	93	149	22	13	7	53	40	49	54	15	.310	.362	.453
CLE96	662	132	210	35	4	14	67	61	82	75	17	.317	.372	.446
CAREER	2821	551	883	133	42	39	261	307	343	327	71	.313	.379	.431

His title as the best leadoff hitter in the game is deserved. Lofton used his incredible speed to lead the league in stolen bases for the 5th consecutive season. He'll take the extra base every time it's offered, and sometimes when it isn't. His baserunning instincts put a great deal of pressure on a defense. And he's not just a slap-hitting speedster, either. Kevin Seitzer was impressed by Lofton's skills when he came over from the Brewers, saying, "He's probably the best leadoff hitter I've ever played with. I played with Willie Wilson, and he was as good as it got. . . . He has great instincts on the bases and there's nobody in

the game who's as good a bunter." He's also an impact player on defense, robbing someone of a home run about as often as Madonna changes her hair or Clinton has to apologize for something. Rumors were swirling that Lofton wanted out of Cleveland after Belle left. Belle can be replaced, but there are no other Kenny Loftons in the big leagues. ■

ALBIE LOPEZ

SLEEPER

SP • BR • TR • 6′2 • 205 • 25 • CLE91/20

	G	GS	IP	H	HR	BB	K	W	L	S	ERA	K/BB	K9	HW9
CLE94	4	4	17	20	3	6	18	1	2	0	4.24	3.0	9.5	13.76
CLE95	6	2	23	17	4	7	22	0	0	0	3.13	3.1	8.6	9.39
CLE96	13	10	62	80	14	22	45	5	4	0	6.39	2.0	6.5	14.81
CAREER	32	25	151	166	28	67	110	9	7	0	5.54	1.6	6.6	13.88

Lopez, 24, has been trying to break into the rotation for 3 seasons now, but he's no closer now than he was in '93. He has the stuff to make it, a 92–95-mph fastball and a good curve. But he just can't make it work in the majors, probably because he's had trouble developing a change-up. Lopez pouted in '95 after he was sent down to Buffalo. He gave up on the season, losing 10 of his 18 starts. The front office started wondering about his makeup. But the Indians are encouraged about the way he handled his demotions in '96—not that that's something any front office wants a player to get *too* good at. The Indians need Lopez to come through for them in '97. They have a big hole in the 5th rotation spot to fill. He's only 25, but unless he gets better command of his pitches and stops giving up the long ball, his career could be with another team. ■

DENNIS MARTINEZ (see Free Agents)

WILLIE MARTINEZ

SLEEPER

SP • BR • TR • 6′2 • 165 • 19 • CLE95

	G	GS	IP	H	HR	BB	SO	W	L	S	ERA	K/BB	K9	HW9
A-	14	14	90	79	5	21	92	6	5	0	2.40	4.4	9.2	10.00

Despite going 0-7 with a 9.45 ERA in '95, Appalachian League managers said Martinez had the best arm and stuff in the league. They didn't have him confused with someone else, because in '96 he moved up to the N.Y.-Penn League where he placed among the league leaders in ERA and strikeouts. Martinez throws a mid-90s fastball with movement, a curve, and a change-up, and looks to have pretty good control. He's raw, but if his first couple of seasons are any indication of his talent, Jacobs Field could be in his future. ■

JACK MCDOWELL

SP • BR • TR • 6′5 • 180 • 31 • CHA87/1

	G	GS	IP	H	HR	BB	K	W	L	S	ERA	K/BB	K9	HW9
CHA94	25	25	181	186	12	42	127	10	9	0	3.73	3.0	6.3	11.34
NYA95	30	30	217	211	25	78	157	15	10	0	3.93	2.0	6.5	11.99
CLE96	30	30	192	214	22	67	141	13	9	0	5.11	2.1	6.6	13.17
CAREER	251	251	1753	1683	152	564	1216	119	77	0	3.73	2.2	6.2	11.54

McDowell was expected to lead the Indians' pitching staff to glory in '96. He started out in fine form, compiling a 2.04 ERA in his first 5 starts. But after that, his season went downhill. Over the next 4 months McDowell would go 8-8 with a 6.26 ERA. He finished the season with 3 victories and a 3.86 ERA in September.

McDowell can thank his competitive nature for his woeful season. He suffered from a strained muscle in his forearm in midseason and on July 22 went on the DL for the first time in his career. But his willingness to conceal it kept him pitching when he should have been treating the injury. As a result, his forkball lost its effectiveness, and McDowell, minus his best pitch, was reduced to pitching on guts for a good chunk of the season.

"There are 3 basic pitching stats: innings, wins, and ERA," McDowell says. "Unless you're Greg Maddux, you can't have all 3." It's hard to argue with McDowell's pitching philosophy, considering the success he's had. He's averaged 16 victories a season over the past 7 years pitching for competitive clubs that could hit, but he has never had much left during the playoffs. There is one other stat that counts: rings. Unless he starts pacing himself better and stops thinking that he alone must pitch the team into the playoffs, he may never get one. ■

KENT MERCKER (see Free Agents)

JOSÉ MESA

RP • BR • TR • 6'3 • 220 • 30 • TOR81

	G	GS	IP	H	HR	BB	K	W	L	S	ERA	K/BB	K9	HW9
CLE94	51	0	73	71	3	26	63	7	5	2	3.82	2.4	7.8	11.96
CLE95	62	0	64	49	3	17	58	3	0	46	1.13	3.4	8.2	9.28
CLE96	69	0	72	69	6	28	64	2	7	39	3.73	2.3	8.0	12.12
CAREER	280	95	780	816	67	307	470	39	52	87	4.48	1.5	5.4	12.96

Answer: Kyle Washington. Question: Who did the Orioles get for José Mesa?

Mesa was fine over the first couple of months of the season. He had a string of 20 consecutive saves from the beginning of the season and a string of 28 dating back to '95. But he hit a stretch in June that saw him blow 3 save opportunities and allow 13 earned runs in 10 innings. His velocity was down, and his control disappeared. Hargrove had no other choice but to replace him as the closer for most of July. Mesa returned to his old self again in late July and was reinstalled as closer. If you take June out of the picture, Mesa had a 2.45 ERA for the season. But that's still more than 1 run higher than his '95 performance. Mesa might not last long as the Indians' closer if he repeats what happened in '96.

His '95 performance came as a complete surprise: A pitcher is given up on by one team to come out of nowhere and emerge as a closer for another, at times an immediately dominating one. Actually, this describes the majority of closers still kicking around in some role today: Rick Aguilera, Rod Beck, Jeff Brantley, Norm Charlton, Dennis Eckersley, Mike Fetters, John Franco, Roberto Hernandez, Trevor Hoffman, John Hudek, Doug Jones, Dan Miceli, Jeff Montgomery, Robb Nen, Bruce Ruffin, Jeff Russell, Heathcliff Slocumb, and John Wetteland. Homegrown closers are very rare: Ricky Bottalico, Troy Percival, Mel Rojas, Mike Timlin, Turk Wendell, Mark Wohlers, and the Billy Wagner/Todd Jones combo platter.

Mesa's failure to repeat his '96 performance also came as a surprise to some. Of those who've been around long enough to judge, many had their best years early if not immediately. He could go the way of Russell and fade quickly—or he could enhance his repertoire and reverse a slow downward slide, as Wetteland has done. The parallels to Wetteland are eerie, so that could be the one to bet on. ■

WILMER MONTOYA

RP • BR • TR • 5'10 • 165 • 23 • CLE92

	G	GS	IP	H	HR	BB	SO	W	L	S	ERA	K/BB	K9	HW9
AA	43	0	51	41	2	28	42	2	5	23	3.38	1.5	7.5	12.26

Montoya signed out of Venezuela in 1993, and after the '94 season he was converted to closer. Montoya doesn't have the stature of a power pitcher or the stamina of a starter, but, like Pedro Martinez, he reaches 90 mph with his fastball nonetheless. He throws an outstanding breaking ball as well. He lost some of his stellar control in his adjustment to Double-A competition last season, but he earned 23 saves anyway on the strength of his stuff. Montoya may need another year or two of seasoning. But he's been very successful in his career so far and is a nice-looking prospect. ■

CHARLES NAGY

AL ELITE

SP • BL • TR • 6'3 • 200 • 29 • CLE88/2

	G	GS	IP	H	HR	BB	K	W	L	S	ERA	K/BB	K9	HW9
CLE94	23	23	169	175	15	48	108	10	8	0	3.45	2.3	5.8	11.87
CLE95	29	29	178	194	20	61	139	16	6	0	4.55	2.3	7.0	12.89
CLE96	32	32	222	217	21	61	167	17	5	0	3.41	2.7	6.8	11.27
CAREER	168	167	1127	1183	95	327	748	74	54	0	3.86	2.3	6.0	12.06

One of the unluckiest pitchers in baseball last summer, Nagy went through a stretch in which he couldn't buy a victory, and it may have cost him a chance to win the Cy Young award. After going 11-1 in his first 14 starts, he went 1-3 in his next 12 despite a slightly improved ERA and HW9. Nagy had 10 no-decisions last season. Eight of those came in that well-pitched, hard-luck stretch from June 21 through August 21. In 2 of those starts, he left with a lead. In 4 of them, the Indians scored 2 or fewer runs. With just average luck, Nagy would have won 3 or 4 of those starts, giving him 20 victories and automatic consideration for the Cy Young.

He finished in the top 10 in victories (4th), ERA (3rd), batting average allowed (6th), hits per 9 innings (6th), walks per 9 (4th), strikeouts (10th), and strikeouts per 9 (10th). It would be pretty hard to find a more complete pitcher. Simply put, Nagy is one of the best starting pitchers in the league and is showing no signs of letting up anytime soon. ■

CHAD OGEA — YOUNG GUN

SP-RP • BR • TR • 6′2 • 200 • 26 • CLE91/3

	G	GS	IP	H	HR	BB	K	W	L	S	ERA	K/BB	K9	HW9
CLE94	4	1	16	21	2	10	11	0	1	0	6.06	1.1	6.2	17.40
CLE95	20	14	106	95	11	29	57	8	3	0	3.05	2.0	4.8	10.53
CLE96	29	21	146	151	22	42	101	10	6	0	4.79	2.4	6.2	11.89
CAREER	53	36	268	267	35	81	169	18	10	0	4.20	2.1	5.7	11.68

The Indians spent half the season looking for a 5th starter. Ogea got a couple of opportunities to claim the job, but he gave up 11 runs in 16.2 innings and fell out of the competition. It took an injury to Dennis Martinez before the Indians gave Ogea another chance, and this time he produced. From July 2 on, he went 7-5 with a 3.90 ERA. He was especially strong in September, when he won 3 games and had a 3.52 ERA. Ogea is a serviceable starter because he has tremendous poise despite having subpar stuff. He never gives in to a hitter, relying on location and pitch selection more than most. Ogea may find a job in the rotation waiting for him in the spring—though a 3.05 ERA in '95 wasn't enough to guarantee him a job for '96. ■

DANNY PEOPLES

1B • CLE96/1 • UNIVERSITY OF TEXAS

	AB	R	H	2B	3B	HR	RBI	BB	SO	SB	CS	BA	OB	SA
A-	117	20	28	7	0	3	26	28	36	3	1	.239	.392	.376

His former coach, Cliff Gustafson, said Peoples had better raw power than any Longhorn ever—including Brooks Kieschnick. He was originally drafted as a first baseman, but since there's a glut of them in the system already, the Indians want to move him to third for the upcoming season. Peoples went down July 31 with a frayed labrum and a partially damaged rotator cuff and had to undergo season-ending shoulder surgery. This may change the Indians' plans to switch his position, at least temporarily. It's quite possible he couldn't have handled the switch anyway as there are doubts about his defense as a whole.

What the front office likes most about Peoples is his desire. He wants to be a complete hitter and says he patterns himself after big leaguers such as Jeff Bagwell and Edgar Martinez. His stock took a slight hit with the injury, but Peoples, if healthy, should prove to be one of the better hitting prospects the Indians have. ■

HERBERT PERRY

1B • BR • TR • 6′2 • 210 • 27 • CLE91/2

	AB	R	H	2B	3B	HR	RBI	BB	SO	SB	CS	BA	OB	SA
CLE95	162	23	51	13	1	3	23	13	28	1	3	.315	.376	.463
CLE96	12	1	1	1	0	0	0	1	2	1	0	.083	.154	.167

When the Indians acquired Julio Franco during the off-season, it really put the kibosh on Perry's chances. But then, like a Hollywood script, Franco is sidelined with a bum hamstring in July, and Perry was . . . stuck on the Buffalo disabled list after knee surgery to repair an old football injury. What a missed opportunity.

Perry could have saved the Indians a reliever (Jim Poole) by claiming the starting job. He wouldn't have been overmatched at the major-league level, and the Indians wouldn't have had to make the trade for Mark Carreon. The club feels Perry is the best defensive first baseman in the system, and he has decent power with a selective eye at the plate. He'll be fine if he's given a chance, but he could get crowded out. ■

ERIC PLUNK (see Free Agents)

ALEX RAMIREZ

OF • BR • TR • 5′11 • 175 • 22

	AB	R	H	2B	3B	HR	RBI	BB	SO	SB	CS	BA	OB	SA
AA	513	79	169	28	12	14	85	16	74	18	10	.329	.353	.513

Ramirez pulled his biscuits out of the bonfire when he hit .323 for co-op Bakersfield in '95. The Indians then promoted him to Double-A Canton/Akron last summer, and Ramirez didn't skip a beat, hitting everything in sight. He has good speed and nice line-drive power. Ramirez has a nice package of skills for such a young player, but his poor plate discipline could end up killing his batting average. He's a long-shot to make a run at the left field spot, but keep an eye out for him this spring. ■

MANNY RAMIREZ — AL ELITE

RF • BR • TR • 6′0 • 190 • 24 • CLE91/1

	AB	R	H	2B	3B	HR	RBI	BB	SO	SB	CS	BA	OB	SA
CLE94	290	51	78	22	0	17	60	42	72	4	2	.269	.357	.521
CLE95	484	85	149	26	1	31	107	75	112	6	6	.308	.402	.558
CLE96	550	94	170	45	3	33	112	85	104	8	5	.309	.399	.582
CAREER	1377	235	406	94	4	83	284	204	296	18	13	.295	.385	.550

Manny Ramirez is an incredibly gifted hitter. He can do it all at the plate: hit for average, hit for power, draw walks, drive in runs, move runners. But

Ramirez is one of the poorest fundamental ballplayers in the game. Because of his speed, he has pretty good range in the field, and he usually catches what he gets to. He also racked up 19 outfield assists. But where Ramirez runs into trouble is when the play requires a split-second decision. He often catches fly balls in a bad position to throw, and he fails to hit the cutoff man.

Overall, though, Ramirez isn't nearly as bad in the field as he is on the bases. Hargrove got into his face after a particularly egregious episode of brain-lock—jogging home from third to score what should have been the go-ahead run, allowing the final out to be made before he reached the plate. But Manny took it like a man. Hargrove: "Manny had every chance to hang his head, but he didn't. He busted his butt the rest of the game." It's nice to hear that a '90s athlete can take a dressing down from his manager, but it might just be that he's getting so much practice at it he now knows how it's done. ■

JOE ROA

SP • BR • TR • 6′1 • 195 • 25 • ATL89/19

	G	GS	IP	H	HR	BB	SO	W	L	S	ERA	K/BB	K9	HW9
AAA	26	24	165	161	19	36	82	11	8	0	3.27	2.3	4.5	10.72

In 8 minor-league seasons, Roa has compiled a 78-41 record. One has to wonder, if he's been averaging almost 10 victories a season for 8 seasons, why isn't he in the majors? Roa isn't a bat-breaker. All 3 of his pitches (fastball, curve and change) are well below average in velocity. He seems to be held back by the prejudice in baseball about young finesse pitchers. Guys like Roa, very intelligent pitchers with exceptional control, are stuck in the minors because they're not seen as crafty enough to succeed right away in the majors—though he wouldn't have done any worse in the Indians' rotation last year than harder throwers such as Albie Lopez or Brian Anderson. ■

KEVIN SEITZER

DH-1B • BR • TR • 5′11 • 185 • 35 • KC83/11

	AB	R	H	2B	3B	HR	RBI	BB	SO	SB	CS	BA	OB	SA
MIL94	309	44	97	24	2	5	49	30	38	2	1	.314	.375	.453
MIL95	492	56	153	33	3	5	69	64	57	2	0	.311	.395	.421
MIL/CLE96	573	85	187	35	3	13	78	87	79	6	1	.326	.416	.466
CAREER	5080	712	1504	271	35	72	589	651	592	80	49	.296	.377	.406

Seitzer has never hit for much power—unless you consider the juiced-ball seasons of '87 and '96, in which he's hit 28 of his 72 career dingers. He's developed into a .300 hitter late in life, after it appeared that his career was over in '93 in Oakland. He was 31, his average had dropped like a stone since his rookie year—from .323 to .304 to .281 to .275 to .265 to .270 to .255—and the A's released him in July. The Brewers picked him up 3 days later, he hit .290 with 7 dingers in the final 47 games, playing every infield position, and you can see what he's done in the 3 years since. With Franco, Williams, and Thome in the mix, it's difficult to see what his role with the Indians could possibly be—other than perhaps a special envoy charged with the task of re-establishing diplomatic relations with the media in Year 1 A.A. (After Albert). ■

RICHIE SEXSON

SOLID PROSPECT

1B • BR • TR • 6′6 • 205 • 22 • CLE93/24

	AB	R	H	2B	3B	HR	RBI	BB	SO	SB	CS	BA	OB	SA
AA	518	85	143	33	3	16	76	39	118	2	1	.276	.331	.444

Sexson broke out in '95 when he hit .306 and slugged 22 homers for Kinston. He stepped up to Double-A Canton/Akron last season, and his offensive production dropped off a bit. But the club thinks he's capable of hitting .280 to.300 in the majors with 30 homers annually. A gangly kid, Sexson is unusually smooth defensively, drawing comparisons to John Olerud. He's also impressed the Indians with his work ethic.

With Julio Franco and Mark Carreon playing first base, the Indians were afforded the luxury of letting Sexson play a full season of Double-A. Now with Matt Williams moving Thome over, he may be available in a trade. ■

PAUL SHUEY — YOUNG GUN

RP • BR • TR • 6'3 • 215 • 26 • CLE92/1

	G	GS	IP	H	HR	BB	K	W	L	S	ERA	K/BB	K9	HW9
CLE94	14	0	11	14	1	12	16	0	1	5	8.49	1.3	13.0	21.15
CLE95	7	0	6	5	0	5	5	0	2	0	4.26	1.0	7.5	15.00
CLE96	42	0	53	45	6	26	44	5	2	4	2.85	1.7	7.5	12.04
CAREER	63	0	71	64	7	43	65	5	5	9	3.93	1.5	8.2	13.55

A high leg kick was blamed for Shuey's inconsistent delivery, his inability to throw strikes, and the fact that baserunners robbed him blind in '95. It was also the reason why he has suffered from hamstring and groin injuries in the past. But Shuey was able to make the adjustment in his motion (which also included abandoning a mini-Tiant body pivot), and he overcame his history of injuries and inconsistency in '96. And when Mesa struggled in midseason, Shuey got the job done as the Indians' closer.

Shuey's repertoire includes a power fastball, a big-breaking curve, and a good split-finger. He throws all 3 pitches low in the strike zone and induces a lot of ground-ball outs. He's nice insurance to have around against the league catching up to Mesa. ■

JIM THOME — AL ELITE

3B • BL • TR • 6'3 • 190 • 26 • CLE89/12

	AB	R	H	2B	3B	HR	RBI	BB	SO	SB	CS	BA	OB	SA
CLE94	321	58	86	20	1	20	52	46	84	3	3	.268	.359	.523
CLE95	452	92	142	29	3	25	73	97	113	4	3	.314	.438	.558
CLE96	505	122	157	28	5	38	116	123	141	2	2	.311	.450	.612
CAREER	1647	315	475	95	12	93	284	310	424	14	10	.288	.404	.530

Thome was a picture of productivity last season, posting career highs in almost every hitting category. He had at least 100 runs, RBI, and walks, becoming the second Indians player to accomplish the feat (Al Rosen did it in 1950). Thome has a lightning-quick swing that allows him to pull, but he also has exceptional power going to the opposite field. Hargrove: "Jimmy is probably the strongest guy on the team. He has pure, raw strength, and as he gains experience he is putting more of his game together."

Strongest guy on the team? Quite a compliment from someone who also managed Albert Belle. One of the reasons Thome is such a good hitter is that he has the plate discipline to make the pitcher come in with something hittable. And he takes a lot of pride in his walks. It's inconceivable that Hargrove would have him hitting in the 7th and 8th spots in the batting order. But Thome spent 139 at-bats in those very spots last season before he was moved up to 3rd in July. Thome was hitting well at the time of the switch, but after he moved up in the order, he exploded. He hit .327 with a .454 on-base average and a .677 slugging percentage batting 3rd. Imagine what he could have done if he had spent the whole season hitting in front of Belle. ■

OMAR VIZQUEL

SS • BB • TR • 5'9 • 155 • 29 • SEA84

	AB	R	H	2B	3B	HR	RBI	BB	SO	SB	CS	BA	OB	SA
CLE94	286	39	78	10	1	1	33	23	23	13	4	.273	.325	.325
CLE95	542	87	144	28	0	6	56	59	59	29	11	.266	.333	.351
CLE96	542	98	161	36	1	9	64	56	42	35	9	.297	.362	.417
CAREER	3481	447	914	134	17	22	284	311	332	116	58	.263	.322	.330

The Indians benefited from his bat in the bottom of the order, where he acted as a pre-leadoff hitter. He reached career highs in batting average and on-base percentage. But his usually stellar defense was short-circuited by a frayed labrum in his shoulder. He decided against surgery in the spring, thinking he could play the season. But his throwing really suffered, and he ended up committing a career high 20 errors. He won his 4th consecutive Gold Glove, but he didn't deserve it—and he knew it. Vizquel had arthroscopic surgery on his shoulder during the off-season, and no damage to the rotator cuff was found. He is expected to be 100% by the spring. ■

CASEY WHITTEN

SF • BL • TL • 6'0 • 175 • 24 • CLE93/2

	G	GS	IP	H	HR	BB	SO	W	L	S	ERA	K/BB	K9	HW9
AAA	12	10	44	54	8	24	35	3	4	0	5.04	1.5	7.2	16.08

In mid-June Whitten missed 3 weeks when he was hospitalized with a vascular condition called Berger's disease that caused clotting in his left hand and right shoulder. Indians representatives said the

condition was caused by Whitten's use of smokeless tobacco. Guess it isn't just for yellow teeth anymore. Whitten is the Indians best left-handed starting prospect. He throws a good 90+ fastball, but he has trouble throwing his slider and curve for strikes. A lefty with his talent may not be in the minors very much longer. ■

MATT WILLIAMS — AL ELITE

3B • BR • TR • 6′2 • 205 • 31 • SF86/1

	AB	R	H	2B	3B	HR	RBI	BB	SO	SB	CS	BA	OB	SA
SF94	445	74	119	16	3	43	96	33	87	1	0	.267	.319	.607
SF95	283	53	95	17	1	23	65	30	58	2	0	.336	.399	.647
SF96	404	69	122	16	1	22	85	39	91	1	2	.302	.367	.510
CAREER	4139	594	1092	179	25	247	732	272	872	29	27	.264	.312	.498

Before the strike ended the baseball season in '94, there were 4 players who had a reasonable shot at breaking Roger Maris's record: Jeff Bagwell, Junior, Prince Albert, and Williams. All have been cursed to some extent ever since, Bagwell and Junior by hand problems; the Prince by an inability to play well with the other children; and Williams by an assortment of ailments. Project Williams's '94, '95, and '96 seasons to 162 games and you realize that injuries and labor strife have likely erased 55 home runs and 165 RBI from his career totals. If he can continue to put up big years, this service interruption probably won't cost him induction into the Hall of Fame. If he can't—well, he and the rest of the union can ask themselves whether it really was worth all that bad karma from throwing away a season on principles only millionaires and lawyers recognize.

Williams wasn't able to return to his lofty levels in '96, producing a more human year of 22 dingers and 85 RBI in 400 at-bats—very human considering that these numbers were met or eclipsed in the same number of at-bats by Ellis Burks, Greg Vaughn, Henry Rodriguez, Geronimo Berroa, Ed Sprague, Todd Hundley, and Bernard Gilkey. His season was ended by arthroscopic surgery on his shoulder. Troubled by injuries, his defense was off a bit in '96, as his fielding percentage declined to the lowest level of his career.

He struck out at his highest rate since '89; if this trend continues, it will be very difficult for him to keep his average at the .300 level. It's a tribute to his ability to take what the pitcher gives him that it ever got up there in the first place, considering that his career batting average in the minors was .279—and much of that was spent in the PCL, where Mike Brumley has put up gaudy numbers. His remarkable resemblance to Harmon Killebrew only gets stronger. There is already talk that, like The Killer, he may be on his way to first base sooner rather than later.

If the Giants weren't such a daffy organization, you'd figure they must have known something about Williams to dump him for so little. The way things work out there, it could just as easily have been Barry saying he wanted the bald guy out of his sandbox. ■

ENRIQUE WILSON — SOLID PROSPECT

SS • BB • TR • 5′11 • 160 • 21 • MIN92

	AB	R	H	2B	3B	HR	RBI	BB	SO	SB	CS	BA	OB	SA
AA	484	70	147	17	5	5	50	31	46	23	16	.304	.346	.390

Wilson was the best fielding shortstop in the Eastern League last summer, and he can produce at the plate as well. He can catch up to just about any fastball, but hitting off his front foot makes him vulnerable to breaking balls. The Indians have Vizquel signed through the year 2022, which means that if Wilson wants a job in Cleveland any time soon, he'll have to give it a shot at second base. Watch him this spring. ■

JARET WRIGHT — GRADE-A PROSPECT

SP • BR • TR • 6′2 • 220 • 21 • CLE94/1

	G	GS	IP	H	HR	BB	SO	W	L	S	ERA	K/BB	K9	HW9
A+	19	19	101	65	1	55	109	7	4	0	2.5	2.0	9.7	10.69

Wright has the best arm in the Indians system. He throws a four seam fastball 95–98 mph, and the Indians are teaching him a two-seamer. His heater is often described as explosive. He complements his fastball with a hard curve and a so-so change-up. As evidence of his stuff, check out how many hits he allowed. He has a great work ethic and an imposing mound presence. ■

■ 1996 AUTOPSY

The Tigers and their fans went into '96 with the understanding that the team was undergoing a major renovation. There was excitement about the new faces in management, including Randy Smith, the wunderkind GM from the Padres, and manager Buddy Bell, a well-respected baseball man stolen from the Indians' coaching staff. While Sparky Anderson had always been loved in Detroit, it was time to move in a new direction and Bell seemed to be an excellent teacher and a determined, hate-to-lose type of guy. For Smith's part, he had already made more moves in the off-season than any Tiger GM in recent memory. A lean season was expected, but the fans weren't expecting the worst team in baseball history. They almost got it.

April 9-18 (9-18, 8 games back)
The Tigers opened on the road in Minnesota with their "ace," Felipe Lira, on the mound. He lasted 3 innings, giving up 6 earned runs. Tigers fans settled in for a long season. But the team bounced back, producing runs with the slugging of Cecil Fielder and Melvin Nieves, and by the 16th were 8-7, 3 games back. Cecil was the story: In Toronto on the 16th, he hit 3 homers, giving him 9 for the season. The team and the town were energized; it seemed impossible, but it looked as if the Tigers could compete overnight. That changed quickly as Fielder cooled off and the Tigers dropped 7 straight, going 1-10 to finish the month. Offense wasn't the problem: Travis Fryman, Mark Lewis, and Melvin Nieves all contributed, and they scored enough runs to win. It was their pitching, the bullpen in particular; the staff couldn't hold any lead, and no one had stepped into the closer's role. Lira managed a few good outings but had little to show for them. Tigers starters threw only 6 quality starts in the entire month, and of those, only 2 were converted into victories.

May 4-23 (13-41, 18 games back)
May was the worst month by a team since Baltimore went 1-21 in April 1988. For an entire month the Tigers faced contenders: Chicago, Cleveland, New York, and Texas. And these teams took the Tigers pitching staff apart. May 11 vs. Texas, Scott Aldred went 1.1 innings giving up 6 hits and 8 runs. May 17 vs. New York, Randy Veres in relief: 0 innings, 3 hits, and 3 earned runs. May 31 vs. Texas, Lira went 3.1 innings, giving up 9 hits and 8 runs. You could say that a pattern was emerging. Meanwhile, Detroit's offense was drying up. They averaged only 3.1 runs a game, which might have been enough for the Braves, but not for a team that would end up with 8 pitchers with ERAs over 8.00. The Tigers dropped 10 games in the standings—and it would have been a lot more than that if the Orioles hadn't been playing almost as badly. The Tigers were on a pace to set the record for the most losses by a major-league club—41 down and 80 to go.

June 10-17 (23-58, 25 games back)
At first glance, a 10-17 month seems pretty good, relatively speaking. It still projects to 102 losses. Omar Olivares, Lira, and Brian Williams each threw a shutout in the month, including Lira and Williams back to back on the 20th and 21st. The starters were beginning to last longer, taking some of the pressure off the bullpen (or, better yet, simply keeping them out of the game). The trade sending John Flaherty and Chris Gomez to San Diego for Andujar Cedeño and Brad Ausmus wasn't as bad as it seemed. Ausmus's work behind the plate helped settle the pitching, although it did little to help the offense. As for Cedeño, he didn't hit the ground running as much as he simply hit the ground, as if thrown from a moving vehicle. Bobby Higginson went on a tear, hitting 3 homers in 3 days, and Tony Clark came up from Toledo to add punch to the lineup.

July 12-14 (35-72, 29 games back)
The team gained a little respect as the starters settled down somewhat, winning enough games to ensure that they wouldn't set a record nobody wanted. In fact, in their first 7 outings, they had 6 quality starts and won 4 of them. But the biggest story came at the end of the month, at the trading deadline. That day, Randy Smith traded Cecil Fielder to the Yankees for Ruben Sierra and top prospect Matt Drews. In another deal, he sent Chad Curtis to the Dodgers for lefty relievers John Cummings and Joey Eischen. Both deals were significant. Cummings and Eischen added depth to the team's weakest spot, the bullpen, and unloading Cecil removed an unhappy player from the clubhouse. Unfortunately, it brought in "the village idiot."

August 14-15 (49-87, 27½ games back)
Riding the excitement of July's personnel changes, the Tigers won 7 of their first 9 games in August against Seattle, Texas, and New York. The pitching staff, bullpen included, held their own, giving up an average of 3.4 runs during that stretch. The offense contributed more than enough to win those games, and there was a general feeling that they had turned the corner. But Kenny Rogers brought them back down to earth with a 12-0 complete-game shutout in New York on the 11th. Rogers held them to 6 hits while Felipe Lira gave up 14 hits and 9 runs in 6.1 innings. This game proved to be a turning point. The party seemingly over before it began, the Tigers dropped 8 straight.

September 4-22 (53-109, 39 games back)
The club essentially went into the tank in the final month. Nobody hit, nobody pitched, and they played 16 games against playoff contenders anxious to pad their win columns: a recipe for disaster. The tailspin left everyone wondering if any real progress had been made as the club quietly closed in on and set a number of "records": the club record for losses (109); the A.L. record for worst ERA (6.38); and major-league records for homers allowed at 241 and grandslams allowed at 14.

■ 1997 DIAGNOSIS

Offense
In 1996 the Tigers had one of the worst offenses in the American League. The average A.L. team scored 872 runs; Detroit scored 783, finishing 11th in the league. They tied for 12th in slugging percentage and were 14th in on-base percentage. They didn't hit significant numbers of singles, doubles, or triples, but they did finish in the middle of the pack in homers with 204. They were 87-for-137 (64%) in their stolen-base attempts (anything below 75% is counterproductive). For '97, the offense is shaping up to be Tony Clark, Fryman, Mark Lewis, Higginson, Pride, and Nieves—which means it won't be much better than it was in '96. It would help to install Bubba Trammell in left, move Nieves to DH, and find at-bats for Phil Nevin. The Tigers' best short-range hitting prospect is second baseman Frank Catalanotto. He would make a fine leadoff or no. 2 hitter. But for now, the Tigers are loaded with mediocrity and no quick fixes.

Defense
Tony Clark is a distinct improvement over Cecil Fielder at first base. The Tigers' main double-play combo, Mark Lewis and the dearly departed Cedeño, were slightly below average. With Cedeño gone, Damion Easley can step in, and he will be an improvement. Fryman is exceptional at third base. The club may go with Phil Nevin at third and Fryman at short, however, sacrificing some defensive prowess for hitting. That may be a mistake, though, with young pitchers on the mound who tend to be too geared up to strike everyone out. It's no coincidence that the Braves' young pitching began to develop as soon as Terry Pendleton and Sid Bream were installed at the corners to settle the infield. In the outfield, center fielder Kimera Bartee has gap-to-gap range and Bobby Higginson has decent range and a fine, albeit sometimes wild, arm. Melvin Nieves, however, is frightening and needs to be converted into a full-time DH as soon as humanly possible. John Flaherty may have hit the tar out of the ball at San Diego, but Ausmus dramatically lowered the team's ERA with his pitch-calling sequences and leadership, and he was better at stopping opposing basestealers (34% to 29%).

Pitching
The Tigers' starting pitching was at or near the bottom in all the major categories, prompting pitching coach Jon Matlack to finally demand his honorable discharge. They did have 10 complete games, which was middle-of-the-pack, but that was probably more a function of complete distrust of the bullpen. They even managed 4 shutouts, which was above-average. This season, there's greater hope. For one thing, unlike '96, baseball fans may actually know the first names of more than two pitchers on their staff. Justin Thompson, if healthy, is the most promising starter the Tigers have had since Jack Morris broke in. In addition, power pitchers such as Mike Drumright, Matt Drews, and Seth Greisinger are on the horizon. Omar Olivares will be available to take the heat off the kids, though he will certainly be dismissed as soon as this team shows any sign of contending. Felipe Lira, Trever Miller, and C. J. Nitkowski could also be adequate stopgaps. Don't except results in '96, but excellent arms are something every team covets and the Tigers have a bunch of them now.

As bad as the rotation was in '96, the bullpen was worse. The Tigers' relief corps(e) was (de)composed primarily of guys with good fastballs and curveballs who couldn't throw strikes. Stuff is irrelevant without control. This was the worst bullpen in the league and in baseball. Look for some addition by subtraction where Mike Christopher (33), Randy Veres (31), and Mike Walker (30) are concerned. These three combined to make 58 appearances, allowing 176 baserunners, 28 dingers, and 90 earned runs in 88 innings! Lefty Williams pitched better than that for the Black Sox in the 1919 World Series and he was trying to lose! In '97, John Cummings and Joey Eischen will provide left-handed depth. José Lima is a decent right-hander. But that's about all they have, and it isn't very much. Might as well let some young arms be the ones to give up a run an inning.

Farm System

In addition to Bubba, Catalanotto, and all those young arms, the Tigers have several other good prospects. Richard Almanzar could be a poor man's Robbie Alomar, with better table manners. Cam Smith has poor command but throws 95. Fausto Cruz should be adequate defensively and has fine power for a middle infielder. And there are sleepers such as outfielders Anton French and Juan Encarnacion. French has blinding speed and Encarnacion is raw, but could be a 5-tool player.

Management and Ownership

Mike Illitch gave free rein to President John McHale, Jr. to select a GM, and Hale went with former Padres GM Randy Smith. Smith has been innovative, bright, and shrewd in his first season as Tigers GM—things no Tigers GM has been accused of in decades. In one year, the team has had a major influx of talent in the minor leagues. Smith is unafraid to pull the trigger on trades—making 12 in '96. Overall, his strategy has been to take a gamble on young players who have talent, but have lost favor—junk bonds, basically, and equally risky. But Smith isn't giving much away, and he's more often getting something in return. In addition, the team has been doing a better job of scouting and drafting.

As for field management, when Buddy Bell is given a major-league team, his abilities can be determined. He's been patient and has taught his players to hustle. With the talent on his roster at the moment, that's all that can be asked.

. . . and whatnot: Worse Than Detroit

In the movie *Airplane!*, those are the words Robert Hays used to describe an especially seedy waterfront dive in an especially seedy port. A fitting quote from a disaster/comedy for the '96 Tigers, who endured the worst season in their 96-year history, losing 109 games. And though they improved during the middle of the season after a dismal start, they reverted in the home stretch, finishing 4-22 in September. This was supposed to be a rebuilding year, but no one signed off on a '62 Mets revival.

But, believe it or not, things are looking up in Detroit. For the first time in many moons, the organization is actually thinking about the future. The new GM, Randy Smith, came to the Tigers after building a winner in San Diego by stocking their organization with young talent. Not so long ago, the Padres were derided for the fire sales that sent talents such as Fred McGriff and Gary Sheffield packing, and it seemed impossible that the club could recover this quickly. Though it would be unreasonable to expect that Smith could do it again that quickly he seems to have already taken steps in that direction.

Raiding mostly from teams he's familiar with—the Padres and Astros—Smith made 12 deals in his first 9 months in Detroit. Some worked out, some didn't. Brad Ausmus was a fine addition; Andujar Cedeño was gone before the end of the season. But it was refreshing enough just to see this much activity. The waters in Detroit have been pretty stagnant in recent years, and some funky stuff was growing on the surface. The strategy of wait-and-see, then scrape together enough loose change from underneath the sofa cushions to bring in Mike Moore and Tim Belcher to "pitch," got very old very quickly.

There have never been more than two legitimate prospects at a time on their farm in recent years, so perhaps getting third-rate hired guns was the best they could do. But even when they had talent down on the farm, they often let it slip away. The most

obvious, and most cited, example is the 1987 deal that sent John Smoltz to Atlanta for Doyle Alexander. The deal worked in the short run: Alexander pitched brilliantly and the Tigers won the division when the Blue Jays choked. But it remains a perfect example of the tomorrow-never-comes mind-set that has consistently left the Tigers with one of the thinnest farm systems in major-league baseball.

All that is changing. Smith has inherited some talent in the minor leagues and brought in some of his own. There are actually pitching prospects—real, live pitchers—in the system! The next step, of course, is to bring them along. The minor-league coaching staffs responsible for molding the talent have remained largely unchanged since Smith took over. Expect him to make some alterations shortly. Improving the farm system would be the final step in his revitalization of the organization and give Tigers fans reason for optimism.

The team is a few years from contending, but finally there is light at the end of the tunnel. Perhaps the '96 Tigers will end up compared to the '65 Mets (50-112), the '88 Braves (54-106), and '79 A's (54-108). From the sub-basement to the postseason in 4 years or less. It's possible—especially since the '65 Mets were worse than Detroit.

RICHARD ALMANZAR *GRADE-A PROSPECT*

2B • BR • TR • 5'10 • 155 • 20 • DET93

	AB	R	H	2B	3B	HR	RBI	BB	SO	SB	CS	BA	OB	SA
A+	471	81	144	22	2	1	36	49	49	53	19	.306	.379	.367

Almanzar is a fine, young Dominican prospect. In a midseason poll of managers he was named the best baserunner and best defensive second baseman in the Florida State League. Offensively, his strikeout-to-walk ratio is already very good, which should allow him to put that speed to use. In recent years the Tigers' team speed has been nonexistent, and they have developed a number of 1-tool speedsters to correct this. Not surprisingly, none of them could ever get on base, and they came and went quickly. Almanzar can reverse this trend. He hit over .300 all year and was the MVP of the F.S.L. All-Star game. Almanzar should start in Double-A and could be up by midseason. ■

BRAD AUSMUS

C • BR • TR • 5'11 • 185 • 27 • NYA87/46

	AB	R	H	2B	3B	HR	RBI	BB	SO	SB	CS	BA	OB	SA
SD94	327	45	82	12	1	7	24	30	63	5	1	.251	.314	.358
SD95	328	44	96	16	4	5	34	31	56	16	5	.293	.353	.412
SD/DET96	375	46	83	16	0	5	35	39	72	4	8	.221	.302	.304
CAREER	1190	153	302	52	6	22	105	106	219	27	14	.254	.317	.363

Ausmus came to the Tigers with Andujar Cedeño for John Flaherty and Chris Gomez after starting very slowly for the Padres (.184 in 103 at-bats). He had been benched for Brian Johnson by mid-May, and the Padres were looking for more offense. They thought John Flaherty might give them that, and got torrid production, including a near-record hitting streak. Ausmus didn't hit anywhere near that level. He's basically a .250-.260 hitter, and not much more than that can be reasonably expected. But Tigers pitchers like how he calls a game, and he will be instrumental in developing their young staff. Shortly after he took over behind the plate, the staff ERA began to go down. Ausmus will feel some pressure from Raul Casanova, who can hit. ■

KIMERA BARTEE

OF • BB • TR • 6'0 • 180 • 24 • BAL93/14

	AB	R	H	2B	3B	HR	RBI	BB	SO	SB	CS	BA	OB	SA
DET96	217	32	55	6	1	1	14	17	77	20	10	.253	.308	.304

Drafted by the Orioles in '93, he was part of the Scott Erickson trade with Minnesota. The Orioles then got him back in the Rule 5 draft, only to have the Tigers grab him back in the Rule 5. Detroit, in their never-ending quest to resurrect Ron LeFlore, is always looking for speed. And Kimera is supersonic. But you can't steal first—and if you want to lead off in the A.L., you have to let a few balls go by. Bartee's strikeout-to-walk ratio is weak and not showing any signs of improvement. He also needs to learn how to be more efficient in his basestealing. His defense is farther along than any part of his game. He has a fine glove and excellent range. ■

RAUL CASANOVA — SOLID PROSPECT

C • BR • TR • 6'0 • 190 • 24 • NYN90/8

	AB	R	H	2B	3B	HR	RBI	BB	SO	SB	CS	BA	OB	SA
DET96	85	6	16	1	0	4	9	6	18	0	0	.188	.242	.341

Raul had a spectacular '94 season at Class-A Rancho Cucamonga, but ankle problems limited him to 89 games in '95, and the Padres unloaded him. In 1996 he picked up where he left off in '94 and he was promoted from Triple-A Toledo on May 24. A wrist injury forced him to undergo surgery and go on the DL in June, but while rehabbing with Double-A Jacksonville in July he went 8-for-24, with 3 homers in 6 games. Raul has good power; and although he doesn't walk enough, he should be a fine hitter. He has good all-around defensive skills and possesses exceptional arm strength. Some observers felt that he appeared lax on defense in the past, but a few weeks with Buddy should cure him of that. ■

FRANK CATALANOTTO — SOLID PROSPECT

2B • BL • TR • 6'0 • 170 • 22 • DET92/10

	AB	R	H	2B	3B	HR	RBI	BB	SO	SB	CS	BA	OB	SA
AA	497	105	148	34	6	17	67	74	69	15	14	.298	.398	.439

Catalanotto's a fine prospect in an organization suddenly loaded with second basemen. He has the best power among them—in fact, he looks like Lou Whitaker offensively. He also adds a little speed and has excellent plate discipline. He started hot last year and made the Southern League All-Star team. His defense isn't drawing accolades, but he looks good anyway. ■

TONY CLARK — YOUNG GUN

1B • BB • TR • 6'8 • 240 • 24 • DET90/1

	AB	R	H	2B	3B	HR	RBI	BB	SO	SB	CS	BA	OB	SA
DET95	101	10	24	5	1	3	11	8	30	0	0	.238	.294	.396
DET96	376	56	94	14	0	27	72	29	127	0	1	.250	.299	.503

The Tigers took Clark with the second overall pick in '90 draft, and they've waited patiently for him to develop. First there was his college basketball career, and then a string of injuries that kept him from playing good portions of 1990-93 (he missed the entire '91 season). Finally, in '94, he managed a full season for Double-A Trenton and hit 21 homers.

Still, there was the small matter of the Big Fella in his way. But the Big Fella became the Bigger Fella, was moved to DH and then to the Yankees, and Tony got an extended look. The Tigers were concerned about his defense, especially his arm, but he showed great improvement in '96. The team now feels he can handle the position. He is strikeout-prone and has a long swing. He shortened it somewhat in '96, but his on-base average is very weak. If it improves, he will move up in the ranks of A.L. first baseman. ■

FAUSTO CRUZ

SS • BR • TR • 5'11 • 165 • 25 • OAK90

	AB	R	H	2B	3B	HR	RBI	BB	SO	SB	CS	BA	OB	SA
OAK95	23	0	5	0	0	0	5	3	5	1	1	.217	.286	.217
DET96	38	5	9	2	0	0	0	1	11	0	0	.237	.256	.289

Cruz, a longtime Oakland prospect, came to the Tigers in the trade for Phil Plantier. He has an excellent defensive reputation and can play second and third. He has good power for a middle infielder, but his average in '96 was unusually low for a .299 career minor-league hitter. All he had to do was dislodge Damion Easley, something many Angels have had no difficulty doing. But the Tigers waived him instead. ■

JOHN CUMMINGS — SLEEPER

RP • BL • TL • 6'3 • 200 • 27 • SEA90/8

	G	GS	IP	H	HR	BB	K	W	L	S	ERA	K/BB	K9	HW9
SEA94	17	8	64	66	7	37	33	2	4	0	5.63	.9	4.6	14.48
SEA/LA95	39	0	44	46	3	17	25	3	1	0	4.06	1.5	5.1	12.89
LA/DET96	25	0	36	48	4	22	29	3	4	0	5.48	1.3	7.2	17.45
CAREER	91	16	191	219	20	92	106	8	15	0	5.33	1.2	5.0	14.67

Of the trades Randy Smith made last year, the one that brought Cummings and Joey Eischen to Detroit was greeted with the most skepticism. Observers felt that the Tigers should have gotten more for Chad Curtis, and they might have. But Buddy wanted Curtis out of the clubhouse immediately, and the Tigers needed help, as always, in the bullpen. Cummings was seen as the weaker of the two

lefties, and management planned to send him to Triple-A, keeping Tom Urbani on the roster. But they gave Cummings a look first, and he impressed quickly. In the end, Urbani got to ride the Greyhound to Toledo. In retrospect, this shouldn't have been so surprising. Cummings was effective with the Dodgers in '95 and was stunned when the Dodgers demoted him. Detroit's bullpen is a little different from L.A.'s, and they won't be so quick to ship him off. But he does need to work on his consistency and eliminate some of those baserunners. ■

MIKE DARR — SLEEPER

OF • BL • TR • 6'3 • 205 • 21 • DET94/2

	AB	R	H	2B	3B	HR	RBI	BB	SO	SB	CS	BA	OB	SA
A+	311	26	77	14	7	0	38	28	64	7	3	.248	.307	.338

Darr is the son of the former major-league pitcher of the same name, and he is considered to be the best pure hitter in the organization behind Daryle Ward. He has excellent power potential and good strike-zone judgment. But he showed nothing in '96, missed the first month of season with a hand injury, and there are questions about his off-field behavior. He needs a lot of work defensively to overcome his weak arm and lack of speed. He could develop into a decent left fielder if he wants it badly enough. ■

ERIC DINYAR

RP • BR • TR • 6'6 • 210 • 23 • DET94/48

	G	GS	IP	H	HR	BB	K	W	L	S	ERA	K/BB	K9	HW9
A+	58	0	66	42	0	35	55	3	3	27	1.78	1.6	7.5	10.55

Dinyar is an imposing type. He uses a sidearm delivery and has an excellent slider and a sinking fastball. His change-up is also effective. He keeps the ball on the ground, which may help him get to Tiger Stadium—and survive once he arrives. ■

MATT DREWS — SOLID PROSPECT

SP • BR • TR • 6'8 • 205 • 22 • NYA93/1

	G	GS	IP	H	HR	BB	K	W	L	S	ERA	K/BB	K9	HW9
AA	15	15	77	66	7	52	77	1	7	0	4.44	13.32	9.0	13.79

If Drews is healthy, he's an 'A.' If he's not, he's merely solid. Drews was the Yankees' top pick in the '93 draft and the *uber*-pitching prospect in their organization. They wouldn't deal him during the pennant race in '95, but they soured on him in '96. He came into the minors with a mid-90s fastball that has fine sinking action, plus a good curve and change-up. His primary weapon has always been that fastball, and he ran into trouble last year when his velocity dropped to the mid-80s after the Yanks jumped him from Class-A to Triple-A. The Tigers, never afraid of a meaty ERA, felt Drews was worth a shot and went after him. Randy Smith said that Drews's problems were due to throwing across his body, and was confident that coaching could correct it. The Tigers have been pleased with his work and how quickly his control improved. More importantly, his strikeout rate has rocketed. He could make the Fielder trade look like John Smoltz for Doyle Alexander in reverse. ■

MIKE DRUMRIGHT — GRADE-A PROSPECT

SP • BL • TR • 6'4 • 210 • 22 • DET95/1

	G	GS	IP	H	HR	BB	K	W	L	S	ERA	K/BB	K9	HW9
AA	18	18	100	80	11	48	109	6	4	0	3.97	2.3	10.9	11.52

The Tigers took Drumright with the no. 11 overall pick in 1995 draft from Wichita State. He has a good fastball that's consistently in the low 90s (and peaks at 95), plus a superb, hard curveball. He's also working on a change-up. In *Baseball America*'s midseason managers' poll, he was rated the best pitching prospect in the Southern League and his curve was rated the league's best breaking pitch. The Tigers have been protective of Drumright's arm, to the point of firing former Jacksonville manager Bill Plummer over it. Plummer was apparently more concerned with victories than development and had Drumright throw nearly 140 pitches in one start. He went on the DL as a precaution and Plummer went on the unemployment line. Drumright should start the year in Toledo. If the Tigers get their wish, he'll be part of a solid rotation with Justin Thompson, Seth Greisinger, and Matt Drews within 2 or 3 years. ■

DAMION EASLEY

SS-2B • BR • TR • 5'11 • 155 • 27 • CAL88/30

	AB	R	H	2B	3B	HR	RBI	BB	SO	SB	CS	BA	OB	SA
CAL94	316	41	68	16	1	6	30	29	48	4	5	.215	.288	.329
CAL95	357	35	77	14	2	4	35	32	47	5	2	.216	.288	.300
CAL/DET96	112	14	30	2	0	4	17	10	25	3	1	.268	.331	.393
CAREER	1166	137	286	50	5	17	116	107	181	27	19	.245	.315	.340

Easley came over to Detroit for Greg Gohr. Hardly an earth-shaking deal. Easley hasn't hit in more than

2 years, and there's little to suggest he'll start now. But his competition may be Fausto Cruz, so he could win by default. ■

JOEY EISCHEN — SLEEPER

RP • BL • TL • 6′1 • 190 • 26 • TEX89/3

	G	GS	IP	H	HR	BB	K	W	L	S	ERA	K/BB	K9	HW9
LA95	17	0	20	19	1	11	15	0	0	0	3.10	1.4	6.8	13.50
LA/DET96	52	0	68	75	7	34	51	1	2	0	4.23	1.5	6.7	14.42

A few years ago, Eischen was the top pitching prospect in the Expos system. He went 14-4 as a starter for Double-A Harrisburg in '93. Obviously his stock has fallen, but not that much. He stepped into Detroit's bullpen last season and did a respectable job. He could cut down on the walks, but his ERA was almost a run lower than that of anyone else on the pitching staff. Eischen has a fastball in the low 90s—exceptional velocity for a lefty—and also has a curve and a change. ■

JUAN ENCARNACION

OF • BR • TR • 6′2 • 160 • 21 • DET92

	AB	R	H	2B	3B	HR	RBI	BB	SO	SB	CS	BA	OB	SA
A+	499	54	120	31	2	15	58	24	104	11	5	.240	.290	.401

The Tigers say he is a 5-tool player, even if his numbers don't. He is good defensively, with an outstanding arm and decent speed. They think with refinement he'll be a major-league right fielder. He had his breakthrough season in '95, but Encarnacion was in a funk most of last year, and he's had trouble hitting breaking balls. Still, given his skills and potential, the Tigers will probably send him to Double-A this year anyway. ■

ANTON FRENCH

OF • BB • TR • 5′10 • 175 • 21 • SL93/14

	AB	R	H	2B	3B	HR	RBI	BB	SO	SB	CS	BA	OB	SA
A+	463	61	122	20	8	5	36	25	80	47	13	.263	.303	.374

French is a raw talent the Tigers acquired from the Braves for Danny Bautista. He's a switch-hitter who hits better from the left side. He's developed some power, but speed is his greatest asset. He's also excellent at bunting for a base hit. Defensively, he has a lot of learning to do and has a weak arm. ■

TRAVIS FRYMAN — CONSISTENT STAR

3B • ER • TR • 6′1 • 180 • 28 • DET87/3

	AB	R	H	2B	3B	HR	RBI	BB	SO	SB	CS	BA	OB	SA
DET94	464	66	122	34	5	18	85	45	128	2	2	.263	.326	.474
DET95	567	79	156	21	5	15	81	63	100	4	2	.275	.347	.409
DET96	616	90	165	32	3	22	100	57	118	4	3	.268	.329	.437
CAREER	3702	517	1013	202	26	127	577	344	818	42	23	.274	.336	.445

Last season was a mixed bag for Fryman. He went to another All-Star game, but that was largely by default. He got off to a sluggish start, and the Tigers had to send somebody to Philadelphia and Tito Fuentes wasn't eligible. But he did score and drive in runs. And his defense continued to be excellent. He has an exceptional arm and great range. Despite the rebuilding efforts in Detroit, Fryman was reportedly the only guy Smith wouldn't consider trading last year. With his attitude and work ethic, that's understandable. But as the off-season began, rumors began flying about a possible trade involving Fryman. Smith reconsidered his previous statements, making Fryman available, but only for the right price. ■

SETH GREISINGER — GRADE-A PROSPECT

RHP • DET96/1 • UNIVERSITY OF VIRGINIA

The Tigers took Greisinger with their first pick after a stellar '96 season, capping a collegiate career that had previously been little more than mediocre. Then he earned a spot on the Olympic team and found himself the no. 2 starter. The American team lost out on the gold, and it was left to Seth to salvage some dignity in the bronze medal game. After a rocky first inning, he retired 19 of the final 21 batters, getting a 10-3 victory against Nicaragua. Greisinger is very poised and polished. He has an excellent curve (*Baseball America* rated his curve as the best college breaking ball last year), a 91–92 mph fastball, and an exceptional change. He can throw all of these pitches for strikes. He could be up as early as this season, but '98 is more likely. ■

DAVE HAJEK

2B • BR • TR • 5'10 • 165 • 29 • HOU89

	AB	R	H	2B	3B	HR	RBI	BB	SO	SB	CS	BA	OB	SA
AAA	508	81	161	31	5	4	64	25	36	9	6	.317	.348	.421

Hajek is a decent fielder who can hit pretty well. Unfortunately for him, the Astros weren't certain he has the range to play shortstop, the arm to play third, or the bat to play outfield. It's second base or sell insurance—and with Biggio there, it was waivers. He's a fine bench player and could start for an expansion team. Or the Tigers. If he were to get a full shot, he'd hit in the .270-.280 range with little power. He wouldn't walk much, but he's better than several guys who have full-time jobs in the majors right now. ■

PHIL HIATT

3B • BR • TR • 6'3 • 200 • 27 • KC90/8

	AB	R	H	2B	3B	HR	RBI	BB	SO	SB	CS	BA	OB	SA
AAA	555	99	145	27	3	42	119	50	180	17	6	.261	.322	.548

Hiatt has proven time and again he can mash Triple-A pitchers. Last season, he was named the best power hitter in the International League. Unfortunately, minor leaguers can strike him out one time out of three. At 28 he may never get the opportunity to play in the majors again (he has 11 dingers and a career batting average of .212 in 372 at bats). ■

BOBBY HIGGINSON

YOUNG GUN

OF • BL • TR • 5'11 • 180 • 26 • DET92/12

	AB	R	H	2B	3B	HR	RBI	BB	SO	SB	CS	BA	OB	SA
DET95	410	61	92	17	5	14	43	62	107	6	4	.224	.329	.393
DET96	440	75	141	35	0	26	81	65	66	6	3	.320	.404	.577

Higginson's development at the plate proved to be one of the bright spots for Detroit. He started the year as part of a right-field platoon with Mel Nieves primarily because he had trouble hitting left-handed pitching in the past. He worked that out last year, managing a .358 on-base average against them. He also increased his power and reduced his strikeouts dramatically. He has a strong but sometimes erratic arm and led the A.L. in assists in '95 with 13. Nobody's talking All-Star now, but he made huge strides in '96 and could be one in the next couple of seasons. ■

GREG KEAGLE

SP-RP • BR • TR • 6'2 • 195 • 25 • SD93/6

	G	GS	IP	H	HR	BB	K	W	L	S	ERA	K/BB	K9	HW9
DET96	26	6	87	104	13	68	70	3	6	0	7.39	1.0	7.2	17.78

The Tigers acquired Keagle from the Padres in the Rule 5 draft in the off-season and he immediately contributed to Detroit's pitching woes. When he went on the DL July 7 with a strained back, his ERA was over 8.00 and his HW9 over 18.00. He was assigned to Triple-A Toledo upon his return and was even worse, posting a 2-3 record and a 10.00 ERA. His fastball is above average with good movement, but his breaking pitches are mediocre and have fooled no one. Either Randy Smith must know something about this guy, or Keagle has 8 × 10s of Smith doing Marge Schott's toenails. ■

MARK LEWIS

2B • BR • TR • 6'1 • 190 • 27 • CLE88/1

	AB	R	H	2B	3B	HR	RBI	BB	SO	SB	CS	BA	OB	SA
CLE94	73	6	15	5	0	1	8	2	13	1	0	.205	.227	.315
CIN95	171	25	58	13	1	3	30	21	33	0	3	.339	.407	.480
DET96	545	69	147	30	3	11	55	42	109	6	1	.270	.326	.396
CAREER	1568	179	425	86	5	21	158	105	276	16	11	.271	.317	.372

Lewis was a pleasant surprise for Detroit fans early in the season, a time when there was little else to be excited about. It seems that many had forgotten that he hit .339 as a reserve with the Reds in '95. The Tigers acquired him along with C. J. Nitkowski for David Wells, and he smashed lefties and easily surpassed his career-high in homers with 11. Buddy Bell loves his work ethic, which is said to be among the best on the team. He isn't a flashy fielder, but he has a good arm and decent range. His hitting tailed off significantly in the second half, however, and he is still prone to strikeouts. There are suddenly a few second-base prospects in the organization, and he will have to produce or he could be out of a job. ■

RICHIE LEWIS

RP • BR • TR • 5′10 • 170 • 31 • MON87/4

	G	GS	IP	H	HR	BB	K	W	L	S	ERA	K/BB	K9	HW9
FLA94	45	0	54	62	7	38	45	1	4	0	5.67	1.2	7.5	16.67
FLA95	21	1	36	30	9	15	32	0	1	0	3.75	2.1	8.0	11.25
DET96	72	0	90	78	9	65	78	4	6	2	4.18	1.2	7.8	14.29
CAREER	197	3	264	251	33	168	224	12	15	2	4.33	1.3	7.6	14.28

It speaks volumes that Lewis was the only pitcher on the staff to yield less than a hit an inning—though he made up for that by walking 6.5 batters per 9 innings—and one of the few to go, on average, 10 innings between dingers, and that he was released at the end of the season. He gets by on a curveball and a sinking fastball, but if he's the best pitcher on your staff, consider yourselves lucky to lose only 109 games. ■

JOSÉ LIMA

RP-SP • BR • TR • 6′2 • 170 • 24 • DET89

	G	GS	IP	H	HR	BB	K	W	L	S	ERA	K/BB	K9	HW9
DET95	15	15	73	85	10	18	37	3	9	0	6.11	2.1	4.6	12.70
DET96	39	4	72	87	13	22	59	5	6	3	5.70	2.7	7.4	13.61

Out of the gate he went 0-4 with a 9.35 ERA, and he wasn't even that good. But after a brief stint at Triple-A to regroup, he returned as a reliever, and as a new pitcher. In his first 21 innings, he went 3-1 with a 2.18 ERA and 25 Ks. José added velocity to his good sinking fastball, hitting 93 mph, which helped set up his best pitch, the circle-change. He also has an average slider. Detroit may try him as a starter again this year, but they should be content with his solid work out of the bullpen. ■

FELIPE LIRA

SP • BR • TR • 6′0 • 170 • 24 • DET90

	G	GS	IP	H	HR	BB	K	W	L	S	ERA	K/BB	K9	HW9
DET95	37	22	146	151	17	56	89	9	13	1	4.31	1.6	5.5	12.76
DET96	32	32	194	204	30	66	113	6	14	0	5.22	1.7	5.2	12.52

Lira had some shining moments last year, earning the title of staff ace by default. In reality, he was erratic at best. Lira has decent stuff, relying on a

split-finger fastball with below-average velocity but good sinking action. He's not afraid to pitch inside and has a good slider. His strikeout totals aren't good, but he has decent control. Last year was his first full season in the bigs, and he may just need time to work on location and consistency, or convincing himself he's a big-league pitcher. ■

DAN MICELI

SLEEPER

RP • BR • TR • 6′1 • 185 • 26 • KC90

	G	GS	IP	H	HR	BB	K	W	L	S	ERA	K/BB	K9	HW9
PIT94	28	0	27	28	5	11	27	2	1	2	5.93	2.5	9.0	12.98
PIT95	58	0	58	61	7	28	56	4	4	21	4.66	2.0	8.7	13.81
PIT96	44	9	85	99	15	45	66	2	10	1	5.78	1.5	7.0	15.24
CAREER	139	9	175	194	27	87	153	8	15	24	5.45	1.8	7.9	14.44

Acquired from the Pirates for Clint Sodowsky, Miceli is coming off a disastrous '96 season. He started from '95's poor late-season numbers (10.61 ERA in his last 9 outings) and quickly went into another tailspin, which landed him in Double-A Carolina in early May. His 3 starts of 3 innings apiece earned him a recall, where he was tried in the rotation for a while—which only served to batter his ego some more. With his stuff, he should be the closer: a 95-mph fastball, a slightly above-average slider, and an adequate change-up. But at times he can't throw strikes, and at other times he leaves his pitches in the middle of the strike zone. Leyland, trying to put a positive spin on the situation after a half-decent cuting from Miceli: "In the past he's been rushing and overthrowing like he's trying to throw the ball through a wall. He has to pitch instead of just trying to throw the ball as hard as he can." The thought of this guy in the AL and in Tiger Stadium is too frightening for words. ■

TREVER MILLER

SP-RP • BR • TL • 6′3 • 175 • 23 • DET91/2

	G	GS	IP	H	HR	BB	K	W	L	S	ERA	K/BB	K9	HW9
DET96	5	4	16	28	3	9	8	0	4	0	9.18	.9	4.5	20.73

Miller went 8-2 for Double-A Jacksonville in '95, but he was mediocre at Triple-A Toledo in '96, and

a human sacrifice in Detroit. The Tigers look at him as a fifth starter or a long reliever. He has a big-breaking curve, an average fastball, and likes to throw sliders. He added the slider in '95 but is still working on it. He keeps the ball down, which is good for Tiger Stadium, and he'll probably get a longer look there this year. ■

TONY MITCHELL

SLEEPER

OF • BB • TR • 6'4 • 225 • 26

	AB	R	H	2B	3B	HR	RBI	BB	SO	SB	CS	BA	OB	SA
AAA	288	45	80	10	4	12	43	41	89	3	2	.278	.367	.465

Mitchell is a big guy and extremely strong. True to that particular product line, he also has excellent power and strikes out a lot. He's a switch-hitter, hit for a decent average in Triple-A Toledo, and also walked quite a bit. He was promoted from Double-A after hitting .312 with 11 dingers in 173 at bats. Defensively, he has a weak arm and limited range. He needs some work, but he could find himself in the outfield mix in Detroit shortly. He's paid his dues: 8 minor league seasons and counting. ■

MIKE MYERS

RP • BL • TL • 6'3 • 195 • 27 • SF90/7

	G	GS	IP	H	HR	BB	K	W	L	S	ERA	K/BB	K9	HW9
DET96	83	0	64	70	6	34	69	1	5	6	5.01	2.0	9.7	14.61

Myers is a lefty who throws hard and has a good arm, but he has been plagued by injuries. He had an excellent strikeout rate last year and earned a shot at the closer role. He allowed too many runners, blew a few saves, and his ERA ballooned. His numbers were pretty good by Tigers standards, but he'll have to work a 1-2-3 inning more than once a week if he's to earn a long-term stay. ■

PHIL NEVIN

SLEEPER

3B • BR • TR • 6'2 • 185 • 26 • HOU92/1

	AB	R	H	2B	3B	HR	RBI	BB	SO	SB	CS	BA	OB	SA
HOU/DET95	156	13	28	4	1	2	13	18	40	1	0	.179	.281	.256
DET96	120	15	35	5	0	8	19	8	39	1	0	.292	.338	.533

Nevin was the no. 1 pick overall in the '92 draft, taken by the Astros. He quickly gained a deserved reputation as cocky, a hothead, and a complainer: joker, joker, and a triple. He was also "big-leaguing" it a bit too much for his minor-league teammates' taste. Evidently, spending the signing bonus on Killer Loop shades to wear at bat wasn't ingratiating him to other, less pretentious Astros farmhands. When Nevin finally made it to the majors, he hit .117, yet still went ballistic on some Astros officials informing him of his demotion. Soon after, the Astros traded him to Detroit for Mike Henneman. When a troubled prospect is traded, it's usually just business. But when it's Detroit, it's personal. Humbled by the ordeal—for now, anyway—Nevin decided to learn how to catch. While playing for Double-A Jacksonville, he allowed 3 passed balls and was yanked from a game at Carolina. Nevin proceeded to go 9 rounds with a bathroom stall in the visitors' clubhouse. Neither the stall nor Nevin was available for comment, and no date has been set for a rematch. He finally exploded on the field in Double-A, and the Tigers were anxious to give that bat another look at major-league pitching. He was impressive in Detroit, and the Tigers used him extensively at third, moving Travis Fryman back to his natural position at short. That experiment was successful, and Nevin will probably see more time at third (and maybe at catcher) this season. ■

MELVIN NIEVES

OF • BR • TR • 6'2 • 185 • 25 • ATL88

	AB	R	H	2B	3B	HR	RBI	BB	SO	SB	CS	BA	OB	SA
SD95	234	32	48	6	1	14	38	19	88	2	3	.205	.276	.419
DET96	431	71	106	23	4	24	60	44	158	1	2	.246	.322	.485
CAREER	750	109	172	31	5	41	106	71	284	3	5	.229	.304	.448

Nieves supplied some power in Tiger Stadium last year, including one shot off Chicago's Matt Karchner on May 17 that cleared Tiger Stadium's right-field roof, only the 25th time that's been done. But

pitches very infrequently made such solid contact with his bat. He's a project, and according to Buddy Bell, he's the analytical type who spends a lot of time going over videotapes. Obviously, the first thing he needs is plate discipline. His defense at the beginning of the year was fairly suspect, but he reportedly had made strides. He still looks pretty bad out there, but they don't pay him for his glove. Hard to believe the player the Padres insisted on having in the McGriff trade is still this raw. ■

C. J. NITKOWSKI

SP • BL • TL • 6'2 • 185 • 24 • CIN94/1

	G	GS	IP	H	HR	BB	K	W	L	S	ERA	K/BB	K9	HW9
CIN/DET95	20	18	71	94	11	35	31	2	7	0	6.66	.9	3.9	16.35
DET96	11	8	45	62	7	38	36	2	3	0	8.08	.9	7.2	19.97

Nitkowski had good strikeout numbers in the minors in '94 and '95 and looked to be progressing nicely. In retrospect, however, the Reds may have rushed him and pinned some unrealistically high hopes on him. Nitkowski has trouble with his command, especially early in games, which has led to some very ugly outings in Detroit. He was effective at Triple-A last year, but that didn't continue when called up. He throws an average fastball that tails in on left-handed batters, but his curveball/change-up combo platter is inconsistent. He uses a good knuckle-curve as his out pitch, and is most effective when he is able to pitch inside. He hasn't always been willing to do that, afraid to make a mistake and end up on *SportsCenter* for the wrong reason. ■

OMAR OLIVARES

SP • BR • TR • 6'1 • 195 • 29 • SD86

	G	GS	IP	H	HR	BB	K	W	L	S	ERA	K/BB	K9	HW9
SL94	14	12	73	84	10	37	26	3	4	1	5.74	.7	3.2	14.90
DET95	16	6	41	55	5	23	22	1	4	0	6.91	1.0	4.8	17.12
DET96	25	25	160	169	16	75	81	7	11	0	4.89	1.1	4.6	13.73
CAREER	182	112	807	824	76	330	427	37	39	3	4.35	1.3	4.8	12.87

Detroit is Olivares's fifth organization. He looked promising for the Cardinals from 1990 to 1993 but

hadn't done much of anything since. The Tigers were willing take a flier on him but didn't expect much. He ended up giving them the most consistent starting pitching they received all year. With a struggling bullpen, this proved to be crucial to the team as it played .500 ball from June through early August. He lost 6 weeks to a severe left hamstring pull, but still led the staff on the mound and in the clubhouse. At this age, unfortunately, he won't get much better. His strikeout rate, once respectable but never stellar, has deteriorated as his walks have increased. Unless the Tigers get major help in the free-agent market, Olivares will survive the off-season shuffle and take a few for the team in '97. ■

SHANNON PENN

2B • BB • TR • 5'10 • 165 • 27 • TEX88/58

	AB	R	H	2B	3B	HR	RBI	BB	SO	SB	CS	BA	OB	SA
AAA	356	65	102	12	4	6	42	26	59	22	11	.287	.356	.393

Penn led the Eastern League with 53 steals in '93 and the International League with 45 in '94. His stolen-base totals have decreased of late, but he was still named the fastest player in the I.L. last season. He has very little power, but he did hit for average. He is known as a solid defensive second baseman, but he wasn't going to make it into the majors on that skill alone. The Tigers have too many of those guys in the system already, and moved him to the outfield. And then to the waiver wire. ■

CURTIS PRIDE

OF • BL • TR • 6'0 • 200 • 28 • NYN86/10

	AB	R	H	2B	3B	HR	RBI	BB	SO	SB	CS	BA	OB	SA
MON95	63	10	11	1	0	0	2	5	16	3	2	.175	.235	.190
DET96	267	52	80	17	5	10	31	31	63	11	6	.300	.372	.513
CAREER	339	65	95	19	6	11	38	36	82	15	8	.280	.349	.469

Pride showed some signs of promise with the Expos, especially in '93, when he hit .326 with 22 homers while playing at 3 levels. But he got caught in a traffic jam of prospects there and his numbers tailed

off until the Tigers picked him up as a free agent last off-season. Pride saw limited time in left field, platooning and losing some time to a shoulder injury. But he showed prowess at the plate with power and speed. Pride was a three-sport athlete at William & Mary, with soccer his best, basketball his favorite, and baseball, at the time, an afterthought. ■

BRANDON REED

SLEEPER

RP-SP • BR • TR • 6'4 • 185 • 22 • DET93/45

	G	GS	IP	H	HR	BB	K	W	L	S	ERA	K/BB	K9	HW9
AA	7	3	26	18	1	3	18	1	0	1	2.08	6.0	6.2	7.27

Reed was a big-time closer at Class-A Fayetteville in '95, earning 41 saves and striking out 78 in 65 innings. Because he couldn't use his change effectively when closing, the Tigers put him in the starting rotation. Initially, the experiment was successful. He was promoted to Double-A Jacksonville, but he developed shoulder problems, and the Tigers shut him down. Reed has an excellent curve and an improving change-up. His fastball has improved as well but is still average at best. He wouldn't be such a long-shot if he hadn't gotten hurt. ■

A. J. SAGER

SP-RP • BR • TR • 6'4 • 220 • 32 • SD88/10

	G	GS	IP	H	HR	BB	K	W	L	S	ERA	K/BB	K9	HW9
SD94	22	3	46	62	4	16	26	1	4	0	5.98	1.6	5.1	15.24
COL95	10	0	14	19	1	7	10	0	0	0	7.36	1.4	6.4	16.71
DET96	22	9	79	91	10	29	52	4	5	0	5.01	1.8	5.9	13.67
CAREER	54	12	140	172	15	52	88	5	9	0	5.59	1.7	5.7	14.40

Sager is an aging sinker-slider pitcher who has always had good control. The Tigers signed him as a free agent in the off-season, and he started the year in Triple-A Toledo. After his call-up, he started out in bullpen, but worked his way into the rotation and did an adequate job—for a Tiger. Bell liked Sager's ability to keep the ball down, an important quality in Tiger Stadium because of the deep infield grass. The influx of kids may crowd him out. ■

CAM SMITH

SOLID PROSPECT

SP • BR • TR • 6'3 • 190 • 23 • DET93/3

	G	GS	IP	H	HR	BB	K	W	L	S	ERA	K/BB	K9	HW9
A+	22	21	114	93	10	71	114	5	8	0	4.59	1.6	9.0	12.99

Smith throws in the mid-90s with good movement. He also has a good breaking ball and change-up, which have helped him to excellent strikeout numbers in the minors. But he gives up a lot of walks and needs to work on his control. He also missed several weeks last year with a sore biceps muscle. He is an emotional sort, and that also has affected his performance. The Tigers feel he's intelligent enough to make the necessary adjustments, though. He'll probably start at Double-A, his ETA is late 1998. ■

JUSTIN THOMPSON

YOUNG GUN

SP • BL • TL • 6'3 • 175 • 24 • DET91/1

	G	GS	IP	H	HR	BB	K	W	L	S	ERA	K/BB	K9	HW9
AAA	13	13	84	74	2	26	69	6	3	0	3.42	2.7	7.4	10.67

Thompson is the Tigers current last, best hope. So close, so much potential, so many injuries. He opened Triple-A Toledo's season with a 7 inning shutout against Norfolk. He followed that with a 2-hit shutout against Richmond on April 10; he fanned 7 and walked 1 in that gem. Thompson ultimately would go 21 innings before giving up his first run. International League managers said he had the league's best breaking ball and was the league's best pitching prospect. In Thompson's major-league debut May 27, he gave up 1 run and struck out 8 in 6 innings. He showed great poise in the majors, but was immediately hampered by a tender elbow, having already missed the entire '94 season with an unrelated elbow problem. After just his second start of the season, he was put on the 15-day DL with what was described as swelling in the left bursa sac—more commonly known as a sore shoulder. If Justin's healthy, his stuff is about even with Al Leiter's—an interesting comparison, given Leiter's injury woes. Thompson consistently hits 93-94 mph

with his fastball, has a sharp-breaking curve that looks like a slurve, and a fine change. There are some concerns about his delivery, which has no leg drive. It puts strain on his arm, not to mention allowing runners to steal at will. But that's about the only complaint anyone has. Hopefully, he won't end up filed under "coulda been a contender." ■

BUBBA TRAMMELL — SOLID PROSPECT

OF • BR • TR • 6'2 • 205 • 25 • DET94/11

	AB	R	H	2B	3B	HR	RBI	BB	SO	SB	CS	BA	OB	SA
AAA	180	32	53	14	1	6	24	22	44	5	1	.294	.369	.483

"You gotta let him in, he's a legacy!" No, he's no relation to Alan, but he is an excellent power prospect. His numbers have increased steadily through 3 years in the minors, culminating in a '96 season full of honors. *Baseball America* rated him the best power prospect in the Southern League, and *Baseball Weekly* named him "Hot Prospect of the Week" in July. He moved up to Triple-A Toledo after the break—after hitting 27 dingers and batting .328 in 83 games at Double-A. He'll be 25 next year and needs to continue to move fast. He'll probably start the season at Toledo, but could move up quickly. ■

TODD VAN POPPEL

SP • BR • TR • 6'5 • 210 • 25 • OAK90/1

	G	GS	IP	H	HR	BB	K	W	L	S	ERA	K/BB	K9	HW9
OAK94	23	23	116	108	20	89	83	7	10	0	6.09	.9	6.4	15.28
OAK95	36	14	138	125	16	56	122	4	8	0	4.88	2.2	8.0	11.80
OAK/DET96	37	15	99	139	24	62	53	3	9	1	9.09	.9	4.8	18.27
CAREER	113	69	442	455	71	271	311	20	33	1	6.23	1.1	6.3	14.78

Oakland's 1st-round pick in '90, Van Poppel was once the highest-touted pitching prospect in the country. He jerked around the lowly Braves, who had the first pick, threatening to go to college if they drafted him, then signed with the mighty A's when they snagged him. He's had that bad karma to overcome, while the Braves have felt their Chipper Jones selection in his place has worked out fairly well. Van Floppel was never able to deal with the hype or show control, and the contract he signed with the A's guaranteed him a spot on the major-league roster by '93. Be careful what you wish for, Todd. He threw himself in to sink or swim, and he sank. After watching him grow up in public for nearly 4 years, including a 1-5, 7.71 ERA start in '96, the A's finally cut him loose. He's a project, but all Detroit had to lose was $20,000. As Randy Smith said, "There's a lot of upside to this and not much downside." He still hits 95, and his curve can be a dandy at times. The Tigers weren't happy with his progress, and now he's the Angels' problem. ■

DARYLE WARD — SOLID PROSPECT

1B • BL • TL • 6'2 • 230 • 21 • DET94/15

	AB	R	H	2B	3B	HR	RBI	BB	SO	SB	CS	BA	OB	SA
A+	464	65	135	29	4	10	68	57	77	1	1	.291	.373	.435

Ward is a first base-prospect stuck behind Tony Clark. For a huge guy he has a great swing. He had a problem with strikeouts, whiffing 101 times in '95. But he improved dramatically in '96. With the way he hit in the Florida State League last season, he has star potential. He is the son of former Twins outfielder Gary Ward. With all those children of the Big Red Machine floating around (Junior, Brian McRae, Eduardo Perez, Ed Sprague, Pedro Borbon), it makes one wonder if the Little Red Machine Twins of the early '80s will produce as much big-league offspring: Lenny Faedo, Jesus Vega, Rob Wilfong, Terry Felton, Pete Redfern, Mark Funderburk, Hosken Powell, Bombo Rivera. The possibilities are limitless. ■

BRIAN WILLIAMS

RP-SP • BR • TR • 6'3 • 205 • 28 • HOU90/2

	G	GS	IP	H	HR	BB	K	W	L	S	ERA	K/BB	K9	HW9
HOU94	20	13	78	112	9	41	49	6	5	0	5.74	1.2	5.7	17.65
SD95	44	6	72	79	3	38	75	3	10	0	6.00	2.0	9.4	14.63
DET96	40	17	121	145	21	85	72	3	10	2	6.77	.8	5.4	17.11
CAREER	164	59	461	515	52	248	310	23	36	5	5.47	1.3	6.1	14.89

Williams is a world-of-potential-type guy with one problem: lefties. He started the year as the closer because Bell thought his fastball was better suited to the role than anything Tipper Gohr had to offer. He blew 2 of his first 4 opportunities, however, and was shifted to the rotation.

Williams throws a good curve and slider, and a mediocre change. Williams showed displeasure when Bell came to the mound to yank him during a start in July, staring at Bell with his hands on his hips. Bell made Williams stand there while he chewed him out for a couple of minutes—shades of that Kodak moment in Shea Stadium when Giants pitcher Jim Barr made the mistake of flipping the ball to Frank Robinson during a pitching change. A real love-hate relationship is said to be growing between these two. A 6.00+ ERA is not very endearing, though, and you can ask Chad Curtis what happens when Buddy's not your buddy. ■

EDDIE WILLIAMS

1B • BR • TR • 6'0 • 175 • 32 • NYN83/1

	AB	R	H	2B	3B	HR	RBI	BB	SO	SB	CS	BA	OB	SA
SD94	175	32	58	11	1	11	42	15	26	0	1	.331	.392	.594
SD95	296	35	77	11	1	12	47	23	47	0	0	.260	.320	.426
DET96	215	22	43	5	0	6	26	18	50	0	2	.200	.267	.307
CAREER	1021	133	261	42	2	36	135	88	185	1	6	.256	.267	.406

Williams is in the twilight of a long, largely undistinguished career. His power has diminished and he's got several holes in his swing. Opposing pitchers have made enough mistakes in recent years to make him look better than he is. But at 32 he's not in the Tigers long-range plans and probably didn't even get a Christmas card from them this off-season. ■

■ 1996 AUTOPSY

The 1995 edition of the Kansas City Royals finished last in the league in runs scored and home runs. The Royals looked to be even thinner on offense in '96 due to the departure of Wally Joyner, Greg Gagne, and Gary Gaetti, the 3 hitters who composed the heart of the lineup. Salary considerations again forced the Royals to do their shopping in the odd-lots section. Despite bringing Mike Macfarlane back into the fold, signing José Offerman and trading for Bip Roberts, manager Bob Boone was having to depend on many 2nd and 3rd-year players to assume important roles within the lineup. And the pitching didn't look like it was going to be anywhere near enough to offset the weak hitting.

April 9-18 (9-18, 8½ games back)
The Royals were swept by the Orioles in the opening series, setting the tone for the rest of the season. Milwaukee swept them in a 4-game series, April 18-21, and the Yankees beat them in 3 out of 4 meetings. The only team the Royals could beat were the hapless Red Sox, who dropped 5 of 6 games to Kansas City in the month. The Royals finished the month dead last in runs, batting average, and slugging average. The pitching was better, albeit marginally. Kevin Appier was inconsistent at the beginning, but it was Chris Haney who really typified the Royals pitching situation. He began the season winless in 3 quality starts and then was demolished in his next 3, to end up 0-4 with a 6.68 ERA in 32 innings.

May 15-12 (24-30, 12 games back)
The best month of the season for the Royals featured a season-high 6-game winning streak, highlighted by a 4-game sweep of the Angels. Later in the month they won 5 in a row, including a series sweep of the Tigers. After a slow start, Appier started rolling again, but it was Mark Gubicza's turn to be inconsistent. He was hammered for 9 runs in 4 innings against Texas May 14 but then came back with a complete-game shutout against them 10 days later. The offense managed to hit just enough to free themselves (if only temporarily) from the run-scoring cellar in the A.L.

June 10-17 (34-47, 15½ games back)
June was one of the best offensive months of the season for the Royals, but the pitching staff squandered the runs they received. The closer, Jeff Montgomery, blew 4 saves in 9 opportunities and had an 8.49 ERA in June. A particularly painful loss came on the 22nd in Baltimore, when the Royals took a 3-0 lead into the ninth inning, only to yield 3 dingers to blow the game. Montgomery gave up two of them—a two-iron by Bobby Bonilla and the game winner to Mark Smith.

July 14-13 (48-60, 17½ games back)
Despite finishing a game above .500, the Royals fell another 2 games off the Central Division lead. The pitching staff got back on track. Their 4.29 ERA of July was exactly a run lower than their ERA for June. Kevin Appier didn't get traded, but got big money instead. He gave up 8 runs in 23.2 innings but won just 2 of his 4 starts. José Rosado also had a fine month, coming up from the minors to post a 2.10 ERA in 4 starts. After flirting with the .300 mark a month earlier, Johnny Damon surpassed it in July, hitting .306. Tom Goodwin hit .330, scored 20 runs, and stole 15 bases.

August 14-15 (62-75, 19 games back)
The warning, "Abandon every hope, ye who enter here," inscribed over the gate of Hell in Dante's *Inferno*, might have been an appropriate scoreboard message in Royal Stadium as the waning dog days of summer continued to take the steam out of the Royals. Kansas City's Royal Stadium is actually quite a nice place to watch a baseball game, thank you very much, but the Royal's plight last season was comparable nevertheless to a hopeless pit of Hell.

September 13-11 (75-86, 24 games back)
See August.

■ 1997 DIAGNOSIS

Offense
Nothing seems to change, as the anemic K.C. offense dragged the team into the cellar and chained it to the furnace yet again. The team led the league with 195 stolen bases but finished last in runs scored (746). Remarkably, one team, the Twins, finished below the Royals in homers. As one might expect, the team's batting average and slugging

average were close to the bottom of the pile as well. One word sums up the Kansas City offense in '96, but morality statutes in 43 states prevent us from using such a term. Is there hope for an offensive turnaround in '97? Johnny Damon and Mike Tucker will have better seasons as they get to know the league's pitchers. Having Chili Davis around increases the odds that Craig Paquette won't lead the team in dingers and RBI. The Royals have some young players who can hit 20 to 25 homers in the majors, such as Joe Vitiello, but sometimes it seems that some big-leaguers don't want to lose their potential by actually producing.

Defense

The loss of Gaetti and Gagne really put the infield in a state of flux. The Royals thought they had acquired a shortstop in the off-season, but Offerman soon proved he couldn't handle the position and was moved to first base. Now all he needs is a sunny disposition and exactly 500 dingers to surpass Ernie Banks among shortstop/first basemen. Hamelin, a disappointment in the field, had to become a full-time designated hitter. Boone had to rely heavily on light-hitting utility players such as Keith Lockhart and David Howard for their gloves. The Royals' young outfield, consisting primarily of Damon, Tucker, and Goodwin, was solid. All 3 players have good range and can track down just about anything that doesn't leave the yard. Damon's arm is the only defensive shortcoming in the outfield. Mike Macfarlane won't lose a team any games behind the plate.

Pitching

The Royals have organizational depth in the pitching department, and it should start paying off in 1997. Bob Boone will continue to hold auditions for spots 2-5 in the rotation. Appier is the best pitcher the Royals have and is locked up through '99. Belcher, if he's still in Kansas City, was very solid in '96, and the Royals need his experience. The Royals hope youngsters José Rosado, and Jim Pittsley, contribute significant innings in '97 so they can deep-six Doug Linton and Chris Haney.

The bulk of the saves will continue to go to Montgomery, but he's getting a little long in the tooth. The Royals are grooming Jaime Bluma to be their closer, and he's already started apprenticing. The bullpen lacked a steady setup man last year, and Bluma will serve in that capacity for now. There's plenty of talented arms in the organization, so the Royals will continue sifting the chaff from the wheat in '97.

Farm System

During the late '80s, the Royals depleted their farm system in an effort to bring another championship to the city before Ewing Kauffman passed away. The Royals have been restocking their system for a few years now. The trickle of prospects that started with Tucker and Damon could soon turn into a flood, and the Royals have reached the point where they would rather give a job to one of their youngsters than break the bank with a risky free-agent signing. Other than converted second baseman Chris Stynes, there isn't much depth in the outfield. Catchers Sal Fasano and Mike Sweeney both saw major-league time last year. But the strength of the organization lies with its young infielders and pitchers. Second baseman Sergio Nuñez is a decent-looking player who can hit, and Gary Coffee is a deep sleeper at first. Mendy Lopez and José Cepeda give the organization third-base depth. Pitchers Pittsley, Bluma, and Jeff Granger will make it to the show, but that doesn't deplete the system. Glendon Rusch's command and makeup outweigh the fact that his stuff isn't overpowering, and he could be in the rotation by midseason. Ken Ray is raw but has a knee-buckling curveball and should develop more velocity as he grows. Bart Evans, another deep sleeper, also has a quality arm.

Management and Ownership

The ownership of the Royals has been unsettled since Ewing Kauffman's death. The team is for sale, but one of the requirements is that any new owner must keep it in Kansas City, so this might take a while to get straightened out. David Glass, the CEO, prefers to maintain a low profile. With that offense, you would too.

GM Herk Robinson could be accused of letting the heart of the team walk out the door as free agents last year, but it's not as if he had a choice. It's tough to win and slash payroll at the same time. In fact, there's only one way to do it, and that's through player development which the Royals appear to be doing well.

Bob Boone brings to his job a unique blend of raw grit and intelligence. It's well known that his playing days were marked by all-out hustle—the same hustle he expects from his players today. But what a lot of people don't know is that Boone was very active in the players' union in its formative years. In fact, he was handpicked by Marvin Miller to serve as a player representative in negotiations because he had earned a degree in psychology. This background helps Boone maintain a stable clubhouse environment and enables him to empathize with the plight of his players without alienating management. Boone is an aggressive field boss who likes to run. He will also field a lot of different lineups throughout the season to squeeze every available bit of production out of his team.

. . . and whatnot: Johnny Damon and George Brett

Ever since he broke into the league a couple of seasons ago, Johnny Damon has drawn comparisons to George Brett. When Brett made his debut 22 years ago, he was touted as a hitter with a sweet left-handed swing who made excellent contact, sent line drives into the gap with regularity, played ball in an old-fashioned, hard-nosed style, and spent little time in the minors. Sound familiar? Those are the same things scouts have been saying about Damon for 2 years. Is Damon on his way to 3,000 hits?

Let's look at their performances at the same age. The general rule of thumb is: The younger a player is when he makes it to the majors, the better he will be. Look down the list of alumni in the Hall of Fame and you will notice that all those players have one thing in common: They were awfully good, awfully young.

Age 18	Level	AB	R	H	2B	3B	HR	RBI	BB	SO	BA	OBA	SLG
Brett	R	258	44	75	8	5	5	44	32	38	.291	.369	.419
Damon	R	192	58	67	13	9	4	24	31	21	.349	.449	.568

Both players started their careers in rookie ball—Brett in 1971 and Damon in 1992—and Damon was actually better.

Age 19	Level	AB	R	H	2B	3B	HR	RBI	BB	SO	BA	OBA	SLG
Brett	A	431	66	118	13	5	10	68	53	53	.274	.353	.397
Damon	A	511	82	148	25	13	5	50	51	83	.290	.359	.419

Their hitting is starting to look eerily similar at the same point of development and in roughly the same level of play (full-season low Class-A leagues). While both show they can take a walk, Brett is showing better plate discipline than Damon at this age. Brett also is striking out less frequently, once every 8 at-bats as opposed to Damon's rate of once every 6 at-bats. But Damon still looks like the better hitter here. He's hitting for a higher average with better power.

Age 20	Level	AB	R	H	2B	3B	HR	RBI	BB	SO	BA	OBA	SLG
Brett	AAA	405	66	115	16	4	8	64	48	45	.284	.360	.402
Damon	A+	472	96	149	25	13	6	75	62	55	.316	.399	.462

Brett made the jump from A-ball to Triple-A in his third year, while Damon advanced to the high Class-A Carolina League. Brett received a September call-up to Kansas City that year. Why did Brett get the promotion to Triple-A in 1973 and why was Damon rotting in the Carolina League in '94? One theory has to do with a different developmental philosophy that has crept into baseball since Brett's days as a phenom. It used to be that if a prospect showed major-league caliber skills he was immediately promoted to a higher level for a trial by fire. Nowadays it's a different story as managers and general managers have to worry about a player's psyche almost as much as his physical health. And then there's the whole issue of service time and free agency—early "learning experiences" can serve only to get a player to arbitration one year earlier.

Age 21	Level	AB	R	H	2B	3B	HR	RBI	BB	SO	BA	OBA	SLG
Brett	Maj	457	49	129	21	5	2	47	21	38	.282	.314	.363
Damon	Maj	188	32	53	11	5	3	23	12	22	.282	.324	.441
	AA	423	83	145	15	9	16	54	67	35	.343	.434	.534

Brett hits the majors by the time he's 21, while Damon sits in Wichita for two-thirds of a season. Damon did get a brief trial in the show as a reward for pummeling Double-A pitchers—and he actually did better than George.

Age 22	Level	AB	R	H	2B	3B	HR	RBI	BB	SO	BA	OBA	SLG
Brett	Maj	634	84	195	35	13	11	89	46	49	.308	.354	.456
Damon	Maj	517	61	111	22	5	6	50	31	64	.271	.313	.368

In Brett's second full season in the big leagues, he led the A.L. in hits and triples. This is also the year Charlie Lau's tutoring of Brett began in earnest. Damon's hitting line is his '96 season, his first full one in the majors. Brett stepped forward while

Damon slipped. If these guys were similar hitters at every stage in their careers except for a season, and Damon's still very young, then he should step forward this season. After all, he's got to make up for that time he wasted in the Carolina League when he could have been whaling away on Double-A pitching. Damon's a hard worker and has been similar to Brett throughout their careers at similar ages. With Damon's penchant for improving himself, expect something like Brett's early .300 seasons with line-drive power—and 30+ steals. Think Kansas City would settle for Brett at 23 . . . (7-67-.333 and a batting title)?

KEVIN APPIER

AL ELITE

SP • BR • TR • 6′2 • 180 • 29 • KC87/1

	G	GS	IP	H	HR	BB	K	W	L	S	ERA	K/BB	K9	HW9
KC94	23	23	155	137	11	63	145	7	6	0	3.83	2.3	8.4	11.61
KC95	31	31	201	163	14	80	185	15	10	0	3.89	2.3	8.3	10.88
KC96	32	32	211	192	17	75	207	14	11	0	3.62	2.8	8.8	11.39
CAREER	222	210	1429	1260	89	494	1168	95	65	0	3.28	2.4	7.4	11.05

Kevin Appier, 29, is still one of the most underrated pitchers in the American League, a credit to his unassuming professionalism and the fact that Kansas City, as a media outlet, is about as happening as the Mir space station. Ask an informed baseball fan about Appier, and there's a good chance she or he will say, "He's a great pitcher, but he's got this funky delivery that's just a rotator-cuff injury waiting to happen." Well, Appier has been turning in 200+ innings (not counting the strike-abbreviated '94 season) since his second full season in '91, and he hasn't shown any signs of letting up yet. His fastball still registers in the 90s and his slider is just devastating. Appier also throws a split-finger and, as a result, is very effective at keeping the ball in the park.

His contract negotiations dragged on throughout the first half of the '96 season, though money wasn't a big issue in the negotiations. The two sides had settled on the dollar amount and length (3 years, $15 million) fairly quickly. The snag occurred when the players' union, unhappy with the salary because they were looking at the contract to be a market-setter, decided to get involved, arguing that the Royals were getting Appier below market value so he should be compensated with a no-trade clause. Appier thought it was a reasonable request. Robinson resisted at first though, and you can hardly blame him. Let's face it: If there's a team in the American League that can't afford to be shackled to a high-paid pitcher (no matter how good he is), it's the Royals. Appier kept the pressure on, compiling a 3.45 ERA with 106 strikeouts in 109.2 innings in the first half, and Robinson finally caved in. The contract includes a 1-year no-trade clause that allows Appier to designate 6 teams he cannot be traded to after the first year is up. If he's traded during the life of the contract, he gets an automatic $400,000 raise. Appier's contract serves as yet another monument to the clout of the Players' Association. Doesn't look like that pendulum is going to be swinging back any time soon. ■

TIM BELCHER

HEADED FOR A FALL

SP • BR • TR • 6′3 • 210 • 35 • NYA84

	G	GS	IP	H	HR	BB	K	W	L	S	ERA	K/BB	K9	HW9
DET94	25	25	162	192	21	78	76	7	15	0	5.89	1.0	4.2	15.00
SEA95	28	28	179	188	19	88	96	10	12	0	4.52	1.1	4.8	13.88
KC96	35	35	238	262	28	68	113	15	11	0	3.92	1.7	4.3	12.48
CAREER	295	274	1821	1721	161	649	1202	109	101	5	3.80	1.9	5.9	11.71

It's been a long time since Belcher's best seasons with the Dodgers, and he's been slipping ever since his trade to Cincinnati in 1992. He left one of the best pitcher's parks in the majors that year and has moved to steadily worse home digs ever since. Not content with torturing himself in Tiger Stadium, Belcher moved to Seattle in 1995. That's like bashing your thumb with a hammer and vowing to correct the problem by swinging harder the next time.

Belcher throws 5 pitches, but they're all below average now. Last season he kept hitters off balance and put together his best season since 1991. At 35 he just doesn't have the stuff to challenge hitters. But if you look at his performance, he held the league to a .281 average (the A.L. hit .277 last year), a .331 OBP, and a .436 slugging percentage, the latter two well below the A.L. averages. His ERA was 10th in the league! Impressive, but don't expect it to happen again. ■

BRIAN BEVIL

SP • BR • TR • 6'3 • 190 • 25 • KC90/28

	G	GS	IP	H	HR	BB	SO	W	L	S	ERA	K/BB	K9	HW9
AAA	12	12	68	62	10	19	73	7	5	0	4.12	3.8	9.7	10.77

Bevil, 25, suffered a setback in '95 when he couldn't handle his first taste of Triple-A ball and lost his prospect status within the organization. He worked on his curve and on keeping his fastball down in instructional league last year and reported to spring training on a mission. Sporting much better command of his 3 pitches, Bevil went 9-2 with a 2.02 ERA during the first half of the season and was named the A.L. starter in the Double-A All-Star Game on June 9. Three days later he was promoted to Omaha, where he fared much better this time around. Aside from his excellent curve, Bevil doesn't have stellar stuff—so he will make his living on the corners. He can help the Royals next season either out of the bullpen or as the 5th starter. ■

JAIME BLUMA

YOUNG GUN

RP • BR • TR • 5'11 • 195 • 24 • KC94/3

	G	GS	IP	H	HR	BB	K	W	L	S	ERA	K/BB	K9	HW9
KC96	17	0	20	18	2	4	14	0	0	5	3.60	3.5	6.3	9.90

Bluma's stocky build and bulldog demeanor make him an excellent closer prospect. Bluma, 24, has been in the bullpen his entire career. He was Wichita State's closer when he was drafted in the 3rd round in '94, and he's been Montgomery's heir apparent since. He has a closer's repertoire: a decent sinking fastball that hits 91 mph, and a slider that was considered the best breaking pitch in the American Association last year. The knocks against him are that his change-up is mediocre, and he doesn't throw inside enough. Bluma has come a long way in a short time and looked effective at the end of the season in K.C. He'll be in the majors to start this season. ■

MELVIN BUNCH

SP • BR • TR • 6'1 • 170 • 25 • KC92/18

	G	GS	IP	H	HR	BB	SO	W	L	S	ERA	K/BB	K9	HW9
AAA	33	27	147	181	32	59	94	8	9	0	6.08	1.6	5.8	14.73

Bunch, 25, had a nifty 4-to-1 strikeout-to-walk ratio going and had climbed steadily through the system when he started the season with Triple-A Omaha, but was still a question mark in the Royals' book because of shoulder problems in '94 and '95. Bunch has an average fastball and a pretty good breaking ball. More importantly, he has excellent command of both pitches. But his lanky frame and awkward delivery create a lot of stress on his shoulder, and that should be a major concern to the Royals. Bunch has the talent and the moxie to make it, but his health history has to make him a long shot for continued success. ■

DARREN BURTON

OF • BB • TR • 6'1 • 185 • 24 • KC90/3

	AB	R	H	2B	3B	HR	RBI	BB	SO	SB	CS	BA	OB	SA
AAA	463	75	125	28	5	15	67	59	82	7	7	.270	.357	.449

Burton is a 24-year-old switch-hitter with an outstanding arm. He was waived in '95 and picked up by the Cubs. He spent half a season with them, hitting .306 at Double-A Orlando. Burton found his way back to the fold last season and put up unspectacular numbers for Omaha. Burton will continue to wait his turn in Triple-A. He would be a capable fill-in if needed but won't get any significant playing time for the Royals. ■

TIMOTHY BYRDAK

SP • BL • TL • 5'11 • 170 • 23 • KC94/5

	G	GS	IP	H	HR	BB	SO	W	L	S	ERA	K/BB	K9	HW9
AA	15	15	85	112	15	44	47	5	7	0	6.91	1.1	5.0	16.58

Byrdak stumbled in Double-A Wichita last season, but the Royals won't lose faith in him just yet. After all, '96 was just his 3rd pro season. He's climbed the ladder quickly. Even though his fastball is below average right now, scouts say his curve and change are of major-league caliber. He could make it to Triple-A Omaha next season if he gets himself back on track. ■

JOSÉ CEPEDA

3B • BR • TR • 6'0 • 185 • 22

	AB	R	H	2B	3B	HR	RBI	BB	SO	SB	CS	BA	OB	SA
A	558	87	161	29	3	3	81	38	44	10	3	.289	.341	.367

The son of Orlando Cepeda, Jose hit .348 in the GCL after signing in '95. He is a natural shortstop, but the Royals moved him to third base due to a lack of depth in the organization. He's now about 2 years away from doing battle with Joe Randa and Lino Diaz in Kansas City—for what that's worth. He

makes good contact at the plate and led the Lansing Lugnuts in hits and runs scored. He also had a 28-game hitting streak early in the season. Incidentally, he kisses his bat before stepping to the plate. Maybe that's why his breath is always pine-tar fresh. Can only imagine how Bob Gibson or Don Drysdale would have greeted his dad if he pulled that stunt. ■

GARY COFFEE — SLEEPER

1B • BR • TR • 6′3 • 235 • 22 • KC94/10

	AB	R	H	2B	3B	HR	RBI	BB	SO	SB	CS	BA	OB	SA
A	393	52	91	17	2	11	59	53	141	6	1	.232	.328	.369

Coffee's 3rd pro season, 1996, was his first playing above the Rookie League level. He has a prodigious power stroke, but is easily fooled by the breaking ball, striking out 141 times last season. He also needs work defensively. Coffee generates tremendous bat speed, and the Royals are starved for a legitimate power threat in their system. The Royals are praying he develops Cecil Fielder's power and not his appetite. Coffee could climb through the system quickly if he learns to hit the curve. ■

JOHNNY DAMON — YOUNG GUN

OF • BL • TL • 6′0 • 175 • 23 • KC92/2

	AB	R	H	2B	3B	HR	RBI	BB	SO	SB	CS	BA	OB	SA
KC95	188	32	53	11	5	3	23	12	22	7	0	.282	.324	.441
KC96	517	61	140	22	5	6	50	31	64	25	5	.271	.313	.368

Damon did not tear up A.L. pitching, but his '96 season did nothing to dispel the notion that he could be an All-Star-caliber center fielder for years. His struggles last year were based almost entirely on his inability to hit left-handed pitching and on Boone's subsequent juggling of his spot in the batting order. Damon hasn't seen an inning of Triple-A baseball, as he was promoted directly from Wichita in 1995 as a 21-year-old, so he still has some holes in his swing. A.L. pitchers have figured out his penchant for low fastballs by now, and they realize he isn't yet quick enough to catch up to the high stuff. That pitching pattern will end soon, though, because by next year he'll be more disciplined and any mistake in his wheelhouse will be going over the fence.

Damon's speed on the basepaths and in center field is unquestionable. He's fast enough to outrun any ball that stays in the park, and his instincts are getting better by the game. His one below-average tool is a weak throwing arm. Damon's mental toughness would do George S. Patton proud. Toronto's Pat Hentgen hit Damon in the face with a pitch on May 31, ending his 10-game hitting streak. Damon started in SkyDome the very next day and stroked a double and a home run. Damon is a no-nonsense ballplayer with a strong work ethic. He is the best ballplayer the Royals have, and he will have a breakthrough season in '97. ■

CHILI DAVIS — HEADED FOR A FALL

DH • BB • TR • 6′3 • 195 • 37 • SF77/11

	AB	R	H	2B	3B	HR	RBI	BB	SO	SB	CS	BA	OB	SA
CAL94	392	72	122	18	1	26	84	69	84	3	2	.311	.410	.561
CAL95	424	81	135	23	0	20	86	89	79	3	3	.318	.429	.514
CAL96	530	73	155	24	0	28	95	86	99	5	2	.292	.387	.496
CAREER	7617	1099	2089	372	29	298	1195	1022	1484	132	93	.274	.357	.448

Chili Dog kept giving heartburn to A.L. pitchers in '96, reaching 2,000 hits along the way—only the 18th switch-hitter to do so. But last year, the league ERA was more than a quarter-run higher than in '95, while Chili's numbers declined. He's at the age where hitters lose it fast— but he's suggested '97 will be his last year, so he might get out before that bill comes due. The Angels unloaded his $4 million salary on the Royals—though they must have been tempted to keep him around long enough for him to break the team record for career RBI. Having Brian Downing at the top of that list is downright embarrassing. ■

LINO DIAZ

3B • BR • TR • 5′11 • 180 • 26 • KC93/30

	AB	R	H	2B	3B	HR	RBI	BB	SO	SB	CS	BA	OB	SA
AAA	266	32	72	13	2	3	28	17	29	0	3	.271	.328	.368

Diaz, 26, is considered the best third base prospect in the system right now, and that tells you how thin the Royals are at the position. He's considered a better hitter than Joe Randa. Unfortunately for the Royals, neither of them has the size or the power customary for the position. Diaz has never been viewed as a topflight prospect but as a contact hitter with smooth defensive skills. He has soft hands and good range. If he sees any playing time this season, he won't embarrass himself. ■

BART EVANS

SLEEPER

SP-RP • BR • TR • 6'1 • 190 • 26 • KC92/12

	G	GS	IP	H	HR	BB	SO	W	L	S	ERA	K/BB	K9	HW9
AA	9	7	24	31	7	36	16	1	2	0	11.84	.4	5.9	24.78

Evans, 26, used to be a highly touted prospect with a Percival-like fastball. After being named Carolina League Pitcher of the Year in '94, Evans went backward in 1995 when his control fell apart and he was bombed in 7 Double-A starts. So the Royals demoted him, shortened his windup and moved him into the bullpen for the remainder of the season.

In '96, his control problems still plagued him at Double-A Wichita but were compounded by a loss in velocity and the discovery of bone chips in his elbow. The chips will be removed in the off-season and Evans will recover, but his 2 wasted seasons will be harder to overcome. ■

SAL FASANO

C • BR • TR • 6'2 • 220 • 25 • KC93/35

	AB	R	H	2B	3B	HR	RBI	BB	SO	SB	CS	BA	OB	SA
KC96	143	20	29	2	0	6	19	14	25	1	1	.203	.283	.343

Fasano impressed everyone in the Arizona Fall League with his defense in 1996 and went into the spring as the primary backup behind Macfarlane. Fasano was hitting .203 with 8 extra-base hits in 143 at-bats when he was demoted to Omaha on July 16 in favor of Mike Sweeney. Perhaps nailing GM Herk Robinson with a foul ball had something to do with that. The Royals believe Fasano has 30-homer potential, but they want to see him learn to hit breaking balls better and cut down on his swing. He was prone to poor conditioning in the past but is now down to 220. The development of Sweeney (23) the past two seasons has already started to push Fasano. Both have great throwing arms and can play solid defense, so whoever hits will get the major-league playing time behind Macfarlane. ■

PAT FLURY

RP • BR • TR • 6'2 • 205 • 24 • KC93/7

	G	GS	IP	H	HR	BB	SO	W	L	S	ERA	K/BB	K9	HW9
A+	45	0	84	66	2	29	67	7	2	5	1.92	2.3	7.2	10.14

Flury made the Royal brass take notice in Class-A Wilmington last year with eye-popping stats. He'd been pitching in the bullpen since he was drafted, with unspectacular results. A marked improvement in his control seems to be the biggest factor in his surge on the Royals' depth chart. ■

TOM GOODWIN

OF • BL • TR • 6'1 • 165 • 28 • LA89/2

	AB	R	H	2B	3B	HR	RBI	BB	SO	SB	CS	BA	OB	SA
KC95	480	72	138	16	3	4	28	38	72	50	18	.288	.346	.358
KC96	524	80	148	14	4	1	35	39	79	66	22	.282	.334	.330
CAREER	1103	176	309	32	8	5	67	84	166	125	46	.280	.335	.337

Goodwin was pushed out of the L.A. system by better-hitting prospects, and it's surprising the same thing hasn't happened to him in Kansas City. Because of his outstanding speed and solid outfield defense, Goodwin has a job. But his short, choppy swing generated only 19 extra-base hits and he doesn't take enough walks to make him worthy of a full-time job as a major-league leadoff man. At 28, Goodwin's chances for stardom are over, but his gaudy stolen-base totals will be enough to keep in the majors for 4 or 5 years. ■

JEFF GRANGER

RP • BR • TL • 6'4 • 200 • 25 • KC93/1

	G	GS	IP	H	HR	BB	SO	W	L	S	ERA	K/BB	K9	HW9
AAA	45	0	77	65	10	29	68	5	3	4	2.34	2.3	7.9	10.99

The Royals drafted this big left-hander with the 5th overall pick in '93 out of Texas A&M, where he used an impressive slider to strike out 150 collegiate hitters in 127 innings. He progressed nicely over the next 2 seasons, but struggled in '95 at Wichita when he tried to overpower everyone and lost command of his slider. He even slipped off the Royals' Top 10 prospects list. Undaunted, Granger reported to winter ball and overhauled his mechanics. He improved his velocity and added a tighter spin on his breaking pitches. He worked out of the bullpen in '96, setting up Jaime Bluma in Omaha, and the move gave Granger a new lease on life. He posted a 2.34 ERA in 45 relief appearances there. Granger is once again in the Royals' pitching plans. ■

BOB HAMELIN

DH-1B • BL • TL • 6'0 • 235 • 29 • KC88/2

	AB	R	H	2B	3B	HR	RBI	BB	SO	SB	CS	BA	OB	SA
KC94	312	64	88	25	1	24	65	56	62	4	3	.282	.388	.599
KC95	208	20	35	7	1	7	25	26	56	0	1	.168	.278	.313
KC96	239	31	61	14	1	9	40	54	58	5	2	.255	.391	.435
CAREER	808	117	195	49	3	42	135	142	191	9	6	.241	.357	.465

In '96, Hamelin reported to spring training and, for a change, he didn't look like Dom DeLuise after a night at the all-you-can-eat barbecue pit. He worked out during the off-season with Royals' conditioning coach Kevin Barr and secured a promise from Bob Boone for more playing time in the field. All for naught, it seems, as he didn't make enough contact to justify a DH role, let alone a starting job in the infield. Besides, Boone wasn't too thrilled with his work around the bag. It's entirely possible the back troubles that plagued him earlier in his career are coming back to haunt him by robbing him of his bat speed. At 29, there's a remote chance he could return to his former self. Chances are, though, he will continue to vindicate those appalled by his '94 Rookie of the Year selection. With Chili in town, there's suddenly nowhere for Hamelin to play. ■

CHRIS HANEY

SP • BL • TL • 6'3 • 185 • 28 • MON90/9

	G	GS	IP	H	HR	BB	K	W	L	S	ERA	K/BB	K9	HW9
KC94	6	6	28	36	2	11	18	2	2	0	7.31	1.6	5.8	15.09
KC95	16	13	81	78	7	33	31	3	4	0	3.65	.9	3.4	12.33
KC96	35	35	228	267	29	51	115	10	14	0	4.70	2.3	4.5	12.55
CAREER	112	106	626	691	68	217	334	31	42	0	4.84	1.5	4.8	13.05

Haney is a typical left-handed finesse pitcher. He throws a below-average fastball, using it to set up his sinker and change-up, and at times the combination can be deadly. The problem with Haney is that he loses command quite frequently and has as many bad days as he does good ones.

Haney had a job in '96 because the Royals were desperate for a left-handed starter. In workhorse fashion, he was able to pile up more than 200 innings. It will be a different story in 1997. José Rosado is already on the scene, and Jim Pittsley and Glendon Rusch are very close to making it as well. Unless Haney becomes "Mr. Dependability" in the off-season, he'll be run out of the rotation. It's more likely that "Mr. Depends" will report to spring training instead. ■

JED HANSEN

2B • BR • TR • 6'1 • 195 • 24 • KC94/2

	AB	R	H	2B	3B	HR	RBI	BB	SO	SB	CS	BA	OB	SA
AA	405	60	116	27	4	12	50	29	72	14	8	.286	.339	.462

Hansen has developed just the way the Royals envisioned when they took him in the 2nd round out of Stanford in '94. He has become an excellent fielder with good range and footwork, and his '96 season at Double-A Wichita earned him a promotion to Triple-A. He's not a star prospect, as his age and level of achievement can testify, but he's not a bad-looking hitter either. The Royals have nothing to lose by bringing him up. Everyone else in their system has gotten a look-see, and 1997 is as good a time as any to give Hansen his. ■

DAVE HOWARD

SS • BB • TR • 6'0 • 165 • 30 • KC86/25

	AB	R	H	2B	3B	HR	RBI	BB	SO	SB	CS	BA	OB	SA
KC94	83	9	19	4	1	13	11	23	3	2	0	.229	.309	.313
KC95	255	23	62	13	4	0	19	24	41	6	1	.243	.310	.325
KC96	420	51	92	14	5	4	48	40	74	5	6	.219	.291	.305
CAREER	1237	127	281	44	12	7	117	108	231	21	15	.227	.290	.299

Howard's offensive numbers tell you all you need to know about what Bob Boone thinks of Jose Offerman's work at short. ■

RICK HUISMAN

RP • BR • TR • 6'3 • 200 • 27 • SF90/6

	G	GS	IP	H	HR	BB	K	W	L	S	ERA	K/BB	K9	HW9
KC96	22	0	29	25	4	18	23	2	1	1	4.60	1.3	7.1	13.33

Huisman was once one of the best pitching prospects in baseball. He was originally chosen by the Giants in the 3rd round of the 1990 draft after leading the nation in strikeouts for Division II Lewis University.

Huisman led the minors in strikeouts in 1991 with 216 and was named the California League Pitcher of the Year. In August 1992, after a fine

season, he had shoulder surgery. The Astros grabbed him off waivers in August 1993 and converted him to relief. They traded him to the Royals for Pat Borders in '95, and Huisman shared late-inning bullpen work with Jaime Bluma in Omaha last season until his call-up in July. Huisman has lost some of the velocity, now hitting 87-90 mph. But he has picked up a nifty split-finger pitch and has a deceptive delivery that ties up left-handed hitters. His addition last season helped stabilize Boone's bullpen, and that should be good enough for a return engagement. ■

JASON JACOME

SP • BL • TL • 6'0 • 180 • 26 • NYN91/14

	G	GS	IP	H	HR	BB	K	W	L	S	ERA	K/BB	K9	HW9
NYN94	8	8	54	54	3	17	30	4	3	0	2.67	1.8	5.0	11.83
KC95	20	19	105	134	18	36	50	4	10	0	6.34	1.4	4.3	14.57
KC96	49	2	47	67	5	22	32	0	4	1	4.72	1.5	6.1	17.02
CAREER	77	29	206	255	26	75	112	8	17	1	5.02	1.5	4.9	14.41

Jacome doesn't have much velocity (mid-80s) but can get his fastball to move pretty well. His best pitch is his curve, which he complements with an average slider and a deceptive change-up. Jacome was a low-round draft choice of the Mets in '91, and his successful climb to the majors was due almost entirely to his pinpoint control. His control abandoned him when the Royals put him in the bullpen last year, which is why his season was less than stellar. But if nothing else, Jacome outpitched Mike Magnante. ■

DOUG LINTON

SP • BR • TR • 6'1 • 190 • 31

	G	GS	IP	H	HR	BB	K	W	L	S	ERA	K/BB	K9	HW9
NYN94	32	3	50	74	4	20	29	6	2	0	4.47	1.5	5.2	16.91
KC95	7	2	22	22	4	10	13	0	1	0	7.25	1.3	5.3	13.09
KC96	21	18	104	111	13	26	87	7	9	0	5.02	3.3	7.5	11.86
CAREER	91	27	237	284	34	96	168	16	16	0	5.85	1.8	6.4	14.43

Unfortunately, that's a career year for Linton in '96. If he gets 18 starts again in '97, the Royals will finish last again in '97. ■

KEITH LOCKHART

2B-3B • BL • TR • 5'10 • 170 • 32 • CIN86/11

	AB	R	H	2B	3B	HR	RBI	BB	SO	SB	CS	BA	OB	SA
KC95	274	41	88	19	3	6	33	14	21	8	1	.321	.355	.478
KC96	433	49	118	33	3	7	55	30	40	11	6	.273	.319	.411

The definition of journeyman. Lockhart paid his dues in spades, logging more than 1,000 minor-league games before getting his shot in '95 with the Royals. A career .306 hitter in the minors before '96, he's been with the Reds, Cardinals, A's, and Padres before Kansas City. Funny thing is, there's no glaring weakness in his game that should have kept him from the majors for so long. ■

MENDY LOPEZ

3B • BR • TR • 6'2 • 165 • 22 • KC92

	AB	R	H	2B	3B	HR	RBI	BB	SO	SB	CS	BA	OB	SA
AA	327	47	92	20	5	6	32	26	67	14	4	.281	.341	.428

Another talented third-base prospect, Lopez, 22, signed as a nondrafted free agent in '92 out of the Dominican Republic. He had a killer GCL season in '94, hitting .364 with 19 steals. Last year wasn't too shabby either, and he was named the best defensive third baseman and possessor of the best infield arm in the Texas League. He's not a topflight prospect yet, but he's young and could still develop some power as his frame fills out. ■

MIKE MACFARLANE

C • BR • TR • 6'1 • 200 • 32 • KC85/4

	AB	R	H	2B	3B	HR	RBI	BB	SO	SB	CS	BA	OB	SA
KC94	314	53	80	17	3	14	47	35	71	1	0	.255	.359	.462
BOS95	364	45	82	18	1	15	51	38	78	2	1	.225	.319	.404
KC96	379	58	104	24	2	19	54	31	57	3	3	.274	.339	.499
CAREER	2901	371	737	178	15	110	414	246	565	11	14	.254	.328	.440

Boone's prodigal son returned to Kauffman Stadium in '96 after a year in Beantown. Macfarlane stands very close to the plate, as he's a pull hitter by nature. But he does so at his peril, and is usually among the league leaders in getting plunked. At 32 Macfarlane still has a few years left, but he will be pushed more and more by Sweeney and Fasano. He's signed through '97, so that looks to be the deadline for Macfarlane's junior associates to be ready. ■

JEFF MARTIN

SP • BR • TR • 6'1 • 200 • 23 • KC95/8

	G	GS	IP	H	HR	BB	SO	W	L	S	ERA	K/BB	K9	HW9
A+	5	5	20	24	3	5	12	0	1	0	4.87	2.4	5.3	12.84

Martin's fastball is average right now and has a tendency to be too straight, but he throws a good curveball and an excellent change-up. Martin is also a good fielder and holds runners well. The Royals need a couple of years to sift through the arms they have stacking up at Double-A and Triple-A, but Martin could force their hand if he keeps pitching the way he has. ■

FELIX MARTINEZ

SS • BB • TR • 6'0 • 170 • 22 • KC93

	AB	R	H	2B	3B	HR	RBI	BB	SO	SB	CS	BA	OB	SA
AAA	395	54	93	13	3	5	35	44	79	18	10	.235	.320	.322

Martinez is a switch-hitting second baseman from the Dominican Republic with excellent speed (he led the Texas League in stolen bases in '95) and good defensive skills. Both his range and his arm are solidly above average, but his 50 errors in '95 raise questions about his concentration. Martinez broke 2 bones in his hand in the Instructional League after the '95 season, and it's possible that the after-effects of the injury hurt him at the plate in '96. ■

JEFF MONTGOMERY — HEADED FOR A FALL

CL • BR • TR • 5'11 • 180 • 35 • CIN83/10

	G	GS	IP	H	HR	BB	K	W	L	S	ERA	K/BB	K9	HW9
KC94	42	0	44	48	5	15	50	2	3	27	4.03	3.3	10.2	12.87
KC95	54	0	65	60	7	25	49	2	3	31	3.43	2.0	6.8	11.77
KC96	48	0	63	59	14	19	45	4	6	24	4.26	2.4	6.4	11.14
CAREER	540	1	701	602	57	235	604	42	39	242	2.86	2.6	7.8	10.74

At 34, Montgomery's effectiveness has begun to erode, and his career might be ending fairly soon. Fatigue and bursitis are starting to limit Montgomery's ability to bounce back from appearances, and Boone must now be careful how he uses him. For example, he was having a rough stretch in early July when he blew 4 saves in 5 opportunities. Boone said he was sticking with Montgomery as his closer, but called all of Montgomery's pitches in his next appearance, a perfect 9th inning July 6. Boone said Montgomery was getting predictable and needed a different pitch-selection pattern.

Montgomery still throws 90 mph but his fastball is pretty straight, so he needs his 2 other pitches (a hard, late-breaking slider and an above-average change-up) working to survive. He got into trouble last year when he couldn't get the slider over, as the .485 slugging average against him attests. The Royals have been grooming Jaime Bluma in the minors, and the perfect scenario would have him setting up Montgomery in '97. Ready or not, Bluma might have to replace Montgomery before the start of 1998. ■

ROD MYERS

OF • BL • TL • 6'0 • 190 • 24 • KC91/13

	AB	R	H	2B	3B	HR	RBI	BB	SO	SB	CS	BA	OB	SA
KC96	63	9	18	7	0	1	11	7	16	3	2	.286	.357	.444

Myers, 24, is a left-handed hitter with good speed and an ability to draw the walk. But he's been in the organization since 1991, and he's watched better prospects such as Damon and Tucker fly by on their way to the majors. Myers would have a better chance of making it in another organization. ■

SERGIO NUÑEZ

2B • BR • TR • 5'11 • 155 • 22

	AB	R	H	2B	3B	HR	RBI	BB	SO	SB	CS	BA	OB	SA
A+	402	60	109	23	6	3	40	38	54	44	11	.271	.339	.381

The Royals loved him for his skill and attitude after a .397-5-24-37 season in the GCL in '94, but a stomach virus in the spring of '95 really knocked the stuffing out of him. Nuñez, 22, has been hurt and underachieving since. He has good speed and good plate discipline. And most importantly, he has time. He may yet win back his place in the Royals' infield plans. ■

JON NUNNALLY

OF • BL • TR • 5'10 • 190 • 25 • CLE92/3

	AB	R	H	2B	3B	HR	RBI	BB	SO	SB	CS	BA	OB	SA
KC95	303	51	74	15	6	14	42	51	86	6	4	.244	.357	.472
KC96	90	16	19	5	1	5	17	13	25	0	0	.211	.308	.456

Nunnally was taken from the Indians as a Rule 5 draftee in '95 and had to spend the entire season on the major-league roster or be offered back. It's easy to see why the Royals wanted him. He's a very aggressive hitter with a savage swing and serious

power. Nunnally also has decent speed, though he gets caught stealing a lot. He strikes out too much because he chases breaking balls in the dirt.

The Royals assigned him to Triple-A to learn how to lay off the junk, but, like Andujar Cedeno and Kurt Cobain, he just couldn't say no. He struck out once every 3.5 at-bats through late July. At 25, Nunnally may be as polished as he's going to get. He may never be able to shorten his swing enough to handle the breaking stuff. But the Royals finished dead last in the majors in home runs last year and desperately need the infusion of power Nunnally might provide. Chances are he'll be hacking away in Kansas City this year. ■

JOSÉ OFFERMAN

1B-2B-SS • BB • TR • 6'0 • 190 • 28 • LA86

	AB	R	H	2B	3B	HR	RBI	BB	SO	SB	CS	BA	OB	SA
LA94	243	27	51	8	4	1	25	38	38	2	1	.210	.314	.288
LA95	429	69	123	14	6	4	33	69	67	2	7	.287	.389	.375
KC96	561	85	170	33	8	5	47	74	98	24	10	.303	.384	.417
CAREER	2528	342	673	98	32	13	207	338	422	85	49	.266	.353	.346

Despite an inability to hit left-handed pitching, Offerman's work at the plate last year was adequate. His plate discipline makes him a pretty good top-of-the-order type, and he can score a lot of runs. Offerman's value plummets though as soon as he has to field a position, and his defensive troubles are becoming the stuff of legend. He has good range at shortstop with decent hands, but forgets what to do with the ball once he gets it in his glove. His errant throws were constant low-lights on *This Week in Baseball* when he was with the Dodgers. Bob Boone spoiled the fun, though, when he found a place for Offerman in the lineup where he wouldn't endanger himself or his fellow man. He moved Offerman to first base in April, and the results have been mixed. By no means is he a natural. He fields the grounders well enough, but throws in the dirt often end up in the dugout. ■

CRAIG PAQUETTE

3B-OF-1B • BR • TR • 6'0 • 190 • 28 • OAK89/7

	AB	R	H	2B	3B	HR	RBI	BB	SO	SB	CS	BA	OB	SA
OAK95	283	42	64	13	1	13	49	12	88	5	2	.226	.256	.417
KC96	429	61	111	15	1	22	67	23	101	5	3	.259	.296	.452
CAREER	1154	138	268	50	6	47	162	49	311	15	7	.232	.263	.408

Paquette began the season with Oakland, but Sandy Alderson got tired of hearing him whine about his lack of playing time and released him in the spring. The Royals picked him up, and hitting coach Greg Luzinski made an adjustment in Paquette's stance, widening it by about 6 inches. This helped him keep his head still and his swing compact. The result was that he led the team in homers despite serving in a utility role. Paquette is a streaky hitter, and he still gets into trouble when he tries to pull everything. He also has a tendency to swing at anything white that flies through the air. But give him credit: His strikeout-to-walk ratio has improved from obscene to merely NC-17. His defense is average, both at third and in the outfield. ■

HIPOLITO PICHARDO

RP • BR • TR • 6'1 • 160 • 27 • KC87

	G	GS	IP	H	HR	BB	K	W	L	S	ERA	K/BB	K9	HW9
KC94	45	0	67	82	4	24	36	5	3	3	4.92	1.5	4.8	14.22
KC95	44	0	64	66	4	30	43	8	4	1	4.36	1.4	6.0	13.50
KC96	57	0	68	74	5	26	43	3	5	3	5.43	1.7	5.7	13.24
CAREER	207	49	508	553	32	182	251	32	26	7	4.36	1.4	4.4	13.02

Pichardo served as the workhorse of the Kansas City bullpen last year, appearing in 57 games. Unfortunately for the Royals, Pichardo was hammered about 57 times. He also has yet to have a season in which he allowed less than a hit per inning. Pichardo throws a fastball in the low-90s that had good movement once upon a time, but now is usually straight and high in the strike zone. To complement it he has an average split-finger pitch that dives into the dirt when it is on. ■

JIM PITTSLEY

SOLID PROSPECT

SP • BR • TR • 6'7 • 215 • 22 • KC92/2

	G	GS	IP	H	HR	BB	SO	W	L	S	ERA	K/BB	K9	HW9
AAA	13	13	70	74	8	39	53	7	1	0	3.97	1.4	6.8	14.46

The Royals were afraid Pittsley would have to have Tommy John surgery after suffering an elbow injury in '95, but it turned out he didn't need it. He instead had a partial tear in the ligaments repaired and spent half the '96 season rehabbing. He throws a 93-mph fastball, 2 curves (hard and slow), and a change-up. All 4 pitches are above average, and he has outstanding command of them primarily because of his smooth mechanics. He's not afraid to work inside either. Pittsley is a great pitching prospect, with the health of his elbow as his only weak point. He should be fully recovered from the surgery and prepared to take his place in the rotation this season. ■

JOE RANDA

3B • BR • TR • 5'11 • 190 • 27 • KC91/11

	AB	R	H	2B	3B	HR	RBI	BB	SO	SB	CS	BA	OB	SA
KC95	70	6	12	2	0	1	5	6	17	0	1	.171	.237	.243
KC96	337	36	102	24	1	6	47	26	47	13	4	.303	.351	.433

Randa has a good-looking swing. He's a contact hitter who has always hit for decent average. For a corner infield position, though, he just doesn't have the power required. In the field he has good hands and decent arm strength, but his range isn't what it should be. Randa just isn't the answer, unless the *Jeopardy* category is "Last Resorts." ■

KEN RAY

SP • BR • TR • 6'2 • 160 • 22 • KC93/16

	G	GS	IP	H	HR	BB	SO	W	L	S	ERA	K/BB	K9	HW9
AA	22	22	121	151	17	57	79	4	12	0	6.12	1.4	5.9	15.51

Ray throws an average fastball, but he complements it with an awesome late-breaking curve that has so much movement he has trouble controlling it. Ray's Double-A Wichita season was his first taste of adversity, so it will be interesting to see how he handles it. ■

BIP ROBERTS

2B • OF • BB • TR • 5'7 • 160 • 33 • PIT82

	AB	R	H	2B	3B	HR	RBI	BB	SO	SB	CS	BA	OB	SA
SD94	403	52	129	15	5	2	31	39	57	21	7	.320	.383	.397
SD95	296	40	90	14	0	2	25	17	36	20	2	.304	.346	.372
KC96	339	39	96	21	2	0	52	25	38	12	9	.283	.331	.357
CAREER	3421	555	1011	166	29	25	284	337	443	230	88	.296	.360	.383

Roberts is an aggressive hitter who can't hit the better fastballs in the league and won't take a lot of walks. Despite this, he hits for a good average because he doesn't try to do too much with a pitch, slapping it to all corners of the field. He also has excellent speed. Unfortunately, Roberts is injury-prone, isn't known for playing through them, and he certainly isn't getting any younger. He can play second and left field, but he might be more valuable, and safer, as a utility player. ■

JOSE ROSADO

YOUNG GUN

SP • BL • TL • 6'0 • 175 • 22 • KC94/12

	G	GS	IP	H	HR	BB	K	W	L	S	ERA	K/BB	K9	HW9
KC96	16	16	106	101	7	26	64	8	6	0	3.21	2.5	5.4	10.78

Rosado's mound presence and pitching savvy took him on a whirlwind tour of the Kansas City system. His meteoric ascension into the Royals' rotation was reminiscent of the rise of Bret Saberhagen and Mark Gubicza in 1984. There isn't much this 22-year-old left-hander didn't do in '96. He began the season in Double-A Wichita, where he allowed no runs in his first 2 starts and was immediately promoted to Omaha. There he went 6-2 with a 3.05 ERA, striking out 64 in 62 innings. He also was named the American Association's best pitching prospect. Shortly after the Royals promoted him to the majors in July, Rosado impressed his new teammates with an 18-inning scoreless streak. In his minor-league career, which has spanned 3 seasons, Rosado has held opponents to a .224 batting average. Even though his fastball is average, it has plenty of movement. Rosado throws 3 pitches for strikes and has tremendous poise for his age. ■

GLENDON RUSCH — SOLID PROSPECT

SP • BL • TL • 6'2 • 170 • 22 • KC93/15

	G	GS	IP	H	HR	BB	SO	W	L	S	ERA	K/BB	K9	HW9
AAA	28	28	170	177	15	40	117	11	9	0	3.98	2.9	6.2	11.51

Rusch features outstanding control and an uncanny ability to work the corners. He throws an 84–87 mph fastball and a decent curve. His stuff is considered mediocre, with the exception of an excellent change-up, but Rusch was considered one of the best pitching prospects in the American Association last year anyway. He's intelligent and has performed at every minor-league level. He could be another Charlie Leibrandt if the Royals are lucky. The Rangers wanted Rusch included in any package for Dean Palmer, but the Royals weren't sure they wanted to give him up. ■

CHRIS STYNES — SOLID PROSPECT

OF-2B • BR • TR • 5'9 • 170 • 24 • TOR91/6

	AB	R	H	2B	3B	HR	RBI	BB	SO	SB	CS	BA	OB	SA
KC95	35	7	6	1	0	0	2	4	3	0	0	.171	.256	.200
KC96	92	8	27	6	0	0	6	2	5	5	2	.293	.309	.359

Stynes was originally drafted by the Blue Jays in the 3rd round of the '91 draft and was acquired by the Royals in the David Cone trade. Stynes looks like the real deal. An excellent contact hitter with gap power, Stynes struck out only 17 times in 284 at-bats in Triple-A Omaha, contributing to a stellar .356 batting average. He's a hard worker and is described by scouts as a "scrapper," which means he's short but hustles. He's a capable fielder, but there are some in the organization who think he lacks the range to play second and want to move him to the outfield. If he gets 450 at-bats, he could surprise everyone. ■

LARRY SUTTON — SLEEPER

1B • BL • TL • 5'11 • 175 • 26 • KC92/24

	AB	R	H	2B	3B	HR	RBI	BB	SO	SB	CS	BA	OB	SA
AA	463	84	137	22	2	22	84	77	66	4	1	.296	.401	.495

Sutton was the Carolina League's MVP in '94 after a monster season at Class-A Wilmington. He missed most of '95 with a fractured elbow but bounced back with a nice season at Wichita in '96. Sutton has solid power, excellent strike-zone judgment, and is pretty good defensively. The problem is that he's 27 and is making his first appearance in Triple-A. For the short term, he looks pretty good. But with his age and level of development, the ceilings in Michael J. Fox's house are higher than his. ■

MIKE SWEENEY

C • BR • TR • 6'1 • 195 • 23 • KC91/10

	AB	R	H	2B	3B	HR	RBI	BB	SO	SB	CS	BA	OB	SA
KC95	4	1	1	0	0	0	0	0	0	0	0	.250	.250	.250
KC96	165	23	46	10	0	4	24	18	21	1	2	.279	.358	.412

Sweeney came to spring training last year in buff condition after an intense off-season weight regimen added almost 30 pounds of muscle to his frame. The bulk didn't cut his flexibility, prompting Royals farm director Bob Hegman to describe him as "a force." He has a quick bat with solid power and can hit breaking balls. More importantly, he has fantastic plate discipline and an excellent work ethic. Defensively, he blocks the plate well and has a strong but erratic arm. He needs some work blocking pitches in the dirt, but he's almost ready. Expect Sweeney to be the starter and Fasano the backup when the Royals are ready to offer Macfarlane a gold watch and a pat on the back. ■

DILSON TORRES

SP • BR • TR • 6'3 • 200 • 26 • TOR90

	G	GS	IP	H	HR	BB	SO	W	L	S	ERA	K/BB	K9	HW9
AA	9	8	56	62	6	13	27	5	3	1	3.88	2.1	4.4	12.13

Torres has enjoyed tremendous success throughout his career—until last season, that is. He gave up a tremendous number of hits as he kept his walks way, way down. Sounds like he might have been wild *in* the strike zone. Torres has an average fastball and a decent slider, but a good split-finger is his out pitch. He also has excellent control. Torres is a little old for the competition at Triple-A, but could be a serviceable middle-relief type if called on. ■

ROBERT TOTH

SP • BR • TR • 6′3 • 200 • 26

	G	GS	IP	H	HR	BB	SO	W	L	S	ERA	K/BB	K9	HW9
AA	9	8	56	62	6	13	27	5	3	1	3.88	2.1	4.4	12.13

Toth throws a fastball, a curve, and a change-up, and has fine command. He also has a pitcher's build and a fluid delivery. He owned a career 2.93 ERA for 6 minor league seasons going into the '96 season, so he knows how to work hitters. He's struggled twice already at Triple-A, but figures to open the season at Omaha. If he finally figures it out, he could be in the majors by season's end. ■

MICHAEL TUCKER

YOUNG GUN

OF • BL • TR • 6′2 • 185 • 25 • KC92/1

	AB	R	H	2B	3B	HR	RBI	BB	SO	SB	CS	BA	OB	SA
KC95	177	23	46	10	0	4	17	18	51	2	3	.260	.332	.384
KC96	339	55	88	18	4	12	53	40	69	10	4	.260	.346	.442

Scouts observing the Royals in spring training predicted that Tucker would have a breakthrough in the power department last year. The regular season started and Tucker had a breakdown instead. The real Tucker is better than he was in '96. He has a graceful swing and quick hands. It just so happens that he battled a wrist injury that put him on the DL in June, and it may very well have played havoc with his hitting. He can't hit the breaking ball well and strikes out too much, but Tucker is young and is still refining his game. The '96 season was a frustrating one for him, but he has the ability to come back strong. ■

JOE VITIELLO

DH-1B • BR • TR • 6′2 • 215 • 26 • KC91/1

	AB	R	H	2B	3B	HR	RBI	BB	SO	SB	CS	BA	OB	SA
KC95	130	13	33	4	0	7	21	8	25	0	0	.254	.317	.446
KC96	257	29	62	15	1	8	40	38	69	2	0	.241	.342	.401

Vitiello had reconstructive surgery on his left knee in '94, which has left him a very slow runner with limited range.He hits for power when he occasionally makes contact, but more often than not he's walking back to the dugout talking to himself. He's Bob Hamelin without the speed. ■

KEVIN YOUNG

SLEEPER

1B-OF • BR • TR • 6′2 • 220 • 27 • PIT90/7

	AB	R	H	2B	3B	HR	RBI	BB	SO	SB	CS	BA	OB	SA
PIT94	122	15	25	7	2	1	11	8	34	0	2	.205	.258	.320
PIT95	181	13	42	9	0	6	22	8	53	1	3	.232	.268	.381
KC96	132	20	32	6	0	8	23	11	32	3	3	.242	.301	.470
CAREER	891	88	209	46	5	21	107	65	201	7	10	.235	.292	.368

Remember when Young was considered the best Pirates prospect among himself, Al Martin, and Carlos Garcia? Well, 3 seasons of brutal strikeout totals and battling with the Mendoza line bought him a ticket out of Pittsburgh and into Kansas City. Soon after the Royals got him and shortened his swing, his power jumped at Triple-A Omaha. Young could be a surprise in '97 if he can resist reverting to the long swing that doomed his Pittsburgh experience. ■

■ 1996 AUTOPSY

Due to the club's 7-25 collapse late in '95—and that minor detail of having little talent and no money to buy any—expectations weren't running high for the new season. A questionable pitching staff was bolstered somewhat by the arrival of free agent Ben McDonald—one of two starters the Orioles had let go, but unfortunately for Milwaukee, the one they signed wasn't going to turn out to be the best pitcher in baseball. B. J. Surhoff was lost to free agency and the team hadn't done much to improve the offense. To go anywhere, they would need career years from Greg Vaughn, John Jaha, Dave Nilsson, Jeff Cirillo, and Jose Valentin. But it wasn't like they were going to combine for 121 dingers and 475 RBI (24 HR and 95 RBI apiece) and a .300 average—were they? If you thought they could, you'd figure they'd win 90 games and take the wildcard. You'd be half right.

April 12-12 (12-12, 4 games back)
The Brewers opened at California with a typical A.L. bang, getting homers from Chuckie Carr, Jeff Cirillo, José Valentin, and Greg Vaughn in a 15-9 victory. But the rest of the week met preseason expectations, as the club went 2-3. The remainder of the month was pretty much the same, as they finished at .500. Playing in the same division as the Indians and the White Sox, this virtually eliminated them from pennant contention already.

May 11-16 (23-28, 10½ games back)
The Brewers played 11 games against division rivals Cleveland and Chicago; they gave up 88 runs and managed 3 victories. Thank you, good night, please drive carefully. The bats cooled off from April; the team batting average dropped to .276, and they slugged only .429. Dave Nilsson became the only Brewer to hit 2 homers in an inning, against the Twins on the 17th. He had another dinger the next day, making him the only converted lefty Australian catcher with a Swedish surname to hit 3 dingers in 2 games.

June 17-11 (40-39, 8½ games back)
The club began to right itself early in the month, going 6-5 against Texas, Cleveland, and Boston. The offense was impressive, scoring 6.4 runs per game in that stretch. For the month, the club slugged .502 with 37 homers and 56 doubles. The pitching staff, especially the bullpen, wasn't doing its part, but the run production was enough to overcome it. Jeff D'Amico arrived in late June and pitched 5.2 scoreless innings in his first start. While it was still early to start talking about the playoffs, the club had almost reached .500, and that puts teams at the edge of wild-card contention these days.

July 12-16 (52-55, 13 games back)
Ben McDonald regained the form he had shown in May, with 5 straight quality starts and won 3 games. D'Amico and Karl were beginning to look like big-league pitchers, and Tim Vanegmond made his first appearances for his new club. In his first 3 games, he was 1-1 with a 4.02 ERA in 15.2 innings. But the fireworks in Milwaukee came at the end of July. Just before the trading deadline, GM Sal Bando sent Greg Vaughn to the Padres for pitchers Bryce Florie and Ron Villone, and outfielder Marc Newfield. How 'bout them Packers?

August 14-16 (66-71, 15 games back)
Any hope of reaching the postseason was crushed early in the month as the club lost 9 straight to Baltimore and Boston, two clubs that were just beginning to get back in the picture. Baltimore outscored them 31-9 in one series. Despite that series, the pitching staff had its best month since April. It was the offense that disappeared. Adjusting to life without Vaughn, the club managed only a .250 average and 131 runs. Newcomer Marc Newfield was one of the only players who made a major impact, hitting .299 with 6 home runs. In one of the few victories a small market team managed over one of the big market greedheads in '96, the Brewers traded Pat Listach and Graeme Lloyd to the Yankees for Gerald Williams and Bob Wickman. Listach arrived in New York with a broken foot and Lloyd quickly developed elbow problems, fueling speculation that the Brewers had unloaded 2 players they knew were injured: What did Bud know and when did he know it? The Brewers denied any wrongdoing, but Yankee GM Bob Watson begged to differ—after waking up screaming at the thought of standing trial in Emperor George's court of final

appeals. All things considered, Steinbrenner took it well—threatening only a public execution of Watson and a limited air assault on Milwaukee, while his hostage-taking incident at the Yankees offices was brief and tastefully done. The Brewers kept smirking and denying, sending Ricky Bones as compensation—which is like sending wilting flowers to the jaywalker you put in the hospital. Steinbrenner wanted a hearing with "Commissioner" Selig to have the trade overturned, a decision Bud would handle fairly and objectively—after Jerry Reinsdorf told him what he should do.

September 14-11 (80-82, 19½ games back)
The club finished in strong fashion, including a surprising sweep of Texas early on and a not-so-surprising sweep of Detroit to close the season. The club can say that progress was made last year, despite the fact that they finished under .500—again—if for no other reason than the brand-new bullpen they acquired from San Diego and the brand-new outfield they put together with young players acquired from Cleveland, San Diego, and the Yankees. They can try out that spin anyway, but see the essay at the end of this section—*Stuck Below .500 with the Milwaukee Brewers Again*—for another perspective.

■ 1997 DIAGNOSIS

Offense
The Brewers fielded a starting lineup of which some rotisserie owners would be hard-pressed to name 4 members other than Greg Vaughn. Who are those guys? Here are some hints.

1. The top nine batting averages in baseball last year: Alex Rodriguez .358, Tony Gwynn .353, Frank Thomas .349, Ellis Burks .344, Paul Molitor .341, Chuck Knoblauch .341, Mike Piazza .336, Lance Johnson .333, and Rusty Greer .332. Who rounds out the top 10?

2. Ken Caminiti led all third baseman with a .326 batting average. Who was second at .325? Jim Thome? Wade Boggs? Chipper Jones?

3. Andres Galarraga knocked in 150 runs, Mo Vaughn 143, Rafael Palmeiro 142, Frank Thomas 134, and Jeff Bagwell 120. What first baseman is next on the list? Mark McGwire? Tino Martinez? Eric Karros? Fred McGriff?

4. Four shortstops knocked in 90 runs: Alex Rodriguez, Cal Ripken, Kevin Elster, and who else? Hint: he stole almost as many bases as these three guys combined. Barry Larkin? Derek Jeter? John Valentin?

The answer to #1 is Dave Nilsson, previously known mostly for contracting some funky disease before the '95 season. He hit .331 with 17 dingers and 84 RBI. The answer to #2 is Jeff Cirillo. And not that many rotisserie owners care about this, but his 46 doubles were topped by only Jeff Bagwell and Alex & Ivan Rodriguez. The answer to #3 is John Jaha. He hit 34 dingers, batted .300, knocked in 118, and scored 108 runs. The answer to #4 is Jose Valentin. He hit 24 dingers, knocked in 95 runs, and stole 17 bases.

Do any of these guys deserve to be mentioned with Frank Thomas, Ken Caminiti, Mo Vaughn, and Alex Rodriguez? Of course not. Are they career years? Probably. Worse still, when you combine these performances with what Marc Newfield and Greg Vaughn combined to do in 151 games (38-126-.291), the Brewers' offense was *still* average last year—finishing 7th in the league in runs, 8th in on-base percentage, and 7th in slugging percentage.

Milwaukee will be hard pressed to maintain this production in '97. Nilsson, Cirillo, Jaha, and Valentin should all be expected to decline in production. Newfield, in his first full season, will find it difficult to maintain the 20 dinger and 90 RBI pace he established at the end of '96. Jeromy Burnitz may develop quickly, but the Mets were counting on that in '94 and he spent most of the season on an extended attitude adjustment in Norfolk.

Defense
Remember how wretched the Red Sox defense was? Remember how much much the Tigers looked like the '62 Mets at various times during the year? Well, the Red Sox had 1 more error than the Brewers, the Tigers 3 more. The Milwaukee infield contributed 90 of the 134 rocks, and it's a tribute to the poise of the pitchers that these resulted in only 73 unearned runs (the Red Sox gave up 114 and the Tigers 88). John Jaha split time with Kevin Seitzer at first, and didn't show the surest hands in the league. Jose Valentin and Fernando Viña showed good range up the middle and turned more than 100 double plays,

but combined for more errors than any other DP combo. Valentin had more errors than any other shortstop in baseball, and only Luis Alicea and Delino DeShields made more errors than Vina at second. Cirillo is versatile enough to be able to play first, second, and third—but his work as a full-time third baseman was nothing special, his fielding percentage better than only Sean Berry, BJ Surhoff, and Chipper Jones. There are about a dozen guys competing for the 3 outfield spots, but the likely combination of Newfield, Burnitz, and Williams won't lose any games for them. Newfield and Williams looked good in their two months in left and center, but Burnitz is trouble waiting to happen in right. Mike Matheny had a decent year behind the plate cutting down base runners, but he hasn't shown much yet as a handler of pitchers.

Pitching

Despite huge question marks at the beginning of the season, the rotation turned in an average year. Their 5.16 ERA was 7th in the league, even better when adjusting for their park. Unlike their offense, which featured some gaudy numbers and little depth, the pitching was average pretty much across the board. Ben McDonald established himself as the leader of the staff, though not with the consistency of a true ace. Scott Karl solidified his status as a major-leaguer, and Jeff D'Amico showed promise after making the leap from Double-A. Cal Eldred also made a solid recovery from Tommy John surgery. No career years here.

Especially early on, the bullpen was the real downfall of the pitching staff. Only Detroit's relievers (5.97) had a higher ERA than Milwaukee's (5.14). They'll begin the season with a much different staff, though, with the addition of Ron Villone, Bryce Florie, and Bob Wickman supporting Mike Fetters, who has established himself as a solid closer. Out of nowhere, Doug Jones showed up to go 5-0 with a 3.41 ERA and a strikeout an inning. Dojo is The Thing That Wouldn't Leave. If not Milwaukee, he'll be throwing slop for someone.

Farm System

Nothing to get too excited about. The Brewers have produced a few players who appear ready for a look in the near future: Todd Dunn, outfield; Tim Unroe, third base; Antone Williamson, third base; and Geoff Jenkins, outfield. All have good power, but none of them are projected to be stars. Ronnie Belliard is also a talented second baseman who could contribute within a year. And reliever Sean Maloney dominated the Texas League last year. Beyond that, the Brewers have some talent, but it's deeper in the system. First-round draft pick Chad Green is a speedster with great range and a decent bat. Valerio de los Santos is not the 4th Tenor or the father of Madonna's child, but a pitcher who threw 97 mph in the Midwest League.

Management and Ownership

Bud Selig wears a lot of hats in his day-to-day existence. As the "acting" commissioner, he is responsible for the operations, or lack thereof, of Major League Baseball—chosen by his peers to be the one who gets to stand at the podium and try to put a positive spin on the foolishness he and his buddies keep concocting. What an honor. He doesn't deserve to be despised, but his and Fehr's cold, unsmiling mugs are embedded in the collective consciousness of baseball fans, forever associated with the worst that team sports has yet to offer. As owner of the Brewers last year, he was embroiled in an often bitter battle over financing for a new stadium—with White Sox owner and all around busybody, Jerry Reinsdorf, finding a way to even get involved with *that.* And as owner of the prototypical "small market" team, Bud tried his best to cover his costs while rattling a cup at his peers in an attempt to shame them into sharing some spare change. One thing he shouldn't have time to do is meddle with the management and personnel of the team, which he doesn't—unless having his daughter do it qualifies as meddling. He got his new stadium, his team has improved, and his payroll has been reduced. For that he deserves credit. But he is the figurehead of the owners and announced the cancellation of the '94 World Series. For that he deserves to be reincarnated as a used car salesman. Oops, been there done that.

GM Sal Bando made some forward-looking moves last season, and, for a change, there were no

significant players declaring free agency and leaving the Brewers empty-handed. He addressed the team's worst concerns in shoring up the bullpen, and he managed to land Marc Newfield in the process. The acquisition of Ben McDonald in the off-season also proved effective. The loss of Greg Vaughn will hurt, but it does reduce the payroll—and he at least managed to get 3 major leaguers for him, rather than a few compensatory draft picks.

Phil Garner has presided over 4 consecutive losing seasons since the team's run at the pennant in '92 in his first season. He has to solidify his bullpen, establish an outfield, and get the infield to tighten up on defense. Expectations will be higher this year than they've been since '93 and rightly so. Garner has talent to work with again and may be out of a job if he doesn't keep the Brewers in the hunt.

. . . and whatnot: Stuck Below .500 with the Milwaukee Brewers Again

The Brewers have been in Milwaukee for 27 years and have managed 10 winning years, 6 of them clustered from 1978–83. Since their surprising 92-70 performance in 1992, they've been 49 games under .500 and never in it. Now they're rebuilding again, but what happened to that '92 team that ran wild on the bases and scared the Blue Jays to death? Wasn't *that* supposed to be the beginning of something? Half of their position players and most of their bench were 27 or younger, and their entire rotation was all under 30. But only 5 players of any significance—Fetters, Eldred, and 3 hitters who combined for only 300 at bats (Jaha, Nilsson, and Valentin)—are still on the team only 5 years later.

Darryl Hamilton, 27, stole 41 bases and hit .298, but was lost to free agency and had a productive year elsewhere. Paul Molitor hit .320, but was lost to free agency and had productive years elsewhere. BJ Surhoff was lost to free agency and had a productive year elsewhere. Dante Bichette was traded to the Rockies for Kevin Reimer, who turned Japanese. On the mound, Jaime Navarro won 17 games, but was lost to free agency and had productive years elsewhere. Chris Bosio won 16 games, but was lost to free agency and ate everything in sight elsewhere. Bruce Ruffin was lost to free agency and had productive years elsewhere. Darren Holmes, 26, saved 6 games with a 2.55 ERA, but was left exposed in the expansion draft and had productive years elsewhere. Dan Plesac was lost to free agency and had productive years elsewhere. Jesse Orosco was lost to free agency and had productive years elsewhere. Ricky Bones, acquired for Gary Sheffield along with Matt Mieske and Jose Valentin, was a bone thrown to the Yankees to try to shut them up about the Listach-Lloyd debacle.

Not all of this team was given away. Starters Bill Wegman and Cal Eldred have been plagued by injuries, and center fielder Robin Yount retired. Pat Listach stole 54 bases and the Rookie of the Year Award from Kenny Lofton, and 4 years later he can't get arrested—but he did help the Brewers acquire Gerald Williams from the Yankees. Reliever Doug Henry was traded to the Mets for second baseman Fernando Vina. It's only of late that the Brewers have stepped up their trading activity: the Listach deal; Greg Vaughn to the Padres for Villone, Florie, and Newfield; and Kevin Seitzer to the Indians for Jeromy Burnitz.

Obviously, the Brewers can't afford to pay top dollar to keep their talent. But they could have done a better job of dealing these players during the season rather than let an entire team just walk out the door. But other than a young, *potentially* talented outfield, a serviceable infielder, and some arms for the bullpen, the Brewers have 4 supplementary draft picks in 1993 to show for their 92-win '92 team. Those picks? Kelly Wunsch, Todd Dunn, Joe Wagner, and Brian Banks. Wunsch is no longer with the organization and Wagner was mediocre in Class-A. Banks and Dunn look like they might be players—but they're both outfielders, and if the Brewers believed in them, would they have blocked them with the 3 outfielders acquired in '96?

Those 4 prospects are a criminal return on a good hitting catcher-third baseman-leftfielder, a Hall of Famer with 733 hits left in his bat (and counting), two solid starters, and four quality relievers. Sounds like Milwaukee hasn't needed revenue sharing as much as they've needed smarter management.

BRIAN BANKS — SLEEPER

OF • BB • TR • 6'3 • 200 • 26 • MIL93/5

	AB	R	H	2B	3B	HR	RBI	BB	SO	SB	CS	BA	OB	SA
AAA	487	71	132	29	7	16	64	66	105	17	8	.271	.356	.458

Banks is one of the best all-around hitters on the Brewers' farm. He's not a great outfielder, and he may get a shot behind the plate. He's developed decent power in his 4-year minor-league career and the Brewers catching job is wide open. ■

RONNIE BELLIARD — SOLID PROSPECT

2B • BR • TR • 5'9 • 175 • 20 • MIL94/8

	AB	R	H	2B	3B	HR	RBI	BB	SO	SB	CS	BA	OB	SA
AA	416	73	116	20	8	3	57	60	51	26	10	.279	.373	.387

At one time Belliard was considered a sleeper in the Brewers' organization. Not anymore. He was voted the Texas League's top second baseman in a mid-season poll of managers. He has good hands and range and is also sweet at turning the double play. Belliard separated his left shoulder and began the season on El Paso's DL, but missed only 8 games. Then, on June 1, he separated his right shoulder and missed 6 games. The oldest recorded victim of separation anxiety, you can either marvel at his resilience or have an office pool about which shoulder goes next and when. At the plate, he has excellent discipline and a little power. His moderate speed helps him stretch some singles and steal a few bases. He's a cousin of big-leaguer Rafael Belliard, although you won't confuse the two at the plate. ■

MARSHALL BOZE

RP • BR • TR • 6'1 • 215 • 25 • MIL90/11

	G	GS	IP	H	HR	BB	K	W	L	S	ERA	K/BB	K9	HW9
MIL96	25	0	32	47	5	25	19	0	2	1	7.79	.8	5.3	20.23

Boze has a reputation as being a real hothead and immature. Reportedly, his attitude and his pitching improved in Triple-A in '95 after he switched from starting to closing—a role better suited for wingnuts. His stint in the majors couldn't have done anything to improve his disposition, though. Through his demotion in early June he was 0-2 with a 7.79 ERA and an HW9 over 20. His stats were slightly skewed by a horrible outing at Toronto on June 30 when he was left out there to die, giving up 10 hits and 8 earned runs in 1.1 innings, but back that out and what was left still wasn't big league caliber. The Brewers haven't given up on him. He throws a fastball and change-up, but the club would like him to develop a better breaking pitch. His numbers in Triple-A look much better, and you can expect to see him in the majors again in '97. ■

BYRON BROWNE

SP • BR • TR • 6'7 • 200 • 26 • MIL91/13

	G	GS	IP	H	HR	BB	SO	W	L	S	ERA	K/BB	K9	HW9
AAA	23	21	107	104	18	73	80	3	9	0	4.66	1.1	6.7	14.84

The jump to Triple-A New Orleans was a bit too much for Browne to handle last year. But he wasn't seriously challenged at lower levels and may just need time to adjust. He throws a fastball that hits 93 mph and a good change-up, so he gets his strikeouts. He also has a slider but is very inconsistent with it. What really jumps out at you, though, are the walks. He gave up about 6 per game, and that was an improvement over previous seasons! Browne needs to fix his control problems before he can move up. He'll get another year in Triple-A to work on it—though New Orleans doesn't seem like the best place for a 26-year-old who has problems with his control. ■

JEROMY BURNITZ

OF • BL • TR • 6'0 • 190 • 27 • NYN90/1

	AB	R	H	2B	3B	HR	RBI	BB	SO	SB	CS	BA	OB	SA
NYN94	143	26	34	4	0	3	15	23	45	1	1	.238	.347	.329
CLE95	7	4	4	1	0	0	0	0	0	0	0	.571	.571	.714
CLE/MIL96	200	38	53	14	0	9	40	33	47	4	1	.265	.377	.470
CAREER	613	117	155	29	6	25	93	94	158	8	8	.253	.356	.442

Originally a Mets prospect, Burnitz is on to his third team in 3 years. Don't be surprised if this westward migration eventually leads him to Yokohama. The Brewers got him a half hour before the August 31 postseason roster deadline last year in a deal with Cleveland for Kevin Seitzer. He won't hit for average, but will occasionally hit a mistake off of a bad pitcher into the parking lot. He drove Mets manager Dallas Green nuts—admittedly a short trip—with his propensity for swinging at bad pitches and not listening to his coaches. Things got so bad at Shea, they opted for Joe Orsulak and Carl Everett rather than have Burnitz around on long trips. He seemed to have settled into a groove for the Indians last year while being used primarily against right-handed pitching. His arrival in Milwaukee makes an already chaotic outfield situation even more so. Jeromy bumped Matt Mieske, a young player having

a solid year, and now several more talented outfielders have arrived. Should make for an interesting spring. If Burnitz lets his hair go and grows a beard, he may get a job simply by garnering the Gorman Thomas/Rob Deer vote in Milwaukee. ■

CHUCK CARR

OF • BB • TR • 5′10 • 165 • 28 • CIN86/9

	AB	R	H	2B	3B	HR	RBI	BB	SO	SB	CS	BA	OB	SA
FLA94	433	61	114	19	2	2	30	22	71	32	8	.263	.305	.330
FLA95	308	54	70	20	0	2	20	46	49	25	11	.227	.330	.312
MIL96	106	18	29	6	1	1	11	6	21	5	4	.274	.310	.377
CAREER	1475	127	376	67	5	9	106	132	225	132	47	.255	.318	.325

Carr spent most of last season on the DL. He went down with a hamstring pull April 22 and was activated May 11, only to return to the DL on May 31, when he blew out his right knee making a spectacular catch in the most disgusting sports highlight since Joe Theismann in all its excruciating, frame-by-frame, once-more-this-time-from-the-reverse-angle glory on *Monday Night Football.* Carr underwent 4½ hours of reconstructive surgery that repaired the anterior cruciate ligament and the hamstring tendon in his knee, and he missed the remainder of the season. His whole career hinges on how he can return from this injury. He's a light-hitting speedster who makes his living covering ground in the outfield and stealing bases. If the speed is gone, his career will have the lifespan of a Snickers bar on Air Force One. And if he can recover, he'll have to compete for a job in a crowded outfield. Bet against him and give him the nod if he beats the odds. ■

JEFF CIRILLO

YOUNG GUN

3B • BR • TR • 6′2 • 190 • 27 • MIL91/11

	AB	R	H	2B	3B	HR	RBI	BB	SO	SB	CS	BA	OB	SA
MIL94	126	17	30	9	0	3	12	11	16	0	1	.238	.309	.381
MIL95	328	57	91	19	4	9	39	47	42	7	2	.277	.371	.442
MIL96	566	101	184	46	5	15	83	58	69	4	9	.325	.391	.504
CAREER	1020	175	305	74	9	27	134	116	127	11	12	.299	.374	.469

At every level of Cirillo's minor-league career, the Brewers have been pleased with his defense and his steady production at the plate. He proved his versa-

tility in '94 by playing every infield position while hitting a respectable .277. Entering the season, the club looked at him as a solid utility infielder, splitting time between second and third. He changed their minds quickly, hitting his way into an everyday job at third. His gap power has improved markedly, and his ability to get on base and his production are equally impressive. These aren't MVP numbers, but he's been a real find for an 11th-round draft pick. ■

JEFF D'AMICO

YOUNG GUN

SP • BR • TR • 6′7 • 250 • 21 • MIL93/1

	G	GS	IP	H	HR	BB	K	W	L	S	ERA	K/BB	K9	HW9
MIL96	17	17	86	88	21	31	53	6	6	0	5.44	1.7	5.5	12.45

In a midseason poll of Texas League managers, D'Amico was voted the best control pitcher. On June 28 he was called up from Double-A El Paso after being named Texas League pitcher of the week. *Gracias y adiós.* At 20 he briefly became the youngest player in the majors. D'Amico didn't take the bigs by storm, but he looked very good for a kid who just jumped 2 levels and couldn't even buy a 6-pack on an off-day. D'Amico is huge and has a heavy 90–91-mph fastball, a forkball, and a good curveball, each with excellent command. He's also working on a change-up. He looks like a good prospect, but there are concerns. First, he needs to watch his weight. The Brewers worry that his mechanics will be erratic because of his size. Second, he missed half of 1993 because of shoulder trouble and all of 1994 after elbow surgery. The Brewers still worry that this might be a recurring problem, even though he has 2 straight solid seasons under his belt. ■

VALERIO DE LOS SANTOS *GRADE-A PROSPECT*

P • BL • TL • 6'4 • 185 • 21

	G	GS	IP	H	HR	BB	SO	W	L	S	ERA	K/BB	K9	HW9
A	33	23	165	164	11	59	137	10	8	4	3.55	2.3	7.5	12.19

De los Santos has hit 97 mph on the gun, and Midwest League managers voted his fastball the best in the league. He also has a decent change-up but needs a breaking ball, which the Brewers are trying to teach him. They got him to stop throwing sidearm, and that increased his velocity. He looks great now with good control, an excellent strikeout-to-walk ratio, and that blazing heat. He needs that breaking ball, but even without it, he's still an intriguing prospect. ■

TODD DUNN *SLEEPER*

OF • BR • TR • 6'5 • 220 • 26 • MIL93/3

	AB	R	H	2B	3B	HR	RBI	BB	SO	SB	CS	BA	OB	SA
AA	359	72	122	24	5	19	78	45	84	13	4	.340	.412	.593

Dunn tore up the Texas League last year, winning the batting title and showing good power and decent speed. He managed to raise his average 50 points from the previous year while moving up a level. That kind of improvement is a pleasant surprise, and is due in part to his learning to handle breaking pitches. The Brewers consider him a 5-tool player and gave him a late September call-up to give him a look. He's got a shot to find himself a spot in the Brewers' outfield next spring. Dunn is getting a little old to be considered a top-rate prospect in Double-A, so he'll have to make his mark soon. ■

CAL ELDRED

SP • BR • TR • 6'4 • 235 • 29 • MIL89/1

	G	GS	IP	H	HR	BB	K	W	L	S	ERA	K/BB	K9	HW9
MIL94	25	25	179	158	23	84	98	11	11	0	4.68	1.2	4.9	12.17
MIL95	4	4	23	24	4	10	18	1	1	0	3.42	1.8	7.0	13.30
MIL96	15	15	84	82	8	38	50	4	4	0	4.46	1.3	5.4	12.85
CAREER	97	97	661	592	73	252	418	45	34	0	3.91	1.7	5.7	11.49

The 1992 Rookie Pitcher of the Year, Eldred lost the '95 season to a career-threatening elbow injury that forced him to undergo Tommy John surgery.

Rehabbing at New Orleans this spring, he decided that he would never, ever throw the number of pitches he did in the past. If he is tired, he says, it's time to come out. He was activated and made his season debut July 14 against the Blue Jays, giving up 3 runs in 7 innings. And his return has pretty much followed that initial success. For a guy who hadn't pitched in a year and a half, he looked pretty good. He averaged only 6 innings in his 15 outings. If that keeps him healthy, and if Florie and Villone can get the ball to Fetters, Eldred will get more wins and do a lot less work than he ever has in the past. And the responsibility of saving the bullpen will fall on the other starters. ■

MIKE FETTERS

CL • BR • TR • 6'4 • 200 • 32 • CAL86/4

	G	GS	IP	H	HR	BB	K	W	L	S	ERA	K/BB	K9	HW9
MIL94	42	0	46	41	0	27	31	1	4	17	2.54	1.1	6.1	13.30
MIL95	40	0	34	40	3	20	33	0	3	22	3.38	1.7	8.7	15.88
MIL96	61	0	61	65	4	26	53	3	3	32	3.38	2.0	7.8	13.42
CAREER	284	6	379	378	28	168	246	15	20	74	3.37	1.5	5.8	12.96

Fetters emerged as the closer for the Brewers in '95 after 4 solid seasons of long relief for them. No one would ever mistake him for Mark Wohlers—for one thing, he doesn't sweat as much. Although he is a big man at 6-foot-4, he isn't dominating. The Brewers were happy with his work and on July 26 gave him a 2-year contract extension worth about $4 million. Fetters is hittable and doesn't get excellent strikeout numbers—but as for living dangerously as a closer, he's nothing compared to Don "Two Pack" Stanhouse, named by manager Earl Weaver for the nicotine fits he prompted, saving 45 games for the '78–'79 Orioles despite walking 103 and striking out only 76 in 148 innings. Fetters hasn't had any real competition for the job thus far and, at that price tag, the job is his for the foreseeable future. ■

BRYCE FLORIE

RP • BR • TR • 6′0 • 185 • 26 • SD88/5

	G	GS	IP	H	HR	BB	K	W	L	S	ERA	K/BB	K9	HW9
SD94	9	0	9	8	0	3	8	0	0	0	.96	2.7	8.0	10.96
SD95	47	0	68	49	8	38	68	2	2	1	3.01	1.8	9.0	11.51
SD/MIL96	54	0	68	65	4	40	63	2	3	0	4.76	1.6	8.3	13.89
CAREER	110	0	146	122	12	81	139	4	5	1	3.70	1.7	8.6	12.51

Florie was an effective but sometimes erratic starter in the Padres' system for a few years before they put him into the bullpen in '94. Ever since, he's been a very reliable middle reliever. His adjustment to the American League was a little rough; through his first 14.2 innings he blew 2 saves, had a 4.30 ERA, and had given up 11 walks. Florie has always given up too many walks, but he gets his share of strikeouts with his sinking fastball, keeping his ERA respectable. Villone's the one the Brewers really liked in that Vaughn trade. ■

RAMON GARCIA

RP • BR • TR • 6′2 • 200 • 27

	G	GS	IP	H	HR	BB	K	W	L	S	ERA	K/BB	K9	HW9
MIL96	37	2	75	84	17	21	40	4	4	4	6.66	1.9	4.8	12.59

Garcia's a longtime White Sox prospect who found his way to the Brewers' bullpen last year. He was a starter on Chicago's farm, and the Brewers were able to use him in long stretches when their starters got clubbed early. He does a decent job keeping guys off base, but the guys who do get on come all the way around. His biggest problem is the long ball: He gave up 17 homers in 75.2 innings. He's also a little inconsistent, a poster child for the randomness of pitching. On June 7 against Boston, he lasted two-thirds of an inning and gave up 4 earned runs; 4 days later, at Texas, he pitched a solid 3 shutout innings for the save. ■

BRIAN GIVENS

SP • BR • TL • 6′6 • 220 • 31 • NYN84/10

	G	GS	IP	H	HR	BB	K	W	L	S	ERA	K/BB	K9	HW9
MIL95	19	19	107	116	11	54	73	5	7	0	4.95	1.4	6.1	14.30
MIL96	4	4	14	32	3	7	10	1	3	0	12.86	1.4	6.4	25.07

Givens started the year on the DL with a sore arm, but came back and looked good during his rehab in New Orleans. He went 5-6 with a 3.57 ERA before

being recalled in early June. He was shelled in Milwaukee, though, and didn't last the month. He may get another chance to impress in the spring, but it may be his last. He's already spent 13 years in the minors—and unlike Crash Davis, doesn't have Susan Sarandon to show for it. ■

CHAD GREEN

SOLID PROSPECT

OF • MIL96/1 • UNIVERSITY OF KENTUCKY

	AB	R	H	2B	3B	HR	RBI	BB	SO	SB	CS	BA	OB	SA
R+	81	22	29	4	1	3	8	15	23	12	3	.358	.455	.543

The Brewers took Green with the 8th overall pick of the amateur draft last year. He is only 5-10 and 180, but he was a top-college tailback recruit. He runs the 60-yard dash in 6.5 seconds. He was considered the fastest player in college baseball in 1996 and *Baseball America*'s choice as the best athlete in the draft, and scouts predict 50 to 60 steals a season in majors. He lacks power, but every other tool is above average. Green played for the Olympic team and then joined Ogden in time for the playoffs, where he hit .385, including a homer that clinched the divisional series. He's a college player, so strong production in that league should be expected. He'll need to be playing in high Class-A this season—and if he puts it together, he'll be a Grade-A player at this time next year. ■

DAVID HULSE

OF • BL • TL • 5′11 • 170 • 29 • TEX90/13

	AB	R	H	2B	3B	HR	RBI	BB	SO	SB	CS	BA	OB	SA
TEX94	310	58	79	8	4	1	19	21	53	18	2	.255	.305	.316
MIL95	339	46	85	11	6	3	47	18	60	15	3	.251	.285	.345
MIL96	117	18	26	3	0	0	6	8	16	4	1	.222	.272	.248
CAREER	1265	207	336	35	20	5	103	76	204	69	16	.266	.307	.337

At one time Hulse showed a lot of promise for the Texas Rangers as a speedy outfield prospect. Injuries have slowed him, though, and his production has been in a nose dive the past few years. The Brewers acquired him in '95, but he hasn't shown anything at the plate for them.

Hulse spent '96 as a utility outfielder and spent June on the DL with a bruised throwing shoulder. He hit a career-high 6 home runs through September 1, but also hit .222 during that time. Bottom line: The Brewers outfield got awfully crowded last year, and if Hulse holds on, it will be a miracle. The highlight of his career is likely to remain the half-dozen balls he consecutively fouled off into the Angels' dugout, until the entire team was huddled down in one corner. ■

JOHN JAHA — HEADED FOR A FALL

1B/DH • BR • TR • 6'1 • 195 • 30 • MIL84/14

	AB	R	H	2B	3B	HR	RBI	BB	SO	SB	CS	BA	OB	SA
MIL94	291	45	70	14	0	12	39	32	75	3	3	.241	.332	.412
MIL95	316	59	99	20	2	20	65	36	66	2	1	.313	.389	.579
MIL96	543	108	163	28	1	34	118	85	118	3	1	.300	.398	.543
CAREER	1798	307	498	86	4	87	302	216	398	31	14	.277	.361	.474

Jaha finally had the big year the Brewers have been waiting for. A long time slugging prospect on Milwaukee's farm, he didn't get a full-time big-league job until 1993, and injuries in '94 and '95 kept him from having a breakthrough year. But he got it together in '96, posting his first 30+ homer, 100+ RBI season. He owned lefties, hitting .371 off them, and was respectable (.279) against righties. He's still prone to strike out, but he's also willing to take a walk. Defensively he can be left alone at first base without causing too much damage, but look for him to see more time at DH.

There were more than a few career years put in back in the juiced ball season of 1987, which is also touched on—for obvious reasons—in Jose Valentin's write-up. Unfortunately for the Brewers, one of them was from another allegedly slugging first baseman from whom big things were expected: Greg Brock knocked in 85 runs and hit .299. Other 27- to 30-year olds who looked briefly as if they were establishing themselves as stars and pulled an Icarus:

	1987	**1988**
Larry Sheets	31-94-.316	10-47-.230
Brook Jacoby	32-69-.300	9-49-.241
Pete O'Brien	23-88-.286	16-71-.272
Lloyd Moseby	26-96-.282	10-42-.239
Mike Davis	22-72-.265	2-17-.196
Greg Walker	27-94-.258	8-42-.247
Ozzie Virgil	27-72-.247	9-31-.256
Mike Pagliarulo	32-87-.234	15-67-.216

Including Brock, that's 9 players, and not another big year out of any of them. Jaha may not disappear completely like Sheets and Jacoby, but he could pull a Tim Wallach. Wallach was 29, went 26-123-.298, then saw his numbers pretty much cut in half in '88. He remained a fairly productive player into his mid-30s, although he did take up residence in the .220s for 3 straight seasons along the way. ■

GEOFF JENKINS

DH • BL • TL • 6'1 • 195 • 22 • MIL95/1

	AB	R	H	2B	3B	HR	RBI	BB	SO	SB	CS	BA	OB	SA
AA	77	17	22	5	4	1	11	12	21	1	2	.286	.391	.494

Jenkins was the Brewers' no. 1 pick in the 1995 draft, but injuries last year have slowed his progress. Early in the season he was sent home to rehab a "loose" right shoulder. He returned in June in Double-A El Paso and eventually landed in Stockton, in the Class-A California League (hitting .348 down there with gap power). He hopes to make up any ground he lost by playing in the Arizona Fall League. When and if Jenkins is healthy, the Brewers look at him as a slugging left fielder. He has a wicked swing but still makes contact. He needs work defensively. Both his range and his arm are considered mediocre-to-average. If he has a successful fall, they may give him a serious look in the spring. ■

DOUG JONES (see Free Agents)

SCOTT KARL

SP • BL • TL • 6'2 • 195 • 25 • MIL92/7

	G	GS	IP	H	HR	BB	K	W	L	S	ERA	K/BB	K9	HW9
MIL95	25	18	124	141	10	50	59	6	7	0	4.14	1.2	4.3	13.86
MIL96	32	32	207	220	29	72	121	13	9	0	4.86	1.7	5.3	12.69

In his first full year in the bigs, Karl survived. His 13-9 record might suggest he did a little better than that, but he received some generous run support (6.1 runs per game). He did provide a lot of quality innings, rarely leaving before the sixth. His ERA was below league average, and his stats were skewed by a few nightmarish

outings. For example, on August 8 against Baltimore, Karl was pummeled early and left out there to die. Either protecting a tired bullpen, figuring they couldn't do any better, perhaps something personal, or knowing Karl was on Davey Johnson's rotisserie team, Garner left him in to endure the following: 6.2 IP, 12 H, 10 ER; his ERA jumped from 4.76 to 5.16. His minor-league history suggests he's a better pitcher than his '96 numbers. Look for an improvement in '97. ■

DANNY KLASSEN

SS • BR • TR • 6'0 • 175 • 21 • MIL93/6

	AB	R	H	2B	3B	HR	RBI	BB	SO	SB	CS	BA	OB	SA
A+	432	58	116	22	4	2	46	34	77	14	8	.269	.335	.352

Klassen tore the right anterior cruciate ligament in his knee during the winter of 1994 and missed most of '95. And his comeback got off slowly last year. But the Brewers consider him a gamer with a strong work ethic. He has a strong arm and good power potential. The club has considered moving him to third, thinking the injury would rob him of range. So far that hasn't been the case. ■

JOSH KLIMEK

SLEEPER

3B • MIL96/10 • UNIVERSITY OF ILLINOIS

	AB	R	H	2B	3B	HR	RBI	BB	SO	SB	CS	BA	OB	SA
R+	253	56	75	17	0	6	51	42	39	5	1	.296	.393	.435

Klimek was the Brewers' 10th-round pick in the '96 draft. He had incredible offensive numbers as a shortstop in college, but he suffered a nasty motorcycle accident that left him with a compound fracture of the left leg. Permanent rods were inserted from his knee to his ankle. Like Gant before him, Klimek did an impressive job of rehabbing and despite a slight loss of speed reportedly returned a much better player. He was projected to go higher but his slight build, the loss of speed, and those unsightly rods scared most clubs away. The Brewers moved him to third and he had a solid season for short-season Helena. The club likes his bat speed, soft hands, and strong arm. If the leg is truly healed, he could be a good prospect, even if he will have trouble getting through airport metal detectors and will be sitting by himself in the dugout during electrical storms. ■

JESSE LEVIS

C • BL • TR • 5'9 • 180 • 28 • CLE89/4

	AB	R	H	2B	3B	HR	RBI	BB	SO	SB	CS	BA	OB	SA
MIL96	233	27	55	6	1	1	21	38	15	0	0	.236	.348	.283

Levis came over from the Indians and soon entered into the mix in Milwaukee with Mike Matheny, bumping Kelly Stinnett out of the way. Of the three, he made the most impact at the plate for the Brewers, which isn't saying much. He showed good plate discipline and had a .348 on-base average, but with absolutely no power. He's shown promise in his minor-league career, including a little pop, and should improve. ■

PAT LISTACH (see Looking for a Game)

MARK LORETTA

2B • BR • TR • 6'0 • 175 • 25 • MIL93/11

	AB	R	H	2B	3B	HR	RBI	BB	SO	SB	CS	BA	OB	SA
MIL95	50	13	13	3	0	1	3	4	7	1	1	.260	.327	.380
MIL96	154	20	43	3	0	1	13	14	15	2	1	.279	.339	.318

Get Back Loretta was a career shortstop before the Brewers moved him to second in the off-season last year. He's got a good glove, and turned in a decent year at the plate, backing up Fernando Viña. He doesn't have much power, though, and never has. Still, he could challenge Viña for the job of Albert Belle's tackling dummy. ■

SEAN MALONEY

SLEEPER

RP • BR • TR • 6'7 • 210 • 25 • MIL93/19

	G	GS	IP	H	HR	BB	SO	W	L	S	ERA	K/BB	K9	HW9
AA	51	0	57	49	1	12	57	3	2	38	1.43	4.8	9.1	9.69

Maloney was dominant for El Paso. He has a good forkball and a fastball that hits 88–89 mph, plus a degree from Georgetown, so he probably knows how to use them—although Yale man Ron Darling used to drive manager Davey Johnson nuts for thinking himself into bases on balls. Texas League managers voted Maloney the top reliever in the league and the Brewers see him as a fine setup man. El Paso has one of the best hitter's parks in pro baseball, so what he could do in that harsh environment makes this guy look for real. ■

MIKE MATHENY

C • BR • TR • 6'3 • 205 • 26 • MIL91/8

	AB	R	H	2B	3B	HR	RBI	BB	SO	SB	CS	BA	OB	SA
MIL94	53	3	12	3	0	1	2	3	13	0	1	.226	.293	.340
MIL95	166	13	41	9	1	0	21	12	28	2	1	.247	.306	.313
MIL96	313	31	64	15	2	8	46	14	80	3	2	.204	.243	.342
CAREER	532	47	117	27	3	9	69	29	121	5	4	.220	.267	.333

Matheny started the season as the Opening Day catcher and played well defensively, but struggled at the plate from day one until mid-August, when he was sent down to Triple-A New Orleans where he continued to struggle. He did show a little power in Louisiana and threw reasonably well in Milwaukee, and that could get him his job back—along with the limited options the Brewers have at this position. ■

JAMIE MCANDREW

P • BR • TR • 6'2 • 190 • 29 • LA89/2

McAndrew had another hard-luck season last year. He had to undergo major surgery in March to repair the medial collateral ligament in his right knee and was out for the year—this after he missed the '94 campaign and after arm trouble knocked him out in 1995 following a couple of good starts in Milwaukee. So in the past three years he's pitched a total of 36.1 innings in the bigs and 104.1 in Double-A. When he was healthy, he looked like a solid starter with good control and command, though without big strikeout numbers. Now he looks like someone who used to have good control and command. ■

BEN MCDONALD

SP • BR • TR • 6'7 • 210 • 29 • BAL89/1

	G	GS	IP	H	HR	BB	K	W	L	S	ERA	K/BB	K9	HW9
BAL94	24	24	157	151	14	54	94	14	7	0	4.06	1.7	5.4	11.75
BAL95	14	13	80	67	10	38	62	3	6	0	4.16	1.6	7.0	11.81
MIL96	35	35	221	228	25	67	146	12	10	0	3.90	2.2	5.9	12.01
CAREER	190	177	1158	1066	125	401	784	70	63	0	3.89	2.0	6.1	11.40

McDonald entered the season under enormous pressure after signing a 2-year, $6 million contract as a free agent. The College Player of the Year in 1989, Ben was once the prize prospect in the Orioles' organization, but has struggled for years with injuries, control, and an inability to remember the book on hitters. He finally emerged as a semireliable no. 2, then took his show on the road . . . and got a pretty nice contract for a guy who'd never posted 15 victories. And initially, he produced. In his first 4 outings he had 4 quality starts and went 3-0. But he was streaky throughout the rest of the season. When he was hot, he was tough—and when he wasn't, it was ugly. His control improved last year and his strikeout-to-walk ratio was impressive, but when he didn't have his good stuff he was decidedly hittable. In his defense, he received little run support in the second half, but an ace has to be more consistent and find a way to win games when his team isn't hitting. In the last year of his contract, he may turn it up a notch. McDonald isn't the smartest player in the majors, but even he knows that the best way for a veteran to get to the postseason is to put up big first-half numbers in a small-market town and hope to get salary dumped into a pennant race. ■

JOSÉ MERCEDES

P • BR • TR • 6'1 • 200 • 26 • BAL89

	G	GS	IP	H	HR	BB	SO	W	L	S	ERA	K/BB	K9	HW9
AAA	25	15	101	109	14	28	47	3	7	1	3.56	1.7	4.2	12.21

After losing 2 months in '94 and most of '95 to injuries, Mercedes was looking more like a Pinto. Starting the '96 season in New Orleans, he pitched well enough to earn an early call-up. He wasn't very sharp in that stint, though, and only lasted with Milwaukee until the end of July (9.18 ERA in 16.2 innings). His numbers at New Orleans suggest he's a better pitcher than that, but not much. He doesn't get many Ks, never has, and gives up a lot of hits. If he can stay healthy and focused, he may be effective in middle relief at some point in his career. ■

MATT MIESKE

OF • BR • TR • 6'0 • 185 • 29 • SD90/17

	AB	R	H	2B	3B	HR	RBI	BB	SO	SB	CS	BA	OB	SA
MIL94	259	39	67	13	1	10	38	21	62	3	5	.259	.320	.432
MIL95	267	42	67	13	1	12	48	27	45	2	4	.251	.323	.442
MIL96	374	46	104	24	3	14	64	26	76	1	5	.278	.324	.471
CAREER	958	136	252	50	5	39	157	78	197	6	16	.263	.321	.448

Mieske tore up the Northwest and California Leagues in '90 and '91, and he's risen quickly since coming over in the Sheffield trade. But he's taken a long time to adjust to big-league pitching. After his production in '96, he could probably argue that he had arrived. Imagine his frustration when, even after the loss of Chuckie Carr and Greg Vaughn, new outfield arrivals left him without an everyday spot. Mieske could earn a starting spot somewhere this year. Odds are, though, he'll continue to be a solid backup. ▪

ANGEL MIRANDA

RP • BL • TL • 6'1 • 160 • 27 • MIL87

	G	GS	IP	H	HR	BB	K	W	L	S	ERA	K/BB	K9	HW9
MIL94	8	8	46	39	8	27	24	2	5	0	5.28	.9	4.7	12.91
MIL95	30	10	74	83	8	49	45	4	5	1	5.23	.9	5.5	16.05
MIL96	46	12	109	116	12	69	78	7	6	1	4.94	1.1	6.4	15.27
CAREER	106	47	349	338	40	197	235	17	21	2	4.49	1.2	6.1	13.80

Miranda entered the Brewers' organization as a promising young reliever in 1987, and the club has tried to make him a starter every year since. But after 12 starts, a 5.19 ERA with only a single quality start in '96, they said enough is enough. Back in the bullpen, he settled down—not world-beating numbers, but solid middle relief. Miranda was once a young stud with a decent fastball and a wicked screwgie. The thermostat on the heat has been lowered a few degrees, but he still has the screwball and can be effective as a reliever. The club should let him settle in there so he can concentrate on his control and not his role. ▪

MARC NEWFIELD — YOUNG GUN

OF • BR • TR • 6'4 • 205 • 24 • SEA90/1

	AB	R	H	2B	3B	HR	RBI	BB	SO	SB	CS	BA	OB	SA
SEA/SD95	140	13	33	8	1	4	21	5	24	0	0	.236	.267	.393
SD/MIL96	370	48	103	26	0	12	57	27	70	1	2	.278	.332	.446

Newfield was one of the Mariners' top prospects for a number of years. He was traded to San Diego for Andy Benes in '95, and then to the Brewers in the Greg Vaughn deal last season—unlike Mark Whiten, who has been traded for Turner Ward, Mark Clark, Scott Cooper, Dave Hollins, released, and dumped for long-shot prospects. Newfield has moved around a lot lately, but it's definitely not a "nobody wants me" type thing; more like "everybody wants me." Newfield led the Padres in spring training with a .475 average, 5 home runs, and 20 RBI in '96, and carried his hot hitting into the season. He credited his success to a hitch he inserted into his swing over the off-season—which is like consciously adding a John Daly backswing to your golf game, but it seems to have worked. That success was continued on his arrival in Milwaukee. He hit .307 with a .508 slugging percentage in 179 at-bats. He's probably the only guy guaranteed a spot in the Brewers' outfield this year—if no other reason than to justify the Vaughn trade—and he has a chance to develop into a star. However, he was arrested in Dearborn, Michigan, in late September for marijuana possession. He apologized and pledged to make good with the fans. At least it wasn't like Steeler running back Bam Morris, who had 6 pounds of the stuff in his trunk—and not even Paul McCartney could get away with claiming that was for personal use. ▪

DAVE NILSSON — YOUNG GUN

OF/DH • BL • TR • 6'3 • 185 • 27 • MIL87

	AB	R	H	2B	3B	HR	RBI	BB	SO	SB	CS	BA	OB	SA
MIL94	397	51	109	28	3	12	69	34	61	1	0	.275	.326	.451
MIL95	263	41	73	12	1	12	53	24	41	2	0	.278	.337	.468
MIL96	453	81	150	33	2	17	84	57	68	2	3	.331	.407	.525
CAREER	1573	223	446	91	8	52	271	169	224	10	11	.284	.351	.451

Nilsson's had a lot of trouble with injuries. He lost a good part of '95 to a lingering malady brought on by an Australian mosquito—the most creative injury since Glenallen Hill fell down a flight of steps in his sleep trying to get away from the spiders he was dreaming were crawling all over him. He was forced out in April '96 with a hairline fracture in his left foot—his 8th time on the DL in 4 years. But when he came back in May, he didn't waste any time commencing his career year. Nilsson's days behind the plate appear to be over. But he's become valuable as a Mickey Tettleton type who can play the outfield, first, and DH, although his defensive skills need

improvement wherever they tell him to stand. As long he can maintain his offensive production, they'll find a place for him. ■

STEVE SPARKS

SP • BR • TR • 6'0 • 180 • 31 • MIL87/6

	G	GS	IP	H	HR	BB	K	W	L	S	ERA	K/BB	K9	HW9
MIL95	33	27	202	210	17	86	96	9	11	0	4.63	1.1	4.3	13.19
MIL96	20	13	88	103	19	52	21	4	7	0	6.60	.4	2.1	15.84

His knuckleball didn't fool anybody last year, and Sparks suffered through start after start until the club finally put him out of his misery in mid-June. At the time he was 3-6 with a 7.48 ERA and 1.69 ratio. As for Sparks's future with the Brewers, it's about degrees of desperation—and Milwaukee is looking less needy lately. Sparks has never had much control or command. He probably won't be back in the starting rotation. But you can never give up on a knuckleballer. After all, Sparks may have only about 20 years left in his career. ■

KELLY STINNETT

C • BR • TR • 5'11 • 195 • 27 • CLE89/11

	AB	R	H	2B	3B	HR	RBI	BB	SO	SB	CS	BA	OB	SA
AAA	334	63	96	21	1	27	70	31	83	3	3	.287	.366	.599

The Brewers got Stinnett from the Mets in January for Cory Lidle and a cheesehead hat. He spent the first few weeks of the season in Milwaukee before being sent down to Triple-A New Orleans to make room for Jesse Levis. Although Stinnett has never looked like much of a power prospect, he hit 27 homers for New Orleans and slugged his way onto the American Association All-Star team. He also earned himself a mid-August call-up for Mike Matheny (hitting .077 in 26 at bats). Stinnett, Levis, and Matheny will be competing for the 2 catching roster spots this spring, and Levis has an inside track on one of them because he's the only lefty. ■

BRIAN TOLLBERG

SP • BR • TR • 6'3 • 195 • 24 • MIL94

	G	GS	IP	H	HR	BB	SO	W	L	S	ERA	K/BB	K9	HW9
AA	26	26	154	183	15	23	109	7	5	0	4.90	4.7	6.4	12.01

Tollberg is a righty with great command, which he used to moderate success last year at El Paso. The Brewers are impressed with his ability to work both sides of the plate. They'll give him a shot in New Orleans this season. Expect his numbers to dramatically improve as he moves from a hitter's paradise to the Dodger Stadium of Triple-A parks. ■

TIM UNROE — SOLID PROSPECT

1B-3B • BR • TR • 6'3 • 200 • 26 • MIL92/29

	AB	R	H	2B	3B	HR	RBI	BB	SO	SB	CS	BA	OB	SA
AAA	404	72	109	26	4	25	67	36	121	8	3	.270	.333	.540

Unroe had himself a big year in a park friendly to pitchers. He's always had decent power, but last year was a major improvement. Defensively, he's competent at either corner, and after 2 full seasons at Triple-A, he has little left to prove there. The challenge will be to find him a spot with Cirillo and Jaha in the way, but expect the Brewers to get him some at bats. ■

JOSÉ VALENTIN — HEADED FOR A FALL

SS • BB • TR • 5'10 • 175 • 27 • SD86

	AB	R	H	2B	3B	HR	RBI	BB	SO	SB	CS	BA	OB	SA
MIL94	285	47	68	19	0	11	46	38	75	12	3	.239	.330	.421
MIL95	338	62	74	23	3	11	49	37	83	16	8	.219	.293	.402
MIL96	552	90	143	33	7	24	95	66	145	17	4	.259	.336	.475
CAREER	1231	210	298	76	12	47	198	148	319	46	15	.242	.322	.438

Valentin's season started ignominiously as he committed 5 errors in his first 8 games, and he finished with 37 errors. He kept his job—and earned a 3 year deal—because he produced at the plate. Half of Ripken's game is better than none. This production was definitely a surprise; he'd never even approached those kinds of numbers in his 9-year career. It's also questionable whether he can do it again. His plate discipline is lacking (145:66 strikeouts-to-walks ratio)

and he tailed off in September. Last year's improvement came out of the blue . . .

. . . like another, even younger, switch-hitting Brewer shortstop who hit 25 dingers, knocked in 95 runs, and batted .252 for Milwaukee in the juiced ball season of 1987: Dale Sveum. Compare his numbers to the switch-hitting Jose Valentin. That can't be making the Brewers feel warm and fuzzy.

Sveum was 1 of only 4 players younger than 25 who had big years in '87 yet proved to be playing well over their heads. The others were Matt Nokes (32-87-.289), Cory Snyder (33-82-.236), and Kal Daniels (26-64-.334 with 26 SBs). Along with these 4, there were 11 young players who looked good and stayed that way—or blossomed into stars. Devon White never hit 24 dingers again, but he got even better as a ballplayer once he got out of Anaheim. At 21, Ruben Sierra (30-109-.263) looked to be on his way to the Hall of Fame, but settled into a long career of decent production instead. Pete Incaviglia (27-80-.271) would go on to hit another 144 dingers (and counting). As for those who would become stars, the Blue Jays had a first base platoon of 23-year-olds who would meet up again in the World Series 9 years later: Cecil Fielder and Fred McGriff combined for 34 dingers in 470 at bats. Mark McGwire debuted with 49 dingers and 118 RBI, overshadowing teammate Jose Canseco's 31 dingers and 113 RBI. Rafael Palmeiro hit 14 dingers in only 221 at bats, but he was overshadowed by college teammate Will Clark's 35 dingers and .308 average. And then there was this 22-year-old named Barry Bonds who hit 25 dingers in his first full season and *his* teammate, Bobby Bonilla, who hit 15 dingers and batted .306.

If past results are indeed the best predictor of future performance, take the big numbers that came from players under 25 in 1996 a bit more seriously than those put up by those like Valentin and Jaha, who are entering or already in their prime years. If the Brewers want to build the case that Valentin's '96 was not a fluke, they can try to ignore the frighteningly similar '87 performances of mid-20s infielders like Juan Samuel (28-100-.272), Jim Presley (24-88-.247), and Jack Howell (234-64-.245), and enter Howard Johnson's year (36-99-.265) into evidence. Hojo followed up '87 with 4 more big years for the Mets before being moved to the outfield and falling off a cliff. Valentin should be so lucky. ■

TIM VANEGMOND — SLEEPER

SP • BR • TR • 6′2 • 180 • 27 • BOS91/17

	G	GS	IP	H	HR	BB	K	W	L	S	ERA	K/BB	K9	HW9
BOS94	7	7	38	38	7	21	22	2	3	0	6.34	1.0	5.2	13.96
BOS95	4	1	6	9	2	6	5	0	1	0	9.45	.8	7.4	22.26
MIL96	12	9	54	58	6	23	33	3	5	0	5.27	1.4	5.5	13.48
CAREER	23	17	99	105	15	50	60	5	9	0	6.00	1.2	5.5	14.08

After 5 years as a promising Red Sox prospect, Vanegmond took advantage of a stipulation in his contract, went free agent, and joined Milwaukee in the off-season. He had some short and shaky stints in Boston, but his minor-league numbers were solid, and he looked like a good risk to the Brewers. He developed quickly for the club last year. Vanegmond attributed his success at New Orleans to getting his 2-seam fastball over the plate. He earned a call-up in mid-July and his presence made Ricky Bones expendable, whom they were able to ship off to New York as compensation for their alleged skulduggery in the Listach affair. Vanegmond didn't post earth-shattering numbers, but he was a league-average pitcher. He won't have a rotation slot reserved for him in the spring, but he'll probably earn one. ■

RON VILLONE — SLEEPER

RP • BL • TL • 6′3 • 230 • 27 • SEA92/1

	G	GS	IP	H	HR	BB	K	W	L	S	ERA	K/BB	K9	HW9
SD95	38	0	45	44	11	34	63	2	3	1	5.80	1.9	12.6	15.60
SD/MIL96	44	0	42	31	6	25	38	1	1	2	3.21	1.5	8.1	11.97

Villone has traveled extensively with Marc Newfield in the past couple of years, accompanying him from Seattle to San Diego for Andy Benes in '95, then to Milwaukee for Greg Vaughn last season. He's definitely the lighter side of that package, but he does bring some tools. He has a mid-90s fastball and an excellent change-up, and he uses them effectively to ring up his share of batters. Villone, like Bryce Florie, found the adjustment to American League hitting a little difficult, but he finished very strongly. His control was horrid, but he was unhittable and had a good strikeout rate. If he throws more strikes this year, he could go from effective to downright nasty. ■

FERNANDO VIÑA

2B • BL • TR • 5'9 • 170 • 27 • NYN90/9

	AB	R	H	2B	3B	HR	RBI	BB	SO	SB	CS	BA	OB	SA
NYN94	124	20	31	6	0	0	6	12	11	3	1	.250	.372	.298
MIL95	288	46	74	7	7	3	29	22	28	6	3	.257	.327	.361
MIL96	554	94	157	19	10	7	46	38	35	16	7	.283	.342	.392
CAREER	1011	165	272	34	17	10	83	76	77	31	11	.269	.341	.366

Vina happens to be an excellent defensive second baseman when he's not brainlocked and standing in the basepath in front of Albert Belle. In addition, he posted his best offensive numbers last year, hitting for average with some power and speed. Viña split time with Mark Loretta last year and may receive some pressure for the job. Loretta's naturally a shortstop, but after Valentin's year at the plate in '96 and his three year deal, it may be difficult to get him out of the lineup. Viña's a tough competitor. If he can survive an elbow that made NHL defensemen cringe, the sight of Mark Loretta in his rearview mirror shouldn't be too much of a concern. ■

TURNER WARD

OF • BB • TR • 6'2 • 200 • 31 • NYA86/18

	AB	R	H	2B	3B	HR	RBI	BB	SO	SB	CS	BA	OB	SA
MIL94	367	55	85	15	2	9	45	52	68	6	2	.232	.328	.357
MIL95	129	19	34	3	1	4	16	14	21	6	1	.264	.338	.395
MIL96	67	7	12	2	1	2	10	13	17	3	0	.179	.309	.328
CAREER	918	130	216	36	7	21	119	120	162	21	7	.235	.324	.358

For the second straight year, Ward lost a good part of the season to the disabled list. Last year it was a shoulder injury; in '95 it was a hamstring. He started the year as a backup in the outfield, and the Brewers have added new young talent out there. He's probably reaching the end of the road—which is exactly where Dante Bichette was in Milwaukee 5 years ago. The Rockies will eventually figure out that they can pick a Turner Ward off the scrap heap and get a reasonable facsimile of Bichette's numbers at a fraction of the price and without that annoying smirk and bad hair. Ward just happened to struggle in Milwaukee a few years too late. ■

BOB WICKMAN

RP • BR • TR • 6'1 • 205 • 28 • CHA90/2

	G	GS	IP	H	HR	BB	K	W	L	S	ERA	K/BB	K9	HW9
NYA94	53	0	70	54	3	27	56	5	4	6	3.09	2.1	7.2	10.41
NYA95	63	1	80	77	6	33	51	2	4	1	4.05	1.5	5.7	12.38
NYA/MIL96	70	0	95	106	10	44	75	7	1	0	4.45	1.7	7.1	14.20
CAREER	235	28	435	444	34	193	273	34	14	11	4.18	1.4	5.6	13.18

Wickman came over to the Brewers at the end of August in the messy Listach trade, and was about the only healthy player in the whole deal. He was competent for the Yankees and provided many solid innings for them. Before this year he had a 27-13 record and a 4.10 career ERA in 4 seasons. He began his career as a starter, but had been used in long relief the past few seasons. He gets his strikeouts, has good control, and induces a lot of ground balls with his hard sinker. ■

GERALD WILLIAMS

OF • BR • TR • 6'2 • 190 • 30 • NYA87/12

	AB	R	H	2B	3B	HR	RBI	BB	SO	SB	CS	BA	OB	SA
NYA94	86	19	25	8	0	4	13	4	17	1	3	.291	.319	.523
NYA95	182	33	45	18	2	6	28	22	34	4	2	.247	.327	.467
NYA/MIL96	325	43	82	19	4	5	34	19	57	10	9	.252	.299	.382
CAREER	687	113	170	49	9	18	87	46	125	19	14	.247	.298	.424

The second-best Williams on the team, Gerald got off to a torrid start for the Yanks last year; through June 2 he was hitting .328 and slugging .555. But by mid-August he'd faded, and New York unloaded him for Listach. A longtime prospect who rarely got playing time, Williams had provided solid backup for a couple of years before briefly taking over the everyday role in left field in New York after Raines went down and before Straw showed up. He did the same in Milwaukee, taking over for the injured Chuckie Carr in center, although he missed a few games himself with a strained shoulder. Defensively, he has good range and has proven he can play in the majors. But he's never shown much at the plate, and was miserable with the bat for the Brewers when he finally got his chance to play regularly. He's already 30 and Yankee GM Bob Watson maintained he wasn't an everyday player while Williams was still on his team, so perhaps the Brewers are expecting too much from him. He has little power and he hasn't made much use of his speed in the

past, though Buck Showalter wasn't known for being a big fan of the stolen base. Under Garner his stolen bases could go up dramatically—if he's playing. ■

ANTONE WILLIAMSON

SLEEPER

1B-DH • BL • TR • 6′1 • 195 • 23 • MIL94/1

	AB	R	H	2B	3B	HR	RBI	BB	SO	SB	CS	BA	OB	SA
AAA	199	23	52	10	1	5	23	19	40	1	0	.261	.326	.397

Williamson has had a rough couple of years since Milwaukee made him their no. 1 pick in '94. He had rotator-cuff inflammation during the Arizona Fall League season in '95, then had arthroscopic surgery to repair a torn labrum in his left shoulder in '96. He then injured his shoulder making a diving stop in a minor-league exhibition game. He's pretty poor defensively at third and the Brewers moved him to first at New Orleans because they were so impressed with Jeff Cirillo's play. Apparently he wasn't so handy there either, because by the end of the season they were using him at DH. Still, he has a sweet swing and seemed to be recovering fine at the plate. Without a glove, though, it may be hard to find a spot in Milwaukee. It remains to be seen if he'll ever be as good as first thought. ■

■ 1996 AUTOPSY

The Twins were the worst team in baseball in '95—but, based on their recent history, that just meant they had a chance to win it all. The front office had been able to buy free agents without bankrupting the team. Paul Molitor had decided to chase 3,000 hits in his hometown. Roberto Kelly was expected to compete with Richie Becker in center. Rick Aguilera had returned, this time as a starter, and was expected to lend veteran poise to the pitching staff. Catcher Greg Myers added experience and a left-handed bat, and Dave Hollins would fill the gap at third until Todd Walker was ready.

But the club was sent reeling 5 days before the season opener when Aguilera developed tendinitis in his throwing arm after lifting a suitcase for his wife. The next day, Puckett woke up with blurred vision. No one knew how long either affliction would last, but both players began the season on the disabled list. The question marks that had already existed were now even more glaring, and the glass was suddenly half-empty. They entered the season needing big contributions from new players and role players.

April 13-12 (13-12, 3½ games back)
For the first time in 6 years, Kevin Tapani didn't take the mound in Minnesota's opener. Instead, Brad Radke got the nod and threw a quality start. Radke would go on to win his first 3 starts, then drop 16 of his next 24 decisions. Frankie Rodriguez was inconsistent. Rich Robertson and LaTroy Hawkins never got it going—combined they were 1-4 with a 6.45 ERA for the month. Dave Stevens saved 5 games, but looked shaky with a 6.48 ERA. Marty Cordova's month made his '95 season look like a warm-up; he hit .403 and slugged .642 with 18 RBI. Chuck Knoblauch played like the All-Star he was and Scott Stahoviak also got off to a good start, easing the club's concerns about first base. The club played well enough to stay above .500 without Puckett and Aguilera. All they had to do was hold it together until they returned.

May 10-16 (23-28, 11½ games back)
The news on Puckett was promising, and it looked like he might return in early June, but Aguilera continued to experience soreness in his rehab starts in Fort Myers. Meanwhile, the club went into a tailspin early in the month. They endured a stretch in which they lost 14 of 19 against California, Milwaukee, Seattle, and Toronto. Rodriguez and Radke both saw good outings slip away, and Robertson contributed, but none of the other starters did. The club gave up on LaTroy Hawkins for the second straight year and sent him down on the 14th. On the bright side, Greg Myers was looking like a solid acquisition as he hit .321 for the month. But the team as a whole slumped horribly. They hit .254 and managed only 97 runs, compared to 175 in April. Not coincidentally, Knoblauch had suffered a fractured knuckle on his left hand and missed several games during the stretch. Already, Cleveland was pulling out of reach.

June 15-13 (38-41 10½ games back)
Puckett underwent his third laser surgery on the 17th, and the doctors didn't expect him to return until August. The club began to seriously contemplate life without him. At least Aguilera was back. His first start was a nightmare, but in the next 3, he allowed 4 runs in 22.1 innings. The Twins won 8 of 10 games against Texas, California, and Oakland. Rodriguez, Robertson, and newcomer Scott Aldred each had 3 quality starts. Aldred would go on to win his first 3 starts for the Twins. Dave Stevens went down with a nerve problem in his elbow, however, and the club began using everyone short of Ron Davis and Doug Corbett to close games.

The offense recovered nicely from its May vacation, hitting .300 and scoring 151 runs. Marty Cordova enjoyed a 23-game hitting streak. For the month, he hit .348 with 2 homers and 22 RBI. Greg Myers continued to hit, and Molitor reached 100 hits. Matt Lawton finally found his bat and was poised to take over right field. The club cooled off later in the month but still played over .500. They weren't gaining any ground on the Indians, but they could entertain wild-card possibilities.

July 13-14 (51-55, 13½ games back)
On the 12th, Kirby Puckett announced his retirement. The latest operation had revealed irreversible damage to his retina. Further, he had glaucoma in both eyes. He retired with a .318 career batting average, 2,304 hits, 207 homers,

1,085 RBI, and 2 World Series titles in his 12 seasons, all with the Twins. On the field, the Twins continued to play .500 ball. The starting rotation was roughed up all month, and the staff had their worst month, with a 6.45 ERA. But the run production was often enough to overcome the deficits. They hit .299, including 69 doubles, and scored 171 runs. Knoblauch hit .402 and scored 40 runs. Dave Stevens found himself back on the disabled list after slicing open his hand punching a wall after blowing a save.

August 16-14 (67-69 13½ games back)
The Twins still weren't out of the race, and they did their best in August to climb back in it. The club won 10 of 11 against California, Oakland, and Toronto in one stretch. Toward the end of the month they were within 3½ games of the wild-card slot. The rotation was a big part of the surge. Aldred, Aguilera, Radke, and Rodriguez combined were 9-5 with a 3.25 ERA. The offense continued to hum, equaling their production in July. Although they weren't given serious consideration by the news media, they were within striking distance, and the team was playing its best ball since April. The biggest news of the month, though, was the 5-year contract Knoblauch signed with club. There had been speculation that he might test the free-agent market. The Twins were now assured that their best player would be around for a long time.

September 11-15 (78-84) 21½ games back
The month started well; they won 7 of 10 against Texas, California, and Oakland. But unfortunately, only so many games can be played against California and Oakland. The remainder of the month included series with Chicago, Cleveland, and Seattle. All three were playoff contenders, and they proved to be too much for the Twins, who dropped 12 of 16 games. It was a disappointing finish, but there were some bright spots. Marty Cordova proved he was no fluke. Paul Molitor reached 3,000 hits on the 18th in Kansas City. The team also set several club records, including highest batting average and most runs scored.

■ 1997 DIAGNOSIS

Offense
They don't call it The Homerdome for nothing; homers were up 12% (and triples up 10% presumably because nothing in the minors, legion ball, high school, Little League, or t-ball prepares someone for playing fly balls off of a Baggie). The Metrodome is a slugger's paradise, but the Twins haven't had a big basher to take advantage of it since Kent Hrbek retired. The Twins offense set several club records last year—batting average, .288; runs scored, 877; hits, 1,633; and doubles, 332—but dingers weren't one of the categories. They were dead last in home runs and 11th in slugging average—which explains why they finished 8th in runs scored. Take away the effect of playing in the Homerdome and they were about 30 runs below the average American League team.

Knoblauch and Molitor were major contributors, but they both had monster years last year and may not be able to repeat them. Marty Cordova could give them a lift if the power he showed in '95 returns. If Todd Walker turns it on in his rookie season, that would change the entire dynamic. But the rest of the offense is made up of decent hitters with moderate or little power—which might work in the NL in 1988, but not in the AL in 1997. Their team speed has improved, but the Twins need to add a slugger to their lineup. They may find help in the free-agent market, or they could look to the farm. Jamie Ogden and Ryan Radmanovich both have excellent power and may be ready to contribute.

Defense
The right side of the infield is solid. Knoblauch is one of the best-fielding second basemen in the game, and both Scott Stahoviak and Ron Coomer handle first well. The left side is a bigger concern. Pat Meares committed 22 errors at short last year, the second-highest total in the A.L. He led the league in '95 with 18. Todd Walker is a natural second baseman playing third, and the club sent him to the Florida Instructional League to work on his defense. Marty Cordova is outstanding in left and getting better. Richie Becker has excellent range

in center and a good arm. He had 18 assists and started 9 double plays last year while making only 3 errors! Roberto Kelly will be back with a year of playing the baggie under his belt. Greg Myers is adequate behind the plate, and was sorely missed in California where adequacy would have been a nice change of pace.

Pitching

The starting rotation improved last year over their performance in '95. But then, the Twins had the worst staff in baseball in '95. In '96 they finished with a 5.48 ERA, 10th in the league. They had 583 strikeouts (10th), but they at least threw strikes (343 walks, 4th in the league). Radke and Rodriguez emerged as legitimate starters who should continue to improve. Rick Aguilera may or may not return to the rotation and is probably more effective out of the bullpen anyway. LaTroy Hawkins has been unsuccessful in the major leagues for 2 straight years and it could be joker, joker, and a triple in '97. Travis Miller, Dan Serafini, and Mark Redman are all excellent prospects who could find themselves thrown to the wolves.

The bullpen was busy last year. They pitched 514 innings, the 5th-highest total in the league. They went 31-16 despite a 4.97 ERA. They recorded just 31 saves, with only Detroit earning fewer. Dave Stevens had trouble with injuries and his temper, but even when healthy and composed he wasn't dominant. Mike Trombley and Dan Naulty pitched very well and will be back this year, though Naulty is more likely to be the one who gets the chance to blow the saves.

Farm System

The Twins have done quite well with their 1st-round draft picks in recent years, and they are close to paying dividends. Dan Serafini has 4 good pitches and is ready to contribute this year. Todd Walker is considered one of the best-hitting prospects in baseball and will start at third. Travis Miller has an excellent slider and mechanics and already had 7 starts last year. Mark Redman is a finesse pitcher who gets a lot out of his change-up. And there are plenty of lower-round picks who are ready to contribute.

Management and Ownership

Carl Pohlad began to turn some of the management duties over to his sons Bob, Bill, and Jim last year. Pohlad is 81, and the way his team seems to slam from worst to first and back again every other year, rattling off the walls like the Jamaican bobsled team, can't be good for the ticker. How this affects the management of the team remains to be seen.

The owners opened up the pocketbooks to sign free agents. More importantly, they gave Chuck Knoblauch a deal he deserved, securing a superstar player and team leader for years to come. They are now gearing up for the battle to acquire a new stadium, one with a retractable dome—and with a right-field wall. Signing Knoblauch was a key move in that drive, indicating to their supporters their commitment to field a winning team.

GM Terry Ryan signed good players last year at reasonable prices. He put an improved club on the field despite the loss of Kirby Puckett. And the Twins could soon see a wave of talent arrive from the minor leagues. The farm system is stocked with talent and, with the possible exception of LaTroy Hawkins, their prospects have been handled very well. Ryan will be tested in the free-agent market this year. The Twins still have holes to fill to reach the next level.

Tom Kelly remains one of the most respected and admired managers in the game. And with the resignation of Jim Leyland last year, he has now been with his current team longer than any other head man in professional sports (which assumes you consider Nebraska football players to be "amateurs"). Kelly had to deal with Puckett's loss more directly than anyone, and still managed to field an improved team that finished just under .500. Considering the adversity they faced in '96, and after being the worst team in baseball in '95, any success was remarkable. Kelly now has to develop some new young talent. The makeup of his team has changed a great deal in the past few years. He has the composure to do it. This, after all, is the man who let Jack Morris talk him into letting him pitch the 10th inning of Game 7 against the Braves in '91, shrugging and saying, "It's just a game."

. . . and whatnot: Kirby Baseball

With only 12 seasons in the big leagues, Kirby Puckett's Hall of Fame induction is likely but not a given. Consider the career length of the hitters inducted into the Hall by the BBWAA in the past 20 years: Mike Schmidt (18), Reggie Jackson (21), Rod Carew (19), Joe Morgan (22), Johnny Bench (17), Carl Yastrzemski (23), Willie Stargell (21), Billy Williams (18), Willie McCovey (22), Lou Brock (19), Luis Aparicio (18), Harmon Killebrew (22), Brooks Robinson (23), Hank Aaron (23), Frank Robinson (21), Al Kaline (22), Duke Snider (18), Willie Mays (22), Eddie Mathews (17), and Ernie Banks (19). The baseball writers haven't inducted a hitter with as few big-league seasons as Puckett since Ralph Kiner (10) in 1975.

They probably will elect Puckett a year after Alam Trammell (20) and Ozzie Smith (19), in his second year of eligiblity—if for no other reason than his wonderful personality. The case can certainly be made for him: five 200+ hit seasons, eight .300+ seasons, three 100+ RBI seasons, a batting title, six gold gloves, two 6-hit games, .308 in the post-season, and two rings. He will likely get in before two players who had longer careers but didn't smile as much: Tony Perez (23) and Andre Dawson (21). Compare the statistics.

Player	G	H	HR	RBI	R	BA	SA	Rings
Puckett	1783	2304	207	1085	1071	.318	.477	2
Dawson	2627	2774	438	1591	1373	.279	.482	0
Perez	2777	2732	379	1652	1272	.279	.463	2

Electing Puckett before Dawson, while continuing to ignore Perez, would represent a significant shift in the baseball writers' opinion of a Hall of Famer. Yet they didn't give even halfhearted consideration to someone who had a lot in common with Puckett. The heart and soul of a ballclub that won 2 World Series. He hit well over .300 in the postseason. He batted .300 three times and knocked in 100 runs three times. He was a great defensive player early in his career. He wasn't built like a ballplayer, but he sure played like one. He won an MVP award—which Kirby never did—but he did more than his share of glowering at the media. And his career was cut short too soon as well.

They'll set a nice precedent when they elect Kirby Puckett.

Too bad they didn't do it first with Thurman Munson.

RICK AGUILERA

SP • BR • TR • 6'5 • 200 • NYN83/5

	G	GS	IP	H	HR	BB	K	W	L	S	ERA	K/BB	K9	HW9
MIN94	44	0	44	57	7	10	46	1	4	23	3.63	4.6	9.4	13.68
BOS/MIN95	52	0	55	46	6	13	52	3	3	32	2.60	4.0	8.5	9.65
MIN96	19	19	111	124	20	27	83	8	6	0	5.42	3.1	6.7	12.24
CAREER	488	89	1033	992	102	284	822	67	62	211	3.48	2.9	7.2	11.12

Aguilera's return to Minnesota was one of the more interesting stories early in the season. Despite his undisputed effectiveness out of the bullpen, the Twins wanted him to bolster the rotation. An integral part of the Twins' 1991 championship team, he was anxious to return and agreed to the experiment.

Aguilera wasn't overmatched, but he's seen better seasons. Injuries had a lot to do with that. He battled tendinitis in his wrist early in the season and suffered a hamstring injury September 7—ironically, this was the night the Twins honored Kirby Puckett before a sellout crowd. The control was still there; he didn't allow many walks and had a good strikeout rate. But he was definitely hittable and averaged only 5.9 innings per start.

Perhaps that can be attributed to the injuries or a readjustment period. The Twins' success in the free-agent market will determine Aguilera's role this year. If they can't land a starter, he'll be back in the rotation. But no one emerged as dominant from the closing committee last year. The club will have higher expectations for '97 and may not want to roll the dice with a young and inconsistent closer. It may be just a coincidence, but Aguilera has been more susceptible to injury as a starter. ■

SCOTT ALDRED

SP-RP • BL • TL • 6′4 • 215 • 28

	G	GS	IP	H	HR	BB	K	W	L	S	ERA	K/BB	K9	HW9
DET/MIN96	36	25	165	194	29	68	111	6	9	0	6.22	1.6	6.1	14.29

Aldred struggled early in the season for the Tigers. In fact, he started 2 games against the Twins, in which they ended up scoring a combined 27 runs. Go figure; Minnesota claimed him off waivers May 28 from the Tigers when he was 0-4 with a 9.35 ERA. He pitched 4.2 scoreless innings out of the bullpen in his debut and started 17 games for the Twins, going 6-5 with a 5.09 ERA. That's not great, but adjusting for the park, that's above average. After years of riding the shuttle between Detroit and Triple-A Toledo, he appears to have found a home. ■

CHAD ALLEN — SLEEPER

OF • MIN96/4 • TEXAS A&M UNIVERSITY

Allen has a reputation as kind of a head case, but he has excellent speed and a good arm. He was also a fine college hitter. He was slowed in his last college season by a bout with mononucleosis, but recovered well enough to hit .403 for Team USA last summer. Then he strained a quadriceps muscle in his second game for Fort Myers, forcing him out for the season. If he can keep it on the rails, he could be a solid no. 2 hitter. ■

RAFAEL ALVAREZ — SOLID PROSPECT

OF • BL • TL • 5′11 • 160 • 20

	AB	R	H	2B	3B	HR	RBI	BB	SO	SB	CS	BA	OB	SA
A	473	61	143	30	7	4	58	43	55	11	9	.302	.363	.421

Alvarez was voted the best defensive outfielder in the Midwest League and had a good year at the plate. After a couple of productive seasons in Fort Wayne, he got a look a brief look at the Florida State League, where he'll start this season. He's got moderate gap power and excellent plate discipline. He can also hit for average and has decent speed. ■

DAVID ARIAS — SOLID PROSPECT

1B • BL• TL • 6′4 • 230 • 21

	AB	R	H	2B	3B	HR	RBI	BB	SO	SB	CS	BA	OB	SA
A	487	89	156	34	2	18	93	52	108	3	4	.320	.389	.509

Arias, who was traded to the Twins from Seattle in the Hollins deal, took a giant leap forward in '96. He's a fine hitter and was voted most exciting player in Midwest League and best defensive first baseman—a pretty rare combo, as Mike Squires, Mike Jorgensen, and Jim Spencer can attest. For whatever reason, it usually doesn't get much duller than a slick-fielding first baseman. ■

MARC BARCELO — SLEEPER

SP • BR • TR • 6′3 • 210 • 25 • MIN93/3

	G	GS	IP	H	HR	BB	SO	W	L	S	ERA	K/BB	K9	HW9
AA	14	13	80	98	7	38	59	3	8	0	5.06	1.6	6.6	15.30

After cruising through the lower levels, Barcelo got rocked in Salt Lake City in '95 and early '96, earning himself another tour through Double-A. He struggled there as well. He was the Twins' "sandwich pick" between the 1st and 2nd round in the '93 draft (compensation for losing John Smiley to free agency), and he looked promising in the Southern League. He has a good fastball and change-up plus a hard slider. There are some real questions about his toughness, though, and he may just need to work on the mental aspect of the game. Right now, to quote Bogie, when he gets slapped he's taking it and liking it. ■

RICH BECKER — YOUNG GUN

OF • BL • TR • 5′10 • 180 • 25 • MIN90/6

	AB	R	H	2B	3B	HR	RBI	BB	SO	SB	CS	BA	OB	SA
MIN94	98	12	26	3	0	1	8	13	25	6	1	.265	.351	.327
MIN95	392	45	93	15	1	2	33	34	95	8	9	.237	.303	.296
MIN96	525	92	153	31	4	12	71	68	118	19	5	.291	.372	.434
CAREER	1022	152	274	51	5	15	112	120	242	34	16	.268	.347	.372

The minor leagues never held much challenge for Becker, but his stints with the Twins in the past 3 years have been more difficult. He stopped switch-hitting in spring training to concentrate on the left side, but his troubles continued early in the season. Through May 19 he was hitting .176, and Roberto Kelly was getting most of

the time in center. But by midseason, Becker had turned that around and established himself as the Twins' center fielder. If you take out his April-May slump, he hit .316 with a .389 on-base average and was 15 for 18 in stolen bases. Becker has good speed and range plus decent power. His minor-league career suggests that the latter part of last season is more indicative of his ability and that he can sustain that kind of production. ■

JASON BELL

SOLID PROSPECT

SP • BR • TR • 6'3 • 205 • 22 • MIN95/2

	G	GS	IP	H	HR	BB	SO	W	L	S	ERA	K/BB	K9	HW9
AA	16	16	94	93	13	38	94	2	6	0	4.4	2.5	9.0	12.54

Bell was an All-American right-hander at Oklahoma State. He's been phenomenal in Class-A over the past 2 years with a 9-4 record and a 1.59 ERA in 124.1 innings. He pitched well in Double-A as well last year. He throws a solid fastball, slider, and change-up. His coaches like his mechanics and excellent command. He's also not afraid to pitch inside. To top it off, he has a reputation as a very good fielder. He is progressing quickly and could be ready to contribute, possibly by this season. ■

BRENT BREDE

SOLID PROSPECT

OF • BL • TL • 6'4 • 190 • 25

	AB	R	H	2B	3B	HR	RBI	BB	SO	SB	CS	BA	OB	SA
AAA	483	102	168	38	8	11	86	87	87	14	6	.348	.446	.528

Brede nearly won the batting title, losing by .003 to teammate Brian Raabe last year. Of the two, Raabe has more power, but with 87 walks, Brede's .447 on-base average left him at the curb. He's also 4 years younger. Brede has good gap power of his own, plate discipline, and fine speed. Bringing back Roberto Kelly for another year may indicate that the Twins don't think he's ready yet. ■

RON COOMER

1B-OF • BR • TR • 5'11 • 195 • 30 • OAK87/13

	AB	R	H	2B	3B	HR	RBI	BB	SO	SB	CS	BA	OB	SA
MIN95	101	15	26	3	1	5	19	9	11	0	1	.257	.324	.455
MIN96	233	34	69	12	1	12	41	17	24	3	0	.296	.340	.511

Coomer was a 30-year-old rookie last year and made the most of what may have been his last shot.

He's naturally a third baseman, but he saw only 9 games there last year. And with the arrival of Todd Walker, his time there may be over. But he proved his versatility filling in at first and in right field—which looks to be his role this year, barring a major free-agent signing. ■

MARTY CORDOVA

YOUNG GUN

LF • BR • TR • 6'0 • 200 • 27 • MIN89/10

	AB	R	H	2B	3B	HR	RBI	BB	SO	SB	CS	BA	OB	SA
MIN95	512	81	142	27	4	24	84	52	111	20	7	.277	.352	.486
MIN96	569	97	176	46	1	16	111	53	96	11	5	.309	.371	.478

Sophomore jinx? Cordova, the 1995 Rookie of the Year, put those concerns to rest and cemented his position as the Twins' left fielder. Though his homer production slipped, he still led the team with 16 and set a club record for doubles with 46. Taking over the cleanup slot in Puckett's absence, he raised his batting average 32 points and turned in the first of what may be many 100+ RBI seasons. The Twins also have been surprised and pleased to see him already become a clubhouse leader at his age. He has an excellent work ethic and power to all fields—a combo that shouldn't be as rare as it is. He's one of the best-kept secrets in baseball. ■

MIKE DURANT

C • BR • TR • 6'2 • 200 • 27 • MIN91/3

	AB	R	H	2B	3B	HR	RBI	BB	SO	SB	CS	BA	OB	SA
MIN96	81	15	17	3	0	0	5	10	15	3	0	.210	.293	.247

A wrist injury to Matt Walbeck gave Durant a chance to play early in the season. He went 3-for-4 in his debut against the Tigers, but his bat cooled after that, and he was sent down in mid-June. He had a solid year at Salt Lake City and could be a decent hitter, though without much power. The job is still open—no one's been a fixture behind the plate in Minnesota since Butch Wynegar. ■

EDDIE GUARDADO

RP • BR • TL • 6′0 • 190 • 26 • MIN90/24

	G	GS	IP	H	HR	BB	K	W	L	S	ERA	K/BB	K9	HW9
MIN94	4	4	17	26	3	4	8	0	2	0	8.47	2.0	4.2	15.88
MIN95	51	5	91	99	13	45	71	4	9	2	5.12	1.6	7.0	14.24
MIN96	83	0	73	61	12	33	74	6	5	4	5.25	2.2	9.1	11.58
CAREER	157	25	276	309	41	118	199	13	24	6	5.74	1.7	6.5	13.92

Once touted as the Twins' lefty starter of the future, Guardado has settled into the role of bullpen workhorse and fan favorite. He's been compared to Al Hrabosky, the Mad Hungarian, because he likes to strut to the mound, talk to himself, and spike his rosin bag. Don't let the ERA fool you—Guardado had an excellent strikeout rate and didn't give up many hits. He throws a 90+ fastball, hard slider, and curveball, and is working on a split-finger pitch. With continued improvement he could find himself back in the rotation. For now, the Twins need his reliability in the bullpen. ■

LATROY HAWKINS

SLEEPER

SP • BR • TR • 6′5 • 195 • 24 • MIN91/8

	G	GS	IP	H	HR	BB	K	W	L	S	ERA	K/BB	K9	HW9
MIN95	6	6	27	39	3	12	9	2	3	0	8.67	.8	3.0	17.00
MIN96	7	6	26	42	8	9	24	1	1	0	8.20	2.7	8.3	17.63

For the second straight year, Hawkins was shelled in the majors. A top prospect since his 15-5 season in the Midwest League in 1993, he's had trouble making the jump to the majors. He complained publicly about the way the Twins have handled him, and said he didn't think he'd ever pitch in the majors for the organization again. He has been moved up rapidly through the system—perhaps too rapidly. Hawkins can become a no. 1 starter. His fastball is quite good for a lefty, with both velocity and movement. He had lost velocity in recent years and his strikeout rate suffered, but he reportedly regained it in the spring of '96 by remaining more upright in his delivery. He also has a good curveball and slider with deceptive motion. There's too much potential here for the Twins to pass up. He'll get another shot in '97. ■

DENNY HOCKING

OF • BB • TR • 5′10 • 180 • 26 • MIN89/52

	AB	R	H	2B	3B	HR	RBI	BB	SO	SB	CS	BA	OB	SA
MIN96	127	16	25	6	0	1	10	8	24	3	3	.197	.243	.268

What a brutal year! Once a top prospect, Hocking was poised to get serious time at short last year when a José Canseco one-hop smash crushed his jaw in the preseason. The drive also lacerated his tongue and knocked out a tooth. Problems with a hernia followed, and he ended up on the DL most of the year. When he did play, he was just one of the guys replacing Puckett in right. But he did look good at Salt Lake City's and he's not out of chances. He's still got a good glove and is decent at the plate, but he's starting to look more like a utility infielder. ■

TORII HUNTER

OF • BR • TR • 6′2 • 205 • 21 • MIN93/1

	AB	R	H	2B	3B	HR	RBI	BB	SO	SB	CS	BA	OB	SA
AA	342	49	90	20	3	7	33	28	60	7	7	.263	.331	.401

Hunter was a teammate of Basil Shabazz, the Cardinals' failed attempt to make a ballplayer out of a superb athlete with a great name. There may be some parallels. Defensively, Torii has a fine arm and very good range. He's very fast, but it doesn't make him a very good baserunner. He also hasn't done much at the plate in the past 2 seasons, hitting for low average with little power. But he's young, in Double-A, and has time to learn how to hit better than Tori Spelling. ■

J. J. JOHNSON

OF • BR • TR • 6′0 • 195 • 23 • BOS91/2

	AB	R	H	2B	3B	HR	RBI	BB	SO	SB	CS	BA	OB	SA
AA	440	62	120	23	3	16	59	40	90	10	11	.273	.341	.448

It took almost 4 years in the minors for Johnson to hit his first 16 homers. He equaled that last year in Double-A and had an impressive stint in Triple-A Salt Lake City. He's shown considerable improvement in the past 2 years, despite the distraction of being the "future consideration" in the trade for Rick Aguilera. His batting average has risen along with his power numbers, which is a very good sign. ■

JACQUE JONES

OF • MIN96/2 • USC

Jones starred for USC and hit .404 for Team USA. In his first game for Class-A Fort Myers, he tripled, doubled, stole a base . . . and sprained his knee, ending a long summer. He's an above-average hitter with moderate power and decent speed. He's also a good defender, although his arm isn't very strong. Some scouts question his power and speed, and are concerned that he won't be able to hit for a high enough average to offset these deficiencies. The power can develop, though, and his 15 home runs last summer were encouraging. ■

ROBERTO KELLY

OF • BR • TR • 6'4 • 185 • NYA82

	AB	R	H	2B	3B	HR	RBI	BB	SO	SB	CS	BA	OB	SA
ATL/CIN94	434	73	127	23	2	9	45	35	71	19	11	.293	.347	.417
MON/LA95	504	58	140	23	2	7	57	22	79	19	10	.278	.312	.373
MIN96	322	41	104	17	4	6	47	23	53	10	2	.323	.375	.457
CAREER	3857	536	1110	190	24	87	442	265	686	220	76	.288	.337	.417

Kelly signed a 1-year deal with the Twins last season, his 5th team in 3 years—a long way from the Yankees "mortgaging their future" to acquire Paul O'Neill. That's a lot of movement for a 2-time All-Star with a .285 career batting average still playing quality defense. Predictably, he turned in another solid year, primarily in the right-field mix and backing up center. Right field is one of the Twins' major concerns, and Kelly played well there for them last year and could handle the job if given it. He's not the long-term answer, but he probably doesn't care; it must just be nice not to spend 2 years in the same city. ■

SCOTT KLINGENBECK

RP-SP • BR • TR • 6'2 • 205 • 26 • BAL92/5

	G	GS	IP	H	HR	BB	K	W	L	S	ERA	K/BB	K9	HW9
BAL/MIN95	24	9	79	101	22	42	42	2	4	0	7.12	1.0	4.8	16.29
MIN96	10	3	28	42	5	10	15	1	1	0	7.85	1.5	4.8	16.67
CAREER	35	13	114	149	28	56	62	4	5	0	7.18	1.1	4.9	16.17

After throwing 3 straight complete games for Salt Lake City last year, Klingenbeck was called up in early August. Three starts with an 11.12 ERA later, they optioned him to Salt Lake City again. Actually, he was up 4 times last year, working mostly from the bullpen. He was more effective in relief, but that is certainly a relative term—for the season he allowed 42 hits in 28.2 innings. Klingenbeck complained that the Twins haven't given him a chance since coming over from Baltimore in the '95 Erickson trade. He's asked for another trade so he can pitch. He has been a promising prospect in the past, but given his current attitude and production, they may want to oblige him. ■

CHUCK KNOBLAUCH

AL ELITE

2B • BR • TR • 5'9 • 175 • 28 • MIN89/1

	AB	R	H	2B	3B	HR	RBI	BB	SO	SB	CS	BA	OB	SA
MIN94	445	85	139	45	3	5	51	41	56	35	6	.312	.381	.461
MIN95	538	107	179	34	8	11	63	78	95	46	18	.333	.424	.487
MIN96	578	140	197	35	14	13	72	98	74	45	14	.341	.448	.517
CAREER	3328	596	1019	184	41	34	333	429	369	214	67	.306	.391	.417

There was much media speculation last season about Knoblauch's future, the fire fueled by a few hints dropped by Chuck himself. All that ended when the Twins resigned him for 5 years at $30 million, the kind of contract the Twins usually reserve for the Kirby Pucketts of the world—and the Yankees dish out to the Kenny Rogerses of the world. Simply put, Knoblauch was as important to the Twins as any player was to his club last year, and his only competition for best second baseman on the planet is Robbie Alomar. Here are their numbers for the past 3 years:

Player	AB	R	H	D	HR	RBI	BB	SB	BA	OBP
Knoblauch	1,561	332	515	114	29	186	217	126	.330	.412
Alomar	1,497	281	468	113	43	198	188	66	.313	.389

Not a whole lot of difference. Both are top defenders and major contributors at the plate. Alomar's stats were boosted by playing for a year in Camden Yards for Baltimore's high-powered offense, an even more favorable environment than the Homerdome. Alomar has more power, but Knoblauch has scored more runs and knocked in nearly as many. Alomar is the flashier defender and can make some stunning plays, but Knoblauch makes all the routine plays all the time. And, like a true ballplayer, he spits only on his own shoes. The Twins' money was well spent. ■

RYAN LANE — SLEEPER

2B-SS • BR • TR • 6'1 • 175 • 22 • MIN93/8

	AB	R	H	2B	3B	HR	RBI	BB	SO	SB	CS	BA	OB	SA
AA	117	13	26	5	1	2	12	8	29	3	4	.222	.270	.333

Lane can play second or short and had a solid season at the plate at Fort Myers. He was equally impressive in '95 for Fort Wayne. He has excellent power for a middle infielder and great speed. These attributes, plus good plate discipline, make him the best shortstop prospect in the Twins' organization. He's still a few years away, but he could develop into an everyday big-leaguer, and there's not much in his way at the moment. ■

CHRIS LATHAM — SOLID PROSPECT

OF • BR • TR • 6'0 • 190 • 23

	AB	R	H	2B	3B	HR	RBI	BB	SO	SB	CS	BA	OB	SA
AAA	376	59	103	16	6	9	50	36	91	26	9	.274	.338	.420

Latham was one of many players who came over to the Twins from the Dodgers in the '95 Kevin Tapani/Mark Guthrie trade. He was selected the most exciting player in the Florida State League in '95 before the trade, and the Twins were satisfied with his production at Salt Lake City. He's a solid switch-hitter with moderate power and outstanding speed. In the outfield he possesses all the tools except a strong arm. ■

MATT LAWTON — SLEEPER

OF • BL • TR • 5'9 • 180 • 25 • MIN91/14

	AB	R	H	2B	3B	HR	RBI	BB	SO	SB	CS	BA	OB	SA
MIN95	60	11	19	4	1	1	12	7	11	1	1	.317	.414	.467
MIN96	252	34	65	7	1	6	42	28	28	4	4	.258	.339	.365

After an impressive showing in the '95 Arizona Fall League, Lawton seemed ready to make a run at the center-field spot in the spring. That didn't happen, and he spent the first half of the season bouncing between Minnesota and Salt Lake City. With right field still unsettled at midseason, he got his chance and ended up playing more games there than any other Twin. He didn't exactly light it up at the plate, but his minor-league stats suggests he can be a good hitter. He's also moved up fast and needs time to adjust. Defensively, he has good range but a below-average arm. ■

PAT MEARES

SS • BR • TR • 6'0 • 185 • 28 • MIN90/15

	AB	R	H	2B	3B	HR	RBI	BB	SO	SB	CS	BA	OB	SA
MIN94	229	29	61	12	1	2	24	14	50	5	1	.266	.310	.354
MIN95	390	57	105	19	4	12	49	15	68	10	4	.269	.311	.431
MIN96	517	66	138	26	7	8	67	17	90	9	4	.267	.298	.391
CAREER	1482	185	391	71	15	22	173	53	260	28	14	.264	.296	.377

After leading A.L. shortstops with 18 errors in only 116 games in '95, Meares didn't show any improvement with 22 last year. And unlike Milwaukee's José Valentin, he didn't make up for it with a strong year at the plate. Actually, his production was about what you'd expect from an average shortstop. He even showed a little power. But he has horrible plate discipline, a problem that hasn't changed over three years with the Twins. He'll be the starter until someone better comes along—but the future will come more quickly for one of their prospects if Meares doesn't get a little less random with the glove. ■

TRAVIS MILLER

SOLID PROSPECT

SP • BR • TL • 6'3 • 205 • 24 • MIN94/2

	G	GS	IP	H	HR	BB	K	W	L	S	ERA	K/BB	K9	HW9
MIN96	7	7	26	45	7	9	15	1	2	0	9.23	1.7	5.2	18.67

Miller was impressive in spring training and almost made the club. In one spring game against the Expos, he struck out 7 in 3 innings. However the Twins wanted him to spend some time in Salt Lake City, where he continued to impress the coaching staff. He was eventually called up in late August. He has an outstanding slider, which he uses as his out pitch; a solid 90+ mph fastball; and a below-average curveball. He has excellent mechanics and a deceptive delivery. He has the kind of problem pitching coaches must like to see once in a while: He throws too many strikes. All of this didn't translate to great success in Triple-A last year or in 7 starts in the majors, but the Twins remain sold on him. ■

PAUL MOLITOR

AL ELITE

DH • BR • TR • 6'0 • 185 • 40 • MIL77/1

	AB	R	H	2B	3B	HR	RBI	BB	SO	SB	CS	BA	OB	SA
TOR94	454	86	155	30	4	14	75	55	48	20	0	.341	.410	.518
TOR95	525	63	142	31	2	15	60	61	57	12	0	.270	.350	.423
MIN96	660	99	225	41	8	9	113	56	72	18	6	.341	.390	.468
CAREER	9795	1644	3014	544	105	220	1149	1004	1130	484	125	.308	.372	.452

When Ted Williams likes you enough to compare your swing to Joe DiMaggio's, who needs 3,000 hits? Molitor decided to return to his hometown in '96 to finish out his career and try to reach that milestone. He was coming off one of his least productive years and was looking at 2 seasons to get his 3,000 hit. But Molitor missed only a single game all season and led the league with 225 hits. He became only the second player since 1950 to drive in more than 100 runs with fewer than 10 home runs (Tommy Herr knocked in 110 for the Cardinals in '85 with 8 dingers and a .302 batting average, while George Kell knocked in 101 for the Tigers in '50 with 8 dingers and a .340 batting average). And, as everyone knows, he reached 3,000 hits with a triple on September 16 against Kansas City. Probably part of the reason he's the only player to reach 3,000 with a triple is that he's one of the few who've reached that milestone without having to hang on to do it—and could get to third without needing an oxygen tank. He shouldn't be expected to repeat that kind of production this year, but if he even comes close, maybe DiMaggio will compare him to Williams—who did 29-72-.316 in his final season, at age 42. ■

GREG MYERS

C • BL • TR • 6'1 • 200 • 30 • TOR84/2

	AB	R	H	2B	3B	HR	RBI	BB	SO	SB	CS	BA	OB	SA
CAL94	126	10	31	6	0	2	8	10	27	0	2	.246	.299	.341
CAL95	273	35	71	12	2	9	38	17	49	0	1	.260	.304	.418
MIN96	329	37	94	22	3	6	47	19	52	0	0	.286	.320	.426
CAREER	1708	172	434	88	6	38	205	113	276	3	8	.254	.298	.379

Myers was the Twins' most productive catcher last year, but that's not saying much. He hit for average and did a good job stopping base stealers. He'll probably end up splitting time with whomever the Twins pick up in the off-season, and then he'll have to worry about Mike Durant. Objects in the side-view mirror, Greg, are closer than they appear. ■

DAN NAULTY

RP • BR • TR • 6'6 • 210 • 27 • MIN92/14

	G	GS	IP	H	HR	BB	K	W	L	S	ERA	K/BB	K9	HW9
MIN96	49	0	57	43	5	35	56	3	2	4	3.79	1.6	8.8	12.32

Naulty was impressive in his rookie season, especially after only a single season at Salt Lake City. He limited hitters to a .207 batting average, the best mark on the Twins' staff. Like Eddie Guardado, he had an excellent strikeout rate, but walks got him in trouble. He has a 91-mph fastball, plus a forkball and a slider. All he needs now is more experience. Naulty was shut down with a circulation problem in his pitching arm in early August, but the Twins expect him to be a big part of the bullpen this season. ■

JAMIE OGDEN

SLEEPER

1B-OF • BL • TL • 6′5 • 215 • 25

	AB	R	H	2B	3B	HR	RBI	BB	SO	SB	CS	BA	OB	SA
AAA	448	80	118	22	2	18	74	45	105	17	2	.263	.332	.442

Ogden's power has increased nicely over his 7-year minor-league career. He's also got good speed for a slugger. He can be inconsistent at the plate, and he strikes out too much. The Twins consider him a fine prospect, though, and have brought him along slowly. No one has clamped down on the first-base job, so watch what he does this spring. ■

JOSÉ PARRA

RP-SP • BR • TR • 5′11 • 160 • 24 • LA89

	G	GS	IP	H	HR	BB	K	W	L	S	ERA	K/BB	K9	HW9
LA/MIN95	20	12	72	93	13	28	36	1	5	0	7.13	1.3	4.5	15.13
MIN96	27	5	70	88	15	27	50	5	5	0	6.04	1.9	6.4	14.79

The jump to the big leagues has been difficult for Parra. He had good control in the minors but it's suffered in a couple of major-league seasons. When he does find the plate, he gets tagged. A move to the bullpen hasn't helped. Another Dodger castoff (see Greg Hansell of the Boston Red Sox), but they usually end up getting it together for someone. ■

A. J. PIERZYNSKI

SOLID PROSPECT

C • BL • TR • 6′3 • 210 • 20 • MIN94/3

	AB	R	H	2B	3B	HR	RBI	BB	SO	SB	CS	BA	OB	SA
A	431	48	118	30	3	7	70	22	53	0	4	.274	.308	.406

Pierzynski. hit .332 for rookie-league Elizabethton in ′95 and .280 with some power over 2 seasons with Class-A Fort Wayne. That's a good average in the Midwest League, and a decent number of homers for Fort Wayne. He has a fairly weak arm, but the Twins feel he's such a good hitter they may keep him at catcher. They won a World Series with Brian Harper, you'll recall. He has the skills to play elsewhere if needed. If he continues to develop, he could be a Tettleton-type player. ■

TOM QUINLAN

3B • BR • TR • 6′3 • 215 • 29

	AB	R	H	2B	3B	HR	RBI	BB	SO	SB	CS	BA	OB	SA
AAA	491	81	139	38	1	15	81	38	121	4	8	.283	.348	.456

Quinlan has always had good power, and he's improved his batting average steadily over a 10-year minor-league career. The improvement has probably come too late. He didn't come to the Twins until ′95, and Todd Walker is installed at third now. Timing, as a drummer named Pete Best could tell you, is everything. ■

BRIAN RAABE

2B • BR • TR • 5′9 • 170 • 29 • MIN90/44

	AB	R	H	2B	3B	HR	RBI	BB	SO	SB	CS	BA	OB	SA
AAA	482	103	169	39	4	18	69	47	19	8	8	.351	.410	.560

Raabe has had little trouble at the plate throughout his minor league career. Last year he won the PCL batting title and earned his second call-up in 2 years. He's got nothing left to prove in the minors, and he's getting too old to stay there. He's never had much power, but he's a good hitter with decent speed. His biggest problems now are Todd Walker and Chuck Knoblauch. ■

BRAD RADKE

YOUNG GUN

SP • BR • TR • 6′2 • 180 • 24 • MIN91/9

	G	GS	IP	H	HR	BB	K	W	L	S	ERA	K/BB	K9	HW9
MIN95	29	28	181	195	32	47	75	11	14	0	5.32	1.6	3.7	12.03
MIN96	35	35	232	231	40	57	148	11	16	0	4.46	2.6	5.7	11.17

Totally Radke's record may not show it, but he was the Twins' most effective starter. He suffered a midseason slump in June and July, during which he was 2-8 with a 5.24 ERA (which is league average when you adjust for the Homerdome). Otherwise, he was 9-8 with a 4.05 ERA and didn't get much support all year (4.9 runs per game—not much for the A.L.). He also led the team with 148 strikeouts. Radke's biggest problem remains the home run; after leading the majors in ′95 with 38 home runs allowed, he gave up 40 last year—and thinks it's funny enough that he's allowed a computer game to dis him about it in a TV commercial. Laughing all the way to the bank, it seems—though it's hard to picture Bob Gibson or Don Drysdale signing on that bottom line. Forget the record and the self-deprecating humor: Radke and Frankie Rodriguez give the Twins a couple of solid arms around which to build a rotation. ■

RYAN RADMANOVICH

SLEEPER

OF • BL • TR • 6'2 • 185 • 25

	AB	R	H	2B	3B	HR	RBI	BB	SO	SB	CS	BA	OB	SA
AA	453	77	127	31	2	25	86	49	122	4	11	.280	.353	.523

Totally Radmanovich had a fine year at the plate last year, displaying excellent power. As you're accustomed to seeing with this product line, he strikes out too much—though his .350 on-base average was decent for a slugger. He can play third or outfield and is too old for Double-A. What he does in Triple-A this season may well be the difference between flying into New York or riding the bus between Tucson and Phoenix. ■

FRED RATH

SOLID PROSPECT

SP • BR • TR • 6'3 • 205 • 24

	G	GS	IP	H	HR	BB	SO	W	L	S	ERA	K/BB	K9	HW9
A+	22	0	29	25	1	10	29	2	5	4	2.79	2.9	9.0	10.86

Rath split time between Fort Wayne and Fort Myers last year and pitched very well in both leagues. Combined, he was 2-7 with a 2.03 ERA. Undrafted, he signed with the Twins after a workout with a scout. He went from throwing in the high 80s in college to the low 90s in the Midwest League after adding 25 pounds of muscle. He's done all he can at this level, and the club will need to move him along quickly to gauge his long-term potential. ■

JEFF REBOULET

IF-OF • BR • TR • 6'0 • 170 • 32 • MIN86/10

	AB	R	H	2B	3B	HR	RBI	BB	SO	SB	CS	BA	OB	SA
MIN94	189	28	49	11	1	3	23	18	23	0	0	.259	.327	.376
MIN95	216	39	63	11	0	4	23	27	34	1	2	.292	.373	.398
MIN96	234	20	52	9	0	0	23	25	34	4	2	.222	.298	.261
CAREER	1016	135	252	46	2	9	100	128	154	13	11	.248	.335	.324

Reboulet defines the term "utility player." He's competent everywhere and played all 4 infield positions last year. He even made 8 appearances in the outfield. But he had his worst year at the plate in 5 years with the Twins and, if it continues, the Twins will probably choose to roll the dice with a rookie who has some upside instead. ■

MARK REDMAN

SOLID PROSPECT

SP-RP • BL • TL • 6'5 • 215 • 23 • MIN95/1

	G	GS	IP	H	HR	BB	SO	W	L	S	ERA	K/BB	K9	HW9
AA	16	16	106	101	5	50	96	7	7	0	3.81	1.9	8.1	12.78

Anything but overpowering, Redman's primary pitch is a straight change-up. His fastball isn't hard, but it moves well. And his curveball was nothing special until the Twins made it into a solid pitch. Redman is a big guy at 6-foot-5 and 215 pounds, but he'll make his living with finesse. The Twins feel he's a very good pitcher and, once he perfects his breaking pitches, will be quite effective in the majors. ■

RICH ROBERTSON

RP • BL • TL • 6'4 • 175 • 28 • PIT90/9

	G	GS	IP	H	HR	BB	K	W	L	S	ERA	K/BB	K9	HW9
PIT94	8	0	15	20	2	10	8	0	0	0	6.89	.8	4.8	17.92
MIN95	25	4	51	48	4	31	38	2	0	0	3.83	1.2	6.7	13.94
MIN96	36	31	186	197	22	116	114	7	17	0	5.12	1.0	5.5	15.14
CAREER	78	35	262	280	28	161	165	9	18	0	5.01	1.0	5.7	15.15

Robertson received less run support (4.4 runs per game) than the other Twins' starters, but that doesn't completely explain his record. When you look at all those walks, you wonder how he kept his ERA as low as he did. Robertson has an average fastball and sinker, and he relies on his change-up as his out pitch. With that repertoire and those results, he may just be afraid to throw strikes because he knows what's going to happen if he does. ■

FRANKIE RODRIGUEZ

YOUNG GUN

SP • BR • TR • 6'0 • 190 • 24 • BOS90/1

	G	GS	IP	H	HR	BB	K	W	L	S	ERA	K/BB	K9	HW9
BOS/MIN95	25	18	105	114	11	57	59	5	8	0	6.13	1.0	5.1	14.66
MIN96	38	33	206	218	27	78	110	13	14	2	5.05	1.4	4.8	12.93

Rodriguez was the price the Red Sox paid to have Rick Aguilera around for a few months. Despite his losing record in '96, he led the team with 13 victories, the most by a Twins pitcher in 4 years. And this in his first full year of starting in the big leagues and his 5th year of pitching. Frank was a star shortstop throughout his amateur career (Marcel Lachemann acknowledged his athleticism and called him the finest defensive pitcher in the game). He had trouble with his control, and his strikeout rate was lower than his minor-league numbers would indicate. But

he's young and learning and has moved up through the minors at a remarkable rate. Another quantum leap forward isn't out of the question in '97. ■

DAN SERAFINI

SOLID PROSPECT

SP • BB • TL • 6'1 • 180 • 23 • MIN92/1

	G	GS	IP	H	HR	BB	SO	W	L	S	ERA	K/BB	K9	HW9
AAA	25	23	131	164	20	58	109	7	7	0	5.58	1.9	7.5	15.29

Serafini has moved through the system quickly, including a brief stint in the majors last year. He had a tough period of adjustment in Salt Lake City last year and his debut in Minnesota wasn't any better, but his minor-league career and pedigree suggest he could be a solid pitcher. He attended Sierra High in San Bruno, California, the same school as Barry Bonds and Gregg Jefferies—so if he grows to be despised in big-league clubhouses, too, it may be time to check the water back home. He has a solid fastball with decent velocity and movement, as well as a good curve, slider, and change. All 4 are ranked at or above major-league average. He also uses a slide-step delivery and is quite effective at shutting down the running game. The Twins like what they see, but want him to use his change-up more. Serafini is one of the Twins' most promising left-handed prospects and is definitely in their short-term plans. ■

SCOTT STAHOVIAK

1B • BL • TR • 6'5 • 210 • 27 • MIN91/2

	AB	R	H	2B	3B	HR	RBI	BB	SO	SB	CS	BA	OB	SA
MIN95	263	28	70	19	0	3	23	30	61	5	1	.266	.341	.373
MIN96	405	72	115	30	3	13	61	59	114	3	3	.284	.376	.469
CAREER	725	101	196	53	3	16	85	92	197	8	6	.270	.353	.418

After Kent Hrbek's retirement, the Twins used 10 different players at first in '95. No one would ever mistake Stahoviak for the man who needed to buy a vowel, but he proved he can play in the majors and provided some stability at first base last year. He made a strong bid for the spot early on: Through early July he'd had only a lone error in 437 chances and was batting .296 and slugging .503. His 13 homers last year matched his career best, and the Twins shouldn't expect much more. He needs to cut down on his strikeouts, but he's solid defensively and does a good job of getting on base. ■

DAVE STEVENS

RP • BR • TR • 6'3 • 210 • 27 • CHN89/20

	G	GS	IP	H	HR	BB	K	W	L	S	ERA	K/BB	K9	HW9
MIN94	24	0	45	55	6	23	24	5	2	0	6.80	1.0	4.8	15.60
MIN95	56	0	65	74	14	32	47	5	4	10	5.07	1.5	6.5	14.68
MIN96	49	0	58	58	12	25	29	3	3	11	4.66	1.2	4.5	12.88
CAREER	129	0	168	187	32	80	100	13	9	21	5.41	1.3	5.4	14.30

The Twins put a lot of faith in Stevens and the bullpen by inserting Rick Aguilera into the starting rotation last year. It was supposed to be Stevens's breakout year, but injuries, inconsistency, and an emotional meltdown kept that from happening. He saved 5 games in April but was messy about it (a 6.48 ERA and a 19.44 HW9). When injuries took their toll, the Twins began closing by committee. He missed most of June with a nerve problem in his right elbow. Then he missed July 21 to August 9 when he cut open his hand punching a wall after giving up a game-winning home run to Cleveland's Alvaro Espinoza.

He returned a much better pitcher, working in long relief. He was 2-1 with 3.49 ERA in 28.1 innings in the last 2 months. For the season, Dave led the team with 11 saves but blew 6. The Twins may look elsewhere for a closer—including back to the future with Aguilera. ■

HECTOR TRINIDAD

SLEEPER

SP • BR • TR • 6'2 • 190 • 23

	G	GS	IP	H	HR	BB	SO	W	L	S	ERA	K/BB	K9	HW9
AA	25	24	138	137	6	31	93	6	6	0	3.84	3.0	6.1	10.93

Trinidad is one of the few players who can say he was traded for a CEO. The Cubs sent him the Twins as compensation for signing Andy MacPhail for their front office in '94. He's anything but a throw-away. He has excellent control, doesn't allow many baserunners, and can finish off hitters. Unless the Tribune Company lets MacPhail start throwing some of its money around, this deal may end up as lopsided as Lou Brock for Ernie Broglio. ■

MIKE TROMBLEY

RP • BR • TR • 6'2 • 200 • 29 • MIN89/14

	G	GS	IP	H	HR	BB	K	W	L	S	ERA	K/BB	K9	HW9
MIN94	24	0	48	56	10	18	32	2	0	0	6.33	1.8	6.0	13.87
MIN95	20	18	97	107	18	42	68	4	8	0	5.62	1.6	6.3	13.82
MIN96	43	0	68	61	2	25	57	5	1	6	3.01	2.3	7.5	11.37
CAREER	141	35	374	398	50	143	280	20	17	8	4.74	2.0	6.7	13.01

Trombley was the grizzled veteran of the Twins' inexperienced bullpen. Fittingly, he had a solid season and led the team with a 3.01 ERA. In fact, he was the only pitcher on the staff with an ERA under 4.00. He had an excellent minor-league career as a starter, but has struggled with the Twins as the club moved him between the rotation and the bullpen. He seems to have finally gotten comfortable out of the bullpen. ▪

JOSÉ VALENTIN

SOLID PROSPECT

C • BB • TR • 5'10 • 190 • 21 • MIN93/7

	AB	R	H	2B	3B	HR	RBI	BB	SO	SB	CS	BA	OB	SA
AA	165	22	39	8	0	3	14	16	35	0	3	.236	.308	.339

José J. Valentin is the younger brother of Brewers shortstop José A. Valentin . . . and the son of unimaginative parents. But they raised good ballplayers. He's fairly raw defensively, except for an outstanding arm. He's also afflicted with a catcher's speed. But he's a very good hitter. In '95 he hit 19 homers playing in Class-A Fort Wayne, in a park that doesn't yield dingers. His numbers tailed off last year, but he'd moved up a couple of levels. Going into '96, he was considered 3 years away. With some luck, he might surface this year. ▪

MATT WALBECK

C • BB • TR • 5'11 • 195 • 27 • CHN87/7

	AB	R	H	2B	3B	HR	RBI	BB	SO	SB	CS	BA	OB	SA
MIN94	338	31	69	12	0	5	35	17	37	1	1	.204	.246	.284
MIN95	393	40	101	18	1	1	44	25	71	3	1	.257	.302	.316
MIN96	215	25	48	10	0	2	24	9	34	3	1	.223	.252	.298
CAREER	976	98	224	42	1	9	109	52	148	7	3	.230	.269	.302

The Twins put pressure on Walbeck in spring training to produce at the plate. A wrist injury slowed him early in the season and he never really recovered. He had a few impressive seasons in the

minors but hasn't shown the Twins anything since they traded Willie Banks for him (in a deal that helped neither team, but merely transferred frustration). The Twins will be looking for a free-agent catcher in the off-season. If they are successful, Walbeck could be the casualty. ▪

TODD WALKER

GRADE-A PROSPECT

3B • BL • TR • 6'0 • 180 • 23 • MIN94/1

	AB	R	H	2B	3B	HR	RBI	BB	SO	SB	CS	BA	OB	SA
MIN96	82	8	21	6	0	0	6	4	13	2	0	.256	.28	.329

The honors piled up for Walker last year on his way to Minnesota. He was voted best batting prospect and the most exciting player in the PCL. He was a second baseman when the Twins drafted him, but with Knoblauch in the way, they moved him to third. After a couple of successful years in the minors, he's considered one of the best-hitting prospects in baseball, and his arrival has been much anticipated. In late August, the Twins cleared the way by trading Dave Hollins—considered a dour influence in the clubhouse (a new code word for "jerk", evidently—in Philadelphia, he was "intense"). He has fine power to all fields and will hit for average and draw walks. He even has decent speed. His September was less than stellar, but give him time. The club is more concerned about his defense and sent him to the Florida Instructional League to work on it. ▪

SCOTT WATKINS

RP • BL • TL • 6'3 • 180 • 26 • MIN92/24

	G	GS	IP	H	HR	BB	SO	W	L	S	ERA	K/BB	K9	HW9
AAA	47	0	50	60	6	34	43	4	6	1	7.69	1.3	7.7	16.81

Watkins recorded 20 saves with a 2.80 ERA for Salt Lake City in '95. He even had a relatively successful debut in Minnesota. But '96 was a different matter. He's always gotten a lot of strikeouts and last year was no exception, but his control disappeared and he got hammered as a result. He's shown a lot of promise in the past, so he'll get another chance in Salt Lake City to return to form. ▪

■ 1996 AUTOPSY

The principal owner expected this team to win, but the fans weren't convinced. Most were outraged that manager Buck Showalter had been fired after getting the Yankees to the playoffs for the first time in 14 years. His replacement, Joe Torre, was perceived as a nice guy who'd finished last too many times. New GM Bob Watson was considered just another Steinbrenner puppet, and he didn't endear himself to the fans by letting Mike Stanley and Randy Velarde go, replacing them with Joe Girardi and Mariano Duncan, respectively. Don Mattingly had retired, and many expected newly acquired Tino Martinez to fold under the pressure of playing in the Bronx and replacing a legend. David Cone had been re-signed, and Kenny Rogers was brought in by The Boss himself, as Steinbrenner overruled his baseball people and their recommendation to throw the $20 million at Chuck Finley. But no one expected much from Jimmy Key and his rebuilt shoulder, and bringing in Dwight Gooden seemed like a transparent attempt to steal the back pages from the Mets. Who next? Darryl Strawberry all over again?

They might have had the payroll of a winner, but to many they didn't have the look of one.

April 13-10 (13-10, half-game ahead)

Torre spent a good portion of the month shuffling his lineup to get Tino Martinez going. Mired in a deep and troublesome batting slump, Tino was booed incessantly by Yankees fans. Meanwhile, Kenny Rogers was the highest-paid player in extended spring training—as the Yankees demoted him to the bullpen, seemingly intent on destroying his psyche before he'd even lost his first game. Gooden took his spot in the rotation and was a disaster (0-3 with an 8.38 ERA in 19.1 innings), his presence on the roster dismissed as another bonehead move commanded by The Boss.

It didn't seem like a big deal at first, but David Cone was also having problems. He started experiencing numbness in his pitching hand and was unable to grip the ball properly. He was examined by a doctor who said he had a "mild circulatory condition." It wouldn't seem so mild in a few days, when his hand turned blue.

May 16-11 (29-21, 1 game ahead)

The Yankees moved 1½ games ahead of the Orioles by taking games in Baltimore on April 30 and May 1. On the 30th, the Yankees won 13-10 in the longest 9-inning game in history (4 hours, 21 minutes). Andy Pettitte was taken off the hook despite allowing 9 runs (8 earned) in 1+ innings. The next day's game took 4 hours, 34 minutes! Pettitte pitched 3 shutout innings (the 13th, 14th and 15th) to get the victory as the Yankees scored 5 runs (4 on Tino Martinez's grand slam) to win 11-6. In the bullpen, Mariano Rivera was unhittable. He had a string of 26 scoreless innings at one point, and for the month a 0.60 ERA in 15 innings. Gooden suddenly looked 10 years younger, going 3-1 with a 2.50 ERA in 36 innings for the month. The highlight of his season was his 2-0 no-hitter against the Mariners on the 14th—pitched while his father was about to have double-bypass surgery. There were 20,786 Yankees fans who paid to see it—and countless others who got in free because they had braved the snow on Opening Day at the Stadium and been treated to free tickets at an upcoming game. This just happened to be one of them.

But Cone appeared to be done for the year, if not for his career, as his circulatory problems were traced to an aneurysm in his right shoulder. Dion James, a reserve outfielder released several days previously, was arrested on a marijuana possession charge. And Steinbrenner continued to make noises about moving the team because attendance was down 1%. Ruben Sierra, who was slumping in the field and at the plate, lost some playing time to Gerald Williams and took it like the team player he is: "I don't have to talk to him [Torre] because he lied to me about playing the outfield. He said that in spring training. I lost 18 pounds to play the outfield and I haven't seen that yet. I don't like people lying to me."

June 18-11 (47-32, 4½ games ahead)

Obviously not content with the club's play getting the headlines, Steinbrenner fired two dozen part-time employees, including clubhouse attendant Charlie Zabransky, 73. Zabransky was a players' favorite, and they took up a collection to rehire him.

Spokesman David Sussman said the firings were because of attendance: "Obviously, a stadium with 16,000 fans doesn't require the same staff as a stadium with 30,000." Obviously a team with media revenues in excess of the total revenues of 18 other teams can afford to pay a 73-year-old clubhouse attendant.

Gerald Williams got a great deal of playing time when Bernie Williams went to Puerto Rico to be with his 5-year-old son, who was undergoing emergency surgery. GM Bob Watson didn't seem all that impressed by the lesser Williams: "He's probably the best 4th outfielder in the league, but an everyday player? No. Gerald is not real proficient against right-handed pitching. And he's not a real good defensive outfielder." Honesty will get you nowhere, Bob. Are you surprised you could only get a utility player with a broken foot for him in a trade?

To round things out in June, Steve Howe, released on the 22nd, was arrested on the 24th for trying to carry a loaded .357 Magnum onto his flight at JFK International.

July 16-10 (63-42, 10 games ahead)
Darryl Strawberry's contract was purchased from the St. Paul Saints of the Northern League July 2 and he was assigned briefly to Triple-A Columbus. Strawberry hit 18 home runs in 29 games for the Saints. He was promoted to New York on July 7 and went right into the starting lineup. He helped the Yankees increase their lead to 10 games as they swept 4 games at Baltimore. In the second game of a doubleheader on the 13th, Strawberry homered twice and drove in 4 as Dwight Gooden improved to 9-4 and the Yankees handed Baltimore's Arthur Rhodes (9-1) his first loss of the season. Straw singled and doubled on the 14th to support Pettitte in his 14th victory.

Steinbrenner was feeling his oats: "All I know is Peter Gammons said it was going to take the Yankees 10 years to recover from our reorganization last winter, from the moves we made with Showalter, Stanley, etc. Well, I like Peter, but I'd have to say it's been a very short 10 years." The only thing worse than Steinbrenner is Steinbrenner on the rare occasions when he happens to be right.

On the 17th, the Yankees lost 12-11 at Fenway as John Wetteland blew his first save since May 11, ending a streak of saves in 25 straight appearances. Gooden, roughed up a bit, went back to his more compact delivery and went through a 24-inning stretch where he allowed 2 runs. With Pettitte's elbow bothering him and Cone out indefinitely, Gooden carried the staff for much of the summer.

On the 31st, Watson traded Sierra and right-hander Matt Drews to the Tigers for Cecil Fielder. The Yankees didn't have much punch, and little from the right side of the plate—and Drews, once an untouchable, must have seemed like a small price to pay to get the "village idiot" out of the clubhouse.

August 13-17 (76-59, 4 games ahead)
Mariano Rivera allowed 7 runs in 2.1 innings to start the month—he only allowed 25 runs all season—but he pitched 16.2 shutout innings the rest of the month. On the 6th, Cecil made his Yankees debut in New York. Strawberry took the headlines, hitting 3 homers. David Cone threw off a mound for the first time since his operation and said he'd be ready by early September.

On the 9th, the Tigers came into town with Sierra, who ripped the Yankees: "If you don't give a [beep] about players, how are you going to win? They don't give a [beep] about people over there, just winning." Obviously, Sierra was much happier now in an environment where winning wasn't expected. It showed: He hit a 3-run homer and a 2-run double to hand Pettitte his 7th loss. Torre, as always, shrugged it off—a vital personality trait for any Yankee manager.

On the 23rd, the Yankees got Graeme Lloyd, a left-handed reliever, and Pat Listach for Gerald "not an everyday player" Williams and Bob Wickman. But Listach arrived with a broken foot, and Lloyd had arm trouble (he'd had a cortisone shot 8 days before the trade). Both Watson and Steinbrenner questioned the ethics of Sal Bando, the Brewers GM. The Brewers tried to make things better by sending Ricky Bones over immediately and promising a minor-leaguer later, though Bando refused to acknowledge any wrongdoing. Evidently Bando must have figured that if Lloyd wasn't healthy enough to get tagged, Bones could fill in capably as a punching bag. With Listach done for the year, the role he was to fill went to Ruben Rivera, who

started his second tour of duty with the team in '96. The Yankees had refused to part with him in July to acquire Denny Neagle. Reggie Jackson had threatened to leave the organization if they traded him—but even that wasn't enough to convince them to part with him.

The bad blood between the Mariners and the Yankees only got worse when Paul O'Neill had his chin buzzed by a fastball in a Seattle blowout, prompting a bench-clearing brawl. Mariano Duncan, a former Red like O'Neill, said: "We got our butts kicked and then they try to hurt somebody. The guy to blame is Lou. He's the biggest [beep] I've ever come across in the game. He doesn't like Paul, he's hated him since 1990 in Cincinnati. I was there, I heard [Piniella] say stuff about him. I don't know why, maybe it bothers him that O'Neill has become the player he is after he got away from Piniella." Piniella tried to downplay the incident, but just managed to stir it up some more: "What [O'Neill] doesn't realize is that he cries too much. If he quit that, he'd be a heckuva ballplayer. He already is a heckuva ballplayer. If he stopped crying, he'd be even better."

The Yankees thought they'd won the division in July, but the Orioles were playing well and the Yankees were coming back to meet them. They missed Wetteland, who'd been out for most of the month with a groin pull. His absence meant the formula of Rivera in the 7th and Wetteland in the 9th was being replaced by the ineffective Jeff Nelson, Lloyd, and newly acquired David Weathers in the 7th, and no lead left for Rivera to protect.

September 16-11 (92-70, won division)

Watson was drawing serious heat from the owner over his trades for Lloyd and Weathers, but he just fanned the flames and tried to bring Torre in with him. "We have the highest payroll in the history of the game. If we can't hold a 12-game lead, then the leadership is responsible. The pilots crash the plane. . . . Joe and I are the pilots. We are the ones who are responsible." Torre shrugged that off, too. He'd lost an older brother earlier in the year, and his other brother, Frank, was in the hospital waiting for a heart transplant. If anyone could remember it was just a game, Torre could.

The team was in a tailspin when Cone returned emphatically on the 2nd with 7 no-hit innings at Oakland. Torre removed Cone with the no-hitter still going to protect his arm, and they ended up with a 1-hitter on an infield single. They dropped a couple of close games to Toronto, then went to Detroit where Ruben Rivera helped turn things around with a game-saving catch in a 9-8 victory. They would go on to sweep the Tigers, with Bernie Williams going deep from both sides of the plate, and would never look back.

On the 20th, the team's showdown series with Baltimore began in bizarre fashion. Watson and umpire crew chief Joe Brinkman had words about the start of the first game. Watson said he told Brinkman the field was unplayable before the game. Brinkman said the conversation never took place. Mike Mussina and David Cone warmed up, the game started, and then was abruptly called. Both pitchers went back to the mound 2 days later, but neither was effective. The Yankees won the first game in extra innings on a Ruben Rivera base hit, and the Orioles ended up dropping 2 of 3. Strawberry had told Torre to play Raines in left because Raines was on a tear. "I'm a player who's more understanding about life," Strawberry said. "I'm not going to die if I don't play." Straw has "gotten his life together" more times than Jimmy Swaggart, but this time it looked like he was indeed back on the rails. The team clinched on the 25th, routing the Brewers 19-2 behind David Cone.

All in all, a perfectly normal season in the Bronx—when a rich, paranoid egomaniac is pulling the strings, these things happen.

October (won the World Series)

The Yankees had only one championship-caliber strength—their bullpen—and they rode it all the way to the end, going 10-1 in games decided by 3 or fewer runs. (See the essay at the end of this section, and the October write-ups for the Texas Rangers, Baltimore Orioles, and the Atlanta Braves, for some of the highlights—or lowlights—depending on your allegiances.)

1997 DIAGNOSIS

Offense

Adjusting for Yankee Stadium, the '96 Yankees had one of the better offenses in the A.L.—about even with Oakland—at 38 runs above the league average. The team doesn't hit for power but is loaded with high-average hitters who draw walks. That'll score runs anywhere. There is no reason to expect much difference in the team's hitting in '97. A couple of the veterans may slip (Boggs, Raines) or be pushed out the door (Boggs, O'Neill), but the Yankees have decent options in the minors if they fail. The team looks to be counting on full seasons from Ruben Rivera and Darryl Strawberry, but penciling in 60 dingers would have to be blamed on the championship afterglow.

Defense

Tino Martinez is no Mattingly at first base, but he makes the routine plays. Pat Kelly is much better than Mariano Duncan, but the Yankees will continue to get Duncan his at-bats. Derek Jeter is a fine athlete and he will continue to improve, but he wasn't much better than average in the field in '97. Wade Boggs is on his last legs, whether he wants to admit it or not. The Yankees brought Charlie Hayes back, and he will be an improvement over Boggs in the field.

Bernie Williams is smooth and graceful in the field and made some great catches in big spots. He is good and will only get better as he heads into his prime. Strawberry in October did the job whether he was asked to play in left field or right field. If (and it's a big if) he keeps this up, the Yankees will be able to get his and Fielder's bats in the lineup at the same time. When healthy, Paul O'Neill is a very good right fielder—he had 7 assists in '96 and made no errors, despite having to play a tricky Yankee Stadium corner. Ruben Rivera will see more time this season, and was very impressive in limited duty in '96.

Neither Girardi nor Leyritz threw particularly well in '96, but Mike Stanley was at the bottom of the league in Boston—and Girardi drew rave reviews for his handling of the pitchers after Stanley's less than stellar work. Rumor had it that David Cone made the replacement of Stanley a requirement if he was to return to the team. The staff's ERA was much higher when Girardi was catching (5.13) than when Leyritz was behind the plate (3.72), but this was due to (1) Leyritz being Pettitte's personal catcher and (2) Leyritz getting a lot of late-inning work in with the relievers, when Girardi was pinch-hit for in close games. Girardi should improve in '97, since he won't have to spend the first half of the season being booed every time he sticks his head out of the dugout.

Pitching

The team's 5 primary starters last season—Andy Pettitte, Kenny Rogers, Dwight Gooden, Jimmy Key, and David Cone—were very good, and all look to be back. Their primary weakness was their durability. The 5 made only 129 of the team's 162 starts (the Braves' top 4, Smoltz, Maddux, Glavine and Avery made 129 starts—and Avery was hurt for a good portion of the season). If Cone can pitch 200 innings and if Pettitte's elbow holds up, the team may improve this season. Brian Boehringer and Ramiro Mendoza could both step in if and when Kenny Rogers finally locks himself in his basement.

The Yankees had the best pitching in the league, and the bullpen was the home of the team's 2 best pitchers: Mariano Rivera and John Wetteland. But Jeff Nelson and Graeme Lloyd are both very good, and David Weathers finally showed what his potential would look like if he ever used it. Rivera's workload last season was disconcerting, and he may not be able to pitch 108 innings in relief again. And if Wetteland signs elsewhere, there is no guarantee that Rivera will be able to repeat his success in the closer role. He struggled when Wetteland was injured in '96. Don't expect another season of dominating performances from the bullpen.

Farm System

The farm system has some decent players in it, but it's pretty thin. At catcher, there's Chris Ashby; infielder D'Angelo Jimenez might be superb, but he's very young and far down in the system; and there's Ruben Rivera, Ricky Ledee, Brian Buchanan, and possibly Jackson Melian (if he's as good as they say) in the outfield. On the mound, there's Katsuhiro Maeda, Eric Milton, and Jay Tessmer. Milton and Maeda come with advanced billing, but neither has done much in the minors yet.

Management and Ownership
George Steinbrenner. You can't say he's controversial, because that would imply that someone out there likes him. He does spend the bucks. Sure, he tries his hand at manipulating this player or that politician, but you know that going in when you choose to do business with him. And you can't say he'll settle for mediocrity. Whose name was invoked in the Angels' clubhouse when California was going through an extended phase of whining and underachievement? The George. Former Yankee Randy Velarde said The Boss would have raised hell if that kind of behavior had taken place in New York. George says that all he cares about is winning—which is almost true. Truth be told, he'd settle for high attendance and close seconds if it meant he'd get more attention.

As for the front office, George is the GM. He just likes to have someone else in the official capacity so he can deflect the blame when his moves don't work. That's how he could cover himself when he let Reggie leave in 1982 and decided to build around Dave Collins—and how he could take credit for Gooden and Strawberry, and avoid the blame for choosing Kenny Rogers over Chuck Finley. Acting GM Bob Watson is only renting the job, and the vote of confidence he finally received soon after the World Series just pushes him that much closer to the edge of the ledge.

Joe Torre is the eye of the hurricane. When any of his players blew a gasket, Torre would be quoted in the paper the next day saying something calm. When Steinbrenner and Watson were trading barbs in the press and saying something to try to drag him into the middle of it, Torre would say only that he was "surprised to hear that." As a manager, he didn't have much to do. If the guy was healthy, Torre would play him. If he was hurt, Torre wouldn't. Mariano Rivera pitched the 7th and 8th every 2 to 3 days; Wetteland came in to pitch the 9th in save opportunities, and Andy Pettitte won 13 games after losses. Torre deserves credit for keeping a calm environment for his players and treating everyone like an adult. He didn't let his players' egos affect the team, and he didn't let his own keep him from hiring Don Zimmer as his bench coach and instructing him to spout strategic options in his ear all season. And he wasn't afraid to take chances in the postseason—walking the winning run on base, benching starters, letting Pettitte bat in the 8th with runners on base—rather than go by The Book. If they didn't work, he'd have opened himself to relentless criticism. They did work and he was the toast of the town. He shouldn't expect to defy the odds again this season. He may be too popular in New York at the moment for George to get away with firing him in midseason, but The Boss is capable of anything.

. . . and whatnot: Avenging 1960
The Yankees won it all despite an October that featured mediocre starting pitching, not much offense, and numerous injuries—Boggs's back, O'Neill's leg, Strawberry's toe, Raines's legs, Rogers's shoulder, and the after-effects of Cone's aneurysm.

When the opposition made a mistake—whether it be a 1st pitch fastball to Mariano Duncan from Mike Henneman in the 9th inning of Game 3 against Texas, a pump fake by Todd Zeile in Game 3 against Baltimore, a decision by Bobby Cox to run Greg McMichael out there in a 2-2 Game 3 against Atlanta, a hanging slider from Mark Wohlers to Jim Leyritz in Game 4, or a dropped fly ball by Marquis Grissom in Game 5— the Yankees cashed it in.

They didn't get a win out of their starting pitching until their 7th playoff game. Overall, their starters went 81.1 innings, yielded 119 baserunners and 14 dingers, struck out 44 while walking 39, and had an ERA of 5.09. That's very similar to the '96 performances of Doug Linton and Zane Smith, just not quite as good.

They went 11-4, in the postseason despite scoring as many runs as they allowed. Tino Martinez had no RBI and hit .188. Paul O'Neill and Wade Boggs nursed injuries and limped through at 13 for 76. Boggs's replacement, Charlie Hayes hit .170, while starting second baseman Mariano Duncan, hit .180. The only regulars to better their season's batting average in October were Derek Jeter (.361), Bernie Williams (.345), and Cecil Fielder (.308). Atlanta outscored them 26-20—making it the 4th time this decade that the Braves have managed to outscore their playoff opponent and still find a way to lose.

Their bullpen kept them in games, and they won the close ones. In games decided by 3 runs or less, they were 10-1. Other than an 8-4 victory in Game

4 against the Orioles, the Yankees didn't have an easy 9th inning all October. The much-derided Graeme Lloyd gave up 1 hit in 5.1 innings, striking out 5 and walking 0 in 8 appearances, and making Ryan Klesko look lost. Lloyd, Rivera, and Weathers combined to pitch 30.2 innings and give up 17 hits and 2 runs, striking out 23 while walking 8 and winning 4 games. Jeff Nelson was the "weak link," actually giving up 3 runs in 10.1 innings. John Wetteland appeared in 12 of 15 games and saved all 7 of his opportunities, redeeming himself for a brutal postseason against Seattle in '95.

They were seemingly on the brink of disaster at all times, summed up very neatly by their 1-0 Game 5 win over the Braves. With the series tied at 2-2, John Smoltz was virtually unhittable and looked to be handing the ball to Greg Maddux to close it out in Game 6. But the Yankees cashed in the lone Braves mistake to scratch out a run. Joe Torre rolled the dice in the 9th, putting the winning run on base so Wetteland could face Luis Polonia. Polonia ripped a gapper, but Paul O'Neill, sore hamstring and all, had been moved five steps to his right by outfield coach José Cardenal just before the pitch and barely managed to get to it for the final out of the game. The next night, Greg Maddux would make 3 bad pitches and the Yankees would hit all of them, while the Braves let Jimmy Key crawl on his hands and knees through 5 innings and hand it to the bullpen. Wanting no part of Tom Glavine in Game 7, they got a chance to close it out and took it.

Coming from New York, with a $60 million payroll, it is hard to view the Yankees as underdogs. But this team, in many ways, didn't play well enough to get through the 1st round. No one must have told them that, just like no one told the 1960 Pirates, who were outscored 55-27, refused to quit and rode the right arm of relief ace Elroy Face to beat the "Team of the Decade" Yankees.

CHRIS ASHBY — SOLID PROSPECT

C • BR • TR • 6'3 • 185 • 22 • NYA92/26

	AB	R	H	2B	3B	HR	RBI	BB	SO	SB	CS	BA	OB	SA
A+	325	55	80	28	0	6	46	71	78	16	4	.246	.388	.388

Ashby is a good young hitter. He has some speed, some power, and a very good eye at the plate. He will be in Double-A this season and could be in Yankee Stadium to stay by next fall. ■

BRIAN BOEHRINGER — SLEEPER

RP-SP • BB • TR • 6'2 • 180 • 28 • CHA91/4

	G	GS	IP	H	HR	BB	K	W	L	S	ERA	K/BB	K9	HW9
NYA95	7	3	17	24	5	22	10	0	3	0	13.75	.5	5.3	24.35
NYA96	15	3	46	46	6	21	37	2	4	0	5.44	1.8	7.2	13.10

What you saw against the Braves in Game 1 of the World Series was typical first-half Boehringer. In the second half of last season, he was sharp – 2-2 with a 3.34 ERA in 32.1 innings. In that stretch the league hit .198 against him with a .279 on-base percentage. His best work came out of the bullpen, so maybe that's where he belongs. He throws 90+ mph and has a good slider and curve. He could be a surprise this season. An extreme fly-ball pitcher, the key to success for him is keeping the ball from being pulled. If the hitters keep flying out to Death Valley, he could be a stud. ■

WADE BOGGS

3B • BL • TR • 6'2 • 195 • 28 • BOS76/7

	AB	R	H	2B	3B	HR	RBI	BB	SO	SB	CS	BA	OB	SA
NYA94	366	61	125	19	1	11	55	61	29	2	1	.342	.433	.489
NYA95	460	76	149	22	4	5	63	74	50	1	1	.324	.412	.422
NYA96	501	80	156	29	2	2	41	67	32	1	2	.311	.389	.389
CAREER	8100	1367	2697	518	55	105	905	1280	630	20	32	.333	.422	.449

Boggs is a decent fielder and can still hit .300, but he has lost almost all of his power. He can still hit singles, but with his speed it's station to station all the way home. He still has a shot at his 3,000 hits, but he's a shadow of his former Fenway self—and he may be getting no. 3,000 elsewhere, as he threatened to do during the '96 pennant race when Charlie Hayes was brought in. If he leaves, the Yankees will further defy the odds by lowering their number of selfish players to 0. ■

BRIAN BUCHANAN — SLEEPER

1B-OF • BR • TR • 6'4 • 220 • 23 • NYA94/1

	AB	R	H	2B	3B	HR	RBI	BB	SO	SB	CS	BA	OB	SA
A+	526	65	137	22	4	10	58	37	108	23	8	.260	.321	.375

During a game in Class-A Greensboro in '95, Buchanan hit the bag at a bizarre angle running to

first and almost took his foot right off. Luckily, the team physician was listening to the game on the radio. He got everything ready at a local hospital, and doctors saved the foot. Buchanan went hardcore during his rehab and played reasonably well at Tampa. He has speed and power. If he can improve his plate discipline, he could be a good one. ■

RICKY BONES (See Looking for a Game)

DAVID CONE — AL ELITE

SP • BR • TR • 6′1 • 185 • 34 • KC81/4

	G	GS	IP	H	HR	BB	K	W	L	S	ERA	K/BB	K9	HW9
KC94	23	23	171	130	15	54	132	16	5	0	2.94	2.4	6.9	9.68
TOR/NYA95	30	30	229	195	24	88	191	18	8	0	3.57	2.2	7.5	11.12
NYA96	11	11	72	50	3	34	71	7	2	0	2.88	2.1	8.9	10.50
CAREER	299	270	1994	1639	154	750	1812	136	80	1	3.16	2.4	8.2	10.78

He didn't care if he never pitched after the '96 postseason, he just wanted the ball in September and October. Shades of Orel Hershiser heading to the bullpen in '88. The lasting image of the World Series will probably be Leyritz's dinger in Game 4, but it's all over before that if Cone doesn't gut it out in Game 3 against Glavine. He's getting up there in age and has pitched a lot of innings over the years, but to his credit, he's not slinging hash up there. His slider still bites, his fastball still jumps, and he still seems to invent a new pitch every week. The combination of the injury, his age, and his past workload makes him questionable for this season. Don't bet against him, though. That's a losing proposition. ■

MARIANO DUNCAN

2B • BR • TR • 6′0 • 185 • 34 • LA82

	AB	R	H	2B	3B	HR	RBI	BB	SO	SB	CS	BA	OB	SA
PHI94	347	49	93	22	1	8	48	17	72	10	2	.268	.306	.406
PHI/CIN95	265	36	76	14	2	6	36	5	62	1	3	.287	.297	.423
NYA96	400	62	136	34	3	8	56	9	77	4	3	.340	.352	.500
CAREER	4338	583	1167	219	37	86	466	189	835	168	54	.269	.303	.396

Duncan saved the Yankees' bacon when both Pat Kelly and Tony Fernandez went down. He was decent defensively, and might have turned in his best season with the bat. What a "unique" hitter he is. Only Slam Duncan could hit .340 with a 77:9 strikeouts-to-walks ratio. How many hitters could bat .367 in 199 at-bats and draw 3 walks? It's true, he had a .367 average in the second half and had a

.369 on-base percentage. That's incredible. But then it's hard for Duncan to walk, considering that he hasn't seen 4 pitches in an at-bat since the Reagan administration. Is he a legitimate .300 hitter? No way—the last time he hit over .300 was in 1990. He's a solid reserve, possibly the best in the league. But eventually the A.L. will figure out not to throw him fastballs and he'll be back in the respectable .280s, where he belongs. ■

TONY FERNANDEZ (See Looking for a Game)

CECIL FIELDER — CONSISTENT STAR

1B-DH • BR • TR • 6′3 • 250 • 33 • KC82

	AB	R	H	2B	3B	HR	RBI	BB	SO	SB	CS	BA	OB	SA
DET94	425	67	110	16	2	28	90	50	110	0	0	.259	.337	.504
DET95	494	70	120	18	1	31	82	75	116	0	1	.243	.346	.472
DET/NYA96	591	85	149	20	0	39	117	87	139	2	0	.252	.350	.484
CAREER	4380	655	1122	168	6	289	879	589	1118	2	5	.256	.346	.495

Big Daddy hits .250 all the time and 450 (feet) every now and then. People seem to focus too much on what he doesn't do, rather than the 765 runs he's knocked in over the past 7 seasons. Yes, he's paid too much (as if that's his fault), though some Tiger fans seemed genuinely offended that he would not take a pay-cut "for the good of the team" (as if a few million here or there was going to vault the Tigers into the pennant race). Yes, he's slow. As you would expect, he's a statue at first base, without the pigeons—but he's a statue with sure hands. Yes, he's fat—but he's also never been on the DL in his career, unlike the chiseled Ron Gant or a sleek greyhound named Eric Davis.

Fielder has also proven to be a team player. He didn't complain when he sat and Straw played—in fact, each was the first out of the dugout to greet the other after a dinger. And when Torre was gutsy enough to bench his woefully unproductive 117-RBI first baseman, Tino Martinez, in the World Series, Fielder made his manager look like a genius. He was one of the few Yankees to hit higher in post-season than in the regular season, and he did it

against Atlanta by shortening his stroke, going the other way with the pitch, and being content with run-scoring singles.

The Yankees may still deal him, if they can find someone willing to take on his massive contract. If he goes, hopefully it will be to an A.L. team, so he can get his ovation when he returns to Yankee Stadium. ■

ANDY FOX — SLEEPER

UT • BL • TR • 6′4 • 185 • 26 • NYA89/1

	AB	R	H	2B	3B	HR	RBI	BB	SO	SB	CS	BA	OB	SA
NYA96	189	26	37	4	0	3	13	20	28	11	3	.196	.276	.265

A good athlete with a strong arm, Fox improved greatly as a hitter in '95 by shortening his swing and going to the opposite field more. In '96 he was hampered by infrequent playing time and was pathetic offensively (his average, on-base percentage, and slugging were similar to what Mariano Rivera *allowed* last season!). With more playing time, his hitting should be fine. He sparked the Yankees' comeback from an 8-0 deficit against the White Sox in May with a hustling infield single, a game many of the players pointed to as a turning point in the season. ■

JOE GIRARDI (See Free Agents)

DWIGHT GOODEN — SLEEPER

SP • BR • TR • 6′3 • 210 • 32

	G	GS	IP	H	HR	BB	K	W	L	S	ERA	K/BB	K9	HW9
NYN94	7	7	41	46	9	15	40	3	4	0	6.31	2.7	8.7	13.28
NYA96	29	29	170	169	19	88	126	11	7	0	5.01	1.4	6.7	13.60
CAREER	334	332	2340	2067	142	739	2001	168	92	1	3.24	2.7	7.7	10.79

From May through June last season he was 10-2 with a 3.43 ERA in 99.2 innings (47 walks, 69 strikeouts). So one can guess what April, August and September looked like. But combine those numbers with Cone's April and September and you've got one of the best pitchers in the league. Last season, Gooden would often pitch backward—throwing his curve early, then flashing his fastball. His command is nowhere near what it once was, but the curve still bites and the fastball can still flummox the opposition. During his no-hitter on May 14, he was hitting 95 mph in the 8th inning. Torre kept him off the postseason roster because he'd "hit the wall" after pitching almost nonstop for more than a year. He could be even better this year. ■

CHARLIE HAYES

3B • BR • TR • 6′0 • 190 • 31 • SF83/3

	AB	R	H	2B	3B	HR	RBI	BB	SO	SB	CS	BA	OB	SA
COL94	423	46	122	23	4	10	50	36	71	3	6	.288	.348	.433
PHI95	529	58	146	30	3	11	85	50	88	5	1	.276	.340	.406
PIT/NYA96	526	58	133	24	2	12	75	37	90	6	0	.253	.300	.375
CAREER	3896	419	1037	199	15	106	527	249	650	38	26	.266	.311	.407

Hayes gave the Yankees solid play after he came over from the Pirates for the stretch drive, and the fact that they chose to bring him back in '97 tells you all you need to know about how much the Yankees think Boggs still has left in the tank. New York was his 4th stop in 3 years, despite the fact that Hayes is a consistent hitter, good fielder, and team player. He's been a victim of his teams' desire to give the third base job to a player a bit more productive or with a bit more upside potential. He's been supplanted by Matt Williams, Dave Hollins, Wade Boggs, Vinny Castilla, and Todd Zeile. ■

MATT HOWARD

2B • BR • TR • 5′10 • 170 • 29

	AB	R	H	2B	3B	HR	RBI	BB	SO	SB	CS	BA	OB	SA
NYA96	54	9	11	1	0	1	9	2	8	1	0	.204	.228	.278

After 6 seasons with the Dodgers' chain and 1 with the Orioles, Howard signed with the Yankees, hoping to finally make it to the majors. His bat caught line-drive-itis, and he came up after a spate of injuries hit the infield. He was pretty much sliced and diced by big-league pitchers. A former replacement player, he wasn't voted a share of the World Series spoils. ■

DEREK JETER — YOUNG GUN

SS • BR • TR • 6′3 • 175 • 22 • NYA92/1

	AB	R	H	2B	3B	HR	RBI	BB	SO	SB	CS	BA	OB	SA
NYA95	48	5	12	4	1	0	7	3	11	0	0	.250	.294	.375
NYA96	582	104	183	25	6	10	78	48	102	14	7	.314	.370	.430

Some scouts had said: Jeter is too error-prone; his arm is too weak; he should play second. Jeter made 56 errors at Class-A Greensboro in '93; after that season, he worked his tail off in the instructional

league and made 25 errors the following year. He played 157 games in the A.L. last season and made 22 errors. Jeter's not a good defensive shortstop yet, but he certainly has the tools to become one. He showed the speed and athleticism necessary for the position. He just needs to improve on the double play and play hitters better. If he does this, he will be—as another scout said—the next Larkin. ■

D'ANGELO JIMENEZ — SOLID PROSPECT

SS • BB • TR • 6'0 • 160 • 19

	AB	R	H	2B	3B	HR	RBI	BB	SO	SB	CS	BA	OB	SA
A	537	68	131	25	5	6	48	56	113	15	17	.244	.317	.343

If Jimenez makes it to Double-A this season—and if he hits better when he gets there—he will be Grade-A. He has gap power, quick feet, good hands, a good arm, fine speed, and factory-installed antilock brakes. Scouts think all he needs is experience. ■

PAT KELLY

2B • BR • TR • 6'0 • 180 • 29 • NYA88/6

	AB	R	H	2B	3B	HR	RBI	BB	SO	SB	CS	BA	OB	SA
NYA94	286	35	80	21	2	3	41	19	51	6	5	.280	.330	.399
NYA95	270	32	64	12	1	4	29	23	65	8	3	.237	.307	.333
NYA96	21	4	3	0	0	0	2	2	9	0	1	.143	.217	.143
CAREER	1599	193	402	91	10	24	173	108	317	48	26	.251	.308	.366

Kelly played 13 games because of a shoulder surgery and a pulled hamstring. Sad to say, but with Duncan hitting .340, Kelly's troubles would have to be categorized as a lucky break for the team. ■

JIMMY KEY

SP • BR • TL • 6'1 • 185 • 35 • TOR82/3

	G	GS	IP	H	HR	BB	K	W	L	S	ERA	K/BB	K9	HW9
NYA94	25	25	168	177	10	52	97	17	4	0	3.27	1.9	5.2	12.27
NYA95	5	5	30	40	3	6	14	1	2	0	5.64	2.3	4.2	13.80
NYA96	30	30	169	171	21	58	116	12	11	0	4.68	2.0	6.2	12.19
CAREER	411	344	2299	2231	225	563	1344	164	104	10	3.50	2.4	5.3	10.94

In the first half, Key hit the DL twice—on May 16 because of his shoulder and on June 11 because of a left calf strain. In the second half, he showed that

he has his stuff back. He is able to play with his fastball, but his basic strategy is to pitch away and change speeds. If he can locate, he can win. Even when he can't locate—as he couldn't in Game 6 of the World Series—he can still find a way to win. Key will never be great aga n, but as long as he's healthy, he'll be a solid no. 3-4 starter. As for handling pressure, obviously starting Game 6 that night wasn't enough for him, since he chose to propose to his girlfriend that afternoon. ■

RICKY LEDEE — SOLID PROSPECT

OF • BL • TL • 6'2 • 160 • 23 • NYA90/16

	AB	R	H	2B	3B	HR	RBI	BB	SO	SB	CS	BA	OB	SA
AAA	358	79	101	22	6	21	64	44	95	6	3	.282	.360	.553

He's Ruben Rivera without the hype. Ledee is the same age as Rivera and doesn't have the arm or the speed, but he can hit—not for average, but he has power and could be a viable option if the Yanks will let him give it a try. ■

JIM LEYRITZ

C-3B • BR • TR • 6'0 • 190 • 33 • NYA85

	AB	R	H	2B	3B	HR	RBI	BB	SO	SB	CS	BA	OB	SA
NYA94	249	47	66	12	0	17	58	35	61	0	0	.265	.365	.518
NYA95	264	37	71	12	0	7	37	37	73	1	1	.269	.374	.394
NYA96	265	23	70	10	0	7	40	30	68	2	0	.264	.355	.381
CAREER	1561	203	416	70	1	57	243	193	349	5	6	.266	.361	.422

Leyritz hit a 2-run homer in the 15th inning of Game 2 against Seattle in '95, then followed that up with a 3-run dinger against Wohlers in Game 4 against Atlanta in '96. Now his teammates don't mind so much those stupid cowboy hats he wears. He's a versatile player who can catch or play first, second, third, or even left field, if need be. As for guts, he's taken a pitch to the head from Randy Johnson and come back for more. What he's worth to a team, statistics can't measure. ■

GRAEME LLOYD

RP • BL • TL • 6′7 • 215 • 29 • TOR88

	G	GS	IP	H	HR	BB	K	W	L	S	ERA	K/BB	K9	HW9
MIL94	43	0	47	49	4	15	31	2	3	3	5.17	2.1	5.9	12.26
MIL95	33	0	32	28	4	8	13	0	5	4	4.50	1.6	3.7	10.13
MIL/NYA96	65	0	56	61	4	22	30	2	6	0	4.17	1.4	4.8	13.32
CAREER	196	0	198	202	17	58	105	7	27	7	4.04	1.8	4.8	11.81

New York fans are quick to give up on someone, but, more than anything else, they love to be proved wrong. Strawberry and Gooden are 2 of the most popular players on the team. And when Jack McDowell flipped off the crowd in '95, then returned to pitch his best baseball of the season, they decided he was a New Yorker after all. Lloyd was the just the latest in a long line. He is a serviceable left-hander with a good slider and a straight fastball who, until he was traded to the Yankees, had a reputation for being rubber-armed. He pitched badly, and suddenly he was being blamed for the Yankees August collapse. It was questionable whether he'd even be on the post-season roster. Many before him—Ed Whitson, Steve Trout—have had nervous breakdowns in New York after a fraction of that adversity. All Lloyd did was roll through the first couple of rounds, then go 8 up 8 down in the World Series in crucial moments—and he deserved the MVP as much as any other member of that bullpen. ■

KATSUHIRO MAEDA

SLEEPER

SP • BR • TR • 6′2 • 215 • 25 • NYA96

	G	GS	IP	H	HR	BB	SO	W	L	S	ERA	K/BB	K9	HW9
AA	9	9	53	49	4	21	30	3	2	0	4.05	1.4	5.1	11.81

Maeda is a raw right-hander from Japan who supposedly throws 96–98 mph. Yankees scouting director Mark Newman said Maeda was one of the 10 hardest throwers in the world. He threw 92–93 mph in his first start. His velocity improved in later starts, but he also said that there was better power hitting in Double-A than there was in Japan. He has spiked blond hair that he dyed orange and that may be purple by the time you read this. ■

TINO MARTINEZ

1B • BL • TR • 6′2 • 205 • 29 • SEA88/1

	AB	R	H	2B	3B	HR	RBI	BB	SO	SB	CS	BA	OB	SA
SEA94	329	42	86	21	0	20	61	29	52	1	2	.261	.320	.508
SEA95	519	92	152	35	3	31	111	62	91	0	0	.293	.369	.551
NYA96	595	82	174	28	0	25	117	68	85	2	1	.292	.364	.466
CAREER	2491	332	676	134	6	113	429	266	394	5	7	.271	.342	.466

Martinez was a fine RBI man last season, but otherwise he was nothing special compared to his peers. Adjusting for Yankee Stadium, here's his batting line and that of an average A.L. first baseman (in the same number of at-bats to make the comparison fair).

	AB	R	H	2B	3B	HR	RBI	BB	K	BA	OBP	SLG
Tino	603	80	173	29	0	24	114	72	86	.287	.362	.456
A.L. avg.	603	96	176	31	1	30	108	80	113	.292	.375	.494

As you can see, Tino's a few RBI better than the average A.L. first baseman, but the average first baseman has a huge edge in runs scored and homers, and beats him in every other category except RBI. The average first baseman didn't bat in the middle of a Yankee lineup that had a .360 on-base percentage. Tino is at the top of the A.L.'s second tier of first basemen. He's a quiet, classy guy who helped the team build its large early lead—and didn't make waves when he was asked to make way for Big Daddy in the World Series. ■

JIM MECIR

RP • BB • TR • 6′1 • 195 • 26 • SEA91/3

	G	GS	IP	H	HR	BB	K	W	L	S	ERA	K/BB	K9	HW9
NYA	96	26	0	40	42	6	23	38	1	1	5.13	1.7	8.5	14.61

Acquired in the Tino Martinez trade, Mecir has a clubfoot (his right) and walks with a permanent limp. The foot is weakly muscled and he cannot drive with it, so he uses his upper body to generate power. He has had a number of hip problems because of the foot. None of it keeps him from being able to pitch like a big-leaguer. He's got a screwball, a hard, sinking fastball, a slider, and a change-up—a repertoire few could match. ■

JACKSON MELIAN

3B-OF • 17 • VENEZUELA

Melian is a Venezuelan third baseman/outfielder who is compared to Ruben Rivera. Named for Reggie Jackson, he was the most coveted international player this past season. He used wooden bats in Venezuela and has great speed and power. He was too young to play in the minors last year, and will start (probably in the GCL) playing in the States

this season. If he's to be the next Andruw, though, he'll have to have an explosive season in 1998. If it's 1999 and he hasn't done much, then he won't be anywhere near that kind of a player. ■

RAMIRO MENDOZA — SLEEPER

SP • BR • TR • 6'2 • 155 • 24 • NYA91

	G	GS	IP	H	HR	BB	K	W	L	S	ERA	K/BB	K9	HW9
NYA96	12	11	53	80	5	10	34	4	5	0	6.79	3.4	5.8	15.28

Mendoza has an excellent sinking fastball, but he could not keep it from hitting major-league bats. He made it to the majors in May, but the Yankees grew tired of watching him get hammered and sent him to Triple-A in mid-July. Torre told Mendoza to stop getting cute and challenge hitters with his sinker and good curve. He returned and had a decent September—1-1, 3.60 ERA. He's going to give up hits, but he has excellent control. ■

ERIC MILTON — SOLID PROSPECT

LHP • NYA96/1 • UNIVERSITY OF MARYLAND

Milton was probably the hardest-throwing left-hander in the draft. His college numbers were mediocre, but he played for a bad team in a Baker Bowl-type stadium. Despite this, he had some dominant performances against some excellent ACC teams. He mixes the fastball with a good curve. He should start at a full-season Class-A team (probably Tampa) and could rise quickly. ■

SHEA MORENZ

OF • BL • TR • 6'2 • 205 • 23 • NYA95/1

	AB	R	H	2B	3B	HR	RBI	BB	SO	SB	CS	BA	OB	SA
A	338	40	84	14	4	2	48	38	92	13	3	.249	.343	.331

Morenz was the 27th overall pick in the '95 draft from the University of Texas at Austin, where he also was the starting quarterback. He has speed and power, but his skills are raw. The Yankees compare him to Kieschnick because of his power potential and strong arm. Kieschnick may be an unfair comparison because Morenz can't handle breaking balls and change-ups drive him nuts. George has a football fetish, which may be the only reason they took him. As you'll recall, he was courting John Elway before he signed with the Broncos. ■

JEFF NELSON

RP • BR • TR • 6'8 • 225 • 30 • LA84/22

	G	GS	IP	H	HR	BB	K	W	L	S	ERA	K/BB	K9	HW9
SEA94	28	0	42	35	3	20	44	0	0	0	2.76	2.2	9.4	11.78
SEA95	62	0	78	58	4	27	96	7	3	2	2.17	3.6	11.1	9.81
NYA96	73	0	74	75	6	36	91	4	4	2	4.36	2.5	11.1	13.49
CAREER	300	0	336	296	25	161	338	17	17	11	3.43	2.1	9.1	12.24

Nelson's a big boy who throws with a three-quarters/sidearm delivery. His fastball hits the low 90s, and he has what one scout calls a "Nintendo slider" because of its outrageous break. He had stretches where he was unhittable, as he was in 1995, but he also lost his control in stretches and teams would move in for the kill. He had a poor first half by his standards, but he was fine in the second half and pitched well in some big spots in the postseason. ■

PAUL O'NEILL — AL ELITE

OF • BL • TL • 6'4 • 205 • 34 • CIN81/4

	AB	R	H	2B	3B	HR	RBI	BB	SO	SB	CS	BA	OB	SA
NYA94	368	68	132	25	1	21	83	72	56	5	4	.359	.460	.603
NYA95	460	82	138	30	4	22	96	71	76	1	2	.300	.387	.526
NYA96	546	89	165	35	1	19	91	102	76	0	1	.302	.411	.474
CAREER	4490	631	1269	271	14	178	756	595	733	69	44	.283	.365	.468

What a hitter. This guy recast himself after coming over from the National League. He was a .250–.280 hitter with good power who struck out too much. Now he's more of a line-drive hitter than a slugger, and his plate discipline and ability to hit for average leave him with few peers in either league. In addition, he remains a smooth defensive right fielder with a solid arm. He's also got a frightening temper and a big contract New York would love to dump. Clearly, he was separated at birth from actor Michael Ontkean (*Twin Peaks, Slapshot*). ■

ANDY PETTITTE — YOUNG GUN

SP • BL • TL • 6'5 • 235 • 24 • NYA90/22

	G	GS	IP	H	HR	BB	K	W	L	S	ERA	K/BB	K9	HW9
NYA95	31	26	175	183	15	63	114	12	9	0	4.17	1.8	5.9	12.65
NYA96	35	34	221	229	23	72	162	21	8	0	3.87	2.3	6.6	12.26

Pettitte throws a bat-breaking cutter considered to be the league's best by a left-hander. When he's

throwing it properly, hitters see a strike and end up flailing at something out of the zone. He also has a very good curve to go with the fastball—when both are working, he is going to win. Pettitte was one of the best in the A.L. last season, but he wasn't even the best pitcher on the staff. Mariano Rivera was. Pettitte's elbow gave him trouble for a good portion of last season. If that continues this spring, it could be the harbinger of a bad year. ■

JORGE POSADA

SLEEPER

C • BB • TR • 6'2 • 205 • 25 • NYA90/24

	AB	R	H	2B	3B	HR	RBI	BB	SO	SB	CS	BA	OB	SA
AAA	354	76	96	22	6	11	62	79	86	3	3	.271	.405	.460

This guy would blow Girardi's doors off as a hitter, but he's suspect defensively. He's been taking the Columbus-Bronx shuttle for the past few seasons, but he needs an emancipation proclamation and a major-league job more than anything. ■

TIM RAINES

OF • BB • TR • 5'8 • 180 • 37 • MON77/5

	AB	R	H	2B	3B	HR	RBI	BB	SO	SB	CS	BA	OB	SA
CHA94	384	80	102	15	5	10	52	61	43	13	0	.266	.365	.409
CHA95	502	81	143	25	4	12	67	70	52	13	2	.285	.374	.422
NYA96	201	45	57	10	0	9	33	34	29	10	1	.284	.383	.468
CAREER	7967	1419	2352	381	109	155	862	1168	838	787	137	.295	.385	.429

Raines had an injury-riddled season. He was placed on the 15-day DL March 21 with a chip fracture in his left thumb, suffered trying to break up a double play in the spring. He returned April 16. But because of persistent soreness in the thumb he was unable to hit right-handed. Raines went back on the DL May 22 with a pulled hamstring. He was activated August 11. He's still a good player, but not what he once was. A great deal of his speed is gone, but he's still a smart baserunner and has excellent plate discipline. For a stretch late in the season and through the first round of the playoffs, he was one of the best players on the team. But he may not have a role on the '97 team. ■

DANNY RIOS

SLEEPER

RP • BR • TR • 6'2 • 210 • 24 • NYA93

	G	GS	IP	H	HR	BB	SO	W	L	S	ERA	K/BB	K9	HW9
AAA	24	0	28	22	1	6	22	4	1	0	1.95	3.7	7.2	9.11

Rios tied for the organization lead with 24 saves in 1995. In '96 he moved to Triple-A and is poised to make a run at a job with the club this season. His control was sharp in Triple-A and he got some strikeouts, so there's no reason to think he can't contribute in New York if he gets the chance. ■

MARIANO RIVERA

AL ELITE

RP • BR • TR • 6'4 • 170 • 27 • NYA90

	G	GS	IP	H	HR	BB	K	W	L	S	ERA	K/BB	K9	HW9
NYA95	19	10	67	71	11	30	51	5	3	0	5.51	1.7	6.9	13.57
NYA96	61	0	107	73	1	34	130	8	3	5	2.09	3.8	10.9	8.99

Since the 1995 divisional series between Seattle and the Yankees, he's been incredible. He doesn't have Percival's control, but he's harder to hit—and almost impossible to homer off of (he allowed 1 all season, to Rafael Palmeiro). He has an explosive 95-mph fastball with late life and a hard-biting slider. He was originally thought of as a starter, but he doesn't have an offspeed pitch and wouldn't fare nearly as well on his second trip through the batting order. There is only one thing to be concerned about: his workload. The Yankees wouldn't have won the division if they hadn't used him as much as they did, but, they were thinking about '96, not "next year." They may lose him to an arm injury as a result, but life's full of trade-offs. ■

RUBEN RIVERA

SOLID PROSPECT

OF • BR • TR • 6'3 • 190 • 23 • NYA90

	AB	R	H	2B	3B	HR	RBI	BB	SO	SB	CS	BA	OB	SA
NYA96	88	17	25	6	1	2	16	13	26	6	2	.284	.381	.443

After a brief stay in the majors, Rivera was demoted to Columbus, where he was ejected from a game July 20. He cleared out his locker after the ejection and disappeared for a day. When he turned up, he found out he had been fined and suspended for a week. His

cousin Mariano was worried that Ruben didn't have his head on straight and was on the verge of throwing his baseball career away. The message was delivered, and he actually returned to the majors to make major contributions to several key victories down the stretch.

But the Yankees have overhyped him, some even comparing him to Mantle. Here is a short list of prospects better than Rivera: Andruw Jones, Vlad Guerrero, Paul Konerko, Karim Garcia, Edgard Velazquez, Ron Wright, Chad Hermansen, Dmitri Young, Nomar Garciaparra, Todd Walker, Darin Erstad, Scott Rolen, Luis Castillo, Enrique Wilson, Todd Helton, Mike Cameron, Richard Hidalgo, Pat Cline, Hiram Bocachica, Richard Almanzar, and Adrian Beltre.

He has speed and power, but his strikeout rate eats up his ability to hit for average. He's never going to hit 500 homers, and he won't be a consistent .300 hitter. If the Yankees are really lucky, Ruben will be Eric Davis—but Mickey Mantle is out of the question. Pretty soon it will be Jackson Melian you'll be hearing about, anyway. ■

KENNY ROGERS

SP • BL • TL • 6'1 • 200 • 32 • TEX82/38

	G	GS	IP	H	HR	BB	K	W	L	S	ERA	K/BB	K9	HW9
TEX94	24	24	167	169	24	52	120	11	8	0	4.46	2.3	6.5	11.91
TEX95	31	31	208	192	26	76	140	17	7	0	3.38	1.8	6.1	11.60
NYA96	30	30	179	179	16	83	92	12	8	0	4.68	1.1	4.6	13.17
CAREER	406	130	1122	1104	113	453	772	82	59	28	4.01	1.7	6.2	12.49

Rogers tried to throw through shoulder pain and keep quiet about it, but having Wade Boggs's strikeouts-to-walks ratio made it pretty obvious to anyone who was watching. He had shoulder surgery after the season. Steinbrenner must be kicking himself—to think he came this close to signing Chuck Finley instead. Finley would've won 20 and helped end the A.L. East race by August. Rogers wasn't awful, but he didn't do what he was signed to do. But then neither did Ed Whitson. At least no Yankee fans have followed Rogers home after games . . . yet. ■

LUIS SOJO

UT • BR • TR • 5'11 • 170 • 31 • TOR86

	AB	R	H	2B	3B	HR	RBI	BB	SO	SB	CS	BA	OB	SA
SEA94	213	32	59	9	2	6	22	8	25	2	1	.277	.308	.423
SEA95	339	50	98	18	2	7	39	23	19	4	2	.289	.335	.416
SEA/NYA96	287	23	63	10	1	1	21	11	17	2	2	.220	.250	.272
CAREER	1698	199	440	68	9	25	160	79	118	20	19	.259	.295	.354

Sojo is a smart player and has a good glove, but he was the least productive offensive player in baseball last season (minimum 250 plate appearances). ■

DARRYL STRAWBERRY

OF • BL • TL • 6'6 • 215 • 35 • NYN80/1

	AB	R	H	2B	3B	HR	RBI	BB	SO	SB	CS	BA	OB	SA
SF94	92	13	22	3	1	4	17	19	22	0	3	.239	.363	.424
NYA95	87	15	24	4	1	3	13	10	22	0	0	.276	.364	.448
NYA96	202	35	53	13	0	11	36	31	55	6	5	.262	.359	.490
CAREER	5045	843	1309	239	36	308	935	750	1237	211	92	.259	.356	.504

Santurce's manager Frankie Thon, said Strawberry had fine bat speed during winter ball in Puerto Rico in 1995-96 and said he'd do some "damage" in the majors. After an incredible performance with the St. Paul Saints of the Northern League—he was on a 100-dinger pace for a 162-game season—Straw signed a contract with the Yankees for $300,000 with a club option for '97. They picked it up and didn't need to think very long about it. If you look at the '96 performance, you'll note it's vintage Straw: an average in the .260s, a good on-base percentage, and a fine slugging percentage. He can still do this for a few seasons.

Even those who want to see him fail would have to admit that, watching him standing calmly in the middle of the locker room celebration, he looked like he's finally turned the corner. He made a mess out of his life and cost himself a chance at the Hall of Fame, but he still answers the bell. ■

BRIEN TAYLOR

SP • BL • TL • 6'4 • 215 • 25 • NYA91/1

	G	GS	IP	H	HR	BB	SO	W	L	S	ERA	K/BB	K9	HW9
A	9	9	16	21	3	43	11	0	5	0	18.73	.3	6.1	35.27

When he was drafted, he was talked up as the next Carlton or Koufax. He got into a brawl in the off-season in '93 and was body-slammed onto his pitching shoulder. Four seasons later, his fastball is 82 when it used to be 95–97. There's no spinning that stat line. What a waste. ■

JAY TESSMER

SOLID PROSPECT

RP • BR • TR • 6′3 • 190 • 24 • NYA95/19

	G	GS	IP	H	HR	BB	SO	W	L	S	ERA	K/BB	K9	HW9
A+	68	0	97	68	2	19	104	12	4	35	1.48	5.5	9.6	8.04

He has mediocre stuff, but he throws sidearm, and it apparently gave Class-A hitters fits. He was dismissed initially, but as the season drew to a close, everyone stopped looking at his stuff and started looking at the results. ▪

DAVID WEATHERS

RP-SP • BR • TR • 6′3 • 205 • 27 • TOR88/3

	G	GS	IP	H	HR	BB	K	W	L	S	ERA	K/BB	K9	HW9
FLA94	24	24	135	166	13	59	72	8	12	0	5.27	1.2	4.8	15.00
FLA95	28	15	90	104	8	52	60	4	5	0	5.98	1.2	6.0	15.60
FLA/NYA96	42	12	88	108	8	42	53	2	4	0	5.52	1.3	5.4	15.33
CAREER	125	57	377	455	34	185	235	17	24	0	5.49	1.3	5.6	15.28

When Mark Hutton went to the Marlins and started pitching like he was Mark Langston, it looked like Bob Watson wouldn't make it until the end of the season. But in the postseason, Weathers became an amalgam of Bob Gibson, John Smoltz, and Babe Ruth. Well, almost. His stuff is decent—an average to average-plus fastball (89–91 mph) that he can sink or 4-seam. He also has a pretty good slider, but his change is in the fetal stage of development. The Marlins still made out on the deal in the long term, but the Yankees have rings, and Weathers is one of the reasons.

JOHN WETTELAND (see Free Agents)

BERNIE WILLIAMS

AL ELITE

CF • BB • TR • 6′2 • 205 • 28 • NYA85

	AB	R	H	2B	3B	HR	RBI	BB	SO	SB	CS	BA	OB	SA
NYA94	408	80	118	29	1	12	57	61	54	16	9	.289	.384	.453
NYA95	563	93	173	29	9	18	82	75	98	8	6	.307	.392	.487
NYA96	551	108	168	26	7	29	102	82	72	17	4	.305	.391	.535
CAREER	2670	430	760	148	27	79	369	348	423	67	39	.285	.368	.449

Williams announced his arrival as a star with a .368-3-13 May and a .362-8-22 June (.695 slugging percentage). One of Bernie's biggest contributions to the team was that he was the yin to the offense's left-handed yang, hitting .376-16-39 in 173 at-bats vs. left-handers (.447 OBP, .694 slugging) and hitting 32% of the Yankees' homers vs. lefties! He didn't run much, but his stolen-base percentage (81%) was excellent. He's in his prime now, so he could top '96. The Yankees would settle for '96 all over again—especially those 6 dingers and 15 RBI in October. ▪

■ 1996 AUTOPSY

Now that manager Tony LaRussa was gone, many expected the A's to lose 100 games the old-fashioned way: through inability and inexperience. New boss Art Howe inherited a pitching staff anchored by the unproven but touted Ariel Prieto, any-day-now Todd Van Poppel, and about a dozen others as familiar to baseball fans as the members of Menudo. It was a real throw-'em-against-the-wall-and-pitch-what-sticks situation now that veterans Dennis Eckersley and Todd Stottlemyre were gone. Subtracting Mike Gallego and Rickey Henderson from the offense didn't help either, and when GM Sandy Alderson dumped Danny Tartabull, too, he was accused of becoming a bit too preoccupied with the team's payroll. Having to go up against the Mariners, the Rangers, and the outstanding-on-paper Angels, the prospect of a train-wreck season was very real.

April 13-12 (13-12, 2½ games back)
The A's opened in Las Vegas because of delayed renovations to Oakland Coliseum. Many assumed the offensive explosion (32 runs in their first 4 games) could be explained away by the Triple-A ballpark, but it continued on the road and back in Oakland. Production came from unexpected quarters, even Mike Bordick, who hit .299, with a .396 on-base percentage and 15 RBI. Scott Brosius was crushing the ball, hitting .369 with 8 homers and a .690 slugging percentage. He was phenomenally patient, drawing 21 walks and getting on base nearly 50% of the time. Jason Giambi wasn't far behind, hitting .344 with 7 doubles, a triple and 3 homers. Even McGwire, who lost most of the month to a torn right arch deluxe—the injury with the grown-up pain—slugged .529 in what would prove to be his worst offensive month of the season. The plot had thickened. If the offense could keep this up—impossible, most thought—the A's could be spoilers if not contenders.

Unfortunately, the pitching was as bad as expected. The staff walked 140 in 231.1 innings while striking out only 145, a truly wretched performance. Doug Johns had 2 great starts, only to follow those with up with 3 lousy ones in which he lasted a combined total of 4 innings, serving as a role model for many of the young hurlers on the staff. No surprise why the bullpen fell apart in the second half—the overwork started here. Carlos Reyes gave up 8 home runs in 33.2 innings but managed a 3-3 record. Meanwhile, de facto ace Ariel Prieto, got no-decisions in 2 quality starts and received about 2 runs a game in support, compared to more than 5 for everyone else.

May 11-16 (24-28, 9½ games back)
The A's rekindled an old flame when their rivalry with Boston flared up yet again, this time over a controversial slide by backup catcher George Williams that broke Wil Cordero's leg. But with both teams now near the bottom of the league, this wasn't the turf battle between two gangs that it used to be—and more like two members of the chess team squaring off in the junior high school playground.

Bordick's time "in the zone" was short, and he hit .165 with a .255 on-base percentage and a .220 slugging percentage in May. These stretches of cluelessness would plague him all season, as he succumbed to 0-for-17, 0-for-21 and 0-for-23 slumps at various points. Brosius also disappeared, but because of injury rather than coming to his senses—and was limited to only 30 at-bats in May and June combined. McGwire turned it up, hitting .356 with 9 homers. But there was no one on base to knock in. Bad timing, because Johns and Prieto stabilized a bit. Johns had 4 quality starts in 6 appearances but managed only a 2-4 record. Prieto was 1-1 with a 4.50 ERA, but went on the DL on the 19th, a day after straining his right elbow against Boston, though no voodoo doll was ever uncovered in the Red Sox clubhouse. Reyes gave up another 6 homers, finishing the month 0-5 with a 7.16 ERA. The fact that the A's let him do that much damage before banishing him to the bullpen showed how sorry their pitching had become only 6 years after Dave Stewart, Bob Welch, Mike Moore, and Scott Sanderson combined to win 79 games. Meanwhile erstwhile closer Mark Acre, did his best imitation of Eck (circa 1986, unfortunately), giving up 15 hits in 9.2 innings, receiving an 8.38 ERA as a parting gift. As Texas and Seattle charged toward the division title, the A's slipped off meekly in the other direction.

June 14-15 (38-43, 10½ games back)
McGwire had an incredible month, hitting .329 with 14 homers and a monstrous .915 slugging percentage—even though he was being pitched around enough to draw 31 walks. He almost single-handedly raised the team on-base percentage to .362 and its slugging percentage to .509. The offense was rolling, batting a season-high .284 with 55 homers. During their second trip to Detroit, the A's hit 10 dingers in a 3-game series—after going deep 9 times in their first series in April. On June 27 they defeated the Angels 18-2, going deep 8 times. Despite this amazing effort, the A's still managed to slip a game farther away in the standings. The pitching was being thoroughly degraded, allowing 115 walks and 296 hits in 258.2 innings, even though they didn't have to face McGwire. Johns went four innings or fewer in three of his five starts, going 1-3, 7.57—at the hands of Kansas City, Toronto, Milwaukee, and California, not exactly the best the league had to offer.

In an effort to find pitchers who could at least get them to the 5th inning, the A's called up several prospects. John Wasdin responded well, beating Roger Clemens and Kevin Appier in his first 2 starts. Bobby Chouinard was less successful, but he impressed the A's management nonetheless. Willie Adams was also called up, but only to make a spot start, as the A's threw him out there to face the Indians. After giving up 2 homers and 4 runs in the first inning, he showed some poise by shutting them down over the next 5. He was sent down after the game, but it was obvious that he'd be back—and at year end he'd made 12 starts and had the best numbers of anyone in the rotation.

July 13-13 (51-56, 6½ games back)
The club slipped by California into third place—or, more accurately, the A's got out of the way as the Angels fell past them. Brosius stormed off the DL with a .343 average, 10 doubles, 7 homers, and 16 walks; McGwire hit 13 homers; and Giambi remained strong, hitting .327 with 14 doubles. It was, however, Jason's last hurrah. His poor performance down the stretch had him refusing to talk to teammates. Steinbach, who quietly had a great year, had his best month of the season, hitting .352 with 10 homers and a .703 slugging percentage. His performance also dropped drastically in August and September as he wore down from all those walks out to the mound. The team went 23 games in a row with at least 1 dinger, and failed to go deep only 3 times all month.

August 15-16 (66-72, 12½ games back)
Brosius was the first hitter to fall victim to the virus sweeping the A's hitters. He hit .314 for the month, but his strikeout-to-walk ratio slipped from an excellent 19:16 in July to a dreadful 26:6. Giambi fell next, hitting no homers and slugging .361. McGwire's power also dropped. This lack of production dropped them 7 games in the standings in May, and in August it dropped them out of contention. They managed to go 15-16 for the month on the strength of their starting pitching—with the notable exception of a 3-game stretch where the A's lost 13-7, 18-5, and 14-3. Prieto, who had come off the DL in July and turned in a promising start, reeled off 6 quality starts, going 8 innings in 4 of them, but was handicapped by poor run support, ending up only 2-2 despite a 2.33 ERA. Even Don Wengert pitched effectively, going 3-2 with a 3.86 ERA. The bullpen didn't contribute much, finally breaking down from overuse.

September 12-12 (78-84, 12 games back)
The offense finished on a downward spiral, though they did manage to break the record of the 1961 Yankees for dingers in a season—more evidence that baseball in the '90s is degenerating into something unrecognizable. The team went deep 3 times in a game 30 times, but only once in September. Howe could choose to look at the glass as half full (the team hovered near .500 despite only a single starter winning 8 games and only 2 having winning records) or half empty (there is no way this team can realistically expect to get 123 dingers and 329 RBI ever again from an injury-prone McGwire, aging Terry Steinbach, and feast-or-famine Geronimo Berroa).

■ 1997 DIAGNOSIS

Offense
Despite reports from Mark McGwire that the ball was flying farther in Oakland Coliseum after the renovations, the data indicate that the Coliseum hasn't changed much and is still an extreme

pitchers' park. There is more foul territory than any other park in baseball and fly balls simply do not carry there. If Dante Bichette had ended up with the A's in 1993, he'd be out of baseball by now. So hitting 243 dingers, as the A's did, is an accomplishment. Nevertheless, the A's scored fewer runs than the Mariners, Indians, Orioles, Rangers, Red Sox, White Sox, Brewers, Twins, and Yankees. The Yankees hit 81 fewer dingers than the A's, the Twins 125 fewer, but these teams had more speed, didn't strike out as much, and hit more than 20 points higher. The comparison between the Yankees and the A's is a fascinating one, because the runs scored are so similar despite completely opposite approaches—making contact versus heel-swinging.

	Runs	1B	2B	3B	HR	BB	SO	BA	SLG	OBP
Yankees	871	1,138	293	28	162	632	909	.288	.436	.360
Athletics	861	945	283	21	243	640	1,114	.265	.452	.344

McGwire was the leader with the bat, and tough hitters such as Geronimo Berroa and McGwire's protégé Giambi, followed his lead. The outfield didn't yield as much as Howe would have liked, and is still unsettled with Matt Stairs, José Herrera, Ernie Young, Phil Plantier, and a number of prospects all bringing something to the table. The corner infielders (McGwire, Brosius, and Giambi) provided a lot of power, but the middle infield was weak. Bordick was mediocre during the best of times for hitters, and Brent Gates continued to be plagued by injuries, leaving Tony Batista as the only offensive bright spot in the middle infield. Steinbach had his best year with the bat, but will be 35 in '97—and Alderson did not offer him arbitration, allowing him to test the free agent waters. If he doesn't return, Izzy Molina and George Williams, who combined for 25 hits in 70 games in '96, will compete for the starting catching spot.

Defense

Only 4 teams made fewer errors than the A's, and 3 of them ended up in the playoffs. Bordick is a standout at short, and Batista kept up with him just fine on the double play. Giambi and Brosius were solid at third, and McGwire was a little below average at first. The outfield wasn't quite so solid. Ernie Young has good range and a strong arm in center. Herrera showed a strong arm in right, but also flubbed a lot of routine plays. He's young, gifted, and tentative. Left field was unsettled all year. Giambi looked lost, Plantier's glove didn't get him to the majors and it won't keep him there, and Stairs is always an adventure; it was rookies Damon Mashore and Brian Lesher who lent some stability during their brief stay. Steinbach has always been one of the best catchers in the game, both at handling a staff and throwing out opposing baserunners.

Pitching

The starters ended '96 with a 47-65 record and a 5.57 ERA. But if you adjust for their pitcher's park, the starters were almost a run worse than the average A.L. team. This should change in '97. Prieto looked good during the second half of '96, his previous poor performances attributed to a sore shoulder caused by his long pitching layoff during and after his defection. He pitched his last 8 starts with a groin pull—and did so effectively—so his toughness and resilience are unquestionable. Willie Adams was the prize of Oakland's staff and was one of the few starters who could be counted on to carry the game into late innings. He consistently threw strikes and succeeded, despite reports that his repertoire was only average and that his velocity wasn't strong (though removal of bone chips in his elbow seems to have corrected this). After Adams, John Wasdin was the most impressive young pitcher; the coaches liked his stuff and his fearlessness. They haven't given up on Steve Karsay yet. And there are plenty of rookies on their way up who can complicate things further: Brad Rigby, Aaron Small, Bret Wagner, Stacey Hollins, and Miguel Jimenez. Art Howe is known for his patience in developing young players; pitching coach Bob Cluck will need to match him sigh for sigh.

The relief corps was much better than the starters, managing a 31-19 record. The A's wouldn't have been close to .500 if the relievers hadn't balanced the terrible starting pitching in the first half, keeping the games close and waiting for McGwire, Berroa, and Steinbach to hit a 3-run homer. Buddy Groom, Mike Mohler and Jim Corsi led the pen, going 17-3. Less impressive was Carlos Reyes, who was dumped from the rotation, only to yield 98 baserunners in 59 relief innings. Billy Taylor was a decent closer—striking out more than a man an inning and averaging fewer than 8 hits per 9—but he rents rather than owns the job.

Farm System
The A's have the fewest scouts in baseball, and GM Sandy Alderson has built, and continues to build, through the acquisition of other team's prospects. The A's have brought along a number of terrific everyday players on their own (McGwire, Steinbach, and José Canseco, to name just 3), but haven't developed a front-line pitcher since Mike Norris—and most of that credit should go to Billy Martin's pitching coach, Art Fowler, and perhaps a certain illegal pitch he was known for teaching.

Management and Ownership
Steve Schott and his partner Ken Hofmann spend more time trying to deal with stadium issues than they'd like to let on, since Alameda County has been bending over backward for Al Davis and the Raiders at the expense of the A's. The A's had to open their season in Cashman Field in Las Vegas. Howe and the players often expressed dismay at the condition of the Oakland Coliseum playing field following football games—Giambi, who is an adventure in a pristine outfield, nearly blew out his knee stumbling around on the loose sod. When the glass put into the new sky boxes was shattered by foul balls—not an issue at football games—the position of the A's well below the Raiders on the Alameda food chain was underscored. The Coliseum people have suggested that the A's are using these as excuses to leave for San José. Renovations, field conditions, and the sound of shattering glass after foul balls aside, the glaring fact remains that the A's had the lowest attendance in baseball, and something has to give.

The Oakland front office is known around the A.L. as one of the savviest in baseball. Sandy Alderson is signed through the 2000 season, and will regain the title of club president in '97. Alderson built a dynasty in the late '80s and is now trying to rebuild it, though he hasn't been all that active in the trade market—especially compared to the Tigers and the Brewers. The failure to deal Rickey Henderson rather than lose him to free agency can be explained, in part, by the uncertainties in ownership (the Haas family sold the team after the '96 season) and field management (LaRussa's status was uncertain until the ownership situation was resolved). But the A's again made no effort to play contenders off one another at the deadline in '96, with Terry Steinbach the card they could have played. He had an excellent year, and his numbers almost guarantee that he'll be too pricey for this year. Alderson seemed to be banking on Steinbach's loyalty. Steinbach may or may not return in '97, but his value in trade terms was at an all-time high. If they lose him, this will prove to have been an enormous missed opportunity.

Art Howe had success with the Astros, helping Biggio, Bagwell, Finley, and Caminiti begin to develop into stars, but couldn't take them to the next level. Unless the A's cement some of their shakier positions, chances are he'll suffer a similar fate in Oakland—helping a team rebuild with dignity, only to be cut loose just when the pieces are in place.

. . . and whatnot: Sympathy for the GM (Part I)
OK, anyone who didn't expect the '96 A's to fold up like a $2 suitcase please stand up. Now, everyone who is related to a team employee please sit back down. The other 3 of you can take your door prize and leave.

The A's were nothing if not shocking in '96. They won 78 games without a 9-game winner on the staff. They lost their core of veteran pitchers and hitters, and it should have crippled them. Eck and Stottlemyre left holes in the staff, while the departure of Rickey and Tartabull gutted the batting order. Alderson didn't get a lot of short-term value for his veterans. Instead, he picked up potential stars such as Bret Wagner, and concentrated on stocking the system with as many other live arms as possible. As a result, draftees such as Willie Adams and Ariel Prieto may have some help in a couple of years.

Alderson filled the holes in the outfield with minor-league veterans such as Ernie Young and fresh-faced prospects such as José Herrera. Jason Giambi was given a lot of elbow room, Tony Batista finally got a chance to play, and Geronimo Berroa dropped jaws around the league with his homers. And though pitching was the downfall of the team, sticking with Prieto bore fruit, and prospects Adams and Jay Witasick got some big-league experience. Unfortunately, other prospects such as Mark Acre, Bobby Chouinard and Steve Wojciechowski used their opportunity to show the A's how much more growing they had to do.

Because of the season's unimpressive finish, many see the '96 A's as a fluke rather than a bonafide success. Maybe they will lose more games in '97 than in '96, but they are heading in the right direction. The A's built themselves a solid foundation last season. This team contended for half the year, and with adjustments they'll be vying for A.L. West pennants before Alderson's contract expires in 2000. No one's claiming that Oakland will be the "Miracle A's"—but they are bearing more than a passing resemblance to the A's of the mid-'80s, a few years before they ended up in the World Series 3 years in a row.

MARK ACRE

RP • BR • TR • 6'8 • 235 • 28 • OAK91

	G	GS	IP	H	HR	BB	K	W	L	S	ERA	K/BB	K9	HW9
OAK94	34	0	34	24	4	23	21	5	1	0	3.41	.9	5.6	12.43
OAK95	43	0	52	52	7	28	47	1	2	0	5.71	1.7	8.1	13.85
OAK96	22	0	25	38	4	9	18	1	3	2	6.12	2.0	6.5	16.92
CAREER	99	0	111	114	15	60	86	7	6	2	5.11	1.4	7.0	14.10

The A's still tout Question Mark as a prospect despite his hittable pitches and lack of command. Acre has a good, 4-seam fastball and average breaking stuff. He will continue to struggle until he masters the breaking ball or can develop a change-up. A's pitching coach Bob Cluck: "He's got to get it through his head that he's not a power pitcher." He was sent down after May, and the A's attempts to revive him at season's end proved fruitless. Unless he can come up with a slider, control, or bad hair, height will be the only thing he has in common with Randy Johnson. ■

WILLIE ADAMS

YOUNG GUN

SP • BR • TR • 6'7 • 215 • 24 • OAK93/2

	G	GS	IP	H	HR	BB	K	W	L	S	ERA	K/BB	K9	HW9
OAK96	12	12	76	76	11	23	68	3	4	0	4.01	3.0	8.0	11.72

Adams pitched effectively in his debut season, showing much better control than the more experienced A's pitchers and posting an outstanding strikeout rate. He took advantage of working in a pitcher's park, going 3-2 with a 2.90 ERA in Oakland. Adams throws an 89–90-mph fastball, and he improved his slider by changing his grip. He also throws a change-up and a good curveball. He's been knocked in the past for being afraid to use his fastball, but that didn't seem to be much of a problem in '96. His control has always been solid, and his confidence was extremely high for a youngster. Pitching for the 1992 Olympic team must have something to do with it, and Oakland seems to breed tough-guy prospects as if they're planning a production of *Guys and Dolls* in the off-season. Considering the pitching woes in Oakland, Adams is an exciting young talent who will be given every opportunity to succeed. Pending the return of Steve Karsay from injury, Adams and Prieto are the cream of this staff. ■

TONY BATISTA

SLEEPER

SS • BR • TR • 6'0 • 180 • 23 • OAK92

	AB	R	H	2B	3B	HR	RBI	BB	SO	SB	CS	BA	OB	SA
OAK96	238	38	71	10	2	6	25	19	49	7	3	.298	.350	.433

Batista hit for both power and average in '96. He's always been a free swinger, but his strikeout-to-walk ratio was a pleasant improvement over his minor-league numbers. He can play both short and second base, has excellent range, and can turn the double play, but he kicks his share of routine grounders. Batista must hit if he's to hold down a job in Oakland. He has more power potential than Gates, but failed to hit well enough to take the job for keeps when Gates went on the DL. ■

ALLEN BATTLE

OF • BR • TR • 6'0 • 170 • 28 • SL91/14

	AB	R	H	2B	3B	HR	RBI	BB	SO	SB	CS	BA	OB	SA
SL95	118	13	32	5	0	0	2	15	26	3	3	.271	.358	.314
OAK96	130	20	25	3	0	1	5	17	26	10	2	.192	.293	.238

Some of Battle's minor-league numbers make him look like Lance Johnson, but he's looked more like Curt Ford in the majors. Battle lost the center-field job to Ernie Young in the spring, and it wasn't due solely to a sore hamstring. Young is younger and has more pop, while Battle is fast but doesn't use it to its full advantage. With kids such as José Herrera and productive utility players such as Matt Stairs in his way, prospects don't look too hot for Battle. ■

MARK BELLHORN

SOLID PROSPECT

2B-SS • BB • TR • 6'1 • 195 • 22 • OAK95/2

	AB	R	H	2B	3B	HR	RBI	BB	SO	SB	CS	BA	OB	SA
AA	468	84	117	24	5	10	71	73	124	19	2	.250	.353	.387

Bellhorn was assigned to Modesto in '95 to begin his minor-league career and spent '96 in Double-A Huntsville. Oakland is in a hurry to develop him. He has a quick first step and possesses an innate sense of positioning. The A's worked on him to be more patient, and it paid dividends. He still strikes out too much, but he did lead Huntsville in walks. He doesn't show much home-run pop, so he'll probably have to make it the majors as a shortstop—though his size has prompted rumors that he will need to shift positions. He was young for his league, and if he's in Triple-A in '97 it will mean the A's are really serious about him. ■

TOM BENNETT

SP • BR • TR • 6'4 • 180 • 20 • OAK95/8

	G	GS	IP	H	HR	BB	SO	W	L	S	ERA	K/BB	K9	HW9
A	6	5	21	17	1	18	17	0	1	0	3.92	.9	7.4	15.25

Bennett looked really good in rookie ball in '95, but his chances for progress were derailed on the first day of spring training when he aired his arm out like it was Game 7. He was shut down and shipped to extended spring training. When healthy, Bennett throws 93–94 mph with good movement. He has a decent change-up, and his curveball is good but inconsistent. Bennett cost himself a season of development and possibly his prospect status by not being able to delay gratification in the spring. Check his velocity and his strikeout totals in '97 to see if he's bounced back. ■

GERONIMO BERROA

DH-OF • BR • TR • 6'0 • 195 • 32 • TOR83

	AB	R	H	2B	3B	HR	RBI	BB	SO	SB	CS	BA	OB	SA
OAK94	340	55	104	18	2	13	65	41	62	7	2	.306	.379	.485
OAK95	546	87	152	22	3	22	88	63	98	7	4	.278	.351	.451
OAK96	586	101	170	32	1	36	106	47	122	0	3	.290	.344	.532
CAREER	1661	255	470	78	6	73	268	163	323	14	11	.283	.347	.469

Berroa had most of his career wasted by organizations such as Toronto, Atlanta, Florida, and Cincinnati before the A's finally rescued him in '94 and let him play. The move has paid enormous dividends, as Berroa has lived up to the expectations established by his many fine minor-league seasons.

Berroa is a below-average fielder, which may have hurt his chances with N.L. clubs. He's better off in a league where he can DH, though he has a good arm and he hustles. Berroa was all about power in '96, helping to reestablish the "Bash Brothers" mystique with help from Mark McGwire, Jason Giambi, Scott Brosius, and Terry Steinbach. Berroa doesn't seem to have the problems with breaking stuff that most sluggers do, so it's not likely that he'll disappear because pitchers stop throwing him fastballs. He twice hit 3 dingers in a game in '96. Because of the A's poor on-base percentage, Berroa managed only 106 RBI with his 36 dingers, 32 doubles, and .290 batting average. If he'd been hitting behind Bagwell and Biggio he would have driven in 150. ■

MIKE BORDICK

SS • BR • TR • 5'11 • 170 • 31 • OAK86

	AB	R	H	2B	3B	HR	RBI	BB	SO	SB	CS	BA	OB	SA
OAK94	391	38	99	18	4	2	37	38	44	7	2	.253	.320	.335
OAK95	428	46	113	13	0	8	44	35	48	11	3	.264	.325	.350
OAK96	525	46	126	18	4	5	54	52	59	5	6	.240	.307	.318
CAREER	2643	273	682	94	15	21	252	240	309	48	31	.258	.324	.329

Bordick had another excellent year with the glove—a good thing, because he had another terrible year at the plate. A strong September got him out of the .220s, but he still ended up barely over .300 in on-base percentage, with only 27 extra-base hits. As bad as he is at the plate, he is indispensable up the middle. His range is still well above average, he positions himself well, and he is excellent on the double play. Good fielding can do a lot for young pitching, keeping them from thinking they have to strike out everyone they face. It might not show in the statistics published every Tuesday in *USA Today*, but Bordick is one of the most valuable players on the team. A service time free agent, many teams were prepared to throw serious money at him if he went on the market. ■

JOHN BRISCOE

RP • BR • TR • 6′3 • 190 • 29 • OAK88/3

	G	GS	IP	H	HR	BB	K	W	L	S	ERA	K/BB	K9	HW9
OAK94	37	0	49	31	7	39	45	4	2	1	4.01	1.2	8.3	12.85
OAK95	16	0	18	25	4	21	19	0	1	0	8.35	.9	9.5	23.00
OAK96	17	0	26	18	2	24	14	0	1	1	3.76	.6	4.8	14.52
CAREER	100	2	139	124	18	129	115	5	5	2	5.70	.9	7.4	16.37

Briscoe has been getting innings out of Oakland's bullpen since 1991, but if these are his prime years, it sure doesn't show. He spent some time back in Triple-A to work on his control and his numbers were reversed: much fewer walks and more hits. He's not afraid of throwing strikes to Triple-A batters. Art Howe probably isn't afraid of him doing that either. ■

SCOTT BROSIUS

3B • BR • TR • 6′1 • 185 • 30 • OAK87/19

	AB	R	H	2B	3B	HR	RBI	BB	SO	SB	CS	BA	OB	SA
OAK94	324	31	77	14	1	14	49	24	57	2	6	.238	.289	.417
OAK95	389	69	102	19	2	17	46	41	67	4	2	.262	.342	.452
OAK96	428	73	130	25	0	22	71	59	85	7	2	.304	.393	.516
CAREER	1509	221	397	75	4	65	208	144	270	25	11	.263	.332	.447

Brosius had a fine season, which was rudely interrupted by injuries at the beginning and middle and a disappointing slump to close out the year. In the last game of spring training he pulled his hamstring stealing second, then was lost for 6 weeks in May and June to an arm injury after being struck by a Mark Gubicza pitch. At the time, Brosius was leading the A.L. in on-base percentage. In the field, Brosius has an average but accurate arm and is a vacuum at third base, a position the A's have been trying to solidify since Carney Lansford retired. Brosius's performance with both bat and glove meant that Jason Giambi was the one who had to shuffle from position to position.

Brosius hit for a much better average than his past performance would indicate, now that he's learned how to handle the breaking stuff that pitchers have been getting him out with for years. His strikeout-to-walk ratio was disturbing, however, falling from 16:21 in April to 26:6 in August. Some bad habits may have resurfaced.

Brosius may never match these numbers again, having never done anything like it before. His career on-base percentage heading into '96 was .306, and '95 was the first time he'd had a percentage higher than .300. His transformation from a role player to a complete hitter in a single year is impressive. Repeating the performance would be even more surprising. ■

ERIC CHAVEZ

3B • OAK96/1 • MOUNT CARMEL HIGH SCHOOL (CA)

Chavez is an impressively built young talent who was considered to be the best pure hitter in the '96 draft. He ended up ditching plans to attend USC, and the A's wasted no time in sending him to instructional ball. The 1997 season will be the first year to see what Chavez can do in the pros, so right now he's more potential than product. The SoCal native said he was "stoked" at the prospect of playing for the A's—which may have prompted A's management to insert a no-street-luge-in-the-off-season clause into his contract. ■

BOBBY CHOUINARD

SP • BR • TR • 6′1 • 190 • 24 • BAL90/6

	G	GS	IP	H	HR	BB	K	W	L	S	ERA	K/BB	K9	HW9
OAK96	13	11	59	75	10	32	32	4	2	0	6.10	1.0	4.9	16.32

Chouinard has spent the past couple of years developing into a very good pitching prospect, but a lack of overpowering stuff has held him back. His control was spotty at Triple-A Edmonton, but he still had an excellent record and a PCL-defying ERA.

His stay in Oakland didn't compare to what Willie Adams was able to do, and Howe couldn't decide how he felt about him—praising him for his toughness early on and then knocking him at the time of his demotion for "killing our bullpen," which is like blaming the '80s pop culture on Boy George. He had some help. If Chouinard can regain his early '96 form, he should have a shot at making the bullpen if not the rotation in '97. ■

JIM CORSI (see Looking for a Game)

STEVE COX

SOLID PROSPECT

1B • BL • TL • 6′4 • 200 • 22 • OAK92/6

	AB	R	H	2B	3B	HR	RBI	BB	SO	SB	CS	BA	OB	SA
AA	381	59	107	21	1	12	61	51	65	2	2	.281	.372	.436

Cox developed from a decent prospect to a stud in '95, primarily because he was injury-free for the first time. He continued his progress in Double-A Huntsville only to break down in the Arizona Fall League. If healthy, he could easily develop into a 20 to 25 homer guy and maybe even better. Cox had a reputation as a hothead, but his attitude seems to have improved as he's risen through the ranks. His defense improved dramatically in '96, making him the class of the Southern League, which will only put a shine on his already bright prospects. Mark McGwire may be a DH in a few years, with Cox the heir apparent at first base. ■

BRENT GATES

SLEEPER

2B • BB • TR • 6′1 • 180 • 27 • OAK91/1

	AB	R	H	2B	3B	HR	RBI	BB	SO	SB	CS	BA	OB	SA
OAK94	233	29	66	11	1	2	24	21	32	3	0	.283	.337	.365
OAK95	524	60	133	24	4	5	56	46	84	3	3	.254	.308	.344
OAK96	247	26	65	19	2	2	30	18	35	1	1	.263	.316	.381
CAREER	1539	179	419	83	9	16	179	141	226	14	7	.272	.331	.369

Gates needed to follow his lackluster '95 season with a breakout year, but injuries cost him the chance. When healthy, he is a good line-drive hitter. He is an average second baseman, so he will need to hit to play. He will face some competition from Tony Batista, so watch how each does in spring training. ■

JASON GIAMBI

YOUNG GUN

1B-OF-3B • BL • TR • 6′2 • 200 • 26 • OAK92/2

	AB	R	H	2B	3B	HR	RBI	BB	SO	SB	CS	BA	OB	SA
OAK95	176	27	45	7	0	6	25	28	31	2	1	.256	.364	.398
OAK96	536	84	156	40	1	20	79	51	95	0	1	.291	.355	.481

Giambi was drafted out of high school by Milwaukee, but he elected to attend college and earned his way onto the '92 Olympic baseball squad. This sweetened his prospects a little, and Oakland took him in the '92 draft. Giambi has developed into a patient hitter with the kind of power you want at the corners. He should hit about .300 with the same

power he displayed this year. He doesn't match up well against lefties, but he hits well enough that a platoon isn't a necessity.

He is fairly versatile on defense, but he doesn't shine anywhere. He shared time with Scott Brosius at third base, but spent just as much time at first base, where he fielded almost every ball his way, and in left field, where he didn't. Giambi has carved out a reputation as a gritty, hardworking player. He has earned the respect and friendship of McGwire, and endorsements like that are hard to come by—even if other teammates were on him about injuries that ended his season prematurely. Can't see where McGwire would have anything to say about that. ■

BEN GRIEVE

GRADE-A PROSPECT

OF • BL • TR • 6′4 • 200 • 20 • OAK94/1

	AB	R	H	2B	3B	HR	RBI	BB	SO	SB	CS	BA	OB	SA
AA	232	34	55	8	1	8	32	35	53	0	3	.237	.338	.384

Grieve continued to live up to lofty expectations in '96, smacking 28 doubles and 19 homers between Class-A and Double-A. He hit .410 in May and left Modesto with a .356 batting average. His batting average collapsed when he moved to Huntsville, but he may have been getting tired by the end of the season. Grieve has a natural swing, and any fears that his power potential had been exaggerated were allayed. He has a good arm for right field, but he's been accused of being too tentative defensively.

In '95 Grieve got impatient when pitchers wouldn't challenge him. He addressed that problem in '96, refusing to give in to the pitcher and taking more walks. There are 5-year veterans who haven't figured that out, so pencil in Grieve for at least 10. ■

BUDDY GROOM

RP • BL • TL • 6′2 • 200 • 31 • CHA87/12

	G	GS	IP	H	HR	BB	K	W	L	S	ERA	K/BB	K9	HW9
DET94	40	0	32	31	4	13	27	0	1	1	3.94	2.1	7.6	12.38
DET/FLA95	37	4	55	81	8	32	35	2	5	1	7.44	1.1	5.7	18.49
OAK96	72	1	77	85	8	34	57	5	0	2	3.84	1.7	6.7	13.90
CAREER	180	15	240	293	28	114	149	7	13	5	5.36	1.3	5.6	15.26

His real first name is Wedsel, which is unfortunate. He is over 30, doesn't have overpowering stuff, and is inconsistent from week to week, which is also unfortunate. He did his best work before the All-Star

break, then went into the tank in August with the rest of the bullpen. He probably just wore out, as he ended up making 72 appearances, behind only Mike Myers, Eddie Guardado, Mike Stanton, Heathcliff Slocumb, Michael Jackson, and Jeff Nelson in the A.L. ■

RAMON HERNANDEZ — SOLID PROSPECT

C • BR • TR • 6′0 • 170 • 20

	AB	R	H	2B	3B	HR	RBI	BB	SO	SB	CS	BA	OB	SA
A	447	62	114	26	2	12	68	69	62	2	3	.255	.355	.403

Hernandez is decent defensively, good at blocking balls in the dirt, and has a good arm. He hits for average and power, but runs like a catcher already. His ability to draw a walk and keep his strikeouts down bodes well for his future. He could be the dark horse who beats out A. J. Hinch for the A's starting job in a few years. ■

JOSÉ HERRERA

OF • BL • TL • 6′0 • 165 • 24 • TOR89

	AB	R	H	2B	3B	HR	RBI	BB	SO	SB	CS	BA	OB	SA
OAK95	70	9	17	1	2	0	2	6	11	1	3	.243	.299	.314
OAK96	320	44	86	15	1	6	30	20	59	8	2	.269	.318	.378

Oakland acquired the services of Herrera and Steve Karsay when they traded Rickey Henderson to Toronto in '93. Karsay could still develop into a fine major-league pitcher, and Herrera had a promising rookie season. Oakland has rushed Herrera, giving him only 92 games above Class-A. He has the tools, but he must exercise more discipline or he'll develop into a 6-hole hitter. He has a strong arm and decent speed. He's been groomed as the A's center fielder, but was pushed to right by Ernie Young. His arm strength should help him if he stays there, but he needs to become more comfortable. When asked what Herrera needed to improve his defense, Howe replied, "You can't coach fear out of a guy." He'll continue to learn on the job in '97, but the Blue Jays have proven that they are not be trusted when it comes to outfield prospects, Berroa notwithstanding. ■

A. J. HINCH — SOLID PROSPECT

C • OAK96/3 • STANFORD UNIVERSITY

Taken in the third round of the '96 draft, Hinch was the catcher at Stanford and a member of Team USA. A potent amateur hitter, he was rewarded with a guaranteed spot on Team USA for not going pro, something USA Baseball would later regret because he couldn't catch due to an arm injury that hampered his throwing. He displays leadership skills and is very athletic. Going into '96, scouts knocked his inconsistent release behind the plate and his inability to pull inside pitches. Despite this, he is an exciting prospect who should develop into an everyday player. There's no guarantee that it will be as a catcher. ■

MIGUEL JIMENEZ — SLEEPER

RP-SP • BR • TR • 6′2 • 205 • 27 • OAK91/14

	G	GS	IP	H	HR	BB	SO	W	L	S	ERA	K/BB	K9	HW9
AA	19	2	38	43	7	27	28	0	4	0	8.84	1.0	6.7	16.73

Back when Karsay was the A's savior apparent, Jimenez appeared to be right behind him in reviving the rotation. Lack of command and a few injuries later, Jimenez had dropped from the picture. While everyone eagerly followed Karsay's recovery, Jimenez was written off. Last year, after a successful stint in Modesto, Jimenez was promoted to Double-A and got clocked. It's getting late, but don't count him out yet. ■

DOUG JOHNS

SP • BR • TL • 6′2 • 185 • 29 • OAK90/21

	G	GS	IP	H	HR	BB	K	W	L	S	ERA	K/BB	K9	HW9
OAK95	11	9	54	44	5	26	25	5	3	0	4.61	1.0	4.2	11.67
OAK96	40	23	158	187	21	69	71	6	12	1	5.98	1.0	4.0	14.58

Johns is a left-hander, but he's a finesse guy with a mediocre fastball who uses an average curveball and change-up as his out pitches. If he doesn't have control, he gets shelled. His first 2 starts were so good that the A's were considering retiring his number, but by July he was in the bullpen, from which he pitched with varying success for the remainder of the season. He'll likely be around in '97, but he'll be crowded out shortly. ■

STEVE KARSAY

SLEEPER

SP • BR • TR • 6'3 • 205 • 25 • TOR90/1

	G	GS	IP	H	HR	BB	SO	W	L	S	ERA	K/BB	K9	HW9
A+	14	14	34	35	2	1	31	0	1	0	2.65	31.0	8.2	9.52

Karsay was once the top pitching prospect in baseball, sporting a 97-mph fastball and a killer curveball. He was felled by an elbow injury before he could prove himself in the majors, and Tommy John surgery kept him out well into '96. He looked strong in the spring of '96, but the A's were cautious, sending him to pitch short-inning starts in Class-A Modesto. Karsay dominated hitters at this level with incredible control and struck out a man an inning. This was more impressive because he was restricted to using 2-and 4-seam fastballs and a change-up and was not allowed to use his curveball. The rehab was not without its scary moments, however, as Karsay did leave one game early and experienced swelling in his elbow afterward. He had more surgery at the end of the '96 season, but he should be ready by the spring of '97. ▪

BRIAN LESHER

OF • BR • TL • 6'5 • 205 • 26 • OAK92/26

	AB	R	H	2B	3B	HR	RBI	BB	SO	SB	CS	BA	OB	SA
OAK96	82	11	19	3	0	5	16	5	17	0	0	.232	.281	.451

Lesher is a big man with power who has some tools, but he doesn't have much plate discipline and is probably a .250 hitter at best. He has good range in both left and right fields. Lesher was called up at season's end and handled lefties while struggling against righties, hitting 5 dingers in 82 at-bats. They might keep him with the club in '97 to spell Giambi against tough lefties. ▪

DAMON MASHORE

OF • BB • TR • 5'11 • 195 • 27 • OAK91/11

	AB	R	H	2B	3B	HR	RBI	BB	SO	SB	CS	BA	OB	SA
OAK96	105	20	28	7	1	3	12	16	31	4	0	.267	.366	.438

Mashore is one of the organization's swiftest players, but he didn't show it in '96, either in Triple-A or the majors. He probably won't be able to hit well enough to ever earn a full-time job in the majors, though players with his speed and glove shouldn't have much trouble finding work somewhere. ▪

MARK MCGWIRE

SUPERSTAR

1B • BR • TR • 6'5 • 250 • 33 • OAK84/1

	AB	R	H	2B	3B	HR	RBI	BB	SO	SB	CS	BA	OB	SA
OAK94	135	26	34	3	0	9	25	37	40	0	0	.252	.413	.474
OAK95	317	75	87	13	0	39	90	88	77	1	1	.274	.441	.685
OAK96	423	104	132	21	0	52	113	116	112	0	0	.312	.467	.730
CAREER	4082	725	1053	171	5	329	860	789	945	7	8	.258	.380	.544

Everybody knows about McGwire's dingers (1 every 8 at-bats) and the runs he drove in (113 in 130 games). These were not the only things that made this season special for him. McGwire hit over .300 for the first time in his career (unless you count his 84-at-bats season in '93), drew more than 100 walks, and slugged over .700—more than 100 points higher than Albert Belle and Frank Thomas.

Defensively, McGwire is an adequate first baseman, and he hit better when playing the field than he did at DH. McGwire took over as the A's career home run leader in '95, and at 329 and counting, it looks as if he's going to retain the title for a very long time. He has good work habits, and the weight lifting he did to take his mind off of his injuries has left him in the best shape of his career. He also has perspective—which is about as rare for a big-leaguer as a .730 slugging average—sitting out a game for the birth of his child while chasing Maris. ▪

IZZY MOLINA

C • BR • TR • 6'1 • 200 • 25

	AB	R	H	2B	3B	HR	RBI	BB	SO	SB	CS	BA	OB	SA
AAA	342	45	90	12	3	12	56	25	55	2	5	.263	.317	.421

Molina is a decent hitter with a cannon arm and the ability to call a game. Unfortunately for the A's, his Triple-A prowess didn't carry over to the majors, where he could barely keep his head above .200. After Steinbach cooled off in August and September, the A's finally gave him a rest and let Molina show what he could do. George Williams had played himself out of the backup role, so the position was ripe for the picking. Molina did not show much. He's not getting any younger, Willie Morales is ready now, and A. J. Hinch is only a couple of years away. ▪

STEVE MONTGOMERY

RP • BR • TR • 6'4 • 210 • 26 • SL92/3

	G	GS	IP	H	HR	BB	SO	W	L	S	ERA	K/BB	K9	HW9
AAA	37	0	56	51	7	12	40	2	0	1	2.89	3.3	6.4	10.13

Montgomery is yet another pitcher who has been billed as the A's next closer. Sure didn't look that way in '96. He's has good command but medicore stuff and no out pitch. Doesn't sound like a closer's résumé. He allowed 31 baserunners in 13.2 innings of work with Oakland, and the only thing that will close is the clubhouse door behind you on the way back to Tacoma. That's not a lengthy enough trial to write him off completely, but it's certainly not cause for optimism. ■

KERWIN MOORE

OF • BB • TR • 6'1 • 190 • 26 • KC88/16

	AB	R	H	2B	3B	HR	RBI	BB	SO	SB	CS	BA	OB	SA
AAA	452	90	104	12	11	2	32	95	115	38	12	.230	.363	.319

Speed is good, speed is right, speed works. Moore's career minor-league stolen-base success rate is 78%, and he led the PCL in steals in '96. As a hitter he can take a walk very well and stretch doubles into triples, but his batting average is very poor. He was hitting .230 in a hitter's league when he was called up, and went 1-16 with the A's. Moore is a decent athlete, but the A's see him only as a utility player. ■

WILLIE MORALES

C • BR • TR • 5'10 • 180 • 24 • OAK93/14

	AB	R	H	2B	3B	HR	RBI	BB	SO	SB	CS	BA	OB	SA
AA	377	54	110	24	0	18	73	38	67	0	2	.292	.362	.499

Morales hits for average, power, and doesn't strike out much. He has more power and a better eye than Izzy Molina, so look for Morales to move up to Triple-A in '97, then get a shot in Oakland. ■

PEDRO MUÑOZ

DH • OF • BR • TR • 5'10 • 210 • 28 • TOR85

	AB	R	H	2B	3B	HR	RBI	BB	SO	SB	CS	BA	OB	SA
MIN94	244	35	72	15	2	11	36	19	67	0	0	.295	.348	.508
MIN95	376	45	113	17	0	18	58	19	86	0	3	.301	.338	.489
OAK96	121	17	31	5	0	6	18	9	31	0	0	.256	.308	.446
CAREER	1708	203	467	75	8	67	252	100	418	11	10	.273	.315	.444

Munoz had his year wasted by injury, hurting his knee and then experiencing a major setback in

rehab days before he should have returned to the A's. In the interim, his spot in the outfield was filled admirably by rookies and veterans alike. They proved that they could get by without him and without missing a beat. The A's should trade him as soon as he goes deep in a spring training game. ■

PHIL PLANTIER

SLEEPER

OF • BL • TR • 5'11 • 195 • 28 • BOS87/11

	AB	R	H	2B	3B	HR	RBI	BB	SO	SB	CS	BA	OB	SA
SD94	341	44	75	21	0	18	41	36	91	3	1	.220	.302	.440
HOU/SD95	216	33	55	6	0	9	34	28	48	1	1	.255	.339	.407
OAK96	231	29	49	8	1	7	31	28	56	2	2	.212	.304	.346
CAREER	1762	247	427	82	3	86	274	224	446	13	12	.242	.332	.439

When Plantier was with Boston, Ted Williams took one look at his deep crouch and massive uppercut and shook his head in disgust. Plantier seemed to be proving Williams wrong in '93, his first year in San Diego, hitting 34 homers and knocking in 100 runs. Many thought that was Plantier's breakout year and that he was going to be spending the next few seasons as a fixture in the outfield with Derek Bell and Tony Gwynn. But he struck out 124 times in 138 games during that career year, and hit only .240. Plantier began to decline in '94, and by '95 the Padres had traded him and the rest of their 40-man roster to the Astros. Since '93 Plantier has maintained his modest numbers, battled the strike zone with varying success, and knocked a few balls out of the yard. The A's were forced to acquire him from the Tigers when McGwire went down, but they had to give up Fausto Cruz, a talented shortstop, to get him. Plantier did not live up to expectations in the short term, but he could pay some dividends. He's not old, and he has incredible, raw power. Oakland can afford to carry him at Triple-A and wait to see if he can turn it around. But Teddy Ballgame is still shaking his head. ■

ARIEL PRIETO

SP • BR • TR • 6'3 • 225 • 27 • OAK95/1

	G	GS	IP	H	HR	BB	K	W	L	S	ERA	K/BB	K9	HW9
OAK95	14	9	58	57	4	32	37	2	6	0	4.97	1.2	5.7	13.81
OAK96	21	21	125	130	9	54	75	6	7	0	4.15	1.4	5.4	13.24

Prieto has an excellent pitcher's build, a fluid delivery, a 90+ mph fastball, and an above-average

slider and change-up. The A's wasted no time with Prieto, bringing him from Class-A to the majors in '95. He responded with poise and command. This year, his first 9 starts were alarming. He lasted 7 innings exactly once in that stretch, and his strikeout-to-walk ratio was 24:24. When he went on the DL with a strained right elbow on May 19, it looked like he was lost for the season. Instead, he came back with one of the best second-half performances in '96. Of 12 starts, 9 were quality, his strikeout-to-walk ratio improved to nearly 2:1; and his ERA dropped from 6.37 to 4.15. In a duel he lost to his idol, Roger Clemens, in August, he impressed everyone, most of all Clemens. There are questions concerning Prieto's age. His papers say he's 26, but rumor has it he's actually 29. If the latter is true, he may be at his best now rather than just coming into his own. ■

CARLOS REYES

RP-SP • BB • TR • 6'1 • 190 • 27 • ATL91

	G	GS	IP	H	HR	BB	K	W	L	S	ERA	K/BB	K9	HW9
OAK94	27	9	78	71	10	44	57	0	3	1	4.15	1.3	6.6	13.27
OAK95	40	1	69	71	10	28	48	4	6	0	5.09	1.7	6.3	12.91
OAK96	46	10	122	134	19	61	78	7	10	0	4.78	1.3	5.8	14.38
CAREER	113	20	269	276	39	133	183	11	19	1	4.68	1.4	6.1	13.68

The A's had counted on Reyes to become an effective starter despite a marked lack of success in this department in years past. He sank to the occasion, going 3-8 for the first 2 months of '96. He was relocated to more familiar turf in the bullpen, but his strikeout-to-walk ratio continued to deteriorate, though he stopped dishing out as many dingers. He's a deceptive pitcher, changing location and selecting pitches intelligently. He possesses a poor fastball with little movement and a soft slider. He has a decent curveball and the best change-up on the A's. ■

BRAD RIGBY

SOLID PROSPECT

SP • BR • TR • 6'6 • 195 • 23 • OAK94/2

	G	GS	IP	H	HR	BB	SO	W	L	S	ERA	K/BB	K9	HW9
AA	26	26	159	161	13	59	127	9	12	0	3.95	2.2	7.2	12.43

Rigby's fastball was voted best in the Class-A California League in '95, and he was also named the top pitching prospect in that league. He has a decent slider and an excellent curveball. His change-up needs improvement, but he could get by on his top 3 pitches. The A's have to feel lucky because Rigby's velocity increased after he turned pro. Although he gave up more hits after moving to Double-A, his strikeout numbers and control were still in line. If Rigby can continue up the ladder to the PCL by midseason, locate his breaking stuff, and retain his comand, he'll be in the A's rotation by '98. ■

AARON SMALL

RP • TR • BR • 6'5 • 210 • 25 • TOR89/22

	G	GS	IP	H	HR	BB	K	W	L	S	ERA	K/BB	K9	HW9
TOR94	1	0	2	5	1	2	0	0	0	0	9.00	.0	.0	31.50
FLA95	7	0	6	7	1	6	5	1	0	0	1.42	.8	7.1	18.48
OAK96	12	3	28	37	3	22	17	1	3	0	8.16	.8	5.5	18.92

Small got a late-season call-up and did not come up big. Instead, he walked everything in sight. The Blue Jays and the Marlins have seen this act before. He's always shown good control in the minors, so you'd think he'd have just thrown it over the plate the third time around just to see what might happen if he did. ■

DEMOND SMITH

SOLID PROSPECT

OF • BB • TR • 5'11 • 170 • 24 • NYN90/6

	AB	R	H	2B	3B	HR	RBI	BB	SO	SB	CS	BA	OB	SA
AA	447	75	116	17	14	9	62	55	89	30	15	.260	.351	.421

Smith became a top prospect in '96. He was a little old for that status in '95, so the A's rushed him through all three Class-A levels that year, and seasoned him in Double-A Huntsville for most of '96 before a last-minute call-up to Triple-A for 3 at-bats. Smith hits for good average, can draw a walk, and has a speed/power package that the A's outfield needed yesterday. He could be in the majors this year. ■

SCOTT SPIEZIO

3B • BB • TR • 6'2 • 195 • 24 • OAK93/8

	AB	R	H	2B	3B	HR	RBI	BB	SO	SB	CS	BA	OB	SA
AAA	523	87	137	30	4	20	91	56	66	6	5	.262	.335	.449

Spiezio has been putting up numbers similar to '96 for several seasons. He's a solid defensive third baseman with very good extra-base hitting skills who can draw a walk and drive in runs. But those kind of numbers in the PCL aren't that big of a deal and won't move Brosius out of his way. ■

MATT STAIRS

OF • BL • TR • 5'9 • 175 • 28 • MON89

	AB	R	H	2B	3B	HR	RBI	BB	SO	SB	CS	BA	OB	SA
BOS95	88	8	23	7	1	1	17	4	14	0	1	.261	.298	.398
OAK96	137	21	38	5	1	10	23	19	23	1	1	.277	.367	.547
CAREER	263	32	69	15	2	11	47	30	45	1	2	.262	.339	.460

A former Expos second-base prospect, Stairs is now a part-time outfielder. But at his age, he's not in the A's long-term plans. If Lesher and Herrara struggle, Howe might have to play him more than he'd like. Or maybe he'll get the last laugh and prove to be the Canadian Rex Hudler. ■

TERRY STEINBACH (see Free Agents)

BILLY TAYLOR

RP • BR • TR • 6'8 • 200 • 35

	G	GS	IP	H	HR	BB	K	W	L	S	ERA	K/BB	K9	HW9
OAK94	41	0	46	38	4	18	48	1	3	1	3.50	2.7	9.4	10.95
OAK96	55	0	60	52	5	25	67	6	3	17	4.33	2.7	10.0	11.54

Taylor was effective for stretches, then pulled a *Hindenburg* in August and September. He was dominated by division rivals Seattle and Texas, racking up his best numbers against the weakest-hitting teams in the league. Taylor is an able pitcher, but because of his age and injury history, he's only a temporary solution to the A's relief woes. ■

MIGUEL TEJADA

GRADE-A PROSPECT

SS • BR • TR • 5'10 • 180 • 20

	AB	R	H	2B	3B	HR	RBI	BB	SO	SB	CS	BA	OB	SA
A+	458	97	128	12	5	20	72	51	93	27	16	.279	.352	.459

Tejada is the A's top position prospect after Ben Grieve, but is a better fielder than Grieve. Tejada has great range and a strong though, at times, erratic arm. With the bat he shows power potential, and he's a speedy runner. He may never hit for a high average, but he should continue to draw walks at the major-league level. His '96 numbers are inflated a bit by Modesto's park and deflated by the month he lost to a thumb injury. He was hitting .290 with 18 homers when he went down. He was the top prospect in the Northwest League in '95 and gained top honors in the California League last year. He's already drawing comparisons to Shawon Dunston. ■

DAVE TELGHEDER

SP • BR • TR • 6'3 • 210 • 30 • NYN89/31

	G	GS	IP	H	HR	BB	K	W	L	S	ERA	K/BB	K9	HW9
NYN94	6	0	10	11	2	8	4	0	1	0	7.20	.5	3.6	17.10
NYN95	7	4	25	34	4	7	16	1	2	0	5.61	2.3	5.8	14.76
OAK96	16	14	79	92	12	26	43	4	7	0	4.65	1.7	4.9	13.44
CAREER	53	25	190	219	28	62	98	11	12	0	4.97	1.6	4.6	13.31

If Telgheder gets 14 starts again in '97, something must have gone terribly wrong. ■

BRET WAGNER

SP • BL • TL • 6'0 • 190 • 23 • SL94/1

	G	GS	IP	H	HR	BB	SO	W	L	S	ERA	K/BB	K9	HW9
AA	27	27	134	125	6	77	98	8	8	0	4.23	1.3	6.6	13.57

Wagner, a former top pitching prospect, had control problems in '96. His decline can be traced to a harsh exercise program that resulted in '95 arm troubles. After his performance dropped off, Oakland was able to secure his services from St. Louis. Wagner has an excellent hard curve, which murders lefties; a good change-up; a hard slider; and a fastball that hits 90 mph. Despite his '96 troubles, his repertoire and command make him one of the better prospects in the organization. If he can regain his preinjury form, the A's will have a starter. Otherwise it might be long relief or insurance sales. ■

JOHN WASDIN

SP • BR • TR • 6'2 • 195 • 24 • OAK93/1

	G	GS	IP	H	HR	BB	K	W	L	S	ERA	K/BB	K9	HW9
OAK95	5	2	17	14	4	3	6	1	1	0	4.67	2.0	3.2	9.00
OAK96	25	21	131	145	24	50	75	8	7	0	5.96	1.5	5.2	13.39

Wasdin shows great command and makeup and has always had very good control. His pitches aren't overpowering, but he throws them for strikes. His fastball can get into the high 80s, and his slider and change-up are average. Wasdin was a solid performer in the PCL but had a rough year in the bigs. If he can learn to pitch inside effectively, he should develop into a fine third or fourth starter. ■

DON WENGERT

SP • BR • TR • 6'3 • 205 • 27 • OAK92/5

	G	GS	IP	H	HR	BB	K	W	L	S	ERA	K/BB	K9	HW9
OAK95	19	0	29	30	3	12	16	1	1	0	3.34	1.3	5.0	13.03
OAK96	36	25	161	200	29	60	75	7	11	0	5.58	1.3	4.2	14.53

Like every other warm body in Oakland, Wengert got his shot in '96. He has a 90-mph fastball and he complements it with a good slider. He had moved quickly through the system in '95, once the A's gave him a chance, but he was a late arrival to the majors. He worked middle relief in April '96 but was pressed into service as a starter by May and took more than a few for the team as he ended up leading the team with 161 unimpressive innings. ■

GEORGE WILLIAMS

C • BB • TR • 5'10 • 190 • 27 • OAK91/26

	AB	R	H	2B	3B	HR	RBI	BB	SO	SB	CS	BA	OB	SA
OAK95	79	13	23	5	1	3	14	11	21	0	0	.291	.383	.494
OAK96	132	17	20	5	0	3	10	28	32	0	0	.152	.311	.258

Williams hits for decent power and consistently had on-base percentages better than .400 during his minor-league career. He was a third baseman by trade until Oakland tried him behind the plate. Williams did not have a good year in '96, his first bid to spend an entire season in the majors. His numbers would be weak standing on their own, but they look positively lame alongside Steinbach's monster season. It didn't help that he never got any regular playing time—he never got more than 40 at-bats in a month. In August the A's called up catching prospect Izzy Molina and demoted Williams. He'll be lucky to find a role on the A's in '97, but he might hit if given another chance. ■

JAY WITASICK

SOLID PROSPECT

RP-SP • BR • TR • 6'4 • 205 • 24 • SL93/3

	G	GS	IP	H	HR	BB	SO	W	L	S	ERA	K/BB	K9	HW9
AA	25	6	67	47	3	26	63	0	3	4	2.3	2.4	8.5	9.86

Acquired in January '96 when the A's traded Dennis Eckersley to St. Louis, Witasick looks like one of the A's better pitching prospects. He's young and throws hard. Because of Oakland's ongoing bullpen woes, they recently converted him from starter to reliever. He has a 95-mph fastball, a hard slider, and a curveball. Art Howe was impressed with Witasick's makeup and thinks he could close in the majors. He looks like a much better possibility for that role than Acre or Taylor. ■

STEVE WOJCIECHOWSKI

SP • BL • TL • 6'2 • 185 • 26 • OAK91/4

	G	GS	IP	H	HR	BB	K	W	L	S	ERA	K/BB	K9	HW9
OAK95	14	7	48	51	7	28	13	2	3	0	5.18	.5	2.4	14.81
OAK96	16	15	79	97	10	28	30	5	5	0	5.65	1.1	3.4	14.23

Wojciechowski started impressively in Oakland, pitching well in his first 6 outings, but things fell apart rapidly after that and he was eventually replaced by Jay Witasick in late May. Like so many of Oakland's pitching prospects, he doesn't have overpowering stuff, and Howe wasn't convinced that he knew how to get people out. He knew how to do that in the PCL—throwing 2 no-hitters in Edmonton after he was demoted. He'll probably get another chance at some point in '97.

ERNIE YOUNG

CF • BR • TR • 6'1 • 190 • 27 • OAK90/15

	AB	R	H	2B	3B	HR	RBI	BB	SO	SB	CS	BA	OB	SA
OAK95	50	9	10	3	0	2	5	8	12	0	0	.200	.310	.380
OAK96	462	72	112	19	4	19	64	52	118	7	5	.242	.326	.424
CAREER	542	83	124	23	4	21	72	61	138	7	5	.229	.313	.402

Young did a more than adequate job in center field despite a lack of range, but his performance at the plate was borderline. His walk total was encouraging, but he struck out too much. If he'd been able to hit close to .270 or .280, he could have been a lead off hitter instead of batting 8th. Herrera was pushed to right field in deference to Young, but Herrera and Kerwin Moore are younger and better suited for center field in the long run. Young and his occasional dinger and more than occasional whiff, however, should continue to provide A's fans with Dwayne Murphy flashbacks in '97. ■

■ 1996 AUTOPSY

The Mariners looked solid coming off their visit to the A.L. Championship Series, though there were plenty of questions. Would Ken Griffey suffer any lingering side effects from his wrist injury—or would he pick up where he left off in the playoffs and take the American League apart? Could Jay Buhner come close to repeating his 121-RBI season? Would the bullpen—old and unreliable—hold together? Would the rotation be anything more than Randy Johnson and whoever was healthy and not currently in manager Lou Piniella's *chateau bow-wow*? Could Paul Sorrento and Russ Davis replace Tino Martinez and Mike Blowers respectively, at the corners? And the biggest long-shot of the bunch: Was Alex Rodriguez—who'd had only 2 postseason at-bats to Luis Sojo's 40 in '95—ready to play in the majors?

March 1-0 (1-0, ½ game ahead)
For the first time in history, a regular season game was played in March. The baseball gods at least put it into 12 innings, so it ended a little after midnight in Cincinnati.

April 15-10 (16-10, tied for first)
The Mariners started hot and heavy, going 12-4 and putting together a club-record 8-game winning streak. During the streak, Dan Wilson hit 5 homers and the team outscored opponents 76-33. Randy Johnson went undefeated (4-0), though his ERA was 3.52 and he wasn't beating the opposition's ace (Steve Sparks, Tipper Gohr, Jim Abbott, and Erik Hanson). The best pitching was being done by Chris Bosio (3-1, 3.09) and reliever Bob Wells, who went 1-0, 1.37 while pitching as many innings as many starters (19.2). Despite the strong work of this troika, the staff was bad (5.56 ERA), and the team gave up 10 or more runs 6 times to teams that weren't exactly elite (Milwaukee, Detroit, and Toronto). But when a team hits a major-league record 44 homers, some messes get covered up.

Injuries would hamper the Mariners all season, and they came early and often. Bobby Ayala, after allowing 16 runs in his first 8.1 innings, rammed his fist through a window in his Chicago hotel room. He needed 9 stitches and ended up on the DL—but Piniella was probably grateful that he'd saved him the trouble of doing it himself. Far more ominous was the sight of Johnson leaving a start late in the month in Milwaukee because of lower back pain. Johnson: "When I landed on my front foot, it felt like a knife being jabbed in my back." The rest of the league didn't feel quite the same way about that—and somewhere in West Virginia, The Krukker must have been pondering a comeback.

May 12-14 (28-24, 5½ games back)
The offense continued its banner run, but the team was slumping, going 4-7 in the initial 11 games of the month. Johnson left his first May start after 2 innings, and his ERA rose to 4.08. He won May 12, but went only 5 innings. He went on the 60-day DL the next day. Chris Bosio would join him there 2 weeks later with a recurring knee injury. One of their more reliable setup men, Tim Davis, went down 3 days later with a fracturated left fibula. There was no truth to the rumor that the pitching corps had become so depleted that Floyd Bannister and Shane Rawley had been offered tryouts. Despite the problems, the Mariners finished May playing better than .500 ball, trying their best to keep the Rangers in sight. After all, an A.L. West team with a long tradition of losing couldn't be counted on to blow an enormous lead two years in a row . . . could it?

June 14-12 (42-36, 5 games back)
They managed to go 14-12 with the best two pieces of the rotation in the shop for repairs. And, of course, there were other injuries: Utility man Alex Diaz went on the 60-day DL with bone spurs in his ankle, and third baseman Russ Davis joined him with a broken leg. But the team's collective heart stopped when Ken Griffey broke his hamate bone June 19 fouling off an Erik Hanson pitch. Junior was holding the bat strangely, trying to gear up for Hanson's curve, and when the ball hit the bat, the force of the impact snapped off the hook of the bone. He was expected to miss 3–5 weeks, and the Mariners' contention hopes were thought by many to be over. Despite Griffey's absence the offense was amazing—just as in '95—scoring 18 runs in Minnesota on the 11th and 19 runs in Toronto on the 28th, covering up for a couple of poorly pitched games by the staff. They had played 78 games and didn't yet have a complete game. Piniella: "We're

not looking for complete games. . . . We're looking for starters to get us into the seventh or eighth inning."

July 16-12 (58-48, 1½ games back)
Norm Charlton was having his problems in the bullpen, blowing 3 straight saves:. "I haven't been able to get anyone out and that is going to change. I will make it change, even if I have to invent a pitch." Careful, Norm—that's how Gaylord Perry got started. There were some positive signs in the bullpen, such as Mike Jackson finally turning it around after struggling most of the year. Piniella was also optimistic about Ayala: "He's back to where he was a couple of years ago and he's going to help us the rest of the way." Hard to tell if that was an assessment, a prediction, or a direct order.

There was plenty of good news in July, as the Mariners climbed back into contention. Bob Wells threw a shutout for the team's first complete game in its 89th attempt. Junior returned on July 8 after missing 20 games. The team had gone 12-8 without him, with Rich Amaral hitting .372 while playing center. Griffey hit .361 for the month, with 11 homers, and slugged .861. Meanwhile, Johnson had the fans buzzing with the news that his back was feeling better. But there was a constant amount of pain hovering around the Mariners all year, so Johnson's had go somewhere. Edgar Martinez, making a rare start at third, rammed into John Marzano going for a pop-up. Martinez bruised several ribs and hit the DL. Piniella offered the party line: "We talked about this team having resiliency, and we'll talk about it some more." Buhner was more blunt: "This sucks. You begin to wonder if we're ever going to get completely healthy."

August 12-17 (70-65, 7 games back)
The Mariners came into August having just acquired Terry Mulholland from the Phillies and Jamie Moyer from the Red Sox for prospects. Even more important than Mulholland and Moyer was the return of Johnson on the 6th. He pitched 2 shutout innings against the Indians in his first appearance in a couple of months. Piniella: "[Pitching in relief] is something Randy suggested. And quite frankly, it makes a lot of sense. . . . When Randy feels ready, he'll go into the rotation."

It never happened. Johnson pitched 9 scoreless innings in his first 3 relief appearances, but was bombed after that. Johnson returned to the DL soon after ex-Mariner Darren Bragg sank a stiletto into the hearts of his former mates with a grand slam at the Fens. It was the first time a left-hander had taken Randy out since Mo Vaughn in 1992. Vaughn downplayed the accomplishment, suggesting that his team hadn't beaten the real Randy Johnson: "He's not throwing that 86- or 88-mph slider."

After going 46-27 at home in '95, the team was now bouncing around near .500 there. They closed out the month on a bit of an up note—the Yankees had come to town and, as is their custom in Seattle, dropped 3 in a row. The Mariners were thinking up new ways to do it to the Yankees in the Kingdome—knocking out Jimmy Key in the first inning of one game after Alex Rodriguez hit a line drive off his elbow that rolled to the wall for a triple!

September 15-11 (85-76, 4½ games back)
The team played well—whipping the division-winning Rangers 4 straight in a critical showdown, holding them to 10 runs. They won 10 in a row from the 12th to the 21st, giving up more than 5 runs only twice, nearly erasing a 9-game lead in the process. But they went back on the road with no margin for error and dropped 3 in a row to the lowly Angels as they were hammered for 28 runs. They fell short for a single reason: Randy Johnson made only 8 starts. Piniella: "We've missed sending a pitcher to the mound who gives us about an 80% chance of winning. The past 2 years, that's about how often we win when Randy pitches." If they'd had The Big Unit all year, they would have been in the playoffs, and—considering how poorly the Yankees play in the Kingdome—would have "probably definitely" been playing the Orioles for the right to go to the World Series. The season that Rodriguez gave the Mariners at shortstop helped negate the injuries the team suffered on offense. There was no pitching equivalent of Rodriguez to pick up the slack for Randy Johnson—not even close.

1997 DIAGNOSIS

Offense

There aren't many teams that have scored more runs per game than the 1996 Mariners. You can begin the short list with the 1927 Yankees of Ruth and Gehrig, and the 1936–37 Yankees of Gehrig and DiMaggio. They outscored the vaunted 1961 Yankees of Mantle and Maris by 20%, and the 1975–76 Big Red Machine by almost as much. No team has scored more runs per game since the 1953 Dodgers of Gil Hodges, Jackie Robinson, Duke Snider, and Roy Campanella.

The Mariners scored 993 runs, and only 6 teams in history have scored more than that (all, by the way, in a 154-game season):

Year	Team	Runs	Highlights
1931	Yankees	1067	Gehrig & Ruth 90 HR, 327 RBI
1936	Yankees	1065	Gehrig & DiMaggio 78 HR, 277 RBI
1930	Yankees	1062	Gehrig & Ruth 92 HR, 347 RBI
1950	Red Sox	1027	Williams 97 RBI in 89 games
1930	Cardinals	1004	Every regular hit .300
1932	Yankees	1002	Gehrig & Ruth 75 HR, 288 RBI
1996	Mariners	993	Griffey & Rodriguez 85 HR, 263 RBI

Worth noting: It's Lou Gehrig that's been on 4 of these teams, not The Babe. And, like the Mariners, these teams didn't always make it to the postseason. The 1950 Red Sox finished 3rd, losing Ted Williams for half the season with a broken elbow, and finding their offense powered by Walt Dropo and Vern Stephens. The 1930 Yankees won 86 games and finished 3rd, 16 games out. The 1931 Yankees finished 2nd, 13½ games out. The 1930 Cardinals lost the World Series. The 1996 Mariners had the worst winning percentage (.528) of the bunch. Only the 1932 and 1936 Yankees went on to win it all.

How will the Mariner offense be in '97? The most recent versions of the '96 Mariners—the '50 Red Sox and '53 Dodgers—declined by more than 20% in runs scored the following year and also dropped in the standings. An across-the-board decline has to be expected for the Mariners as well. Junior could still flirt with 50 homers, but not even the immortals do that year after year. The same goes for Rodriguez, but only Honus Wagner and Ty Cobb were able to hit .350 consistently. Will Buhner again threaten to have more RBI than hits? Will Mark Whiten do what he did over 160 games—meaning 48 dingers and 132 RBI? Sure, and Russ Davis will win the batting title. More likely Whiten will wear out yet another welcome and be on another team by the All-Star break. Edgar is the only one who could be expected to improve, albeit only slightly.

But though their runs scored will decline, it wouldn't matter if the pitching picks them up and they could improve where it really counts: in the standings.

Defense

Paul Sorrento was able to replace Tino Martinez with the bat, but he was an unreasonable facsimile with the glove. Joey Cora is nothing special at second, while Alex Rodriguez is overrated—for now—in the field, his excellent arm notwithstanding. Dave Hollins made 18 errors, far too many for a third baseman, but when Russ Davis was in there, he was worse. The Mariners are a better defensive team in the outfield. With Jay Buhner and Mark Whiten they have decent range in right and left, respectively—good enough when you've got Junior in center—and outstanding throwing arms. Griffey had his best defensive season yet.

Pitching

If you dismiss the Tigers, then the Mariners had the worst starting pitching in the league. This is a testament to the value of Randy Johnson. Without him, the team was lost. The Mariners lost 5 games when they scored 9 or more runs! Piniella looked like he could go postal at any moment: "A fan who leaves his seat for half an inning to use the bathroom is liable to miss 5 runs being scored. And it doesn't matter which half of the inning." This one was even better: "I better see something the last 3 weeks of the season because I will not carry the same staff next year. I'm getting tired of being roughed up all the time." If Johnson's back and healthy, Jeff Fassero adapts to the A.L., Jamie Moyer remains solid, and Salomon Torres and Sterling Hitchcock evolve, the staff should allow 100 fewer runs.

If you adjust for the Kingdome, the Mariners had the core of a decent bullpen: Mike Jackson, Norm Charlton, Rafael Carmona, Tim Davis (and Bob Wells, while he was there). But when the starting rotation is as weak as the Mariners was, it reveals the weak points deeper in the staff. The Angels experienced the same thing. That's why Kevin Gross keeps getting big-league work—by eating up innings, he keeps the good setup men fresh for games the team might win. And deep in the

Mariners staff were punching bags Edwin Hurtado, Rusty Meacham, and Bobby Ayala—all of them ending up being used for 157 innings, mostly in relief, an average of 1 inning every game. Japanese import, Makato Suzuki could contribute in '97, and Ayala should improve—though Piniella may send him elsewhere to get it together. Remember, Piniella is a man whose patience was worn out by one of the most consistent relievers in baseball—Randy Myers—only months after he helped him win a World Series. He stuck him in the rotation to be pummeled, then exiled him to San Diego. A year later, he was wrestling Rob Dibble in the clubhouse. As for Ayala, Piniella may just hire someone to rough him up a bit, then trade him to Detroit.

Farm System

At the moment, the team has two excellent prospects: Ken Cloude, a starting pitcher, and José Cruz, Jr., the team's next left fielder. The rest of the system is pretty thin. It will be difficult to criticize the Mariners personnel people for the next 20 years, after they came away with Junior and Alex Rodriguez with the first picks in the draft. To paraphrase Bill James, if you develop one of those every few seasons, you'll never finish under .500. Gee. Sounds easy, doesn't it?

Management and Ownership

The Mariners ownership group (basically Nintendo) has been quiet and efficient. They spend money, hire people to advocate the building of a shiny new stadium, and leave their staff alone. They've signed the checks when the front office came to them wanting to add pitching for the '95 and '96 stretch drives. They have to be applauded, because unless you live in the Seattle area, you can't name any of the real powers within the ownership. If you live in Houston, New York, or Cincinnati, you know who the owner is and find yourself apologizing for it frequently.

GM Woody Woodward and his scouting guru, Roger Jongewaard, have done a good job with this team. Jongewaard was the one who demanded the team take Ken Griffey when the previous owner was arguing for Mike Harkey. Jongewaard also helped orchestrate the signing of Alex Rodriguez. Woodward has locked in Junior until the year 2000. He also made the trades last season for lefties Mulholland and Moyer, and didn't give up anything the team needed—Desi Relaford, an infield prospect stuck behind Rodriguez, and Darren Bragg, who was about to be displaced by José Cruz's kid. Unfortunately, Jeff Manto for Arquimedez Pozo is looking bad already. Chris Widger wasn't anything the Mariners needed, but packaging Matt Wagner with him for Jeff Fassero may look bad in a few years. Woodward has had to make moves while carefully watching payroll. He's helped his team without busting his budget.

Lou Piniella surrounds himself with veterans. He's slow to acknowledge the value of the kids his team produces and won't go with them if he's in contention—perhaps still scarred from trying to work 22-year-old Scott Scudder into the pitching mix with his championship Reds. No one was second-guessing him at the time, but it makes you wonder what Alex Rodriguez might have been able to do if he'd gotten any chance at all in the '95 postseason. Other than this—and his apparent hatred of relief pitchers—his record in full seasons of work is unassailable: 90-72 and 2nd place in 1986 with the Yankees, with no shortstop, no catcher, and Dennis Rasmussen his only solid starter; 89-73 with the '87 Yankees with a different but equally wretched staff; a title in 1990 with an overmatched Reds team; 90-72 and 2nd place with the '92 Reds after a down year, despite only 99 dingers from his offense; improving the Mariners by 18 games in '93, dragging them above .500 almost by force of will; and into the playoffs in '95 after regressing during the strike year. Based on that, and how little ink he gets compared to LaRussa and Leyland, Piniella may be the most underrated manager in baseball.

. . . and whatnot: A Rod & Mel Ott

It's impressive enough to be starting in the majors at 20, much less win a batting title. Compare Alex Rodriguez's numbers (36-123-.358) to those of Mantle (23-87-.311), Mays (20-68-.274), and Aaron (13-69-.280) at 20. Williams and DiMaggio were still in the bushes at that age. At 20, Honus Wagner wasn't playing, and Rogers Hornsby was batting 45 points below his career average. Ty Cobb hit .350—*almost* up to Alex's level—and won his first batting title. However, in the 40 years of media saturation since Frank Robinson did 38-83-.290 for the Reds in 1956, the best seasons by players who were 20

have come from those who, with the exception of Junior, would turn out to be mere mortals:

Year & Player	G	AB	H	HR	R	RBI	SB	SO	BB	BA	SA
'58 Orlando Cepeda	148	603	188	25	88	96	15	84	29	.312	.512
'65 Tony Conigliaro	138	521	140	32	82	82	4	116	51	.269	.512
'75 Claudell Washington	148	590	182	10	86	80	40	80	32	.308	.424
'78 Bob Horner	89	323	86	23	50	63	0	42	24	.266	.539
'90 Ken Griffey Jr.	155	597	179	22	91	80	16	81	63	.300	.481

Some say Cepeda should be in Cooperstown, but he wouldn't get much p.t. if the Hall of Famers come back from Valhalla to have a pickup game in a field in Iowa someday. Conigliaro was on his way to 500 dingers before he was hit in the eye with a pitch. He had 84—Aaron had 40, Mays had 24, and Ruth had 7—the second most home runs by age 21 of any player in baseball history. More on no. 1 on that list in a bit. Claudell Washington's power numbers aren't all that impressive, but his .308 batting average was fifth in the league behind guys named Carew, Lynn, Munson, and Rice. Bob Horner came right out of college to put up those numbers, and they translate to 42-115 over a full season. Cepeda, Conigliaro, and Washington all needed to hone their plate discipline—as does Rodriguez—which Cepeda did to some extent, Claudell never did, and Conigliaro never got a chance to. Griffey had it and has maintained it, while Horner was the best of the group at it and never lost it.

The hitter whose season at 20 most resembles that of Rodriguez is that of the greatest young baseball player in history—Mel Ott—who did 42-151-.328 for the 1929 Giants. He played 22 years and ended up in the Hall of Fame with 511 dingers, though he would never again match the power and production numbers he put up at 20—and only topped his batting average once, and that was at 21. In his time, he was considered a disappointment.

Despite expansion creating 68 new chances to play regularly since 1968, the number of 20-year-olds playing every day has declined dramatically since the '60s and '70s, probably because of concerns about what the pressures and temptations of big-league life can do to a prospect. Bear that in mind for Rodriguez. After all, his 1996 was the hitting equivalent of what another quiet, self-effacing 20-year-old did on the mound in 1985. Dwight Gooden went 24-4 with a 1.53 ERA, and then failed to endure the pressures of having to live up to it for the rest of his career.

Rodriguez, at least, doesn't have to contend with this nonsense in New York City, and he has a baseball big brother named Griffey who handled it better than Gooden's big brother, Darryl Strawberry.

RICH AMARAL

OF-IF • BR • TR • 6'0 • 175 • 35 • CHN83/2

	AB	R	H	2B	3B	HR	RBI	BB	SO	SB	CS	BA	OB	SA
SEA94	228	37	60	10	2	4	18	24	28	5	1	.263	.333	.377
SEA95	238	45	67	14	2	2	19	21	33	21	2	.282	.342	.382
SEA96	312	69	91	11	3	1	29	47	55	25	6	.292	.392	.356
CAREER	1267	215	351	62	8	9	117	131	191	74	22	.277	.348	.360

Last season Amaral played first, second, third, and left, center and right field and had a .462 OBP as a pinch hitter. Sure he doesn't have any power, but he gets on base and is an excellent baserunner. On a powerhouse team such as Seattle, his job was to set the table, and he did it—and if you project his season to 600 plate appearances, he would have scored 115 runs. ■

BOBBY AYALA

SLEEPER

RP • BR • TR • 6'2 • 190 • 27 • CIN88

	G	GS	IP	H	HR	BB	K	W	L	S	ERA	K/BB	K9	HW9
SEA94	46	0	56	42	2	26	76	4	3	18	2.86	2.9	12.2	10.92
SEA95	63	0	71	73	9	30	77	6	5	19	4.44	2.6	9.8	13.06
SEA96	50	0	67	65	10	25	61	6	3	3	5.88	2.4	8.2	12.08
CAREER	207	14	321	319.2	264	53	175	247	22	22	4.82	3.3	4.9	10.43

Last season left-handers were able to play right through his pitches, hitting .304 and slugging .526 against him. He consistently hits the low 90s with a good splitter. He also has an excuse-me slider, but that pitch often excuses itself over the fence. Ayala used to own lefties—in '95 they hit .229 against him. What to expect this season? He's had several years in the league and has had some success. But it's tough to perform when your boss hates your guts. Piniella has never forgiven him for the two-thirds of an inning he gave him against the Yankees in the '95 playoffs in which he yielded 6 hits, 1 walk, and 4 runs. As this unfolded, Brent Musburger—whose announcing was the most confused on network TV since Reagan's lunar excursion at the '90 All-Star game—observed that Piniella was out to the mound

to offer "words of encouragement" to Ayala. It didn't take a lip-reader to see that something was going on and that Brent didn't know what it was. Look for Ayala elsewhere—and improved—in '97. ■

JAMES BONNICI — SLEEPER

1B • BR • TR • 6'4 • 230 • 25 • SEA90/58

	AB	R	H	2B	3B	HR	RBI	BB	SO	SB	CS	BA	OB	SA
AAA	497	76	145	25	0	26	74	59	100	1	3	.292	.367	.499

Bonnici has put on 50 pounds of muscle since he came into the organization. He's what you might call a "workout freak"—assuming that's where it all came from. He went from hitting no homers in 178 at-bats in rookie ball to slugging .499 in Triple-A Tacoma last season. He signed as a 190-pound shortstop, moved to catcher, and eventually became a 240-pound first baseman who can mash. He's played in pitcher's park after pitcher's park in the minors and has hit well at all stops. He can platoon with Sorrento and get some DH at-bats. If he can get 300+, he should do some major-league damage. Then look for him to break down and endure a rash of bizarre injuries to the back and joints like fellow "workout freaks" Mitchell, Canseco, and Dykstra. ■

CHRIS BOSIO (see Free Agents)

JAY BUHNER — CONSISTENT STAR

RF • BR • TR • 6'3 • 215 • 32 • PIT84

	AB	R	H	2B	3B	HR	RBI	BB	SO	SB	CS	BA	OB	SA
SEA94	358	74	100	23	4	21	68	66	63	0	1	.279	.394	.542
SEA95	470	86	123	23	0	40	121	60	120	0	1	.262	.343	.566
SEA96	564	107	153	29	0	44	138	84	159	0	1	.271	.369	.557
CAREER	3554	570	922	175	16	213	686	499	953	6	22	.259	.353	.497

The great myth is that Seattle's outfield is one of the best defensive units in the game. It's a decent one, but it isn't a trio of Clementes. Buhner has a fine arm, but his range is average at best. But if you are an RBI machine who hits 40 homers a season, you're not getting paid for your glovework. There is nothing fake about those numbers, either—he hit .270-21-65 at home and .273-23-73 on the road last season. Buhner will kick your butt wherever it suits him; it's just a matter of whether you want to put it off or get it over with. And he carries a grudge: The Yankees dealt him for Ken Phelps, and he's been getting medieval on them ever since, capping it off by hitting .458 in the '95 playoffs against them. When he doesn't whiff—which he does 38 percent of the time—he hits .378 and slugs .775 ■

RAFAEL CARMONA — SLEEPER

RP • BL • TR • 6'2 • 185 • 24 • SEA93/12

	G	GS	IP	H	HR	BB	K	W	L	S	ERA	K/BB	K9	HW9
SEA95	15	3	47	55	9	34	28	2	4	1	5.66	.8	5.4	17.04
SEA96	53	1	90	95	11	55	62	8	3	1	4.28	1.1	6.2	14.99

Carmona's command is mediocre at best, but he was a fine reliever last season, as long he was kept away from lefties—whom he made look like Stan Musial. He comes from three-quarters with a fastball that sinks and bores in on righties, a slider, and a circle change-up. His stuff is good (though the slider can be inconsistent), but he has to throw strikes and find a pitch that works on lefties. ■

NORM CHARLTON

RP • BB • TL • 6'3 • 195 • 34 • MON84/2

	G	GS	IP	H	HR	BB	K	W	L	S	ERA	K/BB	K9	HW9
SEA95	55	0	69	46	4	31	70	4	6	14	3.36	2.3	9.1	10.04
SEA96	70	0	75	68	7	38	73	4	7	20	4.04	1.9	8.8	12.71
CAREER	397	37	680	565	49	276	612	40	40	81	3.12	2.2	8.1	11.13

In early August, Charlton blew 4 straight saves, then went to Piniella and asked to pitch middle relief: "I've been killing us. It's like they know what's coming—they whale at my fastball and take my forkball." But no one in baseball has more guts than Charlton, whose career looked to be over when he blew out his elbow in '93 on a pitch that landed somewhere near the on-deck circle. He rallied then—crawling all the way back to the closer's role in '95 after being released by the Phillies. He was ridden hard in the playoffs, yielding 5 hits and 2 runs in 13 innings, winning 2 and saving 2. He ralled in '96, too. His command in September was bad, but he allowed eight hits in 15 innings and no dingers to help the Mariners go down fighting. No one questions this

guy's heart, and when his forkball's on, it's lights out. He's getting up there in years, but this is one reliever even Lou can love. He'll be around until his arm falls off, and then Piniella will probably make him the spiritual advisor to his staff. ■

KEN CLOUDE — *GRADE-A PROSPECT*

SP • BR • TR • 6′1 • 185 • 22 • SEA93/6

	G	GS	IP	H	HR	BB	SO	W	L	S	ERA	K/BB	K9	HW9
A+	28	28	168	167	15	60	161	15	4	0	4.22	2.7	8.6	12.14

Named the best starting pitching prospect in the California League last season (the no. 7 California League prospect overall), Cloude throws 4 pitches, including a fastball that touches 90. He throws inside, is very poised and aggressive, and produced at an extreme hitter's park. Piniella has his eye on him, and he could be moshing in Seattle in September. ■

JOEY CORA

2B • BB • TR • 5′8 • 150 • 31 • SD85/1

	AB	R	H	2B	3B	HR	RBI	BB	SO	SB	CS	BA	OB	SA
CHA94	312	55	86	13	4	2	30	38	32	8	4	.276	.353	.362
SEA95	427	64	127	19	2	3	39	37	31	18	7	.297	.359	.372
SEA96	530	90	154	37	6	6	45	35	32	5	5	.291	.340	.417
CAREER	2558	408	697	104	31	13	208	254	227	96	47	.272	.343	.353

Cora is mediocre defensively, and his on-base and slugging aren't that impressive if you compare him to the league. He's a pretty solid major-league regular, but he is certainly not someone you want to have in the first third of your batting order. The Mariners should find a better hitter to slide into the no. 2 lineup slot—a role José Cruz, Jr., may fill eventually. But if they're looking for another second baseman, they won't find him down on the farm. Any help is a few years away, if it's there at all. ■

DEAN CROW — *SOLID PROSPECT*

RP • BL • TR • 6′5 • 210 • 24 • SEA93/10

	G	GS	IP	H	HR	BB	SO	W	L	S	ERA	K/BB	K9	HW9
AA	60	0	68	64	4	20	43	2	3	26	3.04	2.2	5.7	11.12

Crow throws 96 mph and had 26 saves for a team that won 56 games. He throws strikes, but is hampered because he has a change but no consistent breaking ball. He's working on a split-finger, but it's not there yet. He's a nice-looking reliever and could see the majors this season—and if he harnesses his breaking pitch, he could be dominating. ■

JOSÉ CRUZ, JR. — *GRADE-A PROSPECT*

OF • BB • TR • 6′0 • 190 • 22 • SEA95/1

	AB	R	H	2B	3B	HR	RBI	BB	SO	SB	CS	BA	OB	SA
AAA	76	15	18	1	2	6	15	18	12	1	1	.237	.383	.539

Cruz was taken from Rice University with the no. 3 overall pick in the 1995 draft. Despite hitting only 12 homers among a trio of stops in the minors—as he climbed from Class-A to Triple-A in a single season—he was considered to have the best power among college hitters when he was taken. The no. 2 prospect in the California League last season, he's a 5-tool player with good instincts. The Mariners were concerned his swing was long going into '96 and that he took too many pitches. That perception changed last season when he hit well over .300 at Lancaster and was able to turn that selectivity into a fine on-base percentage. The Mariners project him as their left fielder of the future. He needs to dominate at Triple-A this season to be ready for a major-league job by August. ■

RUSS DAVIS

3B • BR • TR • 6′0 • 170 • 27 • NYA88/26

	AB	R	H	2B	3B	HR	RBI	BB	SO	SB	CS	BA	OB	SA
NYA95	98	14	27	5	2	2	12	10	26	0	0	.276	.349	.429
SEA96	167	24	39	9	0	5	18	17	50	2	0	.234	.312	.377

Some scouts think this guy is a stud, that he's going to hit 25 homers and drive in runs, and the Yankees talked him up so much there was panic in the streets of New York when they finally dealt him. Well, almost. But the games aren't played on paper and Davis was a flop in 1996, missing most of the season with a broken left fibula and not doing much when he was healthy. He's capable of hitting .260 with some punch, but if he doesn't do it in the next couple of years, he probably never will. Davis has good bat speed and an attitude compared to Piniella's, which means that

they should go through half a dozen water coolers and a dozen clubhouse runway lightbulbs by the All-Star break. ■

TIM DAVIS

RP • BL • TL • 5'11 • 165 • 26 • SEA92/6

	G	GS	IP	H	HR	BB	K	W	L	S	ERA	K/BB	K9	HW9
SEA94	42	1	49	57	4	25	28	2	2	2	4.01	1.1	5.1	15.05
SEA95	5	5	24	30	2	18	19	2	1	0	6.38	1.1	7.1	18.00
SEA96	40	0	42	43	4	17	34	2	2	0	4.01	2.0	7.3	12.84
CAREER	87	6	115	130	10	60	81	6	5	2	4.54	1.4	6.3	14.86

He and Russ Davis broke their left fibulas within 10 days of each other. This Davis throws a mediocre fastball, a hard slider, and can upset a hitter's timing with a devastating change-up. Last season he was very good, rebounding from a slow start (0-1, 6.23 in 8.2 innings in April) to go 2-1, 3.44 in 34 innings for the rest of the season. He pitched so well after his injury that Piniella was reportedly considering giving pitching coach Bobby Cuellar a tire iron so he could Nancy Kerrigan the rest of the staff. Davis has been famous for his command, and it became apparent in the season's last couple of months, as he pitched 14.1 innings allowing one walk and striking out 9. If he's healthy, he's one more reason the Mariners' bullpen will be better this season. ■

SCOTT DAVISON

SOLID PROSPECT

RP • BR • TR • 6'0 • 190 • 26 • MON88/5

	G	GS	IP	H	HR	BB	SO	W	L	S	ERA	K/BB	K9	HW9
AAA	17	0	23	13	0	6	23	1	1	9	.39	3.8	9.0	7.43

Drafted as a shortstop by the Expos, Davison throws a fastball that can reach 94–95. He also has good command of his hard slider. His short stint at Triple-A was nothing short of dominating. But he was hammered in his brief major-league time, allowing 6 homers in 9 innings. Davison's old for a prospect, but he played in the Expos chain for 4 seasons before getting his walking papers. If the real Davison shows up this season, he could get 7-10 saves during some Charlton downtime. ■

JEFF FASSERO

SP • BL • TL • 6'1 • 180 • 34 • SL84/22

	G	GS	IP	H	HR	BB	K	W	L	S	ERA	K/BB	K9	HW9
MON94	21	21	138	119	13	40	119	8	6	0	2.99	3.0	7.8	10.36
MON95	30	30	189	207	15	74	164	13	14	0	4.33	2.2	7.8	13.38
MON96	34	34	231	217	20	55	222	15	11	0	3.30	4.0	8.6	10.59
CAREER	262	100	849	782	57	274	750	58	48	10	3.20	2.7	7.9	11.19

Fassero was the best left-hander in the N.L. last season (Tom Glavine was a little better at keeping the ball in the yard, but Fassero had a more distinct edge in keeping runners off base). Fassero doesn't do righties a favor (.292 OBP, .375 slugging allowed last year) and is poison to left-handers (.271 OBP, .270 slugging—he hasn't allowed a homer to a left-hander batter since June 30, 1994, [Barry Bonds], a span of 375.2 innings). Fassero has a sinking fastball that hits the low 90s a fine split-finger (his out pitch) and a slider. He's a ground-ball pitcher, and thrived despite pitching on turf with a mediocre infield. He'll be doing more of the same with Seattle. ■

KEN GRIFFEY

SUPERSTAR

CF • 6'3 • 195 • BL • TL • 27 • SEA87/1

	AB	R	H	2B	3B	HR	RBI	BB	SO	SB	CS	BA	OB	SA
SEA94	433	94	140	24	4	40	90	56	73	11	3	.323	.402	.674
SEA95	260	52	67	7	0	17	42	52	53	4	2	.258	.379	.481
SEA96	545	125	165	26	2	49	140	78	104	16	1	.303	.392	.628
CAREER	3985	695	1204	227	21	238	725	504	634	108	44	.302	.381	.549

There is no doubt that Junior's an exceptional athlete, but in the past he wasn't good at positioning himself in the field, and relied on instinct to catch the ball. This resulted in many spectacular plays on balls that would have been more easily caught if he'd studied the hitters. In an interview in '95, Griffey described his philosophy as "See the ball, catch the ball. See the ball, hit the ball." The latter half of that statement is modesty, but the former was probably more true than he'd want to let on. Last season, athleticism and hustle met maturity and knowledge in center field, so he should get better and better—which might mean making the spectacular look more routine.

Because of the strike—and his injuries in 1995–96—Junior has lost 25 to 40 homers. That doesn't seem like a significant total, but think of this in 10 years when he's chasing Reggie or Mays. It wasn't a complete loss—some guy apparently offered $20,000 for one of the pins taken out of his

wrist in '95. Now that he's entering his prime offensively—a scary thought—how does Junior stack up against the great ones at 26?

Player	AB	R	H	2B	3B	HR	RBI	BB	SO	BA	OB	SA
DiMaggio	3,368	735	1,163	214	69	198	816	336	160	.345	.405	.626
Mantle	3,937	890	1,238	185	50	249	766	803	773	.314	.431	.577
Mays	2,899	525	902	128	63	187	509	361	321	.311	.388	.593
Musial	2,910	552	995	215	71	71	452	379	127	.342	.418	.542
Robinson	3,895	752	1,202	228	36	241	709	468	553	.309	.383	.571
Griffey	3,985	695	1,204	227	21	238	725	504	634	.302	.381	.549
Aaron	4,114	714	1,309	225	57	219	745	341	378	.318	.370	.560

As you can see, the two Yankees are the class of this group. Now, let's describe the discrepancies (i.e., why some guys have a lot more at-bats, and why Ted Williams isn't on the list). DiMaggio is the only player in the group who started playing at age 21. Griffey and Mantle started playing at 19, the rest at 20—seemingly a prerequisite for immortal status. Mays missed most of '52 and all of '53 (when he was 21 and 22, respectively) because he was in the military. Musial missed 1945 (he was 24) for the same reason and had only 47 at-bats when he was 20. Teddy Ballgame started at 21 and missed ages 25-27, as well as 34-35, to serve in the Air Force.

The players most similar to Griffey in this group are Frank Robinson and Henry Aaron. On the strength of his excellent 1996, Griffey is now 19 homers ahead of the Hammer—and only Frank Robinson and Mickey Mantle are ahead of Griffey—so one has to conclude that Griffey has at least 500 dingers in him. Williams missed out on 600 dingers because he was occupied as a fighter pilot. Griffey might miss it because he and his union buddies wouldn't settle for splitting $2 billion right down the middle with their bosses. ■

GIOMAR GUEVARA — SLEEPER

SS • BB • TR • 5'8 • 150 • 24

	AB	R	H	2B	3B	HR	RBI	BB	SO	SB	CS	BA	OB	SA
AA	414	60	110	18	2	2	41	54	102	21	7	.266	.353	.333

Ché Guevara was voted the best defensive shortstop in the Southern League last season. He's not going to be much of a hitter, possibly similar to Cora, but he will field better. It may take a season, and he may stumble at Triple-A and fall off the map, but he will have a chance of unseating Cora within the next couple of seasons. ■

STERLING HITCHCOCK — YOUNG GUN

SP • BL • TL • 6'1 • 200 • 25 • NYA89/8

	G	GS	IP	H	HR	BB	K	W	L	S	ERA	K/BB	K9	HW9
NYA94	23	5	49	48	3	29	37	4	1	2	4.20	1.3	6.8	14.13
NYA95	27	27	168	155	22	68	121	11	10	0	4.70	1.8	6.5	11.95
SEA96	35	35	196	245	27	73	132	13	9	0	5.35	1.8	6.1	14.60
CAREER	94	76	457	503	58	190	322	29	24	2	5.04	1.7	6.3	13.64

Hitchcock's fastball peaks at 90 mph, and he also has an average curve and change-up as well as a good split-finger. Considering how difficult it is to run on Hitchcock and former teammate Andy Pettitte, someone in the Yankee system must be doing something right with the lefties. He had no problems against left-handers, but right-handed hitters ate his lunch and stole his milk money. He worked on doing something about his baby face by growing a goatee in '96. Look for him to improve the rest of his game in '97. ■

DAVE HOLLINS (see Free Agents)

BRIAN HUNTER (see Looking for a Game)

EDWIN HURTADO

RP • BR • TR • 6'3 • 215 • 27 • TOR90

	G	GS	IP	H	HR	BB	K	W	L	S	ERA	K/BB	K9	HW9
TOR95	14	10	77	81	11	40	33	5	2	0	5.45	.8	3.9	14.14
SEA96	16	4	47	61	10	30	36	2	5	2	7.74	1.2	6.9	17.40

Hurtado came to the Mariners with Paul Menhart from the Blue Jays for Bill Risley and Miguel Cairo, in one of those rare trades that hurts both teams. He should be the 11th guy on a 10-man staff—unfortunately he was the 9th pitcher on the Mariners last year, a team so desperate for warm bodies that they actually started him 4 times. ■

RAUL IBANEZ — SLEEPER

OF • BL • TR • 6'2 • 210 • 24 • SEA92/36

	AB	R	H	2B	3B	HR	RBI	BB	SO	SB	CS	BA	OB	SA
AAA	405	59	115	20	3	11	47	44	56	7	7	.284	.530	.430

Ibanez was a very raw defensive catcher who was moved to the outfield in '96 to take advantage of his hitting skills. The Mariners thought so highly of him that they jumped him to Triple-A. Ibanez has gap power and is considered to be the best pure hitter in the organization. ■

MIKE JACKSON (see Free Agents)

RANDY JOHNSON — AL ELITE

SP • BR • TL • 6'10 • 225 • 33 • MON85/2

	G	GS	IP	H	HR	BB	K	W	L	S	ERA	K/BB	K9	HW9
SEA94	23	23	172	132	14	72	204	13	6	0	3.19	2.8	10.7	10.67
SEA95	30	30	214	159	12	65	294	18	2	0	2.48	4.5	12.4	9.42
SEA96	14	8	61	48	8	25	85	5	0	1	3.67	3.4	12.5	10.76
CAREER	232	224	1520	1173	126	780	1709	104	64	2	3.53	2.2	10.1	11.56

Johnson's injury had the greatest impact of any in baseball last season. The Mariners went 16-13 in the games that Johnson would have started if he'd gone every 5th day all year. The Mariners win 80% of the time Johnson starts, so their record in these games should have been 23-6, enough to take the division outright. In fact, this probably understates the case, since that 16-13 record includes 5 wins from Sterling Hitchcock and a win from Jamie Moyer, a couple of their best pitchers. The Mariners' record in any 29 games started by Hurtado, Menhart, Milacki, Meacham, and Wagner was a lot worse than 16-13. However you choose to look at it, Randy Johnson's injury cost Seattle the division and a rematch with the Yankees, again with the home-field advantage to the Mariners.

The word is that the back surgery went fine. Rehabilitation will consist of muscle strengthening as well as balance and coordination exercises. If he can do them without pain, he will be able to start throwing again and should be back at full strength by the spring—and the Mariners will be the favorites to take the division again. ■

EDGAR MARTINEZ — AL ELITE

DH • BR • TR • 5'11 • 200 • 34 • SEA82

	AB	R	H	2B	3B	HR	RBI	BB	SO	SB	CS	BA	OB	SA
SEA94	326	47	93	23	1	13	51	53	42	6	2	.285	.387	.482
SEA95	511	121	182	52	0	29	113	116	97	4	3	.356	.479	.628
SEA96	499	121	163	52	2	26	103	123	84	3	3	.327	.464	.595
CAREER	3276	604	1031	256	11	117	484	555	465	30	20	.315	.417	.507

Martinez has been arguably the best hitter in baseball the past couple of seasons. His doubles totals are exceptional. He also hit .270 with two strikes (see Garret Anderson in the section on the California Angels for some perspective on this performance). So why doesn't Edgar Martinez get more MVP consideration? Because he doesn't play the

field? Because he's overshadowed by Junior? Because his name is Edgar?

In '95, he didn't have the gaudy homer and RBI totals of Mo Vaughn and Albert Belle, but he reached base much more often than they did, and his power was pretty impressive too. Who was more critical to his team? Junior went down for half the season, and Edgar had to carry the Mariners offense (with help from Jay Buhner). Edgar's defense, like Albert's and Mo's, is nothing special, so he can't lose many votes for not owning a glove. If you add the fact that Seattle had to win a playoff to win their division, while Cleveland (by 30 games) and Boston (by 7 games) won more easily, then who was the more valuable player? Edgar Martinez is a magnificent hitter and has incredible plate discipline and very good power. Appreciate how good he is, since many baseball writers don't seem to. ■

JOHN MARZANO

C • BR • TR • 5'11 • 195 • 34 • MIN81/3

	AB	R	H	2B	3B	HR	RBI	BB	SO	SB	CS	BA	OB	SA
SEA96	106	8	26	6	0	0	6	7	15	0	0	.245	.316	.302
CAREER	574	59	135	35	1	6	50	23	99	0	2	.235	.273	.331

If you need a guy who couldn't hit dirt if he fell off a horse, then he's your man. If you need a guy who couldn't throw out Meat Loaf on a straight steal, then he's your man. If you need an everyday catcher, he's not your man. ■

RUSTY MEACHAM

RP • BR • TR • 6'2 • 165 • 29 • DET87/33

	G	GS	IP	H	HR	BB	K	W	L	S	ERA	K/BB	K9	HW9
KC94	36	0	50	51	7	12	36	3	3	4	3.73	3.0	6.5	11.33
KC95	49	0	59	72	6	19	30	4	3	2	4.98	1.6	4.6	13.88
SEA96	15	5	42	57	9	13	25	1	1	1	5.74	1.9	5.4	14.99
CAREER	189	9	302	334	33	81	182	22	14	9	4.20	2.2	5.4	12.36

Meacham has a sinking fastball that has mediocre velocity. He also has a slider and a change-up, but he has had problems in the past with tipping his change-up—not exactly the pitch whose arrival you want to broadcast. Righties and lefties hammered him in the majors, but he was very effective at Tacoma. Meacham still can pitch in the big leagues, but he has to keep his fastball low and on the corners or he won't be doing it anywhere but Arizona or Tampa Bay. ■

PAUL MENHART

SLEEPER

RP • BR • TR • 6′2 • 190 • 28 • TOR90/9

	G	GS	IP	H	HR	BB	K	W	L	S	ERA	K/BB	K9	HW9
TOR95	21	9	78	72	9	47	50	1	4	0	4.92	1.1	5.8	13.73
SEA96	11	6	42	55	9	25	18	2	2	0	7.29	.7	3.9	17.14

He throws 90, and has a good curve and a better change—so the scouts have plenty of nice things to say about him. But the league hit .327 with a .421 on-base percentage and a .571 slugging percentage against him. George Brett had almost identical totals in 1985 and finished second to Don Mattingly in the MVP balloting. If you turn the A.L. into George Brett, you might as well dig a hole and fall in. Menhart has had injury problems in the past—and has undergone Tommy John surgery—but he could be a lot better this season. He certainly can't be much worse. ■

BLAS MINOR

RP • BR • TR • 6′3 • 205 • 31 • PIT88/6

	G	GS	IP	H	HR	BB	K	W	L	S	ERA	K/BB	K9	HW9
PIT94	17	0	19	27	4	9	17	0	1	1	8.05	1.9	8.1	17.05
NYN95	35	0	46	44	6	13	43	4	2	1	3.66	3.3	8.4	11.15
NYN/SEA96	28	0	50	50	10	17	34	0	1	0	4.31	2.0	6.1	12.04
CAREER	146	0	212	218	28	65	178	12	10	4	4.41	2.7	7.6	12.01

Minor has a sinking fastball that checks in at about 86–87 mph and an adequate change and slider. He's also fiddled with a knuckler for the past few seasons. Considering the A.L. of 1996, Minor had a pretty decent year. The only glaring weakness was the number of home runs he allowed—48 projected over a 200-inning season. ■

TREY MOORE

SLEEPER

SP • BL • TL • 6′1 • 200 • 24 • SEA94/2

	G	GS	IP	H	HR	BB	SO	W	L	S	ERA	K/BB	K9	HW9
AA	11	11	54	73	6	33	42	1	6	0	7.71	1.3	7.0	17.78

Moore has a good slider, a 90+ mph fastball, poise, and can change speeds—your typical lefty with the added kicker of an above-average heater. He was pretty good at Class-A Lancaster, which isn't easy to do, but, as you can see, he was violated in Double-A. He'll probably bounce back this season and, with some luck, he'll see the majors this fall. ■

JAMIE MOYER

SP • BL • TL • 6′0 • 170 • 34 • CHN84/6

	G	GS	IP	H	HR	BB	K	W	L	S	ERA	K/BB	K9	HW9
BAL94	23	23	149	158	23	38	87	5	7	0	4.77	2.3	5.3	11.84
BAL95	27	18	115	117	18	30	65	8	6	0	5.21	2.2	5.1	11.50
BOS/SEA96	34	21	160	177	23	46	79	13	3	0	3.99	1.7	4.4	12.54
CAREER	250	198	1276	1372	154	434	756	72	79	0	4.44	1.7	5.3	12.74

Moyer had 7 quality starts in his 11 starts after coming to Seattle from Boston on July 30 for Darren Bragg. Together, he and Mulholland went 10-6 with a 3.99 ERA in 140 innings—which is a good reason why the Mariners stayed in the hunt until nearly the end, and why they gave Moyer a 2-year deal. Moyer survives by cutting and sinking his fastball, keeping it on the corners, then changing speeds with his mediocre breaking stuff and his change (his best pitch). Ideally he's a third or fourth starter. He'll be part of the nastiest left-handed staff outside of The Bronx. ■

TERRY MULHOLLAND (see Free Agents)

GREG PIRKL

1B • BR • TR • 6′5 • 240 • 26 • SEA88/2

	AB	R	H	2B	3B	HR	RBI	BB	SO	SB	CS	BA	OB	SA
AAA	348	50	105	22	2	21	75	14	58	1	1	.302	.337	.557

The Pirkl-ator is a legendary minor-league masher. The guy has legitimate power, but is done in by his impatience at the plate. But before writing him off as a beer league softballer, consider the marketing possibilities of this: He pitched relief in a game at Tacoma and was clocked at 94 mph! Imagine the DH coming in to pitch the 8th. Imagine him pinch-hitting, then moving from first to the mound and back again. The possibilities are intriguing. ■

ALEX RODRIGUEZ

AL ELITE

SS • BR • TR • 6′3 • 190 • 21 • SEA93/1

	AB	R	H	2B	3B	HR	RBI	BB	SO	SB	CS	BA	OB	SA
SEA95	142	15	33	6	2	5	19	6	42	4	2	.232	.264	.408
SEA96	601	141	215	54	1	36	123	59	104	15	4	.358	.414	.631

Rodriguez already may be the most valuable property in baseball. He's a decent fielder with a great arm who will only get better, he's one of the best hitters in the league, *and* he's one of the youngest players in the league. The last couple of players with similar value in the A.L. were Ivan Rodriguez and Ken Griffey—and Alex's performance at the same age is much better. (By the way, Aurelio,

Ivan, and Alex Rodriguez all played in the big leagues as teenagers. Go figure.)

He was hitting .300 in the no. 9 hole in the lineup, but was over .370 when he was moved up in the lineup to hit in front of Junior. As for what Rodriguez will do for an encore, his ability to hit for average could be undermined by his mediocre strikeouts-to-walks ratio. But then again, he did the same thing in the minors and could well be a Puckett-type hacker who can hit .300 cosistently without always making contact. Such players are rare, but it can be done. In all likelihood, Rodriguez's strike-zone judgment should improve. His production will probably fluctuate more so than that of most stars, because he plays the second most taxing position on the field—and will do so on artificial turf for at least a few more years. If he can handle these challenges as well as he did the challenges of playing every day at 20, he can be the Honus Wagner of the 21st century. And if he slumps (by '96 standards) for the rest of his life, he'll still have a career similar to Cal Ripken's. Or Mel Ott's. Hopefully that will be good enough for the Mariners fans and management. ▪

PAUL SORRENTO

1B • BL • TR • 6'2 • 195 • 31 • CAL86/6

	AB	R	H	2B	3B	HR	RBI	BB	SO	SB	CS	BA	OB	SA
CLE94	322	43	90	14	0	14	62	34	68	0	1	.280	.345	.453
CLE95	323	50	76	14	0	25	79	51	71	1	1	.235	.336	.511
SEA96	471	67	136	32	1	23	93	57	103	0	2	.289	.370	.507
CAREER	2226	306	586	116	4	107	386	272	498	5	9	.263	.343	.463

Sorrento came to Seattle and provided exactly the thing he's famous for: left-handed power to burn. The Mariners got someone who was comparable to Tino Martinez—who had a nice season, though it can't be proven that the Mariners suffered at all by losing him. Sorrento drove in his 93 runs for about half Tino's salary, too. He's often useless against a good left-hander, but he is quite potent against a right-handed pitcher (.307-21-82 in 411 at-bats last season). His defense, however, is one cut above that of Dr. Strangeglove, Dick Stuart—a righty who put up Sorrento offensive numbers for the Pirates and the Red Sox in the '50s and '60s but who treated ground balls like venomous snakes. Sorrento will have a starting job somewhere for the next 5 years, simply because he'll come cheap—his flaws are so evident that they cause his strengths to be underrated. ▪

MAKATO SUZUKI

SLEEPER

SP • BR • TR • 6'3 • 195 • 21 • SEA93

	G	GS	IP	H	HR	BB	SO	W	L	S	ERA	K/BB	K9	HW9
AA	16	16	74	69	10	32	66	3	6	0	4.72	2.1	8.0	12.23

Suzuki had arm problems for a couple of seasons, apparently due to an imbalance in the muscles in his arm. He had arthroscopic shoulder surgery and was out until August '95. But he was throwing 95 mph in the Arizona Fall League that year. In '96 he had a sine-wave season, going from peak to valley to peak. He's had trouble changing speeds and throwing a breaking pitch. In the past, he'd worked more on his change, but last season he was working primarily on a curveball. Suzuki's still young, so there's plenty of time to have a solid major-league career. If he's healthy this season, he could emerge and be a factor for the Mariners. ▪

SALOMON TORRES

SP • BR • TR • 5'11 • 165 • 25 • SF89

	G	GS	IP	H	HR	BB	K	W	L	S	ERA	K/BB	K9	HW9
SF94	16	14	84	95	10	34	42	2	8	0	5.44	1.2	4.5	13.82
SEA95	20	14	80	100	16	49	47	3	9	0	6.30	1.0	5.3	16.76
SEA96	10	7	49	44	5	23	36	3	3	0	4.59	1.6	6.6	12.31
CAREER	54	43	258	276	36	133	148	11	25	0	5.30	1.1	5.2	14.27

Torres was rushed to the majors in '93 and thrown into one of the most heated pennant races in recent years, even though what he had in stuff he lacked in mental toughness. In Shreveport, a reporter who covered the Captains, Torres' Double-A team, said that the entire team thought he was gutless and a quitter—which may be redundant, but is certainly not complimentary. Ever since, he's shown flashes of brilliance and then burned out as soon as he got a chance in the majors. He was a tremendous disap-

pointment to the Giants, and San Francisco was ecstatic to dump him on Seattle for Shawn Estes.

Torres has a fine fastball, a good change-up, and a mediocre slider. Scouts feel he has problems mechanically, which straighten out his pitches, and that he pitches backward—trying to establish his slider and change-up first, then trying to get outs with his fastball. Torres was dreadful in Triple-A, but came up late in September and was 3-2 with a 3.06 ERA in 35.1 innings. His strikeouts-to-walks ratio—a leading indicator of success—doesn't fit with his record and his ERA, and hasn't been anywhere near the 4:1 levels he reached in the minors in 1991–92. He's still young and may find his way back to those levels—but with both a fragile psyche and a frail build, he could just as easily go catatonic as arthroscopic, and never see the field again in either case. ■

SAL URSO

RP • BR • TL • 5′11 • 195 • 25 • SEA90/36

	G	GS	IP	H	HR	BB	SO	W	L	S	ERA	K/BB	K9	HW9
AAA	46	0	73	69	5	32	45	6	2	3	2.35	1.4	5.6	12.51

Urso throws a 90–91-mph fastball, a hard slider, and a change-up he uses as an out pitch against righties. His strikeout rate at Tacoma is not overpowering, a function of knowing how to pitch rather than just throwing. He had to nibble at AAA more than Piniella would probably like to see, but it didn't keep him from getting results. It can be done. Tom Glavine's going to the Hall of Fame, and he hasn't thrown a pitch over the plate in 5 years. ■

JASON VARITEK

C • BB • TR • 6′2 • 210 • 24 • SEA94/1

	AB	R	H	2B	3B	HR	RBI	BB	SO	SB	CS	BA	OB	SA
AA	503	63	132	34	1	12	67	66	93	7	6	.262	.350	.406

A client of noted agent and devil incarnate, Scott Boras, the only lasting impact Varitek may make on major-league baseball is as a poster child for the disease of greed. At Georgia Tech he was considered the greatest catcher in modern NCAA history. A star defensively and a superb hitter with an incredible work ethic, he was originally taken by Minnesota, in 1993 with the 21st pick, but he and Boras wanted more money. He eventually ended negotiations with the Twins, played his senior year at Tech, and was drafted as a senior by the Mariners in 1994 with the 14th pick. The Mariners figured they'd sign him for next to nothing—since seniors have no alternative to going pro, therefore no bargaining leverage—while Boras and Varitek decided that they deserved the kind of money the no. 1 or no. 2 overall pick deserved. So there they sat, stalemated, both sides too greedy to see the big picture, until Varitek finally signed in time to play the 1995 season. And here he is now, ready to move to Triple-A after a good but underachieving season at Double-A, and he'll be 25 years old in April. Nobody wins. Seattle gets a top catching prospect who is off to a good start at a career of unfulfilled potential, while Varitek won't make the millions and play in the big leagues as soon or for as long as if he'd signed for less and started playing ball immediately. Well, maybe somebody does win—baseball fans who are weary of shortsighted greedheads, be they players, agents, or management.

Boras gets a smaller commission on Varitek and will probably lose a few clients as a result, but Varitek is the biggest loser in all this. He is only five months younger than grizzled veteran, Ivan Rodriguez, has thrown away a season and a half of professional development he can never get back, and will probably never see the field at an All-Star game. He's a solid hitter and a good defensive catcher, so he can probably last 8 years in the majors. He'll probably put up some big numbers in the PCL and should get a trial in September. He's good enough to make the Mariners feel they could deal Chris Widger, but it doesn't look like he'll be taking any p.t. from Don Wilson any time soon. But he would have been the Twins starting catcher on Opening Day in '97 if he'd made the right decision back in 1993.

It's hard to root for someone to fail, but Varitek could do more for baseball if he does. A few young players will look at him and decide they don't want this to happen to them, regardless of what their agents are hissing in their ears. ■

BOB WELLS

RP-SP • BR • TR • 6′0 • 180 • 30 • PHI88

	G	GS	IP	H	HR	BB	K	W	L	S	ERA	K/BB	K9	HW9
SEA95	30	4	76	88	11	39	38	4	3	0	5.75	1.0	4.5	15.04
SEA96	36	16	130	141	25	46	94	12	7	0	5.30	2.0	6.5	12.94

In the first couple of months, Wells was 4-1, 1.78 ERA in 40.1 innings. For the rest of the season he was 8-5, 6.55, not faring well after he was moved to the rotation. He had elbow surgery in '92, and he hadn't pitched so many innings since 1990. As a starter, he allowed 20 homers in 79.2 innings; in relief he allowed only 5 in 48.2 innings. He's good at shutting down the running game and will give righties fits, but he isn't very successful against lefties—an accurate description of a decent setup man. Given all the injuries the Mariners had to endure in '96, they were forced to use Wells out of position. If they voluntarily put him back out there as a starter in '97, scratch your head and shrug. But don't blink—you might miss something. ■

MARK WHITEN

OF • BB • TR • 6′3 • 235 • 30 • TOR86/5

	AB	R	H	2B	3B	HR	RBI	BB	SO	SB	CS	BA	OB	SA
SL94	334	57	98	18	2	14	53	37	75	10	5	.293	.364	.485
BOS/PHI95	320	51	77	13	1	12	47	39	86	8	0	.241	.324	.400
PHI/ATL/SEA96	412	76	108	20	1	22	71	70	127	17	9	.262	.372	.476
CAREER	2631	396	677	102	20	93	365	313	599	72	37	.257	.337	.417

Whiten has bounced around more than a squash ball, but he surfaced in time to clobber A.L. opponents for Seattle. He went on a rampage, hitting .295-13-40 (.392 OBP, .589 slugging) in August and September. But Seattle is his 5th team in 3 years and his 7th overall—and when a team such as Atlanta decides it does not want a switch-hitting outfielder with power, speed, and a rifle arm on its postseason roster, releasing him after a game-winning pinch-hit home run, one can only conclude that there are intangibles at work. One explanation is that he's a guy you keep around if you want your clubhouse to be as unpleasant as the heyday of the early '80s Expos, when Steve Rogers and Ron Leflore did their level best to divide the most talented team in baseball straight down the middle.

Defensively, Whiten wasn't as great last year as he's been in past years, but he still has that laser hanging from his shoulder. And he still has enough speed to steal 17 bases. If the Mariners don't sign him, his cannon, and his 25 dingers for this season and keep him around until their next outfield prospect is ready, then something is very wrong that statistics won't reveal. ■

DAN WILSON

C • BR • TR • 6′3 • 190 • 28 • CIN90/1

	AB	R	H	2B	3B	HR	RBI	BB	SO	SB	CS	BA	OB	SA
SEA94	282	24	61	14	2	3	27	10	57	1	2	.216	.244	.312
SEA95	399	40	111	22	3	9	51	33	63	2	1	.278	.336	.416
SEA96	491	51	140	24	0	18	83	32	88	1	2	.285	.330	.444
CAREER	1273	123	338	64	5	30	172	87	232	4	5	.266	.313	.394

Wilson was solid in '95 and put it together in '96. He didn't walk, but he hit for power—though he slowed dramatically in the second half—and jelled defensively. He worked well with the pitching staff and shut down the enemy running game, throwing out 39 of 100 would-be base stealers, including both Kenny Lofton and Tom Goodwin. Right after last season ended, Wilson underwent successful surgery to repair a torn meniscus in his left knee. He should be fully recovered by the time spring training starts, and should have another season similar to 1996. ■

BOB WOLCOTT

SP • BR • TR • 6′0 • 190 • 23 • SEA92/2

	G	GS	IP	H	HR	BB	K	W	L	S	ERA	K/BB	K9	HW9
SEA95	7	6	36	43	6	14	19	3	2	0	4.42	1.4	4.8	14.25
SEA96	30	28	149	179	26	54	78	7	10	0	5.73	1.4	4.7	14.07

The Mariners love him. He has 4 pitches with movement—fastball, sinker, slider, and a change with a screwball action against lefties—that he can throw consistently in good parts of the strike zone. He's had excellent command in the minors, and he's shown decent control in the majors. Last season was a "learning experience" for him, and a bit of a disappointment after his gutsy performance in the '95 postseason. His primary problem is figuring out how to contain lefties (.349-15-47 in 304 at-bats last year—a .416 OBP and a .605 slugging average!). If he can't change his arm angle, or better work his change-up into the mix, he'll end up a decent cog in someone's bullpen rather than a front-line starter. ■

■ 1996 AUTOPSY

The Rangers were counting on major production from the offense and improved pitching, but impartial observers felt that not enough runs could be scored to compensate for their pitching and the effects of the withering summer heat in Texas. The contenders in the A.L. West were thought to be the Angels and the Mariners—with the Senators/Rangers, as they had been for their entire 36-year existence, an afterthought.

April 16-10 (16-10, 1 game ahead)
The Rangers opened against Boston with Ken Hill outpitching Roger Clemens, lasting 8.2 innings, giving up 8 hits and no walks, and leading the club to a 5-3 victory. One more out and it would have been the Rangers' first Opening Day complete game since 1989. They went on to win their first seven games, the best start in franchise history. The starting rotation raised eyebrows by throwing 6 quality starts in the stretch, averaging nearly 7 innings per start with a 2.49 ERA. Roger Pavlik won his first 3 starts. Mike Henneman managed to save 5 of his 6 opportunities despite a 6.43 ERA. Offensively almost everyone got off to a good start, but Kevin Elster was ridiculous. Playing for the injured Benji Gil, Elster hit .279 with 5 homers, 8 doubles, and 21 RBI—more than he'd managed over the past 4 years. They started the Baltimore Orioles on a downward slide that would last half the season when they stomped them like MBAs at a Teamster rally, 26-7, on the 19th—43-16 for the 3-game series.

May 18-9 (34-19, 5½ games ahead)
The team entered May hoping to open up their lead, looking at 20 games in the low-rent district: Detroit, Toronto, Minnesota, and Kansas City. They didn't waste any time, winning 8 out of their first 10. Pavlik and Hill threw back-to-back 1-hitters against the Tigers May 3-4. Hill threw 5 quality starts in 5 outings for a 4-1 record and a 1.77 ERA, establishing himself as the staff ace. Pavlik walked 3 batters all month, going 4-1. Kevin Gross and Darren Oliver recovered from shaky Aprils and pitched well. Bobby Witt was the only cylinder who wasn't firing. In the bullpen, Henneman enjoyed his best month, saving 10 games. They were 10-4 in 1-run games through the first 2 months, but that was not going to continue. The offense struggled with injuries, with Dean Palmer missing a few games and Juan Gonzalez most of the month. It didn't keep Texas from jumping out to a 5-game lead. The Rangers won the division in May, and their pitching did it for them. They would play .500 ball the rest of the season.

June 14-13 (48-32, 5 games ahead)
Gonzalez returned early in the month and contributed 11 home runs and 27 RBI. Following his lead, the entire offense took off. Palmer and Ivan Rodriguez each hit .340 and Elster hit .338. Will Clark landed on the disabled list, however, and would struggle all year and into October. Pavlik gave up a lot of runs (24), but received even more support, going 3-1 to bring his record to 10-2. Darren Oliver started to look like a big-league pitcher, and Witt and Kevin Gross were beginning to come around. The team should have done better than 14-13, but they were 2-6 in 1-run games. Rangers fans geared up for yet another long, hot summer that would wilt their pennant hopes.

July 13-14 (61-46, 2½ games ahead)
Gonzalez did his part to stave off the swoon, hitting .407 and slugging .917 with 15 homers and 38 RBI. He became only the 4th player ever to hit 15 in the July heat and was suddenly in serious contention for the MVP. They unloaded some serious offense on some very good pitchers: 8-6 to beat Mark Langston, 8-1 to beat Chuck Finley, 9-2 to beat Jimmy Key, and 15-2 to beat Andy Pettitte. Hill and Pavlik continued to pitch well, and Witt was decent. But the rest of the staff was coming unglued. Gross began developing back problems, and Oliver struggled. The club had tired of Henneman's inconsistency and was closing by committee. They traded for Mike Stanton on the 31st, but that wasn't going to be enough. They could already hear the Mariners footsteps.

August 16-12 (77-58, 7 games ahead)
Gonzalez gave the Yankees a preview of what he would do to them in October, with 7 hits, 3 homers, and 6 RBI in a series to open the month. The team continued its disrespect of front-line starters, beating Juan Guzman 12-1 and then Kevin Appier and Jack McDowell 10-3 on consecutive days. But the future

was being told in their performance in 1-run games—2-5—though they couldn't see it. The Texas defense, not normally known for their prowess, made headlines of their own. From Aug. 4 to 19, the club played 15 games without an error. The streak fell a game short of the major-league record of 16 held by the '92 Cardinals. But the biggest news of the month was the trade for John Burkett. He made an impression immediately, winning 2 games. He and Hill threw back-to-back shutouts in the middle of a 7-game winning streak and held the staff together for the entire month. The streak ensured a winning record and helped them increase their lead over the slumping Mariners. It appeared the Rangers had avoided the slide that everyone had been predicting for the past couple of months—and seen more than once in the past 20 years.

September 13-14 (90-72, won division)
After a 6-3 start the Rangers headed into the stretch on the 11th with a 9-game lead. Then they dropped 3 out of 4 games against Milwaukee and went into the Kingdome for a showdown with the Mariners. Four games later they had been swept, outscored 23-10, their lead down to 2 games. The next night they lost a 10-inning heartbreaker at California when Mike Stanton gave up a 2-strike, game-winning double to Garret Anderson. They had lost 9 of 10 and their lead had dwindled to a game. The offense was MIA and the team seemed primed for a legendary collapse. But Burkett saved their bacon on the 21st with a complete-game, 7-1 victory over California. Hill followed it up with a complete game of his own, winning 4-1. They went on to win 6 of their last 8 to capture the division for the first time in franchise history.

October (lost in divisional series to Yankees)
For a change, the Rangers didn't pack for home at the end of September, heading to New York and the divisional series instead. Burkett had a sterling performance in Game 1, scattering 10 hits and allowing 2 runs in 9 innings. Gonzalez hit a 3-run homer, giving them all the runs they needed. But the bullpen was shaky in the last 3 games, as it had been since June, and squandered leads in all 3—most notably a gem by Darren Oliver in Game 3 that could have buried the Yankees. The hitters were stymied by the Yankees' excellent relievers and continually failed to deliver clutch hits in 3 close defeats: 5-4, 3-2 and 6-4. Juan Gonzalez hit .438 with 5 homers and 9 RBI, but his efforts were undone by Will Clark—who managed 2 singles in 16 at-bats, failed repeatedly in the clutch, allowed the Yankees to start pitching around Gonzalez, and was the main reason why the games were even close enough for the Rangers bullpen to give them away.

■ 1997 DIAGNOSIS

The Rangers had as many decisions to make as any team in baseball in the '96–'97 off-season, with 12 players eligible for free agency and others simply old and in the way. The core of the offense (Gonzalez, Rodriguez, Palmer, Greer) and rotation (Hill, Burkett, Pavlik, Oliver) was locked up for '97. But you'll find most of the rest of the '96 team in the Free Agents and Looking for a Game sections at the back of this book.

Offense
The Rangers scored 928 runs, 56 runs better than the average A.L. team, and tied for 4th in the league. The offense will remain potent this year and could be even better. Gonzalez and Rodriguez have developed into great hitters at their positions. Palmer and Rusty Greer are solid major-league producers. Mickey Tettleton and Will Clark were nicked up last year and could have better seasons this year. Both figure to get more playing time. Slugging prospect Lee Stevens, and perhaps even Bubba Smith, could get a chance to swing for major-league fences.

Defense
The Rangers led the league in defense last year. That's not a misprint, or a hockey reference. Texas gave up only 50 unearned runs—and unearned runs meant the difference in only 7 losses all season. That just makes their Game 2 loss to the Yankees on a Dean Palmer throwing error even more painful. Give a lot of the credit to Johnny Oates, whose Baltimore teams always played tight defense, and who, unlike former manager Kevin Kennedy, was able to sell his players on the benefits of throwing and catching. Will Clark is a decent fielder at first,

though he's slipped significantly. Mark McLemore was allowed to settle in one position and turned in an excellent year at second. No one ever questioned Kevin Elster's glovework. Benji Gil may quickly reclaim his job; he's both more flashy and more erratic—making 45 errors in 132 games in Class-A and 37 in 139 games at Double-A. In fact, the best fielding percentage he's ever managed was in the majors in 1995, and he'll have to prove that wasn't a fluke. Dean Palmer will never win a Gold Glove, but he has a great throwing arm. He'd shown tremendous improvement, and he saved Game 1 against the Yankees with a great diving stop. But after that, he looked lost. Darryl Hamilton doesn't have the range he once had in center, but he's a veteran who knows his position. Rusty Greer is outstanding in left. Juan Gonzalez had a subpar year in right, but he was learning a new position. Ivan Rodriguez is the best behind the plate in baseball. They probably won't be the best defensive unit again in '97, but they shouldn't give away too many games either.

Pitching

The starting rotation was the big question mark going into the season. They weren't spectacular, but they held their own. Their 4.79 ERA was the 5th lowest total in the league. They tied Toronto for 1st with 19 complete games and pitched more than 1,000 innings. Only Kansas City's starters went deeper into the game. Ken Hill gave the Rangers their money's worth and established himself as a legitimate staff ace. John Burkett's arrival and subsequent performance may give Hill a solid rival for the role. Roger Pavlik proved that he is a major-leaguer, and Bobby Witt had a good year as well. But Kevin Gross struggled most of the season and was eventually shut down with back problems. The emergence of Darren Oliver means that Gross won't be missed.

The bullpen had an ERA of 4.32, 5th lowest in the league, but they were undone by inconsistency in the closer role. The Rangers lost 9 games last year in which they led in the ninth inning. Henneman won't be back, and finding a closer will be a major goal in the free-agent market . . . again. Ed Vosberg and Dennis Cook pitched well last year and provide veteran experience. Mike Stanton also has a lot of innings under his belt. Matt Whiteside has struggled but has a lot of potential. And Danny Patterson is a young gun who should get a shot.

Farm System

The Rangers have had one of the thinnest farm systems in recent years. Since taking over in '94, Doug Melvin has gutted it to rebuild from the bottom up. One point of emphasis has been to fill the upper levels with veteran players who can help immediately if needed. Lee Stevens and Bubba Smith are a couple of slugging prospects who fit that bill. They also have some who could be close, such as Julio Santana, Johnathon Johnson, José Alberro, and Patterson. In the lower levels, there is some quality talent, but not in great numbers. Danny Kolb and Eric Moody are a couple of pitchers whose numbers stand out. Part of the consequences of the housecleaning and trades made during the pennant race is a lack of pitching depth. The club has traded away 5 right-handers in recent months. Still, the system is better off than it was last year at this time—and the team got rave reviews for its 1996 draft performance.

Management and Ownership

George W. Bush has now seen 7 years of hard work and patience pay off. The changes he made in the organization, beginning with the new ballpark, have taken time to produce a winner but are beginning to bear fruit. The ballpark has brought fans to the park—though Texas fans did stay away in droves in 1995 after the strike. The resurgence in attendance in '96 has given him the revenues to support a good team. The management staff he put together made sure there was one to support.

GM Doug Melvin was honored last year by *The Sporting News* as their major-league executive of the year. In 2 years, he has brought the Rangers from a 52-62 team to a division winner. His first move was to install his own coaches and he's stood by them. Last season he made several key acquisitions, especially in the pitching staff, who helped make the team more than just a contender. He also has improved the depth of their minor-league talent. Melvin will need to find a closer this year, and several decisions need to be made about older players who helped the team but who will be free agents: Cook, Elster, Gross, Hamilton, Henneman, Stanton, and Jeff Russell.

The Sporting News also hailed Johnny Oates as their manager of the year. Oates did what they said couldn't be done by guiding the Rangers to their first division title ever. The club avoided their annual collapse in the Texas sun—though they gave it their best shot in September. When their lead dwindled to a game, Yankee fans were already groaning about having to go back to the Kingdome in October. Oates didn't panic, and the team held it together to bring home the title. He got the most out of a questionable pitching staff, turning them into one of the most effective rotations in the league. And even more surprising, he helped the Rangers establish themselves as an excellent defensive team.

. . . and whatnot: The Curse of the Senators

Since the Senators abandoned the nation's capital to chase the money in Texas, it's been 25 years, 3,916 games, and 18 managers before they finally got a chance to blow a playoff series. And it took a complete overhaul in the franchise's infrastructure, management, and philosophy just to get this far.

The franchise has a long history of failure and disorganization. In their first season in Texas, they finished 38½ games out—exactly where they'd ended up a year before. Years of futility followed, despite having legends in the dugout: Ted Williams; Whitey Herzog and Billy Martin in the same season, one in which they dropped 105 games; and Eddie Stanky, who resigned after a single game. Even when they fielded decent teams, they couldn't survive the heat and would fade in the stretch.

Their hyped prospects never seemed to pan out: Pete Broberg, Bump Wills, Nelson Norman, Steve Comer, Pat Putnam, Dave Hostetler, Jeff Kunkel, Oddibe McDowell, and the 18-year-old phenom David Clyde, whose psyche was destroyed to sell some tickets. And when they did have gems on their hands, they gave them away: Dave Righetti, Tom Henke, Sammy Sosa, and Wilson Alvarez were all products of this system. Lenny Randle was a good young player they produced and kept, but then he had to go and punch the team's manager in the face. Finally, as if to make this product thoroughly unmarketable, they played in a minor-league facility with more seats in the outfield than in the grandstand.

When George Bush's kid and his partnership took over in 1989, one of their first acts was to put together a deal for a new, fan-friendly stadium to build attendance and cash flow. At the same time, the club finally began to realize the vast Hispanic market that surrounded them, as well as the Latino players who were emerging in major-league systems everywhere, seemingly, but Texas. After the '94 season Bush hired Doug Melvin as the general manager. He immediately fired Kevin Kennedy and replaced him with Johnny Oates, a manager more adept at player development—and at keeping the clean-up hitter from blowing out his arm on the pitcher's mound. Melvin gave him some talent to work with: prospects, veteran free agents, and reclamation projects. Oates took a talented group of individuals and turned them into a cohesive unit. He took youngsters and made them into big-leaguers. He took a collection of aging, marginal, and inconsistent pitchers and turned them into a decent rotation. He took a team with a porous reputation and had them playing solid defense. And by sheer force of will, he kept a team whose death certificate had already been signed from completing one of the biggest chokes in baseball history.

The Rangers may not be making nearly as many mistakes as they have in the past, but they are still paying for ones that took place on the previous administration's watch. And these they may be feeling for the next 10 years. The gaping hole in the bullpen where a closer should be? That would be nicely filled by a guy named Robb Nen, who was traded for something called a Cris Carpenter. The left-handed punch they could have used protecting Juan Gonzalez in the lineup during the playoffs? That could have been more than adequately supplied by Rafael Palmeiro. But after stealing him from the Cubs, they let him go to free agency—so they could sign Will Clark in a misguided attempt at finding a replacement for Nolan Ryan in the good ol' hearts of the good ol' boys in the stands.

If Melvin and Oates can overcome those two legacies in '97 they will really have done something. But apparently the ghosts of the Senators have found their way across the parking lot from Arlington Stadium and into The Ballpark—and are not going quietly.

JOSÉ ALBERRO — SLEEPER

SP • BR • TR • 6'2 • 190 • 27 • TEX91

	G	GS	IP	H	HR	BB	K	W	L	S	ERA	K/BB	K9	HW9
AAA	29	27	171	154	12	57	140	9	9	0	3.47	2.5	7.4	11.11

Alberro had never started a game before '95 in Oklahoma City. He handled himself pretty well, and the experiment continued last year. He wasn't exactly dominant, but he's starting to look like he could be a no. 4 or 5 starter. He has had 3 years of Triple-A experience and 12 games in the majors. Now, with a full year of starting under his belt, he could be ready to contribute in Arlington. ■

MIKE BELL — SOLID PROSPECT

3B • BR • TR • 6'2 • 185 • 22 • TEX93/1

	AB	R	H	2B	3B	HR	RBI	BB	SO	SB	CS	BA	OB	SA
AA	484	62	129	31	3	16	59	42	75	3	1	.267	.329	.442

The Rangers are quite happy with the way Bell has progressed. He has an excellent work ethic, which runs in Buddy's family. He showed good power in Tulsa, especially to the gaps. Defensively he's improved but there are still questions, especially about his arm strength. ■

KEVIN BROWN — SOLID PROSPECT

C • BR • TR • 6'2 • 200 • 23 • TEX94/1

	AB	R	H	2B	3B	HR	RBI	BB	SO	SB	CS	BA	OB	SA
AA	460	77	121	27	1	26	86	73	150	0	3	.263	.373	.496

Despite the depressing reality of trying to win a major-league job behind Ivan Rodriguez, Brown looks like a slugging prospect with a future. He's a big guy with excellent bat speed and raw power. He strikes out too much, and the Rangers would probably like to see a higher batting average in Double-A, but at least he knows how to take a walk. Brown has a strong arm, but he isn't so good at blocking balls yet. He has a reputation as a hard worker and could learn. He sounds eerily like Mickey Tettleton. The Rangers should start giving him some time at first or in the outfield to see if he can handle other positions. And feeding him some of Tettleton's Froot Loops. ■

DAMON BUFORD

OF • BR • TR • 5'10 • 170 • 26 • BAL90/11

	AB	R	H	2B	3B	HR	RBI	BB	SO	SB	CS	BA	OB	SA
BAL/NYN95	168	30	34	5	0	4	14	25	35	10	8	.202	.318	.304
TEX96	145	30	41	9	0	6	20	15	34	8	5	.283	.348	.469

It looked at one time like Buford was the center fielder of the future in Baltimore. But they never gave him much playing time and he didn't make much of the chances he got—whether these came in Baltimore or later with the Mets, after he was traded with Alex Ochoa for Bobby Bonilla's hefty contract and sunny disposition. Buford finally showed some big-league potential in '96. He played in all 3 outfield positions and swung the bat well in only 145 at-bats. The way the Rangers' front-line outfielders are producing, it doesn't look like Buford will crack the starting lineup anytime soon. But if the club decides not to resign Darryl Hamilton, Don's kid would have the first shot at center. ■

JOHN BURKETT

SP • BR • TR • 6'2 • 205 • 32 • SF83/6

	G	GS	IP	H	HR	BB	K	W	L	S	ERA	K/BB	K9	HW9
SF94	25	25	159	176	14	36	85	6	8	0	3.62	2.4	4.8	12.00
FLA95	30	30	188	208	22	57	126	14	14	0	4.30	2.2	6.0	12.69
FLA/TEX96	34	34	222	229	19	58	155	11	12	0	4.26	2.7	6.3	11.63
CAREER	227	221	1407	1462	125	360	872	92	68	1	3.96	2.4	5.6	11.65

Burkett had a fairly rough time of it early in the season for the Marlins, and he was pretty mediocre until the Rangers eventually dealt for him in August. He's always pitched best when the games mattered—with the Rangers in '96, and with the 103-win Giants back in '93. He went 5-2 down the stretch and, on September 21, with the Rangers' lead down to a game after a 5-game skid, he threw a complete game for a 7-1 victory over California that pulled them out of their tailspin. Burkett went on to open the divisional series with a complete-game, 6-2 victory over the Yankees, the Rangers' only win in the series. ■

JORGE CARRION — SLEEPER

DH-SS-SP • TEX96 • NE TEXAS COMMUNITY COLLEGE

	AB	R	H	2B	3B	HR	RBI	BB	SO	SB	CS	BA	OB	SA
A	38	7	11	0	1	0	6	3	10	0	2	.289	.333	.342

That combination of positions makes Biggio's c-cf-2b look pedestrian. Carrion has given the Rangers a problem they don't mind having. So far he's been an excellent hitter and an outstanding pitcher, so they're not sure what to do with him. He hit .309 in

the Gulf Coast League as a DH before his promotion to Charleston, so they were going to let him finish the year as a position player. But they gave him a few appearances and he struck out 19 in 15 innings with a 1.76 ERA. On the mound he hits 95 mph consistently with his fastball, sometimes throwing as high as 98 mph. He was one of the hardest throwers in the college ranks and has been compared to another shortstop/pitcher, Frankie Rodriguez. ■

WILL CLARK

OVERRATED

1B • BL • TL • 6′2 • 190 • 33 • SF85/1

	AB	R	H	2B	3B	HR	RBI	BB	SO	SB	CS	BA	OB	SA
TEX94	389	73	128	24	2	13	80	71	59	5	1	.329	.431	.501
TEX95	454	85	137	27	3	16	92	68	60	0	1	.302	.389	.480
TEX96	436	69	124	25	1	13	72	64	67	2	1	.284	.377	.436
CAREER	5548	914	1667	325	43	218	953	709	920	59	44	.300	.379	.492

Clark battled injuries all year and finally underwent shoulder surgery shortly after his pathetic 2-16 performance in the divisional series against the Yankees. A lot of guys would love to hit over .280 and drive in 74 runs. A lot of guys would also love to make $5 million a year for slapping singles to left. But the *average* first baseman in the A.L. hit 30 dingers and knocked in 100 runs in '96, and The Thrill is now lower than Paul Sorrento on the food chain. Some apologize for Clark's performance by pointing to his "leadership" qualities. Glaring at the pitcher doesn't make you a leader; performance does, and his fall-off in offensive production hinders his ability to play that role. Here is how Clark and Rafael Palmeiro—the man they let go to make room for him—have performed the past 3 years:

Player	BA	AB	R	H	2B	HR	RBI	BB	SB
Clark	.304	1,279	227	389	76	42	244	203	7
Palmeiro	.304	1,616	281	492	102	101	322	211	18

Palmeiro told the Rangers they were crazy when they let him go. Now he's gone out and proved the point. ■

DENNIS COOK (see Free Agents)

CLINT DAVIS

RP • BR • TR • 6′3 • 205 • 27

	G	GS	IP	H	HR	BB	K	W	L	S	ERA	K/BB	K9	HW9
AA	32	0	48	31	3	12	40	3	3	0	1.88	3.3	7.5	8.06

Davis was a promising closer prospect in the Cardinals system, and he looks like a good pickup for the Rangers. He was unhittable for Double-A Tulsa and a brief stint in Triple-A Oklahoma City was also successful. He's capable of pitching longer innings and could eventually provide quality right-handed relief for Texas. ■

EDWIN DIAZ

2B • BR • TR • 5′11 • 170 • 22 • TEX93/2

	AB	R	H	2B	3B	HR	RBI	BB	SO	SB	CS	BA	OB	SA
AA	499	70	132	33	6	16	65	25	122	8	9	.265	.309	.451

Offensively Diaz could be a gem if he works on his plate discipline. He's an outstanding power hitter for a second baseman. The Rangers are concerned about his defense, seeing his problems as more a function of attitude than ability. Can't teach that.

R.A. DICKEY

SLEEPER

SP • TEX96/1 • UNIVERSITY OF TENNESSEE

A lot of significant stories came out of the draft last year; Dickey's was one of the more disturbing. Texas drafted him with the 18th pick of the 1st round. The two parties quickly reached an agreement, and Dickey was set to sign a contract including an $810,000 signing bonus. But the club's orthopedic consultant had seen Dickey's photo on the cover of *Baseball America* and felt that his arm hung unnaturally at his side. The club asked him to take a physical first, and the consultant found evidence of damage to his ulnar collateral ligament. After further tests they found that he had no ligament at all. The Rangers immediately dropped their original offer and he eventually signed for $75,000. There had been concerns about Dickey before this all took place. He generally throws in the low 90s, but his velocity had dropped because he was used so much at the University of Tennessee. His performance for Team USA last summer wasn't stellar, and he isn't known for strong mechanics. But he *is* known as a hard worker. Maybe he'll demonstrate his arm strength by offering to trade jabs with that orthopedic consultant who cost him $735,000. ■

KEVIN ELSTER (see Free Agents)

HANLEY FRIAS

SS • BB • TR • 6′0 • 160 • 23

	AB	R	H	2B	3B	HR	RBI	BB	SO	SB	CS	BA	OB	SA
AA	505	73	145	24	12	2	41	30	73	9	9	.287	.325	.394

Frias has an excellent glove and was voted the top defensive shortstop in the Texas League. His speed has diminished a bit in the past few years, but he still has very good range. He's come a long way at the plate as well. He's steadily improved his average from the .240 range and has developed some gap power. His plate discipline should be his next project. He's already got the tools in the field; if his hitting continues to progress, Benji Gil could be hearing footsteps shortly. ■

SHAWN GALLAGHER — SLEEPER

1B • BR • TR • 6′0 • 185 • 20 • TEX95/5

	AB	R	H	2B	3B	HR	RBI	BB	SO	SB	CS	BA	OB	SA
A	303	29	68	11	4	7	32	18	104	6	1	.224	.280	.356

Despite those numbers, Gallagher is probably the best pure hitter and raw power prospect in the Rangers' system. In high school he tied a national high-school record with a 51-game hitting streak. But he's never been considered much of a prospect because he isn't very skilled in the field. He's a born DH. ■

DAVE GEEVE

SP • BR • TR • 6′3 • 190 • 27 • TEX91/10

	G	GS	IP	H	HR	BB	K	W	L	S	ERA	K/BB	K9	HW9
AA	18	17	83	105	12	23	60	7	6	0	5.55	2.6	6.5	13.94

Geeve improved dramatically throughout his first 3 seasons in the Rangers' system, but ran into a wall when he reached Triple-A in '95. He couldn't recover his form after moving back down to Tulsa either. He has good stuff. At midseason, Texas League managers voted his breaking ball the best in the league. But he struggled with injuries and eventually missed the latter part of the season. He looked promising earlier in his career, but he's had 2 straight lackluster years. ■

BENJI GIL — SLEEPER

SS • BR • TR • 6′2 • 180 • 24 • TEX91/1

	AB	R	H	2B	3B	HR	RBI	BB	SO	SB	CS	BA	OB	SA
TEX95	415	36	91	20	3	9	46	26	147	2	4	.219	.266	.347
TEX96	5	0	2	0	0	0	1	1	1	0	1	.400	.500	.400

Back surgery and the subsequent rehab kept Gil out of the Rangers' lineup at the start of the season. Kevin Elster kept him out of it for the rest of the year. Gil didn't do much to force the issue in Triple-A Oklahoma City either (hitting .223 with 6 dingers and 90 strikeouts in 292 at bats). He's never hit for average, but he has adequate power for a shortstop. And he can be an excellent-fielding shortstop. He was the starter in Texas all year in '95 and it won't be long before he wins the job back. ■

JUAN GONZALEZ — AL ELITE

RF • BR • TR • 6′3 • 185 • 27 • TEX86

	AB	R	H	2B	3B	HR	RBI	BB	SO	SB	CS	BA	OB	SA
TEX94	422	57	116	18	4	19	85	30	66	6	4	.275	.330	.472
TEX95	352	57	104	20	2	27	82	17	66	0	0	.295	.324	.594
TEX96	541	89	170	33	2	47	144	45	82	2	0	.314	.368	.643
CAREER	3130	480	887	172	13	214	659	214	609	16	11	.283	.334	.552

After doctors told Gonzalez he had a better chance of keeping his back healthy if he laid off the weights, he came into spring training 30 pounds lighter (he'd bulked up from 175 to 215 since he first came into the league). As a result, he was able to turn on anything inside and crush it. He started the season well, but really hit his stride in July, when his 15 home runs put him in the company of Joe DiMaggio, Hank Greenberg, and Joe Adcock. For a power hitter he doesn't walk much, an indication that he was getting pitches to hit and going after them aggressively. He set club records for homers and RBI, then hit .438 and homered 5 times against the Yankees in the division series to tie the record for homers in a single playoff series. He also became the second player to homer in 4 consecutive playoff games. He has a new nickname in Arlington, a town unaccustomed to autumnal heroics: "Señor Octubre." And he even got Alex Rodriguez's vote for A.L. MVP, too. ■

RUSTY GREER

LF • BL • TL • 6′0 • 190 • 28 • TEX90/10

	AB	R	H	2B	3B	HR	RBI	BB	SO	SB	CS	BA	OB	SA
TEX94	277	36	87	16	1	10	46	46	46	0	0	.314	.410	.487
TEX95	417	58	113	21	2	13	61	55	66	3	1	.271	.355	.424
TEX96	542	96	180	41	6	18	100	62	86	9	0	.332	.397	.530
CAREER	1236	190	380	78	9	41	207	163	198	12	1	.307	.386	.485

The Rusty Greer Era has begun. Always a promising prospect, Greer had improved steadily for the Rangers as he moved through their system. He had a disappointing season in '95, though, after taking over the everyday job in right field. His average dipped to .271 and the club wanted more production from the left-hander in their left-hander-friendly park. Last season he moved to left and had a breakthrough year. He led the club in hitting and his power increased dramatically. He doubled his doubles and reached the 100 RBI plateau for the first time in his career. Greer always had excellent plate discipline, and he has become a good baserunner and excellent outfielder. He's become the fan favorite at The Ballpark. ■

KEVIN GROSS (see Free Agents)

DARRYL HAMILTON (see Free Agents)

MIKE HENNEMAN (see Free Agents)

GIL HEREDIA

RP • BR • TR • 6′1 • 190 • 31 • SF87/9

	G	GS	IP	H	HR	BB	K	W	L	S	ERA	K/BB	K9	HW9
MON94	39	3	75	85	7	13	62	6	3	0	3.46	4.8	7.4	11.75
MON95	40	18	119	137	7	21	74	5	6	1	4.31	3.5	5.6	11.95
TEX96	44	0	73	91	12	14	43	2	5	1	5.89	3.1	5.3	12.94
CAREER	170	39	402	450	38	89	254	19	21	4	4.34	2.9	5.7	12.07

Heredia's numbers were way off last season. Throughout his career he's always had excellent control and thrown a lot of strikeouts with his superior forkball. Last year his strikeout rate decreased dramatically, while A.L. hitters rung him up for a .301 average. He didn't walk many, but that was more a function of throwing hittable slop than hitting spots. ■

KEN HILL

SP • BR • TR • 6′2 • 175 • 31 • DET85

	G	GS	IP	H	HR	BB	K	W	L	S	ERA	K/BB	K9	HW9
MON94	23	23	154	145	12	44	85	16	5	0	3.32	1.9	5.0	11.04
SL/CLE95	30	29	185	202	21	77	98	10	8	0	4.62	1.3	4.8	13.57
TEX96	35	35	250	250	19	95	170	16	10	0	3.63	1.8	6.1	12.42
CAREER	233	226	1462	1375	103	570	890	90	71	0	3.66	1.6	5.5	11.97

As the Rangers' big free-agent acquisition, a lot was riding on Hill's arm last year. Kenny Rogers was gone, and the club needed Hill to step in and be The Man. In his first full year in the offense-crazy American League, he led the starting rotation in innings pitched, ERA, and strikeouts, and tied for the lead in victories and complete games. He throws hard and needs to keep the ball down to be effective, getting most of his outs on his split-finger. He'll earn $4 million this year in the last year of his deal with Texas, so, if he wants to keep making 100 grand every time he walks out onto the field, he'll need to put good years back to back for the first time in his career. ■

JON JOHNSON

SOLID PROSPECT

SP • BR • TR • 6′0 • 180 • 22 • TEX95/1

	G	GS	IP	H	HR	BB	K	W	L	S	ERA	K/BB	K9	HW9
AA	26	25	174	176	15	41	97	13	10	0	3.56	2.4	5.0	11.20

The Rangers picked up a polished pitcher with their no. 1 pick in '95. Johnson has been compared to Tom Gordon and is considered to be close to major-league caliber right now. His best pitch is an excellent curveball and he has a decent change-up. His fastball is only slightly better than average. Some scouts feel he's never going to be much better than he is now, but others say he has great mechanics and toughness and expect him to continue improving. Johnson pitched well in Tulsa last year, showing good control and a decent strikeout rate. And he pitched a complete-game shutout for Triple-A Oklahoma City. He doesn't look overpowering, but he wouldn't have to be to win 16 games for this team. ■

DANNY KOLB

GRADE-A PROSPECT

SP • BR • TR • 6′4 • 190 • 22 • TEX95/6

	G	GS	IP	H	HR	BB	K	W	L	S	ERA	K/BB	K9	HW9
A+	6	6	38	38	1	14	28	2	2	0	4.26	2.0	6.6	12.32

Kolb has moved from the Rookie League in ’95 all the way to AA at the end of ’96. He started ’96 in Class-A, where he gave up 80 hits in 126 innings while striking out 127. His fastball consistently hits 94, and was voted best in the South Atlantic League last year. He was also voted the top pitching prospect. He also has a good curveball and an improving change-up. If he ever harnesses that power and gains some control, he could be a major stud. And the Rangers know it. The Blue Jays wanted him to be included in a proposed deal for Mike Timlin last year, but the Rangers wouldn’t part with him. ■

MARK LITTLE

SLEEPER

OF • BR • TR • 6′0 • 200 • 24 • TEX94/8

	AB	R	H	2B	3B	HR	RBI	BB	SO	SB	CS	BA	OB	SA
AA	409	69	119	24	2	13	50	48	88	22	10	.291	.377	.455

Little has all the tools to be a big-league center fielder. He was voted the top defensive outfielder in the Texas League, has excellent speed, and has become a good hitter with some power. He’ll probably start the season in Double-A Tulsa, but if he continues to hit, he’ll get a long look in Oklahoma City. ■

MARK MCLEMORE

2B • BB • TR • 5′11 • 195 • 32 • CAL82/8

	AB	R	H	2B	3B	HR	RBI	BB	SO	SB	CS	BA	OB	SA
BAL94	343	44	88	11	1	3	29	51	50	20	5	.257	.354	.321
TEX95	467	73	122	20	5	5	41	59	71	21	11	.261	.346	.358
TEX96	517	84	150	23	4	5	46	87	69	27	10	.290	.389	.379
CAREER	3030	445	782	118	23	22	290	373	457	145	64	.258	.338	.334

Oates saved McLemore’s career in Baltimore and wanted him around in Texas, too. In his second season with the Rangers, McLemore turned in the best year of his career at the plate. He set career highs in hitting, slugging, on-base percentage, walks, stolen bases, and runs scored. They let him play exclusively at second last year—after playing 73 games in the outfield in ’95 and splitting time at second, pretty much the same role he had for 3 years in Baltimore. The stability definitely helped his defense and did a lot to settle the infield. ■

ERIC MOODY

SLEEPER

SP-RP • BR • TR • 6′6 • 185 • 26 • TEX93/24

	G	GS	IP	H	HR	BB	K	W	L	S	ERA	K/BB	K9	HW9
AA	44	5	96	92	4	23	80	8	4	16	3.57	3.5	7.5	10.82

Moody looked strong in Double-A Tulsa after an even better year in ’95 for Class-A Charleston. The Rangers tried him as a closer for a while, and he took to it. They may want to give him some more time in Double-A, especially if the experiment is to continue, but at his age they shouldn’t be afraid of rushing him. If he doesn’t start the season in Oklahoma City, he’ll be there by the end of the year. ■

WARREN NEWSON

OF • BL • TL • 5′7 • 190 • 32 • SD86/4

	AB	R	H	2B	3B	HR	RBI	BB	SO	SB	CS	BA	OB	SA
CHA94	102	16	26	5	0	2	7	14	23	1	0	.255	.345	.363
CHA/SEA95	157	34	41	2	2	5	15	39	45	2	1	.261	.411	.395
TEX96	235	34	60	14	1	10	31	37	82	3	0	.255	.355	.451
CAREER	802	132	208	29	3	24	95	164	234	11	3	.259	.385	.393

Career year #113 for an American League hitter in ’96, for those of you scoring at home. ■

DARREN OLIVER

SP • BR • TL • 6′0 • 170 • 26 • TEX88/3

	G	GS	IP	H	HR	BB	K	W	L	S	ERA	K/BB	K9	HW9
TEX95	17	7	49	47	3	32	39	4	2	0	4.22	1.2	7.2	14.51
TEX96	30	30	173	190	20	76	112	14	6	0	4.66	1.5	5.8	13.83

The Rangers experimented with using Oliver as a starter in ’95, but he broke down with a shoulder injury in June and was lost for the season. Going into ’96, they were ready to try him again in the No. 5 slot. He appears to have passed the audition. Except for a miserable slump during July and August, he pitched remarkably well for a guy in his first full season as a starter. Take those 2 months out and he was 10-2 with a 3.61 ERA.The club stuck with him and he recovered well, finishing out the season 3-0 in September—and a hard-luck loss in the divisional series against the Yankees. ■

LUIS ORTIZ

1B • BR • TR • 6'0 • 190 • 26 • BOS91/11

	AB	R	H	2B	3B	HR	RBI	BB	SO	SB	CS	BA	OB	SA
AAA	501	70	159	25	0	14	73	22	36	0	5	.317	.347	.451

After an extended but disappointing stint in Texas in '95, Ortiz spent most of '96 in Oklahoma City. He got a brief call-up in September, making it the 4th straight year he's seen at least limited major-league playing time. He's an excellent hitter. He's finished over .290 every season in his 6-year minor-league career, and his power numbers have progressed nicely during that time. He's aggressive at the plate, swinging early and often and putting the ball in play. Instead of giving him some time at first or at DH, spelling Clark and Tettleton against lefties, the Rangers cut him loose. ■

DEAN PALMER

3B • BR • TR • 6'1 • 175 • 28 • TEX86/3

	AB	R	H	2B	3B	HR	RBI	BB	SO	SB	CS	BA	OB	SA
TEX94	342	50	84	14	2	19	59	26	89	3	4	.246	.302	.465
TEX95	119	30	40	6	0	9	24	21	21	1	1	.336	.448	.613
TEX96	582	98	163	26	2	38	107	59	145	2	0	.280	.348	.527
CAREER	2390	378	590	113	8	140	396	253	673	27	21	.247	.323	.477

Palmer ruptured the biceps tendon in his left arm swinging at a pitch in '95, easily the most gruesome incident on a baseball field since Roseanne sang the National Anthem. It didn't keep him from getting off to a quick start, hitting .317 with 8 homers and 20 RBI in April. He then went on to turn in a career season. His power has been improving steadily since he broke into the league, and it truly blossomed last year. Defensively, he's the weak link in the infield, though he's come a long way from 59 errors and an .819 fielding percentage in 128 games in Class-A. He led A.L. third basemen in errors in '93 with 29, but held them down to 16 in '96. ■

DANNY PATTERSON — SLEEPER

RP • BR • TR • 6'0 • 185 • 26

	G	GS	IP	H	HR	BB	K	W	L	S	ERA	K/BB	K9	HW9
AAA	44	0	80	79	5	15	53	6	2	10	1.68	3.5	5.9	10.53

They say Patterson throws a "Vulcan" forkball in that the grip looks like Spock's "live long and prosper" sign. He also throws an excellent sinker that produces a lot of ground balls, which impressed Johnny Oates during 4 appearances for Texas last year. Patterson has been masterful in Triple-A over the last 2 years and the Rangers will make room for some younger guys in the bullpen this year. Expect Patterson to be among them. There's even a possibility that he could end up closing for them within a year or two. ■

ROGER PAVLIK

SP • BB • TR • 6'3 • 220 • 29 • TEX86/2

	G	GS	IP	H	HR	BB	K	W	L	S	ERA	K/BB	K9	HW9
TEX94	11	11	50	61	8	30	31	2	5	0	7.69	1.0	5.6	16.37
TEX95	31	31	191	174	19	90	149	10	10	0	4.37	1.7	7.0	12.44
TEX96	34	34	201	216	28	81	127	15	8	0	5.19	1.6	5.7	13.30
CAREER	115	114	671	668	76	315	483	43	33	0	4.61	1.5	6.5	13.18

"Just win, baby," as that guy who used to be Al Davis once said. Pavlik was healthy all year and gave Johnny Oates 34 starts. He's 39-29 since '93 and has proven that he's a major-league talent. He's also become an integral part of the Rangers' rotation. Don't be surprised if he lowers his ERA and goes 12-12—because his 15-8 record is more than a little deceiving. Pavlik was getting more than 6 runs to work with per game and, if he'd been more consistent, he could have won 20. In the month of April, he looked good in his first 3 starts, going 3-0 with a 4.26 ERA and 18 strikeouts in 19 innings. In his next 3 starts, he pitched 10 innings and allowed 17 runs for a 15.30 ERA and no decisions. On the 19th, against Baltimore, he gave up 6 earned runs in 3.2 innings, but the offense bailed him out with 5 home runs to win 26-7. For the month, he was 3-0 with a 7.14 ERA. That was his season in microcosm. He pitched very well and won big in May (4-1, 2.72), then slumped but won in June. His luck ran out down the stretch, and he ended the season on an ugly downslide. ■

IVAN RODRIGUEZ — AL ELITE

C • BR • TR • 5'9 • 165 • 25 • TEX88

	AB	R	H	2B	3B	HR	RBI	BB	SO	SB	CS	BA	OB	SA
TEX94	363	56	108	19	1	16	57	31	42	6	3	.298	.360	.488
TEX95	492	56	149	32	2	12	67	16	48	0	2	.303	.327	.449
TEX96	639	116	192	47	3	19	86	38	55	5	0	.300	.342	.473
CAREER	2667	347	761	158	11	68	340	143	330	19	13	.285	.324	.429

With all due respect to Mike Piazza, Ivan Rodriguez is hands-down the best catcher in baseball. He's been considered the best *defensive* catcher for several years. His arm is unbelievable: He picked off 11 baserunners last year and threw out 49% of attempted basestealers. Only 92 guys even tried to run off of him in 146 games behind the plate! He won his 5th straight Gold Glove in '96. And after 5 years of steady improvement, Rodriguez had an awesome year at the plate. He set a major-league record for catchers with 47 doubles. He was a steady producer all year except for a relatively dismal September, when he hit .214, probably a function of putting in Jim Sundberg innings in the Texas heat. Then he sucked it up and hit .375 in the divisional series.

Defensively, there's no comparison between Piazza and Rodriguez. Offensively, it's closer than most realize. Rodriguez struck out almost half as much, had more extra-base hits (69 to 52), and had his hand in more runs (202 runs and RBI, compared to 192 for Piazza). To be fair, Piazza plays in one of the worst hitters parks in baseball and in a league where pitching isn't optional. Nevertheless, Rodriguez should be getting as much attention as Piazza. Instead, he may be the most underrated player in baseball. ■

JEFF RUSSELL (see Free Agents)

JULIO SANTANA — SOLID PROSPECT

SP • BR • TR • 6'0 • 175 • 24 • TEX90

	G	GS	IP	H	HR	BB	K	W	L	S	ERA	K/BB	K9	HW9
AAA	29	29	186	171	12	66	113	11	12	0	4.02	1.7	5.5	11.49

A converted shortstop, Santana learned to pitch quickly. Perhaps too quickly. In his first couple of seasons, he was dominant at 3 levels, from rookie ball to Double-A. In '95 it was Triple-A and the results were disastrous. Santana recovered a bit last season and appears to be back on track. He probably has the best arm in the Rangers' system and throws a 95–97-mph fastball. He also has an improving slider and a good change-up. He'll be even more effective once he learns to change speeds and takes it out of 5th gear once in a while. Texas was unhappy last year with Santana's physical condition when he arrived in the spring. Sounds like someone for whom things came a bit too easily. If he works harder this winter, he should be ready to join the major-league club this year.

TED SILVA — SLEEPER

SP • BR • TR • 6'0 • 170 • 21 • TEX95/21

	G	GS	IP	H	HR	BB	K	W	L	S	ERA	K/BB	K9	HW9
AA	11	11	75	72	5	16	27	7	2	0	2.99	1.7	3.2	10.51

Silva was the ace of the 1995 College World Series champs, Cal State Fullerton, but was still available in the 21st round. So far, he's been a decent find. He was pretty good in '95 for Class-A Charleston, even better at high Class-A Charlotte, and he continued that success later in '96 in Double-A. He's a poised pitcher with a fine slider, but his stuff is limited. He's only walked 55 batters in 2 minor-league seasons, so at least he knows where it's going. ■

BUBBA SMITH

1B • BR • TR • 6'2 • 225 • 27

	AB	R	H	2B	3B	HR	RBI	BB	SO	SB	CS	BA	OB	SA
AA	513	82	150	28	0	32	94	48	121	0	1	.292	.357	.534

Smith got a lot of ink last year, earning feature stories in both *Baseball America* and *Baseball Weekly*. That's not surprising; he's now won his 3rd league MVP after capturing the Texas League honors last year. Previously, he won the Carolina League MVP while in the Mariners' system in '92, and in '93 with the Reds. Of course, it's a dubious honor to win the MVP in the same minor league 2 years in a row—or to win it 3 times with 3 different organizations. But he's in Texas now with a redneck's name—even if he is from Southern California—and doesn't cost anywhere near what Will Clark does to play that role, so expect the Rangers to give him a shot at some point. ■

MIKE STANTON (see Free Agents)

LEE STEVENS — SLEEPER

1B • BL • TL • 6'4 • 220 • 29

	AB	R	H	2B	3B	HR	RBI	BB	SO	SB	CS	BA	OB	SA
TEX96	78	6	18	2	3	3	12	6	22	0	0	.231	.291	.449

At midseason, American Association managers voted Stevens the top power hitter in the league; by

season's end he was the MVP. But he had a decided advantage: He's been around for 10 years, including extensive big-league experience. His power has developed nicely over the years. Oklahoma City's park doesn't yield many homers, but he hung up some crooked numbers (32-94-.325) with surprisingly good plate discipline for a slugger. Though he started his career as an outfielder, he's now a first baseman/designated hitter type, which may limit his chances in the majors. He looked pretty good in 27 games for the Rangers, though. He'll get another look, especially if Will Clark has a difficult recovery from off-season surgery. ■

KURT STILLWELL (see Looking for a Game)

FERNANDO TATIS — GRADE-A PROSPECT

3B • BB • TR • 6′1 • 175 • 22 • TEX92

	AB	R	H	2B	3B	HR	RBI	BB	SO	SB	CS	BA	OB	SA
A+	325	46	93	25	0	12	53	30	48	9	3	.286	.353	.474

Tatis was Player of the Year in Texas's organization in '95. Last year everyone thought he was done for the season after he damaged a hamate bone in spring training, but he returned in late May. He has excellent power and his plate discipline has improved a great deal in the past few seasons. The Rangers compare him to Pedro Guerrero and he does look like he could hit 30 to 35 homers at his peak. A converted shortstop, Tatis has a good arm but, like Pedro, can be error-prone. Give him time to learn the position. Everything else looks good, so he could move quickly through the system. He's why they were willing to deal Dean Palmer. ■

MICKEY TETTLETON — CONSISTENT STAR

DH • BB • TR • 6′2 • 200 • 36 • OAK81/5

	AB	R	H	2B	3B	HR	RBI	BB	SO	SB	CS	BA	OB	SA
DET94	339	57	84	18	2	17	51	97	98	0	1	.248	.419	.463
TEX95	429	76	102	19	1	32	78	107	110	0	0	.238	.396	.510
TEX96	491	78	121	26	1	24	83	95	137	2	1	.246	.366	.450
CAREER	4654	706	1128	209	16	242	728	946	1295	23	29	.242	.371	.450

Odd as it may seem—except maybe to Yogi Berra—Tettleton is no longer a Mickey Tettleton-type player. The term describes a role that he once clearly defined: the front-line player who can fill in handily at several positions and still provide excellent production at the plate. He was invaluable for the Tigers from 1991 to 1994 playing the outfield, first, catching, and at DH. The term can also be extended to mean a player who will do anything for the team and never complains—the kind of guy sportswriters felt compelled to invent the phrase "giving 110%" for. At what point does inflation drive this up to 120%? Tettleton still plays with the same attitude, but his body no longer lets him roam the field. He played a few games at first last year, but he is now primarily a designated hitter. He's having problems staying healthy, and his numbers tailed off significantly in the second half. Still, he had his most productive season since '93 and may still have some gas left in the tank. He took less money to stay in Texas, so the Rangers cap will likely be the last one he wears. ■

DAVE VALLE (see Looking for a Game)

ED VOSBERG

RP • BL • TL • 6′1 • 190 • 35 • SD83/3

	G	GS	IP	H	HR	BB	K	W	L	S	ERA	K/BB	K9	HW9
OAK94	16	0	13	16	2	5	12	0	2	0	3.95	2.4	8.3	14.47
TEX95	44	0	36	32	3	16	36	5	5	4	3.00	2.3	9.0	12.00
TEX96	52	0	44	51	4	21	32	1	1	8	3.27	1.5	6.5	14.73
CAREER	135	3	131	137	13	63	100	7	10	12	4.05	1.6	6.9	13.73

Vosberg had a decent season last year, but he must have done it with mirrors. He allowed batters to hit .298 off him (righties hit .327), walked almost 4.5 per 9 innings, still led the staff with a 3.27 ERA, and saved 8 of 9. How does that happen? It helps when you don't have John Franco coming in after you (Franco allowed 60% of inherited runners to score, twice that of the average reliever). Vosberg made 24 appearances of 1 inning or more last year and allowed at least 1 baserunner in 20 of them. During a 7-game stretch in June he pitched 7.1 innings, allowing 14 hits, 3 walks, and 0 runs, earned or otherwise. Apparently Vosberg has some John Wetteland in him. ■

MATT WHITESIDE (see Looking for a Game)

BOBBY WITT (see Free Agents)

■ 1996 AUTOPSY

The suits decided in the summer of '95 that they needed to pare payroll and devote more resources to scouting and player development to rebuild their once-proud franchise—at the urging, of course, of the new owners of Labatt's, who didn't know from baseball and had no desire to. Nuclear winter descended on the city of Toronto as team cornerstones Roberto Alomar, Paul Molitor, Devon White, and Al Leiter all left for greener pastures, replaced with the likes of Otis Nixon, Erik Hanson, Paul Quantrill, and Bill Risley. Pitching was still a big question mark going into the season, and the core of the offense was a mix of aging veterans and quality young players who were tantalizingly close to realizing their potential.

April 11-14 (3 games back)
The Jays started their season promisingly enough, winning their first 3 games and scoring 26 runs in the process. Unfortunately, they wouldn't be able to repeat the feat for the rest of April. They went 8-14, mixing in three 3-game losing streaks, and any success they did have was due solely to the offense. Joe Carter, Ed Sprague, and Carlos Delgado led the Jays to a manly .490 slugging percentage, 41 points above the league average. Sprague was a wrecking crew with his 9 home runs and .625 slugging. Carter launched 7 homers and drove in 27 runs. Delgado replaced Olerud in the No. 3 hole and responded with a .333 average, 6 home runs, and 26 RBI.

Juan Guzman was the lone star in the rotation. He put the league on notice by going 3-1 with a 1.88 ERA and earning A.L. pitcher of the month honors. Hanson and Pat Hentgen weren't that bad, but Quantrill contributed an 0-3, 8.17 record and gave up 9 home runs in 5 starts, and Jeff Ware was absolutely undressed in his 2 starts.

May 13-15 (24-29, 6½ games back)
The Jays featured a Jekyll-and-Hyde offense and an unreliable bullpen in May. The hitters scored 72 runs in their first 12 games, but they stumbled over home plate only 31 times in their next 12. Between May 15 and May 26, the rotation allowed 2.4 runs and averaged more than 6 innings per start, but was stuck with a 2-6 record because the offense could manage only 2.6 runs per game. Toronto went 3-9 overall in this stretch.

Olerud finally started hitting, and had a .337 average with 21 RBI, but Carter and Sprague couldn't maintain their 40-50 dinger pace, managing a more reasonable 8 homers between them. Otis Nixon's ancient hamstrings started throbbing about midmonth and Jacob Brumfield was acquired from the Pirates to fill in. Juan Guzman's mighty morphin powers wore off a bit, but Pat Hentgen kicked in a nifty 3.35 ERA, Hanson won 4 games, and Quantrill actually looked like a major-league pitcher for a few starts. Mike Timlin saved 7 games (his best monthly total), but blew 2 and had a less-than-stellar 4.76 ERA.

June 12-15 (36-44, 11½ games back)
Unlike the Blue Jays teams of the mid-80s, the wheels came off in June instead of September or October. Toronto lost 6 in a row to New York and Texas beginning June 6, and by the 15th they had lost 9 out of 10. Overall they were outscored 63-41, and the rotation (1-8, 6.20 ERA in this stretch) was responsible for most of the misery. This 10-game stretch left the Jays 11½ games out of first and essentially killed their season. Even though they won 8 of their next 9 games they couldn't make up any ground at all in the East.

The heart of the batting order again carried the team. Delgado (4 HR), Carter (8 HR) and Sprague (8 HR), drove in 65 of Toronto's 145 runs in June—about 45% of the team's run production. Brumfield hit 5 home runs and Shawn Green hit .517 in limited duty, but the remainder of the lineup contributed nothing.

July 13-14 (49-58, 15 games back)
This was a team out of the hunt, and the Blue Jays played like it. Despite fine performances from Guzman and Hentgen, who went a combined 8-1

in July, the Jays offered little else to cheer about. Guzman, 3-0 with a 1.27 ERA, allowed 30 base-runners in 31 innings. Hentgen went 5-1 with a 2.72 ERA. But Hanson had a 9.51 ERA and Quantrill was banished to the bullpen, where he went 0-2 and contributed 2 of Toronto's 7 blown saves. Timlin hit the wall as well, going 0-3 with 2 blown saves and a 9.72 ERA in 11 games.

The offense continued to produce below-league averages in virtually every category. Unexpected help came from Charlie O'Brien, who hit .328 with 6 homers in 18 games and Shawn Green who hit .339 in 21 games. Otherwise it was the same old story, with the middle 3 hitters carrying the load. Carter had 6 home runs and 20 RBI. Delgado and Sprague both contributed 6 homers apiece despite miserable batting averages.

August 14-15 (63-73, 19 games back)
Toronto's inconsistencies continued to give manager Cito Gaston fits. Two offensive performances stood out: Green continued to pour it on with a .380 average and 10 doubles and Brumfield hit .375 with 23 RBI in 20 games. But that was about it for the hitters. The Blue Jays paid for their dependence on their middle-of-the-order hitters in August as Joe Carter (.138, 9 RBI) and Sprague (.229, 12 RBI) both went on vacation at the same time. Olerud sat out most of the month with a back injury. August was Hentgen's month. He led the pitching staff with a 5-1 record and a 2.61 ERA. Guzman and Hanson were stable, but the "committment to youth" also featured retreads such as Woody Williams and Huck Flener, who each had an ERA above 6.00.

September 11-15 (74-88, 18 games back)
The Blue Jays' pitching staff enjoyed their best month of the season as the hurlers combined for a 3.67 ERA in September. Their performance helped lower their second-half ERA to 4.07, best in the league and almost a full run lower than the first-half. Unfortunately, the hitters decided to go into early hibernation. They scored just 3.5 runs a game and hit.229 with 16 home runs. One of the lone bright spots in September came on the last day of the season, when Pat Hentgen won his 20th game. Juan Guzman had already walked away with the ERA title.

■ 1997 DIAGNOSIS

Offense
With Alomar gone to a division rival, the offensive explosion that characterized the 1996 season passed over everyone in the Toronto lineup not named Ed Sprague. The Blue Jays scored 766 runs. Adjusted for park, they were about 110 runs worse than the league average. Every other team in the league scored more runs, except Kansas City and California. That kind of thing can happen when you have the league's second-worst batting average and finish third from the bottom in strikeouts. Every spot in the batting order contributed more than 100 strikeouts to the team's total, except the 9th spot, which struck out 99 times. About the only positive thing the offense did was finish among the league leaders in stolen bases.

As for 1997, Gord Ash would trade Olerud in a minute if he could find someone to take his salary off the Jays' hands. The problem is where Ash should hide the jar of ether he'd have to use on other GMs when talking trade. Second base will belong to Carlos Garcia in '97. Alex Gonzalez has a stranglehold on shortstop, but the Jays will be expecting more at the plate from him. The Jays have no right to expect any more from Ed Sprague. The Blue Jays would like to see Joe Carter play more at first and DH to rest his 37-year-old body, but both spots are filled at the moment. Otis Nixon will probably be the starting center fielder again, but this time around he'll have Shannon Stewart, not Jacob Brumfield, waiting in the shadows for the eventual hamstring pull. The Jays are hoping to see right fielder Shawn Green improve on his numbers from last year. The 1997 season could be his break-through one, though that's what was being predicted for him in '96.

Defense
The infield defense was a rare strength of the Blue Jays. Despite his gangly appearance, Olerud is as deft a first baseman as you'll find. He has excellent range around the bag and fantastic hands, scooping more dirt than the political desk at the *National Enquirer.* Alex Gonzalez committed 21 miscues, but he has exceptional range, managing to turn 122 double plays despite being teamed with a new second baseman every other day. He is young and

getting better. Tomas Perez and Felipe Crespo split most of the playing time at second after Domingo Cedeño was dealt to the White Sox. While both are adequate in the field (Perez is considered the better fielder), they made a lot of rookie mistakes and suffered greatly from comparisons to their predecessor, Roberto Alomar, the Emily Post of baseball. Ed Sprague, once considered "acceptable" at third base, showed marked improvement in his game and can now be labeled "steady." Joe Carter and Otis Nixon may not be ready for walkers and Metamucil just yet, but they're well into the decline phase of their careers. They lack the range they once had and are becoming much more susceptible to the aches and strains of a long campaign. Shawn Green is a dependable right fielder whose biggest asset is a rifle arm. Shannon Stewart got a late-season call-up last year and could end up replacing Nixon in center this year. Stewart has more than enough range to play center but lacks a strong throwing arm. Charlie O'Brien is a steady hand behind the plate, and Sandy Martinez didn't make it to the majors on the strength of his bat either.

Pitching

This was one of the most underrated staffs in the league. If the team had any hitting—Molitor and Alomar, perhaps—they'd have made a run at the wild-card. Despite a dramatic turn-over that saw two-thirds of their rotation leave since '95, and playing in a hitters' park, they managed to post a team ERA that was about a half-run lower than the league average. The few starters left behind from the '93 championship team, Guzman and Hentgen, were exceptional. But the remaining 3 holes, filled by Hanson, Quantrill, and the Syracuse flavor of the month, required more run production than the Blue Jays hitters could provide. The Jays picked up Luis Andujar from the White Sox in August for Domingo Cedeño, hoping Andujar can stay healthy enough to harness his ability and be their 4th or 5th starter. Marty Janzen, 24, acquired from the Yankees for David Cone, should also be in this rotation. He's got better control than he displayed last season.

Despite getting hung with a lousy record, the bullpen turned out to be a pleasant surprise. Bill Risley was supposed to take over the closer's job last year, but shoulder trouble and a loss of command put him in the outhouse. Plan B closer Mike Timlin, who had a chance to replace Duane Ward 2 years ago, had a fine season . . . if you ignore his July swoon (0-3, 9.72 ERA, 2 blown saves). Setup man Tim Crabtree pitched brilliantly before going down in September with bone chips in his elbow. He suffered from his own effectiveness, actually, as Cito rode him hard and often in the first half. Dan Plesac is a solid lefty addition.

Farm System

Here's the true strength of the ballclub. They Jays have stockpiled a lot of depth at pitching and in the infield over the past 3 years. They're about to put it all to good use. In the 1993 amateur draft, Toronto got three no. 1 draft picks in compensation for losing Jimmy Key, Tom Henke, and David Cone. That draft class yielded first baseman Ryan Jones and three right-handed pitchers: Chris Carpenter, Joe Young, and Jeremy Lee. In the '96 draft, they received two no.1 picks for losing Robby Alomar, and had 7 picks overall in the first 3 rounds. With those picks they came up with future ace Billy Koch, shortstop Joe Lawrence, outfielder Pete Tucci, and third baseman Casey Blake. Those players were added to a system that already had outfielder Shannon Stewart, second baseman Jeff Patzke, and right-handed pitcher Roy Halladay. The Blue Jays have shifted a lot of their resources to player development and will soon be reaping the benefits.

Management and Ownership

Ownership of the Blue Jays is in a state of flux. They're in the process of changing hands in one of those huge corporate deals that eventually becomes an H3O original movie. As a result, nobody in the front office was quite sure just what kind of player payroll they would have.

In the summer of '95 Gord Ash got together with team officials and scouts, and they decided to keep building as they did in the old days. The idea was to pare payroll to free funds for scouting and player development. Ash helped the Blue Jays put a nice rebuilding spin on their cost-cutting, but since when

does rebuilding require you to let a 28-year-old Roberto Alomar walk, when he may be the greatest second baseman to ever play the game? After all, they gave Joe Carter $6.5 million to stick around for another year. Makes you wonder if they knew the real Roberto before he showed it to the world and John Hirschbeck.

The description "even-tempered" doesn't do justice to Cito Gaston. He displays almost as much emotion in the dugout as the cardboard Maytag man in the appliance department at Wal-Mart. But he commands a tremendous amount of respect throughout the organization. Case in point: Frank Viola was given his unconditional release June 5, a couple of days after suggesting that Cito was too easygoing to manage a young team. Gaston manages by the philosophy that his players are like young colts. A tight rein can break their spirit. And he was under orders in '96 to emphasize learning first.

. . . and whatnot: Hentgen and Pettitte

Voting for postseason awards has always favored players on contending teams. That's why Andy Pettitte was considered the virtual lock to win the A.L. Cy Young. Pettitte's pitching led the Yankees into the playoffs and he led the league in wins, so it came as an unpleasant surprise to Joey from Bensonhurst and the rest of the sports radio callers in New York when Hentgen actually won the thing.

Hentgen had a better year. Pettitte edged Hentgen in victories (both received similar support: 5.5 runs for Pettitte, 5.6 for Hentgen). But Hentgen led Pettitte in the following categories: ERA, starts, innings pitched, complete games, shutouts, quality starts, batting-average against, slugging-average against, and strikeouts.

Another way to compare these two is by looking at how they pitched in their victories. Pettitte won 21 games with a 2.64 ERA. In Hentgen's 20 victories he had a 1.81 ERA. SkyDome and Yankee Stadium are roughly similar in their effects on offense, so it's not like Pettitte was pitching in a hitter's paradise and Hentgen was pitching in a cavern.

Finally, consider what each pitcher meant to his respective team's winning percentage.

	Record	Team With	Team Without	Differential
Hentgen	20-10 (.667)	74-88 (.457)	54-78 (.409)	–.048
Pettitte	21-8 (.724)	92-70 (.568)	71-62 (.534)	–.034

Hentgen's 20-10 record had a greater impact on his team's winning percentage than Pettitte's 21-8 record. But with Pettitte out of the rotation, the Yankees wouldn't have won the A.L. East with the resulting .534 winning percentage. And if you replace Pettitte's stats with a league average pitcher's, their winning percentage drops to .527. The Yanks would have finished second to Baltimore in the East, and the Mariners would have walked away with the wild card. Conversely, Toronto's .409 winning percentage without Hentgen would have left them exactly where they finished: fourth place. If you consider just the raw stats, Hentgen clearly had a better season than Pettitte—even if he didn't get to pitch in any games that mattered.

CARLOS ALMANZAR

RP • BR • TR • 6′2 • 165 • 23

	G	GS	IP	H	HR	BB	K	W	L	S	ERA	K/BB	K9	HW9
AA	54	0	95	106	13	33	105	7	8	9	4.85	3.2	10.0	13.22

A right-hander from the Dominican Republic, Almanzar spent his second consecutive season at Double-A Knoxville last year. For most players, that would be an indication that his career has stalled. That couldn't be farther from the truth in Almanzar's case. He stayed there a second season primarily because he was just a season removed from rookie-ball and the Blue Jays wanted to give him a chance to experience success before moving him up. Almanzar is a strikeout pitcher. But what impresses the front office most is his control. As a matter of fact, if his control were any better, he could moonlight as a harem guardian. He'll open the season in Triple-A Syracuse, but he could be a big help to the bullpen down the stretch. ■

LUIS ANDUJAR

SLEEPER

SP • BR • TR • 6′2 • 175 • 24 • CHA90

	G	GS	IP	H	HR	BB	K	W	L	S	ERA	K/BB	K9	HW9
CHA95	5	5	30	26	4	14	9	2	1	0	3.26	.6	2.7	12.00
CHA/TOR96	8	7	37	46	8	16	11	1	3	0	7.05	.7	2.7	15.07

Andujar gave the White Sox every indication he was recovered from '94 elbow surgery and ready to claim a rotation spot in '96. Instead, he sputtered coming out of the gate and fractured his hand while at Triple-A Nashville. The Blue Jays picked him up in the August trade that sent Domingo Cedeño and Tony Castillo to the White Sox. For the Jays, they had nothing to lose—nothing, that is, but an extraneous shortstop and an experienced middle reliever they couldn't afford. It's not a bad gamble, though. He has a decent fastball and slider package and has developed an excellent circle change that he throws deceptively. Andujar might pay off big for the Blue Jays this year. ■

WILLIAM "CASEY" BLAKE

SLEEPER

3B • TOR96/7 • WICHITA STATE UNIVERSITY

	AB	R	H	2B	3B	HR	RBI	BB	SO	SB	CS	BA	OB	SA
A	172	29	43	13	1	2	18	11	40	5	3	.250	.318	.372

Before being taken by the Blue Jays in the 7th round of the '96 draft, Blake was a 1996 Missouri Valley Conference player of the year and two-time All-American. He earned a spot on Team USA after hitting .360 with 22 homers and 101 RBI for the Shockers. Blake is considered a better all-around athlete than Troy Glaus, who started in front of him for Team USA. Glaus has a shade more power, but Blake is far better defensively. ■

TILSON BRITO

SS/2B • BR • TR • 6′0 • 170 • 24 • TOR90

	AB	R	H	2B	3B	HR	RBI	BB	SO	SB	CS	BA	OB	SA
TOR96	80	10	19	7	0	1	7	10	18	1	1	.238	.344	.363

His bat hasn't developed as quickly as the Blue Jays expected, but Brito has the defensive skills to be a fine everyday middle infielder right now. He doesn't have a snowball's chance of displacing Gonzalez at shortstop, but no one has walked away a clear winner in the second-base sweepstakes yet. Brito still has an outside chance for a job, but he'll have to turn his hitting up a notch or he could soon be lost in a sea of younger prospects. ■

JACOB BRUMFIELD

OF • BR • TR • 6′0 • 175 • 31 • CHN83/7

	AB	R	H	2B	3B	HR	RBI	BB	SO	SB	CS	BA	OB	SA
CIN94	122	36	38	10	2	4	11	15	18	6	3	.311	.381	.525
PIT95	402	64	109	23	2	4	26	37	71	22	12	.271	.339	.368
PIT/TOR96	388	63	99	28	2	14	60	29	75	15	4	.255	.311	.446
CAREER	1214	209	323	78	9	28	122	104	215	69	27	.266	.327	.414

Pirates GM Cam Bonifay found out Brumfield was making more than $5 an hour and had to ship him off to the Blue Jays in May for first-base suspect D. J. Boston. Gaston used Brumfield to lead off games, subbing for Otis Nixon. But aside from being the second-best baserunner on the team and having occasional power, Brumfield lacked the hitting skills required for the leadoff spot. Brumfield has proven to 3 teams that he isn't a starter, though he's not ready to admit it. But he's a good fielder with excellent speed and should admirably fill a bench role for someone in '97. ■

MIGUEL CAIRO

SOLID PROSPECT

2B • BB • TR • 6′0 • 160 • 22 • LA90

	AB	R	H	2B	3B	HR	RBI	BB	SO	SB	CS	BA	OB	SA
AAA	465	71	129	14	4	3	48	26	44	27	9	.277	.323	.344

The Mariners acquired Cairo from the Dodgers last year and dealt him to Toronto before he could play a game for them. It looks like they passed up a nifty-looking prospect. He's a contact hitter with a good

eye. He has versatility as well, having played third base in winter ball. Nick Leyva, who managed him at Lara in the Venezuelan League, said he was an excellent leadoff hitter who could ignite the ballclub. He has stolen as many as 44 bases in the minors. Cairo is a very smooth fielder at second base, but he's now on to the Cubs as we go to press. By the time you read this, he could be with his 5th organization in little over a year. ■

CHRIS CARPENTER

SLEEPER

SP • BR • TR • 6'6 • 220 • 21 • TOR93/1

	G	GS	IP	H	HR	BB	K	W	L	S	ERA	K/BB	K9	HW9
AA	28	28	171	161	13	91	150	7	9	0	3.94	1.6	7.9	13.24

One of Toronto's four 1st-round picks in '93, Carpenter has enjoyed rapid progress despite mediocre command. Some might say that he's been rushed. He has an imposing build, a mid-'90s fastball, and a hard-breaking curve—and he gets a lot of strikeouts. The Blue Jays can hardly be blamed for their interest in his advancement. Carpenter possesses tantalizing skills and a fierce competitive attitude. He also has displayed a power pitcher's tendency to get stronger as the game progresses. His penchant for giving up walks may simply be screwed-up mechanics. We're not talking about the next Clemens here, not by a long shot. But one thing is clear: Carpenter might one day be a bat-breaker in the big leagues if he ever draws a bead on the strike zone. ■

JOE CARTER

LF-DH • BR • TR • 6'3 • 215 • 37 • CHN81/1

	AB	R	H	2B	3B	HR	RBI	BB	SO	SB	CS	BA	OB	SA
TOR94	435	70	118	25	2	27	103	33	64	11	0	.271	.317	.524
TOR95	558	70	141	23	0	25	76	37	87	12	1	.253	.300	.428
TOR96	625	84	158	35	7	30	107	44	106	7	6	.253	.306	.475
CAREER	7422	1043	1940	380	48	357	1280	463	1221	219	63	.261	.308	.470

Carter is one of the few players in the league who is a perennial threat to drive in 100 runs. He's also one of the nicest guys in the game. Over the past few years Carter has done his best hitting in the first half, when he's fresh. As the season wears on, his production drops off. This is to be expected, though the problem was much more pronounced last season. He hit .284 with 20 of his 30 homers before the All-Star break. He hit .215 and slugged .380 in the second half. Gord Ash had several opportunities to deal Carter before the trading deadline as contending teams shopped for a power hitter who wouldn't break the prospect bank to acquire. Ash held off. He instead signed Carter to a 1-year extension worth $6.5 million. If the Blue Jays are out of the hunt, Ash will find it much harder (maybe impossible) to resist temptation again this year. But the kids will need someone to learn from, and there is not a single player in baseball who would be a better role model. If he goes, chances are he will have asked Ash to deal him into contention for one more World Series. ■

TIM CRABTREE

RP • BR • TR • 6'4 • 195 • 27 • TOR92/4

	G	GS	IP	H	HR	BB	K	W	L	S	ERA	K/BB	K9	HW9
TOR95	31	0	32	30	1	13	21	0	2	0	3.09	1.6	5.9	12.09
TOR96	53	0	67	59	4	22	57	5	3	1	2.54	2.6	7.7	10.88

After a strong winter league showing and a promising 31-game stint in '95, Crabtree finally earned a job with the big-league club. He opened the season as Timlin's main setup man and was very effective in April and May, posting a 1.09 ERA over 24.2 innings. He looked good in June and July as well, despite blowing 3 of 4 save opportunities. But shoulder tendinitis shut him down in August, and surgery to remove bone chips in his elbow ended his season in September. Control and stamina problems in the minors kept him out of the majors for a while, but he seemed to thrive in '94 after the Blue Jays put him in the pen where he could concentrate on spotting his excellent fastball and refining his curve. If he's healthy, he'll be one of the anchors of the Toronto bullpen. ■

RICKEY CRADLE

OF • BR • TR • 6'2 • 180 • 23

	AB	R	H	2B	3B	HR	RBI	BB	SO	SB	CS	BA	OB	SA
AAA	130	22	26	5	3	8	22	14	39	1	0	.200	.279	.469

He took a step backward in '95 when he couldn't handle a promotion to Double-A Knoxville and was

demoted to Class-A Dunedin. But he got another crack at the Southern League last season and this time around he didn't disappoint. He hit .282 with power for the Smokies before his promotion to Syracuse. Almost as impressive were his 55 walks and .384 OBP. Cradle isn't a bad-looking prospect, but he needs another season or two in Triple-A before he's ready. ■

FELIPE CRESPO

2B • BB • TR • 5'11 • 190 • 24 • TOR90/4

	AB	R	H	2B	3B	HR	RBI	BB	SO	SB	CS	BA	OB	SA
AAA	355	53	100	25	0	8	58	56	39	10	11	.282	.389	.420

Crespo was expected to do battle for the second-base job in the spring, but a strained hamstring landed him on the DL, and he found Tomas Perez and Domingo Cedeño at his position when he got back. His demotion to the minors made sense, since the Blue Jays felt he needed some more work on defense anyway—he's got good hands but mediocre range. Crespo has always been a hitter. In 6 minor-league seasons he's batted lower than .280 only once. In fact, before the season started, scouts were comparing him to Baerga because he's a switch-hitter with a similar build and a smattering of power—and without the belly and the cell phone. With his strike-zone judgment he would fit right in batting second in the Toronto order. ■

CARLOS DEGADO

YOUNG GUN

DH • BL • TR • 6'3 • 205 • 24 • TOR88

	AB	R	H	2B	3B	HR	RBI	BB	SO	SB	CS	BA	OB	SA
TOR94	130	17	28	2	0	9	24	25	46	1	1	.215	.352	.438
TOR95	91	7	15	3	0	3	11	6	26	0	0	.165	.212	.297
TOR96	488	68	132	28	2	25	92	58	139	0	0	.270	.353	.490
CAREER	710	92	175	33	2	37	127	90	211	1	1	.246	.337	.455

By midseason 1995 Delgado had absorbed everything he possibly could in the minors. His bat was screaming to be promoted to the majors, but the Jays let him rot in Syracuse a month longer than he should have. Why, so he could continue slugging .610 off Triple-A pitching? Could it be the Blue Jays didn't believe the numbers they were seeing because Delgado had hit just .215 in his 43-game trial for them the previous year? Hitting coach Willie Upshaw felt that Delgado had become pull-happy in the past, that he overtorqued on inside pitches. He worked with Carlos in the spring to get him to shorten his swing a tad and hit the ball where it was pitched. Delgado started the '96 season hitting in the 6th spot in the order. But when Olerud slumped early on, Delgado was already primed to fill his spot, batting 3rd. With some protection behind him, Delgado punished pitchers to the tune of 6 home runs, a .578 slugging average, and 26 RBI in April. Gaston never once entertained the thought of dropping him in the order. Delgado isn't without his shortcomings. He strikes out a lot, primarily because he occasionally has trouble hitting the curve. This problem is alleviated by his spot in the batting order, as pitchers aren't too keen on the idea of walking Delgado to get to Carter and Sprague. He also has questionable hands around first and will see most of his at-bats as a DH until he refines that part of his game. But Gaston can live with a 25-year-old as his DH, especially one with Delgado's tape-measure power. ■

ROBERTO DURAN

SP • BL • TL • 6'0 • 190 • 24

	G	GS	IP	H	HR	BB	K	W	L	S	ERA	K/BB	K9	HW9
AA	19	16	81	72	8	61	74	4	6	0	5.13	1.2	8.3	14.84

The Blue Jays claimed this Dominican left-hander off waivers from the Dodgers early in the season and assigned him to Dunedin, but it was obvious he didn't belong in A-ball. He went 3-1 with a 1.12 ERA there, striking out 54 in 48 innings and walking just 19. Duran's control left him after a promotion to Double-A Knoxville, though. Hands of Stone throws a low-90s fastball with movement, and his curveball has a good break. The problem is he can't control either very well at this point. All indications point to a pitcher with a live arm, but his development hinges on his harnessing his stuff. Incidentally, Duran's brother convinced his parents to name him Roberto, after the boxer—which is preferable to being named after a bad English hair band. ■

KELVIM ESCOBAR

SOLID PROSPECT

SP • BR • TR • 6'1 • 195 • 20

	G	GS	IP	H	HR	BB	K	W	L	S	ERA	K/BB	K9	HW9
AA	10	10	54	61	7	24	44	3	4	0	5.33	1.8	7.3	14.17

Escobar is a Venezuelan hurler who hits 95 on the radar gun. He also throws a good slider, a great change-up and an occasional forkball. He uses the straight change against lefties and the forkball against righties. Last year he showed greatly improved control and was named the second-best prospect in the Florida State League. He struck out 113 hitters in 110 innings and had a 3.4 K/BB ratio. He struggled after his promotion to Double-A Knoxville and likely will start the season there. Even though Escobar has been in pro ball since 1992, most of his time has been spent refining his pitches in the rookie and short-season leagues. He has had a lot of professional experience at such a young age and the Blue Jays are very anxious to see how he does against higher competition. ■

TOM EVANS — SOLID PROSPECT

3B • BR • TR • 6′1 • 180 • 22 • TOR92/6

	AB	R	H	2B	3B	HR	RBI	BB	SO	SB	CS	BA	OB	SA
AA	394	87	111	27	1	17	65	115	113	4	0	.282	.452	.485

He's a third-base prospect with a quick bat and power. He led the Double-A Knoxville Smokies in strikeouts last season, but he's not a hacker. He got pitched around a lot, but those 115 walks weren't all intentional. Evans was also voted best defensive third baseman in the Southern League last year. His main virtues are his range, soft hands, and an accurate throwing arm. Evans is prone to getting fat—listed weights of athletes are about as accurate as The Warren Report—and has had some knee problems in the past. Unless he keeps his weight down he'll be doomed to experience them again. He has a chance to be the starting third baseman for the Syracuse Chiefs this year and is only a year or two away, if he can cut down on the gravy sandwiches. ■

HUCK FLENER

SP-RP • BB • TL • 5′11 • 175 • 28 • TOR90/10

	G	GS	IP	H	HR	BB	K	W	L	S	ERA	K/BB	K9	HW9
TOR96	15	11	70	68	9	33	44	3	2	0	4.58	1.3	5.7	12.97

Flener had dropped from the list of Toronto prospects after elbow reconstruction surgery in 1994 robbed him of some velocity and his strikeout ratios dropped in 1995. In 1996 he worked his way back into the ballclub's plans by relying on his good off-speed stuff and honing his control. As a reward for his hard work, Flener was called up from Syracuse on July 12 to take some beatings in the 5th rotation spot after Frank Viola, Jeff Ware, and Paul Quantrill were too punch-drunk to continue. He started out well enough, with a 2.39 ERA in 4 July starts. But in August and September Flener wasn't much more effective than the guys he replaced. The Blue Jays also have to be concerned about his elbow—he underwent arthoscopic surgery at the end of the season. ■

ALEX GONZALEZ — YOUNG GUN

SS • BR • TR • 6′0 • 180 • 23 • TOR91/16

	AB	R	H	2B	3B	HR	RBI	BB	SO	SB	CS	BA	OB	SA
TOR95	367	51	89	19	4	10	42	44	114	4	4	.243	.322	.398
TOR96	527	64	124	30	5	14	64	45	127	16	6	.235	.300	.391

Despite his low batting average and 127 strikeouts, Gonzalez is still one of the most promising young players in the league. First and foremost, Gonzalez is a gifted shortstop. He committed 21 errors last season, but that total isn't high considering the fantastic range he displays at the position. And playing with one double play partner all year—Carlos Garcia—will help him. At the plate, Gonzalez has a promising bat for a middle infielder. His quick swing produces line drives. What excites the Blue Jays is the fact that he's still maturing. They think he has 25-homer potential. Gaston would like to see Gonzalez make better contact and not be so easily fooled by breaking pitches. He also showed signs of wear during the second half of the season. After the break, Gonzalez hit .227, and he amassed all but 7 of his 30 doubles in the first half of the season. Gonzalez was once thought to be the best young shortstop in the game. Then, like the favorite nephew at the family reunion, the other Alex came along and stole the attention. Gonzalez has no reason to hang his head, though. He's a Gold Glove candidate with a world of hitting potential. The Blue Jays are looking to build their franchise around him, even if he doesn't hit .360. ■

SHAWN GREEN

YOUNG GUN

RF • BL • TL • 6'4 • 190 • 24 • TOR91/1

	AB	R	H	2B	3B	HR	RBI	BB	SO	SB	CS	BA	OB	SA
TOR95	379	52	109	31	4	15	54	20	68	1	2	.288	.326	.509
TOR96	422	52	118	32	3	11	45	33	75	5	1	.280	.342	.448

Many were predicting greatness for Green, which is why his stats from last season, which aren't bad at all, look so disappointing. He is still a work in progress. As he did in '95, Green struggled in the first half of the season. He hit just .231 and slugged .397 before the All-Star break. After the break, with the Jays out of the race, he hit .335 and slugged .503. Green had a killer July and August, but managed only 16 RBI. It's no fun batting in the bottom third of the order, but Green flat out failed to hit with runners on base. Last season he hit .311 and slugged .507 with no one on base. However, with runners on base, Green hit just .241 and slugged .371.

In the field, Green is a much more polished player. He has a strong arm that he's used to gun down 19 baserunners in the past 2 seasons. He has average range and committed only 2 errors last season, so he probably just needs to work on positioning himself better. Green has a lot going for him, not the least of which is 2 seasons of major-league experience under his belt at age 24. If Green comes out of the blocks hitting next season he could really put up some good numbers. ■

JUAN GUZMAN

AL ELITE

SP • BR • TR • 5'11 • 195 • 30 • LA85

	G	GS	IP	H	HR	BB	K	W	L	S	ERA	K/BB	K9	HW9
TOR94	25	25	147	165	20	76	124	12	11	0	5.68	1.6	7.6	14.75
TOR95	24	24	135	151	13	73	94	4	14	0	6.32	1.3	6.3	14.93
TOR96	27	27	187	158	20	53	165	11	8	0	2.93	3.1	7.9	10.15
CAREER	160	160	1010	918	82	450	865	67	44	0	3.97	1.9	7.7	12.19

After 2 forgettable seasons, Guzman came close to losing his job with the Blue Jays. He ended up signing again with the club, but at the maximum 20% pay cut. Guzman reported to spring training healthy and strong. He was throwing his fastball 96–97 mph and getting the slider up to 87 mph. Guzman let up a bit in May and June, probably slowed by a strained pectoral muscle, but came back strong in July with a 3-0 record and a 1.27 ERA. Basically, Guzman and Hentgen didn't lead the rotation last season—they were the rotation.

Gaston said that Guzman tried to be too fine with his pitches in '95, trying to emulate Greg Maddux. His control did improve noticeably, and throwing to Maddux's catcher, Charlie O'Brien, is the real reason for Guzman finding his command. Having someone that experienced behind the plate meant that he could turn the pitch selection over to him and concentrate on hitting the glove and remembering what three wiggling fingers was the sign for.

Guzman's season ended September 7 when his appendix didn't feel it necessary to play out the string. He should be back at full strength in the spring. When healthy, he is as dominating as any pitcher in the game. If the Blue Jays want him back, they will have to pay full price this year, with or without his appendix. ■

ROY HALLADAY

GRADE-A PROSPECT

SP • BR • TR • 6'5 • 200 • 19 • TOR95/1

	G	GS	IP	H	HR	BB	K	W	L	S	ERA	K/BB	K9	HW9
A+	27	27	165	158	7	46	109	15	7	0	2.73	2.4	6.0	11.15

Drafted no. 1 by the Blue jays in '95, Halladay dominated the Florida State League despite being the youngest player there. He finished 3rd in victories and 5th in ERA. Managers tabbed him as the 3rd-best prospect in the league. His fastball tops out at 94 mph and breaks in on right-handed hitters. He complements the fastball with a good, hard knuckle curve. The Blue Jays will undoubtedly put him on the fast track and promote him to Double-A Knoxville this year. They'll be looking for him to show a little more consistency with his breaking ball, but he's already got one of the best arms in the system. ■

ERIK HANSON

SP • BR • TR • 6'6 • 210 • 31 • SEA86/2

	G	GS	IP	H	HR	BB	K	W	L	S	ERA	K/BB	K9	HW9
CIN94	22	21	122	137	10	23	101	5	5	0	4.11	4.4	7.4	11.80
BOS95	29	29	186	187	17	59	139	15	5	0	4.24	2.4	6.7	11.90
TOR96	35	35	214	243	26	102	156	13	17	0	5.41	1.5	6.6	14.50
CAREER	231	228	1490	1516	126	469	1136	89	81	0	4.04	2.4	6.9	11.99

How did Hanson go from winning 15 games with the Red Sox to losing 17 games with the Blue Jays in a single season? There are two obvious reasons. First, in terms of run support, Hanson went from feast to famine. The Red Sox scored 6.6 runs per game for Hanson in '95. Last year the sorry Blue Jays offense gave him 4.5 runs to work with. Second, Hanson's trademark control abandoned him. Never before had he walked more than 68 in a season. He allowed 4.3 walks per 9 in '96, a far cry from his 2.6 career rate. Hitters, especially right-handers, simply watched his curve go by, and chose instead to wallop his fastball. It's hard to predict success for Hanson in '97. If his curveball isn't working on a particular day, which seems to be the case more often, he becomes a 2-pitch pitcher. And as he demonstrated so vividly last season, his fastball is a meaty snack for ravenous hitters. ■

PAT HENTGEN — AL ELITE

SP • BR • TR • 6'2 • 200 • 28 • TOR86/5

	G	GS	IP	H	HR	BB	K	W	L	S	ERA	K/BB	K9	HW9
TOR94	24	24	174	158	21	59	147	13	8	0	3.40	2.5	7.6	11.22
TOR95	30	30	200	236	24	90	135	10	14	0	5.11	1.5	6.1	14.67
TOR96	35	35	265	238	20	94	177	20	10	0	3.22	1.9	6.0	11.27
CAREER	154	124	914	901	100	352	623	67	43	0	3.94	1.8	6.1	12.34

Hentgen was 7-5 with 3.89 ERA at the end of June, a good record for a mediocre ballclub. But then he turned on the after-burners and was pretty untouchable over the final 3 months of the season. After losing his initial July start, Hentgen reeled off 6 consecutive victories, including a pair of 3-hit shutouts. When the dust cleared, Hentgen had won 10 of his 12 starts in June and July. He earned American League pitcher of the month honors both months, becoming the only pitcher to win the award in consecutive months since Bret Saberhagen in '89. Hentgen's past 3 seasons look a lot like Saberhagen's '87-'89. In '94, Hentgen was on his way to match Saberhagen's 18 win performance of '87 when the strike hit. They both led the league in hits allowed the following year, then had a career year the season after that. Saberhagen won 23 games in '89, but managed only 21 over the next 3 seasons. Fortunately for Hentgen and the Jays, the likelihood of him ending up dumping bleach on reporters in Shea or being dealt for Gregg Jefferies appears slim.

The strength of Hentgen's strong July-September (12-4, 2.58 ERA) allowed him to finish 2nd in the league in wins and ERA, and 3rd in BA allowed (.241) and fewest hits per 9 innings (8.06). Hentgen doesn't have overpowering pitches. His fastball and slider are above average, but he wins by throwing them deceptively and fearlessly. What makes Hentgen such a valuable pitcher, though, is his durability. Since 1993, he has averaged 7 innings per start. Last season he averaged 7.5 innings per start and failed to last 6 innings only once. His 10 complete games easily led the majors. And of his 35 starts, 23 of them (about two-thirds) were quality starts. His iron-man reputation is well deserved. ■

MARTY JANZEN — SOLID PROSPECT

SP • BR • TR • 6'3 • 195 • 23 • NYA91

	G	GS	IP	H	HR	BB	K	W	L	S	ERA	K/BB	K9	HW9
TOR96	15	11	73	95	16	38	47	4	6	0	7.33	1.2	5.8	16.38

Janzen was the principal prospect acquired in the '95 Cone deal. The Blue Jays were hot for him because he's young and can throw 4 pitches for strikes. He throws a fastball that reaches the low '90s, a good curve, a slider, and a circle change. His command is excellent. One minor-league manager compared his command to Kevin Tapani's, and the stats confirm it. Prior to the '96 season, Janzen owned an excellent 3.71 strikeouts-to-walks ratio covering 4 minor-league seasons.

According to Cito Gaston, Janzen has problems keeping his arm speed constant and his mechanics straight. As a result, his fastball can go from excellent to hittable. Scouts also think he should throw his change-up more. Both are very correctable flaws. Janzen had never pitched an inning above Double-A before last season. The jump he

made from Knoxville to the majors was impressive, even if his numbers weren't, and should serve as an indication of just how much the Blue Jays think of him. He doesn't have the pure "stuff" of a rotation ace, but there's no reason why he can't become a very effective second or third starter in the big leagues. ■

RYAN JONES

1B • BR • TR • 6'3 • 220 • 22 • TOR93/6

	AB	R	H	2B	3B	HR	RBI	BB	SO	SB	CS	BA	OB	SA
AA	506	70	137	26	3	20	97	60	88	2	2	.271	.351	.453

Scouts sometimes compare Jones to McGwire because of his powerful lofting swing and red hair. The power has always been evident, as he has hovered around the 20-homer mark since being drafted in '93. Last year he tied for the organizational lead in homers and was recognized as Knoxville's MVP. Jones has really improved his hitting in the past year. He was once a whiff-happy slugger. Now he's making much better contact at the plate, and his patience has improved as well. He drew 45 walks and struck out 124 times in '94, his first full pro season. Last year he improved the ratio to 60 walks and 88 strikeouts. That is the sign of a good hitter. Right now Jones is considered too error-prone to land a major-league job. But if he keeps hitting the way he has, he could be ready to replace Olerud within a couple of years, iron glove or not. ■

BILL KOCH — GRADE-A PROSPECT

SP • TOR96/1 • CLEMSON UNIVERSITY

The Blue Jays took Koch with the 4th overall pick in the '96 draft, making that 2 starters from the same staff taken in the first 4 picks. He was Kris Benson's teammate at Clemson where he fanned 152 batters in 112 innings. He was considered the hardest thrower available. His 2-seam fastball has hit 100 mph on the fast gun, and his excellent slider gets to the plate at 90 mph. He's also developed a circle change that needs some work. While at Clemson, Koch was known as "Captain Chaos." Apparently he's considered kind of a wingnut—no doubt for being so flaky that he would turn down two U.S. national team invites to work on his academics. Well, the Blue Jays don't care if he wears K-Mart clothes and watches *People's Court* religiously. He's big (6'3, 200), has a power arm, and a bright future. ■

BEN LOWE

RP • BB • TL • 5'10 • 185 • 22

	G	GS	IP	H	HR	BB	K	W	L	S	ERA	K/BB	K9	HW9
A	46	1	66	40	2	52	89	2	3	9	2.33	1.7	12.2	12.61

The stats paint a portrait of a pitcher with excellent stuff who desperately needs to learn how to harness it. Lowe allowed just 40 hits in 66 innings last season and averaged a little over 12 strikeouts per 9 innings, very impressive ratios. However, he also gave up 7 walks per 9 innings. Lowe's control is his major weakness right now, and some feel he is too small to pitch in the major leagues. There are plenty of obstacles in his way, so if he wants a chance, Lowe will have to prove them wrong every step of the way. ■

DIEGOMAR MARKWELL

Markwell signed for $740,000 in '96 at the age of 16. His fastball is major-league average right now, but his velocity will improve as he matures. He also features a curve with excellent rotation. He's a very long-term prospect now, but he could be an excellent power pitcher in a couple of years and one of the best names in baseball since Juan Tyrone Eichelberger. ■

SANDY MARTINEZ

C • BL • TR • 6'4 • 200 • 24 • TOR90

	AB	R	H	2B	3B	HR	RBI	BB	SO	SB	CS	BA	OB	SA
TOR95	191	12	46	12	0	2	25	7	45	0	0	.241	.270	.335
TOR96	229	17	52	9	3	3	18	16	58	0	0	.227	.288	.332

He doesn't have much offensive potential, but that's never been a concern with Martinez. It was his defense that got him to the majors, and it will be his defense that keeps him there. The Blue Jays are especially enamored with the way he handles the running game. First-base coach Alfredo Griffin says that Martinez has a stronger throwing arm than Ivan Rodriguez, but adds that Pudge has a faster release and is more accurate. Martinez would be a better fit as a backup

to someone who actually can hit. Charlie O'Brien sure doesn't fit that bill, but Martinez can learn a lot about pitch selection while he's around. ■

JULIO MOSQUERA

C • BR • TR • 6'0 • 165 • 25 • TOR91

	AB	R	H	2B	3B	HR	RBI	BB	SO	SB	CS	BA	OB	SA
AA	318	36	73	17	0	2	31	29	55	6	5	.230	.301	.302

Mosquera was brought up from Double-A Knoxville in August to fill in when Sandy Martinez went down with an ankle injury. Like Martinez, his calling card is defense and a strong throwing arm. In 1995 he led the South Atlantic League in fielding percentage and runners caught stealing. Last year, he was voted the best defensive catcher in the Southern League. Mosquera needs another season in Triple-A Syracuse to develop his bat. He has line-drive power potential, which is more than Martinez can dream of, but needs to work on making consistent contact. It's obvious his glove is ready for the show right now, but the Blue Jays only have enough room on the roster for a couple of catchers with termite-riddled bats at a time. ■

OTIS NIXON

OF • BB • TR • 6'2 • 180 • 38 • NYA79

	AB	R	H	2B	3B	HR	RBI	BB	SO	SB	CS	BA	OB	SA
BOS94	398	60	109	15	1	0	25	55	65	42	10	.274	.360	.317
TEX95	589	87	174	21	2	0	45	58	85	50	21	.295	.357	.338
TOR96	496	87	142	15	1	1	29	71	68	54	13	.286	.377	.327
CAREER	3940	692	1062	116	17	8	246	453	545	498	160	.270	.344	.314

At the ripe age of 38, Otis Nixon is still getting it done. The Blue Jays signed him last season to bat leadoff, and by the time the season ended he had set a career mark for walks and on-base percentage while tying his career high in runs scored. While it wasn't as shocking as Elster knocking in 99 runs, the fact that Nixon turned his game up a notch at his age was surprising, to say the least. Nixon is still considered one of the fastest players in the A.L. Coupled with his defense, Nixon's speed is quite enough to land him a full-time job somewhere. However, while there is truth to the axiom that speed never slumps, nobody ever said that speed never pulls a hamstring. Nixon's age has to make him a gamble. The little injuries will start robbing him of more and more playing time. ■

CHARLIE O'BRIEN

C • BR • TR • 6'2 • 205 • 36 • OAK82/4

	AB	R	H	2B	3B	HR	RBI	BB	SO	SB	CS	BA	OB	SA
ATL94	152	24	37	11	0	8	28	15	24	0	0	.243	.322	.474
ATL95	198	18	45	7	0	9	23	29	40	0	1	.227	.343	.399
TOR96	324	33	77	17	0	13	44	29	68	0	1	.238	.331	.410
CAREER	1751	177	389	94	3	46	210	174	257	1	8	.222	.307	.358

O'Brien's bat has never allowed him to be a full-time catcher. He was brought on board last season to teach Sandy Martinez the finer points of playing catcher, and the Blue Jays couldn't have picked a better tutor. He's a fine defensive catcher with a strong arm. More importantly, pitchers rave about his receiving skills and the way he calls a game. If he stays with the Blue Jays, O'Brien will have a job as Juan Guzman's personal catcher. But he'll probably lose more playing time to his star pupil. ■

JOHN OLERUD

1B • BL • TL • 6'5 • 205 • 28 • TOR89/4

	AB	R	H	2B	3B	HR	RBI	BB	SO	SB	CS	BA	OB	SA
TOR94	384	47	114	29	2	12	67	61	53	1	2	.297	.393	.477
TOR95	492	72	143	32	0	8	54	84	54	0	0	.291	.398	.404
TOR96	398	59	109	25	0	18	61	60	37	1	0	.274	.382	.472
CAREER	3103	464	910	213	6	109	471	514	430	3	8	.293	.395	.471

Olerud had a bipolar season. The highs were really high, and the lows bottomed out. There was no middle ground. Just take a look at his monthly batting averages: April .229, May .337, June .157, July .308, September .176. (In August he was bothered by a bad back and got only 18 at-bats.) The streaky nature of his hitting last season is undeniable. Cito Gaston thought he knew what was causing Olerud's slumps. During a bad stretch in June, he said, "If I knew what was wrong, I'd tell him. I don't think John and I have ever sat down in my office and talked. He's so quiet that half the time you don't know he's there." Apparently Gaston felt that Olerud's unusually even demeanor

left him unable to get fired up over his inability to hit. As if destroying the clubhouse water cooler would have helped him see the ball better—a strategy that has only seemed to work for Paul O'Neill.

Olerud's early hitting woes caused him to lose his spot in the meat of the batting order. His inability to hit left-handed pitchers, a career trend, got him a seat on the bench against them in favor of Delgado. His season stats might not have been that far off his career averages, but if he continues his streaky ways, he could become a part-time player by the end of the year. The Blue Jays will be shopping him around the league, hoping someone will take his salary (11th-highest in baseball last season!) off their hands. ■

JEFF PATZKE — SOLID PROSPECT

2B • BB • TR • 6'0 • 170 • 23 • TOR92/5

	AB	R	H	2B	3B	HR	RBI	BB	SO	SB	CS	BA	OB	SA
AA	429	70	130	31	4	4	66	80	103	6	5	.303	.418	.422

Patzke was originally drafted as a shortstop in the 5th round of the '92 amateur draft, but switched to second base once Alex Gonzalez arrived on the scene. He has some impressive skills. He's a switch-hitter who combines gap-type power with an ability to hit for average and draw a walk. He's also pretty solid defensively. Patzke has to wait his turn on a long list of prospects at second base. But there's no reason to believe that he won't get a shot at the position soon, since everyone except Damaso Garcia and Danny Ainge will be getting a look. He could turn out to be the best of the lot. ■

ROBERT PEREZ

OF • BR • TR • 6'3 • 205 • 27 • TOR89

	AB	R	H	2B	3B	HR	RBI	BB	SO	SB	CS	BA	OB	SA
TOR95	48	2	9	2	0	1	3	0	5	0	0	.188	.188	.292
TOR96	202	30	66	10	0	2	21	8	17	3	0	.327	.354	.406

In another organization, Perez might have had a full-time job last season, but the Jays were committed to developing Shawn Green. He hit pretty well in his limited duty, but that was expected of him. Perez earned the Blue Jays' Player of the Year award in '95 after he won the International League batting title with a .343 average. He hits for average but has very little power. He has speed but doesn't steal often. He has a good arm, but other than that, his fielding is a question mark. Perez will continue to be measured against his potential, and come up short. ■

TOMAS PEREZ

2B • BB • TR • 6'0 • 180 • 23 • MON91

	AB	R	H	2B	3B	HR	RBI	BB	SO	SB	CS	BA	OB	SA
TOR95	98	12	24	3	1	1	8	7	18	0	1	.245	.292	.327
TOR96	295	24	74	13	4	1	19	25	29	1	2	.251	.311	.332

Perez gets the nod over Crespo in terms of defensive ability. A converted shortstop, Perez is often described as brilliant in the field, though a little cocky at times. His bat hasn't come around yet, and that's where Crespo gains the edge. But what do you expect from a 23-year-old in just his 4th pro season? Actually, if you consider he had never seen a pitcher above Class-A before last season, his hitting doesn't look all that bad. As the witch in *Hansel and Gretel* once said, "This kid just needs a little seasoning." Second base looks like it will continue to be a vacancy in 1997. Look for Crespo and Perez to lock horns in the early going and do battle for the job. ■

JOSÉ PETT — SOLID PROSPECT

SP • BR • TR • 6'6 • 190 • 21 • TOR92

	G	GS	IP	H	HR	BB	K	W	L	S	ERA	K/BB	K9	HW9
AAA	20	18	110	134	10	42	50	2	9	0	5.83	1.2	4.1	14.44

Pett is a tall and lanky right-hander who signed with the Blue Jays out of Brazil in 1992. At the time of his signing Pett was throwing 90 mph. Now do the math. Pett was throwing a major-league fastball at age 16! He throws hard but doesn't have a consistent breaking pitch yet—only a change-up. As a result, his strikeout totals over his 3-year career have been very low for a power pitcher. Pett got his first taste of adversity in Syracuse last season as he learned firsthand that every Triple-A hitter can time a fastball. But he was the youngest player in the International League, and he's still high on the club's food chain. The Blue Jays have rushed him

thus far, but he's gone as far as he can go. They'll let him become acclimated to the advanced level before calling him up. The Blue Jays love not only his fastball but his mental approach as well. Evidently, the Pirates did too. ■

PAUL QUANTRILL

SP/RP • BL • TR • 6'1 • 175 • 28 • BOS89/8

	G	GS	IP	H	HR	BB	K	W	L	S	ERA	K/BB	K9	HW9
BOS/PHI94	35	1	53	64	7	15	28	3	3	1	4.92	1.9	4.8	13.42
PHI95	33	29	179	212	20	44	103	11	12	0	4.67	2.3	5.2	12.87
TOR96	38	20	134	172	27	51	86	5	14	0	5.43	1.7	5.8	14.97
CAREER	182	64	553	654	68	169	307	27	44	3	4.47	1.8	5.0	13.39

The Blue Jays signed Quantrill on the cheap last year, assuming he could handle the conversion to starting. You get what you pay for. Quantrill's adventure as a starter resulted in a 4-10 record and a 6.29 ERA. He pulled a turnaround after his demotion to the bullpen, logging a 2.76 ERA in 18 appearances. Quantrill will take the ball every time it's handed to him. He throws a hard slider and a sinking fastball with decent control. But he's not cut out for a starting job because he has a limited repertoire and will get pummeled on his second trip through the batting order. As a starter, he was as miscast as John Wayne in *Genghis Khan*. ■

BILL RISLEY

RP • BR • TR • 6'2 • 215 • 29 • CIN87/14

	G	GS	IP	H	HR	BB	K	W	L	S	ERA	K/BB	K9	HW9
SEA94	37	0	52	31	7	19	61	9	6	0	3.44	3.2	10.6	8.65
SEA95	45	0	60	55	7	18	65	2	1	1	3.13	3.6	9.8	10.95
TOR96	25	0	41	33	7	25	29	0	1	0	3.89	1.2	6.4	12.71
CAREER	110	1	161	125	22	65	159	12	8	1	3.46	2.4	8.9	10.61

Shoulder trouble caused Risley to miss more than 2 months last season, and his pinpoint control escaped him. His first half was essentially ruined by a strained shoulder he suffered in the spring when he made an off-balance throw. He tried to pitch through it, which accounts for his 7.71 ERA in April, but ended up being disabled for a month anyway. By the All-Star break he had given up 16 walks in 18 innings and had a 4.84 ERA. He was able to salvage the second half of his season, holding the opposition to a .191 average. But he went back on the DL with tendinitis in late June and missed all of July. When healthy, Risley is a pretty good setup man. He throws hard and challenges hitters inside like the closer they thought he would be. ■

JUAN SAMUEL (see Looking for a Game)

JOSÉ SILVA

SLEEPER

RP • BR • TR • 6'6 • 180 • 23 • TOR91/9

	G	GS	IP	H	HR	BB	K	W	L	S	ERA	K/BB	K9	HW9
AA	22	6	44	45	3	22	26	2	3	0	4.91	1.2	5	13.70

Silva's numbers aren't eye-popping, but there are two things to consider. First, he was only about a year removed from a very serious car accident. The injuries he sustained kept him out of all but 3 games in '95. He lost an entire season, and '96 was his first step on the road back to prospect status. Second, he was making the switch from starter to reliever. Before the accident Silva threw in the 95–97-mph range but had problems fighting on-the-field injuries. The Jays were happy that his velocity made it back to the mid-90s last season. But they were more excited that he got his mechanics ironed out, for it was suspected that his injury history was caused by a poor throwing motion. On the strength of his fastball, slider, and mound presence, Silva was considered one of the best pitchers in the system. He's part of the price they had to pay for Carlos Garcia, Orlando Merced and Dan Plesac. ■

PAUL SPOLJARIC

RP • BR • TL • 6'3 • 205 • 26 • TOR89

	G	GS	IP	H	HR	BB	K	W	L	S	ERA	K/BB	K9	HW9
TOR96	28	0	38	30	6	19	38	2	2	1	3.08	2.0	9.0	11.61

A conversion to the bullpen has given Spoljaric's career new life. He opened the season in Syracuse, but as soon as the Toronto front office noticed that he had walked 6 and struck out 24 in 22 innings there, they summoned him to the majors. Once there, Spoljaric limited batters to a .214 average and allowed only 5 of 14 inherited runners to score. Spoljaric pitched well enough to be guaranteed a job in the bullpen in '97. But just for good measure, Spoljaric had the foresight to be born on Canadian

soil—though even that couldn't save Denis Boucher's career. ▪

ED SPRAGUE — HEADED FOR A FALL

3B • BR • TR • 6'2 • 210 • 29 • TOR88/1

	AB	R	H	2B	3B	HR	RBI	BB	SO	SB	CS	BA	OB	SA
TOR94	405	38	97	19	1	11	44	23	95	1	0	.240	.296	.373
TOR95	521	77	127	27	2	18	74	58	96	0	0	.244	.333	.407
TOR96	591	88	146	35	2	36	101	60	146	0	0	.247	.325	.496
CAREER	2270	276	567	121	6	82	319	195	472	2	3	.250	.320	.417

The Blue Jays always knew he had power potential, but there wasn't a person on the planet who expected *this.* After a rigorous off-season exercise regimen, Sprague finally put it all together last season. He started the season on a rampage, hitting 9 April homers and driving in 20. He let off a little in May, but stormed right back in June with 8 taters and another 20 RBI. Sprague eclipsed his previous career high in home runs by midmonth and was well on his way to doubling the figure. By the All-Star break he was hitting .269 and had slugged 23 homers. Sprague slumped in the second half of the season, hitting just .223 with 13 homers. His strikeouts went through the roof, but that just meant he grounded into fewer double plays—he led the league in '93 with 23, but had only 7 in '96.

Sprague credits hitting coach Willie Upshaw with refining his uppercut swing, but very few players can maintain this kind of unprecedented power surge when it happens late in their baseball life (29 or older). Some recent examples: Keith Moreland hit 27 at 33 after a previous high of 16, hit 5 the following year, and was done at 35; T-Bone Shelby hit 21 in 120 games at 29 after never having hit more than 11, and only hit 17 the rest of his career; Julio Franco hit 20 in 112 games in '94, then managed only 10 in Japan, and 14 in 112 games in the '96 juiced-ball season; Terry Pendleton came out of nowhere to hit 22 dingers at 30, had another strong season the following year, then rapidly deteriorated. Some exceptions: Mike Stanley hit 26 dingers at 29, exceeding his output for the previous 7 seasons, and has sustained that power ever since—but he'd never played regulary before that; Brian Downing had never hit more than 12 dingers in 9 seasons, but then he hit the weights and jacked 28 at the age of 31 in 1982, and maintained that power until he was 37. Look for Sprague—and his NL counterpart, Jeff King—to fall off significantly in the power department in '97. If they don't, they've beaten the odds. ▪

SHANNON STEWART — GRADE-A PROSPECT

OF • BR • TR • 6'1 • 190 • 23 • TOR92/1

	AB	R	H	2B	3B	HR	RBI	BB	SO	SB	CS	BA	OB	SA
AAA	420	77	125	26	8	6	42	54	61	35	8	.298	.377	.440

He was a raw high school athlete on his way to a football scholarship when Toronto took him in the first round (19th overall) in '92. The Blue Jays have watched his development the past 2 years and are now quite smitten with the young outfielder. They have good reason to be, as Stewart offers a leadoff hitter's package of blazing speed, a high batting average, and refined plate discipline. He led the International League in stolen bases in '96 and won his team's MVP award for the 2nd straight year. He is also a fine center fielder with extraordinary range. Tom Runnels, his manager at Syracuse, says that he could almost cover all 3 outfield positions by himself. He won't hit for much power and his throwing arm is a question mark. But those weaknesses will not keep him from a major-league career. He'll be promoted soon and will eventually push Otis Nixon out of the picture—appropriate, since Stewart is considered Nixon's clone. Stewart is probably the best position prospect in the system, at least in the short term. ▪

MIKE TIMLIN

RP • BR • TR • 6'4 • 210 • 31 • TOR87/5

	G	GS	IP	H	HR	BB	K	W	L	S	ERA	K/BB	K9	HW9
TOR94	34	0	40	41	5	20	38	0	1	2	5.18	1.9	8.6	13.73
TOR95	31	0	42	38	1	17	36	4	3	5	2.14	2.1	7.7	11.79
TOR96	59	0	56	47	4	18	52	1	6	31	3.65	2.9	8.3	10.43
CAREER	267	3	345	328	23	152	295	20	20	43	3.73	1.9	7.7	12.52

It took him 2 seasons, but he finally claimed the closer job the Blue Jays had offered him since the departure of Duane Ward. He won the job in spring training by showing he had regained his sharp-moving fastball. Timlin was pretty effective for the Jays last year,

and if you ignore July, his stats look even better. If you purge that performance from his totals, Timlin would have finished with a 2.61 ERA. Timlin has always been tough on right-handed hitters and last year was no different. He held them to a .191 average because he's not afraid of jamming them inside with his heater. Overall, the league hit .229 off him. He looks like he has finally shrugged off the criticism that he lacks a closer's intensity. Just because he doesn't shoot hitters with his index finger after he strikes them out doesn't mean he can't handle the job. With his 94-mph fastball and slider package, Timlin should be quietly effective again in '97. ■

JEFF WARE

SP • BR • TR • 6'3 • 190 • 26 • TOR91/2

	G	GS	IP	H	HR	BB	K	W	L	S	ERA	K/BB	K9	HW9
TOR95	5	5	26	28	2	21	18	2	1	0	5.47	.9	6.2	16.96
TOR96	13	4	32	35	6	31	11	1	5	0	9.09	.4	3.1	18.52

Ware was a supplemental 1st-round pick in '91, but prior to last season injuries had limited him to 214.2 innings. He was still making up for lost time when the Blue Jays enlisted him as their 5th starter to begin the season. He was shelled unmercifully and found himself back in Syracuse by the end of April. He throws a 4-seam fastball in the upper 80s, a sinker, a curve, and a forkball. The forkball is his out pitch. He is supposed to have good command of his breaking pitches, but it didn't show last season. He walked about 3.7 batters per 9 innings at Syracuse. He's still considered a prospect, though, and the Blue Jays planned to send him to the Arizona Fall League to work on his control. ■

MIKE WHITLOCK

SOLID PROSPECT

1B • BL • TR • 6'3 • 200 • 20 • TOR95/4

	AB	R	H	2B	3B	HR	RBI	BB	SO	SB	CS	BA	OB	SA
A	424	72	107	22	1	20	91	108	132	1	4	.252	.412	.450

Whitlock looked impressive in his first full season. He has serious power that has drawn comparisons to Fred McGriff. Whitlock has a long path to follow before he reaches Crime Dog's territory, but he's on the right track. His main ally at this point is youth. If he has another year like this, he'll be a Grade-A prospect. ■

WOODY WILLIAMS

RP/SP • BR • TR • 6'0 • 190 • 30 • TOR88/28

	G	GS	IP	H	HR	BB	K	W	L	S	ERA	K/BB	K9	HW9
TOR94	38	0	59	44	5	33	56	1	3	0	3.64	1.7	8.5	11.74
TOR95	23	3	53	44	6	28	41	1	2	0	3.69	1.5	7.0	12.23
TOR96	12	10	59	64	8	21	43	4	5	0	4.73	2.0	6.6	12.97
CAREER	103	13	209	192	21	104	164	9	11	0	4.09	1.6	7.1	12.75

Williams spent most of the first half on the disabled list with inflammation in his shoulder. After he got healthy, the Blue Jays put him in the rotation for 10 starts. He won the job by default, not necessarily on the merits of his previous performances. Williams is essentially a 2-pitch pitcher. His fastball is barely adequate because it has little movement, but his curve is nothing special. He will never be more than a utility pitcher, the type who makes emergency starts or comes in when the game has gotten out of hand. ■

KEVIN WITT

SS • BL • TR • 6'4 • 185 • 21 • TOR94/1

	AB	R	H	2B	3B	HR	RBI	BB	SO	SB	CS	BA	OB	SA
A+	446	63	121	18	6	13	70	39	96	9	4	.271	.335	.426

Witt was a high school All-American in '94 and the Blue Jays' 1st-round selection in the draft that year. He made major strides in learning the strike zone in '96. He has good bat speed and an uppercut swing that generates excellent power for a middle infielder. Witt gets a little pull-happy at times, though, and needs to learn to hit to all fields. He is built a lot like Ripken and has the power to justify comparisons between them. But his range at the position is a far cry from Ripken's, so a move to third base is probably in order. ■

National League

■ 1996 AUTOPSY

It wasn't that long ago that the Braves were losing 100 games a year, but after 5 consecutive years of success, they treated postseason play as a birthright. The expectations for the self-proclaimed "Team of the Decade" were nothing short of another World Championship. Suspense would have to come in how many games it would take them to beat the Indians this time.

April 16-11 (16-11, 1½ games back)
The Braves offense got off to a slow start, but by month's end, the team had tied the Atlanta record for victories in April—and it was only the 8th time in 31 seasons that the team had been over .500 for the month. One of the few offensive bright spots was Ryan Klesko (.337-10-20, .747 slugging percentage). Klesko's 10 homers were an Atlanta record (Dale Murphy hit 9 April homers in 1979 and 1985). John Smoltz was 5-1 with a 2.70 ERA in 46.2 innings (51:10 strikeouts-to-walks ratio), and was named the N.L. pitcher of the month. The Braves' top prospect, Andruw Jones, was playing in Class-A Durham. They figured he'd spend the season in the Carolina League and make the majors by 1998 or 1999.

May 19-6 (35-17, 5½ games ahead)
Smoltz went 6-0 with a 1.73 ERA in 41.2 innings (46:11 strikeouts-to-walks ratio) to win N.L. pitcher of the month honors for the second straight month, making him the first since Rick Reuschel in June-July 1977. In his first couple of starts of the month, Greg Maddux allowed late-inning homers, including a grand slam to Benito Santiago in a 6-3 loss. Six earned runs yielded by Maddux? Another sign of The Apocalypse. The media were playing this up, but manager Bobby Cox was having nothing of it: "I think it's a little ridiculous to be worried about Greg." Along with Maddux's "troubles," there were noises about Javy Lopez's catching. Eddie Perez had been catching Steve Avery (who was going well), and some felt Perez should be matched with Maddux, too. Javy's offensive numbers have borne more than a passing resemblance to a young Todd Zeile's. Unfortunately, now his work behind the plate was, too.

Maddux and Lopez aside, the team was clearly worried about David Justice, who dislocated his shoulder swinging at a Denny Neagle pitch and went on the DL. Justice would miss the rest of the season. He had turned down shoulder surgery following the '95 World Series that would have caused him to miss some of the '96 season, opting for weight training and an exercise program.

June 15-13 (50-30, 3 games ahead)
In Maddux's first 13 starts (April, May and his first in June) the team had scored 3 or fewer runs 6 times. He was 5-4 with an ERA of 2.88, 7th in the N.L. Maddux: "It would be frustrating if I was pitching bad. But if you start enough games, there are going to be some when the team is not going to score runs, and that's when you have to win 2-1 or 3-2. I haven't done that." Taking personal responsibility? Accepting adversity? Doesn't he know he's a professional athlete? Then again, Maddux has always had perspective—after all, he took less money rather than play in New York City.

On the 10th, Avery lost 8-3 at Shea. He went 5 innings, allowing 9 hits and 5 runs. The game was notable because of a brawl he touched off. Jose Vizcaino raised his arms and danced on the bases after Todd Hundley homered in the third. "Keep dancing," Avery told Vizcaino as he scored. The next time up, Avery hit Vizcaino in the knee. After the game, Avery and Mets manager Dallas Green stood in separate rooms and talked trash to reporters. Avery: "I don't need some 80-year-old guy telling me he's going to get me somewhere down the road. If they feel they wanted to hit me, go ahead. I'm a big man, I can take it." When told that Green felt that Vizcaino was just excited to be beating the champions, Avery essentially said: Pshaw. "They've got a good young team. But they sometimes get out of hand. They haven't won a World Series and they haven't been to a World Series 3 times in 5 years." At which point Green must have wanted to say: "True. So imagine how excited we would have been if we'd beaten one of their front-line starters rather than just that 26-year-old has-been."

July 15-11 (65-41, 7 games ahead)
On the 13th, Avery hit the DL with a strain of an oblique muscle. On the 16th, Jeff Blauser broke his hand. This was also the month of their Olympic road trip. The one who suffered the most away from home was Fred McGriff. In early June he was hitting

.347 but had hit .187 with 5 homers in his next 171 at-bats. Ryan Klesko had gotten off to a faster home-run start, and now Chipper Jones, who'd heated up in May (he hit .315-8-21, .630 slugging), surpassed him in homers and RBI during the trip. McGriff was no longer the team's dominant offensive weapon.

August 19-10 (84-51, 11½ games ahead)
Avery was the first of the Braves' front-4 to ever go on the DL, but the league wasn't through trying. On the 2nd against the Dodgers, Juan Castro's line drive up the middle hit Smoltz on an exposed part of his glove hand, leaving him with a chip fracture. He didn't even miss a start. On the 7th, Smoltz pitched 5 innings, allowing an unearned run to beat Philadelphia for his 18th victory.

On the 13th, the Braves brought back Terry Pendleton, the man who had played in more post-season games without a World Series championship than any player in history—losing in 7 in 1985, 1987, and 1991, in 6 in 1992, and in the Championship Series in 1993. This would be their big move to strengthen their hitting depth. It wasn't exactly Darryl Strawberry, Cecil Fielder, and Charlie Hayes, but it would have to do. GM John Schuerholz: "We're satisfied that Terry is still able to play at a level that will help us." Cox moved Chipper to short (he'd already volunteered to play right in Justice's absence) and installed Pendleton at third. A few hours later, Andruw Jones appeared in the Braves clubhouse. He would be the youngest man to appear in postseason play since Ken Brett in 1967. His appearance led to the team dumping Mark Whiten after 36 games—he'd lasted only 60 with the Phillies in '96, and was finished in Boston in '95 after only 32—and to David Justice swinging at soft tosses and making noise about being ready for the postseason.

Schuerholz must have felt that the team's most pressing need was a 4th starter, giving up Ron Wright, Jason Schmidt, and Corey Pointer to acquire Denny Neagle from the Pirates. It was a wise use of these prospects—for 1997, that is, if not for their needs in '96 (Neagle started 2 games in the playoffs and the Braves lost both, so he wasn't exactly given a role that Avery couldn't have played). Neagle was already signed through 1997, and he would allow the Braves to show Avery the door and use his money to sign Smoltz—as the Braves went for that 3rd straight World Championship, no doubt.

September 12-15 (96-66, won division)
But the Braves still had a division to win. At the beginning of the month they lost 8 games to also-rans Chicago, Cincinnati, New York, and Colorado. The stretch dropped the Braves to a pedestrian 36-32 on the road. Tom Glavine, 14-1 at Riverfront before the road trip, was shelled in a 12-6 game, allowing 8 earned runs, the most in his 293 career starts. Apparently Reds manager Ray Knight listened to Kevin Mitchell and stacked his lineup with lefties so Glavine couldn't use his change-up so much. Mitchell as a manager? Hmmm. He's got the gut for it, but he'd have to work on actually showing up for the games.

Montreal made things close down the stretch, but couldn't put enough pressure on the Braves or make Bobby Cox make enough decisions. On the 23rd, the Braves beat Montreal 3-1 and said good-bye to Atlanta-Fulton County Stadium at the same time. Tuxedo-wearing ushers and grounds crew worked that day, and Ted Turner asked the crowd to sing "Auld Lang Syne." After the game, former Braves came on the field, introduced by video clips and a spotlight. Among the players: Dale Murphy, Phil Niekro, Bob Horner—and of course—no. 44. And Rick Camp. Rick Camp? And since when was Atlanta-Fulton County Stadium Ebbetts Field? The Braves could have benefited greatly from a resounding "Get over yourselves," but no one in the organization was grounded enough to provide it. It's hard to be humble when you've won your division for the 5th straight time, sharing the record with the 1971-75 A's. Due to the 1994 strike, it took them 6 years to do it.

October (lost World Series in 6 games to Yankees)
The fruits of their regular-season labor gave the Braves a bye in the 1st round of the playoffs—otherwise known as a series against the 1995-96 Dodgers. In the next round, they let the Cardinals push them to the brink of extinction, falling behind 3 games to 1. They could have lost the first game of the series, too, but Cox was bailed out by some dumb luck. A very questionable decision to have the red-hot Chipper Jones bunt in the 8th inning—which would have led to an intentional walk to Fred McGriff and Klesko facing a lefty to try to score the lead run—was forgotten when the Cardinals threw the ball down the right-field line. They came back to win the final 3 games by a combined score of 32-

1, with the lone Cardinals run coming on a Mark Wohlers wild pitch in a close game—after Cox chose to pull a cruising Greg Maddux in the 8th after 80 pitches. They won that game despite Cox painting himself into a corner and needing Rafael Belliard to hit in a crucial situation—when the over-matched Belliard delivered the only big hit of his career. Belliard would make up for that a week later, helping his team lose a game on defense.

Having to win 3 straight games against the Cardinals should have humbled the Braves, but doing so in such convincing fashion did anything but. When they beat the Yankees twice in the Bronx by combined scores of 16-1, they returned home for the coronation. But the Braves' lack of bullpen depth and strategic thinking were both exposed in Game 3 and 4. In Game 3, Greg McMichael—who'd already blown Game 4 against the Cardinals—faced 3 batters and gave up 3 runs in the 8th inning of what had been a close game. In Game 4, Cox pulled a cruising Mike Bielecki and called on Mark Wohlers in the 8th inning of what had been a lopsided game—only to watch him melt down in prime time, getting tagged for a game-tying dinger when he hung his 3rd worst pitch to the Yankees' backup catcher. Cox did his part in extra innings. With runners on first and second, rather than yank the struggling Steve Avery and bring in a righty to turn Bernie Williams around, Cox walked Williams to load the bases. After throwing four wide, Avery now had to try not to walk pinch-hitter Wade Boggs. Boggs is not Boggs anymore, but he still has a great batting eye and the reputation with umpires to go along with it. But then Cox might have thought Avery would be facing Andy Fox—after all, when Boggs was called on to pinch-hit for Fox, the obligatory shot of a muttering, wincing Cox in the dugout could have been captioned: "Damn, they still got that Hall of Famer over there. Next year I gotta start writing this stuff down." Boggs drew a walk. For good measure, Klesko—inserted into the game in a double switch, though it just meant he would have to lead off the bottom of the inning against lefty Graeme Lloyd—followed that by dropping a humpbacked liner hit right to him at first. The Yankees had scored 2 runs and hit only 1 ball out of the infield.

The Braves looked stunned. John Smoltz pitched a gem in Game 5, but Andy Pettitte was better. Atlanta still might have pulled it out, but they couldn't deliver a pinch-hit when it counted. In fact, their bench was hitless in 22 pinch-hit appearances in the postseason. Then again, the bench John Schuerholz assembled was Terry Pendleton, Luis Polonia, and Mike Mordecai. The scenario was repeated in Game 6 in the Bronx, as the Braves lost 3-2 and left the winning runs on base. And the Yankees, just like that, had matched the Team of the Decade with exactly 1 world championship in the '90s.

■ 1997 DIAGNOSIS

Offense

The Braves had the best offense in the N.L. last season. The team hit for a great deal of power, and hit for a good average while drawing a decent number of walks. For '97, expect similar production from the corners (McGriff and Chipper) and catcher (Lopez). Grissom probably won't be able to repeat his year, and Klesko could be better in left—if he isn't losing sleep over the sight of Andruw Jones and Jermaine Dye in his side-view mirrors. It might take him 2-3 seasons, but Jones should develop into a 35-dinger threat.

Defense

As good as the Braves offense is, and as great as its pitching is, its defense was surprisingly inadequate. McGriff makes too many errors for a first baseman—only 4 made more. Mark Lemke is solid and Chipper is versatile, though Jones hasn't yet established himself as a great fielder at any position. And then there's Jeff Blauser. At the most critical position in the infield, he had the lowest fielding percentage, by far, of any full-time shortstop. He had the range of a third baseman in '96, and it was a head-scratcher to see him playing shortstop for a team with championship aspirations. Then again, with his contract, they probably couldn't give him away. The statisticians have numbers that suggest that Klesko is not that bad in left field. ESPN has a blooper reel that suggests otherwise. Coming in for a feet-first sliding catch and ending up with your spikes pointed straight up at the sky and the ball sailing 30 feet over your head isn't going to convince anyone that your DNA isn't hard-coded DH. Grissom is solid in center, though he didn't show it in the World Series. Andruw Jones will be excellent if he plays full-time, and Jermaine Dye will do just fine as

long as the right-field-line umpire doesn't box him out on foul balls. Only Mike Piazza and Mike Stanley had more passed balls than Lopez (who didn't have to handle any knuckleballs), his throwing was average, and his handling of the pitchers isn't well thought of by them. Other than that, he's fine.

Pitching

The entire pitching staff was about 125 runs better than the average N.L. team—so, as is usually the case, this was the best pitching staff in the game last season. Smoltz, Maddux and Glavine were incredible, but the 4th and 5th starters (Avery, Schmidt, Wade, Bielecki, etc.) were mediocre. If you combine Wade and Neagle with the top 3, the Braves look to be even better in '97—but a team can't assume its staff will save 125 runs for them every season.

The bullpen has one strong pitcher—Mark Wohlers—and is desperately in need of depth. Paul Byrd is a big question mark, which Mike Bielecki is going to show up is always an issue, and Brad Clontz is just another McMichael with a little more gas in the tank. Look for the Braves to give some of their hard-throwing prospects—such as Carl Schutz—the chance to become the man responsible for getting the ball to Wohlers. If their starters struggle and can't get them to the 9th with regularity as they've done in the past, this bullpen will cost them the division.

Farm System

Now that Andruw and Jermaine are up and Jason Schmidt and Ron Wright are vapor trails, the Braves don't look so great down on the farm. They don't have any more Grade-A prospects. Randall Simon and Wes Helms are the closest thing the Braves have to top hitting prospects, but neither is a budding superstar. The farm system has been feeding its young to the big club for the past few years and is depleted.

Management and Ownership

Ted Turner used to be a bit more zany and wacky in his younger days. Now he signs the checks, creates cable networks, and is too busy tending buffalo herds on his Montana ranch to do anything other than pay Jane's credit card bills. All that could be asked now is changing the name of Ted Turner Stadium to Henry Aaron Field.

John Schuerholz has continued the '90s tradition of the Braves—overseeing a solid farm system and sending his team into the postseason with glaring weaknesses rather than jeopardize the future. In 1991 the team's closer was Alejandro Peña, in 1992 it was a washed-up Jeff Reardon—until his performance in blowing Games 2 and 3 against the Blue Jays buried him for the rest of the World Series—and in 1993 it was Mike Stanton and Greg McMichael, who helped the team lose 3 one-run games to the Phillies in the playoffs. In 1994 it would have been McMikey again, if they even got there—and a lineup whose best right-handed hitters were Roberto Kelly and José Oliva. In 1995 they finally met up with a team whose bullpen depth and bench were worse, but in 1996 these were exploited all over again. The front office has done a masterful job of building a great team out of essentially nothing. That's an accomplishment not to be minimized. But they'll end up looking back on the '90s and wonder how they came away with so little to show for all those regular-season wins and all that great pitching.

Another weakness that has been glaringly apparent but never addressed is Bobby Cox's inadequacy as a tactician. Cox is a player's manager and, since he is surrounded by winners such as McGriff and Jones, it works. As an in-game manager, he takes very few risks—such as going with a 3-man rotation and making John Smoltz his closer in 1993, for example. He doesn't handle pitchers well. He let Smoltz throw 100 pitches in the game 5 blow-out against the Cardinals, leaving him no option to use him in a close game 7 if necessary. Yet he yanked a virtually unhittable Maddux on low pitch counts twice during the '96 postseason. And he doesn't play chess well with his pinch-hitters, continually being maneuvered by LaRussa and Torre into unfavorable match-ups late in the game.

With his handling of the players and the immense talent of the team, Cox's shortcomings as a tactician don't show up during the regular season. But in a short series against a talented team, Cox is hopelessly overmatched. Felipe Alou would have 3 World Series titles with this team.

. . . and whatnot: Top Prospects' Prospectus

Andruw Jones and Vlad Guerrero. If you just mention their names, GMs and scouts start drooling.

These two are youngsters of rare quality. Several Eastern League scouts have raved about the ability of Guerrero, while Southern/International League observers favor Andruw. The Expos were conservative with Vladimir, moving him from Class-A to Double-A early in the season, then letting him play there until September. The Braves took Andruw on an odyssey that started in the Class-A Carolina League and ended with a trip to the World Series.

But let's look at their performance in Double-A (where we can fairly assess them). Jones is a year younger, and that gives him a distinct advantage. If two players have similar ability and there's an age difference, the younger usually dominates the elder over the course of their careers. But 14 months apart with Guerrero only 21, they are both so young that one could be Frank Robinson and the other could be Hank Aaron. We're going to look at their performance at Double-A to see what they'd probably have hit in the majors.

Player	Age	AB	R	H	2B	3B	HR	RBI	BB	K	BA	OBP	SLG
Guerrero	20	417	84	150	32	8	19	78	51	42	.360	.430	.612
Jones	19	157	39	58	10	1	12	37	17	34	.369	.431	.675

Adjusted for park effects that becomes:

Player	Age	AB	R	H	2B	3B	HR	RBI	BB	K	BA	OBP	SLG
Guerrero	20	423	88	155	34	8	17	82	51	42	.366	.435	.605
Jones	19	155	38	57	9	1	10	36	17	34	.368	.430	.632

Now here are the major league equivalencies for the two players in 500-550 at-bats:

Player	Age	AB	R	H	2B	3B	HR	RBI	BB	K	BA	OBP	SLG
Guerrero	20	535	98	184	41	8	20	92	58	58	.344	.408	.563
Jones	19	528	116	183	28	3	32	109	53	127	.347	.406	.593

Guerrero and Jones are both going to be superstars. Jones is a better all-around hitter and is a year younger, so he's the better prospect, right? Probably, but look at Guerrero's strikeouts-to-walks ratio. His is more in line with a consistent .300 hitter than Jones.

A prediction, assuming they both get a decent amount of playing time: Guerrero hits .300+ this season with lots of doubles and at least 10 homers, while Jones will hit 25+ homers, but his average could be anywhere from .250 up. These equivalencies don't mean these two players will dominate right away (see *21 Guns* in the Montreal Expos section). But as Cal Ripken, Frank Thomas, Jim Thome, and Manny Ramirez could tell you, if you're young and do incredibly well in the minors, you will usually repeat the performance before too long in the majors.

STEVE AVERY (see Free Agents)

DANNY BAUTISTA

OF • BR • TR • 5'11 • 170 • 24 • DET89

	AB	R	H	2B	3B	HR	RBI	BB	SO	SB	CS	BA	OB	SA
DET94	99	12	23	4	1	4	15	3	18	1	2	.232	.255	.414
DET95	271	28	55	9	0	7	27	12	68	4	1	.203	.237	.314
DET/ATL96	84	13	19	2	0	2	9	11	20	1	2	.226	.323	.321
CAREER	515	59	116	18	1	14	60	27	116	9	6	.225	.265	.346

Bautista came to Atlanta from Detroit in a trade for minor-league outfielder Anton French. Then Jeff Parrett hit Bautista in the face with a fastball and his season ended after 20 at-bats with Atlanta. He is the "before" model of Sammy Sosa: speed, power, a good arm, and a complete inability to discern the difference between a ball and a strike. Sosa was more talented and got more at-bats to develop. Bautista now has about a 10% chance of putting together a good career. His bad luck cost him his chance to do it for Atlanta, though. There's too much in his way.

RAFAEL BELLIARD (see Looking for a Game)

MIKE BIELECKI (see Looking for a Game)

JEFF BLAUSER

SS • BR • TR • 6'1 • 180 • 31 • ATL84

	AB	R	H	2B	3B	HR	RBI	BB	SO	SB	CS	BA	OB	SA
ATL94	380	56	98	21	4	6	45	38	64	1	3	.258	.329	.382
ATL95	431	60	91	16	2	12	31	57	107	8	5	.211	.319	.341
ATL96	265	48	65	14	1	10	35	40	54	6	0	.245	.356	.419
CAREER	3442	511	900	170	24	92	391	413	691	56	36	.261	.347	.405

If they were going to arbitration, Orlando Miller, Andujar Cedeño, and José Hernandez would all be comparing their shaky glovework to Blauser's—and his $10 million contract. The Braves gave him that after his disappointing 1994 season—and now they're just hoping he can crawl back to *that* level. His defense hasn't always been this bad, so it should improve. But his offensive numbers are looking a lot like Rafael Ramirez and Andres Thomas in their primes. With the money he's getting, the Braves would be lucky if they could give him away, so expect to see Blauser back at short in '97. But after that, it could be

Chipper, Wes Helms, Tony Graffanino, Marty Malloy, Ed Giovanola, or perhaps even Jerry Royster and Darrel Chaney. ■

PEDRO BORBON

RP • BR • TL • 6'1 • 205 • 29 • CHA88

	G	GS	IP	H	HR	BB	K	W	L	S	ERA	K/BB	K9	HW9
ATL95	41	0	32	29	2	17	33	2	2	2	3.09	1.9	9.3	12.94
ATL96	43	0	36	26	1	7	31	3	0	1	2.75	4.4	7.8	8.25

Borbon went on the 15-day DL with rotator-cuff tendinitis on April 8 last season. On August 22 he went on again with a torn elbow ligament and had Tommy John surgery. When he's on, he has a decent fastball and curveball, but he works off his good change-up. He's not going to return until at least the All-Star break, and possibly not until September. ■

BRAD CLONTZ

RP • BR • TR • 6'1 • 180 • 25 • ATL92/10

	G	GS	IP	H	HR	BB	K	W	L	S	ERA	K/BB	K9	HW9
ATL95	59	0	69	71	5	22	55	8	1	4	3.65	2.5	7.2	12.13
ATL96	81	0	80	78	11	33	49	6	3	1	5.69	1.5	5.5	12.48

Last season he set a Braves record with 81 appearances. Don't get too excited. Here are some pitchers who've been league leaders in this category in recent years: Eddie Guardado, Mike Myers, Steve Reed, Bob Wickman, Greg Harris, Joe Boever, and Barry Jones. He'll never be a closer again until he can get out lefties. Like most righty sidearmers, he's a right-handed hitter's nightmare, but lefties put a pitchfork in him and bale him—a .465 on-base percentage and a .688 slugging average. In the first half he was 5-2 with a 4.30 ERA in 44 innings. In the second half Clontz was 1-1 with a 7.36 ERA in 36.2 innings. The Braves will need to limit the innings and never let him face a lefty without a 5-run lead. ■

JERMAINE DYE

YOUNG GUN

OF • BR • TR • 6'0 • 195 • 23 • ATL93/16

	AB	R	H	2B	3B	HR	R BI	BB	SO	SB	CS	BA	OB	SA
ATL96	292	32	82	16	0	12	37	8	67	1	4	.281	.304	.459

Dye is an excellent defensive right fielder and a decent power hitter. He's especially useful in this lefty-leaning lineup because he can put a charge into left-handed pitchers (.340 OBP, .538 slugging in 93 at-bats in '96). Going into the '96 season, the organization felt he needed to work on hitting breaking balls. This is the key to his development. He has to improve this, or he might well end up another coulda-shoulda-woulda. It might keep him from being among baseball's elite, but he can be one of the league's better players. He played a good deal of the season with a cartilage tear in his right knee, so one thing that can't be questioned is his desire. ■

MIKE EAGLIN

SLEEPER

2B • BR • TR • 5'10 • 170 • 23

	AB	R	H	2B	3B	HR	RBI	BB	SO	SB	CS	BA	OB	SA
A+	466	84	118	25	2	11	54	50	88	23	12	.253	.346	.386

He'll play in the Southern League this season and could come up in September. Eaglin was voted the top defensive second baseman in the Carolina League in '96. He has some power, good speed and a pretty good idea of how to work a pitcher. He'll probably be 25 or 26 by the time he gets a chance (if he's given one), but he could be a perfect replacement for Lemke. ■

TOM GLAVINE

NL ELITE

SP • BL • TL • 6'1 • 190 • 31 • ATL84/2

	G	GS	IP	H	HR	BB	K	W	L	S	ERA	K/BB	K9	HW9
ATL94	25	25	165	173	10	70	140	13	9	0	3.97	2.0	7.6	13.25
ATL95	29	29	198	182	9	66	127	16	7	0	3.08	1.9	5.8	11.27
ATL96	36	36	235	222	14	85	181	15	10	0	2.98	2.1	6.9	11.76
CAREER	298	298	1956	1871	127	664	1212	139	92	0	3.46	1.8	5.6	11.66

Cox in April: "Tom Glavine is throwing as hard as I've ever seen him. He's really popping the ball, throwing it by people." Glavine had his best strikeout rate (nearly 7 per 9 innings) in a full season since 1991, when he won the Cy Young. And in several starts, Glavine was clocked at 92–93 mph. Scouts have always graded his fastball as average, his success due more to a

good curve and a deadly change. He is one of the most consistent pitchers in baseball. If the velocity holds up in '97, he should be a 20-victory threat again. ■

TONY GRAFFANINO — SLEEPER

2B • BR • TR • 6'1 • 200 • 24 • ATL90/9

	AB	R	H	2B	3B	HR	RBI	BB	SO	SB	CS	BA	OB	SA
AAA	353	57	100	29	2	7	33	34	72	11	7	.283	.350	.436

Graffanino missed a lot of the '95 season with back problems, but bounced back last season. He's an excellent defensive second baseman—voted best in the International League in '96. For the most part, Graffanino is the same player as Eaglin, just a year closer to the majors. Cox loves Lemke, but it might behoove Schuerholz and company to commit to one of the younger players to free up some cash. ■

MARQUIS GRISSOM — OVERRATED

CF • BR • TR • 5'11 • 190 • 29 • MON88/4

	AB	R	H	2B	3B	HR	RBI	BB	SO	SB	CS	BA	OB	SA
MON94	475	96	137	25	4	11	45	41	66	36	6	.288	.344	.427
ATL95	551	80	142	23	3	12	42	47	64	29	9	.258	.317	.376
ATL96	671	106	207	32	10	23	74	41	73	28	11	.308	.349	.489
CAREER	3900	616	1096	185	36	89	392	296	507	323	68	.281	.332	.415

Grissom seems to have lost a tremendous amount of his speed over the past 5 years. His steals have declined from 78 to 28, while his success rate has dropped from 86% to 72%. As he gets older, he may not be able to get away with playing so shallow in center field. In many ways, Grissom had his best season in '96, but it still wasn't the amazing performance that's been projected for him for years. His on-base percentage was nothing special for a .300 hitter (let alone a leadoff man). He certainly doesn't have any offensive weaknesses, but he no longer has one exceptional skill. He's still going to be a decent player for a few years. Just don't believe the TBS hype that he's one of the elite players in the league. He's good, but he's not even close to Kenny Lofton or Bernie Williams. ■

STEVE HACKER — SLEEPER

1B • BR • TR • 6'5 • 230 • 22 • ATL95/14

	AB	R	H	2B	3B	HR	RBI	BB	SO	SB	CS	BA	OB	SA
A-	292	45	73	15	1	21	61	26	64	0	0	.250	.318	.524

Hacker was the 1995 NCAA Division I homer champ, hitting .412-37-95 for Southwest Missouri State. He was beaned in July '95, and the ball caved in half his face. He's had three titanium plates inserted near his left eye, and he feels he's got a lot of work to do to regain his hitting ability—but he crushed the ball at Eugene, slugging .524 despite hitting .250. He was a little old for the league, but he sounds like exactly the type of player who doesn't look for excuses to fail. ■

WES HELMS — SOLID PROSPECT

3B • BR • TR • 6'4 • 210 • 20 • ATL94/12

	AB	R	H	2B	3B	HR	RBI	BB	SO	SB	CS	BA	OB	SA
AA	231	24	59	13	2	4	22	13	48	2	1	.255	.306	.381

A nephew of former Red Tommy Helms, Wes has an excellent arm and was voted the best defensive third baseman in the Carolina League in '96. He's an excellent athlete and would be a Grade-A prospect but for his plate discipline. He and former teammate Ron Wright (see the section on the Pittsburgh Pirates) were nicknamed Beavis and Butt-Head and used to delight in pulling scatological practical jokes. The fact that he is a kick boxer helps explain why he still has all his teeth despite this sense of "humor." ■

DAMON HOLLINS

OF • BR • TL • 5'11 • 180 • 22 • ATL92/4

	AB	R	H	2B	3B	HR	RBI	BB	SO	SB	CS	BA	OB	SA
AAA	146	16	29	9	0	0	8	16	37	2	3	.199	.278	.260

A fine athlete, Hollins was shut down after surgery on June 3. Hollins fractured and dislocated his wrist in high school, and the bone healed 7 millimeters too long. A portion of the ulna was sawed off, and the bone was fused. He is a good defensive outfielder with a great arm, and the Braves think he has 25-homer potential. Hollins should be ready by this spring, but he's going to start the season in Double-A Greenville or Triple-A Richmond. ■

ANDRUW JONES — YOUNG GUN

OF • BR • TR • 6'1 • 170 • 19 • ATL93

	AB	R	H	2B	3B	HR	RBI	BB	SO	SB	CS	BA	OB	SA
ATL96	106	11	23	7	1	5	13	7	29	3	0	.217	.265	.443

In 1995 he dominated at his home park in the South Atlantic League, which is a hitter's haven. So there

were some questions coming into '96 if he was the real deal. He was promoted from Class-A Durham to Double-A Greenville at midseason. By July 31 Jones was smacking a 2-run homer in his first game at Triple-A Richmond. In October he was the MVP of Game 1 of the World Series. He was a surreal deal last season—from Class-A to the World Series?

Fred McGriff: "When I was 19, I was in A-ball in Florence, South Carolina. That tells you how special he is. You watch him take batting practice and it's just awesome." Precisely. This kid is a potential Mantle, Aaron, or Mays. You see one of these kinds of players come up every decade or so. The last player who was in Andruw's territory was Ken Griffey's skinny son. Griffey was a .260 hitter when he was 19 and an All-Star (.300-22-80) at 20. If Jones puts up those kinds of numbers in '97, then very little after that will be out of his reach. ■

CHIPPER JONES — NL ELITE

3B-SS • BB • TR • 6'3 • 185 • 24 • ATL90/1

	AB	R	H	2B	3B	HR	RBI	BB	SO	SB	CS	BA	OB	SA
ATL95	524	87	139	22	3	23	86	73	99	8	4	.265	.353	.450
ATL96	598	114	185	32	5	30	110	87	88	14	1	.309	.393	.530

In 1996 Chipper combined the power he developed while weight training to rehabilitate his knee with the ability to hit for average he flashed during his stellar minor-league career. Jones also showed he can still run a bit. His defense is below par at third and short, but injuries have slowed him down a bit. He's an excellent athlete, so he should improve no matter where he plays. As of now, though, comparisons to Eddie Mathews are a bit of a stretch. By 23, Mathews had 153 dingers and 397 RBI—including 47-135-.302 at 21. Nevertheless, as long as Chipper plays 150 games, he's an MVP candidate. Chipper and Andruw may be this generation's answer to Brooks and Frank. The Braves locked him up until 2000 for only $11 million. ■

DAVID JUSTICE

RF • BL • TL • 6'3 • 195 • 30 • ATL85/3

	AB	R	H	2B	3B	HR	RBI	BB	SO	SB	CS	BA	OB	SA
ATL94	352	61	110	16	2	19	59	69	45	2	4	.313	.427	.531
ATL95	411	73	104	17	2	24	78	73	68	4	2	.253	.365	.479
ATL96	140	23	45	9	0	6	25	21	22	1	1	.321	.409	.514
CAREER	2858	475	786	127	16	160	522	45	492	33	31	.275	.374	.499

On the other hand, the Braves are stuck with David Justice for about $13 million through 1998. He was placed on the 15-day DL May 16 with a badly dislocated right shoulder suffered while swinging at a pitch and he never came back. Apparently some teams are interested in Justice's services—and if there are takers, it's time to move him along. He's becoming injury-prone, and has always been one of the more inconsistent stars in the league—his average fluctuating from .250 to .300, his home runs from 20 to 40. He's one of several expendable Braves from the 1991 team—along with Avery, Blauser, and Lemke. From that '91 team, only Smoltz, Glavine, and Wohlers may be left by '97. ■

RYAN KLESKO — OVERRATED

OF • BL • TL • 6'3 • 220 • 25 • ATL89/6

	AB	R	H	2B	3B	HR	RBI	BB	SO	SB	CS	BA	OB	SA
ATL94	245	42	68	13	3	17	47	26	48	1	0	.278	.344	.563
ATL95	329	48	102	25	2	23	70	47	72	5	4	.310	.396	.608
ATL96	528	90	149	21	4	34	93	68	129	6	3	.282	.364	.530
CAREER	1133	183	325	60	9	76	216	144	258	12	7	.287	.367	.557

In the field, Klesko gets bad reads and bad jumps, he often mistimes his leaps, and he falls like a sack of potatoes when he dives for the ball. Among regulars, only Henry Rodriguez—another converted first baseman who can't hit lefties—has less range in left field. He's still young enough to develop into the elite player the Braves brass predicted him to be. At the plate, he's entering his prime right now, and if he's going to become an MVP candidate . . . well, to quote Bobby Bonilla, "Make your move." Klesko could begin by managing more than 6 extra-base hits against lefties, since few MVP candidates get

lifted in big situations in favor of a rookie who happens to stand on the other side of the plate. But don't bet on it. In the World Series, Klesko looked more like a deer in headlights than a franchise player. ▪

MARK LEMKE (see Free Agents)

JAVY LOPEZ — CONSISTENT STAR

C • BR • TR • 6′3 • 185 • 26 • ATL87

	AB	R	H	2B	3B	HR	RBI	BB	SO	SB	CS	BA	OB	SA
ATL94	277	27	68	9	0	13	35	17	61	0	2	.245	.299	.419
ATL95	333	37	105	11	4	14	51	14	57	0	1	.315	.344	.498
ATL96	489	56	138	19	1	23	69	28	84	1	6	.282	.322	.466
CAREER	1131	124	323	42	6	51	159	59	205	1	9	.286	.325	.469

Lopez: "I wish I could be more patient and take more walks, but I can't. Sometimes when I try to be more patient, I lose all my concentration because that's not me." That's too bad, because that's what's going to keep him from consistently hitting .300. As it is, he's rough around the edges, but not far from being among the elite. His game-calling is getting better—during the postseason, he actually got to see the field when Maddux was pitching. He's not smooth behind the plate, but he is improving. His arm is decent enough, but his throwing mechanics need to improve if he's going to throw out more than 30% of runners. If he continues to improve at the plate and in the field in '97, he can move past Santiago (yes, Santiago) on the N.L. catching food chain. ▪

GREG MADDUX — SUPERSTAR

SP • BR • TR • 6′0 • 175 • 30 • CHN84/2

	G	GS	IP	H	HR	BB	K	W	L	S	ERA	K/BB	K9	HW9
ATL94	25	25	202	150	4	31	156	16	6	0	1.56	5.0	7.0	8.06
ATL95	28	28	209	147	8	23	181	19	2	0	1.63	7.9	7.8	7.32
ATL96	35	35	245	225	11	28	172	15	11	0	2.72	6.1	6.3	9.29
CAREER	336	332	2365	2102	119	589	1643	165	104	0	2.86	2.8	6.3	10.24

Maddux had a "terrible year," finishing second to Kevin Brown *in the majors* in ERA. Maddux was distinctly superior to Glavine, for example, but no one said Glavine was having a terrible year. Smoltz and Brown were better than Maddux, but since when has it been a crime to be the third-best pitcher in

the league? Koufax's ERA fluctuated, too. In the table below are 4 Hall of Famers, plus the 2 best pitchers of this generation. Notice that Clemens and Maddux blow Steve Carlton and Bob Gibson away (it would be even more ugly if you adjusted for the DH, with The Rocket's ERA over this stretch closer to 2.35!).

Age	Seaver	Koufax	Clemens	Carlton	Gibson	Maddux
22	2.76	4.47	3.29	2.98	——	3.18
23	2.20	4.06	2.48	2.99	3.32	2.95
24	2.21	3.91	2.97	2.17	5.59	3.46
25	2.81	3.52	2.93	3.72	3.24	3.35
26	1.76	2.54	3.13	3.56	2.85	2.18
27	2.92	1.88	1.93	1.98	3.39	2.36
28	2.08	1.74	2.62	3.90	3.01	1.56
29	3.20	2.04	2.41	3.22	3.07	1.63
30	2.38	1.73	4.46	3.56	2.44	2.72
22-30	2.46	1.87	2.85	3.11	3.13	2.63

Maddux is the most consistent of the bunch. His repertoire doesn't resemble Koufax's, but his career sure has. Unless Maddux retires at 31, as Koufax had to, the N.L. pitcher of the '90s should offically eclipse Koufax as the N.L. pitcher of the 20th century in '97. He's a first-ballot Hall of Famer, 2.72 ERA and all. ▪

MARTY MALLOY — SLEEPER

2B • BL • TR • 5′10 • 160 • 24

	AB	R	H	2B	3B	HR	RBI	BB	SO	SB	CS	BA	OB	SA
AA	429	82	134	27	2	4	36	54	50	11	10	.312	.393	.413

Malloy is the subject of *The Heart of the Game* by Paul Hemphill—a book about the travails of a minor-leaguer. Travails and all, he's still a prospect. He's not going to be Joe Morgan, but he's a fine infielder. The Braves are swimming in a sea of these kinds of players. Malloy is reasonably young and deserves a shot, but he's not alone. ▪

FRED MCGRIFF — HEADED FOR A FALL

1B • BL • TL • 6′3 • 215 • 33 • NYA81/9

	AB	R	H	2B	3B	HR	RBI	BB	SO	SB	CS	BA	OB	SA
ATL94	424	81	135	25	1	34	94	50	76	7	3	.318	.389	.623
ATL95	528	85	148	27	1	27	93	65	99	3	6	.280	.361	.489
ATL96	617	81	182	37	1	28	107	68	116	7	3	.295	.365	.494
CAREER	5129	869	1466	266	18	317	910	812	1135	55	32	.286	.383	.530

McGriff has what Bill James used to call "old players' skills"—plate discipline and power. These

are what McGriff has always brought to the table, but James's thesis was that most good players improve these skills as they age (and as their speed and ability to hit for average diminish). It was also his thesis that players who have "young players' skills" last longer. That doesn't mean Willie Wilson will outlast Harmon Killebrew—it means Hank Aaron would last longer than Joe Adcock. In today's terms, bet the farm on Barry Bonds (who can do it all) playing into his 40s, if he wants to, but don't be so quick to put a buck on Ryan Klesko.

McGriff is still a good player, but he's past his prime. He disappeared in the second half of the season and should be looked at as a .270-28-100 player—when in the past, .290-35-115 was likely. He might have 450 career homers in him, but his shot at 500 is diminishing. The Braves have locked him in for big bucks and should consider trading him before the bottom falls out. If they are willing to go in-division, the Marlins might pony up to install McGriff at first to be Sheffield's big brother again. The two were inseparable in San Diego. ■

GREG MCMICHAEL

RP • BR • TR • 6'3 • 215 • 30 • CLE88/9

	G	GS	IP	H	HR	BB	K	W	L	S	ERA	K/BB	K9	HW9
ATL94	51	0	58	66	1	19	47	4	6	21	3.84	2.5	7.3	13.17
ATL95	67	0	80	64	8	32	74	7	2	2	2.79	2.3	8.3	10.80
ATL96	73	0	86	84	4	27	78	5	3	2	3.22	2.9	8.2	11.61
CAREER	265	0	317	282	16	107	288	18	14	44	2.90	2.7	8.2	11.04

McMichael was smashed in September (5.87 ERA and 17 hits allowed in 7.2 innings). If not for that month, his line would have been a 2.94 ERA in 79.2 innings with only 67 hits allowed. He's not unlike Doug Jones—a pitcher who didn't have great stuff but who was a top closer for a while. McMichael has a mediocre fastball and an excellent change-up, so he has to rely on deception. For most of the season it worked—except September and October. In Shea in '97, that won't matter so much. ■

WONDERFUL TERRIFIC MONDS

OF • BR • TR • 6'3 • 190 • 24 • ATL93/49

	AB	R	H	2B	3B	HR	RBI	BB	SO	SB	CS	BA	OB	SA
AA	110	17	33	9	1	2	14	9	17	7	3	.300	.350	.455

World B. Free's favorite ballplayer. His friends call him Wonder. ■

MIKE MORDECAI

UT • BR • TR • 5'11 • 175 • 29 • ATL89/7

	AB	R	H	2B	3B	HR	RBI	BB	SO	SB	CS	BA	OB	SA
ATL95	75	10	21	6	0	3	11	9	16	0	0	.280	.353	.480
ATL96	108	12	26	5	0	2	8	9	24	1	0	.241	.297	.343

Combine '95 and '96 and project it out to 550 at bats and you've got 15 dingers, 57 RBI, and a .257 batting average with 54 walks. Not bad, and a whole lot cheaper than what Lemke will cost. And in 20 games at second, he showed better hands and better range than Lemke. ■

DENNY NEAGLE

CONSISTENT STAR

SP • BL • TL • 6'4 • 200 • 28 • MIN89/3

	G	GS	IP	H	HR	BB	K	W	L	S	ERA	K/BB	K9	HW9
PIT94	24	24	137	135	18	49	122	9	10	0	5.12	2.5	8.0	12.09
PIT95	31	31	209	221	20	45	150	13	8	0	3.43	3.3	6.5	11.45
PIT/ATL96	33	33	220	226	26	48	149	16	9	0	3.52	3.1	6.1	11.20
CAREER	200	104	755	773	86	229	585	45	39	3	4.10	2.6	7.0	11.95

Neagle lives dangerously with his off-speed stuff, and hitters made him look good at times in '95, but he was deservedly an All-Star that year, and a strong '96 allayed fears that he'd flop. Ironically, it was Cox who snubbed him for the '96 game. Neagle was the lone stand-out on a weak Pirates staff and was as stingy with a walk as Greg Swindell was in his prime. Neagle has a deceptive three-quarters delivery, and former catcher Jason Kendall claimed that Neagle has three speeds on his excellent circle change, "his regular change-up . . . a slower one . . . and a slower one than that." He had Albert Belle yelling at him from the dugout in a spring training game to challenge the hitters, but he is more than content to be what Felipe Alou calls "master of the soft." He'll face most teams' 4th-best pitcher and receive Braves-size run support, so he could win 18 to 20 in '97. ■

TERRY PENDLETON (see Looking for a Game)

EDDIE PEREZ

C • BR • TR • 6′1 • 175 • 28 • ATL86

	AB	R	H	2B	3B	HR	RBI	BB	SO	SB	CS	BA	OB	SA
ATL96	156	19	40	9	1	4	17	8	19	0	0	.256	.293	.404

Perez has backup catcher written all over him. He threw a bit better than Lopez and seems to be more attuned to catching Maddux—though Perez needs to catch the entire staff, and not just Maddux, before his game-calling can be compared to Lopez's. Perez certainly won't disgrace the legacies of Charlie O'Brien and Greg Olson. ■

CARL SCHUTZ — SOLID PROSPECT

RP-SP • BL • TL • 5′11 • 200 • 25 • ATL93/3

	G	GS	IP	H	HR	BB	SO	W	L	S	ERA	K/BB	K9	HW9
AAA	41	7	70	86	4	26	52	4	3	3	5.3	2.0	6.7	14.47

Potentially, Schutz is a left-handed complement to Wohlers. Schutz throws in the 90s with a mid-80s slider. He could be the power arm that their bullpen desperately needs to get the games to Wohlers. ■

RANDALL SIMON — SOLID PROSPECT

1B • BL • TL • 6′0 • 180 • 21

	AB	R	H	2B	3B	HR	RBI	BB	SO	SB	CS	BA	OB	SA
AA	498	74	139	26	2	18	77	37	61	4	9	.279	.331	.448

One of the top defensive first basemen in the minors, Simon is considered to have excellent power potential by the Braves. Double-A Greenville's park really boosts power, but, nevertheless, he has a fine combination of youth and ability. Triple-A Richmond, where Simon will play in '97, is the diametric opposite of Greenville (the park cuts homers in half). If he does well there, he's ready for a job in Atlanta. ■

JOHN SMOLTZ — NL ELITE

SP • BR • TR • 6′3 • 210 • 29 • DET85/22

	G	GS	IP	H	HR	BB	K	W	L	S	ERA	K/BB	K9	HW9
ATL94	21	21	134	120	15	48	113	6	10	0	4.14	2.4	7.6	11.28
ATL95	29	29	192	166	15	72	193	12	7	0	3.18	2.7	9.0	11.16
ATL96	35	35	253	199	19	55	276	24	8	0	2.94	5.0	9.8	9.03
CAREER	266	266	1803	1545	150	627	1528	114	90	0	3.45	2.4	7.6	10.84

Many refuse to acknowledge how good this guy was *before* 1996. He had appeared in 3 All-Star games before last season, led the league in strikeouts in 1992, has been a consistent winner with good ERAs throughout his career, and has been dominant in the post-season. Smoltz used to be the unluckiest of Braves starters, getting mediocre run support and no-decisions in many of his quality starts each season, while hearing all about his unfulfilled potential. For example, in 1993 he went 15-11, but with normal run support he should have gone 17-9. Basically an entire career's worth of misfortune was negated with a single brilliant season. His career won-lost log is now an accurate summation of his career. If you want to place Smoltz's '96 season among the pantheon of great ones, a good comparison would be to Seaver in '69 and Gibson in '70.

Smoltz said in interviews that '96 was his first pain-free season since '91. He was urged to have elbow surgery each off-season, but never did. So he had the surgery and can now locate with control similar to that of Shane Reynolds. That's Seaver and Gibson: 200+ strikeouts and fewer than 2.50 walks per 9 innings. If he hadn't been tagged in some of his losses (see the essay on Brown and Smoltz in the Florida Marlins section), his ERA should have been in the 2.25-2.50 range. In '97, expect the victories to drop, since he can't expect to get enough run support to win 24 times again. Maddux had a lower ERA and went 15-11. ■

TERRELL WADE — YOUNG GUN

SP-RP • BL • TL • 6′3 • 205 • 24 • ATL91

	G	GS	IP	H	HR	BB	K	W	L	S	ERA	K/BB	K9	HW9
ATL96	44	8	69	57	9	47	79	5	0	1	2.97	1.7	10.3	13.55

Wade wrapped up a bullpen spot in the spring of '96 with a 0.79 ERA in 11.1 innings in March. He came to the majors and did the same things he did in the minors: He threw hard, the ball crossed the

plate half the time, and hitters couldn't handle anything they tried to lay a bat on. If the Braves can get him to throw strikes, he could be another Chuck Finley. He's a good fielder with a good change-up. If his curve gets more consistent, it could be very good, too. He's got a world of potential. ■

JUAN WILLIAMS

SLEEPER

OF • BL • TR • 6′0 • 180 • 24 • ATL90/18

	AB	R	H	2B	3B	HR	RBI	BB	SO	SB	CS	BA	OB	SA
AAA	357	55	97	22	2	15	52	51	127	5	4	.272	.361	.471

Williams will strike out like Rob Deer, but he's got good power and can draw walks. When teams are begging for a decent slugger in late July, they should be looking to pick up guys like this instead of trading top prospects for average hitters. The A's rolled the dice and came up a winner with Geronimo Berroa, and Williams could be a similar player if a team gave him 500 at-bats. ■

MARK WOHLERS

NL ELITE

CL • BR • TR • 6′4 • 205 • 27 • ATL88/10

	G	GS	IP	H	HR	BB	K	W	L	S	ERA	K/BB	K9	HW9
ATL94	51	0	51	51	1	33	58	7	2	1	4.59	1.8	10.2	14.82
ATL95	65	0	64	51	2	24	90	7	3	25	2.09	3.8	12.7	10.55
ATL96	77	0	77	71	8	21	100	2	4	39	3.03	4.8	11.7	10.75
CAREER	288	0	295	255	14	127	323	26	14	71	3.29	2.5	9.9	11.65

His best clocking is 103 mph. Last season Wohlers had problems throwing his slider—you know, that thing he threw to Leyritz in Game 4—and, because of this, was getting chewed up by right-handers. The split-finger he throws gives lefties fits, but it isn't that effective against right-handers. That is why his ERA rose dramatically last year. As amazing as it sounds, a pitcher can throw 103-mph strikes and still need another pitch. It took Wohlers about 4 years and that many trips on the Richmond shuttle to figure that out. If he gets the slider back this year, he'll be even better.

Wohlers hinted at being overworked a bit last year, and his inconsistent performance in September and October may have been a function of that. But 77 innings is not an outrageous number, considering that Todd Worrell threw 65 at 37, Robb Nen threw 83, and Trevor Hoffman 88. ■

BRAD WOODALL

SP-RP • BB • TL • 6′0 • 175 • 27 • ATL91

	G	GS	IP	H	HR	BB	K	W	L	S	ERA	K/BB	K9	HW9
ATL95	9	0	10	13	1	8	5	1	1	0	6.10	.6	4.5	18.90
ATL96	8	3	19	28	4	4	20	2	2	0	7.32	5.0	9.4	15.11

Woodall washed out in Atlanta again, only to retun to Richmond (where he's now made 68 career starts) and pitch effectively. He's now 3 years removed from his International League pitcher of the year honors and it's looking like he's more likely to join Derek Lilliquist, Armando Reynoso, Marty Clary, and Pete Smith on the missed-it-by-that-much team than he is of becoming the 5th Beatle with Maddux, Glavine, Smoltz, and Neagle. ■

A. J. ZAPP

1B • ATL96/1 • CENTER GROVE HIGH SCHOOL (IN)

	AB	R	H	2B	3B	HR	RBI	BB	SO	SB	CS	BA	OB	SA
R	161	9	24	9	0	0	5	15	58	0	0	.149	.225	.205

"Our guys to a man say he's the best high school hitter they've ever seen," Schuerholz said of Zapp. "I probably shouldn't say that because we haven't signed him yet." *Baseball America* rated him the best high-school power hitter in the '96 draft. He was horrid in the Gulf Coast League, but so was Chipper in 1990. Jones was brilliant at Class-A Macon the next year, so if Zapp is to show that kind of potential, he better be quick out of the gate. ■

■ 1996 AUTOPSY

A late-season resurgence in '95 and the return of Ryne Sandberg had Cub fans and Bud men believing the team was ready to compete in '96. A core of young pitchers returning from inconsistent seasons, a big hole in their bullpen with the departure of Randy Myers, and a weak offense had the front office downplaying their chances. Meanwhile, the Tribune Company rooted for good weather—which would have more impact on tickets sold and the team's bottom line than the success of the ballclub.

April 13-14 (13-14, tied for first)
The Cubs had to be glad to escape the month a game under .500 and still competing for the division lead. Steve Trachsel did all he could, with a 1.59 ERA spanning 3 starts, but the rest of the rotation was chucking and ducking. Kevin Foster and Jim Bullinger both had ERAs of more than 7.00. Offensively, they fared much better. Ryne Sandberg wasn't hitting for average, but he contributed 5 homers. Mark Grace was on fire, hitting .378 with 15 RBI and 18 runs scored. Sammy Sosa had 6 homers and 18 RBI. Even Scott Servais, usually a slow starter, got into the act, hitting .293 with 6 homers and 20 RBI. All this despite weather at the Friendly Confines that only Mike Ditka could love.

May 9-17 (22-31 4 games back)
Despite losing 6 of their first 10 games, including 5 in a row, the Cubs were still able to stay within a half-game of the division-leading Astros and Reds. Rather than capitalize on this good fortune, they grew more determined to fall out of the race—going 5-11 in their remaining 16 games. The Cubs didn't win a series all month. The best they could manage was a 4-game split against the Astros. A 9-17 record is exactly what happens when a team allows 31 more runs than it scores in only 26 games.

June 16-11 (38-42, 3 games back)
The rotation finally came alive in June. Steve Trachsel won 4 games and had an ERA of 1.59 for the month. Jaime Navarro was also very solid, winning 3 of his 5 starts with a 3.25 ERA. The pitching staff combined to post an ERA of 3.67, their best performance of the season. At the plate, Sammy Sosa continued to carry the club, driving in 22 runs with 10 homers. Sandberg, whose batting average was still well below his standards, had 19 RBI and scored 15 runs. The Cubs won more games in June than in any other month, but were still mired in third place behind the Astros and the Cardinals. Manager Jim Riggleman: "We're lucky to still be in it, but that doesn't make us happy. We can't count on the division staying this way. Someone's going to get hot, and I want it to be us." He was right. Someone did get hot. It just wasn't the Cubs.

July 14-12 (52-54, 4 games back)
The pitching staff returned to normal, which meant only 2 of the 5 starters clicking—and even Trachsel struggled, yielding a half dozen gopher balls over 2 starts. But the team hit .283, their best average all year. Even the bottom of the order started hitting, allowing Brian McRae to drive in 17 runs from the leadoff spot. But despite their best efforts, the Cubs were barely keeping pace with the division leaders. Their best opportunity came at mid-month when the Cardinals came to town and took 3 out of 4. The only solace the bleacher bums could take from the weekend was their ability to dump beer on Ray Lankford and Brian Jordan on consecutive fly balls to the warning track. But in the park where a fan charged the mound, the unprecedented is to be expected.

August 15-13 (67-67, 5½ games back)
The Cubs finally made it back to the .500 mark, a place they hadn't been since May 7. The starters were strong: Navarro (5-0, 2.14), Trachsel (2-1, 3.16), and Castillo (2-2, 3.00) all pitching well, with even Kevin Foster (3-0, 2.14) coming back from the minors to get into the act. But the bullpen, solid all season, started tiring out after lugging a heavy load the first half. Worse still, just when the offense was beginning to fire on all cylinders—Mark Grace hit .366, driving in 22; Brian McRae hit. 340 and scored 26 runs; Luis Gonzalez hit .305 with 19 RBI—the transmission fell out on the highway. On August 21, Sammy Sosa went down for the season with a broken hand. The collective sigh emitted by the Cubs' faithful almost blew the leaves off the ivy in Wrigley.

September 9-19 (76-86, 12 games back)
As expected, the loss of Sosa took all the starch out of the Cubs' pajamas. The offense scored just 111 runs in September, while the pitching staff expe-

rienced sympathy pains and gave up 151. The Cubs finished strong in '95. Just the opposite was true of '96, as they won just 2 of their final 16 games. The drought is at 88 years and counting.

■ 1997 DIAGNOSIS

Offense

The Cubs' offense last season was one of the worst in the league. They didn't hit for average and they didn't get on base. Because of this, they ranked 9th in runs scored despite finishing 4th in the league in homers. Their best players—Sosa, McRae, and Grace—will be back. But Gonzalez is a free agent and third base needs work, so the Cubs need to spend money, get lucky with rookies, and make some shrewd trades if they expect to significantly improve their offense. It will take all three for them to get to where they can do some damage in the playoffs.

Defense

In the A.L., the top 3 teams in fielding percentage made the playoffs (the Rangers, Yankees, and Orioles). In the N.L., the Cubs were the best, followed by the Marlins, with the Phillies percentage points behind the Padres. If you have an explanation for that, our e-mail address is scouting97@aol.com.

The Cubs have some sure-handed players, but most of their fielders lack range. At first, Grace is as good as it gets. He holds down his teammates' throwing errors with his ability to scoop wild throws—getting more than enough practice playing 8 years with Shawon Dunston. Sandberg has lost a step or two in the field, but he makes up for it by positioning himself intelligently. His 6 errors in more than 1,200 defensive innings shows that he hasn't lost his dependable hands. At third, Leo Gomez is harmless and Dave Magadan is a statue, but if either of them have the job next year the Cubs have bigger problems than defense. Rey Sanchez can field but can't hit; José Hernandez can hit but plays grounders as if they're live grenades. The outfield defense is also flawed. Gonzalez was decent, but is on the open market and Brooks Kieschnick will pale in comparison. McRae hustles, but he doesn't have much of an arm or outstanding range. Sosa has a terrific arm (15 assists) but makes too many mistakes showing it off (10 errors). Servais made 11 errors behind the plate, second only to Jason Kendall's 18. He threw out 29% of baserunners, which was about average, trailing Charles Johnson (48%), Kirt Manwaring (45%), Tom Pagnozzi (34%), Rick Wilkins (31%), and Benito Santiago (30%).

Pitching

The Cubs can only really count on Trachsel for '97. They cut the cord with Jaime Navarro, and no one else was very consistent. It looks like they'll be sifting through the wreckage in the spring to come up with a rotation. Kevin Foster, Frank Castillo, and Amaury Telemaco look to have the early advantage over Jim Bullinger, who bitched more aggressively than he pitched in '96.

The Cubs had one of the best bullpens in the National League last year. Their 3.60 ERA was bettered only by the Dodgers, the Expos, the Padres, and the Cardinals, all contending teams. Riggleman went with a bullpen-by-committee approach after the early-season demise of Doug Jones, with Turk Wendell, reluctantly, the closest he had to a go-to guy. All his relievers had to be prepared to pitch in any situation at any time, and for the most part his strategy was successful. Wendell, Terry Adams, and Bob Patterson got the saves last season. If Riggleman chooses one and only one to be The Man—and there's no guarantee he will—it will likely be Adams, because he throws harder. And because Wendell's flakiness gets on his nerves. Turk, it seems, was born more than a bit confused.

Farm System

The system is pretty deep in position prospects at the higher levels and power pitchers at the lower levels. Kevin Orie, a third baseman, is a great prospect, but he gets injured every time he gets out of bed. Brant Brown has a very potent bat but is stuck behind Grace. Pat Cline is a catching prospect who will push Servais soon. Doug Glanville has shown a pretty nice batting stroke at Triple-A Iowa, but he's behind Kieschnick and Robin Jennings. The prime pitching prospect in the organization is young flame thrower named Kerry Wood. Steve Rain is a closer prospect who will be in Triple-A in '97. Jayson Peterson and Todd Noel are also hard throwers, but they're a year or two behind Wood.

Management and Ownership

The Tribune Company owns the Cubs and is very bottom-line-conscious, well aware that they sell out Wrigley all summer whether the team is any good or not. The man making the baseball decisions for the corporation, and trying to wrestle some money out of it, is Andy MacPhail. He is best known for rebuilding the Minnesota Twins into a club that won 2 world championships. And now he's got the mother of all front office tasks: bringing the Cubs their first world championship since 1908.

Ed Lynch is a quiet general manager. He has to be. His predecessor, Larry Himes, was chased out of town by a mob of angry fans with burning torches. Lynch's key moves have included acquiring Servais and Gonzalez from the Astros for Rick Wilkins, prying Brian McRae away from the Royals for Derek Wallace, and picking up Jaime Navarro in the remainders and irregulars bin in the '95 free agent market. The fact that he isn't Larry Himes, coupled with his improvement of the club with these acquisitions, led to Sandberg coming out of retirement. For that alone, Cubs fans will cut him more than his share of slack.

Jim Riggleman has impressed the front office with his ability to communicate with the players. He clears the air without confrontation, and he always lets his ballplayers know what's on his mind. Last season, when Navarro and Castillo ripped him in the press for what they felt to be early hooks, Riggleman's response was even-tempered. Instead of blowing his stack, he sat down with both of them and worked it out together. (Not that he necessarily forgives and forgets. Navarro was petulant all season, and aggravating to manager and teammate alike, so the pitching-thin Cubs waved goodbye to him and his outrageous contract demands during the off-season.) When McRae came out at mid-season and said that the team simply didn't have enough talent to compete, Riggleman's only comment was that McRae was a team leader, respected in the clubhouse, entitled to his opinion, and that he wouldn't "muzzle" his players. Riggleman drew fire last season for not settling on a closer, but you can't argue with the results of his bullpen-by-committee. All in all, he did about as much as he could the past 2 years with teams that simply weren't very good.

. . . and whatnot: Come Back and Go Away

Some years baseball writers have to look so hard to find a comeback player, they end up giving the award to some guy who had to overcome little more than bad representation at the arbitration hearing the year before. In '96 there were more candidates than any time in recent memory, with everyone short of Joe Charboneau and Steve Blass resurrecting his career.

Ordinarily, the Cubs' Ryne Sandberg would have received the award as soon as he stepped on the field. But 1996 was not an ordinary year . . .

Eric Davis had been out of baseball the previous year but returned to hit 26-83-.287 with 23 steals on the rock-hard turf of Riverfront. He hadn't put up those kinds of numbers since 1990. In between, he lacerated his kidney in the final game of that World Series making a diving catch, and was left back in Oakland by Marge Schott to thumb his way home; fell asleep on the bench throughout 1991; returned to L.A. to reunite with Darryl, injure his shoulder, underachieve badly, and irritate Lasorda and the front office so thoroughly that they sent him to Detroit for something called a John DeSilva; in Detroit, he injured his neck, hit $1.83, and retired. No surprise that his comeback in spring training was greeted with a knowing smirk, a patronizing nod, and a "who's next, Chris Brown?" attitude.

Ellis Burks was healthy for a full season for only the 5th time in 10 seasons and the 1st time since 1993, and he put up numbers—even after the Coors fluff is removed—that dwarf the best he'd ever done. He nearly matched the 44 dingers, 147 RBI, and 16 SBs he'd put up in the prior 3 years combined.

If the Dodgers had managed to stumble into the World Series, perhaps Brett Butler could have returned from season-ending ailments twice in the same season. He fought and beat throat cancer, and nearly provided a courage injection in September to the most gutless team outside of Anaheim in the major leagues.

Granted, Ozzie Smith wasn't exactly a team player in 1996, and could be criticized for the most extended farewell since The Who—but he was written off after hitting .199 in 1995, yet hit .282 and contributed to a division-winning ballclub that only made the one mistake of waking the Braves up a game early.

Greg Vaughn had deteriorated to part-time play, managing 17 dingers and .224 with the lowly Brewers—and responded (in the last year of his contract, coincidentally) to hit 41 dingers and set himself up for big cash in 1997 and a Comeback Player award in 1998.

Since last pitching for the Dodgers in 1990, Fernando Valenzuela had bounced around from Palm Springs to Midland to Anaheim to Edmonton to Jalisco (Mexico) to Baltimore to Rochester to Bowie back to Jalisco to Philadelphia and finally San Diego. He was supposed to be little more than a gate attraction in San Diego, but he won 13 games for a pennant winner, including one of the most underrated pressure performances in recent history when he won the first major-league game played in his homeland.

Danny Tartabull managed 27 dingers and 102 RBI in 1994 and 1995 combined, but he put up 27 and 101 for the White Sox in '96. Paul Molitor had his worst season in '95 since he played 13 games for the '84 Brewers—then went on to set a career high in RBI with 113 and to match his career best in batting average at .341 and doubles with 41.

The Yankees alone had four candidates. Darryl Strawberry came back from the St. Paul Saints to hit 11 dingers and play inspired defense on a broken toe in the Series, while Dwight Gooden came back from exile to throw a no-hitter and win 11 games. David Cone had an aneurysm removed from his throwing arm in May—the condition could have been life- or career-threatening—and returned to pitch a 7-inning no-hitter in his first game back, snapping the Yankees out of a late-season funk, and then went on to outpitch Tom Glavine to get the Yankees off the deck in Game 3 of the World Series. Jimmy Key blew out his arm in 1994, but came back in 1996 at age 35 to win 12 games and win the World Series clincher against Greg Maddux.

Dave Hollins had managed 11 dingers, 52 RBI, and 5 trips to the DL in 1994 and 1995, but overcame the best indicator of being washed up—being traded for Mark Whiten—to knock in 78 runs for the Twins and Mariners. Dean Palmer came back from a torn bicep after 36 games in 1995 to hit 38 dingers and knock in 107 runs for the Rangers. Juan Guzman led the A.L. in ERA after going 4-14 with a 6.32 ERA in 1995.

Mark Gardner and Kevin Elster could also be offered for consideration—Gardner was picked off the scrap heap to go 12-7 for the Giants, while Elster was plugged into the Rangers' lineup out of desperation and hit 24 dingers and knocked in 99 runs—but it's not as if either of these guys had ever been there and gone in the first place.

Even if Sandberg didn't bring home the Comeback Player award, the Cubs have the Just Go Away award locked. The list of nominees begins with Tony Tarasco, who went from being the key player in a trade for Marquis Grissom, to going straight up for Sherman Obando and finding himself working on his attitude in the minors, recalled just in time to have a dinger taken away from him by a 12-year-old.

Kevin Mitchell wore out a couple of welcomes in a couple of months as the Red Sox finally realized there weren't enough incentives in the world to coax good ball out of him, and the Reds decided that not showing up for games was not a quality they were looking for in a player.

Andujar Cedeño was exiled to Detroit, couldn't even play his way into the lineup of the worst team in baseball, and somehow found his way back to Houston—the one organization that should know better—no doubt to work with Orlando Miller on flailing at first-pitch breaking balls.

The Astros finally cut their losses on Greg Swindell, yanking his snout out of the feedbag long enough to give him a bus ticket out of town after he took them for $16 million.

The A's finally gave up on the next Tom Seaver, Todd Van Poppel, right after his career year of 1995, when he went 4-8 with a 4.88 ERA.

Steve Howe finally used up all his baseball lives and was promptly nabbed at the airport with a Magnum in his luggage. Nice to know that someone with the self-control of an infant is packing a hand cannon.

And Mark Whiten was dumped by the team with one of the worst offenses in baseball, then dumped by the Braves after a pinch-hit, game-winning dinger.

But the Just Go Away award has to go to Doug Jones, who lost the closer's job in Chicago after 2 games—to a grown man who chain-sucks licorice and hops over foul lines. As always, Dojo landed on his feet, going 5-0 with the Brewers. What doesn't kill him, it seems, just makes him fatter, slower, and still tough to hit.

TERRY ADAMS

YOUNG GUN

RP • BR • TR • 6′3 • 180 • 24 • CHN91/3

	G	GS	IP	H	HR	BB	K	W	L	S	ERA	K/BB	K9	HW9
CHN95	18	0	18	22	0	10	15	1	1	1	6.50	1.5	7.5	16.00
CHN96	69	0	101	84	6	49	78	3	6	4	2.94	1.6	7.0	11.85

Adams was given passing consideration for the closer's role in the off-season, but the club chose instead to go with Doug Jones and, after his release, Turk Wendell, the biggest flake in a baseball dugout since Ted Turner tried to manage the Braves. It's not hard to see why the Cubs think Adams will make a good closer eventually. He's got the repertoire: a mid-90s heater, a hard slider, and a curve that's more for show. Adams stranded only about 67% of the runners he inherited and Riggleman will be looking to see him improve on that before he lets him close full-time. ■

KENT BOTTENFIELD

RP • BR • TR • 6′3 • 235 • 28

	G	GS	IP	H	HR	BB	K	W	L	S	ERA	K/BB	K9	HW9
CHN96	48	0	61	59	3	19	33	3	5	1	2.63	1.7	4.9	11.50

Bottenfield didn't blow anybody away pitching in the Cubs pen, but he was quietly effective last year after his recall from Des Moines. Bottenfield depends on having good control to succeed. Last season he did a good job of keeping the opposition off balance at the plate, but he has a tendency to get hit when he leaves the ball up in the strike zone. He was more effective his first time through the league. This, and his unimpressive performances with the Rockies and Expos a few years back (92 walks and 92 strikeouts in 218 innings), could spell a return to ineffectiveness for Bottenfield in '97. ■

BRANT BROWN

SOLID PROSPECT

1B • BL • TL • 6′3 • 220 • 25 • CHN92/2

	AB	R	H	2B	3B	HR	RBI	BB	SO	SB	CS	BA	OB	SA
CHN96	69	11	21	1	0	5	9	2	17	3	3	.304	.329	.536

Brown is considered a Mark Grace clone, but he has a lot more meat on his bones. He got a chance to fill in when Grace went on the DL earlier in the season, and hit .372 with 4 homers in his brief stay. That didn't keep the Cubs from signing Grace to a long-term deal at the end of the season.

Brown is a fantastic fielder. He has good hands, a good arm and can turn the 3-6-3 double play smoothly. Managers in the American Association liked his play so much, they voted him the league's best defensive first baseman. But he could be forced to make a switch to the outfield, packaged in a trade, or available in the expansion draft this time next year. ■

SCOTT BULLETT

OF • BB • TL • 6′2 • 200 • 28 • PIT88

	AB	R	H	2B	3B	HR	RBI	BB	SO	SB	CS	BA	OB	SA
CHN95	150	19	41	5	7	3	22	12	30	8	3	.273	.331	.460
CHN96	165	26	35	5	0	3	16	10	54	7	3	.212	.256	.297

Bullett is one of the fastest players on the team, has good range and an average arm, but can't hit enough to play every day. He continues to be used as the team's primary pinch hitter despite the fact that his strike-zone judgment isn't very good. If it weren't for the fact that he hit .440 in 18 June games, Bullett's season would have looked even worse than it did. ■

JIM BULLINGER

SP-RP • BR • TR • 6′2 • 185 • 31 • CHN86/9

	G	GS	IP	H	HR	BB	K	W	L	S	ERA	K/BB	K9	HW9
CHN94	33	10	100	87	6	34	72	6	2	2	3.60	2.1	6.5	10.89
CHN95	24	24	150	152	14	65	93	12	8	0	4.14	1.4	5.6	13.02
CHN96	37	20	129	144	15	68	90	6	10	1	6.54	1.3	6.3	14.79
CAREER	148	63	480	473	45	230	301	27	28	11	4.78	1.3	5.6	13.18

"Ears" can't blame his results on Wrigley Field: He had a 5.40 ERA at home and a 7.64 ERA everywhere else last year. He doesn't have any pitch that is considered excellent. He throws a heavy, sinking fastball that tops out at about 86–87 mph. His breaking ball is a little above average, and his change-up is decent. He also doesn't have good command of his pitches *in* the strike zone. Last year his ineffectiveness as a starter forced him to make 17 appearances out of the bullpen. He may end up there permanently, though he went there kicking and screaming. He's a converted shortstop, but his past 3 seasons make it

look like he's done all the learning he's going to do—and that he's moving into the un-learning phase. ■

EARL BYRNE

RP-SP • BL • TL • 6'1 • 165 • 24

	G	GS	IP	H	HR	BB	SO	W	L	S	ERA	K/BB	K9	HW9
AA	11	6	37	36	5	26	30	1	2	0	5.59	1.2	7.3	15.08

Byrne's a left-handed Aussie with pretty good strikeout totals the past few seasons. But at 24, he was a little old for the Florida State League, and he was rocked after his promotion to Double-A Orlando. He also needs quite a bit of work on his control before he can be considered a good prospect. But success is imitated—so every team in baseball will probably try to be like the Yankees and find a future closer to be their setup man; a fat, bald, veteran baseball man to join at the hip with their manager; and a left-handed Aussie out of the bullpen to make Ryan Klesko look like a little leaguer. Unfortunately, most teams' only similarity to the champs will end up being a rich, white, male owner who embarrasses himself whenever he tries to talk baseball in public. ■

LARRY CASIAN

RP • BR • TL • 6'0 • 170 • 31 • MIN87/6

	G	GS	IP	H	HR	BB	K	W	L	S	ERA	K/BB	K9	HW9
CLE/MIN94	40	0	49	73	12	16	20	1	5	1	7.35	1.3	3.7	16.35
CHN95	42	0	23	23	1	15	11	1	0	0	1.93	.7	4.3	14.87
CHN96	35	0	24	14	2	11	15	1	1	0	1.88	1.4	5.6	9.38
CAREER	197	3	200	230	22	68	96	11	10	2	4.23	1.4	4.3	13.41

If Casian weren't left-handed, he would probably be working for a living by now. He has to sneak his fastball past hitters in the dead of night, and his breaking ball has as much bite as a hockey defenseman without his bridge. His best pitch is a change-up, and that's not much better than average. The Cubs have used him very judiciously the past couple of seasons, usually bringing him in for just a batter or two at a time. Casian responded in 1996 with the best season of his career, but he's pitching on borrowed time. You'll never again see ERAs that low from a pitcher who has walked 26 and struck out 26 in 47 innings. ■

FRANK CASTILLO

SP • BR • TR • 6'1 • 180 • 28 • CHN87/5

	G	GS	IP	H	HR	BB	K	W	L	S	ERA	K/BB	K9	HW9
CHI94	4	4	23	25	3	5	19	2	1	0	4.30	3.8	7.4	11.74
CHN95	29	29	188	179	22	52	135	11	10	0	3.21	2.6	6.5	11.06
CHN96	33	33	182	209	28	46	139	7	16	0	5.28	3.0	6.9	12.61
CAREER	146	142	851	861	97	238	585	41	53	0	4.17	2.5	6.2	11.62

Castillo led the Cubs staff in ERA in 1995, but you wouldn't have guessed it by the season he had last year. He used to be obsessed with making the perfect pitch all the time. In '95, it was *just be the ball* as he learned to let go and not worry about making mistakes. After '96, he may need to start worrying a little more.

Castillo throws a solid sinking fastball and a very nice change-up. He also has good control. But he gives up hits like Bob Tewksbury on a bad day, and pitching in Wrigley Field, that can be dangerous to do without a batting practice screen. Last season the opposition hit .288 off Castillo, slugging .471 in the process. Right-handers, in their excitement, were meeting his offerings halfway to the plate—hitting .303 and slugging .517 off him.

Considering how easily the league hit Castillo, he must have assumed hitting wasn't all that difficult. He criticized the Cubs offense for a lack of production after losing to the Astros 8-3 August 16. As it was, only William Vanlandingham, Kevin Jarvis, and Mark Thompson won more games with an ERA as high as Castillo's. This is like Pat Buchanan complaining about intolerance. ■

PAT CLINE

GRADE-A PROSPECT

C • BR • TR • 6'3 • 220 • 22 • CHN93/7

	AB	R	H	2B	3B	HR	RBI	BB	SO	SB	CS	BA	OB	SA
A+	434	75	121	30	2	17	76	54	79	10	2	.279	.373	.475

The best-looking catching prospect in the system, Cline offers an offensive package that is already pretty refined. He hits for good average, and his size gives him tremendous power. Considered the best hitter in the Florida State League, Cline was known last season for launching tape-measure home runs to all fields. His 17 round-trippers set a Daytona Cubs record. Defensively, Cline's best tool is a strong arm.

Like so many young catchers, though, he needs work on the rest—most notably calling a game. But he has an excellent work ethic and has picked up everything they have tried to teach him so far. Cline missed the '94 season with a broken wrist, but from all indications the missed time hasn't hurt him that much. The Cubs think he has the durability and talent to catch 100+ games a year in the majors—and there isn't much in his way. ■

JAIRO DIAZ

RP-SP • BR • TR • 6'2 • 200 • 21

	G	GS	IP	H	HR	BB	SO	W	L	S	ERA	K/BB	K9	HW9
A	25	11	88	80	6	26	84	6	3	0	3.16	3.2	8.6	10.80

Diaz spent time as both a starter and a reliever last season, but the confusion over his role hasn't seemed to have hurt him at all. He has shown the Cubs a pretty good command of the strike zone the past couple of seasons while striking out a batter per inning. He was promoted to the Florida State League last season after his strong performance for Rockford. If he continues to do well at Class-A Daytona, he'll start showing up in Chicago's Top 10 lists. ■

DEE DOWLER

OF • BR • TR • 5'9 • 175 • 25

	AB	R	H	2B	3B	HR	RBI	BB	SO	SB	CS	BA	OB	SA
AA	352	59	98	15	6	6	47	47	42	25	5	.278	.366	.406

Demetrius Dowler is an outfield prospect who tore up the Florida State League for 47 at-bats before his promotion to Double-A Orlando. He can hit for a decent average and has good plate discipline and pretty good speed. But there are 3 knocks against him. At 24, he was a little old for his competition last year. His size limits his potential to hit for power—Jimmy Wynn and Joe Morgan notwithstanding. And finally, there are better outfield prospects in the system already. Unless he starts stealing 60 bases a year, Dowler will find it very difficult to get the Cubs' attention when he raises his hand in class. ■

KEVIN FOSTER

SP • BR • TR • 6'1 • 160 • 28 • MON87/31

	G	GS	IP	H	HR	BB	K	W	L	S	ERA	K/BB	K9	HW9
CHN94	13	13	81	70	7	35	75	3	4	0	2.89	2.1	8.3	11.67
CHN95	30	28	167	149	32	65	146	12	11	0	4.51	2.2	7.9	11.53
CHN96	17	16	87	98	16	35	53	7	6	0	6.21	1.5	5.5	13.76
CAREER	62	58	342	330	58	142	280	22	22	0	4.76	2.0	7.4	12.42

It wasn't looking good for Foster in the early going last season. He was crushed for 11 home runs and had a 7.65 ERA in his first 8 starts—making him a favorite of the Wrigleyville natives who gather with their lawn chairs, baseball mitts, and coolers on Waveland Avenue and wait for Foster's offerings to come back down through the clouds. If the opposition can make it all the way out there, the bleacher bums don't scream at you to throw it back.

There's really nothing wrong with Foster's stuff. He throws a live fastball and a good curve. His fastball is of the 4-seam variety, but when he misses with it, it stays high in the strike zone and gets pounded. He also throws everything hard and doesn't change speeds well at all. Better command and an off-speed pitch could make all the difference. Even though he's 28 years old, he's a lot younger in pitching years, as he was converted to the mound as a third baseman. A lot of the troubles he experienced last season are common to pitchers making the jump from Double-A to Triple-A. Unfortunately, Foster was getting some on-the-job training and his learning experiences showed up on *SportsCenter*. ■

DOUG GLANVILLE

OF • BR • TR • 6'2 • 170 • 26 • CHN91/1

	AB	R	H	2B	3B	HR	RBI	BB	SO	SB	CS	BA	OB	SA
CHN95	83	10	20	5	1	1	10	3	11	2	0	.241	.264	.361

The Cubs thought Glanville really turned his fortunes around in '95 after a MVP-type season in the Puerto Rican winter league. But then someone who prefers to remain nameless (and blameless) gave him the kiss of death, saying of his performance: "He played like Kenny Lofton." Glanville drew comparisons to Eric Davis after his selection in the 1st round of the '91 draft, mainly because of his excellent athletic ability. But his ability hasn't

translated to success at the plate, as he lacks power and plate discipline. His biggest strength has always been his smooth defensive skills. With Gonzalez a free agent, Glanville may be competing with Kieschnick and Jennings for the left field job. He's not likely to beat out Kieschnick—a more recent 1st round pick—but his defensive skills and intelligence (he was an Academic All-American and holds an engineering degree) may be enough to keep him around. ■

LEO GOMEZ

3B • BR • TR • 6′0 • 180 • 31 • BAL85

	AB	R	H	2B	3B	HR	RBI	BB	SO	SB	CS	BA	OB	SA
BAL94	285	46	78	20	0	15	56	41	55	0	0	.274	.366	.502
BAL95	127	16	30	5	0	4	12	18	23	0	1	.236	.336	.370
CHN96	362	44	86	19	0	17	56	53	94	1	4	.238	.344	.431
CAREER	1916	241	466	92	2	79	259	255	399	4	10	.243	.336	.417

Gomez couldn't hit enough to keep the third-base job in Baltimore, and he wasn't supposed to be the starter in '97 for the Cubs either. But then Magadan went down with a hand injury in the spring, and Riggleman had little choice but to give the position to Gomez. Given a chance, Gomez hit .261 and slugged .491 in the first half, enough to keep the position even after Magadan returned. But he's pulled disappearing acts before, and 14-for-86 (.163) over the final couple of months was yet another. It established third base as a question mark in Wrigley yet again—as it's been since Ron Cey waddled off into the sunset, leaving his turf to be manned by Keith Moreland, Vance Law, Manny Trillo, Wade Rowdon, Domingo Ramos, Luis Salazar, Curtis Wilkerson, Chico Walker, José Vizcaino, Gary Scott, Steve Buechele, Doug Strange, Eric Yelding, Eddie Zambrano, Todd Zeile, José Hernandez, Howard Johnson, Magadan, Gomez, and Tyler Houston over the past 10 years. If the Cubs don't make a significant effort to land a big-time bat to play third base and beef up their offense during the '97 off-season, they're not committed to winning.

Gomez has enough power to play the position. He also has the patience to force a pitcher to throw him a fastball. But when he gets one, more often than not he turns it into a lazy fly ball or a 6-4-3 instead of driving it. The only advantage he has over Magadan is his defense, but if the Cubs are deciding between these two again in '97, they're in trouble. Lynch might start taking Hojo's calls. ■

LUIS GONZALEZ (see Free Agents)

MARK GRACE

CONSISTENT STAR

1B • BL • TL • 6′2 • 190 • 32 • CHN85/25

	AB	R	H	2B	3B	HR	RBI	BB	SO	SB	CS	BA	OB	SA
CHN94	403	55	120	23	3	6	44	48	41	0	1	.298	.370	.414
CHN95	552	97	180	51	3	16	92	65	46	6	2	.326	.395	.516
CHN96	547	88	181	39	1	9	75	62	41	2	3	.331	.396	.455
CAREER	4903	696	1514	300	29	91	664	587	388	57	31	.309	.381	.437

Grace has always been criticized for lacking the type of power customary at first base, but his ability to hit for average and get on base more than offsets his scant home-run totals. Grace is one of the best contact hitters in the game. He can catch up to the best fastball, but he has enough balance to stay back on the best curves. He is also a very smart hitter. He studies the way a pitcher works him and adjusts to the patterns. To get him out, pitchers have to mix up their pitches and keep him guessing. If you throw him the same set of pitches twice in a game, Grace will make you pay. Well, more accurately, he'll slap a double down the left field line and Sammy will make you pay.

On defense, he's a Gold Glover. An agile fielder, he saves his team countless throwing errors with his unparalleled ability to scoop throws in the dirt. The Cubs signed Grace to a 3-year deal that will probably ensure that he plays his entire career in the same uniform—and signaled to another team leader and potential free agent, Brian McRae, that they were willing to do what it takes to win. Now about that third baseman . . . ■

TODD HANEY

2B • BR • TR • 5′9 • 165 • 31

	AB	R	H	2B	3B	HR	RBI	BB	SO	SB	CS	BA	OB	SA
CHN95	73	11	30	8	0	2	6	7	11	0	0	.411	.463	.603
CHN96	82	11	11	1	0	0	3	7	15	1	0	.134	.200	.146
CAREER	202	28	50	10	0	3	12	17	29	3	1	.248	.306	.342

Check his batting averages the past 2 seasons; '96 was what the finance guys call a "market correction." ■

JASON HART

RP • BR • TR • 6'0 • 195 • 25 • CHN93

	G	GS	IP	H	HR	BB	SO	W	L	S	ERA	K/BB	K9	HW9
AA	51	0	73	59	11	28	78	3	5	4	3.21	2.8	9.6	10.73

A closer for Class-A Daytona in '95, the Cubs made him a setup man when they promoted him to Double-A Orlando last season. Hart has good control and a nasty slider . But the Cubs think his complementary stuff is mediocre, so he probably won't be a solution for the major-league closer problem. He'll get a chance to show his stuff in Des Moines this year. If he pitches well, he's a good candidate for a September call-up. ■

JOSÉ HERNANDEZ

SS-3B • BR • TR • 6'1 • 180 • 27 • TEX87

	AB	R	H	2B	3B	HR	RBI	BB	SO	SB	CS	BA	OB	SA
CHN94	132	18	32	2	3	1	9	8	29	2	2	.242	.291	.326
CHN95	245	37	60	11	4	13	40	13	69	1	0	.245	.281	.482
CHN96	331	52	80	14	1	10	41	24	97	4	0	.242	.293	.381
CAREER	810	115	190	29	9	24	94	48	228	7	3	.235	.278	.381

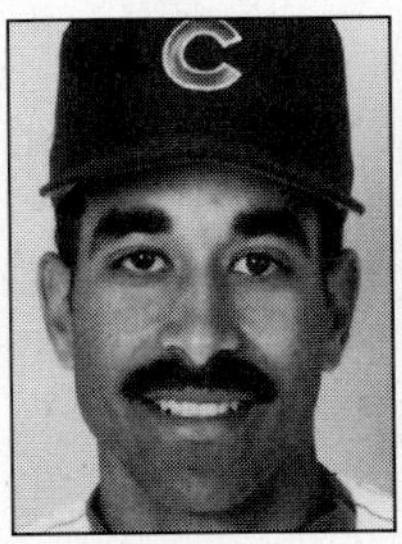

Hernandez was the recipient of more playing time the past couple of years due more to what happened to teammates—Ryno retiring and Rey Sanchez being disabled twice—than anything he'd done. He brings more power to the plate than most utility infielders—swinging hard in case the ball hits the bat—but he misses as many balls with his glove as he does his bat. He can find his way out to second, short, and third base when needed and he knows more or less where to stand, but don't expect much more than that. ■

TYLER HOUSTON

C-3B • BL • TR • 6'2 • 210 • 26 • ATL89/1

	AB	R	H	2B	3B	HR	RBI	BB	SO	SB	CS	BA	OB	SA
ATL/CHN96	142	21	45	9	1	3	27	9	27	3	0	.317	.358	.458

Houston was the 2nd pick in the nation back in '89 and played 7 seasons in the Braves organization. They finally gave up on him last season, dealing him to the Cubbies in June for minor-league pitcher Ismael Villegas. Riggleman, who wasn't quite sure what type of player he was getting, was quickly impressed with Houston's performance at third base. Houston's versatility suits him well, as he doesn't have a great chance of landing a full-time job with the club. Riggleman likes to have him around because he's a left-handed bat with a little power. The Cubs squeezed every bit of offensive potential out of him last year and he'll be hard-pressed to repeat the performance in '97. He never hit more than .279 in the minors, and spent most of his time in the .240s. ■

ELINTON JASCO

2B • BR • TR • 5'10 • 150 • 21 • CHN93

	AB	R	H	2B	3B	HR	RBI	BB	SO	SB	CS	BA	OB	SA
A	464	95	136	11	7	1	43	62	97	48	14	.293	.381	.353

Jasco comes from that great shortstop factory, San Pedro De Macoris in the Dominican Republic, but he was converted to second base shortly after beginning his pro career. Last season he flashed a potent bat and tore up Midwest League basepaths with his outstanding speed. Managers considered him the fastest baserunner in the league. He projects as a top-of-the-order hitter because he draws a lot of walks and can hit for a high average. He is a few years off, but his star is on the rise. ■

ROBIN JENNINGS

SLEEPER

OF • BL • TL • 6'2 • 200 • 24 • CHN91/33

	AB	R	H	2B	3B	HR	RBI	BB	SO	SB	CS	BA	OB	SA
CHN96	58	7	13	5	0	0	4	3	9	1	0	.224	.274	.310

Jennings's career was on the verge of stalling out in '94, so he bulked up in the off-season and posted a very fine season in '95 at Double-A Orlando, hitting .296 and slugging .484. He blew the scouts away in the Arizona Fall League that year and opened the '96 season at Triple-A Iowa. He slugged .528 there and received a promotion to the majors when Sosa went on the DL, but managed to hit only .224 in limited playing time.

Jennings is solid on defense. His arm is outstanding, and he has decent range in right. At the plate he has good power but needs to refine his batting eye. He's easy pickings for pitchers with good breaking stuff. He also has trouble hitting lefties. If there weren't such a glut of outfielders at the major-league level, Jennings would have a good chance to win a job in '97. But Kieschnick is higher on the food chain, so Jennings's best hope may be Arizona or Tampa Bay.

BROOKS KIESCHNICK GRADE-A PROSPECT

OF • BL • TR • 6'4 • 225 • 24 • CHN93/1

	AB	R	H	2B	3B	HR	RBI	BB	SO	SB	CS	BA	OB	SA
AAA	441	47	114	20	1	18	64	37	108	0	1	.259	.315	.431

Kieschnick has rocketed through the system mainly because of his advanced offensive skills. The sum of his experience below the Double-A level? All of 31 at-bats. He probably would have been given the left-field job in '96 had Luis Gonzalez not re-signed with the Cubs. He played most of the season in Des Moines, getting a call-up in late August when Sammy Sosa went down.

Kieschnick has a quick left-handed swing that can produce prodigious home runs. His bat speed allows him time to recognize the breaking ball without being blown away by the fastball. Because of this, he's become known for using the whole field, the mark of a good hitter. He strikes out a lot, about once every 4 at-bats last year in Des Moines, but as he matures as a hitter, that should diminish somewhat. He hit .260 against righties, .255 against lefties, and went deep at the same rate; there's no reason to assume he'll be a platoon player in the majors.

He's no defensive whiz, but Kieschnick has improved his range slightly the past couple of seasons. His main defensive weapon, though, is a strong, accurate throwing arm. After all, he used to be a part-time reliever in college. His defense is of secondary concern. The Cubs are determined to find a spot for his bat in the lineup, because they think he has 30-homer potential in the big leagues. He will get a chance to show that potential in '97. ■

DAVE MAGADAN (see Free Agents)

BRIAN MCRAE NL ELITE

CF • BB • TR • 6'0 • 175 • 29 • KC85/1

	AB	R	H	2B	3B	HR	RBI	BB	SO	SB	CS	BA	OB	SA
KC94	436	71	119	22	6	4	40	54	67	28	8	.273	.359	.378
CHN95	580	92	167	38	7	12	48	47	92	27	8	.288	.348	.440
CHN96	624	111	172	32	5	17	66	73	84	37	9	.276	.360	.425
CAREER	3597	522	966	179	44	59	362	286	564	157	58	.269	.327	.392

McRae has always maintained that he is not a leadoff hitter, but it hasn't kept him from doing his

best to adjust his game to the role. Last season he reached career highs in walks, on-base average, runs scored, and stolen bases. He might not consider himself a leadoff man, but he gets on base, advances himself, and scores runs. He does everything required and then some, adding a bit of power to the role and playing good defense.

What the Cubs like most about McRae, though, is his leadership skills. He's the most aggressive player on the team, both in the field and at the plate. Riggleman: "He plays hard all the time. He doesn't know any other way. He doesn't take at-bats off, and he doesn't jog to first. He's a model for anyone to watch."

Hard to understand why the Cubs would hesitate to lock him up long term, but they finally gave him a 3-year deal in October. Some contenders might have been willing to give him even more money and an extra year, but the opportunity to play in Wrigley and help drag the Cubbies into the playoffs is one of the most attractive in baseball at any price. ■

BOBBY MORRIS

1B • BL • TR • 6'0 • 180 • 24

	AB	R	H	2B	3B	HR	RBI	BB	SO	SB	CS	BA	OB	SA
AA	465	72	122	29	3	8	62	65	73	12	14	.262	.355	.389

He's Hal Morris's younger brother and it shows.They are both left-handed hitters with an excellent batting eye and the ability to pile up base hits in large quantities. Until '96, however, they played different positions. The Cubs found Bobby's defense at second base lacking, so they moved him to first base. He can continue the parallels this spring by charging the mound against José Mesa and getting dropped on his head.

Morris doesn't have a lot of power. In fact, it's virtually nonexistent. His brother made it to the majors as a first baseman with little power, but he didn't have Mark Grace playing in front of him. It was Todd Benzinger in his way. His chances aren't good, especially with Brant Brown also blocking the passing lane.

RODNEY MYERS

	G	GS	IP	H	HR	BB	K	W	L	S	ERA	K/BB	K9	HW9
CHN96	45	0	67	61	6	38	50	2	1	0	4.68	1.3	6.7	13.29

The Cubs released one Myers and signed another. Rodney Myers was a Kansas City farmhand until '96, but he was overshadowed by another player in the system with the same name. The Cubs took a chance on him because he pitches low in the strike zone and generates ground-ball outs. He throws a fastball in the low 90s and complements it with a slider and a circle change.

Often a reliever gets his ERA bent out of shape due to a few ineffective innings in which he gets left out to die. Such was the case last year with Myers. He gave up 10 earned runs in 7 September innings. Once factored out of his pitching line, Myers is left with a respectable 3.72 ERA for the season. But he'll have to improve his control quite a bit if he wants to pitch more significant innings in the future. ■

JAIME NAVARRO (see Free Agents)

TODD NOEL

RHP • CHN96/1 • N. VERMILLION HIGH SCHOOL (LA)

For 3 straight years now, the Cubs have taken a high school fireballer with their initial pick in the draft. (See Adam Eaton of the Philadelphia Phillies for more perspective on the wisdom of this strategy.) Noel is a tall, skinny right-hander who throws 95. His breaking ball is mediocre and his change-up needs a lot of work. But scouts just love his mechanics—he has a smooth, effortless delivery and a loose arm. He's 18, so he's got about 10 years to work on the rest of the stuff.

KEVIN ORIE

GRADE-A PROSPECT

3B • BR • TR • 6'4 • 215 • 24 • CHN93/1

	AB	R	H	2B	3B	HR	RBI	BB	SO	SB	CS	BA	OB	SA
AA	296	42	93	25	0	8	58	48	52	2	0	.314	.403	.480

How's this for spin? True, the Cubs lost Greg Maddux after the '92 season and he went on to win 70 games, 3 Cy Young Awards, hold the league to 2.11 earned runs a game, and walk about as many batters in 4 years as Al Leiter does in a season. But, hey, they used their 1st-round amateur draft compensation pick to snag Kevin Orie. This would be like the Dodgers being pumped about dealing Sandy Koufax for Mike Shannon before the '64 season.

To be fair, Orie is a power-hitting third baseman with excellent bat speed and a smooth swing. He was derailed by torn cartilage in his right wrist in '94, an injury that required surgery to correct. He came back strong in '95 but required surgery on his left wrist after the season. Unfazed, Orie started out at Double-A Orlando in '96, where he hit .314 and slugged .480. He impressed managers enough that they named him the best-hitting prospect in the league in a midseason survey. He was promoted to Triple-A Iowa at the All-Star break, but got in only 48 at-bats before a right-shoulder injury shut him down for the season in late July. He suffered the injury diving for a ball.

Orie is the Cubs' best third-base prospect, and he'll get a chance to prove it in a full season at Triple-A this year. He could end the rotating third-base problem as soon as 1998. He's got a brand-new pair of wrists now, so if he can avoid breaking his neck somewhere along the way, he could be a player.

It is unlikely, however, that he will ever string together 4 of the greatest seasons in baseball history at his position. And, with the Cubs luck, he'll play in Scott Rolen's shadow his entire career—a third-base prospect still on the board when Chicago took Orie. ■

BOB PATTERSON

RP • BR • TL • 6'2 • 195 • 37 • SD82/21

	G	GS	IP	H	HR	BB	K	W	L	S	ERA	K/BB	K9	HW9
CAL94	47	0	42	35	6	15	30	2	3	1	4.07	2.0	6.4	10.71
CAL95	62	0	53	48	6	13	41	5	2	0	3.04	3.2	7.0	10.36
CHN95	79	0	54	46	6	22	53	3	3	8	3.13	2.4	8.8	11.32
CAREER	450	21	537	536	59	158	408	37	33	27	4.04	2.6	6.8	11.63

The Cubs liked his work enough to offer him arbitration after the '96 season. Patterson is a left-handed reliever who came over from the Angels. Pulling his Methuselah act, he contributed one solid outing after another and helped turn the Cubs' pen into one of the best in the National League. Patterson doesn't throw hard at all, but he throws a pretty good curve and screwball combo, and he can throw them for strikes anytime in the count. He makes his living bewildering hitters with stuff that couldn't squash a grape. ■

JAYSON PETERSON

SLEEPER

SP • BB • TR • 6′4 • 185 • 21 • CHN94/1

	G	GS	IP	H	HR	BB	SO	W	L	S	ERA	K/BB	K9	HW9
A	15	15	94	82	8	39	87	4	7	0	3.45	2.2	8.3	11.59

Peterson hasn't done much since the Cubs took him in the 1st round in '94. In fact, going into last season the team was beginning to question his dedication to the game. He's suffered from shoulder problems in the past as well. He really needs to put together a strong season to get back in the organization's plans. ■

STEVE RAIN

SOLID PROSPECT

RP • BR • TR • 6′6 • 225 • 21 • CHN93/12

	G	GS	IP	H	HR	BB	SO	W	L	S	ERA	K/BB	K9	HW9
AAA	26	0	26	17	3	8	23	2	1	10	3.12	2.9	8.0	8.65

Despite his size, Rain has rather mediocre velocity. His fastball tops out at 87–88 mph, but he still sends hitters back to the dugout muttering under their breath because he has excellent movement on his heater and complements it with a good slider, a change-up, and a split-finger pitch. His splitter is his out pitch. He also has pinpoint control. The Cubs have been grooming him as a closer the past couple of seasons, and he has dominated in every league since his move to the bullpen. Last season he made it to Triple-A Iowa, and it looks like he will at least start the season there. If he continues to shine, he could get a call-up by midseason. ■

REY SANCHEZ

SS • BR • TR • 5′10 • 180 • 29 • TEX86/13

	AB	R	H	2B	3B	HR	RBI	BB	SO	SB	CS	BA	OB	SA
CHN94	291	26	83	13	1	0	24	20	29	2	5	.285	.345	.337
CHN95	428	57	119	22	2	3	27	14	48	6	4	.278	.301	.360
CHN96	289	28	61	9	0	1	12	22	42	7	1	.211	.272	.253
CAREER	1630	171	430	69	8	5	112	85	161	18	12	.264	.306	.325

It looked for a while that the return of Sandberg would bump Sanchez from the starting lineup. But then the Cubs let Dunston go—rumor had it that this was a condition of Sandberg's return—and gave him the shortstop job. Sanchez was poised for a good year because, in his words, ". . . I have no pressure on me for the first time in my career because there's no one ready to take my job." Sanchez suffered a hand injury during the first week of the season but tried to play through it because he didn't want surgery. He finally went on the DL in June. He returned in late July but lasted only a couple of weeks before he had to make another trip to the DL when the soreness returned.

Sanchez is a very good fielder, so his switch to shortstop wasn't a surprise. He's really quick, with hands of glue, and his footwork is excellent. And while it may not be apparent with his slap-hitting style, Sanchez does have value at the plate. He may not hit screaming line drives, but he's pretty good at putting the bat on the ball and moving runners over. Riggleman doesn't hesitate putting the hit-and-run on with Sanchez at the plate. With a full winter of rehab, Sanchez should be healthy this season. He will be the starting shortstop again and should hit in the .280 range. ■

RYNE SANDBERG (see Free Agents)

SCOTT SERVAIS

C • BR • TR • 6′2 • 195 • 29 • HOU88/4

	AB	R	H	2B	3B	HR	RBI	BB	SO	SB	CS	BA	OB	SA
HOU94	251	27	49	15	1	9	41	10	44	0	0	.195	.235	.371
HOU/CHN95	264	38	70	22	0	13	47	32	52	2	2	.265	.348	.496
CHN96	445	42	118	20	0	11	63	30	75	0	2	.265	.327	.384
CAREER	1460	143	355	80	1	44	204	109	249	2	4	.243	.306	.390

Servais hit .293 with 6 home runs and 20 RBI in April, feeding false hopes that the offensive strides he made in '95 were for real. But 29-year-old hitters rarely improve that much, and he hit .259 with just 5 homers the rest of the season, and his numbers weren't much better than what he did in 180 fewer at bats in '95. He bats from a distinct crouch at the plate to generate bat speed, but it leaves him with a swing as long as the day is big . . . or something like that. He can pound a pitcher's mistake, but he's much too impatient to be a consistent slugger. Servais is a decent receiver. He works well with pitchers and blocks pitches in the dirt with the best of them. He's not an All-Star, but he's a solid catcher to have around. He'll do more than keep the position warm until Pat Cline is ready. ■

SAMMY SOSA — NL ELITE

RF • BR • TR • 6′0 • 195 • 28 • TEX85

	AB	R	H	2B	3B	HR	RBI	BB	SO	SB	CS	BA	OB	SA
CHN94	426	59	128	17	6	25	70	25	92	22	13	.300	.339	.545
CHN95	564	89	151	17	3	36	119	58	134	34	7	.268	.340	.500
CHN96	498	84	136	21	2	40	100	34	134	18	5	.273	.323	.564
CAREER	3379	503	874	131	29	171	523	232	853	177	70	.259	.310	.466

The Rangers packaged both Sosa and Wilson Alvarez in a deal for Harold Baines at the trading deadline in '89 rather than let the A's get him—only to watch the A's get N.L. batting champ Willie McGee and leave them 16 games back. Baines gave the Rangers 153 games, 16 dingers, and 60 RBI before the Rangers dealt him (to the A's, of course) for Joe Bitker and Scott Chiamparino. Combine those two transactions and you may have the worst trade in baseball history.

Sosa was left off the All-Star roster in favor of Henry Rodriguez. It wasn't the first, last, or biggest mistake Bobby Cox made in 1996, just another one to make you scratch your head and ask yourself how this man even manages to find his way to the ballpark every day. Before Sosa broke his hand in August, he was on pace to hit 52 homers and drive in 130 runs with no protection in the order. Like a lot of power hitters, Sosa is a great low-ball hitter. He can turn a fastball on his shoe-tops into a 450-foot shot in a heartbeat. But his aggressive swing leaves him vulnerable to the high strike and breaking balls. It's scary to think what he could do if he were a little more selective at the plate.

A lot of people assume that his hitting is based purely on natural ability. While he does have a sweet swing, Sosa is also a very hard worker, often taking batting practice twice or three times a day. In his workouts, Sosa uses a bat that is weighted 4 ounces heavier than his 32-ounce game model and balls that weigh 7 ounces, rather than the 6 ounce regulation variety. If he gets any stronger, he may start using a telephone pole and bowling balls. ■

AMAURY TELEMACO — SLEEPER

SP • BR • TR • 6′3 • 180 • 23 • CHN91

	G	GS	IP	H	HR	BB	K	W	L	S	ERA	K/BB	K9	HW9
CHN96	25	17	97	108	20	31	64	5	7	0	5.46	2.1	5.9	12.89

Telemaco put the league on notice in his first start of the season, limiting the Astros to 1 hit in 7 innings

May 16 and earning not one but *two* stupid Berman nicknames for his trouble. He won 2 of his first 3 starts and had a 2.41 ERA going into June. But then rookie inconsistency took over, followed by a trip to the disabled list in August with a strained right shoulder. When healthy, Telemaco throws a 90-mph fastball with good movement, an improving slider, and a change-up. His season may have looked like a step backward, but he's a fine young pitcher and the Cubs think highly of him. ■

OZZIE TIMMONS

OF • BR • TR • 6′2 • 205 • 26 • CHN91/4

	AB	R	H	2B	3B	HR	RBI	BB	SO	SB	CS	BA	OB	SA
CHN95	171	30	45	10	1	8	28	13	32	3	0	.263	.314	.474
CHN96	140	18	28	4	0	7	16	15	30	1	0	.200	.282	.379

At one time Timmons was the best power hitter in the Cubs' minor-league system. But two factors have emerged recently that have severely limited his options. First, his plate discipline has diminished greatly since his promotion to Triple-A in '95. Second, he has shown an inability to hit right-handed pitching. While at Triple-A Iowa last season, Timmons worked on his batting stance. He started squatting a bit lower to enable him to see the low strike better and reach the outside of the plate at the same time. The Cubs have yet to see the results. Unfortunately, it doesn't look like he'll be able to get the playing time he needs to stretch out. That's a catch-22 that spells Diamondbacks in '98. ■

STEVE TRACHSEL — YOUNG GUN

SP • BR • TR • 6′3 • 185 • 26 • CHN91/7

	G	GS	IP	H	HR	BB	K	W	L	S	ERA	K/BB	K9	HW9
CHN94	22	22	146	133	19	54	108	9	7	0	3.21	2.0	6.7	11.53
CHN95	30	29	160	174	25	76	117	7	13	0	5.15	1.5	6.6	14.06
CHN96	31	31	205	181	30	62	132	13	9	0	3.03	2.1	5.8	10.67
CAREER	86	85	531	504	78	195	371	29	31	0	3.78	1.9	6.3	11.85

What did it take for people to start realizing that Steve Trachsel was a winner? It took a winning home record, that's what. It's unfair, but folks were saying that his 3-16 home record was caused by a

mental block and that a trade from Chicago was the only answer. Trachsel responded with a 9-5, 2.58 ERA performance at Wrigley in '96.

Trachsel has the stuff of a very dependable starter. While he doesn't have an overpowering fastball, it has decent movement and he can put it where Servais puts his glove. He also has a decent forkball and a solid slider. His durability allows him to eat innings, and he doesn't lose his cool in pressure situations.

Trachsel has been living with comparisons to Greg Maddux since his first call-up. But it's not a bad bet that the next young pitching phenom to come to Chicago will be called the next Steve Trachsel. ■

PEDRO VALDES

OF • BL • TL • 6'1 • 180 • 23 • CHN90/13

	AB	R	H	2B	3B	HR	RBI	BB	SO	SB	CS	BA	OB	SA
AAA	397	61	117	23	0	15	60	31	57	2	0	.295	.343	.466

Valdes had a fine season in Triple-A, leading his team in hits despite being only 23 years old and competing against much older players. He has a really sweet swing that turns heads. The only thing he needs now is experience. But by the time he gets it, Kieschnick might be a fixture in the Cubs lineup. ■

TURK WENDELL

RP • BB • TR • 6'2 • 180 • 29 • ATL88/7

	G	GS	IP	H	HR	BB	K	W	L	S	ERA	K/BB	K9	HW9
CHN94	6	2	14	22	3	10	9	0	1	0	11.93	.9	5.8	20.52
CHN95	43	0	60	71	11	24	50	3	1	0	4.92	2.1	7.5	14.25
CHN96	70	0	79	58	8	44	75	4	5	18	2.84	1.7	8.5	11.62
CAREER	126	6	176	175	22	86	149	8	9	18	4.50	1.7	7.6	13.34

Other than the fact that he's a full blown nutjob, Wendell is a pretty solid pitcher. Mark Fidrych—whom Wendell is frequently compared to—was goofy, fun-loving, and refused to take himself seriously. Turk . . . well, there comes a point, even for celebrities, where it's no longer "eccentricity" and it's just plain Michael Jackson, Howard Hughes weirdness. Not sure whether that line got crossed with the foul-line-hopping, the obsessive toothbrushing, or his licorice jones, but he's out there where the buses don't run.

Wendell throws the 4 main pitches: fastball, curve, slider, and change. All are about average, though the slider has good bite—he just needs to be more consistent with it. Like most pitchers who can't throw 95, he also needs to keep the ball down to be successful. Wendell served as the closer much of last season, even though Riggleman denied giving the job to anyone and didn't always seem too thrilled to have him around—at one point saying, "Let's face it. Turk's not John Wetteland." True. And Riggleman's not Tony LaRussa. Play the cards you're dealt. Weird or not, Wendell was the best he had out there in '96. Look for him to be used, reluctantly, in save situations in '97. But if he blows a few early, Riggleman won't hesitate to bury him deeper than Doug Jones and Mike Perez. ■

KERRY WOOD

GRADE-A PROSPECT

SP • BR • TR • 6'5 • 190 • 19 • CHN95/1

	G	GS	IP	H	HR	BB	SO	W	L	S	ERA	K/BB	K9	HW9
A+	22	22	114	72	6	70	136	10	2	0	2.91	1.9	10.7	11.18

Wood was considered the best high school arm in the '95 draft, and the Cubs took him with their 1st round pick. He's from Texas, and high schools in that area of the nation have a nasty habit of working their pitchers to death. In fact, shortly before the draft, Wood was called on to throw in both ends of a doubleheader, putting about 200 pitches on his arm that day.

Wood has an excellent repertoire. His fastball was clocked at 98 after he signed, but has leveled off at 93–95 mph. He also has a knee-buckling curve that he can throw for strikes on any count. He dominated the full-season Florida State League at age 18 and was named the best pitching prospect there despite missing some time with a sore elbow. He was mowing down hitters just a short step away from Double-A, a year removed from a point in his life when the most important thing on his mind was who to take to the prom. ■

■ 1996 AUTOPSY

The Reds had won the Central Division in '95, but they returned with a much different team. The off-season shuffle left observers figuring them to finish in the middle of the pack. The most significant change was the arrival of rookie manager Ray Knight. He was considered a fierce competitor and popular with players, but how that would translate to winning was unclear. Ron Gant had left via free agency, as had David Wells and Benito Santiago. Eric Davis was attempting a comeback in the outfield, but no one expected much from him.

April 9-16 (9-16, 3 games back)
The Reds' opener ended tragically 2 minutes into the game when umpire John McSherry collapsed on the field. He was pronounced dead an hour later of "sudden cardiac death." Marge Schott, already condemned for the comments she made in the spring about Hitler, made matters worse by wondering out loud how this could happen to "her." When the season finally did start, the rotation looked shaky and the defense, which had led the league in fielding percentage in '95, committed 17 errors, leading to 22 unearned runs in the first 18 games. Then the club followed that up by dropping the next 8 games. Knight tried 24 different lineups in 24 games, desperate to find the right combination.

May 10-12 (19-28, 4 games back)
Beginning on May 3, the Reds went on a 7-game winning streak that seemed to right the club. But then they dumped the next seven. This set a precedent for a strange season of streaky play. It also left them on the 21st with a 19-24 start, their worst in 10 years. Knight took the losses hard and blamed himself. He offered to resign, but GM Jim Bowden didn't even consider it—not publicly anyway. Nonetheless, Bowden assured the club that changes would be made if the losing continued. On the brighter side, Eric Davis was beginning a sensational comeback. For the month, he hit .370 with 8 home runs and 25 RBI.

June 17-11 (36-39, 2½ games back)
Eric Davis, Reggie Sanders, and Eric Anthony all began the month with injuries, leaving the Reds without any power. But the pitching staff picked up the slack and finished the month with a 7-game winning streak. But the main story of the month was the earthshaking "decisions" arrived at in Cincinnati. Early in the month, Schott invited the team up to her office to vote on changing their mascot from a cow to a gorilla named "Slugger." They took the gorilla. They also voted on whether or not the broadcast team could keep a bust of Elvis in the booth. They voted him out, creating a media sensation. More significantly, Major League Baseball decided to suspend Schott from the operations of her team because of her racist comments. John Allen was named to run the Reds as the "interim CEO."

July 16-12 (52-51, 2½ games back)
Just when the club had started winning, they had to put Willie Greene, Hal Morris and Pete Schourek on the disabled list, all on the same day. Marge Schott sent a threatening memo to her employees assuring them that she was not going to disappear from team operations, as the Lords of Baseball had demanded. When this hit the papers, she got in more trouble. The Lords responded by banning her from Riverfront Stadium and its offices. Approaching the trade deadline, the Reds made a run at Bobby Bonilla. The deal fell through when Orioles owner Peter Angelos decided not to throw in the towel and anger his season-ticketholders. They did, however, acquire Kevin Mitchell from the Red Sox just before the deadline.

August 15-17 (67-68, 6 games back)
On the field, the pitching staff went through its worst slump since April. The offense, reinforced with Mitchell, responded with 44 home runs and scored 157 runs, their highest output of the year. But it wasn't enough, and the club began to slip out of the race for the division. Off the field, where the Reds' saga was much more entertaining, Jim Bowden threatened to X-ray everybody's bats. This was in response to Chris Sabo's suspension for using a corked bat, even though he claimed it was Hal Morris's. Kevin Mitchell, having recently learned a great deal of new medical terminology, suggested they give the bats MRIs as well. Schott, who was not supposed to be talking to the media, told a Denver radio station that the government should "con-

centrate on crack, dope, knives and guns" instead of smoking. "If I had a child, not that you want kids to smoke, I think rather than drugs, I'd rather see them smoke," she said. "We smoked a peace pipe with the Indians, right?"

September 14-13 (81-81, 7 games back)
The Reds opened the month attempting to honor their history by retiring Johnny Bench's jersey. They scheduled the event for September 1, the same day as the Bengals' season opener. A "crowd" of 25,521 were on hand to applaud the greatest catcher in baseball history. The same month, the club allowed Riverfront Stadium to be renamed for a small fee. With their playoff hopes still alive, the club rolled into Los Angeles to start a critical West Coast road trip. They played an error-filled series and were swept. Knight: "I feel like my legs and my back and my neck are broken. This was a must-win game for us. We had a chance to get back within 5 games. We're running out of time." The Reds went 1-8 on the road trip. They were without Reggie Sanders, who had been injured and was out for the season, and Kevin Mitchell, who decided to go on vacation.

■ 1997 DIAGNOSIS

Offense
Despite all the injuries, the Reds had one of the most potent offenses in the N.L. last season. They scored 778 runs, second only to the Rockies. Adjusting for park effects, they were third, behind the Braves and the Astros. Their .256 batting average was good for only 10th in the league, but they made up the difference with 191 home runs.

But there are an awful lot of question marks heading into '97. Can Eric Davis repeat his remarkable year? Or will he even be back? Hal Morris and Barry Larkin also had career years they may be hard-pressed to duplicate. On the other hand, Bret Boone and Reggie Sanders should be better this year. Willie Green and Curtis Goodwin will also play a bigger role. All in all, it is unlikely that the offense will be as potent—if for no other reason than the presence of "village idiot" Ruben Sierra, whom the Tigers will pay nearly $5 million this year just to be rid of him.

Defense
After leading the N.L. in fielding percentage in '95, the defense got off to a rough start but eventually climbed back to the middle of the pack. Barry Larkin had a subpar year, by his standards. Bret Boone was outstanding once again, leading all second basemen in fielding percentage. Hal Morris is a good first baseman, but Jeff Branson played erratically at third and Willie Greene was much worse, making 15 errors in a half-season's worth of work, arguably the worst performance of any third baseman in baseball in '96. Scarier still, it didn't come as a surprise. The outfield performed well—even converted infielder Eric Owens—despite chaotic shuffling all year. Eric Davis wasn't just back at the plate. His fielding wasn't what it once was, but was still very good. Joe Oliver was solid behind the plate and Ed Taubansee showed improvement after a slow start.

Pitching
Taking park effects into account, the Reds' pitching staff was one of the least effective in the league last year. But considering the injuries the starting rotation endured, it was remarkable that they did as well as they did. The starters finished with a 4.55 ERA, the 9th lowest in the league. They pitched 922 innings, the 12th highest total. And their 6 complete games tied them for 10th. José Rijo was out all year. Pete Schourek, their ace, pitched hurt in the first half of the season and missed the second half. John Smiley was pretty steady, but the remainder of the staff struggled because of nagging injuries. Other than Smiley, evidently one of only a trio of untouchables on the team—along with Barry Larkin and Jeff Brantley—the rotation is uncertain going into '97. Mark Portugal has been bought out, Schourek may not be back, and Rijo's rehabbing was not going well at the end of '96. Behind Smiley, that's a recipe for a Dave-Burba-Mike-Morgan-and-two-peanut-vendors-with-command kind of staff.

The Reds' bullpen was a mixed bag. Their 3.96 ERA was the 9th best in the league, but they led the league with 52 saves, building on Jeff Brantley's 44. There isn't much help down on the farm, and nothing to indicate that the bullpen won't be as uneven in '97.

Farm System

The Reds have skimped on their farm system to save money, and it has begun to show. Most noticeably, they decided to drop Princeton, West Virginia, depriving themselves of one of their rookie league teams. They have refused to pay for top amateur prospects and their scouting staff is extremely thin. They've also become one of the last teams to establish a significant international presence. There is some talent in the organization, but most of the prospects are marginal and not close to the majors. With the exceptions of Pokey Reese, Chad Mottola, Steve Gibralter, and Curt Lyons, the farm system will not be able to help the club in the near future.

Management and Ownership

The exploits of owner Marge Schott are legendary, as is her penchant for the timely quote. Her miserly ways have not helped the team compete, and her decision to limit promotions and amenities for the fans have not helped her attendance. Doing so would, of course, give her more capital to work with—but how to explain that to someone who thinks Hitler had some good short-term ideas?

Interim CEO John Allen has turned things around a great deal. A marketing man, he has done little things that should make a difference. Now the Reds have promotions honoring players, rather than Schottzie 02. Now the players have a working whirlpool and don't have to buy their own equipment. Now the stadium displays retired jerseys and championship banners. No surprise that Schott wanted him ousted after only a few weeks at the helm.

GM Jim Bowden is severely hamstrung in almost every area of his responsibilities by the budget he has to work with. Who knows what he could do if he could make a trade without having to convince the other team to pay 90% of the player's salary? To judge him under these circumstances is like trying to get an accurate gauge of a surfer's abilities in Siberia.

Ray Knight had a lot to contend with from day one last year. Injuries were a major problem, as was the media circus that swirled around Cincinnati all season. He held the team together to finish at .500, and that was probably better than they should have done. He's an intense competitor and that may have rubbed off on the team, but it also caused him to appear inconsistent and jumpy as he continually juggled lineups—and to irritate fellow managers who saw him as too much of a cheerleader. The players would also like him to be less forthcoming with the press on their struggles. But he didn't live with his wife before he married her, which is why Marge got rid of Davey Johnson and gave him the job. Kurt Stillwell was nicer to her dog in 1988 than Barry Larkin, but she didn't get her way that time.

. . . and whatnot: Schott in the Dark

Those who believe that baseball is just a business don't understand how the sport could ban Marge Schott for exercising her right to free speech. Reminds you of Scorpio in *Dirty Harry*, wailing, "What about my *riiiiights*?" on the 50-yard line of that empty football stadium. There's not enough sympathy to go around in this world. There sure isn't any to spare for Marge Schott. Frankly, railroading her out of the game was one of the few positive things the baseball establishment has done in recent years.

Some claim she is like so many others in her generation, born in a time when people were free to say whatever they liked as long as it didn't injure another individual. Then again, those nostalgic for those times in America conveniently forget that lynching was bigger down South back then than stock car racing—in part because racist attitudes were tolerated throughout the country.

Some argue that personal injury means a damage to reputation or financial consideration, rather than damaging the collective consciousness of an identification group. Then again, most people who make that argument are white males. So when a group of 27 of the most out-of-touch, rich, white males in the country works together to toss a hate-filled embarrassment like Marge over the side . . . well, it almost makes you proud to be an American.

Was she denied her due process? Sure. So were more than a few African-Americans. Check the racial breakdown on executions sometime—especially those for the crime of rape. Did she commit a crime? No. Neither did the Native Americans. Nice to know the tomahawk chops both ways. Are you afraid that what happened to her puts your own freedoms at risk? Perhaps it does—if you're in the public eye and wish to share your fetish for Nazi armbands with the viewers of *SportsCenter*, that is.

Plenty of lawyers could argue that what was done to Marge was illegal, but that's why they're lawyers. This isn't about laws, it's about what's right. Taking Marge out back and shooting her was a rare indication that there is some hope that maybe we all—most of us, anyway—*can* just get along. The owners didn't use "the best interests of baseball" to justify themselves, but they could have. If we can't agree that Marge Schott has no right to a leadership position in a government-protected monopoly that still, at some level, exists to reinforce what we'd like to believe are our country's values—everyone gets to bat, people judged by how they perform, and a big bucket of money waiting at the end of the rainbow—then maybe there is no common ground after all.

Marge, in her own dimwitted and blundering way, may prove to be a unifying force—someone whose words people of any race, color, creed, or sex can be disgusted by.

PAUL BAKO — SLEEPER

C • BL • TR • 6′2 • 205 • 24

	AB	R	H	2B	3B	HR	RBI	BB	SO	SB	CS	BA	OB	SA
AA	360	53	106	27	0	8	48	48	93	1	0	.294	.381	.436

Bako is a fine defensive catching prospect, but his bat wasn't always impressive. His power has really developed, especially to the gaps. His average isn't bad for a catcher either. The Reds have a few catching prospects, and Bako could get caught in a logjam, but he's got the most complete package and could be the survivor. ■

TIM BELK — SLEEPER

1B • BR • TR • 6′3 • 200 • 26 • CIN92/16

	AB	R	H	2B	3B	HR	RBI	BB	SO	SB	CS	BA	OB	SA
AAA	436	63	125	27	3	15	63	27	72	5	2	.287	.327	.466

Belk is a first baseman in the mold of Hal Morris, and has often been compared to him. He's a very good contact hitter, but without the power expected from major-league first basemen. He's also an outstanding fielder. Last year his average dropped, but he belted a career-high 16 homers so the power may be coming around. Actually, it's kind of amazing that he can stand in there at all. In May '95 he was hit by a pitch in his face, breaking his left cheekbone and eye socket. He had to have plates inserted under and along the lateral wall of his eye orbit. Unbelievably, he returned by late July and finished the season. ■

AARON BOONE — SOLID PROSPECT

3B • BR • TR • 6′2 • 190 • 24 • CIN94/3

	AB	R	H	2B	3B	HR	RBI	BB	SO	SB	CS	BA	OB	SA
AA	548	86	158	44	7	17	95	38	77	21	10	.288	.338	.487

Boone answered a lot of questions about his offensive potential last year. After a successful run through the Arizona Fall League, he returned with renewed confidence. Double-A Chattanooga's Engel Stadium is a pitcher's park that doesn't allow many homers, but he smacked 17 there. More impressively, he hit 44 doubles. He set career highs in several categories, including batting average and RBI, and led the team in 6 categories. As you'd expect, given his gene pool, he's excellent with the glove. If he can maintain his offensive production, it isn't too much of a stretch to picture a couple of Boones in Cincinnati's infield within a couple of years. ■

BRET BOONE

2B • BR • TR • 5′10 • 180 • 27 • SEA90/5

	AB	R	H	2B	3B	HR	RBI	BB	SO	SB	CS	BA	OB	SA
CIN94	381	59	122	25	2	12	68	24	74	3	4	.320	.368	.491
CIN95	513	63	137	34	2	15	68	41	84	5	1	.267	.326	.429
CIN96	520	56	121	21	3	12	69	31	100	3	2	.233	.275	.354
CAREER	1814	224	473	96	9	55	258	117	344	14	11	.261	.310	.415

Boone's offensive production has been steadily declining since his tremendous '94 season. Ray Knight thinks he's overswinging. "He's just trying to hit the ball too hard. He's always had a big man's mentality, thinking he's going to hit 20 home runs. What he's going to do is hit .223 with no production if he continues to swing that way." But Boone is an outstanding defensive second baseman. He had elbow problems early in the season and couldn't throw, but still turned in a terrific season with the glove. He led the league in fielding percentage at second base for the second straight year, but he was again edged out by Craig Biggio for the Gold Glove. The award is supposed to be for defense, but the only thing Biggio does better than Boone is hit and run. ■

JEFF BRANSON

3B • BL • TR • 6'0 • 180 • 30 • CIN88/1

	AB	R	H	2B	3B	HR	RBI	BB	SO	SB	CS	BA	OB	SA
CIN94	109	18	31	4	1	6	16	5	16	0	0	.284	.316	.505
CIN95	331	43	86	18	2	12	45	44	69	2	1	.260	.345	.435
CIN96	311	34	76	16	4	9	37	31	67	2	0	.244	.312	.408
CAREER	1247	147	319	60	9	30	135	104	241	8	3	.256	.311	.391

Branson saw most of his time at third last year in a bizarre, two-lefty platoon with Willie Greene. Branson also spelled Larkin at short and filled in at second. He's solid defensively, but he had a subpar season at the plate for the second straight year. The Reds would like to see Greene take over permanently at third if he can improve his defense, which would leave less innings for Branson this year. But he's still a versatile backup and valuable to the club. ■

JEFF BRANTLEY

CONSISTENT STAR

CL • BR • TR • 5'11 • 180 • 33 • SF85/6

	G	GS	IP	H	HR	BB	K	W	L	S	ERA	K/BB	K9	HW9
CIN94	50	0	65	46	6	28	63	6	6	15	2.48	2.3	8.7	10.24
CIN95	56	0	70	53	11	20	62	3	2	28	2.82	3.1	8.0	9.39
CIN96	66	0	71	54	7	28	76	1	2	44	2.41	2.7	9.6	10.39
CAREER	471	18	712	610	74	295	585	39	30	129	3.05	2.0	7.4	11.44

Brantley broke John Franco's club record for saves (39), set in 1988, and tied Todd Worrell for the league lead. He saved 44 in only 49 opportunities, for a 90% success rate. The Reds rewarded him for 3 years of quality work with a new contract for 3 more, at $2.8 million per year. And when Brantley won the Rolaids Relief Man Award, he took some satisfaction in reminding his former team, the Giants, that he was probably the only man to win the award who had been released. Actually, as is discussed in José Mesa's write-up, most closers still playing haven't taken the job until they've left their first organization. Brantley can talk trash, but the Reds can't. They had Buddy Bell and Van Snider to show for Jeff Russell, Jeff Montgomery, and Trevor Hoffman—and they had John Wetteland for 16 days before trading him for Willie Greene. ■

RAY BROWN

1B • BL • TR • 6'2 • 205 • 24 • CIN94/28

	AB	R	H	2B	3B	HR	RBI	BB	SO	SB	CS	BA	OB	SA
AA	364	68	119	26	5	13	52	52	62	2	1	.327	.412	.533

Of all the Reds' first-base prospects, Brown has the best power. In fact, he's the best hitter. Last season was a nice comeback after a lackluster '95 in Class-A Winston-Salem. His problem is his defense. He's not a very good fielder and has poor range. Still, if he can hit .327 with power in Triple-A Indianapolis, the Reds may overlook his glovework. ■

DAVE BURBA

SP • BR • TR • 6'4 • 220 • 30 • SEA87/2

	G	GS	IP	H	HR	BB	K	W	L	S	ERA	K/BB	K9	HW9
SF94	57	0	74	59	5	45	84	3	6	0	4.38	1.9	10.2	12.65
SF/CIN95	52	9	106	90	9	51	96	10	4	0	3.97	1.9	8.2	11.97
CIN96	34	33	195	179	18	97	148	11	13	0	3.83	1.5	6.8	12.74
CAREER	248	60	586	545	56	277	483	38	35	1	4.13	1.7	7.4	12.62

Several of Cincinnati's hurlers struggled during the early part of the season, which contributed to the club's slow start. Burba was one of them, and he felt compelled to apologize to his new manager. Knight: "He said, 'I'm sorry, I'm not carrying my load.' He was getting frustrated, but he'll never go through a worse streak than he just has." Knight was speaking in mid-June, just after Burba had recorded his first victory of the season. Through June 15, he was 0-8 with a 4.58 ERA. The club considered trading him but wasn't sure anyone would bite. Then he went 5-1 in his next 8 starts, including a 4-0 July with a 2.06 ERA. In the second half he went 8-4 with a 3.57 ERA. He won 9 of 10 games in 1995 after May, as well. Think the Giants would have more use for him now than that defensive back on the Cowboys they gave him up to get? ■

HECTOR CARRASCO

RP • BR • TR • 6'2 • 175 • 27 • NYN88

	G	GS	IP	H	HR	BB	K	W	L	S	ERA	K/BB	K9	HW9
CIN94	45	0	56	42	3	30	41	5	6	6	2.24	1.4	6.6	11.56
CIN95	64	0	87	86	1	46	64	2	7	5	4.12	1.4	6.6	13.66
CIN96	56	0	74	58	6	45	59	4	3	0	3.75	1.3	7.2	12.52
CAREER	165	0	217	186	10	121	164	11	16	11	3.52	1.4	6.8	12.73

Carrasco was disappointing in April after a fine year in '95. In 6 appearances he allowed 17 baserunners in 7.1 innings and had an 8.59 ERA. He was sent down to Indianapolis, then returned in May and rattled off 2 months' worth of excellent work. In his next 17 games he pitched 23.2 innings with a 1.52 ERA and 21 strikeouts. He no longer looks like he'll be a closer in the near future, as the Reds once hoped, but he is an effective member of the bullpen. ■

ERIC DAVIS (see Free Agents)

BROOK FORDYCE

C • BR • TR • 6'1 • 185 • 26

	AB	R	H	2B	3B	HR	RBI	BB	SO	SB	CS	BA	OB	SA
AAA	374	48	103	20	3	16	64	25	56	2	1	.275	.319	.473

Fordyce spent 6 years in the Mets' system before signing with the Reds as a free agent last season. He was a steady riser for the Mets and reached the bigs briefly in '95. He showed fine power at Triple A Indianapolis and hit for his best average since 1992. The Reds were quite pleased with his development. He's also very good defensively, and that could be the edge he needs to break into the lineup in Cincinnati. Look for him to make the roster out of spring training. ■

STEVE GIBRALTER

OF • BR • TR • 6'0 • 190 • 24 • CIN90/6

	AB	R	H	2B	3B	HR	RBI	BB	SO	SB	CS	BA	OB	SA
AAA	447	58	114	29	2	11	54	26	114	2	3	.255	.297	.403

Gibralter had a breakthrough year in '95 and was named an American Association All-Star before a thumb injury ended his season. He has average tools but an outstanding work ethic, and has turned himself into a solid left fielder. Gibralter has looked like a decent hitter with good power in the past, but a shoulder injury slowed him last year. He's scheduled to have surgery on the shoulder in the off-season, which could jeopardize his entire '97 season. He no longer looks like a solution for the Reds in the short term, but if he returns healthy in late '97 or '98, he could be back in their plans. ■

CURTIS GOODWIN

OF • BL • TL • 5'11 • 180 • 24 • BAL91/12

	AB	R	H	2B	3B	HR	RBI	BB	SO	SB	CS	BA	OB	SA
BAL95	289	40	76	11	3	1	24	15	53	22	4	.263	.301	.332
CIN96	136	20	31	3	0	0	5	19	34	15	6	.228	.323	.250

There are those in the Reds' organization who feel that Goodwin is just a notch below Kenny Lofton. Goodwin was voted the fastest and the best baserunner in American Association last year, but there aren't many Kenny Loftons. In fact, there's exactly one. Goodwin has blazing speed, but the Reds don't feel that he takes advantage of it. Jim Bowden said in May that Goodwin was trying too hard to power the ball, when that isn't what they want out of him. They think he could be a 50-steal leadoff hitter, so all they want him to do is get on base. Knight had trouble finding a leadoff hitter last season, and the job would have been Goodwin's if he'd produced earlier. If Goodwin can become a more disciplined hitter and find ways to use his speed, he'll get another chance in '97. ■

WILLIE GREENE

YOUNG GUN

3B • BL • TR • 5'11 • 185 • 25 • PIT89/1

	AB	R	H	2B	3B	HR	RBI	BB	SO	SB	CS	BA	OB	SA
CIN96	287	48	70	5	5	19	63	36	88	0	1	.244	.327	.495
CAREER	486	71	113	13	8	23	84	57	151	0	3	.233	.311	.434

The Reds haven't always been happy with Big Time's work habits, but they never doubted his hitting ability. He has excellent bat speed and generates great power. He is a menace in the field and strikes out too much, which are the main reasons he hasn't nailed down the everyday job yet. But his numbers translate to well over 30 dingers and 100 RBI in a full season's worth of at-bats—despite Knight batting him just about everywhere in the lineup (from 20-50 at bats in every spot in the lineup except leadoff), playing him every day for a week, then benching

him for a couple—so there may be no sitting him anymore. At least against righties. He didn't do much against lefties, hitting .159 with 1 dinger in 44 at-bats. Though his slugging average was half as high against lefties (.273 to .535), his on-base percentage was virtually identical (.321 to .328). He should play every day for a couple of months and bat 6th, and Knight should be wired up to electrodes that will give him a short, sharp shock him if he attempts to bench him or bat him 3rd.

Greene finished the season in style, being named the N.L. player of the week for hitting .320 with 6 homers and 11 RBI. That included 5 home runs in 9 at-bats against the Cubs in Cincinnati's final 3 home games. After the series, Knight said, "Nineteen homers in 287 at-bats, that's impressive. We need to find a spot to play Willie every day." Now he notices. You can be disgusted or amused; it's your choice. ■

LENNY HARRIS

OF-3B-1B • BL • TR • 5'10 • 210 • 32 • CIN83/5

	AB	R	H	2B	3B	HR	RBI	BB	SO	SB	CS	BA	OB	SA
CIN96	287	48	70	5	5	19	63	36	88	0	1	.244	.327	.495
CAREER	486	71	113	13	8	23	84	57	151	0	3	.233	.311	.434

Harris provided solid backup for the Reds for the 3rd straight season since coming over from the Dodgers. Filling in at unsettled positions at third and in the outfield, and frequently playing with pain, he got more than 300 at-bats for the first time since 1992. And he made the most of them. He's also an excellent left-handed pinch hitter, hitting .347 with 13 RBI in 49 plate appearances. ■

THOMAS HOWARD

OF • BB • TR • 6'2 • 200 • 32 • SD86/1

	AB	R	H	2B	3B	HR	RBI	BB	SO	SB	CS	BA	OB	SA
CIN94	178	24	47	11	0	5	24	10	30	4	2	.264	.302	.410
CIN95	281	42	85	15	2	3	26	20	37	17	8	.302	.350	.402
CIN96	360	50	98	19	10	6	42	17	51	6	5	.272	.307	.431
CAREER	1824	235	493	89	20	27	182	112	309	62	38	.270	.312	.385

Howard was important to the club all season as the only true outfielder on the bench. But he might have been a starter if he hadn't entered the season with a broken wrist that sidelined him at the start of the year and kept him from getting it going at the plate

through the first half. That all changed in August, when ToHo started carrying the team. In one series against the Padres, he threw out Tony Gwynn in the 9th inning to preserve a tie and then drove in the winning run in the 13th. The next night he also drove in the game-winner. He finished the series 8-for-14 with 4 RBI. The series capped a stretch in which he had 15 hits in 26 at-bats. You can't stop Thomas Howard, you can only hope to contain him. ■

KEVIN JARVIS

SP • BL • TR • 6'2 • 200 • 27 • CIN91/21

	G	GS	IP	H	HR	BB	K	W	L	S	ERA	K/BB	K9	HW9
CIN94	6	3	17	22	4	5	10	1	1	0	7.13	2.0	5.3	14.24
CIN95	19	11	79	91	13	32	33	3	4	0	5.70	1.0	3.8	14.01
CIN96	24	20	120	152	17	43	63	8	9	0	5.98	1.5	4.7	14.62
CAREER	49	34	216	265	34	80	106	12	14	0	6.00	1.3	4.4	14.37

Ray Knight gave Jarvis a shot at the no. 5 spot in the rotation, replacing Roger Salkeld. Jarvis pitched well in June and July, but the league caught up with him for the remainder of the season. He gave up 59 hits in 36.2 innings in August, which led to an 8.84 ERA for the month. For the season, he was effective as a starter during stretches, but the Reds probably hope he won't have to be back in the rotation this year. ■

MIKE KELLY

OF • BR • TR • 6'4 • 195 • 26 • ATL91/1

	AB	R	H	2B	3B	HR	RBI	BB	SO	SB	CS	BA	OB	SA
ATL94	77	14	21	10	1	2	9	2	17	0	1	.273	.300	.506
ATL95	137	26	26	6	1	3	17	11	49	7	3	.190	.258	.314
CIN96	49	5	9	4	0	1	7	9	11	4	0	.184	.333	.327
CAREER	263	45	56	20	2	6	33	22	77	11	4	.213	.285	.373

Kelly made the roster out of spring training, and Ray Knight talked him up as a potential 25-homer guy. When the bell rang, he didn't play well in the field, and his hitting wasn't much better, so the club demoted him in mid-April. The move was supposed to be temporary. But he got off to a .184 start in 76 at-bats down there. Kelly came back to the majors briefly to fill in for the injured Willie Greene, but that move was also temporary. In July the club brought in George Foster to work with Kelly—but Foster probably just tried to sell him one of his MVP awards. Whatever they discussed, the immediate results weren't positive. Like Reggie Sanders, Kelly

experienced a season he'd like to forget. Unlike Sanders, Kelly has never experienced a season he'd like to remember. His history suggests he's a much better player, and he might at least get his potential back. The results, however, may never come. ■

BARRY LARKIN

NL ELITE

SS • BR • TR • 6'0 • 185 • 32 • CIN85/1

	AB	R	H	2B	3B	HR	RBI	BB	SO	SB	CS	BA	OB	SA
CIN94	427	78	119	23	5	9	52	64	58	26	2	.279	.369	.419
CIN95	496	98	158	29	6	15	66	61	49	51	5	.319	.394	.492
CIN96	517	117	154	32	4	33	89	96	52	36	10	.298	.410	.567
CAREER	4946	828	1476	254	48	135	626	545	483	275	51	.298	.369	.451

Coming off last year's MVP season, Larkin got off to a rough start, with 4 errors in the first 18 games. But he recovered to reclaim his status as the top shortstop in the league. And despite battling nagging injuries, he had an even better year at the plate than in '95. "Last year was his MVP year," said Jim Bowden, "but this year, had we been 8 or 9 games better and in first, he'd probably be an MVP candidate again." In September Larkin became the first shortstop steal 30 bases and hit 30 home runs in a season. "It feels great to finally get it," he said. "I didn't get any sleep at night thinking about it." He credited his power increase to switching to a heavier bat.

Where does Larkin rate? Well, Hank Aaron has seen a few ballplayers in his time. "Looking back on my career at the great shortstops, Pee Wee Reese and some of the other guys who are now in the Hall of Fame," he said, "I can't think of anybody who comes near what Barry Larkin is doing combination-wise—hitting for average, steals, home runs, and fielding. He's a rare specimen to come along in that position."

Now, *that* is something to tell the grandchildren about. ■

CURT LYONS

SOLID PROSPECT

SP • BR • TR • 6'5 • 240 • 22 • CIN92/7

	G	GS	IP	H	HR	BB	SO	W	L	S	ERA	K/BB	K9	HW9
AA	24	24	142	113	8	52	176	13	4	0	2.41	3.4	11.2	10.48

After a great season at Chattanooga last year, the Reds brought Lyons up to bolster their depleted rotation in September. And he looked pretty good for a guy who had just jumped from Double-A, going 2-0 and striking out 14 in 16 innings. He's shown steady improvement down on the farm, especially in his strikeouts and walks. He's increased his velocity and control and now has a very good fastball/change-up combo. There are some things to bear in mind about Lyons. He's never posted an ERA above 3.00, but he's never mowed down hitters at that '96 rate, either. And 1995 was his first year in a full-season league after trying for 3 years to get out of rookie ball. Nevertheless, he currently has the inside track at nailing down the No. 5 spot in the rotation this year. ■

KEVIN MITCHELL (see Free Agents)

MIKE MORGAN

SP • BR • TR • 6'3 • 195 • 37 • OAK78/1

	G	GS	IP	H	HR	BB	K	W	L	S	ERA	K/BB	K9	HW9
CHN94	15	15	80	111	12	35	57	2	10	0	6.69	1.6	6.4	16.41
CHN/SL95	21	21	131	133	12	34	61	7	7	0	3.56	1.8	4.2	11.47
SL/CIN96	23	23	130	146	16	47	74	6	11	0	4.64	1.6	5.1	13.36
CAREER	389	329	2175	2247	192	736	1086	108	155	3	4.02	1.5	4.5	12.34

The Cardinals released Morgan in September, and the Reds picked him up for the league minimum. He had gone 1-5 in his last 7 starts, and 0-4 with a 13.50 ERA in his last 4. But the Reds remembered his 2 starts against them: He was 1-0 with a 2.78 ERA in 13 innings. He was upset with the Cards for dumping him during his slump and was glad to be coming to the Reds. He got his chance at payback when he took the mound in September against the Cards, but he lasted only 5 innings, gave up 2 runs, and took the loss as the Reds were mathematically eliminated from the wild-card race. Expect MiMo back in the Reds rotation next year. Don't expect Tony LaRussa and the Cardinals to be quaking in their boots. His may prove to be one of the longest and most undistinguished careers in baseball history. He's been at this since he was 18 and has had only 2 winning seasons. ■

HAL MORRIS

1B • BL • TL • 6'3 • 200 • 31 • NYA86/7

	AB	R	H	2B	3B	HR	RBI	BB	SO	SB	CS	BA	OB	SA
CIN94	436	60	146	30	4	10	78	34	62	6	2	.335	.385	.491
CIN95	359	53	100	25	2	11	51	29	58	1	1	.279	.333	.451
CIN96	528	82	165	32	4	16	80	50	76	7	5	.313	.374	.479
CAREER	2922	409	902	181	17	71	410	260	406	41	23	.309	.365	.455

Morris could get hurt in a marshmallow bin. Last year's freak injury came in early July. He struggled through May and was just getting it going with a 9-

for-15 streak when he was nailed by the broken barrel of Eric Davis's bat. He was just standing in the on-deck circle minding his own business when the bat broke his elbow.

But the slump in May and the elbow injury were the only negatives in an otherwise excellent season. He set career highs in several categories, most notably home runs. He's still not your prototypical slugging first baseman, but last year was a big improvement over the past 4 seasons. He remains an excellent contact hitter. He's also a decent defensive first baseman. That doesn't mean the Reds won't dump his salary if they get a chance. ■

CHAD MOTTOLA

SLEEPER

OF • BR • TR • 6'3 • 215 • 25 • CIN92/1

	AB	R	H	2B	3B	HR	RBI	BB	SO	SB	CS	BA	OB	SA
CIN96	79	10	17	3	0	3	6	6	16	2	2	.215	.271	.367

The Reds' outfield was unsettled last season and Mottola got a couple of brief stints in the majors. He could be their answer in left or right this year. Mottola was their no. 1 pick in '92 and has been compared to Dale Murphy. He has fine defensive skills, with a cannon arm and good range. Knight: "He's as good a defensive right fielder as I've seen in a long time. I think he's comparable to the Reggies (Sanders) and Larry Walkers. He gets an outstanding jump on the ball and has an accurate throwing arm." His downside so far has been at the plate. His plate discipline has been lacking, and his power hasn't developed as quickly as the Reds would have liked. Still, the outfield is wide open this year, and he could find himself handed a job. ■

JOE OLIVER (see Free Agents)

JOHNNY OLIVER

OF • CIN96/1 • LAKE-LEHMAN HIGH SCHOOL (PA)

	AB	R	H	2B	3B	HR	RBI	BB	SO	SB	CS	BA	OB	SA
R+	143	20	29	5	0	2	13	11	31	3	1	.203	.277	.280

Oliver was the Reds' 1st-round pick in the '96 draft. He was heading for Clemson until the Reds got his attention. He's a speed merchant who looks like he can hit. In his high school senior season last year he hit .648 with 12 homers and stole 25 bases in 26 attempts. The pitching in the Appalachian League was a little better than high school, but give him time to adjust. ■

ERIC OWENS

OF-2B • BR • TR • 6'1 • 185 • 26 • CIN92/5

	AB	R	H	2B	3B	HR	RBI	BB	SO	SB	CS	BA	OB	SA
CIN96	205	26	41	6	0	0	9	23	38	16	2	.200	.281	.229

Owens blossomed as a hitter in '95 and earned the American Association MVP. He tore his right anterior cruciate ligament near the end of the season, though, and showed up in spring last year with a brace on his knee. The Reds kept him on the roster to fill in for the injured Bret Boone. Knight tried him at leadoff for a while, and in left field, but it didn't work out. He was sent down to Indianapolis in May, which began a series of trips back and forth. Owens just didn't make the adjustment to major-league pitching. But the Reds like Owens' attitude and feel he could be a good major-league hitter. That's probably what they were telling other GMs, anyway, as they shopped him around in October. ■

EDUARDO PEREZ

3B-1B • BR • TR • 6'4 • 215 • 27 • CAL91/1

	AB	R	H	2B	3B	HR	RBI	BB	SO	SB	CS	BA	OB	SA
CAL94	129	10	27	7	0	5	16	12	29	3	0	.209	.275	.380
CAL95	71	9	12	4	1	1	7	12	9	0	2	.169	.302	.296
CIN96	36	8	8	0	0	3	5	5	9	0	0	.222	.317	.472
CAREER	416	43	92	17	3	13	58	38	86	8	6	.221	.291	.370

Eduardo, the son of Big Red Machine veteran Tony Perez, came over to the Reds last year after 5 years in the Angels' system. He chewed up Triple-A pitching in Indianapolis, showing more power than he ever had for California. He earned call-ups in June and July, and hit a game-winning homer against Pittsburgh on July 25. It was his first homer for the Reds. Knight: "I had goose bumps all over me. He had this big smile on his face. I've seen his dad run around there a lot of times. It's a special feeling for me." His relationship to one of the most popular Reds in history

may mean an extended look for him this spring, a spot on the roster, and a chance at the first-base job if Morris is dealt. ■

MARK PORTUGAL (see Free Agents)

TIM PUGH

RP • BR • TR • 6′6 • 225 • 30 • CIN89/6

	G	GS	IP	H	HR	BB	K	W	L	S	ERA	K/BB	K9	HW9
CIN94	10	9	47	60	5	26	24	3	3	0	6.04	.9	4.6	16.44
CIN95	28	12	98	100	13	32	38	6	5	0	3.84	1.2	3.5	12.12
KC/CIN96	29	1	51	66	12	23	36	1	2	0	7.22	1.6	6.3	15.68
CAREER	105	56	407	473	51	153	210	24	27	0	4.96	1.4	4.6	13.85

The Reds tried to demote Pugh in May after he'd compiled a 10.57 ERA in 9 appearances, but Kansas City claimed him from waivers. He pitched better there, but not good enough to stay on their roster. They tried to demote in July, and the Reds claimed him back. The Reds tried once again to sneak him through, but Kansas City grabbed him. The Royals figured if they waited until August no one would notice, but the Reds were paying attention. They reclaimed him off waivers again on the 17th. Then they waived him again, but this time the Tigers grabbed him. Which, when you check his numbers, raises the question: What's the point? ■

POKEY REESE

SLEEPER

SS • BR • TR • 6′0 • 160 • 23 • CIN91/1

	AB	R	H	2B	3B	HR	RBI	BB	SO	SB	CS	BA	OB	SA
AAA	280	26	65	16	0	1	23	21	46	5	2	.232	.294	.300

The consensus on Reese is that he's just a healthy year away from making an impression in the majors. Unfortunately, the past couple of seasons have been anything but healthy. He lost time in '95 with a broken ankle and last year with a knee injury. Reese is an outstanding shortstop with a great arm and hands, plus very good range. In '95 he was considered the American Association's best shortstop and infield arm. Of course, if he ever does stay healthy and have a breakthrough year, it's not likely he'll be moving Larkin out of his way. ■

JOSÉ RIJO

SP • BR • TR • 6′3 • 215 • 31 • NYA80

	G	GS	IP	H	HR	BB	K	W	L	S	ERA	K/BB	K9	HW9
CIN94	26	26	172	177	16	52	171	9	6	0	3.08	3.3	8.9	11.98
CIN95	14	14	69	76	6	22	62	5	4	0	4.17	2.8	8.1	12.78
CAREER	332	260	1786	1602	132	634	1556	111	87	3	3.16	2.5	7.8	11.27

The Reds, and N.L. hitters, were kept in suspense most of the season wondering if José would be able to return from Tommy John surgery. He began throwing off the mound in May and it looked like he would be back. Of course, the Reds were more concerned about how they would pay his salary. While on the disabled list, his salary was paid by an insurance policy that cost the club $106,000. But if he returned, they would have to pay his $5.9 million salary. By early July, his recovery had been set back. Rijo was getting tired of the constant questions about his status and began talking about retirement. "I think about it [retirement] every day. I'm running and lifting weights and working hard every day, and it's getting me nowhere." Eventually he was forced to concede that his return wouldn't be in '96. And it still isn't certain that he will return next year. That insurance company might want to send some hitters out to take batting practice against him to see just how bad things really are. ■

JOHNNY RUFFIN

RP • BR • TR • 6′3 • 170 • 25 • CHA88/4

	G	GS	IP	H	HR	BB	K	W	L	S	ERA	K/BB	K9	HW9
CIN94	51	0	70	57	7	27	44	7	2	1	3.09	1.6	5.7	10.80
CIN95	10	0	13	4	0	11	11	0	0	0	1.35	1.0	7.6	10.38
CIN96	49	0	62	71	10	37	69	1	3	0	5.49	1.9	10.0	15.67
CAREER	131	0	183	168	21	86	154	10	6	3	3.88	1.8	7.6	12.49

Ruffin lost much of the '95 season to a knee injury, and last season wasn't the comeback year he was hoping for. He was their top pitching prospect in the early '90s and broke into the league at the tender age of 21. He had a solid season in '94 but has struggled with his control since. But there are signs of life. His stuff is excellent, his strikeout rate was his personal best, and he's still quite young. He could turn out to be one of their better relievers in the near future ■

CHRIS SABO (see Looking for a Game)

ROGER SALKELD

SP • BR • TR • 6'5 • 215 • 26 • SEA89/1

	G	GS	IP	H	HR	BB	K	W	L	S	ERA	K/BB	K9	HW9
CIN96	29	19	116	114	18	54	82	8	5	0	5.20	1.5	6.4	13.03

Salkeld, the former Mariner phenom the Reds received for Tim Belcher, began the season as the no. 5 starter. In June he was 3-1 with a 2.81 ERA and was emerging as the most reliable starter on the staff, but by August the honeymoon was over. Salkeld struggled through a 9.17 ERA in 4 consecutive starts, and divorce proceedings began in mid-September. He may get another look at the rotation this year, but Knight wasn't too happy with his results by the end of the season. ■

REGGIE SANDERS

OF • BR • TR • 6'1 • 180 • 29 • CIN87/7

	AB	R	H	2B	3B	HR	RBI	BB	SO	SB	CS	BA	OB	SA
CIN94	400	66	105	20	8	17	62	41	114	21	9	.263	.332	.480
CIN95	484	91	148	36	6	28	99	69	122	36	12	.306	.397	.579
CIN96	287	49	72	17	1	14	33	44	86	24	8	.251	.353	.463
CAREER	2092	364	573	115	25	92	316	253	547	125	47	.274	.355	.485

Sanders had a breakthrough year in '95 and hoped to prove that it wasn't a fluke in '96. But injuries kept him out of the lineup a good part of the year, and he never had much of a chance. After bruising his knee in spring training, he went down in May with a tear around a disc in his lower back. The injury lingered, and he had trouble with a strained muscle in his ribs. By early June he'd played in only 16 games. And when he was back and healthy, he endured one of those epic slumps that try hitters' souls. Knight even stuck him in the leadoff spot just to shake things up, but that didn't work either. In the second half he hit .219 with 16 RBI. For the season, he hit .177 with runners in scoring position.

In early September he tore a ligament in his thumb, and was done for the season. Sanders: "I'm going to write '1996' on a piece of paper, crumple it up, and throw it into the ocean." Problem is, he'll probably tear his rotator cuff on the follow-through. ■

PETE SCHOUREK

SLEEPER

SP • BL • TL • 6'5 • 195 • 27 • NYN87/3

	G	GS	IP	H	HR	BB	K	W	L	S	ERA	K/BB	K9	HW9
CIN94	22	10	81	90	11	29	69	7	2	0	4.09	2.4	7.7	13.22
CIN95	29	29	190	158	17	45	160	18	7	0	3.22	3.6	7.6	9.62
CIN96	12	12	67	79	7	24	54	4	5	0	6.01	2.3	7.3	13.83
CAREER	161	98	689	714	64	230	482	45	38	2	4.32	2.1	6.3	12.33

Schourek had his season blown out by elbow problems that shut him down in July. It was a major disappointment after his '95 season, in which he came out of nowhere to be the runner-up to Greg Maddux for the Cy Young award. Schourek chose not to have surgery, which makes him a risky proposition in '97. ■

SCOTT SERVICE

RP • BR • TR • 6'6 • 225 • 30 • PHI85

	G	GS	IP	H	HR	BB	K	W	L	S	ERA	K/BB	K9	HW9
SF95	28	0	31	18	4	20	30	3	1	0	3.19	1.5	8.7	11.03
CIN96	34	1	48	51	7	18	46	1	0	0	3.94	2.6	8.6	12.94
CAREER	107	1	144	143	20	63	141	7	5	2	4.50	2.2	8.8	12.87

Service has been released by the Phillies, the Expos twice, played in Japan, waived by the Reds, waived by the Rockies, re-signed by the Reds 9 days later, released by the Reds then re-signed by the Reds 3 months later, traded to the Giants with Deion Sanders, then reclaimed by the Reds in the off-season. And he's only 30. He's from Cincinnati, which might explain why they keep bringing him back. Why they keep letting him go is another question. Service can be overpowering at times, though his control is shaky. It was as good last year as it's ever been, and he was one of the more dependable arms in the bullpen. Figure on him to be released and reclaimed in time for Opening Day. ■

JEFF SHAW

RP • BR • TR • 6'2 • 200 • 30 • CLE86/1

	G	GS	IP	H	HR	BB	K	W	L	S	ERA	K/BB	K9	HW9
MON94	46	0	67	67	8	15	47	5	2	1	3.88	3.1	6.3	11.01
MON/CHA95	59	0	72	70	6	27	51	1	6	3	4.88	1.9	6.4	12.13
CIN96	78	0	104	99	8	29	69	8	6	4	2.49	2.4	6.0	11.07
CAREER	281	19	467	479	53	154	276	19	31	9	4.07	1.8	5.3	12.20

The Reds signed Shaw not quite knowing what to expect. He had been with the Expos and the White Sox in '95 and had not been particularly effective at either stop. But he established himself early for

Cincinnati. Through mid-June his 1.89 ERA was the best on the entire staff. Knight used him early in the season to set up closer Jeff Brantley. Lee Smith's arrival pushed him out of that role, but not because he was ineffective. They simply had to give Smith the more prestigious job. Shaw finished the season with the 2nd-best ERA on the staff behind Brantley and led the bullpen in innings pitched. In early September Jim Bowden gave him a new 2-year contract worth $650,000 per year. ■

RUBEN SIERRA

OF • BB • TR • 6'1 • 200 • 31 • TEX82

	AB	R	H	2B	3B	HR	RBI	BB	SO	SB	CS	BA	OB	SA
OAK94	426	71	114	21	1	23	92	23	64	8	5	.268	.298	.484
OAK/NYA95	479	73	126	32	0	19	86	46	76	5	4	.263	.323	.449
NYA/DET96	518	61	128	26	2	12	72	60	83	4	4	.247	.320	.375
CAREER	6197	870	1675	332	52	232	1024	479	917	130	51	.270	.319	.453

The Reds are paying only about $600,000 of his $5 million salary in '97, and gave up very little to get him, so they shouldn't be complaining when they look under the hood of this sports car in June and don't like what they see. Sierra came over to the Tigers in the addition-by-subtraction trade with the Yankees for Cecil Fielder. The Yanks got rid of Ruben's disruptive attitude, and the Tigers got rid of Cecil's $7.2 million price tag in '97. And that's really all there was to it, from Detroit's point of view. Sierra doesn't exactly make minimum wage either, but that's the price they had to pay to get Matt Drews. Sierra isn't too old at 32, but he's 9 years removed from his only 30-homer season and 5 from his last 25-homer season. He still has the talent, but he's a head case who is more enthralled by his reflection in the mirror than by the success of the team. And his outfield play in '96 was comic even by his standards. ■

JOHN SMILEY

CONSISTENT STAR

SP • BL • TL • 6'4 • 195 • 32 • PIT83/12

	G	GS	IP	H	HR	BB	K	W	L	S	ERA	K/BB	K9	HW9
CIN94	24	24	158	169	18	37	112	11	10	0	3.86	3.0	6.4	11.73
CIN95	28	27	176	173	11	39	124	12	5	0	3.46	3.2	6.3	10.84
CIN96	35	34	217	207	20	54	171	13	14	0	3.64	3.2	7.1	10.82
CAREER	335	254	1753	1658	159	455	1164	115	89	4	3.67	2.6	6.0	10.85

Smiley struggled along with the rest of the staff during their dismal April, but he rebounded to be the staff's most dependable starter. And he inherited the ace role when Pete Schourek went down in July.

Early on, Smiley showed the frustration the Reds were feeling when he accused umpires of squeezing the strike zone on them. He felt the umps were getting back at Marge Schott for her insensitive remarks when John McSherry died on Opening Day. He quickly apologized, but it gave the media the opportunity to stretch out an unfortunate story. After April, he went 12-11 with a 3.22 ERA and a 10.00 ratio. The record could have been much better, but he received the least run support on the rotation, only 4.26 runs per game. The Reds rewarded him in September with a 3-year contract extension worth $3.75 million per year. ■

LEE SMITH (see Looking for a Game)

EDDIE TAUBENSEE

C • BL • TR • 6'3 • 205 • 28 • CIN86/6

	AB	R	H	2B	3B	HR	RBI	BB	SO	SB	CS	BA	OB	SA
CIN/HOU94	187	29	53	8	2	8	21	15	31	2	0	.283	.333	.476
CIN95	218	32	62	14	2	9	44	22	52	2	2	.284	.354	.491
CIN96	327	46	95	20	0	12	48	26	64	3	4	.291	.338	.462
CAREER	1383	161	364	70	6	43	191	120	285	10	7	.263	.321	.416

Taubensee, a .255 career hitter, got off to a torrid start. Through the first 3 weeks, he hit .429 and slugged .694. But not even he was fooled. "Ted Williams has nothing to worry about unless the rest of our games are rained out or we go on strike right now," he said. "I didn't even hit .400 in high school." While Taubensee didn't keep up that pace, he did turn in his best season at the plate, setting set career highs in batting average, RBI, and runs scored. Defensively, though, he had his problems. Through late May he had thrown out only 4 base stealers in 49 tries. Knight suggested he go see Johnny Bench, and that seems to have helped. Taubensee caught 22 in 64 attempts for the rest of the season. That rate isn't stellar, but it is an improvement.

But, as always, the question must be asked: For Kenny Lofton . . .? ■

■ 1996 AUTOPSY

The Rockies and their fans were coming off the high of making it to the playoffs in their third year of existence, the most rapid ascent of any expansion team in history. Management opted to leave well enough alone in '96, making very few changes to their roster and no significant ones—also unheard of for an expansion team after its third year of existence.

April 11-14 (5 games back)
The Rockies won the close ones (10-4 in games decided by two runs or fewer) and got blown out when they lost—including a 21-9 loss to the Expos in Coors on the 28th. Their record in close games was a tribute to Curtis Leskanic, who had a hand in 8 wins, following up his strong '95 by saving 6 games in 6 opportunities in April and going 2-0. Still, manager Don Baylor was concerned: "He hasn't had a clean performance yet, whether it's in a save or a win situation. One day his velocity is great and the next day there is none." Leskanic would blow the only 4 save opportunities he got the rest of the year. The Rockies might have felt they were unlucky to start the year 11-14, but they were outscored 170-128; being outscored by 33% is a tremendous feat—something only the Tigers managed to do in 1996, and should have meant an 8-16 record on the way to a 100 loss season.

The mental state of pitching prospect, Bryan Rekar, was one of the first casualties of the season, even though he didn't show up on the disabled list. He allowed 52 baserunners and 30 earned runs in 19 innings in April—and that included a nifty 4-3 victory over the Cubs in Wrigley—before being talked in off the ledge and sent back to the minors. On the offense, Ellis Burks started off strong (5 dingers, .375 batting average), to which most just nodded their heads and waited for his back to go out. It never would, and his 15 RBI was his lowest total for any month of the season. Eric Young came off the DL on the 22nd, went 2-4, and never looked back.

May 14-11 (25-25, 7 games back)
The Rockies went 1-7 on a road trip in early May—including an 11-0 no-hitter in Florida at the hands of Al Leiter—then returned home to go 7-2. They scored 53 runs in their first 5 games at Coors after managing 21 on the entire 9 game road trip. The hitters were below the Mendoza Line for the trip (.198) with 4 home runs. The Rockies were held to 2 or fewer runs 33 times in '96, 30 times on the road, 5 times in 6 games from May 6th to May 11th. By month-end, the Rockies might have thought they had climbed back into the race, but this road performance had told them their future—and it didn't feature any baseball in October.

Bruce Ruffin took over the closer's role from Curtis Leskanic and never gave it back. Despite a 6.30 ERA, he blew only 1 of his 7 save opportunities. Larry Walker hit for the cycle against Pittsburgh, knocking in 6 runs.

June 15-14 (40-39, 1½ games back)
Everyone hit in June and the team still managed to win only 15 games—as they racked up big numbers during garbage time in several blow outs. The scores looked like Bears-Packers games in the '70s, as the Rockies lost 12-8, 16-8, and 13-10, while winning 14-7, 19-8, 13-12, 10-6, 11-3, 13-1, 13-4, and 16-15. All but 2 of those games were at Coors Field Welcome to Arena Baseball. Dante Bichette (11-39-.375), Ellis Burks (9-31-.389), Vinny Castilla (12-28-.370), Andres Galarraga (8-27-.318), and Eric Young (1-18-.388) were all hot at the same time. They did most of this damage without Walker, who ran into the center field wall against the Braves on the 9th, separated his shoulder, and wouldn't return for 2 months—but that only gave John Vander Wal a chance to show just how good an ordinary player can look when he plays at altitude. Project his June numbers to 550 at bats and you get 30 home runs and 150 RBI. Sound familiar, Dante? The team hit .315 for the month with 51 dingers, and had an on-base percentage of .385 and a slugging percentage of .533—an entire lineup of Manny Ramirezes.

Despite all of this, the team managed to go only 3-9 on the road, scoring only 28 runs in the 9 losses. Baylor wasn't thrilled about going 1-5 on the road against the Mets and Phillies: "We go out on the next trip (to San Francisco and Los Angeles) and play like this, and we're buried. That will be like throwing dirt over your grave. They don't even need to shovel. You shovel yourself." They would open the month of July on that road trip and go 2-5.

Many Rockies were looking at their offensive numbers and thinking nothing more could be asked of them, so near the end of the month, an unimpressed Baylor had to reintroduce his team to defense and fundamentals: "If we did some more of the little things right, we could be 4 or 5 games ahead right now. This (practice session) is sort of a refresher course for everybody."

The staff wasn't significantly worse in June than any other month—except for the bullpen, which blew 9 of 15 save opportunities. Darren Holmes was the worst of the bunch, giving up 4 homers in 14 innings and losing 3 games. He would be virtually unhittable for the rest of the season. Rekar returned briefly to make 4 starts. He outpitched Curt Schilling, 4-1, but then got lit up all over again and was sent back down. Mark Thompson was similarly abused, going 0-3 while yielding 55 baserunners and 6 dingers in 28 innings. Kevin Ritz somehow managed to go 4-0, despite walking 19 and striking out only 17 in in 41 innings. He beat Paul Wagner 2-0 in Three Rivers, then became the beneficiary of 14 runs against Doug Drabek, 11 against a rehabbing Bobby Munoz and the Phillies, and 13 runs against Pedro Astacio. The game against Astacio was the first of a twisted 4-game series against the Dodgers at the end of the month, in which the Rockies scored 52 runs and gave up 33. Rockie hitters hit .416 with 12 home runs.

July 14-14 (54-53, 2½ games back)
The Rockies went 11 home games in a row in which they scored at least 7 runs, which tied a record previously held only by the 1938 Yankees. That team played at sea level, outscored the Rockies for the year despite a lower batting and slugging average, struck out nearly 500 fewer times, won their third World Series in a row, and featured 3 Hall of Famers—and 2 of the greatest ever—in its starting lineup: Bill Dickey, Lou Gehrig, and Joe DiMaggio. Hopefully these 2 teams will never again be mentioned in the same sentence.

Quinton McCracken slapped enough singles and drew enough walks to hit .350 for the month with a .422 on-base percentage. Armando Reynoso began to fall apart after a solid three months of work. He gave up 9 dingers in 27 innings and his K/BB ratio, which had been an outstanding 53:19, deteriorated to 11:10. Another phenom pitcher was called up from the minors to face big league hitters in Coors Field. Jamey Wright struggled, but fared much better than Rekar, earning his first major league win in Denver, beating Osvaldo Fernandez, 4-3. After Wright was touched up for 3 runs in his first inning at Coors, Baylor had to tell him: "Rekar gave up 7. You only gave up 3. Lighten up."

August 16-14 (70-67, 6 games back)
On a road trip at mid-month, they faced 3 of the best pitchers in baseball on consecutive days: John Smoltz, Al Leiter, and Kevin Brown held them to 10 hits as the Rockies lost 4-1, 5-0, and 2-1. Their last stop on that trip was Cincinnati, where Baylor took exception to Reds manager, Ray Knight, who he felt had found a way to celebrate good times more obnoxiously than his players. Baylor: "When they come to our ballpark, we'll find out who the cheerleaders are. I'm taking notes." Baylor was probably more bothered by the fact that August was the month when the Rockies needed to make a run at the playoffs, only to drop 7 of 8 in the middle of an 11 game road trip. Larry Walker retuned to hit .295 with 4 dingers, but the team had played .500 ball without him and continued to play .500 ball with him. Galarraga had his best month of the season, hitting .344 with 12 home runs and 33 RBI.

September 13-12 (83-79, 8 games back)
The Rockies were hungover from '95, played like it all year, and never more so than September—a month in which Hideo Nomo, in Denver, with the Rockies still in the hunt, and pitching most of the game from the stretch due to the wet condition of the mound, no-hit the Blake Street "Bombers." Walt Weiss finished slowly, hitting .240 after July and watching the future, Neifi Perez, get an extended audition at short. Eric Young slumped in every aspect of his game in September, hitting .247, failing to draw walks, and getting caught stealing 5 times in 9 attempts. They mailed in the last two weeks of the year, dropping 8 of 12, 6 to the Triple-A Giants.

Interestingly, the workhouses of the bullpen—Darren Holmes, Mike Munoz, Steve Reed, and Bruce Ruffin—finished strong. They combined to strike out 45, walk only 13, and yield only 30 hits and 9 runs over 44 innings. They were 4-1 with 6 saves, blowing holes in the theory that Baylor

overworks his relievers—and helping make the case that the bullpen is the only genuine strength this time may have.

■ 1997 DIAGNOSIS

Offense

The home and road splits reveal the extent to which the Blake Street Bombers are a mirage.

	AB	R	H	2B	3B	HR	BA	SA
Home	2909	658	997	189	26	149	.343	.579
Road	2681	303	610	108	11	72	.228	.357

Below is what their offense actually looked like, and what it should have looked like if this team had to play under normal conditions. When you adjust for the fact that the Rockies get to play 81 games in Coors Field and the rest of the league gets to play 6, their offense drops from 2nd best in the National League to the bottom. Bottom, as in "below the Phillies."

	AB	R	H	2B	3B	HR	BA	SA
Actual	5590	961	1607	297	37	221	.287	.472
Adjusted	5379	632	1249	222	23	150	.232	.366

One-third of this team's run production was due solely to its park. Here is what Dante, Vinny, Andres, Ellis, and EYo would have put up if they played 6 games a year at Coors. In a juiced ball year, only Ellis Burks was anything close to special.

	HR	RBI	BA
Dante Bichette	20	89	.256
Ellis Burks	37	108	.295
Vinny Castilla	28	84	.262
Andres Galarraga	32	100	.251
Eric Young	2	44	.228

On the morning after, in the harsh light of day, Murderers' Row is looking a lot more like Sean Berry, Jeff King, Benito Santiago, Henry Rodriguez, and Jody Reed. There's a very good reason most of these superstars were available in the expansion draft. They aren't superstars.

Dante is known for bristling at hearing the truth. Baylor doesn't: "What the media writes isn't distorted. It's fact. I see the numbers. I see the big drop-off. I don't think the media is being unfair. And until it changes, they're going to continue to write about it."

See *Into Thin Air* at the end of this section for more on Coors Field and its effect on the Rockies.

Defense

Baylor was disappointed with the team's defense all year: "One of the things I was most proud of last season was our defense. This year, we're not playing the same type defense. Too many nights, we've had 3- and 4-error games. We had 6 once. We never had that last year. . . . When you play bad defense, you're always holding your breath. . . . It's not just the errors. It's the plays that don't show up as errors. It's like we're not even prepared when the ball is hit."

Only the Mets made more errors in the N.L. than the Rockies. There are no defensive standouts on this team. Jeff Reed and Jayhawk Owens combined for 20 errors and 18 passed balls, and a cardboard cut-out of Carlton Fisk would block balls in the dirt more effectively. The team was so dissatisfied with their work that they resorted to a waiver maneuver that brought Steve Decker in from San Francisco for Trenidad Hubbard—which did little but give the Rockies 3 inadequate catchers rather than just 2. Castilla and Galarraga are decent at the corners; they combined for 34 errors—which was topped by only Sean Berry and Jeff Bagwell with 38—but the Rockies staff is dominated by groundball pitchers, so their infield gets more chances than any team in baseball. Young has improved dramatically (just to become average) at second, but Walt Weiss had a tough year. His 30 errors and .957 fielding percentage put him near the bottom with Orlando Miller, Mark Grudzielanek, José Valentin, and Shawon Dunston. He didn't get his hands on that many balls, considering his pitching staff, as he begins to lose a step or two in the field. Both Eric Young and Vinny Castilla were at or near the top for their position in total chances handled per game—and neither of them is considered by experts to have the range of a Joe Morgan or Brooks Robinson—while Weiss was only in the middle of the pack.

The outfield isn't in much better shape. Ellis Burks was the only player to benefit from the musical gloves that put him in left, Walker in center, and Dante in right. Walker doesn't have the range for center, and his collision with the wall that cost him two months had Baylor second-guessing his decision to put him there. Bichette is bad in right and getting worse; his ratio of 4 assists to 9 errors (6 in September alone) was the weakest of any regular outfielder in baseball. The only outfielders with more errors all had far more assists: Albert Belle (10

errors, 11 assists), Kenny Lofton (10 errors, 13 assists), Brian Hunter (12 errors, 11 assists), Sammy Sosa (10 errors, 15 assists), and Raul Mondesi (12 errors, 11 assists). Dante has been accused of thinking his "big" bat excludes him from putting in an honest day's effort with the glove, and his play in left in '95 prompted Baylor to call him the dumbest player he'd ever seen. Dante likes to compare himself to Ted Williams as a hitter, but it's as disinterested defensive outfielders that they have something in common. Things will improve if Baylor does as expected and puts Walker back in right, Burks in center, and Bichette in left.

Pitching

The gap between the home and away totals of the pitchers does not match that of the hitters. The hitters struggle on the road, but the pitchers are absolutely traumatized at home and they seem to carry the scars with them on road trips. Here are the starters:

	W	L	ERA	BB	K	HW9
Rekar (Home)	1	2	12.62	15	8	21.14
Rekar (Away)	1	2	4.88	11	17	13.34
Reynoso (Home)	6	4	4.81	24	40	13.50
Reynoso (Away)	2	5	5.13	25	48	12.50
Ritz (Home)	8	4	5.93	47	57	14.79
Ritz (Away)	9	7	4.65	58	48	14.04
Thompson (Home)	5	4	6.41	39	46	15.64
Thompson (Away)	4	7	4.32	35	53	12.45
Wright (Home)	2	1	6.38	20	22	14.67
Wright (Away)	2	3	3.67	21	23	14.14

All the pitchers' numbers are wretched at Coors, as would be expected, but their road numbers are pretty lousy, too. (Only Reynoso was better at home, and they traded him.) Are these pitchers that bad (Ritz, Reynoso) or inexperienced (Wright, Rekar, and Thompson), or are they all shell-shocked? The Rockies better hope it's the former. They can do something about that. If it's the latter, they'll continue to score runs, draw fans, and play .500 ball indefinitely. A bad sign: some of their young pitching prospects at Colorado Springs in the PCL looked shell-shocked, too, after playing under more normal conditions for most of their careers: Garvin Alston, Mike DeJean, Rob Pedraza, John Thomson, and Jake Viano, just to name 5. See their write-ups for the gruesome details. If it was possible, the Rockies would be wise to have their minor leaguer pitchers play at altitude from Rookie-ball to Triple-A, so they wouldn't continually eat their young when promoting them to Colorado Springs and Denver.

The Rockies bullpen has managed to develop a relative immunity to Coors Field that defies explanation. Perhaps it's a function of not having to wait around for 5 days after getting lit up, thinking about it. Maybe it helps that there are no rookies in the bullpen—the kids in the rotation (Wright, Thompson, Rekar, and swing-man Roger Bailey) had the biggest home/away gaps on the staff. Perhaps it helps to just go as hard as you can for as long as you can, rather than to try to pace yourself. Or maybe relievers are just crazy enough to handle adversity better.

	W	L	S	ERA	BB	K	HW9
Holmes (Home)	5	1	0	4.28	11	37	13.28
Holmes (Away)	0	3	1	3.65	17	36	11.43
Leskanic (Home)	4	0	2	5.87	15	36	15.03
Leskanic (Away)	3	5	4	6.62	23	40	14.27
Munoz (Home)	2	0	0	6.95	7	24	15.14
Munoz (Away)	0	2	0	6.35	9	21	13.50
Painter (Home)	3	0	0	5.81	12	26	13.65
Painter (Away)	1	2	0	5.95	13	22	15.56
Reed (Home)	1	1	0	3.02	13	29	9.29
Reed (Away)	3	2	0	5.13	6	22	11.34
Ruffin (Home)	6	2	12	3.96	19	37	12.63
Ruffin (Away)	1	3	12	4.05	10	37	8.91

Leskanic, Munoz, and Painter were equal opportunity b.p. pitchers home or away. Ruffin and Holmes weren't that much worse in Coors, while Reed was significantly *better* at home. Colorado has consciously gone after groundball pitchers, and there are more in the bullpen (Ruffin and Munoz the most extreme), but being a groundball pitcher is no guarantee of success. Ritz and Wright struggle at home while veteran flyball pitchers Reed and Reynoso come as close to thriving as a pitcher can, after struggling prior to 1996.

Maybe the only variable that really matters here is age. Perhaps it's no coincidence that the best pitchers on the staff in '96 have all turned 30.

Farm System

Baylor: "What have we got at Triple-A? Mostly guys who already have been here. Guys down there are struggling." Not exactly. They actually have a few terrific prospects: outfielder Edgard Velazquez, first baseman Todd Helton, and shortstop Neifi Perez will be the core of this team by the end of the century. If pitchers Jamey Wright and Doug Million were in any other organization, it would be very tempting to rave about their prospects. Until a young pitcher can establish himself as a big leaguer in Colorado, however, it has to be assumed that it can't be done. The Rockies continually emphasize pitching in the draft (13 of their first 14 picks in '96), but they may have to wait a lot longer for the payoff than they expect. If '96 is any indication, Coors Field may delay the development of young pitchers into consistent performers by 3-to-5 years—and in some cases, forever.

Management and Ownership

Who said owning a baseball team is difficult? Just sell out every game you play and sign the checks. According to Financial World, the Rockies estimated revenues are topped by only the Yankees, Orioles, and Dodgers. They're part of a government-protected monopoly with an entire time zone to themselves. Who couldn't make money under those conditions?

GM Bob Gebhard was criticized in '96, both in the press and in the clubhouse, for not pulling the trigger on a deal that would help the Rockies win in '96. He wouldn't part with any of his top prospects to come away with a pitcher or a catcher. Gebhard: "I tried to make a deal. I couldn't find one that made sense. . . . Every general manager out there knows we need pitching, so they ask for more than they do from other teams. And every National League pitcher we talked about, I have to see how they pitched in Coors Field. Most of the guys who were out there (available in a trade), their numbers weren't very good." Uh, Bob, name one starting pitcher whose Coors Field numbers *are* good. Walter Johnson would get torched if he pitched in Denver.

Manager Don Baylor is a motivator and one of the better young managers in baseball, but his team and the conditions in which they have to play is leaving him a bit frayed around the edges. Baylor was nailed 267 times with pitches without incident. The first time he charges the mound, it might be on a pitching change.

. . . and whatnot: Into Thin Air

A number of fans don't buy this Curse of the Bambino stuff as an explanation for the Red Sox failure to win anything since before the Bolshevik Revolution. They suggest it has nothing to do with selling Babe Ruth to the Yankees, and everything to do with playing in a park that distorts the game. A case can certainly be made that Fenway has caused the Red Sox to consistently overrate their hitters and underrate their pitchers—most notably their left-handed starters, as Bob Ojeda and John Tudor can attest. Coors Field may similarly doom the Rockies, but to mediocrity rather than Game 7 tragedies. The real park effect of Coors Field may be that it will cause the Rockies to continually do what the Red Sox have been doing for most of the century.

People think of Coors Field as a home run park, but it is the only stadium in baseball that increases singles, doubles, triples, and homers. A tiny park will increase homers and decrease everything else. A spacious park will take away dingers, but increase doubles and triples. A park with nooks and crannies will turn doubles into triples. In Coors, there is no trade-off. It takes a park at altitude where fly balls travel 10% farther, routine line drives reach the outfield so fast they get through to the wall, and breaking balls don't break, to help every single aspect of the offensive game. And that's why what the Rockies do in Denver is something that looks like baseball, smells like baseball, but is anything but baseball.

Coors is so extreme, it affects road games. The Rockies were 55-26 at home, 28-53 on the road. At first, Baylor seemed to be trying to convince himself that the road woes were simply due to bad habits: "At home, our approach is good. We go the other way and use the whole field. We can do that on the road, too. I think sometimes we get on the road and we hear the fans talking about the Blake Street Bombers and the light air at Coors Field, and we try to pull the ball and hit homers to prove we can hit them anywhere." But as the year progressed, it never got better than April: 6-6 on the road in April, 4-9 in May, 3-9 in June, 3-11 in July, 7-10 in August, and 5-8 in September.

As the season continued, Baylor grew even more disgusted by his team's play on the road: "It's beyond a physical thing. It's mental. . . . It's the most frustrating thing I've ever witnessed. When you have a worse record on the road than the Detroit Tigers, that's a tough one."

Coors certainly does foster bad habits, as well as mess with the heads of players—especially young starting pitchers who get pummelled, then sit around thinking about it for the next week. But yet another issue the Rockies face is how to field a lineup that can consistently hit big league pitching when it only sees it half the year. They get used to seeing AA-caliber breaking pitches in the thin air, then have to hit the road and see big league sliders again. Dante: "I really believe that it takes a few days to make adjustments once we leave Coors Field. We saw these same pitchers last weekend, and I swear to God they're different here than they were there. They don't pitch the same. They're tougher. Their breaking balls break more." Consider these batting averages in the first games of road trips: Bichette (.178), Burks (.211), Galarraga (.132). These 3 Bombers managed 2 dingers and 12 RBI in 121 at bats in their first game after playing fast-pitch softball at Coors—and the team went 3-8.

The Rockies have put a lot of effort into signing and developing young pitchers—in part, because they know they won't be able to get many front-line pitchers in the free agent market to voluntarily destroy their Cooperstown credentials, and in part, because they may think they have a great offense. They don't. And even if they did have front-line hitting talent, it remains to be seen whether Bonds or Griffey could adjust to the difference in pitching quality when they went back out on the road.

All of this could keep this team from ever being serious contenders for anything but the most statistical asterisks.

GARVIN ALSTON

RP • BR • TR • 6'1 • 185 • 25 • COL92/10

	G	GS	IP	H	HR	BB	K	W	L	S	ERA	K/BB	K9	HW9
AAA	35	0	34	47	3	27	36	1	4	14	5.77	1.3	9.4	19.40

Alston got a brief trial in Colorado and was tagged in 6 brief appearances. His numbers suffered dramatically after being promoted from New Haven. In Double-A in '95, his ERA was 2.84 and his HW9 was 9.86. He throws hard—his fastball is in the low 90s—but he had trouble with the rest of package (slider, curve, change-up). He's struggled in the past after being promoted, so he may just need another year to acclimate himself. ■

ERIC ANTHONY (see Free Agents)

ROGER BAILEY

RP-SP • BR • TR • 6'1 • 180 • 26 • COL92/3

	G	GS	IP	H	HR	BB	K	W	L	S	ERA	K/BB	K9	HW9
COL95	39	6	81	88	9	39	33	7	6	0	4.98	0.8	3.7	14.11
COL96	24	11	83	94	7	52	45	2	3	1	6.24	0.9	4.9	15.82

To get batters out in '97, Bailey will rely on a sinking fastball to induce groundballs, a change-up to keep hitters off-balance, and a trade. His ERA at Coors was 6.65 in '95, and it's up to 7.12 in '96. Unfortunately, his road ERA has increased from 2.80 to 5.55. His nibbling is not just a Coors thing. In his career, he's walked 50 and struck out only 42 on the road. He hasn't overpowered hitters since low Class-A in '92, so there's nothing to suggest he'll ever be anything more than a 9th or 10th pitcher on a staff. ■

JASON BATES

IF • BB • TR • 5'11 • 185 • 26 • COL92/7

	AB	R	H	2B	3B	HR	RBI	BB	SO	SB	CS	BA	OB	SA
COL95	322	42	86	17	4	8	46	42	70	3	6	.267	.355	.419
COL96	160	19	33	8	1	1	9	23	34	2	1	.206	.312	.288

Bates lost the starting job to Eric Young in '95 when he injured his wrist, and hasn't been a factor since. He contracted an infection early in '96 that caused an alarming swelling in his knee. Bates: "It's like the movie *Outbreak*. It's an unidentified something or other." It might also be an explanation for some pretty sad offensive numbers. Bates *slugged* .184 on the road. Project his home numbers to 500 at bats and he's not much better than Mark Lemke. If he doesn't have a good spring, he could be looking for work. ■

ROBBIE BECKETT

RP • BR • TL • 6′5 • 240 • 24 • SD90/1

	G	GS	IP	H	HR	BB	K	W	L	S	ERA	K/BB	K9	HW9
AA	33	7	62	55	8	61	62	7	3	0	5.11	1.0	9.2	16.93

The Padres finally gave up on their former 1st-round draft pick and he was claimed on waivers by the Marlins and ended up with the Rockies. Like Jason Grimsley, Beckett throws hard (mid-90s) and randomly. Believe it or not, that stat line represents an improvement, as he actually gave up fewer than a walk per inning. He also cut his wild pitches from 25 in '93 (1 every 3.1 innings) to 7 in '96 between Double-A, Triple-A, and the majors. A lefty who throws this hard will always get his share of second, third, and fourth chances—and he'll need it after walking 9 in 5.1 innings in a brief trial with the Rockies. Every now and then, one of these pitchers gets it together—like Robb Nen, who had walked 26 and struck out 12 in 23 innings when the Rangers finally got rid of him—so Beckett should be kicking around for a few more years. ■

DANTE BICHETTE — OVERRATED

RF • BR • TR • 6′3 • 235 • 33 • CAL84/17

	AB	R	H	2B	3B	HR	RBI	BB	SO	SB	CS	BA	OB	SA
COL94	484	74	147	33	2	27	95	19	70	21	8	.304	.334	.548
COL95	579	102	197	38	2	40	128	22	96	13	9	.340	.364	.620
COL96	633	114	198	39	3	31	141	45	105	31	12	.313	.359	.531
CAREER	3629	527	1056	222	18	157	629	174	661	119	54	.291	.327	.492

An impostor snuck onto the field during pre-game warm-ups at the 1979 All-Star Game. After enjoying himself shagging flies with the pitchers, he walked up to Indians relief pitcher, Sid Monge, and said, "You know, I don't belong here." Monge laughed and said, "Neither do I." It's too bad Bichette doesn't treat his good fortune with similar humility. Instead, he arranges an audience with Ted Williams to talk hitting. That's like Macauly Caulkin inviting himself over to Laurence Olivier's to compare notes—and it's simply Reason #96 why baseball fans who care about credit going where credit belongs find the sight of Dante Bichette on the foul line at All-Star games to be an ongoing source of displeasure.

Dante had a problem with being called "the poster boy" for Coors Field by Bob Costas during the '96 All-Star Game. His rebuttal: "It was an unfair statement, and he seemed to be saying the hitting difference was something limited to me and the Colorado Rockies. You look around baseball and the same could be said about anyone. Most players hit better at home than they do on the road." True, but most players don't go from 22-99-.366 at home to 9-42-.253 on the road. And it's not like '96 was an aberration; from '93-'95, Bichette did 57-189-.369 at home and 31-123-.269 on the road. Costas might be a bit precious and self-absorbed, but he also, in this instance, happens to be right.

Ringo Starr. John Grisham. Dante Bichette. Moderately talented, at best, but in the right place at the time. And Ringo's the only one of the bunch who can't seem to take himself or his success seriously. Dante was 2 years away from serving up cold slices and sodas with too much ice at a pizza parlor in Daytona if it hadn't been for expansion. He was 29, his career totals worked out to 14-64-.254 for a full season, he'd never hit above .300 at any professional level, and the Brewers were willing to deal him for Kevin Reimer, who the Rangers had been willing to leave exposed in the expansion draft. Every team in baseball has at least one outfielder who would outproduce Bichette if given the chance to play left field in Colorado.

As Bichette's offense has improved, his defense has deteriorated rapidly. He once had a very strong arm but it's a memory now, and his assists have declined from 14 to 10 to 9 to 4 in the past 4 seasons. He used his bad knee as an excuse for his limited range in right field, but it didn't stop him from getting thrown out stealing 12 times in his quest to do 30/30. He underwent knee surgery in the off-season, but he'll be back in '97 for the second year of a 3-year, $11 million deal. If he goes on the DL, however, Edgard Velazquez may take his job and never give it back. ■

HEATH BOST — SLEEPER

RP • BR • TR • 6′4 • 200 • 22 • COL95/18

	G	GS	IP	H	HR	BB	K	W	L	S	ERA	K/BB	K9	HW9
A	41	0	76	45	3	19	102	5	2	15	1.30	5.4	12.1	7.58

If you think those numbers are good, he struck out 42 and walked 3 in low Class-A in 1995. He earned a promotion to Double-A New Haven and was similarly dominant in his brief trial. Despite those numbers, he hasn't cracked any Top 10 lists. He was a low round pick from a small college, was a bit old

for his league, and doesn't put up big numbers on the radar gun—but if he produces like that in New Haven, he'll be in the majors before the year is out. ■

MARK BROWNSON

SP-RP • BR • TR • 6′2 • 175 • 21 • COL93/30

	G	GS	IP	H	HR	BB	K	W	L	S	ERA	K/BB	K9	HW9
AA	37	19	144	141	10	43	155	8	11	3	3.50	3.6	9.7	11.50

Brownson throws his fastball in the mid-90s, a nasty slider, and a big breaking curveball—all of which he can get over for strikes. Too bad he tips all those pitches off with his wind-up, a herky-jerky motion that has him practically leaping off the rubber on his fastball, much less so on his slider, and barely even pushing off on his curveball. It didn't affect him too badly in a late August game against the Reading Phillies, where he gave up 5 soft singles, walked none, and struck out 12 in 8 innings. But major leaguers anywhere will pummel anything when they know it's coming, but the thought of tipping your pitches in Coors Field ... well, the Rockies should be humane enough not to ever let that happen until they work on his motion. ■

JOHN BURKE

RP • BB • TR • 6′4 • 220 • 27 • COL92/1

	G	GS	IP	H	HR	BB	K	W	L	S	ERA	K/BB	K9	HW9
COL96	11	0	16	21	3	7	19	2	1	0	7.47	2.7	10.9	16.09

Local hero Burke finally earned a promotion to the Rockies, despite an ERA around 6.00 with Colorado Springs. He has a good fastball, an even better curveball, and a decent change-up, but he has trouble with his control. He's also been hampered by shoulder injuries throughout his career, and, despite being used primarily as a starter, he has only gotten 100 innings in a season once (1993). He pitched better with Colorado Springs out of the bullpen, and his strikeout rate for the Rockies was unprecedented for him. By the time he's 30 and numb to the pain of pitching in Coors, he might be something. ■

ELLIS BURKS

LF • BR • TR • 6′2 • 200 • 32 • BOS83/1

	AB	R	H	2B	3B	HR	RBI	BB	SO	SB	CS	BA	OB	SA
COL94	149	33	48	8	3	13	24	16	39	3	1	.322	.388	.678
COL95	278	41	74	10	6	14	49	39	72	7	3	.266	.359	.496
COL96	613	142	211	45	8	40	128	61	114	32	6	.344	.408	.639
CAREER	4333	731	1255	247	48	177	662	427	772	141	63	.290	.355	.491

Ellis Burks has had a star-crossed career, having spent 35 weeks on the DL, so who's to begrudge him some stats inflation? Besides, of all the "Blake Street Bombers," he's the only one who showed the ability to hit outside of Colorado. He did 23-79-.390 at home, but 17-49-.291 on the road isn't too shabby. He also showed no signs of wearing down, hitting .348 after the All-Star break. The Rockies locked him up for 2 years and $9 million at the end of the year and will now keep their fingers crossed that he can play a full season again; he's only ever done it once before, in 1990 with the Red Sox. Gebhard credited Burks' success to hard work: "It started in the offseason. Ellis worked very hard to get in better condition. He was in here (Coors) hitting and working out all the time." Burks credits it to not having to play center field. He'll reluctantly return to center field in '97, where he fears that his back and hamstrings won't be able to hold up to the grind of that position. ■

VINNY CASTILLA

OVERRATED

3B • BR • TR • 6′1 • 200 • 29 • ATL90

	AB	R	H	2B	3B	HR	RBI	BB	SO	SB	CS	BA	OB	SA
COL94	130	16	43	11	1	3	18	7	23	2	1	.331	.357	.500
COL95	527	82	163	34	2	32	90	30	87	2	8	.309	.347	.564
COL96	629	97	191	34	0	40	113	35	88	7	2	.304	.343	.548
CAREER	1644	233	488	89	10	84	252	86	249	13	16	.297	.333	.516

Gee, how could the Braves let this guy get away? Amazing how an organization as consistently excellent as Atlanta's could fail to see that a guy with 34 dingers in his 399-game minor league career would develop into a 40-homer-a-year guy. If Castilla was still with the Braves, he might have made their postseason roster—assuming he hadn't been released in the past 3 years. But he plays in a park where routine flyballs travel 360 feet and curveballs don't break, so he goes to the All-Star Game and Sammy Sosa stays home. Eventually, the Rockies front office will figure out that you don't need to pay 7-figure salaries for this kind of production.

Castilla did 27-74-.345 at home, 13-39-.259 on the road—and this was an improvement. Prior to

'96, he'd gotten about 500 at bats both in Colorado and on the road, putting up 29-85-.353 at home and 15-53-.234 under less friendly circumstances. He's one of the most aggressive hitters in the league, living off fastballs, and hitting 21 of his home runs on the first pitch. He also continues to start and end slow: 64 of his 84 home runs with the Rockies have come during June, July, and August. Like Bichette, Castilla won't be able to afford any extended trips to the DL. ■

BRENT CROWTHER

SP-RP • BR • TR • 6'4 • 220 • 24 • COL94/10

	G	GS	IP	H	HR	BB	K	W	L	S	ERA	K/BB	K9	HW9
AA	25	12	86	109	10	30	54	3	7	1	6.20	1.8	5.7	14.60

Crowther only has average velocity, but his fastball and slider both dive into the ground (25 wild pitches in 261 innings in '95). He had a huge '95 in Class-A, with 12 consecutive victories and 4 shutouts, but Double-A batters in '96 had a lot easier time laying off his pitches and making him throw strikes. His pitches may have a lost of bit of their action, too, as he only uncorked 4 wild pitches in '96. ■

MIKE DEJEAN

RP • BR • TR • 6'2 • 205 • 26 • NYA92/24

	G	GS	IP	H	HR	BB	K	W	L	S	ERA	K/BB	K9	HW9
AAA	30	0	40	52	3	21	31	0	2	1	5.13	1.5	6.9	16.29

De Jean has a fastball, slider, and forkball, and all of it worked a bit better at sea-level in Double-A. In '95–'96, DeJean had 31 saves and a 3.04 ERA in 100 innings in Double-A. This earned him a promotion to Triple-A, where his control, which was never great, deteriorated. Assuming he can figure out Colorado Springs, there's no guarantee he'll ever be able to figure out Coors Field. ■

ANGEL ECHEVARRIA

OF • BR • TR • 6'4 • 215 • 25 • COL92/17

	AB	R	H	2B	3B	HR	RBI	BB	SO	SB	CS	BA	OB	SA
AAA	415	67	140	19	2	16	74	38	81	4	3	.337	.393	.508

There were some questions about Echevarria's ability to hit the breaking ball coming into '96. At first glance, it looks like he figured it out. But his Double-A performance in '95 in a much tougher park in a pitchers' league was far more impressive. He hit 21 home runs, knocked in 100 runs, and hit .300. Despite his batting average going up 37 points in '96, Echevarria's slugging average actually went down. His defense isn't great, either, so he may not end up being anything more than a spare part in Colorado. ■

MIKE FARMER

SP • BR • TL • 6'1 • 195 • 28 • PHI89

	G	GS	IP	H	HR	BB	K	W	L	S	ERA	K/BB	K9	HW9
COL96	7	4	28	32	8	13	16	0	1	0	7.71	1.2	5.1	14.46

Farmer is a fastball/change-up pitcher who the Rockies took in the Rule 5 Draft from the Phillies. He had nerve surgery in his elbow in '94, struggled in '95, and was called up in '96 for some big league punishment. Farmer is a former replacement player, motivated by his 18-month-old son's need for an operation. Baylor: "After a year or so you have to rethink your position. We still don't have a labor agreement. It's not like we're talking about Charles Manson." The Rockies accepted him, but, unfortunately, so did the National League. ■

ANDRES GALARRAGA

OVERRATED

1B • BR • TR • 6'3 • 235 • 35 • MON79

	AB	R	H	2B	3B	HR	RBI	BB	SO	SB	CS	BA	OB	SA
COL94	417	77	133	21	0	31	85	19	93	8	3	.319	.356	.592
COL95	554	89	155	29	3	31	106	32	146	12	2	.280	.331	.511
COL96	626	119	190	39	3	47	150	40	157	18	8	.304	.357	.601
CAREER	5474	788	1561	306	26	247	911	350	1328	99	54	.285	.336	.486

Baylor on this Blake Street Bomber: "He's always swung at bad pitches. . . . But now it's each at-bat day in and day out. He's undercutting the ball. That makes his swing slow." After an 0-29 slump, Baylor said: "He's swinging at balls that never were strikes. He's swinging at pitches that are way inside. He doesn't know where the strike zone is now." Has any hitter in baseball history been described in those terms by his manager in the same season in which he hit 47 home runs and batted .304? But then, how many washed-up hitters, 4 years removed from 10-39-.243 at 31, have risen from the dead to hit .370 or knock in 150 runs? Only one, and only because Jason Thompson, Nate Colbert, and Bob Robertson never got a chance to play in Coors Field. The obligatory home/away breakdown for The Big Cat: 32-103-.359 at home, 15-47-.245 on the road. *103*

RBIs in 79 games at home? Prior to '96, the best Galarraga had ever done in a *season* was 106. Maybe the Rockies were put on this earth to finally teach us that statistics lie—because in Galarraga's case, his record couldn't be more deceptive if he was running for public office. ■

DERRICK GIBSON — SOLID PROSPECT

OF • BR • TR • 6'2 • 240 • 22 • COL93/13

	AB	R	H	2B	3B	HR	RBI	BB	SO	SB	CS	BA	OB	SA
AA	449	58	115	21	4	15	62	31	125	3	12	.256	.313	.421

Bo Jackson used to play running back for Auburn. This guy played linebacker. He's got an impressive package of tools, but he's very raw. Despite good speed, especially for his size, his defense is nothing special and as a basestealer . . . well, maybe he shouldn't bother. He has a big swing, but his head flies out; with his strength, he could cut down on his swing and the ball would still jump off of his bat. In a hitters' park in '95 in Class-A he did 30-30, but he struck out 136 times while walking only 29. That was an improvement over '94, when he whiffed 102 times in 73 games. He stands right on the plate like Don Baylor, but Baylor never hit below .300 or struck out 100 times at any level of the minors. He's built like Frank Thomas, but The Big Hurt was in the majors after 593 minor league at bats. You'll be hearing the comparisons to both of them, but he hasn't earned them yet. ■

TODD HELTON — GRADE-A PROSPECT

1B • BL • TL • 6'2 • 195 • 23 • COL95/1

	AB	R	H	2B	3B	HR	RBI	BB	SO	SB	CS	BA	OB	SA
AA	319	46	106	24	2	7	51	51	37	2	5	.332	.425	.486

Helton was the no. 8 pick in the 1995 draft from the University of Tennessee and he won the Dick Howser Award as Top College Player. Unfortunately, the winner of that award is not guaranteed much of a big league career. Winners since 1981 have included the anonymous (Mike Sodders, Jeff Ledbetter, and Casey Close); the frustrating (Mike Kelly, David McCarty, and Phil Nevin); the mediocre (Dave Magadan, Oddibe McDowell, Pete Incaviglia, John Olerud, and Ben McDonald); and Robin Ventura. Now it's up to Helton, Brooks Kieschnick, and Jason Varitek to make an impact. Helton is the best bet to put up some big numbers, and not just because of Coors Field. Helton has an excellent swing, power to all fields, and a good glove. If he can begin to pull the ball more his power numbers should improve. He earned a promotion to Triple-A and hit .352 in 21 games. If you don't believe he can steal the job from Galarraga if given the chance, The Big Cat didn't make it to Double-A until he was 24, hit .269, and struck out 103 times. Don't expect Helton to hit 47 dingers in the big leagues, but he could win a few batting titles in Denver before he's through. He had to leave the Arizona Fall League after only 6 games to have bone spurs removed from his heel, but he's expected to be ready to go in the spring. ■

DARREN HOLMES — SLEEPER

RP • BR • TR • 6'0 • 200 • 30 • LA84/16

	G	GS	IP	H	HR	BB	K	W	L	S	ERA	K/BB	K9	HW9
COL94	29	0	28	35	5	24	33	0	3	3	6.35	1.4	10.6	18.94
COL95	68	0	66	59	3	28	61	6	1	14	3.24	2.2	8.3	11.86
COL96	62	0	77	78	8	28	73	5	4	1	3.97	2.6	8.5	12.39
CAREER	316	0	374	368	30	149	336	19	20	52	4.09	2.3	8.1	12.44

Holmes could have been the Brewers closer if they hadn't left him unprotected in the expansion draft (at the age of 26 after a season in which he had a 2.55 ERA and allowed less than 10 baserunners per 9 innings). He has an impressive collection of pitches: a cut fastball, a slider, and a very good, sharp breaking curveball which he can go to late in the count. He was the best pitcher on the staff in the second half; he had a 2.41 ERA and allowed 32 hits in 41 innings, while striking out 36 and walking 15. He could probably be a quality closer for another team—or the Rockies, again, if Ruffin falters and Leskanic fails to regain his '95 form—but don't be surprised if he ends up in the rotation instead. ■

BOBBY M. JONES

RP • BR • TL • 6'0 • 175 • 24 • MIL91/44

	G	GS	IP	H	HR	BB	K	W	L	S	ERA	K/BB	K9	HW9
AAA	57	0	89	88	8	63	78	2	8	3	4.97	1.2	7.9	15.33

Jones never had serious control problems until he reached Colorado Springs in '95 and started nibbling. He walked more than 7 batters per 9 innings in '95 and was tagged for a 7.30 ERA. He walked more than 6 batters per 9 innings in '96 as

the Rockies converted him into a full-time reliever. He did hold lefties to a .226 batting average, so he may have a future as a one-batter-per-appearance type in the big leagues. ■

TERRY JONES

OF • BB • TR • 5'10 • 165 • 26 • COL93/40

	AB	R	H	2B	3B	HR	RBI	BB	SO	SB	CS	BA	OB	SA
AAA	497	75	143	7	4	0	33	37	80	26	14	.288	.337	.318

Jones is the fastest player in the organization, but . . . 1) he doesn't hit the ball on the ground enough, 2) he managed only 11 extra base hits in the PCL, which makes Tom Goodwin look like Ken Griffey, 3) his stolen base success rate has dropped from 80% to 65%, 4) he doesn't walk enough, and 5) he strikes out too much. If you think he can find a role on the Rockies, bear in mind what Trenidad Hubbard did at 26 in AAA: .310 with 34 steals and 22 extra base hits. Hubbard was up to 12 dingers and .363 before he was through, and still couldn't fetch more than Steve Decker in a trade. ■

DAVE KENNEDY

1B • BR • TR • 6'4 • 215 • 26 • CAL91/6

	AB	R	H	2B	3B	HR	RBI	BB	SO	SB	CS	BA	OB	SA
AAA	333	46	85	27	0	11	50	36	82	1	2	.255	.332	.435

Kennedy blew out his arm as a pitcher for the Angels and gave it a shot as a hitter. But .255 in Colorado Springs isn't going to get anyone's attention, and the Rockies will want Todd Helton playing first for the Sky Sox in '97. ■

MIKE KUSIEWICZ

SLEEPER

SP • BR • TL • 6'2 • 185 • 20 • COL94/5

	G	GS	IP	H	HR	BB	K	W	L	S	ERA	K/BB	K9	HW9
AA	14	14	76	83	4	27	64	2	4	0	3.30	2.4	7.5	12.97

Kusiewicz is a pitcher, not a thrower. At his age, he should gain some velocity as he matures. As it is, his fastball already has movement. He also has excellent control, can change speeds, and hits spots. He may be the most promising 2-4 starting pitcher in the minors. ■

CURTIS LESKANIC

RP • BR • TR • 6'0 • 180 • 28 • CLE89/7

	G	GS	IP	H	HR	BB	K	W	L	S	ERA	K/BB	K9	HW9
COL94	8	3	22	27	2	10	17	1	1	0	5.64	1.7	6.9	15.11
COL95	76	0	98	83	7	33	107	6	3	10	3.40	3.2	9.8	10.65
COL96	70	0	73	82	12	38	76	7	5	6	6.23	2.0	9.4	14.78
CAREER	172	11	250	251	28	108	230	15	14	16	4.89	2.1	8.3	12.92

Probably no other pitcher frustrated Baylor in '96 more than Leskanic. Baylor (commenting on a Leskanic fastball that didn't show much movement until it landed for a game-winning home run): "If it doesn't break, then it's just a nothing fastball." Sounds like Baylor has spent some time in Dallas Green's diplomatic corps. Leskanic pitched a lot of innings in '95 and he broke down in '96 in late May (he was on pace for 86 appearances and 92 innings). He missed most of June, but didn't look much better over the final 3 months of the season and Baylor didn't exactly take it easy on him. If he regains some of his lost velocity in '97, he might rebound—but there was nothing in his history to indicate he was capable of his '95 numbers, so don't expect him to make it all the way back. He'll have to recover from arthoscopic elbow and shoulder operations performed during the off-season. ■

TAL LIGHT

SOLID PROSPECT

3B • BR • TR • 6'3 • 205 • 23 • COL95/8

	AB	R	H	2B	3B	HR	RBI	BB	SO	SB	CS	BA	OB	SA
A+	234	29	55	10	0	13	36	19	59	3	1	.235	.305	.444

Light led NCAA Division I with 106 RBI in '95 while with Oklahoma State. Between Asheville and Salem, he hit 25 home runs, knocked in 87 runs, and hit .278. At his age, Castilla was splitting time between the South Atlantic and the Southern Leagues, and was hitting 13 home runs and batting .257. In any other organization, Light would have his work cut out for him. With Colorado, he might just need a chance to play. He could be challenging for the third base job as early as '98, especially if he can make the pitchers throw him more strikes. ■

CHRIS MACCA

SOLID PROSPECT

RP • BR • TR • 6'2 • 185 • 22 • COL95/3

	G	GS	IP	H	HR	BB	K	W	L	S	ERA	K/BB	K9	HW9
AA	28	0	34	18	0	18	33	3	1	15	1.34	1.8	8.8	9.63

Macca throws 95, slinging it from a three-quarter/sidearm delivery that looks like an elbow injury waiting to happen. But he's been unhittable since he turned pro, racking up 30 saves between Asheville and New Haven in '96, holding hitters to a .157 batting average and recording a 1.20 ERA. The Rockies may want to see what he can do in Denver as soon as this year. ■

CHANDLER MARTIN

SP • BR • TR • 6'1 • 180 • 23 • COL95/6

	G	GS	IP	H	HR	BB	K	W	L	S	ERA	K/BB	K9	HW9
A+	13	13	69	80	5	53	59	2	8	0	5.87	1.1	7.7	17.35

Martin throws a circle-change-up, a good curveball, and can spot his fastball. He was untouchable in Class-A Asheville, where he went 9-0 with a 2.20 ERA. Salem was his first taste of adversity, and it was a fairly low level for a pitcher to begin nibbling. He could disappear from the radar screen in '97. ■

QUINTON MCCRACKEN

SLEEPER

OF • BB • TR • 5'8 • 170 • 27 • COL92/25

	AB	R	H	2B	3B	HR	RBI	BB	SO	SB	CS	BA	OB	SA
COL96	283	50	82	13	6	3	40	32	62	17	6	.290	.363	.410

Rotisserie players were scratching their collective heads in '96 over whether to roll the dice on Trenidad Hubbard or Quinton McCracken as the player most likely to get p.t. when Ellis Burks went down. Walker went down instead, the smaller, younger McCracken got the job, and Hubbard got shipped out to one of the worst hitters' parks in baseball.

QMC is a former cornerback and second baseman from Duke. He's a better hitter from the left side. He's patient at the plate, a fast runner, and a decent defensive player. If he could cut down a bit on his uppercut to better utilize his speed, and blow the cobwebs off of his infielders mitt, there's no reason he couldn't put up Eric Young numbers in Colorado. Their PCL numbers at 25 are virtually identical. ■

DOUG MILLION

SOLID PROSPECT

SP • BL • TL • 6'4 • 175 • 21 • COL94/1

	G	GS	IP	H	HR	BB	K	W	L	S	ERA	K/BB	K9	HW9
AA	10	10	54	54	2	40	40	3	3	0	3.15	1.0	6.6	15.57

It took Million more than 1-1/2 seasons to get out of high Class-A and he didn't show much in Double-A. Nevertheless, scouts still think he is one of the top prospects in the Rockies system. He has a good fastball and change-up and one of the best breaking balls in the minors, though he has had difficulty controlling his stuff. He's walked 6.5 batters per 9 innings in the past 2 years. He is asthmatic and has worked hard to put on weight, but to date all he's gotten for his trouble is a shoulder strain in '95. If his learning curve is this flat in the minors, who knows how long it might take him to figure out Coors Field. ■

MIKE MUNOZ

RP • BL • TL • 6'2 • 190 • 31• LA86/3

	G	GS	IP	H	HR	BB	K	W	L	S	ERA	K/BB	K9	HW9
COL94	57	0	45	37	3	31	32	4	2	1	3.74	1.0	6.4	13.58
COL95	64	0	43	54	9	27	37	2	4	2	7.42	1.4	7.7	16.95
COL96	54	0	44	55	4	16	45	2	2	0	6.65	2.8	9.2	14.50
CAREER	286	0	220	240	22	124	162	11	13	5	5.40	1.3	6.6	14.89

Munoz consistently threw strikes for the first time in his career, and his strikeouts increased significantly. But challenging hitters isn't always rewarded at Coors, and Munoz was hit for a .302 average for his efforts. He turns over his change-up and uses a forkball to try to get batters to beat the ball into the ground. It doesn't always work, home or away. He owned lefties in '96, holding them to a .200 average. Unfortunately, he only faced them one-third of the time. The rest of the time it was righties and they hit .352 against him. ■

DAVID NIED

SP • BR • TR • 6'2 • 185 • 28 • ATL87/14

	G	GS	IP	H	HR	BB	K	W	L	S	ERA	K/BB	K9	HW9
AAA	16	16	62	116	16	32	53	3	8	0	12.27	1.7	7.7	21.37

Nied was the Rockies first pick in the expansion draft and started their first game ever, in Shea Stadium against Dwight Gooden. In '96, he was demoted all the way down to high Class-A where he

finally got it back on the rails. The Rockies called him back up in September and he got beat up and battered around; in his last 8 major league appearances, he's pitched 9.2 innings, given up 16 hits, 11 walks, 3 dingers, and 18 runs. Gebhard: "I'm not ready to give up on David Nied yet. I believe he's going to pitch in the majors again, and we're going to be the ones who give him that chance." Nied didn't want that chance, and got out of Colorado as soon as he was eligible, signing with the Reds in November. ■

JAYHAWK OWENS

C • BR • TR • 6'1 • 215 • 28 • MIN90/3

	AB	R	H	2B	3B	HR	RBI	BB	SO	SB	CS	BA	OB	SA
COL95	45	7	11	2	0	4	12	2	15	0	0	.244	.286	.556
COL96	180	31	43	9	1	4	17	27	56	4	1	.239	.338	.367
CAREER	323	54	75	16	2	11	36	38	104	5	1	.232	.318	.396

Not to nitpick, but the Rockies didn't like his offense *or* his defense. He hit .308 at home and only .145 on the road, and struck out once every 3 at bats. He made 9 errors in 68 games, giving him the lowest fielding percentage of any catcher who'd played as many games—and his 7 passed balls in 460 innings was far too high a number for someone who doesn't catch a knuckleballer. With the Rockies staff, how many opportunities does a catcher even get to pass a ball? As for his handling of the pitchers, the ERA when he was catching was a full run higher than when Jeff Reed was behind the plate. He's more reason to distrust PCL numbers: He got 652 at bats at Colorado Springs from '93 to '95, and hit 24 home runs, knocked in 135 runs, and batted .288. The PCL stat to focus on should have been the 183 strikeouts. He didn't bring the batting average up the road to Denver, but he did bring the whiffs. His brief trial in '95 convinced the front office that they could let Joe Girardi go. His extended trial in '96 convinced them they needed to try to buy a catcher in the free agent market. Owens is not long for Denver, and if he can't stick here, you'd have to conclude that his career may be over. ■

LANCE PAINTER

RP • BL • TL • 6'1 • 195 • 29 • SD90/25

	G	GS	IP	H	HR	BB	K	W	L	S	ERA	K/BB	K9	HW9
COL94	15	14	73	91	9	26	41	4	6	0	6.11	1.6	5.1	14.41
COL95	33	1	45	55	9	10	36	3	0	1	4.37	3.6	7.2	13.00
COL95	34	1	50	56	12	25	48	4	2	0	5.86	1.9	8.6	14.56
CAREER	92	22	208	254	35	70	141	13	10	1	5.67	2.0	6.1	14.01

Painter is a sidearming lefty who doesn't have overpowering stuff. Since he isn't particularly tough on lefties, it doesn't even look like he'll be able to stick as a one-batter-per-appearance type for the Rockies. Like Owens is the poster child for what the PCL does to mediocre hitters, Painter serves the same function for what the low minors can do to mediocre pitchers. In Rookie ball and Class-A, he looked like the second coming of Steve Carlton. He struck out 104, walked 15, and allowed only 45 hits in 72 relief innings in the Northwest League. He followed that up by going 14-8 as a starter with a 2.30 ERA while striking out a batter per inning with command. Most of the rest of his career has been spent in the state of Colorado, and he's not showing any signs of taking to it. In fact, he's nibbling more and more each year, his walks per game now up to 4.5. Painter needs a change of scenery. At what point will Rockies pitchers begin to insist on a yes-trade clause? ■

ROB PEDRAZA

SP • BR • TR • 6'2 • 210 • 27

	G	GS	IP	H	HR	BB	K	W	L	S	ERA	K/BB	K9	HW9
AA	19	18	122	115	10	21	74	7	3	0	2.95	3.5	5.5	10.03

Pedraza doesn't have great stuff, but throws strikes and knows how to pitch. It works until he gets to Colorado Springs. In his past 2 tours of New Haven, he's gone 20-6 with a 3.10 ERA. He spent time in the PCL both years, pitching 61 innings, giving up 99 hits and 60 earned runs. If you were in the Rockies front office, would you give someone with his resumé a chance to get lit up in Denver? Or showcase him in New Haven? ■

NEIFI PEREZ

SOLID PROSPECT

SS • BB • TR • 6'0 • 175 • 22 • COL92

	AB	R	H	2B	3B	HR	RBI	BB	SO	SB	CS	BA	OB	SA
AAA	570	77	180	28	12	7	72	21	48	16	13	.316	.337	.444

If Perez could hit, he'd be a Grade-A prospect. But other than his time in the PCL, he's never hit above .260. In the majors, he won't draw walks and he won't do much more than slap singles, even in Coors. He hit .156 with a .156 on-base percentage in a 17-game trial with the Rockies in September. He is very fast, but doesn't yet know how to steal bases. He will stay in the majors on the strength of his good glove, great range, and strong arm. Salt Lake manager, Phil Roof, compared him to Ozzie Smith. Baylor: "I hope no one says, 'here's the next Ozzie Smith', like Rey Ordonez has had to deal with. Because he's not there yet. If he hits, it will be a tremendous plus." For financial reasons, Walt Weiss or Eric Young will likely be gone and Perez will be in the starting lineup. If he's at shortstop, look for the Rockies to turn even more than their league-leading 139 double plays in '97 behind their groundball pitching staff. ■

BEN PETRICK

SOLID PROSPECT

C • COL95/2 • GLENCOE HIGH SCHOOL (OR)

	AB	R	H	2B	3B	HR	RBI	BB	SO	SB	CS	BA	OB	SA
A	446	74	105	24	2	14	52	75	98	19	9	.235	.350	.392

Petrick was drafted in '95, but didn't play as a professional until '96. He is a very strong defensive catcher—compared by some observers to Ron Karkovice. A running back in high school, he has good speed for a catcher. Petrick will be 20 in '97, but it hasn't been common of late for catchers to be regulars in the major leagues before 23—with the notable exceptions of Ivan Rodriguez and Jason Kendall. With nothing in front of him, expect Petrick to be an exception and claim the job before the turn of the century. ■

JEFF REED

C • BL • TR • 6′2 • 190 • 34 • MIN80/1

	AB	R	H	2B	3B	HR	RBI	BB	SO	SB	CS	BA	OB	SA
SF94	103	11	18	3	0	1	7	11	21	0	0	.175	.254	.233
SF95	113	12	30	2	0	0	9	20	17	0	0	.265	.376	.283
COL96	341	34	97	20	1	8	37	43	65	2	2	.284	.365	.419
CAREER	2101	170	508	91	7	28	184	230	328	4	5	.242	.316	.332

Reed was taken with the 12th pick in the 1980 draft (a guy named Daulton was still available in the 25th). From that high school class, though, only Reed, Danny Tartabull, and Darryl Strawberry are still getting at bats 17 years later. After 12 years in the big leagues, Reed had 20 home runs. After 57 games in Coors, he's got 7 more. The Rockies will buy themselves a catcher and Reed's playing time will decline. ■

STEVE REED

RP • BR • TR • 6′2 • 210 • 31 • SF88

	G	GS	IP	H	HR	BB	K	W	L	S	ERA	K/BB	K9	HW9
COL94	61	0	64	79	9	26	51	3	2	3	3.94	2.0	7.2	14.77
COL95	71	0	84	61	8	21	79	5	2	3	2.14	3.8	8.5	8.79
COL96	70	0	75	66	11	19	51	4	3	0	3.96	2.7	6.1	10.20
CAREER	284	0	323	299	43	99	243	22	12	9	3.54	2.5	6.8	11.09

Reed is a submariner, so he's much more effective against righties than lefties. Despite the fact that he's not a groundball pitcher, he was the most effective on the staff at Coors in '96. If he can put up those kind of numbers in Colorado, you have to wonder whether he could be Kent Tekulve or Dan Quisenberry if he pitched somewhere else. ■

BRYAN REKAR

SP • BR • TR • 6′3 • 210 • 24 • COL93/2

	G	GS	IP	H	HR	BB	K	W	L	S	ERA	K/BB	K9	HW9
COL95	15	14	85	95	11	24	60	4	6	0	4.98	2.5	6.4	12.60
COL96	14	11	58	87	11	26	25	2	4	0	8.95	1.0	3.9	17.52

Rekar dominated at Double-A in 1995, was even better after being promoted to Colorado Springs, and had an ERA below 5.00 as a rookie in Denver—so the organization had high hopes in '96 that he would be the first of their pitching prospects to establish himself in the majors. Instead, he may be the next, after David Nied, in what will be a long line of demoralized pitching prospects. It is hard to overstate how brutal he was in home games. Here, projected to 500 at bats, is the hitting line of the batters who faced him in Coors (and, since it's pretty tough to find that combination of power and batting average, the closest we could come to a similar season from a big league hitter):

	AB	R	H	2B	3B	HR	RBI	BB	SO	BA	SA
B. Rekar '96	500	158	201	25	7	32	148	53	28	.401	.669
R. Hornsby '25	504	133	203	41	10	39	143	83	39	.403	.756

Basically, he made every hitter he faced look like the greatest second baseman to ever play the game—only a more difficult to strike out version of him. Obviously, Rekar is not this bad. He has a fastball, slider, and change-up, but his out pitch is his curveball. He uses his curve to set up his fastball and, usually, his location is exceptional. He lost that location in '96—and a healthy bit of his confidence—and you can see the results. If he's not scarred for life from facing The Rajah batter after batter in '96, he could be a quality pitcher. ■

ARMANDO REYNOSO

SP • BR • TR • 6'0 • 205 • 30 • ATL90

	G	GS	IP	H	HR	BB	K	W	L	S	ERA	K/BB	K9	HW9
COL94	9	9	52	54	5	22	25	3	4	0	4.82	1.1	4.3	13.15
COL95	20	18	93	116	12	36	40	7	7	0	5.32	1.1	3.9	14.71
COL96	30	30	168	195	27	49	88	8	9	0	4.96	1.8	4.7	13.07
CAREER	98	93	533	608	72	182	282	33	32	1	4.73	1.5	4.8	13.34

Armando Reynoso has rebounded from Tommy John surgery in 1994, though he hasn't been able to go as deep into games. He throws just about everything (slider, change-up, forkball, curveball, fastball) and he continually changes his arm angle to try to confuse hitters. His biggest strength may be his ability to take one on the chin at Coors and come back to pitch effectively 5 days later—and that will no longer be needed now that he's a Met. This lack of a gap between his home/away performance suggests that Reynoso, surprising as it sounds, won't be significantly more effective pitching for a different team in '97. ■

KEVIN RITZ

SP • BR • TR • 6'4 • 195 • 31 • DET85

	G	GS	IP	H	HR	BB	K	W	L	S	ERA	K/BB	K9	HW9
COL94	15	15	73	88	5	35	53	5	6	0	5.62	1.5	6.5	15.15
COL95	31	28	173	171	16	65	120	11	11	2	4.21	1.8	6.2	12.28
COL96	35	35	213	236	24	105	105	17	11	0	5.28	1.0	4.4	14.41
CAREER	131	110	637	689	52	329	403	39	46	2	5.19	1.2	5.7	14.38

Other than his won-loss record, Ritz's numbers look like that of a pitcher on his way out of the game, not one looking for a fat contract. But the Rockies will be bringing him back and he won't be cheap. He eats innings and he's willing to pitch at Coors,

and that can even make a pitcher who walks as many as he strikes out a valuable commodity. He coaxes his share of groundballs with a sinking fastball and a deceptive circle change. He throws a few too many fat, first pitch fastballs. His were fatter than most in '96: batters hit .424 and slugged .757 on his first pitch. ■

BRUCE RUFFIN

CL • BB • TL • 6'2 • 215 • 33 • PHI85/2

	G	GS	IP	H	HR	BB	K	W	L	S	ERA	K/BB	K9	HW9
COL94	56	0	55	55	6	30	65	4	5	16	4.04	2.2	10.6	13.89
COL95	37	0	34	26	1	19	23	0	1	11	2.12	1.2	6.1	11.91
COL95	71	0	69	55	5	29	74	7	5	24	4.00	2.6	9.6	10.95
CAREER	446	152	1245	1327	89	547	812	60	80	56	4.19	1.5	5.9	13.55

Ruffin came to the Rockies from the Brewers, where he was 1-6 with a 6.67 ERA. Prior to that, he was a source of frustration to the Phillies, where he was 42-58, primarily as a starter who couldn't throw strikes, and who deteriorated rapidly after a promising rookie season in 1986. In 4 years with the Rockies, he's had an ERA of 3.74 and 53 saves. He has a limited repertoire—a hard slider and sinking fastball—which makes him better suited to relief. Considering what he did and where he did it, he may have been the most underrated pitcher in the N.L. in '96. ■

BRET SABERHAGEN

SP • BR • TR • 6'1 • 195 • KC82/19

The Rockies gave up two good arms (Juan Acevedo and Arnold Gooch) and about $5 million to get 9 starts and 2 wins out of Saberhagen—who never wanted to be in Colorado in the first place, rarely traveled with the team, and put more work into keeping the Rockies from picking up his option after the '96 season than he did into rehabbing his shoulder. The Rockies granted him his wish, but only after Saberhagen claimed he was being "pushed into" shoulder rehab

by GM Bob Gebhard. Saberhagen finally underwent reconstructive surgery in May '96, and another 12 months of downtime was considered "optimistic." His arm is clearly a question mark. But after these difficulties with the Rockies and his charming use of bleach in the Mets clubhouse, there aren't nearly as many questions about his character. ■

MIKE SAIPE

SP-RP • BR • TR • 6'1 • 190 • 23 • COL94/12

	G	GS	IP	H	HR	BB	K	W	L	S	ERA	K/BB	K9	HW9
AA	32	19	138	114	12	42	126	10	7	3	3.07	3.0	8.2	10.17

Saipe is the latest pitching prospect to arrive in New Haven and put up some attractive numbers. Unlike some other pitchers who did so only to blow up in Colorado Springs, Saipe has actually improved all aspects of his game—control, ERA, wins—as he's risen through the system. So don't be surprised if he actually survives the PCL. ■

BILL SWIFT

SP • BR • TR • 6'0 • 180 • 35 • SEA84/1

	G	GS	IP	H	HR	BB	K	W	L	S	ERA	K/BB	K9	HW9
SF94	17	17	109	109	10	31	62	8	7	0	3.38	2.0	5.1	11.56
COL95	19	19	105	122	12	43	68	9	3	0	4.34	1.6	5.8	14.14
COL96	7	3	18	23	1	5	5	1	1	2	5.40	1.0	2.5	13.97
CAREER	360	181	1389	1420	84	430	661	79	63	27	3.54	1.5	4.3	11.99

The Rockies paid Bret Saberhagen $5 million for 9 starts, and to date they've paid Swift $8 million for 22 starts. Unlike Saberhagen, Swift at least tried to come back in '96, but he had no velocity and he eventually had the shoulder operated on for the second time within a year. He came back to pitch in September, even though he admitted he wasn't anywhere close to 100%. Swift: "I feel like I need to be out there. I'm getting paid a lot of money." But once the team dropped out of contention, they shut him down again, this time because of tricep tightness. Swift had been on the DL 11 times in his career coming into '96, and he's only pitched 200 innings once at any level, so expect an honest effort but limited results from Swift in '97. ■

MARK THOMPSON

SP • BR • TR • 6'2 • 205 • 25 • COL92/2

	G	GS	IP	H	HR	BB	K	W	L	S	ERA	K/BB	K9	HW9
COL95	21	5	51	73	7	22	30	2	3	0	6.53	1.4	5.3	16.76
COL96	34	28	169	189	25	74	99	9	11	0	5.30	1.3	5.3	14.00
CAREER	57	35	229	278	34	104	134	12	15	0	5.74	1.3	5.3	15.01

Thompson was being penciled into the Rockies '97 rotation during the off-season, despite an erratic '96 and difficulties in coping with Coors Field that were more pronounced than any starter except Rekar. Thompson has a slider/fastball package, and needs to stay on top of his fastball to make it sink. He felt that he was finally back to where he was in '93 before his arm operation, but his numbers since—most notably his strikeouts and walks—have never approached what he'd done before the injury. Sounds like wishful thinking. ■

JOHN THOMSON

SP • BR • TR • 6'3 • 175 • 23 • COL93/7

	G	GS	IP	H	HR	BB	K	W	L	S	ERA	K/BB	K9	HW9
AAA	11	11	70	76	6	26	62	4	7	0	5.04	2.4	8.0	13.18

Thomson was promoted to Colorado Springs in mid-season after going 9-4 with a 2.86 ERA at Double-A. He responded with the worst numbers of his career. Welcome to the club. Thomson needed a second stint at New Haven before he figured things out there, so maybe he'll be able to improve in '97. He'll have to do so with a fastball that's not very fast, but moves, and erratic breaking stuff. ■

JOHN VANDER WAL

OF-1B • BL • TL • 6'2 • 200 • 30 • MON87/3

	AB	R	H	2B	3B	HR	RBI	BB	SO	SB	CS	BA	OB	SA
COL94	110	12	27	3	1	5	15	16	31	2	1	.245	.339	.427
COL95	101	15	35	8	1	5	21	16	23	1	1	.347	.432	.594
COL96	151	20	38	6	2	5	31	19	38	2	2	.252	.335	.417
CAREER	851	106	214	36	11	25	125	103	176	14	7	.251	.332	.408

Vander Wal went 28-87 (.322) as a pinch-hitter in '95, but in '96 managers began to bring in lefties to get him out of the game, limiting him to only 16-56 (.286). He hasn't been able to produce when he's in the starting lineup: He did 2-18-.232 as a starter, 3-13-.286 in half as many at bats coming off the bench. The injury to Larry Walker gave him a chance to show

what he could do if he played regularly, and the answer was: not get a chance to pinch-hit. ▪

EDGARD VELAZQUEZ — *GRADE-A PROSPECT*

CF • BR • TR • 6'0 • 170 • 21 • COL93/10

	AB	R	H	2B	3B	HR	RBI	BB	SO	SB	CS	BA	OB	SA
AA	486	72	141	29	4	19	62	53	114	6	2	.290	.365	.484

Velazquez is the Rockies long-term answer in center field. He has good range in the outfield and a strong arm. He hasn't yet used his speed to turn himself into a stolen base threat, but his success rate was over 60% for the first time in '96. At the plate, his high step and big stride translate into power and strikeouts. He is frequently compared to Manny Ramirez and to his uncle, Roberto Clemente. Ramirez made his debut at 21 and was a star by 23. That's not out of the question for Velazquez. He could put up some ungodly numbers in Colorado Springs this year, and be ready to replace Ellis Burks in 1999 when his 2-year deal is up. His numbers in Coors could be those of a superstar, strikeouts and all. ▪

JACOB VIANO

RP-SP • BR • TR • 5'10 • 170 • 23 • COL93/11

	G	GS	IP	H	HR	BB	K	W	L	S	ERA	K/BB	K9	HW9
AA	23	5	45	39	6	24	32	4	3	0	4.84	1.3	6.4	12.70

Viano is yet another Rockies pitcher whose progress stalled upon being promoted to Triple-A. After saving 19 games with a 3.38 ERA, an excellent strikeout rate, and good control in New Haven in '95, he was crushed at Colorado Springs. He gave up 7 home runs and 25 runs in 21 innings, while walking 13 and striking out 12. Upon being demoted back to New Haven, he couldn't even pitch well there. In addition to a damaged psyche, Viano will need to overcome the bias against short pitchers. Right now, he's a longshot. ▪

LARRY WALKER — *CONSISTENT STAR*

CF • BL • TR • 6'3 • 225 • 30 • MON84

	AB	R	H	2B	3B	HR	RBI	BB	SO	SB	CS	BA	OB	SA
MON94	395	76	127	44	2	19	86	47	74	15	5	.322	.394	.587
COL95	494	96	151	31	5	36	101	49	72	16	3	.306	.381	.607
COL96	272	58	75	18	4	18	58	20	58	18	2	.276	.342	.570
CAREER	3132	522	892	196	25	153	543	333	604	132	40	.285	.359	.510

Walker missed most of June and July and half of August with a broken collarbone. He then shut it back down again in September, though the Rockies

were technically in a pennant race. He is a tremendous talent, but is he a bit too laidback to ever lead his team into the World Series? No other major leaguer in the history of the game has ever been enough of a space cadet to give a live ball to a fan during an inning when there were men on base, rounding them at will. This year, he repeatedly pestered Don Baylor to yank him from games so he could watch the Colorado Avalanche play for The Cup. Perhaps Don Baylor wouldn't mind this kind of stuff from a middle reliever who is around to keep everybody loose. But from the most talented player on the team . . . ?

Walker is the best hitter to ever player for the Rockies, so most expected him to put up outrageous numbers in Coors. His offense has actually declined. Consider what he's done in '94, '95, and '96 when you project each season to 500 at bats:

	AB	R	H	2B	3B	HR	RBI	BB	SO	BA	OB	SA
Walker '94	500	96	161	56	3	24	109	59	94	.322	.394	.587
Walker '95	500	97	153	31	5	36	102	49	73	.306	.381	.607
Walker '96	500	107	138	33	7	33	107	37	107	.276	.342	.570

Walker hits more home runs, but he was just as productive in a pitchers' park with the Expos '94 lineup as he was on a team that scored 961 runs in '96. He's less selective at the plate, doesn't get on base as much, and his slugging average has actually declined. The argument can be made that playing in Coors is hurting him on the road more than it's helping him at home. Consider his road numbers, projected to 500 at bats, for the past 2 seasons: 24-85-.268 (with 65 walks and 66 strikeouts) in '95, 24-51-.142 (with 28 walks and 126 strikeouts) in '96 Is Coors Field, and the bad habits it fosters, turning him into Rob Deer? ▪

WALT WEISS

SS • BB • TR • 6′0 • 175 • 33 • OAK85/1

	AB	R	H	2B	3B	HR	RBI	BB	SO	SB	CS	BA	OB	SA
COL94	423	58	106	11	4	1	32	56	58	12	7	.251	.336	.303
COL95	427	65	111	17	3	1	25	98	57	15	3	.260	.403	.321
COL96	517	89	146	20	2	8	48	80	78	10	2	.282	.381	.375
CAREER	3475	440	891	122	18	19	274	472	469	76	28	.256	.347	.318

The Rockies were looking to trade Weiss in the '97 off-season, both to dump his salary and to make room for Neifi Perez. Even Weiss, a groundball hitter with less power than the Commissioner's Office, had his numbers inflated by Coors: 3-16-.227 with a .305 slugging average on the road, 5-32-.337 with a .444 slugging average at home. His age, that road performance, and his deteriorating play at short (his errors were up from 16 to 30 while his range declined), may prove to make that salary a tough one to unload. ■

JAMEY WRIGHT

SOLID PROSPECT

SP • BR • TR • 6′6 • 205 • 22 • COL93/1

	G	GS	IP	H	HR	BB	K	W	L	S	ERA	K/BB	K9	HW9
COL96	16	15	91	105	8	41	45	4	4	0	4.93	1.1	4.4	14.43

Wright is the Rekar of '97: the young pitcher with unlimited potential who has blown through the organization, pitched well at Colorado Springs, and made it out of Coors Field with all his teeth. He may fare better than Rekar did in his second year, simply because no one could fare worse. And because he has the best arm in the organization. He has a 93-mph fastball with exceptional sinking action (described as a "sinking bowling ball"), a four-seamer that can occasionally touch 96, and a hard slider. His pitches are very tough to drive; he gave up only 19 extra base hits in '95, while in '96 he had a 0.81 ERA in New Haven and a 2.72 ERA in Colorado Springs, yielding only 3 home runs in 60 PCL innings. On the down side, he doesn't change speeds well and the National League hit .295 against him *on the road*. He injured his knee in July, but pitched through it. He underwent arthoscopic surgery in the off-season and will be 100% by the spring. With his stuff, he'd be a Grade-A Prospect if he pitched for any other team. ■

ERIC YOUNG

2B • BR • TR • 5′9 • 180 • 29 • LA89/46

	AB	R	H	2B	3B	HR	RBI	BB	SO	SB	CS	BA	OB	SA
COL94	228	37	62	13	1	7	30	38	17	18	7	.272	.378	.430
COL95	366	68	116	21	9	6	36	49	29	35	12	.317	.404	.473
COL96	568	113	184	23	4	8	74	47	31	53	19	.324	.393	.421
CAREER	1784	309	528	74	22	25	193	205	127	154	58	.296	.376	.404

It took the Rockies longer than it should have to realize Norman Bates wasn't the answer at second base, and to let Eric Young play every day. Young was motivated by the Rockies going after Biggio in the '95-'96 off-season: "Of course that hit home for me. Once everytl ing was said and done, it inspired me to come out and perform. Hopefully, I'll be the All-Star caliber player they were looking for." He may be similarly motivated by the Rockies shopping him in the '96–'97 off-season, and the disinterest with which he was being greeted by other General Managers as we went to press—many of whom questioned whether he could produce outside of Coors. Wherever he ends up, he may have to reiterate what he said in '96 on his way to the All-Star game: "All I ever wanted is for somebody to say, 'You're our man at second base.' And you know what? The Rockies still haven't said that to me."

Other teams had every right to be skeptical of Young's ability to put up big numbers in their parks. He had the greatest home/away differential of any player on the Rockies: 7-55-.412 at home, 1-19-.219 on the road. Since he's been a Rockie, he's been Ty Cobb in Denver and Jody Reed everywhere else. Home or away, he finished very slowly in '96. Young was hitting .352 through June after going .388 for the month. In July he hit .331, in August .316, and in September .247 (when he was thrown out 5 times out of 9 trying to steal). He's worked hard to go from being a low round draft pick by the Dodgers to the All-Star Game, but he simply isn't a legitimate hitter and wouldn't be able to hold the starting job for many other big league clubs, if any. ■

■ 1996 AUTOPSY

With a new and improved playoff system that rewards mediocrity and boosts September TV ratings, the Florida Marlins were thinking wild-card in the spring. Added to an already decent staff were free agents Al Leiter and Kevin Brown—and yet another Cuban defector with a fastball, Livan Hernandez, seeking political asylum and hard currency. The rest of the league scoffed at the money thrown at such unestablished starters, but their pitching looked like a genuine strength if not an underpaid one. Offensively, their hopes depended on Gary Sheffield staying healthy, Charles Johnson developing into a consistent hitter, their young double play combination of Quilvio Veras and Kurt Abbott continuing to progress, and veterans Terry Pendleton and Devon White having one more September run left in them. If the fans, players, and suits knew that Gary Sheffield and Kevin Brown would be in serious contention for MVP and Cy Young hardware, and that Robb Nen would solidify his position as one of the best closers in baseball, then they'd probably have turned that expectations knob all the way up to 11 and wondered just how far behind them Atlanta would finish.

April 11-16 (11-16, 6½ games back)
The Marlins started the season pitching reasonably well, but they weren't hitting. The team hit .220 and slugged .352—which is basically a line-up of 8 Dave McCartys. Jeff Conine was hitting .222 with only 1 dinger, a .280 on-base percentage, and a .278 slugging average; to put that dreadful showing in perspective, that's about what Kevin Brown held N.L. hitters to all season. Hideo Nomo had a big strikeout day against Florida, throwing back 17 Fish in his second-best outing of the season. Gary Sheffield hit 11 dingers but managed only 17 RBI, frequently greeted at home plate by only the on-deck hitter and the batboy—and often it was hard to tell the difference. The league had yet to discover that there was absolutely no reason to pitch to him unless the score was tied and the bases loaded in the bottom of the 9th. Leiter and Brown combined for an ERA in the low 2s in 76 innings, but a lack of run support held them down to a record of 6-4. Pull those two "overpaid" and "unestablished" starters out of the rotation and the team ERA was 4.70. It was a fitting beginning to a season of mixed results and extended frustration.

May 16-11 (27-27, 9 games back)
The hitting improved and, somehow, the pitching did as well, as the Marlins crawled back to .500. They even won 9 in a row and 13 of 15. Brown and Leiter pitched 63 innings with a 2.15 ERA but managed to go only 4-4. Leiter no-hit the Rockies on little more than 100 pitches, 80% of them fastballs, retiring the last 20 he faced. In the bullpen, Robb Nen finally got some consistent work and he came alive, allowing no runs in 14 innings, winning a game, saving 7, and striking out 20 while walking only 3. He had hitters missing his hard, diving slider by a foot. Conine had his tear ducts unclogged; his vision improved, and he started hitting, going long 8 times with 23 RBI. As always, Sheffield continued to be one with the ball. Only his stolen base numbers were down, and that was due to sore legs as he took the pain in his pursuit of playing a full 162 games. Yet he remained unappreciated by the fans, whose opinions were shaped by a largely hostile media—and it was wearing thin on the only hitter who was showing up for work everyday. "I can take those 17 homers elsewhere," he explained. "If the fans don't want me here, I don't have to be here." Shortstop Kurt Abbott also didn't have to be there, and was sent down to Charlotte. Second baseman Quilvio Veras would be the next to disappear, succumbing to a hamstring injury from which he was slower to recover than Bill Parcells from open-heart surgery.

June 12-14 (39-41, 11 games back)
The cycle of forward, backward continued in June. Again it was the offense that failed, but this time it was a lack of clutch hitting rather than the complete system crash that took place in April. Despite both hitting .360, Conine and Colbrunn managed only 27 RBI between them; in '96, a team needed about that from each of its no. 3 and no. 5 hitters in a good month. If they had gotten more timely hitting, those 8 one-run losses could have been turned into wins and they'd have gone 20-6 for the month. Sheffield was on pace to walk nearly 150 times, an N.L. record. The Braves walked him 4 times in one

game. Sheffield: "I know guys are trying hard and want to help out. It's a tough situation. But if we had a Fred McGriff on deck, do you think they wouldn't pitch to me? It's a situation we have to address. I'm not the GM, I'm a player." Dombrowski would begin to "address" it by putting his franchise, the best offensive player in the league, on the trading block—and not even being very discreet about it.

July 10-17 (49-58, 16½ games back)
The team finally started to hit in July, but the team ended wheels up in the ditch anyway. The pitching staff had its first off month (5.03 ERA), as Leiter came back to reality. Brown was still impeccable with a 2.20 ERA in 45 innings—but his team got him 2 wins for his efforts. After being hit on the shin with line drives in consecutive starts and injuring his ankle fishing (yes, that's right), he was hit by a swinging fungo bat during warm-ups; there was no truth to the rumors that the team asked this good luck charm to fly on a separate plane. As the team faded from even the diluted contention of the '90s, two things were now glaringly apparent: They could not hit right-handed pitching and if the pitching failed, the game was over, Sheffield or not. All of which, of course, is the manager's fault. With attendance down and 8 digits worth of red ink projected by the bean counters, Dombrowski scrambled to higher ground, stepping on the neck of his manager, Rene Lacheman, in the process.

August 16-13 (65-71, 19½ games back)
With John Boles now in the dugout, the Marlins suddenly began to hit—which, of course, is the manager's doing. Experts pointed to tighter discipline and team unity as the sources of the team's ability to score runs. If the rest of the staff, other than Nen and Brown, had been better, the team would have done better than 16-13—but that might have been too much to expect after John Burkett was dispatched to Texas and Boles had to do everything short of calling fans down out of the stands to pitch. After a midseason assurance from Dombrowski that he would not be traded, Sheffield heard his name in trade rumors again and—after a season of being pitched around by the opposition and jerked around by management—he understandably went ballistic. "I don't have to like [Dombrowski] and he doesn't have to like me. He wants to blame it on the players, rather than say, 'I put this team together.' . . . He'll have to answer for his own problems. He put the team on the field." Apparently Dave didn't have to answer for much. He discussed his future with Huizenga and, after a pat on the back and a Fresca from his boss, said, "I'm set. I'm signed through 1998. I've already had my conversation with the owner. I'm set. We're already planning for next year."

September 15-11 (80-82, 16 games back)
The team finished the season on an upswing and nearly made it back to .500. Starters Mark Hutton and Rick Helling, acquired from the Yankees and Rangers, respectively, looked marvelous in teal; they went 7-2 and allowed only 61 hits in 84 innings. Luis Castillo was solidifying his hold on the second-base job, only to hurt his shoulder and have to be shut down. Kurt Abbott tried his best to give back the third-base job, pressing at the plate in a brutal September. And there was even a Livan Hernandez sighting. After spending much of the season spending his signing bonus on fast food, Livan shed 18 pounds, threw 3 scoreless innings, and raised expectations again.

■ 1997 DIAGNOSIS

Offense
Despite Sheffield's best efforts, the Marlins had an offense that was buried in the bottom third of the N.L. This team didn't hit for average, didn't draw walks, and didn't hit for power—although Sheffield was near the top in all of these categories. In addition, the team did not run very much, due to Quilvio's hamstring injury and Sheffield's aching legs. Things could improve dramatically if they put Conine at first, if the left-handed-hitting Billy McMillon—or a free agent bopper—is given the left-field job, and if Luis Castillo can shake off his shoulder troubles and establish himself as a true leadoff man.

Defense
Charles Johnson had one of the best throwing seasons for a catcher since such stats have been

kept. At one point he'd thrown out 21 of 37 base-runners (1 in 3 is average, and 50% is outstanding), and only 7 of 28 had made it safely when he attempted a throw. Colbrunn is good at first, but they wouldn't lose much by putting Conine there; in fact, they'd probably add by subtraction by getting Jeff out of left field where he is a menace. Castillo and Renteria drew raves for the defense and may quickly become the best double-play combination in the league. A healthy Veras is a good-fielding second baseman, too, and Ralph Milliard is even better. Abbott's limited range makes him better suited to third base. Even Devon White in his prime couldn't cover up for Conine, and White is a few years past that and accelerating downhill. Gary Sheffield is an average fielder at his third position; he has a good arm, but he is hampered a bit by management's edict that he not injure himself by diving for balls anymore.

Pitching
After adjusting for ballpark—as must always be done, thanks to Coors Field taking the entire league through the looking glass and making the Rockies mediocre offense look like the 1927 Yankees—the Marlins had the second-best starting pitching in the N.L. behind the Braves. Brown and Leiter could pitch with Smoltz and Maddux or any other duo in the National League—but unfortunately the Marlins were often left with a Pat Rapp and a Hammond Cheese to pitch with Glavine and Avery. There are more than a few pitchers waiting to take these spots in the chorus line, most notably Hutton and Helling and possibly Kurt Miller. Although Alex Fernandez and Steve Avery are reportedly on the team's short list of free agents, if the Marlins could acquire only one impact player they would be better off with a power hitter to protect Sheffield.

When 5 of the 6 best ERAs on the staff belong to starters, that usually means a pitiful bullpen rather than an outstanding rotation. Such was the case in Miami, where Robb Nen's set-up men could be more accurately described as let-up men. Even with Nen's 1.95 ERA, the bullpen was at 4.37, second-worst in the league. There is hope—if Matt Mantei can rebound from serious arm troubles, Bill Hurst can emerge, Jay Powell can evolve, and a capable lefty can be found sometime, anywhere.

Farm System
A lot of the team's top youngsters have made it to the majors already: Renteria, Castillo, McMillon, Milliard. The system's top prospect is now outfielder Mark Kotsay, their '96 1st-rounder, 9th overall, out of CalState-Fullerton. He's expected to start the season at Double-A. There's also outfielder Todd Dunwoody, who looks solid. If Livan Hernandez is healthy and svelte, he could finally earn a return on the investment. But in general, what's left down on the farm is a lot of players who *could* be solid major-leaguers rather than potential superstars.

Ownership and Management
Wayne Huizenga has owned the Marlins since their inception. He hired a GM (Dombrowski) who was considered one of the brightest young architects in the game, left him alone, and signed the checks on some big free agents. But by midseason Huizenga wasn't showing up for games anymore, his infatuation with the overnight success of the Panthers of the NHL and his frustration with the apparent success of the expansion brethren Rockies gnawing at him. Something had to give and it was Rene Lacheman, not Dombrowski. With Jim Leyland on-board, the GM won't be able to deflect the criticism any longer. If the Marlins struggle in '97, Dave better get his résumé together.

. . . and whatnot: Leiter & Brown vs. Maddux & Smoltz
The rumbling started early in the season, as John Smoltz finally started to put together the monster season that's been predicted for him since 1990: Kevin Brown, the unluckiest pitcher in baseball, would win the Cy Young going away if it weren't for his inept team. His ERA (1.89) was more than a full run lower than Smoltz's. But let's not just look at those two, let's throw in the other two starters at the top in ERA—Al Leiter and some guy named Maddux.

Pitcher	IP	ERA	Runs Saved
Brown	233	1.89	60.1
Maddux	245	2.72	40.6
Leiter	215.1	2.93	30.6
Smoltz	253.2	2.94	35.8

The N.L. ERA was 4.21 last season. **Runs Saved** is how many runs each pitcher saved compared to an average pitcher. Saving his team 60 runs is a tremendous performance by Brown, and quantifies just what it means to be more than 2 runs a game better than the average pitcher. Given that, Brown wins hands down, right? Not yet. That big difference in ERA—was it due to Smoltz and Brown pitching similarly when they won, but Smoltz getting beat up more when he lost? Below is a chart of the number of times each pitcher started and allowed a certain number of runs.

Pitcher	0 runs	1 run	2 runs	3 runs	4 runs	5 runs	6+ runs
Brown	8	7	6	5	4	2	0
Maddux	5	7	9	4	5	3	2
Leiter	6	7	7	4	4	5	0
Smoltz	5	8	7	6	3	2	4

Smoltz allowed 4-plus runs 9 times, Leiter 9 times, Maddux 10 times, and Brown 6 times. Here are the pitchers' records when they allowed fewer than 4 runs a start.

Pitcher	W	L	ERA
Brown	16	7	1.26
Maddux	13	6	1.53
Smoltz	22	2	1.71
Leiter	15	4	1.71

Brown certainly wasn't the unluckiest of the group. Maddux took those honors. Here are their records when they allow four runs or more. As you can see, there were only 6 "cheap" wins for all of these pitchers.

Pitcher	W	L	ERA	IP	H	R	ER	BB	K
Brown	1	4	4.99	39.2	43	26	22	9	24
Maddux	2	5	6.21	62.1	78	48	43	9	47
Leiter	1	8	7.28	47	58	41	38	32	45
Smoltz	2	6	7.55	53.2	73	53	45	16	59

Even when Brown and Maddux were bad, they weren't *that* bad. But it's obvious that when Smoltz was bad, he was terrible. Overall, Maddux and Leiter were brilliant, but Smoltz and Brown pitched at a dazzling level for a greater number of innings. John Smoltz's problem was that he was worse on his bad days than the other guys. But conversely, when he was on (which was 80% of the time), he pitched better than the competition. He kept runners off base and the ball in the yard as well as or better than anyone in the league. He pitched more innings than Brown and led the league in strikeouts. Smoltz's ERA was higher, because when he was off, he was way off. He matched Brown pitch for pitch when they were both going well. When they struggled, neither of them won, but Brown's line looked a little prettier. Maybe the better-hitting Braves would have been able to find a way to win some of Brown's off starts, but it's hard to vote against someone who went 24-8 for a team playing games that meant something.

Interestingly, however, similar logic did not hold in the AL where the Kevin Brown of the league beat the ace on the best team. (See Toronto Blue Jays).

KURT ABBOTT

SS-3B • BR • TR • 6'0 • 170 • 27 • OAK89/15

	AB	R	H	2B	3B	HR	RBI	BB	SO	SB	CS	BA	OB	SA
FLA94	345	41	86	17	3	9	33	16	98	3	0	.249	.291	.394
FLA95	420	60	107	18	7	17	60	36	110	4	3	.255	.318	.452
FLA96	320	37	81	18	7	8	33	22	99	3	3	.253	.307	.428
CAREER	1146	149	289	54	17	37	135	77	327	12	6	.252	.305	.426

In early May, Abbott went on the disabled list because of "dizziness," eventually blamed on allergies. By the time he was better, Edgar Renteria had stolen his job and Abbott was in Charlotte. In mid-June, Abbott was brought back up to play second, but he spent more time backing up Renteria at short. Then, in August, he moved to third when Pendleton was traded. That was his best chance to solidify a starting job, and he didn't do it. To make things worse, he turned down the club's repeated requests to play winter ball to work on it

Offensively, Abbott has one strength: He can hit the ball a mile, on the rare occasions that he makes solid contact. He has decent speed, too and impresses scouts by flying down the line—though he's unable to translate this skill into stolen bases. He struck out nearly 5 times for every walk drawn. At his age, it becomes less likely that he will improve this significantly, and it will end his career prematurely.

Abbott is fundamentally flawed—the prototypical "tools" player who can't refine his skills enough to become a stud. He is useful, but if the Marlins can find a decent third-base prospect, there might be no room at the inn for an average fielder who tries to pull everything. ■

JOEL ADAMSON

SP • BL • TL • 6'4 • 180 • 25 • PHI90/7

	G	GS	IP	H	HR	BB	K	W	L	S	ERA	K/BB	K9	HW9
AAA	44	8	98	108	15	28	84	6	6	3	3.78	3.0	7.7	12.53

Adamson has 4 pitches, but none of them is exceptional. He gets hit, then pitches his way out of big innings. He has had arm trouble, missing nearly two months in 1995 with tendinitis in his pitching shoulder. He does have excellent control and can shut down lefties, so his best bet for a major-league career is to be used like Tony Fossas—pitching spot relief, facing one or two lefties at a time. The Marlins tried to call up Adamson in May of '95, but he was nowhere to be found. Adamson: "I felt possibly that if not that week or month, I'd get another call-up later that season. I guess they were teaching me a lesson and it worked." ■

ANTONIO ALFONSECA

SP • BR • TR • 6'4 • 160 • 24 • MON89

	G	GS	IP	H	HR	BB	K	W	L	S	ERA	K/BB	K9	HW9
AAA	14	13	72	86	6	22	51	4	4	1	5.53	2.3	6.4	13.56

Alfonseca has six fingers on each hand, but that doesn't mean he's twice as good as "Three-Finger" Mordecai Brown. He throws his fastball in the low 90s and has a fine hard slider. In the past, he had poor command and was rattled easily. His frail physique (6-foot-4, 160 pounds) makes durability a question mark, as does elbow trouble in '95. In '96 Alfonseca threw strikes for a change and got battered in the process. At his age he's got some time to get it together and have a career, but there are plenty of guys just like him at Double-A and Triple-A who'd like to get off the bus and fly first class for a change. ■

ALEX ARIAS

UT • BR • TR • 6'3 • 185 • 29 • CHN87/2

	AB	R	H	2B	3B	HR	RBI	BB	SO	SB	CS	BA	OB	SA
FLA94	113	4	27	5	0	0	15	9	19	0	1	.239	.298	.283
FLA95	216	22	58	9	2	3	26	22	20	1	0	.269	.337	.370
FLA96	224	27	62	11	2	3	26	17	28	2	0	.277	.335	.384
CAREER	901	94	243	36	5	8	94	86	98	4	2	.270	.338	.347

Arias has found his level. He is a good-hit, average-glove utility infielder. He's not outstanding at anything, but he doesn't have any glaring weaknesses either—which means he should have a long career as a bench player somewhere, even if he does get crowded out in Florida by all those middle-infield prospects. Like a good umpire, if you don't notice him, he's doing his job. ■

MIGUEL BATISTA

RP • BR • TR • 6'0 • 160 • 26

	G	GS	IP	H	HR	BB	K	W	L	S	ERA	K/BB	K9	HW9
AAA	47	2	77	93	4	39	56	4	3	4	5.38	1.4	6.5	15.43

Batista's fastball is only a notch below Robb Nen's and about even with Jay Powell's. Despite that kind of hard stuff, he was beaten like a redheaded mule at Triple-A. He'll be 26, so he's not too old to get it together—provided that finding the plate ceases to be a random event. ■

JOSH BOOTY

3B • BR • TR • 6'3 • 210 • 21 • FLA94/1

	AB	R	H	2B	3B	HR	RBI	BB	SO	SB	CS	BA	OB	SA
A	475	62	98	25	1	21	87	46	195	2	3	.206	.275	.396

Booty has bat speed, good power, handled his '95 move to third base easily, and had the best arm in the Midwest League (he was a heavily recruited quarterback). Scouts like his makeup and think the rest of his tools are all above average. He was Florida's 1st-round pick in '94 and at the time got the biggest signing bonus ($1.6 million) in baseball history. But he is, at best, a mediocre prospect. He never saw a curveball while playing high school ball in northwestern Louisiana and can't hit one today. His strikeout rate is abysmal (he "led" professional baseball by whiffing 195 times) and he's going to have to hit well over .200 to make it to South Florida. He might end up being one of the most disappointing 1st-round selections in recent history, the reincarnation of Jay Schroeder, another quarterback who couldn't hit a curveball—though Jay didn't cost $1.6 million. Does this sound like $1.6 million worth of ballplayer?: "I swing just as hard when I have two strikes on me as if I have one strike or no strikes. Striking out is part of the game. I don't let it get to me." So much for adjusting your approach depending on the count. He can't bag this and go play football until after 1999, or he forfeits the signing bonus. Perhaps the Marlins should save themselves the headache, meet him halfway now, and cut him loose. ■

KEVIN BROWN

NL ELITE

SP • BR • TR • 6'4 • 195 • 32 • TEX86/1

	G	GS	IP	H	HR	BB	K	W	L	S	ERA	K/BB	K9	HW9
TEX94	26	25	170	218	18	50	123	7	9	0	4.82	2.5	6.5	14.19
BAL95	26	26	172	155	10	48	117	10	9	0	3.60	2.4	6.1	10.62
FLA96	32	32	233	187	8	33	159	17	11	0	1.89	4.8	6.1	8.50
CAREER	245	153	1684	1664	103	509	1018	105	84	0	3.52	2.0	5.4	11.61

Kevin Brown was exceptional in 1996 and was easily the best free-agent pickup in either league. The Marlins won 20 of his starts and scored only 11 runs for him in his losses. He has modest strikeout totals for the kind of stuff he has, suggesting that he's perfectly willing to get hitters out with 1 pitch rather than 3 or more. He has a sinking fastball that hits 94-96 mph, a hard slider, uses a cut fastball to handle lefties, and throws all his pitches for strikes. In '96, Brown consistently kept the ball down and hitters were unable to drive his pitches. As one scout put it (prior to the Alomar incident): "He's a pitcher you salivate for."

He has a great work ethic, but he's been labeled a hothead, moody, and selfish in the past. Other polite phrases included "clubhouse lawyer," which is GM-speak for being capable of independent thought. Now that he's excelling, these vices are suddenly virtues. Boles: "This guy, he's an animal. If I got into a fight in an alley, he'd be my no. 1 draft pick to stand with me. . . . I wish we could bottle this and ship it out to pitchers in our organization. . . . He's a killer. He goes for the jugular. I've never seen anybody this much of a perfectionist. He gets upset when he gets a guy out, because the pitch wasn't exactly where he wanted it. I love this guy."

Brown's career has never been incredibly consistent, and he'll be 32 in '97. His control has likely changed for the better, but it is unreasonable to expect his performance to stay at this level—where only Maddux has resided in recent years. An across-the-board decline in all of his numbers should be expected—but a decline from those levels doesn't mean he won't be making another All-Star appearance. ■

LUIS CASTILLO — *YOUNG GUN*

2B • BR • TR • 5′11 • 150 • 21 • FLA92

	AB	R	H	2B	3B	HR	RBI	BB	SO	SB	CS	BA	OB	SA
FLA96	164	26	43	2	1	1	8	14	46	17	4	.262	.320	.305

Castillo was voted the fastest baserunner and best defensive second baseman in the Eastern League. and he didn't miss a beat coming to the majors. One scout said: "He's got a chance to be an above-average big leaguer, quick hands, quick feet, can turn the double play for you. He needs to learn how to hit. . . . Right now, all he's thinking about is contact and running. After a while, people will get wise to him and start bringing the infield in, but he can fly and he can disrupt a defense. If [Robbie] Alomar's a 10 defensively, Castillo's a 7. Castillo is a 7 out of 10 as a prospect right now; he could be an 8 or a 9." In fact, his defensive stats (albeit in a half-season's sample) are superior to Alomar's—who some believe is preoccupied with cheating to his left so he can make pretty plays for *SportsCenter.*

Castillo has shown excellent growth in one season. He had no power in '95, hitting .326 with 4 doubles, 4 triples, and no homers, then missed the second half of that season with a separated shoulder. If Castillo hits the weights and starts driving the ball, his ceiling could be very high. Unfortunately, just after the season ended, he had surgery on his left shoulder. There's a chance this condition could be chronic. Though he is expected to be healthy this spring, it might affect his throwing and his all-around play. ■

GREG COLBRUNN

1B • BR • TR • 6′0 • 190 • 27 • MON87/8

	AB	R	H	2B	3B	HR	RBI	BB	SO	SB	CS	BA	OB	SA
FLA94	155	17	47	10	0	6	31	9	27	1	1	.303	.345	.484
FLA95	528	70	146	22	1	23	89	22	69	11	3	.277	.311	.453
FLA96	511	60	146	26	2	16	69	25	76	4	5	.286	.333	.438
CAREER	1515	174	423	75	3	51	230	68	239	23	13	.279	.317	.434

Colbrunn has decent power and hits the ball hard to all fields. He doesn't strike out very much, but he doesn't walk either. He is in his prime and is capable of returning to his 20+ homer level of '95. But in the '90s, that kind of prime isn't good enough. Mark Grace is distinctly superior to Colbrunn as both a hitter and a fielder, yet he gets knocked regularly for power that is modest at best. First base is a tough gig; among N.L. first basemen, only David McCarty and Butch Huskey were worse in '96 than Colbrunn, and McCarty is not even a regular. McGriff, Grace, Morris, Bagwell, Karros, Segui, Jeff King, Joyner, and Mabry are all better than what the Marlins put out there in '96. ■

JEFF CONINE — *CONSISTENT STAR*

LF • BR • TR • 6′1 • 205 • 30 • KC87/58

	AB	R	H	2B	3B	HR	RBI	BB	SO	SB	CS	BA	OB	SA
FLA94	451	60	144	27	6	18	82	40	92	1	2	.319	.373	.525
FLA95	483	72	146	26	2	25	105	66	94	2	0	.302	.379	.520
FLA96	597	84	175	32	2	26	95	62	121	1	4	.293	.360	.484
CAREER	2237	304	667	116	15	81	372	230	470	6	8	.298	.362	.472

Over the past three seasons, Jeff Conine has been very reliable—hitting .300 with an on-base percentage around .370 and slugging around .500. He struck out more in '96 than he has in the past, but the rise wasn't dramatic. He is a solid defensive first baseman and one of the worst defensive left fielders in baseball. Conine will turn 31 in June, but players of his caliber will usually hold it together for several more years and at least one more guaranteed contract. He had a dry eye problem early in the year, which was eventually corrected by some opthalmological duct work. Prior to that, he considered wearing glasses but vetoed goggles. Conine: "I'll hit .220 before I have to look like Sabo." Baseball in the '90s in 10 words. ■

WILL CUNNANE

SP • BR • TR • 6′2 • 165 • 22 • FLA92

	G	GS	IP	H	HR	BB	K	W	L	S	ERA	K/BB	K9	HW9
AA	25	25	152	156	15	30	101	10	12	0	3.74	3.4	6.0	11.04

Cunnane throws strikes with a 2-seam fastball and a 4-seam fastball. Both pitches are slightly above average, and the four-seamer can touch 90. Cunnane also has a slider and a change-up. He is not a Grade-A prospect, but if he comes up this season, he certainly can be no worse than Hammond was as a starter in '96. ■

VIC DARENSBOURG

RP • BL • TL • 5'10 • 165 • 26 • FLA92

	G	GS	IP	H	HR	BB	K	W	L	S	ERA	K/BB	K9	HW9
AAA	47	0	63	61	7	32	66	1	5	7	3.69	2.1	9.38	13.22

Darensbourg missed the '95 season after having bone chips removed from his elbow. When he's right, he throws a hard-moving, low-90s fastball. In the past, he didn't have much of a breaking ball, but based on his strong performance at Triple-A, he's doing something right. He's a lefty, so the Marlins will find room for him in '97. ■

TODD DUNWOODY — SOLID PROSPECT

OF • BL • TL • 6'2 • 185 • 21 • FLA93/7

	AB	R	H	2B	3B	HR	RBI	BB	SO	SB	CS	BA	OB	SA
AA	552	88	153	30	6	24	93	45	149	24	19	.277	.337	.484

One scout said: "[Dunwoody] has a chance to be a pretty good player. Decent fielder, just a solid player, certainly not a top guy. He's a 5 out of 10." He is a good young player with a strong arm and nice range in the outfield. In addition, he has solid power and has enough speed to steal 20+ bases. If he had better plate discipline and was a year younger, that 5 might be an 8. ■

CHRIS HAMMOND (see Looking for a Game)

RICK HELLING — SLEEPER

SP • BR • TR • 6'3 • 215 • 26 • TEX92/1

	G	GS	IP	H	HR	BB	K	W	L	S	ERA	K/BB	K9	HW9
TEX94	9	9	52	62	14	18	25	3	2	0	5.88	1.4	4.3	13.85
TEX95	3	3	12	17	2	8	5	0	2	0	6.57	.6	3.8	18.75
TEX/FLA96	11	6	47	37	9	16	42	3	3	0	4.39	2.6	8.0	10.13
CAREER	23	18	111	116	25	42	72	6	7	0	5.34	1.7	5.8	12.80

Helling has always been a good prospect. He was inconsistent as a rookie—like just about every pitcher except Dwight Gooden—and the Rangers overreacted by burying him in the minors and going with the consistently mediocre Kevin Gross. Helling dominated at Triple-A, throwing a perfect game along the way. He came to Florida in the deal for John Burkett, and was outstanding in his September trial (27.2 innings, 14 hits, 7 walks, and 26 strikeouts). He has a low 90s fastball, an excellent slider, and has command of both pitches. If he goes into the third spot in the rotation, he could win 12-15 games with any kind of offensive support. ■

FELIX HEREDIA — SOLID PROSPECT

RP • BL • TL • 6'0 • 165 • 20

	G	GS	IP	H	HR	BB	K	W	L	S	ERA	K/BB	K9	HW9
AA	55	0	60	48	3	15	42	8	1	5	1.50	2.8	6.3	9.45

At the start of '96, Heredia was the second-youngest player in Double-A. He was very good at Portland, though his strikeout numbers weren't where a reliever's need to be. He throws in the low 90s with late life on his fastball and dominates lefties. His manager, at Portland, Carlos Tosca, feels Heredia will gain a few miles per hour as he matures. He wasn't great in his Florida call-up, but he could be back in the majors by mid-season. ■

LIVAN HERNANDEZ — SOLID PROSPECT

SP • BR • TR • 6'2 • 220 • 22 • FLA96

	G	GS	IP	H	HR	BB	K	W	L	S	ERA	K/BB	K9	HW9
AAA	10	10	49	61	3	34	45	2	4	0	5.14	1.3	8.3	17.45

In the spring, Dave Dombrowski said of Livan: "We're looking at the kind of arm strength that can project him to be at the top of a rotation." He signed a $2.5 million contract, lost velocity in the spring, and had celebrated troubles with Triple-A and Double-A hitters. Unlike fellow Cuban Osvaldo Fernandez, whose difficulties could be attributed to the distraction of being separated from his family and fearing for their safety, Livan was done in by gluttony. His troubles were blamed on velocity that hadn't come as advertised, which was in turn blamed on the spare tire around his waist. He pitched a lot better late in the season, and the Marlins claimed he dropped 18 pounds by September. One scout begged to differ: "I saw him at the end of the year. If he lost any weight, it was in his toe. He was as big as a house." The house factor notwithstanding, this scout liked what he saw: "His fastball is live with good late movement. . . . He has a slider and a curve. They're probably going to eliminate one of the pitches, (but) they're both good, above-average major-league pitches. (But)

let's face it, if he carries all that weight, he'll break down." Sounds like the next Sid Fernandez. If he moves into your town, go in with some friends and open a Wendy's franchise. ■

BILL HURST

RP • BR • TR • 6'7 • 215 • 26

	G	GS	IP	H	HR	BB	K	W	L	S	ERA	K/BB	K9	HW9
AA	45	0	49	45	3	31	46	2	3	30	2.20	1.5	8.4	13.96

The Cards released Hurst in '92 after he had "Tommy John" surgery. He was out of baseball until '95, when the Marlins found him coaching high school baseball and made him their closer at Brevard County in the Florida State League. There he flashed a fastball that could hit 98 and a biting slider that hit 90. Hurst's control is wretched and he's going to have to improve it dramatically to make the majors. One scout said: "He has as good an arm as there is. (But) you have to be leery of him because of his history. He still has to learn how to pitch. Control isn't the right word, I think command is the right word. Command to me is you can throw a pitch anywhere you want to throw it, anytime you want to throw it. He can't do that." ■

MARK HUTTON

SLEEPER

SP • BR • TR • 6'6 • 240 • 27

	G	GS	IP	H	HR	BB	K	W	L	S	ERA	K/BB	K9	HW9
NYA/FLA96	25	11	86	79	9	36	56	5	3	0	4.18	1.6	5.9	12.03

Hutton came over from the Yankees for David Weathers. He throws a 94-96 mph sinking fastball. Joe Torre was very impressed with him in March, but if you know the trading habits of Steinbrenner's puppets, you know why he's now a Marlin. In 1989 the Yankees had an outstanding young pitching staff: Doug Drabek, Jose Rijo, Jim Deshaies, and Tim Belcher. Unfortunately, it was all in the N.L., and it was Andy Hawkins, Walt Terrell, Dave LaPointe, and Greg Cadaret chucking and ducking in the Bronx. Hutton's long history of injuries is troublesome, but he looked very good at the end of the year for Florida. Given his experience as an Australian rules football player back home, there's not much about the game of baseball that should be the least bit frightening to him. ■

CHARLES JOHNSON

C • BR • TR • 6'2 • 215 • 25 • FLA92/1

	AB	R	H	2B	3B	HR	RBI	BB	SO	SB	CS	BA	OB	SA
FLA95	315	40	79	15	1	11	39	46	71	0	2	.251	.351	.410
FLA96	386	34	84	13	1	13	37	40	91	1	0	.218	.292	.358

Charles Johnson is the best defensive catcher in baseball, even better than Ivan Rodriguez. He handles pitchers well and his throwing is on another plane than the rest of the league. Unfortunately, his offense continues to lag far behind his defense. The 1995 season had been a successful all-around one for him, and the Marlins figured they could work with him on shortening his swing in '96. Unfortunately, Johnson's swing stayed long and he got pull-happy. He kept swinging at bad pitches, didn't drive the ball, and was rarely on base. He missed some time during the second half when he stretched a ligament in the middle finger of his throwing hand. Johnson's arm and ability to work with pitchers are so good that he could hit a soft .200 every year and be guaranteed a job. His upside is much better than that, though one scout is pessimistic about his ability to reach it: "He's gonna be what he is. . . . (He) has a long swing, (and) it's very hard to shorten a guy's swing, especially a power guy. He has the strength, but the bat speed isn't there yet. And it might never be there." ■

MARK KOTSAY

GRADE-A PROSPECT

OF • FLA96/1 • CAL STATE-FULLERTON

	AB	R	H	2B	3B	HR	RBI	BB	SO	SB	CS	BA	OB	SA
A	60	16	17	5	0	2	8	16	8	3	0	.283	.436	.467

Kotsay is one of the greatest college players in modern history. He was the heart and soul of Cal State Fullerton during the school's impressive recent run in the College World Series. Kotsay was also a mainstay of Team USA during their abortive attempt to win Olympic gold. Some scouts routinely dismiss him, acknowledging he's a fine line-drive hitter but saying his only true skill is his desire. He went undrafted out of high school, then put on 25 pounds in college and emerged as an impact player. Scouting director Orrin Freeman: "He's a slender, wiry, strong guy who will make you marvel at how the ball comes off his bat. You'll say, 'Gee, where

does that strength come from?'" He is unselfish and clutch—those 6th and 7th tools often missing from 5-tool players—and he is a potential superstar. ■

ANDY LARKIN

SLEEPER

SP • BR • TR • 6'4 • 180 • 22 • FLA92/25

	G	GS	IP	H	HR	BB	K	W	L	S	ERA	K/BB	K9	HW9
AA	8	8	49	45	6	10	40	4	1	0	3.10	4.0	7.3	10.03

Larkin had surgery to repair a partially torn medial collateral ligament in his right elbow in '95 and missed most of that season and a good portion of '96. Before the surgery, he threw a 93-mph sinker, and had a late-breaking curveball that at times was unhittable. He also had great control, was poised, and worked hard. He came back late in the season and pitched poorly at Brevard County before being promoted to Double-A. He's down to 87-88, but scouts like his makeup and think he might get some of that velocity back this season. ■

AL LEITER

NL ELITE

SP • BL • TL • 6'3 • 210 • 31 • NYA84/2

	G	GS	IP	H	HR	BB	K	W	L	S	ERA	K/BB	K9	HW9
TOR94	20	20	111	125	6	65	100	6	7	0	5.08	1.5	8.1	15.40
TOR95	28	28	183	162	15	108	153	11	11	0	3.64	1.4	7.5	13.28
FLA96	33	33	215	153	14	119	200	16	12	0	2.93	1.7	8.4	11.38
CAREER	146	116	737	643	54	428	639	49	44	2	3.94	1.5	7.8	13.08

Leiter has an excellent fastball that hits the mid-90s and moves wickedly. When he has control of the fastball and his excellent tight-breaking curve, he can carve up good-hitting teams. Though Leiter continues to walk 5 batters per 9 innings, his strikeouts per 9 innings are up from fewer than 6 to more than 8. If the hitter isn't patient, he'll have much more trouble against Leiter in '96 than he would have in '93.

Leiter has come back from all kinds of arm misery. He has spent 10 years in major-league baseball and hasn't pitched 750 innings despite being a starter almost his entire career. He's been hurt so often that he has never gotten his innings. He is learning on-the-job how to be a 200-inning stopper, while trying to learn how to throw strikes. It's unrealistic to expect him to do all this at once. It's also highly unlikely that Leiter will ever get those walk totals down anyway. So he'll always have a few starts per season where he's knocked out by the third because his poor mechanics leave him unable to throw strike 1. Even after his no-hitter, Lacheman commented: "He gets a 6-run lead after the first and walks the first hitter and hits the second. But that's the way he pitches. He's a 'top-step' guy. He always keeps you on the top step of the dugout." ■

LOU LUCCA

3B • BR • TR • 5'11 • 210 • 26 • FLA92/32

	AB	R	H	2B	3B	HR	RBI	BB	SO	SB	CS	BA	OB	SA
AAA	273	26	71	14	1	7	35	11	62	0	3	.260	.296	.396

Lucca's an original Fish—a member of Florida's first draft in '92, the starting third baseman in the first game in the organization's history, and the only member of that starting lineup still with Florida. In the past, Lucca hit for a decent average, got on base, and showed line-drive power. In '96 he took a flying backward leap. He didn't draw any walks, struck out a lot and his average sank. With the void now at third base in Miami, he picked the wrong time to start hitting like Rafael Ramirez. He may well bounce back, but he'd better do it fast unless he wants to remain trapped in Triple-A. ■

MATT MANTEI

SLEEPER

RP • BR • TR • 6'1 • 180 • 23 • SEA91/25

	G	GS	IP	H	HR	BB	K	W	L	S	ERA	K/BB	K9	HW9
FLA95	12	0	13	12	1	13	15	0	1	0	4.73	1.2	10.1	16.88
FLA96	14	0	18	13	2	21	25	1	0	0	6.38	1.2	12.3	16.69

Despite control problems, Mantei rode his 97-mph fastball through the minors on the fast track. Lacheman considered him the best arm in the organization behind Nen. Unfortunately, all's not peaches and cream. Mantei was shut down for the season in mid-June with 3 tears in the rotator cuff. He's got a lot of rehab in front of him, most likely won't be ready by Opening Day, and his chances of big-league success have diminished. But you never, ever want to completely dismiss someone with an arm like Mantei's. ■

BILLY MCMILLON — SOLID PROSPECT

OF • BL • TL • 5′11 • 170 • 25 • FLA93/8

	AB	R	H	2B	3B	HR	RBI	BB	SO	SB	CS	BA	OB	SA
FLA96	51	4	11	0	0	0	4	5	14	0	0	.216	.286	.216

He didn't do much in a brief trial with the Marlins, but he has nothing left to prove in the minors. If he can hit .350 in Triple-A Charlotte, it's time to find out what he can do in Miami. He has no arm and, because of his age, is not on the same planet as Andruw Jones or Vladimir Guerrero. But an offense as anemic as Florida's—especially from the left side—needs all the help it can get. ■

KEVIN MILLAR — SLEEPER

3B • BR • TR • 6′1 • 195 • 25

	AB	R	H	2B	3B	HR	RBI	BB	SO	SB	CS	BA	OB	SA
AA	472	69	150	32	0	18	86	37	53	6	5	.318	.375	.500

Millar doesn't have a real good arm, is slow and getting up there in years for a Double-A ballplayer, but he can hit. He's got solid power, and his decent strikeout-to-walk ratio suggests he'll be able to hit for average in the majors. He dramatically improved after moving to third and is now the best prospect they have at the position. Barring a free agent acquisition, watch him and Abbott go eye to eye this spring and see which one blinks first. ■

KURT MILLER — SLEEPER

SP • BR • TR • 6′5 • 200 • 24 • PIT90/1

	G	GS	IP	H	HR	BB	K	W	L	S	ERA	K/BB	K9	HW9
FLA96	26	5	46	57	5	33	30	1	3	0	6.80	.9	5.9	17.60

For the first time in several seasons, Miller looked like the exceptional power pitcher the Pirates drafted in 1990. He threw 94 mph when he turned pro. He lost a great deal off his fastball, got roped, and was sent to winter ball before the 1996 season to improve his curveball. Last spring the Marlins were impressed because he again was hitting the low 90s and was throwing inside. If he continues to show this kind of velocity, command, and attitude this spring, he could make the rotation. ■

RALPH MILLIARD — SOLID PROSPECT

2B • BR • TR • 5′10 • 160 • 23 • FLA92

	AB	R	H	2B	3B	HR	RBI	BB	SO	SB	CS	BA	OB	SA
FLA96	62	7	10	2	0	0	1	14	16	2	0	.161	.312	.194

Milliard was the second native of Curaçao to reach the majors, after Hensley Muelens. Given Andruw Jones's arrival, it's very doubtful that Milliard will hold any career hitting records for the island. The Marlins like him, but Luis Castillo appears to have already displaced him. They like his strong arm, good range, and soft hands in the field, but aren't as high on his instincts. But the choice between Milliard and Castillo isn't as easy as it may look. Castillo may be a better fielder and has a distinct edge in speed, although Milliard is not exactly Cecil Fielder. Castillo has gotten it done in the majors, while Milliard has struggled. Both players have excellent plate discipline. Milliard's edge is in his power potential: He has moderate power, while Castillo's is practically nonexistent. It's not out of the question that Milliard could win the job—or even end up at third base. ■

ROBB NEN — NL ELITE

CL • BR • TR • 6′4 • 200 • 27 • TEX87/34

	G	GS	IP	H	HR	BB	K	W	L	S	ERA	K/BB	K9	HW9
FLA94	44	0	58	46	6	17	60	5	5	15	2.95	3.5	9.3	9.78
FLA95	62	0	65	62	6	23	68	0	7	23	3.29	3.0	9.4	11.77
FLA96	75	0	83	67	2	21	92	5	1	35	1.95	4.4	10.0	9.54
CAREER	205	4	262	238	20	107	259	12	14	73	3.54	2.4	8.9	11.85

His 98-mph fastball may be only second-best in the league behind Mark Wohlers, but Nen is better than the Braves closer. In fact, only Trevor Hoffman is better in the N.L. After a solid '95, he took it up a notch in '96. His pitches have such great action that it was almost impossible to drive the ball off him. In addition to his fastball and a late-diving slider reminiscent of Ron Guidry's back in '78 (when he was a god), Nen

worked hard on his change-up during the '95 off-season to give hitters a different look. Some scouts question his mechanics and are concerned he'll blow his arm out, but that's a problem with many power closers and may just be wishful thinking from N.L. East organizations that can see this team's headlights getting larger in the rearview mirror. ■

YORKIS PEREZ

RP • BL • TL • 6'0 • 180 • 29 • MIN83

	G	GS	IP	H	HR	BB	K	W	L	S	ERA	K/BB	K9	HW9
FLA94	44	0	40	33	4	14	41	3	0	0	3.54	2.9	9.2	10.56
FLA95	69	0	46	35	6	28	47	2	6	1	5.21	1.7	9.2	12.33
FLA96	64	0	47	51	2	31	47	3	4	0	5.29	1.5	9.0	15.68
CAREER	180	0	138	121	12	75	138	9	10	1	4.69	1.8	9.0	12.77

Perez has a sinking fastball with average velocity. He mixes in a slider and forkball, and with this combination, he can pile up the strikeouts. His problems in '96 were due to his control, or lack thereof. Very few pitchers are gifted enough to get away with not throwing strikes and none of them are named Yorkis. No one was jacking him last season (he allowed 2 homers in 47.2 innings), but it didn't matter, considering the number of baserunners he allowed (the league had a .374 OBP against him). So, for Lacheman, watching Perez blowing a lead was a slow and messy bleeding rather than something quick and merciful. Perez never hit the DL, but he had a 3.66 ERA before the All-Star break and an 8.62 ERA after. Smells like someone trying to throw through the pain. ■

JAY POWELL

YOUNG GUN

RP • BR • TR • 6'4 • 220 • 25 • BAL93/1

	G	GS	IP	H	HR	BB	K	W	L	S	ERA	K/BB	K9	HW9
FLA96	67	0	71	71	5	36	52	4	3	2	4.54	1.4	6.6	13.56

Powell is yet another Marlins reliever with a mid-90s fastball. Powell's fastball sinks and he mixes in an 88-mph slider. He went down in late April with a strained rib-cage muscle. After coming back in early May, his numbers—especially his walks—were mediocre. Nevertheless, he's the best they've got in the bullpen after Nen. He's only a 1- or 2-inning guy, and he has no off-speed pitch, but set-up men who only go through the lineup once can get away with just the hard stuff. He'll only get better. ■

PAT RAPP

SP • BR • TR • 6'3 • 195 • 29 • SF89/15

	G	GS	IP	H	HR	BB	K	W	L	S	ERA	K/BB	K9	HW9
FLA94	24	23	133	132	13	69	75	7	8	0	3.85	1.1	5.1	13.60
FLA95	28	28	167	158	10	76	102	14	7	0	3.44	1.3	5.5	12.61
FLA96	30	29	162	184	12	91	86	8	16	0	5.10	.9	4.8	15.27
CAREER	101	98	566	583	42	281	323	33	39	0	4.18	1.1	5.1	13.74

Rapp has a fastball he can sink, cut, or ride. The problem is, his riding fstball frequently gets ridden back in the other direction. He also has a curveball, slider and change, but these pitches are nothing special. He was superb down the stretch in '95, but had back surgery the following off-season. Throwing across his body puts him at risk for other injuries. Despite getting hit harder than Curly or Larry, he does keep the ball down and in the park. He does himself in with his poor control, allowing patient-hitting teams to "walk" him to the showers. ■

EDGAR RENTERIA

YOUNG GUN

SS • BR • TR • 6'1 • 170 • 21 • FLA92

	AB	R	H	2B	3B	HR	RBI	BB	SO	SB	CS	BA	OB	SA
FLA96	431	68	133	18	3	5	31	33	68	16	2	.309	.358	.399

When Kurt Abbott got dizzy, Renteria, the fourth Colombian to play in the majors, stepped into the breach and stayed there. He impressed Lacheman very quickly: "Edgar Renteria, in the 10 or 12 games he's played for us, has been the best defensive shortstop we've had here." He also hit in 22 straight games, showing that he's no one-trick pony. Sheffield loves him: "This guy is unbelievable. He is one guy I can say is a franchise player. Usually I don't give a guy that kind of credit this early, but this guy is for real." This turned out to be mutual admiration. Soon after he arrived, Renteria was cocking his bat like Sheffield and wearing a thick gold chain like Gary as well—just the kind of meaningless stuff that scares the

suits. Maybe they put Sheffield on the block because they feared that Renteria's fashion statements meant that Gary was being a "bad influence" on the kids.

By the way, Renteria's family claims he's actually 20, not 21. They say they lied about his age so he could sign a year early. He's already got incredible potential. If he's only 20, he could turn into Robin Yount. ■

VICTOR RODRIGUEZ — SOLID PROSPECT

SS • BR • TR • 6'2 • 185 • 20 • FLA94/2

	AB	R	H	2B	3B	HR	RBI	BB	SO	SB	CS	BA	OB	SA
A+	438	54	120	14	4	0	26	32	42	20	7	.274	.324	.324

Rodriguez gets mixed reviews in the field, but there is more consensus on his hitting. The Marlins wanted him to bulk up and become a better offensive player. He certainly didn't drive the ball much, but his selectivity improved, driving his average up 39 points despite his move to a much tougher league for hitters. With his youth and plate discipline, all he needs to do is hit the weights and he could become Grade-A prime. And give the Marlins more middle-infield decisions to make. ■

JOHN ROSKOS — SOLID PROSPECT

1B • BR • TR • 5'11 • 200 • 22 • FLA93/2

	AB	R	H	2B	3B	HR	RBI	BB	SO	SB	CS	BA	OB	SA
AA	396	53	109	26	3	9	58	67	102	3	4	.275	.385	.424

The Marlins moved him from catcher to first base and started comparing him to Greg Colbrunn—but don't hold that against him. He's young, his plate discipline is improving, and he is already a decent hitter. If he keeps progressing, he could become a major-league star. ■

TONY SAUNDERS — SLEEPER

SP • BL • TL • 6'1 • 190 • 22 • FLA92

	G	GS	IP	H	HR	BB	K	W	L	S	ERA	K/BB	K9	HW9
AA	26	26	168	121	10	62	156	13	4	0	2.63	2.5	8.4	9.82

Saunders had trouble with his elbow in '94 and '95 but bounced back in '96. He's extremely hard to hit and struck out more than 8 per 9 innings. Despite 18 months of arm trouble, his control is sharp and he looks very good. He was in line for a September call-up, but Livan ended up taking his spot. ■

GARY SHEFFIELD — NL ELITE

RF • BR • TR • 5'11 • 190 • 28 • MIL86/1

	AB	R	H	2B	3B	HR	RBI	BB	SO	SB	CS	BA	OB	SA
FLA94	322	61	89	16	1	27	78	51	50	12	6	.276	.380	.584
FLA95	213	46	69	8	0	16	46	55	45	19	4	.324	.467	.587
FLA96	519	118	163	33	1	42	120	142	66	16	9	.314	.465	.624
CAREER	3215	517	937	172	13	159	550	440	361	112	52	.291	.380	.501

To say Gary Sheffield had an active '95 off-season would be an understatement. He was shot in the left shoulder during an apparent carjacking attempt. He had surgery on an inflamed bursa sac in his right shoulder. He was slapped with a restraining order after the mother of his 2-year-old son, who lives in Arizona, said she received threatening calls and letters. According to reports, she found two bullets and a note at her door warning her to let Sheffield see their son. Should it have come as a surprise that he looked awful in spring training?

Sheffield appeared to be on his way to a disappointing season after 2 injury-plagued years. Much to the dismay of most sportswriters and talk show hosts in Miami, he had the best season of his career instead. In April he tied a major-league record by hitting 11 homers. He drew an exceptional number of walks and hit for average while not striking out. He never slowed down, never slumped, and was one of the best offensive players in the league. How does someone playing outside of Philadelphia get booed for that?

Sheffield has a reputation for not hustling, but the Marlins told him not to dive for balls so he could stay healthy—but that didn't stop him from running the bases like a fiend in '96. As for being a troublemaker, Boles directly and succinctly addressed those allegations: "I haven't had any problems with Gary Sheffield. If we had more Gary Sheffields, we'd be in the playoffs. He's played hard every game." He played with pain in an effort to play all 162 games, until the wear and tear of Dombrowski taking him on and off the trading block finally demotivated him enough to have a seat. With protection in the order, he can hit 50 home runs and bat .330—at least with the baseball they used in '96. ■

MARC VALDES

SP • BR • TR • 6′0 • 170 • 25 • FLA93/1

	G	GS	IP	H	HR	BB	K	W	L	S	ERA	K/BB	K9	HW9
FLA96	11	8	48	63	5	23	13	1	3	0	4.81	.6	2.4	16.10

Valdes is another in a growing line of star-crossed 1st-round picks by the Marlins. He had the swagger and the attitude in '95 but couldn't back it up. Pitching coach Larry Rothschild: "If you're going to come in by storm, you better perform right away. Confidence is one thing. False bravado is another." Nothing much to swagger about with the Marlins in '96, as he walked 23 and struck out only 13 in 49 innings. He pitched very well in AA, but struggled badly in AAA. Boles offered his assessment: "He went to Triple-A and thought he was a power pitcher. I don't know why he changed. The problem is when he throws too hard, the flatter his ball gets." Makes you wonder what exactly it was the Marlins saw when they drafted him. ■

QUILVIO VERAS

SLEEPER

2B • BB • TR • 5′9 • 170 • 25 • NYN89

	AB	R	H	2B	3B	HR	RBI	BB	SO	SB	CS	BA	OB	SA
FLA95	440	86	115	20	7	5	32	80	68	56	21	.261	.384	.373
FLA96	253	40	64	8	1	4	14	51	42	8	8	.253	.381	.340

Veras went down in early May with hamstring troubles and this injury cost him his starting job. During Veras's injury and prolonged recovery, the Marlins auditioned Ralph Milliard and Luis Castillo. Veras's injury reduced his range significantly while keeping him from stealing bases at even a mediocre rate. He still had his great batting eye but wasn't hitting for much average or power and found himself playing at Triple-A Charlotte in mid-August. Veras is still young, his hamstring will heal, and he could again become a solid leadoff man and defender. It's a lot less crowded at second base in San Diego. ■

BRYAN WARD

SLEEPER

SP • BL • TL • 6′2 • 210 • 25 • FLA93/20

	G	GS	IP	H	HR	BB	K	W	L	S	ERA	K/BB	K9	HW9
AA	28	25	147	170	23	32	124	9	9	0	4.91	3.9	7.6	12.40

Ward is a lefty with a 91-mph fastball and a good slider. He kills lefties and has shown good command throughout his minor-league career. He got hit in Double-A, but with his stuff and Florida's desperate search for left-handed arms, he could easily turn it up this season and make the Marlins. ■

DEVON WHITE

HEADED FOR A FALL

CF • BB • TR • 6′2 • 180 • 34 • CAL81/2

	AB	R	H	2B	3B	HR	RBI	BB	SO	SB	CS	BA	OB	SA
TOR94	403	67	109	24	6	13	49	21	80	11	3	.270	.313	.457
TOR95	427	61	121	23	5	10	53	29	97	11	2	.283	.334	.431
FLA96	552	77	151	37	6	17	84	38	99	22	6	.274	.325	.455
CAREER	5494	866	1435	283	64	148	599	391	1146	271	71	.261	.314	.417

White was pretty solid last season across the board. He had a good slugging percentage, a good stolen-base percentage, and his on-base percentage was fine (as long as he's not asked to lead off). All of it exceeded his career totals, but at his age and with his reliance on his legs, that won't last long. He's no longer blindingly fast, though he did steal 20+ bases for the time since 1993. He's defying the odds and will fall off a cliff soon. He's a similar player to Willie McGee, whose last season as a regular was at the age of 34—so it's too bad the Marlins don't have half as many center-field prospects as they have middle infielders. ■

RANDY WINN

OF • BR • TR • 6′2 • 175 • 22 • FLA95/3

	AB	R	H	2B	3B	HR	RBI	BB	SO	SB	CS	BA	OB	SA
A	514	90	139	16	3	0	35	47	115	30	18	.270	.340	.313

Winn is a former basketball player at the University of Santa Clara and was the fastest college baseball player in the '95 draft. He has excellent range in center field and an average arm. He's compared to Kenny Lofton—but he's not even anywhere near the *hoops* player Lofton was. But then Todd Van Poppel was compared to Tom Seaver. And Lofton could put up those offensive numbers before the first day of summer. ■

■ 1996 AUTOPSY

The Astros were considered the favorite to win the Central. Cincinnati had been decimated by Marge's salary cutting, while St. Louis seemed to be relying too much on creaky veterans like Dennis Eckersley and Gary Gaetti. Clearly, the smart money was on the balanced attack and solid pitching of the Astros. But Houston has been falling short quite a bit since they let a certain native son and gubernatorial shoo-in leave town to pitch 2 no-hitters, earn his 300th win, and strike out his 5,000th batter in Arlington.

April 13-14 (13-14, tied for first)
The Astros looked like an A.L. team in April—plenty of hitting, but pitching optional. Hampton (2-2, 2.65 ERA in 34 innings) was brilliant, and Kile (3-2, 5.22, 29.1) finished the month strong—but Drabek had 2 wheels in the ditch and would soon settle into that rut. The starters, on average, were out before the 6th inning was over, and hot starts by Bagwell (.337-8-24), Brian Hunter (322-0-8, 19 runs), Orlando Miller (.329-4-16, slugging .553) and Bell (322-3-23) couldn't overcome it. They ended the month a game under .500, but tied for first in a division that would be embarassingly bad throughout the first half of the season.

May 14-14 (27-28, 2 games ahead)
Bagwell exploded in May (.360-10-31), as did Biggio (.308-4-12, 22 runs), and the pitching improved. For a change—but not for long—Todd Jones looked like a closer (2-0, 1.23 ERA with 7 saves in 9 opportunities). Darryl Kile continued the dominance he showed in late April, going 3-1, 2.35. And Shane Reynolds flashed his exquisite control (3-2, 3.27), striking out 48 while walking only 5. But that didn't keep the team from running in place at 14-14, as they lost 6 of 8 games decided by a single run. In one of those close losses, back-up catcher Jerry "Turn Your Head and" Goff returned to the majors and went deep in his first and only game—but gave the game away with 6 passed balls and was released a few days later. GM Gerry Hunsicker wasn't blaming the team's performance on Terry Collins . . . yet. Hunsicker: "You can't blame the manager. He comes out here with as much intensity and fire as anybody in the league. I'm not sure some of the players have that competitive fire." May also featured the Astros' first games against St. Louis in a showdown of divisional "leaders." The Cardinals would sweep and the Astros would have no idea their future had just been told.

June 15-12 (42-40, tied for first)
The Astros started another 3-game series at St. Louis on May 31, hoping to exact some revenge. What they got was swept yet again. In the series finale, Kile pitched well, despite being the first pitcher since 1957 to nail 4 batters in a single game. (Dock Ellis plunked the first 3 Reds he faced in a game once, but got tossed before he could hit for the cycle.) In 6 games the Cardinals had won 6 times, outscoring the Astros 31-18. But Houston, at 27-30, remained in a tie for first in the division with St. Louis. This division was the laughingstock of baseball, if not of professional sports—with shades of the "glory" days of the Norris Division in the NHL in the late 70s and the A.L. Worst of the late '80s. Bagwell: "Guys look up at the scoreboard and see the Cubs lost or the Reds lost and think, 'Oh, well, we lost, but it's no big deal.' That attitude is not going to last, because some team in this division is going to get hot and win 8 or 10 games in a row. That team better be us." In an attempt to put themselves in position to do just that, the Astros called up Billy Wagner—who wasn't fazed in the least by big-league hitting—and cut Greg Swindell, choking down the cold leftovers of his $4.5 million salary. Swindell: "I know I didn't pull my load, and they had a right to do what they did. But I feel this year I wasn't given a very good shake. Obviously, the way I pitched out of the bullpen, that wasn't for me." Millionaire ballplayer's logic: If I fail in a minor role, I deserve a chance to redeem myself in a more important role. If you paid a guy $18 million to get fat and go 30-34 on good teams falling just short, and then had to listen to him whine about being paid the final $2.7 million to just go away . . . well, collusion and union-busting would be on your agenda, too.

July 15-12 (57-52, ½ game back)
The Astros scored 31 fewer runs than they allowed, but went 15-12. They were outscored 46-10 in 4 losses and they were 9-4 in 1-run games, winning 4 in a row that way against the Braves and Padres at one point. They did this despite Bagwell losing

momentum (.230-2-8) along with the rest of the lineup except Biggio (.347-1-13). Disaster seemed imminent when Todd Jones hit the DL, but the Astros got great relief pitching from Xavier Hernandez (3-0, 2.57 ERA in 14 innings) and Billy Wagner stepped into the closer's role, getting 5 saves in 7 opportunities (1-0, 3.14 ERA). They acquired Kirt Manwaring for Rick Wilkins, growing tired of both Wilkins's .2-teens average and his subsequent pouting. Evidently, Manwaring is quite used to hitting .215 and doesn't let it bother him.

August 17-11 (74-63, 2½ games ahead)
The Astros finally got around to retiring Nolan Ryan's number in August—but it's doubtful the ceremony will do anything about The Curse. The Astros finally began to make a serious run at the postseason, with Bagwell (.369-6-23), Berry (.333-1-19), Biggio (.333-4-13, 29 runs), and Hunter (.318-2-9, 21 runs) all producing. Reynolds (4-1, 1.88 ERA, 3 walks, 34 strikeouts), X-man (1-0, 3.38, 4 saves in 5 opportunities), and Wagner (0-1, 1.93, 2 saves) carried the staff. Then, on the 23rd the Cards came to the Astrodome. Game 1 was an Astrodome special—Houston nemesis Donovan Osborne pitched 7 shutout innings, edging Darryl Kile 1-0 on Ray Lankford's homer. Kile struck out 9 in 8 innings, but it wasn't enough. Todd Stottlemyre had dominated Houston twice, and he pitched a quality start again on the 24th, but Reynolds pitched a complete-game 5-hitter—his 16th and final victory—and Houston finally beat them, 3-1. In game 3, Donne Wall won his 8th game, allowing 3 hits in 7 innings, and Bagwell was 3-for-4 with a homer as the Astros won 4-1. With the Cardinals on the ropes and the Astros going in for the kill, the suddenly gutty Andy Benes rallied St. Louis in game 4, winning his 14th game and striking out 10 in 7 innings. Hampton pitched valiantly, but the Cardinals won 3-2, the Astros lead was down to a half-game, and Houston was already looking forward to a September showdown in Busch Stadium.

September 8-17 (82-80, 6 games back)
Houston came into Busch in front by 1½ games and willing to settle for 1 of 3 and leaving town with a lead. In game 1 on Labor Day, Houston jumped to a 3-0 lead in the first and built a 7-3 lead, only to lose in extra innings 8-7. Ozzie Smith had his last big day in the majors, going 3-for-5 with 4 RBIs and 4 runs scored. In game 2, the teams traded runs in the early innings before St. Louis scored 4 two-out runs in the 7th. They added 4 more in the 8th as staff ace Shane Reynolds melted down when it mattered. In game 3, the Astros played their first game as a second-place team since July. The Cardinals gave their ace, Andy Benes, an early lead and he was on cruise control. He'd kept the Cards off the ropes in August, he had his foot on the Astros' necks in September, and he wasn't about to let them back up. The Astros had finished their season series 2-11 against St. Louis. They lost in '95 because they couldn't beat the Reds. History had repeated a few hundred miles to the west in '96. They would go 5-12 in their next 17 games, going out not with a bang but a whimper.

■ 1997 DIAGNOSIS

Offense
The Astrodome remains one of the best pitcher's parks in baseball, even with lower and closer fences. The dead air holds down extra base hits, but the artificial turf gives back some doubles. Astros pitchers have always looked better than they really are, while hitters such as Jose Cruz and Terry Puhl never got their due. What Bagwell is able to do in this park is far more impressive than anything anyone has done in Colorado. Adjust for the park and the Astros offense was second only to the Braves, and the Rockies are down with the Phillies, Marlins, and Cubs. As good as their offense was in 1996 (and they scored more runs than any Houston team ever has, and featured gaudy numbers from Bagwell, Berry, Biggio, and Bell), it wasn't as good as the team effort of the '95 Astros. That team scored 16 fewer runs in 18 fewer games with only 2 players with more than 8 home runs and no one with 90 RBI. In '95, *everyone* contributed—not just the B-Boys.

Defense
Not good. Only the Mets and the Rockies committed more errors in the N.L., and only the Mets and the Giants gave up more unearned runs. They have many stars with the bat, but no one really did much with the glove in '96. Bagwell and Biggio are normally very good, but Bagwell had an off year and Biggio wore down, even if the Gold Glove

voters didn't notice. The shortstops—O, Ricky Manyerrors, and Andujar Cedeño (with that name, you knew he'd find his way back to Houston)—were even worse. This instability on the right side certainly must have had some effect on Biggio but doesn't explain all of his difficulties. Sean Berry quietly played in about as much pain as Ken Caminiti, but his shoulder troubles resulted in 22 errors in 132 games—far too many rocks for a third baseman. In the outfield, Brian Hunter's inability to harness his speed into solid defense has been a source of tremendous frustration for the Astros. Derek Bell has a strong arm and frequently turns routine fly balls into great plays, leading many to rate him much better as a fielder than he is. Manwaring was very solid behind the plate, but with his wheels and his stick, he better be.

Pitching

What the Rockies are to offense, the Astros are to pitching. Here are some home/away ERA splits for Astros starters: Hampton (3.45/3.75), Reynolds (3.34/4.01), Kile (3.79/4.60), Wall (3.62/5.28), and Drabek (3.64/5.64). They combined to give up one run less per game at home (3.56/4.61).Reynolds and Hampton are solid pitchers in any locale. No one can ever tell which Kile is going to show up, whether it's a road game in San Diego (where he held the Padres to 1 run and 5 hits in 8 innings at Jack Murphy on April 28) or a home game in Houston (where he gave up 10 runs in 3.2 innings on April 10). Drabek can still flash some of his old form when in the Dome, but he looked finished on the road. As for Wailing Wall, he's been good at Tucson—and you can't understate how impressive that is—but he hasn't done much in the majors anywhere but the Dome. It's too soon and he was too inconsistent to tell what Wall's long-term tendencies will be. Billy Wagner may end up in the rotation, but he doesn't have an off-speed pitch yet and may become the National League's answer to Mariano Rivera instead.

Four different pitchers held the closer's job for some time during '96, and the set-up men were often old and ineffective (Anthony Young, Gregg Olson, Jeff Tabaka, and Jim Dougherty made 67 appearances, walking 54 while striking out only 51 and yielding 90 hits in 76 innings). As for '97, here's the positive spin: If Hudek can finally make his way back to close out the games, Wagner can own the 7th and 8th, and John John-stone, Mark Small, and Manuel Barrios develop, it could actually be a strength. The more realistic spin: If Todd Jones, who has problems with both his shoulder and his head, is expected to close . . . if Wagner has to start, or is rudely awakened on his 3rd time through the league . . . if Hudek has more body parts removed to wear around his neck . . . well, it could be a train wreck.

Farm System

Hunsicker doesn't think much of it: "I don't see much help in the next couple of years coming out of our farm system." It's rare to find a GM downplaying his prospects—the Blue Jays and Mets have done the exact opposite for years—and it's a disputable assertion anyway. In the outfield, the team has Bob Abreu and Richard Hidalgo. If you were to throw Hidalgo in right and Abreu in left for Houston, in 2 years you probably wouldn't miss Derek Bell, or the melange of left fielders the team's been using. There's also Ramon Castro, a raw but superbly talented young catcher; Russ Johnson, a good hitter who could strengthen the infield; and a slew of young shortstops led by Jhonny Perez and Julio Lugo. The pitchers include Scott Elarton and Oscar Henriquez, who hits 96 mph, and Chris Holt, who could immediately help the rotation.

Management and Ownership

These days, an owner is judged on his or her ability to get a new ballpark. On that score, Drayton McLane has succeeded. He was able to exert enough influence (i.e., extort the taxpayers with a threat to move the team to Virginia) to get support for a new stadium—with grass and a retractable roof—to be ready by the year 2000. In addition to doing whatever it takes to get his sky boxes, he also can't be accused of being cheap. Despite getting burned by throwing big money at Drabek and Swindell, it didn't keep him from throwing money at Biggio and Bagwell. But the owner can't do anything about a team's record against its key divisional rival—except fire a competent manager after the obligatory vote of confidence, and hire a broadcaster to replace him in what amounts to a transparent publicity stunt.

General Manager Gerry Hunsicker didn't do much to impress anyone last season. He traded for Gregg Olson, Kirt Manwaring, Danny Darwin and Andujar Cedeno—not exactly the "missing pieces" for a pennant run—giving up prospects and Rick Wilkins in return. At year end, Hunsicker brought in Larry Dierker to manage. Dierker was good for some yuks in *Ball Four*, a terrific pitcher, and well liked in the Houston area. But the other times that teams have brought announcers out of the booth to run the place, the results were disastrous (GM Ken Harrelson in Chicago, Manager Jerry Coleman in San Diego). He's being used by an owner more interested in heightening public interest in the Astros than he is in winning a pennant in '97. McLane is doing a good imitation of Goldilocks with his managers. Howe was too soft. Collins was too hard. Dierker will be just right—at least until the ink is dry on the politicians' agreement to buy him a new stadium with the taxpayers' money.

At least Dierker had the sense to hire Bill Virdon as his bench coach. There are managers far more seasoned than Dierker who should consider bringing in an experienced baseball man—one of those guys who can't relate to big leaguers anymore, but knows the X's and O's and how the game should be played.

. . . and whatnot: Lies, Damned Lies, and Statistics

In his player write-up, it is argued that Derek Bell is one of the most overrated hitters in the game. Here is the rest of the Lies-and-Statistics Team—players with talent who put up fairly big numbers, but who just aren't as good as these statistics suggest. Most of the Rockies lineup could be included—Dante Bichette, Andres Galarraga, Vinny Castilla, and Eric Young are all mirages—though only one has been named to this team. It's no coincidence that all this "talent" was available to an expansion team 4 years ago and the Marlins ended up with none of it. Every spot they take up on an All-Star roster should be accompanied by a grievance filed by someone who misses out on incentive money because of it.

Mike Stanley. The Yankees were vilified for letting Stanley go before the '96 season—but his weak defense wasn't missed while his offense was fairly ordinary for someone playing in the AL and in Fenway Park. He's gone from being underrated to overrated in 4 years, but that's what playing in New York will do.

Tino Martinez. Other than Travis Fryman and Derek Bell, he had the lowest slugging percentage of any player with 100+ RBI. His gaudy RBI totals were a function of batting in the middle of an order that had the third highest on-base percentage in baseball. Consistency is also very valuable, but isn't measured. Martinez has been streaky throughout his career and 1996 was no exception—as he virtually disappeared during April and September, and didn't manage an RBI in the post-season.

Eric Young. The perception of Coors Field as a power hitter's paradise is only half-true. This is the only park in baseball that inflates singles, doubles, triples, and dingers. Eric Young shouldn't have hit 8 dingers or knocked in 74 runs, but he also shouldn't have hit .324. His performance on the road made Delino DeShields look productive, his defense, though greatly improved, remains inconsistent, and he gets caught stealing too much—yet he seems surprised that the Rockies *still* have not committed to him as their second baseman.

Jose Valentin. He has been locked up for three years by the Brewers, despite being a menace in the field and an undisciplined hitter. He's young and might improve, but his production in '96 was a function of swinging hard in case he made contact. *John* Valentin is an honorable mention, nearly playing his way out of a job on a mediocre team despite hitting nearly .300.

Wade Boggs. He hit .311, his 14th .300+ season in 15 years. But batting average may be the most misleading statistic in baseball, as it fails to accurately measure the ability to get on base or to hit for extra bases. Boggs has been little more than foul balls and slap singles the past four years, and—unless Steve Avery is pitching, the bases are loaded, and the season is on the line—doesn't even draw walks the way he used to. Boggs may have hit .311, but he wasn't much more productive than Terry Pendleton in '96.

Ryan Klesko. A terrific slugger against right-handers who hits the ball real hard on TBS once in a while, he hasn't hit well enough against lefties to play every day. Or to do much against tough left-handed relievers when it's close and late—other than to make Bobby Cox make decisions, or to

wave at sweeping breaking balls when he does get a chance to hit in prime time. He doesn't help his case by being one of the worst defensive players in baseball.

Tom Goodwin. On offense, he is as one-dimensional as it gets. He doesn't walk. He doesn't hit for power. He doesn't even hit doubles. He stole 66 bases, which was second only to Kenny Lofton in the majors—but he gave back a lot of the gains by being caught 22 times. Of the 20 baserunners who stole at least 30 bases, Goodwin is only 1 of 4 who failed at least 25% of the time (along with Eric Young, Dante Bichette, and Royce Clayton).

Derek Bell. Here are 20 players whose batting and slugging averages were close to or better than Bell's—and who would have arguably knocked in at least as many runs as Bell if they hit behind Bagwell and Biggio all year: Jermaine Dye, Orlando Merced, Tom Pagnozzi, John Mabry, Thomas Howard, Greg Colbrunn, Alex Ochoa, Butch Huskey, Luis Gonzalez, Darrin Fletcher, Brian Johnson, Eddie Murray, Troy O'Leary, Jeff Kent, Jeromy Burnitz, Matt Mieske, Michael Tucker, Craig Paquette, Bob Hamelin, and Dave Hollins.

This team might be full of All-Stars, but there's no guarantee they'd make it to post-season. And if they did, they wouldn't take their division by as many games as you might expect.

BOB ABREU — GRADE-A PROSPECT

OF • BL • TR • 6'0 • 160 • 23 • HOU90

	AB	R	H	2B	3B	HR	RBI	BB	SO	SB	CS	BA	OB	SA
AAA	484	86	138	14	16	13	68	83	111	24	18	.285	.391	.461

Abreu is an excellent young hitter who doesn't have anything left to learn at Triple-A. This is the second straight season he's spent at Tucson, and both times he's hit around .290 with plenty of extra-base hits. He's a decent right fielder with a strong arm, but is probably the left fielder of the future in deference to Richard Hidalgo. Abreu is emotional and gets down on himself, but he might just be sick of Tucson. That can happen. If his triples and doubles turn into home-run power as he develops, Abreu could be the Astros' cleanup hitter for the next decade. If not, he would fit nicely between Biggio and Bagwell in the lineup. ■

CHAD ALEXANDER — SOLID PROSPECT

OF • BR • TR • 6'0 • 190 • 22 • HOU95/3

	AB	R	H	2B	3B	HR	RBI	BB	SO	SB	CS	BA	OB	SA
A	435	68	115	25	4	13	69	57	108	16	11	.264	.350	.430

The organization considers Alexander to be a "pure" hitter. That's scout-speak for not looking like Mark Johnson at the plate. Or Dave Winfield, for that matter. Alexander's strikeout rate isn't that of a "pure" hitter, but he was playing in a pitcher's league in a pitcher's park. He has decent power and should do better in high-A, or in Double-A. ■

JEFF BAGWELL — SUPERSTAR

1B • BR • TR • 6'0 • 195 • 28 • BOS89/6

	AB	R	H	2B	3B	HR	RBI	BB	SO	SB	CS	BA	OB	SA
HOU94	400	104	147	32	2	39	116	65	65	15	4	.368	.451	.750
HOU95	448	88	130	29	0	21	87	79	102	12	5	.290	.399	.496
HOU96	568	111	179	48	2	31	120	135	114	21	7	.315	.451	.570
CAREER	3091	545	950	206	18	144	589	500	567	78	30	.307	.406	.525

Bagwell wasn't thrilled with the effort his team was putting in during '96. In May, the team was under .500 and in first place, and their best player was saying: " Players should be giving 100% every time out, but sometimes we aren't doing that. I think some guys are just happy to be in the big leagues, collect their check every 2 weeks, and go home." Not him. At one point he was leading the league in 3 offensive categories, yet criticized himself for his strikeouts. He's tough, too. Though the team was eliminated with a week to go, he played all 162 games in '96—after 3 hand injuries and 2 labor disputes kept him from doing that from '93 to '95. Bagwell: "So as long as I can put my uniform on with both hands—which I can do this year—I'm going to be out there." Bagwell is the finest first baseman in the National League. And it's not too much of a stretch to say he's the best first baseman in baseball. Defensively, he's much better than Frank Thomas. As an offensive player, he's complete. Last season, he hit for power and average, drew walks, and stole 21 bases in 28

attempts. He's been doing this since 1991. He combines power with an eye similar to Rickey Henderson's: He has the on-base percentage of a leadoff man and the slugging percentage of Albert Belle. Adjusting for his park, he hit .335 last season and slugged .600 with a .464 on-base percentage—the numbers of a young DiMaggio. ■

MANUEL BARRIOS

SLEEPER

RP • BR • TR • 6′0 • 145 • 22 • HOU93

	G	GS	IP	H	HR	BB	K	W	L	S	ERA	K/BB	K9	HW9
AA	60	0	68	60	4	29	69	6	4	0	2.37	2.4	9.1	11.72

Barrios throws hard and was effective at Double-A, striking out a batter per inning and holding the opposition to fewer than 8 hits per 9. He made the jump from the low-Class-A Midwest League to the Texas League last season, and the only thing that really suffered was his control. This bodes very well, as most pitchers can't survive this kind of jump. Unfortunately, he'll have to continue to refine his game at Tucson, which is working the high wire without a net. It's probably going to take him most of the season to do it, so don't expect him in Houston until September. ■

DEREK BELL

OVERRATED

RF • BR • TR • 6′2 • 200 • 28 • TOR87/2

	AB	R	H	2B	3B	HR	RBI	BB	SO	SB	CS	BA	OB	SA
SD94	434	54	135	20	0	14	54	29	88	24	8	.311	.354	.454
HOU95	452	63	151	21	2	8	86	33	71	27	9	.334	.385	.442
HOU96	627	84	165	40	3	17	113	40	123	29	3	.263	.311	.418
CAREER	2244	302	636	106	9	62	341	146	443	116	29	.283	.333	.422

This guy has great ability. He could be something special, but he's 28 and has yet to have a season that reflects this ability. His RBI count was nice in '96, but he hit .233 with 3 homers in 219 at-bats with runners in scoring position and .260 with 6 homers in 339 at-bats with runners on. Is this the portrait of an RBI machine? Or of a decent hitter who happens to bat behind Bagwell and Biggio? He was eventually dropped from the cleanup spot late in the season, only to whine that he was being dissed by his manager. Do the math, Derek. If the Astros had a real cleanup hitter—say, one who hit .300 with runners in scoring position instead of .219, and could manage more dingers than Orlando Merced—he'd have knocked in 150 runs. And the Astros would have gone to the playoffs. Bell's batting average was sexy in '95, but he drew walks so infrequently that his on-base percentage was ordinary. And his weak performance in the '96 stretch drive finished him off more than 70 points lower in '96. In the field, he has a strong arm but doesn't position himself well, and he doesn't use his speed effectively enough. He's got talent, but once you go inside the numbers you realize he's yet to have a great year. ■

SEAN BERRY

3B • BR • TR • 5′11 • 200 • 31 • KC86

	AB	R	H	2B	3B	HR	RBI	BB	SO	SB	CS	BA	OB	SA
MON94	320	43	89	19	2	11	41	32	50	14	0	.278	.347	.453
MON95	314	38	100	22	1	14	55	25	53	3	8	.318	.367	.529
HOU96	431	55	121	38	1	17	95	23	58	12	6	.281	.328	.492
CAREER	1504	198	420	99	7	57	249	129	270	43	17	.279	.340	.468

Berry has power and hits for average, but like Derek Bell, he can't draw a walk and had his RBI numbers inflated from the luxury of hitting behind Bagwell and Biggio. He's a useful part of an offense, but he gave back more than a few of those runs with his 22 errors as he played with a torn rotator cuff in his throwing arm. He made 9 errors in his first 16 games, but only 13 in his next 116 games after getting shot up with cortisone. He went back to Dr. Feelgood twice more during the season to stay in the lineup. Pain has a purpose, and this just makes you wonder what kind of damage he did while he was comfortably numb—though the suits were assuring him otherwise. He went under the knife in the off-season, but, healthy or not, he's probably going to face some competition at third base from Russ Johnson in the near future. ■

CRAIG BIGGIO

NL ELITE

2B • BR • TR • 5'11 • 185 • 31 • HOU87/1

	AB	R	H	2B	3B	HR	RBI	BB	SO	SB	CS	BA	OB	SA
HOU94	437	88	139	44	5	6	56	62	58	39	4	.318	.411	.483
HOU95	553	123	167	30	2	22	77	80	85	33	8	.302	.406	.483
HOU96	605	113	174	24	4	15	75	75	72	25	7	.288	.386	.415
CAREER	4485	728	1279	245	28	94	464	550	646	221	72	.285	.371	.415

According to *Baseball America*'s midseason survey and the Gold Glove voting, Biggio is still considered the best defensive second baseman in the league. But when you move beyond reputation, you will find that during the past 2 seasons his range was below average. His offense has fallen off, too, and may never return to his lofty '95 levels. His stolen-base efficiency also dropped a bit last season, suggesting that he might be wearing down. He had nothing left in September, slumping badly when it counted. He got plunked by pitches 26 times—many of them early in the year while he was struggling at the plate, turning into pitches to take one for the team. "Anything to get on base," as Biggio succintly put it. He plays about 100 games a year on plastic concrete. Finally, he is not a very big guy—certainly not as big as his numbers. Add it all up: Biggio is a terrific player, but either he was playing through injuries last season, or he will be in '97 if the Astros don't give him a few home games off. ■

DOUG BROCAIL

RP • BL • TR • 6'5 • 220 • 29 • SD86/1

	G	GS	IP	H	HR	BB	K	W	L	S	ERA	K/BB	K9	HW9
SD94	12	0	17	21	1	5	11	0	0	0	5.82	2.2	5.8	13.76
HOU95	36	7	77	87	10	22	39	6	4	1	4.19	1.8	4.6	12.74
HOU96	23	4	53	58	7	23	34	1	5	0	4.58	1.5	5.8	13.75
CAREER	98	38	289	326	36	97	169	11	22	1	4.64	1.7	5.3	13.17

Brocail has decent stuff: a pretty good fastball and slider, as well as a curve and a split-finger pitch. He can't change speeds well and can't handle lefties. In '95, lefties cuffed him around; in '96, they keyed his car before ransacking his house. He can be pretty effective against right-handers, but his ability evaporates as soon as he leaves the comfort of the Astrodome. If he doesn't come up with something to give lefties a harder time, the Astros have plenty of options, and he's as good a candidate as any to fall by the wayside. He broke down early in '96 due to shoulder "instability." Haven't seen that word in the DL listings since Dibble, and it wasn't Rob's arm that was the problem. Brocail had to have his shoulder scoped, and he returned well ahead of schedule—though the exploratory surgery revealed a "minor fraying" of the biceps tendon. So if he pulls a Dean Palmer some time next year, and ends up rolling around on the carpet with his bicep up by his armpit, he can jack that doctor up and ask him just what he meant by "minor fraying" of that rope that holds his arm together. ■

JOHN CANGELOSI

OF • BB • TL • 5'8 • 150 • 34 • CHA82/4

	AB	R	H	2B	3B	HR	RBI	BB	SO	SB	CS	BA	OB	SA
NYN94	111	14	28	4	0	0	4	19	20	5	1	.252	.371	.288
HOU95	201	46	0	5	2	0	18	1	42	21	5	.000	.024	.045
HOU96	262	49	69	11	4	1	16	44	41	17	9	.263	.378	.347
CAREER	1635	281	410	56	15	10	112	309	262	147	57	.251	.377	.322

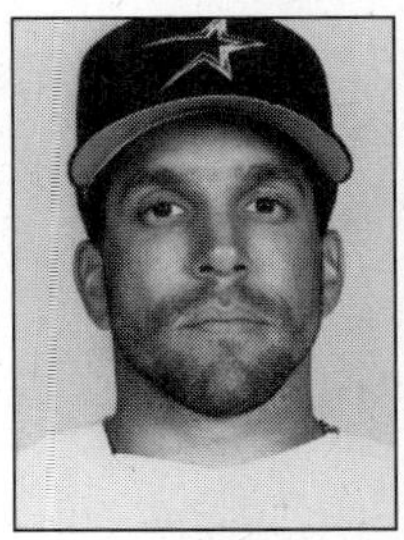

Cangelosi is the perfect Astrodome hitter: He takes a lot of pitches and slaps the ball on the ground, taking advantage of his speed. He can't drive the ball, and he isn't a great baserunner, but he'll score 50 runs a season if he gets 250 to 300 at-bats. At the very least, he's a great bench player. And he's got guts. Who can forget . . . August 12, 1996. Montreal's Jeff Juden (6-foot-8, 265 pounds) squares off against Cangelosi (who's giving away 1 foot and 115 pounds) in Montreal. Juden looks like some psychovillain from Rocky VII taking on Macauly Caulkin. Juden comes in swinging roundhouse rights, but *right there*: Down goes Juden. And the diminutive one is on top, pummeling the side of the big man's head. Give Cangelosi credit for guts, craziness, or both. It was the closest the Astros came in '96 to going down swinging. ■

RAMON CASTRO

SOLID PROSPECT

C • BR • TR • 6′3 • 195 • 21 • HOU94/1

	AB	R	H	2B	3B	HR	RBI	BB	SO	SB	CS	BA	OB	SA
A	314	38	78	15	0	7	43	31	61	2	0	.248	.317	.363

The first Puerto Rican high school player taken in the 1st round of the amateur draft, Castro has a great arm and great potential as a hitter. He's a raw defensive player but showed flashes of ability. He hit reasonably well in the Midwest League—which is not something to dismiss quickly . He didn't strike out excessively, and he showed some power and the ability to take a walk. He won't be one of the greats, but there is a lot to like about him. ■

ANDUJAR CEDEÑO

SS • BR • TR • 6′1 • 170 • 27 • HOU86

	AB	R	H	2B	3B	HR	RBI	BB	SO	SB	CS	BA	OB	SA
HOU94	342	38	90	26	0	9	49	29	79	1	1	.263	.334	.418
SD95	390	42	82	16	2	6	31	28	92	5	3	.210	.271	.308
SD/DET/HOU96	335	30	71	6	3	10	38	15	70	5	3	.212	.247	.337
CAREER	2051	221	485	98	13	47	223	143	488	26	17	.236	.292	.366

Joaquin Cesar—love child of two of the craziest hombres ever to pull on Houston's early '80s rainbow pajamas—has shown good power potential in the minors and in '93 for the Astros. But he did a whole lot of nothing once the league figured out never to throw him a strike. Go ahead and give him a full-time job again—what's 450 outs among friends? Still, the Astros saw something they like—even if Tigers GM Randy Smith gave up on him about 15 minutes after he stepped off the plane from San Diego. If nothing else, it's a good sign for Detroit that Tiger Stadium is no longer the end of the line. ■

RYAN CREEK

SP • BR • TR • 6′1 • 180 • 24 • HOU92/35

	G	GS	IP	H	HR	BB	K	W	L	S	ERA	K/BB	K9	HW9
AA	27	26	142	139	9	121	119	7	15	0	5.26	1.0	7.5	16.48

After a successful season at Jackson in 1995, Creek returned there in '96 and threw up an airball. When he's right, he has a good fastball and an inconsistently brilliant curve. He can be effective against lefties, because his fastball has a cutting action. Creek's control is as bad as it gets—Brad Pennington and Steve Dalkowski laugh at this guy. But maybe Creek was hurt last year, so don't write him off just yet. ■

DANNY DARWIN (see Looking for a Game)

DOUG DRABEK (see Free Agents)

SCOTT ELARTON

SOLID PROSPECT

SP • BR • TR • 6′8 • 225 • 21 • HOU94/2

	G	GS	IP	H	HR	BB	K	W	L	S	ERA	K/BB	K9	HW9
A+	27	27	172	154	13	54	130	12	7	0	2.92	2.4	6.8	10.86

Elarton is huge and has a decent fastball that should improve as he matures. He also has an excellent curveball. His problem is his lanky build, which accentuates any minor flaw in his delivery. As for other third-string centers in baseball uniforms, it took Randy Johnson several years to work out his delivery, and Eric Hillman never could. Elarton's strikeout rate isn't there yet, but just about everything else that matters is. He was promoted to Jackson for the Texas League playoffs and ended up pitching the title-winning game against Wichita. If the kinks get worked out in the spring, the major-league timetable could be accelerated. ■

TONY EUSEBIO

C • BR • TR • 6′2 • 180 • 29 • HOU85

	AB	R	H	2B	3B	HR	RBI	BB	SO	SB	CS	BA	OB	SA
HOU94	159	18	47	9	1	5	30	8	33	0	1	.296	.320	.459
HOU95	368	46	110	21	1	6	58	31	59	0	2	.299	.354	.410
HOU96	152	15	41	7	2	1	19	18	20	0	1	.270	.343	.362
CAREER	698	83	200	38	4	12	107	63	120	0	4	.287	.343	.404

Eusebio is a useful player. He's a righty who can handle righties. He can't drive the ball, so he's content to slap rugburners all day. His playing time was cut by more than 50% in '96 because of injuries and poor throwing; N.L. runners were 30-for-39 (76.9 % success rate) against him. He's a good second catcher and will show up on *SportsCenter* more than most, as he gets his share of big hits. ■

ALEJANDRO FREIRE

SLEEPER

OF • BR • TR • 6′1 • 170 • 22

	AB	R	H	2B	3B	HR	RBI	BB	SO	SB	CS	BA	OB	SA
A+	384	40	98	24	1	12	42	24	66	11	7	.255	.309	.417

In a pitcher's park in a pitcher's league, Freire showed decent power. His on-base percentage was

horrible, but this has been better in the past, and he did make good contact. This is the season where he shows what he's made of. He'll be at Double-A Jackson, a pitcher's park in a hitter's league. A lot like the Astrodome, only with fans. If he can perform like he did in '95 (.305-15-65, 50 Ks, and 83 walks), he's the real deal. ■

CARLOS GUILLEN

SLEEPER

SS • BR • TR • 6'0 • 150 • 21

	AB	R	H	2B	3B	HR	RBI	BB	SO	SB	CS	BA	OB	SA
A	112	23	37	7	1	3	17	16	25	13	6	.330	.405	.491

Guillen was hurt for a lot of last season, but he has decent power, a rifle arm and good speed. What he did in his short time at Quad Cities did nothing to dispel the favorable reviews. If he does this again in a full season, he will probably be a Grade-A prospect. ■

RICKY GUTIERREZ

SS • BR • TR • 6'1 • 175 • 26 • BAL88/2

	AB	R	H	2B	3B	HR	RBI	BB	SO	SB	CS	BA	OB	SA
SD94	275	27	66	11	2	1	28	32	54	2	6	.240	.321	.305
HOU95	156	22	43	6	0	0	12	10	33	5	0	.276	.321	.314
HOU96	218	28	62	8	1	1	15	23	42	6	1	.284	.359	.344
CAREER	1087	153	281	35	8	7	81	115	226	17	10	.259	.334	.325

Gutierrez is not a good enough fielder to play every day, but he won't hurt you too much defensively, is an improvement over Orlando Miller, and he can hit pretty well for a middle infielder. He's always hit lefties, but had a festival against them last season. A ground-ball hitter, he certainly didn't have a problem at the Dome, hitting .348 on the home turf and .217 on the road. But he can't match Miller's power, so O will continue to get the majority of the playing time. ■

MIKE HAMPTON

YOUNG GUN

SP • BR • TL • 5'10 • 180 • 24 • SEA90/6

	G	GS	IP	H	HR	BB	K	W	L	S	ERA	K/BB	K9	HW9
HOU94	44	0	41	46	4	16	24	2	1	0	3.70	1.5	5.3	13.60
HOU95	24	24	150	141	13	49	115	9	8	0	3.35	2.3	6.9	11.40
HOU96	27	27	160	175	12	49	101	10	10	0	3.59	2.1	5.7	12.60
CAREER	108	54	369	390	32	131	248	22	22	1	3.78	1.9	6.0	12.71

Hampton is an extreme ground-ball pitcher, and is the Astro who would be most helped by a better

defensive infield. He was very consistent last season: home/road, grass/turf, day/night, lefty/righty, it didn't matter—he was effective regardless of the situation. There were only 3 disturbing things, all of which could be related: (1) the high number of hits he allowed; (2) his poor second-half performance; and (3) injuries that cut his innings pitched last season. He has a mediocre fastball, but he can cut it, sink it, ride it, do everything short of make it disappear en route. He also has a decent curve and slider, and an adequate change. Some scouts compare his arsenal and technique to those of Tom Glavine. That's not as ridiculous a comparison as it sounds. He's young, and in a great park. If the Astros shore up the left side of their infield and he stays healthy, he could take a major step forward. ■

CHRIS HATCHER

OF • BR • TR • 6'3 • 220 • 28

	AB	R	H	2B	3B	HR	RBI	BB	SO	SB	CS	BA	OB	SA
AAA	348	53	105	21	4	18	61	14	87	10	8	.302	.333	.540

Superficially, this guy looks good, but it's pretty much an illusion. He's been at Tucson for 3 years now and if you take the air out of his numbers, you're looking at a guy who'll hit .260 with 10 or 11 homers and about 8 walks in 300 at-bats. He won't slug .400 and he won't have an onbase percentage over .300. And that's not good. ■

OSCAR HENRIQUEZ

SLEEPER

RP • BR • TR • 6'4 • 175 • 23 • HOU91

	G	GS	IP	H	HR	BB	K	W	L	S	ERA	K/BB	K9	HW9
A+	37	0	34	28	0	29	40	0	4	15	3.97	1.4	10.6	14.56

Weird things continue to happen to Astros pitchers. Don Wilson commits suicide, James Rodney Richard has a stroke, John Hudek has circulatory problems and disposable ribs, and Larry Dierker gets the manager's job with no experience. Henriquez nearly died from myasthenia gravis (a condition that paralyzes muscles), missing '94 and half of '95 because of surgery to correct this. He's working on a change and a curve, but at the moment he doesn't have anything other than his 95–96 mph fastball.

But if he can build on that, he could develop into a good pitcher. ▪

XAVIER HERANDEZ (see Free Agents)

RICHARD HIDALGO — GRADE-A PROSPECT

OF • BR • TR • 6′2 • 175 • 21 • HOU91

	AB	R	H	2B	3B	HR	RBI	BB	SO	SB	CS	BA	OB	SA
AA	513	66	151	34	2	14	78	29	55	11	7	.294	.341	.450

No one will mistake Hidalgo's speed for Kenny Lofton's, and no one will mistake his batting eye for Edgar Martinez's. Those are the extent of his flaws. He's a very good fielder with an excellent arm. He hits for average and has line-drive power. He's a very good young hitter, and as he matures, his power should increase dramatically. As a prospect, he's similar to Raul Mondesi. He's not as fast and his arm isn't *that* good, but he's a similar hitter and has a good chance of being a *much better* one because of his strike-zone judgment. Hidalgo doesn't walk much, but he cut his strikeouts from 76 to 55 between 1995 and 1996 while walking the same amount. Mondesi never made that kind of improvement at any level. Some Astros fans might see a bit of José Cruz in him. They aren't too far off. ▪

CHRIS HOLT — SOLID PROSPECT

SP • BR • TR • 6′4 • 205 • 25 • HOU92/4

	G	GS	IP	H	HR	BB	K	W	L	S	ERA	K/BB	K9	HW9
AAA	28	27	186	208	11	38	137	9	6	0	3.62	3.6	6.6	11.88

Holt was voted the best control pitcher in the Pacific Coast League and has the basic 3 pitches: fastball, curveball, and straight change. His stock rose within the organization after he dominated in winter ball after the '95 season. Holt has a "heavy" fastball that sinks and touches 90 mph. Scouts say he lacks confidence in his other pitches, relying too much on his fastball. They also feel it isn't a dominant pitch, merely a good one. He will get a good chance to take Drabek's spot this spring and could be a pleasant surprise. ▪

JOHN HUDEK — SLEEPER

RP • BB • TR • 6′1 • 200 • 30 • CHA88/10

	G	GS	IP	H	HR	BB	K	W	L	S	ERA	K/BB	K9	HW9
HOU94	42	0	39	24	5	18	39	0	2	16	2.97	2.2	9.0	9.68
HOU95	19	0	20	19	3	5	29	2	2	7	5.40	5.8	13.1	10.80
HOU96	15	0	16	12	2	5	14	2	0	2	2.81	2.8	7.9	9.56
CAREER	76	0	75	55	10	28	82	4	4	25	3.60	2.9	9.8	9.96

When Hudek is right, he can bring it in the 95–96 mph range with excellent movement. Unfortunately, he wasn't anywhere close to that in his '96 rehab and brief comeback. He's suffered from all kinds of injuries over the past 2 seasons—primarily because of his ribs. He fractured 2 in the same month in 1996 and had part of one removed in 1995. He made a necklace out of that one and wears it to remind him of the procedure. Be grateful it wasn't another, more personal operation. He is impossible to forecast without a Ouija board. He could be on the shelf most of the year, or he could be closing games again. ▪

BRIAN HUNTER — OVERRATED

CF • BR • TR • 6′4 • 180 • 26 • HOU89/3

	AB	R	H	2B	3B	HR	RBI	BB	SO	SB	CS	BA	OB	SA
HOU95	321	52	97	14	5	2	28	21	52	24	7	.302	.346	.396
HOU96	526	74	145	27	2	5	35	17	92	35	9	.276	.297	.363

The Astros hate Hunter's defense. They feel he's got bad hands and uses poor judgment. Though his error rate is high—several due to simply dropping fly balls—his range is well above-average and at times he can outrun his mistakes. Collins: "He needs to take the same attitude in the field that he has at the plate and running the bases." The Astros should be focusing on his on-base percentage. He is a rally-killer. He has to draw walks, or he has minimal value. At his age, the chances of him dramatically improving his batting eye aren't great. He once was compared to Lofton. If he continues to underachieve, he may end up getting compared to what they got for Kenny Lofton: Eddie Taubansee. ▪

MARK JOHNSON — SOLID PROSPECT

RHP • HOU96/1 • UNIVERSITY OF HAWAII

The 19th overall pick in the '96 draft, Johnson looks like a good one. He has excellent command and throws a consistent 93-mph fastball and a dominating slider. He also has a decent change-up. Johnson had mediocre numbers in college, but his coach blamed that on poor team defense. The Astros think he could do anything: start, set up, or close. No plans yet for mop-up or take-one-for-the-team-you're-being-left-out-there-to-die duty. ■

RUSS JOHNSON — SOLID PROSPECT

SS • BR • TR • 5'10 • 185 • 24 • HOU94/3

	AB	R	H	2B	3B	HR	RBI	BB	SO	SB	CS	BA	OB	SA
AA	496	86	154	24	5	15	74	56	50	9	4	.310	.382	.470

If Russ was younger, he'd be Grade-A. Nevertheless, the more you look, the more you like. He was at Double-A in '95 and '96, but the difference between his 2 seasons is mind-boggling. In '95, his average was weak, his power middling, and his defense questionable. In '96, his average was over .300 and his power was better. The jury is still out on his defense, but he did play last season at shortstop. At LSU, he teamed with the Twins' Todd Walker to form what was probably the best double-play combo in NCAA history. Like Walker, Johnson will probably be moved to third. Johnson's not quite as good as Walker, but he has a long but realistic shot at the Astros' third-base job in '97—especially if they tell Berry, "Thanks for taking all those cortisone shots for us last year, but we won't be joining you at that arbitration hearing. Don't let the door hit you in your blown-out throwing arm on your way out." ■

JOHN JOHNSTONE — SLEEPER

RP • BR • TR • 6'3 • 195 • 28 • NYM87/20

	G	GS	IP	H	HR	BB	K	W	L	S	ERA	K/BB	K9	HW9
AAA	45	1	55	59	2	22	70	3	3	5	3.42	3.2	11.4	13.18

Johnstone has good stuff, including an excellent curve, and pitched very well at Triple-A. His control wasn't great, but his strikeout rate was dominating. He didn't do much with the Astros in '96 (5.54 ERA in 13 innings), but he deserves another shot at a bullpen job with the big club. With the quality of the team's relief pitching in '96, they have nothing to lose by flipping him the keys and letting him take it for a spin. ■

TODD JONES

RP • BL • TR • 6'3 • 200 • 28 • HOU89/2

	G	GS	IP	H	HR	BB	K	W	L	S	ERA	K/BB	K9	HW9
HOU94	48	0	72	52	3	26	63	5	2	5	2.72	2.4	7.9	9.74
HOU95	68	0	99	89	8	52	96	6	5	15	3.07	1.8	8.7	12.82
HOU96	51	0	57	61	5	32	44	6	3	17	4.40	1.4	6.9	14.68
CAREER	194	0	266	230	20	125	228	18	12	39	3.28	1.8	7.7	12.01

If you're wondering why Todd Jones has struggled so much, it might have something to do with the fact that he was what the Astros got in the draft as compensation for losing Nolan Ryan to the Texas Rangers. In April and May, Jones pitched 30 innings, allowing 29 hits (1 homer), struck out 28, walked only 12, and had an ERA of 3.00. From June on, Jones struck out 16, walked 20, and had an ERA of 5.93. Tojo's first clue that something might not be right came in August, when his arm popped out of the socket a few times in a game at Wrigley. "No, skip, I'm fine. It's just that my arm might detach on my next pitch. That's not a balk, is it?"

If he's on, he's great. His ongoing problems against left-handers are offset by the stomping he gives to right-handers. But after the All-Star break, he's consistently been slapped around like Tyson's bum-of-the-month. Hello, McFly—the guy's arm is falling off! He pitched 173 innings in the 2 Fehr-shortened seasons of '94 and '95, and he was on pace to put in around 225 in 2 full seasons. Unless they've already blown him out, the Astros have to look at him as a 50-60 inning pitcher, going an inning at a time. As for his confidence, about as important to a closer as a fastball with movement, that might be beyond repair. His pitching coach has suggested he's "talked himself" into bad games. As Tojo puts it: "It's never easy when I go out there." Jones simply doesn't have the attitude to be a closer and may never have it. He could learn something from Doug Jones. Dojo had *nothing,* and if he got ripped, he'd be in the clubhouse the next day flipping through a *Road & Track* without a thought or care in his head. ■

DARRYL KILE

SP • BR • TR • 6′5 • 185 • 28 • HOU87/30

	G	GS	IP	H	HR	BB	K	W	L	S	ERA	K/BB	K9	HW9
HOU94	24	24	147	153	13	82	105	9	6	0	4.57	1.3	6.4	14.38
HOU95	25	21	127	114	5	73	113	4	12	0	4.96	1.5	8.0	13.25
HOU96	35	33	219	233	16	97	219	12	11	0	4.19	2.3	9.0	13.56
CAREER	175	148	944	920	70	468	768	52	58	0	4.12	1.6	7.3	13.23

Kile defies every expectation. After 2 extended, failed trials in '91 and '92, he had lost his prospect status among many. So he goes 15-8 and throws a no-hitter in '93. Expected to move to the ranks of the elite, he went 13-18 in '94 and '95 with an ERA pushing 5.00. In '96 Kile managed to do all of this in the same season. In his best 9 starts he went 4-1 and gave up 52 hits in 70 innings, striking out 74 batters and walking only 19 with an ERA barely over 1.00. Surprisingly, nearly half of these gems were on the road. At his worst, also evenly split home and away, he was 0-4 with 46 hits, 15 walks, and only 16 strikeouts in 16.2 innings and an ERA of 16.20 and HW9 of 32.95. With numbers like this, the existence of an evil twin cannot be discounted. Kile has an incredible curve, a good fastball, and a split-finger, so there's absolutely no reason why he couldn't dominate for years. If he could become more consistent with his stuff and find a way to throw his breaking pitches for strikes when he's behind in the count, a Cy Young award would not be out of the question. Those who claim to know which Kile is going to show up on any given day are kidding themselves. This is as random and extreme as it gets and you couldn't blame any manager who simply chose to leave him in the clubhouse and go with 24 guys rather than put up with the *agita*. ■

JULIO LUGO

SOLID PROSPECT

SS • BR • TR • 5′11 • 155 • 21

	AB	R	H	2B	3B	HR	RBI	BB	SO	SB	CS	BA	OB	SA
A	393	60	116	18	2	10	50	32	75	24	11	.295	.350	.427

He was young and very impressive in the Midwest League. As a hitter, the only thing he lacks is good strike-zone judgment, and that could easily improve. Of all the players that Houston had at Quad City, he's probably the best, with Chad Alexander a close second. ■

KIRT MANWARING (see Free Agents)

DERRICK MAY

OF • BL • TR • 6′4 • 210 • 28 • CHN86/1

	AB	R	H	2B	3B	HR	RBI	BB	SO	SB	CS	BA	OB	SA
CHN94	345	43	98	19	2	8	51	30	34	3	2	.284	.340	.420
MIL/HOU95	319	44	90	18	2	9	50	24	42	5	1	.282	.333	.436
HOU96	259	24	65	12	3	5	33	30	33	2	2	.251	.330	.378
CAREER	1822	218	506	90	9	42	270	133	198	26	11	.278	.327	.406

May is not a star, but he's got a refreshing attitude. When the Astros sat him to play Mouton full-time, even though May was outproducing him, he took it like a man: "James needs to get in a groove, and I'm comfortable coming off the bench." Then he went out and produced as a pinch hitter. He got back in the starting lineup eventually, but he'll be making way for Hidalgo and Abreu next. But someone will always find room for a team player who hits left-handed. ■

TONY MCKNIGHT

SP • BL • TR • 6′5 • 205 • 19 • HOU95/1

	G	GS	IP	H	HR	BB	K	W	L	S	ERA	K/BB	K9	HW9
R	8	5	22	28	1	7	15	2	1	0	6.23	2.1	6.2	14.54

McKnight was taken with the 22nd pick in the '95 draft. He was a badly abused high school right-hander from Arkansas, who was once asked to throw 200 pitches in one game. The Astros put him on a conditioning program and he was supposed to be 100% coming into 1996. He wasn't, pitching only a few innings and doing poorly in them. If he's OK, he throws 92-93. What his high school coaches did to him was sick and wrong, but he has a chance (albeit slim) of overcoming it. ■

MITCH MELUSKEY

C • BB • TR • 5′11 • 185 • 23 • CLE92/12

	AB	R	H	2B	3B	HR	RBI	BB	SO	SB	CS	BA	OB	SA
AA	134	18	42	11	0	0	21	18	24	0	0	.313	.396	.396

Initially considered a raw catcher, Meluskey came over from the Cleveland organization for Buck McNabb, a John Cangelosi clone, in what looked like an off-off-Broadway performance of the Lofton-for-Taubansee tragedy. Meluskey had never hit in the past, so his '96 performance was a pleasant surprise. He started the year at Kissimmee and hit

.333 in 231 at bats before being promoted. He also dramatically improved defensively. He doesn't look great, but his stock within the Astros organization rocketed last season and he might get a big-league job this year. They must really be determined to show that they can get the better of the Indians in a trade. ■

ORLANDO MILLER

SS • BR • TR • 6'1 • 180 • 28 • NYA87

	AB	R	H	2B	3B	HR	RBI	BB	SO	SB	CS	BA	OB	SA
HOU95	324	36	85	20	1	5	36	22	71	3	4	.262	.319	.377
HOU96	468	43	120	26	2	15	58	14	116	3	7	.256	.291	.417

'Do is inconsistent defensively, he can't reach base, and he may be the professional athlete most likely to commit a felony on the playing field. As he came through the minors his nickname was El Diablo because of this volatile temper. In the field, he makes errors and doesn't position himself properly. At the plate he lunges at everything and is worthless if you pitch him inside. At his age, he's not going to learn the things that will turn him from a subpar hitter into a good hitter. But just when you're about to write him off . . . well, here's Biggio: "What's amazing about him is that he can look terrible on one pitch by swinging and missing by a mile, then hit the next pitch 500 feet." Unfortunately, that sounds a lot like Andujar Cedeño. 'Do did gut it out through a lot of pain this year, taking a cortisone shot in the shoulder and playing on sore knees, so his offensive numbers might improve a bit even if his sunny disposition doesn't. ■

RAY MONTGOMERY

SLEEPER

OF • BR • TR • 6'3 • 195 • 27

	AB	R	H	2B	3B	HR	RBI	BB	SO	SB	CS	BA	OB	SA
AAA	360	70	110	20	0	22	75	59	54	7	1	.306	.407	.544

He looks like a good expansion pick—like Geronimo Berroa would have been if the Marlins had ever let him play. He's more likely a .260 hitter than a .300 hitter, but he's got power and really can work a pitcher. He'll go deep in the count waiting for his pitch or taking a walk. He's at his peak physically and needs 400-plus at-bats to show what he can do. ■

ALVIN MORMAN

SLEEPER

RP • BL • TL • 6'3 • 210 • 28 • HOU91/44

	G	GS	IP	H	HR	BB	K	W	L	S	ERA	K/BB	K9	HW9
HOU96	53	0	42	43	8	24	31	4	1	0	4.93	1.3	6.6	14.36

Once a top prospect, Morman used to throw a fine curve and 2-seam and 4-seam fastballs. The 4-seamer used to peak at 94 mph. Two seasons of arm trouble later, he has a *decent* fastball, his curve is now more of a slurve, and he has a straight change-up. So he's not the pitcher he once was, but at the end of the season he was pretty good. From April to July, he was 1-1 with a 5.74 ERA and 34 hits allowed (8 homers) in 31.1 innings (18 walks, 19 strikeouts). In August and September he was 3-0, 2.53 with nine hits allowed (no homers) in 10.2 innings (6 walks, 12 strikeouts). It's quite possible that it's taken him all this time to get it together after his injuries. If that's the case, expect him to pitch like he did at the end of the season. He was never much of a control pitcher, but he had electrifying stuff and could be a pleasant surprise. ■

TONY MOUNCE

SP • BL • TL • 6'2 • 185 • 22 • HOU94/9

	G	GS	IP	H	HR	BB	K	W	L	S	ERA	K/BB	K9	HW9
A+	25	25	156	139	7	68	102	9	9	0	2.25	1.5	5.9	11.97

He's a lefty, he's young, and his ERA has declined steadily as he's climbed from the Rookie League to high Class-A in 3 years. He's gone 29-19 in the process. The bad news: he can't throw 90 and can't control his breaking stuff. His K/BB ratio has declined steadily from 4:1 to 1.5:1, his strikeouts-per-nine from 10.9 to 5.9. He may already have hit his ceiling. ■

JAMES MOUTON

OF • BR • TR • 5'9 • 175 • 28 • HOU91/12

	AB	R	H	2B	3B	HR	RBI	BB	SO	SB	CS	BA	OB	SA
HOU94	310	43	76	11	0	2	16	27	69	24	5	.245	.315	.300
HOU95	298	42	78	18	2	4	27	25	59	25	8	.262	.326	.376
HOU96	300	40	79	15	1	3	34	38	55	21	9	.263	.343	.350
CAREER	908	125	233	44	3	9	77	90	183	7	22	.257	.328	.341

During major-league rookie orientation in 1994, players were asked to name their favorite player. When it reached him, this guy blurted, "James Mouton!" Well, McLane, Hunsicker, and Collins certainly wouldn't offer that answer. The Astros were showcasing Mouton in May, then dropped him to

Tucson in June (though he was immediately recalled when Derrick May pulled a hamstring). Well, it's the thought that counts. Management is this close to throwing up their hands and shipping him out, confident in the ability of Abreu and Hidalgo to fill his shoes, and tired of Mouton's underachievement and tantalizing inconsistency. He hit .339 against lefties and did nothing against righties, but the Astros aren't willing to settle for platoon duty from him. Some other team might be able to steal him. n

GREGG OLSON (see Looking for a Game)

JHONNY PEREZ — GRADE-A PROSPECT

SS • BR • TR • 5'10 • 150 • 20 • HOU93

	AB	R	H	2B	3B	HR	RBI	BB	SO	SB	CS	BA	OB	SA
A+	322	54	87	20	2	12	49	26	70	16	16	.270	.329	.457

Yes, that's the correct spelling. The slugging percentage he had at Kissimmee is correct, too. His strikeout-to-walk ratio is pretty weak and he might try breaking for second *before* the ball has left the pitcher's hand, but that's about it for the flaws. He's 20 and will be in the Texas League. If he can do well there, it's only a matter of time before he hits well in the majors. And at his age, he has star potential. ■

EDGAR RAMOS — SOLID PROSPECT

SP • BR • TR • 6'4 • 170 • 22

	G	GS	IP	H	HR	BB	K	W	L	S	ERA	K/BB	K9	HW9
AA	12	12	66	63	2	29	52	4	5	0	4.88	1.8	7.1	12.48

Ramos signed with the Astros at 16. He started last season in the Florida State League, went 9-0 with a 1.51 ERA, and was promoted to the Texas League. He has a deceptive motion and throws a good change-up, a sinking fastball, an improving curveball and a slider. Astros coaches compare him to Greg Maddux. This makes him the 150th minor-leaguer compared to Maddux, and none of them is on his way to 4 consecutive Cy Young awards or helping lower the major league ERA to 2.00. Florida State League managers said he was the best control pitcher in the league last season. Despite his Double-A numbers, he is a very good prospect. He was promoted despite back problems and was pitching in pain during his first few starts. He was shut down after going 0-2 with a 13.50 ERA in 11.1 innings. He returned and went 4-3, 3.11 in 55 innings to finish his season there. Ramos could pitch in the majors this season. ■

SHANE REYNOLDS — NL ELITE

SP • BR • TR • 6'3 • 210 • 29 • HOU89/5

	G	GS	IP	H	HR	BB	K	W	L	S	ERA	K/BB	K9	HW9
HOU94	33	14	124	128	10	21	110	8	5	0	3.05	5.2	8.0	10.81
HOU95	30	30	189	196	15	37	175	10	11	0	3.47	4.7	8.3	11.10
HOU96	35	35	239	227	20	44	204	16	10	0	3.65	4.6	7.7	10.21
CAREER	111	85	588	604	47	114	509	35	29	0	3.57	4.5	7.8	10.99

When Shane Reynolds developed his split-finger (with a lot of help from then-minor-league pitching coach Brent Strom), he went from also-ran prospect to major-league ace. Reynolds: "Without the splitter, I'd be struggling in the minor leagues." His manager wasn't crazy about him using it, falling into the camp of those who feel it's a pitch that destroys arms shortly after it salvages careers. But it was easy to talk himself into ignoring those fears when Reynolds was on his way to a 16-win season with a strikeout-to-walk ratio of 4.6. He also has a solid fastball and a good curve to go with that splitter.

Reynolds did have his problems, though. He was 0-3, 5.15 in 36.2 innings in September. Of course, there also was the disparity between his home ERA and his road ERA, something most Astros starters show. And then there were his problems with righties. Right-handers hit .283 and slugged .433 against Reynolds. They hit .266 against him in '95 and also had a higher slugging percentage and on-base percentage than lefties did. Scouts say this is because the splitter is a much more effective pitch against left-handers.

Reynolds is in his prime, has a work ethic, and with his combination of grounders and strikeouts is the perfect Astrodome pitcher. He's not in the same class as Maddux, Smoltz, or Brown, but he's getting closer. ■

MARK SMALL

RP • BR • TR • 6'3 • 205 • 29 • HOU89/17

	G	GS	IP	H	HR	BB	K	W	L	S	ERA	K/BB	K9	HW9
HOU96	16	0	24	33	1	13	16	0	1	0	5.92	1.2	6.0	17.23

Small has a good curveball, a decent fastball, and a split-finger. He was very good at Triple-A in the PCL last season (2.08 ERA with 36 strikeouts in 39 innings), so he's better than he showed in his brief stint with the Astros. ■

BILL SPIERS

3B • BL • TR • 6'2 • 190 • 30 • MIL87/1

	AB	R	H	2B	3B	HR	RBI	BB	SO	SB	CS	BA	OB	SA
MIL94	214	27	54	10	1	0	17	19	42	7	1	.252	.316	.308
NYN95	72	5	15	2	1	0	11	12	15	0	1	.208	.314	.264
HOU96	218	27	55	10	1	6	26	20	34	7	0	.252	.320	.390
CAREER	1982	263	503	69	19	22	215	152	309	59	27	.254	.308	.341

Spiers got his career out of intensive care in '96, where it's been since '91 when he hit 8 dingers and batted .283 for the Brewers. He provided a decent left-handed bat off the bench and, unlike Berry, was able to make the throw from third without needing a relay man. He's not good for as many laughs on the bench as Mike "Mothra" Simms, who has had live insects pulled from his ear in the dugout, but is much more likely to see the field in '97. ■

JEFF TABAKA

RP • BR • TL • 6'2 • 195 • 33 • MON86/2

	G	GS	IP	H	HR	BB	K	W	L	S	ERA	K/BB	K9	HW9
PIT/SD94	39	0	41	32	1	27	32	3	1	1	5.27	1.2	7.0	12.95
SD/HOU95	34	0	30	27	2	17	25	1	0	0	3.23	1.5	7.5	13.20
HOU96	18	0	20	28	5	14	18	0	2	1	6.64	1.3	8.1	18.87
CAREER	91	0	91	87	8	58	75	4	3	2	4.94	1.3	7.4	14.33

Not even a lefty can stay in the majors with those kind of numbers. Look for Smokeless Tabaka to be moving on to his 4th organization in 4 years in '97, assuming any team will return his calls. ■

BILLY WAGNER

YOUNG GUN

P • BL • TL • 5'10 • 180 • 25 • HOU93/1

	G	GS	IP	H	HR	BB	K	W	L	S	ERA	K/BB	K9	HW9
HOU96	37	0	51	28	6	30	67	2	2	9	2.44	2.2	11.8	10.22

When Wagner was first called up, Hunsicker saw him as a set up man. "I see him as someone who can get us from the 6th inning to the ninth." After getting a chance to close in '96, set up is how he might be used in '97 now that Mariano Rivera has redefined the role. Wagner already has the second-hardest left-handed fastball in the game behind

Randy Johnson's—though he's about a foot shorter. He was moved into the closer's role by the Astros down the stretch, but he can throw in the 90s throughout a game so he has the stuff to be a starter. Then again, his lack of a reliable off-speed pitch—yet—makes his repertoire look like Rivera's. "Where should we have him excel?"—a nice problem for the Astros to have. Wagner's curveball has been inconsistent in the past, but last season it was often excellent. He also dramatically improved his change-up at Triple-A last year. His control is weak, but he held lefties to an .087 batting average, righties to .177, so he'll continue to see a lot of hitters trying to work a walk. If he can throw strikes and keep the ball in the park, he could be positively untouchable this season. ■

DONNE WALL

SP • BR • TR • 6'1 • 180 • 29 • HOU89/20

	G	GS	IP	H	HR	BB	K	W	L	S	ERA	K/BB	K9	HW9
HOU95	6	5	24	33	5	5	16	3	1	0	5.55	3.2	6.0	14.25
HOU96	26	23	150	170	17	34	99	9	8	0	4.56	2.9	5.9	12.24

Wall has so many pitches, what's coming on 3-0 is impossible to anticipate. He has excellent control, throws mid-to-high 80s, and has a decent curveball and change-up. Pitching coach Brent Strom: "Donne doesn't have that one outstanding pitch that will get him out of jams. But he has a good pace. He works quickly and changes speeds. He'll give up his hits and put the ball in play, but he doesn't walk people." He started off 6-0 but finished 9-7. He fell apart in July before rallying in August (3-1, 2.76 ERA in 32.2 innings). But he did his part in the September collapse that got his manager axed, going 0-3 with a 9.35 ERA. If he can get his ERA under 4.50 on the road, he may be here to stay. If he can't, he may just be another Vern Ruhle who lived large briefly, and only in the 8th Wonder of the World. ■

ANTHONY YOUNG

RP • BR • TR • 6′2 • 200 • 31 • NYN87/39

	G	GS	IP	H	HR	BB	K	W	L	S	ERA	K/BB	K9	HW9
CHN94	20	19	114	103	12	46	65	4	6	0	3.92	1.4	5.1	11.76
CHN95	32	1	41	47	5	14	15	3	4	2	3.70	1.1	3.3	13.39
HOU96	28	0	33	36	4	22	19	3	3	0	4.59	.9	5.2	15.80
CAREER	181	51	459	471	41	167	245	15	48	20	3.90	1.5	4.8	12.51

AYo has gone 10-13 in his past 3 seasons to raise his career record to 15-48. He must be getting some of the good luck he never got when he went 5-35 for the Mets, because he's losing it. His strikeout-to-walk ratio, which was never great, is deteriorating, and he's becoming much more generous about putting runners on base despite moving to a much friendlier ballpark. Looks like it might be time to close the book on the unluckiest ballplayer since Terry Felton (career record: 0-16). ■

■ 1996 OUTLOOK

The Dodgers, coming off a disappointing playoff sweep, went into '96 with strong pitching, a solid and potentially powerful offense, and a defense strengthened greatly by the presence of Greg Gagne at short in place of José Offerman. There wasn't much to stop the Dodgers from taking the West. San Francisco was a speed bump, Colorado still hadn't convinced the schedule makers to let them play all their games at home, and San Diego would need to wring every drop out of their roster to make things fly. L.A.'s hopes were set on winning their first post-season game since 1988 and taking it from there.

April 14-14 (14-14, 3½ games back)
When Ramon Martinez pulled a groin muscle on the frozen tundra of Wrigley Field, Chan Ho-mania struck L.A.—just as Nomo-mania had in '95. Park went 2-1 in his 4 starts, posted a 2.25 ERA, and struck out 27 in 24 innings. Unfortunately, he walked 21. Nomo did his part to take back the spotlight, striking out 17 Marlins.

Delino DeShields also got off to a good start: "This is the best I've felt since I've been in L.A. What I'm striving for is consistency—not to try and do it all, but to do it consistently." He didn't know how right he'd prove to be, for the wrong reasons. Mike Piazza made headlines with his April power outage, getting his first extra-base hit in his 56th at-bat and knocking his first dinger in his 66th. Of course, he offset this by hitting .370, a pace he would maintain through May as well.

May 15-12 (29-26, 5½ games back)
The team was in the cellar in almost every offensive category. Hitting coach Reggie Smith took it the hardest, frustrated at his inability to solve the problem. "I've been taking it home with me," Smith said. "I'll go home, turn on the computer and go over each guy's at-bats and play it back in my head. I've been falling asleep at 3, 4 o'clock each morning. I never should have let it get this far." Smith wasn't shouldering all the blame, however, complaining that the hitters showed an "unwillingness to experiment," something he said that all great hitters are willing to do. Outside of Piazza, who was rolling along just fine, the number of "great" hitters on the team could be counted on no hands. Karros, for instance, was hitting just over .200 and barely slugging .400. Karros insisted that things would improve and said "my role is to drive in runs."

June 13-14 (42-40, 1 game back)
Coming on the heels of Brett Butler's throat cancer diagnosis, manager Tommy Lasorda suffered a mild heart attack and was admitted to the hospital the next day. Dodgers bench coach Bill Russell took over as interim manager amid rumors concerning the possibility of Lasorda's retiring. Russell knew where he stood in the Dodgers' scheme, diplomatically handling his new status. "Sure it's an audition," he said. "A lot of people are going to look at it like that. I'd like to make a big impression. You prepare like any game. The only thing is, I'm the boss now."

The team continued at .500, and despite the fact that San Diego went 9-19 in June, the Dodgers still couldn't take over the lead in the West. Piazza admitted that he was uncomfortable behind the plate following his May knee injury, but refused to admit that catching was shortening his career and that a position change was in order.

Chan Ho Park had his own troubles, but it was with his teammates. As is the case with most rookies, he was the victim of a clubhouse prank. But this one went awry. He went to his locker after a game to find his suit in tatters. The punch line was that he was supposed to wear a disco outfit through the airport on the way home. As it turns out, he pitched a fit, throwing chairs about the clubhouse and cursing the players because the suit was a gift from his mother and had great sentimental value. Was he supposed to understand that we cut up each other's clothes in this country to show that we like each other? Park apologized, but the Dodgers should have been considerate enough to apologize to him. Instead, the handler of the pitchers, Mike Piazza, criticized Park in the press—his statements sounding more like a teenager dismissing a classmate for being uncool than the team leader he is supposed to be.

July 15-11 (57-51, ½ game back)
The Dodgers played well, despite the uncertain situation in the dugout and the eventual retirement of Lasorda in a tearful news conference July 29. GM

Fred Claire was saved the ignominious chore of firing a beloved manager. The Dodgers acquired Chad Curtis from the Tigers to try to fill Butler's hole in center field and leadoff, and signed Tim Wallach to replace Mike Blowers, who'd blown out his knee rounding third and was done for the year. They'd been interested in Todd Zeile, Ed Sprague, and Terry Pendleton, but had to settle for what was left of Wallach.

August 17-10 (74-61, 1 game back)
Team morale continued to worsen. Bill Russell benched Raul Mondesi after he was late for batting practice at a game in Pittsburgh. Mondesi was also fined, and ordered to come out early for batting practice in the next game. Russell denied that a feud was brewing, but Mondesi did struggle at the plate for a few days after the incident. The biggest blow was Brett Butler's abortive comeback. He sparked the club for a few games, but his return was brief and ended with a season-ending hand injury in September.

September 16-11 (90-72, 1 game back)
Martinez, Nomo, and Valdes compiled a 10-1 record with a 2.24 ERA. More than anything, this trio put the team in the playoffs. On the 17th, Nomo went into Coors Field and threw a no-hitter in a pennant race. That he threw from the stretch for most of the game due to the poor condition of the mound made it all the more impressive. The case could be made that it was one of the most astounding pitching performances in the history of the game. Even Bob Dole was impressed by what those Brooklyn Dodgers were up to these days. The regular season ended anti-climactically, when the Dodgers gave back the lead they'd fought hard to get—dropping 3 straight at home to the Padres to end the regular season, and backing into the playoffs as the wild-card.

October (lost division series in 3 games to the Braves)
Why did they bother? If it was possible to lose a 3-game series in 2, the Dodgers would have found a way to do it. L.A. could only muster three runs against the Braves and ran their postseason losing streak to 6 games. On paper, they matched up well with the Braves: strong starting pitching and a better bullpen, with some dangerous hitters to help them steal enough close games to win the series. But Piazza had nothing left, looking as lost at the plate as he ever has as a professional. For the second consecutive season, the Dodgers were among the biggest underachievers in baseball.

■ 1997 OUTLOOK

Offense
The Dodgers offense was well below average, scoring 53 fewer runs than the average N.L. team. Piazza, Mondesi and Karros led the offense, but the rest was a mess. Even after adjusting for the tremendous pitchers park in which they play, they were 10th in the league in runs scored. By September, Todd Hollandsworth was the 8th player to be tried in the leadoff spot. The bottom half of the order was a pastiche of Fonvilles, Kirbys, Curtises, Castros—guys who could play their position but provided little at the plate. Once the Dodgers add prospects such as Paul Konerko and Karim Garcia to the mix, the offense will improve immediately.

Defense
The infield defense was much improved in '96, due almost exclusively to Greg Gagne's presence and José Offerman's absence. No one else in the infield stood out, for either good reasons or bad. The outfield defense was equally solid. Hollandsworth was as good with the glove as he was with the bat, while Mondesi's arm remained a potent weapon in right field. Roger Cedeño lacked focus in his tour of center field, and will need to improve if he wants to take the job full-time. Piazza isn't good enough behind the plate to risk him to injury and deterioration, and should be given a third or first baseman's mitt sooner rather than later.

Pitching

The Dodgers rotation was among the best in the game. The fact that they edged the Braves for best ERA in the league is more a tribute to their pitcher's park. The heart of the rotation—Nomo, Martinez, and Valdes—is excellent, and young. If Chan Ho Park matures enough to start regularly, the Dodgers would be one of the scariest teams to face in the league.

Despite injuries and age, Todd Worrell remains one of the best closers in the N.L. His setup was provided by Antonio Osuna, who has an excellent fastball and fearless presence. He looks like the likely successor to Worrell, if that day ever comes. Along with Park and Osuna, Darren Dreifort, who pitched well after a lengthy rehab assignment, was a glimpse of the future.

Farm System

The Dodgers have an excellent farm system. No team has as many blue-chip prospects right now, and they consistently produce more big-leaguers than any other team. Their cast-offs could stock entire pitching staffs (see Greg Hansell in the Boston Red Sox section). Ironically, if there is fault to be found at the moment, it is that none of the top prospects is a pitcher. The Dodgers have one of the best foreign scouting arms in the biz, having signed Nomo, developed Park, Valdes, and Mondesi (to name a few major-leaguers), and are developing Onan Masaoka, Adrian Beltre, Wilton Guerrero, and Karim Garcia. The Dodgers have baseball academies in the Dominican Republic, Venezuela, and Australia. Peter O'Malley has worked to popularize baseball in Nigeria, China, Korea, Italy, Nicaragua, the Netherlands, and Russia. If Antarctica ever produces a kid who can throw 90, it's the Dodgers who'll find him.

Management and Ownership

Peter O'Malley has always been a far-sighted owner. He allows his employees to run day-to-day operations while he concentrates on making his organization stronger. This has resulted in the development of a far-reaching prospect empire which other teams have only recently begun to emulate. The Yanks' acquisition of Katsuhiro Maeda (the Japanese Billy Idol) was directly linked to the success of Nomo. O'Malley's teams have been successful, reaching the post-season the last two years, but he is poised to unleash a team that could contend for years to come. Not to mention that the Dodgers are frequently listed as one of the best companies to work for in the country.

GM Fred Claire is a fairly savvy customer, rarely getting burned on a trade, and following his creed of developing prospects rather than trading for pennants. He insists that he's building an empire, and the fact that the Dodgers have contended despite inconsistent offense is a testament to the pitching staff he has built. A glance at the minor-league juggernaut he's helped develop tells you he's not full of hot air. His is a team on the rise, and needs only a character infusion (as Kirk Gibson provided in 1988) to get them over the hump.

Tommy Lasorda was beloved by his players and fans. He is a generous and gregarious free spirit who loves the game with a rare passion. He was also an incorrigible cheerleader and maudlin sentimentalist. He was a tremendous motivator, but he wasn't much of a tactician and he frequently overworked his starting pitchers. Bill Russell seems to be an able replacement. He kept the team from completely imploding, disciplined players when necessary, and made the tough substitutions. Any rumors that he was strictly interim were dismissed when the organization gave him a 2-year contract—unheard of in L.A. Russell should give the team a new look: serious, focused, and workmanlike—more like Walter Alston than Tommy Lasorda.

. . . and whatnot: Chemistry 101

Mark Guthrie: "If you say, 'No, [chemistry] doesn't matter,' then you've never played on a team with chemistry." Eric Karros: "I don't think you have to hang together, or even like each other that much. But wanting to win has to be foremost." Delino DeShields: "There's a lot of good guys in here, but it's no secret that we don't hang together. A lot of guys don't even talk to each other."

The quotes above, by veteran players, are indicative of the mess that was the Dodgers clubhouse last year. A lack of chemistry contributed to a lackluster offense, a .500 record for most of the year, and disciplinary problems with young players. There is a marked lack of leadership on the Dodgers. The best player, Mike Piazza, is not the sort of take-charge player who leads a squad. Eric Karros is not a people person, to say the least. Raul Mondesi? Showing up for batting practice every day would be a good start. Nomo? His best friend on the team is Valdes, and neither can communicate in the other's native tongue.

The team is seemingly divided on every possible line. Veterans and rookies. Americans and foreigners. Pitchers and hitters. After the pitching staff carried them into the postseason, and almost led them past the Braves in Game 1 by giving up only 2

runs, Eric Karros used some bizarre form of pretzel logic to conclude: "I understand Ramon [Martinez] said the hitters have got to start scoring some runs. Well, it works both ways. They've got to hold the other team down, too." Piazza, failing to recognize his role as the 11th member of the pitching staff, sided with the hitters: "I've heard people say we're not hitting, but we haven't been pitching real well, either. We've made some very poor pitches. Any pitch that's hit out of the ballpark is a bad pitch." And who called that pitch? Mike Scioscia?

The team was rudderless. Even their pranks seemed overdone and cheerless, as if forced camaraderie was going to solve their problems. Most teams hide the rookie's suit and make him dress strangely. The Dodgers sliced and diced Park's, and then were angry and bewildered when he blew up. They couldn't see how the joke would appear mean-spirited to a stranger in a strange land, or anyone who lives in The Real World. Chances are, it was only a handful of players involved in the monkeyshines, while the rest watched bemusedly. If, as it seems, Karros and Piazza were behind it, how likely is it that the rest of the team would raise an objection, no matter how they felt? Is this the leadership that the veteran players provide?

Bill Russell should be an agent of change. There will be no more after-game dinners in his office, and no preferential treatment for stars. Russell is a keen observer who knows his players' strengths and weaknesses. He benched the experienced but struggling DeShields in the postseason. He disciplined the talented but immature Mondesi. If the players will not provide leadership, he'll have to pick up the slack—or beg Fred Claire to get Eric Karros off his hands and airlift in Joe Carter.

The number of nationalities represented in the clubhouse, in the major-league equivalent of the Tower of Babel, is only part of the problem—and a convenient excuse. But not for long. The Dodgers are the best at finding international talent. No doubt they'll soon become the best at helping these players assimilate. Having some veteran leaders with character, regardless of their homeland, would be a good start.

BILLY ASHLEY

OF • BR • TR • 6'7 • 220 • 26 • LA88/2

	AB	R	H	2B	3B	HR	RBI	BB	SO	SB	CS	BA	OB	SA
LA95	215	17	51	5	0	8	27	25	88	0	0	.237	.320	.372
LA96	110	18	22	2	1	9	25	21	44	0	0	.200	.331	.482

Ashley had few at-bats, but they amply illustrated the type of hitter he is. He didn't hit for average, was on a pace for approximately 40 homers, and struck out like a demon. He did draw a lot of walks, giving him a good on-base percentage (for Dodger Stadium). Ashley was frustrated last season and demanded a trade. But his expectations are unrealistic. He's a poor defensive player, and he was very weak against right-handers last season. He should grit his teeth and prepare to get about 200 at-bats a year. ■

PEDRO ASTACIO

SP • BR • TR • 6'2 • 175 • 27 • LA87

	G	GS	IP	H	HR	BB	K	W	L	S	ERA	K/BB	K9	HW9
LA94	23	23	149	142	18	47	108	6	8	0	4.29	2.3	6.5	11.42
LA95	48	11	104	103	12	29	80	7	8	0	4.24	2.8	6.9	11.42
LA96	35	32	211	207	18	67	130	9	8	0	3.44	1.9	5.5	11.68
CAREER	148	108	732	697	63	231	483	41	38	0	3.60	2.1	5.9	11.41

Had the Dodgers retained Kevin Tapani, Astacio probably would have been relegated to the bullpen. He got a chance, though, barely beating out Chan Ho Park for a rotation spot. He made the most of it, showing good control and keeping his record over .500. His ERA was in line with the rest of the staff, almost a full run below league average. Astacio doesn't have the best reputation with Dodger management, but he made strides in this area as well. In the past he was known as a slow worker and for his histrionics on the mound. Pitching coach Dave Wallace squelched that, convincing the high-strung hurler that dancing and fist-pumping expend valuable energy, and that they don't win friends and influence people. And he convinced him that by working faster, his fielders would be less likely to slip into comas behind him.

Astacio slings the ball at batters. He throws a very good sinker and straight change, and he can change speeds on his good curve. In some ways

he's reminiscent of teammate Ramon Martinez, but he throws about 5 mph slower. When Park or other candidates are ready to start, Astacio will be on the bubble. Only Candiotti is less sure of his footing. ■

HOWARD BATTLE

3B • BR • TR • 6'0 • 195 • 25 • TOR90/5

	AB	R	H	2B	3B	HR	RBI	BB	SO	SB	CS	BA	OB	SA
AAA	391	37	89	24	1	8	44	21	53	3	8	.228	.267	.355

Like most former Blue Jays prospects, the talk of ability has turned to questions of work ethic. Toronto has these guys on a conveyor belt: Sign them, tout them, and deal them to the N.L. They're well into double figures with this product line, with really only Derek Bell working out. Battle looked like a stud at 19 in low Class-A, but all trends are negative after three years in Triple-A. He was rudely shunted aside by the Phillies when Scott Rolen blew through town, another welcome officially worn out. ■

ADRIAN BELTRE — GRADE-A PROSPECT

3B • BR • TR • 5'11 • 175 • 19 • LA96

	AB	R	H	2B	3B	HR	RBI	BB	SO	SB	CS	BA	OB	SA
A+	244	48	75	14	3	16	59	35	46	4	3	.307	.406	.586

Beltre is the Dodgers' next Karim Garcia/Roger Cedeño-caliber prospect. He lacks their speed, but he looks like a more polished hitter and has more power. He also addresses the team's problems at third base. Even though '96 was his first season in the United States, the Dodgers started him in a full-season league. He rewarded their confidence by becoming the top prospect in the Sally League, drawing glowing reviews for his hitting, defense, and arm. He's very mature for his age, displaying better plate discipline than hitters in their 20s. He sometimes tries to do too much, but that doesn't keep him from being one of the best all-around prospects in the game. ■

MIKE BLOWERS (see Looking for a Game)

MIKE BUSCH

3B • BR • TR • 6'5 • 240 • 28 • LA90/4

	AB	R	H	2B	3B	HR	RBI	BB	SO	SB	CS	BA	OB	SA
LA95	17	3	4	0	0	3	6	0	7	0	0	.235	.235	.765
LA96	83	8	18	4	0	4	17	5	33	0	0	.217	.261	.410

Busch is another in the long line of Dodger third-base candidates who have not panned out. He was supposed to be a savior, but he's really just the second coming of Dave Hansen. Busch's status couldn't have been improved by serving as a replacement player in '95. With the Dodgers locker room not being the warmest of havens, the problem is only exacerbated. He could be writing for the next Albuquerque travel guide. ■

BRETT BUTLER

CF • BL • TL • 5'10 • 160 • 39 • ATL79/22

	AB	R	H	2B	3B	HR	RBI	BB	SO	SB	CS	BA	OB	SA
LA94	417	79	131	13	9	8	33	68	52	27	8	.314	.411	.446
NYN/LA95	513	78	154	18	9	1	38	67	51	32	8	.300	.377	.376
LA96	131	22	35	1	1	0	8	9	22	8	3	.267	.313	.290
CAREER	7837	1307	2278	269	128	54	560	1087	867	543	247	.291	.377	.378

Butler went on the 15-day DL May 3 for surgery to remove his tonsils. He was diagnosed with tonsillitis 5 days before spring training but was told that antibiotics could reduce the swelling and allow him to play. The symptoms continued to worsen as the season progressed, and Butler was in an awful slump when he decided to have the surgery. When the doctor removed the tonsil, a tumor the size of a plum was found in his right tonsil. Butler had surgery to remove his lymph nodes and tissue surrounding them and then had radiation treatments 5 times a week for 6 weeks. He worked like a possessed man to return, and incredibly began taking batting practice in August. The team rallied around him and he made his comeback at the beginning of September. Unfortunately, another blow was dealt when he broke his hand 5 days into his comeback. The chances of Butler making a full recovery and coming back in '97 are scant—but few would bet against him when he puts his mind to something. ■

TOM CANDIOTTI

SP • BR • TR • 6'3 • 205 • 39 • KC80

	G	GS	IP	H	HR	BB	K	W	L	S	ERA	K/BB	K9	HW9
LA94	23	22	153	149	9	54	102	7	7	0	4.12	1.9	6.0	11.94
LA95	30	30	190	187	18	58	141	7	14	0	3.50	2.4	6.7	11.61
LA96	28	27	152	172	18	43	79	9	11	0	4.49	1.8	4.7	12.73
CAREER	359	346	2317	2226	185	750	1507	126	135	0	3.54	2.0	5.9	11.56

The 1996 season looks like the beginning of the end for Candiotti, but knuckleballers can make such

judgments look rash. His success over the years can be attributed to his great control. This is a fleeting commodity in his trade (witness the struggles of Tim Wakefield), and he's one of the best because he actually knows where his pitches are going. But the drop in his strikeouts from '95 to '96 is alarming. He'll probably pitch for several more years, but it's doubtful that he'll end his career wearing Dodger blue. ■

JUAN CASTRO

SS • BR • TR • 5'10 • 165 • 24 • LA91

	AB	R	H	2B	3B	HR	RBI	BB	SO	SB	CS	BA	OB	SA
LA95	4	0	1	0	0	0	0	1	1	0	0	.250	.400	.250
LA96	132	16	26	5	3	0	5	10	27	1	0	.197	.254	.280

Castro was not the first choice for a call-up when Billy Ashley went on the DL, but the other candidates in Triple-A Albuquerque were injured and he won by default. And 132 at-bats later, he demonstrated why he wasn't their first choice. He could have another shot for playing time in '97, but he's bench fodder at best. ■

ROGER CEDEÑO — SOLID PROSPECT

OF • BB • TR • 6'1 • 165 • 22 • LA91

	AB	R	H	2B	3B	HR	RBI	BB	SO	SB	CS	BA	OB	SA
LA95	42	4	10	2	0	0	3	3	10	1	0	.238	.283	.286
LA96	211	26	52	11	1	2	18	24	47	5	1	.246	.326	.336

Cedeño is probably the fastest player in the organization, and one of the fastest players in the N.L. Brett Butler taught him a lot in spring training and during the season. He has gap power and potential Gold Glove defense but had trouble judging fly balls hit straight at him when playing center. For all his speed he's short on baserunning savvy. He's still one of the best prospects in the organization, but he looked a lot more raw than L.A. had let on. He showed his youth against the Giants when he stole second in the ninth inning of a game that the Dodgers were winning by 9 runs. He thought he'd been given the green light by first-base coach Reggie Smith. Teammates were split on the decision, Karros saying that he'd have been ticked off, too, and DeShields chalking it up to youthful exuberance. The Giants weren't so divided. They all wanted to kill him. ■

DAVE CLARK (see Looking For a Game)

CHAD CURTIS (see Looking for a Game)

DELINO DESHIELDS (see Free Agents)

DARREN DREIFORT — SLEEPER

RP • BR • TR • 6'2 • 205 • 24 • LA93/1

	G	GS	IP	H	HR	BB	K	W	L	S	ERA	K/BB	K9	HW9
LA96	19	0	23	23	2	12	24	1	4	0	4.94	2.0	9.4	13.66

In spite of the fact that he had Tommy John surgery in '94 and showed a lack of stamina and lack of command last year, Dreifort may have the organization's best arm. He showed great velocity in Triple-A, and scouts think he could make the transition to starter. That's a questionable call, and the Dodgers will most likely continue to view him as a possible heir to Worrell, or the lead setup man. Dreifort isn't just any sleeper—he's in the Steve Karsay category of extraordinary pitchers who've been derailed by injuries but could rise up and smite the league at any time. His elbow should be much stronger in '97. When he's right, he throws a 96-mph fastball with wicked movement. Don't count him out. ■

CHAD FONVILLE

UT • BB • TR • 5'6 • 155 • 26 • SF92/11

	AB	R	H	2B	3B	HR	RBI	BB	SO	SB	CS	BA	OB	SA
MON/LA95	320	43	89	6	1	0	16	23	42	20	7	.278	.328	.303
LA96	201	34	41	4	1	0	13	17	31	7	2	.204	.266	.234

Somewhere along the line in '96, he made the transition from utility to futility. If he hadn't, he might have the second base job right now. ■

GREG GAGNE

SS • BR • TR • 5′11 • 185 • 34 • NYA79/5

	AB	R	H	2B	3B	HR	RBI	BB	SO	SB	CS	BA	OB	SA
KC94	375	39	97	23	3	7	51	27	79	10	17	.259	.314	.392
KC95	430	58	110	25	4	6	49	38	60	3	5	.256	.316	.374
LA96	428	48	109	13	2	10	55	50	93	4	2	.255	.333	.364
CAREER	5159	663	1311	276	47	102	547	336	1001	106	91	.254	.302	.385

Gagne saves runs, even if he doesn't create them at the plate. He was a tremendous improvement over José Offerman at shortstop, and when he went down for an extended chunk of the season, Juan Castro was able to remind the fans what it used to be like. Gagne re-signed, but he didn't seem too wild about playing for the Dodgers—like fellow former-Twin Mark Guthrie, he knows what it's like to actually play for a team that likes each other and wants to win. ■

KARIM GARCIA — *GRADE-A PROSPECT*

OF • BL • TL • 6′0 • 200 • 21 • LA92

	AB	R	H	2B	3B	HR	RBI	BB	SO	SB	CS	BA	OB	SA
AAA	327	54	97	17	10	13	58	29	67	6	4	.297	.353	.529

Garcia had a rough time last year. His attitude was fine in the spring, as it had been throughout his career, but after rotting in Triple-A for another year, he began to get fed up. When he took an unscheduled vacation in mid-season after a brief call-up to the majors, they got angry and demoted him all the way down to Double-A to remind him who had the hammer.

Garcia was voted the no. 6 prospect in the PCL, and should have been higher. He has an excellent arm (second only to Mondesi's in the organization) and has excellent instincts (even if he is error-prone). He has decent speed and excellent power potential. Garcia feels he's ready to play in the bigs, and he's right. Cedeño and Hollandsworth are good, but Garcia is better. If he straightens out and the Dodgers give him a shot in '97, here's yet another Rookie of the Year. ■

WILTON GUERRERO — *GRADE-A PROSPECT*

2B • BR • TR • 5′11 • 155 • 22 • LA91

	AB	R	H	2B	3B	HR	RBI	BB	SO	SB	CS	BA	OB	SA
AAA	425	79	146	17	12	2	38	26	48	26	15	.344	.383	.454

Guerrero isn't the stud prospect his younger brother Vlad is, but he's gold nonetheless. He's fast, hits for average, and has a great eye. On defense he shows good range and a strong arm but is hampered by poor concentration. It's nice that the Dodgers have a solid prospect who doesn't play outfield, and they're counting on Guerrero to be what Offerman was supposed to be. The team switched Guerrero to second base from short and were ecstatic over the results. He could end up at there at the major-league level this year—meaning that games against Montreal are going to be even more competitive than ever (what with the Martinez brothers and the Guerreros). ■

MARK GUTHRIE

RP • BR • TL • 6′4 • 195 • 31 • MIN87/7

	G	GS	IP	H	HR	BB	K	W	L	S	ERA	K/BB	K9	HW9
MIN94	50	2	51	65	8	18	38	4	2	1	6.14	2.1	6.7	14.64
MIN/LA95	60	0	62	66	6	25	67	5	5	0	4.21	2.7	9.7	13.21
LA96	66	0	73	65	3	22	56	2	3	1	2.22	2.5	6.9	10.73
CAREER	330	43	582	611	52	205	463	31	32	9	3.93	2.3	7.2	12.62

Guthrie has been very effective since joining the Dodgers in '95, helping to anchor the team's long relief. Despite a drop in his strikeout rate, his control was excellent as he averaged just 2.7 walks per 9 innings. But his future is questionable because of his mechanics. He has a high leg kick and throws across his body, both of which tend to disable pitchers eventually. His pitches are solid, however, and he's great when he can keep the ball low. He relies on a forkball and a sinking fastball, and he doesn't let many balls leave the park. He also has a curve that breaks in a big way, but hitters can lay off it most of the time. He may find himself in the starting rotation in '97. ■

TODD HOLLANDSWORTH — *YOUNG GUN*

LF • BL • TL • 6′2 • 195 • 23 • LA91/3

	AB	R	H	2B	3B	HR	RBI	BB	SO	SB	CS	BA	OB	SA
LA95	103	16	24	2	0	5	13	10	29	2	1	.233	.304	.398
LA96	478	64	139	26	4	12	59	41	93	21	6	.291	.348	.437

Hollandsworth is going to have a tough time in '97. Considering the ups and downs of former top-rookie teammates Eric Karros and Raul Mondesi after winning the Rookie of the Year award, Hollandsworth should concentrate his energies on following in the footsteps of Mike Piazza. Piazza is

one of the few Dodger rookie stars to actually blossom into a veteran superstar. Hollandsworth is an intense and focused player who has been compared to former Dodger Kirk Gibson—albeit a somewhat more hygienic version. Hollandsworth brings speed to the field, and can play well in left or center. He's not a true power hitter, but 20–25 homers a year wouldn't be out of the question. ■

MICHAEL JUDD — SOLID PROSPECT

RP-SP • BR • TR • 6'2 • 200 • 21 • NYA95/9

	G	GS	IP	H	HR	BB	SO	W	L	S	ERA	K/BB	K9	HW9
A	44	8	84	62	4	23	98	6	4	13	2.90	4.3	10.5	9.14

The Dodgers made a great deal trading Billy Brewer, 29, to the Yankees for Judd, a hot young commodity. As well as Judd was pitching for Greensboro at the time of the trade, he looked even better pitching for Savannah. He lowered his ERA significantly and continued to knock the bat out of hitters' hands while maintaining excellent control. He improved dramatically in '96, so '97 could see him become the Dodgers' top minor league closer. ■

ERIC KARROS — CONSISTENT STAR

1B • BR • TR • 6'4 • 205 • 29 • LA88/5

	AB	R	H	2B	3B	HR	RBI	BB	SO	SB	CS	BA	OB	SA
LA94	406	51	108	21	1	14	46	29	53	2	0	.266	.310	.426
LA95	551	83	164	29	3	32	105	61	115	4	4	.298	.369	.535
LA96	608	84	158	29	1	34	111	53	121	8	0	.260	.316	.479
CAREER	2743	355	724	137	8	123	431	215	480	16	9	.264	.317	.454

Karros had a breakout year in '95, and while his '96 performance wasn't as good, he still held his ground in terms of power and RBI. He also hit .276 with runners in scoring position and .300 with the bases loaded. It's worth noting that hot-hitting prospect Paul Konerko was asked to switch to third, so it's not looking like Karros is going anywhere any time soon—though his departure would probably do wonders for the team's attitude. While he seems to be satisfied just driving in runs, the team would like him to get on base a little more frequently. Unless that changes, no team should bat him higher than fifth or sixth in the order. ■

WAYNE KIRBY

OF • BL • TR • 5'10 • 185 • 33 • LA83/13

	AB	R	H	2B	3B	HR	RBI	BB	SO	SB	CS	BA	OB	SA
CLE94	191	33	56	6	0	5	23	13	30	11	4	.293	.341	.403
CLE95	188	29	39	10	2	1	14	13	32	10	3	.207	.260	.298
CLE/LA96	204	26	55	11	1	1	12	19	19	4	3	.270	.333	.348
CAREER	1102	172	285	49	8	14	115	87	147	43	20	.259	.314	.356

In '94, Kirby had people wondering what he could do if he ever got a chance to play every day. In late '96, he showed them. Now he's in the way of Karim Garcia and Roger Cedeno—just to name a few—so he'll be a bench player again in '97. ■

PAUL KONERKO — GRADE-A PROSPECT

3B • BR • TR • 6'3 • 210 • 21 • LA94/1

	AB	R	H	2B	3B	HR	RBI	BB	SO	SB	CS	BA	OB	SA
AA	470	78	141	23	2	29	86	72	85	1	3	.300	.397	.543

Konerko is one of the best-hitting prospects in the game, and he has a great attitude, having switched from catcher to first base and now to third base without complaining. The damage he did in the Texas League—a proving ground for hitters—was criminal (he garnered top-prospect honors as a result). Power, average, and patience at the plate are the marks of his prowess. He has exceptional balance at the plate and hardly ever looks fooled. Konerko was the Dodgers' 1st-round pick in '94, and he's probably ready to hit in the majors now. Don't expect the Dodgers to buy much more than a short-term solution at third base in the off-season, if anyone. ■

JESUS MARTINEZ

SP • BL • TL • 6'2 • 145 • 23 • LA90

	G	GS	IP	H	HR	BB	SO	W	L	S	ERA	K/BB	K9	HW9
AA	27	27	162	157	7	92	124	10	13	0	4.4	1.3	6.9	13.86

Martinez is a decent pitching prospect, but he doesn't share his brothers' talent. He throws hard, but he lacks their command. The Dodgers fell in love with the idea of having three hard-throwing brothers on the staff, but Pedro's trade to Montreal and Jesus' slow development have burst that bubble. Expect the Dodgers to give him every chance to succeed. He may even turn out to be okay. Just don't expect the second coming of Ramon. Two in one gene pool was impressive enough. ■

RAMON MARTINEZ — CONSISTENT STAR

SP • BR • TR • 6′4 • 185 • 29 • LA84

	G	GS	IP	H	HR	BB	K	W	L	S	ERA	K/BB	K9	HW9
LA94	24	24	170	160	18	56	119	12	7	0	3.97	2.1	6.3	11.44
LA95	30	30	206	176	19	81	138	17	7	0	3.66	1.7	6.0	11.23
LA96	28	27	168	153	12	86	133	15	6	0	3.42	1.5	7.1	12.80
CAREER	229	225	1495	1319	126	595	1103	106	69	0	3.47	1.9	6.6	11.52

Martinez got off to a bad start in '96, tearing his right groin muscle running to first base against Chicago on April 6th in a series in which temperatures for all 4 of the games were around 30 degrees. Martinez returned on May 14th and immediately put to rest any fears that he had lost his edge, going 3-0 with a 2.81 ERA for the month. Martinez was one of the most consistent pitchers on the staff, pitching equally well at home or on the road, winning 15 games despite walking 4.5 per 9 innings and having to strand more than his share of baserunners. He was also crucial down the stretch, going 4-0 with a 2.45 ERA in September.

Martinez has a solid repertoire. He throws a plus fastball that sinks and moves in on righties, occasionally cutting it versus lefties. He also has an outstanding circle change, a mediocre curve, and a slider that's strictly for show. His consistency has come with learning to throw his fastball and change-up with the same arm motion. Although Nomo had a very good sophomore year, Martinez still is the Dodgers' ace. They both had great crunch-time performances, but Martinez's experience gives him the edge. Of course, they'll both have to watch out for Valdes usurping the role. This is one of the best three-man rotations in baseball. And as Valdes matures, they could become the best. ■

ONAN MASAOKA — SOLID PROSPECT

SP • BR • TL • 6′0 • 190 • 19 • LA95/3

	G	GS	IP	H	HR	BB	SO	W	L	S	ERA	K/BB	K9	HW9
A	13	13	65	55	7	35	80	2	5	0	4.29	2.3	11.1	12.46

Masaoka, from Hawaii, is one of the best young lefties in the organization. He throws a 91–92-mph fastball with sharp movement, a rudimentary curveball, and a circle change-up. He was young by Savannah standards but responded with decent control and a high strikeout rate. He's got a lot of growing to do, but he already throws hard and projects to become a star. ■

RAUL MONDESI — OVERRATED

RF • BR • TR • 5′11 • 210 • 26 • LA88

	AB	R	H	2B	3B	HR	RBI	BB	SO	SB	CS	BA	OB	SA
LA94	434	63	133	27	8	16	56	16	78	11	8	.306	.333	.516
LA95	536	91	153	23	6	26	88	33	96	27	4	.285	.328	.496
LA96	634	98	188	40	7	24	88	32	122	14	7	.297	.334	.495
CAREER	1690	265	499	93	22	70	242	85	312	56	20	.295	.311	.501

"[The 1996 season] is going to be the greatest year of my career. Write it down. It's going to happen." When a guy who can't do much in the outfield but throw (his 12 errors led the league and his range was average) and can't hit breaking stuff starts beating his breast in the press, look out. Mondesi is the type of player who says things twice as loud to convince himself that they're true. He has tremendous potential and could be among the league's elite. He is strong, can hit for average, and possesses the best arm in the N.L. His physical tools are unquestioned, especially by the league. After leading the N.L. in assists the past couple of years, he had only a single assist through June 16th. Nobody wanted to run on his arm.

"I can't believe it sometimes. I say, 'Please, go. Give it a try.' But no one wants to run on me," complained Mondesi. His mental tools and maturity, however, are constantly questioned. When he bragged about his new tattoo—a cannon with a plume of smoke coming from the barrel—most had to turn away to hide their smiles. All season, Mondesi talked about how he liked to go out and have a really good time after a good game—which might explain why he put so few of them back to back. He is among the best at his position, but Dodgers management and fans are disappointed because he's not *the* best. If he can screw his head on straight, and develop more patience at the plate, he could be—but that doesn't sound likely for a grown man with a cannon tattooed on his arm. ■

HIDEO NOMO

NL ELITE

SP • BR • TR • 6'2 • 210 • 28 • LA95

	G	GS	IP	H	HR	BB	K	W	L	S	ERA	K/BB	K9	HW9
LA95	28	28	191	124	14	78	236	13	6	0	2.54	3.0	11.1	9.52
LA96	33	33	228	180	23	85	234	16	11	0	3.19	2.8	9.2	10.46

There were many rumors that Nomo had lost it in '96, but he overcame them and the sophomore jinx to post the best record on the staff. The most worrisome report was that he had lost several miles off his fastball, dropping it from 90 mph to 86. Because of this, hitters were laying off his forkball and making him throw a weak fastball for strikes. Nomo attributed his struggles to the league having adjusted to him. The coaching staff pointed at bad mechanics, saying that Nomo's were out of whack and that they'd get him back on track.

None of this was being bandied about in April, when he threw consecutive 3-hitters, striking out 17 Marlins in the second start. This was a strikeout short of the franchise record of 18 shared by Ramon Martinez and Sandy Koufax. And none of this was being bandied about in the last third of the season, when he went 6-2 for August and September including a no-no in Coors. He was awesome at home, posting a 2.75 ERA in 18 starts. He remained one of the top strikeout artists in the league. Pretty good for a guy with an 86-mph fastball, huh?

Nomo's bread and butter is his forkball, complemented by his regular fastball. He has a weak curve, but it's strictly a conversation piece. He owns just about every deceptive throwing technique in the book, from changing release points to varying the length of his stretch. He did indeed deserve the Rookie of the Year in '95, and he has established himself now as the real deal—one of the best pitchers in the game. ■

ANTONIO OSUNA

YOUNG GUN

RP • BR • TR • 5'11 • 160 • 23 • LA91

	G	GS	IP	H	HR	BB	K	W	L	S	ERA	K/BB	K9	HW9
LA95	39	0	44	39	5	20	46	2	4	0	4.43	2.3	9.4	12.07
LA96	73	0	84	65	6	32	85	9	6	4	3.00	2.7	9.1	10.39

Osuna is a power pitcher, and like many of his cohorts, he doesn't throw a high percentage of strikes. Rather, he goes deep in the count and even-

tually coaxes a strikeout or induces the batter to put a strike into play. Osuna's arsenal is fearsome. His fastball was voted third-best in the N.L., and he improved his curve after working with Sandy Koufax. Osuna complements the two pitches with a good change-up. He will throw his fastball to anyone, anytime. Although his stats in the second half of the season were a bit rocky at times, he showed how dominant he can be by throwing 18.1 innings of scoreless ball in May. He held batters to a .220 average and a .296 on-base percentage. It wouldn't be surprising to see him refine his control and lower the latter number even more. Osuna is one of the best young pitchers in the majors. There has been talk the past couple of years of his assuming the closer duties, and he'll learn a lot setting up Worrell. ■

CHAN HO PARK

YOUNG GUN

RP-SP • BR • TR • 6'2 • 185 • 23 • LA94

	G	GS	IP	H	HR	BB	K	W	L	S	ERA	K/BB	K9	HW9
LA96	48	10	108	82	7	71	119	5	5	0	3.64	1.7	9.9	12.74

The Dodgers have been accused of rushing Park, and the reviews of his '96 season have been mixed as a result. His supporters point to his great strikeout rate (the highest on the staff) and his success as a spot starter. His detractors emphasize his nearly 6 walks per 9 innings (also the highest) and his reluctance to throw inside. Park is young, but he's neither as polished nor as raw as his proponents and detractors think. He is all of the above—in others words, one of the top pitching talents in the N.L. who is learning in the best classroom that baseball can provide. Park may be shaky at times, but he showed poise with runners on and got himself out of a lot of jams. The trend has been to second-guess organizations who ripen their prospects in the show, but recent cases such as Piazza, Hollandsworth, Valdes, and Mondesi have been proven successes. Chances are that Karim Garcia will be added to that list in '97. Instead of handling these grade-A talents with kid gloves, the

Dodgers tend to adopt a sink-or-swim approach that may bruise egos, but which let's them find out what these guys are made of sooner rather than later.

Park's fastball is one of the best, hitting 98 mph. His slider is quite effective and he throws a curve in the low 80s. The curve usually doesn't land for strikes, but he showed increased success with it by year's end, as he did with his improving change-up. Park's lack of command accounts for most of his problems. He needs to move his pitches in and out, working the corners so batters can't lay off his fastball. He should make big strides in '97, and will likely be in the rotation for good the minute he cuts his walks down to 4 a game. ■

MIKE PIAZZA

NL ELITE

C • BR • TR • 6'3 • 200 • 28 • LA88/61

	AB	R	H	2B	3B	HR	RBI	BB	SO	SB	CS	BA	OB	SA
LA94	405	64	129	18	0	24	92	33	65	1	3	.319	.370	.541
LA95	434	82	150	17	0	32	93	39	80	1	0	.346	.400	.606
LA96	547	87	184	16	0	36	105	81	93	0	3	.336	.422	.563
CAREER	2002	319	653	78	2	128	409	203	336	5	10	.326	.388	.559

Piazza is one of the best singles and dingers hitters in baseball. Obviously, when he sold his soul to the devil, doubles weren't included in the deal. The primary threat to his remaining that type of hitter is his position. His frequent injuries cut into his playing time in '94 and '95, and the Dodgers wisely gave him more time off in '96—but not much. When he screwed up his knee on a bad slide into second last year, he insisted that he catch despite admissions that the injury was bothering him behind the plate. Piazza argues that he makes a difference behind the plate, and he has learned to handle the staff well. But his throwing is just about the worst in the league. It isn't surprising to see that 20 consecutive runners have successfully stolen on him. It's time for him to realize that his contribution to this team is with the bat, not the glove. If a catcher is going to win the batting title, hit 50 homers, or even achieve the Triple Crown in the next five years, Piazza would be the man. But he's more likely to accomplish those at third base or first base. ■

SCOTT RADINSKY

RP • BL • TL • 6'3 • 205 • 29 • CHA86/3

	G	GS	IP	H	HR	BB	K	W	L	S	ERA	K/BB	K9	HW9
CHA95	46	0	38	46	7	17	14	2	1	1	5.45	.8	3.3	14.92
LA96	58	0	52	52	2	17	48	5	1	1	2.41	2.8	8.3	11.93
CAREER	374275.2		313	70	131	218	72	21	334.623.42			.3	2.1	8.28

It looked like Radinsky's career was over when he had lack-luster outings in '93 and '95 and lost all of '94 to Hodgkin's Disease. The White Sox thought they smelled toast and he landed in L.A., where he returned to his pre-injury form. Radinsky was tougher on lefties than on righties, but he held hitters to a .264 batting average overall. His strikeouts were in line with his peak years, and he was still strong in September, posting a 2.25 ERA. The Dodgers took a risk, and it paid off. Despite the history of injury, Radinsky is a battler who's got a lot of miles left on his arm and more guts than most. ■

GARY RATH

SP • BL • TL • 6'2 • 185 • 24 • LA94/2

	G	GS	IP	H	HR	BB	SO	W	L	S	ERA	K/BB	K9	HW9
AAA	30	30	180	177	13	89	125	10	11	0	4.19	1.4	6.2	13.28

Rath was an All-American at Mississippi. Before David Yocum came along, he was considered the best lefty pitcher in the organization. The key difference between them is that Rath relies on a good curveball, while Yocum throws hard. Rath's fastball is only in the mid-80s, but it moves well. The Dodgers haven't started a left-handed pitcher since they had Bobby Ojeda, so he may get a long look in the spring. If he can cut down on his walks he'll at least get a look to join Radinsky and Guthrie in the bullpen's southpaw faction. Do you think that the righties and lefties mingle in this clubhouse, or is that just another dividing line? ■

BRIAN RICHARDSON — SOLID PROSPECT

3B • BR • TR • 6'2 • 190 • 21 • LA92/10

	AB	R	H	2B	3B	HR	RBI	BB	SO	SB	CS	BA	OB	SA
AAA	355	52	87	17	2	9	43	32	89	4	1	.245	.310	.380

Richardson played most of the year in Triple-A at a tender age and didn't look overmatched. He's not as talked about as the other Dodger outfield prospects, but he's top-notch nonetheless and may wind up as trade bait. ■

ADAM RIGGS

2B • BR • TR • 6'0 • 190 • 24 • LA94/22

	AB	R	H	2B	3B	HR	RBI	BB	SO	SB	CS	BA	OB	SA
AA	506	68	143	31	6	14	66	37	82	16	6	.283	.339	.451

Much was made of Riggs's performance in '95, and he was the California League MVP as a result. He was converted to second base from the outfield and the organization hoped they had a hitter they could use to fill a hole. Unfortunately, he proved in '95 that the transition would be rough, with a league-worst 41 errors. He has poor hands and range and his arm was no great shakes even when in the outfield. He should be in Triple-A in '97, and could be in the majors by the time he's 25. ■

ISMAEL VALDES — YOUNG GUN

SP • BR • TR • 6'3 • 185 • 23 • LA91

	G	GS	IP	H	HR	BB	K	W	L	S	ERA	K/BB	K9	HW9
LA94	21	1	28	21	2	10	28	3	1	0	3.18	2.8	9.0	9.95
LA95	33	27	197	168	17	51	150	13	11	1	3.05	2.9	6.9	10.01
LA96	33	33	225	219	20	54	173	15	7	0	3.32	3.2	6.9	10.92
CAREER	87	61	451	408	39	115	351	31	19	1	3.19	3.1	7.0	10.44

The Dodgers have had a good feeling about Valdes from the start. Considering he started in Rookie ball in '91 and missed all of '92, they still motored him through the system, playing him at Double-A, Triple-A, and the major-league level in '94. He hasn't skipped a beat at any stage of his development, and he may be the most underrated pitcher in the N.L. His calling card is pinpoint control of a good sinker that kills both lefties and righties. He doesn't have full command of his repertoire yet, but his change-up is outstanding and his curveball is good. He saves a hard slider for lefties. He's comparable in many ways to Greg Maddux. No, that's not a misprint. Valdes shares the focus of the Cy Young winner, throwing hard into late innings and working deliberately with runners on. The Dodgers wouldn't have been in the postseason without him, as he joined Nomo and Ramon Martinez with an excellent September record. He's much younger than those two, and he's the most likely of the trio to garner Cy Young attention in the near future. ■

TODD WORRELL

CL • BR • TR • 6'5 • 215 • 37 • SL82/1

	G	GS	IP	H	HR	BB	K	W	L	S	ERA	K/BB	K9	HW9
LA94	38	0	42	37	4	12	44	6	5	11	4.29	3.7	9.4	10.50
LA95	59	0	62	50	4	19	61	4	1	32	2.02	3.2	8.9	10.02
LA96	72	0	65	70	5	15	66	4	6	44	3.03	4.4	9.1	11.76
CAREER	552	0	633	548	53	224	567	48	46	221	2.89	2.5	8.1	10.97

L.A. has been lucky with Worrell. Few thought he'd come back from the arm injuries that felled him in his prime, and fewer yet thought he'd return strongly from his '94 shoulder surgery. Instead, he's been among the best closers in baseball, converting 44 saves in 53 opportunities in '96 and throwing consistently in the 90s. He occasionally hits 96 mph. Worrell throws a couple of good fastballs—a sinking 2-seamer and a rising 4-seamer—but has junked his slider in favor of a slurve, perhaps to save wear and tear on his arm. He sometimes throws a weak change-up to mix things up. He's a horse—one of the very few closers to actually get better with age, despite the injuries he's endured (see Jose Mesa in the Cleveland Indians section). ■

DAVID YOCUM

SP • BL • TL • 6'0 • 175 • 22 • LA95/1

	G	GS	IP	H	HR	BB	SO	W	L	S	ERA	K/BB	K9	HW9
A+	7	7	15	22	1	7	8	0	2	0	6.14	1.1	4.9	17.80

Yocum was the no. 20 pick in the '95 draft. He's a lefty from Florida State with a great curveball and a good fastball, which gets as high as 92 mph. The Dodgers want him to slow down the fastball and make it sink more. Much of '96 was lost when he went on the DL in the Florida State League and didn't return until early August. If his arm is strong in '97, he's probably the Dodgers' best lefty prospect. ■

■ 1996 AUTOPSY

Manager Felipe Alou looked at his team's situation and said: "It's going to be a long year. In today's baseball, it's tough to compete with teams that spend $60 million a year. It's not fair." The Expos at least know how to make a run at it. Check out the Milwaukee Brewers—*Stuck Below .500 with the Milwaukee Brewers Again*—for an example of how not to do it.

April 17-9 (17-9, 1½ games ahead)
Montreal looked like the Cleveland Indians in April—without the insensitive logo. The team hit .303 and went deep in 11 straight games. The streak ended, ironically, at Coors Field—as did Rondell White's chances for a breakthrough season. He bruised his spleen crashing into the center field wall on the 27th and was gone until after the All-Star Break.

May 14-14 (31-23, 5 games back)
By early May, the Expos were 13-3 at home, the best record in baseball. But by the end of the month, the Braves had already taken control of the division—something they usually wait until late September to do. The offense was struggling, despite solid performances from Mark Grudzielanek (.324-2-7, 23 runs) and Henry Rodriguez (11 homers). The month ended with Jeff Fassero getting into a cat-fight with umpire Charlie Williams. Fassero felt Williams blew a call on Wally Joyner's double down the first-base line on the 27th. Fassero: "That's Charlie Williams at his finest. In Pittsburgh he missed a couple of ball-strike calls that cost me a couple of runs. Some of the guys said he wasn't really paying attention, like he wasn't watching the play." Crew Chief Bruce Froemming: "Typical sour grapes from a guy who is struggling and looking for an alibi. He's 3-5, making two-plus million dollars a season. He should concentrate on improving." By year end, this kind of player-umpire interaction would look like a love-in. Closer Mel Rojas was struggling, being taken out of a game after walking the first batter he faced. Felipe Alou said it was a mechanical problem. Rojas: "It's all in my head, no place else. They only say 'mechanical' when you're not doing well." Set-up man, Tim Scott, wanted a chance to be the man to pitch the ninth, but Alou didn't share his enthusiasm.

June 16-10 (47-33, 3 games back)
The team had lost 16-of-20 by the beginning of the month and Alou held a closed-door meeting on the 5th—a day after Gary Sheffield said the Expos "looked dead." The offense was still sputtering and Rodriguez was cooling off, too. He hit his 22nd homer on the 19th. He hit No. 21 17 days earlier. Rodriguez hit 25 homers in the Expos' first 75 games, but would hit 11 in the team's remaining 87 games. Alou: "This type of team that you see right now is really the kind of team we are. All those home runs in April? That wasn't really us. That was outrageous, an outrageous team."

July 11-15 (58-48, 7 games back)
On July 3, as the Expos were starting a series with Atlanta before the All-Star break, GM Jim Beattie was discussing making moves in case of injury. Less than an hour later, David Segui fractured his right thumb on a bad pick-off throw from Urbina. In that same game, Tim Scott gave up the winning homer to Chipper Jones in the eighth inning. Alou: "There's a difference between pitching in the seventh inning or the ninth inning." Scott was traded a few days later to the Giants for Mark Leiter.

Alou did stand up for Henry Rodriguez, though, after he and Sammy Sosa were initially left off the All-Star team because Bobby Cox thought they struck out too much. Alou: "Babe Ruth struck out a lot, too. I guess that means he wouldn't have been able to make this year's All-Star team." Speaking of Babe Ruth, Rondell White came back from the minors talking about a prospect he'd seen named Vladimir Guerrero. White said that Guerrero was the best player he'd ever seen.

August 14-14 (72-62, 11½ games back)
Mark Leiter made his debut on the 1st. He allowed three homers in five innings and was booed off the field. In his next start on the 7th, he allowed three runs in six innings getting the victory over the Astros. Kerrigan worked with Leiter on his leg kick and he never looked back. But in a key game against the Padres, Pedro Martinez left his game in the bullpen and got shelled, perhaps a result of warming up for more than 50 minutes before the

game. "We needed a big game out of him and then he does that," one Expo said. "A lot of guys in here were mad at him." The Expos went on to be swept in that series, going 1-5 on their West Coast swing.

September 16-12 (88-74, 8 games back)

The offense continued to misfire: Fletcher (.163-0-2) and Lansing (.236-0-3) could point to a long season and playing through pain. Part-timer Shane Andrews (.073) couldn't use that excuse, having given back the starting third base job every time he got it. Vladimir Guerrero got the call and hit the first of what will be many big league dingers. His first just happened to be off Mark Wohlers. That's called serving notice. But the team continued to lose games it needed to win. On the 20th vs. the Braves, Dave Leiper gave up a game-winning double to Fred McGriff. He thought he should have been watching the action, not participating in it: "I spent most of the year in Triple-A and the guys I got out are mostly home now. Before that, I had a horsebleep year with a horsebleep team (the Phillies). In fact, I've just been horsebleep, period. But in this situation, when you're trying to make the playoffs, you need to go with the guys who've been here all year." Come in off the ledge, Dave. On the 28th, the Expos were eliminated from the wild-card race. From August 16th through to the 28th of September, the Expos played 18 games against the teams they needed to beat: Los Angeles, San Diego and Atlanta. They went 5-13 and went home.

And the work began on trimming a payroll ($15 million) that was already one of the lowest in baseball.

■ 1997 DIAGNOSIS

Offense

The offense put up more than could be expected, considering what they had to work with. Mark Grudzielanek hit .306; Henry Rodriguez had a year he may never come close to repeating, hitting 36 home runs and knocking in 103 runs; and Mike Lansing scored 99 runs (as did Grud). But the team ended up outscoring only the Dodgers, Marlins, and Phillies because Moises Alou, Rondell White, Cliff Floyd, and Shane Andrews, for reasons ranging from injuries to missed opportunities, all put up less than had been hoped for—the 4 of them averaging 13 dingers and 57 RBIs, which in '96, were Tom Pagnozzi numbers. David Segui and Darrin Fletcher had that season, too, but that was to be expected. Vlad may develop into .320-25-100 eventually, but he'll only be 21. Read the essay at the end of this section—*21 Guns*—to see how likely that will be to happen right away.

Defense

The Expos allowed only 63 unearned runs in '96, lowest in the NL. But this was more a tribute to the pitchers than the fielders, because the team made 126 errors (only 8th in the league). David Segui wasn't as good as his flashy reputation in '96 (Jose Offerman and Mark Johnson had higher fielding percentages). Mike Lansing and Mark Grudzielanek play hard, but neither of them have very good range and they've been at or near the bottom in double plays turned the past 2 years. Lansing had sure hands in '96, but Grud's 27 errors and .959 fielding percentage put him in Orlando Miller's neighborhood. Shane Andrews had a decent year in the field, but nothing special. Things aren't much better in the outfield. Henry Rodriguez may actually be worse than Ryan Klesko in the field. Rondell White and Moises Alou only made 3 errors between them, but neither showed exceptional range. Catching may be the weakest link, where Fletcher threw out only 20% of runners, prompting the Expos to acquire defensive specialist, Chris Widger, from the Mariners. It is impressive that the Expos pitchers were as successful as they were with no defensive stand-outs playing behind them.

Pitching

Montreal had the 3rd best starting pitching in the league (behind Atlanta and Florida, after adjusting for home parks). But Jeff Fassero is gone and a young prospect named Matt Wagner is in his place. Mark Leiter was turned around by pitching coach Joe Kerrigan, but Kerrigan's gone to Boston and Leiter decided to test the free agent waters. Pedro Martinez may be the only one they can count on in

'97. Rheal Cormier was a decent No. 3 starter, Carlos Perez should be able to return from his injury, and Jose Paniagua could be ready for a full-time job. Ugueth Urbina got some starts, but will probably move to the bullpen. This leaves Tavo Alvarez, Everett Stull, and Neil Weber duking it out for what's left. Omar Daal and Jeff Juden were relievers in '96, but they also may get a chance at the rotation in '97.

The bullpen was excellent last season, which is why they may look there for some starters. Closer Mel Rojas had an incredible second half, as did Juden, Dave Veres, and Barry Manuel. Mike Dyer pitched well, too, so depth shouldn't be a problem. Since Kerrigan's been there, it rarely has. If the staff blows up in '97, you'll know just how important he was.

Farm System

Every year, this team operates on a shoestring, but it contends. This is a testament to the team's minor-league system which is extraordinarily well-run. Lately, the team has been squeezing out pitchers (Urbina, Paniagua are the two prominent examples) and there are more on the way: Shayne Bennett, Everett Stull, J.D. Smart, Neil Weber, and Derek Aucoin all throw hard and could blossom within 2-3 seasons. Offensively, Vlad Guerrero and Hiram Bocachica are excellent (Guerrero could be the best prospect in baseball—see the Atlanta Braves for a comparison of Vladimir and Andruw). New GM Jim Beattie took a hit when John Patterson, the No. 5 pick overall last season, was one of 3 1st-rounders who used a loophole to become free-agents available to the highest bidder. Don't bet on that being Montreal.

Management and Ownership

The Expos are owned by a limited partnership of 13 investors and the city of Montreal. Claude Brochu has been president of the team since 1986 and oversaw its transfer to the current group in June 1991. Brochu has overseen a team that doesn't cough up much for its major-league roster, placing its emphasis on player development. They've got half of the equation down, and the World Series teams of '95–'96 were very grateful for the talent Montreal has been unable to keep.

GM Jim Beattie is a former major-leaguer with an undergraduate degree from Dartmouth and an MBA from the University of Washington—and he's managed to overcome both. He spent several years as the Mariners director of player development and since he took over the Expos, his major moves have been getting rid of Wil Cordero before he became arbitration-eligible (for Cormier, Shayne Bennett and a David Segui clone named Ryan McGuire) and dealing Jeff Fassero for Chris Widger and Matt Wagner (who should perform capably in the brief time they're here, before having to be salary dumped in the year 2000). But none of those trades will matter if Beattie can't bring Felipe Alou back to the dugout.

Alou is smart, a good strategist and no one has done more with a roster of question marks than he has. But if he's back, he'll be without the pitching coach who turned Jeff Fassero into the best lefty in the NL in '96, who actually was getting through to Jeff Juden, who turned around Mark Leiter's season after a week with him, who consistently gets production out of raw rookies (Perez, Paniagua, Urbina) . . . You get the idea. When the time comes for the Expos to enter a season with neither of these gentlemen in the dugout, you could finally see that long overdue 100-loss train-wreck.

. . . and whatnot: 21 Guns

Going into '97, it is assumed by many that Vlad Guerrero will step into the Expos starting lineup and hit .300 with power and production. Maybe he will. But there are two things working against him. One is that Jim Beattie is no fool, and he must be tempted to bury him for another year in Triple-A so that he becomes arbitration-eligible a year later and a year closer to his prime. The other is how rare it's been for a 21-year-old in the NL to play regularly, put up big numbers immediately, and keep them there until Cooperstown. Johnny Bench was the last to do it.

Here are the most recent 21 year old National Leaguers who played regularly. It's a star-crossed bunch, to say the least: Edgar Renteria (5-33-.309), Cliff Floyd (4-41-.281), Wil Cordero (10-58-.248), Delino DeShields (4-45-.289), Roberto Alomar (7-56-.295), Gregg Jefferies (12-56-.258), Benito Santiago (18-79-.300), Darryl Strawberry (26-74-.257), and Tim Raines (5-37-.304). And before you

pencil Vlad in for a better year than any of those, here's what Barry Bonds did as 21-year old rookie:

	AB	R	H	2B	3B	HR	RBI	SB	BA
'86 Bonds	413	72	92	26	3	16	48	36	.223

The best, most Vlad-like numbers are Santiago's—and, until this year, he never approached them again and hasn't had his stuff out of storage since '92. Raines had some off-the-field troubles early in his career, but has been quite literally a rock solid citizen ever since. The same can't be said for Alomar, Bonds, Jefferies, and Strawberry, who've established themselves as stars while hitting more than a few immaturity speed bumps along the way. As for the Expos, they've tried this 21-thing before, but have nothing to show yet from Cliff Floyd—and Pedro Martinez, Rheal Cormier, and a couple of prospects to show for that young double play combination of DeShields and Cordero.

As you can see, throwing the kids in to see if they can swim hasn't been too popular recently (see *A Rod and Mel Ott* in the Seattle Mariners). It was a bit more common in the '70s, but the crop of kids who came up then were an uneven bunch, too. You've got to go through: Bob Horner (33-98-.314, washed up at 29); Terry Puhl (3-35-.289, on the bench by 28); Garry Templeton (8-79-.322, talking about 2,000 hits from each side of the plate and falling just a bit short); Larry Parrish (10-65-.274 and a solid 15-year career); Gary Carter (17-68-.270 and an outside shot at the Hall of Fame); Greg Gross (0-36-.314, a role player at 24); Derrel Thomas (5-36-.230, a utility man at 26); Dave Roberts (5-33-.244, hit .167 in 113 games at 23); Tim Foli (2-35-.241 and a solid 16-year career); Greg Luzinski (18-68-.281 and a solid 15-year career); Cesar Cedeno (22-82-.320 with 55 SBs, and all downhill from there); Chris Speier (8-46-.235 and a not quite Foli-esque 19-year career); Ted Simmons (7-77-.304, one of the best switch-hitters to ever play the game); Wayne Garrett (1-39-.218 as part of a miracle); Richie Hebner (8-47-.301 and a solid 18-year career); until you get to first-ballot Hall of Famer Johnny Bench (26-90-.293) in 1969.

But if you think they don't make them like they used to, consider what Roberto Clemente, a player Guerrero is frequently compared to, did in his first 5 seasons:

	AB	R	H	2B	3B	HR	RBI	SB	BA
1955 (20)	474	48	121	23	11	5	47	2	.255
1956 (21)	543	66	169	30	7	7	60	6	.311
1957 (22)	451	42	114	17	7	4	30	0	.253
1958 (23)	519	69	150	24	10	6	50	8	.289
1959 (24)	432	60	128	17	7	4	50	2	.296

If Guerrero does that for the next 5 years, the Expos might be able to afford him when he becomes eligible for free agency. But there's always the chance that Andruw and Vladimir will be the second coming of 21 Guns named Hank (27-106-.314) and Frank (29-75-.322), who made noise immediately and stayed loud for about another 21 seasons. If it happens, be sure to appreciate it. You can see how rare it is.

MOISES ALOU — CONSISTENT STAR

RF • BR • TR • 6'3 • 185 • 30 • PIT86/1

	AB	R	H	2B	3B	HR	RBI	BB	SO	SB	CS	BA	OB	SA
MON94	422	81	143	31	5	22	78	42	63	7	6	.339	.397	.592
MON95	344	48	94	22	0	14	58	29	56	4	3	.273	.342	.459
MON96	540	87	152	28	2	21	96	49	83	9	4	.281	.339	.457
CAREER	2149	343	627	138	16	84	373	183	304	53	21	.292	.348	.488

The consensus around the league is that Alou is a goner. He's going to go free agent and sign elsewhere for the big bucks. The Expos will let him go and drop Vladimir into his spot. Is Alou worth the money? Probably not. He's a good ballplayer, but not a superstar. He's a superb defensive outfielder and a solid hitter, but he'd be better suited as a member of the supporting cast—batting 2nd or 5th, rather than 3rd or cleanup. He'll show a good deal more power if he switches to a hitter's park, and if he can avoid a slump like he suffered in May and June, he'll return to the .300s. He's a fine athlete and an upstanding citizen, but he's not worth $5 million. ■

TAVO ALVAREZ — SLEEPER

SP • BR • TR • 6'3 • 235 • 25• MON90/2

	G	GS	IP	H	HR	BB	K	W	L	S	ERA	K/BB	K9	HW9
MON95	8	8	37	46	2	14	17	1	5	0	6.75	1.2	4.1	14.59
MON96	11	5	21	19	0	12	9	2	1	0	3.00	.8	3.9	13.29

Alvarez didn't get serious about staying in shape until he had rotator-cuff troubles in '95. He strained his right hamstring and went on the 15-day DL May

15, and when he got healthy he was optioned to Triple-A Ottawa. He didn't impress in the minors (4-9 with a 4.70 ERA), but he could be a contender in the Expos rotation if he watches his doughnut intake. When he's right, he's got a 90-plus fastball and he has good command. ■

SHANE ANDREWS

3B • BR • TR • 6'1 • 215 • 25 • MON90/1

	AB	R	H	2B	3B	HR	RBI	BB	SO	SB	CS	BA	OB	SA
MON95	220	27	47	10	1	8	31	17	68	1	1	.214	.271	.377
MON96	375	43	85	15	2	19	64	35	119	3	1	.227	.295	.429

How to Fall into Disfavor by Shane Andrews. Part I: Hit .263-11-39 (.338 OBP, .483 slugging) in the first half, then go .181-8-25 in the second. Part II: Tell management you're going to miss 2 days for your grandfather's funeral and then decide you want 4 without telling anyone, shortly after expressing your excitement about being given the full-time job at third. Part III: Maintain a 190-strikeout pace for a full season (600 at bats). During Shane's June hot streak (he hit .321-6-19 that month), he was promoted from the No. 8 hole to the No. 6 hole. He went 2-for-5 in his first game in the slot. Andrews: "There are times where you don't get much to hit in the eighth spot. I have to think that moving up in the order will improve the quality of pitches I see. . . . I'm learning (from hitting coach Tommy Harper) there are times when the pitcher has to pitch to you, when you're going to get something good to hit. When that happens, you have to drive the ball as hard as you can." Did Andrews really absorb these lessons? Well, pitchers got 2 strikes on him 53% of the time in '96 and he was toast by then, hitting .117. Andrews was quickly moved out of the No. 6 hole after going 1-for-15 in his next few starts there. Alou benched Andrews in late August, saying: "I need players who put the ball in play, make contact. If you can't make contact, then I can't use you." Andrews is a decent defensive player, and he can adjust enough to become a decent hitter, but right now he's in trouble. He has to work the count more or look for work. ■

DEREK AUCOIN

RP • BR • TR • 6'7 • 225 • 27 • MON89

	G	GS	IP	H	HR	BB	SO	W	L	S	ERA	K/BB	K9	HW9
AAA	52	0	75	74	6	53	69	3	5	3	3.96	1.3	8.3	15.24

Aucoin has 2 solid pitches: a hard slider and a fastball in the 90s. He has no command, but doesn't see where that's his fault. "I'm working on so much stuff that every time out, it seems like I'm trying something new. It's just hard to get a rhythm going. Maybe next time out I'll try throwing with my left hand." If Aucoin can throw strikes, he's a pitcher. If he can't, they can't even use him for b.p. ■

SHAYNE BENNETT

RP • BR • TR • 6'5 • 200 • 24

	G	GS	IP	H	HR	BB	SO	W	L	S	ERA	K/BB	K9	HW9
AA	53	0	93	83	6	35	89	8	8	12	2.53	2.5	8.6	11.46

Bennett is an Aussie who came from the Red Sox in last season's Wil Cordero trade. He has a 90-plus fastball and an 86-mph forkball. The Expos want Bennett to sharpen his curve, but he looks pretty good as is. He's ready for a tryout now. ■

YAMIL BENITEZ

OF • BR • TR • 6'2 • 195 • 24 • MON89

	AB	R	H	2B	3B	HR	RBI	BB	SO	SB	CS	BA	OB	SA
AAA	439	56	122	20	2	23	81	28	120	11	4	.278	.319	.490

Benitez has good range and a decent arm. Despite mediocre stolen-base totals, he has good speed. Benitez has almost everything you'd want in a player except he has a serious uppercut, can't hit breaking balls, strikes out too much, and rarely draws a walk. Other than that, he's fine. He's a fourth outfielder or an expansion pick. ■

HIRAM BOCACHICA GRADE-A PROSPECT

SS • BR • TR • 5'11 • 165 • 21 • MON94/1

	AB	R	H	2B	3B	HR	RBI	BB	SO	SB	CS	BA	OB	SA
A–	267	50	90	17	5	2	26	34	47	21	3	.337	.419	.461

Bocachica has the best infield arm in the organization. He also has good range, but made too many errors—attributed by his coaches to mental lapses rather than a lack of ability. He had surgery to remove fragments from his elbow in early June—he was leading the Florida State League in batting average and on-base percentage when he went on the DL. He was a DH after the surgery and finished

very strongly. If he starts off playing well at Harrisburg, he could be moved to third and push Shane Andrews out of the way. Or they may choose to hold him back until Grudzielanek is on his way out the door in a few years. ■

RHEAL CORMIER

SP • BL • TL • 5′10 • 185 • 29 • SL88/8

	G	GS	IP	H	HR	BB	K	W	L	S	ERA	K/BB	K9	HW9
SL94	7	7	39	40	6	7	26	3	2	0	5.45	3.7	6.0	10.83
BOS95	48	12	115	131	12	31	69	7	5	0	4.07	2.2	5.4	12.68
MON96	33	27	159	165	16	41	100	7	10	0	4.17	2.4	5.7	11.66
CAREER	168	107	712	767	72	147	425	38	38	0	4.13	2.9	5.4	11.55

All season long the team was mystified by his poor performance in the first inning. In the first inning, the league hit .309; during innings 2-6, they hit .256. The Expos tried to get Cormier to change the way he prepares for starts because of this, but he showed no improvement—in fact, he got worse. Scouts don't like Cormier because he doesn't have good stuff—a mediocre sinker, slider and a forkball—and he has to have very good command to win. Don't expect much more than 150 innings. He's never pitched 200 innings in his career and might well have hit the wall in the second half (2-5 with a 5.26 ERA). ■

OMAR DAAL

SLEEPER

RP • BL • TL • 6′3 • 185 • 25 • LA90

	G	GS	IP	H	HR	BB	K	W	L	S	ERA	K/BB	K9	HW9
LA94	24	0	13	12	1	5	9	0	0	0	3.29	1.8	6.2	11.71
LA95	28	0	20	29	1	15	11	4	0	0	7.20	.7	5.0	19.80
MON96	64	6	87	74	10	37	82	4	5	0	4.02	2.2	8.5	11.48
CAREER	163	6	156	151	17	78	121	10	8	0	4.61	1.6	7.0	13.21

Daal was acquired acquired from the Dodgers in the '95 off-season, and came into the spring of '96 having pitched brilliantly in winter ball. He had improved his command and was able to spot his solid curveball. He credited Kerrigan with adjusting his delivery to keep his head level, saying this led to the improved control. He had walked 41 batters in his 69 career innings going into '96 (5.4 per nine) and cut that to 37 in 87.1 innings (3.8 per nine). He then went out and put up a 2.98 ERA in 51 innings from April through July, allowing only 38 hits with a 2.1 strikeout-to-walk ratio (45/21). In August and September he pitched 36 innings and had a 5.50 ERA, allowing 36 hits and six homers. Write it off to fatigue after pitching so many innings as a starter in the winter leagues. Daal may still be a competent candidate for the rotation. If it turns out he can't pitch the innings, he's still a quality left-hander in the pen. ■

MIKE DYER

RP • BR • TR • 6′3 • 200 • 30 • MIN86/4

	G	GS	IP	H	HR	BB	K	W	L	S	ERA	K/BB	K9	HW9
PIT94	14	0	15	15	1	12	13	1	1	4	5.87	1.1	7.8	16.16
PIT95	55	0	74	81	9	30	53	4	5	0	4.34	1.8	6.4	13.50
MON96	70	1	75	79	7	34	51	5	5	2	4.40	1.5	6.1	13.55
CAREER	155	13	236	249	19	113	154	14	18	6	4.61	1.4	5.9	13.80

They call him The Unabomber—his photo is included by way of explanation. Dyer credited Kerrigan at the beginning of the season for helping him improve his split-finger and his curveball. He didn't seem to help his consistency. He was 2-4, 6.19 ERA in 36.1 innings from June through August—3-1, 2.97 in April, May and September. As for improvement, it would be hard to find another pitcher who had more identical seasons from '95 to '96. ■

DARRIN FLETCHER

C • BL • TR • 6′2 • 195 • 30 • LA87/6

	AB	R	H	2B	3B	HR	RBI	BB	SO	SB	CS	BA	OB	SA
MON94	285	28	74	18	1	10	57	25	23	0	0	.260	.314	.435
MON95	350	42	100	21	1	11	45	32	23	0	1	.286	.351	.446
MON96	394	41	105	22	0	12	57	27	42	0	0	.266	.321	.414
CAREER	1814	166	472	100	5	46	260	139	177	0	4	.260	.316	.397

In consecutive months, Fletcher hit .333, .176, .313, .254, .325, and .163. This and his weak defense (he only threw out 20% of baserunners) led the Expos to acquire Chris Widger from the Mariners. He'll do fine as half of a platoon with a better defensive catcher like Widger, and the Expos picked up his option, bringing him back to do just that. ■

CLIFF FLOYD *SLEEPER*

OF • BL • TL • 6'4 • 220 • 24 • MON91/1

	AB	R	H	2B	3B	HR	RBI	BB	SO	SB	CS	BA	OB	SA
MON94	334	43	94	19	4	4	41	24	63	10	3	.281	.332	.398
MON95	69	6	9	1	0	1	8	7	22	3	0	.130	.221	.188
MON96	227	29	55	15	4	6	26	29	52	7	1	.242	.337	.423
CAREER	661	81	165	35	8	12	77	60	146	20	4	.250	.318	.381

Remember when he was supposed to be "Frank Thomas with speed." During spring, the Expos were concerned that Floyd wasn't show full range of motion in the wrist that was shattered on a play at first base in '95. He only got piecemeal playing time, and in September, Floyd started complaining about the way he was used: "We have too many outfielders here and I don't know if it's going to get better next year. I have to be playing every day. Here I am, (24) years old, and I'm a role player . . . I just don't get it, the guys who are involved in these decisions all played at one time, right? Don't they know what this does to your confidence?" Some scouts don't like Floyd's long swing, and of course management can't like his whining. But Floyd could provide a perfect replacement for Henry Rodriguez, who the Expos would love to deal before he turns into a pumpkin at midnight. ■

BRAD FULLMER *SOLID PROSPECT*

OF • BL • TR • 6'1 • 185 • 22 • MON93/4

	AB	R	H	2B	3B	HR	RBI	BB	SO	SB	CS	BA	OB	SA
AA	98	11	27	4	1	4	14	3	8	0	0	.276	.311	.459

Fullmer tore a rotator cuff in the spring of '94 and missed that season. He debuted as a pro by hitting .323 in Class-A in '95, and .303 in high Class-A in '96 before his promotion to Harrisburg. He's currently a line-drive hitter (only 17 dingers in 946 minor league at bats), but management thinks he could hit for power. If you get to see him, note his stance—he stands at the plate with his feet together and keeps wiggling his fingers. Shades of John Wockenfuss. ■

VLADIMIR GUERRERO *GRADE-A PROSPECT*

OF • BR • TR • 6'2 • 195 • 21 • MON93

	AB	R	H	2B	3B	HR	RBI	BB	SO	SB	CS	BA	OB	SA
AA	417	84	150	32	8	19	78	51	42	17	10	.360	.438	.612

In 1996, the Eastern League tabbed Guerrero as its best defensive outfielder, best batting prospect, best power hitter, the owner of the league's best outfield arm, and its most-exciting player. Unfortunately, he wasn't the league's best pitching prospect and he wasn't its best managing prospect, so he'll have to work on that in the off-season. Here's what two scouts say:

"He's the best player I've seen in my five years covering the Eastern League. He plays hard, he's not a dog. He reminds me of Roberto Clemente. A bad-ball hitter, free-swinger, a rifle in the outfield. He does something every time to make you like him more. . . . I saw him get hit in the kneecap (with a pitch) in one game. The next time up, he hit one to right that got outta the park real fast." Another said: "The only hitter I've seen in the Eastern League who was better was Manny Ramirez." He's an incredible talent and he will be a star as long as he's healthy Maybe he'll even be Frank Thomas with speed. ■

MARK GRUDZIELANEK *YOUNG GUN*

SS • BR • TR • 6'1 • 185 • 26 • MON91/12

	AB	R	H	2B	3B	HR	RBI	BB	SO	SB	CS	BA	OB	SA
MON95	269	27	66	12	2	1	20	14	47	8	3	.245	.300	.316
MON96	657	99	201	34	4	6	49	26	83	33	7	.306	.340	.397

No one compares Grudzielanek to Frank Thomas. No, he gets burdened with comparisons to Paul Molitor. Not only was Grud a big Molitor fan as a kid, but he has adopted his stance. His batting stance in '95 was more of a crouch, and he hit .245. This year, hitting coach Tommy Harper has him more upright in his stance, and the difference is evident in the numbers. Alou on Grud: "He can eventually be a Ryne Sandberg, Paul Molitor or Jay Bell-type of player." Oh well, 2 out of 3 ain't bad. But are all these Molitor comparisons fair? If you're talking about grit, hustle and love of the game, sure. If you're talking about 3,000 hits, forget it. Here's what they did at 22, Grudzielanek's 2nd year as a pro and Molitor's 3rd.

Age 22	LG	AB	R	H	2B	3B	HR	RBI	BB	SO	B.A.	OB	SA
Grud	MW	496	64	122	12	5	5	54	22	59	.246	.278	.321
Molitor	A.L.	584	88	188	27	16	9	62	48	48	.322	.373	.469

Hitting .322 in the A.L. is 2000 light years from hitting .246 in the Midwest League. He'll turn 27

this year (the age at which Molitor got his 900th hit), so he's at his physical peak—and '97 and '98 could be as good as it gets for him. ■

JEFF JUDEN

SLEEPER

RP • BR • TR • 6'7 • 245 • 26 • HOU89/1

	G	GS	IP	H	HR	BB	K	W	L	S	ERA	K/BB	K9	HW9
PHI94	6	5	27	29	4	12	22	1	4	0	6.18	1.8	7.3	13.63
PHI95	13	10	62	53	6	31	47	2	4	0	4.02	1.5	6.8	12.19
SF/MON96	58	0	73	61	8	34	61	5	0	0	3.32	1.8	7.5	11.69
CAREER	83	18	187	166	22	88	148	8	11	0	4.29	1.7	7.1	12.24

No longer "Baby Huey"—an old nickname earned in one of his 3 previous organizations—Juden rallied and turned into a major-league pitcher last season (he had a 4.92 career ERA going into 1996). Kerrigan worked his magic after the Giants cut him loose (shortly after Juden challenged a groundskeeper to a fight after being accidentally sprayed with a hose), and Juden responded with a 2.25 ERA in 36 innings from July through September (4.22 ERA in April through June).The Expos see him as a possible closer, but Juden sees himself as a starter—a much more likely role for him in '97. Juden: "I still have the arm strength. . . . And I think I'm young enough. Maybe when I'm 10 years older, and can't last eight or nine innings, it will be time to become a closer." Let's take it one step at a time, Baby Eck. Like getting your 4th career win as a starter. ■

MIKE LANSING

2B • BR • TR • 6'0 • 180 • 28 • MON91

	AB	R	H	2B	3B	HR	RBI	BB	SO	SB	CS	BA	OB	SA
MON94	394	44	105	21	2	5	35	30	37	12	8	.266	.328	.368
MON95	467	47	119	30	2	10	62	28	65	27	4	.255	.299	.392
MON96	641	99	183	40	2	11	53	44	85	23	8	.285	.341	.406
CAREER	1993	254	548	120	7	29	195	148	243	85	25	.275	.331	.386

In many ways, Lansing is another Grudzielanek. He's a fiery player, fast, a line-drive hitter, and not a great fielder. Like the rest of his team, he started off white-hot. He hit .383 in April, but hit .237 in 219 at bats in August and September as he was nagged by injuries but refused to come out of the lineup. Lansing was signed by the Expos from an independent team, made it to the majors at 25, never hit over .300 in the minors and never showed much power. What he's accomplished in the majors has been due to sheer force of will. He'll turn 29 in April and it would be unfair to expect anymore than what he did in '96. ■

MARK LEITER (see Free Agents)

BARRY MANUEL

RP • BR • TR • 5'11 • 185 • 31

	G	GS	IP	H	HR	BB	K	W	L	S	ERA	K/BB	K9	HW9
MON96	53	0	86	70	10	26	62	4	1	0	3.24	2.4	6.5	10.05

Manuel started throwing from the stretch full time in late June because he saw better movement on his pitches with the shorter delivery. In August and September, he pitched 27.1 innings (2.31 ERA), allowing 21 hits, striking out 21 and walking only 2. Keep doing what you're doing. If the control he displayed in the second half is for real (six walks in 35.1 innings), he's getting close to Eckersley's neighborhood. He's a little old to be establishing himself, he won't have Kerrigan to work with him, and he hasn't had a season like that since high Class-A in 1990. Don't be surprised if he can't repeat it in '97. ■

PEDRO MARTINEZ

NL ELITE

SP • BR • TR • 5'11 • 170 • 25 • LA88

	G	GS	IP	H	HR	BB	K	W	L	S	ERA	K/BB	K9	HW9
MON94	24	23	144	115	11	45	142	11	5	1	3.42	3.2	8.9	10.00
MON95	30	30	194	158	21	66	174	14	10	0	3.51	2.6	8.1	10.39
MON96	33	33	216	189	19	70	222	13	10	0	3.70	3.2	9.2	10.79
CAREER	154	89	670	544	56	239	665	48	31	3	3.40	2.8	8.9	10.52

Martinez still isn't very beefy, but he's actually put on 20 pounds since he first arrived in the majors throwing heat. His fastball is a 7 on the scouts' grading scale (1-8, with 8 being Wohlers and Randy Johnson)—he cuts the fastball to get lefties, and runs it in on right-handers. He's got that nice change, and his curve is getting a lot better. He has command of his stuff and isn't

afraid to throw inside. That adds up to 27 wins in 2 years with numbers that could have gotten him 40 wins with a better team. Any fears that he might be mellowing as he ages were dispelled late in the season in a game against the Phillies; Martinez was suspended for 8 games for charging the mound and throwing his helmet at Mike Williams after Williams threw inside to him. Evidently, Pedro prefers to give rather than receive. If the Expos had still been in it on the final weekend, this stunt may have kept him from being available to pitch his team into the playoffs. ■

SHERMAN OBANDO — SLEEPER

OF • BR • TR • 6'4 • 215 • 27 • NYA87

	AB	R	H	2B	3B	HR	RBI	BB	SO	SB	CS	BA	OB	SA
MON96	178	30	44	9	0	8	22	22	48	2	0	.247	.332	.433

Alou: "He can be a devastating hitter. It isn't his bat that has made us reluctant to start him." That's a very polite way to say that he can't field—which is ironic, considering that's what caused them to sour on Tony Tarasco, who they traded to the Orioles for Obando. Obando is a thumper. In the International League in '94, Obando hit .330-20-69 in 403 at-bats (he led the league with 36 doubles and slugged .603). He'd be better off back in the A.L. where fielding is optional. ■

JOSÉ PANIAGUA — YOUNG GUN

SP • BR • TR • 6'1 • 160 • MON90

	G	GS	IP	H	HR	BB	K	W	L	S	ERA	K/BB	K9	HW9
MON96	13	11	51	55	7	23	27	2	4	0	3.53	1.2	4.8	13.76

Paniagua has a mid-90s fastball and a deadly slider. His velocity is a bit below Urbina, but his fastball has much better movement. Paniagua has problems changing speeds and his command is mediocre. If he can't develop an off-speed pitch, he may find himself in the bullpen. He's raw, but he proved he can pitch in the majors last season. It may take him one or two seasons before he establishes himself, but he's got a Grade-A arm. ■

CARLOS PEREZ — SLEEPER

SP • BL • TL • 6'3 • 195 • 25 • MON87

	G	GS	IP	H	HR	BB	K	W	L	S	ERA	K/BB	K9	HW9
MON95	28	23	141	142	18	28	106	10	8	0	3.69	3.8	6.8	10.85

In March 1996, Perez went on the DL with "tendinitis" in his left shoulder. An MRI was performed in mid-April and it showed a small tear in a muscle under his left armpit. He had a torn labrum and a partially torn rotator cuff and he ended up missing the season. Perez is expected to be ready for the spring, and is currently doing rehab to regain full range of motion on his post-strikeout gesticulations. His injury probably cost the Expos one or two games in the standings and possibly the wild-card. ■

HENRY RODRIGUEZ — HEADED FOR A FALL

OF-1B • BL • TL • 6'1 • 205 • 29 • LA85

	AB	R	H	2B	3B	HR	RBI	BB	SO	SB	CS	BA	OB	SA
LA94	306	33	82	14	2	8	49	17	58	0	1	.268	.307	.405
LA/MON95	138	13	33	4	1	2	15	11	28	0	1	.239	.293	.326
MON96	532	81	147	42	1	36	103	37	160	2	0	.276	.325	.562
CAREER	1298	158	333	77	4	57	204	84	315	3	2	.257	.302	.454

Rodriguez's season wasn't as unprecedented as many think. He was the Texas League MVP in 1990 (hitting .291-28-109 at age 22). Rodriguez was always a good hitter who'd never gotten the chance to play every day. He hit the weight room hard before the 1996 season and has added 25 pounds of muscle since he made it to the majors. But he's not a great bet to have as good a season this year. He's a bit old in baseball years to be establishing himself as a star, and very few hitters can maintain .276 batting averages with a Rob Deer strikeout pace. It would be more realistic to expect 20 dingers and a .250 average, which is why the Expos wanted to deal him sooner rather than later. As a fielder, he's Ryan Klesko on carpet, which is a scary thought. ■

MEL ROJAS

CONSISTENT STAR

CL • BR • TR • 5'11 • 195 • 30 • MON85

	G	GS	IP	H	HR	BB	K	W	L	S	ERA	K/BB	K9	HW9
MON94	58	0	84	71	11	21	84	3	2	16	3.32	4.0	9.0	9.86
MON95	59	0	67	69	2	29	61	1	4	30	4.12	2.1	8.2	13.16
MON96	74	0	81	56	5	28	92	7	4	36	3.22	3.3	10.2	9.33
CAREER	385	0	509	423	35	179	418	29	23	109	3.04	2.3	7.4	10.64

In the first half of the season, Rojas had a 5.19 ERA in 43.1 innings; in the second half, he had a 0.96 ERA in 37.2 innings and the league hit .125 as he converted 24 of 25 saves. He temporarily lost the closer role in late May because his mechanics were fouled up and Felipe Alou questioned his confidence. Part of what turned Rojas around was following Kerrigan's advice and using his fastball as a first pitch instead of the forkball. Both pitches are very good (his fastball hits 92-94). He is one of the players that Jim Beattie identified as a must keeper, despite the interest the Marlins had in him to set up Nen and the belief held by many that Ugueth Urbina is ready for a shot at closing games. His nickname is Desmond Tutu, which is even better than Dyer's—evidence that someone in the clubhouse is watching something other than *SportsCenter* and the financial reports. ■

JON SAFFER

SLEEPER

OF • BL • TR • 6'2 • 200 • 23 • MON92/5

	AB	R	H	2B	3B	HR	RBI	BB	SO	SB	CS	BA	OB	SA
AA	487	96	146	26	4	10	52	78	77	8	16	.300	.401	.431

It's a longshot, but it's possible that Saffer could work his way into the outfield mix in Montreal. As a hitter, there's little he can't do; he hits for average, knows the strike zone, and has decent power. With a few seasons in the N.L. he could become the leadoff hitter this team is desperately seeking. His 8-16 (SB-CS) stolen base numbers were an aberration—he was 53-29 prior to '96. Shades of Craig Biggio, who went 15-17 in 1993—109-36 before and 97-19 since. ■

F.P. SANTANGELO

OF-3B-2B • BB • TR • 5'10 • 165 • 29 • MON89/20

	AB	R	H	2B	3B	HR	RBI	BB	SO	SB	CS	BA	OB	SA
MON95	98	11	29	5	1	1	9	12	9	1	1	.296	.384	.398
MON96	393	54	109	20	5	7	56	49	61	5	2	.277	.369	.407

Santangelo was asked to play center when Rondell went down, and had a .369 OBP at the position and played good defense. When Andrews slumped late in the year, he got some time at third. Alou likes his work at second, too. He doesn't have great speed, but he works the count and will force the pitcher to make good pitches. He worked hard to turn himself into a major-leaguer and with his versatility, will likely remain one even if he never matches those offensive numbers again. ■

DAVID SEGUI

SLEEPER

1B • BB • TL • 6'1 • 170 • 30 • BAL87/19

	AB	R	H	2B	3B	HR	RBI	BB	SO	SB	CS	BA	OB	SA
NYN94	336	46	81	17	1	10	43	33	43	0	0	.241	.308	.387
NYN/MON95	456	68	141	25	4	12	68	40	47	2	7	.309	.367	.461
MON96	416	69	119	30	1	11	58	60	54	4	4	.286	.375	.442
CAREER	2182	287	597	122	6	48	283	234	254	10	13	.274	.343	.401

Segui is yet another 2-hole hitter on a team full of 2-hole hitters. There aren't too many candidates for the 5- or 6-hole, but there are plenty who have decent on-base percentages and a little power.

He and J.T. Snow are very similar players—switch-hitting glove men at first base—but the unappreciated Segui is a better player. He can hit from both sides of the plate, makes better contact, and is more consistent. Segui is supposedly past his prime, but expect him to return to his '95 levels if not exceed them. He had a strong second half (.429 OBP, .480 slugging), and is finally at the stage where he knows the league and is playing every day. ■

FERNANDO SEGUIGNOL

OF • BB • TR • 6'5 • 180 • 22 • NYA93

	AB	R	H	2B	3B	HR	RBI	BB	SO	SB	CS	BA	OB	SA
A	410	59	98	14	5	8	55	48	126	12	13	.239	.327	.356

This is what the Expos got for John Wetteland. Seguignol has some skills—he's young, plays good defense, has some speed, some power and draws a decent number of walks. But he's a raw player who's going to take a long time to make the majors, if he ever does. If you have a top-flight closer, you have to get more than this. Evidently the Expos couldn't even afford to showcase Wetteland until June and auction him off to the highest bidding contender. So far, thanks to former GM Kevin Malone, they have Seguignol, the 31-year old Esteban Yan, Sherman Obando, Henry Rodriguez, Kirk Bullinger (Jim's brother, only with less potential), and Darond Stovall (deep on the outfield depth chart) to show for Wetteland, Marquis Grissom, Ken Hill, and Larry Walker. ■

EVERETT STULL *SLEEPER*

SP • BR • TR • 6'3 • 195 • 25 • MON92/3

	G	GS	IP	H	HR	BB	SO	W	L	S	ERA	K/BB	K9	HW9
AAA	13	13	70	87	7	39	69	2	6	0	6.33	1.8	8.9	16.28

Stull earned a promotion from Double-A after going 6-3 with a 3.15 ERA, striking out 81 and walking 52 in 80 innings. He was in the best shape of his career in '96, coming off of a wretched '95 in which he went 3-12 with a 5.54 ERA. He hits 96 with his fastball, has a slider with wicked action, a good, hard curve, and terrible mechanics. Until he gets that straightened out, expect inconsistency. ■

UGUETH URTAIN URBINA *YOUNG GUN*

SP-RP • BR • TR • 6'2 • 170 • 23 • MON90

	G	GS	IP	H	HR	BB	K	W	L	S	ERA	K/BB	K9	HW9
MON95	7	4	23	26	6	14	15	2	2	0	6.17	1.1	5.9	15.65
MON96	33	17	114	102	18	44	108	10	5	0	3.71	2.5	8.5	11.53

U^3 has a superb fastball (97 mph) and an excellent change. He worked hard on his slider last season and it's starting to pay off. He started the season in the rotation, but ended it pitching exceptionally in relief (1.99 ERA, 25:5 strikeout-to-walk ratio in 22.2 innings). Beattie on Urbina's role in '97: "We'd like

to see Ugueth spend another year in the setup role." To progress, he'll need to develop a pitch to use against lefties (they hit .315 and slugged .511 vs. him; righties hit .153 and slugged .306). His control is decent (excellent as a reliever), his stuff is great, and he's got the strikeouts to prove it. He could establish himself as one of the better pitchers in the league in '97. ■

DAVE VERES

RP • BR • TR • 6'2 • 195 • 30 • OAK86/4

	G	GS	IP	H	HR	BB	K	W	L	S	ERA	K/BB	K9	HW9
HOU94	32	0	41	39	4	7	28	3	3	1	2.41	4.0	6.1	10.10
HOU95	72	0	103	89	5	30	94	5	1	1	2.26	3.1	8.2	10.40
MON96	68	0	77	85	10	32	81	6	3	4	4.17	2.5	9.5	13.66
CAREER	172	0	221	213	19	69	203	14	7	6	2.97	2.9	8.3	11.48

Veres battled a sore arm for the first half of the year, but finished up with a 2.30 ERA in his last 31.1 innings, which is more like what he did for the Astros in '94 and '95. Veres has average stuff, a riding fastball, a slider, and a split-finger, but is able to locate well enough to strike out a batter an inning. Unless his arm troubles resurface, expect that strong second half to carry over into '97. ■

JOSÉ VIDRO *SOLID PROSPECT*

3B • BB • TR • 5'11 • 175 • 22 • MON92/6

	AB	R	H	2B	3B	HR	RBI	BB	SO	SB	CS	BA	OB	SA
AA	452	57	117	25	3	18	82	29	71	3	1	.259	.300	.447

Vidro plays short and second as well as third. Don't be surprised if he makes a run at the third base job by the end of July. He's more dangerous from the left side and his power has been getting better and better as he's climbed the ladder—he'd only hit 17 home runs in his first 4 minor league seasons. ■

MATT WAGNER *YOUNG GUN*

SP • BR • TR • 6'5 • 215 • 24 • SEA94/3

	G	GS	IP	H	HR	BB	K	W	L	S	ERA	K/BB	K9	HW9
SEA96	15	14	80	91	15	38	41	3	5	0	6.86	1.1	4.6	14.51

Wagner came over from Seattle in the Fassero deal. If it weren't for a herniated disc when he pitched at Iowa State, he wouldn't have been on the board when the Mariners took him in the 3rd round in the 1994 draft. Going into last season, he had the best fastball in the Mariners system. He also has a good

breaking ball and a solid change. He was healthy last season, had a fine year at Triple-A, and had a "learning experience" at the major-league level. He pitched well in some of his starts and survived the PCL, so there's no reason why he can't pitch better baseball in pitcher-friendly Stade Olympique this season. ■

NEIL WEBER — SOLID PROSPECT

SP • BL • TL • 6'5 • 205 • 24 • MON93/8

	G	GS	IP	H	HR	BB	SO	W	L	S	ERA	K/BB	K9	HW9
AA	18	18	107	90	8	44	74	7	4	0	3.03	1.7	6.2	11.27

Weber has a moving fastball that occasionally hits 94, which is the territory of a young Chuck Finley. His other pitches—currently a curveball and a change-up—are still in development, but have pretty good potential. Weber was shut down because of shoulder soreness during the regular season, but was shipped off to the instructional league and was fine there. He could get the chance to win a spot in the rotation in '97. ■

LENNY WEBSTER

C • BR • TR • 5'9 • 200 • 32 • MIN85/21

	AB	R	H	2B	3B	HR	RBI	BB	SO	SB	CS	BA	OB	SA
MON94	143	13	39	10	0	5	23	16	24	0	0	.273	.370	.448
PHI95	150	18	40	9	0	4	14	16	27	0	0	.267	.337	.407
MON96	174	18	40	10	0	2	17	25	21	0	0	.230	.332	.322
CAREER	751	84	191	45	1	16	84	87	104	1	2	.254	.337	.381

Webster's got a fine arm, nailing 19-of-50 (38 percent) baserunners, but his knees are shot. And if you can't squat, you can't catch ■

RONDELL WHITE — YOUNG GUN

CF • BR • TR • 6'1 • 205 • 25 • MON90/2

	AB	R	H	2B	3B	HR	RBI	BB	SO	SB	CS	BA	OB	SA
MON94	97	16	27	10	1	2	13	9	18	1	1	.278	.358	.464
MON95	474	87	140	33	4	13	57	41	87	25	5	.295	.356	.464
MON96	334	35	98	19	4	6	41	22	53	14	6	.293	.340	.428
CAREER	978	147	284	65	10	23	126	79	174	41	14	.290	.348	.448

In the spring, Felipe Alou was predicting a 30 homer, 40 steal season for Rondell. All chances of that ended when White suffered a bruised shoulder, spleen and kidney diving into an outfield wall on April 27. Rondell has great tools and was a superstar in the minors, but .300 with 25 homers until he becomes arbitration-eligible could be more reasonable to expect than what Felipe penciled him in for. If you can live with his bad throwing arm, you can live with his weaknesses—because it's a short list and that's the only thing on it.

CHRIS WIDGER — SOLID PROSPECT

C • BR • TR • 6'3 • 195 • 25 • SEA92/3

	AB	R	H	2B	3B	HR	RBI	BB	SO	SB	CS	BA	OB	SA
AAA	352	42	107	20	2	13	48	27	62	7	1	.304	.355	.483

Widger was one of the most coveted prospects in the game and it took Jeff Fassero to pry him away from the Mariners. He has an excellent rapport with his pitchers and a strong arm. At first the Mariners drafted him strictly for his bat, but have fallen in love with his glove. His swing is long, and he might not be much of a hitter in the majors when he gets his shot—that .304 average in Triple-A was 28 points higher than his previous best and was put up in a hitters' league. He's 3 years older than Jason Kendall and only 2 years younger than Dan Wilson—which makes you wonder why he's getting everyone so hot and bothered, and why the Mariners were so reluctant to deal him. The Cubs' Pat Cline looks like a much better prospect, but only close friends and family even know who he is. ■

■ 1996 AUTOPSY

It was all about expectations.

A trio of young Mets pitchers were surrounded by a tremendous amount of hype in the weeks leading up to Opening Day. After impressive call-ups in '95, Jason Isringhausen and Bill Pulsipher were to be joined by phenom Paul Wilson, and they would pitch the team to glory. The Mets also handed the starting shortstop job to rookie glove-sensation Rey Ordoñez, another youngster. His defensive prowess was supposed to make third basemen obsolete.

They signed Lance Johnson, who would serve as table-setter, and dealt for Bernard Gilkey, who would finally get the chance to drive in runs in the middle of the order. Finally, they expected Carl Everett and Edgardo Alfonzo to develop into everyday players, while Butch Huskey was supposed to shed his extra weight and start pounding the ball the way he did in the minors.

Manager Dallas Green summed it up best in the spring: "If you have young players, you sometimes have to live with their inconsistency because that's how they learn at this level. But I'll tell you this: We're going to be a better club as the year goes on. And I have the same high expectations that everyone else has."

April 11-13 (11-13, 5 games back)

The major downfall of the Mets in the early part of the season involved pitching and defense. The team hit better than expected the first month, batting .287 and slugging .559, led by the potent bats of Bernard Gilkey (7 homers, 23 RBI) and Todd Hundley (8 homers, 21 RBI). But the pitching staff, supposedly their strength, first suffered the loss of Bill Pulsipher to season-ending surgery and then had to endure the performances of Wilson and Bobby Jones, who both had 7.71 ERAs. And when the pitching wasn't pathetic, starters were being hung with tough luck. For example, Mark Clark, their best pitcher in April, had a 3.60 ERA but a 1-2 record to show for it. The pitchers weren't exactly being helped by a defense whose errors led to 24 unearned runs for the month—an average of 1 per game.

May 11-17 (22-30, 13 games back)

On May 3, Dallas Green left Paul Wilson in to close out a 2-1 gem over the Cubs. Green likes to try to make men out of his young pitchers, but Sammy Sosa burned him this time, hitting a 3-run dinger to win the game with 2 out in the bottom of the 9th. If Wilson gets Sosa, he would have been 2-1. Instead he was 1-5 by the end of the month, as the Mets lost his next 4 starts. But as May came to an end, the pitching started ironing itself out. During one late May stretch, Mets pitchers threw 3 shutouts in 4 games.

Offensively, the Mets hit just .239 in May and scored 93 runs, their lowest total all season. Gilkey and Johnson did their part, but Rico Brogna (.187) disappeared, and the rookies weren't much help. Everett and Huskey appeared to be competing to see who could be the first to get Dallas Green to take a swing at one of them.

June 15-13 (37-43, 13 games back)

The Mets battled for respectability in June. Mark Clark emerged as the ace of the staff and led the Mets with a 4-1, 2.34 ERA record. Isringhausen either threw a gem or got creamed, and Wilson went down with a shoulder injury. The hitters picked up the pace in June. They scored 124 runs despite hitting just 22 home runs for the month. The main cause of this power outage was the loss of Brogna for the season. But they hit 57 doubles, their best monthly total, and got much more aggressive on the basepaths, swiping 25 bases. Johnson and Gilkey hit better than .300 and Hundley slugged 8 homers.

July 15-13 (52-56, 14 games back)

The Mets approached the .500 mark in early July—only to have remarks from the front office about wild-card contention escape to the press. They responded by losing 8 of 9 games, yielding most of the ground they had made up. Near the end of the losing streak, Hundley and Franco ripped their teammates while standing in an empty clubhouse just a little more than an hour after a game. The team had become too accustomed to losing. Despondency was settling in.

Then, on the last day of the month, GM Joe McIlvaine pulled off a major deal, sending Jeff Kent and José Vizcaino to the Indians for Carlos Baerga and Alvaro Espinoza. It was an attempt to improve the ballclub, mostly the defense, for the stretch drive. But little did he know the potholes that lay before the Mets on that drive.

August 8-20 (60-76, 24½ games back)
As in April, most of the blame for the Mets' 20 losses should have been credited solely to the pitching staff and to the defense. The combination of shoddy pitching (100 walks allowed) and loose fielding (27 unearned runs) led to the Mets giving up 159 runs in August, and the offense just couldn't keep up. Jones (4.81 ERA) and Isringhausen (5.54 ERA) were ineffective, but Paul Wilson (0-5, 8.32 ERA, 8 dingers allowed) really fell apart. On August 6, hard-luck Mark Clark had his 5th shutout thrown *against* him—including ones by Danny Darwin and Jim Bullinger.

The Mets had fallen by the wayside, and somebody had to take the blame. On August 26, Joe McIlvaine pulled the plug on Dallas Green's tough-love experiment. Green and pitching coach Greg Pavlick were fired and replaced by Bobby Valentine and Bob Apodaca from their Triple-A Norfolk affiliate. Green was fired a week after he criticized Isringhausen and Wilson in the press, saying, "It sounds very harsh and very negative, but what have they done to get here? These guys really don't belong in the big leagues."

September 11-15 (71-91, 25 games back)
The team's season was not salvageable, so Valentine went about getting to know his players, evaluating needs, and auditioning talent. There were some bright spots. Hundley and Johnson set plenty of league and team records in September, Paul Wilson gave the club hope for next year by posting a 1.76 ERA, and they beat Kevin Brown and Greg Maddux on consecutive days.

But Isringhausen remained the poster boy for the Mets' season. Just as the Mets put the finishing touches on a season that saw them below .500 for the 6th consecutive season, Isringhausen blew his arm out and needed surgery that would put him in question for Opening Day '97. Wilson went under the knife in the off-season, making the Mets 3-for-3 with their phenoms.

■ 1997 DIAGNOSIS

Offense
The Mets tied Atlanta for the best batting average in the league, but in runs scored, the only stat that really matters, they ranked 10th. They were too dependent on individual players for the bulk of their offense. Lance Johnson generated all the team speed, Todd Hundley supplied the power, and Gilkey drove in the runs. There's no reason why the offense shouldn't be much better in '97. Carlos Baerga will have a full season to prove himself again, and the right-field situation may have finally been resolved with the arrival of Ochoa (though he was being dangled in trade offers all winter). Alfonzo and Huskey may finally have positions to call their own.

Defense
The Mets led the National League in errors in '96, but Kent is gone and Ordoñez should settle down. Ordoñez is the key to the Mets' infield. He was erratic at times (27 errors), but he was more often spectacular. Ozzie Smith made 25 errors in his first season, and he seemed to do a decent job of adjusting. Ordoñez's range is astounding, and he's in the upper class of the league in turning the double play. Who he is teamed with could change easily as the Mets plan on either Alfonzo playing second and Baerga playing third, or vice versa. Butch Huskey won't be nearly as agile as Brogna around first base. Bernard Gilkey was fantastic last season. His 18 outfield assists led the league, and he made only 6 errors; a 2:1 ratio of outfield assists to errors is a terrific season. Lance Johnson tracked down just about everything hit at him last season, but he did contribute 12 errors to the team's league-leading total. It was a career high, came after 2 seasons in which he made a total of 3 errors, and it should come down considerably in '97. Right field should be significantly improved if Alex Ochoa can hold down the job, with the days of going from first to third on singles against the Mets coming to an end. Hundley is solid behind the plate, but the Mets will need to do a better job of spelling him. He may have to learn how to play third base if he wants to play in 153 games again.

Pitching
Two of the 5 Mets starters were young hurlers who couldn't live up to their billing. Two of the 5 were forgotten hurlers who pitched way above their potential. Pete Harnisch was the only one who did what was expected of him, while Pulsipher did nothing, breaking down before the season even

started. Mark Clark, cast off by the Indians, was the ace of the staff last year but will be hard pressed to repeat his performance. Bobby Jones pitched capably, but that may be the best he can do. Wilson and Isringhausen both had seasons to forget. They're still great-looking prospects with tremendous stuff who could be ready to dominate in '97.

Mets relievers finished with a 3.85 ERA, which was just a bit below the league average. But relievers' ERA lies more than most statistics (see *Lies, Damned Lies, and Statistics* in the Houston Astros section for some others); the Mets ushered in nearly 40% of inherited runners, compared to less than 35% for the league. McIlvaine claims that teams called about every member of their bullpen at some time during '96, but this may say less about the Mets relievers and more about the pathetic state of big-league pitching in the 28-team major leagues. Franco wasn't as good as his numbers looked and he can't keep it up very much longer, even though the Mets are willing to bet $5.5 million that he's got 2 years left in him. Derek Wallace has come from practically nowhere to contend for the job, and will be in a setup role in '97. The Mets need to sort through their right-handers and come up with a supporting cast.

Farm System

Two outfielders stand out in the hitting corps. Terrence Long is one of the system's best hitting prospects but is a few years away. Jay Payton, though hurt for a good part of last year, is farther along and also excites with his bat. Some good arms are scattered throughout the lower ranks of the system as well. But they aren't very experienced and will need time. Arnold Gooch and Nelson Figueroa are foremost in the Mets' plans, though don't expect the Mets to be so aggressive with these young pitchers.

Management and Ownership

Fred Wilpon and Nelson Doubleday have been known to work toward opposing goals at times. A recent example: Wilpon didn't think much of Doubleday's pal Green, when McIlvaine hired him. Doubleday, in turn, opposed bringing in Valentine and preferred that the Mets ask permission to talk with Jim Leyland. They might not get along, but they've always provided the cash to sign free agents and draft picks. The Mets haven't had to slash development costs either because of their patronage. It had to be hard pouring money down the sinkhole for the returns they'd been getting. They will be rewarded pretty soon when their system starts paying off.

General Manager Joe McIlvaine's hands were tied in the Dallas Green firing. McIlvaine had to fend off speculation he would fire Green since the middle of June. He stayed with his manager longer than some GMs would have. He faced a September 1 deadline for extending Green's contract, and then Green shot his mouth off about Izzy and Wilson not belonging in the big leagues, making the decision for him. McIlvaine's free agent signings of Lance Johnson, and his trades for Gilkey and Mark Clark panned out better than he planned. It was the homegrown talent that failed—though he was about the only Mets official not trumpeting the arrival of Wilson, Izzy, and Pulsipher. High expectations are one of the prices the Mets pay for the hefty cash that sports-radio WFAN (all 50,000-watts and 24-hours of it) pays to broadcast their games, hype their prospects, and get their managers fired. Perhaps it's no coincidence that Dwight Gooden and Ron Darling joined the rotation in 1984, at 19 and 23, and thrived—3 years *before* sports-radio existed.

Bobby Valentine had managed Norfolk for 2½ seasons (broken up by a stint in Japan) before being named manager of the Mets. He's had a chance to see most of their prospects develop, so they went with the devil they knew. He's had to live down a reputation in baseball for being a know-it-all. One American League manager even said that he would burn out his pitching staff to beat Valentine's Rangers. But he brings to the job a certain loyalty to the players that was sorely needed. When asked about his philosophy of handling players, he very artfully said, "When somebody has the same uniform on I have, I believe in him."

. . . and whatnot: 1968 and the "E" Word

As spring training approached last season, all attention on the Mets was focused on the 3 top young power pitchers from the minors who were supposed to carry the team into contention. Dallas Green said he expected 15 wins from Isringhausen

and that Pulsipher would be "right there." Meanwhile, *Baseball America* was saying that Wilson could be the "next Roger Clemens."

Paul Wilson, Jason Isringhausen, and Bill Pulsipher were considered by many Mets fans as the reincarnations of Tom Seaver, Jerry Koosman and Nolan Ryan. Three young pitchers who had come up from the minors in 1968 and led the Mets to a division title and a World Series victory the very next season.

It's easy to see the similarities. Isringhausen was Seaver—the most developed of the trio who, like Seaver, had tasted success the previous season. Pulsipher was Koosman—lefties who had debuted the previous season as well, only not with the same amount of visibility. And finally, Wilson was Ryan—the young stud who threw gas.

Some would argue that the assessment of the youngsters was fair, based on the talent level they displayed. After all, Wilson and Pulsipher had wicked mid-90s fastballs, and Isringhausen was known for his knee-buckling curve. And it's not like they hadn't all been consistently successful in their careers before. But to get an idea of just what they were up against, here's what Seaver, Koosman, and Ryan did in 1968.

Pitcher	W	L	ERA	IP	H	BB	SO
Seaver	16	12	2.20	278	224	48	205
Koosman	19	12	2.08	264	221	69	178
Ryan	6	9	3.09	134	93	75	133

The numbers Isringhausen, Pulsipher, and Wilson put up in '95 didn't compare to these incredible stats, even when you realize that the late '60s were the height of the greatest pitchers' era in baseball history. Did anybody really expect the trio to dominate the way Seaver, Koosman, and Ryan did? Is it any wonder they failed to meet expectations? Mets fans are spoiled when it comes to pitching. More than a few had penciled in the following for Wilson, Pulsipher, and Isringhausen in '96:

Pitcher	W	L	ERA	IP	H	BB	SO
Isringhausen	25	7	2.21	273	202	82	208
Pulsipher	17	9	2.28	241	187	68	180
Wilson	13	12	3.42	234	192	81	154

(Wilson has been changed from Ryan to Gary Gentry to make the fantasy all the more compelling.)

Too bad the trio of young arms didn't come through. As in '69, the Braves and Orioles were waiting in the postseason—and a Subway Series could have decided, once and for all, whose fans—Yankees or Mets—could be more fat, drunk, and stupid during lopsided losses.

JUAN ACEVEDO — *SLEEPER*

SP • BR • TR • 6'2 • 220 • 26 • COL92/14

	G	GS	IP	H	HR	BB	SO	W	L	S	ERA	K/BB	K9	HW9
AAA	19	19	103	116	15	53	83	4	8	0	5.96	1.6	7.3	14.82

Acevedo was the price the Rockies had to pay for the privilege of having Bret Saberhagen cash checks and watch game shows. Acevedo brought expectations with him, but his stock underwent a major market correction in '96. He was considered one of the best pitching prospects in the system and a candidate for a rotation job in the spring, but when Dallas Green got a chance to see him in an April exhibition game against the Mets he questioned his mental makeup and his stuff, saying, "He's not ready to pitch in the big leagues." Sounds familiar, doesn't it? Acevedo strained a hamstring and ended up in the minors.

He throws a couple of fastballs in the 90-mph range, a 2-seamer and a 4-seamer. He also has a good slider and a split-finger that serves as his out pitch. Pulsipher and Isringhausen are questionable for the start of the season, and Acevedo might again receive serious consideration for a job. He'll have a better chance this year now that Green is out of the picture. A switch to the bullpen might also be an option. ■

EDGARDO ALFONZO — *YOUNG GUN*

2B-3B-SS • BR • TR • 5'11 • 185 • 23 • NYN91

	AB	R	H	2B	3B	HR	RBI	BB	SO	SB	CS	BA	OB	SA
NYN95	335	26	93	13	5	4	41	12	37	1	1	.278	.301	.382
NYN96	368	36	96	15	2	4	40	25	56	2	0	.261	.304	.345

Alfonzo kicked butt for 4 seasons in the minor leagues before joining the big-league roster in '95. He hasn't set the world on fire in his 2 seasons of part-time play with the Mets, but he hasn't been overmatched either. In fact, his continuing development as a hitter was one of the main reasons McIlvaine felt he could part with José Vizcaino in

the deal for Baerga. He wanted badly to find Alfonzo a regular spot in the lineup, and second base seemed a natural fit.

Within the organization, Alfonzo is considered a coach's dream. He has solid tools across the board, including good power potential for a middle infielder, and a fantastic attitude. And as he gets older (remember, he's only 23) he should be able to hit .300 regularly. ■

CARLOS BAERGA

2B • BR • TR • 5'11 • 200 • 28 • SD85

	AB	R	H	2B	3B	HR	RBI	BB	SO	SB	CS	BA	OB	SA
CLE94	442	81	139	32	2	19	80	10	45	8	2	.314	.333	.525
CLE95	557	87	175	28	2	15	90	35	31	11	2	.314	.355	.452
CLE/NYN96	507	59	129	28	0	12	66	21	27	1	1	.254	.293	.381
CAREER	3692	550	1100	193	15	105	571	199	378	48	15	.298	.338	.444

The trade of Baerga crushed many a hard-core Indian fan and confused some analysts. Why would the Indians mess with the chemistry of the team in midseason by trading their clubhouse leader? Aside from the fact that he just wasn't hitting, GM John Hart felt Baerga hadn't worked hard enough to rid himself of the extra weight he lugged into spring training. He felt Baerga's defensive lapses in '96 were partly due to the extra tonnage and ordered him to participate in postgame workouts. The fact that Baerga was spotted chatting on his cellular phone during batting practice probably didn't help his cause, either. In fact, some believed it had been surgically attached to his left ear. Carlos just wore out his welcome in Cleveland.

Baerga, however, offered his own explanation of the trade a few days later. When the Indians were still in the hunt for Roberto Alomar's services in the off-season they brought up the idea of moving Baerga to third base. Baerga refused. "Ever since then, all I've heard is that I'm overweight," he said. Hart responded in his own defense, "This was strictly a baseball deal. We felt we were limited at second base." They were limited by a high-priced prima donna who wouldn't do the extra work required to shed some extra pounds to help get his team to another World Series. Can't blame Baerga for being confused—he's been known to stare lovingly at his own reflection, so he obviously likes what he sees.

His days as a second baseman may be over, but his days as a leader and an All-Star may be, too. That cellular phone came with him to Shea, and he didn't seem all that broken up about sitting out September with an abdominal strain. The Mets think this deal is Keith Hernandez all over again. More likely, it's George Foster all over again. ■

RICO BROGNA

1B • BL • TL • 6'2 • 200 • 26 • DET88/1

	AB	R	H	2B	3B	HR	RBI	BB	SO	SB	CS	BA	OB	SA
NYN94	131	16	46	11	2	7	20	6	29	1	0	.351	.380	.626
NYN95	495	72	143	27	2	22	76	39	111	0	0	.289	.342	.485
NYN96	188	18	48	10	1	7	30	19	50	0	0	.255	.318	.431
CAREER	840	109	242	49	5	37	129	67	195	1	0	.288	.340	.490

Brogna had major problems with a partial tear in his shoulder early in the season and eventually required season-ending surgery to repair it. The fact that he was hurt explains his low batting average. But there's more to it.

Brogna's .298 career average coming into the '96 season was clearly a misleading stat. He's a very aggressive hitter with the strikeout ratios to match, and quite frankly, pitchers have only just begun to exploit that weakness. He struck out once every 3.8 at-bats last season. Not exactly Tony Gwynn territory.

It's not that Brogna doesn't have attractive skills. His power alone makes him a worthwhile player to have on the roster. He's also an excellent fielder. But he can't hit left-handers, and he swings as freely as Hef in the '70s. Because of this, he probably won't hit better than .280. He'll drive in a healthy amount of runs, but his career batting average is due for a fall. Fortunately for him, the Phillies didn't trade five players to get him. ■

PAUL BYRD

RP • BR • TR • 6'1 • 185 • 26 • CLE91/4

	G	GS	IP	H	HR	BB	K	W	L	S	ERA	K/BB	K9	HW9
NYN95	17	0	22	18	1	7	26	2	0	0	2.05	3.7	10.6	10.23
NYN96	38	0	46	48	7	21	31	1	2	0	4.24	1.5	6.1	13.48

Byrd went on the DL at the beginning of the season with a bulging disc in his back and was out until early June. He was largely ineffective his first month back. He rebounded with a 3.11 ERA in July and August, but wore out again in September. Byrd throws hard and throws strikes, but he didn't have the repertoire to make a go of it as a starter when he was in the Indians system. The Mets switched him to the bullpen in '95, and he thrived. The Braves traded Greg McMichael for him and are counting on him to rebound from his back woes in '97. If he can, he'll build a solid career in middle relief. ■

MARK CLARK

SP • BR • TR • 6'5 • 225 • 28 • SL88/11

	G	GS	IP	H	HR	BB	K	W	L	S	ERA	K/BB	K9	HW9
CLE94	20	20	127	133	14	40	60	11	3	0	3.82	1.5	4.3	12.26
CLE95	22	21	124	143	13	42	68	9	7	0	5.27	1.6	4.9	13.43
NYN96	32	32	212	217	20	48	142	14	11	0	3.43	3.0	6.0	11.25
CAREER	127	110	709	746	80	202	384	45	37	0	4.14	1.9	4.9	12.03

The Mets traded Ryan Thompson and Reid Cornelius to Cleveland for Clark on the eve of opening day. It seems that with the signing of Jack McDowell the Indians felt they didn't need the services of an erratic pitcher who had tantalized with his potential in '94, then let them down big-time in '95. Did the Indians get hosed on this trade? Just inflicting Thompson on themselves is bad enough, but losing a quality pitcher in the process just makes it worse.

Clark became the ace of the Mets' staff by default last season. He led the team in victories and ERA when everyone expected him to be pitching in Triple-A. He's always had good control (and last season it was exquisite), but 1996 was a banner year for him in strikeouts. One of the reasons for his improvement is that Clark actually threw harder with New York than he did with the Indians. His sinking fastball, which used to top out in the mid-to-upper 80s, registered as high as 91 mph last season. He mixes in a slider, a split-finger and a changeup to keep hitters off balance.

The Mets were very pleased with Clark's performance last season. With two of their three young studs questionable for the start of the 1997 season, they are thankful to have the depth. But don't expect him to be the ace of the staff again this year, as he may find it too difficult to maintain his velocity and duplicate his strikeout performance. ■

JERRY DIPOTO

RP • BR • TR • 6'2 • 200 • 28 • CLE89/2

	G	GS	IP	H	HR	BB	K	W	L	S	ERA	K/BB	K9	HW9
CLE94	7	0	15	26	1	10	9	0	0	0	8.04	.9	5.4	21.51
NYN95	58	0	78	77	2	29	49	4	6	2	3.78	1.7	5.7	12.23
NYN96	57	0	77	91	5	45	52	7	2	0	4.19	1.2	6.1	15.89
CAREER	168	0	227	251	8	114	151	15	12	13	3.88	1.3	6.0	14.47

DiPoto came back from having a cancerous thyroid gland removed in March 1994 and has made 115 appearances the past 2 seasons. That says a lot about his resiliency. But don't be fooled by his 7-2 record. He wouldn't have won so many games if the Mets had not scored a whopping 7.9 runs per 9 innings while he was in the ball game. After all, we're talking about a pitcher who allowed a .298 average and let the opposition on base to the tune of almost 16 baserunners per 9 innings. DiPoto got kicked around like Bob Packwood at a NOW rally. ■

ALVARO ESPINOZA

UT • BR • TR • 6'0 • 170 • 35 • HOU78

	AB	R	H	2B	3B	HR	RBI	BB	SO	SB	CS	BA	OB	SA
CLE94	231	27	55	13	0	1	19	6	33	1	3	.238	.258	.307
CLE95	143	15	36	4	0	2	17	2	16	0	2	.252	.264	.322
CLE/NYN96	246	31	66	11	4	8	27	10	37	1	3	.268	.303	.443
CAREER	2406	249	617	104	9	22	194	74	312	12	18	.256	.281	.335

In 112 A.L. at-bats, Espinoza hit .223 and slugged .401. But after the Mets acquired him in the Baerga deal, he went nuts, hitting .306 and slugging .478 in 134 N.L. at-bats. Nobody should expect Espinoza to repeat his offensive performance of '96. He'll still be used as a defensive replacement, but he'll see a lot more breaking balls from now on. The lumber he carried last year will turn back into plywood at midnight.

After all, he fits in nicely with the last couple of shortstops to play for both the Mets and Yankees: Kevin Elster and Rafael Santana. ■

CARL EVERETT

OF • BB • TR • 6′0 • 190 • 26 • NYA90/1

	AB	R	H	2B	3B	HR	RBI	BB	SO	SB	CS	BA	OB	SA
FLA94	51	7	11	1	0	2	6	3	15	4	0	.216	.259	.353
NYN95	289	48	75	13	1	12	54	39	67	2	5	.260	.352	.436
NYN96	192	29	46	8	1	1	16	21	53	6	0	.240	.326	.307
CAREER	551	84	134	22	2	15	76	64	144	13	5	.243	.328	.372

Once considered a power/speed threat, Everett was given yet another chance to win the right field job early in the season as the Mets hoped his athleticism would take over. But he failed to hit after returning from a strained quadriceps in April and fell out of favor with the front office. Both Green and McIlvaine complained about his lack of intensity, and the Mets started shopping him around the league. They found no takers. When asked if a rare start for Everett in late May was meant to entice a trade, Green said, "You don't showcase a .190 hitter."

Everett isn't too old to salvage his career, but he'll have to do so with another organization. His future with the Mets is as precarious as Nate Newton on the high wire. Alex Ochoa impressed the team with his performance last season and will get the outfield job the Mets envisioned Everett filling. Everett, if he's still around, will ride the pine behind him. If there's any justice, the Blue Jays will end up with him. They've scattered these high-potential, low-result athletes all over the big leagues. It's time they get in on the fun of living with one. ■

NELSON FIGUEROA — SOLID PROSPECT

SP • BB • TR • 6′1 • 165 • 22 • NYN95/30

	G	GS	IP	H	HR	BB	SO	W	L	S	ERA	K/BB	K9	HW9
A	26	25	185	119	10	58	200	14	7	0	2.04	3.4	9.7	8.60

Figueroa dominated the Sally League, striking out 200 batters and winning the league's Pitcher of the Year award. He began the season with a 29-inning scoreless streak that included a 2-hitter and a 4-hitter. Figueroa throws a couple of fastballs (a 2-seamer and a 4-seamer), a curve, a slider, and a nasty split-finger that serves as his out pitch. He's been throwing the splitter since high school. He doesn't throw any of his pitches very hard (which is why he went so deep in the draft) but is intelligent and adept at changing speeds. He's also quite durable. Figueroa will move quickly if given the chance. ■

JOHN FRANCO — HEADED FOR A FALL

CL • BL • TL • 5′10 • 180 • 36 • LA81/6

	G	GS	IP	H	HR	BB	K	W	L	S	ERA	K/BB	K9	HW9
NYN94	47	0	50	47	2	19	42	1	4	30	2.70	2.2	7.6	11.88
NYN95	48	0	51	48	4	17	41	5	3	29	2.44	2.4	7.2	11.47
NYN96	51	0	54	54	2	21	48	4	3	28	1.83	2.3	8.0	12.50
CAREER	712	0	876	806	48	336	648	72	57	323	2.57	1.9	6.7	11.73

The 1996 season was a milestone for Franco. On April 29 he recorded his 300th save, becoming the only left-hander to reach that total. He topped it off by recording his lowest ERA since 1992. In between, there were more than a few ugly moments. He blew 8 saves, allowed 60% of inherited runners to score, and was hit for a nearly .300 average by righties.

Franco is the unofficial team captain of the Mets. He is unafraid to call a team meeting, and he can get away with ripping his teammates in the press. The Mets needed Franco around for at least another season until Derek Wallace gets his feet wet, but Franco wouldn't come back for fewer than 2 years. They'll pay him nearly $6 million, though he's a lot closer to done than his ERA indicates. ■

MIKE GARDINER

SP • BB • TR • 6′0 • 200 • 31 • SEA87/18

	G	GS	IP	H	HR	BB	SO	W	L	S	ERA	K/BB	K9	HW9
AAA	24	24	146	125	18	38	125	13	3	0	3.21	3.3	7.7	10.05

Gardiner's fastball is nothing special, but he has a nasty split-finger pitch that he used to strike out 125 Triple-A hitters. International League managers said he had the best control in that league in '96. But there are a couple of things to consider with Gardiner. First, he's 31 years old. Second, he bombed out in Detroit's bullpen in '95, with an ERA higher than Ben Blomdahl, Pat Ahearne, and C. J Nitkowski. ■

BERNARD GILKEY

LF • BR • TR • 6′0 • 170 • 30 • SL84

	AB	R	H	2B	3B	HR	RBI	BB	SO	SB	CS	BA	OB	SA
SL94	380	52	96	22	1	6	45	39	65	15	8	.253	.336	.363
SL95	480	73	143	33	4	17	69	42	70	12	6	.298	.358	.490
NYN96	571	108	181	44	3	30	117	73	125	17	9	.317	.393	.562
CAREER	2704	427	783	170	21	82	367	296	416	97	54	.290	.362	.459

Gilkey has always hit for decent average, so last season's batting average shouldn't come as much of a surprise. But the power and the run production . . . well, Gilkey will probably be considered the poster boy for the juiced ball. After never hitting more than 17 homers in his career, he hit 30 last season, becoming the offensive force behind the Mets—even more so than Hundley. What was this all about? Well, the run production can be explained by the presence of Lance Johnson at the top of the order. But the dingers? His home yard when he was with the Cardinals, Busch Stadium, is known for deflating home-run totals, while Shea is neutral. With the Cardinals, Gilkey was always miscast as a top-of-the-order hitter. When he came to the Mets, they saw that he hit .300 with runners in scoring position the past 5 seasons and made him a no. 3 hitter. Besides, they reasoned, with more protection behind him, Gilkey could afford to swing away. Last season Gilkey hit an incredible .406 with runners in scoring position. Still those two factors may not be enough to explain a 72-point jump in his slugging average. That's where the juiced-ball factor (or whatever you want to call it) comes in. In a normal offensive season, Gilkey might have hit 18 to 22 homers batting in the 3rd spot. But 1996 was far from normal. Last season was a career year for Gilkey, so look for his performance to decline.

The possibility of '96 being a career year didn't keep the Mets from locking him in for 4 years for $20 million, though they generally frown on deals longer than 3 years. That's what having Bobby Bonilla offering to show reporters The Bronx while Bret Saberhagen sprays them with bleach will do. Todd Hundley becomes a free agent after the '97 season and had stated that his decision on whether to stay would depend on what the Mets do with Gilkey. ■

ARNOLD GOOCH

SOLID PROSPECT

SP • BR • TR • 6′2 • 195 • 20 • COL94/6

	G	GS	IP	H	HR	BB	SO	W	L	S	ERA	K/BB	K9	HW9
A+	26	26	168	131	7	51	141	12	12	0	2.58	2.8	7.6	9.77

Acquired in the Saberhagen trade with the Rockies, Gooch is much better than his 12-12 record suggests. He carves up hitters with a couple of pitches: an upper-80s fastball that has a sinking motion, and a very effective curve. He's still working on a change-up, but he's done just fine so far without it. His low hit totals are indicative of just how good his stuff is. Last year, he was the youngest player in the Florida State League All-Star game, and his ERA ranked 3rd overall. He's an excellent-looking pitcher and McIlvaine loves him, so expect to see him in the big leagues soon. Besides, with a name like that, he's got to make it. But if Chris Berman dubs him Arnold "Gooch-ie Gooch-ie Goo," he should be led to the gallows. ■

JASON HARDTKE

2B • BB • TR • 5′10 • 175 • 25

	AB	R	H	2B	3B	HR	RBI	BB	SO	SB	CS	BA	OB	SA
NYN96	57	3	11	5	0	0	6	2	12	0	0	.193	.233	.281

He bounced from the Indians to the Padres and finally to the Mets in his 6-year minor-league career. That's not exactly the signs of a super prospect, but Hardtke's got a lot going for him. He's a switch-hitter with line-drive power and a good eye at the plate. He also plays solid defense. Like Wally Joyner, he plays better than he looks. Knee injuries have hindered him the past couple of seasons. Last year it was a strained medial collateral ligament that kept him out about a month. It's too bad, though. Hardtke could be a good utility player in the big leagues, but his injury history makes it a long shot that he will win a starting job. ■

PETE HARNISCH

SP • BB • TR • 6′1 • 195 • 30 • BAL87/3

	G	GS	IP	H	HR	BB	K	W	L	S	ERA	K/BB	K9	HW9
HOU94	17	17	95	100	13	39	62	8	5	0	5.40	1.6	5.9	13.17
NYN95	18	18	110	111	13	24	82	2	8	0	3.68	3.4	6.7	11.05
NYN96	31	31	194	195	30	61	114	8	12	0	4.21	1.9	5.3	11.87
CAREER	217	216	1345	1227	136	509	981	71	75	0	3.79	1.9	6.6	11.62

Harnisch missed the first couple of weeks of the season after surgery to repair torn cartilage in his right shoulder. His fastball didn't return to the upper

80s until July. When it did, Harnisch's performances improved greatly, but his team gave him little support. In August and September Harnisch had a 3.54 ERA in 11 starts but had a 2-5 record.

The shoulder problems he experienced the past couple of years have robbed him of his once-formidable fastball. But last season was a promising start in his transition from thrower to pitcher. As his strikeouts have dropped, so have his walks. Harnisch isn't the intimidator he used to be, but his competitiveness is unmatched. His bulldog mentality makes him think he can throw his fastball by anybody in the league. However, those 30 home runs he gave up last year should be enough to convince him that his heater doesn't smoke as it used to. Until he starts nibbling the corners and changing speeds a lot more, Harnisch's pitches will leave more vapor trails over Shea Stadium than the jets leaving LaGuardia. ■

DOUG HENRY

RP • BR • TR • 6'4 • 185 • 33 • MIL85/8

	G	GS	IP	H	HR	BB	K	W	L	S	ERA	K/BB	K9	HW9
MIL94	25	0	31	32	7	23	20	2	3	0	4.60	.9	5.8	15.95
NYN95	51	0	67	48	7	25	62	3	6	4	2.96	2.5	8.3	9.31
NYN96	58	0	75	82	7	36	58	2	8	9	4.68	1.6	7.0	14.16
CAREER	288	0	329	309	35	147	258	14	26	74	3.94	1.8	7.1	12.47

Henry was never considered much of a pitcher when he was with the Brewers, even when he was their default closer in '92. Most people wrote him off with a "if he's not a closer, he's nothing" attitude. A trade to the Mets in '94 gave him a chance to pitch without the specter of failed expectations hanging over him. He emerged as a solid setup man in '95, and he led the team in appearances in '96 despite getting into only 5 games in September. And regardless of what his ERA says, Henry was relatively effective. The difference between Henry's 4.68 ERA and a 3.71 ERA is 4.2 innings in September. He got crushed for 12 hits and 10 runs in those fateful innings. Take those stats out of his season totals and what you have is a decent journeyman reliever who was ridden hard and often by Dallas Green and who got a well-deserved vacation once Valentine and Apodaca arrived. ■

TODD HUNDLEY

NL ELITE

C • BB • TR • 5'11 • 170 • 27 • NYN87/2

	AB	R	H	2B	3B	HR	RBI	BB	SO	SB	CS	BA	OB	SA
NYN94	291	45	69	10	1	16	42	25	73	2	1	.237	.303	.443
NYN95	275	39	77	11	0	15	51	42	64	1	0	.280	.382	.484
NYN96	540	85	140	32	1	41	112	79	146	1	3	.259	.356	.550
CAREER	2008	254	478	93	5	91	299	200	453	8	5	.238	.311	.425

Nobody expected Hundley to break Roy Campanella's home-run record for catchers, but there were indications that he was poised for a breakthrough year.

Consider that Hundley probably would have hit 30 homers with 100 RBI in '95 if he hadn't gone down with a badly sprained left wrist that July. He had off-season surgery to correct the problem, but one of the unforeseen benefits was that it forced him to build up the muscles protecting his wrist. Another factor was a change Hundley made in his batting stance. Once a dead-pull hitter with an open stance, Hundley closed it off quite a bit and started hitting to all fields.

Hundley's biggest weakness remains his inability to hit lefties. Last season he hit just .196 from the right side of the plate. Batting left-handed, though, he hit 35 homers and had a .620 slugging percentage. Hundley shouldn't be a platoon player, regardless of his lefty/righty splits. He is considered one of the better defensive catchers in baseball because of his work with the pitchers and his ability to block those 58-foot sliders and forkballs.

He could use some time off, however. Hundley went into the tank after he hit his 41st dinger—going 6-41 with 2 RBI, 3 extra-base hits, and 13 strikeouts—so he was either out of gas or celebrating too much. For his sake, the hope is it's the former. ■

BUTCH HUSKEY

1B-OF • BR • TR • 6'3 • 245 • 25 • NYN89/7

	AB	R	H	2B	3B	HR	RBI	BB	SO	SB	CS	BA	OB	SA
NYN95	90	8	17	1	0	3	11	10	16	1	0	.189	.267	.300
NYN96	414	43	115	16	2	15	60	27	78	1	2	.278	.319	.435

Huskey wowed the front office at the onset with his power, setting a Mets spring training record with 9 home runs. But when the bell rang, he stayed in his corner. Things went downhill quickly and he had to fight off Carl Everett, Chris Jones, and Kevin Roberson for the starting right fielder's job. Green dropped him into the 7th spot in the batting order in early May, and by June the Mets were looking to trade Huskey because he was out of options and couldn't be demoted to Triple-A without exposing him to waivers.

Given a chance at first base when Brogna went down, Huskey hit .339 with 7 homers and 20 RBI in July. He had a knee injury that forced him to miss August, but he returned in September and slugged .492. Huskey has made it hard for the Mets to get rid of him. The flashes of power he showed them is reminiscent of what Carlos Delgado did with the Blue Jays in '95. ▪

JASON ISRINGHAUSEN — *YOUNG GUN*

SP • BR • TR • 6'3 • 195 • 24 • NYN91/46

	G	GS	IP	H	HR	BB	K	W	L	S	ERA	K/BB	K9	HW9
NYN95	14	14	93	88	6	31	55	9	2	0	2.81	1.8	5.3	11.52
NYN96	27	27	171	190	13	73	114	6	14	0	4.77	1.6	6.0	13.84

Dallas Green predicted 15 wins for Isringhausen. Then Green and the rest of the front office ripped him in the press for his mental approach when he failed to meet their expectations. Izzy certainly wasn't helping his case any acting like he was vegging out in front of MTV most of the season. When Harnisch starting pitching well again in July, Green told Isringhausen to pay close attention to the veteran's starts so that he could learn how he sets up his fastball. Later, when Isringhausen was asked what he'd learned, he couldn't come up with anything. He then came back after his July 24 start in Colorado, in which he gave up 14 hits and 6 runs in 6 innings, and said he thought he pitched well.

Green got himself fired when he told the press that Isringhausen didn't belong in the big leagues—but the situation should never have been allowed to develop. The Mets should have done the right thing and quietly sent their demoralized young pitcher back to Norfolk in June. And the story doesn't exactly have a happy ending—for now. In late September Isringhausen was diagnosed with a torn labrum in his shoulder and bone chips in his elbow. He underwent 2 arthroscopic procedures to correct the problems, and a long off-season of rehab awaits. Apparently he pitched with pain for a good chunk of the season and just didn't tell the trainers—another youthful mistake he has to pay a stiff price for. Or another young pitcher wanting to show Dallas Green he was a man.

Isringhausen started throwing a cut fastball last season, which will make his other pitches that much more effective. He's got fantastic stuff when he's healthy. And if he can straighten out his head, he could be a very good major-league pitcher. But he may never be what the Mets initially expected. Having produced Tom Seaver, Nolan Ryan, and Dwight Gooden, this organization and its fans are spoiled. ▪

LANCE JOHNSON — *CONSISTENT STAR*

CF • BL • TL • 5'10 • 160 • 33 • SL84/6

	AB	R	H	2B	3B	HR	RBI	BB	SO	SB	CS	BA	OB	SA
CHA94	412	56	114	11	14	3	54	26	23	26	6	.277	.321	.393
CHA95	607	98	186	18	12	10	57	32	31	40	6	.306	.341	.425
NYN96	682	117	227	31	21	9	69	33	40	50	12	.333	.362	.479
CAREER	4300	604	1258	139	99	26	403	247	304	282	84	.293	.330	.389

His 1995 season was supposed to be the career one for Lance Johnson. After all, 1996 was a new league, he was 32, and he was in the first year of his contract, not the last. But of all the unexpected hitting performances turned in by Mets hitters, Johnson's may well be the most outstanding. Already a very consistent hitter when he came over from the White Sox, Johnson torqued it up with his best season ever in batting average and on-base average. He also bested his career slugging average by more than 100

points. But a couple of accomplishments really make his season stand out. After leading the American League 4 of the previous 5 years in triples, Johnson had 21 last season, the highest total in the N.L. since 1930. He also became the first player ever to lead both leagues in hits over a season. And for good measure, he did it in consecutive seasons.

Bobby Valentine got folks all worked up by hitting Johnson in the third spot in the lineup for 17 September at-bats. But it was much ado about nothing. Johnson is the Mets' leadoff hitter because there's no one else in the system, or possibly in baseball, who puts the ball in play more often. Suprisingly, the front office threw $10 million at him to extend his contract for 2 years through 1999. ■

BOBBY JONES

SP • BR • TR • 6'4 • 210 • 27 • NYN91/2

	G	GS	IP	H	HR	BB	K	W	L	S	ERA	K/BB	K9	HW9
NYN94	24	24	160	157	10	56	80	12	7	0	3.15	1.4	4.5	11.98
NYN95	30	30	195	209	20	53	127	10	10	0	4.19	2.4	5.9	12.09
NYN96	31	31	195	219	26	46	116	12	8	0	4.42	2.5	5.4	12.23
CAREER	94	94	612	646	62	177	358	36	29	0	3.94	2.0	5.3	12.10

Jones doesn't throw very hard at all. He's a finesse pitcher who relies on changing speeds with a varied repertoire to be successful. His durability the past couple of seasons has been a refreshing change of pace for Mets fans, but he can't continue to survive allowing as many homers as he does.

The 1996 season was the second consecutive one of decline for Jones, yet he managed to hold onto his rotation job because he was able to stay healthy and out of the spotlight. Next season he won't have the same luxury. The Mets will be counting on him to improve on his mediocre numbers. If he can't, there's always another phenom in the minors to hype, promote, and demoralize. ■

TERRENCE LONG

SLEEPER

OF • BL • TL • 6'1 • 180 • 21 • NYN94/2

	AB	R	H	2B	3B	HR	RBI	BB	SO	SB	CS	BA	OB	SA
A	473	66	136	26	9	12	78	36	120	32	7	.288	.342	.457

He's a raw athlete with great ability. A 21-year-old, left-handed hitter, he has a sweet—but long—swing that could generate a .300 average and 20 homers in the majors some day. He also has great speed. Fans in Binghamton and Norfolk should be anxiously waiting for his arrival in the very near future. ■

TERRELL LOWERY

SLEEPER

OF • BR • TR • 6'3 • 175 • 26 • TEX91/2

	AB	R	H	2B	3B	HR	RBI	BB	SO	SB	CS	BA	OB	SA
AAA	193	25	45	7	2	4	21	22	44	6	3	.233	.312	.352

The Mets traded Damon Buford to the Rangers for Lowery in January '96. The deal was initially prompted because the organization thought it needed a replacement for Lance Johnson after the '97 season. Lowery, though not as advanced as Buford, has a higher ceiling. He was out of action most of the '95 season with an Achilles tendon injury, but he made up for lost time last year. He hit well with Binghamton but wasn't quite ready for Norfolk. Now that Johnson's been extended through 1999, Lowery will have to be lucky to find a position with the Mets. ■

BRENT MAYNE

C • BL • TR • 6'1 • 195 • 28 • KC89/1

	AB	R	H	2B	3B	HR	RBI	BB	SO	SB	CS	BA	OB	SA
KC94	144	19	37	5	1	2	20	14	27	1	0	.257	.323	.347
KC95	307	23	77	18	1	1	27	25	41	0	1	.251	.313	.326
NYN96	99	9	26	6	0	1	6	12	22	0	1	.263	.342	.354
CAREER	1212	113	301	56	3	9	125	106	192	6	13	.248	.309	.322

Mayne was the 13th pick in the '89 draft—taken ahead of Mo Vaughn, Tim Salmon, Jim Thome, Marty Cordova, Chuck Knoblauch, John Olerud, Ryan Klesko, Jeff Bagwell, Shane Reynolds, Denny Neagle, and Trevor Hoffman. The New York Jets have had better drafts. Mayne's bat never developed and his arm is weak. Other than those two minor details, he's fine. Managers like him because of his hard-nosed style. He also works well with pitchers and is adept at handling balls in the dirt. He had surgery after the season to remove a bone spur in his shoulder, so his throwing should improve in '97. No spurs found in his bat, unfortunately. ■

ETHAN MCENTIRE

SP • BL • TL • 6'1 • 195 • 21 • NYN93/12

	G	GS	IP	H	HR	BB	SO	W	L	S	ERA	K/BB	K9	HW9
A	27	27	174	123	10	61	190	9	6	0	2.22	3.1	9.8	9.52

McEntire is a left-handed pitcher who helped the Columbia pitching staff become the most dominating in the league. As his hits allowed and strikeouts suggest, he has excellent stuff. As his walks suggest, he can't always control it. He got a lot of attention in '96, but he isn't considered as advanced as someone such as Nelson Figueroa. ■

DAVE MLICKI

RP • BR • TR • 6'4 • 190 • 28 • CLE17/90

	G	GS	IP	H	HR	BB	K	W	L	S	ERA	K/BB	K9	HW9
NYN95	29	25	160	160	23	54	123	9	7	0	4.26	2.3	6.9	12.04
NYN96	51	2	90	95	9	33	83	6	7	1	3.30	2.5	8.3	12.80
CAREER	87	34	285	289	37	109	229	15	16	1	3.98	2.1	7.2	12.57

Mlicki was poised to win a rotation spot with the Indians, but shoulder surgery sidelined him for the '94 season. He did well in the Mets rotation in '95, but stamina was a concern. He was moved to the bullpen, where he would be able to maintain his low-90s fastball better. He responded with a fine season in which he improved his control and had an ERA about a quarter of a run better than that for a league-average reliever. But the most significant contribution he made to the Mets bullpen was that he allowed just 5 of the 27 runners he inherited to score. Mlicki was one of the few bright spots in the Mets bullpen last year and should be solid again in '97. ■

ALEX OCHOA

YOUNG GUN

RF • BR • TR • 6'0 • 185 • 25 • BAL91/3

	AB	R	H	2B	3B	HR	RBI	BB	SO	SB	CS	BA	OB	SA
NYN95	37	7	11	1	0	0	0	2	10	1	0	.297	.333	.324
NYN96	282	37	83	19	3	4	33	17	30	4	3	.294	.336	.426

For some reason, the Mets downplayed Ochoa's talent midway through the season, admitting that they had overestimated his potential and that he wasn't a Grade-A prospect. It could be that the Mets were finally realizing that their practice of hyping their prospects was coming back to haunt them. But after downgrading him publicly, they offered him around in trades during the off-season. McIlvaine apparently got his cue cards reversed.

By the time the Mets finally called up Ochoa in June, he was leading the International League in hitting. In fact, in a midseason poll, Ochoa was named the best batting prospect in the league. The league's coaches also said he had the best arm there. Of course they did—no one in the *majors* has a better one. Ochoa won the Mets starting right-field job last season with his performance, both in the minors and in the majors. He proved himself as a run producer in Norfolk. And immediately following his promotion to New York, he hit .400 in his first 7 games, with 4 doubles and 6 RBI. Then, on July 3, he celebrated his independence from Triple-A early by becoming the first Mets player to hit for the cycle since Kevin McReynolds in 1992. ■

REY ORDOÑEZ

YOUNG GUN

SS • BR • TR • 5'9 • 160 • 25 • NYN93

	AB	R	H	2B	3B	HR	RBI	BB	SO	SB	CS	BA	OB	SA
NYN96	502	51	129	12	4	1	30	22	53	1	3	.257	.289	.303

Ordoñez defected from Cuba in 1993 by jumping over the outfield fence during the World University Games in Buffalo. He's scaled the Mets organizational depth chart just as quickly, landing the starting shortstop job last season. The fielding prowess everyone expected was there in abundance. Ordoñez displayed fantastic range, while his glove work would make an L.A. crime-scene expert proud. But he doesn't have the plant-and-throw ability of more experienced fielders such as Gagne and Larkin yet, so he was responsible for an inordinate amount of errors last season. However, that's about the only thing that's keeping him from winning the Gold Glove. Ordoñez has an accurate arm and very smooth footwork around the bag. He led the league in double plays turned last season, and odds are he can do it again. The Mets will be patient with his bat. He's merely a singles hitter. But it's rare that a shortstop of his caliber comes along so they won't mind hiding his bat in the bottom of the order. ■

JAY PAYTON — SOLID PROSPECT

OF • BR • TR • 5'10 • 190 • 24 • NYN94/3

	AB	R	H	2B	3B	HR	RBI	BB	SO	SB	CS	BA	OB	SA
AAA	153	30	47	6	3	6	26	11	25	10	1	.307	.363	.503

He was considered one of the top hitting prospects in the organization until he went down with an elbow injury in '95. He had Tommy John surgery to replace an elbow tendon in September of that year but was able to come back and log 153 at-bats as a DH. He's got good speed, a line-drive swing, and doesn't strike out very often. Managers like him because he's a really hard worker. The Mets have had to temper their rhetoric regarding their prospects, but Payton makes it hard for them to keep their lips buttoned. ▪

ROBERT PERSON

RP-SP • BR • TR • 5'11 • 180 • 28 • CLE89/24

	G	GS	IP	H	HR	BB	K	W	L	S	ERA	K/BB	K9	HW9
NYN95	3	1	12	5	1	2	10	1	0	0	.75	5.0	7.5	5.25
NYN96	27	13	89	86	16	35	76	4	5	0	4.52	2.2	7.7	12.23

In his attempts to land a job the past couple of seasons, Person bounced between the rotation and the bullpen. The results have been mixed, to say the least. He bombed out of the big-league bullpen in April and spent a little more than a month in Triple-A. A return to the rotation seemed to suit him in Norfolk. When the Mets recalled him in June, it was to replace the injured Paul Wilson in the rotation. In his first start, Person shut out the Cardinals for 7 innings, allowing 3 hits and 1 walk. He's not a big guy, but he throws hard. His fastball averages 92-94 mph, and he has a curve that he throws at about 82 with great movement. His change-up is rudimentary at best, which is why the Mets moved him into the bullpen to begin with. That's probably the best place for him. ▪

ROBERTO PETAGINE — SLEEPER

1B • BL • TL • 6'1 • 170 • 25 • HOU90

	AB	R	H	2B	3B	HR	RBI	BB	SO	SB	CS	BA	OB	SA
SD95	124	15	29	8	0	3	17	26	41	0	0	.234	.367	.371
NYN96	99	10	23	3	0	4	17	9	27	0	2	.232	.313	.384

Even though he didn't hit for beans after his recall, Petagine should prove to be a great pickup for the Mets. He has hit his brains out in the minors the past couple of seasons, but he can't seem to put it together in the big leagues. He's a high-average hitter with power and great plate discipline. Those skills alone should be enough to earn him a job. But he is also a very good defensive first baseman, making him even more attractive. What does Petagine have to do to earn a job? First, he's got to prove he can hit major-league pitching. Then find a way to take out Huskey. If Shawn Eckardt is hanging around Port St. Lucie in March, Huskey better watch his back. ▪

BILL PULSIPHER

SP • BL • TL • 6'3 • 210 • 23 • NYN91/3

	G	GS	IP	H	HR	BB	K	W	L	S	ERA	K/BB	K9	HW9
NYN95	17	17	126	122	11	45	81	5	7	0	3.98	1.8	5.8	11.93

Pulsipher went on the DL March 22 with a torn ligament in his left elbow. The injury, which occurred during a March 18 exhibition game, was his second elbow injury in less than a year. Pulsipher had a similar injury in '95, but it wasn't as severe and wasn't in exactly the same spot. Pulsipher blamed it on jumping into spring too hard, too soon. Mets coaches speculated that his delivery might have caused the injury. Regardless of the cause, Pulsipher underwent season-ending surgery the week of April 20. As strange as it may sound, he might have been the lucky one. At least he didn't have people in the front office calling him a head case every fifth day. He wasn't considered to have the same ceiling as Wilson or Isringhausen a year ago. Now that he's had big-time elbow surgery, his ceiling is coming down. If he can pick up a ball, he

might pitch in a winter league. The Mets are just hoping he can regain his excellent moving fastball by the spring. They will follow Pulsipher's progress very closely. And very quietly. ■

ROBERT STRATTON

OF • 96/1 • SANTA BARBARA HIGH SCHOOL (CA)

The 13th overall pick in the '96 draft, Stratton has tremendous power that terrified his opponents, a compact swing, a pretty good arm, and decent speed. Scouting director John Barr says, "If everything comes together, he's a 5-tool player who'll hit in the middle of the lineup." Keep an eye on him. Unlike Stanley Jefferson and Shawn Abner, this one might be the goods. ■

DEREK WALLACE — SLEEPER

RP • BR • TR • 6'3 • 200 • 25 • CHN92/1

	G	GS	IP	H	HR	BB	K	W	L	S	ERA	K/BB	K9	HW9
NYN 96	19	0	24	29	2	14	15	2	3	3	4.01	1.1	5.6	16.08

Wallace became the most promising pitcher in the organization after pitching brilliantly at Norfolk. He pitched so well, he was named the top reliever in International League. A longtime Cubs prospect, he found his way to New York from Kansas City in the Jason Jacome trade. He had a 4-seam fastball with little movement that he tried to throw past everyone. He also threw a slider, which needed improvement. When the Mets got him, though, they taught him a 2-seam fastball that moves and a split-finger they think might put him over the top. They hope he can close out games at the major-league level. He'll set up Franco in '97, and he's their best bet to be his eventual replacement. ■

MIKE WELCH — SLEEPER

RP • BL • TR • 6'2 • 195 • 24 • NYN93/3

	G	GS	IP	H	HR	BB	SO	W	L	S	ERA	K/BB	K9	HW9
AA	46	0	51	55	4	10	53	4	2	27	4.59	5.3	9.4	11.47

Welch was voted the best reliever in the Eastern League last season despite questionable stuff. He has a fastball that's slightly above average and a mediocre slider. What sets him apart is that he likes to challenge hitters inside, pitching with no fear at all. He reminds folks of Eckersley. He also has Eck's great control. Hopefully he watched The Eck enough in '96 to know not to taunt the opposition until the 4th game is won. ■

PAUL WILSON — YOUNG GUN

SP • BR • TR • 6'5 • 235 • 24 • NYN94/1

	G	GS	IP	H	HR	BB	K	W	L	S	ERA	K/BB	K9	HW9
NYN 96	26	26	149	157	15	71	109	5	12	0	5.38	1.5	6.6	13.77

Wilson was the best pitching prospect in the game coming into the '96 season. The Mets knew what they had in Wilson, and so did the rest of the baseball world. He's got the size, and when healthy he has perfect mechanics, a superhuman fastball and slider combo, and outstanding command of the strike zone. So why did his season look like landfill? Rookie season jitters, outrageous expectations, and a bout with shoulder tendinitis in June did Wilson in. He got hit early on and lost confidence in his fastball. A chain reaction of bad things started happening when Wilson tried to nibble the corners with the heater and started giving up walks. He had only 9 quality starts last year, but in them he went 4-1 with a 1.90 ERA. In the other 17 starts he went 1-11 with an 8.13 ERA.

Wilson only needs to do one thing: trust in the almighty fastball. In his best start of the season, he threw 8 shutout innings against the Giants May 30, allowing just 3 hits and walking none. He threw 100 pitches, 73 for strikes. After the game, Hundley noted, "He has the kind of stuff where he can throw the ball down the middle of the plate and not worry. His fastball has so much juice on it nobody's going to hit it real hard." There's no reason in the world why Wilson can't come back and become the bat-breaker everyone predicted him to be, though his off-season shoulder surgery was a bad ending to a bummer of a year. ■

■ 1996 AUTOPSY

With their entire starting rotation injured, a young, unproven bullpen, no clean-up hitter, and Lenny Dykstra & Darren Daulton each with one foot in the DL, the phaithful went into 1996 expecting the worst. And, for a change, they weren't disappointed.

April 13-11 (13-11, 3 games back)
Despite an unsettled lineup, the worst offensive performance in baseball, and their team leader, Daulton, essentially waving a white flag on his career, the Phillies managed to keep their noses above .500. Mike Grace went 4-0, the bullpen was better than anyone could have reasonably expected, and Dykstra was near .300 and on pace to do 20/20. But Gregg Jefferies ripped up his thumb in the 3rd game of the year and went down for 2 months, Mark Whiten followed up his strong 1995 second half by hitting .215, and they even lost pitching coach Johnny Podres for the year, due to a heart ailment.

May 13-15 (26-26, 9 games back)
Grace kept up his terrific pitching in May, shutting out both Greg Maddux and Kevin Brown within a span of 10 days. Curt Schilling came off the DL throwing strikes. Ricky Bottalico was 14-for-14 in save opportunities. Pete Incaviglia was downright sleek and aerodynamic at the plate (9/20/.312), even though, in the field, he continued to beep when he backed up. But Dykstra went down near the end of the month and, as always, the team fell apart without him—going 30 games under .500 over the next 4 months. Their Triple-A manager, Butch Hobson, was arrested on cocaine charges and should have entered his lineup card into evidence to support a plea of not guilty by reason of despair.

June 6-21 (32-47, 17½ games back)
They ran straight down in June, losing 21 of 27 for the month and 12 of 13 during one stretch. Pitching and defense had carried this weak-hitting team in April and May, but after yielding only 14 unearned runs in the first 2 months, they allowed 22 in June. The good news: Mike Williams earned his 1st win in his 9th start. The bad news: Todd Zeile disappeared after a good start, hitting .214 with 8 RBI; they lost Grace and Sid Fernandez for the year, the holes plugged by Bobby Muñoz in a futile comeback bid and overmatched rookies like Carlos Crawford and Rafael Quirico; they shipped Lee Tinsley back to Boston after he failed to hit his cholesterol count. Jefferies came back ahead of schedule, but the team had played its best baseball without him.

July 11-16 (43-63, 22 games back)
The tension between manager Jim Fregosi and GM Lee Thomas was heightened when Fregosi announced: "Right now we need to get better players and I have no control over that." As bad as it was—and it included dropping 13 of 14—it could have been worse if they hadn't managed to win 5 of 6 single run games. Bottalico got back on track after a difficult June, but it was Ken Ryan's turn to struggle out of the bullpen, giving up 33 baserunners in 14 innings with a 6.43 ERA, 2 losses, and 2 blown saves.

August 11-19 (54-82, 30½ games back)
In a year where even Kevin Elster and Rex Hudler had corked biceps, the Phillies went 8 games without a dinger, going 1-7. They only managed 13 for the month—a good total for just about any A.L. first baseman—and were outscored by 50% (162-108). Schilling talked guaranteed money and multiple years, then went out and got it done on the field, striking out 56 and walking 8 in 44 innings. After dispatching Terry Mulholland to Seattle in July, Zeile and Inky went to Baltimore for 2 prospects. On why more deals weren't done, Thomas said, "What teams were offering us was nothing and I couldn't take nothing." No, just Garrett Stephenson, Calvin Maduro, and Desi Relaford—a reasonable facsimile of nothing.

September 13-13 (67-95, 29 games back)
The Phillies managed to go .500 in September, though it helped that they played only 4 games against playoff teams. Benito Santiago hit 3 dingers in a game against the Cubs and reached 30 for the year, just about guaranteeing a price for his services

the owner won't be willing to pay. Catching prospect Bobby Estalella made a bid for the job in only 17 at-bats, going deep twice in a season-ending series against the Mets. Scott Rolen looked impressive at times, before a broken arm ended his season with his rookie-of-the-year eligibility for 1997 still intact.

■ 1997 DIAGNOSIS

Barring a slew of shrewd trades and aggressive free-agent signings, the Phillies shouldn't expect to do much better than what they managed to cough up in 1996. This is a bad team that hasn't bottomed out yet.

Offense

The worst in the National League. While the rest of the league was binging and indulging, the Phillies were at the bottom in both batting average and slugging percentage. In clutch situations—runners in scoring position and 2 men out, close and late—they hit in the 2-teens. Strictly trailer park fare: The table didn't get set and the meat of the order was nothing but fillers and extenders. The team's leadoff hitters were near the bottom in the N.L. in on-base percentage, while its clean-up hitters trailed the pack in slugging average.

If Rico Brogna can't stay healthy, Jefferies may return to first base—since Gene Schall and Jon Zuber aren't even very impressive at Triple-A. PeeWee Jeffman goes 3-for-5 in a loss and is all smiles, offering to buy the house a round of Frescas; he is the anti-Daulton and his teammates would rather see Dutch on crutches at first base. Morandini and Stocker are good fielders, but the lamest multi-year DP combo in the N.L. since the days of Glenn Hubbard and Rafael Ramirez. The third-base job is Scott Rolen's for the next 5 years—or 4, depending on the next work stoppage and service time dispute. If the Phillies leave Jefferies out in left to twist in the wind, they should expect a decline in his offensive numbers. Ricky Otero and Wendell Magee can't play center field every day, and Dykstra is done. Eisenreich will put up numbers regardless of his role, but the team needs to find a clean-up hitter somewhere and right field might be his home. *They have no legitimate outfield prospects at any level of the minors.*

Defense

They had no stars on offense, and their defense was pedestrian at best. Santiago was rejuventated behind the plate, throwing better than he had in years. They were solid in the infield, though first base was a revolving freak-show. Brogna will be a big improvement. But the staff was full of fly-ball pitchers and their outfield defense was brutal. Eisenreich was sound, but Otero was downright scary, and Inky and Jefferies would have been better off bringing lacrosse sticks out to left field.

Pitching

The staff kept the team respectable in April and May but declined precipitously during the summer. Grace and Schilling, who were healthy at the same time for 15 minutes, combined to go 16-12 with one of the lowest ERAs in the league. The rest of the starting rotation was a ragged patchwork quilt of 100% polyester, with Williams, Fernandez, Mike Mimbs, and Rich Hunter combining to go 15-36 with an ERA of 5.33. The rotation will be Curt Schilling and the first four guys who can throw batting practice without hearing something pop. Best case: Mike Grace and Bobby Muñoz rebound, Mike Williams finally moves to the next level, and either Matt Beech, Rich Hunter, Calvin Maduro, or Ryan Nye evolve. Worst case: Same old Mike Williams and Mike Mimbs combo platter and a sore-armed veteran, overmatched rookie goulash.

The bullpen was one of the team's only bright spots, led by Ryan and Bottalico's 42 saves, and supported capably—believe it or not—by Ricardo Jordan, Jeff Parrett, and Russ Springer. A team as bad as the Phillies may not have the luxury of keeping Ken Ryan around to set up Bottalico. He's one of the few players they can trade who might bring back something more than a fistful of dog-eared baseball cards. Russ Springer was overpowering at times and wouldn't embarass himself in Ryan's role.

Farm System
Arguably the worst in the majors. Their only solid prospect, Scott Rolen, is already at third base and being penciled in as a perennial All Star. They have no potential star position players at the upper levels, just a few dingers and lots of strikeouts, or soft .300s. There are some decent looking pitchers in Double-A and Triple-A (Bronson Heflin, Ryan Nye, and Keith Troutman), some interesting looking pitchers in A-ball who need to prove themselves at the higher levels (Rob Burger, Dave Coggin, and Randy Knoll), and their latest attempt at an impact 1st-rounder (hard-throwing 18-year-old, Adam Eaton).

Ownership and Management
The Phillies have the largest single-team market in baseball and can draw nearly 2 million and bank their $50 million even with the defective product they put out there for consumption in 1996. So why spend another $10 million to win more games, draw more fans, and maybe make it back and then some in gate receipts and beer? This is a business, after all, that's not a risk-free proposition, and this company has gotten fat, lazy, and disinterested.

And that's not the worst thing that's been said about them. Owner Bill Giles began to endure a dirtstorm of criticism in 1996 about the front office's alleged racism—something that's swirled around the Phillies since they fielded an all-white lineup in the 1993 World Series. Giles even barged in on a focus group of minority fans venting their collective spleens, then broke down in tears after they reiterated their frustrations to his face. Ironically, GM Lee Thomas was criticized in St. Louis for the exact opposite—signing "too many" black players, whatever that's supposed to mean. Giles, however, has never been active in the free-agent market, and the few big signings (Lance Parrish, Gregg Jefferies, Todd Zeile) have been very white. Maybe Giles is not a racist; perhaps he's just cheap and clueless.

In Philadelphia, Thomas has been a brilliant trader, which is reason enough to keep him on the payroll—even if the farm system has deteriorated precipitously on his watch. Thomas built the 1993 World Series team by recognizing character and fleecing his fellow GMs. He was laughed at when he gave Daulton big money after hitting .196 in 1991. He snagged Kruk from the Padres for Chris James, then took Dave Hollins from them in the Rule 5 Draft. He stole Dykstra from the Mets for Juan Samuel, and Schilling from the Astros for a soft pretzel. He stole Mitch from the Cubs for Chuck McElroy and Bob Scanlan. He turned an aging Steve Bedrosian into Dennis Cook, Charlie Hayes, and Terry Mulholland. The 1993 Phillies were probably the best example of building through theft since Gabe Paul built the mid-'70s Yankees by turning a bag of used baseballs into Chris Chambliss, Willie Randolph, Graig Nettles, Lou Piniella, and Mickey Rivers.

Jim Fregosi was openly auditioning for the California job in late '96. He was fired at season's end and was replaced by Terry Francona, who will be the youngest manager in the big leagues. Fregosi's time in Philadelphia had eerie parallels to his first tour of duty with the Angels, when he took a team of veterans to the playoffs, then oversaw its rapid deterioration in subsequent years. The Angels got Nolan Ryan for Fregosi in a player trade. If the Phillies can do half as well with this latest exchange, they'll be in great shape.

. . . and whatnot: Sympathy for the GM (Part II)
In '93, the scratching, spitting, and slobbering Phillies came this close to denying both the precious, well-bred Braves and the *nouveau riche* Blue Jays from world championships. Now that Philadelphia has landed in the basement three years later, down there with the forgotten keg buckets, assumptions are quickly becoming conventional wisdom: The '93 team was a fluke, and Lee Thomas doesn't know what he's doing. But conventional wisdom is fast food for your brain. An argument can be made that the Phillies of '93 were not a fluke—and instead one of the unluckiest teams in recent memory.

People remember that team as Mitch, Kruk, Dykstra, and Daulton, but personalities aside, its most striking feature was its young pitching. In '93, all four division winners got 30 wins from pitchers 26 or younger, something that hasn't happened

before or since. And none had a young threesome with more wins than Curt Schilling, Tommy Greene, and Ben Rivera. Of the 112 playoff teams since '69, only 12 have gotten as many wins out of starting pitchers 26 or younger. With the exception of the '69 Mets and '93 Phillies, all these teams won their divisions again during the next 3 years—though the Mets were at least competitive. One has to go back to the '61 Reds to find a young staff with more wins that didn't return to the postseason within 3 years (though the Reds were more a victim of an undiluted postseason than bad luck, and didn't drop below .500 until they traded Frank Robinson for Milt Pappas).

So what derailed the '93 Phillies? The starters blew out their arms. Daulton and Hollins couldn't stay healthy. Kruk fought back against cancer, only to succumb to the attitudes of his fellow union members. Dykstra suffered the curse of muscle-bound baseball players, otherwise known as a bad back. The young players on the bench—Wesley "Big Life" Chamberlain, Ricky Jordan, Todd Pratt, Ruben Amaro, and Tyler Green—didn't develop. Check the numbers: as Joe Carter finished the least dignified home run trot in baseball history, half the Phillies' roster was poised to do a full-gainer off a performance cliff.

Other than being lulled to sleep by Kevin Stocker playing over his head, ignoring Dykstra's wretched personal life and overnight muscles when giving him a guaranteed, big-money contract, and dumping a brat like Jefferies into a clubhouse full of men, most of this team's deterioration can't be traced to Lee Thomas. The Phillies have holes everywhere, an atrocious farm system, and racial tension with their fans. But if they decide they don't need a horse trader with Thomas's record, some other team will take him. Expect him to then fleece the Phillies on a few deals—and that won't be bad luck for Philadelphia, that will be dumb luck.

MARLON ANDERSON

2B • BL • TR • 5'10 • 190 • 23 • PHI95/2

	AB	R	H	2B	3B	HR	RBI	BB	SO	SB	CS	BA	OB	SA
AA	314	38	86	14	3	3	28	26	44	17	9	.274	.330	.366

Anderson is considered an excellent defender, solid leadoff man, hard worker, stolen-base threat, and potential .300 hitter. He was promoted from Clearwater after stealing 26 bases in 27 attempts and striking out only 18 times in 257 at bats. He could be ready even before Morandini's 3-year, $6 million deal mercifully ends. ■

MATT BEECH

SP • BL • TL • 6'2 • 190 • 25 • PHI94/7

	G	GS	IP	H	HR	BB	K	W	L	S	ERA	K/BB	K9	HW9
PHI96	8	8	41	49	8	11	33	1	4	0	6.97	3.0	7.2	13.16

A year out of A-ball, Beech beat Greg Maddux in his debut. It was his only win, but even if that's his career total, it sure beats telling the grandkids about the time you took some fratboy deep in an intramural softball game. Beech throws in the high 80s and in the strike zone, mixing in a curve and a slider. There'll be some more ugly "learning experiences" along the way, but he could easily make the rotation in '97 and evolve. ■

MIKE BENJAMIN (see Looking for a Game)

RON BLAZIER

RP • BR • TR • 6'6 • 215 • 25 • PHI89

	G	GS	IP	H	HR	BB	K	W	L	S	ERA	K/BB	K9	HW9
PHI96	27	0	38	49	6	10	25	3	1	0	5.87	2.5	5.9	13.96

Fregosi: "He doesn't back off. He throws strikes and isn't intimidated by major-league hitters." Bear in mind that (1) Blazier came back to earth with a moist thud soon after this statement, and (2) Fregosi's pitching sound-bites invariably boil down to two statements: If things are going well, it's because the pitcher is challenging the hitters, and if things aren't going well, it's because the pitcher isn't being aggressive enough. There's a lot to be said for aggressiveness. That's why they serve red meat in clubhouses and not quiche. There's also a lot to be said for brains and finesse. Ted Williams used to scream at Yankee junkballer Eddie Lopat to throw

him a fastball. Lopat would smirk, serve up some more slop, and watch Williams try to pull another outside curveball into the teeth of the shift. Taking a young pitcher without enough pitches or good enough stuff and telling him to be aggressive is like telling your buddy with the bad hair, yellow teeth, and coffee breath to be direct and demanding with the supermodels in the ski lodge. That's not the kind of advice Blazier would have gotten from pitching coach Johnny Podres if he'd been around. Blazier looked quite good in Double-A and Triple-A, but the National League hit .310 with power against him whether he threw the first pitch for a strike or not. So much for aggressiveness. ■

TOBY BORLAND

BR • TR • 6′6 • 185 • 27 • PHI87/26

	G	GS	IP	H	HR	BB	K	W	L	S	ERA	K/BB	K9	HW9
PHI94	24	0	34	31	1	14	26	1	0	1	2.36	1.9	6.9	11.90
PHI95	50	0	74	81	3	37	59	1	3	6	3.77	1.6	7.2	14.35
PHI96	69	0	90	83	9	43	76	7	3	0	4.07	1.8	7.6	12.59
CAREER	143	0	198	195	13	94	161	9	6	7	3.68	1.7	7.3	13.13

Borland is a sidearmer who keeps the ball down and relies on hitters chasing pitches out of the strike zone. The league only hit .239 against him (righties only .210). Expect Borland to continue to improve. His first taste of Triple-A was in '92, and he ended up with a 7.24 ERA. By '94 it was down to 1.68, with only 1 baserunner per inning. In a brief stint in '95, he was unhittable. He'll be a valuable arm out of some team's bullpen for several years. ■

RICKY BOTTALICO — YOUNG GUN

CL • BL • TR • 6′1 • 200 • 27 • PHI91

	G	GS	IP	H	HR	BB	K	W	L	S	ERA	K/BB	K9	HW9
PHI95	62	0	87	50	7	42	87	5	3	1	2.46	2.1	9.0	9.52
PHI96	61	0	67	47	6	23	74	4	5	34	3.19	3.2	9.9	9.39

Bottalico was snagged as a free agent from the Greater Hartford Twilight League after spending his college days as a catcher. He throws in the mid-90s and combines that with a nasty slider that can make batters look like duffers trying to return serve. With two men on in the bottom of the 9th of a 1-run game against the Dodgers in May, Bottalico struck out Piazza, Karros, and Mondesi. It put the Phillies at 21-21 and was probably the high-water mark of the season. He converted 34 of 38 saves in all, despite being slowed in the second half of the season by tendinitis and a lack of opportunities. As good as he was in '95, he was even better in '96, and he's only 27. With Ryan setting him up, the bullpen is the only strength this team has. ■

ROB BURGER — SLEEPER

SP • BR • TR • 6′1 • 190 • 21 • PHI94/10

	G	GS	IP	H	HR	BB	K	W	L	S	ERA	K/BB	K9	HW9
A	27	26	160	129	9	61	171	10	12	0	3.38	2.8	9.6	10.69

Burger throws in the low- to mid-90s, has a good curveball, and is working on a change-up. He did well in the South Atlantic League, striking out more than a batter an inning with decent command. When considering both stuff and results, he could be the best pitching prospect currently in the system. ■

ESSEX "GAS" BURTON

2B • BR • TR • 5′9 • 155 • 27

	AB	R	H	2B	3B	HR	RBI	BB	SO	SB	CS	BA	OB	SA
AA	381	66	116	19	5	1	30	37	56	40	12	.304	.367	.388

Stuck behind Ray Durham and Norberto Martin, Gas stole 211 bases in A-ball before the White Sox finally let him have a look at Double-A pitching. It's singles and walks and not much else, but when you steal 60 bases, a lack of extra-base hits can be overlooked. He hit .300 for Reading in '96 and deserves a shot, but he may never get it. ■

DAVE COGGIN — SOLID PROSPECT

SP • BR • TR • 6′4 • 195 • 20 • PHI95/1

	G	GS	IP	H	HR	BB	K	W	L	S	ERA	K/BB	K9	HW9
A	28	28	169	156	12	46	129	9	12	0	4.31	2.8	6.9	10.74

Coggin was a supplemental pick in the 1st round of the '95 draft, compensation for "losing" Danny Jackson. He throws in the low 90s and has a good curveball, attitude, and mechanics. He's only 20, and the Phillies are 4 levels away, but the young arms in this organization won't have to wait until the next millennium to have beer dumped on them in Philly. ■

CARLOS CRAWFORD

SP • BR • TR • 6'1 • 185 • 25 • CLE90/51

	G	GS	IP	H	HR	BB	K	W	L	S	ERA	K/BB	K9	HW9
AAA	28	25	159	169	15	63	89	9	10	1	4.54	1.4	5.0	13.16

The Phillies plucked him from the Indians' farm system and, after his brutal season in Triple-A and brief disaster in Philadelphia, they'll probably wish they kept the receipt. No threat to Wahoo Sam's status as the greatest Crawford in baseball history. ▪

DARREN DAULTON

DL • BL • TR • 6'2 • 195 • 35 • PHI80/25

	AB	R	H	2B	3B	HR	RBI	BB	SO	SB	CS	BA	OB	SA
PHI94	257	43	77	17	1	15	56	33	43	4	1	.300	.380	.549
PHI95	342	44	85	19	3	9	55	55	52	3	0	.249	.359	.401
PHI96	12	3	2	0	0	0	0	7	5	0	0	.167	.500	.167
CAREER	3235	443	787	176	17	123	525	553	652	44	9	.243	.355	.422

Eight surgeries on his left knee, one ill-advised ride home with Nails, and one beautiful-when-she's-angry ex-wife, and it's a torn ACL on the *right* knee that has likely ended Daulton's career. Some suggest that Daulton hasn't officially retired because that might keep him from getting the $5 million left on his contract. Put that in athlete-speak and you get:" . . . I haven't retired. I feel I have to honor my contract. Nobody is putting any pressure on me but myself." Even throwbacks like Daulton are now able to convince themselves that riding exercise bikes in Clearwater and cashing paychecks constitute "honor." Or maybe it's just alimony making a man do funny things. ▪

DAVID DOSTER

2B • BR • TR • 5'10 • 185 • 26 • PHI93/27

	AB	R	H	2B	3B	HR	RBI	BB	SO	SB	CS	BA	OB	SA
PHI96	105	14	28	8	0	1	8	7	21	0	0	.267	.313	.371

He didn't do much in Triple-A, looked frustrated at the plate after a 21 dinger season in Double-A in '95, and wouldn't even have gotten a September call-up if Rolen hadn't been injured. He's a decent defensive player and may stick in the majors for a few years as that utility infielder who goes deep in game two of a rain-delayed twi-nighter in August off some random Pirates middle reliever. ▪

LEN DYKSTRA

OF • BL • TL • 5'10 • 190 • 34 • NYN81/12

	AB	R	H	2B	3B	HR	RBI	BB	SO	SB	CS	BA	OB	SA
PHI94	315	68	86	26	5	5	24	68	44	15	4	.273	.404	.435
PHI95	254	37	67	15	1	2	18	33	28	10	5	.264	.353	.354
PHI96	134	21	35	6	3	3	13	26	25	3	1	.261	.387	.418
CAREER	4559	802	1298	281	43	81	404	640	503	285	72	.285	.375	.419

Even the wretched '96 Phillies were a .500 ballclub when Dykstra played; the bottom didn't fall out until he pulled a rib cage muscle in May, his ninth time on the DL since '91. He was healthy for 4 straight years from '86 to '89, then quickly added 25 pounds of muscle before the '90 season and it's been a dramatic improvement in performance yet only 2 full seasons in 7 years since. In June he had an operation to repair nerve damage in his back, pretty much ending his career. When his guaranteed contract finally ends in '98, the Phillies will have paid him nearly $30 million for 700 at-bats. Good work if you can get it. ▪

ADAM EATON — SOLID PROSPECT

RHP • PHI96/1 • SNOHOMISH HIGH SCHOOL (WA)

The Phillies gave Eaton a $1.1 million bonus after 51 impressive innings in high school and hitting 95 on the gun a few times. It's hard to argue against throwing big money and high expectations at 1st-round 18-year-olds, since the Mariners came away with Junior and A Rod doing just that. But they're harder to sign because they have the opportunity to attend one of those, you know, academical institutions. And though the majority of 1st-round picks continue to be high-schoolers, those coming out of college are more likely to become impact major-leaguers. Which of the following teams do you want to bet the family jewels on—the one with Junior, A Rod, a handful of head cases and rag-arms, or the one with all those dingers and 15 good pitchers to choose from?

First round at 18: c, Kendall; 1b, Tony Clark, Brogna, Jefferies; 2b, Delino; ss, Alex Rodriguez, Jeter, Blauser, Dunston, Jay Bell, Clayton; 3b, Chipper, Shane Andrews; of, Junior, Manny Ramirez, McRae, Straw, Sheffield, dh, Baines; sp,

Gooden, Avery, Appier, Tommy Greene, Mike Morgan.

First round at 21: c, Charles Johnson; 1b, Thomas, Palmeiro, McGwire, Tino Martinez, Will Clark; 2b, Knoblauch, Biggio; ss, Larkin, Weiss; 3b, Matt Williams, Ventura, Jeff King, Sprague, Wallach; of, Bonds, Carter, Burks, Surhoff; dh, Molitor; sp, Kevin Brown, Mussina, The Rocket, Alex Fernandez, Jack McDowell, Dizzy Benes, Daffy Benes, McDonald, Swift, Osborne, Hamilton, rp, Roberto Hernandez, Billy Wagner, Todd Worrell, Plesac.

The difficulty 1st-round 18-year-old pitchers have making it big underscores the importance of the mental aspects of the game over the blessing of a Nuke Laloosh arm. Consider *Baseball America*'s "Phenom Roll Call" of teenage pitchers, a who's who of tragedy, irrelevance, and underachievement: Paul Pettit, Lew Krausse, J. R. Richard, David Clyde, Bill Gullickson, John Peters, Van Poppel, and Brien Taylor. James Rodney was on his way to the Hall of Fame—the others should have followed Gullick-*san* to Japan.

Adam Eaton shouldn't spend the $1.1 million in one place. ■

JIM EISENREICH

OF • BL • TL • 5′11 • 195 • 37 • MIN80/16

	AB	R	H	2B	3B	HR	RBI	BB	SO	SB	CS	BA	OB	SA
PHI94	290	42	87	15	4	4	43	33	31	6	2	.300	.371	.421
PHI95	377	46	119	22	2	10	55	38	44	10	0	.316	.375	.464
PHI96	338	45	122	24	3	3	41	31	32	11	1	.361	.413	.476
CAREER	3511	435	1037	199	36	49	430	278	371	99	38	.295	.345	.414

Eisenreich is a true hero and it overshadows the fact that he is one of the most fundamentally sound players in the major Leagues. He wears out righties and, though he rarely plays against them, he still manages to slap enough singles to hit .300 against lefties. He has a compact swing and is one of the best in baseball with 2 strikes. He doesn't make defensive mistakes. He is 21 for 22 in steals over the past 2 seasons. Though his career was interrupted in his early 20s and he never played regularly until he was 30, he collected his 1,000 hit in '96. He is the rarest of birds, a fan favorite in Philadelphia—the city that booed Santa Claus and Mike Schmidt. So popular, in fact, that he was one of the few veterans not available in a trade during '96. So for being such a good egg, he earns an extended stay in the City of Brotherly Resentment. Now, Alanis, *that* is ironic. ■

BOBBY ESTALELLA SLEEPER

C • BR • TR • 6′1 • 200 • 22 • PHI92/22

	AB	R	H	2B	3B	HR	RBI	BB	SO	SB	CS	BA	OB	SA
AA	365	48	89	14	2	23	72	67	104	2	4	.244	.365	.482

Estalella looks better long-term than Lieberthal, showing flashes of that in the season's final weekend at Shea. He's bigger, has more power, can do the job behind the plate, and is only 22. He needs to make better contact, but he did just that after going from Spartanburg to Clearwater. ■

SID FERNANDEZ (see Free Agents)

WAYNE GOMES

RP • BR • TR • 6′0 • 215 • 24 • PHI93/1

	G	GS	IP	H	HR	BB	K	W	L	S	ERA	K/BB	K9	HW9
AA	67	0	64	53	7	48	79	0	4	24	4.48	1.6	11.1	14.13

The fourth player taken in the '93 draft, the Phillies tried to make Gomes a starter after he gave up 5 hits and struck out 24 in his first 15 relief innings as a professional. He throws in the mid-90s and has the best curveball in the Eastern League. Too bad he doesn't know where either pitch is going. His walks per 9 innings dropped from 6 to 5 in '95, then climbed toward 7 in '96. That he was Reading's closer proves—along with the brief return of Thingwild—that someone in the organization wanted Fregosi to have a nervous breakdown. ■

MIKE GRACE

SP • BR • TR • 6′4 • 210 • 26 • PHI91/10

	G	GS	IP	H	HR	BB	K	W	L	S	ERA	K/BB	K9	HW9
PHI95	2	2	11	10	0	4	7	1	1	0	3.18	1.8	5.7	11.45
PHI96	12	12	80	72	9	16	49	7	2	0	3.49	3.1	5.5	9.90

Injuries to the entire Phillies rotation gave Grace his chance in '96. He went 7-2 during April and May with a radical approach to pitching: throwing strikes and keeping the ball down. Then his arm gave out on him again—he missed all of '93 due to injury and has already had three elbow operations—and his career may be

over. Despite all the prior trouble Grace had with his arm, his fastball was in the low-90s in '96 before he broke down. File Grace away with another terrific unknown named John Fulgham—guys who had the stuff, showed it briefly, but never got their full quarter's worth on the ride. ▪

TOMMY GREENE

SP • BR • TR • 6'5 • 225 • 30 • ATL85/1

	G	GS	IP	H	HR	BB	K	W	L	S	ERA	K/BB	K9	HW9
AAA	5	5	31	31	3	7	26	2	0	0	3.77	3.7	7.5	11.03

Greene put up some impressive numbers at Class-A and Triple-A as he tried to overcome shoulder and back ailments. He had to do it with his slider and his experience because his fastball may be gone for good. In a game against Norfolk in August, Greene pitched 7 effective innings without getting a single batter to swing and miss at his fastball. He's 30 and he's won only 2 games since '93, so don't assume he can bring that Triple-A ERA with him back to Philadelphia. ▪

BRONSON HEFLIN — SLEEPER

RP • BR • TR • 6'3 • 200 • 25 • PHI94/37

	G	GS	IP	H	HR	BB	K	W	L	S	ERA	K/BB	K9	HW9
AAA	30	0	38	25	4	3	23	4	0	12	2.61	7.7	5.4	6.63

Those numbers are as close as you're going to find to Greg Maddux. The scouts says Heflin has an average fastball and a good slider, which means he's put up Maddux numbers with Maddux stuff. This degree of control is a new thing for him. As early as the first half of '96, he was walking 15 batters in 29 innings in Reading. He's worth watching in spring training to see which Heflin shows up. ▪

DAN HELD

1B • BR • TR • 6'0 • 200 • 26 • PHI93/42

	AB	R	H	2B	3B	HR	RBI	BB	SO	SB	CS	BA	OB	SA
AA	497	77	121	17	5	26	92	60	141	3	8	.243	.347	.455

Held's power numbers have improved each year, but his average has dropped into the .240s as his strikeouts continue to climb. He's Glenn Murray without the speed and with a couple of good wrists. ▪

RICH HUNTER

SP • BR • TR • 6'1 • 180 • 22 • PHI93/14

	G	GS	IP	H	HR	BB	K	W	L	S	ERA	K/BB	K9	HW9
PHI96	14	14	69	84	10	33	32	3	7	0	6.49	1.0	4.2	15.25

Hunter's fastball is in the low 80s, so he works the black and changes speeds. He's only 22 and climbed from low-A to Double-A in '95, going 19-2 in the process with an ERA below 3.00 at all 3 stops. He was rushed to the majors in '96 and looked worse than his 3-7 record. But he made it around the league and still has most of his teeth, so the Phillies might have a crafty righty on their hands if they can wait a few years. ▪

GREGG JEFFERIES — OVERRATED

1B-OF • BB • TR • 5'11 • 175 • 29 • NYN85/1

	AB	R	H	2B	3B	HR	RBI	BB	SO	SB	CS	BA	OB	SA
SL94	397	52	129	27	1	12	55	45	26	12	5	.325	.391	.489
PHI95	480	69	147	31	2	11	56	35	26	9	5	.306	.349	.448
PHI96	404	59	118	17	3	7	51	36	21	20	6	.292	.348	.401
CAREER	4192	581	1224	231	21	98	525	361	268	169	48	.292	.351	.427

Jefferies has played about the same number of positions as unimpressively as Pete Rose. He *is* Rose, only with the bad and the good bleached out. Take the gambling jones and the desire to win away from Rose, and all you're left with is a 5'11, stat-conscious switch-hitter who hits doubles and can't field no matter where you put him. Sound familiar?

Consider the results of the teams Jefferies has played for. He became a regular for the '89 Mets, they lost 15 more games than the '88 division-winner, and the unraveling of the franchise began. He went to the Royals in '92, they lost 10 more games, and he was shipped back out a year later for Felix José. Now that he's "matured," it takes 2 years for his anti-Midas touch to take effect. The Cardinals were a .512 team before he arrived, .465 when they let him leave, and back in the playoffs now that his presence has been exorcised; the Phillies were at .470 before he arrived and now they're down in the

.4-teens. Why do you suppose "unnamed players" are always complaining about commitment and chemistry every place he's been? PeeWee Jeffman must be the biggest drag to have around since the days when Al Oliver was holding forth on his Hall of Fame credentials in the Expo dugout.

Jefferies has a lifetime batting average hovering around .300 from both sides of the plate and more than 1,200 hits at age 29, so he brings some skills to town. He can still steal a base. He's very tough with 2 strikes; in fact, it's rare that he even swings and misses. Met fans will recall that his best tantrums were after pop-ups, not strikeouts. He doesn't walk either, putting the ball in play nearly 9 at-bats out of 10. He's been hit with only 6 pitches in the past 6 years, but that doesn't include batting practice. He's another multimillionaire who thinks stats equate to leadership, but his refusal to take one for the team or work the count prompted a blasting from Fregosi when Jefferies swung at the first pitch in the 9th inning of a game in which the Phillies trailed 7-4.

What were the Phillies thinking when they gave Jefferies $5 million a year and tossed him into a clubhouse full of guys who took his lunch money when he was a kid? And what was Jefferies thinking when he signed on the bottom line? The '94 Phillies made the '89-'91 Mets—grown men who sawed PeeWee's game bats in half—look like Peace Corps volunteers. By '96 he'd already worn out the welcome. He was available in the right deal, even before he whined about his only friend, Todd Zeile, being shipped out to Baltimore. After that one, Lee Thomas said he "should worry about playing left field and leave the rest to us." They'll be trying to give him away in '97. ■

KEVIN JORDAN

2B-1B • BR • TR • 6'1 • 185 • 27 • NYA90/20

	AB	R	H	2B	3B	HR	RBI	BB	SO	SB	CS	BA	OB	SA
PHI95	54	6	10	1	0	2	6	2	9	0	0	.185	.228	.315
PHI96	131	15	37	10	0	3	12	5	20	2	1	.282	.309	.427

Jordan hit reasonably well when the Phillies plugged him in at first after Jefferies tore up his thumb. And he played errorless defense at an unfamiliar position until he injured his knee. But if the Phillies believed in him as a second baseman, they wouldn't have made Morandini financially secure for life. They don't like his defense at all, so it looks like he's the next Ricky Jordan—a Phillies infielder who can hit but never gets to play. ■

RICARDO JORDAN

RP • BL • TL • 6'0 • 180 • 26 • TOR90/37

	G	GS	IP	H	HR	BB	K	W	L	S	ERA	K/BB	K9	HW9
TOR95	15	0	15	18	3	13	10	1	0	1	6.60	.8	6.0	18.60
PHI96	26	0	25	18	0	12	17	2	2	0	1.80	1.4	6.1	10.80

Apparently, Ricky Jordan, still frustrated by lack of playing time, has become a lefthanded relief pitcher. He wasn't good at Triple-A in '95 and was even worse in Toronto. His numbers were a bit more interesting in '96, though they have always been sloppy—a strikeout an inning without command and ERAs that look like projections of Junior's lifetime home-run totals. Out of nowhere, he came up with an amazingly low ERA for the Phillies, despite continuing control problems. He held the league to a .202 batting average, lefties to a .176 on-base percentage. But in his second time around the league with the Mets, he may very well get a harsh dose of reality. ■

RYAN KARP

SP • BL • TL • 6'4 • 205 • 26 • NYA92/7

	G	GS	IP	H	HR	BB	K	W	L	S	ERA	K/BB	K9	HW9
AAA	7	7	41	35	1	14	30	1	1	0	3.07	2.1	6.6	10.76

Shoulder surgery may have short-circuited a career of left-handed spot-starting, mop-up, and bullpen food runs. Karp will be 27 in April, he's never been able to consistently control his stuff, and his only major league action was 1 game in '95 when he walked 3, struck out 2, and heaved a wild pitch in 2 innings of work. ■

RANDY KNOLL

SOLID PROSPECT

SP • BR • TR • 6'4 • 190 • 20 • PHI95/3

	G	GS	IP	H	HR	BB	K	W	L	S	ERA	K/BB	K9	HW9
A	22	22	151	111	7	31	144	10	7	3	2.09	4.6	8.6	8.46

After a brief and ugly '95, Grassy Knoll blew through the South Atlantic League in '96 and didn't break stride after being promoted to Clearwater. He gets it done with breaking balls and by changing speeds, and has the command to be able to throw junk behind in the count. The test for Knoll will be in Double-A and Triple-A, where the righties don't

moonwalk out of the batter's box when he throws a spinner. ■

MIKE LIEBERTHAL

C • BR • TR • 6′0 • 180 • 25 • PHI90/1

	AB	R	H	2B	3B	HR	RBI	BB	SO	SB	CS	BA	OB	SA
PHI94	79	6	21	3	1	1	5	3	5	0	0	.266	.301	.367
PHI95	47	1	12	2	0	0	4	5	5	0	0	.255	.327	.298
PHI96	166	21	42	8	0	7	23	10	30	0	0	.253	.297	.428
CAREER	292	28	75	13	1	8	32	18	40	0	0	.257	.303	.390

Fregosi: "I think he's really come into his own. He's grown up. He's going to be an every-day, big-league catcher someday." Lieberthal's season was shortened by knee surgery that is not considered career-threatening. His '96 offensive performance projects to 20 dingers in 500 at-bats, though he's not that big and has never showed this punch in the minors. He makes contact and knows the strike zone, but the Phillies shouldn't expect anywhere near Santiago's offensive numbers when and if they hand him the job. ■

CARLTON LOEWER

SP • BB • TR • 6′6 • 220 • 23 • PHI94/1

	G	GS	IP	H	HR	BB	K	W	L	S	ERA	K/BB	K9	HW9
AA	27	27	171	191	24	57	119	7	10	0	5.26	2.1	6.3	13.05

Loewer was the Phillies' 1st-round pick in '94, but his numbers look more like someone who's already made the big, guaranteed cheese. For someone with a low 90s fastball with movement, a good curve, and an improving change-up, he sure gives up a lot of runs. He's got Schilling's build and Lefty's name, so God help him when he finally makes it to the Vet and doesn't win his first 10 starts. ■

CALVIN MADURO

SOLID PROSPECT

SP • BR • TR • 6′0 • 175 • 22 • BAL91

	G	GS	IP	H	HR	BB	K	W	L	S	ERA	K/BB	K9	HW9
AA	19	19	124	116	8	36	87	9	7	0	3.26	2.4	6.3	11.00

This Aruba native has a low 90s fastball and can control his change-up and curve. His performance in the low minors was very impressive, and by '96 he was up to Triple-A and still striking out a batter an inning with command. He's still very young, but then there's not much blocking his path, and he looked good in his brief time with the Phillies in September. ■

WENDELL MAGEE, JR.

OF • BR • TR • 6′0 • 225 • 24 • PHI94/12

	AB	R	H	2B	3B	HR	RBI	BB	SO	SB	CS	BA	OB	SA
PHI96	142	9	29	7	0	2	14	9	33	0	0	.204	.252	.296

Magee climbed steadily through the Phillies system, producing at each stop, before getting an extended look in Philadelphia in September. Though he didn't hit much, he showed some power when the pitcher hit his bat with the ball. He's raw, but is—as the college football color men say on TV—ath-uh-letic. Wendell should be one of the Phillies five outfielders in '96, if for no other reason than the great name. ■

CHAD MCCONNELL

OF • BR • TR • 6′1 • 180 • 26 • PHI92/1

	AB	R	H	2B	3B	HR	RBI	BB	SO	SB	CS	BA	OB	SA
AA	385	70	95	18	1	12	50	40	119	6	5	.247	.345	.392

The absence of impact players in the Phillies organization is due in large part to 1st-round bricks like McConnell (and Lieberthal . . . and Tyler Green . . . and Gomes . . . and Loewer . . . and Reggie Taylor, just to name the ones still in the organization). McConnell has had operations on his knee, back, and shoulder, limiting him to fewer than 400 at-bats every season as a professional. When he's played, he's hit .250 without much power or speed. He's been at Reading for three years now, but his learning curve has flat-lined. ■

MIKE MIMBS

SP • BL • TL • 6′2 • 180 • 28 • LA90/24

	G	GS	IP	H	HR	BB	K	W	L	S	ERA	K/BB	K9	HW9
PHI95	35	19	136	127	10	75	93	9	7	1	4.15	1.2	6.2	13.37
PHI96	21	17	99	116	13	41	56	3	9	0	5.53	1.4	5.1	14.27

The trash talk scouting report says to tell him his brother is ugly. When Mimbs was 1-6, Fregosi said he had a chance of pitching himself onto the '97 staff if he stopped falling behind hitters and became more "consistent." Mimbs is nothing if not consistent: He hasn't thrown

strikes at any level. He cut down a bit on the nibbling and threw more strikes in '96, but the league hit nearly .300 off him as a result. Some suggest his future is in left-handed middle relief, but he was mugged by the few lefties who faced him. It won't say much for the '97 team if he does end up in the rotation after going a very messy 2-3 after a direct challenge from his manager. ■

JASON MOLER

3B • BR • TR • 6'1 • 195 • 27 • PHI92/3

	AB	R	H	2B	3B	HR	RBI	BB	SO	SB	CS	BA	OB	SA
AA	374	59	92	22	0	18	59	54	50	4	5	.246	.343	.449

Moler is a converted catcher who ended up playing third, short, left, and first at Reading, so he has a future as a utility man. He makes good contact and gets his share of extra-base hits, but he's 27 and Doster is a younger, better version of him. ■

MICKEY MORANDINI

2B • BL • TR • 5'11 • 170 • 30 • PHI88/4

	AB	R	H	2B	3B	HR	RBI	BB	SO	SB	CS	BA	OB	SA
PHI94	274	40	80	16	5	2	26	34	33	10	5	.292	.378	.409
PHI95	494	65	140	34	7	6	49	42	80	9	6	.283	.350	.417
PHI96	539	64	135	24	6	3	32	49	87	26	5	.250	.321	.334
CAREER	2558	320	672	116	39	19	193	219	401	82	23	.263	.327	.361

As a wise old cabbie once said, "If you're playing ball and calling yourself Mickey, you better be good." Maybe it would be easier to give Morandini his due if he called himself Mike. He faded after the All-Star break, stopped hitting, stopped running, and started talking contract. Not the soundest of strategies, but it worked. When The Mick was locked in until '99 for $2 million a year plus incentives, it showed how far the Phillies and the Braves have diverged since they met in the playoffs in '93. The Braves suffered injuries to Gant, Justice, and Avery without blinking; they made some deals, called up some prospects, and suddenly Ron, Dave, and Steve are wondering why they're behind Chipper, Jermaine, and Denny in the lunch line. Meanwhile, the Phillies find themselves having to cling to the likes of Morandini—a lighter-hitting Mark Lemke who runs. Six million dollars for 3 dingers and .250 at the age of 30 in a juiced-ball year? This wealth transfer is very questionable, especially since second base is one of the few positions where the Phillies have a number of alternatives who can hit .250 for minimum wage. He's a good fielder and one of the few members of the team who doesn't aggravate the suits, so maybe the moral of this $6 million story is that it's the bland who will inherit the earth. ■

BOBBY MUÑOZ

SLEEPER

SP • BR • TR • 6'8 • 250 • 29 • NYA88/15

	G	GS	IP	H	HR	BB	K	W	L	S	ERA	K/BB	K9	HW9
PHI94	21	14	104	101	8	35	59	7	5	1	2.67	1.7	5.1	11.77
PHI95	3	3	15	15	2	9	6	0	2	0	5.74	.7	3.6	14.40
PHI96	6	6	25	42	5	7	8	0	3	0	7.82	1.1	2.9	17.62
CAREER	68	23	190	206	16	77	106	10	13	1	4.26	1.4	5.0	13.40

If this horse hadn't needed shooting, Mulholland for Muñoz would have gone down as more Lee Thomas thievery. But shoulder problems and transplanted elbow ligaments kept Muñoz from bringing it in '96. In 25 innings he walked 7, struck out 8, and yielded 42 hits and 5 dingers before they mercifully shut him down and gave his spot in the rotation to Wayne Twitchell. If he has his velocity back in the spring, he's worth watching. If not, hide the children and shield your eyes. ■

GLENN MURRAY

OF • BR • TR • 6'2 • 200 • 26 • MON89/2

	AB	R	H	2B	3B	HR	RBI	BB	SO	SB	CS	BA	OB	SA
PHI96	97	8	19	3	0	2	6	7	36	1	1	.196	.250	.289

There's no reason to be excited about a major leaguer who hits .230, joins the strikeout century club in August, and hasn't even managed a 30-home-run season in 5 full tries. Murray is the *minor-league* version of this. He didn't give the Phillies much before heading to the doctor with wrist problems. A ligament was torn and a bone was too long; he had the ligament fixed, but put off the bone shave for now. If it turns out to be necessary this spring, he could be done for '97. He's better off getting a head start on his beer-league softball career anyway. He's the Reds' problem now. ■

RYAN NYE — *SOLID PROSPECT*

SP • BR • TR • 6'2 • 195 • 23 • PHI94/2

	G	GS	IP	H	HR	BB	K	W	L	S	ERA	K/BB	K9	HW9
AAA	14	14	81	97	10	30	51	5	2	0	5.02	1.7	5.7	14.17

Nye has an average fastball, a sinker, a good slider, and a change-up. He's 32-13 in his minor-league career, with a K/BB ratio over 3—though he's yet to show this at Triple-A. He was promoted from Double-A, where he was 8-2 with a 3.84 ERA and struck out a batter an inning. He's only 23 and probably shouldn't go north with the team—unless the starters suffer another group cuff tear. ■

RICKY OTERO

OF • BB • TR • 5'7 • 150 • 24 • NYN90/45

	AB	R	H	2B	3B	HR	RBI	BB	SO	SB	CS	BA	OB	SA
NYN95	51	5	7	2	0	0	1	3	10	2	1	.137	.185	.176
PHI96	411	54	112	11	7	2	32	34	30	16	10	.273	.330	.348

They call him "Flea," but given the imaginative way he played the outfield and ran the bases in '96, "Skates" would have been more appropriate. Possessed by the spirit of Lonnie Smith, he managed to match all of Lonnie's best moments—except stopping at second base to cost his team a World Series. Otero was thrown out stealing when he stopped running hard, thinking the batter had walked. He was picked off first when he tried to call time by lifting the hand that was on the base. He got bad jumps on flyballs to make routine plays look spectacular. He made long runs to get to balls on the warning track and forgot to lift his glove to catch them once he got there. He even made one of those vintage Lonnie Smith 30-foot throws straight into the turf. They finally cut down his playing time soon after Skates II ran headlong into the wall in San Diego, and then bruised his face diving for a ball in the outfield. By doing so, the Phillies probably saved his life. Otero was one of those players who was in the right place at the right time to show how limited his skills are. At least he won't have to grow old wondering what if . . . ■

JEFF PARRETT (see Looking for a Game)

J. R. PHILLIPS

1B-OF • BL • TL • 6'1 • 185 • 26 • CAL88/3

	AB	R	H	2B	3B	HR	RBI	BB	SO	SB	CS	BA	OB	SA
PHI95	231	27	45	9	0	9	28	19	69	1	1	.195	.256	.351
SF/PHI96	104	12	17	5	0	7	15	11	51	0	0	.163	.250	.413
CAREER	389	41	72	15	1	18	50	31	138	2	1	.185	.246	.368

When asked how he planned on using the newly acquired Phillips, Fregosi said: "To say hello to him and go from there." Can't fault him for being underwhelmed. Phillips was a bush leaguer for *4 years* before he saw the north slope of .200. Since then, he can be counted on to put up big enough numbers in Triple-A to merit the good table at all the best nightspots in Scranton/Wilkes-Barre—and to do nothing in the show. He simply gives away too many strikes to be a successful major league hitter. He'll be 27 in April and it may be time to start thinking about Plan B. ■

DESI RELAFORD

SS • BB • TR • 5'8 • 155 • 23 • SEA91/4

	AB	R	H	2B	3B	HR	RBI	BB	SO	SB	CS	BA	OB	SA
AAA	402	39	85	16	1	5	43	31	77	17	7	.211	.269	.294

When the Phillies got Relaford from the Mariners for Mulholland, he went from being behind Alex Rodriguez on the depth chart to staring up at Kevin Stocker. You'd think that kind of pressure change would give him the bends. It's his excellent glove that makes him a prospect, his bat having only seen the sunny side of .300 once—in A-ball after a demotion. He makes contact and has speed, so there's no reason he can't learn to bunt big-league pitching and bang grounders into the carpet. He's young, a switch-hitter, and can steal a base, so Stocker's job may be his sooner rather than later. Stocker on Relaford's acquisition: "I didn't believe they were looking for a shortstop and then this happened. I am disappointed they would get a shortstop." Too bad. It's called Darwinism, Kevin. ■

SCOTT ROLEN — *YOUNG GUN*

3B • BR • TR • 6'4 • 210 • 21 • PHI93/2

	AB	R	H	2B	3B	HR	RBI	BB	SO	SB	CS	BA	OB	SA
PHI96	130	10	33	7	0	4	18	13	27	0	2	.254	.322	.400

Scott Rolen is not the next Mike Schmidt. It's slowly dawning on the Phillies' fans that they treated the best player they'll live to see like a three-legged

greyhound at a North Tampa dog track. But that's no reason to saddle Rolen with the responsibility of giving them their shot at redemption. Rolen has the tools and the attitude to be a star—one scout described him in early '96 as "the best player in the minor leagues today." If he plays like a healthy Dave Hollins, Phillies fans should shower him with love—though if you've ever been in the Vet's upper deck on a muggy night in July, you know these people are not a James Taylor demographic.

Rolen is the only real prospect the Phillies have in their entire system and they moved Pee Wee Jeffman to left, and Todd Zeile to first and then down I-95 to make room for him. Though he was only 21 and a year removed from A-ball, he looked like he was there to stay, both at the plate and in the field, until a Steve Trachsel pitch broke a bone in his arm. He finished the year with 130 at-bats, just enough to keep him eligible for rookie of the year in '97—so the marketing department won't have to find some other poor sap a year out of Spartanburg to hype. ■

KEN RYAN

RP • BR • TR • 6'3 • 200 • 28 • BOS86

	G	GS	IP	H	HR	BB	K	W	L	S	ERA	K/BB	K9	HW9
BOS94	42	0	48	46	1	17	32	2	3	13	2.44	1.9	6.0	11.81
BOS95	28	0	32	34	4	24	34	0	4	7	4.96	1.4	9.6	16.31
PHI96	62	0	89	71	4	45	71	3	5	8	2.43	1.6	7.2	11.73
CAREER	186	0	226	198	13	120	191	12	14	30	3.18	1.6	7.6	12.66

When Ryan was the local hero in Boston, he was handed the closer role and he gave it right back. He threw hard, high, and straight, ended up back in the minors, and was bumped from the playoff roster for a 24-year-old named Joe Hudson. Either he found Philadelphia a breath of fresh air, or it helped to be pitching in what were essentially exhibition games instead of a pennant race. Ryan retired the first 30 right-handers he saw in '96. Though he has closer's stuff, there's no guarantee he'll ever be one—he converted only 8 of 13 save opportunities. Ryan wouldn't be the first to take the zero if that role came his way again. Mike Perez was unhittable in '92 and '93 for the Cardinals when the games didn't matter and he wasn't The Man. ■

BENITO SANTIAGO (see Free Agents)

GENE SCHALL

1B • BR • TR • 6'3 • 190 • 26 • PHI91/4

	AB	R	H	2B	3B	HR	RBI	BB	SO	SB	CS	BA	OB	SA
PHI95	65	2	15	2	0	0	5	6	16	0	0	.231	.306	.262
PHI96	66	7	18	5	1	2	10	12	15	0	0	.273	.392	.470

After Jefferies went down, Schall got another opportunity to play regularly. Nine games into the experiment, the Phillies were mailing him back to Scranton/Wilkes-Barre. Fregosi: "I tried to give the job to Schall, but he didn't do the job. If he hit a few balls hard he might still be here." After a soft .230 in '95, Schall hit a soft .260 in his first tour in '96. He showed more punch against Triple-A call-ups in September, but he'll be 27 in '97, he's not much with the glove, and those Hal Morris numbers he's put up in the minors have never even been hinted at in Philadelphia. His last chance may very well have been in '96 so he got two more than some and one more than most. ■

CURT SCHILLING

SP • BR • TR • 6'5 • 205 • 30 • BOS86/2

	G	GS	IP	H	HR	BB	K	W	L	S	ERA	K/BB	K9	HW9
PHI94	13	13	82	87	10	28	58	2	8	0	4.48	2.1	6.4	12.62
PHI95	17	17	116	96	12	26	114	7	5	0	3.57	4.4	8.8	9.47
PHI96	26	26	183	149	16	50	182	9	10	0	3.19	3.6	8.9	9.79
CAREER	232	121	988	880	80	291	800	52	52	13	3.49	2.7	7.3	10.67

The biggest game in Schilling's season came in early September when he made his 22nd start, triggering a clause that guaranteed him $3.5 million for '97. Schilling was on the DL for the early part of the season after right shoulder surgery—like nearly every other veteran pitcher on the roster—but he was the only one to make it back. A diplomatic Fregosi: "He's been amazing, but out of all the pitchers we have had try and come back from surgery, he was really the only one who was a good pitcher before being hurt." Ouch.

Schilling was much better than his 9-10 record. He struck out a batter an inning with command, threw well into the 90s, managed 9 complete games, wasn't afraid to use his split-finger, and produced a 3.19 ERA in a hitter's year. Despite his performance, the abysmal play of the team ground him down: "I have never been this low. I have never been through anything like this before on any team. This is one of those times you find out what people are made of." Funny, you didn't hear comments like this before Jefferies showed up. ■

KEVIN SEFCIK

UT • BR • TR • 5'10 • 175 • 26 • PHI93/33

	AB	R	H	2B	3B	HR	RBI	BB	SO	SB	CS	BA	OB	SA
PHI96	116	10	33	5	3	0	9	9	16	3	0	.284	.341	.379

Sefcik works hard and can play 3 positions, but his .284 batting average for Philadelphia in 100+ at-bats may just set him up for the same kind of unrealistic offensive expectations that Stocker couldn't meet. Sefcik is a little guy who makes contact, but he doesn't have any punch, doesn't have enough speed to be a basestealing threat, and is too impatient at the plate. His numbers in '97 will look like what player/manager Pete Rose put up during male menopause, penciling his own name into the lineup as he pursued Ty Cobb with more regard to career stats and point spreads than putting the best team on the field. ■

SCOTT SHORES

OF • BR • TR • 6'1 • 190 • 25 • PHI94/5

	AB	R	H	2B	3B	HR	RBI	BB	SO	SB	CS	BA	OB	SA
AA	398	52	91	19	8	11	51	46	133	19	10	.229	.315	.399

He has some power and speed, but he's never hit above .254, he's already 25, and he's striking out once every 3 at-bats at Double-A. He's got to make a quantum leap in '97 if he wants to position himself for that brief, Rick Bosetti expansion career commencing in '98. ■

ANTHONY SHUMAKER

RP • BL • TL • 6'5 • 225 • 23 • PHI95/23

	G	GS	IP	H	HR	BB	K	W	L	S	ERA	K/BB	K9	HW9
A+	31	0	29	42	1	12	25	5	3	3	5.52	2.1	7.7	16.57

Shumaker earned a promotion to Clearwater after being dominant at Piedmont, striking out 51, walking 10, and yielding only 16 hits in 33 innings. The Phillies may find themselves in desperate need of a lefty reliever in '97, so don't be surprised if they have to reach this deep into the organization to find one. In other words, it's going to be another long year in Philadelphia, and Shumaker might get to play a part in some of its messier chapters. ■

RUSS SPRINGER

RP • BR • TR • 6'4 • 195 • 28 • NYA89/6

	G	GS	IP	H	HR	BB	K	W	L	S	ERA	K/BB	K9	HW9
CAL94	18	5	45	53	9	14	28	2	2	2	5.52	2.0	5.6	13.38
CAL/PHI95	33	6	78	82	16	35	70	1	2	1	5.29	2.0	8.1	13.50
PHI96	51	7	96	106	12	38	94	3	10	0	4.66	2.5	8.8	13.49
CAREER	130	27	296	332	48	129	235	7	20	3	5.56	1.8	7.1	14.01

Springer throws hard and high—which is a high-risk, high-reward proposition without much margin for error. He's one of the most pronounced fly-ball pitchers in the big leagues. Some others? Belcher, Bere, Lilliquist, Mahomes, Van Poppel, and VanLandingham are a representative sample. Fly-ball pitchers crash hard when they lose a foot on their fastball. That's why the more successful ones are those who get to work an inning at a time: Beck, Brantley, Henke, Lee Smith, Dave Stevens, Wetteland, and Worrell the Elder. Springer the reliever struck out 73 and walked 24 in 63 innings. Springer the starter struck out 21 and walked 14 in 34 innings. This is not an accident. If he is ever asked to pitch 5 innings in a major-league game again, someone should lose his job. ■

GARRET STEPHENSON

SP • BR • TR • 6'4 • 185 • 25 • BAL92/18

	G	GS	IP	H	HR	BB	K	W	L	S	ERA	K/BB	K9	HW9
AAA	23	21	122	123	13	44	86	7	6	0	4.81	2.0	6.4	12.35

Acquired along with Maduro in the Inky/Zeile fire sale, Stephenson looks a lot less promising. In fact, he's little more than a warm body—a replacement for a player who neither side realized had been released the day before. He has an average fastball and relies on his change-up and curve, and, unlike Maduro, has had to do a lot of chucking and ducking at Double-A. The Phillies look like they're going to throw all these young arms at the wall in '97 and pitch the ones that stick. Stephenson slides to the floor first. ■

KEVIN STOCKER

SS • BB • TR • 6'1 • 175 • 27 • PHI91/2

	AB	R	H	2B	3B	HR	RBI	BB	SO	SB	CS	BA	OB	SA
PHI94	271	38	74	11	2	2	28	44	41	2	2	.273	.383	.351
PHI95	412	42	90	14	3	1	32	43	75	6	1	.218	.304	.274
PHI96	394	46	100	22	6	5	41	43	89	6	4	.254	.336	.378
CAREER	1336	172	348	59	14	10	132	160	248	19	7	.260	.351	.348

Since hitting .324 in a fluke '93, Stocker's gotten lazy and his average has dropped to .273 then .218 and finally .191 during the first half of '96. Recognizing that he might not even be able to find work with a team as bad as the Phillies, he impersonated a big-leaguer in the second half, raising his average to .254 and playing well in the field. He's a switch-hitter who can't hit righties, which means he's not much of a switch-hitter at all, and can't be counted on for anything more than .250 and solid defense, at best. ■

BRIAN STUMPF

RP • BL • TR • 6'3 • 200 • 24 • PHI94/45

	G	GS	IP	H	HR	BB	SO	W	L	S	ERA	K/BB	K9	HW9
A+	56	0	59	54	3	32	48	1	6	26	3.36	1.5	7.3	11.59

The Phillies found Stumpf at a local community college. He's racked up 66 saves after only 2-1/2 seasons in the minors, but his ERA has risen 1 run with each new level and he's no longer blowing away the hitters. He'll probably get a chance to close some games at Reading in '97, but that may be the end of the line for him. ■

REGGIE TAYLOR

OF • BL • TR • 6'1 • 180 • 20 • PHI95/1

	AB	R	H	2B	3B	HR	RBI	BB	SO	SB	CS	BA	OB	SA
A	499	68	131	20	6	0	31	29	136	36	17	.263	.305	.327

Taylor has speed, a good arm, no punch, and a hole in his bat. Player personnel director Unser: " . . . he is learning well defensively. The concern I have is that he doesn't dig a hole for himself at the plate. If he stays aggressive, he will be okay." Does that sound like a review of the 14th player taken in the '95 draft? Apparently the Phillies have filled another spot on the All-Airport team—the players who look great going through customs but couldn't hit a slider with a snowshoe. As Kruk said while dunking a glazed doughnut in his beer, "Lady, I'm not an athlete. I'm a ballplayer." You can have Glenn Braggs and his cut-off jerseys, Delino and his slam dunks. Take the quick wrists and the 20/15 vision. ■

KEITH TROUTMAN

RP • BR • TR • 6'1 • 200 • 23 • LA92/17

	G	GS	IP	H	HR	BB	K	W	L	S	ERA	K/BB	K9	HW9
AA	52	1	73	62	7	40	73	6	3	1	3.31	1.8	9.0	12.52

The Phillies grabbed Troutman from the Dodgers system, where he put up some ungodly K/BB numbers in relief in Great Falls, Yakima, and San Antonio. His command wasn't quite as good at Reading, but he's only 23. He could be getting meaningful innings sooner rather than later. ■

DAVID WEST (see Looking for a Game)

MIKE WILLIAMS

SP • BR • TR • 6′2 • 190 • 27 • PHI90/14

	G	GS	IP	H	HR	BB	K	W	L	S	ERA	K/BB	K9	HW9
PHI94	12	8	50	61	7	20	29	2	4	0	5.01	1.5	5.2	14.57
PHI95	33	8	87	78	10	29	57	3	3	0	3.29	2.0	5.9	11.07
PHI96	32	29	167	188	25	67	103	6	14	0	5.44	1.5	5.6	13.74
CAREER	99	54	384	406	50	145	227	13	25	0	4.87	1.6	5.3	12.91

Williams is another one who frustrated Fregosi with an unwillingness to challenge hitters, but the league was hitting .385 on his first pitch. How aggressive would you be if throwing first-pitch strikes undressed you like Charlie Brown by line drives back through the box? The Phillies have been running Williams out there for 5 years now. He actually showed signs of promise at times in '95 and '96, finishing strong both seasons, but chances are Philadelphia will run out of patience before he ever strings together 6 good starts. ■

GARY YEAGER

RP • BR • TR • 6′1 • 190 • 23 • PHI95/27

	G	GS	IP	H	HR	BB	SO	W	L	S	ERA	K/BB	K9	HW9
A	40	1	81	73	2	19	66	5	2	6	2.68	3.5	7.4	10.27

Ordinarily, there's not much reason to pay attention to late round draft picks out of college who've been dumped in the low minors, no matter how good their numbers may look. They'll be old for their leagues and their organizations will tend to move them slowly because of the other, more expensive prospects in front of them. But with the Phillies, those rules don't apply. It's grab a bucket and start bailing, and they can't afford to turn away any able-bodied men. Rich Hunter was 2 years removed from pitching mop-up in the lowest level of their system when he found himself served up to big leaguers on a platter. Matt Beech was 2 years from the NY-Penn League when he found himself staring down Greg Maddux. A late round draft pick out of a small college, Yeager went 9-4 with a 2.56 ERA in Piedmont and looked just as good at Batavia in '96. If he continues to pitch like this, he'll be in Reading before the '97 season is done. Another rash of injuries on the big club and Yeager could find himself in Philly. And he may ask himself, "Well, how did I get here?" ■

JON ZUBER

1B • BL • TL • 6′1 • 175 • 27 • PHI92/11

	AB	R	H	2B	3B	HR	RBI	BB	SO	SB	CS	BA	OB	SA
PHI96	91	7	23	4	0	1	10	6	11	1	0	.253	.296	.330

He's old, skinny, slow, and hits singles. ■

■ 1996 AUTOPSY

The Pirates hadn't looked promising going into a season since Barry Bonds and Doug Drabek left town to follow the money, but no team with Jim Leyland running it can ever be counted out. Yet with ancient veterans such as Danny Darwin and Zane Smith in the starting rotation, no impact players on the offense, and Mike Kingery and Charlie Hayes the best they could do in the free-agent market, just getting the Pirates out of last place would probably have merited a Manager of the Year award.

April 12-14 (12-14, ½ game back)
The Pirates were hanging around the leaders in a very weak division thanks to pitching that was better than expected. In 26 games the starters threw 14 quality starts, going 10-4. Denny Neagle followed up his strong '95 with a solid April. Paul Wagner was particularly effective, raising hopes that he was finally transforming all that talent into results. Zane Smith, defying all reasonable expectations, also got off to a strong start. But Dan Miceli had fallen and couldn't get up. He was a few feet short on his fastball, lost the job of closer, and never came close to getting it back—and the Pirates would finish the season with 8 different pitchers earning at least 1 save.

May 9-18 (21-32, 5 games back)
The team fell apart in May, undone by weak defense and unreliable middle relief. Darwin was especially victimized by his team's ineptitude, with his 4 quality starts resulting in 2 losses and 2 no-decisions. Wagner kept rolling until he was pulled from a start on the 19th after 3 shut out innings. Arm troubles would soon shut him down for the season. Miceli spent some time in Double-A to get it together, dominated during his brief stay, then promptly reverted to form upon his return. Center field, unsettled since Andy Van Slyke left, continued to be a problem. Now out of Colorado, Mike Kingery suddenly looked like the .250 hitter he'd always been. Jacob Brumfield didn't get to play every day and sulked. Midre Cummings was briefly given the job in one last chance to establish himself as the impact player they thought they'd gotten for John Smiley, but he was the same old lazy and ineffective Midre who was on his way to being washed up at 25. Jay Bell proclaimed the team only 5 players away from being a contender but volunteered no inside information on the availability of Bonds, Bonilla, Drabek, Smiley, and Wakefield.

June 15-12 (36-44, 5 games back)
With no team taking charge of the division, the Pirates remained in contention despite being on pace to lose nearly 90 games. If the division had been better or if the Pirates had been worse, the rebuilding process could have started earlier. Instead, the Pirates felt obligated not to throw in their cards. But when their staff ace, Denny Neagle, injured his back while taking a shower, it should have been seen as a neon sign that this was not going to be an odds-defying team of destiny. Management distracted the fans briefly with sketches of a 35,000-seat, baseball-only park overlooking the Allegheny River, and tried its best to gloss over those minor, nagging details —the $200 million price tag, the consistent inability of the Pirates to generate revenue regardless of the quality of the product, and the fact that Forbes Field was torn down only 25 years before and replaced by a carpeted petri dish because the old park, with capacity of 36,000, was too small.

July 12-15 (48-59, 8½ games back)
No one was left from the original starting rotation except Denny Neagle. John Ericks was in the minors after he was waived and went unclaimed—unclaimed during a season when Frank Viola got 6 starts. Smith had been released, as management came to its collective senses. Darwin was traded to the Astros with about 15 pitches left in his arm and incentive clauses about to kick in. Wagner, long accused of being soft, was told to throw through the pain and he promptly blew out his elbow. Miceli, who hadn't started a game since high school, was thrown out there for the same type of punishment that Lou Piniella meted out to Randy Myers in 1991. With Brumfield given away to the Blue Jays just to get him out of the clubhouse, Kingery reeling in offensive numbers a third-string catcher would throw back, and Midre Hustle still in an upright coma, the Pirates finally gave the center-field job to Jermaine Allensworth. Meanwhile, Jay Bell couldn't hit a barn with a bass fiddle, collecting 16 hits and slugging .247. His nosedive couldn't come at a more inopportune time: With a price tag of $4.8

million per year through 1997 and the Pirates looking to rebuild, the suits wanted to deal him to a contender but couldn't give him away.

August 56-79 (8-20, 17 games back)
As the Pirates went 8-20, dropping 14 of 16 at one point, Leyland wouldn't point the finger at any of his players: "Who am I going to yell at? Al Martin, who plays so hard every day? Dave Clark, who's ready to do whatever we ask every day? Jay Bell, who plays almost every inning, plays dog tired, and never complains? I'm proud of them."

The offense remained what it had been all season, but the staff had a 5.25 ERA and allowed 409 baserunners in 252 innings—well over 15 per 9 innings, 2 more than the average N.L. team. Dan Plesac, who had just been signed to a 1-year extension, lost 4 games in 2 weeks. So it probably wasn't all that surprising that the waived-and-unclaimed John "I thought I was dead in this organization" Ericks was now the team's closer. And as mediocre as the hitting was and as bad as the pitching was, their timing was worse. About the only stretch of good pitching the Pirates produced was on the 18th and 19th, when the hitters went 16-93 and the team lost 2-1 in 14 innings against the Braves, then 2-1 in 13 innings against the Astros.

The Pirates were able to eradicate all vestiges of their April rotation, dealing Neagle to the Braves and the manager who snubbed him for the All-Star game, for 3 prospects. They also sent Charlie Hayes to the Yankees for a minor league pitcher. Owner Kevin McClatchy was a bit bewildered by the negative reaction all this salary dumping was prompting: "This isn't the Chicago Bulls we're breaking up here."

September 17-10 (73-89, 15 games back)
Jermaine Allensworth contributed as much as anyone to the Pirates' best month of the season, suggesting that the Pirates leadoff problems might be over. The team hit .283, almost 20 points higher than in any other month. They also stole 30 bases and had an excellent strikeouts-to-walks ratio of 154:119 (the average N.L. team was 170:91 in September). The pitching was also sharp, posting a 3.95 ERA and allowing only a hit an inning. They won 11 in a row, finishing 14-4 to avoid a 90-loss season. Perhaps Leyland should have resigned in April.

■ 1997 DIAGNOSIS

Offense
The Pirates did what they could with the spare parts they had lying around. They hit for a decent average, drew walks, and struck out less than any other team in the league. They had gap power, hitting more doubles than any other team in the league, but outhomered only the Phillies and the Astros. In '97, Jason Kendall could develop into an excellent no. 2 hitter—if he could draw walks as he did in the minors. He already has displayed astonishing bat control, striking out 30 times in 414 at-bats. The outfield could be on the upswing, with Allensworth digging his hooks into the center-field position. The infield, unfortunately, is heading in the other direction. Chad Hermansen is their best infield prospect, and he could be playing in the majors come September. Drawing fewer fans than any team except the A's and the Brewers, and losing $8 million in the process, the Pirates won't be going after big free agents. As a result, their offense will stagnate at best. Even if they were going to be active in the free-agent market, the likes of Darren Lewis and Otis Nixon were turning their noses up at the Pirates last year. With plans to trim the payroll to $19 million—and the savings having to come from dumping members of the offense, where 80% of the salaries are currently invested—they will almost certainly be worse.

Defense
Hardly anyone in the Pirates infield was playing his best position in '96. Consider Leyland's and Berifay's options last year: Garcia would perform better at short than at second, at least until Hermansen is ready, although this phenom is really better suited to third, while King is considered to be a better second baseman than Garcia, which could open up first base for Mark Johnson, where King had to play because shoulder problems made him a nightmare at third, but then maybe they'd be better off with Orlando Merced at first, even though for most of the year he was the best defensive outfielder among a weak bunch, yadayadayada. It was beginning to look like an Escher painting, or one of those unsolvable trick puzzles to keep the munchkins

quiet in the backseat on a long trip. They solved the problem by dealing Garcia and Merced to Tornoto. Al Martin is a hard worker and team leader but not much of a fielder. Allensworth comes with good reviews in center, but he fell asleep out there at times in '96. He could have learned a few things watching Brian McRae in the final week of the season; though the Cubs were eliminated, McRae ran into the wall to make a great catch in center field in Pittsburgh, then in Wrigley turned a ground single up the middle to Allensworth into a double. Kendall is a work in progress at catcher. Leyland liked the way he called games but was not happy with his throwing—though he thinks that's due to mechanics, not arm strength.

Pitching

The Pirates used 18 starting pitchers in '96, and about half of them were relievers pressed into the rotation out of desperation. Neagle, Darwin, and Jon Lieber were really the only ones who didn't have to hang their heads in shame on those long walks from the mound to the dugout. The Pirates' top prospect, right-hander Kris Benson, probably won't be a factor until '98, but it's not inconceivable that he could pull an Andy Benes and go through the system in a single season. Benes really didn't learn anything in the minors except that he could get out minor-league hitters, and scouts are saying the same thing about Benson. But the more likely scenario is Lieber, Esteban Loaiza, Chris Peters, Jason Schmidt, and temporary closer Francisco Cordova. Wagner isn't expected back until August, and what he'll bring with him is impossible to anticipate. Unlike the offense, there's a lot of upside to the pitching—because it's so random in general, and because it was so bad in '96.

Hard to tell what their bullpen will do—they traded it. Pitching coach Ray Miller has gone back to the Baltimore Orioles, a transition that did not attract as many headlines as Leyland's departure but could be significant nevertheless. He's been replaced by Pete Vuckovich, the suave and debonair ace of the '82 Brewers.

Farm System

Pitcher Kris Benson and shortstop Chad Hermansen are the closest to being sure things in the organization. But despite the limited funds the Pirates have to throw around, the farm system is one of the strongest in baseball. Other players to watch include left-hander Jimmy Anderson, shortstop Lou Collier, and outfielders José Guillen and T. J. Staton. But the surprise of the system could be shiny new pitching phenom Elvin Hernandez, who looks good now and will look even better if he can repeat his '96 performance.

Management and Ownership

California newspaper magnate Kevin McClatchy bought the team in '96. He has a vision for the Pirates, but reality frequently intrudes. He wants a $200 million stadium downtown, but securing the financing will be a very high bar to clear. He told Bonifay to grab the best player available in the '96 draft with the no. 1 pick, and Kris Benson was snagged and promptly signed for $2 million. Though they had only a $3 million budget for all their draft picks, they were still able to sign their first 14, a performance only the Indians and Devil Rays could match. Unfortunately, some of the investors—clearly unfamiliar with baseball since Brien Taylor—gulped at the money that went to Benson and walked away. This, and operating losses well in excess of projections, forced McClatchy to slash the payroll—though he had originally promised to increase it gradually. McClatchy must be slowly coming to the realization that his plan for the Pirates sounds good but simply won't work. Baseball in Pittsburgh may be steeped in tradition, but as a business it's a lousy investment. Any year in Pittsburgh could be the last.

The trading tactics of GM Cam Bonifay weren't making him any friends in San Diego. Padres GM Kevin Towers on the Orlando Merced talks, after thumbing his nose at the Pirates and acquiring Greg Vaughn: "We keep going back and forth and I got tired of their bull [puckey]." Bonifay also wasn't doing a very good job at keeping his trade offers discreet—especially his failed attempts to deal his clean-up hitter, Jeff King—and knowing the team's best players were being peddled on the sidewalk for loose change couldn't have been good for morale. He also makes a habit of going after raw "tools" players rather than players who have one or two refined skills and less athletic ability. The Braves

don't look very good going through the airport, but they win games. The Pirates organization has too many fine athletes who can't hit, and pitchers with good stuff but a questionable ability to pitch. What they will have in '97 is a new logo, 3 new uniform styles, and 3 new caps—as they chase the merchandising cheese and sit out the pennant race.

Gene Lamont won't have to deal with the pressure of expectations he had to endure with the White Sox, but he will have to show an extraordinary amount of patience or he'll traumatize the kids and burn holes in his stomach. That's what it will take to survive the experience in the short term; if he wants to be competing for the division with this team in the year 2000, he'll need to show he can develop young players and not simply restrain from strangling them.

. . . and whatnot: Come Back, Jim. Jim, Come Back. Remember the movie *Shane*, where the quiet gunman rolls into the little town, saves the townfolk, and then leaves because he knows in his gut that he just doesn't belong there anymore? Too bad for Leyland that he didn't stick with plot and leave with Bonds and Drabek, rather than stay put with that annoying brat and his family for *Shane II*.

Leyland's best Pirate teams were a faint memory by 1996. Guys such as Martin, Merced, and King are a nice addition to any team, but they hardly compare to the core of Bonds, Bonilla, and Van Slyke that the Pirates hadn't been able to keep. The rotation that had once featured Doug Drabek and John Smiley was now led by Neagle, Paul Wagner, and Danny Darwin—2 eventually dealt to N.L. rivals, the other shut down by a serious elbow injury.

Leyland did what he could in '96. He pushed and prodded, tried every arm in the organization's depth chart—and a few peanut vendors with arm speed and command—wrung runs out of a mediocre offense, contended right up to the midseason break, never blamed his players for not being talented enough, and never lost his temper. As late as mid-August there was no hint that Leyland wouldn't be back in Pittsburgh in '97, doing it all over again. Most reports from Three Rivers contained his musings on the future of young players in development such as Jermaine Allensworth, John Lieber, and no. 1 pick Kris Benson. That all ended when practical realities—low attendance, uneasy investors—forced team owner Kevin McClatchy to make a business decision that lengthened the Pirates' rebuilding process by a few more years.

McClatchy is taking a lot of heat now for promises he should have known he couldn't keep, but give him credit for releasing Leyland from his contract when he couldn't deliver him the players he needed.

Leyland deserves another chance at the postseason, and he thinks he can make that happen in Florida with a team that is by no means a sure thing. But the Fish are a lot closer to the promised land than the Pirates, where even conservative estimates give them 3 or 4 years before they can contend again, if at all—and maybe not in Pittsburgh when the time comes.

Leyland leaving is just the beginning. And by the time the Marlins are playing in October, it won't be Jim the town is calling back. It will be an entire 40-man roster and a fleet of moving vans.

JERMAINE ALLENSWORTH — YOUNG GUN

CF • BR • TR • 6'0 • 180 • 25 • PIT93/2

	AB	R	H	2B	3B	HR	RBI	BB	SO	SB	CS	BA	OB	SA
PIT96	229	32	60	9	3	4	31	23	50	11	6	.262	.337	.380

Allensworth was the 34th overall pick, drafted from Purdue, in the '93 draft—the Pirates compensation pick for losing Doug Drabek. If everything breaks right he should hit in the .290s with gap power. It's taken him a while to get to the majors, so it's unlikely he'll develop into a perennial All-Star. His hitting on arrival in the majors (.262 batting average and .337 on-base percentage) was better than expected and impressive enough to make center field appear to be one less thing to worry about. He had poor strikeouts-to-walks ratios in the past and has done a commendable job in developing a better eye at the major-league level—though he's no threat to Rickey Henderson. Allensworth's speed is a godsend to a team that's desperate enough to have Jeff King stealing home. Allensworth looks more like a leadoff man than anyone else in the organization, and, at the moment, it's his job to lose. Unfortunately, the same could have been said about Omar Moreno, Marvell Wynne, Jacob Brumfield, Mike Kingery, and Midre Cummings in the days before and after Andy Van Slyke. ■

JIMMY ANDERSON — SOLID PROSPECT

SP • BL • TL • 6'1 • 180 • 21 • PIT94/9

	G	GS	IP	H	HR	BB	SO	W	L	S	ERA	K/BB	K9	HW9
AA	17	16	97	92	3	44	79	8	3	0	3.34	1.8	7.3	12.62

Anderson was successful at Double-A after beginning the season with an eye-opening tour of the Class-A Carolina League (1.93 ERA). His fastball can hit 90 and his slider is exceptional. On the down side, he has a slight build, he occasionally loses command, and he has a temper. But at his age, there's still time for all of the above to improve. Reports are that he's working to add a change-up. Next to Benson, he's the best they've got. ■

TREY BEAMON

OF • BL • TR • 6'3 • 195 • 23 • PIT92/2

	AB	R	H	2B	3B	HR	RBI	BB	SO	SB	CS	BA	OB	SA
PIT96	51	7	11	2	0	0	6	4	6	1	1	.216	.273	.255

The Pirates had big plans for Beamon after he won the Southern League batting title in '94 at age 20, but concerns about his work ethic and a batting average heading south (even in the hitter's paradise of the PCL) weren't in the script. Beamon looked uninspired in his September call-up, finishing below both Kingery and Midre in the team's final statistics—and that's like sleeping on the sidewalk without even being able to find a warm grate. Like Allensworth, he has speed, makes contact, and has no power, but the team probably can't get away with two of those guys in the same outfield. Beamon will be hitting the weights this off-season, so check his extra-base hits this spring. ■

JAY BELL — HEADED FOR A FALL

SS • BR • TR • 6'0 • 180 • 31 • MIN84/1

	AB	R	H	2B	3B	HR	RBI	BB	SO	SB	CS	BA	OB	SA
PIT94	424	68	117	35	4	9	45	49	82	2	0	.276	.353	.441
PIT95	530	79	139	28	4	13	55	55	110	2	5	.262	.336	.404
PIT96	527	65	132	29	3	13	71	54	108	6	4	.250	.323	.391
CAREER	4529	663	1202	249	46	83	461	457	867	64	41	.265	.335	.396

Yes, headed for a fall—as in worse than '96. Since becoming a full-time player in 1990, Bell has been extremely consistent in his fielding, power, and batting average—rarely hitting double-digit homers or straying far from his .272 career batting average. He has been an underrated hitter and an overrated fielder. Pittsburgh's pitchers have always yielded ground balls, so Bell has usually had far more balls hit to him than other N.L. shortstops, which distorts his numbers. Several factors may point to a continued decline in the next couple of years: (1) The drop in Bell's batting average is directly attributable to a drop in his success against left-handers. He came into the season hitting .311 against them in his career and was hitting .233 against them by season's end. (2) His .250 batting average is somewhat of a mirage, the result of a late-season thrust, obscuring the fact that he spent much of the season in the 2-teens. (3) Bell's slugging average is deteriorating as well. He's not getting as many doubles and homers as he did

in the early '90s. At nearly $5 million a year through '97, the Pirates couldn't give him away in '96. With orders to cut the payroll to $19 million, they'll continue to try to unload him and will have to get nothing and like it in return. ■

KRIS BENSON
GRADE-A PROSPECT

RHP • PIT96/1 • CLEMSON UNIVERSITY

The no. 1 overall pick in the draft last season, Benson had an incredible college season that was derailed when Miami crushed him twice in the College World Series. He throws a solid 90s fastball that peaks at 95, an excellent knuckle-curve, and a fine change-up. He has exceptional control and some scouts say he could jump straight into the majors—though 1998 is the current projection. He has durability and can throw strikes, though he can be wild *in* the strike zone. In addition to his troubles in the College World Series, he had a mediocre performance in his Olympic starts for Team USA. Benson's skills are in your face, but his troubles in prime time suggest a need for some extended work in A and Double-A. Any success there will continue to turn up the volume on the hype that he could be the best college pitching prospect since Roger Clemens. The Pirates scraped together $2 million for him, $1.84 million more than what they had to pay 10 years ago when they snagged Jeff King with the no. 1 pick in the draft. ■

D.J. BOSTON

1B • BL • TL • 6'7 • 230 • 25 • TOR90/39

	AB	R	H	2B	3B	HR	RBI	BB	SO	SB	CS	BA	OB	SA
AA	321	47	90	16	4	8	48	49	61	5	3	.280	.377	.430

Daryl's brother, D.J., has struggled with prospect status for years and lost the battle. Seasons past have seen him lose his power, then regain it, only to lose his ability to hit for average. But he had a decent season in Double-A Carolina after Pittsburgh acquired him from Toronto for Jacob Brumfield, perhaps a carryover from the work Toronto hitting coach Willie Upshaw did on Boston's weight shift and looping swing. It's unlikely he'll ever make the impact once projected for him, but he could be a platoon possibility at first base—which sounds a lot like Willie Upshaw. ■

ADRIAN BROWN
SLEEPER

OF • BR • TR • 6'0 • 185 • 23 • PIT92/48

	AB	R	H	2B	3B	HR	RBI	BB	SO	SB	CS	BA	OB	SA
AA	341	48	101	11	3	3	25	25	40	27	11	.296	.345	.372

Brown is an outfield prospect with a good arm and outstanding speed. He looked great at Class A Lynchburg, hitting .321 and stealing 18 bases in 215 at-bats, before being promoted to Double-A Carolina. He doesn't walk much but doesn't strike out, either. Power is the only club he doesn't have in his bag, but if Beamon or Allensworth falter, this late round longshot may be Plan C. ■

JASON CHRISTIANSEN

RP • BR • TL • 6'5 • 230 • 27 • PIT91

	G	GS	IP	H	HR	BB	K	W	L	S	ERA	K/BB	K9	HW9
PIT95	63	0	56	49	5	34	53	1	3	0	4.15	1.6	8.5	13.34
PIT96	33	0	44	56	7	19	38	3	3	0	6.70	2.0	7.8	15.33

Youth breeds inconsistency. Christiansen was demoted to develop into a starter after yielding 33 runs in 33 relief appearances, then was shut down because of shoulder soreness. Left-handed hitters hit him with blows to the body, while righties followed that up with shots to the head. His strikeout rate was pretty good, but he pitched like he was getting paid per baserunner allowed. He has a decent fastball that can top 90 and has a curveball and change-up. But his best pitch is a hard slider, which, last year, was about as effective as a knife in a gunfight. Considering his collapse at the end of '95 due to overuse, last year's ineffectiveness shouldn't have come as a shock. Now it's a question of whether both his arm and his psyche can rebound. ■

LOU COLLIER
SOLID PROSPECT

SS • BR • TR • 5'10 • 170 • 23 • PIT92/33

	AB	R	H	2B	3B	HR	RBI	BB	SO	SB	CS	BA	OB	SA
AA	443	76	124	20	3	3	49	48	73	29	9	.280	.355	.359

Chad Hermansen may be the top shortstop prospect in the system, but Collier is a level closer to the majors, a better fielder, and may be the reason Hermansen ends up at third. Collier has a good arm, is smooth on the double play, but makes a few too many errors. At the plate Collier hits for average,

takes a walk, and has developed into a solid on-base guy. With his speed and developing power, he has the makings of an effective leadoff hitter. They won't sit Bell, because that will eliminate any possibility of dumping his salary. But if they can move Bell, Collier may find himself in the majors. ■

STEVE COOKE

SP • BR • TL • 6'6 • 235 • 27 • PIT89/35

	G	GS	IP	H	HR	BB	SO	W	L	S	ERA	K/BB	K9	HW9
AA	12	12	54	56	3	26	45	1	5	0	4.36	1.7	7.5	13.75

Three years ago, Jim Leyland was calling Steve Cooke the best pitching prospect Pittsburgh ever developed. But Cooke's numbers deteriorated drastically in '94, and he made all of 2 minor league starts in '95 because of a sore left shoulder. His shoulder troubles continued into '96. He began the season on the 15-day disabled list and was transferred to the 60-day DL in late April. He returned June 18 and made a few brutal starts in Double-A. Cooke is a finesse fly-ball pitcher. His top pitch is a change-up which he complements with a nice curveball. Right now things don't look good for him, but the Pirates starting rotation will be as unsettled in '97 as it was in '96, and he'll probably get his chance to serve up some dingers. ■

FRANCISCO CORDOVA

RP-SP • BR • TR • 5'11 • 165 • 24

	G	GS	IP	H	HR	BB	K	W	L	S	ERA	K/BB	K9	HW9
PIT96	59	6	99	103	11	20	95	4	7	12	4.09	4.8	8.6	11.18

Cordova was one of Pittsburgh's few pleasant surprises this year when he unexpectedly stepped up to share the closer role for a while with Dan Plesac after Danny Miceli imploded. Cordova never pitched in the minors but had an excellent record with the Mexico City Red Devils. His top pitch is a solid 90s fastball, his control was excellent in Pittsburgh, and his strikeout rate is improving. Because he is from rural Mexico and converses in a local dialect, he has trouble speaking Spanish, much less English. But the Pirates had little trouble communicating their satisfaction with his relief performance. Nevertheless, his future might be as a starter. Leyland: "I said from spring training that he had the equipment to be a starter. He's got a loose, live arm, and he throws strikes. We used him in the bullpen because we thought that was the best way to get him some experience up here. Until he comes up with a good straight change, left-handed hitters are going to give him trouble. He needs to work on some things, but I don't think there's any question he can be a starter." ■

CHRIS CORN

SP • BR • TR • 6'2 • 170 • 25 • NYA94/21

	G	GS	IP	H	HR	BB	SO	W	L	S	ERA	K/BB	K9	HW9
A+	26	25	170	145	10	38	109	12	4	0	2.91	2.9	5.8	9.67

Acquired from the Yankees in a trade for Charlie Hayes, Corn's chief attribute is his stamina. Despite a 90-mph fastball, he has a reputation as a finesse type, like Neagle, relying on his circle change for strikes. His curve has good movement but ends up in the dirt more often than not. His future is probably in relief—he was much more successful after the Yanks converted him to the bullpen. He's a little old for a Class-A pitcher and he doesn't fit in with Bonifay's new "power" approach to prospect acquisition—but how much would you give up to rent Charlie Hayes if you already had Wade Boggs? ■

MIDRE CUMMINGS

OVERRATED

OF • EB • TR • 6'1 • 190 • 25 • MIN90/2

	AB	R	H	2B	3B	HR	RBI	BB	SO	SB	CS	BA	OB	SA
PIT94	86	11	21	4	0	1	12	4	18	0	0	.244	.283	.326
PIT95	152	13	37	7	1	2	15	13	30	1	0	.243	.303	.342
PIT96	85	11	19	3	1	3	7	0	16	0	0	.224	.221	.388
CAREER	359	40	81	15	2	6	37	21	73	1	0	.226	.268	.329

Cummings didn't have an awful year in Triple-A (8-55-.304), but it wasn't much by PCL standards and just another in a long string of disappointments. He has consistently fallen short of the organization's expectations, and his reputation as a jake endures. He's done everything short of dressing down to business casual for Friday games. He has also lost his strike-zone judgment, hasn't been doing much with his speed, and is not going

to get to Pittsburgh by virtue of his fielding. He didn't even merit a September call-up in '96, and may be another organization's source of pride and joy by spring training. But if Leyland can't motivate you, no one can. ■

KANE DAVIS

SP • BR • TR • 6'3 • 180 • 21 • PIT93/16

	G	GS	IP	H	HR	BB	SO	W	L	S	ERA	K/BB	K9	HW9
A+	26	26	157	160	12	56	116	11	9	0	4.29	2.1	6.6	12.36

Davis has 3 tough pitches: a low 90s fastball, a hard slider, and a straight change-up. His record and ERA weren't stellar, but his strikeout rate was encouraging, and his control was decent. It wouldn't be shocking to see him get a look in '97, though it remains to be seen whether he'll be the 15th starting pitcher they use or only the 11th. ■

ELMER DESSENS

P • BR • TR • 6'0 • 190 • 25 • PIT95

	G	GS	IP	H	HR	BB	SO	W	L	S	ERA	K/BB	K9	HW9
PIT96	15	3	25	40	2	4	13	0	2	0	8.28	3.3	4.7	15.84

Dessens was purchased from the Mexican League and may be on his way back. He led the Southern League in ERA in '95, but was easy to hit, and his fastball was far from dominating. As you would expect, his major-league debut included few walks, few strikeouts, and lots of hits. ■

ANGELO ENCARNACION

C • BR • TR • 5'8 • 180 • 23 • PIT90

	AB	R	H	2B	3B	HR	RBI	BB	SO	SB	CS	BA	OB	SA
AAA	263	38	84	18	0	4	31	10	19	6	2	.319	.349	.433

Encarnacion had a good year at the plate, hitting for average with line drive-power. He is a fine defensive catcher with an excellent arm but is considered mediocre at handling pitchers. He has good speed for a catcher, he's young, and he'll be a capable back-up. ■

JOHN ERICKS

RP • BR • TR • 6'7 • 220 • 29 • SL88/1

	G	GS	IP	H	HR	BB	K	W	L	S	ERA	K/BB	K9	HW9
PIT95	19	18	106	108	7	50	80	3	9	0	4.58	1.6	6.8	13.42
PIT96	28	4	46	56	11	19	46	4	5	8	5.79	2.4	9.0	14.65

Ericks went from his manager saying, "You can't afford to carry anybody who can't get people out"

after demoting him in April, to closing games in the second half. But then the Pirates have used just about everyone except Enrique Romo and Odell Jones to close games during the 90s. He throws a low-90s fastball with a mediocre curveball, slider, and change-up. Once upon a time he threw in the high 90s, but injuries have robbed him of his velocity. He's been accused of thinking too much on the mound, though you wouldn't assume that from looking at him. ■

CARLOS GARCIA

2B • BR • TR • 6'1 • 185 • 29 • PIT87

	AB	R	H	2B	3B	HR	RBI	BB	SO	SB	CS	BA	OB	SA
PIT94	412	49	114	15	2	6	28	16	67	18	9	.277	.309	.367
PIT95	367	41	108	24	2	6	50	25	55	8	4	.294	.340	.420
PIT96	390	66	111	18	4	6	44	23	58	16	6	.285	.329	.397
CAREER	1782	240	496	83	15	30	174	96	266	60	30	.278	.320	.392

Garcia has been solid in his tenure with the Pirates, but he's another relatively high-priced player who is on the trading block. He has good bat speed but doesn't have the selectivity to realize his potential as a hitter. He hasn't been able to utilize his speed, mainly because of injuries such as a nagging hamstring problem that placed him on the DL for good parts of May and July '96. When healthy, Garcia is a fine second baseman who shows good hands, range, and a strong arm. In Toronto, he may find hmiself in a pennant race for the first time. ■

FREDDY GARCIA

SOLID PROSPECT

3B • BR • TR • 6'2 • 185 • 24 • TOR91

	AB	R	H	2B	3B	HR	RBI	BB	SO	SB	CS	BA	OB	SA
A+	474	79	145	39	3	21	86	44	86	4	2	.306	.358	.534

Pittsburgh took him from Toronto in the '94 Rule 5 draft, but that meant they had to jump him from Class-A to the majors in '95 and leave him for the season in order to keep him. He didn't exactly thrive and was returned to Class-A in '96. He's a disciplined hitter with great power—he tied teammate José Guillen for the league lead in

homers—who can also hit for average. He struck out a lot, but not at an alarming rate. He has a strong arm at third base and can make the plays. He could get another chance at major-league pitching at some point in '97. ■

JOSÉ GUILLEN

GRADE-A PROSPECT

OF • BR • TR • 5'11 • 165 • 20 • PIT92

	AB	R	H	2B	3B	HR	RBI	BB	SO	SB	CS	BA	OB	SA
A+	528	78	170	30	0	21	94	20	73	24	13	.322	.357	.498

Guillen is a great prospect. He is young and has power, speed, and an arm that has been compared to Dave Parker's and Robert Clemente's by some scouts. He earned Carolina League MVP honors, hitting well over .300 with power, driving in almost 100 runs, and stealing 24 bases. Jeff Banister, the Lynchburg manager, projects Mondesi numbers for him—25 dingers, 25 steals—to go with the Mondesi arm. ■

CHAD HERMANSEN

GRADE-A PROSPECT

SS • BR • TR • 6'2 • 185 • 19 • PIT95/1

	AB	R	H	2B	3B	HR	RBI	BB	SO	SB	CS	BA	OB	SA
A+	226	41	57	11	3	14	41	38	65	11	3	.252	.377	.513

Hermansen was the 10th overall pick in the '95 draft, and deservedly so. Chipper Jones comparisons are outrageous this early on, but they do share many of the same qualities. He's a composed player who hits for average and power, has advanced quickly, and seems to hit better the higher he ascends. He easily held his own with older prospects such as Guillen and Garcia in Lynchburg after being promoted from Augusta. He has speed and can steal a few bases. Talk around Three Rivers is that despite his solid defense, his size may necessitate a shift to third or even the outfield. With his bat, they'll find a place for him somewhere. ■

ELVIN HERNANDEZ

SOLID PROSPECT

SP • BR • TR • 6'1 • 165 • 19 • PIT94

	G	GS	IP	H	HR	BB	SO	W	L	S	ERA	K/BB	K9	HW9
A	27	27	158	140	13	16	171	17	5	0	3.14	10.7	9.76	8.96

Hernandez came out of nowhere to have one of the best minor-league seasons of '96. His record, control, and strikeout numbers were overwhelming. Nobody would have predicted such a breakout season based on his '95 stats (2.89 ERA, 6-1 record, and only 54 Ks in 80 innings of work). He isn't big, but he's young and should fill out. Considering how many innings he worked this year, the Pirates must make sure he doesn't get overworked in '97 as he attempts to follow Benson all the way to Pittsburgh. ■

JOHN HOPE

SP • BR • TR • 6'2 • 205 • 26 • PIT89/3

	G	GS	IP	H	HR	BB	SO	W	L	S	ERA	K/BB	K9	HW9
AAA	23	21	125	147	11	49	71	4	7	0	4.82	1.4	5.1	14.11

Hope had an excellent start in '95 at Triple-A, going 7-1 with a PCL-leading 2.49 ERA, but he struggled in '96. He once threw 90+, but has lost velocity since shoulder surgery. Now he keeps the ball down and uses exceptional control. He's getting old and, with the kids coming up, he won't exactly be the center of attention. He may get his last, best chance in Pittsburgh in '97. ■

MARK JOHNSON

1B • BL • TL • 6'4 • 230 • 29 • PIT90/20

	AB	R	H	2B	3B	HR	RBI	BB	SO	SB	CS	BA	OB	SA
PIT95	221	32	46	6	1	13	28	37	66	5	2	.208	.326	.421
PIT96	343	55	94	24	0	13	47	44	64	6	4	.274	.361	.458

Comparisons to Balboni and Pagliarulo abound. He strikes out a lot because he guesses when he's at the plate, but he made surprising strides toward rectifying the problem in '96. It helped that the former Dartmouth QB cut down on the leg lift and hitch that made for one of the most unorthodox swings since Mel Ott. Leyland found as much time as he could for him, especially in the latter half of the season, mainly facing righties. This should continue to be the case this season. In the outfield he looked more like a nose tackle than a quarterback. At first base he was adequate. ■

JASON KENDALL

YOUNG GUN

C • BR • TR • 6'0 • 170 • 22 • PIT92/1

	AB	R	H	2B	3B	HR	RBI	BB	SO	SB	CS	BA	OB	SA
PIT96	414	54	124	23	5	3	42	35	30	5	2	.300	.372	.401

In a scouting survey, Fred Kendall, Jason's dad and a former major-league catcher himself, ranked his son

behind Mike Piazza and Todd Hundley on a list of the N.L.'s best catchers. High praise, even if it is from your Dad. Kendall has drawn rave reviews for his defense at every level he's played. Dan Plesac said Kendall is a good target with soft hands, and he seems to work well with all the Pirates pitchers. After one game in April, Wagner said: "I throw whatever he puts down. . . . I don't care if he's 21 or 41, he's a smart kid." But Jim Leyland warned, "Let's not get him in the Hall of Fame yet."

He's a tough out, whiffing only 30 times in 414 at-bats. In fact, he hit over .250 with 2 strikes, a remarkable performance at any age but stunning at 21. He currently has shown little power, but he runs well enough to hit in the top of the order.

There were scary rumors that Kendall had heard something pop in his shoulder while playing in the '95 Arizona Fall League, but his arm appeared fine in the spring. At best, his arm is good but not overpowering. He threw out 30% of runners in the minors a couple of times but looks like he might nail 25% in the majors—perhaps higher if he can iron out some mechanical difficulties. Any shortcomings in Kendall's game can and should be weighed against his age. He's a hard-nosed player with a high ceiling. He's got perennial All-Star written all over him—especially since someone has to represent the Pirates. ■

JEFF KING — HEADED FOR A FALL

1B-2B-3B • BR • TR • 6'1 • 185 • 32 • PIT86/1

	AB	R	H	2B	3B	HR	RBI	BB	SO	SB	CS	BA	OB	SA
PIT94	339	36	89	23	0	5	42	30	38	3	2	.263	.316	.375
PIT95	445	61	118	27	2	18	87	55	63	7	4	.265	.342	.456
PIT96	591	91	160	36	4	30	111	70	95	15	1	.271	.346	.497
CAREER	3161	419	817	173	16	99	493	296	405	47	25	.258	.320	.417

King had the best offensive season on the team by several light-years, with no protection in the lineup. He made some adjustments at age 28 to improve his bat speed and has been a consistent hitter since. His domination of lefties made him better than average, but when that goes, so will he. He could maintain

his production for the next couple of years, but he can roll off the table anytime—especially if his back troubles return. (See Ed Sprague of the Toronto Blue Jays for a discussion of unprecedented power outbursts at the age of 29 or older.) King still falls into stretches of passiveness at the plate—prompting Leyland to bench him for 2 games at one point in '96, no doubt forcing him to eat red meat and watch Chuck Norris movies in the clubhouse.

What King may lack in aggressiveness, he makes up for in attitude. He appears to be one of the few major-league players who haven't completely lost touch with reality. Leyland: "This is a perfect example of a content player. He knows he could have gotten more money on the open market last winter, but he's happy in Pittsburgh, and he's happy with his salary. He likes the area, his family likes it, and he'd like to stay and finish his career here. He feels very comfortable in these surroundings. He's a happy player, and there's something to be said for that." No doubt, Fehr & Loathing at the union office will be looking into this immediately. ■

JON LIEBER — SLEEPER

SP • BL • TR • 6'3 • 220 • 26 • KC92/5

	G	GS	IP	H	HR	BB	K	W	L	S	ERA	K/BB	K9	HW9
PIT94	17	17	108	116	12	25	71	6	7	0	3.73	2.8	5.9	11.74
PIT95	21	12	72	103	7	14	45	4	7	0	6.32	3.2	5.6	14.63
PIT96	51	15	142	156	19	28	94	9	5	1	3.99	3.4	6.0	11.66
CAREER	89	44	323	375	38	67	210	19	19	1	4.43	3.1	5.9	12.31

Lieber was hurt by righties and emotionally scarred by lefties in '95. Both performances improved in '96. He brings a decent sinker that hits 90-91 on the fast gun, a cut fastball, an average slider, and a weak change-up to the mound. He needs all 4 pitches to get outs, and late in the season he was doing just that. He may be the ace of the staff in '97. Neagle didn't emerge until his 4th year either. ■

ESTEBAN LOAIZA

SLEEPER

SP • BR • TR • 6′4 • 190 • 25 • PIT91

	G	GS	IP	H	HR	BB	K	W	L	S	ERA	K/BB	K9	HW9
PIT95	32	31	172	205	21	55	85	8	9	0	5.16	1.5	4.4	13.60
PIT96	10	10	52	65	11	19	32	2	3	0	4.96	1.7	5.5	14.52

Loaiza has been an extremely frustrating player for Leyland and the Bucs. He's managed to pitch himself out of major-league starting jobs the past 2 years. In '95 he tied for the N.L. lead in starts and led the league in runs allowed with 115. He has been a bust in terms of command and poise on the mound. But Loaiza's stuff is unquestioned, cited as the organization's best by the Pirates and major-league scouts. He has excellent sinking action on his 90-mph fastball, complemented by a great tight-breaking slider, a decent curveball, and a change-up. He really needs to trust his pitches instead of trying to blow away every batter. And a little work wouldn't hurt either. Leyland—who never blasts his players in the press, and who spent 7 years with Barry Bonds and only tried to fight him once—on Loaiza: "I'm not saying he's lazy, but I'd like to see him exert himself a little more. You just don't know what you're going to get from one start to the next." Don't exactly have to read between those lines. An ankle injury might have hampered his velocity early in the season, but he made it back to the majors eventually and wasn't that bad. ■

RICH LOISELLE

SLEEPER

P • BR • TR • 6′5 • 225 • 25 • SD91/39

	G	GS	IP	H	HR	BB	K	W	L	S	ERA	K/BB	K9	HW9
PIT96	5	3	20	22	3	8	9	1	0	0	3.05	1.1	4.0	13.46

Loiselle was the pitcher acquired for Danny Darwin last season, and it looks like they got a lot for a guy with very few grains of sand left in the top half of his hourglass. Loiselle throws a good 4-seam fastball and a 2-seamer. His mechanics are strong and he's improved his breaking ball and change-up. His performance in Calgary was also strong. He'll be in the Pirates rotation at some point in '97 if he has more than 2 pitches working. Otherwise he'll be in the bullpen and may get a chance to close some games. ■

AL MARTIN

LF • BL • TL • 6′2 • 220 • 29 • ATL85/7

	AB	R	H	2B	3B	HR	RBI	BB	SO	SB	CS	BA	OB	SA
PIT94	276	48	79	12	4	9	33	34	56	15	6	.286	.367	.457
PIT95	439	70	124	25	3	13	41	44	92	20	11	.282	.351	.442
PIT96	630	101	189	40	1	18	72	54	116	38	12	.300	.354	.452
CAREER	1837	305	529	103	17	58	212	174	391	89	38	.288	.350	.457

Martin looks like a platoon candidate on paper, but only the strat-o-matic crowd plays the games there. He played every day, and his dismal performance against lefties (he hit .132 against them in '95) improved to a more respectable level north of the Mendoza Line in '96. His overall numbers look like a career year. He's a good baserunner with the ability to swipe 20 to 25 bases consistently. Though he's not much in the field, he's great in the clubhouse. Leyland: "Al Martin can play for me every day of the week. . . . He plays so hard and gives you everything he's got. He runs every ball out like it's the last one he'll hit in his life. He's one of my all-time favorites. I'll be proud to say that I managed Albert Martin." The Pirates locked him in through 1999, so it appears that Martin is the one they want around the rookies. ■

ORLANDO MERCED

RF • BB • TR • 6′0 • 180 • 30 • PIT85

	AB	R	H	2B	3B	HR	RBI	BB	SO	SB	CS	BA	OB	SA
PIT94	386	48	105	21	3	9	51	42	58	4	1	.272	.343	.412
PIT95	487	75	146	29	4	15	83	52	74	7	2	.300	.365	.468
PIT96	453	69	130	24	1	17	80	51	74	8	4	.287	.357	.457
CAREER	2613	396	739	146	19	65	394	339	423	35	18	.283	.364	.428

Merced would have been traded if he hadn't been injured as the deadline approached, and he will probably be dealt during the off-season in yet another salary dump. He continues to get little respect, but consider this: (1) The Padres wanted him for their pennant drive; (2) he continues to contribute regardless of where the Pirates play him in the field or bat him in the order; and (3) Leyland wouldn't have kept him around if he was lazy, gutless, or disruptive. He could be a terrific role player on a good team, like Roy White, flaws and all, was for the Yankees in the late '70s.

When Merced and Garcia were both healthy, the team went 49-47—24-42 with either one of them out. ■

RAMON MOREL

SLEEPER

RP • BR • TR • 6′2 • 170 • 22 • PIT91

	G	GS	IP	H	HR	BB	K	W	L	S	ERA	K/BB	K9	HW9
PIT96	29	0	42	57	4	19	22	2	1	0	5.36	1.2	4.7	16.29

Morel had consistently good strikeout rates until he hit the majors. His fastball hits the low 90s but has dropped disturbingly into the mid-80s on several occasions. Whether this indicates motion or mechanical problems is debatable, but it's not a good sign. Morel has a mature repertoire, throwing a curveball, slider, and change-up in addition to his fastball. Coaches expect him to develop more velocity as he gets older. Believe it when you see it, but if it happens, the results could be impressive. ■

KEITH OSIK

C • BR • TR • 6′0 • 185 • 28

	AB	R	H	2B	3B	HR	RBI	BB	SO	SB	CS	BA	OB	SA
PIT96	140	18	41	14	1	1	14	14	22	1	0	.293	.361	.429

Like most replacement players, Osik was forgotten by ownership as soon as the strike was resolved. Despite putting up excellent numbers in Triple-A Calgary in '95, he was not called up. His acceptance by the Pirates in '96 was aided by team leader Al Martin: "I wish he wouldn't have [become a replacement player], but who am I to judge? . . . All I know is that he is a guy who can help this team win, and anyone who can help this team win is welcomed with open arms in this clubhouse." When Osik did get a shot backing up Kendall in '96, he performed well despite losing a month to a hand injury and having to contend for playing time with Encarnacion. Osik also can play third base and the outfield, so he should get 200 at bats as the new John Wehner. Like Kendall, the Pirates weren't thrilled with his throwing but liked how he handled pitchers. Pitching coach Ray Miller: "[Kendall and Osik] both have an innate ability to set up hitters. They both study. We only called 2 pitches for them in the first 15 games." ■

CHRIS PETERS

SOLID PROSPECT

SP • BL • TL • 6′1 • 170 • 25 • PIT93/40

	G	GS	IP	H	HR	BB	K	W	L	S	ERA	K/BB	K9	HW9
PIT96	16	10	64	72	9	25	28	2	4	0	5.63	1.1	3.9	13.64

Peters has the best curveball in the organization, and there is talk that he is being groomed for the lefty closing role—provided Grant Jackson or Rod Scurry isn't available. He displayed excellent control in the minors and keeps the ball down. But in the majors, batters got the ball up—way up—and it took his final few starts to salvage his season. Before that strong finish, Leyland wasn't sounding very impressed: "His command hasn't gotten much better. I like him a lot and I think he has a bright future. This might be a case where he got here a little too quick. As far as whether he's ready for the big leagues right now, that's a little bit up in the air." ■

CHARLES PETERSON

OF • BR • TR • 6′3 • 200 • 22 • PIT93/1

	AB	R	H	2B	3B	HR	RBI	BB	SO	SB	CS	BA	OB	SA
AA	462	71	127	24	2	7	63	50	104	33	10	.275	.345	.381

Peterson is another of those raw, athletic outfield prospects Pittsburgh can't seem to say no to. His fielding is terrific: He's quick, his range is excellent, and he has a fine arm. He manages good base-stealing numbers year after year, but his hitting is less impressive. His average is decent and he draws an adequate number of walks, but he strikes out too much. With Beamon, Allensworth, and Brown all in his way, he might have to settle down in Calgary. ■

DAN PLESAC

RP • BL • TL • 6′5 • 210 • 35 • MIL83/1

	G	GS	IP	H	HR	BB	K	W	L	S	ERA	K/BB	K9	HW9
CHN94	54	0	54	61	9	13	53	2	3	1	4.61	4.1	8.8	12.32
PIT95	58	0	60	53	3	27	57	4	4	3	3.58	2.1	8.6	12.00
PIT96	73	0	70	67	4	24	76	6	5	11	4.09	3.2	9.8	11.69
CAREER	607	14	772	715	69	271	681	43	50	148	3.54	2.5	7.9	11.49

After 5 years as Milwaukee's closer, Plesac has been used in recent years as a setup man who can shut down left-handers. When asked to share the closer role with Francisco Cordova for a while, he showed he hadn't forgotten how it's done. Plesac throws a strong

fastball that he can cut or sink, a deceptive palmball, and a slider (his out pitch). He's lost some velocity because of shoulder injuries, but he throws consistently in the high 80s. He would have been dealt in '96, but he didn't clear waivers—so they had to wait until November to deal him to Toronto. ■

COREY POINTER

SLEEPER

C • BR • TR • 6'2 • 205 • 21 • ATL94/2

	AB	R	H	2B	3B	HR	RBI	BB	SO	SB	CS	BA	OB	SA
A-	233	46	57	12	3	14	39	35	88	10	2	.245	.349	.502

Hip Pointer was the throw-in in the Neagle trade. He's got lots of pop, draws walks and has speed, but his strikeout rate is high. The Pirates dumped him in the N.Y.-Penn League, one of the lowest leagues around, and he fared poorly—but he's only 21 this season and could rise quickly. ■

MATT RUEBEL

SP • BL • TL • 6'2 • 180 • 27 • PIT91/4

	G	GS	IP	H	HR	BB	K	W	L	S	ERA	K/BB	K9	HW9
PIT96	26	7	58	64	7	25	22	1	1	1	4.60	.9	3.4	13.79

Ruebel throws in the mid-80s with a good change-up and curveball. Bonifay compares him to Neagle, but his '96 numbers don't flatter the comparison. He has a hard slider but uses it sparingly. His control is decent, but he's the type of solid but uninspiring pitcher most teams let "ripen" in the minors for extended periods. The Pirates don't have that luxury, so he'll get another chance in '97. ■

MATT RYAN

RP • BR • TR • 6'5 • 190 • 25 • PIT93/28

	G	GS	IP	H	HR	BB	SO	W	L	S	ERA	K/BB	K9	HW9
AAA	51	0	53	70	4	28	35	2	6	20	5.30	1.3	6.0	16.75

Ryan was the closer at Triple-A Calgary, though his strikeouts-to-walks ratio doesn't look like anything Rich Gossage would settle for even now. His best pitch is an 88-mph sinker, which he developed after breaking a finger. Some scouts rave about this pitch, but AAA hitters weren't overwhelmed by it and he never got a chance to pitch for the '96 Pirates—which says a lot. ■

CHANCE SANFORD

2B • BL • TR • 5'10 • 165 • 24 • PIT92/29

	AB	R	H	2B	3B	HR	RBI	BB	SO	SB	CS	BA	OB	SA
AA	470	62	115	16	13	4	56	72	108	11	11	.245	.341	.360

Sanford displayed home-run power in previous seasons, but he was more of a line-drive hitter in '96. He's used his speed and aggressiveness to stretch more than a few singles into doubles, and his triples were off the chart in '96. He strikes out too much and he's not great defensively at second base, but that could describe Tony Phillips when he first arrived in Oakland. ■

JASON SCHMIDT

YOUNG GUN

SP • BR • TR • 6'5 • 185 • 24 • ATL91/7

	G	GS	IP	H	HR	BB	K	W	L	S	ERA	K/BB	K9	HW9
ATL95	9	2	25	27	2	18	19	2	2	0	5.76	1.1	6.8	16.20
ATL/PIT96	19	17	95	108	10	53	74	5	6	0	5.77	1.4	7.0	15.23

Schmidt has one of the best power arms in the league and is not far away from being a dominant N.L. starter. His fastball reaches the mid-90s, he sets it up with great breaking stuff, and he's working on a complementary change-up. Although the organization considered him unpolished, they still felt that he should learn at the major-league level and inserted him in their rotation upon arrival. The results were promising, as he threw strikes and didn't take too many blows to the head. His development isn't always going to be pretty, and he will be facing much better pitchers than he did out of the 5-hole in Atlanta. At least there won't be 50,000 howling fans in the stands as he tries to evolve into a staff ace. And if he doesn't want to be The Man, he can always comfort himself with this mantra: "Benson is coming. Benson is coming. Benson is coming." ■

CLINT SODOWSKY

SP • BL • TR • 6'3 • 180 • 24 • DET91/11

	G	GS	IP	H	HR	BB	K	W	L	S	ERA	K/BB	K9	HW9
DET95	6	6	23	24	4	18	14	2	2	0	5.01	.8	5.5	16.43
DET96	7	7	24	40	5	20	9	1	3	0	11.84	.5	3.4	22.47

Sodowsky got off to a great start in Triple-A Toledo (6-1, 2.99 ERA) and received a much-heralded call-up in June. He received a rude welcome (1-3, 11.84 ERA), and was sent back down to finish the year

solidly for Toledo. He throws an adequate sinking fastball and an outstanding change-up, but reportedly he has a problem with tipping it. In 1995 Sodowsky received Sparky's kiss of death: "This guy is going to be a no. 1 pitcher on a good staff. He's the best young pitcher they've brought in here since Dan Petry." And Danny Bautista was going to be the next yadayadayada. If Sodowsky wins 20 games in his career, it will be a miracle. ■

T. J. STATON — *SOLID PROSPECT*

OF • BL • TL • 6'3 • 200 • 22 • PIT93/10

	AB	R	H	2B	3B	HR	RBI	BB	SO	SB	CS	BA	OB	SA
AA	386	72	119	24	3	15	57	58	99	17	7	.308	.403	.503

Staton is another Pittsburgh prospect whose power exploded in '96. His speed was at the same impressive levels as '95, and his strikeouts-to-walks ratio was solid. Most promising was his ability to adjust to Double-A pitching without a hitch. He did slow down the during the second half of last season, but he looks awfully good. Staton played in the '96 Arizona Fall League, and he could really turn some heads in '97 if he doesn't wear down. ■

DALE SVEUM

3B • BB • TR • 6'3 • 185 • 33

	AB	R	H	2B	3B	HR	RBI	BB	SO	SB	CS	BA	OB	SA
AAA	343	62	103	28	2	23	84	33	71	2	1	.300	.365	.595

Sveum, who once hit 25 dingers for the Brewers (see the Milwaukee Brewers for a discussion of the 1987 juiced ball year and the eerie parallels between Sveum and José Valentin), has crawled all the way back to the light after managing only 43 hits in his last 241 major-league at-bats. He had one of the better minor-league seasons in the entire organization, and it looks like there's still life in his bat after hitting .353 in 34 September at bats in Pittsburgh. ■

PAUL WAGNER

SP • BR • TR • 6'3 • 205 • 29 • PIT89/13

	G	GS	IP	H	HR	BB	K	W	L	S	ERA	K/BB	K9	HW9
PIT94	29	17	119	136	7	50	86	7	8	0	4.59	1.7	6.5	14.06
PIT95	33	25	165	174	18	72	120	5	16	1	4.80	1.7	6.5	13.42
PIT96	16	15	81	86	10	39	81	4	8	0	5.40	2.1	9.0	13.88
CAREER	128	75	520	548	50	208	406	26	40	3	4.60	2.0	7.0	13.08

A late bloomer, Wagner is in only his fourth year of major-league service. Prior to '96 Wagner not only

dodged success but also embraced failure, leading the league in losses in '95. Until early '96, scouts couldn't agree as to why he wasn't clicking on the mound, some insisting that he was throwing in lieu of pitching while others cited his inability to change speeds. Wagner's control has historically been poor and he's never had an ERA under 4.20 as a major-league starter. He throws a good fastball that gets into the 90s and bores in on right-handers, occasionally cuts his fastball, and has a slider that ranks just below his heater. He has a curveball, but it generally gathers dust. He dominated early in '96 but was halted in June by pain in his biceps tendon. Perceived by his teammates and his organization as a bit of a gimp when it came to injuries, he was encouraged to throw through the pain. He was shut down soon after, underwent surgery to repair damage to his elbow ligaments, and isn't expected back by the Pirates until midseason. Opening Day isn't out of the question, but don't bet the baby's milk money on it. ■

RON WRIGHT — *GRADE-A PROSPECT*

1B • BR • TR • 6'0 • 215 • 21 • ATL94/9

	AB	R	H	2B	3B	HR	RBI	BB	SO	SB	CS	BA	OB	SA
AA	232	39	59	11	1	16	52	38	73	1	0	.254	.360	.517

The Yankees wouldn't give up Ruben Rivera to get Neagle. Wright is what it took for the Braves to get him. It's tough to find a better power prospect in minor-league baseball. He followed a 32-homer performance in '95 with a 36-homer encore in '96 in Class-A and Double-A. He needs to improve his batting average, but he drew enough walks to offset his high strikeout rate. Bonifay hasn't ruled out the possibility of Wright arriving in Pittsburgh this year, which is a sign that the organization feels they have to produce immediate results from the fire sale of '96. They'd be best to start him at Triple-A, await proof that he can get on base at an acceptable rate, and let him get more intimate with his glove than he had been in the past, and then bring him up in May or June. With his youth and power, he could easily hit 400 homers in the majors, and Neagle could be the answer to a trivia question. ■

■ 1996 AUTOPSY

In an effort to avoid another 4th place finish in the National League Central, the Cardinals made major renovations in the off-season. When GM Walt Jocketty finally got the cash to spend, like Marla Maples on her own personal *Wheel of Fortune*, he didn't choose to take any of it on a gift certificate. By the time Jocketty was through, the Cards looked like a different team: the Oakland A's. The Cardinals imported manager Tony LaRussa at a cost of $1.5 million. But he didn't come alone. His entourage consisted of pitching coach Dave Duncan, Todd Stottlemyre, Dennis Eckersley, and utilityman Mike Gallego. But the retooling wasn't limited to Oakland. Jocketty also brought in Ron Gant, Andy Benes, Gary Gaetti, and Royce Clayton. The one glaring weakness of the team was its age. Gaetti, Eck, Ozzie Smith, Mike Morgan and Danny Jackson were all on the back nine. But LaRussa certainly had a lot more to work with than Joe Torre had been given the year before.

April 12-15 (12-15, 1 game back)
The Cardinals were very fortunate in April. They were 3 games under .500, allowed 32 runs more than they scored, were out-homered 33-19, and still finished the month a game behind the division leader. The Cardinals started the month 11-7, scoring first in 14 of those 18 games. But a precursor to their falloff was the fact that 7 of those games were decided by a run and 3 were extra-inning affairs. "I knew it wasn't going to be easy," LaRussa quipped, "but I didn't think every game was going to be sudden death."

The Cards went 1-9 in the final 10 games. The brothers Benes were not exactly carbon copies of each other. Alan emerged as the front-line starter the club expected him to be, going 3-1 in his first 6 starts, but big brother Andy went 1-3. However, the Cardinals' bullpen blew 6 of 13 save opportunities. And the offense was short-circuited by the absence of Brian Jordan, who stayed behind in spring training because of an injured thumb.

May 12-14 (24-29, 2 games back)
Although they were 5 games below .500, the Cardinals went into June only 2 games behind the leaders in the Central. From May 5 to 19 the Cardinals lost 10 of 13. Ray Lankford said the team was panicking. Tom Pagnozzi said, "We can't do anything right. Even when we were bad, we weren't this bad. We deserve to be 20 games out." Players could even be heard sniping about LaRussa's intense style.

But then the Cardinals fought back to near respectability, winning 7 of 10. The offense finally started scoring, even with Gaetti and Gant gone for part of the month. But the Cards were still being victimized by inconsistent pitching and bad defense. The pitching staff had a 5.08 ERA and 4 blown saves in May, and the defense saddled them with 12 unearned runs. If it weren't for 4 victories against Houston in May, the Cardinals would have have had even more ground to make up.

June 17-10 (41-39, tied for the lead)
St. Louis's pitching was responsible for the team's streak up the standings in June. Combined, the staff allowed 97 runs, good for a 3.20 ERA. The starting pitchers, considered the strength of the team going into the season, began performing to their capabilities, with the front-4 winning 12 games. Donovan Osborne was 3-1 with a 1.96 ERA; Alan Benes 3-1, 2.65; Andy Benes 3-1, 3.59; and Todd Stottlemyre 3-3, 4.20. Two games over .500 and tied for the lead? If the divisions were as they'd been, 3 St. Louis would have been buried behind the Expos and there would be no reason for Cardinals fans to come out to the park. The wild-card and three divisions may dilute the postseason, but it does wonders for attendance—and that's what it's really all about, isn't it?

July 15-11 (56-50, ½ game ahead).
Defense and dingers helped spark the Cardinals in July. After starting the season with 59 errors in their first 50 games, the team made 16 errors in their next 37 games. Gant, Gaetti, and Pagnozzi combined for 17 homers, and the Cardinals hit a total of 32, their best month of the season. Their output was given a boost by a trip to Wrigley. The Cardinals hit 7 homers there July 12—4 off Steve Trachsel—and added 3 more the next day. But most importantly, they continued to get solid performances out of their rotation. Led by Andy Benes's 4 victories—back from oblivion after starting the season 1-7—the staff

compiled a 3.99 ERA in July, solidifying itself as one of the best in the league. But the bullpen provided no relief, with Eckersley suffering from a sore elbow most of the first half. Through the end of July the Cardinals bullpen had blown 19 saves. Things were so bad, the front office approached Tom Henke about coming out of retirement. When rebuffed, no doubt they tried to reach Bruce Sutter and Lindy McDaniel.

August 15-15 (71-65, 2½ games back)
The Central became a race in August, as Houston roared back with a 17-11 record. The Cardinals could only spin their wheels and watch them go by. The bullpen came around, compiling 9 saves in 10 opportunities, and the rotation continued to produce. Andy Benes almost single-handedly carried the team, winning 6 games with a 2.92 ERA. But the offense disappeared when the rest of the rotation pitched. Alan Benes had a 3.69 ERA and Donovan Osborne had a 2.52 ERA, but they combined for just 4 victories in 12 starts.

The Cards nearly tied the Astros again near the end of the month, but let the opportunity slip through their fingers when they split a 4-game series with Houston and then were swept in a 3-game set by Florida at home. It was looking like a real nail-biter in the Central, and the Cardinals offense had LaRussa down to his cuticles.

September 17-9 (88-74, 6 games ahead)
The nail-biter turned out to be a manicure (see September in the Houston Astros section). St. Louis began the month sweeping the Astros 8-7 (in 10 innings), 12-3, and 6-4. The Cardinals walked away with a 1½-game lead in the Central that they wouldn't relinquish. They went 14-9 the rest of the way, led by a pitching staff that compiled a 3.55 ERA. LaRussa's crew clinched the division September 24 in a 7-1 victory against Pittsburgh. And Houston? Houston's Christmas gift to the Cardinals came early in the form of an 8-17 record when the games mattered most.

It was dominance over their divisional foes that made the difference for St. Louis. Against National League Central teams, the Cardinals went 37-15. Their record versus the rest of the league was 51-59. If the Cards had the same winning percentage against their division, they'd have gone 24-28 vs. the Central and would have finished 75-87.

October (lost in 7 games to Atlanta in championship series)
LaRussa on the Cardinals season, after losing 15-0 in Atlanta in Game 7 and being told what a great season it was for his team: "Almost great. If I could change anything, I would have changed the type of game it was. It took them 7 to beat us. But we earned more than getting embarrassed." The team was 1 win away from the World Series, only to have the Braves outhit them 46-17 (all 17 were singles) and outscore them 32-1 in the final 3 games, their lone run coming on a wild pitch. It was the third time a Cardinals team had blown a 3-1 lead in post-season. They did it in 1968 when Mickey Lolich beat them twice in 4 days, as the Tigers outscored them 22-5 and beat Bob Gibson in Game 7 when center fielder Curt Flood played a Jim Northrup flyball in the 7th into a triple. They did it in 1985, as the Royals outscored them 19-2, including 11-0 in Game 7, prompting John Tudor to punch a fan (the spinning variety) and Joaquin Andujar to be ejected for challenging the home plate umpire to a duel.

As impressive as a Cardinals victory over the Braves would have been in '96, it might not have equalled what St. Louis would have done if a blown call hadn't been made in the bottom of the 9th inning of Game 6 in '85. If St. Louis had held on to beat Kansas City 1-0 in that game, they would have taken the Series despite scoring only 13 runs and managing only 35 hits. Even the hopelessly over-matched Pirates of 1960 (see *Avenging 1960* in the New York Yankees section) managed 17 runs and 49 hits in the first 6 games of that World Series.

■ 1997 DIAGNOSIS

Offense
The Cardinals have shifted the focus of their offense from the speed-oriented teams of the past to the power-game prevalent in baseball today. They signed Ron Gant and Gary Gaetti, who combined to hit 53 home runs in '96. The Cardinals hit 142 home runs, up by 35 from '95, but not enough to keep pace with the rest of the league. Only 3 N.L. teams hit fewer—the Astros, Phillies, and Pirates.

Despite the lack of power, the team's slugging average trailed only the Rockies (but not really—when you consider that Busch Stadium is a pitchers park and Coors Field is a video game), the Braves, the Mets, and the Reds. The Cards finished 4th in the league in stolen bases. And for the first time in the history of the team the Cardinals had three 20-home-run men and three 20-stolen-base men on their roster at the same time. Gaetti and Gant hit the home runs, Jordan and Clayton stole the bases, and Lankford did both. The Cardinals offense could best be described as "in transition." The infusion of power won't happen overnight, and there's enough team speed left over to give the St. Louis fans Bake McBride and Tony Scott flashbacks.

Defense

John Mabry has made the conversion from outfield to first base quite well, committing just 8 errors in 138 starts there. Second baseman Luis Alicea lost his job temporarily to Mike Gallego in midseason because of erratic defense, a problem that has plagued him in the past. Royce Clayton displayed great range and much improved hands at short, perhaps just from drinking the same Gatorade as Ozzie. Gaetti's range at third is rapidly diminishing, but the 4-time Gold Glove winner still has the hands and the arm. Ray Lankford has good hands in center, but his speed should translate into better range. Ron Gant has an average to below-average arm, but he tracks the ball well and is dependable making the routine plays. Brian Jordan is the best of the lot. His amazing athleticism takes over in the field, his instincts are improving daily, and he is very comfortable playing center field when needed. Jordan recorded only 9 assists in '96, which is a function of the respect his arm is earning around the league. Tom Pagnozzi was solid as ever behind the plate, but he opted for free agency in the '96 off-season (and remained unsigned as we went to press).

Pitching

The rotation was the strength of the team as the Cardinals squeezed a 66-50 record out of their starters. Only Atlanta and Los Angeles got more victories out of their rotation. The Cardinals haven't had a rotation this strong in years—29 years to be exact. The brothers Benes, Todd Stottlemyre, and Donovan Osborne gave them four 13-game winners for the first time since 1967 (Bob Gibson, Steve Carlton, Nelson Briles, and Dick Hughes). What Duncan could do if he had a Gibson to work with is a scary thought. As it is, he turned a reputedly soft Andy Benes into the backbone of the staff—just as he'd turned the reputedly soft Todd Stottlemyre into a big-time pitcher the year before. St. Louis looks to have all of the front-4 back for '97, and are planning to give the remaining rotation spot to either Danny Jackson or prospect Eric Ludwick.

Bullpen is where the most tinkering will be done. There is something wrong when the relievers have a combined ERA of 3.45 yet blow half their save opportunities. The fact that Walt Jocketty tried to woo Henke out of retirement says a lot, too. Eckersley will return, but he's losing his effectiveness quite rapidly and is running on guts and fumes. They're bringing back the oldest player in baseball, Rick Honeycutt, as well. T. J. Mathews will likely return to the setup role he filled so admirably last season, and he'll close if Eck breaks down. Mark Petkovsek seems to have found his niche in the bullpen—slopping up wins—as has Cory Bailey—by keeping the games close and the ball in the yard.

Farm System

The Cardinals have an above-average farm system, stocked to the rafters with pitching. Alan Benes made his debut last summer, but there's plenty more where he came from. The best of the bunch is Matt Morris. He's a workhorse with a power pitcher's build (6-5, 210) and a 95-mph fastball. And there's also Mike Busby, another big guy (6-4, 215) who throws hard and just needs a little fine-tuning. And a long shot whose odds are dropping is Britt Reames, a converted position player who toyed with Midwest League hitters all season, allowing just 97 hits in 161 innings. Braden Looper, the club's 1st-rounder in '96, will emerge as a big-name pitching prospect in '97. Offensively, Dmitri Young has finally begun to fulfill his vast potential and is the best position prospect in the system. But he won't be for long, as the Cards have plans for him this summer in the big leagues.

Management and Ownership

The 1996 season was a landmark one for the St. Louis Cardinals. It was the first season since 1953 in

which a member of the Busch family was not sitting in the owner's box. The Anheuser-Busch company sold the team, its biggest advertising venue—sparing fans the spectacle of the Budweiser jingle being played during the 7th-inning stretch. A partnership led by Bill DeWitt, Jr., bought the team during the off-season. DeWitt has baseball bloodlines. His father once owned the St. Louis Browns, and Bill, Jr., was once the batboy for the team. An interesting side note: It was DeWitt's uniform that was used to outfit midget pinch-hitter Eddie Gaedel. From batboy to owner. Quite an odyssey. It was Busch who let loose with the cash to sign Gant and company, in an attempt to build the value of the club before putting it up for sale. But DeWitt didn't blink at taking those contracts on, so there's no indication he won't spring for more free-agent help if it's needed.

Walt Jocketty was able to work without harsh financial restrictions for the first time in his regime, and the results were more than he could have asked for. Ron Gant hit 30 homers and had 82 RBI despite losing 5 weeks to injury. Gary Gaetti hit 23 homers and had 80 RBI. Eckersley saved 30 games. Andy Benes won 18 games. Todd Stottlemyre won 14 games. But Jocketty has got his work cut out for him in the off-season. He needs to find a leadoff hitter, a second baseman, and some bullpen help. If he's half as successful with this year's acquisitions, the Cardinals will repeat.

In '96 Tony LaRussa won his 3rd Manager of the Year award with his 3rd different team. He's credited with giving the Cardinals "instant credibility" when he came over from the A's. A lot of LaRussa's success stems from the way he prepares a team. He's a stickler for conditioning and pregame workouts. He sets the rules and expects them to be followed, no exceptions. While some have chafed at his style, there's no arguing with the results. Apparently he can even intimidate an umpire into calling an appeal play his way on the road, as he displayed in the playoffs against Atlanta. But part of LaRussa's success over the years has been due to pitching coach Dave Duncan, who came over with him from the A's. There's nobody in the game better at rediscovering lost pitchers. Just look at what he's done with Osborne and Andy Benes this year. And that's not even considering what he's done with Todd Stottlemyre, who might very well be hanging curves for the Ham Fighters if it weren't for him.

Anyone who doesn't want LaRussa managing their ballclub isn't interested in winning, and that was a significant chunk of St. Louis when Ozzie Smith got too wrapped up in himself to just go away quietly. The fact that LaRussa kept Ozzie from ripping the team apart is reason enough to give him the Manager of the Year award. Here are some others . . .

. . . and whatnot: Cardinal Sins

Go back to the beginning of the season, and you'll find a St. Louis clubhouse divided by as many cliques as a New England boarding school. Even Walt Jocketty noticed. "Everywhere you looked, there were different factions all over the place," he said. "I mean, no one was even mingling." And Ozzie Smith, who had accused LaRussa of lying to him about his role, wasn't the only guy unhappy about the new guy in charge. Who was this dude, they asked themselves, and why was he insisting on turning the Cardinals into the midwestern version of the Oakland A's? So many new players. So many new routines. Extra batting practice. Extra fielding drills. Extra conditioning. Extra work, period. More than a few were probably reiterating Canseco's lament when he was finally dealt from the A's: "All this team cares about is winning."

The team was on the verge of breaking apart. Mike Gallego summed it up. "Some players weren't happy with the way he went about his business. It took a while for people to get used to LaRussa's way. There were a lot of people who didn't understand him and really didn't like him."

In late May, the reputedly self-absorbed LaRussa decided it wasn't the team who failed, it was he. "I blame myself first and stop there," he said. "If they're not playing well, there's something I'm not doing. I've got to start figuring out what I can do better. . . . My biggest mistake was that I pushed and pushed trying to get these guys ready to play, where I almost forgot how important it was just to have a good atmosphere to play in." Hard to imagine those words coming from Jimmy Johnson or Pat Riley, a couple of other coaches whom LaRussa supposedly bunks with at the egomaniacs convention.

The change was almost immediate. Suddenly he was allowing previous sins such as card games and music in the clubhouse. And most importantly, he

became more communicative. "I wasn't communicating with them before and after games," he said. "I was only talking to them during games, and that was my fault. . . . Nowadays you need to explain and discuss what you're doing and why more than you used to."

Truth be told, LaRussa was probably galled by the fact that a group of players who hadn't won anything—except the A's he brought with him—didn't want any part of putting in the effort needed to succeed. And the one Cardinal who had won something, Ozzie Smith, was revealing a side of himself he'd never shown before, undercutting his manager because he had the gall to play a younger version of him. LaRussa was used to dealing with professionals, having single-handedly turned the A's into that as soon as he took over in 1986. Dealing with these '90s athletes—monsters of someone else's creation—must have come as a cold, harsh blast of reality. But rather than try to beat a winning attitude into them after the first efforts were resisted, LaRussa was shrewd enough to find a new approach. He admitted his "mistakes" and gave himself a chance to start fresh. And it worked.

He got them a game from the World Series, primarily by using his team's biggest strength—himself—to expose the biggest Atlanta weakness: Bobby Cox (see October in the Atlanta Braves section). And along the way, Brian Jordan had emerged as someone who'd have looked like he belonged in an A's jersey. If Jordan fills Ozzie's "leadership" role in the clubhouse in '97, it will accelerate the transformation of the Cardinals into a team LaRussa won't have to apologize to for showing them what it takes to win.

LUIS ALICEA (see Free Agents)

MANUEL AYBAR

SLEEPER

SP • BR • TR • 6'1 • 165 • 22

	G	GS	IP	H	HR	BB	SO	W	L	S	ERA	K/BB	K9	HW9
AA	20	20	121	120	10	34	83	8	6	0	3.05	2.4	6.2	11.45

Originally drafted as a strong-armed shortstop out of the Dominican Republic, Aybar was converted into a pitcher in '94 because he couldn't hit. Since then, he's compiled a 2.96 ERA in 76 starts, climbing from the rookie leagues to Triple-A (where he struck out 25 and walked only 7 in 5 starts) by age 21. He's not much of a strikeout pitcher, but he's got great control—and he's a good-hitting pitcher. ■

COREY BAILEY

RP • BR • TR • 6'1 • 210 • 26 • BOS91/15

	G	GS	IP	H	HR	BB	K	W	L	S	ERA	K/BB	K9	HW9
SL 96	51	0	57	57	1	30	38	5	2	0	3.00	1.3	6.0	13.74

Bailey is a former Boston farmhand who has put up some impressive save totals in the minors, but he's no closer. He doesn't have the required control and is too vulnerable to right-handed hitters. Bailey is still relatively young (26), so the Cardinals can use him to eat innings. His most valuable role in the bullpen will be saving better relievers from being overworked. ■

BRIAN BARBER

SP • BR • TR • 6'1 • 175 • 24 • SL91/3

	G	GS	IP	H	HR	BB	SO	W	L	S	ERA	K/BB	K9	HW9
AAA	11	11	50	49	12	26	33	0	6	0	5.62	1.3	6.0	13.59

Once one of the better pitching prospects in the system, Barber must now work his way back into the Cardinals' plans. He used to throw a 93-mph fastball with good movement. But in '95 he lost velocity, and it never came back. The Cardinals diagnosed him with an inflamed ulnar nerve in the spring and shut him down for most of the season. Barber credits the loss of his fastball with turning him into more of a complete pitcher. He says it made him concentrate more on his slider and change-up. Nice spin, but if he doesn't regain the 5 mph he's lost, he may never get the opportunity to show his refinement in the majors. ■

DAVID BELL

SLEEPER

3B-2B • BR • TR • 5'10 • 170 • 24 • CLE90/9

	AB	R	H	2B	3B	HR	RBI	BB	SO	SB	CS	BA	OB	SA
CLE/SL95	146	13	36	7	2	2	19	4	25	1	2	.247	.275	.363
SL96	145	12	31	6	0	1	9	10	22	1	1	.214	.268	.276

Acquired in the deal that sent Ken Hill to the Indians in '95, Bell has a number of things going for him. First, he's the son of Detroit manager Buddy Bell and the grandson of former major-leaguer Gus Bell—so he's inherited a great work ethic, unusual smarts for someone his age, and pretty good

instincts. Second, he's versatile in the field with excellent hands. He's playing major-league-caliber defense at second and third right now, and he'll only get better. And third, he's pretty young (24 years old) for a third-year big-leaguer. As a hitter, he's got a disciplined eye at the plate, and the Cardinals think he will develop some line-drive power. He's a lot like his dad at the plate—a .280 hitter with the potential to hit 15 homers. The plan for Bell is to let him serve another year of apprenticeship under Gaetti, then give him the third-base job in '98. ■

ALAN BENES — YOUNG GUN

SP • BR • TR • 6'5 • 215 • 25 • SL93/1

	G	GS	IP	H	HR	BB	K	W	L	S	ERA	K/BB	K9	HW9
SL95	3	3	16	24	2	4	20	1	2	0	8.44	5.0	11.3	15.75
SL96	34	32	191	192	27	87	131	13	10	0	4.90	1.5	6.2	13.15

Benes might have a higher ceiling than his big brother for a couple of reasons. First, he has an incredibly strong competitive desire, a mental toughness that Andy has been accused of lacking—until this year, anyway. Creighton called on him to pitch the final game of the College World Series as a freshman, and he was beaten in a close game by Tyler Green. And second, his stuff is as good as, if not better than, his brother's. His fastball, which gets up to 90 mph on the slow gun, has a good sinking action. But he also throws a cutter that he can work to either side of the plate. His hard slider, which reaches 85–87 mph is also a pretty nifty pitch. He's working on a change-up, and will throw an occasional lollipop curve to keep hitters honest. He missed a good chunk of the '95 season with forearm stiffness, but impressed the front office in the fall when he led the Arizona Fall League with 6 victories, 62 strikeouts, and a 1.78 ERA. Given a starting job in the spring, Benes did nothing in '96 to make the Cardinals regret their decision, winning 13 games in the bottom half of the rotation. Brothers hadn't combined for 30 wins on the same staff since Jim and Gaylord Perry won 38 for the 1974 Indians. Daffy Benes may soon pass brother Dizzy as the no. 1 pitcher in the St. Louis rotation. ■

ANDY BENES — NL ELITE

SP • BR • TR • 6'5 • 235 • 29 • SD88/1

	G	GS	IP	H	HR	BB	K	W	L	S	ERA	K/BB	K9	HW9
SD94	25	25	172	155	20	51	189	6	14	0	3.86	3.7	9.9	10.78
SD/SEA95	31	31	181	193	18	78	171	11	9	0	4.76	2.2	8.5	13.48
SL96	36	34	230	215	28	77	160	18	10	1	3.83	2.1	6.3	11.42
CAREER	235	232	1528	1415	151	512	1241	94	87	1	3.70	2.4	7.3	11.35

After starting off the season with a couple of no-decisions and a victory, Benes lost his next 7 starts and by mid-June was 3-8 with a 5.25 ERA. But starting June 19, Andy won 10 consecutive decisions and was 15-2 through the end of the season—his only losses coming at Coors Field. In that 10-victory stretch, Benes pitched 90.2 innings, giving up 76 hits, 28 earned runs (2.78 ERA), and 25 walks while striking out 57. Obviously, Benes turned a corner in '96. But the question remains: What made the difference?

One theory, and it's a good one, goes like this: Dave Duncan said he had a hard time helping Benes early in the season because he just didn't know him or his pitching style. But after getting to know him, Duncan realized that Benes just needed to learn to finish what he started—not games, but innings. Benes had a bad habit of going strong in the first half of a game, then giving up a couple of hits in the later innings and looking into the dugout for a rescue. Beginning June 19, no relief was forthcoming. The second part of Benes's season became one long gut-check. In the 21 games he started after that point, Benes was pulled in the middle of an inning just 3 times, with one of those occasions being his final start of the season in which they used him for just two-thirds of an inning. The tough-love approach seems to have worked. Not quite Bob Gibson—who pitched the entire 1968 season without being pulled in mid-inning—but not too shabby either.

Benes is a pure power pitcher and doesn't change speeds. He has a good fastball, a hard slider that breaks in on the fists, and command of both. He was hit pretty hard in '95 because he started nibbling and pitching away from hitters. That's suicide for a pitcher with his stuff. He got behind in the count a lot and served up a good deal of meatball specials. In '96 the nibbling stopped and

Benes went after hitters with a previously unseen toughness. Challenging hitters resulted in a career-worst 28 home runs being given up, but on the whole, they didn't seem to hurt him. And taters didn't keep Ferguson Jenkins or Catfish Hunter from winning 20 games every year. ■

JEFF BERBLINGER

SLEEPER

2B • BR • TR • 6'0 • 190 • 26 • SL93/8

	AB	R	H	2B	3B	HR	RBI	BB	SO	SB	CS	BA	OB	SA
AA	500	78	144	32	7	11	53	52	66	23	10	.288	.360	.446

Berblinger had a very nice season in the Texas League last summer. He hit for power, was aggressive on the basepaths, and refined his plate discipline. His reputation is that of a speedy second baseman with great range and average hands. If it weren't for the fact that he's 26 years old, he'd be a great prospect. As it is, he is still a viable possibility for the Cardinals if the '96 Delino shows up in St. Louis. ■

MIKE BUSBY

SOLID PROSPECT

SP • BR • TR • 6'4 • 215 • 24 • SL91/18

	G	GS	IP	H	HR	BB	SO	W	L	S	ERA	K/BB	K9	HW9
AAA	14	14	72	89	11	44	53	2	5	0	6.38	1.2	6.6	16.63

Even though he got clobbered in Triple-A Louisville and spent the last month of the season on the DL, Busby is still held in high esteem by the Cardinals. He's young, throws a 93-mph fastball, and his slider bites like a piranha. His change-up is average, but he's working on it. Busby just needs a little tweaking before he's ready for a full major-league trial. One more season in Louisville ought to do it. ■

ROYCE CLAYTON

SS • BR • TR • 6'0 • 175 • 27 • SF88/1

	AB	R	H	2B	3B	HR	RBI	BB	SO	SB	CS	BA	OB	SA
SF94	385	38	91	14	6	3	30	30	74	23	3	.236	.295	.327
SF95	509	56	124	29	3	5	58	38	109	24	9	.244	.298	.342
SL96	491	64	136	20	4	6	35	33	89	33	15	.277	.321	.371
CAREER	2281	243	581	92	22	24	219	166	432	99	41	.255	.306	.346

Clayton improved almost every area of his game last season despite the Ozzie Smith distraction. He cut his strikeouts, stole more bases, and improved his fielding. In the field, his hands are soft, and he has fantastic range, especially to his left. The one shortcoming in his defense is an average throwing arm, but he compensates for it with a quick release—just like Ozzie. At the plate, Clayton is an extreme

ground-ball hitter who can leg out hits with his speed. When he hits the ball in the air it's often to the opposite field. He doesn't possess good bat speed, so if he should pull a pitch, it's either because he guesses what's coming or the pitcher hangs a curve. Clayton will have the shortstop job all to himself this year. He'll still have the pressures of replacing a legend, but at least the legend won't be dressing in the locker next to him and whining about playing time. ■

KRIS DETMERS

SOLID PROSPECT

RP • BB • TL • 6'5 • 215 • 22 • SL93/22

	G	GS	IP	H	HR	BB	SO	W	L	S	ERA	K/BB	K9	HW9
AA	27	0	163	154	15	70	97	12	8	0	3.35	1.4	5.3	12.35

Whoever scouted this guy deserves a medal. Detmers, a tall, lanky lefty, was taken as a draft-and-follow in '93. The Cardinals just love him. His fastball is average, but his curve is considered the best breaking ball in the organization. He led the Florida State League in strikeouts in '95, but he had trouble with his command last year in Double-A Arkansas, and the K's really dropped. Despite this, he won 12 games for the Travelers. Now that Bret Wagner has been traded, Detmers is the best left-handed pitcher in the organization. ■

DENNIS ECKERSLEY

SP • BR • TR • 6'2 • 190 • 42 • CLE72/3

	G	GS	IP	H	HR	BB	K	W	L	S	ERA	K/BB	K9	HW9
OAK94	45	0	44	49	5	13	47	5	4	19	4.26	3.6	9.6	12.67
OAK95	52	0	50	53	5	11	40	4	6	29	4.83	3.6	7.2	11.52
SL96	63	0	60	65	8	6	49	0	6	30	3.30	8.2	7.4	10.65
CAREER	964	361	3193	2981	332	722	2334	192	165	353	3.48	3.2	6.6	10.44

Many folks were predicting the end for The Eck last year. He was 41, coming off 3 consecutive subpar (for him) seasons, and changing leagues. But he was able to find the fire for one more 15-rounder, appearing in 63 games and earning 30 saves for the 7th time. His stellar control was even better than usual. It's hard to imagine what the Cardinals would have

done without him. Without Eck in a closing situation last season the bullpen blew 19 saves, converting fewer than half of their chances.

But there are definite signs that his effectiveness is ending. For example, the league hit .264 off him within his first 15 pitches. Once he got past the 15-pitch limit, though, the batting average against him ballooned to .326. If he doesn't get the first 3 batters out, things turn ugly. He'll be back, so the youngsters will get another chance to learn from the Zen master. ▪

TONY FOSSAS

RP • BL • TL • 6'0 • 195 • 39 • TEX79/12

	G	GS	IP	H	HR	BB	K	W	L	S	ERA	K/BB	K9	HW9
BOS94	44	0	34	35	6	15	31	2	0	1	4.76	2.1	8.2	13.24
SL95	58	0	36	28	1	10	40	3	0	0	1.47	4.0	10.0	9.50
SL96	65	0	47	43	7	21	36	0	4	2	2.68	1.7	6.9	12.26
CAREER	450	0	340	336	30	137	260	14	14	7	3.68	1.9	6.9	12.52

The LaRussa/Duncan tandem really milked the best performances out of their veteran relievers last year, and Fossas is yet another example. Fossas doesn't throw hard enough to break a pane of glass anymore, and he throws a sloppy breaking ball that is below average at best. But he effectively changes speeds and throws a sinking fastball that induces grounders aplenty. That's how he has maintained his effectiveness the past 2 seasons.

The turning point in his season came when Fossas got a call from a woman in his church congregation. She had never called him before in the 18 years he knew her. She read him an inspirational Bible verse, and Fossas took it as a sign. Right after the call, he rattled off 16 consecutive scoreless appearances—which may prompt the stats geeks to create a new situational category: pre- and post-epiphany. ▪

MICAH FRANKLIN

OF • BB • TR • 6'0 • 195 • 24 • NYN90/3

	AB	R	H	2B	3B	HR	RBI	BB	SO	SB	CS	BA	OB	SA
AAA	468	75	111	28	4	22	84	67	131	5	5	.237	.343	.455

Franklin is the Mark Whiten of the minor leagues. The Cardinals are his 5th organization, and his 4th in 3 years—despite hitting dingers at every stop. He was released by the Mets at 19, only 2 years after being their 3rd pick in the draft. He was traded for Brian Hunter (the fat one) after hitting 31 dingers. He was released by the Pirates—have they ever released anyone?—after hitting 21 dingers and batting .293 in two-thirds of a season. And the Tigers gave up on him after 53 games. Don't exactly have to read between those lines. ▪

JOHN FRASCATORE

SLEEPER

SP-RP • BR • TR • 6'1 • 210 • SL91/28

	G	GS	IP	H	HR	BB	K	W	L	S	ERA	K/BB	K9	HW9
AAA	36	21	156	180	22	42	95	6	13	0	5.18	2.3	5.5	12.78

Frascatore throws hard (96 mph), but sure doesn't get to hear the catcher's glove pop very often. He also has a good slider and cut fastball. But the Cardinals are disappointed that he isn't blowing people away with his stuff and after his season at Louisville, they have even more reason to be upset with him. If you're 26 and can't get Triple-A hitters out with a 96-mph fastball, you do not pass go and you do not collect $200. Younger, hotter pitchers will start blowing by him on their way to the majors unless he gets his act together. ▪

GARY GAETTI

3B • BR • TR • 6'0 • 185 • 38 • MIN79

	AB	R	H	2B	3B	HR	RBI	BB	SO	SB	CS	BA	OB	SA
KC94	327	53	94	15	3	12	57	19	63	0	2	.287	.328	.462
KC95	514	76	134	27	0	35	96	47	91	3	3	.261	.329	.518
SL96	522	71	143	27	4	23	80	35	97	2	2	.274	.326	.473
CAREER	7725	985	1975	376	36	315	1155	534	1398	88	60	.256	.307	.436

Gaetti may not have duplicated his awesome '95, when he hit 35 homers for the Royals with little or no protection in the lineup, but it was unreasonable to expect that kind of season again at his age. But he certainly didn't show any signs that he's ready to throw in the towel either. At 38 he plays more like a 28-year-old, only with more experience. Gaetti has always been an aggressive hitter, and nothing will change that. And even though his bat is slowing, he can still turn on a high fastball. If he struggles, John Mabry may get some time at third with Dmitri Young playing first. But Gaetti has a habit of proving people who think he's washed up wrong. Just ask the Angels. ▪

MIKE GALLEGO (see Looking for a Game)

RON GANT

LF • BR • TR • 6′0 • 190 • 32 • ATL83/4

	AB	R	H	2B	3B	HR	RBI	BB	SO	SB	CS	BA	OB	SA
CIN95	410	79	113	19	4	29	88	74	108	23	8	.276	.386	.554
SL96	419	74	103	14	2	30	82	73	98	13	4	.246	.359	.504
CAREER	4021	668	1052	191	33	206	650	447	806	193	80	.262	.336	.479

Gant's season was broken up by a hamstring pull that sidelined him for 5 weeks in May and June. He also suffered a torn rotator cuff by sliding headfirst into home on August 30. But despite the lost time and the debilitating effects of the shoulder injury, he still had enough in him to jack 30 balls out of the park and drive in 82 runs. Gant goes to the plate to pull the ball out of the park, nothing more. To get him out, a pitcher has to throw him sliders off the plate and hope he lunges for them. He looks to turn on anything from the middle of the plate in, and if a pitcher makes the mistake of coming inside—but not quite inside enough—he'll make the pitch a souvenir in a hurry.

Once a threat to hit 30+ doubles a season, Gant has hit just 33 the past couple of seasons. The leg injury that cut his Atlanta career short has robbed him of most of his speed. It didn't rob him of his desire. If anything, by releasing him, the Braves may have motivated him for the rest of his career. No one wanted that playoff series against Atlanta more than Gant. Perhaps it's some consolation that pushing them as far as they did may have set his former team up for its eventual defeat. ■

MIKE GULAN

3B • BR • TR • 6′1 • 190 • 26 • SL92/2

	AB	R	H	2B	3B	HR	RBI	BB	SO	SB	CS	BA	OB	SA
AAA	419	47	107	27	4	17	55	26	119	7	2	.255	3.080	.461

Gulan was the organization's Player of the Year in '95 and is often touted as their best third-base prospect, but he is overrated. He has big-time power and is a fine fielder, but strikeouts have become a concern. His strikeouts-to-walks ratio would make Greg Maddux proud and, at 26, there are major league All-Stars who'd need him to buy them beer. He'll probably get some major-league playing time in the next year or two, but don't expect him to stick. ■

CHRIS HAAS

3B • BL • TR • 6′2 • 210 • 20 • SL92/1

	AB	R	H	2B	3B	HR	RBI	BB	SO	SB	CS	BA	OB	SA
A	421	56	101	19	1	11	65	64	169	3	2	.240	.347	.368

Haas was one of the top young power hitters in the 1995 draft, taken with the Phillies pick as compensation for Jefferies, but some question his bat speed. His strikeouts are unbelievable—and, if it's a vision problem, perhaps he should start swinging at the ball in the middle. He has mediocre range at third, but his hands are adequate and he's got a good arm. He's hit the weights to improve his physique, but he's seen as one of those Kevin Mitchell types who could eat his way out of the game if he doesn't watch it. This prospect is very raw. ■

ANDY HALL

2B • BB • TR • 6′0 • 175 • 22 • SL95/16

	AB	R	H	2B	3B	HR	RBI	BB	SO	SB	CS	BA	OB	SA
A	446	80	134	29	5	4	68	75	90	21	7	.300	.414	.415

Hall is a switch-hitting second baseman with plenty of plate discipline and a smooth swing that generates line-drive power. He can also scoot on the bases. He's already a prospect, but if he does this for another summer, he'll be in the Cardinals' top 10. ■

RICK HONEYCUTT

RP • BL • TL • 6′1 • 190 • 42 • PIT76/17

	G	GS	IP	H	HR	BB	K	W	L	S	ERA	K/BB	K9	HW9
TEX94	42	0	25	37	4	9	18	1	2	1	7.20	2.0	6.5	16.56
OAK/NYA95	52	0	45	39	6	10	21	5	1	2	2.96	2.1	4.2	9.80
SL96	61	0	47	42	3	7	30	2	1	4	2.85	4.3	5.7	9.38
CAREER	795	268	2157	2178	185	656	1036	109	143	38	3.71	1.6	4.3	11.82

Not a bad career for a guy who was traded for both Dave Pagan and Ken Clay before he even made the big leagues. Nobody but Duncan and LaRussa could have gotten this kind of performance out of Honeycutt—just look at what he did in '94 without them. But he'll turn 43 this season. And during a 12-game stretch last season, he allowed 10 of 21 batters to reach base.

Such bouts of ineffectiveness are not promising. Repent, the end is near. ■

DANNY JACKSON

SP • BR • TL • 6'0 • 205 • 35 • KC82

	G	GS	IP	H	HR	BB	K	W	L	S	ERA	K/BB	K9	HW9
PHI94	25	25	179	183	13	46	129	14	6	0	3.26	2.8	6.5	11.51
SL95	19	19	100	120	10	48	52	2	12	0	5.90	1.1	4.7	15.12
SL96	13	4	36	33	3	16	27	1	1	0	4.46	1.7	6.7	12.24
CAREER	336	311	2004	2012	122	788	1193	110	122	1	3.89	1.5	5.4	12.57

DayJay missed most of the season due to late-January ankle surgery, and when he returned, he was limited to 4 starts and 9 relief appearances. Nobody really knows what to expect from Jackson, as he's had more ups and downs in his career than John Travolta. But the Cardinals are on the hook for another season of his contract, so he'll duke it out with Eric Ludwick for the 5th rotation spot. Jackson may prove to be Duncan's biggest challenge yet. ■

BRIAN JORDAN

CONSISTENT STAR

OF • BR • TR • 6'1 • 205 • 30 • SL88/3

	AB	R	H	2B	3B	HR	RBI	BB	SO	SB	CS	BA	OB	SA
SL94	178	14	46	8	2	5	15	16	40	4	3	.258	.320	.410
SL95	490	83	145	20	4	22	81	22	79	24	9	.296	.339	.488
SL96	513	82	159	36	1	17	104	29	84	22	5	.310	.349	.483
CAREER	1597	229	459	83	17	59	266	89	286	63	25	.287	.331	.472

The common baseball wisdom holds that position players don't develop much after age 27. However, Brian Jordan is anything but common. He's an impressive athlete with a nice combination of power and speed, just coming into his own at age 30. It leaves one to wonder how good he would have been if he had not flirted with a football career.

Jordan suffered a fractured thumb in the spring and opened the season on the DL. In fact, he suffered from torn ligaments in the thumb most of the season, which is why he missed out on the 30/30 season so many had predicted for him. Jordan has a quick, short stroke that allows him to catch up to any fastball in the league. An excellent low-ball hitter, he doesn't get cheated in any at-bat. He's aggressive and won't draw many walks, but with his power, the Cardinals will accept a high strikeout total. With nobody on, Jordan hit .265, but with runners on the bases, he hit .367. When the bases were loaded, he hit an incredible .684. His 13 bases-loaded hits were the most in the majors since 1989.

He rises to the occasion more than any other position player on the team. He helped turn around the Cardinals' season—and Andy Benes's—with an incredible diving catch in the 9th against the Phillies in a game in June. They won 3-2 in the bottom of the ninth. Then, 5 days later in Atlanta, Bobby Cox went by the righty-righty book—and against the don't-walk-a-beanpole-to-load-the-bases-and-face-an-insulted-football-player book—by having Smoltz put Mabry on to face him. Jordan hit his first pitch, a high fastball, about 30 feet over the fence in dead center. He established himself in '96 as the best Falcons defensive back ever to play major-league baseball. ■

RAY LANKFORD

CONSISTENT STAR

CF • BL • TR • 5'11 • 180 • 29 • SL87/3

	AB	R	H	2B	3B	HR	RBI	BB	SO	SB	CS	BA	OB	SA
SL94	416	89	111	25	5	19	57	58	113	11	10	.267	.359	.488
SL95	483	81	134	35	2	25	82	63	110	24	8	.277	.360	.513
SL96	545	100	150	36	8	21	86	79	133	35	7	.275	.366	.486
CAREER	3141	516	845	186	40	104	437	407	755	178	85	.269	.353	.453

Lankford possesses a tantalizing package of skills. He's got an excellent power stroke, but his swing is long and he refuses to shorten it when he's behind in the count. In addition, he suffers from a vulnerability to left-handed pitchers, having hit just .246 against them last season. He's got wonderful speed that some thought would translate into 50+ stolen bases a year. But he's not very good at reading pitchers, so he doesn't get good jumps.

The scouting report on Lankford says that right-handers can throw him hard stuff outside and he'll either chase it or hit ground balls to second. Lefties can work him away with breaking balls, inducing weak fly balls to left field. But if anybody, either righties or lefties, challenges him on the inside part of the plate, he'll punish them. Lankford isn't a

superstar player, but he is one of the better hitters in the National League. And if the Cardinals can find a decent leadoff hitter to bat in front of him, Lankford has a chance for 100 RBI. ■

BRADEN LOOPER — GRADE-A PROSPECT

RHP • SL96/1 • WICHITA STATE UNIVERSITY

Looper was the Cardinals' 1st round pick (no. 3 overall) in the '96 draft. He was the closer for the Wichita State team that made it to the College World Series last summer. Looper lost in his CWS appearance, but before that, he was 4-0 with 12 saves and a 1.09 ERA in 22 appearances during the regular season. He walked 12 and struck out 60 in 50 innings. Looper was considered the second-hardest thrower in the draft, next to Billy Koch. Looper's fastball has been clocked at 97 mph, and he complements it with a good slider and change-up. The Cardinals shut him down for the summer after drafting him. They moved him to the Arizona Fall League, which means the team has him on the fast track—and it's possible he could see action in St. Louis this season. ■

ERIC LUDWICK — SLEEPER

SP • BR • TR • 6'5 • 210 • 25 • NYN93/2

	G	GS	IP	H	HR	BB	SO	W	L	S	ERA	K/BB	K9	HW9
AAA	11	11	60	55	4	24	73	3	4	0	2.83	3.0	10.9	11.79

Ludwick was one of the players acquired from the Mets in the Bernand Gilkey deal in the spring of '95, and the Cardinals are considering him for a rotation spot in '97. He's a big guy who throws in the mid-90s with a good slider. He has good command, but his mechanics are those of an injury-prone pitcher. He strained his right elbow in the spring and was shelved until July. But he regained his health enough to strike out 11 batters per 9 innings in Triple-A Louisville in '96. If he stays healthy, he could be a big surprise in '97, especially if he pitches well enough to break camp with the team in spring. ■

JOHN MABRY

1B • BL • TR • 6'4 • 195 • 26 • SL91/10

	AB	R	H	2B	3B	HR	RBI	BB	SO	SB	CS	BA	OB	SA
SL95	388	35	119	21	1	5	41	24	45	0	3	.307	.347	.405
SL96	543	63	161	30	2	13	74	37	84	3	2	.297	.342	.431

Mabry has the arm, build, and foot speed (or lack thereof) of a pitcher. Going into '96, the Cardinals thought Mabry would develop more power, but so far he's been more of a doubles and RBI guy than a home-run producer. He has a short, quick swing, so he doesn't get overmatched by good fastballs very often. He also has the potential to handle the breaking ball. LaRussa likes Mabry's approach to at bats: "I don't think I've seen him throw one away."

An outfielder all his career, Mabry was asked to make the conversion to first base. His footwork is a little slow and he's still hesitant on throws. But he may not have to worry about playing first much longer. The Cardinals are considering moving him to third base in order to fit first baseman Dmitri Young into the lineup. It might be good for Mabry, as he has a strong and accurate throwing arm. But that would make two position switches in two seasons, and they can't keep doing that and expect his production at the plate not to suffer. ■

ELIESER MARRERO

C • BR • TR • 6'1 • 180 • 23 • SL93/3

	AB	R	H	2B	3B	HR	RBI	BB	SO	SB	CS	BA	OB	SA
AA	374	65	101	17	3	19	65	32	55	9	6	.270	.330	.484

Marrero is an enticing prospect with great tools. He came into his own last year against older competition in the Texas League. He was named the league's no. 3 prospect as well as its top defensive catcher. He showed off a strong and accurate throwing arm by nailing a superb percentage of would-be basestealers last year. His work at the plate was also praised, especially considering that he played in a pitcher's park. Fairly or unfairly, Marrero has gotten the reputation as being somewhat of a jake. He'll have to work that tag off at Triple-A in '97. ■

T. J. MATHEWS

RP • BR • TR • 6'2 • 200 • 27 • SL92/36

	G	GS	IP	H	HR	BB	K	W	L	S	ERA	K/BB	K9	HW9
SL95	23	0	29	21	1	11	28	1	1	2	1.52	2.5	8.7	9.93
SL96	67	0	83	62	8	32	80	2	6	6	3.01	2.5	8.7	10.18

Mathews did a fantastic job as LaRussa's primary setup man last season, limiting the opposition to a

.203 batting average in 83.2 innings. He was tough with runners on, allowing only 6 of his 36 inherited runners to score, a *very* impressive performance. His main weapon is a sinking fastball that he brings to the plate at 91 mph. He also uses a deceptive delivery that especially fools right-handed hitters. He's working on a split-finger and a knuckle-curve, but he needs to refine them. Mathews may be the closer of the future, but he didn't help his candidacy much when he blew 5 of his 11 save opportunities last season ▪

WILLIE MCGEE

OF • BB • TR • 6'1 • 185 • 38 • NYA77

	AB	R	H	2B	3B	HR	RBI	BB	SO	SB	CS	BA	OB	SA
SF94	156	19	44	3	0	5	23	15	24	3	0	.282	.337	.397
BOS95	200	32	57	11	3	2	15	9	41	5	2	.285	.311	.400
SL96	309	52	95	15	2	5	41	18	60	5	2	.307	.348	.417
CAREER	6809	929	2028	314	89	73	764	395	1070	330	113	.298	.336	.402

His speed is gone now, but McGee still has value to a ballclub as a pinch hitter and spare outfielder. His presence in the clubhouse can be a stabilizing influence for a young team. But the Cardinals are old as dirt and in desperate need of an infusion of youth. ▪

MIGUEL MEJIA

OF • BR • TR • 6'1 • 155 • 22

	AB	R	H	2B	3B	HR	RBI	BB	SO	SB	CS	BA	OB	SA
SL96	23	10	2	0	0	0	0	0	10	5	3	.087	.087	.087

Mejia is a 22-year-old outfield prospect the Cardinals acquired in the Rule 5 draft from the Orioles last year. Now that they own him free and clear, Mejia will be on his way back to the minors. He's a capable fielder with a good arm. His main asset, however, is his speed. He stole 52 bases in '95 between High Desert and Bluefield. The Cardinals want him to become a switch-hitter, and he spent most of last season learning how. He's a couple of years away, but if you want a preview of what will be, just look at Detroit's Kimera Bartee. The two are similar players under similar circumstances. ▪

MATT MORRIS

GRADE-A PROSPECT

SP • BR • TR • 6'5 • 210 • 22 • SL95/1

	G	GS	IP	H	HR	BB	SO	W	L	S	ERA	K/BB	K9	HW9
AA	27	27	167	178	14	48	120	12	12	0	3.88	2.5	6.5	12.18

Morris was the no. 12 pick in the 1995 draft, taken from Seton Hall University, and he was considered the hardest thrower in college in 1995. He throws a solid 92–95-mph fastball and an excellent curveball. He's very raw and needs to work on his mechanics and his command. If it weren't for that, he could have made the majors last year out of spring training. He was one of their last cuts. He's got the talent and the desire to join Alan Benes in headlining the Cardinals pitching staff within 2 or 3 years. He's simply the best pitching prospect they have. ▪

DONOVAN OSBORNE

SP • BB • TL • 6'2 • 195 • 27 • SL90/1

	G	GS	IP	H	HR	BB	K	W	L	S	ERA	K/BB	K9	HW9
SL95	19	19	113	112	17	34	82	4	6	0	3.81	2.4	6.5	11.63
SL96	30	30	198	191	22	57	134	13	9	0	3.53	2.4	6.1	11.27
CAREER	109	104	646	649	71	176	403	38	31	0	3.71	2.3	5.6	11.49

Osborne started the '96 season on the DL, but at least this time it was unrelated to his arm. He suffered a hairline fracture of his ribs in a car accident and was forced to miss the first couple of weeks of the season. He struggled to find his rhythm during the first 2 months, but went 9-6 the rest of the way with a 3.21 ERA—despite a drunk-and-disorderly arrest and a cut on his thumb from a champagne bottle during the division-clinching celebration. His comeback solidified his reputation as one of the better young pitchers in the N.L.

It's a testament to modern surgery and Osborne's work ethic that he hasn't lost any velocity from the rotator cuff surgery that caused him to miss all of '94 and half of '95. His fastball still gets up to 90 mph, and it has good movement. He also throws a hard slurve and a Sparky Lyle-type slider. Osborne's breaking ball isn't always sharp, so he can't make any mistakes with it or else it gets launched into orbit. But last year his control was tip-top. He also has a tendency to get out of whack with his

delivery—and he sure didn't look like he wanted to be out there in Game 7 against the Braves. Dave Duncan should be able to help out in both areas. ■

TOM PAGNOZZI (see Free Agents)

MARK PETKOVSEK

RP-SP • BR • TR • 6'0 • 185 • 31 • TEX87/3

	G	GS	IP	H	HR	BB	K	W	L	S	ERA	K/BB	K9	HW9
SL95	26	21	137	136	11	35	71	6	6	0	4.00	2.0	4.7	11.23
SL96	48	6	88	83	9	35	45	11	2	0	3.55	1.3	4.6	12.06
CAREER	104	28	267	283	31	83	136	20	9	0	4.58	1.6	4.6	12.33

Petkovsek is proof that a pitcher doesn't have to be a flame-thrower to succeed. He won 11 last year, mostly in long relief, by throwing strikes and upsetting the timing of hitters. The velocity on his fastball is below average, but Petkovsek gets hitters to pound it into the ground because it has a nice sinking action. His best pitch, however, is a big-breaking curveball that he'll throw on any count. Hitters can't sit on a 3-1 fastball with Petkovsek, and that works in his favor a great deal of the time. But Petkovsek isn't a good bet to repeat his '96 performance. He's 31 years old, and an ERA of about 4.00 would be more realistic. And 11 victories and a .846 winning percentage are out of the question. ■

BRITT REAMES — SOLID PROSPECT

SP • BR • TR • 5'11 • 170 • 23 • SL95/17

	G	GS	IP	H	HR	BB	SO	W	L	S	ERA	K/BB	K9	HW9
A	25	25	161	97	5	41	167	15	7	0	1.9	4.1	9.3	7.71

Reames's fastball is only average, but he has a knee-buckling curveball that dropped jaws and over-matched Midwest League hitters all season. With it, he led the league in strikeouts and ERA and gave up a hit about as often as Steinbrenner shares credit or takes blame. League managers voted him the best pitching prospect with the best curve and the best control. ■

CHRIS RICHARD — SLEEPER

1B • BL • TL • 6'2 • 185 • 22 • SL95/14

	AB	R	H	2B	3B	HR	RBI	BB	SO	SB	CS	BA	OB	SA
A+	460	65	130	28	6	14	82	57	50	7	3	.283	.369	.461

Richard is a slugging first baseman who showed an unusual amount of plate discipline for a player in just his second pro season. He looked like a natural-born run producer as well. Drafted out of Oklahoma State (where he hit .336 and slugged .626), Richard had a great year at the plate for a 22-year-old in the Florida State League. He also impressed managers enough in the field to be named the league's top defensive first baseman. He has the talent and desire to handle the promotion to Double-A Arkansas. Another season like '96 and he'll be one of the more coveted hitting prospects in the system. ■

KERRY ROBINSON — SLEEPER

OF • BL • TL • 6'0 • 175 • SL95/34

	AB	R	H	2B	3B	HR	RBI	BB	SO	SB	CS	BA	OB	SA
A	440	98	158	17	14	2	47	51	51	50	26	.359	.422	.475

Because he played for a small college, Robinson slipped to the 34th round of the '95 draft. But after the season he had in the Class-A Midwest League last year, he won't go unnoticed again. He had an All-Star season for Peoria, winning the league's batting title and swiping 50 bases with his blazing speed. But almost as impressive as his stolen-base total was his strikeouts-to-walks ratio. He doesn't have much power yet, but leadoff hitters with extra-ordinary speed don't need it. A little more refinement of his defense and he could be challenging for a job within a couple of years. ■

DANNY SHEAFFER

C • 3B • BR • TR • 6'0 • 185 • 35 • BOS81/1

	AB	R	H	2B	3B	HR	RBI	BB	SO	SB	CS	BA	OB	SA
COL94	110	11	24	4	0	1	12	10	11	0	2	.218	.283	.282
SL95	208	24	48	10	1	5	30	23	38	0	0	.231	.306	.361
SL96	198	10	45	9	3	2	20	9	25	3	3	.227	.271	.333
CAREER	814	77	186	33	5	13	99	52	105	5	8	.229	.276	.329

It's hard to believe, but Sheaffer was th 20th overall pick back in 1981. But he never developed with the bat and has been relegated to backup duty the past several years. He's a sound defensive catcher and if Pagnozzi signs elsewhere, he may get playing time out of desperation. ■

TODD STOTTLEMYRE

SP • BL • TR • 6'3 • 195 • 31 • TOR85

	G	GS	IP	H	HR	BB	K	W	L	S	ERA	K/BB	K9	HW9
TOR94	26	19	140	149	19	48	105	7	7	1	4.22	2.2	6.7	12.66
OAK95	31	31	209	228	26	80	205	14	7	0	4.55	2.6	8.8	13.26
SL96	34	33	223	191	30	93	194	14	11	0	3.87	2.1	7.8	11.46
CAREER	271	239	1571	1601	171	587	1061	97	88	1	4.34	1.8	6.1	12.53

Stottlemyre's competitiveness has always hindered him in the past. He'd try to do more than he was capable of, wanting to strike out every hitter he faced, preferably on 3 pitches and swinging—that is, until Duncan got hold of him and convinced him to stay within himself and let his pitches do the work. He got Stottlemyre to be more aggressive with his fastball, junk his curve, and concentrate on throwing the slider more. The result was 14 victories for Oakland in '95 and a huge boost in his confidence that bled over into '96.

Stottlemyre's fastball is above average in velocity and has a nasty sinking motion. His slider is a plus pitch. The curve and change-up aren't as refined, but he throws all his pitches with excellent mechanics which adds to their effectiveness. All of this doesn't necessarily mean he's ready to take over as the ace of the staff. He still has questionable control and gives up a lot of home runs. But he's one of the best no. 2 or no. 3 starters around. He owes Dave Duncan and Tony LaRussa a lot—they're responsible for turning his career around when he was close to flunking out at the major-league level. If they ever leave town, Stottlemyre should be a stowaway in their luggage. Again. ■

MARK SWEENEY

1B-OF • BL • TL • 6'1 • 195 • 27 • CAL91/10

	AB	R	H	2B	3B	HR	RBI	BB	SO	SB	CS	BA	OB	SA
SL95	77	5	21	2	0	2	13	10	15	1	1	.273	.348	.377
SL96	170	32	45	9	0	3	22	33	29	3	0	.265	.387	.371

Sweeney has excellent judgment at the plate and makes the pitchers work. Sweeney has a role with the Cardinals as their primary backup and pinch hitter. His batting average is bound to improve—it was around .300 for much of the season—but he won't hit for power. Like Mabry, he could be a surprise in the bottom of the order if given the playing time, as he can get on base a lot more than the typical no. 7 or 8 hitter. ■

DMITRI YOUNG

SOLID PROSPECT

1B • BB • TR • 6'2 • 240 • 23 • SL91/1

	AB	R	H	2B	3B	HR	RBI	BB	SO	SB	CS	BA	OB	SA
AAA	459	90	153	31	8	15	64	34	67	16	5	.333	.378	.534

Young finally got his career back on track last season and emerged as the best position prospect in the system. He had suffered from on- and off-field problems throughout '95, getting into a barroom brawl and then, later in the season, climbing into the stands in Wichita to punch out some racist fans who had been heckling him. Instead of a medal, he got a 20-game suspension—and if that's a fair punishment, Roberto Alomar should have been given jail time. Young also had suffered from weight problems in the past, leaving some within the organization with the impression that he was a headcase DH-wanna-be.

But the Cardinals sent him to winter ball after the '95 season and, with all the conflict and turmoil behind him, he won the Mexican Pacific League batting title, successfully making the transition to first base in the process. Back in the States in '96, Young was a changed man. He displayed an excellent work ethic, made great strides in his defense at first, and kept his weight down for the whole season. The Cardinals felt he finally grew up last year. To top off his stellar season, Young received a call-up to the majors and a spot on the postseason roster, and got the hit that put the Cardinals within a game of the World Series.

After all he's been through, people have the tendency to forget that Young is just 23 years old. A switch-hitter with excellent power and an ability to hit for average make him one of the most coveted prospects around. The Cards will find a spot for him on the roster, even if it means eventually moving John Mabry to third base. Young has a dangerous bat and could provide excellent protection in the no. 5 spot in the lineup. The 1996 season was his minor-league breakthrough year. The 1997 season may be his major-league breakthrough year. ■

■ 1996 AUTOPSY

In April, Tony Gwynn said: "We have a team capable of winning the division, and this is the first time in a long time I can say it and mean it. We have 25 players, a manager, coaches and trainers trying to accomplish something that hasn't been done here since 1984." Many observers greeted that with indulgent smiles and wrote it off to jock-speak. The team was improved—adding Rickey Henderson, Wally Joyner, and Bob Tewksbury, while the only loss of any real significance was Bip Roberts—but they seemed to be lacking the power and pitching depth they'd need to keep pace with the rest of the West. The Padres had finished 4 games under .500 the year before, the team had hit more home runs than only the Astros, Cardinals, and Phillies, and Andy Ashby and Trevor Hoffman had been their only front-line pitchers. And they were only 3 years removed from the firesale that stripped their lineup of Fred McGriff and Gary Sheffield. Leap-frogging the Rockies and Dodgers to take the division seemed like a pipedream.

April 17-10 (2½ games ahead)
The Padres lost their home opener in extra innings to the Cubs, then won 8 of their next 10. They outscored their opponents 145-108 for the month, despite being outhomered 27-13. The team's defense contributed to the fast start, yielding only 8 unearned runs. It was the bullpen that carried the team—with Tim Worrell, Doug Bochtler, Trevor Hoffman, and Bryce Florie combining to pitch 50.1 innings, allowing 28 hits, and striking out 58 with an ERA of 1.43. This dominance covered up for a number of trouble spots: Tony Gwynn missed 8 games with an inflamed right heel and had to take a cortisone shot; Rickey was hitting .212 (although his on-base percentage was .409), was 2-for-5 in stolen base attempts, and missed some time with a pulled rib cage muscle; Steve Finley was hitting .218, but his on-base percentage was a decidedly un-Rickey .298; Brad Ausmus was hitting .211; and Andujar Cedeno had 2 extra base hits.

Marc Newfield filled in for Henderson, hit a team-leading 3 home runs, and knocked in 12 runs, while Craig Shipley got some time at shortstop and hit .448. Catcher Brian Johnson and first baseman Archi Cianfrocco combined for 17 RBI in only 59 at bats. Manager Bruce Bochy: "Our bench is doing more than any club expects from its role players."

The team didn't seem too concerned about the lack of power, Gwynn's injury, or the slow starts by several of its players. Joyner: "We are this good." Ken Caminiti: "This is a great team."

May 17-10 (34-20, 5½ games ahead)
The Padres scored 16 fewer runs than they did in April, but they were able to expand their lead because the pitching staff was even better than they'd been the month before. The staff allowed more than 5 runs only 3 times. They already had 15 wins combined out of Andy Ashby and Joey Hamilton (after getting only 18 from them in all of 1995). It was the bullpen, though, that remained the strength of the team. They were firing on all 6 cylinders: Hoffman, Worrell, Bochtler, Florie, Sanders, and Blair. They pitched 70.2 innings, allowed 38 hits, struck out 75, and had an ERA of 1.40. They needed to. Cedeno (.180) and Ausmus (.125) continued to struggle, and Gwynn had 48 singles but only 8 extra base hits. Not often you hear this from a big leaguer hitting .350: "No complaints, no excuses. I just stink." Henderson hit .209 for the month and began to hear boos in San Diego. Former teammate, Todd Stottlemyre, offered some left-handed words of encouragement: "He's still very capable of showing up and carrying a club offensively."

Injuries limited Caminiti to 35 at bats. He took 2 cortisone shots to kill the pain in his left shoulder, but was also bothered by hamstring and hip injuries, and a lower abdominal strain so severe it was originally thought to be a hernia. Caminiti after trying to play through it: "I couldn't walk for two days. I walked out to the parking lot and fell down. I was pretty scared then." Tragically, Mike Sharperson was killed in an auto accident in Las Vegas on his way to join the Padres to replace Caminiti, who never did go on the DL all year.

June 9-19 (43-39, 1 game ahead)
Everything the Padres had gained in April and May they gave back in June. The slide began on June 2, the same game the team's leading RBI man, Wally Joyner, injured his thumb sliding into second base. He'd be out for nearly 6 weeks. They dropped that

game and 15 of their next 17. Their defense collapsed, yielding 20 unearned runs during those 17 games (after allowing only 17 in the first 2 months). They were shut out 3 times, lost in extra innings 3 times, and their pitching was tagged for 8 or more runs 7 times (after allowing that many runs only 4 times in the first 2 months). " One of their 2 wins came on a heroic performance by Tony Gwynn, going deep for the first of only 3 times in '96, off of lefthander Tony Fossas with 2 out in the bottom of the 9th inning, despite excruciating pain in his heel.

The happiness was short-lived. They dropped their next 8 and Andy Ashby went on the DL with a bad shoulder. They pulled out of the slide shortly after GM Kevin Towers dealt the slumping Ausmus and Cedeno to Detroit for John Flaherty and Chris Gomez. Caminiti broke out of a 12-game slump, during which the team dropped 10 games as he went 4-48 with 0 RBI—including an 0-7 in an extra-inning loss to the Cubs. It also helped to play the Giants, who they swept in San Francisco by a combined score of 31-12.

If a first place team going 9-19 wasn't strange enough, Steve Finley hit 9 home runs and knocked in 25 runs for the month. His previous best for a *season* was 11 home runs.

July 15-12 (58-51, ½ game ahead)

Tony Gwynn went down again in early July, this time to an Achilles tendon injury, possibly caused by the cortisone shot he took in his heel. They recalled the anti-Gwynn to replace him: Rob Deer. Deer was hitting .225 with 91 strikeouts in 209 at bats in the PCL. The team's streakiness continued—a 5-game winning streak at home (again, 4 courtesy of the Giants), a 5-game losing streak on the road (including 4 straight in Colorado, one of them when the bullpen blew a 9-2 lead in the seventh inning), then another 4-game winning streak. Wally Joyner came back ahead of schedule for the series in Colorado, saying, "Coors Field is calling me." But Andy Ashby, who had already been on the DL twice, continued to have trouble with his velocity. He was limited to 6 starts in June and July.

Carrying the team was John "Flash" Flaherty, who brought a career batting average of .229 to San Diego and promptly reeled off a 27-game hitting streak—second only to Benito Santiago's 34-game hitting streak in 1987 for catchers. Ever. Flash's previous best was 6 games. He overshadowed the other new Padre, Chris Gomez, who hit .298 in July with 16 RBI. Caminiti hit .357 and knocked in 26 runs, but he was only getting warmed up.

The Padres were winning games in every conceivable way. They beat the Marlins 3-0 in 11 innings, then came back the next day to pound out a 20-12 victory. Two days later, Scott Sanders out-dueled Kevin Brown 5-3, then Fernando Valenzuela beat Greg Maddux 2-1 the following day. The next day, at the trading deadline, they acquired Greg Vaughn from the Brewers for relievers Bryce Florie and Ron Villone, and potential star outfielder, Marc Newfield.

August 18-10 (76-61, 1 game ahead)

The Padres had their best month of the season in August, but the Dodgers stayed right with them. The pitching (3.02 ERA) was nearly as good as it had been in May (2.89), this time on the strength of the starters—despite being without Andy Ashby for the month. Hamilton, Sanders, and Fernando went 11-2 with an ERA of 2.24. Trevor Hoffman saved half of the team's victories, yielding 0 runs and 5 hits in 14.1 innings. Their defense was excellent once again, this time yielding only 6 unearned runs, only 1 of them coming in a loss (a 10-4 blow-out). Rickey Henderson, woken up by the acquisition of Vaughn, regained his starting job with a .338 batting average and .463 on-base percentage. Vaughn had 6 home runs, but was hitting .178.

The month included the first major league games ever played in Mexico, as the Padres took on the Mets in Monterrey. Fernando pitched, and won, the first game of the series, but Ken Caminiti stole the show in the final game. Stricken with Montezuma's Revenge, all Caminiti needed was an I.V. and a Snickers bar to get him ready by game-time. He hit 2 home runs in an 8-0 victory. Bochy: "I've never been around anyone tougher. He just played with pure guts." Bob Tewksbury: "That's the most incredible thing I've ever been around in baseball. Talk about inspiration. Damn. Unbelievable. Absolutely unbelievable."

After the I.V. and Snickers bar, Caminiti played in 37 games, batting .399 with 16 home runs and 47 RBI. Who needs speed and steroids?

September 15-10 (91-71, won division by 1 game)
The Padres were outscored 108-102 in September, but still found a way to win 15 of 25 on their way to their second division title, and their first in 12 years. They were an incredible 8-2 in 1-run games. The Padres swept a 3-game series with Pittsburgh, winning 6-5, 6-5, and 8-7, all in the bottom of the 9th. The tension of the pennant race, something San Diego fans and players alike are unfamiliar with, even got to happy-go-lucky Tony Gwynn. He got on his manager for pitching to Barry Bonds late in the game on the 17th, allowing Bonds to go deep in a 9-7 Giants win. Then, responding to just this type of "constructive criticism" from the people who pay his salary, Gwynn offered this advice to the *San Diego Union-Tribune*: "Tell the fans to go bleep themselves. They aren't out here all bleeping year and now they're critics. We're in a pennant race and all of a sudden they're GMs and managers. The majority of people don't have the slightest idea of what's going on." No, Tony. Why don't you tell them yourself. While you're at it, you can tell them why, when you were injured the team played .590 ball (23-16), and when you were healthy the Padres were only a .553 team.

It wasn't Gwynn and his singles and his nervous tension who was carrying the team to the playoffs, anyway. It was Steve Finley, who hit 9 homers in a month *again*; Trevor Hoffman, who saved 9 of the games and won 2 others, striking out 28 in 18 innings; and Caminiti, who hit .375 and knocked in 23 runs—going 6-11 with a game-winning double in the season-ending series with L.A. that decided the Dodger-Padre battle for the division and the Piazza-Caminiti battle for the MVP.

October (lost in division series in 3 games to the Cardinals)
The Padres had to overcome a lot just to get to the playoffs, but it was over before they knew it. Greg Vaughn was limited to a pinch-hitting role, going 0-3, while Joyner and Finley were held to 2 hits in 21 at bats. Rickey Henderson got on base and Ken Caminiti hit 3 home runs, but the team hit .238 as the Cardinals swept them in 3 close games, 3-1, 5-4, and 7-5.

■ 1997 DIAGNOSIS

Offense
The Padres offense was one of the best in the N.L., scoring 771 runs in a pitchers' park, 7 fewer than the Reds, who led the non-Coors league. Their offense was driven by unglamorous elements: singles, doubles, walks, on-base percentage, and making contact. They didn't hit many home runs, didn't run very often or very successfully, left more runners on base than any team in the league, and grounded into more double plays than any team in the league. Ironically, the team with the best on-base percentage in the non-Coors league was shutout more often than every team except the Giants, Dodgers, and Marlins.

Things don't look good for '97, because of the age of their position players and the number of big years on the '96 team (see *Old Players and Peaking Careers* at the end of the section). Their power was only average and was also heavily concentrated; basically it was Finley and Caminiti. These two hit nearly 50% of their team's home runs. Not even Bonds/Williams or Sheffield/Conine dominated their team's offense to this extent. Only Hundley and Gilkey with the Mets compared to Finley and Caminiti. There is only one thing that would be more surprising than 2 players in their 30s—one who had never hit 30 home runs, the other who had never hit 15—combining for 70 home runs. That would be for them to do it again. If they bring him back, it's quite possible that Finley, Caminiti, *and* Vaughn won't hit 70 home runs.

Defense
GM Kevin Towers made a number of moves (Joyner, Gomez, and Henderson in, Williams, Cedeno, Roberts, Nieves, and Plantier out) that strengthened the team's defense, and the team responded by moving from 6th in the league to 3rd, and cutting its unearned runs from 83 to 66.

Wally Joyner was a distinct improvement over Eddie Williams at first—only Jeff King and John Olerud had a higher fielding percentage. Jody Reed was solid at second, and Quilvio Veras will have better range, even if he does kick a few routine plays that Reed would have handled. Chris Gomez isn't spectacular, but he stabilized shortstop when he replaced Andujar Cedeno. Caminiti, despite all the aches and pains, actually lowered his errors in

'96, while he made plays at third no human being, be he named Pie, Brooks, or Graig, has ever made. If you missed them, make sure you catch the Plays of the Decade in late-December 1999 for the one where he threw out a runner while sitting on the third base line.

In the outfield, Greg Vaughn was a very underrated left fielder. He may not be anywhere near as fast as Rickey, but he has better range—and a much better arm. Steve Finley is one of the best in center, but Tony Gwynn's range continues to deteriorate in right field.

Brad Ausmus was one of the best defensive catchers in the N.L. in '95, but his throwing declined (he threw out 42% of base-stealers in '95, down to 32% with San Diego in '96) and he had more passed balls in 46 games in '96 than he did in all of '95. John Flaherty was brought in to provide more offense, but his defense wasn't as much of a drop-off as would have been expected. The Tigers raved about Ausmus's handling of the pitchers—the ERA when he was behind the plate dropped from 7.04 to 5.50—but the Padre ERAs didn't increase significantly (3.92 to 4.06) when Flaherty took over.

Pitching

Pitching coach Dan Warthen gave his staff shirts that read: "Strike one, work fast, change speeds." It worked. The staff's walks per game dropped from 3.6 to 3.1, but this wasn't a function of throwing strikes and running over to back up third base. Hits allowed stayed flat, home runs dropped, and strikeouts increased. The personnel on the staff was virtually identical, so give Warthen some credit for bringing the young pitchers along. The team's ERA dropped from 4.13 to 3.72, which was the main reason the team went from 70-74 to 91-71.

Joey Hamilton established himself as a front-line starter, while Scott Sanders finally showed what he could do if he was healthy for an extended period of time. Andy Ashby showed that his '95 emergence was no fluke—but his ongoing shoulder troubles don't bode well for '97. Bob Tewksbury and Fernando Valenzuela managed to put together productive years for what may be the last time; both were free agents in the off-season, and the Padres may choose to go with Sean Bergman or lefty prospect, Heath Murray, in '97.

The Padres bullpen was the deepest in baseball, and it allowed them to deal young arms Ron Villone and Bryce Florie to get Greg Vaughn, and Dustin Hermanson for Quilvio Veras in the off-season, without missing a beat. The bullpen is where the leap forward for the Padres took place. Hoffman went from 3.88 and 31 saves to 2.25 and 42 saves, and his strikeout rate went through the roof. Doug Bochtler's appearances increased from 34 to 63, while his ERA dropped from 3.57 to 3.04. Tim Worrell was finally healthy; he started out in the bullpen and went from 13 uneven innings to 121 outstanding ones (9-7 with a 3.05 ERA). As a reliever, he was more dominating than Hoffman, if that's possible. Scott Sanders also started off in the 'pen and shook off elbow woes, lowering his ERA from 4.30 to 3.38. The Padres will still have a deep bullpen in '97—especially if Dario Veras continues to evolve, and if Warthen can get Andres Berumen to throw strike one, work fast, and change speeds.

Farm System

The Padres farm system is not done feeding young pitchers to the parent club. Marc Kroon is next in line. Reliever Andres Berumen also has talent, but he'll be more of a project. Lefties Heath Murray and Shane Dennis could challenge for a spot in the rotation. First baseman, Derrek Lee, and catcher, Ben Davis, were sought in trades throughout '96, but San Diego had no interest in dealing them. GM Kevin Towers: "It sure is nice to sit in the stands and have the other scouts salivating over your players."

Ownership and Management

Padre ownership is more committed to doing what it takes to win than it's been in years, and the fans are responding. Attendance at Jack Murphy Stadium was up 85% from 1995. They are also finally putting some effort into attracting the Latino market. It remains to be seen whether they can maintain these attendance levels if the '97 squad plays .500 ball and is only on the fringes of wild-card contention.

GM Kevin Towers has built on the strong foundation Randy Smith left behind before heading to Detroit. He took a big risk when he dealt three

prospects to bring in Greg Vaughn for the stretch drive. Unfortunately, Vaughn didn't produce in San Diego, the team didn't go far in the playoffs, and the outfielder's initial salary demands were $1 million per year higher than what they were willing to pay *before* he hit .206 for 2 months. In the off-season, Towers was feeling pressure to justify the loss of Villone, Florie, and Newfield, while also recognizing the damage Vaughn could do to his team's fortunes if he was signed for big money and failed to produce. The only way Towers may think he can win will be if he brings Vaughn back and the slugger puts up big numbers, but that's not all that likely to happen (see Vaughn's write-up in the Free Agents section). It wouldn't be the first time Villone and Newfield were traded to rent a disappointment for a few months; that's what the Mariners had to give up in '95 to get Andy Benes.

Bruce Bochy took a team to the playoffs that had no history of winning (only Valenzuela, Gwynn, and Henderson had been to the World Series); endured subpar performance from key players (Ausmus and Cedeno were both below the Mendoza Line and disappointing in the field at the time they were traded; Henderson had his lowest batting average as a big leaguer; Vaughn never did adjust to the league); suffered through an epic slump (16 of 18 in June); was nearly decimated by injuries (Joyner, Gwynn, and Ashby all missed significant time, and Caminiti, if he was human, should have); and had all the elements in place for a September clubhouse meltdown (4 star players for 3 outfield positions, while Gwynn questioned the manager's in-game moves and blasted the fans). Other than that, Bochy really didn't have to do much.

. . . and whatnot: Old Players and Peaking Careers

The Padres were an old team in 1996, as they were in 1984, the only other time they've made it into post-season. In 1985, the team slipped back to .500 and finished 12 games back. In 1986, they were under .500 and 22 games back. In 1987, they were back in last place, 25 games back. What happened to the 1984 team, and what is the past the Padres may condemn themselves to repeat? Old players and peaking careers. It's a dangerous combination, and it can very quickly transform a pennant-winner into something unrecognizable.

Old Players. Three key players on the '84 team were near the end of their careers: Steve Garvey (35), Graig Nettles (39), and Rich Gossage (32). Garvey had some productive years left, but his batting average and RBI in 1984 were as high as they'd ever get again, and he was through three years later (replaced by the anti-Garvey, John Kruk, who they'd later trade for Chris James). Graig Nettles would hang around for 2 more semi-productive years, but third base would remain a black hole, manned by Randy Ready, Chris Brown, Luis Salazar, Mike Pagliarulo, Scott Coolbaugh, and Jack Howell until Gary Sheffield arrived in 1992. Gossage had one more Gossage-like year, before giving way to Lance McCullers, Mark Davis, Craig Lefferts, Larry Andersen, Randy Myers, and Gene Harris. It was a new closer every year, before Trevor Hoffman was acquired in 1994. All of this is what the management consulting types call a "succession planning breakdown."

Peaking Careers. Alan Wiggins, 26, played second base for the '84 Padres, stole 70 bases, and scored 106 runs. He spent '85 in rehab, ended up in Baltimore in '86, was out of baseball by '88, and died in 1991. Tim Lollar and Mark Thurmond combined for 25 wins. The only lefty duo in the N.L. that could top that was Jerry Koosman and Steve Carlton. Thurmond would go 10-18 over the next 1½ seasons and be dealt to the Tigers for Dave LaPoint with 9 wins left in him. Lollar had already shown signs of regression after going 16-9 in 1982, so they dealt him after the '84 off-season. Good idea. For Lamarr Hoyt. Bad idea. The large, expensive, and troubled Hoyt had one good year for San Diego before his life fell apart

The '96 Padres had even more old players and more peaking careers than the '84 squad.

Old Players. The current Padres need to have successors identified for Wally Joyner (35), Fernando Valenzuela (36), Tony Gwynn (37), Rickey Henderson (38), and Ken Caminiti (34). The future at first base is Derrek Lee, and Heath Murray may be a lefthanded starter in San Diego as soon as '97. But you have to look all the way down in Rookie ball to find an outfield prospect (Vernon Maxwell), and he is raw and not very Gwynn-like (45 strikeouts and 49 hits in 194 at bats). As for a lead-off man, the

front office hopes Quilvio Veras will be the answer, but some Padres weren't convinced. Finding a replacement for the battle-scarred Caminiti at third base won't be as important as finding someone else who will be willing and able to step forward as a team leader. Maybe that burden will evenutally fall on Derrek Lee or Ben Davis, though both of them will find themselves preoccupied simply with making contact with big league pitches when their time comes.

Peaking Careers. San Diego also has several players who are poised for significant drop-offs in production, and not all of them are the aging veterans described above. Tony Gwynn's production may quickly become that of a heavier, more injury-prone Wade Boggs. His slugging percentage, if you can call it that, has been declining steadily and his 3 home runs was a career low for a 100-game season. Ken Caminiti's development as a player late in his baseball life is unprecedented, and his body has been abused, so the inevitable decline will most likely be sudden and steady. John Flaherty, 29, and Steve Finley, 32, are also coming off of career years. If they use a significant chunk of their limited resources to re-sign Greg Vaughn, who'll turn 32 in July, they shouldn't expect 41 home runs and 117 RBI from him, either. On the mound, Joey Hamilton and Andy Ashby are one of the most talented tandems in baseball, but both pitchers have been troubled by sore shoulders. Hamilton is young and may have his best years ahead of him. Ashby is a much better bet to be spending significant time in the shop for repairs in '97 and beyond.

The '84 Padres had two young hitters coming into their own (Tony Gwynn and Kevin McReynolds, both 24) while the '96 Padres had a very old offense. Of the playoff teams, they were the only one that did not get signficant production from a player in his 20s—not to mention the complete absence of any talented kids like Derek Jeter, Chipper Jones, Andruw Jones, Jermaine Dye, Todd Hollandsworth, and Manny Ramirez. The '97 Padres have better prospects coming through their system than the '84 Padres did (Kruk and Benito Santiago in the pipeline and little else). The future is bright for this team.

But 1997 isn't.

GABE ALVAREZ

SOLID PROSPECT

SS • BR • TR • 6'1 • 185 • 23 • SD95/2

	AB	R	H	2B	3B	HR	RBI	BB	SO	SB	CS	BA	OB	SA
AA	368	58	91	23	1	8	40	64	87	2	3	.247	.361	.380

Alvarez has a great arm, but his range may force a move to third base eventually. He was a star at USC and those numbers don't show what he can do as a hitter. He hit .344 and slugged .528 in Rancho Cucamonga in '95. A stress fracture in his foot in '96 kept him out in June and July, and when he returned he was unable to drive the ball. The Padres really like him as a hitter, in part because of how well he can handle breaking balls already. ■

ANDY ASHBY

SP • BR • TR • 6'5 • 190 • 29 • PHI86

	G	GS	IP	H	HR	BB	K	W	L	S	ERA	K/BB	K9	HW9
SD94	24	24	164	145	16	43	121	6	11	0	3.40	2.8	6.6	10.31
SD95	31	31	192	180	17	62	150	12	10	0	2.94	2.4	7.0	11.34
SD96	24	24	150	147	17	34	85	9	5	0	3.23	2.5	5.1	10.86
CAREER	159	116	709	723	80	235	483	32	44	1	4.20	2.1	6.1	12.16

Ashby has a good sinking fastball, a cut fastball, and a hard curveball. He was always considered to have a live arm, but he couldn't throw strikes in Philadelphia and his curveball wouldn't break in Colorado. Randy Smith stole him from the Rockies (along with Doug Bochtler and Brad Ausmus) for Bruce Hurst and Greg Harris. He pitched very well in '96, when he was healthy, though he was hitting the wall after 75 pitches—something that hadn't been a problem for him in San Diego before '96. It was probably a function of his shoulder problems; he went on the DL twice with what was eventually determined to be "frayed shoulder cartilage." Ashby tried to throw through the pain in the September pennant race, despite a lack of velocity, and was hung with a 4.78 ERA that pushed him over 3.00 for the year. He's only thrown 200 innings once (in 1991, and he spent most of the following year on the DL). As good as Ashby is, he has to be viewed as a quesiton mark in '97. ■

SEAN BERGMAN

SLEEPER

SP-RP • BR • TR • 6′4 • 205 • 26 • DET91/6

	G	GS	IP	H	HR	BB	K	W	L	S	ERA	K/BB	K9	HW9
DET94	3	3	17	22	2	7	12	2	1	0	5.60	1.7	6.3	15.29
DET95	28	28	135	169	19	67	86	7	10	0	5.12	1.3	5.7	15.73
SD96	41	14	113	119	14	33	85	6	8	0	4.37	2.6	6.8	12.10
CAREER	81	51	305	357	41	130	202	16	23	0	4.96	1.6	6.0	14.37

The Padres love Bergman's stuff if not his results. He has a good 92–94-mph fastball that both sinks and tails, and a hard slider. He doesn't trust it enough, though. Warthen on Bergman's troubles: "I think he is thinking too much and trying too hard." He also needs to work more on his off-speed stuff, and work it into his repertoire without losing his aggressiveness. The Padres have not given up on him by any means, and he will get a chance to win a spot in the rotation in '97. He was much more effective, however, as a reliever, only having to go through the lineup once. He spent the second half of the season in the bullpen, and had a 2.84 ERA with 16 strikeouts and 4 walks in 25 innings. ■

ANDRES BERUMEN

RP • BR • TR • 6′2 • 210 • 25 • KC89/28

	G	GS	IP	H	HR	BB	K	W	L	S	ERA	K/BB	K9	HW9
AAA	50	0	71	73	4	58	59	4	7	1	6.11	1.0	7.5	16.69

Berumen has a good, 4-seam fastball and an even better slider that he has no command of whatsoever. He got an extended trial in San Diego in '95, but walked the ballpark. As you can see, things didn't get any better in Las Vegas. In desperate need of an off-speed pitch, he's working on a change-up and the results have been messy. The Royals left him unprotected in the expansion draft, and the Marlins sent him to the Padres in the Sheffield deal. If he doesn't harness his potential, he'll be on to his 4th organization sooner rather than later. If he does get it together, then Warthen will continue to build the case that he is one of the better young pitching coaches in baseball. ■

WILLIE BLAIR

RP • BR • TR • 6′1 • 185 • 31 • TOR86/11

	G	GS	IP	H	HR	BB	K	W	L	S	ERA	K/BB	K9	HW9
COL94	47	1	77	98	9	39	68	0	5	3	5.79	1.7	7.9	16.00
SD95	40	12	114	112	11	45	83	7	5	0	4.34	1.8	6.6	12.39
SD95	60	0	88	80	13	29	67	2	6	1	4.60	2.3	6.9	11.15
CAREER	260	50	609	672	69	218	406	25	41	4	4.73	1.9	6.0	13.15

If that's the worst pitcher in your bullpen, then you're in pretty good shape. Like most pitchers on the staff, Blair throws hard and throws strikes. Unlike most pitchers on the staff, he was very erratic. In May and August, he was unhittable, yielding 16 hits in 28.2 innings, walking 4 and striking out 22 with an ERA of 1.26. In his other 40 appearances, he was meat: 1-6 with a 6.22 ERA. Historically, his effectiveness diminishes the longer the appearance, though that hasn't stopped teams from trying to use him as a starter. That trend continued in '96, as hitters hit .400 off of him after 30 pitches. If he was limited to one inning per appearance, his numbers might improve dramatically. If the Padres want him to eat innings to save the rest of the bullpen, they'll have to live with the occasional ugly outing that will result. He was involved in the Kenny Lofton trade, so maybe he's the one the Astros really wanted, not Ed Taubansee. ■

DOUG BOCHTLER

YOUNG GUN

RP • BR • TR • 6′3 • 205 • 26 • MON89/9

	G	GS	IP	H	HR	BB	K	W	L	S	ERA	K/BB	K9	HW9
SD95	34	0	45	38	5	19	45	4	4	1	3.57	2.4	9.0	11.40
SD96	63	0	65	45	6	39	68	2	4	3	3.02	1.7	9.4	11.62

Bochtler has a deceptive motion, a hard fastball, and he throws high in the strike zone and can get away with it. He held the league to a .195 batting average (.117 after the All-Star break), and is equally tough against lefties and righties. If not for a brutal June, Bochtler's numbers would have been in Mariano Rivera's league: 53 innings, 27 hits, 55 strikeouts, and a 1.72 ERA. He got stronger as the year went on and the pressure increased, so look for Bochtler to further establish himself as one of the best set-up men in the N.L. in '97. ■

HOMER BUSH

SLEEPER

2B • BR • TR • 5′11 • 180 • 24 • SD91/8

	AB	R	H	2B	3B	HR	RBI	BB	SO	SB	CS	BA	OB	SA
AAA	116	24	42	11	1	2	3	3	33	3	5	.362	.388	.526

Bush's season ended when he broke his right tibia, leaving him with some bizarre numbers (a .526 slugging average with 3 RBI, a 33:3 K/BB ratio) and a lost year of development. They expected Bush back for August, but he never returned. The Padres liked him enough to put him on the major league DL, which meant a pro-rated chunk of the big league minimum salary. They also had him travel with the team to expose him to a pennant race. On the other hand, they gave up a good young arm in Dustin Hermansen to get Quilvio Veras, who is only 1½ years older than Bush and now in his way. Like Veras, Bush is a leadoff man with excellent speed who is getting better in the field, but Homer had a lot more reason to be optimistic this time last year, when he was healthy and only Jody Reed and Luis Lopez were in his way. He still might beat Veras out eventually, just don't expect it to happen right away. ■

KEN CAMINITI

NL ELITE

3B • BB • TR • 6′0 • 200 • 33 • HOU84/4

	AB	R	H	2B	3B	HR	RBI	BB	SO	SB	CS	BA	OB	SA
HOU94	406	63	115	28	2	18	75	43	71	4	3	.283	.352	.495
SD95	526	74	159	33	0	26	94	69	94	12	5	.302	.380	.513
SD96	546	109	178	37	2	40	130	78	99	11	5	.326	.408	.621
CAREER	4513	592	1233	250	15	141	669	445	757	62	32	.273	.338	.429

After the '94 strike, the Astros and Padres made a major deal involving Caminiti and healthy chunks of each other's 40-man rosters. Now that some time has elapsed and some of the principals have moved along in trades for other players—such as Andujar Cedeno for Chris Gomez—here's what it boils down to in '96: **San Diego**—Caminiti (40-130-.326), Finley (30-95-.298), Gomez (3-29-.262); **Houston**—Derek Bell (17-113-.263), Ricky Gutierrez (1-15-.284), and Doug Brocail (4.58). The Astros had financial reasons for making that deal, but it's starting to look almost as bad as . . . well, Lofton for Taubansee (and Blair).

Caminiti's development at his age (he'll turn 34 in April) is unprecedented. Here are the only other hitters to win their first MVP at the age of 33 or older: Willie Stargell (32-82-.281 at 39), Harmon Killebrew (49-140-.276 at 34), Ken Boyer (24-119-.295 at 33), Elston Howard (28-85-.287 at 34), Hank Sauer (35-121-.270 at 35), Dolph Camilli (34-120-.285 at 34), Charlie Gehringer (14-96-.371 at 34), Lou Gehrig (49-152-.354 at 33), and Gabby Hartnett (13-91-.344 at 34). Worth noting: 1) Only Lou Gehrig's (yup, Lou Gehrig's) numbers can match up with Caminiti's in '96; 2) Stargell, Killebrew, Gehringer, Gehrig, and Hartnett were all wrapping up Hall of Fame careers, and these weren't even their career years; 3) Boyer, Howard, Sauer, and Camilli were consistent stars who had already had several years similiar to their MVP seasons. As rare as it is for a hitter to put up Caminiti's numbers at any age, no one in history has ever done it at 33 after such a nondescript career. Not bad for a guy who didn't even hit 40 home runs in 4 minor league seasons.

Caminiti is the best defensive third baseman in baseball, and the toughest player at *any* position. There are no modern baseball players to compare him to, unless Emmitt Smith and Mark Messier have decided to try the 2-sport thing since we've gone to press. Despite an abdominal strain that had management begging to let them put him on the disabled list, and a left shoulder injury that turned out to be a completely torn rotator cuff, and a partly torn biceps tendon, Caminiti finished stronger than any player in either league. After the All-Star Break (he didn't make the team), he hit 28 home runs, knocked in 81 runs, and hit .360. He hit 13 home runs and knocked in 48 runs with 2 strikes on him. Ray Knight: "He plays every day and is as hard-nosed as anybody. The best player in the league is still Barry Bonds. But Ken Caminiti is the MVP."

He was operated on in October and is expected to be out until as late as the All-Star Break. With his track record, there's no reason not to expect him back by Opening Day. ■

ARCHI CIANFROCCO

IF-OF • BR • TR • 6′5 • 215 • 30 • MON87/7

	AB	R	H	2B	3B	HR	RBI	BB	SO	SB	CS	BA	OB	SA
SD94	146	9	32	8	0	4	13	3	39	2	0	.219	.252	.356
SD95	118	22	31	7	0	5	31	11	28	0	2	.263	.333	.449
SD96	192	21	54	13	3	2	32	8	56	1	0	.281	.315	.411
CAREER	984	107	245	44	7	29	154	50	258	8	2	.249	.290	.396

Cianfrocco played every position in '96, including 1 game at catcher. This versatility is going to keep him around, as will the numbers he continues to put up for the Padres in limited play: 63 RBI in his last 310 at bats. He's slow, he doesn't have a particularly quick bat, rarely draws a walk, and strikes out too much—but he finds a way to produce. If Caminiti isn't ready by Opening Day, Cianfrocco should get some playing time at third. ■

BEN DAVIS

SOLID PROSPECT

C • BB • TR • 6′4 • 195 • 20 • SD95/1

	AB	R	H	2B	3B	HR	RBI	BB	SO	SB	CS	BA	OB	SA
A+	353	35	71	10	1	6	41	31	89	1	1	.201	.264	.286

Davis is considered by some to be the best high school catching prospect drafted in the last 20 years. He hits for power from both sides of the plate, has a good arm, and has already demonstrated leadership skills. He was hampered by calcium deposits in his throwing elbow in '96, but he played through it. Unless he makes a quantum leap in '97—probably at Double-A Memphis—the Rockies' catching prospect, Ben Petrick, has a better chance to be playing in the majors by the age of 21.

SHANE DENNIS

SLEEPER

SP • BR • TL • 6′3 • 200 • 25 • SD94/7

	G	GS	IP	H	HR	BB	K	W	L	S	ERA	K/BB	K9	HW9
AA	19	19	115	83	11	45	131	9	1	0	2.27	2.9	10.3	10.02

Dennis finally convinced the Padres brass that he was for real in '96. Towers still thinks he needs to work on his breaking stuff—but if he doesn't clear a spot for him on the 40-man roster, Dennis will be working on that for whatever team grabs him in the Rule 5 Draft.

STEVE FINLEY

CONSISTENT STAR

CF • BL • TL • 6′2 • 180 • 32 • BAL87/14

	AB	R	H	2B	3B	HR	RBI	BB	SO	SB	CS	BA	OB	SA
HOU94	373	64	103	16	5	11	33	28	52	13	7	.276	.329	.434
SD95	562	104	167	23	8	10	44	59	62	36	12	.297	.366	.420
SD96	655	126	195	45	9	30	95	56	88	22	8	.298	.354	.531
CAREER	4019	612	1130	177	64	77	387	318	478	207	72	.281	.335	.415

The book on Finley had been that he was a good breaking ball hitter who could be overmatched by hard fastballs. As he gets older, his bat, if anything, is speeding up. He became a genuine home run threat, and it wasn't from going deep during garbage time. His late game heroics won two games in a week during the September pennant race—one with 2 outs and an 0-2 count in the bottom of the 9th.

Think the Orioles might like to undo that Glenn Davis deal for Finley, Curt Schilling, and Pete Harnisch? Just when you think Finley has taken it as far as he can, he raises his game to another level. He played high school ball in Kentucky where the bright future was assumed to belong to teammate Terry Shumpert. When he made it to the majors, he was supposed to be a 5th outfielder. When he ended up with the Astros and was given the chance to play every day, he was supposed to be a singles hitter. Now, just when the league had gotten comfortable with him as a Gold Glover with gap power, he outproduces every center fielder in the non-Coors league. He continues to provide excellent defense, playing a shallow center field and rarely getting burned on gappers. He has never really been vulnerable to lefties and he still isn't; he's been hitting around .270 against them since he came to the N.L., .326 in '95. His days of stealing 30 bases may be over—in part because his outstanding production caused Bochy to drop him into the 3-hole for roughly half of his at bats, and there wasn't much reason to run in front of Caminiti. Finley adapted his game to the role he was asked to play, striking out a bit more when batting third, but driving the ball; he raised his slugging average nearly 100 points to .593 from his numbers in the 2-hole. This from what had been a table-setter, who, coming into '96, had a career slugging average of only .392.

It's hard to imagine Finley getting any better than '96, however. The best way to forecast his numbers

for '97 is to figure out what his manager *wants* him to do. Finley hasn't disappointed any of them yet. ■

JOHN FLAHERTY

C • BR • TR • 6'1 • 195 • 29 • BOS88/25

	AB	R	H	2B	3B	HR	RBI	BB	SO	SB	CS	BA	OB	SA
DET95	354	39	86	22	1	11	40	18	47	0	0	.243	.284	.404
DET/SD96	416	40	118	24	0	13	64	17	61	3	3	.284	.314	.435
CAREER	901	87	226	51	1	24	112	41	132	3	4	.251	.286	.390

Flaherty once hit .289 in half a season at New Britain, but, prior to '96, that was the extent of his highlight film. With a career average of .223 and a personal best 6-game hitting streak coming into '96, he was on the short list of least likely candidates for a 27-game hitting streak—second longest for a catcher ever. When he and Gomez were traded for Ausmus and Cedeno, it was assumed that the Padres were giving up a lot of defense behind the plate to get a little more offense. They got even more offense than they expected, and didn't lose all that much on defense. Bochy, a former catcher, liked the fit between Flaherty's personality and that of his staff: "One thing we wanted to get was a little more aggressive. We wanted them to establish the fastball. That's the pitch that really establishes other pitches. It goes with John, too. He's an aggressive, intense kid. He's rubbed off on the pitchers."

It's often assumed that trading is a zero-sum game where somebody wins and somebody loses. That was certainly true with Gomez and Cedeno. But with Ausmus's bat coming around a bit in Detroit, and the pitchers responding to his approach, the other half of that trade looks like it helped both teams. ■

CHRIS GOMEZ

SS • BR • TR • 6'1 • 185 • 25 • DET92/3

	AB	R	H	2B	3B	HR	RBI	BB	SO	SB	CS	BA	OB	SA
DET94	296	32	76	19	0	8	53	33	64	5	3	.257	.336	.402
DET95	431	49	96	20	2	11	50	41	96	4	1	.223	.292	.355
DET/SD96	456	53	117	21	1	4	45	57	84	3	3	.257	.347	.333
CAREER	1311	145	321	67	4	23	159	140	261	14	9	.245	.323	.355

Gomez was rushed through the Tigers system, getting less than 500 at bats and hitting only .250 in the minors. He showed no punch on the farm and,

as you can tell from his slugging average, what he's displayed in the majors has declined steadily. He's always made the pitchers go deep into the count, but he is making more contact now, and working out more walks. He's also hanging in better against righties, raising his average against them from .201 to .262. But his bat isn't why they got him. Towers: ". . . we made the change at shortstop, not so much for offense but because we wanted more consistency at the position—somebody who's going to catch the routine balls, somebody who's going to leave his feet to stop a ball. . . . Gomez is no Gold Glover, or anything. But most of the time, the plays he's supposed to make, he makes. I feel very comfortable when the ball is hit to him. I can't say I used to feel that way. And when he throws the ball, I have a pretty good idea it's going to be somewhere Wally has a chance to catch it. I couldn't say that, either." That's a very polite way of describing how brutal it was to watch Cedeno in the field on a daily basis. Must be nice for Gomez to be following in his footsteps, rather than Alan Trammell's.

The Padres have a number of shortstop prospects, so they may only be renting him the position for a year at a time. Expect him to face an annual battle every spring for the starting job. ■

CHRIS GWYNN (see Looking for a Game)

TONY GWYNN — CONSISTENT STAR

RF • BL • TL • 5'11 • 215 • 36 • SD81/3

	AB	R	H	2B	3B	HR	RBI	BB	SO	SB	CS	BA	OB	SA
SD94	419	79	165	35	1	12	64	48	19	5	0	.394	.454	.568
SD95	535	82	197	33	1	9	90	35	15	17	5	.368	.404	.484
SD96	451	67	159	27	2	3	50	39	17	11	4	.353	.400	.441
CAREER	7595	1140	2560	411	82	90	854	664	361	296	116	.337	.389	.448

Gwynn needs 440 hits to reach 3,000, but he won't necessarily be crossing that finishing line in full stride, When the effect of the labor unrest is taken into account (which looks to have cost him 100 hits and what would have been 2 more 200+ hit seasons), his hits per year

projects to a decline from 243 in '94 to 222 in '95 to 159 in his injury-riddled '96. If he can play 2 full seasons at his '94–'95 levels, look for him to be slapping a memorable single to left in September '98 on his way to his 9th batting title. But if injuries continue to wear him down, he could be slapping that single in the year 2000 at 39 as a part-time player. Gwynn doesn't like to hear about his weight, but he only played 116 games in '96, losing 8 to a heel injury in April, and another 31 in July and early-August to an Achilles tendon problem. He had the ankle cleaned out in the off-season, but it could just be a knee or the other ankle in '97. Gwynn: "I don't see any skinny guys out there hitting .320 every year." True, but you also don't see too many athletes 30 pounds overweight staying productive into their late-30s. Otherwise, the discussion right now might be about Gwynn's chances at 4,000 hits. ■

JOEY HAMILTON — YOUNG GUN

SP • BR • TR • 6'4 • 230 • 26 • SD91/1

	G	GS	IP	H	HR	BB	K	W	L	S	ERA	K/BB	K9	HW9
SD94	16	16	108	98	7	29	61	9	6	0	2.98	2.1	5.1	10.58
SD95	31	30	204	189	17	56	123	6	9	0	3.08	2.2	5.4	10.81
SD96	34	33	211	206	19	83	184	15	9	0	4.17	2.2	7.8	12.32
CAREER	81	79	524	493	43	168	368	30	24	0	3.50	2.2	6.3	11.35

Hamilton is one of the hardest throwing starting pitchers in baseball (clocked as high as 98), but unlike most power-pitchers, he does not challenge hitters up in the zone. He has a sinking fastball—along with a slider, curve, and improving change-up—and he tries to gets hitters to wave at balls in the dirt or beat the ball into the ground. Like most groundball pitchers, he's much less effective on astroturf—going 1-4 in 6 starts with a 5.17 ERA.

Hamilton's 15-9 record obscures the fact that he was one of the few Padre pitchers to take a step back in '96. He tried to blow hitters away, and as his strikeouts increased, so too did his walks. On average, he was at 100 pitches through 6 innings (Andy Ashby, who is more effective with less dominating stuff, goes just as deep into the game as Hamilton, but throws, on average, 12 fewer pitches a game—and that will add up over the course of a season to about 4 more starts worth of pitches taken out of your arm). Hamilton won 9 more games in '96 than he did in '95 not because he progressed, but because he got 5 runs to work with rather than 3.6.

In August, Hamilton complained of shoulder soreness, but the MRI was negative. He pitched through it, but struggled early in games because he had trouble getting loose. His strikeouts-to-walk ratio was only 26:25 in the 1st inning, compared to 158:58 in the rest of the game. If he can stay healthy and use his great stuff more efficiently, he could be John Smoltz. At 25, they were **awfully** similiar.

	W	L	ERA	K/BB	K9	HW9	HR9
Smoltz	15	11	3.62	2.1	7.7	11.38	.8
Hamilton	15	9	4.17	2.2	7.8	12.32	.8

Smoltz pitched more innings (244) and held opponents to a lower batting average (.230 to .256). He wasn't afraid to challenge hitters at the letters. He also had a better slider, and a splitter that Hamilton doesn't have. As Smoltz has improved his command of his stuff—cutting his walks in half—he's become a Cy Young winner. It's not likely that Hamilton will ever have a season like Smoltz had in '96 (few have), but he's got the stuff to be a 20-game winner. He's just got to figure out how to use it more effectively. ■

RICKEY HENDERSON — NL ELITE

LF • BR • TL • 5'10 • 195 • 38 • OAK76/4

	AB	R	H	2B	3B	HR	RBI	BB	SO	SB	CS	BA	OB	SA
OAK94	296	66	77	13	0	6	20	72	45	22	7	.260	.411	.365
OAK95	407	67	122	31	1	9	54	72	66	32	10	.300	.407	.447
SD96	465	110	112	17	2	9	29	125	90	37	15	.241	.410	.344
CAREER	8328	1829	2450	412	59	244	887	1675	1191	1186	280	.287	.406	.435

Henderson said all the right things when he was benched in favor of Greg Vaughn in August: "Our job is to play baseball and win. And that's what I'm looking for, to go out and win ballgames and pull for everyone." But he admitted he was "disappointed" and "hurt." And he had every right to be. Henderson's batting average may have dropped 60 points in '96, but his on-base percentage actually went up. He played more games and scored a lot more runs, even if he didn't do it by hitting singles. Here are the players in the N.L.

who got on base more often than Henderson: Gary Sheffield (.465), Barry Bonds (.461), Jeff Bagwell (.451), and Mike Piazza (.422). If you're looking for another leadoff man who got on base more often, there isn't one. Henderson didn't know the pitchers yet, so he worked them even more than he usually does and drew walks. In fact, when he tried to become more aggressive in the second half, his batting average went up and his on-base percentage (and slugging average) went down. Even without swinging the bat, Henderson was one of the best players in the National League last year.

If they bring Vaughn back for big bucks, Henderson will either end up a $2 million 4th outfielder or get salary-dumped on another team. And the Padres will probably be scratching their heads when their offense sputters. Even at 37, Henderson scored every 5 times to the plate. Quilvio Veras is good at that, too. But he's not *that* good. Few are. If Rickey has a starting job in '97—and shows up regularly for work—he'll get on base and score runs. And, based on this soliloquy, he may even start going deep again: "My bulk is from situps and pushups. I might decide to lift weights this year. I'll be in here saying, 'I can hit 50.' I'd be way bigger, because if I hit the weights, they'll say, 'Sure enough, Rickey, you should go back into football.' You'll see me and say, 'Mr. America just arrived.' " ■

DUSTIN HERMANSON — SLEEPER

RP • BR • TR • 6'3 • 195 • 24 • SD94/1

	G	GS	IP	H	HR	BB	K	W	L	S	ERA	K/BB	K9	HW9
AAA	42	0	46	41	3	27	54	1	4	21	3.13	2.0	10.6	13.30

Hermanson was the first of the Class of '94 to reach the majors, and didn't fare well. Bochy: "It was probably the first time in a long time, maybe ever, he really didn't have a lot of success. He lost a little confidence. Sometimes kids, especially high draft choices, feel too much pressure to perform. It's not too easy to perform up here." He got cuffed around again in a brief trial with the Padres in '96 (8.56 ERA), but most of that ugliness was due to one particularly wretched outing in Monterrey when Bochy tried to leave him to go 3 innings for the save in a laugher against the Mets—only to sweat out a messy 9th in a 15-10 victory.

Hermanson was traded to the Marlins for Quilvio Veras in November. He has an excellent fastball that hits 98, a good slider, an evolving change-up, inconsistent mechanics, and isn't known for listening attentively in class. If the Marlins can get through to him, Hermanson-Nen will be the N.L.'s answer to Rivera-Wetteland. ■

TREVOR HOFFMAN — NL ELITE

CL • BR • TR • 6'0 • 205 • 29 • CIN89/11

	G	GS	IP	H	HR	BB	K	W	L	S	ERA	K/BB	K9	HW9
SD94	47	0	56	39	4	20	68	4	4	20	2.57	3.4	10.9	9.48
SD95	55	0	53	48	10	14	52	7	4	31	3.88	3.7	8.8	10.53
SD96	70	0	88	50	6	31	111	9	5	42	2.25	3.6	11.4	8.28
CAREER	239	0	287	217	30	104	310	24	19	98	3.14	3.0	9.7	10.07

The Padres locked up Hoffman for 3 years for $8.4 million—an absolute steal, considering what the Mets will be paying John Franco for the next 2 years. He may very well have established himself as the best closer in baseball in '96. Hoffman has a good fastball, but gets his strikeouts on an exceptional slider. The league hit .161 against him. Day/night, left/right, grass/turf, home/away, he was unhittable. He got to two strikes on a batter 190 times and gave up 17 hits. Take out one miserable outing in Coors in July and his ERA would have been 1.67. Not bad for a converted shortstop that the Reds didn't think was worth protecting in the expansion draft. ■

BRIAN JOHNSON — SLEEPER

C • BR • TR • 6'2 • 200 • 29 • NYA89/15

	AB	R	H	2B	3B	HR	RBI	BB	SO	SB	CS	BA	OB	SA
SD94	93	7	23	4	1	3	16	5	21	0	0	.247	.283	.409
SD95	207	20	52	9	0	3	29	11	39	0	0	.251	.287	.338
SD96	243	18	66	13	1	8	35	4	36	0	0	.272	.290	.432
CAREER	543	45	141	26	2	14	80	20	96	0	0	.260	.288	.392

Johnson is smart, hard-working, and one of the more underrated players in the National League. The knock on him is his defense, but it continues to improve. Johnson: "I believe in what I can do—offensively and defensively. A lot of times, catchers are stereotyped: good-hitting catcher, good defensive catcher. I disagree. I think my game's pretty balanced."

At the plate, he's an aggressive, pull-hitter, who doesn't believe in working the pitcher. If Flaherty's

offense returns to where it's been, Johnson might take playing time from him, just as he did Ausmus early in 1996. He hit .328 against lefties, so the Padres may consider working him in at first base to spell Joyner on occasion; he's already played a handful of games there in his career. If it was up to hitting coach, Merv Rettenmund, he'd be playing everyday: "He has the ability to hit with Piazza for batting average."

Come back to us, Merv. ■

WALLY JOYNER — HEADED FOR A FALL

1B • BL • TL • 6′2 • 200 • 34 • CAL83/3

	AB	R	H	2B	3B	HR	RBI	BB	SO	SB	CS	BA	OB	SA
KC94	363	52	113	20	3	8	57	47	43	3	2	.311	.386	.449
KC95	465	69	144	28	0	12	83	69	65	3	2	.310	.394	.447
SD96	433	59	120	29	1	8	65	69	71	5	3	.277	.377	.404
CAREER	5538	784	1601	319	20	166	854	629	627	55	30	.289	.361	.444

Joyner had a big year at the right time (1991), and stepped into a very generous deal with the Royals. He didn't seem to enjoy the attention it attracted to him, and he was pleased to be traded from Kansas City for Bip Roberts: "No one here is pushing for the limelight, and everyone roots for everyone else." Limelight? In Kansas City? And no one pushing for it in Southern California? Sounds like Joyner got his cue cards reversed.

Joyner played well for the Padres until he injured his thumb sliding and missed 6 weeks. He hit .321 and slugged .500 before the injury, .245 and .333 after. He disappeared in the playoffs, and he struggled all year against lefties—hitting a soft .214 against them, 60 points below his '95 levels. As the Padres debated whether or not to bring Vaughn back, you have to wonder whether they considered throwing in a first baseman's mitt with the deal. ■

BRANDON KOLB — SOLID PROSPECT

SP • BR • TR • 6′1 • 190 • 23 • SD95/4

	G	GS	IP	H	HR	BB	K	W	L	S	ERA	K/BB	K9	HW9
A	27	27	181	170	7	76	138	16	9	0	3.42	1.8	6.8	12.21

Kolb throws 92–94 and was considered to be the best pitching prospect in the South Atlantic League. Considering the numbers he put up, it sounds like Kolb has more potential than results at the moment. The Padres aren't exactly rushing him through the system—there are still 3 levels between him and San Diego—but it's a name to remember. ■

MARC KROON — SOLID PROSPECT

RP • BR • TR • 6′2 • 195 • 23 • NYN91/4

	G	GS	IP	H	HR	BB	K	W	L	S	ERA	K/BB	K9	HW9
AA	44	0	47	33	4	28	56	2	4	22	2.89	2.0	10.80	11.68

Former GM Randy Smith stole Kroon from the Mets in a deal for Frank Seminara, and he tried to steal him back in '96, but the Padres refused to include him in the deal for Gomez and Flaherty. Kroon throws well into the 90s, but needed to work on his other pitches (slider and change-up) to be an effective starter. It's not a coincidence that he improved dramatically when they made him into a one-inning closer. He may be the next hard thrower in the Padre bullpen, especially if they end up using Bergman in the rotation. He would have been called up in September last year if he hadn't torn ligaments in his right thumb. Look for his name this spring. ■

DERREK LEE — SOLID PROSPECT

1B • BR • TR • 6′5 • 220 • 21 • SD93/1

	AE	R	H	2B	3B	HR	RBI	BB	SO	SB	CS	BA	OB	SA
AA	500	98	140	39	2	34	104	65	170	13	6	.280	.360	.570

Lee is an excellent athlete who'll probably be doing damage in the big leagues as early as 1998. With what little there is in front of him, the Padres only excuse for holding him back would be to delay his arbitration-eligibility. In addition to the strikeouts—which are growing more frequent as he climbs the ladder and the pitchers get better at changing speeds—there are questions about how often the game gets his full attention. Most consider him a Grade-A Prospect, but it's hard to justify that kind of accolade for someone who strikes out once every 3 at bats. After all, here are some big leaguers who were making that many left turns in Double-A: Eric Anthony, Billy Ashley, Jim Edmonds, Kirk Gibson, J.R. Phillips, Darryl Strawberry, and Lee Tinsley. As you can see, it can be overcome—but no one ever accused Edmonds and Gibson of lacking intensity as they have Lee. Strawberry, like Lee, came through Double-A at 20—so perhaps Derrek can put up 30 dingers and .250 after all. At the moment, it looks like a 50/50 proposition at best. ■

SCOTT LIVINGSTONE

1B-3B • BL • TR • 6'0 • 190 • 31 • DET88/2

	AB	R	H	2B	3B	HR	RBI	BB	SO	SB	CS	BA	OB	SA
DET/SD94	203	11	54	13	1	2	11	7	26	2	2	.266	.289	.369
SD95	196	26	66	15	0	5	32	15	22	2	1	.337	.380	.490
SD96	172	20	51	4	1	2	20	9	22	0	1	.297	.331	.366
CAREER	1356	158	397	68	4	17	159	81	163	8	11	.293	.329	.386

He only saw as much time as he did because of Joyner's injury. If Caminiti takes the pain again in '97 and recovers from surgery by Opening Day, there may not be a role for Livingstone other than pinch-hitter. He had 19 pinch-hits (.311) and 11 RBI in '96. ■

LUIS LOPEZ

2B • BR • TR • 5'11 • 175 • 26 • SD87

	AB	R	H	2B	3B	HR	RBI	BB	SO	SB	CS	BA	OB	SA
SD94	235	29	65	16	1	2	20	15	39	3	2	.277	.325	.379
SD96	139	10	25	3	0	2	11	9	35	0	0	.180	.233	.245

Lopez took the zero in '95 when he ripped his elbow ligament diving for a ground ball in spring training. He got another shot in '96, but you'd hope he took some souvenirs with him because it doesn't look like he'll be back. ■

VERNON MAXWELL

OF • SD96/2 • MIDWEST CITY H.S. (OK)

	AB	R	H	2B	3B	HR	RBI	BB	SO	SB	CS	BA	OB	SA
R	194	41	49	6	4	0	17	31	45	15	4	.253	.374	.325

The Padres were delighted to find Maxwell still on the board halfway through the 2nd round—feeling like they had come away with two no. 1 picks. They lured him away from Tennessee—the school wanted him to play safety. Maxwell has all of the tools, though the only refined aspects of his game at the moment may be his hitting eye and his base-stealing. But the Padres don't have a lot of outfield prospects, so Maxwell could be moved quickly through the system. ■

JUAN MELO

SLEEPER

SS • BR • TR • 6'3 • 185 • 20 • SD93

	AB	R	H	2B	3B	HR	RBI	BB	SO	SB	CS	BA	OB	SA
A+	503	75	153	27	6	8	75	22	102	6	8	.304	.345	.429

Melo was the top defensive shortstop in the California League, because of his good hands and outstanding arm. His range, however, may mean a move to third base as he moves through the system. He's filled out since they signed him at 17, and it shows in his numbers. ■

HEATH MURRAY

SOLID PROSPECT

SP • BL • TL • 6'4 • 205 • 23 • SD94/3

	G	GS	IP	H	HR	BB	K	W	L	S	ERA	K/BB	K9	HW9
AA	27	27	174	154	13	60	156	13	9	0	3.21	2.6	8.1	11.07

Believe it or not, those numbers include a poor second half, something he blames on trade rumors—his name came up frequently as the Padres shopped for a hitter in July. He throws a tailing, high-80s fastball, an excellent change-up, and decent breaking pitches—and has command of all of it. There could be some big league "learning experiences" in his future in '97. He may be the first solid lefty starter the Padres have developed since Dave Dravecky. ■

JODY REED

2B • BR • TR • 5'9 • 170 • 34 • BOS84/8

	AB	R	H	2B	3B	HR	RBI	BB	SO	SB	CS	BA	OB	SA
MIL94	399	48	108	22	0	2	37	57	34	5	4	.271	.362	.341
SD95	445	58	114	18	1	4	40	59	38	6	4	.256	.348	.328
SD96	495	45	121	20	0	2	49	59	53	2	5	.244	.325	.297
CAREER	4442	560	1209	261	10	27	384	532	392	37	42	.272	.351	.354

Every N.L. team that made it to the postseason in '96 did so with a mediocre second baseman. All 4 may very well have different players out there in '97. The job will be Quilvio's to lose, and Reed can look back on the last 3 years of limited and declining production and kick himself *one more time* for the $10 million contract he turned down from the Dodgers (after hitting 2 home runs and batting .276) because his agent told him he could get more on the open market. He ended up having to take six-figures to play in Milwaukee. If Aesop lived today, his fables might have professional athletes in them instead of geese and golden eggs. ■

SCOTT SANDERS

SLEEPER

SP-RP • BR • TR • 6'4 • 220 • 28 • SD90/2

	G	GS	IP	H	HR	BB	K	W	L	S	ERA	K/BB	K9	HW9
SD94	23	20	111	103	10	48	109	4	8	1	4.78	2.3	8.8	12.24
SD95	17	15	90	79	14	31	88	5	5	0	4.30	2.8	8.8	11.00
SD96	46	16	144	117	10	48	157	9	5	0	3.38	3.3	9.8	10.31
CAREER	95	60	397	353	48	150	391	21	21	1	4.08	2.6	8.9	11.40

Unlike Hamilton, Sanders is more of a classic strikeout pitcher. He challenges hitters with his 95 mph fastball, then looks to put them away with his hard slider. His slider is much more effective against righties; lefties find it easier to take the pitch for ball 4. He struck out 1 in 3 righties he faced—101 strikeouts and only 18 walks. Most teams these days will want to use an arm like his in late-inning relief, but the Padres have enough hard-throwers in the bullpen that they don't need him down there. It didn't look like Sanders would be doing any pitching in '96 this time last year, as he was slated for elbow reconstruction. He never had it and ended up putting together the best season of his career. If he stays healthy and pitches in the rotation, he could lead the league in strikeouts. ■

CRAIG SHIPLEY

UT • BR • TR • 6'1 • 190 • 34 • LA84

	AB	R	H	2B	3B	HR	RBI	BB	SO	SB	CS	BA	OB	SA
SD94	240	32	80	14	4	4	30	9	28	6	6	.333	.362	.475
HOU95	232	23	61	8	1	3	24	8	28	6	1	.263	.291	.345
SD96	92	13	29	5	0	1	7	2	15	7	0	.315	.337	.402
CAREER	1059	115	288	47	5	13	102	35	149	32	12	.272	.301	.363

Shipley was sidelined by injuries for most of '96 and doesn't seem to have a role in '97, but that doesn't take away what he's done the past 3 years. In a season's worth of at bats he's hit .301 with 8 home runs, 61 RBI, and 19 stolen bases—and that looks a lot like what Gregg Jefferies and Mike Lansing put up in '96. ■

BOB TEWKSBURY (see Free Agents)

JASON THOMPSON

1B • BL • TL • 6'4 • 200 • 25 • SD93/9

	AB	R	H	2B	3B	HR	RBI	BB	SO	SB	CS	BA	OB	SA
AAA	387	80	116	27	0	21	57	51	93	7	5	.300	.386	.532

Thompson has a good glove at first and, when Joyner went down, he was called up to San Diego for a 13-game trial. He went deep twice, but struck out 14 times in 49 at bats and hit only .224. He'll be 26 in June, which is getting up there for a minor leaguer, and those numbers in the PCL don't translate to enough big league production to take Wally Joyner's job or block Derrek Lee's path. It doesn't look like he's going to match the 208 career dingers of the original 6'4, lefty, first baseman named Jason Thompson. ■

FERNANDO VALENZUELA (see Free Agents)

GREG VAUGHN (see Free Agents)

JORGE VELANDIA

SLEEPER

SS • BR • TR • 5'9 • 160 • 22 • DET92

	AB	R	H	2B	3B	HR	RBI	BB	SO	SB	CS	BA	OB	SA
AA	392	42	94	19	0	9	48	31	65	3	7	.240	.295	.357

Velandia could play shortstop in the major leagues right now. The question has been whether he could hit well enough to stay there. His numbers in Double-A Memphis were a a big improvement over what he's done in the past at any level, which makes him an interesting name to watch for this spring. ■

DARIO VERAS

SOLID PROSPECT

RP • BR • TR • 6'1 • 155 • 24 • LA93

	G	GS	IP	H	HR	BB	K	W	L	S	ERA	K/BB	K9	HW9
SD96	23	0	29	24	3	10	23	3	1	0	2.79	2.3	7.1	10.55

Veras is a former Dodger pitching prospect, which is reason enough to pay attention to his prospects. He put it together at Double-A and Triple-A—walking 15 while striking out 77 in 83 innings—and was part of the reason the Padres felt comfortable enough to deal Florie, Villone, and Hermanson. ■

TIM WORRELL

SLEEPER

RP-SP • BR • TR • 6′4 • 215 • 29 • SD89/19

	G	GS	IP	H	HR	BB	K	W	L	S	ERA	K/BB	K9	HW9
SD94	3	3	14	9	0	5	14	0	1	0	3.68	2.8	9.0	8.96
SD95	9	0	13	16	2	6	13	1	0	0	4.73	2.2	9.0	15.23
SD96	50	11	121	109	9	39	99	9	7	1	3.05	2.5	7.4	11.01
CAREER	83	30	249	238	22	93	178	12	15	1	3.94	1.9	6.4	11.96

More proof never to count a Worrell out when he has an arm injury. His brother, Todd, blew out his arm in 1989, missed 2 entire seasons, pitched uneven relief for 3 years, then re-emerged 6 years after the injury to have what are probably his best years as a pro. Tim blew out his elbow in 1994 just as he was beginning to establish himself as a major league pitcher, put up some sloppy numbers in 1995 in minor league rehab stints, only to work himself back into the Padres plans in '96. A flyball pitcher, he fared *much* better in relief in '96, limiting the opposition to a .137 batting average in 58 untouchable innings (compared to .315 as a starter). In roughly the same number of innings as a starter, he gave up 53 more hits, 5 more dingers, and 21 more runs. The Padres returned him to the bullpen when Ashby came back, and they should keep him there. ■

■ 1996 AUTOPSY

Undone by awful pitching and an injury to Matt Williams in '95, the Giants finished 10 games under .500 and 11 games back. So when the team brought in starting pitchers Allen Watson from St. Louis and Osvaldo Fernandez from Cuba, hopes were raised that they might be able to keep their opponents from scoring 5 runs a game. Reality was a little harsh.

April 14-12 (2½ games back)
If you told the Giants they'd open the season in Atlanta with a pasting of Greg Maddux and end the first month 1 game up on the Dodgers and 2½ on the Rockies, they'd have taken it and run with it. Unfortunately, April was as good as it got for the Giants, and it wasn't very good at that. It was their only month with a winning record all season, and it ended with them 2½ games behind a team with a gate attraction as its 5th starter. The team hit 39 homers in April, on pace to break the '61 Yankees' record. Barry Bonds hit 11 and Williams was at .350. Rod Beck was 5-for-5 in save opportunities and had given up only 3 hits in 10 innings. Then there was the defense, which was supposed to be a strength but was yielding an unearned run a game.

May 12-14 (26-26, 7 games back)
Baker pulled a hitless Bonds in a blowout, ending a career-best 14-game hitting streak. Far be it from anyone to accuse Barry of sulking, but he would go 7 for his next 46 with two RBI, and it would be exactly one month before he hit another home run. The Giants were 25-22 and in second place when Glenallen Hill fractured his wrist. He would be gone for 10 weeks and the Giants would go 21-41. Mark Gardner and Watson continued to carry the staff, but their efforts were undermined by Lee Harvey Osvaldo, Mark Leiter, and William VanLandingham, who were giving up dingers at an alarming rate (17 in 85 innings). The staff gave up 4 grand slams in 5 games. Beck continued to be solid when they could get to him, having given up only 1 run in 22 innings.

June 10-17 (36-43, 5½ games back)
The wheels came off as they closed the month with a 10-game losing streak. Beck was the losing pitcher in 3 of the 10, coming back to earth with a thud. The absence of Hill from the lineup was having an effect on Williams, who hit .154 during the streak. The team hit 20 dingers, while the staff served up 40. It was now *the staff* that was threatening to match the '61 Yankees.

July 10-17 (46-60, 10 games back)
After snapping their losing skid with two victories against the Rockies, they dropped another 7 in a row and 11 of their next 13—4-21 over a 25 game stretch. Dusty Baker: "Guys are sleepwalking out there. . . . If you ain't hungry, you ain't going to play." To make matters worse, they lost their two best starters—Gardner to appendicitis, Watson to elbow troubles—for 3 weeks. This gave prospect Shawn Estes an opportunity, and he threw 7 shutout innings in his debut. They thought they were adding by subtraction when they sent Leiter off to serve up his *circuites* north of the border—only to watch the Expos raise the dead. As for Osvaldo, his mind was on his family back home with Fidel: After starting off 3-0, he was 4-10. The team stopped hitting in July, going .242 for the month. Everyone except Bonds and Williams was available in a trade, but apparently Carreon, Manwaring, and Leiter were the only ones anyone wanted badly enough.

August 12-15 (58-75, 16 games back)
Troubled by injuries all season, the Giants lost three every-day players in August when Shawon Dunston, Stan Javier, and Williams all went down. Rob Thompson had already fallen and still couldn't get up. Catcher Tom Lampkin went down before the month was over. The team's starting lineup looked like the replacements came back and Bonds crossed the picket line. The staff served up its 10th salami, a National League record.

September 10-19 (68-94, 23 games back)
The Giants backed up the truck in September, dumping their Double-A and Triple-A lineups on Dusty Baker's front lawn and instructing him to build something with it. But other than a totally unexpected 330 out of Bill Mueller, there wasn't much there there. The rest of the "prospects" finished the year with 11 dingers and a .231 average in nearly 750 at-bats. Barry set a record for mean-

ingless stolen bases in getting his 40/40 in the last series of the season.

October
Bonds again went hitless.

■ 1997 DIAGNOSIS

Things look dismal in the short term, not much better in the long. At the end of the '96 season, the team was basically two Hall of Famers, a closer they should trade before he blows up, and 22 other guys they'd trade straight up for any 22 players on any other major-league team. Hank Aaron and Eddie Mathews played together for 13 years and never came close to finishing below .500. The same can be said for Mays and McCovey. Bonds and Williams have finished under .500 three of their four seasons together! Perhaps to spare themselves more of this embarrassment, they decided they'd rather go into '97 with two glorified utility infielders, a head-case pitcher, and a free agent hitter to be named later than with Williams. The Giants will look back on the Bonds years in San Francisco like the Knicks do on Patrick Ewing's wasted days in New York.

Offense
Only the no. 3 and no. 4 slots in the Giants' order outperformed the league. The team didn't hit when it was close and late, and only the Philadelphia/Wilkes-Barre Phillies were less clutch. In fact, the Giants didn't hit when it was late regardless of the score. Or against lefties. Or at night. Contributing to the problems in the midnight hour, Bonds showed for the first time a big difference in his day/night performance, hitting almost 100 points lower after dark. Injuries had a lot to do with this all-around lame effort but weren't the only explanation—despite all the spinning the front office did. Things won't be much better in '97, even if the Giants do deliver the promised impact free agent with the money they'd been paying Williams.

Defense
Other than the Rockies of the Arena Baseball League, the Giants gave up more runs than any team in the league. Contributing to this was a defense that gave up more unearned runs than any team but the Astros. The Giants sure made the most of their errors, giving up nearly one unearned run per rock—compared to the Expos, who gave up about half that. But if you were as shell-shocked as the Giants' starters, you'd melt down, too, if someone drop-kicked a double-play ball across the infield with Gary Sheffield headed to the plate. Williams was an unexpected culprit, having his worst fielding season in the majors. Also pitching in were Kim Batiste, Steve Scarsone, and Thompson, who combined for 29 errors (and a .214 batting average) in a full season's worth of "work." With Williams gone, Bonds is now the only standout on a once superb fielding team. For his 11-year career, his ratio of assists to errors is more than 2:1; through their first 11 seasons, Joe DiMaggio (1.5:1) and Willie Mays (1.7:1) weren't able to match that.

Pitching
Some teams put the ball over the plate and give up home runs as a result. Others get burned by nibbling and filling the bases. The Giants managed to do both. The pitching was a crime, but Osvaldo did not act alone. The entire staff was doing the Exorcist neck twist all year, watching their pitches disappear behind clouds 194 times—only 4 fewer than the Rockies' staff! The relievers cleared the bases when they came into the game, allowing 40 percent of inherited runners to score before Tim Scott and Jim Poole arrived—compared to a league average of 33%. The league was swinging as soon as they stepped into the box, hitting over .350 on the first pitch—the worst in the NL outside of Colorado. This after the Giants traded the best shortstop the team has produced since Alvin Dark to strengthen the staff. The Royce Clayton deal reminds one of what Frank Robinson said when the Cubs traded Lee Smith for Calvin Schiraldi and Al Nipper: "They traded a horse and got two ponies." The Giants traded a greyhound and got three puppies. They do have a horse to deal, however: Rod Beck.

The Giants could get by with a committee of closers until Russ Ortiz is ready, and Beck would fetch an attractive package on the open market. He has put in his share of innings over the past five seasons and, at times, he looks like he's been ridden hard and put away wet. He wouldn't be the first closer to lose it in a hurry, as the accounting firm of Dibble, Thigpen, and Thingwild can certify, so the Giants should give Texas a call before his value dips.

Farm System

No longer a dust bowl, but not exactly the Fertile Crescent either. Other than the outfield, pickings are pretty thin in Double-A and Triple-A. Things look better in Class-A-ball, but then things often look better down there. The farm system has been in sorry shape for years, unable to produce a front-line starter since the '60s and not much but Williams, Clayton, Chili Davis, and Will Clark in the past 15 years. The Giants say they are serious about fixing the minors, and adding a third Class-A ball team is a good start. That's gives them 7 bush-league teams, if you count the parent club.

Management and Ownership

The Giants were purchased before the '93 season for $100 million. The owners would have been better off putting it in a stock fund and playing mah-jongg in the Keys. They'd have earned a better return and would not have to deal with all the ancillary nonsense that comes with owning a big-league ballclub (watching Barry Bonds spend your money, having to engage in a frank exchange of views with the evil geniuses pulling the players' strings, Marge Schott espousing her political philosophy in front of the help . . .).

No team was more damaged by the strike than the Giants. Attendance has plummeted below '92 levels and is now seventh worst in the majors, only above the Pirates in the N.L. Hopes are now being pinned on a new ballpark. Yet another team trying to convince themselves that, if they build it, they will suddenly have Lofton leading off and Belle batting clean up. At least these guys are trying to pay for it by fleecing private investors, not the taxpayers. Believe it when you see it.

Personnel director Brian Sabean was brought in to fix the minor-league system and will eventually assume the GM role from Bob Quinn. Fortunately for the Giants, there's not much left for Quinn to give away while he's still got the big office. That's not to say he won't find a way to throw some more of Magowan's millions at another Cuban pitcher whose age is a mystery and whose stuff is straightforward.

Dusty Baker became the first Giant's manager in history to keep his job after three consecutive losing seasons. It will be 4 and counting this time next year.

. . . and whatnot: The Wrath of the Gods

Ever wonder why the baseball gods have let the Giants off light for leaving the Polo Grounds to chase the money in San Francisco? Well, they haven't. And it's more than just floods in 1962 and an earthquake in '89 the two times they made it to the World Series—losing to hated rivals both times. Their best season in California, '93 was part of the curse, too. To what extent is just now becoming apparent.

The '93 Giants won more games (103) than any second-place team in divisional history, losing to the Braves on the last day of the season. It was the most second place wins since the 1954 Yankees tried to keep pace with the Indians. Twenty-six teams have won 100 games since divisional play began and the Giants have, by far, the worst winning percentage in the following three years (.456), the only team below .500. Only two other 100-win teams have failed to make postseason play in the following three years: the 1969 and 1988 Mets.

But the Giants are also the second-worst team during the three years before they won 100 (.477), ahead of only the 1969 Mets. The '69 Mets and the '93 Giants are also the only two to have losing records the season before they won 100 games. The Giants improved even more dramatically than the Miracle Mets: 31 more wins, compared to 27. The success of the 93 Giants was, in many ways, as ridiculous as that of the '69 Mets. It should have been their first title since they went west, and a miraculous and heartwarming one at that, a year after the locals thought they'd lost the team to St. Petersburg. But the gods brought the tomahawk down instead.

A casual observer might ask what the front office has done in the years since to ruin that team. But if held together, they wouldn't even have come close to 90 victories in '96. Behind highly unlikely 20-game winners Swift and Burkett, the starting staff featured Bud Black, Bryan Hickerson, and Trevor Wilson. Half of their starting lineup—Thompson, Manwaring, Willie McGee, and Darren Lewis—are shadows of their former selves.

That's not to say management didn't help accelerate the decline. They let Will Clark go because they couldn't afford to overpay both him and Thompson, letting Texas open the vault to get a good ol' boy into their Latino-dominated lineup. The shortstop went out for three questionable pitchers.

Their center fielder (Lewis) and a solid pitcher (Dave Burba) went to Cincinnati to rent a distracted cornerback for a few months. They got next to nothing for their two best starters (Burkett and Swift) and two of their best relievers (Brantley and Michael Jackson).

And the fans, deprived of their miracle and awaiting the next natural disaster, will continue to get nothing and have to like it.

RICH AURILIA

SS-2B • BR • TR • 6′0 • 170 • TEX92/24

	AB	R	H	2B	3B	HR	RBI	BB	SO	SB	CS	BA	OB	SA
SF95	19	4	9	3	0	2	4	1	2	1	0	.474	.476	.947
SF96	318	27	76	7	1	3	26	25	52	4	1	.239	.295	.296

Aurilia was given the shortstop job in December, then had it taken back when Dunston was signed in January. He took over at second halfway through the season when Thompson's hip gave out from all those left turns to the dugout from the batter's box. He ended up back at short when Dunston's face broke. Now the job's been taken back by Jose Vizcaino. Aurilia's numbers were uninspiring and won't get significantly better. Defensively he's sure-handed but has limited range. ■

LORENZO BARCELO

SP • BR • TR • 6′4 • 205 •19

	G	GS	IP	H	HR	BB	SO	W	L	S	ERA	K/BB	K9	HW9
A	26	26	153	138	19	46	139	12	10	0	3.54	3.0	8.2	10.85

Barcelo struck out a batter an inning in A-ball and managed to win 8 games for a lousy team. He's only 19, so expect the Giants to dub him their latest next Marichal if Fausto Macey doesn't work out. ■

KIM BATISTE (see Looking for a Game)

JOSE BAUTISTA (see Looking for a Game)

ROD BECK

CONSISTENT STAR

CL • BR • TR • 6′1 • 215 • 28 • OAK86/13

	G	GS	IP	H	HR	BB	K	W	L	S	ERA	K/BB	K9	HW9
SF94	48	0	48	49	10	13	39	2	4	28	2.77	3.0	7.3	11.61
SF95	60	0	58	60	7	21	42	5	6	33	4.45	2.0	6.5	12.57
SF96	63	0	62	56	9	10	48	0	9	35	3.34	4.8	7.0	9.58
CAREER	343	0	393	337	45	85	340	14	24	162	2.89	4.0	7.8	9.66

There's no other position in sports where athletes have better harnessed the power of their physical appearance than closer—and Rod Beck is certainly no exception. He has a funny-looking mustache, bad hair, and 5 pitches he throws hard for strikes: a fastball, split-finger fastball (his out pitch), sinker, slider, and curve. But unlike a truly devastating closer, he doesn't blow hitters away, and he can be taken out of the yard. He's lost something off his fastball and has to rely on location now.

If you look for a clue to the future in his minor-league numbers, you'll find those tea leaves murky at best. He was primarily a starter and wasn't used to close until he reached Triple-A. His numbers in the minors don't approach his best in the majors. One would be hard-pressed in '90 to predict stardom in San Francisco for the big boy sleeping at the back of the bus on the way home from Albuquerque. ■

MARVIN BENARD

OF • BL • TL • 5′10 • 180 • 26 • SF92/50

	AB	R	H	2B	3B	HR	RBI	BB	SO	SB	CS	BA	OB	SA
SF95	34	5	13	2	0	1	4	1	7	1	0	.382	.400	.529
SF96	488	89	121	17	4	5	27	59	84	25	11	.248	.333	.330

Mike Felder lives. Benard, the sixth Nicaraguan to play in the majors, filled in admirably when Hill and Javier went down with injuries. He wasn't expected to match Hill's power production but was a better alternative in the leadoff spot than Javier. He stole 25 bases in 36 attempts and managed a .333 on-base percentage (closer to Lance Johnson than you might think). His play shouldn't have come as a surprise, since he's hit .300 at every level of the minors and .382 in a September '95 call-up. Benard struggled against left-handers, and if he gets behind in the count, he's over. He'll have to improve in those areas to beat back the prospects for playing time. ■

DARIN BLOOD

SOLID PROSPECT

SP • BL • TR • 6'2 • 205 • 22 • SF95/3

	G	GS	IP	H	HR	BB	SO	W	L	S	ERA	K/BB	K9	HW9
A+	27	25	170	140	4	71	193	17	6	0	2.65	2.7	10.2	11.17

Blood is a starter with a closer's name. He jumped two levels in '96 and thrived, leading the minors in wins. He strikes out more than a batter an inning with decent command, relying more on his curveball and slider than his fastball. ■

BARRY BONDS

SUPERSTAR

LF • BL • TL • 6'1 •185 • 32 • PIT85/1

	AB	R	H	2B	3B	HR	RBI	BB	SO	SB	CS	BA	OB	SA
SF94	391	89	122	18	1	37	81	74	43	29	9	.312	.426	.647
SF95	506	109	149	30	7	33	104	120	83	31	10	.294	.431	.577
SF96	517	122	159	27	3	42	129	151	76	40	7	.308	.461	.615
CAREER	5537	1121	1595	333	51	334	993	1082	871	380	110	.288	.404	.548

"He's a 9-year-old kid in the body of an extraordinary 28-year-old athlete." A Pirate exec said this about Barry Bonds in '92. That means in '96 Barry began to enter emotional puberty. Now a 13-year-old kid, he became the first player to be ejected from a game in which he reached the 300-homer, 300-stolen base club—and just how petulant does one of the greats have to be to be accorded that little respect? The N.L. hasn't seen a dis like it since the Phillies brought Wesley "Big Life" Chamberlain's mother to the Vet for Mother's Day, only to send her son to the minors immediately after the game. Personality aside, his skills are undeniable. His batting average has been around .300, his on-base percentage over .400, and his slugging percentage over .500 all decade.

To his credit, he raised his level of play after becoming financially secure. Ask a dog like Von Hayes about that. Bonds plays with pain, has been on the disabled list only once in his career, and set a Giants record for consecutive games played. His vision, like that of most top baseball players, is freakish; one of his off-season workouts is to take batting practice with tennis balls that have numbers written on them—but only to swing at the odd-numbered ones. His bat is still as quick as anyone's, generating just as much power from 185 pounds as a behemoth like McGwire or a pantload like Fielder. Hitting the weights in the off-season got his bench press up to 315 but didn't do much to his stat line—in a year where Greg Vaughn, Ellis Burks, and Todd Hundley hit 40 dingers, you can't credit his muscles for the blip in his power numbers. Given how injury-prone musclebound beasts like McGwire, Canseco and Juan Gonzalez seem to be—not to mention the cautionary tale of a 5-tool player like Ruben Sierra deteriorating to little more than a dinger threat after falling in love with the reflection of his physique—perhaps Barry should leave well enough alone. ■

STEVE BOURGEOIS

SP-RP • BR • TR • 6'1 • 220 • 24 • SF93/23

	G	GS	IP	H	HR	BB	K	W	L	S	ERA	K/BB	K9	HW9
SF96	15	5	40	60	4	21	17	1	3	0	6.30	.8	3.8	18.23

Steve Middleclass was a replacement player and pitched like one, allowing more than 2 baserunners per inning. He was equally bad as a starter and a reliever. The league hit .355 against him, .425 once they saw 30 pitches. His 12-3 record at Shreveport in '95 wasn't as good as it looked, and it saddled him with unrealistic expectations. ■

JAMIE BREWINGTON

SP • BR • TR • 6'4 • 180 • 25 • SF92/10

	G	GS	IP	H	HR	BB	SO	W	L	S	ERA	K/BB	K9	HW9
AAA	35	17	110	130	14	72	75	6	9	1	7.02	1.0	6.1	16.51

Brewington had one good year in the minors and was rushed to the majors in '95, where he was nothing special. He walked as many as he struck out and his ERA was well over 4.00, though he did manage to win 6 games. After a brutal spring in '96 the Giants sent him to Triple-A where he walked more than he struck out and had an ERA of well over 6.00. Brewington throws hard but is inconsistent. At times his fastball is in the 90s with movement, but other times it's straight and slow. He was brought up in '95 because he was mulching Texas League hitters. If he could harness his stuff, he could do the same in the N.L. Don't hold your breath. ■

JAY CANIZARO

2B • BR • TR • 5′10 • 175 • 23 • SF93/6

	AB	R	H	2B	3B	HR	RBI	BB	SO	SB	CS	BA	OB	SA
SF96	120	11	24	4	1	2	8	9	38	0	2	.200	.260	.300

Canizaro was going to have a chance at the Giants' second-base job in '97, but his play in late '96 may make Jeff Kent start to look viable at second. He has some punch and some speed but was overpowered at times by Triple-A pitching and got thoroughly abused in the majors. He's still young and could develop into a player similar to Robby Thompson—hopefully without the war wounds. He has a cannon arm, is good on the double play, and has good range. He was used as a backup shortstop wherever he played in the minors. ■

DAN CARLSON

SP-RP • BR • TR • 6′1 • 185 • 27 • SF93

	G	GS	IP	H	HR	BB	SO	W	L	S	ERA	K/BB	K9	HW9
AAA	33	15	147	135	18	46	123	13	6	1	3.44	2.7	7.5	11.11

Carlson had two big years in Class-A and Double-A in '91 and '92, going 31-16 and striking out 320 in 370 inn-ings. He got low-level minor-leaguers out with an average fastball and the ability to spot his curveball. Since then, he's been fairly ordinary and was tried in relief in '96. He performed adequately out of the bullpen, but nothing to suggest, at 27, that he'll ever be anything more than a third or fourth option or a spot starter—the guy the bullpen coach sends to make the food run when the starter is going well. ■

MIKE CARUSO

SOLID PROSPECT

SS • BB • TR • 6′0 • 165 • 18 • SF96/2

	AB	R	H	2B	3B	HR	RBI	BB	SO	SB	CS	BA	OB	SA
A-	312	48	91	13	1	2	24	16	23	24	10	.292	.324	.359

Caruso is a switch-hitting shortstop, leadoff man, and all-around good egg from Florida who gave up a scholarship at Miami to go pro. He tied for the Northwest League lead in stolen bases. His manager, Shane Turner: "He's the best young player in this league and he's getting better." ■

DOUG CREEK

RP • BL • TL • 5′10 • 205 • 28 • SL91/7

	G	GS	IP	H	HR	BB	K	W	L	S	ERA	K/BB	K9	HW9
SF96	63	0	48	45	11	32	38	0	2	0	6.52	1.2	7.1	14.43

What does this guy bring to the table except a nickname Chris Berman can't use on basic cable? On the basis of 6.2 outstanding major-league innings by age 27, the Giants decided they had to have him in the Clayton trade. He then went out in '96 and walked almost as many as he struck out and, like everyone on the staff, served up his share of dingers. ■

DEIVI CRUZ

SS • BR • TR • 6′0 • 175 • 21

	AB	R	H	2B	3B	HR	RBI	BB	SO	SB	CS	BA	OB	SA
A	517	72	152	27	2	9	64	35	49	12	5	.294	.342	.406

Overmatched at the plate at Burlington in '95, Cruz put together a decent year there in '96. He set a league record for shortstops with a .980 fielding percentage, and his manager believes he could play defense in the majors right now. He's only 21, needs to do more with the bat, and is stuck behind several good prospects—and in front of Mike Caruso, the team's no. 2 pick in '96. ■

JACOB CRUZ

SOLID PROSPECT

OF • BL • TL • 6′0 • 175 • 24 • SF94/1

	AB	R	H	2B	3B	HR	RBI	BB	SO	SB	CS	BA	OB	SA
SF96	77	10	18	3	0	3	10	12	24	0	1	.234	.352	.390

Cruz was taken with a supplemental 1st round pick as compensation for losing Will Clark. Cruz ended up in the majors briefly, but was returned to Phoenix to play every day. He has a good arm, some power, and hit for a decent average in Shreveport and Phoenix. He's been successful stealing 11 times in 27 attempts, so maybe someone should get the hint. He has a chance to make the team in '97 as a reserve, though outfield is the only position where the Giants are deep. His manager likens him to Dave Martinez, but he could develop into a better hitter. He was the only September call-up who put up numbers that even remotely suggest he could become an impact player. ■

WILSON DELGADO

SLEEPER

SS • BB • TR • 5′11 • 165 • 21

	AB	R	H	2B	3B	HR	RBI	BB	SO	SB	CS	BA	OB	SA
A+	462	59	124	19	6	2	54	48	89	8	3	.268	.337	.348

The Giants got Delgado from Seattle in the Salomon Torres trade. He's a terrific fielder, but his average dropped from .300 to .250 after he was promoted to San Jose. Full-time employment in the majors is a few years away and at the moment it doesn't look like he'll hit much when and if he gets there. Could be worse: He could be back in Seattle, behind Alex Rodriguez instead of Rich Aurilia. The glove is there and he's young enough to improve his hitting, so keep an eye on him. ■

RICH DELUCIA

RP • BR • TR • 6′0 • 180 • 32 • SEA86/6

	G	GS	IP	H	HR	BB	K	W	L	S	ERA	K/BB	K9	HW9
CIN94	8	0	10	9	4	5	15	0	0	0	4.22	3.0	13.4	12.52
SL95	56	1	82	63	9	36	76	8	7	0	3.39	2.1	8.3	10.87
SF96	56	0	61	62	8	31	55	3	6	0	5.84	1.8	8.1	13.71
CAREER	217	49	498	486	72	217	378	5	40	1	4.70	1.7	6.8	12.70

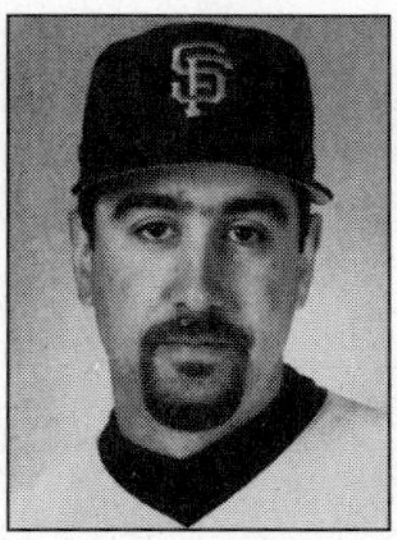

If you've got a 31-year-old pitcher coming off the best season of a mediocre career, based solely on the strength of one good month, get the Giants on the phone. Though there is no talk of this, the next mistake the Giants can make is to move DeLucia back to the rotation—since he can't get lefties out and his numbers are dramatically better as a reliever than as a starter. Yet another fly-ball pitcher who fares better in smaller doses. ■

DON DENBOW

SLEEPER

OF • BR • TR • 6′4 • 215 • 23 • SF93/3

	AB	R	H	2B	3B	HR	RBI	BB	SO	SB	CS	BA	OB	SA
A+	97	19	36	8	3	6	19	17	30	1	1	.371	.466	.701

Denbow was Burlington's answer to Rob Deer in '95, striking out 143 times in 326 at-bats while hitting .178. He raised his average 100 points in '96, but he still screws himself into the ground 40% of the time. Like Deer, he goes too deep in the count, taking too many good pitches and swinging at too many bad ones. He does draw more than his share of walks and has good speed—so he has that going for him, which is nice. ■

MARK DEWEY

RP • BR • TR • 6′0 • 185 • 32 • SF87/23

	G	GS	IP	H	HR	BB	K	W	L	S	ERA	K/BB	K9	HW9
PIT94	45	0	51	61	4	19	30	2	1	1	3.68	1.6	5.3	14.11
SF95	27	0	31	30	2	17	32	1	0	0	3.13	1.9	9.3	13.65
SF96	78	0	83	79	9	41	57	6	3	0	4.21	1.4	6.2	13.01
CAREER	205	0	248	243	18	102	168	12	7	8	3.66	1.6	6.1	12.52

Like DeLucia, Dewey is useless against left-handed hitters and pitches better when not being used on consecutive days—which isn't exactly a description of your ideal middle reliever. Do they really need two of these guys in the same bullpen? If they plan to keep only one, Dewey made their decision for them in July. A fundamentalist Christian, he enraged some locals by sitting out the ceremonies at AIDS Awareness Day at Candlestick. He even wore his red ribbon sideways, in the shape of that Christian fish you see on the back of cars doing 55 in the left lane on the interstate. ■

SHAWON DUNSTON (see Free Agents)

SHAWN ESTES

YOUNG GUN

SP • BR • TL • 6′2 • 200 • 24 • SEA91/1

	G	GS	IP	H	HR	BB	K	W	L	S	ERA	K/BB	K9	HW9
SF95	3	3	17	16	2	5	14	0	3	0	6.75	2.8	7.4	11.12
SF96	11	11	70	63	3	39	60	3	5	0	3.60	1.5	7.7	13.11

Estes has an outstanding left-handed curveball and a low-90s fastball. The questions are about his makeup. In the spring, Bob Quinn called him a "wild horse." Then, early in '96, Shawn was in Phoenix and Baker was saying: "Estes is a great talent who never won until last year and this year (in the minors). He's got to learn how to win there before he can win up here. Everybody wanted to push Estes here from the beginning, but it's more than just winning. It's . . . how you handle adversity, how you handle your teammates if they make a couple of errors. There's a maturation point you have to get to before you come up here. That's why he's still down there."

Sure looks like he's figuring it out. He'll be the ace of the staff sooner rather than later. ■

OSVALDO FERNANDEZ — SLEEPER

BR• TR • 6'2 • 190 • 28-42 • SF96

	G	GS	IP	H	HR	BB	K	W	L	S	ERA	K/BB	K9	HW9
SF96	30	28	171	193	20	57	106	7	13	0	4.61	1.9	5.6	13.15

In July, Dusty Baker could have a T-shirt printed that says: "My GM went to Cuba and all I got was this lousy pitcher." While their competitors cackled, the Giants signed Osvaldo to a $3 million deal—a lot of scratch for someone who never faced major-league pitching before and whose real age is a mystery (Marlins GM Dave Dombrowski claims Fernandez is 42!) Early on, Osvaldo looked like an even bigger bust than his detractors predicted, going 1-10 from May through July as he threw it over the plate and ran for cover. But in August and September—once it became apparent that he would shortly be reunited with his family, still back home in Cuba—Fernandez was 3-2 with an ERA of 2.77, yielding only 3 dingers in 52 innings. They should get more for their money from Osvaldo in '97. ▪

JOE FONTENOT — SOLID PROSPECT

SP • BR • TR • 6'2 • 185 • 20 • SF95/1

	G	GS	IP	H	HR	BB	SO	W	L	S	ERA	K/BB	K9	HW9
A+	26	23	144	137	7	74	124	9	4	0	4.44	1.7	7.8	13.19

Fontenot's only 20 and on his way to Double-A in '97. He was a first-round draft pick in '95, and they managed to lure the local hero away from LSU. He has good stuff but doesn't have command of it yet. Younger than Fausto Macey and a better bet to make an impact in the majors at some point. He has a good fastball and an exceptional curve. ▪

KEITH FOULKE — SLEEPER

SP • BR • TR • 6'1 • 195 • 24 • SF94/10

	G	GS	IP	H	HR	BB	SO	W	L	S	ERA	K/BB	K9	HW9
AA	27	27	182.2	149	16	35	129	12	7	0	2.76	3.7	6.4	9.09

Is Bob Knepper really the best the Giants have produced in the past 20 years? Might Foulke be the acorn the blind squirrels have found? After a terrific season in Class-A-ball, he continued to throw strikes and keep hitters off base in Double-A. In fact, the biggest criticism his pitching coach had of him was that he threw too many strikes, rather than trying to get the batter fishing when he got ahead in the count. His stuff isn't outstanding, but the 9-inning average for his career is 8 hits, 3 earned runs, 8 strikeouts, and fewer than 2 walks. If he does it in Triple-A, he could be pressed into the rotation before the season ends even if his fastball doesn't make sexy numbers on the Jugs gun. ▪

MARK GARDNER — HEADED FOR A FALL

SP • BR • TR • 6'1 • 190 • 35 • MON85/8

	G	GS	IP	H	HR	BB	K	W	L	S	ERA	K/BB	K9	HW9
FLA94	20	14	92	97	14	30	57	4	4	0	4.87	1.9	5.6	12.42
FLA95	39	11	102	109	14	43	87	5	5	1	4.49	2.0	7.7	13.41
SF96	30	28	179	200	28	57	145	12	7	0	4.42	2.5	7.3	12.92
CAREER	200	156	992	971	120	373	738	53	55	1	4.39	2.0	6.7	12.19

Bryant, Caldwell, Montefusco, Halicki, Blue, Alexander, Laskey, Krukow, LaCoss, Reuschel, Burkett, Wilson, Portugal, and Leiter. Add Gardner to the illustrious list. These are the names of the pitchers who have led this team in victories since 1972. Gardner was signed by the Giants after the Marlins cut him, at John Burkett's suggestion. His career season, at age 34, is more proof of the randomness of pitching—as if any more was necessary after what Danny Jackson did in '94 at age 32 after being woeful for the entire Bush administration. After his bout with appendicitis, he returned to the rotation to add his name to the less than illustrious list of San Francisco "aces" since Juan Marichal (see team essay). Given the slim pitching pickings, the Giants may well be penciling Gardner in for 15 victories in '97—just as they did for Leiter in '96. Then again, the Cubs penciled Mike Bielecki in for 20 after his career year in '89 and got 8. The Giants should be so lucky. The only sure thing with Gardner is, win or lose, there'll be plenty of souvenirs for the bleacher bums. ▪

JULIAN HEREDIA

RP • BR • TR • 6'1 • 190 • 27

	G	GS	IP	H	HR	BB	SO	W	L	S	ERA	K/BB	K9	HW9
AAA	52	2	69	71	12	23	59	0	5	4	4.91	2.6	7.7	12.23

Heredia is 27 and continues to strike out nearly a batter per inning in the minors with good control, but he's yet to see any major-league action. He even

looked good in the spring in '96. A sidearmer, he's tougher on righties than lefties. Originally buried in the Angels system, he's now somehow buried in an organization with even thinner pitching. Give him his chance. ■

SANTOS HERNANDEZ

RP • BR • TR • 6'1 • 172 • 24

	G	GS	IP	H	HR	BB	SO	W	L	S	ERA	K/BB	K9	HW9
A	61	0	67	39	4	13	79	3	3	35	1.89	6.1	10.7	7.02

Hernandez was the closer for Burlington, having a hand in well over half of the team's wins. He struck out 55 and walked 10 in 47 innings, having posted similar numbers for Burlington in '95. He was voted the best reliever in the Midwest League. At 23 he was fairly old for the league, so there's no guarantee he will continue to have this kind of success as he moves on to San Jose, Shreveport, and beyond. ■

GLENALLEN HILL

OF • BR • TR • 6'3 • 210 • 32 • TOR83/9

	AB	R	H	2B	3B	HR	RBI	BB	SO	SB	CS	BA	OB	SA
CHN94	269	48	80	12	1	10	38	29	57	19	6	.297	.365	.461
SF95	497	71	131	29	4	24	86	39	98	25	5	.264	.317	.483
SF96	379	56	106	26	0	19	67	33	95	6	3	.280	.344	.499
CAREER	2308	326	607	116	13	107	351	182	522	83	31	.263	.318	.464

When Hill fractured his left wrist, the team went 21-41 and Bonds grumbled about the front office's failure to make a trade to keep him motivated. Hill was on his way to a 30-dinger, 100-RBI season before the injury, numbers that would have exceeded his career-best performance in '95. He continues to make a living off left-handed pitching. He can run, too—stealing 51 bases in 65 attempts since he came over to the N.L. in late '93. But his speed doesn't translate to great range in the outfield, and he makes too many errors. He disappears a bit late in the game and in clutch situations, and he isn't very selective. He's back up to striking out once every 4 at-bats—though he's a long way from his 4 year stretch in the minors when he struck out 666 (yes, 666) times in 2,000 at-bats. Somehow he climbed from Class-A to Triple-A in the process—but then that was the '80s, and excess was in vogue. ■

TRENIDAD HUBBARD

OF • BR • TR • 5'8 • 185 • 30 • HOU86/12

	AB	R	H	2B	3B	HR	RBI	BB	SO	SB	CS	BA	OB	SA
COL95	58	13	18	4	0	3	9	8	6	2	1	.310	.394	.534
COL/SF96	89	15	19	5	2	2	14	11	27	2	0	.213	.307	.382
CAREER	172	31	44	10	3	6	26	22	37	4	1	.256	.344	.453

The Giants outfield is crowded, he's 30, he was hitting .217 in Colorado, and the Rockies were willing to give him up for Steve Decker. Other than that, all indicators look great. ■

JESSE IBARRA

1B • BB • TR • 6'3 • 195 • 24 • SF94/7

	AB	R	H	2B	3B	HR	RBI	BB	SO	SB	CS	BA	OB	SA
A+	498	63	141	38	0	17	95	63	108	5	1	.283	.366	.462

Ibarra put up huge numbers in the Midwest League in '95 but wasn't able to match them in San Jose. His batting average dropped nearly 50 points and he hit half as many dingers. He's 24, still in Class-A-ball, and he strikes out too much. First base is wide open in San Francisco and Ibarra has some ability, but don't expect him to be catching Iron Butterfly at the Fillmore West any time soon. ■

STAN JAVIER

OF • BB • TR • 6'0 • 185 • 33 • SL81

	AB	R	H	2B	3B	HR	RBI	BB	SO	SB	CS	BA	OB	SA
OAK94	419	75	114	23	0	10	44	49	76	24	7	.272	.349	.399
OAK95	442	81	123	20	2	8	56	49	63	36	5	.278	.353	.387
SF96	274	44	74	25	0	2	22	25	51	14	2	.270	.336	.383
CAREER	3170	483	822	145	23	33	297	341	532	169	32	.259	.332	.351

Every time Javier has had a chance to play regularly he's produced, though that hasn't kept him from changing his address 6 times in the past 10 years. Despite a slow start, frequent injuries, and an early exit, Javier put up some decent numbers for the Giants. It helped when they moved him out of the leadoff spot, a role to which he's not particularly suited; he's put up his best numbers hitting second. The modest power he displayed during his second stint in Oakland proved to be a fluke. His ability to steal efficiently is not—he's been successful at least 85% of the time in 8 of the last 10 years. He's a switch-hitter who can put up numbers from either side of the plate, though he's a better hitter from the right

side. He lives off the first pitch and is basically a .250 hitter if he doesn't connect immediately. He may very well get crowded out by the prospects in '97. ■

MARCUS JENSEN

C • BB • TR • 6'4 • 195 • 24 • SF90/3

	AB	R	H	2B	3B	HR	RBI	BB	SO	SB	CS	BA	OB	SA
AAA	405	41	107	22	4	5	53	44	95	1	1	.264	.338	.375

Jensen is a taller, switch-hitting version of Kirt Manwaring: His defense is strong and he hits .250 without much power. He has had some injury problems throughout his minor-league career, but may well be handed the starting job in '97. Catchers hitting tends to improve with age—unless you're Mike Piazza and have sold your soul to the devil—so it's quite possible that the power numbers could come. ■

DAX JONES

OF • BR • TR • 5'11 • 185 • 25 • SF92/1

	AB	R	H	2B	3B	HR	RBI	BB	SO	SB	CS	BA	OB	SA
SF96	58	7	10	0	2	1	7	8	12	2	2	.172	.269	.293

Daximilian has no power and only decent speed, so don't expect him to be an impact player. Most of the Phoenicians who got the call didn't do much in San Francisco, and Jones did less than any of them. There's no guarantee he will even make the 25-man roster in '97. ■

JEFF KENT

3B-1B • BR • TR • 6'1 • 185 • 29 • TOR89/20

	AB	R	H	2B	3B	HR	RBI	BB	SO	SB	CS	BA	OB	SA
NYN94	415	53	121	24	5	14	68	23	84	1	4	.292	.341	.475
NYN95	472	65	131	22	3	20	65	29	89	3	3	.278	.327	.464
NYN/CLE96	437	61	124	27	1	12	55	31	78	6	4	.284	.330	.432
CAREER	2125	296	583	118	11	78	318	140	415	16	18	.274	.327	.450

Kent is making a career out of being on the wrong end of unpopular trades. He went to the Mets for David Cone to the Blue Jays, then left for Carlos Baerga, and finally came from Cleveland for Matt Williams. While with the Mets in the early part of '96, Jeff Kent tried to make the transition from second base to third. He committed four errors in the first week and said, "I hope the table is not set with china because I'm playing with Tupperware right now." One of the reasons the Mets were willing to give up his power was that they were tired of his shoddy defense. He provides solid pop for a second baseman, but at the corner infield positions he comes up short. He'll get a chance to pale in comparison to Matt Williams at third, watch groundballs scoot by him at second, or put up second baseman's numbers at first. ■

FAUSTO MACEY

SP •BR • TR • 6'4 • 185 • 21

	G	GS	IP	H	HR	BB	SO	W	L	S	ERA	K/BB	K9	HW9
AA	27	26	157	165	22	47	62	10	7	0	4.3	1.3	3.6	12.15

A great name, but the Giants think Macey can be another Juan Marichal, which pretty much seals his fate. He's 21 and people rave about his arm, but the only thing all that impressive about his Double-A numbers were the 10 wins—which means next to nothing, as Roger Pavlik and Kevin Brown will tell you. He throws strikes, but only fans about 3 per 9 innings. If the Giants are patient, maybe he'll develop, but he's a few years away and more likely the next Salomon Torres. ■

DAVID MCCARTY

1B • BR • TL • 6'5 • 215 • 27 • MIN91/1

	AB	R	H	2B	3B	HR	RBI	BB	SO	SB	CS	BA	OB	SA
MIN94	131	21	34	8	2	1	12	7	32	2	1	.260	.322	.374
MIN/SF95	75	11	17	4	1	0	6	6	22	1	1	.227	.289	.307
SF96	175	16	38	3	0	6	24	18	43	2	1	.217	.294	.337
CAREER	731	84	164	30	5	9	63	50	177	7	9	.224	.281	.316

Going into '96, McCarty's major-league career was 600 at-bats with 6 dingers, 49 RBI, a .226 average, and 145 strikeouts. He was a bit more productive in '96, and actually looked like a major-leaguer in July, when he played regularly and hit .300. Other than that, it was pretty much more of the same. He also managed to sprain his ankle while stumbling toward the bathroom in the dark. He always put up big numbers down on the farm, but when you see a minor leaguer who struck out as often as McCarty did—a little over once every 5 at-bats—forget that he hit over .300. If minor-league pitching can make you wave at air that much, major-league pitching will take you home and beat you up in front of your family. ■

DOUG MIRABELLI

C • BR • TR • 6'1 • 205 • 26 • SF92/5

	AB	R	H	2B	3B	HR	RBI	BB	SO	SB	CS	BA	OB	SA
AA	380	60	112	23	0	21	70	76	49	0	1	.295	.419	.521

Mirabelli put up good numbers at Shreveport, but he backed up Marcus Jensen down there in '95, is 2 years older than he, and doesn't switch-hit. He got called up to San Francisco first, but only so Jensen could play in the Triple-A playoffs. ■

BILL MUELLER — SLEEPER

3B • BB • TR • 5'11 • 175 • 26 • SF93/17

	AB	R	H	2B	3B	HR	RBI	BB	SO	SB	CS	BA	OB	SA
SF96	200	31	66	15	1	0	19	24	26	0	0	.330	.401	.415

Mueller is a switch-hitting infielder with a good eye who hits for average and draws walks. He's not very big and doesn't hit for power, and that .330 average could raise expectations to a level he can't meet. Nevertheless, he's the best Mueller to play for the Giants in the past 40 years and could end up at second base. ■

CALVIN MURRAY

OF • BR • TR • 5'11 • 185 • 25 • SF92/1

	AB	R	H	2B	3B	HR	RBI	BB	SO	SB	CS	BA	OB	SA
AAA	311	50	76	16	6	3	28	43	60	12	6	.244	.341	.363

Murray strikes out too much, but he's getting better at drawing walks. He didn't merit a call-up in September, but he does play center field and willl be worth watching in the spring to see if he can beat the odds and make the team. He was the Giants' no. 1 pick in '92—the same year they got Marvin Benard with their 50th pick. He's a bit old for Triple-A to be an exceptional big-leaguer, but he's got ability. ■

RUSS ORTIZ — GRADE-A PROSPECT

CL • BR • TR • 6'1 • 190 • 22 • SF95/4

	G	GS	IP	H	HR	BB	SO	W	L	S	ERA	K/BB	K9	HW9
AA	26	0	26	22	0	21	29	1	2	13	4.05	1.4	10.0	14.77

In A-ball, Ortiz gave up 1 earned run in 37 innings—that's an ERA of 0.25—while striking out 63. That's more than 15 per 9 innings. Your best bet was to keep the bat on your shoulder; he walked 20 while yielding 16 hits. He did this same routine in the Northwest League in '95, where he gave up 2 earned runs in 34 innings. He got cuffed around a bit after being promoted to Double-A, but he'll probably have that league figured out by July. He throws in the high 90s with good location, and has a hard curveball with a quick break. He is apparently working on a change-up, though the other teams in the league have filed a temporary restraining order. ■

DAN PELTIER (see Looking for a Game)

RICKEY PICKETT — SLEEPER

BL • TL • 6'0 • 185 • 27 • CIN92/29

	G	GS	IP	H	HR	BB	SO	W	L	S ERA	K/BB	K9	HW9
AA	29	0	48	35	4	35	51	4	1	22.77	1.5	9.5	13.07

Wicked Pickett came over in the Deion Sanders deal and is even less likely to produce for the Giants than Prime Time. He was in line for a job as a lefty in the Giants bullpen, but their acquisition of Jim Poole tells you how close they think he is to being ready. He's a one-pitch pitcher who throws in the 90s and all over the place. If he ever harnesses his stuff yadayadayada. That's what they said about Brad Pennington. He started the year in Triple-A, got abused, and was returned to Shreveport, where he continued to regress. ■

JIM POOLE

BL • TL • 6'2 • 190 • 30 • LA88/8

	G	GS	IP	H	HR	BB	K	W	L	S ERA	K/BB	K9	HW9
BAL94	38	0	20	32	4	11	18	1	0	06.64	1.6	8.1	19.32
CLE95	42	0	50	40	7	17	41	3	3	03.75	2.4	7.4	10.26
CLE/SF96	67	0	49	44	5	27	38	6	1	02.93	1.4	7.0	13.01
CAREER	253	0	226	185	22	97	173	15	7	33.18	1.8	6.9	11.22

Regardless of how he's frequently been used, he's shown that he can do more than face one lefty at a time. He's very tough on lefties, but righties don't fare that much better against him. Poole stranded 3 of 4 inherited runners, which isn't bad at all. ■

DANTE POWELL — SOLID PROSPECT

OF • BR • TR • 6'2 • 185 • 23 • SF94/1

	AB	R	H	2B	3B	HR	RBI	BB	SO	SB	CS	BA	OB	SA
AA	508	92	142	27	2	21	78	72	92	43	23	.280	.371	.465

After making the jump from Class-A to Triple-A, Powell improved in nearly every offensive category. He still strikes out too much, but at least he's getting

selective enough to draw some walks. With his speed, he can quickly turn bases on balls into doubles. He'll be 23 on Opening Day and would probably be better off honing his skills at Triple-A in '97—but his potential may earn him a promotion before he's ready. He's got the 5-tool label, can play center field, and is the most likely of the Giants' crop of outfield prospects to be a star in the big leagues eventually . . . if he wants it. Apparently he's mailed in more than his share of 0-fers. Jack Hiatt, Giants director of player development on Dante Powell in '95: "On given days, he put on some real shows, but on other given days, to put it quite frankly, he was just average." ■

ARMANDO RIOS

SLEEPER

RF • BL • TL • 5'9 • 180 • 25 • SF94

	AB	R	H	2B	3B	HR	RBI	BB	SO	SB	CS	BA	OB	SA
AA	329	62	93	22	2	12	49	44	42	9	9	.283	.365	.471

Rios put up big numbers in A-ball in '95, including 51 stolen bases, then followed that up with more dingers and many, many fewer stolen bases in Shreveport. He has been voted the best arm in both the Texas League and the California League. He merits watching in Triple-A. ■

KIRK RUETER

SP • BL • TL • 6'3 • 190 • 26 • MON91/19

	G	GS	IP	H	HR	BB	K	W	L	S	ERA	K/BB	K9	HW9
MON94	20	20	92	106	11	23	50	7	3	0	5.17	2.2	4.9	12.62
MON95	9	9	47	38	3	9	28	5	3	0	3.23	3.1	5.4	9.00
MON/SF96	20	19	101	109	12	27	46	6	8	0	4.01	1.7	4.1	12.11
CAREER	63	62	326	338	31	77	155	26	14	0	3.89	2.0	4.3	11.45

After Rueter was traded to the Giants, Expos pitching coach Joe Kerrigan said Rueter's high-80s velocity had declined. The lefty with the funniest-looking ears this side of Jim Bullinger—reason enough to print the out-of-date picture—claimed otherwise. With 12 dingers in 81 innings in Montreal, it's frightening to think what would happen if he ever did start to lose it. He's still young, but his stuff isn't all that great, and it's becoming evident that his rookie success was a fluke—so he and VanLandingham should have plenty to talk about. ■

STEVE SCARSONE (see Looking for a Game)

TIM SCOTT (see Looking for a Game)

BENJI SIMONTON

1B-OF • BR • TR • 6'1 • 225 • 24 • SF92/3

	AB	R	H	2B	3B	HR	RBI	BB	SO	SB	CS	BA	OB	SA
AA	469	86	117	25	1	23	76	101	144	6	4	.249	.389	.454

Anyone who strikes out one-third of the time in Double-A will flail away in the majors. Even with all his strike-outs, he's never managed any better than 28 dingers in a season, and that was in A-ball. Lest you think this no-field, big-swing man-child could find a home with the Red Sox, they've already claimed him once and returned him. ■

CHRISTOPHER SINGLETON

OF • BL • TL • 6'2 • 195 • 24 • SF93/2

	AB	R	H	2B	3B	HR	RBI	BB	SO	SB	CS	BA	OB	SA
AA	500	68	149	31	9	5	72	24	58	27	12	.298	.333	.426

Another young outfielder without much power and good speed (he was a wide receiver at Nevada), Singleton would have to leap past several players to make the Giants in '97. A hacker who makes contact, he's better off spending the year in Triple-A learning the strike zone. His average has climbed from .250 to .300 in two seasons, so there's reason for optimism. He had knee surgery in spring training but still made Shreveport's opening day line up, so he's got the work ethic. ■

STEVE SODERSTROM

SLEEPER

SP • BR • TR • 6'3 • 215 • 24 • SF93/1

	G	GS	IP	H	HR	BB	SO	W	L	S	ERA	K/BB	K9	HW9
AAA	29	29	171	178	13	58	80	7	8	0	4.41	1.4	4.2	12.40

Not to be confused with the attractive female golfer, Steve is the much more common 1st-round flop. Injuries hampered him at the beginning of his career, but he was healthy and ineffective in Triple-A in '96. He throws hard, but his strikeouts were way down at Phoenix, where his ERA hovered near 5. They called him up anyway and he won ugly twice against David Neid in the same week. As for whether Soderstrom can ever get things straightened out against someone other than Endless Aching Neid, Joaquin Andujar said it best: "You never know." ■

JULIAN TAVAREZ

RP-SP • BR • TR • 6′2 • 165 • 23 • CLE90

	G	GS	IP	H	HR	BB	K	W	L	S	ERA	K/BB	K9	HW9
CLE95	57	0	85	76	7	21	68	10	2	0	2.44	3.2	7.2	10.27
CLE96	51	4	80	101	9	22	46	4	7	0	5.36	2.1	5.2	13.83
CAREER	117	12	203	236	24	57	133	16	12	0	4.52	2.3	5.9	12.99

For Julian Tavarez, 1996 was a season to forget. He started off pitching poorly, then found himself in the doghouse because he wasn't listening to his coaches instructions and failed to make personal appearances. And on May 31, Tavarez demonstrated his personal defense training on umpire Joe Brinkman, flipping him to the ground in a brawl in Milwaukee. The Indians demoted him for a short time in July to get centered. When Tavarez returned, his attitude was much improved, but his pitching wasn't. The Indians tried him in the rotation in July, but he allowed 15 runs in 14 innings and finished out the second half with a 6.14 ERA. To make it a truly wasted year, he was traded from the penthouse to the outhouse. Tavarez has an excellent repertoire and he will lend inconsistency to a young staff in San Francisco in '97. ■

ROB THOMPSON (see Looking for a Game)

DOUG VANDERWEELE

SP-RP • BR • TR • 6′3 • 200 • 26 • SF91/7

	G	GS	IP	H	HR	BB	SO	W	L	S	ERA	K/BB	K9	HW9
AAA	41	3	89	101	13	35	42	4	2	0	5.36	1.2	4.2	13.75

Vanderweele is 27, he's bounced up and down the Giants' system, he's never done anything to get the pulse pounding, and the big club probably isn't ready for another right-handed Vanderwhatever. You can find him in the minor-league register alongside Matt Vanderbush, Jon Vandergriend, Bill Vanderwel, Ryan Vandeweg, Tim Vanegmond, and Jules Vanlanduyt. Yet another one who's in no danger of bringing honor and glory to the tulip people. ■

WILLIAM VANLANDINGHAM SLEEPER

SP • BR • TR • 6′2 • 210 • 26 • SF91/3

	G	GS	IP	H	HR	BB	K	W	L	S	ERA	K/BB	K9	HW9
SF94	16	14	84	70	4	43	56	8	2	0	3.54	1.3	6.0	12.11
SF95	18	18	122	124	14	40	95	6	3	0	3.67	2.4	7.0	12.10
SF96	32	32	181	196	17	78	97	9	14	0	5.40	1.2	4.8	13.62
CAREER	66	64	388	390	35	161	248	23	19	0	4.45	1.5	5.7	12.77

When a team with pitching as thin as the Giants begins to shop around a healthy 26-year-old, it

speaks volumes. They not be the only ones who've given up on him; VanLaunchingpad himself seemed to be throwing up his hands at times in '96. He often wore that young pitcher look of anger and confusion you used to see on Mark Wohlers's sweaty mug. Not surprisingly, the Giants are more concerned about his head than his arm. With many young pitchers, it's a question of figuring out how to harness good stuff and throw it for strikes. When the planets line up and Darryl Kile does it, he can be as good as just about any pitcher in the league, which is one of the reasons the Astros have given him about as many chances as Steve Howe. VanLandingham doesn't have Kile's stuff, but he has a very good fastball with excellent move-ment. If he can develop better command of his other pitches, he could be something. ■

MIKE VILLANO

RP • BR • TR • 6′1 • 200 • 25 • SF94/25

	G	GS	IP	H	HR	BB	SO	W	L	S	ERA	K/BB	K9	HW9
A+	39	2	88	48	2	33	133	7	1	8	.72	4.0	13.6	8.28

Was he loading up his pitches with bong water? Villano gave up 7 earned runs in 88 innings, and thanks to Russ Ortiz, he wasn't even the best pitcher on the team! He's a converted catcher with a fastball, slider, and change-up, and he doesn't tip his pitches. He was 25, which is very old for A-ball, but that's an incredible performance at any age at any level. ■

JOSE VIZCAINO

2B • BB • TR • 6′1 • 180 • 29 • LA86

	AB	R	H	2B	3B	HR	RBI	BB	SO	SB	CS	BA	OB	SA
NYN94	410	47	105	13	3	3	33	33	62	1	11	.256	.310	.324
NYN95	509	66	146	21	5	3	56	35	76	8	3	.287	.332	.365
NYN/CLE96	542	70	161	17	8	1	45	35	82	15	7	.297	.341	.363
CAREER	2503	294	688	86	25	12	217	172	353	42	32	.275	.321	.344

Vizcaino reached career highs in batting average and on-base average in '96, and just missed his career mark in slugging percentage. The Indians acquired him from the Mets for Carlos Baerga because he doesn't treat defense as optional, doesn't have a spare tire around his waist, and doesn't have

a cell phone surgically attached to his left ear during batting practice. The Giants may move Vizcaino back to shortstop in '97. ■

ALLEN WATSON

SP • BL • TL • 6'3 • 195 • 26 • SL91/2

	G	GS	IP	H	HR	BB	K	W	L	S	ERA	K/BB	K9	HW9
SL94	22	22	115	130	15	53	74	6	5	0	5.52	1.4	5.8	14.31
SL95	21	19	114	126	17	41	49	7	9	0	4.96	1.2	3.9	13.18
SF96	29	29	185	189	28	69	128	8	12	0	4.61	1.9	6.2	12.55
CAREER	88	85	501	535	71	191	300	27	33	0	4.90	1.6	5.4	13.04

Before the '96 season, Watson was dismissed as a "journeyman" by an N.L. GM critiquing the Clayton trade. Then he was dissed by umpire/loose cannon/power-mad pantload Joe West, who told Watson to shut up after Watson cursed out himself. Add in some elbow problems in July and you'd figure '96 was another train wreck for a pitcher once touted as a star by the Cardinals. Instead, Watson had his best season in '96—the first half of it, anyway. The most obvious improvement in Watson's game could be seen in his strikeouts. He struck out 49 batters in 114 innings in '95, walking nearly the same amount. This from a guy who, in the minors, had strikeout-an-inning stuff, with command. In '96, this was a more respectable 128 in 186 innings. Like most Giants' starters, he is a fly ball pitcher prone to the 'tater: He gave up 1 every 7 innings, a ratio that has steadily deteriorated since he came to the majors. A major cause for concern is his performance after his elbow injury in July. He came back from the DL throwing in the low 90s against the Braves, his best velocity since his rookie season, and looked quite good in his first three starts. But his finish was about as weak as the Dodgers'. He went 7 innings only once in his last 9 starts after doing that 14 times in his first 20 starts. He put off surgery in '96, but that bill may be ready to come due in '97. ■

RICK WILKINS

C • BL • TR • 6'2 • 210 • 29 • CHN86/23

	AB	R	H	2B	3B	HR	RBI	BB	SO	SB	CS	BA	OB	SA
CHN94	313	44	71	25	2	7	39	40	86	4	3	.227	.317	.387
CHI/HOU95	202	30	41	3	0	7	19	46	61	0	0	.203	.351	.322
HOU/SF96	411	53	100	18	2	14	59	67	121	0	3	.243	.344	.399
CAREER	1819	246	458	87	6	72	234	250	476	9	12	.252	.344	.425

Wilkins hit .213, was useless against lefties, struck out once every 3 at-bats for the Astros, then rode the bench for a while behind Tom Lampkin in San Francisco—which tells you all you need to know about how low his stock had fallen. Out of nowhere, he hit 8 dingers, knocked in 36 runs, and batted .289 in his last 50 games—but it still might not have been enough to play his way onto this cost-conscious, last-place team in '97. ■

KEITH WILLIAMS

OF • BR • TR • 6'0 • 190 • 24 • SF93/9

	AB	R	H	2B	3B	HR	RBI	BB	SO	SB	CS	BA	OB	SA
AAA	398	63	109	25	3	13	63	52	96	2	2	.274	.354	.450

Williams has put up good numbers at every level in the minors, though his batting average dropped below .300 at Phoenix in '96. He hasn't run much since A-ball, and he strikes out too much. He'll be 25 in April and, like Ozzie Timmons, he could probably hit 15 dingers for someone if he got the chance. Doesn't look like it will be in San Francisco ■

DESI WILSON

1B • BL • TL • 6'7 • 230 • 28

	AB	R	H	2B	3B	HR	RBI	BB	SO	SB	CS	BA	OB	SA
SF96	118	10	32	2	0	2	12	12	27	0	2	.271	.338	.339

He's 6-foot-7, 230, and has a low-post game, but his stats would make you think of Mark Grace with some speed. Despite his Billy Ashley build, he stole at least 10 bases every season in the minors, including 29 in A-ball. The Giants got him from the Rangers for Burkett. Hoops came first for him, so he got a late start—making it to the majors at 28 after hitting well above .300 in Phoenix. He keeps his weight back throughout the swing, managing only 4 extra base hits in his 41-game call-up. If he could have found a way to turn loose the power his frame could generate, the first-base job would have been his. ■

Free Agents

In many ways, the free agent market has begun to resemble rotisserie drafts, as life imitates obsession. Here's what was available during the winter of '96–'97.

LUIS ALICEA

2B • BB • TR• 5′ 9 • 165 • 31 • SL86/1

	AB	R	H	2B	3B	HR	RBI	BB	SO	SB	CS	BA	OB	SA
SL94	205	32	57	12	5	5	29	30	38	4	5	.278	.373	.459
SL95	419	64	113	20	3	6	44	63	61	13	10	.270	.367	.375
SL96	380	54	98	26	3	5	42	52	78	11	3	.258	.350	.382
CAREER	1693	251	510	99	29	22	217	252	322	42	26	.301	.342	.433

A second baseman who doesn't hit for average or power but can draw walks can be a valuable asset. But not when he hits .234 in the leadoff spot and plays defense the way Alicea did last summer. He committed 18 errors in the first half of the season, losing his job to Mike Gallego at the All-Star break. He regained his position after hitting .320 in 15 July games and he made just 6 errors the rest of the season. But it's a telling fact that the Cards were shopping for Pittsburgh's Jeff King during the stretch drive. It's Delino's turn to hit .234 in the leadoff spot in St. Louis. ■

ERIC ANTHONY

OF • BL • TL • 6′2 • 195 • 29 • HOU86/34

	AB	R	H	2B	3B	HR	RBI	BB	SO	SB	CS	BA	OB	SA
SEA94	262	31	62	14	1	10	30	23	66	6	2	.237	.297	.412
CIN95	134	19	36	6	0	5	23	13	30	2	1	.269	.327	.425
CIN/COL96	185	32	45	8	0	12	22	32	56	0	2	.243	.535	.481
CAREER	1925	241	444	78	6	76	264	205	473	22	14	.231	.304	.396

The Reds sold Anthony to the Rockies at the end of July, deciding they'd rather have Kevin Mitchell in their lineup. He's gotten a full season's worth of at bats in the past 3 years and hit 27 dingers, knocked in 75 runs, and hit .246. That's about what he's done everywhere he's been and it hasn't been good enough for anyone. He's not much of a fielder and can't hit lefties, so he better get good at pinch-hitting or work on a knuckleball. ■

STEVE AVERY

SP • BL • TL • 6′4 • 180 • 26 • ATL88/1

	G	GS	IP	H	HR	BB	K	W	L	S	ERA	K/BB	K9	HW9
ATL94	24	24	151	127	15	55	122	8	3	0	4.04	2.2	7.3	10.84
ATL95	29	29	173	165	22	52	141	7	13	0	4.67	2.7	7.3	11.29
ATL96	24	23	131	146	10	40	86	7	10	0	4.47	2.2	5.9	12.78
CAREER	203	201	1222	1180	103	371	815	72	62	0	3.83	2.2	6.0	11.42

With Denny Neagle and Terrell Wade in the fold, there's no need for the Braves to pay him $4 million. The Braves need that money to commit to their top starters—something Avery hasn't been since 1993. Scouts believe his problems stemmed from trying to emulate Glavine and Maddux, pitching off his change-up instead of his fastball—so he may be helped, in a strange way, by getting away from them. Avery was brilliant in April and May (6-4, ERA below 3.00) but was lit up in June and September (0-5, with an ERA over 9.00). He was out for most of July and August with a strained muscle in his side. Pitching coach Leo Mazzone said in late June that a mechanical problem was causing Avery to leave his pitches over the middle of the plate, but he wished he'd had that problem in Game 4 against Boggs with the bases loaded. ■

HAROLD BAINES

DH • BL • TL • 6′2 • 195 • 38 • CHA77/1

	AB	R	H	2B	3B	HR	RBI	BB	SO	SB	CS	BA	OB	SA
BAL94	326	44	96	12	1	16	54	30	49	0	0	.294	.356	.485
BAL95	385	60	115	19	1	24	63	70	45	0	2	.299	.403	.540
CHA96	495	80	154	29	0	22	95	73	62	3	1	.311	.399	.503
CAREER	8366	1113	2425	416	48	323	1356	877	1225	33	31	.290	.355	.467

Baines is perhaps the only player, besides Michael and Magic, to put back on a number already retired by his team. No offense, but he never established himself as merely "Harold," so you have to wonder how desperate the Sox must have been for attendance to substitute Baines Day for White Sox Floppy Sunhat Day. Despite his age, he still swings quality wood. He is a good low-ball hitter and will demolish a pitcher who dares work him inside. Consistency? Baines hit .300 in every month except

June. His main priority last season was to provide protection for Frank Thomas. Pitchers still walked the Big Hurt more than 100 times last season, including 26 intentional passes, but it was a far better situation than in '95, when runners on base and anything less than a 5-run lead meant Thomas was thrown an automatic 4 outside. And with Thomas on base in front of him all year, Baines responded with his best season since 1985. Don't expect to be able to put up those numbers in many other lineups. ■

STAN BELINDA

RP • BR • TR • 6'3 • 185 • 30 • PIT86/10

	G	GS	IP	H	HR	BB	K	W	L	S	ERA	K/BB	K9	HW9
KC94	37	0	49	47	6	24	37	2	2	1	5.14	1.5	6.8	13.04
BOS95	63	0	69	51	5	28	57	8	1	10	3.10	2.0	7.4	10.30
BOS96	31	0	28	31	3	20	18	2	1	2	6.59	.9	5.8	16.35
CAREER	376	0	434	363	42	184	360	32	20	74	3.90	2.0	7.5	11.34

Belinda's career has run straight down since he yielded that pinch-hit single to Francisco Cabrera in Game 7 of the '92 playoffs against the Braves. He should be in his prime, but his numbers in '96 were anything but. With his sidearm delivery, he should be able to provide quality innings for a team that needs a pitcher to get out tough righties who aren't named Cabrera. ■

BOBBY BONILLA

OF-DH • BB • TR • 6'3 • 230 • 34 • PIT81

	AB	R	H	2B	3B	HR	RBI	BB	SO	SB	CS	BA	OB	SA
NYN94	403	60	117	24	1	20	67	55	101	1	3	.290	.374	.504
NYN/BAL95	554	96	182	37	8	28	99	54	79	0	5	.329	.388	.576
BAL96	595	107	171	27	5	28	116	75	85	1	3	.287	.363	.491
CAREER	5786	916	1643	333	54	245	965	719	931	37	47	.284	.361	.487

When Bonilla learned that Davey Johnson planned to use him as a designated hitter, it was the first of many well-publicized tiffs in the Orioles' clubhouse. He considered himself a position player and let everybody know it. Apparently, he was right—at least with the bat, if not the glove. He slumped through the first couple of months as a DH, but when Johnson gave in and moved him to right, he responded. As a DH early in the season, Bonilla hit .221 with 2 home runs in 163 at-bats. As a right fielder, he hit .304 with 25 home runs and 89 RBI in 401 at-bats. He's a butcher defensively, but that's the sacrifice any team will have to make to keep his bat going. The Marlins may make that sacrifice back at third base where he started. Judge his worth to Florida not just on his numbers, but on how many fewer walks Gary Sheffield draws. ■

CHRIS BOSIO

SP • BR • TR • 6'3 • 235 • 33 • MIL82

	G	GS	IP	H	HR	BB	K	W	L	S	ERA	K/BB	K9	HW9
SEA94	19	19	125	137	15	40	67	4	10	0	4.32	1.7	4.8	12.74
SEA95	31	31	170	211	18	69	85	10	8	0	4.92	1.2	4.5	14.82
SEA96	18	9	60	72	8	24	39	4	4	0	5.93	1.6	5.8	14.38
CAREER	309	246	1709	1742	162	481	1059	94	93	9	3.97	2.2	5.6	11.71

Since 1994 Bosio's had major problems with his right knee, and he can't find his stuff or his command. It's no coincidence that he also can no longer look down and see his toes. Since the Mariners threw big bucks at him after going 30-20 in '91–92 for Milwaukee, he's 27-31 with 5 trips to the DL. If he walks to the mound this spring and his butt still looks like a couple of strange bulldogs in a bag, then he might not even manage last year's numbers in '97. ■

SHAWN BOSKIE

SP • BR • TR • 6'3 • 205 • 30 • CHN86/1

	G	GS	IP	H	HR	BB	K	W	L	S	ERA	K/BB	K9	HW9
SE/CH/PH94	22	15	90	92	15	30	61	4	7	0	5.06	2.0	6.1	12.19
CAL95	20	20	111	127	16	25	51	7	7	0	5.64	2.0	4.1	12.32
CAL96	37	28	189	226	40	67	133	12	11	0	5.32	2.0	6.3	13.95
CAREER	184	118	775	853	114	262	434	42	54	0	4.92	1.7	5.0	12.95

For two straight seasons, Boskie has started strong, only to be annihilated in the second half. He's always been successful as a reliever and struggled as a starter. Before '96 he'd never thrown more than 129 innings in a season—but he threw 189 last season and had to make 28 starts, because the other options were so unattractive. Not surprisingly, he hit the wall in July—his ERA from July through September was 6.50 (it was

4.23 overall). In fact, his career ERA in September is in the 8s. He's a competent pitcher, but he's better suited as a 1-inning-per-appearance guy who pitches about 75 to 90 innings a year. He's also a fly ball pitcher during the worst of times for fly ball pitchers—and he was taken deep 40 times last year, roughly twice per 9 innings. ■

MARK CARREON

1B • BR • TL • 6′0 • 195 • 33 • NYN81/7

	AB	R	H	2B	3B	HR	RBI	BB	SO	SB	CS	BA	OB	SA
SF94	100	8	27	4	0	3	20	7	20	0	0	.270	.324	.400
SF95	396	53	119	24	0	17	65	23	37	0	1	.301	.343	.490
SF/CLE96	434	56	122	34	3	11	65	33	42	3	4	.281	.339	.449
CAREER	2012	246	557	108	5	69	289	140	246	12	11	.277	.327	.438

Carreon was busy proving he could be an everyday player in San Francisco when the Indians came out of nowhere July 9 and scooped him up for a ride to the postseason. Julio Franco, had just landed on the 15-day DL with a hamstring injury two days earlier, and John Hart needed to find a major-league first baseman fast. Carreon hit .324 for the Indians in 38 games before he landed on the DL after fouling a ball off his knee. He could only watch from the dugout during the pennant drive and the playoffs. Carreon worked hard to cut down his strikeouts the past two seasons and better contact at the plate is the primary reason why he earned a full-time job last year. It's probably back to being a spare part in '97. ■

ROGER CLEMENS

SP • BR • TR • 6′4 • 230 • 34 • BOS83/1

	G	GS	IP	H	HR	BB	K	W	L	S	ERA	K/BB	K9	HW9
BOS94	24	24	170	124	15	71	168	9	7	0	2.85	2.4	8.9	10.32
BOS95	23	23	140	141	15	60	132	10	5	0	4.18	2.2	8.5	12.92
BOS96	34	34	242	216	19	106	257	10	13	0	3.63	2.4	9.6	11.97
CAREER	383	382	2775	2359	194	856	2590	192	111	0	3.06	3.0	8.4	10.43

Roger Clemens is not the pitcher he used to be, but he's still one of the best in the game. He struggled with his velocity in the first half and reached the All-Star break at 3-8, 5 games under .500 for the first time in his career. But during that time his ERA was 4.04 and the A.L. ERA was 5.10. He had 134 strikeouts in 131.1 innings. And he left 6 games with a lead, only to have the bullpen blow 5. And as usual, he could sue the offense for non-support. Throughout his career, Red Sox hitters have taken the night off to watch him pitch. He finished the season again with the lowest run support in the rotation (4.4 runs per game). On top of that, he had to deal with trade rumors, greatly exaggerated rumors of his demise, and being outbid for JFK's golf clubs.

After the All-Star break, Clemens kicked his salary drive into gear and went 7-5 with a 3.15 ERA, more than 1.5 below the league average. He threw a compete-game shutout against the Tigers, fanning 20 to tie his own record set a decade ago. Buddy Bell said it was more impressive than a no-no. "The no-hitters I've been involved with or seen, there was luck involved. This was a dominating performance. I think it was the best pitching performance I've ever seen."

With the victory, Clemens tied Cy Young for the club records for victories (192) and shutouts (38). He was asked if he was tired after the 151-pitch game. "When you're chasing the guy they named the pitching award after, you don't get tired," Clemens replied. Uh, Roger, wasn't it the Orioles and Yankees you were supposed to be chasing? And hadn't you thrown a lot fewer than 151 pitches when you asked out of Game 6 of the '86 World Series to leave it to Calvin Schiraldi to hold a 3-2 lead?

Clemens wants to reach 300 victories, and he's still got a lot of pitching left to do to get there. Watch this off-season to see if he goes to the highest bidder, or takes less to go to a contender. ■

DENNIS COOK

RP • BL • TL • 6′3 • 185 • 34 • SF85/18

	G	GS	IP	H	HR	BB	K	W	L	S	ERA	K/BB	K9	HW9
CHA94	38	0	33	29	4	14	26	3	1	0	3.55	1.9	7.1	11.73
CLE/TEX95	46	1	57	63	9	26	53	0	2	2	4.53	2.0	8.4	14.05
TEX96	60	0	70	53	2	35	64	5	2	0	4.09	1.8	8.2	11.31
CAREER	295	71	689	649	92	253	425	37	30	3	3.93	1.7	5.6	11.78

Cook hasn't pitched 70 innings since his rookie year in 1992, but he led the Rangers' staff in appearances last year. He was a starter most of his career and didn't start working out of the bullpen full-time until '94. He couldn't find a home as a starter; Texas is his 7th team in 12 years, and he became a free agent after the '96

season. In 2 years with Texas he's gone 5-4 with a 4.06 ERA. Last year he limited hitters to a .214 average. Those aren't Mariano Rivera numbers, but that's solid relief work for the A.L. ■

ERIC DAVIS

OF • BR • TR • 6′3 • 190 • 34

	AB	R	H	2B	3B	HR	RBI	BB	SO	SB	CS	BA	OB	SA
DET94	120	19	22	4	0	3	13	18	45	5	0	.183	.290	.292
CIN96	415	81	119	20	0	26	83	70	121	23	9	.287	.394	.523
CAREER	4110	746	1076	169	20	231	728	603	1096	329	54	.262	.357	.481

Davis retired from baseball with a herniated disc in his neck after the '94 season and that, it was assumed, was that. But he wanted to return, and Cincinnati took the chance. He was their best player for most of the season, staging the unlikeliest of comebacks (see *Come Back and Go Away* in the Chicago Cubs section), returning to a standard of play he hadn't displayed in 8 years. Those are solid numbers for a 27-year-old, much less a 35-year-old who'd been out of the game for a year. He still has tremendous speed and played decent defense in center. ■

DELINO DESHIELDS

2B • BL • TR • 6′1 • 170 • 28 • MON87/1

	AB	R	H	2B	3B	HR	RBI	BB	SO	SB	CS	BA	OB	SA
LA94	320	51	80	11	3	2	33	54	53	27	7	.250	.357	.322
LA95	425	66	109	18	3	8	37	63	83	39	14	.256	.353	.369
LA96	581	75	130	12	8	5	41	53	124	48	11	.224	.288	.298
CAREER	3399	501	894	120	39	38	292	457	679	301	102	.263	.351	.355

DeShields was brutal. His slugging percentage was awful, even for a middle infielder, and he made 451 outs. This is not the way to win friends and influence people. He tried to be a leader in a clubhouse that desperately needed one, but nobody knows you when you're down and out. He was still a great base stealer, with a success rate of more than 80%. He also scored a lot of runs despite his poor on-base percentage. But his days in L.A. were over when he was replaced by Juan Castro in Game 2 of the divison series. LaRussa and the Cardinals will try to resurrect his career, though he's not going to be the solution to their lead-off problems. ■

MIKE DEVEREAUX

OF • BR • TR • 6′0 • 195 • 33 • LA85/5

	AB	R	H	2B	3B	HR	RBI	BB	SO	SB	CS	BA	OB	SA
BAL94	301	35	61	8	2	9	33	22	72	1	2	.203	.256	.332
CHA/ATL95	388	55	116	24	1	11	63	27	62	8	6	.299	.342	.451
BAL96	323	49	74	11	2	8	34	34	53	8	2	.229	.305	.350
CAREER	3655	483	930	166	33	105	472	286	623	84	55	.254	.308	.404

Devereaux returned to the Orioles after a year with the White Sox and the Braves. He left just long enough to get a World Series ring, then signed to play right field for the O's. When Johnson installed Bonilla in right, Devereaux was left with a backup role and played the entire outfield. His production did little to change the situation. Gillick took his cost-cutting shears out in the off-season, and Devereaux will likely take a pay cut or go elsewhere. ■

DOUG DRABEK

SP • BR • TR • 6′1 • 185 • 34 • CHA83/11

	G	GS	IP	H	HR	BB	K	W	L	S	ERA	K/BB	K9	HW9
HOU94	23	23	164	132	14	45	121	12	6	0	2.84	2.7	6.6	9.71
HOU95	31	31	185	205	18	54	143	10	9	0	4.77	2.6	7.0	12.60
HOU96	30	30	175	208	21	60	137	7	9	0	4.57	2.3	7.0	13.78
CAREER	344	335	2257	2140	196	606	1454	137	112	0	3.41	2.4	5.8	10.9

Drabek was one of the best pitchers in the league as recently as 1994. But he was dreadful in '96, has taken a lot of Drayton McLane's money to go 38-42 with 38 no-decisions, and got a $1 million buy-out this off season just to go away. His fastball is gone, so he tries to change speeds on it and lob slop curves. When he's on, his curveball is a thing of beauty, but it's rarely there anymore. Drabek was too much of a man to blame his performance on a chronically sore hamstring that bothered him all year and kept him from following through on his pitches. You may recall he ripped it running the bases in the 1991 playoffs, though it didn't keep him from taking the mound in Game 6 and losing to Avery 1-0 in a game that could have put the Pirates in the World Series. Hard to keep the ball down with bad legs, and that was exactly what did in Drabek during '96. If a team is in need of a 4th starter and leader, and is aware that he'll get clocked a good deal of the

time then they could do a lot worse than Drabek. But he's pitching on guts and guile now, not on the stuff that made him a Cy Young winner. ■

SHAWON DUNSTON

SS • BR • TR • 6'1 • 175 • 34 • CHN82/1

	AB	R	H	2B	3B	HR	RBI	BB	SO	SB	CS	BA	OB	SA
CHN94	331	38	92	19	0	11	35	16	48	3	8	.278	.313	.435
CHN95	477	58	141	30	6	14	69	10	75	10	5	.296	.317	.472
SF96	287	27	86	12	2	5	25	13	40	8	0	.300	.331	.408
CAREER	4438	533	1186	220	46	103	473	176	746	154	64	.267	.296	.407

Dunston took less money and a 1-year deal to play in the Bay Area. He was hitting .300 when he broke his face, and had 8 stolen bases in 82 games without getting caught. If San Francisco had kept him, he might have been able to teach Bonds a few things about rising to the occasion instead of whining or fading away. When the Cubs were playing games that mattered in '89, Dunston brought both his hitting and fielding to another level. When he was asked to lead off for them, his on-base percentage went up 50 points. In '95, when he was being written off due to back ailments, he had his best season. His average consistently rises when it's late and close; in '96 he was 1 of only 2 players to take Robb Nen out of the yard.

Though he's a free swinger, he's not an automatic out with 2 strikes; he hit .275 in such situations in '96, with more hits than strikeouts. He made 15 errors in half a season, but his range is still good and his arm remains one of the best. As for how he plays the game, he sparked a win in May when, groin injury and all, he beat the pitcher to first with a head-first dive on an 8th inning infield grounder that should have been an easy out. Dusty Baker adored him.

KEVIN ELSTER

SS • BR • TR • 6'2 • 200 • 32 • NYN84/2

	AB	R	H	2B	3B	HR	RBI	BB	SO	SB	CS	BA	OB	SA
NYA/PHI95	70	11	13	5	1	1	9	8	19	0	0	.186	.272	.329
TEX96	515	79	130	32	2	24	99	52	138	4	1	.252	.317	.462
CAREER	2189	256	498	112	9	59	282	203	405	14	7	.228	.292	.368

After playing only 49 major-league games from 1993 to 1995, Elster started the '96 season filling in for an injured Benji Gil. He wound up turning in a

remarkable year and resurrecting his career. He got out off the blocks fast in April, hitting .279 with 5 homers and 8 doubles, and he led major-league shortstops with 21 RBI. By early May, Johnny Oates had decided to stick with Elster whether Gil was healthy or not. For the season, Kevin set career highs for just about everything that can be measured. Defensively he was outstanding, making all the routine plays and a few spectacular ones. He was the anchor of a very solid infield. But he's still Kevin Elster, and Benji Gil is still the Rangers' shortstop of the future. ■

SID FERNANDEZ

SP • BL • TL • 6'1 • 220 • 34 • LA81/4

	G	GS	IP	H	HR	BB	K	W	L	S	ERA	K/BB	K9	HW9
BAL94	19	19	115	109	27	46	95	6	6	0	5.15	2.1	7.4	12.13
BAL/PHI95	19	18	92	84	20	38	110	6	5	0	4.56	2.9	10.8	11.93
PHI96	11	11	63	50	5	26	77	3	6	0	3.43	3.0	11.0	10.86
CAREER	306	299	1861	1417	190	713	1740	113	96	1	3.35	2.4	8.4	10.30

Thanks to the center-field camera, pitchers get more air-time for their butts than do NFL cheerleaders or UPN bimbos. But that hasn't kept El Sid from allowing his butt to expand more rapidly than that gluttonous little brat in *Willy Wonka.* People in the real world have to squeeze in exercise time between work and family; this guy is a professional athlete who works once every 5 days, can't swing a dead cat without hitting a piece of exercise equipment, and still looks like Carvel's Fudgie the Whale ice cream cake. Check out a Met old-timers game in 2011 and you'll see Sid getting pushed out to the first-base line in a wheelbarrow. A poster child for underachievement, Fernandez made his 7th trip to the DL in '96. And if you think arm troubles have nothing to do with weight, try to throw hard for an hour in a lead-lined Santa suit and tell the doctor where it *doesn't* hurt. He used to run out of gas at 90 pitches; now he goes toes up at 75. Graft his arm onto someone with self-discipline and Hall of Fame wouldn't have been out of the question. Any outing could be his last, and it probably won't be in Philadelphia. They've seen this rehab movie too many times already. ■

JOE GIRARDI

C • BR • TR • 5′11 • 195 • 32 • CHN86/5

	AB	R	H	2B	3B	HR	RBI	BB	SO	SB	CS	BA	OB	SA
COL94	330	47	91	9	4	4	34	21	48	3	3	.276	.321	.364
COL95	462	63	121	17	2	8	55	29	76	3	3	.262	.308	.359
NYA96	422	55	124	22	3	2	45	30	55	13	4	.294	.346	.374
CAREER	2417	273	660	101	17	20	235	157	340	35	22	.273	.321	.354

In the early part of the season, the New York fans were sarcastically calling him Joltin′ Joe Girardi-o and booing him incessantly. But to his credit, he moved from Denver and *raised* his average 30 points. He may have the best speed of any catcher in baseball, though he is an average hitter at best. But that isn′t why they got him. The pitchers adore him. Now the New York fans do, too—even before he became the most unlikely player since Jim Northrup to deliver a critical triple off of an immortal in a World Series-deciding game. ▪

LUIS GONZALEZ

LF • BL • TR • 6′2 • 180 • 29 • HOU88/5

	AB	R	H	2B	3B	HR	RBI	BB	SO	SB	CS	BA	OB	SA
HOU94	392	57	107	29	4	8	67	49	57	15	13	.273	.353	.429
HOU/CH95	471	69	130	29	8	13	69	57	63	6	8	.276	.357	.454
CHN96	483	70	131	30	4	15	79	61	49	9	6	.271	.354	.443
CAREER	2767	370	748	171	31	74	411	280	410	67	50	.270	.341	.435

Gonzalez has a smooth swing that generates very solid line-drive power. It tends to get a little long, so he constantly has to remind himself to shorten it. To get him out, pitchers have to throw him breaking balls on the first pitch, but Gonzalez has the plate discipline to let them go by and often gets ahead in the count. He likes to hit balls low in the strike zone, but he can get caught chasing the ball up high as pitchers get him to "climb the ladder." Most of his time was spent hitting in the 5th spot in the batting order, where he offered Sammy Sosa decent protection. Unfortunately, the Cubs had no one to protect Gonzalez. Getting Gonzalez and starting catcher Scott Servais for Rick Wilkins is one of the more underrated swindles in the past 5 years. ▪

MIKE GREENWELL

LF • BL • TR • 6′0 • 200 • 33 • BOS82/6

	AB	R	H	2B	3B	HR	RBI	BB	SO	SB	CS	BA	OB	SA
BOS94	327	60	88	25	1	11	45	38	26	2	2	.269	.348	.453
BOS95	481	67	143	25	4	15	76	38	35	9	5	.297	.349	.459
BOS96	295	35	87	20	1	7	44	18	27	4	0	.295	.336	.441
CAREER	4623	657	1400	275	38	130	726	460	364	80	43	.303	.368	.463

Greenwell struggled early in the season, as did most of the club, and went on the disabled list in May with a torn ligament between his fingers. When he returned in July, he hit a hot streak but couldn′t sustain it through August. Rumors began to fly about his future. As his struggles continued, it became clear that, one way or another, he wouldn′t be in a Red Sox uniform in ′97. Greenwell asked Duquette to trade or release him if he was no longer in the team′s plans, but the GM left him hanging. So one of the final two members of the ′86 World Series team turned the volume up to 11 down the stretch. On September 2 in Seattle he went 4-for-5 with 2 homers to drive in all 9 runs for the Red Sox in a 9-8 victory. He went on to hit .366 with 21 RBI for the month. Shortly after the season ended, Duquette released a brief missive to the press. It read: "The Red Sox appreciate Mike Greenwell′s long tenure in a Red Sox uniform. He built a name for himself with his play in Boston." With that he was designated for assignment and out the door. Nice send-off for an 11-year veteran and one of only four guys to play as much left field in Boston since 1939. Meanwhile, the Red Sox fans must want to send their own brief missive to Duquette: "So when exactly does the genius stuff start?" ▪

KEVIN GROSS

SP • BR • TR • 6′5 • 215 • 35 • PHI81

	G	GS	IP	H	HR	BB	K	W	L	S	ERA	K/BB	K9	HW9
LA94	25	23	157	162	11	43	124	9	7	1	3.60	2.9	7.1	11.75
TEX95	31	30	183	200	27	89	106	9	15	0	5.54	1.2	5.2	14.21
TEX96	28	19	129	151	19	50	78	11	8	0	5.22	1.6	5.4	14.02
CAREER	462	365	2462	2489	226	966	1707	140	157	5	4.08	1.8	6.2	12.63

Gross battled back problems throughout the latter half of the season, spent some time on the DL, and eventually missed the postseason with a herniated

disc. Through June he was 8-5 with a 4.96 ERA. After a painful July and the arrival of John Burkett, he only saw 2 more starts. His Grossness has never been dominant, but he has been steady and durable. He's a free agent and will be eating innings for someone's staff this year, but with the arrival of Burkett and the emergence of Darren Oliver, it won't be in Texas. ■

DARRYL HAMILTON

CF • BL • TR • 6′1 • 180 • 32 • MIL86/11

	AB	R	H	2B	3B	HR	RBI	BB	SO	SB	CS	BA	OB	SA
MIL94	141	23	37	10	1	1	13	15	17	3	0	.262	.331	.369
MIL95	398	54	108	20	6	5	44	47	35	11	1	.271	.350	.389
TEX96	627	94	184	29	4	6	51	54	66	15	5	.293	.348	.381
CAREER	2820	417	821	123	25	29	304	260	281	124	45	.291	.351	.383

Hamilton suffered through a series of leg injuries, then went through reconstructive shoulder surgery in '94. He lost a lot of speed and struggled at the plate through '95. But after signing with the Rangers last year, he seems to have made it all the way back. He led off for the club all year, and set career marks for runs scored, doubles, and at-bats. He's still a good contact hitter and even contributed a little power. His plate discipline is also decent, although a club would probably like a few more walks out of the leadoff spot. Don't expect him to ever steal 20+ bases again. Defensively his range has diminished since '93, but he has an excellent glove and didn't have an error all season. ■

MIKE HENNEMAN

RP • BR • TR • 6′4 • 205 • 35 • DET84/4

	G	GS	IP	H	HR	BB	K	W	L	S	ERA	K/BB	K9	HW9
DET94	30	0	34	43	5	17	27	1	3	8	5.19	1.6	7.1	15.85
DET/HOU95	50	0	50	45	1	13	43	0	2	26	2.15	3.3	7.7	10.44
TEX96	49	0	42	41	6	17	34	0	7	31	5.79	2.0	7.3	12.43
CAREER	561	0	732	686	47	271	533	57	42	193	3.21	2.0	6.6	11.77

Texas hoped they could squeeze one more good year out of free agent Mike Henneman last year. He saved 31 games for them, but how he managed to do it with an ERA like that is mind-boggling. By the All-Star break he had blown 6 saves and had a 7.90 ERA. For the remainder of the season he got only 10

opportunities and saved all of them. But the Rangers limited him to 14.2 innings in the second half and traded for Mike Stanton, not exactly votes of confidence. They trusted him with Game 3 against the Yankees and he blew it on the first pitch, an inexcusable fastball over the heart of the plate to first ball, fastball Mariano Duncan, the kind of mistake a rookie might make. That kind of brainlock is reason enough for Texas to let him walk. ■

XAVIER HERNANDEZ

RP • BL • TR • 6′2 • 185 • 31 • TOR86/4

	G	GS	IP	H	HR	BB	K	W	L	S	ERA	K/BB	K9	HW9
NYA94	31	0	40	48	7	21	37	4	4	6	5.85	1.8	8.3	15.53
CIN95	59	0	90	95	8	31	84	7	2	3	4.60	2.7	8.4	12.60
CIN/HOU96	61	0	77	77	13	28	81	5	5	6	4.67	2.9	9.5	12.26
CAREER	373	7	563	527	55	214	485	34	25	34	3.89	2.3	7.8	11.85

For 2 straight seasons, the X-man has carved up N.L. right-handers like meat loaf. Unfortunately, N.L. left-handers turn him into the same. Righties hit .236; lefties hit .300 with a .383 onbase percentage and a .530 slugging percentage. He'll have to prove he can contain lefties when games are out of reach before he ever faces one when the game is on the line. ■

DAVE HOLLINS

3B • BB • TR • 6′1 • 195 • 30 • SD87/6

	AB	R	H	2B	3B	HR	RBI	BB	SO	SB	CS	BA	OB	SA
PHI94	162	28	36	7	1	4	26	23	32	1	0	.222	.328	.352
PHI/BOS95	218	48	49	12	2	7	26	57	45	1	1	.225	.391	.394
MIN/SEA96	516	88	135	29	0	16	78	84	117	6	6	.262	.377	.411
CAREER	2290	404	592	116	13	83	352	352	467	20	17	.259	.366	.429

Hollins is what he's always been—a switch-hitter who can't hit left-handed, and an intense player who can produce if he stays healthy. The starting job is his in California until he injuries himself. George Arias may have taken it by the time he gets back. ■

REX HUDLER

UT • BR • TR • 6'1 • 180 • 36 • NYA78/1

	AB	R	H	2B	3B	HR	RBI	BB	SO	SB	CS	BA	OB	SA
CAL94	124	17	37	8	0	8	20	6	28	2	2	.298	.326	.556
CAL95	223	30	59	16	0	6	27	10	48	13	0	.265	.310	.417
CAL96	302	60	94	20	3	16	40	9	54	14	5	.311	.337	.556
CAREER	1604	242	429	91	10	51	157	67	285	106	43	.267	.300	.432

Hudler was nothing short of amazing on the field. He played second, first, left field and center field—with offensive numbers similar to those of Jim Edmonds: slugging .556 and scoring 60 runs in 302 at-bats. If it happens with Philadelphia in '97, the league office will have to saw him in half to check for cork. Hard to tell what his role will be in Philadelphia. The Phillies might be looking too much at the price tag and not enough at the product. ▪

MIKE JACKSON

RP • BR • TR • 6'2 • 225 • 32 • PHI84

	G	GS	IP	H	HR	BB	K	W	L	S	ERA	K/BB	K9	HW9
SF94	36	0	42	23	4	11	51	3	2	4	1.49	4.6	10.8	7.23
CIN95	40	0	49	38	5	19	41	6	1	2	2.39	2.2	7.5	10.47
SEA96	73	0	72	61	11	24	70	1	1	6	3.63	2.9	8.8	10.63
CAREER	623	7	810	639	83	346	721	47	51	44	3.33	2.1	8.0	10.94

Jackson started the season in a mediocre fashion, which he blamed on not knowing the hitters and being unable to locate his pitches. Left-handers, it seemed, had no problem locating his pitches. His strikeout rate and his control were fine throughout his slump, so it was no surprise when he rallied in the second half. He has a fine fastball/slider combo—so good that scouts don't think he should use his split-finger, and wonder if that's why he's been getting hurt so many times during his career. He doesn't have many effective years left, but '97 should be one of them. ▪

DOUG JONES

RP • BR • TR • 6'3 • 195 • 39 • MIL78/3

	G	GS	IP	H	HR	BB	K	W	L	S	ERA	K/BB	K9	HW9
PHI94	47	0	54	55	2	6	38	2	4	27	2.17	6.3	6.3	10.17
BAL95	52	0	46	55	6	16	42	0	4	22	5.01	2.6	8.2	13.89
CHN/MIL96	52	0	63	72	7	20	60	7	2	3	4.28	3.0	8.6	13.12
CAREER	578	4	784	802	49	179	639	50	60	242	3.21	3.6	7.3	11.26

Don't pile the dirt on him yet. DoJo was actually quite effective in Milwaukee after the Cubs gave up on him. He's been let go by 4 teams (the Indians, Astros, Orioles, and Cubs) and gotten the last laugh each time. ▪

MARK LEITER

SP • BR • TR • 6'3 • 200 • 33 • BAL83/4

	G	GS	IP	H	HR	BB	K	W	L	S	ERA	K/BB	K9	HW9
CAL94	40	7	95	99	13	35	71	4	7	2	4.72	2.0	6.7	12.69
SF95	30	29	195	185	19	55	129	10	12	0	3.82	2.3	6.0	11.08
SF/MON96	35	34	204	219	37	69	164	8	12	0	4.94	2.4	7.2	12.70
CAREER	213	115	875	888	116	305	633	46	50	3	4.49	2.1	6.5	12.27

When the Expos got Leiter, Joe Kerrigan said he and the Expos scouts had detected several flaws in Leiter's delivery that were causing him to keep his pitches up in the strike zone. Leiter definitely needed the help because the league was demolishing him. Kerrigan decided to concentrate on Leiter's leg kick and managed to alter it so he wasn't finishing high. Leiter didn't turn into Jeff Fassero, but he had a 5.19 ERA with San Francisco and a 4.39 ERA with the Expos. Leiter still has decent stuff. His fastball hits 91-92, and he has a nice slider. He may have to follow Kerrigan to Boston if he wants to maintain his late-season success. ▪

MARK LEMKE

2B • BB • TR • 5'10 • 170 • 31 • ATL83/27

	AB	R	H	2B	3B	HR	RBI	BB	SO	SB	CS	BA	OB	SA
ATL94	350	40	103	15	0	3	31	38	37	0	3	.294	.363	.363
ATL95	399	42	101	16	5	5	38	44	40	2	2	.253	.325	.356
ATL96	498	64	127	17	0	5	37	53	48	5	2	.255	.323	.319
CAREER	2788	306	692	104	14	30	237	309	275	9	18	.248	.321	.328

Last season Lemke was a decent fielder and a drain offensively. A drain not by comparing him to an average N.L. hitter, but by comparing him to a league-average *second baseman.* And why Cox was batting him and his .323 on-base percentage second—an OBP lower than Alex Arias, Kevin Stocker, Brent Mayne, Billy Ashley, Dave Silvestri, Luis Alicea, Tom Lampkin,

Jody Reed, and Rob Deer—is a question whose answer is probably beyond human comprehension. Lemke has developed a deserved reputation as a clutch post-season performer and an old-fashioned grinder—someone who takes the game seriously and always hustles but doesn't have great talent. And shouldn't get big money. ■

DAVE MAGADAN

3B • BL • TR • 6'3 • 190 • 34 • NYN83/4

	AB	R	H	2B	3B	HR	RBI	BB	SO	SB	CS	BA	OB	SA
FLA94	211	30	58	7	0	1	17	39	25	0	0	.275	.386	.322
HOU95	348	44	109	24	0	2	51	71	56	2	1	.313	.428	.399
CHN96	169	23	43	10	0	3	17	29	23	0	2	.254	.360	.367
CAREER	3271	421	944	174	11	32	389	566	415	9	7	.289	.391	.378

Third base has been a revolving door in Chicago for quite some time now. Since Ron Santo last played for them in 1974, the Cubs have employed 74 players there. Magadan was brought in during the off-season to stop that revolving door, but instead, he spun it faster. That shouldn't have come as a surprise to the Cubs, since Magadan is baseball's answer to porta-QB, Dave Krieg.

Magadan spent the first couple of months of the season on the DL after undergoing surgery to remove a bone spur in his left hand. It took a while to get his bat going, and he ended up sitting behind Leo Gomez. Magadan has one of the best batting eyes in baseball, so he'll always get good pitches to hit. He's often been criticized for being too selective at the plate, but maybe that's why he took a .290 career batting average into 1996 after 10 seasons. The biggest problem with Magadan is his fielding, or lack thereof. He can't run, catch, or throw, and that could make it a bit difficult for any team but the Red Sox to find a spot for him. ■

KIRT MANWARING

C • BR • TR • 5'11 • 185 • 31 • SF86/2

	AB	R	H	2B	3B	HR	RBI	BB	SO	SB	CS	BA	OB	SA
SF94	316	30	79	17	1	1	29	25	50	1	1	.250	.308	.320
SF95	379	21	95	15	2	4	36	27	72	1	0	.251	.314	.332
SF/HOU96	227	14	52	9	0	1	18	19	40	0	1	.229	.300	.282
CAREER	2217	179	544	86	12	16	211	163	355	8	9	.245	.307	.317

Behind the plate he's one of the best. He threw out 37 of 83 opposition baserunners (45%), and Astros

pitchers fell over themselves complimenting him on his game-calling ability soon after he arrived—which says just as much about how well Rick Wilkins must have been doing that. Unfortunately, he is the slowest player in the NL and arguably the worst hitter in the big leagues. ■

DENNIS MARTINEZ

SP • BR • TR • 6'1 • 185 • 41 • BAL73

	G	GS	IP	H	HR	BB	K	W	L	S	ERA	K/BB	K9	HW9
CLE94	24	24	176	166	14	44	92	11	6	0	3.52	2.1	4.7	10.73
CLE95	28	28	187	174	17	46	99	12	5	0	3.08	2.2	4.8	10.59
CLE96	20	20	112	122	12	37	48	9	6	0	4.50	1.3	3.9	12.78
CAREER	630	548	3860	3723	356	1117	2070	240	182	6	3.63	1.9	4.8	11.28

Martinez could only manage 20 starts for the Indians last season, but they took all he could give and were grateful. In his first 12, Martinez was 8-2 with a 4.13 ERA. But he hit the wall, going 1-4 in his last eight starts with a 5.30 ERA, failing to make it to the 6th in all but one of them. He went down June 28 with a strained flexor tendon in his elbow and, after a 3-game comeback attempt in August, was done for the season. Martinez's velocity isn't much of a factor anymore. He depends more on his wits and his control. Martinez is three victories shy of Juan Marichal's record for victories by a Latin-American pitcher, so he'll be back in '97 for one last go-round. ■

KENT MERCKER

SLEEPER

SP-RP • BL • TL • 6'1 • 175 • 29 • ATL86/1

	G	GS	IP	H	HR	BB	K	W	L	S	ERA	K/BB	K9	HW9
ATL94	20	17	112	90	16	45	111	9	4	0	3.45	2.5	8.9	10.85
ATL95	29	26	143	140	16	61	102	7	8	0	4.15	1.7	6.4	12.65
BAL/CLE96	24	12	69	83	13	38	29	4	6	0	7.04	.8	3.8	15.77
CAREER	257	66	584	523	62	280	455	35	31	19	3.91	1.6	7.0	12.37

The Indians took a chance on Mercker July 21 when they acquired him from the Orioles for Eddie Murray. The trouble he experienced with Baltimore, namely his 7.76 ERA, was the direct result of a mysterious drop in velocity. Once consistently in the low-90's, his fastball tailed off to the low-80's. The Indians assigned Mercker to Triple-A Buffalo after the trade to iron out his mechanics. After 3 starts

there, the Indians reported that his velocity had returned and promoted him. Mercker pitched out of the bullpen for the remainder of the season, yielding a 3.08 ERA in 10 appearances. Mercker knows how to pitch, but he never really developed his breaking stuff enough to succeed in the rotation. If the Indians keep him in the bullpen, there's no reason why he can't return to the form he displayed with Atlanta a few years back. ■

KEVIN MITCHELL

OF • BR • TR • 5′11 • 245 • 35

	AB	R	H	2B	3B	HR	RBI	BB	SO	SB	CS	BA	OB	SA
CIN94	310	57	101	18	1	30	77	59	62	2	0	.326	.429	.681
BOS/CIN96	206	27	65	15	0	8	39	37	30	0	1	.316	.420	.505
CAREER	3948	609	1135	216	24	228	728	473	682	29	32	.287	.364	.528

To say Kevin Mitchell had a turbulent season would be a gross understatement.

He was signed to an incentive-laden deal in the off-season by Boston to add power to their already formidable line-up, but missed most of the early part of the season with constant injuries. It got to the point where he apologized to his teammates and the fans in Fenway for being unable to play and letting them down. They could have told him, "Don't be silly, Kevin. You let us down when you *do* play." By the time the Reds traded for him in late July, he had only 92 at-bats and 2 homers for the Red Sox.

He's never hit in the A.L., so it wasn't too much of a surprise that he improved with the Reds. Through mid-September he was hitting .325 with 6 homers and 26 RBI in 114 at-bats. But he developed a viral throat infection while the club was in San Diego, where Mitchell lives. He showed up in the clubhouse in pajamas and slippers, so Knight sent him home. That was on a Sunday. The club gave him permission to stay home and meet them in Pittsburgh on Tuesday. When he didn't show by Wednesday, with no contact or explanation, GM Jim Bowden suspended him for the rest of season. Evidently he'd received death threats from a San Diego gang, but it was never determined that this had any bearing on his absence. The offense sputtered on the road trip without any power threat, and the club's wild-card hopes dwindled.

Eric Davis spoke for the team when he said, "He might feel like he had to do what he had to do, but sometimes you can't think about yourself all the time. Sometimes you have to think of your team and teammates, and who you go to war with. . . . You don't want to put it all on one guy, but he was an integral part of the team, and was swinging the bat well. He let the whole club down."

Would you bring him back? ■

TERRY MULHOLLAND

SP • BR • TL • 6′3 • 200 • 34 • SF84/2

	G	GS	IP	H	HR	BB	K	W	L	S	ERA	K/BB	K9	HW9
NYA94	24	19	120	150	24	37	72	6	7	0	6.49	1.9	5.4	14.02
SF95	29	24	149	190	25	38	65	5	13	0	5.80	1.7	3.9	13.77
PHI/SEA96	33	33	202	232	22	49	86	13	11	0	4.68	1.8	3.8	12.52
CAREER	263	230	1520	1617	149	379	792	81	89	0	4.30	2.1	4.7	11.82

The second of a couple of lefties Seattle picked up for the stretch run, Mulholland wasn't up to Jamie Moyer's standards, but still went 5-4, 4.67 in 69.1 innings in August and September. Considering that Seattle starters had a 5.70 ERA overall, Mulholland was a star. He has mediocre stuff (but it's come back a little since his horrendous '95 season) and he has that awesome pickoff move (making him impossible to run on). But he could collapse at any moment—like Jake and Elwood's police cruiser at the end of *The Blues Brothers*. Doesn't look like he'll be leaving that mess in Seattle. ■

JAIME NAVARRO

SP • BR • TR • 6′4 • 210 • 30 • MIL87/4

	G	GS	IP	H	HR	BB	K	W	L	S	ERA	K/BB	K9	HW9
MIL94	29	10	89	115	10	35	65	4	9	0	6.62	1.9	6.6	15.16
CHN95	29	29	200	194	19	56	128	14	6	0	3.28	2.3	5.8	11.25
CHN96	35	35	236	244	25	72	158	15	12	0	3.92	2.2	6.0	12.05
CAREER	247	215	1479	1563	124	446	810	91	77	1	4.10	1.8	4.9	12.22

Navarro was the glue that held the rotation together last season. When the Cubs needed him last season, he was there. His 5-0, 2.14 ERA record in August almost single-handedly kept the team in the wild-card race. Navarro finished 4th in the National League in innings pitched and averaged about 6.75 innings per start. He induces a lot of ground balls, considered a necessity in Wrigley Field. To achieve that, he throws 2 fastballs low in the strike zone: a heavy sinker and a riding 4-seamer. He also throws a "slurve" with good movement and an occasional split-finger pitch. He has good control, and despite a reputation for letting himself get out of shape, he's very durable.

He's a fierce competitor, but concentration and poise on the mound have been problems for him in the past. He has a tendency to lose it if an ump blows a call. His temperament serves him well if he uses it as a motivational tool—he was greatly disappointed that Milwaukee gave up on him, and vowed he would make them regret their decision. He admits that he still thinks about it before every start. But this doesn't always work to his advantage: Upset at being pulled early from a game in Houston, Navarro pulled a Jeff George, exploding at Riggleman, with the dugout camera capturing every moment. Later in the season, he and Frank Castillo joined forces to complain to the press about being pulled early. Can't we all just get along? You guys are playing major-league baseball in Wrigley Field. What more could you want out of life? ■

JOE OLIVER

C • BR • TR • 6'3 • 215 • 31 • CIN83/3

	AB	R	H	2B	3B	HR	RBI	BB	SO	SB	CS	BA	OB	SA
CIN94	19	1	4	0	0	1	5	2	3	0	0	.211	.286	.368
MIL95	337	43	92	20	0	12	51	27	66	2	4	.273	.332	.439
CIN96	289	31	70	12	1	11	46	28	54	2	0	.242	.311	.405
CAREER	2396	225	595	127	2	70	350	180	445	7	8	.248	.301	.391

The Reds signed Oliver, a 7-year veteran who had left the Reds in '95, to platoon with Eddie Taubensee. Oliver didn't have an outstanding year, but he did a solid job. Mired in an 0-for-20 streak in late August, he broke out of it by hitting a grand slam and a 3-run double, both off Rockies reliever John Burke. After the game, a reporter asked him if scouting reports had helped him. "Advance scouting?" Oliver replied. "This is Cincinnati; we don't have advance scouting . . . or post-scouting, either. Our scouting is just watching the guy warm up."

Oliver throws better than Taubansee (28% to 23% at throwing out baserunners) and is more adept at handling the pitchers better (4.14 ERA v. 4.52). He wants more playing time in '97. If he stays with Cincinnati, look for him to get more at bats. ■

TOM PAGNOZZI

C • BR • TR • 6'0 • 190 • 34 • SL83/8

	AB	R	H	2B	3B	HR	RBI	BB	SO	SB	CS	BA	OB	SA
SL94	243	21	66	12	1	7	40	21	39	0	0	.272	.327	.416
SL95	219	17	47	14	1	2	15	11	31	0	1	.215	.254	.315
SL96	407	48	110	23	0	13	55	24	78	4	1	.270	.311	.423
CAREER	2686	236	687	141	11	42	302	174	406	18	21	.256	.301	.363

The skinny on Pagnozzi in the past was that he wasn't much of a hitter because his bat speed could be timed with a sundial. But he was put on a conditioning program that seems to have solved that problem, at least for the time being, and he responded by setting a career high with 13 home runs. A fine defender, Pagnozzi is one of the best in the league at calling a game and handling pitchers. He's had to work hard over the years to quicken his release on his throws and it continues to work for him (he cut down 34% of baserunners in '96). Wherever he winds up, he is still capable of contributing to a team on defense, even if his hitting in '96 wasn't for real. ■

ERIC PLUNK

RP • BR • TR • 6'5 • 210 • 33 • NYA81/4

	G	GS	IP	H	HR	BB	K	W	L	S	ERA	K/BB	K9	HW9
CLE94	41	0	71	61	3	37	73	7	2	3	2.54	2.0	9.3	12.42
CLE95	56	0	64	48	5	27	71	6	2	2	2.67	2.6	10.0	10.55
CLE96	56	0	77	56	6	34	85	3	2	2	2.43	2.5	9.9	10.51
CAREER	528	41	936	799	86	538	878	60	46	34	3.62	1.6	8.4	12.85

Plunk has been the most reliable reliever in the Cleveland bullpen for the past 5 seasons. In recognition of his value to the organization, Hargrove made sure he was on the mound September 17 when they clinched the division title. Plunk is a classic setup guy. A hard thrower, he's been using a basic three pitch combo for a number of years now and has them refined to perfection. He's got a fastball, a slider and a curve, and he can throw all of them for strikes. ■

MARK PORTUGAL

SP • BR • TR • 6′0 • 190 • 34 • MIN80

	G	GS	IP	H	HR	BB	K	W	L	S	ERA	K/BB	K9	HW9
SF94	21	21	137	135	17	45	87	10	8	0	3.93	1.9	5.7	11.82
SF/CIN95	31	31	181	185	17	56	96	11	10	0	4.01	1.7	4.8	11.98
CIN96	27	26	156	146	20	42	93	8	9	0	3.98	2.2	5.4	10.85
CAREER	286	227	1496	1431	155	529	949	92	76	5	3.83	1.8	5.7	11.79

Portugal pitched very well through stretches, but elbow and hamstring injuries affected his performance and forced him to miss numerous starts. They could also end up costing him a lot of money. He had a clause in his contract that would have kicked in an extra year on his contract, at $4.5 million, if he had pitched a certain amount of innings. The injuries caused him to fall short, and the Reds bought him out at $400,000. Portugal: "I'm confident that I'll be able to pitch next year, if not here, elsewhere. I'd like to play here, whether it's under the current terms or new terms. I think this team can win. I've made a lot of money in this game, and winning is more important to me right now." By the time you read this, he will have signed with someone for '97 and you can judge his sincerity. ▪

JEFF RUSSELL

RP • BR • TR • 6′3 • 210 • 35 • CIN79/8

	G	GS	IP	H	HR	BB	K	W	L	S	ERA	K/BB	K9	HW9
BOS/CLE94	42	0	40	43	5	16	28	1	6	17	5.09	1.8	6.3	13.25
TEX95	37	0	32	36	3	9	21	1	0	20	3.03	2.3	5.9	12.66
TEX96	55	0	56	58	5	22	23	3	3	3	3.38	1.0	3.7	12.86
CAREER	589	79	1099	1065	100	415	693	56	73	186	3.75	1.7	5.7	12.12

Struggling with a back injury, Russell signed a minor-league contract with Texas in the spring of '96, and they were uncertain that he would join the team at all. But he made it back and provided some effective spot relief. He was even part of the closing committee after Henneman lost the club's confidence, saving 3 games while blowing 4. At one time, Russell was one of the premier closers in the game, but '96 could have been his swan song. ▪

RYNE SANDBERG

2B • BR • TR • 6′2 • 190 • 37 • PHI78/20

	AB	R	H	2B	3B	HR	RBI	BB	SO	SB	CS	BA	OB	SA
CHN94	223	36	53	9	5	5	24	23	40	2	3	.238	.312	.390
CHN96	554	85	135	28	4	25	92	54	116	12	8	.244	.316	.444
CAREER	7938	1264	2268	377	76	270	997	733	1166	337	103	.286	.346	.454

After 17 months away from the game, many observers wondered if Sandberg would be able to get his swing back. He was starting to lose his bat speed, and the wrist injury he suffered in '93 had robbed him of power. But Ryno's triumphant return is a credit to his professionalism as a player and his intelligence as a hitter. It wasn't the most successful return of a no. 23 to a Chicago starting lineup, but impressive nonetheless. Because of his advancing age and slowing bat, Sandberg looks for pitches he can drive early in the count. If he gets an early offering in the middle of the plate or inside, he will put it over the fence. But when the count goes deep, Sandberg will go to the opposite field.

He's lost a lot of range in the field. But he isn't a liability yet because he knows how to position himself to compensate, and his hands are as steady as ever. Sandberg will continue to slow, but he supplies more power from a second baseman than the Cubs have a right to expect. They should consider themselves lucky to have his veteran influence in their clubhouse for as long as he wants to play. Anyone who doesn't root for the Cubs to get him into the playoffs one more time has the heart of a corporate lawyer. ▪

BENITO SANTIAGO

C • BR • TR • 6′1 • 185 • 32 • SD82

	AB	R	H	2B	3B	HR	RBI	BB	SO	SB	CS	BA	OB	SA
FLA94	337	35	92	14	2	11	41	25	57	1	2	.273	.322	.424
CIN95	266	40	76	20	0	11	44	24	48	2	2	.286	.351	.485
PHI96	481	71	127	21	2	30	85	49	104	2	0	.264	.332	.503
CAREER	4425	507	1161	198	25	150	595	274	813	77	57	.262	.306	.420

The Phillies were Benito's 4th team in 5 years, and there's still no guarantee he'll be able to take the Velvet Elvises out of storage anytime soon. It would

have been 5 in 5 if the Orioles had been willing to part with Jeffrey Hammonds—even though Santiago was only 31, was throwing as well as he had in years, and outproduced every catcher in the league except Hundley and Piazza. Despite his best efforts to establish diplomatic relations with the nation of Philadelphia—even professing a love for the cheesesteak early in the season—Benito remained unappreciated. He has actually been a very consistent player over the past 10 years, yet no one wanted him putting up his numbers for them. Then in '96 he was getting talked up for a Gold Glove again . . . team leader Curt Schilling was telling the club to sign him. . . . Colorado and Baltimore were reportedly very interested in throwing money at him over the winter. But Giles hesitated when he could have locked him in for less money and fewer years than his market value. Letting Benito walk will simply add fuel to the allegations of racism and stupidity that swirled around the front office all year. ■

MIKE STANTON

RP • BL • TL • 6'1 • 190 • 29 • ATL87/13

	G	GS	IP	H	HR	BB	K	W	L	S	ERA	K/BB	K9	HW9
ATL94	49	0	45	41	2	26	35	3	1	3	3.55	1.3	7.0	13.38
ATL/BOS95	48	0	40	48	6	14	23	2	1	1	4.24	1.5	5.2	13.95
BOS/TEX96	81	0	78	78	11	27	60	4	4	1	3.69	2.2	6.9	12.11
CAREER	407	0	388	372	36	149	293	23	25	56	3.90	2.0	6.8	12.08

When the Rangers had given up on Mike Henneman as their closer, they went out and traded for Mike Stanton to join their bullpen committee. In 32 appearances with Texas, he was 0-1 with a 3.22 ERA. He limited batters to a .261 batting average and was especially effective against left-handers. Lefties like him will have a job in the big leagues until rigor mortis sets in. ■

TERRY STEINBACH

C • BR • TR • 6'1 • 195 • 35 • OAK83/9

	AB	R	H	2B	3B	HR	RBI	BB	SO	SB	CS	BA	OB	SA
OAK94	369	51	105	21	2	11	57	26	62	2	1	.285	.327	.442
OAK95	406	43	113	26	1	15	65	25	74	1	3	.278	.322	.458
OAK96	514	79	140	25	1	35	100	49	115	0	1	.272	.342	.529
CAREER	4162	498	1144	205	14	132	595	307	689	15	18	.275	.328	.426

Steinbach had his best year ever, despite a late-season slump. Like many A's, it was his power numbers that got the most attention. His previous high of 16 homers (during his rookie year) was more than doubled. Everyone's power numbers were inflated in '96, and his obscured some trouble spots. Half of his homers came in his most productive months of June and July. His overall numbers began to look a bit more reasonable after an extended slump in August and September. Having started 130 games behind the plate and appearing in 137, wearing down should not come as a surprise.

Steinbach still is one of the best receivers in the game. He handles his pitchers well, plays good defense, and is consistently ranked among the best in the league in runners caught stealing. If Steinbach simply returns to past form in '97, as is likely, he'll still be one of the best catchers in the game. But he could be doing that on another team in '97. While he's attracted to the idea of playing on one team for his career, he will be sought after by teams as rich as the Orioles and as persuasive as his hometown Twins. It will be a blow to the A's if they lose such a talented and classy player, especially since they could have traded him during the '96 season while his value was peaking. If he escapes and the A's take the zero, a lot of fingers will be pointed at GM Sandy Alderson. ■

KEVIN TAPANI

SP • BR • TR • 6'0 • 180 • 33 • OAK86/2

	G	GS	IP	H	HR	BB	K	W	L	S	ERA	K/BB	K9	HW9
MIN94	24	24	156	181	13	39	91	11	7	0	4.62	2.3	5.3	12.69
MIN/LA95	33	31	190	227	29	48	131	10	13	0	4.96	2.7	6.2	13.03
CHA96	34	34	225	236	34	76	150	13	10	0	4.59	2.0	6.0	12.48
CAREER	231	225	1460	1541	152	349	919	92	75	0	4.18	2.6	5.7	11.65

Tapani is the prototype for pitchers who do more with less. None of his pitches has a lot of velocity, but he does a lot with his fastball. He cuts it, sinks it, turns it over, makes it sit up and beg. He throws a split-finger pitch that drops off the table, a slider, and a pretty good change-up. He makes his living mixing his pitches

and throwing them for strikes. He is also a very durable pitcher. He had to miss a start in April, marking the first time in 161 starts that he missed a start due to injury. Even then, Tapani was back the next time his spot in the rotation came up, and he didn't miss a start the remainder of the season. His 13 victories were the most he's had since 1992 when he was with the Twins—but he had a 5.23 ERA in his no-decisions. He benefited from a combination of good fortune and a good offense in his wins—and if you're looking for another omen that Tapani's losing it, you only need to look as far as the number of home runs he gave up. ■

DANNY TARTABULL

RF • BR • TR • 6'1 • 205 • 34 • CIN80/5

	AB	R	H	2B	3B	HR	RBI	BB	SO	SB	CS	BA	OB	SA
NYA94	399	68	102	24	1	19	67	66	111	1	1	.256	.360	.464
NYA/OAK95	280	34	66	16	0	8	35	43	82	0	2	.236	.335	.379
CHA96	472	58	120	23	3	27	101	64	128	1	2	.254	.340	.487
CAREER	5004	754	1366	289	22	262	925	764	1358	37	30	.273	.368	.497

Tartabull played like he had something to prove last season. He started the season slowly, with a .229 average and 5 home runs by the end of May. But from June on, Tartabull hit .268 and slugged .536. He hit 22 home runs and collected 76 RBI in that span. In September he was a wrecking crew, with 8 homers and 24 RBI. And his play in the field, criticized in the past as indifferent or personally dangerous, was much improved. Tartabull has proven that he still has a couple of years left in him, although a repeat of '96 would probably be too much to ask—especially the injury-free part. ■

BOB TEWKSBURY

SP • BR • TR • 6'4 • 200 • 36 • NYA81/19

	G	GS	IP	H	HR	BB	K	W	L	S	ERA	K/BB	K9	HW9
SL94	24	24	155	190	19	22	79	12	10	0	5.32	3.6	4.6	12.30
TEX95	21	21	129	169	8	20	53	8	7	0	4.58	2.7	3.7	13.19
SD96	36	33	206	224	17	43	126	10	10	0	4.31	2.9	5.5	11.66
CAREER	250	226	1489	1669	111	241	660	95	76	1	3.80	2.7	4.0	11.54

Tewksbury is another "master of the soft," who lets the hitters swing the bat and makes his fielders do the work. He held opponents to a .275 average,

after being knocked around at .287 for the past 5 years and .319 in his dismal '95. Though he was only 10-10, it was his best season since he went 17-10 in St. Louis in '93. But he followed his traditional trend of wearing down—or getting figured out by the league—by year end, going 3-5 after the All-Star Break. Since '91, he's been 48-30 before the Break, 26-24 after. And though he struck out more than 100 batters for the first time in his career, he walked more batters than games started for the first time since 1990. It's been a good run—he's persevered through 146 minor league starts and overcome being traded for Steve Trout—but don't be surprised if whatever team ponies up for him comes away with the '95 model instead. ■

FERNANDO VALENZUELA

SP • BL • TL • 5'11 • 200 • 36 • LA79

	G	GS	IP	H	HR	BB	K	W	L	S	ERA	K/BB	K9	HW9
PHI94	8	7	45	42	8	7	19	1	2	0	3.00	2.7	3.8	9.80
SD95	29	15	90	101	16	34	57	8	3	0	4.98	1.7	5.7	13.50
SD96	33	31	171	177	17	67	95	13	8	0	3.62	1.4	5.0	12.84
CAREER	435	406	2840	2612	214	1105	2013	171	141	2	3.50	1.8	6.4	11.78

The Padres wanted Fernando to draw crowds at home games, but he ended up being on the short list of effective NL lefty starters (only Jeff Fassero, Tom Glavine, John Smiley, Al Leiter, Mike Hampton, and Donovan Osborne were better). He's a far cry from the mid-80s, he's been reduced to nibbling, and if he's 36, so's Jane Fonda—but compare '95–'96 to his best season:

	IP	H	BB	K	W	L	ERA
1986	269	226	85	242	21	11	3.14
1995–96	261	278	101	154	21	11	4.10

He's a shadow of what he once was—except for the results. ■

GREG VAUGHN

:LF • BR • TR • 6'0 • 195 • 31 • MIL86

	AB	R	H	2B	3B	HR	RBI	BB	SO	SB	CS	BA	OB	SA
MIL94	370	59	94	24	1	19	55	51	93	9	5	.254	.345	.478
MIL95	392	67	88	19	1	17	59	55	89	10	4	.224	.317	.408
MIL/SD96	516	98	134	19	1	41	117	82	130	9	3	.260	.365	.539
CAREER	3385	548	828	161	14	179	588	445	792	66	41	.245	.333	.459

It will be tough for some owner to restrain himself from throwing at least $5 million a year at a guy who hit 40 dingers, but 1996 is as good as it's going to get for Vaughn (his previous best was 30-97-.267 in '93). He didn't adjust well to the N.L., hitting .206 in 43 games, and he remains vulnerable to breaking balls. He does work hard, and he fetched more on the open market during the '96 pennant race than the Brewers would have expected after he managed only 36 dingers and 114 RBI in the previous *two* seasons. But he could very well put up numbers in '97 that Billy Ashley could match in the same number of at bats. ■

DAVID WELLS

SP • BL • TL • 6'3 • 225 • 33 • TOR82/2

	G	GS	IP	H	HR	BB	K	W	L	S	ERA	K/BB	K9	HW9
DET94	16	16	111	113	13	24	71	5	7	0	3.96	3.0	5.8	11.10
DET/CIN95	29	29	203	194	23	53	133	16	8	0	3.24	2.5	5.9	10.95
BAL96	34	34	224	247	32	51	130	11	14	0	5.14	2.5	5.2	11.97
CAREER	348	178	1412	1396	165	371	922	90	75	13	3.99	2.5	5.9	11.26

Wells was one of the main off-season acquisitions for the Orioles last year and was expected to fall into the no. 2 spot behind Mussina. He was streaky, but pitched very well during stretches. He got the least run support on the rotation, which would help explain the losing record. Going into the final month, he was 10-13 with a 4.72 ERA, the lowest mark on the rotation. He was roughed up in September, though, which skewed his final stats. He rebounded to pitch well in the playoffs, going 2-0 with a 4.43 ERA in 3 starts. He was criticized for his work habits early in the season, but he's an old dog who's not going to learn new tricks. He's also one of the more colorful players in the game. He'll be an integral part of someone's rotation again this year. ■

JOHN WETTELAND

CL • BR • TR • 6'2 • 215 • 30 • LA85

	G	GS	IP	H	HR	BB	K	W	L	S	ERA	K/BB	K9	HW9
MON94	52	0	63	46	5	21	68	4	6	25	2.83	3.2	9.7	9.56
NYA95	60	0	61	40	6	14	66	1	5	31	2.93	4.7	9.7	7.97
NYA96	62	0	63	54	9	21	69	2	3	43	2.83	3.3	9.8	10.70
CAREER	370	17	511	392	43	174	556	28	33	180	2.92	3.2	9.8	9.97

Remember when Torre brought Wetteland in for Pettitte in Game 5? Chipper was on third with 1 out? Wetteland got Lopez easily enough on a grounder to third. Then Klesko pinch hit for Andruw. Wonder why they intentionally passed Ryan?

	AB	HR	RBI	Avg.	OBP	SLG
Klesko vs. right	389	31	81	.301	.390	.604
Wetteland vs. left	144	7	24	.285	.340	.507

There was a good chance that Klesko would have turned on a Wetteland pitch and Atlanta would have had a 3-2 Series lead before the games in Gotham. Wetteland's failure vs. lefties in '96 is unprecedented. Here are his lefty/righty splits from 1991–95:

	AB	HR	RBI	Avg.	OBP	SLG
vs. right-handers	471	7	45	.204	.270	.306
vs. left-handers	601	13	68	.191	.270	.295

His fastball has always had great velocity, but it's straight. His technique is to spot the fastball and use that awesome hard curve the get his strikeouts. He was the second best reliever on the staff last year and not as good as his save totals might suggest. And he has a disturbing habit of making *every* 9th inning interesting. He didn't dodge as many bullets in '95 and may not in '97. ■

BOBBY WITT

SP • BR • TR • 6'2 • 205 • 32 • TEX85/1

	G	GS	IP	H	HR	BB	K	W	L	S	ERA	K/BB	K9	HW9
OAK94	24	24	135	151	22	70	111	8	10	0	5.04	1.6	7.4	14.73
FLA/TEX95	29	29	172	185	12	68	141	5	11	0	4.13	2.1	7.4	13.24
TEX96	33	32	199	235	28	96	157	16	12	0	5.41	1.6	7.1	14.96
CAREER	312	306	1899	1821	165	1121	1616	112	119	0	4.62	1.4	7.7	13.94

It says a lot about a team's pitching staff when they basically use only 6 starters all year and the worst

ERA on the rotation is only 0.42 runs worse than the league average. Unfortunately for Witt, that mark happened to be his. He had a season much like teammate Roger Pavlik, but even less consistent and with a little less run support to paint over the holes. ■

TODD ZEILE

3B-1B • BR • TR • 6′1 • 190 • 31 • SL86/3

	AB	R	H	2B	3B	HR	RBI	BB	SO	SB	CS	BA	OB	SA
SL94	415	62	111	25	1	19	75	52	56	1	3	.267	.348	.470
SL/CHN95	426	50	105	22	0	14	52	34	76	1	0	.246	.305	.397
PHI/BAL96	617	78	162	32	0	25	99	82	104	1	1	.263	.348	.436
CAREER	3610	468	949	197	13	109	523	444	567	34	33	.263	.342	.415

Zeile started at third most of the year for the Phillies until much-heralded prospect Scott Rolen was called up. He was moved to first, but he was a free agent at the end of the year and one of the few players on the Phillies anyone wanted. The Orioles wanted right-handed power, so they traded for him and Pete Incaviglia in late August. He made a great first impression on the Orioles, hitting 5 homers, and playing solid defense at third—at least until Game 3 of the playoffs against the Yankees, when an ill-advised pump fake allowed the lead run to score and gave Mussina the excuse to crumble. The Orioles would never have the lead in the series again. Ripken will be moving to third and Zeile will be heading out of town for the 4th time in 2 years. ■

■ SERVICE TIME FREE AGENTS

These are players who became free agents once a labor agreement was finally reached and service time was granted.

Moises Alou (see Montreal Expos)
Mike Bordick (see Oakland A's)
Tony Castillo (see Chicago White Sox)
Alex Fernandez (see Chicago White Sox)
Thomas Howard (see Cincinnati Reds)
Brent Mayne (see New York Mets)
Tim Naehring (see Boston Red Sox)
Mel Rojas (see Montreal Expos)
Craig Shipley (see San Diego Padres)
Mark Whiten (see Seattle Mariners)

Looking for a Game

Many of these guys will be watching the games on TV in '97. But Kevin Elster's 99 RBI would have been buried in here this time last year, as would Mark Gardner's 12 wins, and the returns of Eric Davis and Straw Man.

KIM BATISTE

UT • BR • TR • 6'0 • 193 • 29

	AB	R	H	2B	3B	HR	RBI	BB	SO	SB	CS	BA	OB	SA
SF96	130	17	27	6	0	3	11	5	33	3	3	.208	.235	.323

Batiste had his 15 minutes of fame in the '93 post-season, when he established himself as the worst-fielding defensive replacement in baseball history. His 130 at-bats in '96 should have gone to someone from Triple-A. If they don't in '97, the Senate should hold hearings. ■

JOSÉ BAUTISTA

RP • BR TR • 6'1 • 205 • 32 • NYN81

	G	GS	IP	H	HR	BB	K	W	L	S	ERA	K/BB	K9	HW9
CHN94	58	0	69	75	10	17	45	4	5	1	3.89	2.6	5.9	11.99
SF95	52	6	100	120	24	26	45	3	8	0	6.44	1.7	4.1	13.14
SF96	37	1	69	66	10	15	28	3	4	0	3.36	1.9	3.6	10.56
CAREER	280	49	632	662	98	157	305	30	40	3	4.46	1.9	4.3	11.66

Don't let Bautista's ERA fool you. He ushered in the inherited runners like a maître-d', then got serious once he was buying. He has a good splitter, a weak fastball, and mediocre breaking stuff. Throughout his career, hitters have owned him during his first 15 pitches and when runners are in scoring position. Not exactly what you look for in a reliever. ■

RAFAEL BELLIARD

SS • BR • TR • 5'6 • 160 • 35 • PIT80

	AB	R	H	2B	3B	HR	RBI	BB	SO	SB	CS	BA	OB	SA
ATL94	120	9	29	7	1	0	9	2	29	0	2	.242	.264	.317
ATL95	180	12	40	2	1	0	7	6	28	2	2	.222	.255	.244
ATL96	142	9	24	7	0	0	3	2	22	3	1	.169	.179	.218
CAREER	2210	207	488	52	14	1	138	135	366	43	16	.221	.272	.258

Belliard couldn't lay off a first pitch if he had a bomb strapped to him. His reasoning is simple: The best pitch most hitters get to see is the first one, and big-leaguers tend to hit about .333 on them if they

make contact. This is mostly a function of marginal pitchers being browbeaten by their managers and pitching coaches to be "aggressive"—after all, pitching coaches have their statistics, too, and they harp on how low batting averages drop when you get ahead in the count (to about .200). Many pitchers respond by throwing first-pitch fastballs over the heart of the plate—especially to lightweight shortstops. So, if you were as overmatched as Belliard, you'd probably take your chances with the first blur you saw that wasn't coming at your head, too. The patron saint of good-field, no-hit utility men, Belliard makes Mark Belanger look like Tony Gwynn. At 35, his range is dipping, so he might soon become the patron saint of former major-league good-field, no-hit utility men. ■

MIKE BENJAMIN

UT • BR • TR • 6'3 • 195 • 31 • SF87/3

	AB	R	H	2B	3B	HR	RBI	BB	SO	SB	CS	BA	OB	SA
SF94	62	9	16	5	1	1	9	5	16	5	0	.258	.343	.419
SF95	186	19	41	6	0	3	12	8	51	11	1	.220	.256	.301
PHI96	103	13	23	5	1	4	13	12	21	3	1	.223	.316	.408
CAREER	740	92	148	31	4	17	64	48	163	24	2	.200	.259	.322

When a pitching-starved team like the Phillies deals a young, hard-throwing Jeff Juden for a low-grade utility infielder, it tells you all you need to know about what a joy Jeffrey must be to have in the backseat on long trips. Benjamin went down for the year in '96 with a stiff neck after a surprisingly productive 100 at-bats. Someone younger will have the job of carrying Stocker's and Morandini's bags in '97. ■

MIKE BIELECKI

RP • BR • TR • 6'3 • 195 • 37 • PIT79

	G	GS	IP	H	HR	BB	K	W	L	S	ERA	K/BB	K9	HW9
ATL94	19	1	27	28	2	12	18	2	0	0	4.00	1.5	6.0	13.33
CAL95	22	11	75	80	15	31	45	4	6	0	5.97	1.5	5.4	13.31
ATL96	40	5	75	63	8	33	71	4	3	2	2.63	2.2	8.5	11.51
CAREER	297	178	1173	1180	107	475	723	67	66	3	4.18	1.5	5.5	12.70

Bielecki hit the weights in the off-season before '96 and came into the spring strong as an ox. The results? Apart from the bloody nose the N.L. gave him in June (6.52 ERA in 9.2 innings), he held the league to a 2.45 ERA or less in each month. He even tossed 23.2 solid innings as a starter (3.42 ERA in 5 starts) when Avery went down. And he was throwing harder than he ever had in his career in Game 4 of the World Series, striking out the side with runners on base and cruising through 2 innings. At his age there's no guarantee he'll be able to maintain this level. ■

MIKE BLOWERS

3B • BR • TR • 6'2 • 190 • 31 • MON86/10

	AB	R	H	2B	3B	HR	RBI	BB	SO	SB	CS	BA	OB	SA
SEA94	270	37	78	13	0	9	49	25	60	2	2	.289	.348	.437
SEA95	439	59	113	24	1	23	96	53	128	2	1	.257	.335	.474
LA96	317	31	84	19	2	6	38	37	77	0	0	.265	.341	.394
CAREER	1695	210	439	86	6	60	267	184	449	6	8	.259	.332	.423

Blowers didn't adjust to the N.L. at the plate, suffering a major power outage, striking out frequently, and looking a whole lot more like the '94 Blowers. His '95 season was a fluke and his '96 season ended when he blew out his knee running third, so don't expect him to be handed a third base job anywhere. He'll have to earn everything he gets in '97. ■

RICKY BONES

SP • BR • TR • 5'10 • 175 • 27 • SD86

	G	GS	IP	H	HR	BB	K	W	L	S	ERA	K/BB	K9	HW9
MIL94	24	24	170	166	17	45	57	10	9	0	3.43	1.3	3.0	11.17
MIL95	32	31	200	218	26	83	77	10	12	0	4.63	.9	3.5	13.55
MIL/NYA96	36	24	152	184	30	68	63	7	14	0	6.22	.9	3.7	14.92
CAREER	166	149	944	1016	131	325	356	51	62	0	4.72	1.1	3.4	12.78

His ERA and HW9 over the past 3 years are what you call a negative trend. He doesn't have hard stuff and he relies on keeping batters off balance. Those kind of pitchers are supposed to get better with age, but the league has been learning him far more than he's been learning the league. He may need to try the N.L. if he wants to get back to his 1994 form. ■

PAT BORDERS

C • BR • TR • 6'2 • 190 • 33 • TOR82/6

	AB	R	H	2B	3B	HR	RBI	BB	SO	SB	CS	BA	OB	SA
TOR94	295	24	73	13	1	3	26	15	50	1	1	.247	.284	.329
KC/HOU95	178	15	37	8	1	4	13	9	29	0	0	.208	.246	.331
SL/CAL/CHA96	220	15	61	7	0	5	18	9	43	0	2	.277	.306	.377
CAREER	2693	234	685	142	10	62	300	129	434	6	8	.254	.288	.384

Borders earned his frequent-flier miles last year. In June the Cardinals traded him to the Angels, who traded him a month later to the White Sox. He should think about hanging out a shingle: "Will catch for food." He doesn't have much of a stick left, but he's really good at working with pitchers and can block pitches in the dirt almost as well as the batting practice backstop. ■

DAVE CLARK

OF • BL • TR • 6'2 • 210 • 34 • CLE83/1

	AB	R	H	2B	3B	HR	RBI	BB	SO	SB	CS	BA	OB	SA
PIT94	223	37	66	11	1	10	46	22	48	2	2	.296	.355	.489
PIT95	196	30	55	6	0	4	24	24	38	3	3	.281	.359	.372
PIT/LA96	226	28	61	12	2	8	36	34	53	2	2	.270	.364	.447
CAREER	1690	217	448	66	8	57	248	189	372	17	12	.265	.337	.415

In '93 and '94, Leyland got Dave Clark 500 at bats and Clark gave him back 21 dingers, 92 RBI, and a .280 batting average. His average has been in a steady decline since then, but he did manage 22 extra-base hits in part-time play in '96, which was only 5 fewer than Gregg Jefferies managed in 400+ at bats and more than James Mouton produced in 300. Somebody will want this left-handed bat on their bench in '97. ■

JIM CORSI

RP • BR • TR • 6'1 • 210 • 35 • NYA82/24

	G	GS	IP	H	HR	BB	K	W	L	S	ERA	K/BB	K9	HW9
OAK95	38	0	45	31	2	26	26	2	4	2	2.20	1.0	5.2	11.40
OAK96	57	0	73	71	6	34	43	6	0	3	4.03	1.3	5.3	12.93
CAREER	222	1	319	296	20	127	179	13	16	5	3.24	1.4	5.0	11.93

There's nothing really special that Corsi does, but he is effective. With the league exploding around him, he just kept throwing sinkers and inducing grounders. As always, lefties gave him a hard time, but he squelched right-handers, and he ended the year as one of the few Oakland pitchers with respectable numbers. ■

CHAD CURTIS

CF • BR • TR • 5'10 • 175 • 28 • CAL89/45

	AB	R	H	2B	3B	HR	RBI	BB	SO	SB	CS	BA	OB	SA
CAL94	453	67	116	23	4	11	50	37	69	25	11	.256	.317	.397
DET95	586	96	157	29	3	21	67	70	93	27	15	.268	.349	.435
DET/LA96	504	85	127	25	1	12	46	70	88	18	11	.252	.341	.377
CAREER	2567	401	680	118	13	60	268	298	410	161	79	.265	.343	.391

Curtis went from being traded straight-up for Tony Phillips to not even being offered a contract by the Dodgers after being dumped by the Tigers for two questionable arms (John Cummings and Joey Eischen) because Buddy Bell got tired of his whining. He's always been overrated as an offensive player—his on-base percentage has never been where it should be for a leadoff man, and his stolen base success rate has consistently been below 70%. But he dropped off in all categories and wore out two welcomes. Even his defense suffered in '96, as his .960 fielding percentage was the worst of his career and second worst among center fielders to Brian Hunter, while his assists have dropped from 16 in '92 to only 5. He's got a lot of work to do to revive his career, but it will be very surprising if he gets the chance to do that as a regular with a contender. ■

MILT CUYLER

OF • BR • TR • 5'10 • 175 • 28 • DET86/2

	AB	R	H	2B	3B	HR	RBI	BB	SO	SB	CS	BA	OB	SA
DET94	116	20	28	3	1	1	11	13	21	5	3	.241	.318	.310
DET95	88	15	18	1	4	0	5	8	16	2	1	.205	.271	.307
BOS96	110	19	22	1	2	2	12	13	19	7	3	.200	.299	.300
CAREER	1380	224	326	45	23	9	116	120	273	77	26	.236	.303	.322

Cuyler signed with Boston when the Tigers cut him after the '95 season—probably because Duquette wanted either him or Cole, but couldn't keep them straight. He has excellent speed, and the Tigers waited several years for him to blossom as a hitter. But it turned out that he just had excellent speed. Cuyler got the chance to start in center when Kevin Kennedy soured on Dwayne Hosey in early April. They were in the middle of their horrible start, and that just shows how desperate things had gotten. ■

DANNY DARWIN

SP-RP • BR • TR • 6'3 • 190 • 41 • TEX76

	G	GS	IP	H	HR	BB	K	W	L	S	ERA	K/BB	K9	HW9
BOS94	13	13	75	101	13	24	54	7	5	0	6.30	2.3	6.5	14.99
TOR/TEX95	20	15	99	131	25	31	58	3	10	0	7.45	1.9	5.3	14.73
PIT/HOU96	34	25	164	160	16	27	96	10	11	0	3.79	3.6	5.3	10.26
CAREER	652	322	2710	2594	272	780	1769	158	161	32	3.72	2.3	5.9	11.20

By now, Darwin is left with a below-average fastball, a mediocre curve, a decent slider and a pretty good circle change-up. He pitched well enough for the Pirates that they could lure Rich Loiselle away from the Astros for him at mid-season. Then he arrived in Houston and pitched as he did in '95. Very. Badly. The highlight of his stay was sparking one of the great baseball brawls in recent history, plunking Henry Rodriguez—who simply has not earned the right to style as much as he does. In the '70s when Darwin came up—pitching with Ferguson Jenkins, Jon Mat-lack, and Dock Ellis back in the Pleistocene Epoch—Henry would have had that message delivered back in April and a few feet closer to his head. As for Darwin, he should have retired right then and made it his closing word on the state of baseball in the '90s. But now it's past time to take the receiver off the hook and go fishing. ■

MARK EICHHORN

RP • BR • TR • 6'3 • 210 • 36

	G	GS	IP	H	HR	BB	K	W	L	S	ERA	K/BB	K9	HW9
BAL94	43	0	71	62	1	19	35	6	5	1	2.15	1.8	4.4	10.27
CAL96	24	0	30	36	3	11	24	1	2	0	5.04	2.2	7.2	14.08
CAREER	563	7	885	825	49	270	640	48	43	32	3.00	2.4	6.5	11.13

After missing 1995 with arm trouble, Eichhorn returned to the A.L. and did a credible job. Remove one horrid appearance in June from his numbers (1.1 innings, 7 hits, 5 earned runs) and his ERA drops to 3.72. He spent a great deal of time on the DL with an inflamed rotator cuff. He still could be a decent long reliever, and if he goes through the lineup once, that funky delivery of his will improve the numbers of the pitchers who follow him. ■

TONY FERNANDEZ

2B-SS-DL • BB • TR • 6′2 • 175 • 34 • TOR79

He got the Mets to trade him in '93 by pretending to have arm trouble, then went deep in the hole and came up firing in his first game for Toronto. This year he complained bitterly for a trade after learning he was being bumped for a 21-year-old rookie named Derek Jeter who played like he did when he was 21. One scout summed it up well: "He's a pain in the ass." ■

MIKE GALLEGO

2B • BR • TR • 5′8 • 160 • 36 • OAK81/2

	AB	R	H	2B	3B	HR	RBI	BB	SO	SB	CS	BA	OB	SA
NYA94	306	39	73	17	1	6	41	38	46	0	1	.239	.327	.359
OAK95	120	11	28	0	0	0	8	9	24	0	1	.233	.292	.233
SL96	143	12	30	2	0	0	4	12	31	0	0	.210	.276	.224
CAREER	2888	368	693	109	12	42	281	325	457	24	31	.240	.322	.330

Gallego suffered a torn hamstring in the spring and was feared lost for the season. But he came back in July and swiped the starting job away from Luis Alicea. Of course, he couldn't hit enough to keep it, and found himself back on the bench by August. His recurring leg injuries and inability to hit for average make him nothing more than a utility player. The only things that have kept him around are his occasional power and his fielding ability at second base. And the power looks likes it's next to go. ■

JASON GRIMSLEY

SP-RP • BR • TR • 6′3 • 180 • 29 • PHI85/10

	G	GS	IP	H	HR	BB	K	W	L	S	ERA	K/BB	K9	HW9
CLE94	14	13	82	91	7	34	59	5	2	0	4.57	1.7	6.5	13.71
CLE95	15	2	34	37	4	32	25	0	0	1	6.09	.8	6.6	18.26
CAL96	35	20	130	150	14	74	82	5	7	0	6.84	1.1	5.7	15.50
CAREER	101	68	425	450	35	263	283	18	25	1	5.40	1.1	6.0	15.10

Grimsley throw hard and randomly. Asked to comment on his league-leading 13 hit batsmen, Grimsley explained, "I'm not a machine out there.

My pitches have been known to sometimes get away from me." Some team should turn him into a modern-day Ryne Duren. Put thick, Coke bottle glasses on him, a flask in his hip pocket, and send him weaving out to the mound to squint in at the catcher and heave his first warm-up pitch off the screen. And as the hitter steps reluctantly into the box, the catcher can mutter under his breath the refrain of the *Friday the 13th* serial killer: *Jason, Jason, Jason* . . . ■

CHRIS GWYNN

OF • BL • TL • 6′0 • 220 • 32 • LA85/1

	AB	R	H	2B	3B	HR	RBI	BB	SO	SB	CS	BA	OB	SA
LA94	71	9	19	0	0	3	13	7	7	0	2	.268	.333	.394
LA95	84	8	18	3	2	1	10	6	23	0	0	.214	.272	.333
SD96	90	8	16	4	0	1	10	10	28	0	0	.178	.260	.256
CAREER	1007	119	263	36	11	17	118	71	171	2	4	.261	.308	.369

Not even having a brother on the team with 2,560 base hits is going to keep you around with numbers like this. Hard to believe that this Gwynn's the one to go in the 1st round, while Tony was still around in the 3rd. Compare Chris's career to Tony's 1987:

	AB	R	H	2B	3B	HR	RBI	BB	SO	SB	BA
Tony '87	642	107	218	36	13	7	54	82	35	56	.370
Chris	1007	119	263	36	11	17	118	71	171	2	.261

That's almost as good as Hank and Tommie Aaron:

	AB	R	H	2B	3B	HR	RBI	BB	SO	SB	BA
Hank '59	629	116	223	46	7	39	123	51	54	8	.355
Tommie	994	102	216	42	6	13	94	86	145	9	.229

CHRIS HAMMOND

RP-SP • BL • TL • 6′1 • 190 • 30 • CIN86/6

	G	GS	IP	H	HR	BB	K	W	L	S	ERA	K/BB	K9	HW9
FLA94	13	13	73	79	5	23	40	4	4	0	3.07	1.7	4.9	12.57
FLA95	25	24	161	157	17	47	126	9	6	0	3.80	2.7	7.0	11.40
FLA96	38	9	81	104	14	27	50	5	8	0	6.56	1.9	5.6	14.56
CAREER	159	125	764	801	73	278	457	43	49	0	4.39	1.6	5.4	12.71

In 1995, Hammond stepped forward, pitching with fine control and using his solid change-up to keep hitters off-balance. In 1996 it was 2 steps back and 3 flights down. In a 4.1 inning stretch between late April and early May, he allowed 19 earned runs. He suffered an

ear infection and injured his neck while stretching in his hotel room—but the starts he missed as a result were probably his biggest contributions to the team. His previously solid strikeout-to-walk ratio of 1995 went south. Hammond has to change speeds to survive, so he'll have to re-establish his curveball and change-up. With his middling stuff, there's little room for error.

The Marlins took a gamble after a series of dreadful starts (2-6, 10.60 ERA in 35.2 innings in 9 games) and threw him into the bullpen. The difference was dramatic, as Hammond went 3-2 with a 3.38 ERA in 45.1 innings. His ratios weren't great (49 hits allowed—a .282 average against), but he struck out 32 while walking only 14. Someone will take a chance on him. ■

BRIAN R. HUNTER

1B-OF • BR • TL • 6'0 • 225 • 29 • ATL87/8

	AB	R	H	2B	3B	HR	RBI	BB	SO	SB	CS	BA	OB	SA
CIN/PIT94	256	34	60	16	1	15	57	17	56	0	0	.234	.277	.480
CIN95	79	9	17	6	0	1	9	11	21	2	1	.215	.312	.329
SEA96	198	21	53	10	0	7	28	15	43	0	1	.268	.327	.424
CAREER	1122	134	266	64	5	49	193	83	233	3	6	.237	.288	.434

When Hunter was with the Pirates in '94, after wearing out his welcome in Atlanta, his stretching regimen quite literally involved standing with his hands on his knees and checking to see if Leyland was looking. He managed 42 dingers in the N.L.—including a 1st-inning, Game 7 blast off of a positively terrified John Smiley in the '91 playoffs. But he was hitting mistakes, only to swing at 3-0 pitches in the dirt in his next at-bat. No surprise that he lasted less than half a season with Leyland. He dropped some weight in '96—once it dawned on him that his career and his 6-figure paychecks could be history at 28—and Piniella was able to coax some decent production out of him. He should kick around as a right-handed DH for the next few years, but he's already blown the only chances he'll ever get to play regularly. ■

PETE INCAVIGLIA

OF • BR • TR • 6'1 • 225 • 32

	AB	R	H	2B	3B	HR	RBI	BB	SO	SB	CS	BA	OB	SA
PHI94	244	28	56	10	1	13	32	16	71	1	0	.230	.278	.439
PHI/BAL96	302	37	73	9	2	18	50	30	89	2	0	.242	.318	.464
CAREER	4049	527	1002	189	21	201	641	347	1221	33	26	.247	.311	.453

Baltimore traded for Incaviglia and Todd Zeile in August, looking for some right-handed power as they chased the Yankees down the stretch. He had 16 homers and 42 RBI in 99 games for the Phillies. His impact was immediate: He hit a grand slam on the 31st off Jamie Moyer in his first game for the Orioles. And he continued to hit well in a backup role. But about 5 minutes after the season ended, he was out of a job. ■

CHAD KREUTER

C • BB • TR • 6'2 • 200 • 32 • TEX85/5

	AB	R	H	2B	3B	HR	RBI	BB	SO	SB	CS	BA	OB	SA
DET94	170	17	38	8	0	1	19	28	36	0	1	.224	.327	.288
SEA95	75	12	17	5	0	1	8	5	22	0	0	.227	.293	.333
CHA96	114	14	25	8	0	3	18	13	29	0	0	.219	.308	.368
CAREER	1158	145	274	59	4	28	128	157	280	2	4	.237	.328	.367

Kreuter's season ended July 19 after he severely dislocated and fractured his left shoulder in a collision at the plate. The pain was so bad, Kreuter passed out in the shower. While he's capable behind the plate, he doesn't hit well enough to be anything other than a backup. It's too soon to tell if the shoulder injury will mess up his throwing, but it's a safe bet it will. A switch-hitting catcher is a rare commodity, which is why teams keep taking chances on him. But his platoon differential (.270 vs. lefties, .195 vs. righties last season) suggests that he's as much of a switch-hitter as Carlton Fisk. ■

PAT LISTACH

CF • BB • TR • 5'9 • 170 • 29 • MIL88/5

	AB	R	H	2B	3B	HR	RBI	BB	SO	SB	CS	BA	OB	SA
MIL94	54	8	16	3	0	0	2	3	8	2	1	.296	.333	.352
MIL95	334	35	73	8	2	0	25	25	61	13	3	.219	.276	.254
MIL96	317	51	76	16	2	1	33	36	51	25	5	.240	.317	.312
CAREER	1640	237	420	61	11	5	137	156	314	112	36	.256	.322	.316

Listach has been spiraling downward since beating out Kenny Lofton for the 1992 Rookie of the Year award. After injuries in '93, a lost '94 (only 16 games played), and .219 in '95, trade rumors surrounded Listach as the Brewers broke spring camp. A deal with the Yankees for Scott Kamieniecki was close to completion but fell through. He appeared to be turning it around, hitting .271 through June 28, but predictably, he strained his throwing shoulder and

landed on the DL. Then things got interesting on August 23, when he was traded in a package to New York and arrived with a broken foot. The Brewers neglected to mention this detail to Yankee GM Bob Watson before completing the deal. The Brewers claim they didn't know, and Steinbrenner took the news with his typical composure. Listach may be able to contribute at the plate and his defense is solid, but his body definitely isn't. ■

GREGG OLSON

RP • BR • TR • 6'4 • 210 • 30 • BAL88/1

	G	GS	IP	H	HR	BB	K	W	L	S	ERA	K/BB	K9	HW9
ATL94	16	0	14	19	1	13	10	0	2	1	9.20	.8	6.4	20.47
CLE/KC95	23	0	33	28	4	19	21	3	3	3	4.09	1.1	5.7	12.82
DET/HOU96	52	0	52	55	7	35	37	4	0	8	5.02	1.1	6.4	15.57
CAREER	411	0	450	383	22	225	415	24	26	172	2.94	1.8	8.3	12.15

The Astros took on Olson as a "what have we got to lose?" project. Not to mention the fact that he was related to the financial adviser of Mark Johnson, their 1st-round pick who hadn't yet signed on the bottom line. Olson's once-incredible curve still breaks marvelously, but nowhere near the plate. His fastball, once a solid 90-plus mph pitch, now checks in at 85 mph. He didn't do much for Houston. Then again, Johnson finally signed, so maybe they got exactly what they wanted out of him. ■

STEVE ONTIVEROS

SP • BR • TR • 6'0 • 180 • 36 • OAK82/1

Ontiveros is 36 and has had 5 elbow operations, including not 1 but 2 reconstructions. He has been on the DL 12 times as a professional, including a streak of 9 consecutive seasons from 1984 through 1992. He has missed entire seasons twice, in '92 and '96. But he hasn't thrown in his cards yet. The odds of him making it back can't be any higher than the odds of two unrelated men named Steve Ontiveros playing in the big leagues. ■

JEFF PARRETT

RP • BR • TR • 6'3 • 200 • 35 • MIL83/9

	G	GS	IP	H	HR	BB	K	W	L	S	ERA	K/BB	K9	HW9
SL95	59	0	76	71	8	28	71	4	7	0	3.64	2.5	8.4	11.72
SL/PHI96	51	0	66	64	2	31	64	3	3	0	3.41	2.1	8.7	12.95
CAREER	491	11	724	672	61	345	616	56	43	22	3.80	1.8	7.7	12.64

Parrett looked washed up in *1991*. The Phillies signed him after the Cardinals released him and he ended up yielding only 2 dingers in 66 innings. He struck out a batter an inning with command; in fact, his K/BB ratio in '95 and '96 is by far the best it's ever been. Nevertheless, he's 35, he let a few too many inherited runners run up the bill on someone else's tab, and he's pretty flammable when he's behind in the count. But give him the nod for not going quietly. ■

DAN PELTIER

1B • BL • TL • 6'1 • 200 • 28

	AB	R	H	2B	3B	HR	RBI	BB	SO	SB	CS	BA	OB	SA
SF96	59	3	15	2	0	0	9	7	9	0	0	.254	.328	.288

Peltier blamed his release by the Rangers on his refusal to be a replacement player. Granted, the Rangers have a long and unenviable history of mistakes, but how about Dan-o taking some personal responsibility? He's a first baseman without much punch, and the Rangers are already paying one of those guys several million dollars. ■

TERRY PENDLETON

3B • BB • TR • 5'9 • 195 • 36 • SL82/7

	AB	R	H	2B	3B	HR	RBI	BB	SO	SB	CS	BA	OB	SA
ATL94	309	25	78	18	3	7	30	12	57	2	0	.252	.280	.398
FLA95	513	70	149	32	1	14	78	38	84	1	2	.290	.339	.439
FLA/ATL96	568	51	135	26	1	11	75	41	111	2	3	.238	.290	.345
CAREER	6682	823	1808	337	39	136	900	459	916	124	58	.271	.316	.394

Compare Pendleton's '96 numbers to those of the average N.L. third baseman—who hit 20 dingers, knocked in 84 runs, hit .268, and had an on-base percentage of .330 and a slugging average of .435. He still can field, but his bat is gone. The competition in the N.L. is pretty fierce, but here are the only third basemen Pendleton outproduced in '96: David Bell, Kim Batiste, Matt Franco, and Tim Wallach. He's not much of a player anymore, so he's much more likely to get that elusive ring as a coach. ■

CHRIS SABO

3B • BR • TR • 6′0 • 185 • 35 • CIN83/2

	AB	R	H	2B	3B	HR	RBI	BB	SO	SB	CS	BA	OB	SA
BAL94	258	41	66	15	3	11	42	20	38	1	1	.256	.320	.465
CHA/SL95	84	10	20	6	0	1	11	4	14	3	0	.238	.283	.345
CIN96	125	15	32	7	1	3	16	18	27	2	0	.256	.354	.400
CAREER	3354	494	898	214	17	116	426	274	460	120	49	.268	.326	.445

In recent years there have been few players as popular in Cincinnati as Chris Sabo. Don't ask why—some things defy explanation. He did supply one of the more comical incidents last season, depending on your perspective. In late July he hit a pop-up to short in a game in Montreal, shattering his bat. Small chunks of cork flew out of the bat as the barrel landed halfway down the third-base line. Sabo got a 7-game suspension from the league, despite halfhearted claims that it was an old Hal Morris model he found in a pile of equipment. Couldn't he at least have blamed someone no longer with the team—like Billy Hatcher? ■

JUAN SAMUEL

OF/DH • BR • TR • 5′11 • 180 • 36 • PHI80

	AB	R	H	2B	3B	HR	RBI	BB	SO	SB	CS	BA	OB	SA
DET94	136	32	42	9	5	5	21	10	26	5	2	.309	.364	.559
DET/KC95	205	31	54	10	1	12	39	29	49	6	4	.263	.360	.498
TOR96	188	34	48	8	3	8	26	15	65	9	1	.255	.319	.457
CAREER	5936	846	1542	280	98	157	686	423	1401	378	132	.260	.315	.419

Samuel's gotten to the point in his career where he no longer can contribute full-time to the lineup, but he's a great influence to have in the clubhouse. He works his butt off every day, and Samuel was such a good influence on the rookies last season that Sprague started calling Samuel "Molitino," in reference to the hard-working Paul Molitor. Some team could use him in their day care center until he decides to start coaching. ■

STEVE SCARSONE

UT • BR • TR • 6′2 • 170 • 29 • PH86/2

	AB	R	H	2B	3B	HR	RBI	BB	SO	SB	CS	BA	OB	SA
SF94	103	21	28	8	0	2	13	10	20	0	2	.272	.330	.408
SF95	233	33	62	10	3	11	29	18	82	3	2	.266	.333	.476
SF96	283	28	62	12	1	5	23	25	91	2	3	.219	.286	.322
CAREER	752	101	183	39	4	20	80	59	237	5	8	.243	.303	.386

Your basic Charles Grodin-looking utility infielder. He played like Robby Thompson in '96, though the Giants didn't have to pay him $5 million to hit .220 and strike out a lot. He continues to hit much better against left-handers and owns enough gloves to play all four infield positions, though they all clank. ■

TIM SCOTT

RP • BR • TR • 6′2 • 185 • 30 • LA84/2

	G	GS	IP	H	HR	BB	K	W	L	S	ERA	K/BB	K9	HW9
MON94	40	0	53	51	0	18	37	5	2	1	2.70	2.1	6.3	11.71
MON95	62	0	63	52	6	23	57	2	0	2	3.98	2.5	8.1	10.71
MON/SF96	65	0	65	65	8	30	47	5	7	1	4.70	1.6	6.5	13.13
CAREER	259	0	292	278	22	126	237	23	12	5	3.85	1.9	7.3	12.45

Other than a brutal July, Scott was fairly effective in '96. His biggest weakness is that Cecil Fielder is a threat to steal against him—runners are 67 for 77 against him in his career! He got run out of Montreal after whining about not getting a chance to close games, the Giants waived him in the off-season, and now he'll get a chance to reluctantly hand the ball to Jeff Brantley in Cincinnati. ■

LEE SMITH

RP • BR • TR • 6′6 • 270 • 39 • CHN75/2

	G	GS	IP	H	HR	BB	K	W	L	S	ERA	K/BB	K9	HW9
BAL94	41	0	38	34	6	11	42	1	4	33	3.29	3.8	9.9	10.65
CAL95	52	0	49	42	3	25	43	0	5	37	3.47	1.7	7.9	12.31
CAL/CIN96	54	0	55	57	4	26	41	3	4	2	3.76	1.6	6.7	13.57
CAREER	997	6	1268	1105	87	478	1236	71	91	473	2.99	2.6	8.8	11.24

When the Reds traded Chuck McElroy for Lee Smith in late May, it could have been a disaster for the Reds, but it wasn't. Smith hated it in California. He felt the club had promised him the closer's job, but reneged when Troy Percival emerged while he was hurt. Could Smith accept the set up role in Cincinnati when he couldn't in California? "Don't worry about me," Smith said. "I'm just glad to come to your ballclub. . . . Thank you for rescuing me."

And as far as the Reds were concerned, he behaved himself and pitched quite well. He adapted to his new role and became the club's main middle reliever. Perhaps it wasn't the role as much as it was his teammates. (See the California Angels for a glimpse of the worst clubhouse in baseball.) But by the end of the season, it was clear that he wasn't happy. He wants to close somewhere, and if that

isn't possible, he at least wants to pitch closer to his Louisiana home. He's going to the Hall of Fame. If he retires now, he'll get there that much sooner. ■

KURT STILLWELL

SS • BB • TR • 5'11 • 185 • 31

	AB	R	H	2B	3B	HR	RBI	BB	SO	SB	CS	BA	OB	SA
TEX96	77	12	21	4	0	1	4	10	11	0	0	.273	.364	.364

Some may recall that in 1988, when the Reds shortstop job was up for grabs, Marge Schott lobbied hard for Stillwell over Barry Larkin because Kurt was nice to her dog. Well, Schottzie 02 wouldn't cross the street these days to mark his territory on Stillwell's spikes and Larkin's on his way to Cooperstown. ■

ROBBY THOMPSON

2B • BR • TR • 5'11 • 170 • 34 • SF83/1

	AB	R	H	2B	3B	HR	RBI	BB	SO	SB	CS	BA	OB	SA
SF94	129	13	27	8	2	2	7	15	32	3	1	.209	.290	.349
SF95	336	51	75	15	0	8	23	42	76	1	2	.223	.317	.339
SF96	227	35	48	11	1	5	21	24	69	2	2	.211	.301	.335
CAREER	4612	671	1187	238	39	119	458	439	987	103	62	.257	.329	.403

Robby Thompson was finishing up the best season of his career in '93 when a Trevor Hoffman fastball rearranged his face. Like many who've suffered this stroke of bad luck, he hasn't been the same player since: Dickie Thon, Paul Blair, Tony Conigliaro, Ray Chapman. Thompson was hitting .312 with 19 dingers and playing Gold Glove defense when he was beaned. He's managed .220 with 15 dingers and 166 strikeouts in the 3 years since. His fielding percentage dipped to its lowest point since '87. He no longer steals, either. He probably doesn't even take out the garbage well anymore. Thompson's decline has also been blamed on shoulder problems. Then again, there hasn't been a muscle he hasn't pulled at one time or another. Though he claimed to feel great in the spring, he added hip problems, whiplash, and food poisoning to his list of ailments in '96. Whatever the cause, he's over. As if to underscore the point, his monthly batting averages from April through July went from .283 to .235 to .193 to .139 and done for the year in August. ■

DAVE VALLE

C • BR • TR • 6'2 • 200 • 36 • SEA78/2

	AB	R	H	2B	3B	HR	RBI	BB	SO	SB	CS	BA	OB	SA
BOS/MIL94	112	14	26	8	1	2	10	18	22	0	2	.232	.348	.375
TEX95	75	7	18	3	0	0	5	6	18	1	0	.240	.305	.280
TEX96	86	14	26	6	1	3	17	9	17	0	0	.302	.368	.500
CAREER	2775	314	658	121	12	77	350	258	413	5	7	.237	.314	.373

On most teams, the no. 2 catcher can expect to play a good number of games. Not so for the Rangers, where Ivan Rodriguez is a workhorse behind the plate and Valle caught only 35 games. He hit well when he played, showing good power and plate discipline. And he got the job done defensively when they needed him. It's been 3 years since he's seen 100 at-bats, and he may never again. But he's a fine veteran presence who can be relied on when he gets the call. ■

DAVID WEST

RP • BL • TL • 6'6 • 250 • 32 • NYN83/4

	G	GS	IP	H	HR	BB	K	W	L	S	ERA	K/BB	K9	HW9
PHI94	31	14	99	74	7	61	83	4	10	0	3.55	1.4	7.5	12.27
PHI95	8	8	38	34	5	19	25	3	2	0	3.79	1.3	5.9	12.55
PHI96	7	6	28	31	0	11	22	2	2	0	4.76	2.0	7.1	13.48
CAREER	198	78	567	518	64	304	433	31	38	3	4.59	1.4	6.9	13.05

Remember when West was the phenom and Aguilera was the afterthought in the Viola trade? He didn't look much better than Bobby Muñoz in his return from the DL and went right back on with a strained right groin after sprinting to the all-you-can-eat buffet without properly stretching. The Phillies wouldn't have picked up his $1.5 million option without a gun to the head. ■

MATT WHITESIDE

RP • BR • TR • 6'0 • 185 • 29 • TEX90/25

	G	GS	IP	H	HR	BB	K	W	L	S	ERA	K/BB	K9	HW9
TEX94	47	0	61	68	6	28	37	2	2	1	5.02	1.3	5.5	14.16
TEX95	40	0	53	48	5	19	46	5	4	3	4.08	2.4	7.8	11.38
TEX96	14	0	32	43	8	11	15	0	1	0	6.68	1.4	4.2	15.17
CAREER	181	0	247	263	27	92	150	10	9	9	4.48	1.6	5.5	12.93

At one time Whiteside looked like the Rangers' closer of the future. In '91 and '92 he saved 58 minor-league games and 4 in the majors. But he has struggled since, and it looked like he was "devolving" into more of a setup or long-relief pitcher. Last season was his worst in 5 years with the club, and they sent him down to Triple-A Oklahoma City early on. They even used him as a starter in 7 games, which he hadn't done since 1990. He'll be back in Texas in '97. ■

SURVEY

You can help make *The Scouting Report* even better. Please take the time to tell us what you think.

1. Please rate each feature on how INFORMATIVE it is, on a scale of 5 (excellent) to 1 (poor).

Teams		**Players**	
1996 Autopsy	______	Major Leaguers	______
1997 Diagnosis	______	Minor Leaguers	______
. . . and whatnot	______	Stat Lines	______

2. Please rate each feature on how ENTERTAINING it is, on a scale of 5 (excellent) to 1 (poor):

Teams		**Players**	
1996 Autopsy		Major Leaguers	______
1997 Diagnosis	______	Minor Leaguers	______
. . . and whatnot	______		

3. Are you in a rotisserie or fantasy league? Yes ☐ No ☐

   If so, is this your primary resource for draft preparation? Yes ☐ No ☐

4. Would you like to have *The Scouting Report* available in electronic format in the future?

   Yes ☐ No ☐ If yes, how (web site, CD-ROM, diskette, etc.)?

   ____

   ____

   ____

5. Which of the following would you prefer to have more of in the *The Scouting Report: 1998*?

   ☐ Statistical analysis/comparisons
   ☐ Anecdotes and observations
   ☐ "Eyes-on" scouting reports

6. Anything you'd like to see that we haven't provided?

   ____

   ____

   ____

Mail to us at: Mountain Lion Inc., P.O. Box 257, Rocky Hill, NJ 08553
E-mail us at: scouting97@aol.com